HOT SEAT

FRANK RICH

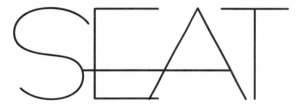

THEATER CRITICISM FOR

THE NEW YORK TIMES,

1980–1993

RANDOM HOUSE

NEW YORK

All of the reviews in this book were originally published in *The New York Times*
or *The New York Times Magazine*.

Grateful acknowledgment is made to the following for permission to reprint previously published material:

Hal Leonard Corporation: Excerpt from "There Is More to Love," music by Andrew Lloyd
Webber, lyrics by Don Black and Charles Hart. Copyright © 1989 by The Really Useful Group
Ltd. All rights for North America controlled by R&H Music Co.; excerpt from "Love Changes
Everything," music by Andrew Lloyd Webber, lyrics by Don Black and Charles Hart. Copyright
© 1988 by The Really Useful Group Ltd. All rights for North America controlled by R&H Music
Co.; excerpt from "Love Is a Chance," music and lyrics by Walter Marks. Copyright © 1964 and
renewed by Walter Marks. All rights controlled by MPL Communications, Inc. International
copyright secured. All rights reserved. Reprinted by permission of Hal Leonard Corporation.

Warner Bros. Publications U.S. Inc.: Excerpt from "Hello Little Girl," by Stephen Sondheim.
Copyright © 1988 by Rilting Music, Inc.; excerpt from "Beautiful," by Stephen Sondheim.
Copyright © 1984 by Rilting Music, Inc.; excerpt from "Putting It Together," by Stephen Sondheim. Copyright © 1984 by Rilting Music, Inc.; excerpt from "Opening Doors," by Stephen
Sondheim. Copyright © 1981 by Rilting Music, Inc. All rights on behalf of Rilting Music, Inc.,
administered by WB Music Corp. All rights reserved. Used by permission of Warner Bros. Publications U.S. Inc., Miami, FL 33014.

Williamson Music: Excerpt from "Intermission Talk," by Richard Rodgers and Oscar
Hammerstein II. Copyright © 1953 by Richard Rodgers and Oscar Hammerstein II. Copyright renewed. International copyright secured. All rights reserved. Reprinted by permission
of Williamson Music, owner of publication and allied rights throughout the world.

Library of Congress Cataloging-in-Publication Data
Rich, Frank.
Hot seat : theater criticism for The New York Times, 1980–1993 / Frank Rich.
p.   cm.
Includes index.
ISBN 0-679-45300-8 (alk. paper)
1. Theater—New York (State)—New York—Reviews.
PN2277.N5R53   1998   792.9'5'097471—dc21   98-22683

Random House website address: www.randomhouse.com/atrandom
Printed in the United States of America on acid-free paper
4 6 8 9 7 5

Book design by J. K. Lambert

To my wife, Alex,
whom I love even more than the theater
—

and to Wendy Wasserstein and Rafael Yglesias,
who never asked the title of the play
before agreeing to go

CONTENTS

INTRODUCTION

When I joined *The New York Times* in 1980, Broadway still offered light comedies with aging stars playing philandering spouses, the Morosco Theatre had yet to give way to a towering Marriott hotel, and no one was known to have died of AIDS. When thirteen years later I moved on, the talk of Broadway was the epic "gay fantasia" known as *Angels in America,* Disney was just getting ready to produce its first Broadway musical, and Neil Simon, Broadway's signature playwright for three decades, was about to be forced by economic realities to flee to Off Broadway.

Or to look at it from a more mundane angle: When I joined the *Times,* I was about to turn thirty-one and my first son had just been born. Thirteen years later, I had lived through the dissolution of my first marriage and the hopeful beginning of a second, and had seen two sons grow toward their teens as I entered middle age.

Where these two stories intersect is often hard to pinpoint, but no doubt they do at times in the course of these pages, which chart (largely) the New York theater as seen through my eyes over that period. The theater kept changing, and so inevitably did my vision of it as life took me in various directions that had nothing to do with my job but no doubt had some bearing on my execution of it. (Some of these intersections I wrote about in a 1994 *Times Magazine* valedictory called "Exit the Critic," which concludes this collection.) Such is the subtext of this book. The text, though, is the reviews themselves—written under deadline, for better and worse, come hell in my private life or high water on Broadway, without much time for the luxury of reflection. That's the job of a daily journalist, whatever the beat. (During my tenure as drama critic, the press generally covered the last preview of a production; my deadline was around 3 p.m. the following day.)

Rereading these pieces now, nearly four years after I left drama reviewing to write about a larger world as a *Times* op-ed columnist—and some seventeen years after I wrote my earliest reviews for the *Times*—I encountered some great nights and great artists that remain indelible, as if I'd only been covering them yesterday. I also discovered plays I no longer remembered, actors whose faces I could no longer place, artists of exciting promise who vanished without explanation soon after their highly praised debuts. (And who may just turn up in the opening credits of tonight's network sitcom.) I also encountered younger incarnations of myself—sometimes immature, sometimes brash, sometimes wince-inducing, sometimes naive, sometimes more sensible than I had recalled. You'll see other real-life characters evolve in these pages as well: Some theater artists grew up (and others fell by the wayside) over the fifteen theater seasons spanned by my thirteen and a half years on the aisle.

The sheer volume of what I saw was enormous. The 330-odd pieces in this book represent barely a quarter of my output as drama critic for the *Times*. In selecting reviews—and, occasionally, essays about some broader theatrical themes that I wrote as Sunday pieces or as a "Critic's Notebook" for the daily paper—I have, of course, tried to include those of plays and musicals that (in my view) are the era's best (and, in some cases, its notorious worst). But I've included others because they illustrate some aspect, controversial or not, of what it's like to be in the hot seat, which the job of chief drama critic of the *Times* perennially is. I've also included some reviews of shows that were not red-letter events in theatrical history but do give some flavor of the cavalcade of New York theater during the 1980s and early nineties. Most plays I saw—most plays of any period—are neither triumphs nor turkeys. Most are in between, and they often reveal the temper of the theater more accurately than do the relatively anomalous hits and bombs. Those middling, typical shows are by necessity wildly underrepresented here in favor of better-known productions, but I hope the sampling will give at least a sense of the routine norm of the drama critic's life.

No one—or almost no one except stagestruck kids like I once was—sits down and reads a collection of reviews from start to finish, but anyone brave or foolish enough to try will find a narrative here. I've tried to assemble an anthology that captures New York theater at a time of change and that traces that theater's major careers, on stage, in the wings, and behind the scenes. In the eighties, Broadway lost whatever claim it still had as a source for American theater; it became instead a showplace for theater that originated elsewhere: Off Broadway, theater companies throughout the United States, England. This was also a decade in which the English usurped Broadway's most original creation, the musical, and in which AIDS killed off many important theatrical artists in their prime even as it became in itself a spur to theatrical imagination. These shifts in the theater are articulated in greater detail in "Exit the Critic"—as are the ins and outs of my own career—but for this book I have also provided brief postscripts to individual reviews, to give an additional context or relevant anecdote where appropriate, and also to express my second thoughts about my own judgments. In the Appendix, the reader will also find some lists in which I answer some constant questions I've never forced myself to address before. Such as: What were the best plays I saw? The worst? The ones I most overrated and underrated?

The passing of time has given me more perspective on these questions, on my own work, on the theater itself. I can't imagine being a daily critic again—I enjoy having my nights back—but I can't imagine a life in which I didn't go to the theater constantly. That's been the case with me since late childhood and always will be. But these days I'm a little more selective in what I choose to see. Sometimes I even wait for the reviews.

New York City
August 1998

A NOTE ON THE TEXT

The text of each review is printed in full. The general essays included in this collection—"Critic's Notebooks," etc.—sometimes appear in excerpt. A few scattered sentences have been recopyedited; occasionally a clarifying phrase or note has been added in brackets.

I reviewed several productions more than once, if not incessantly—first, at an American regional theater, or British theater, or Off Broadway; and then again if the play transferred to Broadway; and then perhaps again if there were major cast changes during the run. For this collection, I have chosen what I regard as the best, or most representative, review (and, in a few cases, reviews) of these productions. Overall I've tended to favor the New York incarnations of these shows.

The pieces are published in chronological order because that best illustrates the historical saga of theater during this period. The reviews are divided by season. Exactly when a new theater season begins is not tightly defined but I've followed the generally accepted practice of the *Best Plays* series and begun each season on June 1 (just as Tony Awards are handed out for the previous season). The date listed with each piece is the date it was published in *The New York Times*—usually the morning after a production's designated opening night in the case of Broadway shows and Off Broadway shows. (Off Off Broadway and out-of-town productions were often reviewed on a catch-as-catch-can basis.) Sometimes, of course, pieces were simply held until a slower news day when an editor could jam them into the paper, a common newspaper practice that was generally regarded by producers as part of the *Times*'s conspiracy against the theater.

Another way to use this book, of course, is to track specific plays or artists through the Index. Or to look at the lists in the Appendix, which will direct the reader by date and title to some of the best plays and performances as well as some of the most fabulous fiascoes.

With each review I've also listed the theater where the play was put on—as the theater was named at the time of the review. Some Broadway houses were renamed in the eighties: The Uris becomes the Gershwin;

the 46th Street becomes the Richard Rodgers. Others were torn down, leased to nontheatrical tenants (the Mark Hellinger most sadly), or fell into disuse. Off Broadway, some major companies (the Roundabout, the Manhattan Theatre Club) moved at least once; some (the Hudson Guild, the Circle Repertory Company) folded. But following the theatrical tradition of regeneration, others came along to take their place—and still do so, every season.

FIRST SEASON

Spring 1980

Jim Dale (center) and
Glenn Close (bottom right) in *Barnum*

MARLON BRANDO SAT RIGHT HERE

BOLTAX THEATRE, APRIL 17, 1980

Say this about playwright Louis La Russo II: The man is sincere. Though Mr. La Russo's latest exercise in kitchen-sink melodrama, *Marlon Brando Sat Right Here,* is a virtual compendium of sentimental bromides, the author always dishes out the clichés with a completely straight face. The result is a rather weird evening in the theater. Mr. La Russo's large collection of stereotyped characters is forever talking gravely about matters of life, love, and death, but somehow it is hard to resist the temptation to laugh.

Marlon Brando, which opened last night at the Boltax, is not quite as perversely amusing as last season's La Russo offering, *Knockout,* but it comes close. This time out, the setting is a Hoboken, N.J., greasy spoon frequented by Italian-American longshoremen; the date is 1955. We are in the spring of everyone's discontent. Only a year before, the play's various drifters and losers had tasted the glamour of Hollywood: Marlon Brando had come to town to shoot *On the Waterfront.* Now the movie people are gone and show no signs of ever coming back. The regulars at Gracie's waterfront dive suddenly realize in one long night full of epiphanies that the most exciting days of their lives are behind them.

Mr. La Russo tells this story in a manner that might be described as paint-by-numbers Saroyan. First he has each character tell the audience his or her lifelong dreams; then those dreams are methodically obliterated. A sour, failed singer (Paul Sorvino) wants to reclaim the affections of Gracie (Janet Sarno), whom he had loved and lost eighteen years before. The local fruit peddler (Leonard D'John) aspires to movie stardom. The appropriately named Fat the Miser (Hy Anzell) wants to go to bed with an equally obese neighborhood woman (Rose Roffman).

There are so many homely hopes to be enumerated that the evening is well gone before the playwright can get around to dashing them. Mr. La Russo tries to wrap things up fast by abruptly injecting his drama with bizarre plot twists. Two characters are murdered, another attempts rape, one man suddenly learns he has terminal cancer and a teenage boy discovers he is illegitimate. Given the play's generally soppy tone, such lurid developments are not so much tragic as absurd.

For all this frantic activity, the actors do not have much to play. Since almost everyone on stage has a heart full of gold and a mind of mush, the performances range from broad to broader. Most of the time, the cast must recite truisms that announce the play's point of view rather than dramatize it. The first act isn't even half over before someone laments that "maybe we expected too much and we dreamt too hard." From there it's on to such lines as "No matter what we do, we all end up alone" and "The smart people are the ones who know how to survive."

Mr. Sorvino fares a bit better than the rest of the crowd by underplaying when possible; as the play's director, he manages to keep the busy traffic moving efficiently through Dick Young's authentic-looking set. Yet the only truthful moment of the evening occurs when Mr. Anzell announces to the assembled that "in twenty-five years, it'll all look like a big joke." Who needs to wait twenty-five years?

≡ *This was my first review for the* Times *and the only show I ever reviewed at a dinner theater—in the incongruous setting of SoHo. Even now I feel as if I hallucinated the whole experience. It was pouring rain, I took the wrong subway and ended up sprinting across deserted streets in lower Manhattan to a theater I never saw or heard of again after this night.*

I had been assigned this review to begin a long apprenticeship as sort of a floating theater, movie, and TV critic—with an eventual expectation I'd do theater full-time and maybe someday succeed Walter Kerr. I was halfway through writing this piece when I was summoned into the office of the editor who'd hired me, Arthur Gelb, and told that I was being immediately assigned to theater full-time because Walter had taken seriously ill the night before. It was the height of the season, and I soon found myself in a baptism by fire, reviewing big Broadway shows in tandem with the second-string drama critic, Mel Gussow.

BARNUM
St. James Theatre, May 1, 1980

Is there anything that Jim Dale can't do? Mr. Dale, who roared into town last night in a new musical called *Barnum,* is not your everyday song-and-dance man. Oh, he sings just fine—in the bright style of the old British music hall—and he can kick up his legs until his feet nearly collide with his forehead. But, for this fellow, such gifts are merely a point of departure. During the course of a busy evening, Mr. Dale shows off enough tricks to make all but a Houdini dizzy. He leaps from a trampoline, he rides a unicycle, he walks a tightrope, he conducts a marching band, he dons a carrot-colored wig and plays the clown. Yet his best stunt may be the simplest of them all. When the curly-haired Mr. Dale comes forward to address the audience, his arms spread wide as if to embrace the St. James Theatre's entire second balcony, he immediately transforms a gargantuan circus of a show into his own joyous playpen. This man can create magic—the magic of infectious charm— even on those rare occasions when he's standing still.

With a human wonder like Mr. Dale all about, it would be ungracious to belabor the shortcomings of the musical that tries (not too hard) to contain him. *Barnum* has plenty of other virtues besides its star, but, to get the bad news out of the way fast, it doesn't have a book. Mark Bramble, the writer, tries to create a sympathetic portrait of P. T. Barnum, the nineteenth-century circus man and self-styled Prince of Humbug, and he tries to use show business as an all-purpose metaphor for the vagaries of life. But such shades of, respectively, *The Music Man* and *Gypsy* don't amount to much, and neither does the half-hearted love triangle on which Mr. Bramble hangs his story. In *Barnum,* the mercifully brief libretto—or the tattered scraps that remain of it—is but stitching designed to yank us from one musical number to the next.

Given the numbers, we certainly don't mind being yanked. Cy Coleman, the composer, is in top form. Having flirted with operetta in *On the Twentieth Century,* he has now returned to the snazzy showbiz idiom of *Little Me* and *I Love My Wife. Barnum* simply bursts with melodies— ballads, marches, ragtime strut numbers, burlesque turns—and they have been orchestrated to raise the rafters by the incomparable Hershy Kay. (They are also gamely conducted by Peter Howard, who often finds his band disbanded into every pocket of the theater.)

Perhaps Michael Stewart's lyrics are a bit prosaic—rainbow colors and that sort of thing—but since he has no legitimate characters to write for, he can't be blamed for supplying all-purpose words. Besides, one of the unspoken advantages of writing the score for a bookless musical is that almost every song can be plucked from the show's context and sung in a saloon.

For Joe Layton, the director-choreographer, the principal mission of the evening is to keep the numbers whizzing by as fast as possible. Too many pauses might deflate the whole precariously balanced enterprise. Mr. Layton, whose last effort was the funereal *Platinum,* seems to have studied up on Gower Champion in the interim (notably the Champion of *Carnival!*). His staging is a veritable riot of sleight-of-hand effects. He not only keeps his company changing in and out of a seemingly endless supply of vivid Theoni V. Aldredge costumes, but he also has them swing on ropes, fall through midair, and charge through the audience streaming balloons, handbills, and confetti. Only in the middle of the second act, when Mr. Bramble bids adieu to most of his ostensible characters and unveils a political subplot, does the energy noticeably flag.

One of the by-products of Mr. Layton's Herculean efforts is to make a cast of nineteen seem about a hundred strong. While Mr. Dale may account for about half of that number, some talented supporting players do emerge. Glenn Close, as the earthbound wife who unaccountably wants Barnum to get a factory job, is a winning partner to Mr. Dale in two duets. There are also spirited contributions from Marianne Tatum, as a rich-voiced Jenny Lind, and Terri White, as the springiest 160-year-old gospel singer one might ever hope to see. Leonard John Crofoot, the show's inevitable Tom Thumb, hoofs up a storm to a song with the perhaps inevitable title of "Bigger Isn't Better." Mr. Crofoot is nimble, but no midget, and how *Barnum* reduces him to the proper stature is one of the show's wittier gags.

If there is anyone who deserves to share Mr. Dale's star billing, however, it is the designer, David Mitchell. His circus-ring set extends above the St. James's proscenium, into the boxes, and then adds a few boxes of its own. There is a candy-striped curtain, yards of red-white-and-blue bunting, and, way back upstage, the glimmer of a mammoth tent. When circumstances require it, Mr. Mitchell is not averse to sending scenery flying from all directions, including the floor. Yet the set is more than a collection of pretty gimcracks. Its roseate, gaslight glow and golden crown of letters spelling out "America" suggest another, deeper entertainment: one that really explores the life and times of P. T. Barnum.

Barnum is not that musical. It is, in its hero's vernacular, a humbug: a relentless flow of acts that provides the illusion of miracles rather than the miracles themselves. But if it is not the greatest show on earth—or even the greatest musical on Forty-fourth Street—*Barnum* and its crack ringleader nonetheless deliver an evening of pure, exhilarating fun.

≣ *This was the first "big"—i.e., highly publicized—Broadway show I reviewed. I later heard that* Barnum *had had enormous problems during previews, and that word of mouth on it had been poor, and that therefore my review had demonstrated to the industry that I didn't know what I was talking about. But, having watched so many productions go through grow-*

ing pains as they tried out in Washington when I was a child, I knew that most shows were a mess in their earliest stages. Which is why the word of mouth is bad for virtually every show in previews—and why I tried not to hear about it and always disregarded it. As for Barnum, *it became a hit, running two years.*

A COUPLA WHITE CHICKS
SITTING AROUND TALKING
Astor Place Theatre, April 17, 1980

Susan Sarandon and Eileen Brennan are having such a terrific time down at the Astor Place Theatre that it would be a pity not to join them. The occasion of the actresses' merriment is a very slight but often very funny play that goes by the overly cute, if descriptive, title of *A Coupla White Chicks Sitting Around Talking.* John Ford Noonan, the author of the evening, does not have much of import to say, but when Ms. Sarandon and Ms. Brennan talk, we listen. By turning idle cleverness into comic plunder, these two women have made Mr. Noonan the luckiest playwright in town.

At first *White Chicks* appears to be a cross between the old J. D. Salinger story about confessional housewives, "Uncle Wiggily in Connecticut," and an unusually smart sitcom. It ends up as a vaguely feminist retread of *The Odd Couple.* Set entirely in a well-equipped Westchester kitchen (spiffily designed by Charles Cosler), the play describes a loquacious week in the life of two sharply contrasting housewives. Maude (Ms. Sarandon) is a no-nonsense, straight-laced WASP who is governed by the precepts of *House and Garden* magazine. Hannah Mae (Ms. Brennan) is a vulgar, sexed-up émigré from Austin, Tex., who has just moved in next door. At first grudgingly, and then wholeheartedly, these two opposites become the best of friends. Along the way, you can be certain that the life-embracing Hannah Mae indoctrinates the uptight Maude on the pleasures of carnal abandon.

What prevents Mr. Noonan's play from soaring is not the familiarity of the materials, but his inability to dip beneath the surface of his characters. Hannah Mae seems the genuine article—a good-hearted Sunbelt slattern—but her underlying loneliness is grafted on rather than dramatically earned. She is a character who has been written far more insightfully by Preston Jones and James McClure [in their Texas plays]. Mr. Noonan's caricatured rendition of the more genteel Maude comes right out of such facile television shows as *Soap*. A few stereotypical buzz-words—Book-of-the-Month Club, tag sale, *Scruples*, League of Women Voters—do not a dreary suburban matron define.

Within these self-imposed limits, however, Mr. Noonan is quite a skillful jokesmith. He has a fine ear for language, a knack for the throw-away line, and a sense of timing that is pretty much faultless. None of this goes unnoticed by the director, Dorothy Lyman, who has given *White Chicks* a highly slick finish. The production's only flaw is the stars' occasional self-indulgent tendency—which should be checked at once—to point up their own gags.

Hannah Mae is the showier role, and who knows better what to do with a showy role than Ms. Brennan? Wearing a wild array of garish out-fits (some of which could well wallpaper a tropical nightclub) and drip-ping in costume jewelry (all of which jingle-jangles), this actress is a Vesuvius of rebel yells and outlandish homespun wisdom. Ms. Brennan, who once upon a time sang soprano in musicals, now delivers lines in a rasp so gravelly it may soon turn to concrete. Yesteryear's Little Mary Sunshine is rapidly evolving into a delightfully horsey, latter-day Ruth Gordon.

An even greater revolution is Ms. Sarandon. For those of us who as-sociate her with dreary roles in dreary movies, the actress we see in *White Chicks* comes as a shock. Ms. Sarandon, it turns out, is a rubber-faced comedienne with considerable resources of both charm and craft. It is worth seeing *White Chicks* just to watch her explode. One of the ex-plosions begins the play: As Maude folds laundry and bakes cookies to the beat of the Rolling Stones' "Gimme Shelter," the sallow, bored housewife slowly but exponentially transforms her dull daily routine into a hilarious, closet disco fantasy. It is topped later on when the newly lib-erated Maude dons a smashing red dress and does a deliriously sexy jig of victory on the wreckage of her own kitchen. However transitory the other merits of *White Chicks*, it's a sure thing that Ms. Sarandon is here to stay.

SUNDAY ESSAY: NICHOLS AND MAY IN VIRGINIA WOOLF
NEW HAVEN, MAY 4, 1980

It is the happiest possible reunion. Here, after far too many years of waiting, are Mike Nichols and Elaine May—finally together again, alive and well, on the very same stage. They look pretty much as we remember them, too. Maybe Mr. Nichols has been dealt a few curves by middle age, but he still has those eyes whose mad glint belies the innocence of his deadpan cherub's face. Maybe Ms. May has gained a few facial shadows, but her curly mane is still pleasingly unkempt and her body remains a triumph of angularity; she is a Jules Feiffer cartoon woman sprung to life.

Just seeing these two performers in the same place at the same time, we involuntarily start playing back some of the funniest bits in the canon of modern cabaret humor. We imagine Ms. May, as the most metallic-voiced of telephone operators, depriving a lost motorist of his very last dime. We hear Mr. Nichols, as the most fatuous of late-night talk-show hosts, questioning the starlet "Barbara Musk" about her very close friendship with "Albie" Schweitzer.

But no. This legendary pair has not reunited to ply us with all their old, cherished routines or to bring back the glory days of Second City; indeed, they have not even come back as the comedy team of Nichols and May. When the lights come up on the stage at New Haven's Long Wharf Theatre, the couple are inhabiting one of the most famous of theatrical living rooms. For a six-week run that is scheduled to conclude next Sunday, Mr. Nichols and Ms. May are playing George and Martha in Edward Albee's *Who's Afraid of Virginia Woolf?*

No wonder, then, that the audience's initial feelings of delight soon give way to morbid curiosity. Except for occasional, brief appearances, this pair has not been a team since they went off to pursue separate Broadway and Hollywood careers in the early sixties. They have never acted together in a play in New York. But what really makes their reemergence at the Long Wharf seem audacious is their choice of vehicle—not to mention what they do with it.

One might picture Mr. Nichols and Ms. May trying out a comedy of their own invention, or maybe having a go at a *Plaza Suite* or *Same Time, Next Year.* Instead they have plunged right into a demanding classic of the American theater. *Virginia Woolf* is not a play built for two slumming stars on an ego trip; indeed, anyone who undertakes it now—even in New Haven, far from the glare of Broadway—is asking to be measured against a formidable corps of illustrious predecessors. What's more, a new George and Martha must contend with the problem of the work's familiarity. Is it still possible for any actors to make *Virginia Woolf* seem fresh?

Mr. Albee's lethal drama has had quite a lively history over the past eighteen years. The original production, directed by Alan Schneider and starring Uta Hagen and Arthur Hill, was one of the pivotal events of post–World War II theatrical history. Though Mr. Albee had had success as the Off Broadway author of such avant-garde playlets as *The Zoo Story* and *The American Dream,* no one quite expected his first full-length drama to turn out the way it did. In one bold stroke, the writer seemed to inherit the mantle of Eugene O'Neill. He had written his own and original *Long Day's Journey into Night*: an alcohol-fueled, psychological striptease that revealed all the rage of a battling couple while simultaneously upholding that marriage's right to exist.

It was an exhausting, lacerating, and, for many, shocking night of theater. Mr. Albee had not only presented an extraordinarily corrosive view of modern marital bliss, but he had used rough language that was new to Broadway. Some audiences—and critics—had trouble getting past the four-letter words, especially those that came out of Ms. Hagen's mouth. The reviewer for New York's largest circulation newspaper [John Chapman of the *Daily News*] suggested that Mr. Albee be "taken out behind the literary woodshed and spanked." The Pulitzer Prize committee, despite protests, chose to withhold an award for drama rather than bestow one on a play that some of its members apparently regarded as "dirty."

Other theatergoers debated different aspects of *Virginia Woolf* that seem equally arcane now. Were George and Martha named after George and Martha Washington, and, if so, what did that mean? (Only a few years ago Mr. Albee disingenuously attempted to clear up this matter by telling an interviewer that his play actually was "an examination of whether or not we, as a society, have failed the principles of the American revolution.") Did the couple actually have a son or not? (They did not.) Were the characters disguised homosexuals? (The latter question, when answered yes, allowed heterosexuals to view the play from a very safe remove; it was like saying that Willy Loman's tragedies are the occupational hazards of traveling salesmen.)

When the film version of *Virginia Woolf,* minus a few deleted expletives, appeared in 1965, the reaction and debates were not much different, although they were more widespread. The director of the movie, of course, was Mike Nichols, in his debut as a filmmaker. Since Mr. Nichols had only directed comedies on Broadway, and since his adaptation starred Richard Burton and Elizabeth Taylor, purists feared that he would gut the power of the original. For the most part, he did not. The movie was shot, with self-conscious gravity, in black and white, and the stars did not deviate markedly from the tone of the original production's characterizations. Yet, in retrospect, Mr. Nichols did somewhat bring out the play's wit, which had been present but not dominant on stage. Ms. Taylor's game performance, looked at today, is funnier than one remembers. At the time, it was so surprising to see a movie goddess gray her hair and speak rudely that the shock effect largely neutralized her lighter moments.

By the time Mr. Albee directed the play himself, on Broadway in 1976, it was no longer possible to duplicate the impact of the Hagen-Hill and Taylor-Burton versions. The drama's once-inflammatory vision and language had long since been absorbed by American popular culture. Mr. Albee's promise as a writer had faded; the novel dramatic techniques of his best play had become the common currency of such hits as Mart Crowley's *The Boys in the Band* and Jason Miller's *That Championship Season*. But Mr. Albee did have a new and somewhat incendiary idea: He gave the drama an unusually playful production. Colleen Dewhurst's Martha was a savvy, sexy earth mother; as her victim, Ben Gazzara was wry and at times jocular. There were more laughs than anyone had found in *Virginia Woolf* before, or at least enough to put a fresh face on an otherwise standard, and somewhat becalmed, reading of the play.

As visitors to the Long Wharf have been discovering, Mike Nichols and Elaine May have decided to go Mr. Albee at least one better. Hardly do the lights come up than the audience is laughing as hard as it would at any production of *Same Time, Next Year*. Without altering a line of the text, the stars transform a Strindbergian duel of the sexes into a knock-out battle of wits.

And though it's impossible not to be unsettled by this production at first, any fears that this *Virginia Woolf* might be a vanity show soon subside. The actors are in character. When Mr. Nichols tells Ms. May that "there isn't an abomination award you haven't won," we begin to see the impotent anger of a defeated associate professor in New Carthage College's history department. Martha's swift rejoinder—"If you existed, I'd divorce you"—comes back with such a guttural snap that we immediately accept Ms. May as the barracuda daughter of the college's iron-fisted president. The precise comic rhythms are not just the practiced style of two comedians; they testify to the long years that George and Martha have spent united in unholy wedlock. It's as if Mr. Albee had consciously set out to write the ultimate Nichols and May routine back in 1962.

But, of course, he didn't, and this new reading subtly but dramatically alters the play's meaning. Now, as in years past, Mr. Nichols and Ms. May remain accomplices in comic mayhem; they are just too jocular to be aiming Mr. Albee's darts at each other. So they shoot them instead at their dreary nocturnal guests: the square junior faculty member Nick (James Naughton) and his dim wife, Honey (Swoosie Kurtz). If Mr. Nichols has a nasty expletive to deliver, he lobs it like a tennis ball right into Honey's court. (When it lands, Ms. Kurtz lets loose with a squeal.) Ms. May's periodic carnal taunts leave her partner unperturbed, but send Mr. Naughton reeling.

The play's first act sustains this approach with no apparent strain. Yet, as the evening wears on, the laughs are not really there to be had and we find ourselves getting a bit hungrier for blood: Martha and George do declare "total war" on each other eventually; adultery, humiliation, and other cruel forms of psychological brutality are their chosen weapons. After such a hilarious start, we begin to worry if the director, Arvin Brown, and his cast can bring about the necessary shift of dramatic gears. It is not for nothing that Mr. Albee titles his last two acts "Walpurgisnacht" and "The Exorcism."

At first this difficult transition is cleverly negotiated. The second act works quite well in its own peculiar way. Since George and Martha still refuse to go for each other's throats, the focus switches almost entirely to their victims. The director finesses the shift by providing the Nick and Honey of one's dreams. Mr. Naughton complements his hosts' rapid-fire delivery with a slightly doltish lethargy; he is a cool jock who is pushed by constant prodding into anger. He also may be the first Nick ever to capture the character's ambition, boorishness, and casual ruthlessness without falling into clichéd Sammy Glick mannerisms or sacrificing the role's humor. Mr. Naughton's slow-boiling, robustly heterosexual biologist gives a whole new beat to the play.

Once Nick goes into the kitchen to tryst with Martha, it is Ms. Kurtz's turn to let loose with some fireworks. As the soused and sick Honey, she manages miraculously to straddle all the play's moods at once. Her provincial naivete is both appalling and funny, but booze has given her the utter lucidity of the truly mad. Though Honey cannot articulate the source of her sorrow, Ms. Kurtz's grinning fool's face shows us that she has grasped the internal logic of the night's horrors.

And when Mr. Nichols moves in for the kill, dredging up Honey's repressed memories of her long-ago hysterical pregnancy, her pain rises up in a flash and simply tears into the audience. Perched on the couch, Ms. Kurtz first loses control of her limbs and then her voice and then the rest of her torso; her whole body seems to shriek. By the end of Act 2, she is a battered pink pulp, lying in an abandoned heap on the floor. Mr. Nichols, towering above her, arrives at his most powerful moment: His face set in an eerie jack-o'-lantern grin, he announces his chilling plot to wreak final revenge on Martha. Well after the lights go down and plunge him into darkness, we retain the image of the fire rising in his steely eyes.

Unfortunately, once the new day begins to dawn in the last act, this grueling momentum is lost; the exorcism that Mr. Albee promises does not quite materialize. When George finally tells Martha that their fictive son is dead, Mr. Nichols italicizes his lines: He isn't committing a ritual killing, but is instead playing a tart practical joke. When Ms. May retreats into convulsive sobs, the reaction doesn't seem justified; shouldn't she, like us, know that George is only having waspish fun? Her transformation from braying tyrant to fearful, vulnerable child is so well done that the play's final moments are moving anyway. Yet somehow we feel that this George and Martha have never gone, as Mr. Albee puts it, "to the marrow." The emptiness that the dead son symbolizes—and that paradoxically binds this warring couple together—has not been made terrifyingly real.

One could blame the occasional failures of this *Virginia Woolf* on lapses in the performances, but that really would not be fair: On its own terms, the production is almost entirely consistent. What Mr. Brown and his actors have done is face up to the fact that the drama can no longer deliver the same devastating revelations it did in another time. This worldly-wise *Virginia Woolf* seems a concerted effort to find a solution to the problem: What if George and Martha are in fact a happily married couple who play grotesque games merely to while away the night? If such an interpretation robs Mr. Albee's work of some of its emotional power, it pays unexpected dividends as well. Certainly it is hard to feel too cheated at the Long Wharf these nights. We arrive expecting to watch two rusty stand-up comics do a novelty act. We leave having seen four thinking actors shed startling new light on one of the great dark plays of our time.

≡ *This Sunday piece came about when Arthur Gelb stormed into the culture department demanding to know why we weren't reviewing this production, which was widely publicized but off-limits to critics. Informed by an underling that Nichols and May had specifically requested no press coverage, Arthur witheringly asked, "Well, they're selling tickets, aren't they? Buy one." And so we did, albeit well into the run, after the show presumably had found its footing.*

SECOND SEASON

1980—81

Jane Seymour, Ian McKellen, and Tim Curry in *Amadeus*

Dale is an attractive young Chinese American who has made it in golden Los Angeles. He's not rich, he explains, but he is definitely "upper middle." He has mastered the art of ordering hors d'oeuvres at Scandia and knows just where to hang out in West Hollywood. Late at night, he takes his hot sports car out on the Ventura Freeway, downshifts, and flies with the wind. Still, it hasn't been easy for Dale to escape the "yellow ghosts" of his childhood. "My parents tried to cage me up in their Chineseness," Dale says. "I had to work hard to be a human being just like everybody else."

FOB, the new play at the Public Theater, tells what happens when Dale must confront the ethnic roots he thought he had severed. The subject of the evening is a very old one: the price that minorities pay to assimilate in mainstream America. But David Henry Hwang, the play's twenty-two-year-old author, is too rambunctious to tell a familiar story in a tired way. In *FOB*, he deals with three distinct cultures, Chinese American, American, and Chinese, and writes in at least that many theatrical styles. Though the result is an unwieldy, at times spotty work, Mr. Hwang hits home far more often than he misses. Surely, *FOB* is the first show that has ever attempted to marry the conventional well-made play to Oriental theater and to mix the sensibilities of Maxine Hong Kingston and Norman Lear.

The clashes unfold in the backroom of a grungy Chinese restaurant, where Dale (Calvin Jung) has come to while away an evening with his cousin Grace (Ginny Yang), a journalism student at the University of California at Los Angeles. Dale is rather nonplussed to discover that Grace's date for the night is an FOB, a "fresh off the boat" immigrant named Steve (John Lone). Dale doesn't think much of FOBs. Indeed, he regards them as "clumsy, ugly, greasy, loud, stupid," the sort of losers who congregate at community colleges and Bee Gees concerts. And

Steve is more than willing to live down to Dale's expectations. He bows and scrapes like a B-movie coolie, grins idiotically, and speaks only in broken English malaprop. When Dale tries to give Steve helpful lessons in how to carry himself like John Travolta, the FOB seems more inclined to emulate Olivia Newton-John.

Yet if Steve is an FOB, he's no fool. His behavior is but a pose designed to taunt and challenge his complacent antagonist. Away from Dale, Steve is a regal, eloquent man who regards himself as an exiled Chinese god of "warriors, writers, and prostitutes." Although his own past is somewhat conflicted—his father was a souvenir tycoon in Hong Kong—he refuses to give up the legacy of yellow ghosts for the materialistic promises of white ones. In a community full of ABC's, or American-born Chinese, clad in leisure suits and blue jeans, he would rather maintain his "fobbishness."

Mr. Hwang describes the communications gap between Steve and Dale with true comic verve. In the hilarious climax of Act 1, the men try to one-up each other by seeing who can stomach the largest doses of Szechuan hot sauce. Dale regards spicy food as low-class and refers to Chinese pancakes as "those Burrito things."

Other aspects of *FOB* are sketchy. Though sensitively played by Ms. Yang, Grace is not fully written: She is supposed to be torn between the poles represented by the men, but more often she just seems vague. In Act 2, the playwright attempts a daring gamble that doesn't quite pay off. He swings away from Western naturalism by having his characters act out their subconscious mythological fantasies as full-blown Chinese theater. This literal reconciliation of past and present makes sense intellectually, but it has not yet been artfully woven into the body of the play.

The production, which is abetted by Lucia Hwong's native music and Mr. Lone's martial choreography, could not be better. As Dale, Mr. Jung creates a complex striver who is appealing and intelligent as well as snide; Mr. Lone is a whirlwind of graceful energy as the alternately farcical and commanding title character.

The director of the evening is Mako, best known to New York audiences for his performance in the musical *Pacific Overtures*. Here, he brings sharp timing to the play's American comic rhythms and precise visual imagery to its Oriental theatrics. If West and East don't precisely meet in *FOB*, they certainly fight each other to a fascinating standoff.

≡ *So began the New York career of the very young David Henry Hwang (which would reach a peak with* M. Butterfly) *and the acting career of John Lone (later to be discovered by the movies and to play the title role in*

Bertolucci's The Last Emperor). *Here was Joseph Papp's multiculturalism at its most inspired. A more typical Papp stunt of cross-cultural shake and bake, intriguing but wrong-headed, is described below.* (For a career retrospective of this most influential of New York producers, see "Joseph Papp, The Last of the One-Man Shows," page 824.)

SUNDAY ESSAY: AN AFRICAN AMERICAN MOTHER COURAGE

JUNE 15, 1980

When it comes to sheer guts, no play this season can beat the new version of Bertolt Brecht's *Mother Courage and Her Children* at the Public. Director Wilford Leach has staged an elaborate and iconoclastic revival: The cast is black, and the script has been adapted from Brecht by the African American playwright Ntozake Shange. About the production, which ends its run today, there will be no quibbles here. Who wouldn't want to see Gloria Foster and Morgan Freeman play all the great roles in theatrical literature? This *Mother Courage* features some of the best actors, black or white, in New York; they give the play a passionate reading.

But what play are they doing? The text of Ms. Shange's *Mother Courage* amounts to a whole new show, and it raises some troubling questions. What are an adapter's responsibilities to the original work? What are a playwright's obligations to history? Is it right to call a play *Mother Courage* when it in many ways violates the spirit of the drama we associate with that title? The motivations behind Ms. Shange's adaptation may well be pure, but the result is a case study of what can happen when an exercise in literary adaptation goes wildly astray.

Certainly the adaptation cannot be objected to in principle. Brecht would have approved; he was fond of rewriting classic theatrical texts himself. And certainly Ms. Shange, the author of *For Colored Girls,* would seem the ideal candidate to redo *Mother Courage.* Like Brecht, she is a poet with a radicalized political consciousness. It can even be argued that Ms. Shange is entitled to move the play's setting from seventeenth-century Middle Europe to another time and place; it all depends on how and why the relocation is done. By resetting Brecht's play in post–Civil War America and making the title character an emancipated slave, Ms. Shange has landed in a quagmire. She ends up betraying Brecht and distorting American history.

To understand what has gone wrong in Ms. Shange's *Mother Courage* it helps to remember the original. Shameful as it seems, *Mother Courage* has had only one other major local production since Brecht wrote it in 1939, and that was the short-lived Jerome Robbins staging (with Anne Bancroft and Barbara Harris) in 1963. Even so, the play lives on as a classic of the modern repertory. By telling the story of Mother Courage and the adventures of her three children on the fringes of the Thirty Years' War, Brecht created a damning picture of capitalism's spiritual ravages at their most extreme.

Mother Courage is a small-time businesswoman who runs a wagon canteen. She survives a holocaust by exploiting both war and peace, victors and vanquished, for modest financial sustenance. She is neither villain nor heroine, but is, as Brecht put it, "a great living contradiction." Though she will do anything to assure her children's survival, she nonetheless loses her two sons when she haggles too long over business deals. And yet she just can't help herself. In her world, profiteering is the only game in town, the only way to feed her family. She is the ultimate product of a bankrupt status quo: The system has stripped her of the right to make moral choices and stripped her human virtues of their meaning. As the critic Richard Gilman has written, Mother Courage's final trudge forward at the end of the play is no cause for celebration: She is "a survivor only in the narrowest bodily sense."

Such is the depth of Brecht's ironic vision that *Mother Courage* easily transcends simple categorizations; it's not just an antiwar play or a Marxist tract or a tribute to the human spirit.

Ms. Shange's version is another matter: The antiwar aspects are muted, the Marxism is skewed, sentimentality is embraced, and a bizarre element of antiblack propaganda is thrown into the mix. Much of this stems from Ms. Shange's strange choice of wars. Her *Mother Courage* is set in the Southwest territories of 1866–77, and it principally concerns a disconnected series of skirmishes in which American troops completed the clearing of the West by slaughtering the Indians.

In contrast to Brecht's Thirty Years' War—a religious struggle waged by equally culpable antagonists who together wreaked havoc on a helpless peasantry—the battles of Ms. Shange's play are conflicts involving clearly defined good guys and bad guys. This immediately alters Brecht's point in a substantial way. In his *Mother Courage*, war (or, for that matter, peace) is a meaningless state that serves no purpose except to perpetuate a malevolent ruling class. It doesn't matter which side Mother Courage has financial dealings with, for both sides are the enemy. Everyone is out to grind her down; she is the trapped, innocent victim of an entire system.

In Ms. Shange's version, Mother Courage is thrust into a class and racial war where the antagonists are anything but interchangeable. The bad guys are the government soldiers, the ruling class, and their victims are a defenseless proletariat, the Indians. As a result, Ms. Shange's protagonist, unlike Brecht's, does have a moral choice. And for her Mother Courage, the choice should be clear; she has, after all, just lived through the Civil War. If she now does business with the oppressive Army, she is a villain; if she refuses, she is a heroic resister. Either way, Brecht's complex work is transformed into a simplistic melodrama about right and wrong.

Worse still, Ms. Shange's Mother Courage, as well as her two sons, capitulate to the bad guys. The sons (one of whom is half-Indian, no less) join up with the Colored Cavalry—the so-called Buffalo Soldiers who were recruited by whites to fight against the Indians—and the mother does business with their superiors. While these actions parallel the text of the original play, their meaning becomes quite different in the context Ms. Shange has chosen. When Brecht's Mother Courage says "in business you ask what price, not what religion," it is a nihilistic fact of life. When Ms. Shange's Mother Courage, at the same point in the play, implies that she would just as soon trade with rebel whites as anyone else, she is consciously siding against her own interests. She is no longer a pawn of historical forces beyond her control but an active counterrevolutionary siding with whites against her own people.

Perhaps Ms. Shange would insist that her Mother Courage had to capitulate to whites to survive, just as Brecht's Mother Courage had to serve all comers to keep going. But is it really true that freed slaves, in the aftermath of the Civil War, had no option but to become collaborators in a new campaign of white genocide against the Indians? It would take a rather jaundiced reading of American history to claim so.

Some blacks did, of course, join the Buffalo Soldiers. But during part of the time that Ms. Shange's play covers, many more were active participants in Reconstruction governments in much of the South. When blacks later lost their freedom to a new, white supremacist South, it was not because the former slaves abandoned their democratic ideals for easy cash or because they left the South to fight Indians out West. The blacks' government was taken away from them—by whites—in a violent spree of vigilantism. As W.E.B. Du Bois wrote in *Black Reconstruction*, "The white laborer joined the white landholder and capitalist and beat the black laborer into subjection through secret organizations and the rise of a new doctrine of race hatred." In Ms. Shange's *Mother Courage*, such a secret organization, the Ku Klux Klan, finally does show up (in the next-to-last scene)—and Mother Courage's daughter valiantly warns a neighboring black town of their arrival—but by then we've had an entire evening of watching cowardly blacks sell themselves out to white interests for simple expediency's sake.

To fulfill her mission of resetting *Mother Courage* in black America, Ms. Shange seems to have seized on some events that superficially correspond to those of Brecht's play without carefully considering how those events would square with the true meaning of the original text. Once the events were chosen, they became an idée fixe from which she refused to depart. By grafting far-from-representative black sellouts on to the epic theater of *Mother Courage,* Miss Shange has condemned a whole generation of black people by inference. If a white had written this play, he would have, quite rightfully, been accused of racism.

If Ms. Shange had reshaped the entire work, she might have solved some of these problems. But she has not done that; she has only retranslated the play into black English. Perhaps if there were major white characters in this *Mother Courage*—her versions of Du Bois's landowners and capitalists or the greedy bigots of Lillian Hellman's *The Little Foxes*—we could see why some blacks did have no choice but to become collaborators with their enemy. This fact can't be explained away by the social system dramatized in Brecht's play—which is still the only one to be found in Ms. Shange's version—because the system that prevailed in the Thirty Years' War is not an accurate description of Reconstruction America. So confusing is Ms. Shange's mixture of Brecht and Indian wars that on the night I saw her play, an audience of blacks and whites was actually cheering Mother Courage at the end. This shouldn't happen in an honest production of Brecht's drama—one that upholds the writer's so-called "alienation effect"—and it certainly shouldn't happen in Ms. Shange's version, where Mother Courage is demonstrably evil.

However much the audience might blamelessly misread it in the theater, it seems that Ms. Shange really did set out to concoct a *Mother Courage* that vilified its central characters. In an article in *The Village Voice* of May 19, she says so: "My *Mother Courage* begins with the first thirty years of struggle by the first mass of freed slaves to become American, the first thirty years of our culpability in the genocidal activities of the cavalry, the exploitation of non-English speaking peoples, the acceptance of the primacy of the dollar. If I must come to terms with being a descendant of imperialist assimilationists who were willing if not eager to murder and destroy other people of color, in the name of a flag that represents only white folks, then let me use a vehicle conceived in the heartland of one of history's most cruel ideologies, Nazism."

According to this historical perspective, a *Mother Courage* about Jews of the Nazi era would be one that focused on the handful of Jews who survived the death camps by collaborating with their captors; a *Mother Courage* about blacks who fought in the Vietnam war would focus on those gung-ho black GI's who survived by piling up the largest Vietnamese body counts. By all means there are plays to be written about such people, and Ms. Shange might write a great one. But *Mother Courage* is not that play.

Perhaps the writer's true modus operandi is revealed elsewhere in the same piece, where she says that her choice of *Mother Courage* for adaptation was "arbitrary" (from a list that also included *Death of a Salesman, Cat on a Hot Tin Roof,* and *Marat/Sade*) and that her intention was to attack the "oppressive authority figure" of white culture by making a "demon classic bend to my will." She adds that by tackling Brecht she would also resolve a personal dilemma: She had forgotten about her own work and was involved "in fruitless combat with myself" about "the works of dead white men." On this point she is entirely right. Such combat is fruitless. A black writer indeed has no obligation to answer to white writers, living or dead, and for Ntozake Shange it seems a waste of talent and energy to do so.

CRITIC'S NOTEBOOK: WHAT MAKES A PLAY SEEM DATED?

JULY 6, 1980

Revivals aren't merely a trend this season; they're a flood. They just keep coming, and not even the summer can slow them down. In the past few weeks, *Look Back in Anger, The Man Who Came to Dinner,* and *The Sound of Music* have been added to a roster of golden oldies that already accounts for a lion's share of the current shows in town. Nor is a letup anywhere in sight: Richard Burton returns in *Camelot* this week, and new productions of *My Fair Lady, Brigadoon,* and *Can Can* are promised for next season. There's nothing wrong with this revival fever, I guess, although an overdose of nostalgia can be disorienting. See two vintage shows on one Saturday, and you may well go home wondering why orchestra seats no longer cost five dollars and Jimmy Walker isn't still Mayor.

If this season's large-scale revivals have one trait in common, it's that most of them cannot rightfully be considered classics. Producers are not bringing us big new productions of Shakespeare and Chekhov, but are instead remounting the relatively recent Broadway hits (and, at times, flops) of the 1930s, forties, fifties, and early sixties. And that's a tricky matter. In this restless century, nothing dates faster than fashions in popular, commercial art. Last year's rage—whether in theater, music, movies, television, or fiction—can often prove to be next year's crashing, embarrassing bore. As Ira Levin wittily puts it in *Deathtrap,* "Nothing recedes like success."

Not all of the current revivals have aged badly, of course, and even those shows that do look a bit geriatric have their charms. But it is fascinating, and at times startling, to see what holds up and what does not. The old plays now on view rely heavily—and often exclusively—on theatrical conventions, social customs, and sociological issues that are indigenous to the periods when they were originally produced. As those periods fade into history, the plays can age exponentially. Sometimes one aspect of a drama can erode before another: Style and content don't necessarily disintegrate at the same rate. Sometimes a musical, like *Peter Pan* or especially *Oklahoma!,* can camouflage its anachronisms with a score full of good songs. Still, in one way or another, for better or for worse, time has warped all the current revivals into new and often peculiar shapes.

West Side Story and *Look Back in Anger* are among the youngest shows being revived, and, oddly enough, they have undergone the greatest sea change. It's hard to believe it now, but both were considered rather revolutionary works when they first arrived in New York in 1957. In *Anger,* the British playwright John Osborne was releasing a howl of rage. His drama was designed to savage the genteel British theater of his day, as well as the floundering, antiquated, bankrupt society that he held responsible for that theater. The young American collaborators who created *West Side Story* had a related intent. By placing angry, alienated teenagers—rougher, New York versions of Mr. Osborne's hero, Jimmy Porter—at the center of a musical, they hoped to shake up the dramatic and stylistic traditions of Broadway's generally lightweight song-and-dance shows.

Looked at today, these works often seem not so much angry as quaint. Indeed, for me, Mr. Osborne's play almost looks benign. Jimmy Porter's mocking tirades against the legacy of Edwardian England, against his wife's bourgeois background, against the H-bomb, sound like pretty tame stuff next to the political and theatrical rhetoric that followed in the sixties. Subsequent British dramatists—notably Simon Gray (*Butley*) and Frederic Raphael (*The Glittering Prizes*)—have created far more eloquently bitter protagonists than Mr. Osborne's prototype. Since many of Jimmy's most lacerating speeches are aimed at his wife, his mother-in-

law, and his wife's best female friend, his anger no longer seems motivated by proletarian political conviction but by distasteful, old-style
misogynism. Nor is the language at all shocking by present standards. If
anything, Mr. Osborne's characters seem a little prim: At one point they
waltz around, but refuse to say, the dread word *abortion*. Perhaps some of
the blandness of the play could be blamed on the becalmed production at
the Roundabout, but one wonders: If Malcolm McDowell cannot bring
off Jimmy Porter, who could? Mr. McDowell is a fine actor, and, in movies
like *If . . .* and *A Clockwork Orange*, he has played latter-day incarnations
of Osborne's angry young man to the hilt.

Without that burning rage at its core, one must look for other compen-
sations. Edward Albee's *Who's Afraid of Virginia Woolf?* has also lost some
of its verbal sting, but it survives, as the recent Mike Nichols–Elaine May
revival at the Long Wharf proved, thanks to its profound human comedy.
In the case of *Look Back in Anger,* there isn't much to hold on to. The supporting characters are thin and the dramaturgy is surprisingly creaky and
old-fashioned. In terms of its structure, Mr. Osborne's play is intrinsically
no different from the plays it was revolting against. Much of the action is
propelled by the devices of drawing-room drama—phone calls, telegrams,
sudden revelations of secrets—and its central love triangle is contrived out
of thin air. In retrospect, it seems that the real breakthrough in the British
theater of the late fifties was being brought off by Harold Pinter, whose
first plays (among them, *The Birthday Party* and *The Dumb Waiter*) were
written the same year *Anger* opened in New York.

The language and violence of *West Side Story* have also paled. These
days it's hard for me to imagine how my parents thought this show too
"adult" for an eight-year-old when it passed through Washington, D.C.,
during its original pre-Broadway tryout. In 1980, even daytime television
contains more rude shocks than this musical at its harshest. Time has
also played another, even crueler trick on *West Side Story:* The sociology
and liberal faith of Arthur Laurents's book are now fairly meaningless.
Today's audiences no longer see juvenile delinquency as a rumble between white-ethnic and Puerto Rican street gangs; we no longer feel that
ghetto tragedies can be overcome by pleas for tolerance and understanding.

Even so, I think the show's creators have performed a great service by
refusing to update it for present-day audiences. For one thing, an intricate musical falls apart with too much tinkering—as was demonstrated
a few years back by the rewritten, all-black, disco-orchestrated revival of
Guys and Dolls. But, more important, we have the rare opportunity—
maybe our last opportunity—to see Jerome Robbins's original staging as

re-created by the choreographer himself. However dated the story it serves, Mr. Robbins's work looks as farsighted now as ever. Maybe even more so.

It's not the individual show-stopping numbers, good as they are, that had such a radical and lasting impact on the musical theater, but Mr. Robbins's ability to set almost the entire evening to dance movement. To take just one example: When, in Act 1, Maria tries on her new dress, she goes into a twirl of delight that sets the whole show moving. Her friends start to spin with her, streamers fall from above, the set changes (without us really registering it) and suddenly we have joined the entire company in the midst of a big number, "The Dance at the Gym." It's all happened as fluidly and gracefully as a movie dissolve, with none of the awkward transitional dialogue that usually pockmarked pre-Robbins musicals. Watching the breakthroughs of *West Side Story* today offers pleasures that weren't available in 1957: We can now see the genesis of the staging techniques used in such subsequent musicals as *A Chorus Line, Sweeney Todd,* and *Evita.*

There were no modern stylistic flourishes in George S. Kaufman and Moss Hart's *The Man Who Came to Dinner* and Paul Osborn's *Morning's at Seven,* which were, respectively, a huge hit and a respectable flop of the 1939–40 season. These are both traditional, well-made, three-act, one-set comedies written on an elaborate, highly populated scale that not even Neil Simon would attempt these days.

Seeing *The Man Who Came to Dinner* now, the transparency of the thirties screwball comedy technique comes to the fore. When Kaufman and Hart have such unlikely goods as penguins and a mummy case delivered to the Stanley household in Ohio, we know darn well they're laying comic booby traps. As a result, it's impossible to respond to these gags with the innocent delight that audiences did forty years ago. During Act 1 of *The Man Who Came to Dinner*—as in Act 1 of BAM's recent revival of Charles MacArthur's 1942 *Johnny on a Spot*—we wait somewhat impatiently for the playwrights to set all their jokes in motion. When the punch lines finally pay off, as they do at the end of Acts 2 and 3, we're treated to a joyful, old-time fireworks display. Maybe we're too sophisticated to believe that fireworks are magic, but the sparks are still bright.

Perhaps the biggest loss in *The Man Who Came to Dinner* is its satirical thrust. Kaufman and Hart were sending up their Algonquin Round Table friends, all of whom were famous then, but not all of whom are well known now. Their title character (played by Ellis Rabb at Circle in the Square) was a thinly disguised stand-in for Alexander Woollcott, and Woollcott even played the role on the road. Noël Coward (Roderick

Cook) and Harpo Marx (Leonard Frey) are also among the play's principal players. The script is forever dropping such celebrity names as William Beebe, Rube Goldberg, Zasu Pitts, Margaret Bourke-White, Jock Whitney, and Judge Crater. As these names cease to be household words, the once-snappy lines that contain them begin to wilt.

If box-office success is any indication, *Morning's at Seven* looks better now than it did in 1939. Not as jokey as the Kaufman-Hart play, it seemed undernourished by comparison a generation ago. Now we don't at all mind the absence of continuous laughter, and the play's sorrowful underpinnings have become more accessible. Mr. Osborn's elderly characters are at once desperately lonely and incapable of articulating their despair; two of them seem to be on the verge of nervous breakdowns. Such pain is just as much a part of life now as it was in 1939, and it's far more openly talked about. The play's vanished setting, a picturesque small town of the 1920s, isn't dated, because the writer's concerns aren't tied to it; *Morning's at Seven* could just as easily take place in a 1980 retirement condominium. Nor is the well-made style of the work a distraction: Mr. Osborn uses the old conventions to reveal the interior lives of his characters rather than to build a perpetual joke machine.

That's why, if I had to guess which one of these revivals might be revived again forty years from now, I'd put my money on *Morning's at Seven*. Political passions, sociological imperatives, and topical gags come and go. The human condition—dramatized simply and honestly—has a way of always looking fresh.

THE PIRATES OF PENZANCE
DELACORTE THEATER, JULY 30, 1980

Yes, the New York Shakespeare Festival's production of *The Pirates of Penzance* does sound crazy. One needn't be an orthodox Savoyard to wonder what two American rock singers, Linda Ronstadt and Rex Smith, are doing smack in the middle of one of Gilbert and Sullivan's most beguiling operettas. Or to wonder why they are surrounded by an eclectic crew of Broadway and West End actors, all belting to the electronic strains of a small, stringless pit band. But if this *Pirates of Penzance* at first seems like a misbegotten ship of fools, I'll be damned if it doesn't sail. If I were you, I'd run to Central Park's Delacorte Theater on your first free moonlit night and save any doubting questions for the morning after.

This may not be a perfect *Penzance* or a purist's *Penzance* or a D'Oyly Carte *Penzance*, but it delivers a dizzying amount of pleasure. The euphoria begins with the first arrival of the pirates' ship, complete with trompe l'oeil fireworks, and rarely subsides until the celebratory, waltz-happy finale. Though Wilford Leach, the director, and William Elliott, the conductor and orchestrator, have kidded around with Gilbert and Sullivan a bit, they have not transformed the show into a rock musical or, God forbid, attempted to update it. In the ways that really count, this production upholds the spirit and often the letter of the original.

The show still glides on Arthur Sullivan's glorious melodies, which are, by turns, lilting, parodistic, and thunderous. W. S. Gilbert's lyrics still dazzle us with their verbal pyrotechnics and sly wit; his libretto's outrageous Dickensian plotting and gentle satirical sallies are all intact. Despite the American accents and the set's crowning co-portraits of Queen Victoria and Rutherford B. Hayes, we are thrust right back into the romantic nineteenth-century England of seafaring mates, helmeted bobbies, and fair, pastel-gowned maidens. If the clever Mr. Leach and his equally witty choreographer, Graciela Daniele, have also thrown in a whiff of twentieth-century burlesque, some silent-movie slapstick, and a ramp right out of Broadway's *Hello, Dolly!*, their whirligig labors are never at war with the text. The show's seemingly ill-matched parts eventually come together to form a crazy quilt of rambunctious merriment. As Gilbert might say, this successful blending of old and new is a most ingenious paradox.

The wild casting, it turns out, is generally first-rate and at times inspired. My childhood memories of latter-day D'Oyly Carte companies are dim, but I wonder if the comic Gilbert and Sullivan leads could have ever been in better hands than they are at the Delacorte. Leading the fray is George Rose, who was born to play "the very model of a modern Major General." He doesn't disappoint. Wearing a white colonial outfit that makes him look like an overdressed croquet player, Mr. Rose stops the show with his tongue-twisting ditty about his vast store of knowledge "vegetable, animal, and mineral." Not only does he enunciate every juicy word, right down to that tricky "commissariat," but he also kicks up his legs like a toy soldier, twirls a red parasol, and prances about the stage in the aristocratically wacky manner of Beatrice Lillie. This man is surely one of the comic treasures of the literate theater.

Kevin Kline, cast as the clumsily swashbuckling Pirate King, at times recalls Mr. Rose's impersonation of Captain Hook in the revival of *Peter Pan*. But Mr. Kline also demonstrates here, as he did in *On the Twentieth Century*, that he is a musical actor of extraordinary gifts. A deft pratfall artist with an ability to convey deadpan innocence, narcissism, and self-deprecating irony at the same time, the handsome, big-voiced Mr. Kline is blessed with the best qualities of Ben Turpin, Errol Flynn, Chevy Chase, and Alfred Drake. As Mr. Kline's sidekick Ruth, that piratical "maid of all work," Patricia Routledge is illuminated by her characteristically daffy, befuddled glee. Like Mr. Rose, she should be embargoed from ever returning to her native England.

You were worrying about the evening's wandering rock stars? Well, I was never too worried about Ms. Ronstadt, especially having heard her crystalline version of Sigmund Romberg's "When I Grow Too Old to Dream" on a recent album. Her wholesome beauty is just right for the moony ingenue, Mabel, and her voice, at least to these untrained ears, can skyrocket. True, she doesn't seem to know the first thing about acting, but acting is not the order of the evening. Once she appears, a lacy vision in white, to sing "Poor Wandering One," it's enough to turn any slave of duty into a slave of love.

Mr. Smith, a bubblegum singer of Top 40 renown, makes up for his limited vocal range by bringing a lot of self-effacing charm to the role of Mabel's naive and proper suitor. He plays Frederic with the perfect note of farcically youthful ardor; his uncomplicated earnestness gives the show its essential sentimental core. But Mr. Smith is more than a straight man: To "Oh, is there not one maiden breast," he adds a teasing, funny taste of Elvis Presley.

The high-spirited supporting cast is often up to the level of the stars, but not always. The female chorus is too campy and vocally brash to handle the quicksilver delights of "Let us gaily tread the measure." The show has other irritants as well, most notably a tinny sound system that wreaks havoc on Ms. Ronstadt's high notes and adds blaring treble to Mr. Elliott's bright orchestrations.

The evening also needs an overture, new or old, and could live without "Sorry Her Lot," an *H.M.S. Pinafore* song that has been gratuitously tossed into Act 2 to provide Ms. Ronstadt with a contemporary-sounding ballad. Another added number—"My Eyes Are Fully Open" from *Ruddigore*—gives Ms. Routledge and Mr. Kline and Mr. Smith a delightful opportunity to match Mr. Rose in the evening's elocutionary sweepstakes.

Mr. Leach and Ms. Daniele are so single-mindedly devoted to fun that their show's occasional lapses hardly matter. When the pirates march on the audience to bellow out "With catlike tread," their vocal and physical dynamism could chase away a hailstorm. When the police sergeant, played by the rubber-limbed and metallic-voiced Tony Azito, leads his cowardly troops in constabulary song, it's as if the Keystone Kops were in collaboration with Jerome Robbins at his most whimsical. When Ms. Ronstadt and Mr. Smith, bathed in the dewy glow of Jennifer Tipton's lighting, exchange the tender "Fa-la, lalas" of "Ah, leave me not to pine," their sweet passion could make a cynic blush. Maybe the New York Shakespeare Festival has forsaken Shakespeare this season, but it has nonetheless given us a rhapsodic midsummer night's dream.

≡ *The Papp–Kevin Kline connection was to be one of the most sustaining partnerships of both the New York Shakespeare Festival and the New York theater in general until—and even a bit after—Papp's death in 1991. Though many actors who make it in the New York theater go to Hollywood rarely to return, from John Barrymore and John Garfield to Meryl Streep and Kathy Bates, Kline was a notable and consistent exception. (When the Festival started to fall into chaos in Papp's wake, Kline dropped everything to come back and undertake one last Shakespearean role.)*

In the winter, Pirates *moved indoors—to Broadway's largest and least commodious house, the Uris (later renamed the Gershwin)—and played surprisingly well, piling up a long run that was later duplicated with another cast in Gilbert and Sullivan's home turf of London. But a movie version directed by Leach and again starring Kline captured none of the magic of the stage show and disappeared within days of its release.*

CRITIC'S NOTEBOOK: KENNETH TYNAN DIES
AUGUST 15, 1980

Of all the beautiful and witty sentences that poured out of Kenneth Tynan, perhaps the one that best emblemized his gift was that famous line of 1956, "I doubt if I could love anyone who did not wish to see *Look Back in Anger*." What makes the sentence so moving, then and now, is its author's passion for the theater he believed in and his ability to convince us that such theater is of life-and-death importance. Since Mr. Tynan was committed to the theater of literacy, of intellectual daring, and of social change, his criticism was invariably a force for good. Since he wrote so well, his reviews have a life apart from the plays that inspired them. To take only one example: Who remembers anything about *Flower Drum Song* these days except that Mr. Tynan called it "a world of woozy song"?

He died July 26 in Los Angeles, his adopted home during the last years of his life. Los Angeles is no theater town, but Mr. Tynan's enthusiasms stretched to encompass the cultural landscape at hand. Out West, he wrote a *New Yorker* profile of Johnny Carson that also amounts to a definitive description of the esthetics of the electronic stage. His lyric love song to Louise Brooks—another *New Yorker* profile collected in the book *Show People*—reclaimed for audiences today both the life and art of a mysterious silent-movie actress. Though Mr. Tynan was desperately ill as he reported and wrote these pieces, who would have guessed? His exuberant prose gave no quarter to his pain.

A few years ago, I had the pleasure of watching Kenneth Tynan hold court to a dinner party at his penultimate home, high in the peach-hued precincts of Beverly Hills. His health was failing, but he still looked like the handsome, youthful Oxford iconoclast of legend. In his airy expatriate's salon, Mr. Tynan rattled off stiletto-sharp observations on such diverse subjects as politics, sex, British royalty, and the sharks of Hollywood. The laughter subsided only when he gently and painstakingly quizzed his younger daughter, then all of ten, on the merits of the current television season. The father treated his child as an equal, and fetchingly enough, she improvised a critical wrap-up in the distinctively eloquent and self-confident Tynan voice.

Since Mr. Tynan's death, his friends—led by Christopher Isherwood, Shirley MacLaine, and Penelope Gilliatt—have memorialized him in Los Angeles. Another service will take place September 18 in London, the city where he first made his reputation and which he liked to shock. A publisher could pay Kenneth Tynan a further tribute by bringing out some of his books—notably the 1961 collection, *Curtains*—that are now out of print. No one who loves the theater should be deprived of any of his words.

≣ *As a child growing up two hundred miles from New York, with at first limited access to the theater, there were two critics I discovered early whom I could count on to tell me what I was missing: Tynan in* The New Yorker *and Walter Kerr, then in the* New York Herald-Tribune. *They were a mutual admiration society, I discovered: In* Curtains, *Tynan wrote (in a 1958 piece) that Kerr was the "cogent best" of Broadway's critics because he combined "a style that is vivid and popular (in the best sense of the word) with a background of scholarship."*

Curtains, sadly, remains out of print. A posthumous effort by Tynan's widow, Kathleen, to republish his reviews in America—which I agreed to edit at her request—never found a publisher before the project was aborted by Kathleen's own illness and death. I also wish Walter's daily reviews— especially the 1963 collection The Theater in Spite of Itself, *written at his and the* Trib's *peak—were back in print; they are a model of newspaper criticism.*

Walter died in 1996. By then I'd long been friends with him and his wife, the writer Jean Kerr. In a Sunday piece for the Times, *I wrote a reminiscence that read in part:*

> Kerr was a critic to race the pulse and make you kill to get a ticket. He was drunk on theater, and, God, could he write. If you wanted to know what it was like to be in a Broadway house on a particular night—the sights, the emotions, the fury, the laughs—then he was your man. . . . Kerr (like Tynan) showed it was possible to write reviews for a mass-circulation publication (even on the barbarously short deadlines he detested) that were neither journalistic hack work nor stuffy academic grade-giving but something fresh and new and pleasurable in themselves. . . .
>
> The *Trib* died in 1966, just as the thriving Broadway that Kerr had chronicled began to fade as well. He moved somewhat warily to the *Times,* where he came up with the idea of dividing the paper's newly enlarged critical power by writing Sunday essays—a second opinion, after the opening night critic weighed in. . . .
>
> When I took over the daily job nearly fifteen years after he arrived on West Forty-third Street, I was more than a little intimidated at the prospect of sharing the theater beat with a man I had revered from almost the moment I fell in love with the theater. But in person Walter was shy, unpretentious, and supportive—though never to the point that he would soft-pedal a tart opinion or suffer a fool gladly. . . . The dinners I spent listening to Walter and Jean finish each other's stories about their adventures in the theater were so full of love, laughter, humanity, and drama—not to mention cigarette smoke—that they play on in memory now as brightly as the opening nights that are fixed forever in Walter's incandescent prose.

42ND STREET
Winter Garden Theatre, August 26, 1980

If anyone wonders why Gower Champion's death is a bitter loss for the American theater, I suggest that he head immediately to the Winter Garden, where *42nd Street* opened last night. This brilliant showman's final musical is, if nothing else, a perfect monument to his glorious career. Indeed, *42nd Street* has more dancing—and, for that matter, more dancers—than Mr. Champion has ever given us before. As it fortunately happens, this show not only features his best choreography, but it also serves as a strangely ironic tribute to all the other musicals he has staged over the past two decades. Here and there in *42nd Street*, one happily finds witty homages to such memorable past Champion showstoppers as the telephone number from *Bye Bye Birdie*, "Put On Your Sunday Clothes" from *Hello, Dolly!*, and "When Mabel Comes In the Room" from *Mack and Mabel*. See Mr. Champion's work in *42nd Street* and try not to weep.

The excuse for the dances, of course, is the 1933 film that started Warner Bros. on its binge of backstage movie musicals during the Depression. In truth, the screen version of *42nd Street* did not have that many musical numbers, but David Merrick, the show's producer, has solved that problem by outfitting his stage extravaganza with a whole crop of other hits from the Harry Warren–Al Dubin song catalogue. With the aid of the best Robin Wagner sets, Tharon Musser lighting, and Theoni V. Aldredge costumes that Mr. Merrick's money can buy, Mr. Champion has been given an unparalleled opportunity to let his considerable imagination go berserk.

You name it, this choreographer does it. For "The Shadow Waltz," he has sent his uncommonly graceful legions of chorus people gliding gaily in silhouette across a nearly empty stage. (It's the "Dancing" number from *Hello, Dolly!* with an added layer of wit.) For "You're Getting to Be a Habit with Me," he's done his own, showbiz version of Jerome Robbins's ballet "The Concert." There's a chorine-filled castle of mirrors for "Dames," the requisite larger-than-life silver dollars for "We're in the Money," a breakaway train (shades of *Sugar*) for "Shuffle Off to Buffalo." That tribute to the jungle-gym "Telephone Hour" of *Bye Bye Birdie* opens Act 2: Singers occupy three stories of backstage dressing rooms to deliver "Sunny Side to Every Situation." And, impossible as it seems, Mr. Champion goes on to top it all with the title song. When the whole cast comes on to do "42nd Street" on the musical-within-the-musical's climactic opening night, we are treated to a tap-and-blues fantasy that simultaneously joshes and celebrates such an unlikely duo as George Balanchine and Busby Berkeley.

Unfortunately, as has frequently been the case for Mr. Champion in recent seasons, nothing else in his latest show comes close to matching the style and sheen of his handiwork. In adapting the film script to the stage, Michael Stewart and Mark Bramble have written a curious non-book; it's not for nothing that the *Playbill* describes the libretto simply as "lead-ins and crossovers." The writers have kept most of the original's plot about a chorus girl who steps in for a Broadway star. They have even kept many of the most famous punch lines intact. Nonetheless, the gritty, slam-bang rhythm that gave the movie its charm is almost completely lost.

Part of the problem is the addition of all those numbers, which are so good and plentiful that they make the story seem an unwanted intrusion into the action. But an even greater difficulty has to do with the simple matter of tone. Mr. Stewart and Mr. Bramble have not really spoofed the old Warners musicals in the winning manner of such latter-day parodies as the Off Broadway hit *Dames at Sea* or the recent film *Movie Movie*. And yet they haven't exactly played the old clichés straight, either. When we watch their characters overcome quintessential showbiz adversities to bring their musical to Broadway, it's hard to know whether we are to laugh or to cheer or merely to float off on a cloud of nostalgia. For the most part, we simply grin and bear the forced gaiety of the plot-advancing scenes while waiting for Mr. Champion to get his dancers tapping once more.

Given the show's uncertain attitude, the evening's stars are often left stranded. Jerry Orbach, in the Warner Baxter role of the sardonic, desperate director, fares the best: In Act 2, when he must get his show on the road, he delivers his knock-'em-dead speeches with raucous relish. His final reprise of the title song is so full of unexpected sarcasm and melancholy that for a brief instant he even summons up the bittersweet spirit of the original film.

Tammy Grimes, as the impossible leading lady who fatefully breaks her ankle, is a forceful, blowzy-voiced grande dame; she sings in the same fetchingly guttural manner one recalls from her musical comedy debut in *The Unsinkable Molly Brown* in the early sixties. And yet, even when she lands in a wheelchair for her long-awaited bitchy farewell, the writers deprive her of a big comic scene. Wanda Richert, as the overnight star who becomes Ms. Grimes's nemesis, is a precise, madcap dancer with an appealing belter's voice. No doubt she has charm, too, but the show's shortchanging of the movie's romantic subplot gives her little chance to show it off.

Then again, perhaps no performers can be expected to compete with this show's dance numbers or with the tragic real-life drama that surrounded the opening at the Winter Garden last night. The flaws of *42nd Street* are undeniably real and damaging. But, for now at least, they are nothing next to Gower Champion's final display of blazing theatrical fireworks.

≡ *The story of this action-packed opening night can be found near the end of this volume, in "Exit the Critic," the farewell reminiscence I wrote for the* Times Magazine *after I left the drama critic's job. As for my review, I never wrote so fast in my life—not because the piece was written on a tight opening-night deadline but because I had to rewrite it from top to bottom about twenty minutes before that deadline. Arthur Gelb, who had originally decreed that I leave any discussion of Champion's death to an accompanying news story written by the drama reporter, John Corry, had an abrupt (if not atypical) change of heart and decided that I had to lead with Champion's death after all.*

42nd Street received raves from virtually every critic except me and proved, of course, an enormous hit. But in an almost ritualistic acting out of the shift of power on Broadway in the 1980s, Merrick's show soon had to vacate its original home, the Winter Garden, to make way for the incoming Cats *and then had to leave its next home, the Majestic, to make way for* The Phantom of the Opera—*both British spectacles by Andrew Lloyd Webber that required major architectural changes in hallowed old Broadway theaters. During the summer of the* Phantom *renovation,* 42nd Street *moved just across Forty-fourth Street to the St. James—once home to Merrick's office and the site of the producer's biggest previous hit,* Hello, Dolly!, *in the 1960s. For a few weeks, at least, the producer conspired to retain a* 42nd Street *marquee at both houses, making it virtually impossible for any tourist visiting the theater district to escape the show's logo. Once* Phantom *did open, Merrick pushed back his show's curtain time so that his barkers could usher disappointed* Phantom *ticket seekers across the street to buy tickets for* 42nd Street *instead. By then Merrick was a stroke victim.* 42nd Street *was his last lavish production and his last hit.*

TRICKS OF THE TRADE

BROOKS ATKINSON THEATRE, NOVEMBER 7, 1980

*T*ricks of the Trade, Sidney Michaels's Central Intelligence Agency melodrama, which opened at the Brooks Atkinson last night, calls itself "a romantic mystery." Well, the only mystery about this play is why George C. Scott elected to star in it. It's true that Mr. Scott has not always been a genius when it comes to picking material—remember *The Savage Is Loose?*—but he has really outdone himself here. *Tricks of the Trade* is so limp it makes the cold war seem slightly less exciting than *Bowling for Dollars.*

Mr. Scott is cast as Dr. August Browning—wonderful name!—an East Side shrink whose office looks like a Rock Hudson bachelor pad in a

1961 Doris Day movie. Dr. Browning, who early on confesses he never went to medical school, has unorthodox methods: He doesn't care about his patients' childhood memories or dreams, and he isn't averse to doing crossword puzzles in the midst of a seventy-five-dollar-an-hour session. But he's a man of wide interests. He also owns a restaurant on Fifty-third Street and dabbles in espionage work for "the Agency."

Tricks of the Trade is about what happens when Dr. Browning takes on a new patient, Diana Woods, played by Trish Van Devere. Diana is rather strange. She won't say where she lives or talk about her parents. More alarming still, she pays her bills in cash, thereby forfeiting her tax deduction. Dr. Browning gets suspicious. Is it possible that Diana is the assassin who killed his best Agency pal in Prague last year? Is it possible that she's Nadia, the feared Russian agent? Is it possible that she will lure the good doctor to bed? One thing is certain: It is more than possible that you won't care who she is or what she does.

In any case, there is lots of talk about moles and leaks and secret lists and plane tickets to Zurich and microfilm—not to mention the occasional invocations of the dread East Germany. Much of this talk takes place on the phone, and some of it is recited by two nefarious gentlemen in raincoats (Lee Richardson and Geoffrey Pierson) who pop up now and again. There is also a large stock of red herrings, whose fishy smell is strong enough to carry from the stage of the Atkinson clear out to Forty-seventh Street. For his climax, Mr. Michaels has come up with a triple-twist ending that I wouldn't give away even if I understood it.

The playwright's method of dramaturgy is quite strange. The entire story is unbelievable, right down to the smallest details. (The doctor won't sell his posh Manhattan co-op because he's fearful of a financial loss.) Then there are the matters of structure and dialogue. *Tricks of the Trade* is a series of brief, perfunctory scenes, each of which has two purposes: to add a single plot point and to allow Ms. Van Devere to change into yet another one of Albert Wolsky's endless supply of hideous red and purple costumes. For humor, there are some doctor's-couch jokes that date almost as far back as Smith and Dale. And each scene ends with Mr. Michaels's idea of a dramatic punch line: a sudden thunderclap perhaps, or the swatting of a fly, or Mr. Richardson's immortal insult to the hero, "Chiropractor!" Act 1 concludes with Ms. Van Devere disrobing in near total darkness; it was the only time the audience gasped.

It says something about the level of the acting that the stars, who are married in real life, never convince us that their characters' eventual romantic attachment is real. Under Gilbert Cates's static direction, both performances are unusually irritating. Ms. Van Devere, who has been quite charming in films like *Where's Poppa?* and *Movie Movie,* here delivers every line in the same grating singsong. It's unfortunate that Mr. Michaels has given her the recurring bits of dialogue: "I don't know who I am"; "I'm just walking through it."

Mr. Scott does an extremely relaxed version of the Ernest Hemingway he did so well in the film *Islands in the Stream.* Portly and wheezy, he gets to play drunk, to smoke cigarettes, and to sing a raspy "My Funny Valentine." For some reason, even in his more intimate tête-à-têtes with Ms. Van Devere, he delivers many of his lines in the heavenly direction of the balcony. It's too late for prayers now.

A LESSON FROM ALOES
PLAYHOUSE THEATRE, NOVEMBER 18, 1980

In *A Lesson from Aloes* the playwright Athol Fugard transports the audience into a landscape of seemingly unrelieved bleakness. The year is 1963. The setting is the Port Elizabeth, South Africa, home of Piet (Harris Yulin), a middle-aged Afrikaner, and his wife, Gladys (Maria Tucci). This couple's lives are as threadbare as their home. Piet, an ex–bus driver who once helped fight the failed antiapartheid revolution, has now retreated into a private botanical hobby: He collects different varieties of aloes, an ugly, thorn-covered shrub. Gladys, recently released from a mental hospital, is bitter and withdrawn. There's no love, no money, no fresh air. Old political friends, silenced by government intimidation, have vanished from sight. As Gladys puts it, the end of the world may already be at hand.

But Gladys is wrong. In *A Lesson from Aloes,* Mr. Fugard once again reveals his remarkable talent for tracking down the pulsebeat of life in a world that even God seems to have abandoned. In the literal sense, that world is the misbegotten land of South Africa, but such are the power and truth of Mr. Fugard's writing that his best plays transcend even the political tragedy of his native country. *Aloes* is one of his best plays, maybe his very best. It arrived in full, staggering force at the Playhouse last night, in an absolutely perfect production directed by the author.

Piet and Gladys are not the only characters of the evening. In Act 2, the couple is paid a visit by Steve (James Earl Jones), a charismatic political comrade of Piet's from the old days. Outwardly, Mr. Fugard's three South Africans seem to be strikingly different from one another. Piet is a calm, often-abstracted man who likes to recite English poetry. The pasty-faced Gladys is high-strung to the point of hysteria. Steve is a warm and boisterous figure, bubbling over with hearty laughter and savage angers. Nonetheless, the three have a lot in common. Like the thorny aloe, they all have been cruelly warped by their homeland—and yet they all somehow find the means to survive.

A Lesson from Aloes is the story of how these characters got to where they are now and how they chose their respective paths to survival. It's not a pleasant tale. Steve, recently released from jail, is moving his family to England, leaving his life and home behind "like a pile of rubbish." Gladys, her spirit forever destroyed by a violent police raid, is eager to enter the hell of total madness. She tells Steve: "They've burnt my brain as brown as yours." Piet clings to a stubborn idealism: "Social injustice is man-made and can be unmade by men." But there are no longer any people or evidence to support his view.

Exile, madness, utter loneliness—these are the only alternatives Mr. Fugard's characters have. What makes *Aloes* so moving is the playwright's insistence on the heroism and integrity of these harsh choices. Short of Beckett, it's hard to think of a contemporary playwright who so relentlessly and unsentimentally tracks down humanity in the midst of apocalypse. And, like Beckett, Mr. Fugard sets forth his drama in spare, direct, at times even witty dialogue.

If there's anything wrong with his plays, it's a slight tendency to start slowly in his first acts and to spell out his metaphors. Act 1 of *Aloes* is not immune to these flaws—it feels about ten minutes too long. But that's a very small price to pay, given what follows. When Mr. Jones arrives in Act 2 for an ostensibly celebratory farewell, Mr. Fugard plunges through layer after layer of his characters' inner darkness—only to arrive, miraculously, at a climax that floods the theater with light.

At the Playhouse, it's all but impossible to separate the actors from the play. It doesn't detract from Ms. Tucci's and Mr. Jones's achievements to say that Mr. Yulin dominates the evening. His is the quietest character; in a way Piet is defined by the peaceful silence that surrounds him. Even when his old friend Steve accuses him unjustly of political hypocrisy (and worse) or his wife assaults him in a fit of viciousness, he has "nothing to say." When Piet does talk—of his plants or the salad days of his political passion—Mr. Yulin shows us the kind, humorful man he still is. Nor is he at all sanctimonious when he uselessly attempts to persuade the others that the antiapartheid cause still lives. Mr. Yulin's idealism, like Mr. Fugard's, is expressed as simple dignity; it's a state of grace.

Ms. Tucci is rending as Gladys, a woman torn by centrifugal forces. In Act 1 she clings to her last companion, her diary, as if holding on to the book might prevent her from flying apart. In Act 2, Gladys's fluttery neuroticism gives way to a harrowing eruption of nihilistic bile. Mr. Jones is no less commanding in the smaller role of Steve. A high-spirited, playful figure at first, he is every bit the magnetic, inspirational leader Piet has advertised him to be. Once the wine wears off and his prison memories flood back, Mr. Jones's rakish slouch becomes the whipped yet unbowed countenance of a man who has only narrowly escaped his torturers.

The performances alone do not sum up Mr. Fugard's direction. With the help of Michael H. Yeargan's sad, dusty set and William Armstrong's sun-baked lighting, the playwright has also filled *Aloes* with poignant images: Steve ripping up his beloved father's photograph to break with his past, or Gladys mechanically setting a festive picnic table in a doomed effort to dispel her gloom. The most powerful image, perhaps, is the last: a tableau of the deserted Piet sitting by himself, contemplating his prized aloe. It's a simple moment, yet at once shattering and uplifting. In *A Lesson from Aloes,* Mr. Fugard summons up the full agony and triumph of people who have lost everything except the gift of staying alive.

DEAD END KIDS
PUBLIC THEATER, NOVEMBER 19, 1980

ead End Kids, the new Mabou Mines production at the Public Theater, seeks to solve a most difficult theatrical problem: How is it possible to create a political play about an overfamiliar subject without boring the audience? The subject of *Dead End Kids* is nuclear holocaust—and, as President Carter recently discovered, that grave peril doesn't grab the American public the way it once did. If we haven't exactly learned "to stop worrying and love the bomb," as *Dr. Strangelove* once promised we would, we may have learned to live with it. And, even if we haven't, who wants to go to a theater and hear lectures about Hiroshima, SALT, or Three Mile Island?

There are no such lectures in *Dead End Kids.* This free-form work, which was conceived and directed by JoAnne Akalaitis, has indeed given agitprop theater a fresh, exciting beat. By dramatizing historical and scientific facts with corrosive imagery and grotesque humor, Ms. Akalaitis has found a way to make us think about the unthinkable all over again. *Dead End Kids*—the title encapsulates both the evening's rough-house style and charnel-house content—is subversive in the best sense of the word.

Or such is the case once we get to the show's scabrous second half. The first half is more noble than involving. It's basically a series of sketches that attempt to live up to the evening's subtitle, "a history of nuclear power." Ms. Akalaitis fills her expansive stage space, which sometimes encompasses at least seven different playing areas, with dreamy tableaux and costumed figures that are meant to take us from the alchemists to Madame Curie to J. Robert Oppenheimer. Books are strewn everywhere; scientific knowledge, it seems, can be the mother of rubble. True, but the scenes go on too long—especially an updating of *Faust*— and the intellectual synapses are too often blurred by runaway theatrical gimmickry.

Still, there are two sequences that gnaw at us before the intermission. In the first, two American generals read aloud an actual Government report on an early atomic bomb test; as they do, a chorus of eavesdroppers snickers at the unintended sexual imagery in the generals' macho nuclear jargon. Later, the entire cast dons military garb to sing and dance to "Hubba, Hubba," a peppy postwar pop song about how the United States whipped the Japanese. As choreographed by Gail Conrad, the number looks like something out of an old-time Hollywood musical. It's fun, yet disturbing. Isn't there something wrong with a society that can effortlessly absorb mass death into the rhythms of the hit parade?

As it happens, that number propels *Dead End Kids* to the heart of its true, chilling subject. This is not a show about the history of science, but about the bomb's fallout over the last thirty-five years. And not so much the radioactive fallout as the social fallout. In the second half, Ms. Akalaitis bombards us with artifacts and images (some of them almost subliminal) to suggest that our whole culture, as well as our health, has been battered by the continuing threat of nuclear war—not only our pop music, of course, but also our moral and sexual values, our everyday landscape and behavior.

The set pieces that follow—some documentary, some invented—are sickly funny, as they must be. We see an absurd Atomic Energy Commission propaganda film, undoubtedly shown to a generation of school kids, about the suburban pleasures (golf, station wagons) of that "mile-high city, Los Alamos." Another bit features a bored gum-chewing teacher drilling a Cub Scout on the detonation devices of a red-white-and-blue hydrogen bomb. In the longest and most shocking sequence, a vulgar, Las Vegasesque comic does a routine featuring a dead chicken, a female audience volunteer, and the actual text of a National Academy of Sciences tome titled *Effects of Radioactive Fallout on Livestock in the Event of Nuclear War.*

Through it all, the pace accelerates. Actors fly in and out of doors along the theater's back wall. Blistering lights pop on and off. Laboratory garments and apparatus float in and out of the action like hallucinatory visions. By the time Ms. Akalaitis unleashes her heaviest arsenal—percolating Geiger counters, toy bombs, seat-shaking rumbles—we've already been made half-crazy. It's not just the fear of death that gets to us, but also the show's slapstick portrait of an America gone berserk.

It's all staged with tight precision, and an inventiveness that doesn't flag once the show finds its way. With the additional aid of slide shows, voice-over recitatives, and an avalanche of props, Ms. Akalaitis creates a dense circus out of the surreal bric-a-brac that has entered our lives since the invention of the fallout shelter. There's even a lobby display of high-school science-fair projects celebrating fission and "nuclear-powered coffee pots."

The performers are good—especially Ellen McElduff, who is the evening's sexy, all-purpose comedienne. The show's real achievement, though, is its success as political theater. *Dead End Kids* provokes a jaded audience by arguing that the bomb, in a sense, has already been dropped. Agree or disagree, you're likely to leave the Public heatedly debating the point.

≡ *JoAnne Akalaitis was an imaginative, if uneven, director; this was one of her most inspired efforts and later became a film. Years later a dying Joseph Papp would quixotically choose her as his successor at the New York Shakespeare Festival, with unhappy and short-lived results.*

THE AMERICAN CLOCK
BILTMORE THEATRE, NOVEMBER 21, 1980

Sometimes it seems as if there's just no justice in the world—or at least in the world of the theater. Last spring, when it opened at the Spoleto Festival in Charleston after New York previews, Arthur Miller's *The American Clock* was a flawed but powerful play about the Great Depression of the 1930s. Mr. Miller was in touch with his best themes again; he seemed on the verge of creating an epic, tragic statement about a family caught in the midst of the collapse of the American Dream. Last night, Mr. Miller's drama arrived at the Biltmore with an extensively rewritten script, a new director, and a partially new cast. The result is a tragedy of another sort. Upsetting as it seems, the once beautiful pieces of *The American Clock* have been smashed almost beyond recognition.

What's gone wrong? It's almost too sad to talk about. Mr. Miller has tinkered with his play to the point of dismantling it. While he has reduced some of its unnecessary sprawl, he hasn't solved its structural problems; he also has injected too much sentimentality, thematic signposting, and slapdash comedy. Vivian Matalon, a director who knows better, has coarsened the evening by staging it in an emphatic, bellowing style that plunges even the well-written scenes into melodrama or burlesque. Though there are still two strong, if diminished, performances by Joan Copeland and John Randolph, they now must play against William Atherton, who has been absurdly miscast in the play's third crucial role.

The three stars play the Baums, a family that is not unrelated to those of Miller plays from *All My Sons* and *Death of a Salesman* through *The Price*. Moe (Mr. Randolph) is a proud patriarch whose spirit has been all but broken by economic disaster. Rose (Ms. Copeland) is a strong, complex woman who loves her husband but has a limited tolerance for human weakness. Their son, Lee (Mr. Atherton), is an aspiring writer who also serves as the evening's narrator. It is Mr. Miller's notion, potentially a great one, that the Baums' story can help tell the story of America itself during the traumatic era that gave birth to our own.

As it happens, neither tale is told well in *The American Clock*: Indeed, the Baums and history fight each other to a standoff. The play was loosely inspired by Studs Terkel's *Hard Times,* and Mr. Miller has struggled gamely but vainly to duplicate the book's oral-history technique. In his initial version, the evening's historical segments were thrown in like minidocumentaries: The story of the Baums would come to a halt and we'd suddenly see a scene showing the suffering of other, unrelated Depression victims. In the new version, such digressions are instead force-fed into the family's scenes. Where before there was an onstage confrontation between farmers and bankers, now a farmer turns up at the Baums' Brooklyn home and tells them of the confrontation. This is not an improvement.

Either way, the non-Baum characters—from patrician Wall Street titans to a redneck sheriff to poor blacks—are written as superficial archetypes. As before, they slow down and fractionalize Mr. Miller's domestic drama. The Baums' story, meanwhile, has now been expanded without being deepened. The familial relationships are often sketched in or announced rather than fully dramatized, and they are cluttered with additional deadwood characters. As acted by a shrill, hand-waving supporting cast, the assorted Baum relations and neighbors seem to have wandered in from a Norman Lear sitcom.

Mr. Atherton's Lee, on the other hand, seems to have floated in from a Princeton club. An autobiographical stand-in for the author, the son must set the tone for the evening. His confrontations with his parents, especially his mother, are ostensibly the most important in the play. His journey through the thirties, especially his brush with leftism, should give the evening its historical perspective. That's all gone here. There's little feeling in Mr. Atherton's performance. He is far too preppie and arch to pass as the son of Moe and Rose or as a foe of social injustice. Worse still, when the actor reads Mr. Miller's flashback narration, he adopts a smart-aleck manner that seems to mock the lines.

Not that Mr. Atherton is responsible for all of the evening's wrong notes. Some of the play's more portentous historical transitions sound like *March of Time* newsreels: "All of a sudden, quick as death, the lights went dark in the casino." There's a running gag about Lee's college plans that cheapens the play's father-son relationship. The maudlin interludes are merciless. One minor character exists solely so he can commit suicide in Act 2; a bit later, there's a sloshy and extraneous scene showing Moe and Rose in their golden years.

Though Ms. Copeland and Mr. Randolph are buffeted by these forces, Mr. Miller has given them some lovely moments. Rose does have too many repetitive, histrionic fits, including a painful one in which she brays at an unseen President Roosevelt, but Ms. Copeland touchingly straddles that boundary between hysterical laughter and tears. Her best monologue opens Act 2: Sitting at her piano and singing in a frayed voice, she plays her favorite Gershwin songs in a valiant yet doomed effort to bring back her wealthy, pre-Crash days. In an underwritten role, Mr. Randolph shows us the impact of Moe's slide down the economic ladder by gradually aging his posture, his face, and his voice. By the end, he seems an ideal candidate to play a brilliant Willy Loman.

The sadness, of course, is that Moe could have been as towering a character as Willy and that Rose could have been, as her son ultimately suggests, a woman who embodies the contradictions of an entire nation. Ms. Copeland and Mr. Randolph have the gifts to play those roles; Mr. Miller has the inspiration for a potentially soaring play that could contain them. It's a bitter loss for the theater that *The American Clock* has arrived on Broadway unwound.

≡ *With few exceptions, almost every play that was transferred to Broadway after enjoying initial success at a regional theater or Off Broadway or in London was the worse for wear by the time it reached the bright glare of the Great White Way. What went wrong? Usually key actors would leave and be replaced by less felicitous second choices—or a set would be glitzed up—or a production would be broadened or coarsened to play in a much larger house. (That a play would be rewritten for the worse—as was in part the case with* The American Clock—*was a rarity.) There were some exceptions, though: Tom Stoppard and Mike Nichols vastly improved the text and the casting of* The Real Thing *as it made its way from the West End to Broadway, and every August Wilson play was substantially rewritten and cut to positive effect between its premiere at Yale and its New York debut. And occasionally a play—Marsha Norman's* 'night, Mother, *for instance— would actually come across exactly on Broadway as it did at its less pretentious out-of-town premiere.*

HOW I GOT THAT STORY
SECOND STAGE, DECEMBER 9, 1980

Amlin Gray's *How I Got That Story* is an explosion of young talent—in writing, directing, and acting—and a bracing demonstration of what such talent can do when everything goes right. Though this play calls for only two actors and a minimal set, it has an epic sweep. Mr. Gray's subject is the American adventure in Vietnam. One of the actors, Daniel Stern, plays a young reporter who goes to cover the war; the other, Bob Gunton, plays all the people that the reporter meets overseas. But this evening is not, as one might fear, a political chalk talk or merely a hipper version of last season's dreary *Billy Bishop Goes to War.* By turns painfully funny and just plain painful, *How I Got That Story* recaptures both the black comedy and the bottomless tragedy of Vietnam—and it does so with the simple magic of pure theater.

The play is the season's opening production at the Second Stage, an Off Off Broadway company that gained attention last spring with its revival of Michael Weller's *Split.* Like the Weller play, Mr. Gray's is directed by one of the theater's artistic directors, Carole Rothman. On the basis of this effort, Ms. Rothman can hold her own with most of the best directors in town. Even leaving aside her work with her two actors, one still is dazzled by the world she has brought to life on her tiny stage. With the aid of a few screens and props designed by Patricia Woodbridge, this director effortlessly whips the audience from Southeast Asia's cities and villages to its jungles and minefields. We are even taken on a bombing mission—an effect Ms. Rothman and her lighting designer, Victor En Yu Tan, achieve for roughly one-millionth the cost of a similar sequence in *Apocalypse Now.*

Mr. Gray's comedy in some ways parallels Francis Ford Coppola's movie, with a little of Evelyn Waugh's novel *Scoop* thrown in for good measure. Its plot, stripped down to its essentials, is familiar. As the innocent reporter ventures deeper and deeper into a nominally fictional country named Amboland, he gradually realizes that both his employer, the Trans Pan Global wire service, and his government are backing a corrupt Asian regime. Mr. Gray, writing in short, punchy scenes, steadily revitalizes this tale until his prototypical pilgrim's progress takes us in shocking directions we don't fully expect.

Some of the writing is surrealistically witty. When the reporter meets the inscrutable Madame Ing, the queen of the Imperial Palace, she lambastes *Time* magazine for not crowning her woman of the decade and gives her guest a most sobering warning: "We will never be perfectly inscrutable to you until we have killed you and you do not know why."

The reporter also meets a GI who gives a riotous demonstration of the swear words he has learned in battle and a photographer whose proudest achievement is a photo of his own arm being blown off. In one of the evening's most inventive scenes, the reporter tries to gauge the feelings of the common people by dutifully interviewing a bar prostitute. As the hero mistakes the woman's sexual come-ons for political opinions—and vice versa—a farcical cultural clash becomes a metaphor for the entire American experience in Saigon.

In Act 2, the farce escalates into horror. When the newly radicalized reporter quits his job, he falls into an exitless nowhere zone worthy of *Catch-22*. Now a gung ho guerrilla partisan, he is captured by the guerrillas—only to be told by them that he is a decadent observer who has "no right" to live in the country. But it's too late; the reporter, like so many Americans who went to Asia, has become addicted to his new home. As he searches desperately, in brothels and orphanages, for a way to connect to the society that spurns him, *How I Got That Story* finds its own entry point into the chilling heart of the American-Vietnamese darkness.

That darkness is brilliantly illuminated by the twenty-one characters created by Mr. Gunton. This actor, who originated the role of Juan Perón in the Broadway production of *Evita*, seems to have a boundless imagination. Not only does he nail down a widely diverse crew of people—from Trans Pan Global bureaucrats to soldiers of all stripes to Asians of every social class—but he also moves among his various parts with a split-second precision that is breathtaking. More amazing still, he plays the various ladies of the evening, including that touching, childish prostitute, without resorting to wigs, makeup, or campy mannerisms. At one point, he even impersonates Madame Ing as she impersonates a male guerrilla leader. We never stop suspending disbelief.

Mr. Stern, who played one of the young heroes in the film *Breaking Away,* is almost as impressive. Tousle-haired and gawky, he's at first an amusing innocent abroad, a naïf from Dubuque who can hardly work a tape recorder. When he witnesses a monk's self-immolation, he keeps his distance from the pain by yelling at himself: "You're just reporting this!" Once he is swept away by all the brutality he sees, the actor becomes a madman torn between hysterical panic and a bombed-out tranquillity. He ends up a pitiable, homeless zombie—a faceless "Yankee dressed up like a gook."

The playwright has a word, "imprintment," to describe his hero's sad fate: It's what happens when a reporter "goes to cover a country and the country covers him." But, of course, reporters were not the only ones to be imprinted during the Vietnam War; the readers back home were, too. That's why *How I Got That Story* transcends its many, intricate parts to embrace the larger story of the Vietnamization of America during the 1960s. While that story isn't a scoop in 1980, the Second Stage has abundantly proved that an old nightmare can still be brought back to stunning life.

AMADEUS
Broadhurst Theatre, December 18, 1980

Contrary to its title, Peter Shaffer's *Amadeus* is not really about Wolfgang Amadeus Mozart. Nor is it really about its central character, Antonio Salieri, the hack court composer who knew Mozart in eighteenth-century Vienna and later claimed, falsely, to have murdered him. Though these men are Mr. Shaffer's antagonists, the real subject of *Amadeus* is God. And it is He who is murdered in the angry and thrilling play that arrived in Peter Hall's triumphant production at the Broadhurst last night.

Amadeus is a black comedy that's just about as black as they come. To be sure, Mr. Shaffer has his witty fun with musical history. Working from documentary materials, he has created a scabrous portrait of the private Mozart and a speculative thriller about the composer's brief, unhappy life. But this play's mission isn't to titillate us with antique musicological gossip. The wicked plot of *Amadeus* is merely a means for the playwright to present his view of the world—and a most contemporary and nihilistic view it is. If Mr. Shaffer shatters the audience's idealized illusions about his title character, he then goes on to smash our romantic illusions about ourselves.

Our guide through this dark hall of mirrors is Salieri, who's constantly on stage, from the moment we enter the theater. It's a marathon role, and not just because of its length: The play's flashback structure requires him to jump back and forth between his youth and dotage. Paul Scofield originated the part at Britain's National Theatre, and it is our good fortune that another astonishing actor, Ian McKellen, is playing it here. As he struggles within Mr. Shaffer's metaphysical maze, Mr. McKellen gives a towering performance. In conjunction with the playwright's bristling language, this actor's voice—by turns waspish, deathly, pathetic, and evil—provides the play with its true musical score.

It is Mr. Shaffer's dramatic conceit—supported by a clever manipulation of circumstantial evidence—that the envious, ungifted Salieri conspired to poison Mozart's career, if not Mozart himself. True or not, this hypothesis allows the playwright to set up a dynamic confrontation between mediocrity and genius. Salieri is a religious and moral man who had given himself to God so that he might realize his sole ambition, to be a great composer. Mozart (Tim Curry) is a foul-mouthed, graceless libertine who has realized that very ambition without even trying. This unjust paradox is what drives Salieri to take revenge. Once he realizes that Mozart's music reduces his own to "lifeless scratches," he sets out to destroy the "obscene child" who is the incarnation of God's voice.

Because Salieri was in fact the more successful of the two composers during their lifetime, it's plausible that he did somehow impede Mozart's career. But in itself this plot is not all that interesting: Indeed, Salieri's shadowy attempt to sabotage *The Marriage of Figaro*, though amusingly contrived, brings about one of the evening's few noticeable sags. It's the injuries that Salieri inflicts on himself, not his nemesis, that shake us. When he discovers that there is no connection between virtue and the talent he covets, Salieri must confront the most profound emptiness— the one that comes when man ceases to believe that he lives in a rational universe governed by a divine plan. By obsessively plunging into that void, Salieri escalates his plight until he arrives at a tragic rendezvous with madness.

Mr. McKellen undergoes a remarkable transformation as he takes the character down this apocalyptic path. Before he meets Mozart, he's a sophisticated, if sadly servile, figure, regaling the audience with sardonic asides about his doltish royal employers and self-mocking soliloquies about his passion for sweets. After Salieri's first, almost mystical encounter with his rival's music, his posture and voice begin to warp in agony. In one trembling, hallucinatory moment, the contemplation of Mozart's scores sends him collapsing to the floor in a dead faint.

As Salieri progressively violates his pious past by careening into viciousness and degradation, there are many high-voltage scenes. In one of them, Mr. McKellen slowly turns ashen as he listens to the giddy Mozart improving a Salieri composition at the piano. Clumsily trying to seduce Mozart's wife (the comely Jane Seymour) later on, Mr. McKellen rises from his initial sexual ardor to explode in a wounding paroxysm of self-hatred. In a climactic scene inspired by the mysterious history of Mozart's Requiem, Salieri goes to his enemy's house dressed as a specter of death. Hiding behind a grim mask, Mr. McKellen becomes a hideous, eerie devil who can't separate his own fearful nightmares from those he is trying to bring to his prey. As he disintegrates in defeat, we see the birth of the aged, cackling Salieri, slack-jawed and stooped, who is the evening's narrator.

Just the same, Mr. Shaffer's protagonist is moving, even likable. He's so hapless in everything he does, from composing music to plotting foul play to preparing for his own death, that his failures take on a Chekhovian aura of tragicomedy. He's also smart: In one of the evening's other paradoxes, Salieri reveals himself to be the only man in Vienna who recognizes both Mozart's musical gifts and his own lack of them. Nor is Mozart truly despicable, at least as delineated in the impressively fine-tuned performance by the braying yet sensitive Mr. Curry. For all the young man's foul language, sadomasochistic sexual proclivities, gross manners, and arrogance, he gains a feverish grandeur as he approaches his drunken, impoverished death. In Mr. Shaffer's scheme, both men are victims of fates they are helpless to control. To the extent that we identify with them, their helplessness before the irrationality of fate becomes our own.

The entire supporting cast is good, with particularly notable contributions from Ms. Seymour, Patrick Hines's toadlike Count Orsini-Rosenberg, and Nicholas Kepros's dim-witted Emperor Joseph II. With the aid of John Bury's inventive production design, which creates an ingenious stage-within-the-stage, Mr. Hall molds his large company into painterly tableaux that vividly portray a distant, rococo world.

The director cannot, however, cover up the un-Mozartean passages in Mr. Shaffer's otherwise glorious writing. As in *Equus*, this playwright has a tendency to use stylized devices (in this case, drawn from opera) as an excuse both to provide point-blank exposition and to understate his secondary characters. In *Amadeus*, Constanze Mozart is an ambiguous plot pawn; the various members of Viennese society are either one-joke caricatures or superfluous narrators designed to score easy points. Mr. Shaffer is also flummoxed by Mozart's father, who is dragged into the text (but never on stage) in a last-minute effort to provide a gratuitous Freudian analysis of his son's life and opera librettos.

Though these weaknesses, as well as the play's blurred multiple endings, may take a toll in a less-than-great production of *Amadeus,* they don't much mar the excitement at the Broadhurst. We still leave the theater possessed by the chilling central image that Mr. Shaffer and Mr. McKellen have created. That image is of Salieri keeling over in pain, crying out for deliverance from an inscrutable God.

Amadeus may be a play inspired by music and death, but it fills the theater with that mocking, heavenly silence that is the overwhelming terror of life.

TRUE WEST
PUBLIC THEATER, DECEMBER 24, 1980

Some day, when the warring parties get around to writing their memoirs, we may actually discover who killed *True West,* the Sam Shepard play that finally opened at the Public Theater last night. As the press has already reported, this failure is an orphan. Robert Woodruff, the nominal director, left the play in previews and disowned the production. Mr. Shepard has also disowned the production, although he has not ventured from California to see it. The producer Joseph Papp, meanwhile, has been left holding the bag. New Year's will be here shortly, and one can only hope that these talented men will forgive and forget.

At least their battle has been fought for a worthwhile cause. *True West* seems to be a very good Shepard play—which means that it's one of the American theater's most precious natural resources. But no play can hold the stage all by itself. Except for odd moments, when Mr. Shepard's fantastic language rips through the theater on its own sinuous strength, the *True West* at the Public amounts to little more than a stand-up run-through of a text that remains to be explored. This play hasn't been misdirected; it really looks as if it hasn't been directed at all.

You know a play has no director when funny dialogue dies before it reaches the audience. Or when two lead actors step on each other's lines and do "business" rather than create characters. Or when entrances and scene-endings look arbitrary rather than preplanned. Or when big farcical sequences—an avalanche of Coors beer cans, for instance—clatter about the stage creating confusion rather than mirth. Or when an evening's climax—the mystical death embrace of two fratricidal brothers— is so vaguely choreographed it looks like a polka. All these things and more happen at the Public.

It's a terrible shame. *True West* is a worthy direct descendant of Mr. Shepard's *Curse of the Starving Class* and *Buried Child*. Many of his persistent recent themes are present and accounted for—the spiritual death of the American family, the corruption of the artist by business, the vanishing of the Western wilderness and its promised dream of freedom. If the playwright dramatizes his concerns in fantastic flights of poetic imagery, that imagery always springs directly from the life of the people and drama he has invented. Mr. Shepard doesn't graft symbols onto his plays. He's a true artist; his best works are organic creations that cannot be broken down into their constituent parts.

The brothers of *True West* are both hustlers, or, if you will, modern-day cowboys who have lost their range. Lee (Peter Boyle) is a drifter and petty burglar, and the younger Austin (Tommy Lee Jones) is a screenwriter. The play is about what happens when the two men reunite in their mother's ticky-tacky suburban Los Angeles home. By the end of the evening, they have stolen each other's identities and destroyed the house, and yet they can never completely sever the ties that bind. Like the heroes in the "true life" Hollywood movie western they write during the course of the play, Lee and Austin are "two lamebrains" doomed to chase each other eternally across a desolate, ever-receding frontier.

Mr. Shepard is an awesome writer. When Lee and Austin lament the passing of the West they loved (and that maybe never existed), they launch into respectively loopy, nostalgic monologues about the film *Lonely Are the Brave* and the now-extinct neighborhood of their youth. Amusing as they are, these comic riffs are also moving because they give such full life to Mr. Shepard's conflict between America's myths and the bitter, plastic reality that actually exists. Lee can no longer distinguish the true West from the copy he finds in a movie; Austin discovers that his childhood memories are inseparable from the vistas he sees on cheap postcards. Looking for roots, Mr. Shepard's characters fall into a void.

The playwright also provides motifs involving dogs, crickets, desert topography, cars, household appliances (especially toasters and television sets), and the brothers' unseen, destitute father. As the play progresses, these images keep folding into one another until we are completely transported into the vibrant landscape of Mr. Shepard's imagination. Such is the collective power of this playwright's words that even his wilder conceits seem naturalistic in the context of his play. We never question that Lee would try to destroy a typewriter with a golf club or that the family patriarch would lose his false teeth in a doggie bag full of chop suey.

True West slips only when Mr. Shepard, a master of ellipses, tries to fill in his blanks. Does he really need lines like "There's nothing real here now, least of all me" or "There's no such thing as the West anymore"? The movie-industry gags, most of which involve a producer in gold chains (Louis Zorich), are jarring as well. Mr. Shepard's witticisms about development deals and agents have been written funnier by Woody Allen and Paul Mazursky, and they bring *True West* down to earth.

Still, these judgments must be tentative. It's impossible to evaluate a play definitively when it hasn't been brought to life on stage. There's nervous energy at the Public, but it leads nowhere. Mr. Boyle, a loping, ill-shaven figure in baggy clothes, is engagingly sleazy for a while, but his performance trails off into vagueness and repetition just as it should begin to build. Mr. Jones is kinetic and finally frantic as he tries and fails to get a handle on the screenwriter. We never believe that these actors are mirror image brothers locked into a psychological cat-and-mouse game. Theatergoers who venture to the Public must depend on their own imaginations to supply the crackling timing and the violent tension that are absent.

Who's to blame? Please address your inquiries to the Messrs. Shepard, Woodruff, and Papp. And while you're writing, demand restitution. These men owe New York a true *True West.*

≡ True West *would indeed be revived in 1982 in an exciting Off Broadway production that made stars of its two heretofore unknown (in New York) leads, John Malkovich and Gary Sinise, and of the Chicago theater troupe, the Steppenwolf Theater Company, that staged it. It's the best Shepard play of the post-1980 phase of his career.*

MACBETH

VIVIAN BEAUMONT THEATER, JANUARY 24, 1981

To put it simply, there can be no *Macbeth* without Macbeth. Such is the sad case with the Lincoln Center Theater Company's production of the play, which opened Thursday night. The evening is by no means without its incidental merits. Sarah Caldwell, the director, has conceived a commanding physical production that at times solves the problems of the Vivian Beaumont's vast stage. Her supporting cast is often outstanding, and Shakespeare's text rings through the huge auditorium with nary a word lost. But without a Macbeth, the audience might just as well go home. Ms. Caldwell has erected a gargantuan theatrical contraption only to leave out the motor that would make it fly.

The nominal Macbeth of the evening is Philip Anglim, the young actor who triumphed as the physically deformed "Elephant Man." Here he tries to play one of the most demanding mental cripples in theatrical literature and sinks without a trace. The problem is not his youth: There have been other young Macbeths. Nor is it his voice: Declaiming diligently from his diaphragm, Mr. Anglim is capable of sounding the bass notes that are essential to the character. What's missing from this performance are merely the bread-and-butter qualities of good acting: feeling, stage presence, physical, vocal, and facial expressiveness.

I don't know what this actor is up to in *Macbeth,* and I doubt that he does, either. In the early scenes, he is so shifty-eyed and bonkers that one expects him to be arrested for suspicion of murder before he actually commits one. He shows us none of Macbeth's equivocation or false faces until the Banquo's ghost scene, at which point his sudden, quirky smiles earn unwanted laughs. As he charges into his doom, his performance changes not a whit: There is no discernible difference between his flat, pop-eyed reading of the dagger speech and his final droning of the "Tomorrow, and tomorrow, and tomorrow" monologue.

It's not that Mr. Anglim is misinterpreting the hero; there is no interpretation here at all. This is a Macbeth bereft of emotions—unless utter, dead coldness counts as such. The star's eyes neither make contact with those of his fellow actors nor look inward. His face is fixed in a blank, unchanging pose of mild nervousness, as if he feared he might be late for a train. His voice rarely varies in tone, and his body, which was so expressive as John Merrick, clumps about woodenly. His one, tardy attempt to summon up passion is the beginning of a sob on the line with which he greets news of his wife's death ("She should have died hereafter"). It's debatable whether the then-dazed Macbeth would start to cry at that point; in any case, Mr. Anglim turns his back on the audience rather than letting us see even the most tentative stirring of his heart.

There are lots of ways to play this tragically ambitious Scotsman—sympathetically, neurotically, wittily, or even (in desperation) as a one-note blackguard. It says a lot about Mr. Anglim's Macbeth that he not only fails to inspire pity but that he also fails to arouse even the easy response of pure hatred. He is instead a strolling vacuum that swallows up the rest of the production. Though Miss Caldwell must bear partial responsibility for her star's performance, she deserves better.

Ms. Caldwell does, however, inflict some wounds of her own on this *Macbeth*. In her debut as a theater director, she at times betrays her roots as an iconoclastic opera impresario. Much of the staging is too stately, and there are sequences that sacrifice the text for pointless visual conceits. The banquet table in the ghost scene is set perpendicular to the audience, thereby making it impossible for us to see the reactions of the guests to Macbeth's "strange infirmity." The goings-on surrounding Duncan's murder unfold on a high, *Sweeney Todd*–style bridge that puts the actors out of visual reach and also causes them to do a lot of breathless running up and down stairs.

Indeed, most of the Beaumont's Act 1 (three acts of Shakespeare) can be written off. Mr. Anglim is on stage much of the time, and his performance constricts the range of Maureen Anderman's well-considered Lady Macbeth. Duncan (Neil Vipond) and the drunken porter (Roy K. Stevens) are both inadequate, and surprisingly enough, Miss Caldwell does nothing of interest with the witches. These weird sisters include a man, whatever that means, and they sing some of their verses to *Exorcist* music that merely blurs the words.

But, in Act 2, Duncan and the Porter are gone, and so, for much of the time, are Macbeth and the witches. As a result, Ms. Caldwell's *Macbeth* starts to get going. Kaiulani Lee proves to be an extraordinary Lady Macduff: In her single scene, her voice careers from anger to grief to horror, and her murder provides the evening's only gooseflesh. J. Kenneth Campbell's fierce (if overslouchy) Macduff, James Hurdle's coolly cynical Ross, and, especially, John Vickery's magnetic, quixotic Malcolm transform their difficult reunion scene in England into a compelling battle of complex sensibilities. Freed of Mr. Anglim, Ms. Anderman's Lady Macbeth becomes a somewhat harrowing sleepwalker—a pale, frazzled Edvard Munch figure imprisoned in nihilistic pain.

With the considerable aid of the handsome black-and-steel void of a set by Herbert Senn and Helen Pond, Ms. Caldwell also creates some rending images. Ms. Anderman ascends to her bedroom on a labyrinthine, winding staircase that mirrors the turmoil of her soul. The attacking army, camouflaged by Birnam Wood, comes to Dunsinane from the smoky rear of the stage like a haunted, advancing forest. The subsequent battle scenes cascade forward in mad bursts of violence that are faithful to the jagged rhythms of Shakespeare's shortest, most abruptly composed tragedy.

But by then the impassive Mr. Anglim has reappeared to die, like a crumpled toy soldier, in the distracting midst of Ms. Caldwell's sound and fury. One would like to say that nothing became this *Macbeth* like the protagonist's leaving it—but in this doomed production, I'm afraid, Macbeth never even arrived.

≡ *Since its inception in 1965 the Vivian Beaumont Theater, the stepchild of the Lincoln Center complex, had brought many major theatrical figures to grief. The original Robert Whitehead–Elia Kazan regime burned out after a few seasons, as did its immediate successor, the team of Jules Irving and Herbert Blau, and, in the 1970s, Joseph Papp. The Richmond Crink-ley regime arrived in the fall of 1980 with a seemingly foolproof debut—Blythe Danner in* The Philadelphia Story—*that fell flat. Then came this* Macbeth, *which received universal pans. Though Crinkley had assembled an impressive artistic board that included Woody Allen and Liviu Ciulei as well as Sarah Caldwell, his own qualifications for running an institution of this size and prominence were hazy (aside from a close connection to some of the theater's board members) and he didn't even devote full time to the job, choosing to do some Broadway producing on the side. He fled soon enough.*

But to the amazement of everyone in the theater, the Vivian Beaumont would be successfully revived later in the decade, by the director Gregory Mosher (formerly of Chicago's Goodman Theater) and the producer Bernard Gersten (Papp's longtime partner at the New York Shakespeare Festival), to become one of the most active and successful theatrical operations in town more than twenty years after its stillbirth. The streak continued with Mosher's successor, André Bishop (formerly of Playwrights Horizons).

PENGUIN TOUQUET
PUBLIC THEATER, FEBRUARY 2, 1981

Richard Foreman, the director, doesn't dream big dreams. He dreams mesmerizing small ones and then inflates them until they fill the stage. In *Penguin Touquet,* his new theatrical piece, Mr. Fore-man is dreaming about spinning waiters, bearded saxophone players, blind men, large gray rocks, scissors-crazed barbers, fish soup, a town called Great Poetry—and, yes, penguins. Are his dreams any more pro-found than yours or mine? No, but then you and I are not capable of turn-ing our subconscious ramblings into an evening of hallucinatory theater. Mr. Foreman is. *Penguin Touquet* may not be an intellectual revelation, but it's surely one of the season's most audacious displays of fantastic stagecraft.

Although this production unfolds in the Public Theater's spacious Newman Theater, it doesn't much depart from Mr. Foreman's past antics at his own tiny Ontological-Hysteric playhouse. Once more the proscenium is bisected by string; the leading lady is still the alluring Kate Manheim. In *Penguin Touquet,* which runs a refreshingly taut eighty minutes, there is also a story of sorts. Ms. Manheim plays Agatha, a latter-day Dorothy who searches for an ontological Oz. The wizard is a psychiatrist (David Warrilow), who may or may not have the power to lead her into a "different form of life."

Well, let's not be literal-minded. What counts most here is Mr. Foreman's gift for shaping actors, scenery, sound, lighting, and architectural space into a cascade of animated images that have their own internal flow and logic, their own cause and effect. Some of the images are funny or beautiful or frightening, and many are haunting. In *Penguin Touquet,* Mr. Foreman has managed to fold the spooky visual styles of Magritte and de Chirico, as well as Brechtian theatrical technique, into a show that occasionally recalls, of all things, that old psychoanalytical musical, *Lady in the Dark.*

The action unfolds in a mysterious funhouse of a set, designed by Mr. Foreman and Heidi Landesman, which looks like a cross between a giant eye chart, a Left Bank Paris bistro, and a chessboard. It is decorated with incomplete words (DIFFEREN, RESOULTI), and its components are always on the move. The stage frame is bordered by lights of all kinds, which sometimes blind the audience. The sounds include snippets of movie music, pounding heartbeats, rhythmic chants ("I am on fire, am I not!"), loud breathing, and deafening electronic blasts. Mr. Foreman long ago went on record to the effect that the artistic experience must be an ordeal.

Yet *Penguin Touquet* is not painful, and it's rarely boring. The best vignettes really do have the lucidity and power of dreams. In one of them, Agatha pounds a piano keyboard with one of the ubiquitous rocks, only to be told by a godlike voice that "The rock can't make a career of playing the piano" and that it will soon be "pulverized, mixed with other things, and turned into a road." The indomitable Agatha asks, "Where will the road lead?"—but she gets no answer. Instead, the cast breaks into spastic gestures that suggest some mass electrocution of the psyche.

I was also fond of a sequence in which Agatha starts to whistle a symphony, ends up whistling a popular tune, and soon gets swept away in a frenzied tap dance. Somewhat later the penguins appear—they may or may not symbolize sexual terror—and the lighting (superbly designed by Pat Collins) dims into a spooky twilight that promises a carnal hurricane.

Another motif of *Penguin Touquet* is gold. Disgusted to find some nuggets in his soup, Mr. Warrilow plaintively asks, "Would you mind if I broke down and cried?"

As always, Mr. Foreman plays manic tricks with time. The actors' movements frequently speed up or slow down, silent-movie style, and the one poor soul who attempts to wear a watch gets his wrist burned. The evening's choreography is unfailingly precise; the associative links between segments are so clear that we never lose our way in the director's iconographic map. We're ready for anything: heads of cabbage, chandeliers, a huge snowman. When characters are struck by nose-bleeds, we accept the attacks as Mr. Foreman's equivalents to a conventional play's emotional catharses. Indeed, when the bleeding Agatha retreats from her self-discoveries at the end, we're even moved. Her final, questioning refrain—"When you see something out of the corner of your eye, do you really see it?"—perfectly expresses the melancholy of a dreamer awakened.

Though acting is not required, the performers are an integral part of the fun. Ms. Manheim is a splendid girl-woman, capable of both primal rages and sexy flights of daffiness. The spindly Mr. Warrilow, dressed like a sepulchral floorwalker of the soul, is a grave deadpan comedian who can break into funny paroxysms of mock vomiting. Gretel Cummings is quite amusing as a "grande dame" who erupts orgasmically when she walks across the stage with an old-fashioned radio between her ankles.

And what does it all mean? Mr. Foreman provides the audience with a combination glossary/plot summary that explains his symbols and re-caps his concern with such philosophical polarities as mind and body, nature and culture, feeling and thought, and so on. Be assured that there's little new or surprising in any of it. But one doesn't attend this show to discover the meaning of life, or even the meaning of the title, *Penguin Touquet*. One goes instead to watch Mr. Foreman transform his idiosyncratic stream of consciousness into a flood of theatrical magic.

INADMISSIBLE EVIDENCE
ROUNDABOUT THEATRE, FEBRUARY 24, 1981

In 1965, Nicol Williamson came to New York and scored a huge personal triumph as Bill Maitland, the angry antihero of John Osborne's *Inadmissible Evidence*. Last night, Mr. Williamson returned to town in his career-making role—and the evidence on display at the Roundabout suggests that history is about to repeat itself. This marathon performance is a daring, uncompromising feat: Mr. Williamson ushers us into the consciousness of one of the postwar theater's most unappetizing characters and simply refuses to let us escape. If *Inadmissible Evidence* is an evening of almost pure pain, it is honest pain, truthful pain—pain that is raised by brilliant acting to the level of art.

Mr. Osborne's play, which is by no means flawless, tells the story of a particularly bad day in its protagonist's thirty-nine-year-old life. Bill is a London lawyer and, as he tells us, an "irredeemably mediocre" man. He is bored with his wife and children. His legal practice is a dreary monotony of divorce cases. His sex life consists of an endless series of petty, casual affairs in which he "inflicts more pain than pleasure." As if things weren't bad enough, Bill has begun to notice that taxi drivers speed past him when he tries to hail a cab.

Inadmissible Evidence is, for the most part, an extended monologue for the panicked Bill. Discovering that he can no longer keep "everything in place," he starts to fall apart. As delivered by Mr. Williamson, Bill's lengthy diatribe is not the teary wallow in self-pity or self-hatred that one might expect: It's a lawyer's objective tallying of the facts of his own bankrupt life. By thinking through every specific gesture of his character, the actor gives a performance that is beyond pity and is far too complex to devolve into a sentimental archetype. He shows us Bill clearly for what he is; the case is presented without prejudice.

Mr. Williamson is something to see. Standing tall in a pin-striped three-piece suit, he enters the stage in darkness, then stands weaving in a blinding spotlight, like Archie Rice in Mr. Osborne's *The Entertainer*. His voice sputters and whinnies as words tumble out in babbling incoherence. He searches his vest pockets for his pills and then sends his long hands flying up to his temples—as if he were trying to push his spilling brains back into his skull. When Bill tells us that his eyes are like "oysters," we look at his heavy, flickering lids and know just what he means.

In his office a bit later, Bill is not unlike Butley in the Simon Gray play that Mr. Osborne undoubtedly influenced. Mr. Williamson sits behind his desk and hurls verbal darts at all comers—fellow lawyers, secretaries, clients. Yet he doesn't even have the courage of his own bile. When his dull, humorless aide (a properly pallid Philip Bosco) suddenly announces that he may soon leave for another firm, Mr. Williamson explodes with a withering insult—only to turn ashen a second later and beg like a child for forgiveness. It's soon clear that Bill doesn't know what he's doing: His steady torrent of words—whether malicious, circumspect, or witty—increases in velocity until, finally, it's a harrowing buzz that just can't be stopped. Mr. Williamson is drowning so quickly that he wouldn't see a life preserver even if someone bothered to toss him one.

Though it's hard for anyone else on stage to get a word in edgewise, there are some other decent performances here. Elaine Bromka is upsetting as a discarded lover who tries and fails to hurt Bill in their final confrontation, and Anthony Heald is woundingly pathetic as both a colorless law clerk and a crumbling homosexual client. Anthony Page, who also directed the original production, hasn't cast the other roles so well, but then those characters aren't well-written, either. Though *Inadmissible Evidence* isn't dated, as Mr. Osborne's *Look Back in Anger* proved to be in its Roundabout revival last season, it still suffers from structural failings. The otherwise well-constructed Act 1 is somewhat blighted by its mystical courtroom prologue. The overlong Act 2 collapses into unduly repetitive scenes in which Bill's mostly interchangeable loved ones and clients each desert him in turn.

But one cannot take away the tough-mindedness that Mr. Osborne has brought to the creation of Bill Maitland. Without ever asking us to like this man, without ever trying to redeem him, the playwright does find a common ground where the audience and his hero can meet. One doesn't have to pity Bill or share his emptiness to understand and identify with his feelings of psychological vertigo: We all reel, at times, from the sweaty fear that we may, in the end, be completely alone in the world. It is Mr. Osborne's achievement that *Inadmissible Evidence* takes us right up to the edge of that darkest of voids. Then Mr. Williamson comes along and, with the most terrifying of ease, pushes us in.

SOPHISTICATED LADIES
LUNT-FONTANNE THEATRE, MARCH 2, 1981

In the course of his extraordinary career, Duke Ellington did just about everything with jazz that any mortal could be expected to do. Yet, strangely enough, there was one goal that eluded this giant of American music right up to his death in 1974: He never had a hit Broadway show to call his own.

Well, it sure looks as if he has one now. *Sophisticated Ladies*, the new musical revue at the Lunt-Fontanne, is an Ellington celebration that just won't quit until it has won over the audience with dynamic showmanship. It's not a perfect entertainment—let's save the flaws for later—but it rides so high on affection, skill, and, of course, stunning music that the lapses don't begin to spoil the fun. What's more, this is the only Broadway revue of recent vintage that operates on a truly grand scale. There's a lavishness in this show's physical production (right up to the last spangle on the last top hat) and in its depth of performing talent (right down to the last member of the chorus) that actually squares with current Broadway ticket prices. Ellington, who had an extravagant style to go with his genius, would undoubtedly be pleased.

Indeed, there are times in this evening of three dozen songs when he might be beside himself. That certainly seems the only fitting response to the show's star, the esteemed Gregory Hines. It's no secret that Mr. Hines may be the best tap dancer of our day, but he's never had a chance to show himself to quite the advantage that he does here. Wearing slicked-backed hair, a series of sleek evening outfits, and a raffish smile, he's more than a dancer; he's the frisky Ellington spirit incarnate. And, like the show's unseen hero, he seems to be able to do everything—including, at one point, a solo on the drums.

His singing is raspy, but so charged with feeling that he makes that wistful Ellington–Billy Strayhorn ballad "Something to Live For" the evening's most moving number. The show's funniest song also belongs to him: On "I'm Just a Lucky So-and-So," Mr. Hines comes out carried by a human Checker cab and proceeds to trade giddy notes with his vehicle of transportation. (Don't ask questions; you have to see for yourself.) As for his tap dancing, what more is there to say? In his big Act 2 solo, Mr. Hines provides a one-man tour of his calling. He sweeps about gently and then lets loose with cataclysmic force; he takes big leaps and then tucks in his wings for a dazzling display of terpsichorean precision. This man is human lightning, and he just can't be contained.

But don't think that *Sophisticated Ladies* is a one-man show. Gregg Burge, a lithe fellow with an insouciant grin, would be the standout tapper in any other musical. He and the chorus turn themselves into a silver-lamé airplane for "Caravan," and, when smoke pours onto the stage, you wouldn't be surprised if they actually took flight. A little before that, Mr. Burge and Mr. Hines exchange high kicks on "It Don't Mean a Thing (If It Ain't Got That Swing)." By the end of this joyous song, the two men are both leapfrogging so deftly about each other that one has no choice but to call their informal dancing duel a draw.

Forced to choose between the two sultry female singers of the evening, I'd also have to equivocate. When Phyllis Hyman, a cool tomcat of a woman, applies her powerful, smoky voice to "In a Sentimental Mood," she immediately transports the audience to a Fifty-second Street saloon of yesteryear at three in the morning. Terri Klausner, last seen playing *Evita* at Wednesday matinees, is likewise no slouch in the smoke department. Slithering about in a dress of midnight blue and silver to sing "Hit Me with a Hot Note and Watch Me Bounce," she uses a bluesy, guttural attack to send us bouncing on every line. It's unfortunate that Ms. Klausner is often paired with the show's one wrong-note performer, P. J. Benjamin, who has here come down with a distracting case of the cutes.

Even Mr. Benjamin wouldn't attempt to distract us from the other star of the evening, Judith Jamison, and no wonder. The towering, charismatic Ms. Jamison, on furlough from Alvin Ailey, is a commanding work of art just when she's standing still. Too much of the time, perhaps, she does just stand there—as if the show's creators were too intimidated to figure out what to do with her. But Ms. Jamison sings well when asked, especially when lounging luxuriantly across a red piano for "I Love You Madly." More important, she gives the evening a presence that no one else can provide. Beaming and sassy, wearing one spectacular Willa Kim costume after another, she becomes a mesmerizing incarnation of 1920s Cotton Club glamour. By the time she descends a staircase, a vision in white, to Mr. Hines's rendition of *Sophisticated Lady*, she'll take your breath away.

Ms. Jamison also makes something sweet out of an inadequately conceived mock-ballet solo that accompanies Priscilla Baskerville's lush soprano reading of "Solitude." While the show's three choreographers— Donald McKayle, Michael Smuin (of the San Francisco Ballet), and Henry LeTang (for tap)—have generally done a sprightly job of re-creating (if not reinventing) old-time Harlem razzmatazz, you'll notice such occasional imaginative sags, as well as a few repetitions. You'll notice, too, a lack of wit in the lyrics that often accompany Ellington's melodies; there are not the opportunities for humor here that Fats Waller's songbook offered *Ain't Misbehavin'*. While the music is as vibrantly played as it is sung—Mercer Ellington's big band is on stage— the inexcusably raucous amplification, "designed" by Otts Munderloh, at times violates its spirit.

The evening's flaws duly noted, we should count the other blessings. Tony Walton has created a handsome set (not unlike the one he did for *Chicago*) with a floating bandstand, a Deco frame, and high-flying explosions of neon. Jennifer Tipton, that wondrous lighting designer, has sculpted romantic, soulful, and glamorous spaces out of thin air. Ms. Kim's costumes are so profuse and brightly hued that they transform the cast into an ever-changing satin rainbow. That's just how it should be when you've got Duke Ellington to back up your rainbow with pure musical gold.

LOLITA

Brooks Atkinson Theatre, March 20, 1981

After weeks of delays, Edward Albee's *Lolita* finally opened at the Brooks Atkinson last night, and all one can do is wonder why it did. This show is the kind of embarrassment that audiences do not quickly forget or forgive. It's not just that *Lolita* is incompetent or boring or that it lays waste to a masterpiece of modern literature: Those are pardonable sins that have been known to occur in Broadway theaters. What sets *Lolita* apart from ordinary failures is its abject mean-spiritedness. For all this play's babbling about love, it is rank with indiscriminate—and decidedly unearned—hate.

Lolita bills itself as an adaptation of Vladimir Nabokov's novel about Humbert Humbert, a professorial European émigré whose sexual obsession with a twelve-year-old girl sends him crisscrossing America in a frenzy of passion that leads to madness and murder. The book is a funny and finally tragic evocation of a man's desire to possess his irretrievable past, of the modern American landscape, of the beauties and limits of the English language. Last and least, it is a book about sex: The lovers' carnal adventures are described with sensitivity and only then in the early stages of Humbert's parodistically confessional memoir.

Mr. Albee's *Lolita* is something else. Aside from odd verbatim lines (usually ripped out of context), all that remains of Nabokov's novel at the Atkinson is its most accessible feature, its mildly salacious plot. And even that is so ineptly told—usually by means of flat-out narration or announcements—that it often seems to be taking place offstage. (By Act 2, the action is so remote and truncated it seems phoned in from another solar system.) There are vague attempts to pay lip service to the deeper, passionate concerns of the novel—the play's hollowed-out Humbert periodically wails earnestly about his mad love and invites our pity—but the evening is mainly a slapdash compilation of jokes. The jokes are Mr. Albee's, not Nabokov's, and they are a perfect amalgam of the witless and the tasteless.

The only benign gags, perhaps, are the playwright's sadly sophomoric attempts to match Nabokov's intricate word games and ironic literary conceits. Instead of the book's dense, Joycean poetic fabric, we get idle alliterative doodles typified by Humbert's non sequitur "Better bugs in the basement than buggery in the bedroom." Literature is represented by a character named "a certain gentleman" (Ian Richardson) who shadows Humbert (Donald Sutherland) throughout the evening and is apparently meant to be a stand-in for Nabokov. This well-dressed fellow—who also resembles the narrator of Mr. Albee's grim adaptation of *The Ballad of the Sad Café*—tries desperately to give the evening highfalutin airs. When he refers, at one typical point, to a house of "double perfumes and cracked mirror images," he allows Mr. Albee to reduce a major imagistic motif of the novel to a single, cryptic, pretentious line.

When it comes to sex, Mr. Albee reveals a sensibility that would be right at home on network television. This *Lolita* isn't more explicit than Nabokov's (despite the addition of four-letter words); it's just more smirky. Each time Humbert and Lolita (Blanche Baker) try to engage in a sex act, they are interrupted either by a supposedly farcical intruder or by that certain gentleman, who brings down a curtain and coyly asks us to invoke our imaginations. The most famous sexual incident of the book—in which Humbert has an orgasm while Lolita sits innocently on his robed lap—is painful to witness. Mr. Sutherland gasps and pants and bobs like a fleabag comic cavorting at a stag dinner.

If there's a point to the would-be sex scenes in Mr. Albee's *Lolita*, it is an unpleasant one: The writer is not out to titillate, but to render the erotic impulse ridiculous. The ridicule doesn't stop there. Charlotte Haze (Shirley Stoler), Lolita's vulgar yet handsome mother in the book, has been transformed into "sort of a pig." She's a screechy circus freak in a loud muumuu—a caricature of female sexuality that sends a shudder of revulsion through the theater. Worse still, Mr. Albee has given the mother a black maid who has no dramatic function beyond recalling the heyday of *Amos 'n' Andy*. We also get a wisecrack in which Humbert accuses Charlotte of being an "anti-Semite (who) differentiates between Jews and kikes." The line is meaningless except as an attempt to get a sleazy laugh on the word "kikes."

Frank Dunlop has directed these proceedings with a slam-bang crudeness that one associates with long-running London sex-farces. He isn't helped much by the hideous and awkward set, designed by the usually smart William Ritman, that forces the actors to stumble about slanted panels and odd heaps of furniture. Nor is any attempt made to duplicate Nabokov's witty, abstracted backdrop of crazy-quilt American motels and suburban communities. Even Alan Jay Lerner's 1971 musical comedy version of *Lolita,* which folded in Boston on its way to Broadway, got the scenery right.

The cast must fend for itself. As the narrator, Mr. Richardson is, as always, ineffably urbane even when reciting gibberish. In the title role, here a minor figure, the twenty-four-year-old Ms. Baker does a clever job of impersonating the downy nymphet; she deserves a more substantial stage vehicle soon. The others—who also include Clive Revill imitating Peter

Sellers's movie characterization of Clare Quilty—fare badly. One feels especially sorry for Mr. Sutherland, a very fine actor who here is asked to yuk at his own bad jokes, to affect prissy hand gestures, and to flounce about like a broken puppet. It's as if he's parodying one of his rare bad screen performances—his other pedophile, in Bernardo Bertolucci's *1900*.

But Mr. Sutherland and company will survive this carnival. And so, needless to say, will Vladimir Nabokov's novel. About Mr. Albee, it's hard to be so sanguine. This playwright, who promised and delivered great things two decades ago, has in recent years abandoned his gifts. Now he's gone further: In *Lolita*, Mr. Albee has forsaken the humane impulse that is the minimal, rock-bottom essential of art.

≣ *Edward Albee, the contemporary American playwright I most admired as a theater-infatuated youth, did the least and worst work of his career during my years as drama critic. Only two new plays of his made it to New York: his adaptation of* Lolita *and* The Man Who Had Three Arms. *In the mid-1990s, after I'd switched jobs, I met him for the first time and enjoyed a spirited discussion with him about* Lolita *in which he explained some of the behind-the-scenes insanities that he had had to put up with at the hands of its producer. If he was angry with me for this review all these years later, he was too polite to say so. (I'm happy to report that my experience with Albee was typical: The awkwardness that usually inhibits even non-adversarial meetings between artists and critics evaporated quickly in most such encounters once I left criticism behind.)*

By the time of our meeting, Albee's career-revivifying Three Tall Women *had arrived Off Broadway—and it would soon be joined by Gerald Gutierrez's fine Broadway revival of the 1966* A Delicate Balance *starring George Grizzard, Rosemary Harris, and Elaine Stritch, and far superior to the original version (starring Hume Cronyn and Jessica Tandy) that I'd seen in the mid-sixties. I keep waiting for a revival of my favorite neglected Albee work—the 1971* All Over, *a Broadway failure that proved stageworthy when Peggy Ashcroft and Angela Lansbury appeared in Peter Hall's production of it for the Royal Shakespeare Company in London that year.*

WOMAN OF THE YEAR
PALACE THEATRE, MARCH 30, 1981

I wrote the book on class," sings Lauren Bacall in her new musical, *Woman of the Year*, and you had better believe it. This star's elegance is no charade, no mere matter of beautiful looks and gorgeous gowns. Her class begins where real class must—in her spirit—and only then makes its way to her angular physique, her big, sensuous eyes, and that snapdragon of a voice. Even when her leading man, Harry Guardino, dumps a pot of water over her head, she remains not only mesmerizing, but also completely fresh. As hard and well as Ms. Bacall works in *Woman of the Year,* she never lets us see any sweat.

That's why this actress is a natural musical-comedy star. By making life and art look as easy and elegant as a perfect song, Ms. Bacall embodies the very spirit of the carefree American musical. She also, as a result, makes extraordinary demands on her theatrical collaborators. When we see Ms. Bacall on stage, we want the entertainment that contains her to come together as simply and delightfully as her performance. If it doesn't, we're going to notice the esthetic gap between the star and her vehicle very fast.

Woman of the Year, which opened at the Palace last night, is an amiable show that suffers from such a gap. It boasts other assets besides Ms. Bacall—most crucially a tuneful score by John Kander—but it often huffs and puffs to achieve effects that its leading lady can pull off with a flick of her regal head. And, even then, it doesn't always deliver. While this show never drops below a certain, hard-nosed level of Broadway professionalism, neither does it rise to a steadily exciting pitch. Its creators are most fortunate to have a star who crackles whether they light a fire under her or not.

The musical has been adapted by Peter Stone from the tender and funny Ring Lardner Jr.–Michael Kanin screenplay that first brought Katharine Hepburn and Spencer Tracy together in 1942. Mr. Stone's book isn't up to his source material, but it doesn't disfigure it. This *Woman of the Year* is still a modern battle between the sexes: the story of how a man's man, Sam Craig (Mr. Guardino), and a fabulously successful career woman, Tess Harding (Ms. Bacall), try to build a marriage around their powerful egos.

Mr. Stone has, by necessity, made his heroine and hero older than the originals. He has changed their professions as well. Tess, formerly a newspaper columnist, has been smartly reinvented as a superstar broadcast journalist modeled on Barbara Walters. Sam has been transformed from a sportswriter into a cartoonist—an alteration that proves a mixed blessing. Though Sam's new career allows the musical to mix screen animation with live action for amusing results, it backs the book into some unfortunate corners early on. In order to bring about a first meeting for his leads, Mr. Stone must have Tess recite a television editorial against comic strips—a phony bit that introduces the heroine on an obnoxious note. When Sam reacts with outrage—he objects to cartoons being called "funnies"—we wonder how a cartoonist can be so humorless.

This jerry-built conflict is eventually and mercifully shoved aside, at which point the book's other problems present themselves. Though there are a few funny jokes scattered about—especially one that details the one surefire way to get a table at Pearl's restaurant—the batting average is not high. Mr. Stone seems to believe that the dropping of fading famous names—from G. Gordon Liddy to Marie Osmond—automatically provokes laughs. He's also insisted on recounting so much of the movie's plot that he bloats the show into overlength in Act 1.

The book's top-heaviness is compounded by its inefficient, old-fashioned structure. Mr. Stone's song cues announce themselves like sirens—and then give way to numbers that tend to illustrate the action rather than advance it. Nor is there a first-rate choreographer present to take up the slackened forward drive. Tony Charmoli, who staged the dances, all too clearly hails from television. While his numbers have energy, they're simplified, variety-special versions of dances that have been done better by Bob Fosse (in his slouch-hat vein) and Michael Bennett (in *Company*). There's even a gratuitous Russian kickline that recalls the Jerome Robbins of *Fiddler on the Roof.*

Yet Mr. Kander's accompanying music is sprightly indeed. From the moment we hear the cheering overture (superbly orchestrated by Michael Gibson), it's clear that the score is flush with melodic ballads and showbiz brio. Ms. Bacall gets to whoop it up with some male barflies in a trademark Kander rouser in Act 1 and then returns to the same bar to harmonize sweetly (in her fashion) with a pair of cleaning women in Act 2. For Mr. Guardino and his animated alter ego (a cat named Katz), there's a charming, sardonic duet that, if anything, seems too brief. While Fred Ebb's lyrics are sometimes routine (especially in the inadequate title song), they ascend to witty heights in the prolific comedy turns. Ms. Bacall and Marilyn Cooper, as a hilariously frumpy housewife, bring down the house when they try to decide whose "grass is greener" late in Act 2.

Robert Moore, a good comedy director, has cast able clowns (Roderick Cook, Grace Keagy) in the minor roles and punched up every joke he can. He hasn't quite succeeded in providing Ms. Bacall with an evenly matched leading man. Though Mr. Guardino is skillful, his blandness recalls the salad days of Sydney Chaplin. Until Sam arrives at a touching Act 2 ballad, we're unclear about why Tess finds him so fascinating. Even then, we don't believe that she would consider, however briefly, abandoning her career for him.

The production's design could also use some spiffing up. Tony Walton's elaborate sets are clever yet colorless, and Marilyn Rennagel's lighting is gloomy. The usually inspired costume designer Theoni V. Aldredge has done well by her star, only to dress the rest of the cast in varying shades of drab. But that may be the point. The people who concocted this musical know what their show is really about. Ms. Bacall is on hand virtually the whole time, and she's vibrant whether no-nonsense or tipsy, domineering or moony, dry or wet. If *Woman of the Year* is tired around the edges, it is always smart enough to keep its live wire center stage.

≣ *This mediocre show ran two years to large, often full houses with Bacall and her successor, Raquel Welch—longer than the original Broadway runs of* West Side Story, Death of a Salesman, *and* Gypsy, *among many other earlier hits—but never paid back its investors in full. Thus it introduced an ominous new phenomenon to the Broadway theater: the "hit" that turns out to be a flop. Like other long-running, often Tony-winning examples of flop "hits" to follow—*Jerome Robbins' Broadway, The Will Rogers Follies, Sunset Boulevard, Victor/Victoria—*Woman of the Year *exposed the perilously inflated, if not completely absurd, state of Broadway economics.*

How could a show play to crowded houses at high ticket prices for two years and still fail to make a profit on its Broadway run? Very simply. If weekly operating costs are out of hand, even those huge ticket sales will barely cover them—let alone return a significant profit on top of that. A musical that requires an initial investment of, say, $10 million or more to bring to Broadway in the late 1990s might require ticket sales approaching $500,000 a week just to meet its weekly costs—a figure that includes star and cast and crew and musicians' salaries, royalties to the authors, theater rent, print and TV advertising. If the show meets or exceeds that $500,000 in ticket sales each week, it may well be playing to large, perhaps even near-full houses, and can run indefinitely. But the production will go into profit only if its business exceeds that $500,000 level long enough to pay back in weekly installments the $10 million-plus initial outlay that got the show to Broadway in the first place.

A flop "hit," in other words, is a production that runs two years or longer because it meets its weekly break-even figure of $500,000 (to continue with my hypothetical example) but rarely exceeds it. When it finally closes—after its weekly gross has dropped well below that break-even point—such a show has happily provided two years of income to its employees, two years of rent to the theater owner, and lots of money to The New York Times and other advertising venues. But it has paid back little or none of the $10 million its backers put up to create the show.

Given these odds, who in his right mind would invest in a Broadway show? Mainly (a) large corporations that can afford to roll the dice; (b) hedging Broadway theater owners who will collect weekly rent that may exceed in total whatever they throw in (and lose) as an initial investment; (c) those eternal romantics, people who have money to burn and are irrationally intoxicated with the glamour of show business in general and Broadway in particular. Every season produces at least one unexpected gusher that defies the odds and keeps the dream of backing a real hit alive.

THE DANCE AND THE RAILROAD
NEW FEDERAL THEATER, MARCH 31, 1981

David Henry Hwang, a twenty-four-year-old Chinese American playwright, is a true original. A native of Los Angeles, born to immigrant parents, he has one foot on each side of a cultural divide. He knows America—its vernacular, its social landscape, its theatrical traditions. He knows the same about China. In his plays, he manages to mix both of these conflicting cultures until he arrives at a style that is wholly his own. Mr. Hwang's works have the verve of well-made American comedies and yet, with little warning, they can bubble over into the mystical rituals of Asian stagecraft. By at once bringing West and East into conflict and unity, this playwright has found the perfect means to dramatize both the pain and humor of the immigrant experience.

In *FOB*, his play at the Public Theater last spring, Mr. Hwang wrote about an assimilated Chinese American who meets and mocks a "fresh-off-the-boat" immigrant in a Los Angeles restaurant. His new play, *The Dance and the Railroad*, is a leaner, more accomplished dramatization of a similar story. The setting is again California, but the time is a century earlier. *Railroad*, now at the Henry Street Settlement's New Federal Theater, tells of two Chinese laborers who are toiling to build the transcontinental railroad in 1867.

Lone, the more worldly of the pair, has been in America two years. In China, he had spent his childhood studying to be an actor in the Chinese opera—only to have his promising career cut short when his impoverished parents sold him into servitude. Even now, after putting in ten hours with his work gang each day, Lone goes to a vacant mountaintop at night to practice his theatrical gymnastics. He believes that as long as he makes his muscles work for himself as well as the railroad, he will not be merely another coolie slave.

If Lone is proud and cynical, his companion is a naive dreamer. Ma has been in California only four weeks, and he still believes all the propaganda. Ma thinks that American mountains are made of gold, that the "white devil" can be "civilized" by the Chinese, and that he'll soon amass a fortune that will send him home in luxury. He never doubts that his new life is "the best of both worlds."

Railroad, which runs about an hour, consists of a series of encounters between the two men as they wait out a strike. Ma admires Lone's acting acrobatics and asks his newfound friend to teach them to him. Lone finds Ma something of a fool, but he tries to teach him anyway. As the two men whirl and leap about the stage in their informal practice sessions, they talk more and more about their past lives in China, their visions of the future, and the progress of their ongoing revolt against their white bosses.

Much of the action is humorous—especially when Ma is trying, ineptly, to imitate the dazzling grace of Lone's gymnastic tricks. But there's an underlying sadness, too, as we watch these lonely men clinging to old customs in a new frontier that tempts them with whiskey, gambling, and out-of-reach riches. That sadness rises shatteringly to the surface in the play's final section, in which Ma and Lone improvise their own Chinese opera about their harrowing sea journey to America and their subsequent adventures in the ostensible promised land. By the end of this often funny burlesque, the two characters have subtly traded positions until finally we wonder if the wise Lone might not be the real slave, the real fool, the man who has lost the illusions of both his worlds.

The play's production is as witty, poetic, and affecting as the writing. The director and star is John Lone, who performs his namesake role. Mr. Lone, who also appeared in *FOB,* is a magnetic figure: a stunning acrobat, mimic (of everything from ducks to Americans), and actor who precisely conveys his character's mixture of princely arrogance and unspoken despair. Tzi Ma, as the awkward, childish Ma, is a fine comic foil. It says a lot about these two performers that they let us hear every note in Mr. Hwang's startling and far-ranging theatrical voice.

≡ *Surely this was the most unusual audience with which I ever saw a play I was reviewing. The production was performed in a tiny playhouse at the Henry Street Settlement House, as part of its cultural mission to bring theater to housing-project residents. The weekday afternoon crowd was almost all women and their very young children. Everyone was held rapt. And before long, Joseph Papp moved the production intact to the Public Theater,*

where it enjoyed an extended run in tandem with another new and inter-
esting Hwang play, Family Devotions.

MARCH OF THE FALSETTOS
PLAYWRIGHTS HORIZONS, APRIL 10, 1981

When the best two musicals of the season (*The Pirates of Pen-*
zance, Sophisticated Ladies) are both the work of dead songwriters, you know that the American musical theater is in trouble.
Indeed, I can't even remember the last time I attended a musical—on
Broadway or Off—that introduced a new composer or lyricist of serious
promise. And that's why I had trouble believing my ears at a new show
with the unlikely title of *March of the Falsettos*. This one-hour musical,
which is now running in the small upstairs space at Playwrights Horizons, tells its story through twenty songs by William Finn. The songs are
so fresh that the show is only a few bars old before one feels the unmistakable, revivifying charge of pure talent.

Who is William Finn? He's the author of a previous Off Off Broadway
musical, *In Trousers,* which, to my eternal damnation, I haven't seen. According to the program, he was awarded the Hutchinson Fellowship for
Musical Composition at Williams College—a prize that Stephen Sondheim also received once upon a time. The program further states that
Mr. Finn is collaborating with Joan Micklin Silver, the director, on a musical version of her film *Hester Street*. This confirms my view that Mrs.
Silver tends to be one of the first people in New York to spot young writers and performers who are going places.

Falsettos has been staged by James Lapine, whose own play *Table Set-*
tings was a hit at Playwrights Horizons last season. It's a small show that
tells of Marvin (Michael Rupert), a rueful fellow who leaves his wife (Alison Fraser) and preteen son (James Kushner) for a male lover (Stephen
Bogardus). If this central idea sounds like a variation on Christopher
Durang's recent comedy, *Beyond Therapy,* a further twist recalls Charles
Ludlam's *Reverse Psychology.* No sooner does Marvin leave home than
his ex-wife takes up with his psychiatrist, a very funny eighty-bucks-an-
hour cad named Mendel (Chip Zien).

However slight and predictable the raw materials, Mr. Finn has transformed them into a show that is funny and tender on its own contained,
anecdotal terms. The title notwithstanding, there's nothing cute, campy,
or precious about *Falsettos*. Nor is there any propaganda. The show's

hetero- and homosexual couples both suffer from the same anxieties, loneliness, and neuroses. The evening's most touching relationship isn't sexual at all. Marvin, who wants to keep his tight-knit family even after he's left it, is obsessed with retaining the affection of his bright, chess-playing child. It isn't easy. "My father's a homo," sings the anguished son, who then goes on to worry about his chromosomes.

Yet the real story here is Mr. Finn's score. The music in this show is honest-to-God music. It's played by a lovely seven-piece band, conducted by Michael Starobin, that is long on woodwinds and strings and bereft of synthesizers. There are no Broadway or rock mannerisms—just a continuous flow of original, unpredictable melodies that run from melancholy ballads to eccentric comic riffs. At times Mr. Finn's writing recalls the feeling and substance of Leonard Bernstein's analysand musical, *Trouble in Tahiti* (especially in a number called "Marvin at the Psychiatrist," which is billed as a "three-part mini-opera"). One also thinks of the British songwriter Alan Price (*O Lucky Man*) and, occasionally, of Mr. Sondheim. But there are so many musical surprises here that one never doubts that Mr. Finn is his own man.

The lyrics are of a slightly lesser order, but, at their best, they suggest what Woody Allen might be like if he'd gone into the songwriting game. Words like "linguini" and "smarmy" turn up in the most amusing of contexts. The opening number, "Four Jews in a Room Bitching," is funnier than its title suggests, as is the title song, a flat-out showstopper about male role-confusion. When the characters sing about the difficulties of being in love, the lyrics' openhearted passion often overrides their occasional technical deficiencies and descents into ordinary sentiment.

Mr. Finn's songs are sung by uniformly appealing performers, who are blissfully unamplified and up to the demands of the often intricate choral work. Mr. Rupert's sad, befuddled hero and Mr. Zien's parodistic shrink are particularly engaging. Mr. Lapine's wildly resourceful staging—which uses only a few movable pieces of furniture for a set—has a zippy, slam-bang sense of confidence that has been lacking in most bigger musicals this season. And no wonder. *March of the Falsettos* is that rare musical that actually has something to be cocky about.

≡ *This show was playing under such obscure circumstances—in a less-than-100-seat upstairs room at Playwrights Horizons, with no advertising or ABC listing—that it was initially ignored by nearly all critics. I went only because the title captured my attention and I had a free night when another show postponed. By a decade later,* Falsettos *and its sequel,* Falsettoland, *would become, in various forms and productions, the theater's signature response to the AIDS crisis.*

THE FLOATING LIGHT BULB
Vivian Beaumont Theater, April 28, 1981

Because the author's name is Woody Allen, we bring a certain set of expectations to *The Floating Light Bulb,* the new play that opened at the Vivian Beaumont last night. For the last five years, beginning with *Annie Hall,* Mr. Allen has been steadily staking out fresh territory as a filmmaker: He has insisted on being adventurous in each new movie, even at the risk of making a fool of himself.

So it's only natural that one expects *The Floating Light Bulb* to take him to another plateau—if not in terms of achievement, then at least in terms of daring. Hit or miss, we expect him to bring us a surprise. And that's why one is startled—and, yes, disappointed—by the conventional, modest, and at times pedestrian family drama that Mr. Allen has written. *Light Bulb* doesn't pick up where *Stardust Memories* leaves off; rather, it picks up where Mr. Allen's active playwriting career left off—with his last Broadway play, *Play It Again, Sam,* in 1969. For whatever reasons, Mr. Allen has decided to keep the cinematic and theatrical sides of his talent on two distinctly separate tracks.

Light Bulb is nothing to be embarrassed about, especially in the skillful production directed by Ulu Grosbard at Lincoln Center, but it could easily be mistaken for a journeyman effort by a much younger and less-experienced writer. This is an earnest autobiographical play that recycles, to much less invigorating effect, some of the material in *Annie Hall.* There are a few laughs, a few well-wrought characters, and, in Act 2, a beautifully written scene that leads to a moving final curtain. But most of the time *Light Bulb* is superficial and only mildly involving. As a serious playwright, Mr. Allen is still learning his craft and finding his voice.

Like so many young American plays, this one is overly beholden to the early Tennessee Williams. The setting is a lower-middle-class household in the Canarsie of 1945, but the milieu is pure *Glass Menagerie.* Instead of Amanda Wingfield, the mother is Enid Pollack (Beatrice Arthur), a proud, nagging woman who once dreamed of being a dancer (for *George White's Scandals*) and who now, like Amanda, is reduced to hounding neighbors with telephone business schemes to make ends meet. In place of Amanda's pleurisy-afflicted daughter Laura, Mr. Allen has provided a stuttering teenage son—Paul (Brian Backer), a bright, shy ugly duckling who retreats from life by practicing magic tricks in his grim bedroom. There's also a gentleman caller, a talent manager played by Jack Weston, who arrives in Act 2 to raise and then dash the Pollock family's last hopes.

Mr. Allen's family does vary slightly from Mr. Williams's. The father, a petty gambler and philanderer named Max (Danny Aiello), hasn't fled the coop yet, though he's on his way out the door. The family also contains a younger brother, Steve (Eric Gurry), who seems to exist only to provide Act 1 with wisecracks. Indeed, it's when Mr. Allen departs from *The Glass Menagerie* that *Light Bulb* is at its weakest: Neither Max nor Steve nor Max's illicit girlfriend (Ellen March) are much more than cogs in the action.

The others fare better. As played with commanding assurance and wit by Beatrice Arthur, the mother is a dynamic survivor—so much so that she at times recalls Ethel Merman's Rose in *Gypsy*. She's not overly vulnerable—we don't quite believe she's the alcoholic the script suggests—and yet we ultimately care about her. Left alone and bereft in her shabby living room at the end, Ms. Arthur suddenly goes white with fear. For a second, she really does seem the mother of the stammering, cowering son who is both the repository and victim of her failed aspirations.

That son is somewhat self-pityingly written, but he, too, finally touches us. When his mother yanks him out of his bedroom to perform his tricks for the visiting agent, the boy shivers and hyperventilates from panic. Mr. Backer, who glancingly resembles Mr. Allen in manner, does very well by the role: With his dark, drooping eyelids, frail posture, and incongruous magician's turban, he makes us see the almost terminal loneliness of a scared and loveless child.

But the best character is Mr. Weston's. This manager arrives at the Pollacks' apartment ostensibly to audition the son, but in fact to make eyes at the mother. Mr. Allen clearly knows such small-time showbiz hustlers to their bones. Mr. Weston is full of big talk—he has met Jimmy Durante and Cesar Romero—but his own clients turn out to be fleabag acts that play "the mountains." Still, he's more than a tired flimflam artist; he's also a sad, overgrown momma's boy who lacks the courage to seize the moment with Enid. Mr. Weston, by turns craven, pathetic, and funny (especially when imitating his prime client, a talking dog), brings Act 2 to fully rounded life.

The remaining performances, most notably Mr. Aiello's brusque, selfish Max, are good, too, but Mr. Weston has the luck to have the only sustained scene in the play. Act 1 is a series of splintered, underwritten episodes that are mainly designed to get the plot going. Once Mr. Weston leaves Act 2, Mr. Allen veers mechanically toward his inevitable conclusion. If the ending works better than it deserves to, that's because the playwright has made the most of his two best images—Paul's magic wand and a recurring anonymous phone call.

The play's other images and themes are pedantic. The son's floating light bulb magic trick—his own glass menagerie, as it were—is too archly set up as a metaphor for life's illusions. When characters talk of their various failed dreams or doomed hopes (a winning longshot bet for the father, a big star for the agent), they do so point-blank and repetitively. Instead of announcing these warmed-over poetic conceits again and again, Mr. Allen might have paid more attention to writing scenes that dig deeper and actually flesh out the relationships among the Pollacks. It's his refusal to take that next step that makes his drama seem like mock Williams, O'Neill, and Miller rather than the real thing.

Given the play's modest attainments, it might have been better served by a workshop airing in less pretentious circumstances. Santo Loquasto's towering, evocative tenement set, Pat Collins's brooding lighting, and Mr. Grosbard's sensitive, fluid staging all promise an evening as grandiose as *Death of a Salesman*. While this full-dress production was probably inevitable, it still doesn't seem right. Like any other, less-famous playwright, Woody Allen deserves the chance to develop his promising but unfinished *Light Bulb* away from Lincoln Center's harsh glare.

≡ *I begged to get out of reviewing this show. I had known Woody Allen through the years—though hardly intimately enough to call him "a friend"—and thought that this should disqualify me from reviewing this play as my friendships with Wendy Wasserstein and Jonathan Reynolds disqualified me from reviewing theirs. Arthur Gelb would have none of it; this was just too big an opening, he said, and I didn't know Woody so well that I would lose my objectivity. In this, he was right.*

Some of the reviews for The Floating Light Bulb *were more favorable than mine. Perhaps I was overcompensating to avoid any hint of favoritism. After this piece ran, I didn't hear from Woody for years. By then, he'd returned to the theater with a very funny play,* Central Park West, *that dominated a bill* (Death Defying Acts) *also containing one-acts by Elaine May and David Mamet.*

THE LITTLE FOXES
MARTIN BECK THEATRE, MAY 8, 1981

It may have taken a long time for her to get to Broadway, but she has arrived in high style. In Lillian Hellman's *The Little Foxes,* Elizabeth Taylor has found just the right vehicle to launch her career as a stage actress. And she rewards the role of Regina Giddens, that malignant Southern bitch-goddess, with a performance that begins gingerly, soon gathers steam, and then explodes into a black and thunderous storm that may just knock you out of your seat. Throw in a snappy supporting cast—led by Maureen Stapleton in a rending portrait of a fading, dipsomaniacal plantation belle—and you can begin to picture the crackling entertainment that opened at the Martin Beck last night.

Entertainment—that's what *The Little Foxes* most abundantly is. The story of an avaricious family of turn-of-the-century Southern entrepreneurs, Ms. Hellman's 1939 play is not long on emotional and intellectual niceties. The good characters are saintly, the bad ones dastardly, and they fight a battle to the literal death. Indeed, at its cold heart, *The Little Foxes* is essentially a plain old-fashioned thriller with a less-than-staggering moral tacked on. (Money, power, and moral cowardice are the roots of all evil.) But what a thriller! If there are few subtleties in this play, neither are there any dud scenes. Ms. Hellman knows how to tell a story at a breathtaking clip and how to stack her theatrical deck with well-placed narrative bombshells (from a rifled safe-deposit box to an out-of-reach medicine bottle). Most of all, she knows how to throw her actors the prime red meat of bristling language. If *The Little Foxes* is Broadway melodrama, it's as good as the genre gets.

Or so it is in the hands of people who know how to milk it for every last gasp, thrill, and laugh that it's worth. Count Ms. Taylor in that company. Maybe Regina, like all the play's other roles, doesn't require great acting or trenchant soul-searching; it's all at the surface. But it does require the tidal force of pure personality. This is a woman who would kill her husband, barter her daughter, and double-cross her brothers to get her hands on the ruling interest in a cotton mill—even as she maintains the façade of a charming, sexy grande dame. No doubt it's superfluous to point out that Ms. Taylor has charm, grandeur, and sex appeal. The news here is that she has the killer instinct, too—and the skill to project it from a stage. When she lets loose in Acts 2 and 3, crashing about to knock down every human obstacle in her omnivorous path, we never question that this is one woman who gets what she wants, when she wants it, at any price. Ms. Taylor makes us hate her guts—God bless her.

The star is not so effective in Act 1, when Regina is still trying to keep her iron fist hidden in a velvet glove. As she prattles flirtatiously with the visiting Chicago moneybags (a properly smug Humbert Allen Astredo), her true, calculating intentions flicker too blatantly in those gleaming violet eyes. Yet once Regina's principal antagonist—her dying, estranged husband, Horace (Tom Aldredge)—returns home from the hospital, Ms. Taylor rises to the bait. When Horace resists her brief, coquettish efforts to enlist him in her business scheme, her giggly, girlish demeanor hardens in a flash to a mean, narrow-eyed barracuda's glare. And then we see just how wonderful the casting is, for Ms. Taylor is no cardboard harridan. Regina perfectly taps this actress's special gift—first fully revealed in the film version of *Who's Afraid of Virginia Woolf?*—for making nastiness stinging and funny at the same time.

His weak Southern accent aside, Mr. Aldredge is the star's perfect foil. A frail man with red-rimmed eyes, he looks like a goner, and he conveys all of the heroic Horace's rueful intelligence. Heart ailment or no, he can also match Ms. Taylor blow for blow in those blistering battles where they dredge up the putrid ruins of their long-dead marriage. His quiet moments are better still. When Mr. Aldredge sits forlornly apart from the others to sift through some worthless old mementos that remain in his looted safe-deposit box, he shows us the serene, almost senile face of a man who's taking a private final tally of an entire lifetime.

There are other strong performances, too. Anthony Zerbe's Uncle Ben, with his boozily slitted eyes and phony good-ole-boy manners, is a fiendish, pickled specimen of white-trash-turned-tycoon. As nephew Leo, the littlest of the foxes, Dennis Christopher (best known as the bicyclist hero of the film *Breaking Away*) is so weak and amoral that he seems to lack a skeleton as well as a soul or mind. Novella Nelson and Joe Seneca, as the household's black retainers, pack dignity and humor into their brief, often portentous appearances. Only Joe Ponazecki, as the sweaty, sniveling Uncle Oscar, and Ann Talman, as Regina's increasingly bold daughter Alexandra, could be sharper. Mr. Ponazecki's voice lacks shading and Ms. Talman, after her strong last speech, relaxes into ambiguity at the final curtain.

As Mr. Ponazecki's battered wife, Ms. Stapleton is a wonder. True, playing the role of Aunt Birdie is a little like stealing: A kind, gentle drunk who hasn't had "one whole day of happiness in twenty-two years," Birdie exists mainly to be abused by the others and earn our sympathy. But this actress digs beneath the surface to give *The Little Foxes* a tragic, Chekhovian dimension. As she reminisces about her idyllic plantation childhood or confesses her hatred for her own son, Ms. Stapleton's light voice trills in and out of coherence, finally to hit bottom in sudden, guttural sobs. Her lonely eyes float in and out of focus as well, often disappearing entirely into impenetrable shadows. And when, at one point, Ms. Stapleton raises her hand violently in unexpected recollection of a painful, buried memory, it doesn't matter that there's no line to announce precisely what that memory is. Such is this actress's talent that she can conjure abject terror out of silence and thin air.

Austin Pendleton, who played Leo in Mike Nichols's 1967 Lincoln Center revival of this play, was clearly born to direct it. Using overlapping conversations and vibrant blocking, he gives Ms. Hellman's artifice the relentless flow of real life. His old-style theatrical flair—abetted by Andrew Jackness's Gothic set, Florence Klotz's matching costumes, and Paul Gallo's grim lighting—is often delicious. The three male villains usually move together, hovering like buzzards above their prey. In Horace's heart-attack scene, the director sends Mr. Aldredge and wheelchair crashing into the Giddenses' grand staircase—an effect that catapults the stricken man halfway up the stairs and sends the audience's nerves flying with him.

I also loved a moment in Act 1 when Ms. Taylor suddenly marches downstage center to face her quarreling family from a lofty distance, then shuts them all up in mid-sentence by placing her hands on her hips and yelling "Why don't you all go home!" When this star commands her guests to go home, you had better believe they go.

Elizabeth Taylor, meanwhile, looks very much like someone who's on the stage to stay.

≡ *This was, to put it mildly, a minority view of this production. Walter Kerr wrote a hilarious, and devastating, pan of Taylor's performance in the* Sunday Times. *I have no memory of why I was so dazzled, but watching a failed revival of* The Little Foxes *at Lincoln Center in 1997, in which Stockard Channing, an ideal Birdie, was miscast as Regina, the Taylor version started to come back to me; it may well not have been as good as I thought it had been, but in retrospect it certainly had its moments (especially Maureen Stapleton's). This play is not as easy to do—as foolproof—as it looks.*

LENA HORNE: THE LADY AND HER MUSIC
Nederlander Theatre, May 13, 1981

About midway into the first half of her show at the Nederlander, Lena Horne does the one thing we know she's going to do before we even arrive at the theater. Sliding into her best Metro-Goldwyn-Mayer stance, she looks up into a spotlight and proceeds to sing the hell out of "Stormy Weather." The moment doesn't disappoint. As Ms. Horne has already demonstrated in the evening's warm-up numbers—"From This Moment On," "Where or When," "Can't Help Lovin' Dat Man"—she's in transcendent voice and, at age sixty-three, as beautiful and elegant as ever. You can be sure that she sings "Stormy Weather" so it will stay sung.

Still, there's something disconcerting about her decision to give us this treat so early in the evening. It's an unspoken rule of recitals like this that a singer saves her trademark number for the evening's ultimate, or at least penultimate, spot. The star still has a good hour of singing to go after "Stormy Weather," and we begin to worry how in the world she can possibly top her most famous showstopper.

But Lena Horne—as we should have learned by now—is nobody's fool. Late in her show's second half, just after a racy "Love Me or Leave Me," she announces her next number by saying "I had to grow into this song." And then what does she do? Why, she sings "Stormy Weather" all over again. Only this time she sings it as if she had just grown into it, as if she had never sung it before. Before she even hits the first lyric, she lets loose with a gospel cry that erupts from her gut with almost primeval force. Then she bobs gently up and down, staring into her hand mike, letting the words pour out. By the time she tells us that "it's raining all the time"—packing about a dozen torrential notes into the word *raining*—she is blind with sweat and tears. And so is the audience. Not only have we heard a great singer top what we thought to be her best work, but we've also witnessed an honest-to-God coup de théâtre.

If that second "Stormy Weather" is the indisputable high point of *Lena Horne: The Lady and Her Music,* the riches of the evening scarcely end there. Ms. Horne is out to prove something in this revue, and it's not merely that her talents and looks are unbruised by the years that have passed since she first danced across a Cotton Club stage an era ago. She doesn't simply present herself as a survivor—a favorite device of older stars who come back to Broadway—but as an artist who is still growing, who is only now reaching the peak of her powers. Ms. Horne proves her point handily in a show that, for all its high-spirited fun, also turns out to be surprisingly moving.

Ms. Horne accomplishes this feat without the aid of lectures or phony schmaltz. She provides only a few autobiographical anecdotes, all of which are told with good humor even though they frequently deal with racist indignities she suffered in Hollywood. Most of the time, she just sings down front, to the accompaniment of a superb onstage band under the direction of Harold Wheeler. In *Lena Horne: The Lady and Her Music,* Ms. Horne seems to be saying that the lady is her music: She transforms each song, however familiar, into an intensely personal story that we've never quite heard before.

Though all her celebrated gestures are there—the clipped diction, the naughty grins, the finger-snapping sassiness—she's singing with an abandon, range, and feeling that weren't apparent even as recently as her last New York appearance with Tony Bennett. Letting her fists fly, she punches up "I Got a Name" with defiance, if not outright anger. For "I'm Glad There Is You," she surprises us by suddenly breaking out of her smoky, twangy register to embrace a top note with a bell-clear soprano. For "The Lady Is a Tramp," she's so down and dirty she's practically crouching on the floor: On the lyric "I'm flat/that's that," her voice becomes an instrument as peppery as Louis Armstrong's horn.

On other occasions, she teaches us just about everything there is to know about styling a song. No matter how many thousand times you've heard "The Surrey with the Fringe on Top," it's possible you've never quite heard Oscar Hammerstein's lyrics until you hear Ms. Horne spell them out, point by point, in the best pianissimo manner of her Waldorf period. "I Want to Be Happy" is sung with shifting rhythms and colors until it's a standard reborn. Ms. Horne introduces "Bewitched" as "a sad song about an old broad—with money." Then she shows us what she means by turning from bitterness on the phrase "half-pint imitation" to a debutante's kittenish rapture on "Now I'm like sweet-seventeen a lot."

It must be noted that not all of the show is as well-styled as Ms. Horne's music. The choreographer Arthur Faria, working with a trio of talented singer-dancers but cramped floor space, contributes a Cotton Club routine that looks pretty wan next to the one in *Sophisticated Ladies*. Though Thomas Skelton's lighting is fine, either he or the set designer, David Gropman, has made too much of a fetish of exposed klieg lights. As is the habit of fashion designers who create costumes for the stage, Giorgio Sant'Angelo has supplied Ms. Horne with glamorous outfits that are impractical, even cumbersome, in performance.

Yet these are at most minor irritations in an evening of generally undiluted triumph. Maybe the star is looking back at her old days—clear back to four decades ago, when Fats Waller taught her songs at the piano—but she emphatically isn't living in them. For both Lena Horne and the audience, the excitement is beginning all over again—right now.

≡ *Here's an example of how easy it is for a critic to disregard his prejudices. I fought vehemently against reviewing this show, arguing that it was a nightclub act that should be covered by the paper's pop music or jazz critic. But because Horne was playing in a Broadway theater, Arthur Gelb insisted that I do it. I was not particularly a fan of Lena Horne's and went to the theater grudgingly—only to be disarmed within minutes after she appeared on stage.*

CLOUD 9
THEATRE DE LYS, MAY 20, 1981

loud 9, a new comedy by a British writer named Caryl Churchill, may not transport the audience all the way to Cloud 9—but it surely keeps us on our toes. The evening's subject is sexual confusion, and Ms. Churchill has found a theatrical method that is easily as dizzying as her theme. Not only does she examine a cornucopia of sexual permutations—from heterosexual adultery right up to bisexual incest— but she does so with a wild array of dramatic styles and tricks.

Her first act, which is part bedroom farce and part Waughian satire, unfolds in the darkest colonial Africa of 1880. Act 2, a foray into sometimes sentimental agitprop, takes place in a London park of the present day. Though a few characters appear in both halves, the holdovers age only twenty-five years during intermission, rather than a full century. As if this weren't mad enough, the seven actors change roles for Act 2—and don't necessarily play characters of their own age or gender.

Ms. Churchill, as you might gather, is one daft writer. *Cloud 9*, now at the De Lys, has real failings, but intelligence and inventiveness aren't among them; we're always interested in what the playwright is up to, no matter what the outcome. And in her director, Tommy Tune, she has found the most helpful possible ally. Working with just the right, delicate balance of rowdiness and sensitivity—as well as with an unusually good cast—Mr. Tune often succeeds in giving a seriously overlong evening the illusion of flight.

In Act 1, the director sends his company dashing about the sliding doors of Lawrence Miller's clever set to create a nonstop round-robin of sexual liaisons. This half of *Cloud 9* is about what happens when a very proper colonial British family receives a visit from a pith-helmeted explorer named Harry Bagley (Nicolas Surovy). While the natives outside the camp are getting restless, they have nothing on the rakish Harry. He's really been too long in the bush. Grabbing every clandestine opportunity he can, this explorer seduces the household's wife (played by a man), schoolboy son (played by a woman), and obsequious black servant (played by a white)—all before getting married to the governess, a lesbian.

What makes this carnal circus funny is the contrast between the characters' manners and deeds. No matter what they do, Ms. Churchill's colonials act and talk like true-blue, genteel Victorians. When Harry is caught in a homosexual act, he apologizes by explaining that he is merely the helpless victim of "a disease worse than diphtheria." When his host engages in his own dalliance with a local widow, the fully clothed couple reach orgasm with a stiff-upper-lip reticence worthy of a Westminster debate.

The joke does wear thin too quickly. Once we understand that Ms. Churchill is stripping bare the hypocrisies of an oversatirized era, Act 1 becomes stalled. The transsexual casting is also problematic: Though the male and female impersonations are amusing, not smirky, they nonetheless serve the unwanted function of announcing the jokes. Nor is the story's farcical structure so strong that it pulls up the slack. Instead of the ingenious clockwork of, say, an Alan Ayckbourn play, Ms. Churchill provides a progression of overly similar scenes that steadily reveal each character's particular proclivity.

Act 2 has its own problems—and pleasures. We reencounter three members of the 1880 family, as well as four new characters, and find that, in 1980, they are as liberated as their predecessors were repressed. But progress presents its own difficulties. The homosexual schoolboy of 1880, now hitting middle age, is so confused by his love for both his sister and an insolent young male lover that he worries that he might be a lesbian. His sister, meanwhile, is torn between her ostensibly enlightened husband (a writer at work on "a novel about women from the woman's point of view") and a woman who propositions her in the park.

Ms. Churchill covers this and much more territory by relying on tender monologues. The speeches are very well written, but one hungers for stronger interchanges between the characters. An element of ideological Pollyannaism also creeps in, for the playwright provides most of her lost souls with happy endings. Is everyone really so much better off in the swinging 1980s? It seems a waste that Act 2's wittiest conceit—the ghostly return of characters from Act 1—is mainly used to draw mawkish parallels between now and then.

Yet the acting buttresses the writing considerably. Despite the cast's showy sex changes, Mr. Tune keeps the performances at a realistic level: He goes for the heart of Ms. Churchill's play even as he gives full polish to its surface pranks. Some actors are best in Act 1 (Mr. Surovy, Don Amendolia) and some in Act 2 (Veronica Castang, Concetta Tomei). Others shine throughout. Zeljko Ivanek does a fine transformation from fluttery colonial wife to wary young street hustler. Jeffrey Jones, a pompous twit of a father in Africa, is sad and sweet when he turns up in London as the forlorn homosexual son.

Perhaps the standout performance comes from E. Katherine Kerr, who in Act 2 inherits the mother's role. Looking and sounding not unlike

England's present queen, Ms. Kerr delivers a beautiful closing speech in which she graphically describes how she overcame her sheltered 1880 upbringing to take her rightful place in a modern, feminist world of infinite possibilities. "If there isn't a right way to do things," she explains, "you just have to invent one."

By the end, we're terribly moved by this middle-aged woman's brave attempt to reinvent herself—just as we're moved by Caryl Churchill's attempt to reinvent the comedy of manners so that it might do such a heroine justice.

≡ *Tommy Tune is best known for his work as a director of musicals, with each successive one proving less ambitious than the one that came before— but in this production he revealed a talent for edgy comedy that he never again tapped. Later Churchill plays brought to New York, mainly by Joseph Papp, were staged exclusively and no less successfully by British directors, including Les Waters* (Fen), *Max Stafford-Clark* (Serious Money), *and Mark Wing-Davey* (Mad Forest).

THIRD SEASON

1981—82

Roger Rees, David Threlfall, and the cast of
The Life and Adventures of Nicholas Nickleby

If Dreiser had lived in the age of Beckett, he just might have written *American Buffalo*. Like many of Dreiser's novels, David Mamet's brilliant play is a violent vision of the dog-eat-dog jungle of urban American capitalism. But if Dreiser sent his doomed proletarian losers loping through sprawling narratives and larger-than-life events, Mr. Mamet does the exact reverse by following the fashions of modern drama. *American Buffalo* is as reductivist as *An American Tragedy* is expansive. Instead of a big story and torrents of grand prose, Mr. Mamet's play provides only an inconsequential anecdote and declarative sentences of one-syllable words. Yet by the time *American Buffalo* is over, it, too, has pounded away at the American dream of success until it is left in soiled, hideous tatters.

Mr. Mamet can also be quite funny—a fact that wasn't entirely apparent in Ulu Grosbard's tough 1977 Broadway staging of this work. Mr. Grosbard's production hissed like a rattlesnake: Audiences came away startled, even shocked, by the scatological language and the violence that erupts in Act 2. The new revival starring Al Pacino, which opened at the Circle in the Square (Downtown) last night, leaves another impression, for Arvin Brown, the director, shows us the other side of Mr. Mamet's verbal coinage. When the play's three men hatch their ill-fated get-rich-quick "business" scheme—the robbery of a rare Buffalo nickel—their pathetic machinations now seem more absurd than vicious. The play's meaning, impressively enough, remains unchanged: Funny or horrifying, *American Buffalo* is still a tale of men who are eternally trapped on the bottom rung of the Social Darwinist ladder.

The setting is a junk shop, and Mr. Mamet's underclass hustlers, like the wares of their hangout, are the discarded junk of their country. These men keep hoping for a big score—for "real classical money"—but they don't have any idea of how to make a living, let alone a killing. They plan their crime in great detail, only to have it derailed by their own incompetence, the no-show of a key accomplice, and their endless paranoia and infighting. When it ultimately becomes clear that they have failed, tempers flare and the men briefly pummel one another. Though they like to believe, as one of them puts it, that the "free enterprise system" has saved them from savagery, they are allowed no such salvation. These would-be con artists are still lost in the American wilderness and, like the proverbial buffalo, doomed.

The key role, now as before, is Teach, the most volatile and conniving member of the group. In Mr. Grosbard's version, Robert Duvall was taut and mean in the part: After fumbling away his burglary, his self-hatred drove him to lash out like a killer. Mr. Pacino, by contrast, is slovenly and abstracted. With his baggy clothes and pasty, ill-shaven face, he's a tabby rather than an alley cat. And he's very, very funny. This is this actor's first fully rewarding performance on stage or film since *Dog Day Afternoon*.

In Act 1, when Teach is first trying to horn in on his friends' heist, Mr. Pacino is all darting, jittery hand gestures and phony bravado. Like the others, he spouts dim-witted syllogisms about the nature of business, loyalty, and friendship, yet his behavior is so itchy that we always realize that Teach neither knows nor means what he says. He only wants to cut his friends out of the action, and, because his friends may be dumber than he is, he almost gets away with it. Mr. Pacino has an uncommon knack for revealing the inner workings of a slippery lowlife's restless mind.

As the night wanes and the robbery drifts further out of reach, the actor swerves gently into farce. When Teach tries to revive the scam by placing a pointless phone call to the putative victim, Mr. Pacino provides the sort of beautifully timed ineptitude one associates with Art Carney's old television persona on *The Honeymooners*. Even Teach's ultimate eruption into anger mixes humor with malice. Mr. Pacino's dark eyes, now swimming deep in their sockets, show us his rage, but his ineffectual, sloppy blows are the comically self-punishing thrashings of a wild animal banging his own cage.

A few minor mannerisms have crept into the star's performance since this production was first performed at New Haven's Long Wharf Theatre last fall. Mr. Pacino makes a fetish of his tilted posture in Act 1, and at times he overly stylizes lines that speak for themselves. There has also been a falloff in Mr. Brown's pacing in the evening's early stages; the pauses in the rapid-fire dialogue occasionally widen into gaps. But Clifton James, who plays the fat, middle-aged junk store owner, and especially Thomas Waites, as his young junkie gofer, are much improved. While they don't blot out the memory of Kenneth McMillan and John Savage in the Broadway production, they are now both giving fresh, clean performances that prove the perfect kindling for Mr. Pacino's sparks.

The play, though, is the thing. Working with the tiniest imaginable vocabulary—words like "nothing," "great," and "no," as well as those of four letters—Mr. Mamet creates a subterranean world with its own non-literate comic beat, life-and-death struggles, pathos, and even affection. He does so despite the fact that his characters are the slimy protozoa of a society, eking out a fruitless existence in a figurative cave. Mr. Mamet believes that these people have a right to our attention and compassion, because their story, like it or not, is tied to our own. In *American Buffalo*, he has created a deceptively small-scale tragedy that is packed with the power to explode the largest of American myths.

GROWN UPS
American Repertory Theatre,
Cambridge, Mass., June 18, 1981

At this late date, it's no secret that our favorite hostile cartoonist, Jules Feiffer, is also a serious writer. No sooner do we laugh at the pop-art killings of his play *Little Murders* or the empty seductions of his film *Carnal Knowledge* than we are stung by the pricks of painful truth. But in *Grown Ups,* the Feiffer play now having its premiere at Harvard's American Repertory Theatre, he has reversed his usual method and taken his seriousness a step further: Now the pain comes first and then, somehow, the laughter. It's a big step—maybe a giant one. By forcing the audience to crawl through an emotional hell to get to his punch lines, Mr. Feiffer has written a drama of wrenching impact without sacrificing one note of his bracing comic voice.

To put it simply, *Grown Ups* is the ruthlessly honest, no-holds-barred dissection of the American Jewish family that recently has eluded both Arthur Miller (in *The American Clock*) and Woody Allen (in *The Floating Light Bulb*). It also contains Mr. Feiffer's most sustained theatrical writing to date: *Grown Ups* doesn't unfold in the short takes of a cartoonist or screenwriter, but in three relentless acts, each more virulently pitched than the last. At Harvard, John Madden has directed the play with a vengeance that would do honor to O'Neill.

The protagonist is Jake, a middle-aged success played by Bob Dishy. A hotshot reporter for *The New York Times,* Jake is blessed with a likable wife (Cheryl Giannini), a bright eight-year-old daughter (Jennifer Dundas), and a comfy Upper West Side apartment. His parents (Barbara Orson and George Martin) can never see enough of him and bask in his every "accomplishment." Told that such celebrities as David Halberstam and John Kenneth Galbraith are providing dust-jacket blurbs for her son's forthcoming Random House book, Jake's mother overreacts to the point of declaring "I'm so excited I can hardly breathe." She shows no interest, however, in the book's actual contents.

The book is about how the Cold War led to "the moral and ethical disintegration of the American Dream." In *Grown Ups,* it's Jake who is disintegrating, taking his portion of that dream with him. The play begins calmly, with the hero joining his suffocating mother and his Willy Loman of a father at the New Rochelle home of his married sister (Karen MacDonald), who is an also-ran for the parents' affections. But in Act 2, set a year later, a quiet evening at home with Jake and his wife, Louise, suddenly erupts into a marital battle of obscene dimensions.

The final act, which follows without intermission, is a Sunday brunch in which the entire family settles the scores of a lifetime: As Jake and his sister finally air their long-repressed grievances with the parents, the parents go after each other, too. The tidal wave of anger accelerates so quickly that it takes an Ibsen thunderbolt to end the play. While Mr. Feiffer doesn't ask Jake to commit suicide or slam a door, you can be sure he provides a startling contemporary equivalent of his own.

The playwright's analysis of his childish grown-ups is Freudian: Each character's misery is tied up with that of his childhood, and there's no escape. (As Jake points out, even the murder of his parents would be a "short-range solution" to his anguish.) The play lives, however, in the specific details that flesh out its conventional theme. In one of the evening's most violent turns, Jake turns on his doting father and cries: "You never supported me until I made it at the *Times.* I had to make it with strangers to be accepted by my own family." Not even in *Carnal Knowledge* did Mr. Feiffer so combustively explode intimate relationships to dramatize the pathology of the American obsession with success.

The evening's laughs are always hard-won. It's only after we learn that a character has a drinking problem that we can hear that the bottle is hidden "on the sixth shelf, behind William Shirer." It's only after his sobbing wife has shouted "I want to die!" that Jake injects a wisecrack into their brawl. As Jake's parents endlessly repeat their ceremonial familial greetings—"So what's new?" or "When can I see my granddaughter?"—

Mr. Feiffer rips away the humorous tribal clichés like scabs to get at the festering resentments underneath.

There is other virtuosic writing as well. The entire first act is subtext: as the characters exchange pointless anecdotes and family gossip in a kitchen, the play's complex nexus of conflicts is set up almost entirely by what is not said. Act 2 is an unerringly precise journey through the circular, deadlocked debates that define a rotting marriage. In Act 3, Mr. Feiffer finds just the right innocuous incident to trigger his final storm: Jake's mother bristles with hurt upon discovering that her granddaughter already owns the gift book *The Cat in the Hat* that she had "shopped like a dog for."

Working with the same talented set designer, Andrew Jackness, with whom he collaborated on Arthur Kopit's *Wings,* Mr. Madden pulls out all the stops. I won't soon forget his choreography of the last act, in which the characters alternately meet chin-to-chin or drift into shadowy isolation as their lives come undone. One climactic twist is almost too awful to watch: Jake's daughter marches innocently out of her bedroom, carrying her Dr. Seuss books, only to find herself smack in the deadly crossfire of her father and grandfather. Oblivious to her arrival, the enraged men twist their knives in deeper.

While virtually the whole cast is strong, *Grown Ups* is a particular triumph for Mr. Dishy, whose accomplished comic style here expands as much as Mr. Feiffer's. Perhaps the evening's most powerful passage occurs when he tries to silence his wife's recriminations by shoving his book's loose galleys, one by one, off his desk, all the while yelling "Stop! Stop! Stop!" Though the repeated word chokes in the actor's throat, it keeps coming and coming, as uncontrollably as vomit.

In the same scene, a calmer Jake tries to comfort his awakened daughter. "Don't be afraid of people fighting," he tells her. "It doesn't mean anything." But of course the fighting in *Grown Ups* means everything—and there's no comfort for anyone. Looking in Mr. Dishy's frightened eyes, we can see, as he does, that there's blood all over his living room's nice parquet floor.

SUNDAY ESSAY: BROADWAY CAN LIVE WITHOUT TV
JULY 19, 1981

The Greek theater had its gods and the Elizabethans had their kings, but who, pray tell, does our theater celebrate? If the past season is any indication, our cosmic icons include the following, all of whom were at least mentioned, sometimes personified, and occasionally worshiped in new plays and musicals: Miss America, Marie Osmond, June Lockhart, Bob Newhart, Barbara Walters, and Merv Griffin. Perhaps that's how it should be. If culture inevitably reflects the society that spawns it, surely it must, these days, reflect the primacy of television in American life. If we don't have a Zeus or a Henry V to look up to, did the Greeks and Elizabethans have a Johnny Carson?

Don't laugh. Our presidents may come and go, our gods may periodically be declared dead by philosophers, but it's hard to imagine that anything, including the fall of Fred Silverman, will dim the tube. Television is our national wallpaper, the one constant in our firmament. Some people love television; some hate it so much they hold it responsible for all social ills short of California's fruit flies. But even those who hate TV love to hate it. And even those who don't watch it are far from indifferent to its spell.

Speaking as someone who enjoys watching television—and not just British imports on Channel 13—I nonetheless find myself worrying increasingly about the medium's impact on the theater. That impact is spreading on all fronts. A growing number of comedy writers—somehow convinced that theater audiences will pay thirty dollars for what they can see at home for free—emulate the devices of television series in constructing their plays. Others drop the names of television's personalities and its advertised commercial products into their scripts to induce Pavlovian chuckles or maybe guffaws of recognition from the audience. Nor are these habits by any means confined to Broadway. This was the season that Elizabeth Swados, in her musical version of Lewis Carroll's *Alice in Wonderland* at the Public, could not resist plying us with a few bars from a television cat-food jingle.

While one might charitably think that these writers are parodying TV, they're often just exploiting it. Television provides a ready-made shorthand that can save writers the difficulty of writing their own characters and jokes. The result is not just a coarsening of the theater, but an assault on the very definition of theater. To the extent that network television's rigid lexicon of gags, formats, and proper names extends to playwriting, the theater loses its direct contact with human experience: Life enters the stage twice, not once removed, and it enters via a foreign, electronic jargon that is further and further adrift from English. Throw in the wanton use of amplification in Broadway houses, and some of these entertainments seem entirely canned. Can canned laughter be far behind?

Certainly one wonders after seeing *Woman of the Year,* a musical whose virtues do not include its book by Peter Stone. In adapting the

1942 screenplay by Ring Lardner Jr. and Michael Kanin (originally written for Katharine Hepburn and Spencer Tracy) to the musical stage, Mr. Stone transformed the heroine from a Dorothy Thompson–like newspaper columnist to a Barbara Walters–like television journalist. There's nothing wrong with that notion in principle, but there's much to be desired about the librettist's execution of it.

Rather than taking an ironic approach to his television milieu, Mr. Stone merely milks it, adoringly, for its iconography and celebrities. Famous television names—from Rona Barrett to Marvin Hamlisch—are worked slavishly into what seems like every line of his script, for the sole purpose of idle name-dropping. The *Today* show is replicated on stage as *The Early Bird Show* without any credible attempt at parody. Mr. Stone reaches his lowest ebb when his hero, a cartoonist played by Harry Guardino, must explain his marital separation from the heroine. Mr. Guardino tells his pals, "It was like being married to *60 Minutes* and *That's Incredible* all in one." Besides being close to a non sequitur, the line transforms the musical's potentially moving plot (it was so in the film) into dehumanized talk-show patter. A non–television watcher who sees *Woman of the Year* may need a copy of *TV Guide* to explicate the show's text.

If Mr. Stone is the splashiest recent practitioner of this kind of nonwriting, he's not alone. At the Public last fall, one found a musical revue, *Girls, Girls, Girls,* whose every sketch (including one dealing with suicidal depression) depended on a knowledge of such television trivia as *Spin and Marty.* Even sadder was Broadway's short-lived *Bring Back Birdie*: In that musical, whose finale was a Grammy Awards show, the set consisted primarily of mobile banks of television monitors which often offered simultaneous (and pointless) broadcasts of the live action. This was depressing theater coming from the creators of *Bye Bye Birdie*—the giddily satirical 1960 musical in which Paul Lynde's nutty hymn to Ed Sullivan forever altered our view of one of TV's patron saints.

In nonmusical comedies, television's impact is more insidious still, for these plays imitate network shows while pretending not to. And they don't even copy the best of the breed. The models aren't *The Mary Tyler Moore Show* or *Lou Grant* or *M*A*S*H*—TV series that offer a large assortment of often multifaceted characters, a multitude of sets, a smattering of social relevance, and week-to-week variations in tone. Instead we get Broadway plays that imitate the real junk of prime time—namely, those situation comedies that are tied to one principal set, three or four major one-note characters, and toilet and jiggle jokes.

All too typical was the recently departed *Wally's Cafe,* which told of three hash slingers' adventures over forty years in a California desert hamburger stand. This play managed to echo both CBS-TV's *Alice* (also about loudmouths in a greasy spoon) and ABC-TV's *Three's Company* (also about two women and one man in close quarters). For added spice, Sally Struthers, a star of the now defunct series *All in the Family*, played one of the lead roles—a doxy whose funniest speech proved to be an account of how she accidentally castrated a man with a misaimed gun.

What distinguishes situation comedy from theatrical comedy is not only the level of taste, but also the substitution of gimmicks for true comic writing that springs from character. The first telltale gimmick to present itself in these plays is invariably the set. In *Wally's Cafe*, the diner was shaped like a huge hamburger (complete with bun and pickle) and underwent sputtering changes to show the passing of decades at the end of each scene. In *It Had to Be You*, another short-lived Broadway sitcom of the spring, the set was a cutesy Greenwich Village apartment that could fly on and off the stage in a clever flash. *Mixed Couples*, a dreary James Prideaux comedy of last winter, took place in a fastidiously designed 1920s airplane hangar.

The plays that inhabited these gimmicky sets didn't have plots—just facile sitcom situations that the sets could define with little additional help from the playwright. And, indeed, the basic premise was exactly the same in each show: Feuding couples were trapped, respectively, in a desert hamburger stand, a snowed-in apartment, and a fogged-in airplane hangar. The characters were pretty much identical, too. Each play offered heroines (played by Rita Moreno, Renee Taylor, and Geraldine Page) who were, in varying degrees, nagging shrews. Of course, these women weren't real characters, but types summed up by a single, instantly recognizable personality trait. This, too, is television practice, for half-hour network shows often feel compelled to establish their characters immediately and loudly to gain the restless viewer's fragile attention. These plays' authors further imitated their TV prototypes by closing their vulgar comedies with an unearned, sentimental message. The message was the same each time—learn to love thyself—and was usually tacked on as abruptly and tearfully as those codas that once concluded episodes of *Father Knows Best*.

Lest we think that all commercial Broadway comedies are inevitably doomed to follow this format, it must be remembered that one, Jean Kerr's *Lunch Hour*, stubbornly chose to be a play, rather than a sitcom, last season. Though this comedy, too, was a light entertainment about warring couples and though it starred a television actress (Gilda Radner), Mrs. Kerr provided an honest-to-God farcical plot (with a double-twist ending) and well-rounded principal characters who revealed their feelings and grew up as the evening progressed. The playwright was working in the tradition of Philip Barry and S. N. Behrman, not *Laverne and Shirley*.

We can also be grateful that last season brought a few plays that actually chose to examine television's social impact—and did so without becoming, themselves, part of the problem. In *Coming Attractions*, at Playwrights Horizons, Ted Tally wrote a satire about a Son of Sam–like mass-murderer who becomes a media celebrity. While the play stretched itself thin, it contained one scabrous scene, in which the killer, as well as a Middle Eastern terrorist–cum–nightclub comic, were guests on a television talk show. The show's fawning host (Jonathan Hadary), a gold-lamé narcissist replete with open shirt and hand mike, was all too glad to welcome such outlaws into his den for small talk. After all, on television, a star of any kind is still a star. Especially to Tom Snyder, who in fact booked Charles Manson as a guest on his *Tomorrow* show some months after Mr. Tally's play opened.

It's also hard to forget JoAnne Akalaitis's American version of Franz Xaver Kroetz's *Request Concert*, an avant-garde, dialogueless work about a lonely woman who comes home from work and, for seventy minutes, prepares for bed. In this play, a bona fide television show was actually part of the action: At one point, the woman turned on a working television set and fitfully watched whatever program was on. The set was positioned so the audience could only hear it, not watch it, but we could nonetheless see its reflected, chilly glare on the heroine's face. That haunting, solitary image—a devastating portrait of alienation in the midst of our supposedly utopian electronic village—demonstrated just why and how television can be a subject for the contemporary theater. A subject, yes; an esthetic, no.

THE HOTEL PLAY
LA MAMA ANNEX, AUGUST 28, 1981

While Wallace Shawn's unabashedly nasty farce, *The Hotel Play*, may not be everybody's idea of a play, it is unassailable as a mad theatrical stunt. This seventy-five-minute outing, which ends its brief, limited run at the La Mama Annex Sunday night, has the largest cast to be seen on a New York stage in memory: There are seventy-odd players, of whom over fifty have speaking roles. Even if you loathe *The Hotel Play*—and be warned, you might—you're unlikely to get totally bored. At the very least, you can kill the time reading the cast biographies in the voluminous program.

Once you dip into those bios, you'll discover that the occupants of Mr. Shawn's hotel—a mildly seedy resort in the tropics—are no shleppers. The cast of *The Hotel Play* not only includes some first-rate actors— Griffin Dunne, Michael Murphy, Mark Linn-Baker, among others—but also nonactors on holiday: three playwrights (Ed Bullins, Christopher Durang, Wendy Wasserstein), two *New Yorker* cartoonists (Frank Modell, Jim Stevenson), a fiction writer (Ann Beattie), a movie producer (Dominick Dunne), a jewelry product manager (Aimee Simons), a sales engineer (Charlie Peruzzi), and a whole gaggle of artists and children. If anyone's still looking for Judge Crater, La Mama may be just the place to renew the search.

These performers aren't just milling around, either, and they're not holding a private party under the guise of theater. John Ferraro, the director in charge of managing the mob, has pulled the troops together with high style. As Mr. Shawn's addled tourists drift in and out of Michael Moran's authentic-looking, two-story set (lobby and bar below, bedrooms above), Mr. Ferraro keeps the timing sharp and the traffic brisk; with the help of Richard Weinstock's music and Gregory C. MacPherson's lighting, he adroitly transforms a far-flung collection of blackout bits into a ceaseless flow of life. And when virtually the entire cast comes on stage at once for cocktail hour, the director orchestrates a carnival of overlapping action that's worthy of Robert Altman's *Nashville*. As the actors are live, rather than screen images, the effect is unusually joyous.

Mr. Shawn's play, meanwhile, is not joyous and doesn't mean to be. Written before *Our Late Night* and *Marie and Bruce*, this work is unmistakably their precursor. Here, as in his later, tidier, and more scatological efforts, Mr. Shawn is unveiling a misanthropic view of humanity that, tropics or no, admits no sunshine. The hotel's married guests abuse and humiliate each other and their children with unstinting cruelty; the single guests devour and degrade each other, in and out of bed. Many of the vacationers "feel sick" (usually to their stomachs), and words like *putrid, nauseated,* and *disgusting,* as well as the epithets *pig* and *hog,* set the tone. When the characters exchange comic anecdotes, they are invariably about mutilation and death. We hear about a terminally ill pathologist who purchases an artificial lung and an electric neck, and of another fellow who swallowed a live rat that chewed his heart "into a hundred pieces."

Because the playwright is willing to go for broke to realize his vision— and honorably refuses to make any concessions to so-called good taste—

he at times achieves a pungent, heightened form of reality that remakes the meaner alienations of modern life into ferocious comedy. The most absurd gags curdle so quickly that they even tumble over into pathos. A desperate-eyed Michael Murphy, clad in a kimono, is actually touching as a psychiatrist who finds that he vomits every time he sees an attractive woman. Elizabeth McGovern, so striking as Timothy Hutton's persistent girlfriend in the film *Ordinary People,* grabs us here when she offhandedly starts worrying about the color of her shoes while a sadistic lover gives her a fast, postcoital dismissal.

The evening's most horrifying—and best—vignette is reserved for the playwright and Ann Lange. Mr. Shawn and Ms. Lange play a Strindbergian couple whose hatred boils over in an insult barrage that finally leads the wife to threaten to kill herself. But the husband won't even allow his spouse suicide as a weapon in their marital war. "I don't fear in the slightest the sight of your dead body," shrieks Mr. Shawn, before going on to describe the various ways (depending on the method of suicide) such a corpse might look. Ms. Lange—heretofore a tough antagonist—then falls apart with a rapidity that is too convincing and excruciating to be safely categorized under the distancing rubric of black comedy.

But the incendiary, even dangerous, cataclysms of *The Hotel Play* are too few and scattered. The rest of the time, the jokes about death, sex, tourism, and bodily functions repeat themselves. We contemplate the narrow spectrum of Mr. Shawn's verbal and theatrical palette, and monotony sets in. By the end, there's nothing left for the playwright to do but hammer his point home. This he does in a graphic suicide scene in which, predictably, the female victim's bedmate ignores the bloody mayhem to go calmly about his own selfish business. While this climax gives the work a formal shape, it still seems that the essence and real merits of *The Hotel Play* could be conveyed by any randomly selected twenty-minute passage.

Given the fact that a large role in this play evaporates in roughly a minute, it's no surprise that some cast members don't register. Among those who do are Griffin Dunne in the one continuing role of a cunning hotel clerk, Tom McDermott as a mother-infatuated poet, and Tom Costello as a self-made millionaire boar hunter whose father had been "a lavatory attendant in a sewer." The outstanding nonactors afoot are Mr. Durang, as a cackling, madras-outfitted cashier, and Mr. Bullins, as a diner who is fond of saying "Thank you ever so much" with eerily exaggerated politeness. The vacationer you may most identify with, however, is the one (Richard Peterson) who announces that every mean-spirited person on stage makes him sick. "I wish there were some dogs and cats staying in this hotel," he announces, and, after a while, we come to know just how he feels.

A TALENT FOR MURDER
Biltmore Theatre, October 2, 1981

Before we get to the sorry heart of the matter let's pause for a fond salute to Claudette Colbert. In *A Talent for Murder,* the Jerome Chodorov–Norman Panama play that arrived at the Biltmore last night, this star is quite a surprise.

Or so she is for this theatergoer, who missed her last Broadway appearance in *The Kingfisher*. It's not merely that the actress, now in her late seventies, still looks hearty, with her big Betty Boop eyes, curly light hair, and shimmering array of bright Bill Blass gowns. What's really pleasing is the fact that her low, one-of-the-boys voice remains intact as well—effortlessly hurling asides like pool balls into every pocket of the house. This is no grande dame preserved in aspic to impersonate the coy ingenue of *It Happened One Night.* This is the sardonic Colbert revealed by Mitchell Leisen and Preston Sturges in *Midnight* and *The Palm Beach Story*—a lady of piquant, irrepressible, ever-so-amusing common sense.

But I do worry about her judgment in scripts. Aside from its brevity (Act 2 is a sneeze), Ms. Colbert's latest vehicle has but one virtue: It allows its star to be on stage virtually the entire time. That's not enough. *A Talent for Murder* wants to be a mystery or a comedy—and the audience has the right to demand that it be so, too. But, as whodunits go, this play is one big piece of Swiss cheese, minus the cheese. And, as for the comedy—well, not only has Ms. Colbert known better, but so have Mr. Chodorov (the coauthor of *My Sister Eileen*) and Mr. Panama (coauthor of the Hope-Crosby *Road to Utopia*).

The star plays Anne Royce McClain, a successful mystery novelist "second only to the immortal Agatha." Confined to a wheelchair by various ailments, she lives in a Berkshires estate called Twelve Oaks, surrounded by her $15.7 million art collection and her extended family. Anne's relatives wouldn't mind killing her (or each other) to get their hands on a Matisse or two—and they're not bashful about revealing their intentions. Indeed, when the heroine describes her household as "a nest of vipers," she's only being polite.

Anne's son is the "gutless, impotent" editor of an "ineffectual little quarterly" who openly refers to his mother's sixty-eight novels as "drivel."

Sonny's wife is a greedy, blackmailing philanderer who wants to lock her mother-in-law away in an old-age home. Anne's other child, a daughter who suffered brain damage in an airplane crash, is married to a Maserati salesman fond of seducing fifteen-year-old girls. In their spare time, you may not be pleased to hear, this crowd likes to take in the concerts at Tanglewood.

In any case, it isn't easy to care who does what to whom—especially after we meet the actors cast as the villains. As cloddishly directed by Paul Aaron, they're all leering, sneering varmints who would disgrace a high-school production of *The Lottery*. Not that better performances would make a great difference. One must totally subscribe to the powers of luck—and, at times, clairvoyance—to believe that this play's crimes could even be committed. When the culprits are anticlimactically revealed, they seem to have been chosen by lot. Nor are the authors successful in their efforts to place Ms. Colbert in frightening jeopardy; our only real fear is that she might die of boredom.

That mild concern extends to two other cast members: the savvy Shelly Desai, who makes the most of an Indian butler who uses the word "chutzpah" (one of the evening's bigger jokes), and to Jean-Pierre Aumont, playing a live-in doctor who was once Anne's Parisian lover. All Mr. Aumont, a good actor, gets to do here is wander aimlessly about Oliver Smith's typically well-executed drawing-room set. Wearing a blazer, ascot, and frozen smile, he looks like nothing so much as a maître d' presiding over a restaurant full of empty tables.

Ms. Colbert is kept slightly busier. She puffs on cigars, takes "belts" of brandy, opens and closes her vault, rattles off the sales figures of her books (hardcover and paperback), and, on one occasion, lets fly with a four-letter expletive. But, really! While no one expects Ms. Colbert, now or ever, to play *Medea*—or even *The Little Foxes*—surely she can find a stage vehicle, however light, that gives her more to drive than a wheelchair.

THE LIFE AND ADVENTURES
OF NICHOLAS NICKLEBY
PLYMOUTH THEATRE, OCTOBER 5, 1981

A nd so, after eight and a half hours of *The Life and Adventures of Nicholas Nickleby*, we go home with an indelible final image. The time is Christmas, and a grand Victorian happy ending is in full swing. Carolers are strewn three stories high about the stage, singing "God Rest Ye Merry Gentlemen." Families have been reunited, couples joined together, plot ends neatly tied. And our young picaresque hero, Nicholas, has vanquished the two enemies who have stalked him for five acts—his usurious uncle, Ralph, and the cruel Yorkshire schoolmaster, Wackford Squeers.

But is all right with the world? Not entirely. For as Nicholas sings along with everyone else, he spots, crouching far downstage center, a starving boy. At first our hero tries to ignore the sight, but he can't. So he walks over to the youth, lifts him up into the cradle of his arms, and then stands to face the audience.

As the singing and lights dim, Nicholas stares and stares at us—his eyes at once welling with grief and anger—and what do we feel? What we feel, I think, is the penetrating gaze of Charles Dickens, reaching out to us from the nineteenth century, imploring us to be like his hero at this moment—to be kinder, better, more generous than we are. "If men would behave decently, the world would be decent"—that's how Orwell distilled Dickens's moral vision. It's a vision that can still inflame us— and does—at the very end of the Royal Shakespeare Company's marathon dramatization of Dickens's third novel.

This climax is one of maybe a dozen such moments in this production, which officially arrived yesterday at the Plymouth. Working with thirty-nine members of a great acting company, two ceaselessly imaginative directors, Trevor Nunn and John Caird, periodically reveal that they can indeed translate Dickens into pure theater. To show how "wealthy and poor stood side by side" in a nascent industrial world, for instance, they give us a horrifying, mimed image of lower-class humanity pressed flat against the window of a restaurant where the wealthy dine. When Nicholas is swallowed up by the city's "huge aggregate of darkness and sorrow," the directors choreograph a mob that all but eats him alive. Such staging techniques are not new in this post-Brechtian era—one thinks of Paul Sills [of Story Theater] and the Becks [of The Living Theatre]—but they are at times exquisitely consolidated here to root out the soul of Dickens's book, and to re-create the cinematic techniques (from crosscutting to dissolves) of his narrative.

The novel's atmosphere—that dense and sweeping social canvas of a Victorian universe—also receives its due. With the aid of unbeatable costume and lighting designers, John Napier and David Hersey, the directors effortlessly move us from teeming London to the dark gloom of Yorkshire to the bucolic countryside of Devonshire. The set consists only of platforms, scaffolding, cagelike balconies, and ratty bric-a-brac, but it extends by catwalks and planks through both levels of the theater. When the actors fan out into every nook and cranny—sometimes merging together to impersonate coaches or even walls—bodies and light sculpt the large space until a vanished England falls into place.

What does not fall into place, I must report, is a sustained evening of theater. We get an outsized event that sometimes seems in search of a shape. While the high points of this *Nicholas Nickleby* are Himalayan indeed, they are separated by dull passages which clog the production's arteries. The problem is not the length of work per se—it's the use of that length. In adapting a long novel to the stage, the British playwright David Edgar has chosen a strategy that is as questionable as it is courageous.

Unlike so many stage and film adapters of Dickens, Mr. Edgar has gone whole hog: He gives us at least a glimpse of every plot development and character (over fifty of substance and two hundred altogether) in the original book. But how is this possible, even in an adaptation of this length? Many of the characters in Dickens's novels—especially the subsidiary ones—are not revealed through dialogue or action, but by the steady accretion of the writer's vitally observed details. In the theater, those details can only be conveyed if each actor is given enough stage time to communicate them through performance—or if a narrator reads Dickens's descriptions aloud. While Mr. Edgar does use narration here (distributed cleverly among the entire cast), he generally uses it to fill in plot rather than to supply characterizations (except in the case of a few major figures). And eight and a half hours is not enough time for all the minor characters to occupy center stage as they can in an eight-hundred-page novel.

So Mr. Edgar gives some of them short shrift. The milliner Manatalini and her profligate husband, the Keswigs family, the cameo artist Miss La Creevy, and the accountant Tim Linkinwater—among others—receive television's *Masterpiece Theater* treatment: They appear in proper costume, in animated tableaus, but they whisk away so fast that they blur. The difficulty is not that they don't measure up to the book—that's not required—but that they don't add up to anything much at all, whether one has read Dickens or not.

Individually, their brief scenes aren't bothersome, but, collectively, they pile up as dead weight—especially in the four-hour part one. There are two theoretical ways to solve this dilemma: to make *Nicholas Nickleby* twice as long as it is, or to cut some of these people out and take care of their plot functions (if any) by adding to the spoken narration. The latter, far more preferable route can be accomplished—if a scenarist is willing to exercise fully his right of esthetic selectivity.

When it is dealing with its major characters—those that do have the time to reveal all their human twists—*Nicholas Nickleby* is far more effective. (Part two moves faster precisely because the action increasingly narrows its focus to the principal players.) And the cast fixes some of these roles with images that will endure as long as we can remember them. To the protagonist—a lesser Dickens hero, who, unlike Pip or David Copperfield, doesn't really grow much during the narrative—Roger Rees brings so much flaring sensitivity and intelligence that he takes the goo out of the young man's righteousness. Similar miracles are worked on his best friends. Though at times overmilked for curtain scenes, David Threlfall's Smike—a frail, stuttering wastrel whose lame body is bent almost into a Z—is the perfect apotheosis of those oppressed souls Dickens championed. As the tipsy clerk Newman Noggs, a fallen gentleman afraid of his own every move, Edward Petherbridge elevates a comic type with rending poetry.

The two major villains are equally impressive; they never devolve into mere heavies. Alun Armstrong finds Brueghelesque comedy in the sadistic schoolmaster, and John Woodvine turns Uncle Ralph into a near-Shakespearean tragic figure. When this cool, imperious businessman must finally confront the humane impulses he's suppressed for a lifetime, we see a man unravel to the terrifying point where the audience's loathing must give way to a compassionate embrace.

Through no fault of the actors or Mr. Edgar, some of the saintly characters are not so memorable. Nicholas's beloved Madeline, his sister Kate, and his beneficent saviors, the Cheerybles, don't register in the novel, either. In the secondary roles, most of the company handles its multiple assignments as sharply as the script allows. Not surprisingly for a man of the stage, Mr. Edgar gives the fullest treatment by far to those supporting characters who belong to the fleabag acting troupe that Nicholas joins in Portsmouth. These provincial theatrical hams are all hilariously rendered, and their bowdlerized performance of *Romeo and Juliet* ends part one on a high parodistic note that echoes the mechanicals' *Pyramus and Thisbe* in *A Midsummer Night's Dream*.

Interestingly enough, both the *Romeo and Juliet* and the production's brilliant crowning moment are the creations of Mr. Edgar. One wishes he had taken more such liberties, for these inventions are more Dickensian in spirit than many of the scenes in which he tries to be literally faithful to the book. Yet if this mammoth show re-creates the breadth and plot of a Victorian novel without consistently sustaining its exhilarating mixture of pathos and comedy, one must treasure those instances when it does rise to the full power of Dickens's art. The rest of the time *Nicholas Nickleby* is best enjoyed—and, on occasion, endured—as a spectacular display of theatrical craft.

≡ *I was too tough on* Nicholas Nickleby, *which was deemed the theatrical experience of a lifetime by most of my colleagues (including one whose snoring was so loud that I had to ask the management to either wake him up or change my seat). While I think my assessment of the play itself remains valid—indeed, it has rarely been revived in the past decade—I overemphasized that judgment to the point where I didn't give full value to the production's theatrical flavor. Perhaps I was in revolt against the* Masterpiece Theater*–style hard sell that preceded the show's arrival in New York. The pitch played heavily on snob appeal and Anglophilia; for a while the* Playbill *for* Nickleby *had the cachet in Manhattan living rooms of a coffee-table book.*

*For the Shuberts and Nederlanders—the rival Broadway theater owners who normally fought like the Hatfields and the McCoys but banded together to cosponsor the New York engagement—*Nickleby *was not a profit-making venture (even at sellout, it could at best break even). It was an image-burnishing publicity coup, and, best of all, from their point of view, a Trojan Horse (I would realize only later) to introduce the idea of a hundred-dollar ticket price (for all sections of the house, back of the mezzanine included). In this,* Nickleby *indeed changed Broadway history: Top prices soon skyrocketed for all shows and the concept of selling most of the balcony for the same price as front orchestra seats is now standard.*

Five years later the RSC sent Nickleby *to Broadway again with an equally talented cast and the now no-longer-novel hundred-dollar top. I wrote a far more enthusiastic appraisal—I went to it twice, in fact, and even my five-year-old son lasted for seven hours, to my utter amazement—and the other critics were as cheering as they had been the first time. But all those theatergoers who had bitterly complained about not being able to get into* Nickleby *during its initial limited engagement failed to show up. Yesterday's news, the show closed prematurely after only a few weeks of sparse attendance, its hundred-dollar seats frequently going begging at the half-price TKTS booth.*

MARLOWE

RIALTO THEATRE, OCTOBER 13, 1981

W hen everything goes right in a musical, the audience feels a rush of exhilaration that is the quintessence of Broadway. And what happens when everything goes wrong? Well, when everything goes wrong, another kind of giddiness sets in—that same slaphappy feeling that comes when Laurel and Hardy send a grand piano crashing down a flight of stairs.

Such is the perverse pleasure offered by *Marlowe*, a wholly ridiculous show that is much more fun to sit through than many merely mediocre musicals. Like such famous Broadway fiascoes as *Kelly, Rachael Lily Rosenbloom*, and *Rockabye Hamlet*, this one has the courage to meet vulgarity far more than halfway. If *Marlowe* isn't quite a classic of its kind, that's a matter of size, not content. Tacky-looking and sparsely populated, this show lacks the splendor and expenditure of Broadway's all-time fabulous wrecks.

Connoisseurs of theatrical disaster will still find much amusement in the self-described rock musical that opened last night at the Rialto. In attempting to give us a song-and-dance account of that madcap Elizabethan playwright, Christopher (Kit) Marlowe—the one who had "the devil market cornered"—the coauthors, Leo Rost and Jimmy Horowitz, have left no folio undefaced. The insanity begins with the opening scene, in which Queen Elizabeth I (Margaret Warncke) dispatches a lover with the line "Don't forget your codpiece!"

A little later, there's a musical number in which Marlowe, "Willie" Shakespeare, and Richard Burbage get stoned on marijuana provided by Sir Walter Raleigh—who has passed it on from his good friend Pocahontas. Act 2 reaches its peak when the hero (Patrick Jude) returns from the grave on a cloud of dry-ice smoke. Wearing a silver-lamé jumpsuit—tight enough to reveal a bulky microphone battery-pack above his navel—he imparts the evening's message in a song called "The Madrigal Blues": "Make love to life, and you will find death a friend."

Though it pays lip service to Marlowe's renegade anticlerical views, the libretto is principally concerned with his love life. As the authors have it, their hero stole a woman, Emelia Bossano (Lisa Mordente), from Shakespeare—and never mind the other characters' conjecture that Marlowe tended to "prefer the boys." According to the *Playbill*, "the story of this drama is essentially true and accurate, except for minor adjustments in time for dramatic purpose." This may come as a surprise to some scholars, who will discover, in addition to the other "minor adjustments," that the authors have changed the generally accepted location and perpetrator of Marlowe's murder.

Don Price, the director, has assembled the very cast the material demands. With his open shirt, glittery vest, and leopard boots, the pelvis-thrusting Mr. Jude would be the toast of any small-town shopping-center disco. The rumpled, mini-skirted Ms. Mordente has two expressions to go with Mr. Jude's one, and she reacts to her lover's death with all the sorrow of a sixteen-year-old who's discovered a small run in her stocking. Lennie Del Duca Jr.'s spurned Shakespeare—"I've sweated sonnets for you," he tells Ms. Mordente—is so retiring and slow-witted that we always believe the authors' contention that he was the Globe's foremost nerd.

The scraggly chorus of Elizabethan "chroniclers," wearing Day-Glo tights, performs dance routines that might be ragged run-throughs for a Jordache jeans commercial. They inhabit a balconied set that suggests just how sixteenth-century England might have looked had cellophane, aluminum foil, and Con-Tac paper only been invented back then. The soundalike "rock" songs recall high-school band improvisations, circa 1965. Because of the acoustical feedback, static, and rumbles, the lyrics are often garbled. The few that do surface—"Good guys and bad guys couldn't deny / Marlowe was king of the gadflies"—make one regret the loss of even a single verse.

≣ *Very few shows misquoted me in their advertisements—the practice is far more common in movie ads—but* Marlowe *was one of the few, running an ad in the* Times *purporting that I had declared this musical "more fun than Laurel and Hardy."*

Actually, maybe that wasn't so inaccurate after all. Few can afford to produce flops like this anymore: While a small musical could still slip into a small Broadway house at a cost of a few hundred thousand dollars in the early 1980s, fifteen years later it would take at least $4 million to produce a show on even the shoddy scale of Marlowe.

SISTER MARY IGNATIUS
EXPLAINS IT ALL FOR YOU
PLAYWRIGHTS HORIZONS, OCTOBER 22, 1981

Anyone can write an angry play—all it takes is an active spleen. But only a writer of real talent can write an angry play that remains funny and controlled even in its most savage moments. *Sister Mary Ignatius Explains It All for You* confirms that Christopher Durang is just such a writer. In this one-act comedy he goes after the Catholic Church with a vengeance that might well have shocked the likes of either Paul Krassner or Lenny Bruce, and yet he never lets his bitter emotions run away with his keen theatrical sense.

Sister Mary Ignatius, the second half of a Durang double bill that opened at Playwrights Horizons last night, is both the most consistently clever and deeply felt work yet by the author of *A History of the American Film* and *Beyond Therapy*. Originally produced by the Ensemble Studio Theater two years ago, it has the sting of a revenge drama, even as it rides waves of demonic laughter. The play is also terribly honest, for Mr. Durang knows better than to give himself a total victory over his formidable antagonist. With pointed rue, he must finally leave the church bloodied but unbowed.

Sister Mary Ignatius (Elizabeth Franz) is an aging teacher conducting an assembly in the auditorium of Our Lady of Perpetual Sorrows School. She seems, at first, a reasonably kindly pedant. As she lectures her students on the "physical torments" of hell, her voice quivers with self-contentment, her mouth curls heavenward in a self-righteous smile. Nor is her *Going My Way* demeanor challenged by the impish student questions she reads from file cards. "Was Jesus effeminate?" asks one of her charges. "Yes!" replies Ms. Franz, cheerily closing off any further debate.

For about half the play's length, Mr. Durang uses his glibly dissembling protagonist to illustrate what he regards as church hypocrisies. Sister Mary must do some fancy and unconvincing footwork to explain how supposedly "infallible" dogma could have been changed overnight by her least favorite pope, John XXIII. She instructs her star pupil, the seven-year-old Thomas (Mark Stefan), to read "a partial list" of sinners going to hell—and the roll call includes Zsa Zsa Gabor, Christine Keeler, David Bowie, Betty Comden, and Adolph Green. The nun also tends to fondle little Thomas just a shade too playfully—thus allowing Mr. Durang to score his wicked points about the hidden sexual quotient of ostensibly sinless celibacy.

Eventually, however, we see that there is one question that does throw Sister Mary: "If God is all powerful, why does He allow evil in the world?" And the playwright forces the nun to confront that issue when four grown-up former students show up to stage a Joseph-and-Mary pageant, complete with camel, for her current flock. The visitors all hated their despotic teacher; they soon try to settle the score by making her defend God and his rules in a world where rape and cancer seem to justify such sins as abortion and agnosticism.

Mr. Durang successfully escalates this comic confrontation to a literally violent climax that strips the nun's moral authority bare even as it allows her to retain her crippling psychological power over her students, past and present. As the playwright sees his villain, she will tolerate no failings in others—but will gladly use Church law to rationalize even murder when it suits her own authoritarian purposes. In making his extreme case, Mr. Durang receives strong help from the director, Jerry Zaks, who wisely keeps his actors in realistic bounds. The entire cast is first-rate, including Mr. Stefan's catechism-reciting choirboy, and Ms. Franz is brilliant. After her real—and insane—personality is revealed, she still remains all too frighteningly human.

Mr. Zaks and company also do very well by the evening's curtain-raiser, *The Actor's Nightmare.* In this sketch, the playwright gives us what his title promises—a hero, appropriately named George Spelvin (Jeff Brooks), who suddenly finds himself on stage in a play he has never rehearsed. The premise lets Mr. Durang show off his gift for theatrical and showbiz satire, for the play-within-the-play proves to be an ever-changing amalgam of *Private Lives, Hamlet, A Man for All Seasons,* and the collected works of Beckett. Who but this writer would imagine that Godot will someday arrive—reeking of garlic and telling stewardess jokes?

The nebbishy, deadpan Mr. Brooks may be the least likely melancholy Dane since Jack Benny in *To Be or Not to Be;* he is most amusing as he calls on *Kiss Me, Kate* lyrics and other half-remembered theatrical lines to ad-lib his way through his jam. Like the playwright and cast, the designers—Karen Schulz, William Ivey Long, and Paul Gallo—run joyously amok plundering the styles of four centuries of theater. If *The Actor's Nightmare* finally runs out of jokes too early and fails in its effort to deepen its hero, it gets us as ready as possible for the unstoppably virulent comic nightmare that's soon to come.

CRIMES OF THE HEART
JOHN GOLDEN THEATRE, NOVEMBER 5, 1981

Beth Henley's *Crimes of the Heart* ends with its three heroines—the MaGrath sisters of Hazelhurst, Miss.—helping themselves to brick-sized hunks of a chocolate birthday cake. The cake, a "super deluxe" extravaganza from the local bakery, is as big as the kitchen table, and the sisters laugh their heads off as they dig in. The scene is the perfect capper for an evening of antic laughter—yet it's by no means the sum of *Crimes of the Heart.* While this play overflows with infectious high spirits, it is also, unmistakably, the tale of a very troubled family. Such is Ms. Henley's prodigious talent that she can serve us pain as though it were a piece of cake.

Prodigious, to say the least. This is Ms. Henley's first play. Originally produced at Louisville's Actors Theatre, it won the Pulitzer Prize and

New York Drama Critics Circle Award after its New York production last winter at the Manhattan Theatre Club. Last night that production arrived, springier than ever, at the Golden, and it's not likely to stray from Broadway soon. Melvin Bernhardt, the director, has fulfilled Ms. Henley's comedy by casting young actors whose future looks every bit as exciting as the playwright's.

Crimes is set "five years after Hurricane Camille" in the MaGrath family kitchen, a sunny garden of linoleum and translucent, flowered wallpaper designed by John Lee Beatty. The action unfolds during what the youngest sister, twenty-four-year-old Babe (Mia Dillon), calls "a bad day." Babe knows whereof she speaks: She's out on bail, having just shot her husband in the stomach. And Babe's not the only one with problems. Her twenty-seven-year-old sister Meg (Mary Beth Hurt), a would-be singing star, has retreated from Hollywood by way of a psychiatric ward. Lenny (Lizbeth Mackay), the eldest MaGrath, is facing her thirtieth birthday with a "shrunken ovary" and no romantic prospects. As if this weren't enough, Old Granddaddy, the family patriarch, is in the hospital with "blood vessels popping in his brain."

A comedy, you ask? Most certainly—and let's not forget about the local lady with the "tumor on her bladder," about the neighbor with the "crushed leg," about the sudden death by lightning of Lenny's pet horse, Billy Boy. Ms. Henley redeems these sorrows, and more, by mining a pure vein of Southern Gothic humor worthy of Eudora Welty and Flannery O'Connor. The playwright gets her laughs not because she tells sick jokes, but because she refuses to tell jokes at all. Her characters always stick to the unvarnished truth, at any price, never holding back a single gory detail. And the truth—when captured like lightning in a bottle—is far funnier than any invented wisecracks.

Why did Babe shoot her husband? Because, she says, "I didn't like his looks." Why, after firing the gun, did she make a pitcher of lemonade before calling an ambulance? Because she was thirsty. Why did she carry on with a fifteen-year-old black boy during the months before her crime? "I was so lonely," explains Ms. Dillon, "and he was goooood." Why has Babe's lawyer, a young, sheepish Ole Miss grad (Peter MacNicol), taken on such a seemingly hopeless case? Because Babe won his heart when she sold him poundcake at a long-ago church bazaar—and because he believes in "personal vendettas."

You see Ms. Henley's technique. She builds from a foundation of wacky but consistent logic until she's constructed a funhouse of perfect-pitch language and ever-accelerating misfortune. By Act 3, we're so at home in the crazy geography of the MaGraths' lives that we're laughing at the slightest prick of blood. At that point Ms. Henley starts kindling comic eruptions on the most unlikely lines—"Old Granddaddy's in a coma!"—without even trying. That's what can happen when a playwright creates a world and lets the audience inhabit it.

We're not laughing at the characters, of course, but with them. We all have bad days, when we contemplate—or are victims of—irrational crimes of the heart. In this play, Ms. Henley shows how comedy at its best can heighten reality to illuminate the landscape of existence in all its mean absurdity. But the heightening is not achieved at the price of credibility. The MaGraths come by their suffering naturally: It's been their legacy since childhood, when their father vanished and their mother hanged herself—and her pet cat—in the cellar. *Crimes of the Heart* is finally the story of how its young characters escape the past to seize the future. "We've got to figure out a way to get through these bad days here," says Meg. That can't happen for any of us until the corpses of a childhood are truly laid to rest.

Like the compassionate author, the director makes us care deeply about the MaGraths, crimes and all. Mr. Bernhardt is completely in touch with the play's strong family feelings; he turns a funhouse into a love-suffused, sisterly home that fills the Broadway vacuum left by the departure of *Morning's at Seven*. Though he can't quite whip the evening's slight overlength and the routine writing of the two secondary characters, you'll probably be too busy enjoying the four principal players to care.

It's great fun to watch Ms. Mackay's spinsterish Lenny blossom from a moody, self-pitying fussbudget into a self-possessed woman; the actress walks a tremulous line between hilarity and hysteria as she goes. As Meg, the loose, selfish sister who blossomed too early, Ms. Hurt proves she's a powerfully sexy comedienne as well as a good actress. A battle-scarred, rueful adult, she also lets us see the golden, headstrong teenage girl who once liked to shock her peers by mocking the March of Dimes posters at Dixieland Drugs.

Ms. Dillon and Mr. MacNicol are priceless as the accused Babe and her green lawyer. Perhaps the baby-faced Mr. MacNicol is so because his awkward little boy's demeanor—slow molasses voice, misbuttoned suit, and toothy, open-mouthed grin—is in such ridiculous contrast to the no-nonsense professional manner he adopts to impress his client. Perhaps Ms. Dillon—speaking in an excitable girlish yelp—delights us because she's guileless when contemplating murder yet naughty on the subject of birthday cakes. But why try to pin them down? Just be grateful that we have a new writer from hurricane country who gives her characters room to spin and spin and spin.

THE DRESSER
BROOKS ATKINSON THEATRE, NOVEMBER 10, 1981

The dark and jagged set of Ronald Harwood's play *The Dresser* is the ratty backstage area—moldy dressing rooms, cramped corridors and wings—of a crumbling theater somewhere in the British provinces. The time is 1942, and the stink of death is in the air. Outside, there are howling sirens, signaling another Luftwaffe bombing raid. Inside, skulking about the gloom, are Mr. Harwood's central characters—two men who seem to have scant reason to live.

Sir (Paul Rogers) is an aged Shakespearean actor-manager, now reduced to touring third-rate towns with a war-depleted troupe of "old men, cripples, and nancy-boys." His mind and body are failing fast, yet tonight he is to give his 427th performance as King Lear. Norman (Tom Courtenay), his dresser, is supposed to ready Sir for the show, yet he's scarcely better off. A sepulchral, middle-aged homosexual who's spent sixteen years in near-feudal servitude to his master, he seems to gain his sole spiritual nourishment from the pint bottle he keeps in his back pocket. Whatever friends he has are long gone, ghosts left behind at other lonely theaters along the road.

But while Sir and Norman are pathetic, they're bound together by a common cause: An audience is in the house, and the show must go on. *The Dresser,* which arrived at the Atkinson last night, is about how Sir, Norman, and the rest of their fleabag company somehow rise above air raids and personal calamities to perform their *Lear.* If it's a stirring evening—and it most abundantly is—it's not because Mr. Harwood has written a flawless play, or one that runs particularly deep. It's because this writer and his two glorious stars burn with a love of the theater that conquers all.

Why do Sir and Norman go on with the show? Because, for them, the stage really is the one safe haven where even the dreariest realities of life can always be escaped. As we watch these theater people practice their total childlike faith in the transcendent powers of make-believe, we rediscover that feeling in ourselves. The primal impulse that makes Sir and Norman go on is the same one that first sent us to the theater as an audience.

Mr. Harwood does more, too. A one-time dresser to the late actor-manager Donald Wolfit, the playwright has crammed *The Dresser* with perfectly observed, devilishly entertaining backstage lore. Sir's hammy provincial troupe is the final, seedy inheritor of the nineteenth-century theatrical tradition epitomized by Vincent Crummles's roving company in *Nicholas Nickleby*—and it's just as hilarious in its noble yet chaotic pursuit of the Bard. Most important, Mr. Harwood has written a moving, platonic love story for Sir and Norman—two irascible men who can't live without each other any better than they can live without the theater.

It is the author's conceit—sometimes too explicitly stated—that Sir and Norman's private backstage drama parallels the onstage one between Lear and his fool. The crotchety old star sees himself as royalty—even if, to his eternal displeasure, he has yet to be knighted—and he regards Norman as a peon who exists only to do his every bidding. But now that Sir is in decline, he needs the dresser as a nursemaid and confessor—a role the younger man plays very well, even as he bridles at his boss's parsimony and abuse. Yet Norman needs Sir, too: When the old actor takes to the stage, the dresser basks in his performance as if it were his own. Once their theatrical tradition—and war-torn England itself—fall into ruin, it's only a matter of time before the men come together in madness and affection.

To be sure, *The Dresser* isn't *King Lear,* but the stars play it as if it were. In Sir, Mr. Rogers has his first good New York role since *The Homecoming* [in 1967]. Often deflated and confused to the point of tears, he suddenly rises to full imperious height at the prospect of a full house or an autograph seeker. He rails at the heavens about the glories of Shakespeare, then behaves like a petulant child when crying out for chocolates, bad-mouthing his theatrical rivals or recalling his rejection by Hollywood. ("They haven't built a camera large enough to record me!") And while Mr. Rogers is a broken-down old wheezebag in his soiled street clothes and unkempt white mane, he does achieve a star's grandeur once dressed in full Lear regalia. We believe, as Norman says, that "once he's assumed the disguise, he's a different man"—ennobled by the only passion he knows.

Mr. Courtenay, never less than a brilliant actor, has outdone himself here. His Dresser is so seamless that it's impossible to tell, for instance, at what point he ceases to be tipsy and becomes roaring drunk. Dressed in black, his long fingers in perpetual flutter, the spindly Mr. Courtenay starts off as a prototypical backstage queen. He coddles his boss in the disingenuous, singsong voice of a nanny, prattles blithely on about his trivial theatrical memories, then darts like a snake when another member of the company intrudes upon his turf. But Norman is not really a bitchy conniver. Once he nears the stage, his face loses its lines and radiates the utter sweet innocence of a child at his first pantomime. He says of the theater: "Here's beauty. Here's spring and summer. Here pain is bearable"—and that simple credo, as delivered by Mr. Courtenay, raises a fundamentally silly man to a state of grace.

Full-bodied as the performances are, the frailties of the play are nonetheless visible. Mr. Harwood tends to explain his jokes and, especially in an Act 2 confrontation between Sir and his long-suffering actress wife (well done by Rachel Gurney), to announce his emotional points. His ending—though much redeemed by Mr. Courtenay's volcanic final speech—is sentimental melodrama, not tragedy. Luckily, these real weaknesses are usually counterbalanced by the author's wit and high-charged theatricality.

That theatricality, whether chilling or farcical, is always captured by the director, Michael Elliott, and a strong supporting cast that includes Douglas Seale as the worst understudy ever to play Lear's Fool and Lisabeth Bartlett as an ambitious ingenue. Laurie Dennett's set, Stephen Doncaster's costumes, and Beverly Emmons's haunted-house lighting are first-rate. But what you'll most remember about *The Dresser* is its stars, who give their blood to prove that all the world can indeed be a stage.

MERRILY WE ROLL ALONG
Alvin Theatre, November 17, 1981

As we all should probably have learned by now, to be a Stephen Sondheim fan is to have one's heart broken at regular intervals. Usually the heartbreak comes from Mr. Sondheim's songs—for his music can tear through us with an emotional force as moving as Gershwin's. And sometimes the pain is compounded by another factor—for some of Mr. Sondheim's most powerful work turns up in shows (*Anyone Can Whistle, Pacific Overtures*) that fail. Suffice it to say that both kinds of pain are abundant in *Merrily We Roll Along*, the new Sondheim–Harold Prince–George Furth musical that opened at the Alvin last night. Mr. Sondheim has given this evening a half-dozen songs that are crushing and beautiful—that soar and linger and hurt. But the show that contains them is a shambles.

Merrily We Roll Along has been adapted by Mr. Furth from the second George S. Kaufman–Moss Hart collaboration, a Broadway curiosity of 1934. While the new version is rewritten and updated, it repeats the defects of the original text—even as it adds more of its own. Now, as before, *Merrily* is about three best friends who reach the top of the

Broadway-Hollywood showbiz whirl only to discover, in two cases, that their lives are empty, petty, and loveless. The gimmick is to tell the story backwards. The central plot begins with the principals at a present-day party, where they're at their lowest, most jaded ebb. We end up at a high-school graduation, where the hero vows to uphold all the pure ideals we've spent the evening watching him betray.

Mr. Furth blunts the shock effect of the original play's structure by enclosing it within a conventional flashback, and, even so, he fails to solve its major dramatic failure. We never do learn why the characters reached the sad state they're in at the outset. While a busy story—often built around unconvincing, melodramatic twists—does tell us how the three friends fell apart, that's not enough.

We keep waiting for some insight into these people that might make us understand, if not care, about them, but all we get is fatuous attitudinizing about how ambition, success, and money always lead to rack and ruin. Like Kaufman and Hart—but unlike Harold Pinter in the similarly designed *Betrayal*—Mr. Furth abandons his emotional issues entirely once he moves far back in time. Act 2 is all anticlimactic plot exposition—an undramatized, breathless recap of the red-letter events that first brought the friends to fame.

There's another difficulty as well, for the book's tone often seems as empty as its characters. Mr. Furth's one-line zingers about showbiz, laced with unearned nastiness, are as facile as those he brought to *The Act* (1977) and *The Supporting Cast* (1981). He defines the show's principal female character, an alcoholic writer (Ann Morrison), by giving her labored retreads of the wisecracks he wrote for Elaine Stritch in his book for the Sondheim-Prince *Company.* Meanwhile, the emotional basis of the friendship between the two heroes, a composer (Jim Walton) and a lyricist (Lonny Price)—or between them and the heroine—is never established at all. We're just told, repeatedly, that they're lifelong friends.

Perhaps the libretto's most unfortunate aspect, however, is its similarity to James Goldman's far fuller one for the Sondheim-Prince *Follies.* That 1971 musical also gave us bitter, middle-aged friends, disappointed in love and success, who reunite at a showbiz party, then steadily move back through time until they become the idealistic kids they once were. Forced to contemplate the esthetic gap that separates these two like-minded shows, we see that not only the characters are rolling backward this time out.

Follies had everything the new version does not—most notably a theatrical metaphor that united all its elements, from its production design and staging and choreography (by Michael Bennett) to its score. It also used the effective trick of assigning each major character to two actors, one middle-aged and one young, so that past and present could interweave at will to potent effect. With one passing exception, the roles in *Merrily* are always played by young actors, no matter what the characters' ages or how high the toll in cuteness.

While Mr. Prince often finds brilliant unifying concepts for his shows, even the ones that don't work, he's come up with a flat one here—school. Eugene Lee's set is a high tech jungle gym of bleachers, surrounded by gym lockers, that looks as if it's left over from *Runaways*. When it is augmented by skyline projections, it becomes a decimated version of the set from *Company*—a parallel that's reinforced by the staging of the party scenes and the dramatic uses of platforms. As has been true of some other recent Prince shows, the choreography, by Larry Fuller, is uninspired to the extent that it exists at all.

Although Mr. Sondheim's lyrics seem less airborne than usual, as do Jonathan Tunick's brassy, Jule Styne–esque orchestrations, the score only occasionally falls to the show's level. There are two songs, "Rich and Happy" and "It's a Hit!," that are as glib as the book, and one parody number about the Kennedys (a sixties composition of the heroes) that may be intended as a satirical pastiche of such parodies, but is unfunny in any case.

The other, sublime numbers give the three appealing principal players their only opportunities to reveal their talent. Mr. Price, in the most sympathetic role, is a charming, Woody Allen–esque fellow who brings fire to the show's angriest song ("Franklin Shepard, Inc.") and a plaintive undersell to its most conventional ballad ("Good Thing Going"). Mr. Walton, likable, if less than charismatic, as an innocent-gone-sour, gives a rush of sweetness to "Not a Day Goes By," a relentless song of unrequited love that matches its equivalent, "Too Many Mornings," in *Follies*. Ms. Morrison's heroine, attractively plump and sassy, sparks what may be the show's richest song, the trio "Old Friends."

With the exception of Sally Klein, as a jettisoned first wife, the rest of the cast is dead wood until the penultimate number, an ironic, idealistic anthem titled "Our Time." At that point, Mr. Sondheim's searing songwriting voice breaks through once more to address, as no one else here does, the show's poignant theme of wasted lives. But what's really being wasted here is Mr. Sondheim's talent. And that's why we watch *Merrily We Roll Along* with an ever-mounting—and finally upsetting—sense of regret.

≡ *A decade earlier, Stephen Sondheim had been the first person in the theater to give me encouragement as a drama critic. I had reviewed the pre-Broadway tryout of* Follies *for my college paper,* The Harvard Crimson, *in 1971, and he wrote me a letter about the piece, which led to us meeting and having some memorable and (for me) hugely educational conversations about the theater. Because part of my* Follies *review was published in a memoir that Harold Prince wrote in the early seventies, it was assumed around Broadway—I eventually learned—that Sondheim and Prince had something to do with my being hired by the* Times. *It wasn't true; I hadn't been in touch with either of them in years, though Sy Peck, the* Times *cultural editor when I arrived, told me that he had received a copy of my* Follies *review when I was still in college, possibly from Prince, suggesting me as a potential theater critic. The suggestion had promptly been forgotten, and Arthur Gelb, who hired me, had no knowledge of the incident when I asked him about it.*

I was and am a huge admirer of both Prince and Sondheim, but, with the single and major exception of Sondheim's Sunday in the Park with George, *was often disappointed by their new shows during my years as drama critic. Whether I liked Sondheim's shows or not, we never communicated throughout my thirteen years on the job—and when I needed to interview him and Prince for a book I was writing about their frequent collaborator, the set designer Boris Aronson, I sent a proxy (Aronson's widow, Lisa) to do it so no one would be uncomfortable. Since leaving the job, I've reencountered Sondheim, who has the sharpest perspective on the theater I've ever encountered; we picked up our conversations where'd we left off twenty-plus years earlier.*

Merrily picked itself up, too. Sondheim and George Furth revised it several times for productions stretching from La Jolla, California, in the mid-eighties to Off Broadway's York Theatre in the mid-nineties, usually with adult actors in the leads. All were superior to the original production, but none quite worked. For one example, see page 710.

For one example, see page 710.

THE WEST SIDE WALTZ
ETHEL BARRYMORE THEATRE, NOVEMBER 20, 1981

Ernest Thompson has written a tired play in *The West Side Waltz*, which opened at the Barrymore last night, but be assured that his star goes ahead and puts on her own vital show without him. Katharine Hepburn is at hand here, and Katharine Hepburn, in all her wonder, is what you'll get.

The actress ostensibly plays Margaret Mary Elderdice, an aging, widowed pianist who lives in a dreary Upper West Side apartment and wears dowdy cardigans that fall below her knees. While the playwright maintains that Margaret Mary is originally from Iowa, don't worry: Ms. Hepburn's pronunciation—just hear the word "pooper-scooper"—remains the apotheosis of Yankee. It's also suggested that the heroine's health is failing—it's Mr. Thompson's wont to give her a new orthopedic appliance in nearly each scene—but don't believe that, either. Ms. Hepburn, to say the least, is still yare.

Just how yare is first apparent not only in her robust face—gleaming eyes and those unmatchable cheekbones, all framed by a halo of graying curls—but also in her comic timing. When an overprotective neighbor tells her that it's too cold to walk in Central Park, Ms. Hepburn waits one half-beat and announces, "I'll run!" The sheer finality of her delivery makes a so-what line very funny—and our laughter is capped by hers, which is contagious and openmouthed and more-than-halfway aimed at herself. A little later, Margaret Mary is told of a man who is "gay," and at first Ms. Hepburn pretends not to know the current usage of that word. But the light soon dawns—brighter than any sunrise. "Oh, ga-aa-aay," she says—and we see the same triumphant smile of mischief she gave James Stewart in *The Philadelphia Story* as she feigned not to know the location of his hometown of South Bend.

Then come the passion, the stubbornness, the vulnerability. Mary Margaret's best friend has killed herself, and someone asks why. "Because she's a fool!" cries Ms. Hepburn, flying into a contained rage, complete with small fists. Then she adds, "I won't forgive her for that," and her low, vehement voice quiets any fears that she might have softened her stand against spiritual weakness. Yet, as always, she's not really sanctimonious—she can fall off her pedestal, too. When a young woman doesn't immediately accept Margaret Mary's offer of a job, the actress's face drains of color in morbid fear of rejection. It's a glimpse of her Mary Tyrone, trying to retrieve lost love in the long shadows of a New London night.

Beautiful moments, all—and all Katharine Hepburn. Let's be grateful that Mr. Thompson feeds her lines and stays out of her way. Be grateful, too, that *The West Side Waltz* improves on the season's previous star vehicle, Claudette Colbert's *A Talent for Murder,* by placing its heroine in a wheelchair for only a scene or two instead of the entire evening.

But *The West Side Waltz* is otherwise a tedious retread of Mr. Thompson's previous effort, *On Golden Pond.* Once again this writer gives us an elderly protagonist, isolated and a bit embittered by old age, who learns to live again after a young companion (Regina Baff, as a would-be actress) moves in for an extended stay. And once again Mr. Thompson stands up boldly for the old verities. "Human beings are not meant to be alone." "If you want something in life, you have to go out and get it!" "Don't sell yourself short."

It's Mr. Thompson who sells people short. Rather than create characters, he gives us types (two here have burlesque accents), walks them through contrived situations and then steps in to resolve their lives with divinely ordained happy endings. *The West Side Waltz* wants to be warm and poignant, but it's so coolly calculating it might have been written by computer. Margaret Mary's one flaw, selfishness, must be corrected by the final curtain—and, ipso facto, it is. Her companion must gain her self-confidence—and so she does. The other major character, a prim, virginal violinist played by Dorothy Loudon, is a prig for two hours, then kicks up her heels just before we go home.

These transformations aren't credible because they aren't dramatized. They either take place magically between scenes or are announced as faits accomplis. The play's only real conflict—a fight between Margaret Mary and her companion—springs up out of nowhere and blows over about ten minutes later. In a similarly arbitrary manner, Mr. Thompson suddenly bestows a lover on one character in Act 2; his heroine's money problems, much discussed early on, simply fade away. Life is always neat and easy here: All six scenes end with Ms. Hepburn playing a waltz at her piano and saying the same curtain line ("Now we're cooking"). Such television-style tidiness cries out for commercial breaks.

The jokes are cheap and often compromise the characters, such as they are. (Would Ms. Loudon's blue-nosed spinster really boast, "I've never even had my period"?) Mr. Thompson's comic shtick, here as before, is to have elderly characters say—or overhear—expletives or sexual innuendoes. This time he's also added some Neil Simon gags about such New York indignities as cockroaches and underheated apartments. Most of these are recited by a Rumanian—and inevitably malaprop-prone—superintendent.

Although Ms. Loudon doesn't subside into broadness until Act 2 and David Margulies somewhat redeems the super with sweetness, the acting of the supporting cast is generally as mannered and thin as the writing. Noel Willman's direction contains no surprises: You just keep waiting for him to move his characters to the piano so each scene can end. But the star does keep you guessing about which part of her persona she'll reveal next—and there are more parts to her than most mere mortals around. While *The West Side Waltz* never gives us cause to look away from Katharine Hepburn, you might not be able to take your eyes off her even if it did.

≡As Hepburn's generation of theater performers—the generation that first played Broadway before World War II—has grown extinct, so has this kind of boulevard play: a star vehicle designed only to be played by one actor, after which it will disappear forever. I saw several such productions in the early eighties—they were farewell performances, really. The performance of this sort that haunts me most came from Eva Le Gallienne, although the play that prompted it, To Grandmother's House We Go, lingers in memory as a title and nothing more.

A SOLDIER'S PLAY
NEGRO ENSEMBLE COMPANY, NOVEMBER 27, 1981

In the first scene of Charles Fuller's *A Soldier's Play*, the opening production of the Negro Ensemble Company's new season, we see a middle-aged black Army officer stumbling about in shadows. The man, Tech. Sgt. Vernon Waters (Adolph Caesar), is drunk and raving and half-bent to the ground. "They still hate you!" he screams in a gravelly, barrel-chested voice. "They still hate you!" Then two shots ring out, and Waters collapses in a mortal heap.

What happens next is what you might expect. Another black officer, Capt. Richard Davenport (Charles Brown), is sent to the scene of the crime—Fort Neal, La., in 1944—to find out who murdered Waters. Davenport conducts his inquiry in the usual manner of courtroom dramas: As he interviews each potential suspect, the scenes that led to the fateful gunshots are reenacted until the guilty party is at last unmasked. But there is nothing usual about the way Mr. Fuller has written his play. By the time he reaches his resolution, it's clear that the identity of the culprit isn't what really matters here at all. What does matter, it turns out, is the meaning of the victim's cryptic last words—for what Mr. Fuller has written is a relentless investigation into the complex, sometimes cryptic pathology of hate.

A Soldier's Play is, to put it simply, a major breakthrough for the promising author of *The Brownsville Raid* and last season's *Zooman and the Sign*. This is, in every way, a mature and accomplished work—from its inspired opening up of a conventional theatrical form to its skillful portraiture of a dozen characters to its remarkable breadth of social and historical vision. It's also a play that speaks to both blacks and whites without ever patronizing either group. Mr. Fuller writes characters of both races well—and he implicates both in the murder of Sergeant Waters.

As befits a work that uses the conventions of a whodunit, almost all the characters on stage—and some offstage—could have committed the crime. Fort Neal contains its share of racist white rednecks; the local town has an active chapter of the Ku Klux Klan. As Captain Davenport quickly discovers, many of Sergeant Waters's soldiers might have also had their motives. Though black, Waters was a tyrant who frequently addressed his recruits as "shiftless, lazy niggers." He spewed contempt for rural Southern blacks in particular, accusing them of causing whites to look on the entire race as "fools."

But Waters isn't as simple as he seems in the play's early flashbacks. For all his venom and cruelty, he was also a prideful man who refused to toady to whites and who often wanted the best for his fellow blacks. "Who the hell was he?" asks the prosecutor in frustration as the evidence comes in—and it soon becomes apparent that the case can't be solved until that question is resolved.

As the answer comes, Mr. Fuller uses it to illuminate the behavior of every black character in the play, as well as the white society they inhabit. Waters is psychotic, all right, but the basis of his warped, cruel behavior is self-hatred, not hatred—and the cause of that self-hatred is his own recognition of the bankruptcy of his efforts to please whites. Much as he's tried to bury his black roots and as far as he's gone in the Army, Waters just can't escape the demon of racism—that sinking feeling that, for all his achievements, they still hate you. And in Waters's distorted personality, his men see a magnified, mirror image of what they most fear and hate in themselves—the fear of being destroyed by allowing white racism to define the ambitions of one's life.

While we can see why the men might have been tempted to murder Waters, Mr. Fuller recognizes such an act for what it is—both a symbolic and literal form of self-destruction. The playwright took this same moral position in *Zooman,* which told the story of a contemporary black community that was too cowardly to identify a murderer in its midst. Here, as before, the playwright has compassion for blacks who might be driven to murder their brothers—because he sees them as victims of a world they haven't made. Yet he doesn't let anyone off the hook. Mr. Fuller demands that his black characters find the courage to break out of their suicidal, fratricidal cycle—just as he demands that whites end the injustices that have locked his black characters into the nightmare.

At the same time, Mr. Fuller places his new play in a historical context that gives it a resonance beyond its specific details. As the investigation proceeds, another, larger drama is played out; the soldiers, who have not seen any wartime action, wait in desperate hope that they may get orders for overseas, so that they can prove that "colored boys can fight" Hitler as well as white boys can. But in the playwright's view, this aspiration is just another version of Waters's misplaced ambition to deny his blackness by emulating whites—and just as likely to end in tragic, self-annihilating doom.

Douglas Turner Ward, the director, has given *A Soldier's Play* a superlative production, lyrically linking the drama's time-leaping scenes as well as capturing its period flavor and barracks humor. The entire cast is excellent. Mr. Brown, as the impassioned yet rational prosecutor, is a perfect stand-in for the evenhanded playwright. Larry Riley gets to show off his strong voice, as well as his characteristic sweetness, in the role of a blues-singing soldier who is Waters's principal goad. Denzel Washington, who recently scored as Malcolm X in *When the Chickens Come Home to Roost,* is equally effective here as another, cooler kind of young renegade. Peter Friedman brings full honesty to a white officer who is at once capable of making racist insults and of apologizing for them.

In the principal role, Mr. Caesar is able to make Waters a hateful Queeg one moment and a sympathetic, pitiful wreck the next. It's a fascinating performance, full of contradictions that always leave the audience on edge. As such, it emblemizes Mr. Fuller's play, which tirelessly insists on embracing volatile contradictions because that is the way to arrive at the shattering truth.

≡ *This was a high-water mark for the Negro Ensemble Company and Charles Fuller, who won the Pulitzer Prize for this play, which later became an effective movie,* A Soldier's Story. *But the NEC had financial woes within the decade and Fuller, unlike such cast members as Denzel Washington, Samuel L. Jackson, and Peter Friedman, rarely surfaced again in the New York theater.*

**SUNDAY ESSAY: SHOULD WE
EXPECT MAGIC IN THE THEATER?**
DECEMBER 7, 1981

In one of the high points of *Nicholas Nickleby,* the title character and his best pal, the deformed wastrel Smike, join up with Vincent Crummles's provincial acting troupe. Nicholas and Smike are quite excited to undertake life on the stage—but they're a little disconcerted once they lay eyes on the shabby playhouse where they must make their debut in *Romeo and Juliet*. More than a little. Smike is shocked. "Is this the theater?" he asks Nicholas, disappointment rising in his frail voice. "I thought it would be ablaze with light and finery."

Smike's line brings down the house with the laughter of recognition— or so it did at the performance of *Nicholas Nickleby* I attended, which was full of critics and other folk who spend most waking minutes think- ing about the theater. People who love the stage always enter a theater expecting to find the illusory world that Smike does. And then, like him, they are so often crushed when the magic doesn't happen. Both the childlike wonder and the heartbreak of the theatrical calling, the ecstasy and the agony, are there in the orphan's one wonderful line.

That line has stayed with me for two months now—but, with each passing day, it seems more rueful than funny. *Nicholas Nickleby* was the first major opening of the Broadway season, and it was indeed ablaze with light and finery. Since then? We've been as disillusioned as Smike. There have been only three other worthwhile efforts, and all of them, like *Nickleby*, are remountings of productions first done elsewhere: *The Dresser*, also from London, and *Mass Appeal* and *Crimes of the Heart*, both from Off Broadway's Manhattan Theatre Club.

As for the rest, one doesn't know whether to laugh or cry. Three flop musicals in one week. Two shoddy star vehicles propelled by wheelchair. One "drama" about an unseen polar bear. The second revival of *Camelot* in as many years; the dreariest Shaw revival (*Candida*) in recent memory. Not to mention a so-called rock musical, *Marlowe*, in which the title character, William (Willie) Shakespeare, and Richard Burbage were to be seen puffing marijuana backstage at the Globe!

If you see too many of these shows, you may have trouble remember- ing what it was that attracted you to the theater in the first place. It's lucky for Broadway that only critics have had to see all of them. It's also fortunate that two of the season's four good plays do remind audiences of the theater's real power in the most explicit way possible—by putting the world of the theater itself on stage.

We feel that power at the end of part one of *Nickleby*, when Smike fi- nally gets his chance to act in *Romeo and Juliet*. Smike discovers that the theater is up to his expectations, after all. No sooner does this decrepit, bent orphan take to the stage than he glows and smiles for the first time since we've met him, as if acting were an instant panacea for all his con- siderable ills. His transformation is just like those moments in François Truffaut's film *The Last Metro* when the hero, a Jewish actor-manager in hiding from the Gestapo, somehow manages to forget all his woes as soon as he hears actors performing on the stage above his underground sanctuary.

A similar miracle occurs in Ronald Harwood's *The Dresser,* which also takes place during World War II and involves a fleabag British touring company about to perform a *King Lear* as disheveled as the Crummleses' *Romeo and Juliet.* In lieu of Smike, we get the pathetic wastrel of Mr. Harwood's title—Norman (Tom Courtenay), an alcoholic backstage aide de camp to a failing actor-manager known as Sir (Paul Rogers). When Norman is suddenly sent onstage to inform the audience about an ongoing German air raid, he, too, is transformed by his theatrical debut: A drunken nitwit becomes a radiant sprite. It's a moving moment because in the joy of this childish man, as in Smike, we see that primal, preintellectual impulse that first sent most of us into a theater when we were children: the promise of refuge, of transfiguration, of a make-believe world ablaze with light and finery.

As plays, neither *Nicholas Nickleby* nor *The Dresser* is a perfect creation: They both tend to meander here and there into unprofitable subplots. But next to most of Broadway's recent offerings, they are models of dramatic efficiency. This has been a season in which playwrights seem to have forgotten even the basic grammar of their craft. Too many new plays and musicals have been riddled by structural flaws so severe that the possibility of drama is foreclosed from the outset.

In *Ned and Jack,* for instance, Sheldon Rosen waited until Act 2 before he disclosed the full dilemma of one of his title characters—the terminal nature of the illness that would eventually reduce the playwright Ned Sheldon to total mortification. By leaving this matter unaddressed for so long, Mr. Rosen sent the audience out for intermission with the impression that *Ned and Jack* might be an evening composed entirely of idle chitchat. Is it any wonder that some audience members didn't return for Act 2?

In *The First,* the musical about Jackie Robinson, the authors of the libretto (Joel Siegel and Martin Charnin) waited until almost the end of Act 1 to have their hero sign with the Dodgers. Why? The only reason seemed to be that the authors want first to tell us the story of that colorful manager, Leo Durocher. Because Durocher was suspended before Robinson's first season, *The First* could keep the manager center stage only by putting the title character on hold for a while. When the libretto finally does get around to its ostensible concern—Robinson's courageous attempts to overcome racism in major-league baseball—the evening is too far gone to do it justice.

There have been other entertainments—*A Talent for Murder* and *The West Side Waltz*—that are so shapeless they could begin or end with virtually any scene. In the case of *Murder,* a would-be suspense thriller, even the unmasking of the murderer failed to provide the play with a climax. As the curtain fell, you had to double-check the *Playbill* to make absolutely certain that there wasn't another, real final scene, complete with double whammy dénouement still to come—and you could hear fellow theatergoers rustling the program's pages to do exactly that.

When it comes to structural calamities, however, the season's champion is likely to remain *Merrily We Roll Along*. This George Furth–Stephen Sondheim–Harold Prince musical told its story backward, as did the 1934 George S. Kaufman–Moss Hart play from which it was adapted. This trick can work—as Harold Pinter proved in *Betrayal*—but only if it is used to dig into the psychological roots of the characters. In the case of each *Merrily*, the authors were so in love with the notion of telling a busy plot in reverse order that they never got around to the underlying purpose of the exercise. We knew little more about the emotional lives of the characters at the end than we did upon first meeting them.

Given the particular nature of this show's characters, this failing was especially grievous. *Merrily* was about hugely successful theater people who are the antithesis of Smike or Norman—they're generally jaded and embittered by their stage careers. If there's no explanation for their discontent, their unhappiness can't be moving—it quickly curdles into frivolous, bratty, and off-putting self-indulgence. This was as true in 1934 as in 1981. Indeed, a sarcastic note sent by the screenwriter Herman J. Mankiewicz (*Citizen Kane*) to George S. Kaufman back then is just as damning of the new *Merrily* as it was of the first: "Here's this wealthy playwright"—a songwriter in the musical—"who has repeated success and has earned enormous sums of money, has mistresses as well as a family, an expensive townhouse, a luxurious beach house and a yacht. The problem is: How did the son of a bitch get into this jam?"

The problems of the new *Merrily* didn't end there. Although it had roughly a third as many cast members as the 1934 version (which had ninety-one, or more than twice as large a population as *Nicholas Nickleby*), it still seemed too large and hectic. The big and ugly set, the many minor players and chorus members, were only pointless detractions from the intimate central story, which involved three principal characters and at most three crucial secondary ones. Might *Merrily* have had more of a fighting chance if it had been done on the scale of, say, *March of the Falsettos?* At least then its authors might have been able to get a focus on their work's many ailments.

Yet, for all the clutter heaped on top of it, one aspect of *Merrily* was worthwhile—the score. On the day the show closed, I found myself irresistibly drawn to the Alvin to listen to part of it again. True, there are few sadder theatrical experiences than watching a flop musical in its death throes—especially in a house haunted by memories of such happier Sondheim occasions as *A Funny Thing Happened on the Way to the Forum* and *Company*. One couldn't help but feel as crushed as Smike when he first arrived at that gloomy provincial theater. But the passion of Mr. Sondheim's music remained unmistakable—it poured out of the wreckage. While it alone wasn't enough to make the Alvin seem ablaze with light and finery, it did leave one with the hope that the magic of a full-fledged Sondheim musical will one day return.

DREAMGIRLS
IMPERIAL THEATRE, DECEMBER 21, 1981

When Broadway history is being made, you can feel it. What you feel is a seismic emotional jolt that sends the audience, as one, right out of its wits. While such moments are uncommonly rare these days, I'm here to report that one popped up at the Imperial last night. Broadway history was made at the end of the first act of Michael Bennett's beautiful and heartbreaking new musical, *Dreamgirls*.

Dreamgirls is the story of a black singing group that rises from the ghetto to national fame and fortune during the 1960s. Like the Supremes, to which they bear more than a passing resemblance, the Dreams have their share of obstacles to overcome on the way up. At the end of Act 1, the heroines are beginning to make it in Las Vegas, but there's some nasty business to be dealt with backstage. The act's hard-driving manager, Curtis (Ben Harney), has come into the Dreams' dressing room to inform Effie, who is both his lover and the group's best singer, that she is through.

Effie is through because the Dreams are at last escaping the showbiz ghetto of rhythm and blues to cross over into the promised and lucrative land of white pop. To take the final leap, the Dreams must change their image—to a new, more glamorous look and a "lighter" sound. Effie no longer fits: She's fat, and her singing is anything but light. And Curtis's bad news does not end there. Not only does he have a brand-new, svelte Dream in costume, ready to replace Effie on stage, but he also has chosen another Dream to replace Effie in his bed.

It's at this point that Jennifer Holliday, the actress who plays Effie, begs Curtis to let her stay, in a song titled "And I Am Telling You I'm Not

Going." Ms. Holliday is a young woman with a broad face and an ample body. Somewhere in that body—or everywhere—is a voice that, like Effie herself, won't take no for an answer. As Ms. Holliday physically tries to restrain her lover from leaving, her heart pours out in a dark and gutsy blues; then, without pause, her voice rises into a strangled cry.

Shortly after that, Curtis departs, and Ms. Holliday just keeps riding wave after wave of painful music—clutching her stomach, keeling over, insisting that the scoundrel who has dumped her is "the best man I'll ever know." The song can end only when Mr. Bennett matches the performer's brilliance with a masterstroke of his own—and it's a good thing that Act 1 of *Dreamgirls* ends soon thereafter. If the curtain didn't fall, the audience would probably cheer Jennifer Holliday until dawn.

And, with all due respect to our new star, there's plenty more to cheer. Just as Ms. Holliday's Act 1 solo is one of the most powerful theatrical coups to be found in a Broadway musical since Ethel Merman sang "Everything's Coming Up Roses" at the end of Act 1 of *Gypsy,* so *Dreamgirls* is the same kind of breakthrough for musical stagecraft that *Gypsy* was.

In *Gypsy,* the director-choreographer Jerome Robbins and his collaborators made the most persuasive case to date (1959) that a musical could be an organic entity—in which book, score, and staging merged into a single, unflagging dramatic force. Mr. Bennett has long been Mr. Robbins's Broadway heir apparent, as he has demonstrated in two previous *Gypsy*-like backstage musicals, *Follies* (which he staged with Harold Prince) and *A Chorus Line.* But last night the torch was passed, firmly, unquestionably, once and for all. Working with an unusually gifted new composer, Henry Krieger, and a clever librettist, the playwright Tom Eyen—as well as with a wholly powerhouse cast and design team—Mr. Bennett has fashioned a show that strikes with the speed and heat of lightning.

He has done so in a most imaginative way. *Dreamgirls* is full of plot, and yet it has virtually no spoken scenes. It takes place in roughly twenty locations, from Harlem to Hollywood, but it has not one realistic set. It is a show that seems to dance from beginning to end, yet in fact has next to no dance numbers.

How is this magic wrought? *Dreamgirls* is a musical with almost forty numbers, and virtually everything, from record-contract negotiations to lovers' quarrels, is sung. More crucially, Mr. Krieger has created an individual musical voice for every major player and interweaves them all at will: In one cathartic backstage confrontation ("It's All Over"), the clashing of seven characters is realized entirely in musical terms.

What's more, the score's method is reinforced visually by Robin Wagner's set. Mr. Wagner has designed a few mobile, abstract scenic elements—aluminum towers and bridges—and keeps them moving to form an almost infinite number of configurations. Like the show's voices, the set pieces—gloriously abetted by Tharon Musser's lighting and Theoni V. Aldredge's costumes—keep coming together and falling apart to create explosive variations on a theme.

Linking everything together is Mr. Bennett. He keeps *Dreamgirls* in constant motion—in every conceivable direction—to perfect his special brand of cinematic stage effects (montage, dissolve, wipe). As if to acknowledge his historical debt to Mr. Robbins, he almost pointedly re-creates moments from *Gypsy* before soaring onward in his own original way.

Some of his images are chilling. In Act 1, an exchange of payola money between two men blossoms into a surreal panorama of mass corruption that finally rises, like a vision out of hell, clear to the roof of the theater. Throughout the show, Mr. Bennett uses shadows and klieg lights, background and foreground action, spotlighted figures and eerie silhouettes, to maintain the constant tension between the dark and bright sides of his dreamgirls' glittery dreams.

And in that tension is the emotional clout of the show. Like its predecessors among backstage musicals, *Dreamgirls* is about the price of success. Some of that price is familiar: broken love affairs, broken families, broken lives. But by telling the story of black entertainers who make it in white America, this musical's creators have dug into a bigger, more resonant drama of cultural assimilation. As the Dreams blunt the raw anger of their music to meet the homogenizing demands of the marketplace, we see the high toll of guilt and self-hatred that is inflicted on those who sell their artistic souls to the highest bidder. If "dreams" is the most recurrent word in the show, then "freedom" is the second, for the Dreams escape their ghetto roots only to discover that they are far from free.

This upsetting theme is woven into the evening's very fabric. Mr. Krieger gives the Dreams songs that perfectly capture the rhythm-and-blues music of the fifties, and then replays them throughout the evening to dramatize (and satirize) the ever-changing, ever-more-emasculated refining of the Motown sound. (Indeed, the Dreams' signature number is used to clock their personal and esthetic progression much as "Let Me Entertain You" was used in *Gypsy*.) Mr. Eyen has supplied ironic, double-edged lyrics (notably in a song called "Cadillac Car"), and Harold Wheeler's subtle, understated orchestrations are sensitive to every delicate nuance of the Dreams' advance through recent pop-music history.

Perhaps inevitably, the cast's two standouts are those who play characters who do not sell out and who suffer a more redemptive form of anguish: Ms. Holliday's Effie and Cleavant Derricks, as a James Brown–like star whose career collapses as new musical fashions pass him by. Like Ms. Holliday, Mr. Derricks is a charismatic singer who conveys wounding, heartfelt innocence. When, in Act 2, he rebels against his slick new Johnny Mathisesque image by reverting to his old, untamed Apollo shenanigans during a fancy engagement, he gives *Dreamgirls* one of its most crushing and yet heroic solo turns. But everyone is superb: Mr. Harney's Machiavellian manager, Sheryl Lee Ralph's Diana Ross–like lead Dream, Loretta Devine and Deborah Burrell as her backups, Obba Babatunde as a conflicted songwriter, and Vondie Curtis-Hall as a too-honest agent.

Is *Dreamgirls* a great musical? Well, one could quarrel with a few lapses of clarity, some minor sags, the overpat and frantic plot resolutions of Act 2. But Mr. Bennett and Ms. Holliday have staked their claim to greatness. And if the rest of *Dreamgirls* isn't always quite up to their incredible level, I'm willing to suspend judgment until I've sampled the evidence another four or five times.

≡ *This show was not rapturously greeted by most of the press and seemed to baffle older Broadway audiences. It enjoyed a long run but did not do well on the road; some in the theater feel that white audiences resisted it. What those who didn't see* Dreamgirls *missed is the most spectacular staging I've ever seen of any musical—an endlessly inventive and largely abstract choreographing of stage space that can't be found in the show's text or score.*

As was also the case with A Chorus Line, *few involved with this production went on to the careers it promised. Holliday's subsequent singing career, largely carried out away from Broadway, was erratic. Michael Bennett never completed another musical and died of AIDS in 1987.*

CRITIC'S NOTEBOOK: THE CASE FOR
KEEPING FEIFFER'S GROWN UPS OPEN
JANUARY 15, 1982

It's sad news that Jules Feiffer's *Grown Ups* may close tomorrow night, a scant five weeks after its premiere. Or so it is if you feel, as I do, that this is an exceptionally rewarding play in a top-flight production. Why is it closing? Maybe it's because the reviews were mixed. Maybe it's because of the snow. Maybe it's because *Grown Ups* is one of the few Broadway productions this season that has not blitzed us day and night with radio and television jingles.

It's also possible—and I'm only raising the question—that a play like *Grown Ups* is doomed to fail in the current Broadway climate. The serious plays that have succeeded on Broadway in recent seasons tend to fall into one of several categories—all of which exclude *Grown Ups.* They have big-name movie stars to get them going (Christopher Reeve in *Fifth of July*); they are British imports with largely British casts (*Amadeus, Nicholas Nickleby, The Dresser*); they are plays that, in the current fashion of television movies, deal with the dilemmas of the physically afflicted (*Children of a Lesser God, Whose Life Is It Anyway?, The Elephant Man, The Shadow Box*). Though exceptions slip in—a *Talley's Folly* or *Crimes of the Heart*—they usually do so with the boost of a Pulitzer Prize.

Grown Ups is superior to some of these hits and inferior to others, but it has little in common with most of them. Mr. Feiffer's comic, psychological dissection of a warring Jewish American family is about everyday people with common problems that can't be easily explained by medical science—and that can't be viewed from a safe distance. It is written in an iconoclastic, jagged, plotless manner: Mr. Feiffer refuses to resolve the issues he raises and send us home at peace, because he feels that painful truths can't be tied up into neat theatrical endings. In this sense, *Grown Ups* has more in common—in style, if not always in achievement—with Athol Fugard's *A Lesson from Aloes* and Harold Pinter's *Betrayal* than with the dramatic hits of recent seasons. *Aloes* and *Betrayal*, which had disappointing Broadway runs, were not hits.

But one must take a longer view. In the short time since its Broadway failure, *Aloes* has been produced, it seems, by every major regional theater in the country—from Los Angeles's Mark Taper Forum to Washington's Arena Stage. *Betrayal*, too, has seen many American productions and is soon slated to become a film. Mr. Feiffer's own 1967 play, *Little Murders,* went on from a scant seven-performance Broadway run to successful revivals by the Royal Shakespeare Company and Off Broadway's Circle in the Square before becoming a Hollywood movie. . . .

One of the most provocative aspects of *Grown Ups*—and let me remind you that there are still three performances to be caught at the Lyceum—is that almost nothing happens on its surface. As theater people say, it's a play that's nearly all subtext—much in the Pinter manner.

This becomes clear quickly in Act 1, set in a sunny New Rochelle kitchen, in which Mr. Feiffer has his characters repeat the same innocuous anecdote about an ill-fated dinner party three times. If the anecdote is trivial, what's actually happening is not. By constantly switching the family member who's telling the story, as well as the listeners, the playwright uses language, pauses, and reactions to lay out the festering antagonisms that will bring his characters to blows later on. By doing so indirectly, instead of through the conventional means of narrative exposition, he achieves lifelike verisimilitude. In real life, people do tend to bury their feelings in chitchat. It's mainly in plays—lesser plays than *Grown Ups*—that people announce forthrightly every thought in their heads.

It's also amusing how Mr. Feiffer uses books—and his characters' attitudes toward books—as another indirect means for creating drama in *Grown Ups*. The play's family brawls are triggered by trivial conversations about a Miss Marple mystery (Act 2) and library cards (Act 3). The anguished hero, a *New York Times* reporter played by Bob Dishy, is writing a book about "the moral and ethical disintegration of the American Dream"—and one of the play's most devastating moments occurs when his proud, success-crazed parents jump for joy at seeing a proof of its dust jacket: Though they're thrilled to see their son's name in large type on the cover, the parents don't care remotely about the book's contents. We suddenly understand just why the hero takes no pleasure in his parents' pride in his achievements.

Perhaps Mr. Feiffer's most daring use of indirection involves the characters' Jewishness. One allusion to the "Old Country" aside, the playwright never says directly that his characters are Jewish—and his director, John Madden, doesn't always say so expressly in his casting. This is particularly true in the case of Frances Sternhagen, at first glance an odd choice to play a domineering Jewish mother. Ms. Sternhagen is dressed in Bergdorf chic; she doesn't sling Yiddish; her manner resembles that of a Park Avenue grande dame rather than that of the comic Jewish mothers created on stage and screen by such actresses as Shelley Winters and Beatrice Arthur.

But the Jewishness is there, nonetheless. It's there in Mr. Feiffer's precisely observed English, which often observes Old Country cadences: It's not for nothing that the mother, addressing her son, says "She's a little cold, your wife" instead of "Your wife is a little cold." (Arthur Miller used a similar technique in *Death of a Salesman*, in which Willy Loman's unspoken ethnic background was conveyed through lines like "I'm tired to the death.") And by casting an actress who is elegant and prim, Mr. Madden has heightened the central point of Mr. Feiffer's play. The hero of *Grown Ups* is enraged at his mother precisely because she values her immigrant's dreams of worldly success above everything, including love. It makes sense that the mother epitomizes the values she champions—that she has the elegant manners and style of a woman who has succeeded in assimilating herself into the mainstream of upper-middle-class American life.

≡ *I quickly learned how hard it was even for the* Times *to motivate audiences to go see a drama on Broadway. With poor reviews from everyone else,* Grown Ups *had no chance—and this piece succeeded in extending its run only a month, for a total engagement of only eighty-three performances. That serious theater was an endangered species on Broadway no matter how praising the reviews in the* Times *or elsewhere became apparent when plays that received universally favorable notices failed financially in subsequent seasons: the Royal Shakespeare Company's* All's Well That Ends Well, *August Wilson's* Ma Rainey's Black Bottom *and* Joe Turner's Come and Gone, *the Steppenwolf Theater Company's* The Grapes of Wrath, *among many others. Even* Angels in America, *the best received and most profusely awarded drama of the eighties and nineties, only barely broke even in its nineteen-month Broadway run.*

Grown Ups was filmed for television, but it doesn't turn up in revival; the opinion of the plays' many harsh critics has thus far turned out to be posterity's verdict. Meanwhile, both Feiffer and Robert Brustein, who first produced* Grown Ups *in Cambridge, became among my own harshest critics when, it turned out, I did not prove a loyal fan of all their subsequent efforts.*

OTHELLO
WINTER GARDEN THEATRE, FEBRUARY 4, 1982

By the end of the *Othello* that opened on Broadway last night, you will, I think, ache for James Earl Jones's noble Moor—a massive mountain of strength reduced to so much dust in his smothered Desdemona's boudoir. But up until then, you may ache even more for Christopher Plummer's Iago.

Mr. Plummer, a sensational actor in peak form, has made something crushing out of Shakespeare's archvillain. He gives us evil so pure—and so bottomless—that it can induce tears. Our tears are not for the dastardly Iago, of course—that would be wrong. No, what Mr. Plummer does is make us weep for a civilization that can produce such a man and allow him to flower. We weep because the distant civilization that nurtured Iago is all too similar to the one that has given us a Hitler or two of our own.

This *Othello,* a revamped version of the one that originated in Stratford, Conn., last summer, has more than its Iago to offer. Although there is one glaring casting error—Dianne Wiest's Desdemona—the production at the Winter Garden is a vigorous conventional reading of Shakespeare that usually hurtles forward with headlong speed. But it's simply impossible to take one's mind—or eyes—from Mr. Plummer, because his work here is awesome.

Lithe and trim in his tight-fitting tunics and leather boots, he's a bristling hornet of a man; even his hair, mustache, and angular joints seem as sharp as porcupine quills. His voice is brittle, even metallic, but never so much so as to betray Iago's true designs on his prey. Obsequiously commiserating with Othello—or good-naturedly prodding Cassio to take a fateful drink—Mr. Plummer wittily accomplishes the crucial task of making Iago a double-edged blade: We never doubt that his victims would mistake his poisonous deceptions for the devotion and counsel of an honest friend.

Left alone to address the audience, Mr. Plummer ceases to be the consummate Machiavelli and shows us another man. When he vows to turn Desdemona's "virtue into pitch," his eyes burn and his arm whips through empty space as if to stir a witch's cauldron. Weaving "the net that shall enmesh them all," he turns the word *enmesh* into a shudder that seems to envelop the audience like a web. Yet he doesn't stop there. The most scary aspect of this villain is that his malignancy really does seem motiveless.

While Mr. Plummer indicates Iago's resentment of Cassio by referring to the lieutenant's Florentine origins and "proper" bearing with effete, high-pitched condescension, he also makes it clear that Cassio is but a minor irritant in his case against all mankind—a fly easily swatted away. While Mr. Plummer pays lip service to the sad speculation that his wife Emilia may be unfaithful, it's apparent that he doesn't really care. His is a sexless Iago who playfully kisses men and women alike because he has no use for either. He may tolerate Emilia's fond caresses if that's what it takes to pry away Desdemona's handkerchief, but, once he has what he wants, he shuts off his affection as if he were slamming a steel trap.

Who is the Iago who exists underneath the many cynical poses? I think we see him most clearly in Mr. Plummer's eerie moments of utter stillness. "I hate the Moor!" he booms in the opening scene, to reassure the foolish Roderigo (a wonderfully slimy Graeme Campbell) that they are indeed allies against Othello. But when Mr. Plummer repeats the same line to himself a few moments later—or tells us "I am not what I am"—the words are said quietly, enigmatically, as if they come from an icy, impenetrable netherworld. It is Mr. Plummer's special gift that he gives us peeks into a nihilistic void of a soul—a mysterious, inexplicable blackness that is horrifying precisely because it cannot be explained away.

If Mr. Jones's imposing hero isn't quite as multidimensional, he is still impressive, and, in his hushed final collapse, daring. Against the dissonantly buzzing gadfly of Mr. Plummer, he provides a ramrod-straight Othello of resonant, exotic musicality—especially in the early speech when he tells the autobiographical saga by which he wooed his wife.

Mr. Jones's ease and authority as a military commander seem his by birthright, even as he maintains the uneasy aloofness of an outsider. Later on, his bass, chest-thumping eruptions upon summoning up his "black vengeance" shake through both his body and the house like tribal exorcisms. When he finally realizes what his vengeance has wrought, he droops to deliver his "O! O! O!" in a disembodied rumble, as if his voice were racing his body to the grave.

What he does not make credible—and, God knows, Shakespeare gives him little aid—is Othello's all too sudden transformation from self-assured leader to jealous madman. This is in part because Mr. Jones sometimes seems to overintellectualize the role to the point where Othello's "free and open nature" is masked by stolidity. Yet the actor's major handicap is his Desdemona.

Ms. Wiest, a good actress in contemporary plays, affects an arch, put-on sweetness here that is often conveyed with pinched smiles and a candied voice; in the slapping scene, her sorrow, too, seems a bit secondhand. If there's not a flowing, openhearted Desdemona to balance Iago, an Othello can't easily dramatize the hero's violent swings between the author's poles of good and evil.

The rest of the cast, well-costumed by Robert Fletcher, is fine: Kelsey Grammer's noble but not syrupy Cassio; David Sabin's aggrieved Brabantio; Patricia Mauceri's saucy, tender Bianca; Raymond Skipp's rational Lodovico; and Robert Burr's fatuous Duke of Venice. Aideen O'Kelly's Emilia is outstanding. She keeps her secret sadnesses and fears to herself until the climax, at which point her calm voice and maternal demeanor break apart in quivering despair.

While the direction is credited to Peter Coe, Zoe Caldwell took over his chores during the later stages of the production's pre-Broadway tour. A few hokey freeze-frames aside, the staging is vibrant and fluid—most notably in the prefigurative hurly-burly that takes us from Venice to Cyprus and in the fight scenes (choreographed by B. H. Barry) that erupt during Cassio's drunken binge.

David Chapman and Marc B. Weiss, who also did inventive work on *The First* this season, have contributed evocative scenery and lighting. Mr. Chapman's oval-shaped, balconied set, with its ever-changing configurations of poles and canvas drapes, makes full use of the Winter Garden's vast stage, as well as of its orchestra pit. Mr. Weiss fills a huge cyclorama with burning sunsets and inky nights that join Mr. Plummer in beckoning us directly into hell.

THE DINING ROOM
PLAYWRIGHTS HORIZONS, FEBRUARY 15, 1982

In one of the many vignettes that make up A. R. Gurney Jr.'s new play, *The Dining Room,* an aunt proudly poses with her collection of Waterford crystal for a photo-snapping nephew. The aunt is all smiles and coos. She's most pleased that the nephew has left his studies at Amherst to come down and take her picture.

But eventually she makes the mistake of asking the boy just why it is that he's taken such a sudden interest in both her and her stemware. And, to her horror, she discovers that he is doing an anthropology class project on "the eating habits of vanishing cultures." The nephew has chosen "the WASPs of the Northeastern United States" as his subject. His aunt's crystal fingerbowls, he explains, demonstrate "a neurotic obsession with cleanliness associated with the guilt of the last stages of capitalism."

Mr. Gurney's play, now occupying the tiny theater upstairs at Playwrights Horizons, is a similar anthropological study, though not nearly so stern or dry. *The Dining Room* is set in an archetypal WASP dining room—austere dark wood table and sideboard, parquet floor, sterile white walls, Oriental rug—and it offers a series of snapshots of a vanishing culture. In each scene we meet the members and servants of a different WASP family, as they gather together for holidays, birthdays, or dinner parties, or fall apart by dint of arguments, infidelities, deaths, or changing mores. While the characters belong to various generations and various twentieth-century decades, they are all exemplars of an insular upper-middle-class way of life that social history has outrun.

The Dining Room isn't flawless, but it's often funny and rueful and, by the end, very moving. Mr. Gurney, a novelist as well as a playwright, was the author of one of the Public Broadcasting Service's John Cheever dramatizations (*O Youth and Beauty*), and he learned some lessons well. If he doesn't share Mr. Cheever's gift for subtlety, he does share his compassion and ability to create individual characters within a milieu that might otherwise seem as homogenous as white bread. Though dozens of people whirl in and out of Mr. Gurney's metaphorical dining room, they all come through as clearly and quickly as the voices we hear in a Cheever story like "The Enormous Radio."

In part, this is because the director, David Trainer, has assembled a wonderful cast. The six actors are constantly required to switch ages as well as characters, and they do so to perfection. It's no surprise, perhaps, to find the commanding, stentorian Remak Ramsay in the role of an oppressive Depression-era father lecturing his children on grammar and manners. But Mr. Ramsay is equally effective as a stooped old grandfather, as a guilt-ridden suburban philanderer, and even as a young schoolboy who suddenly becomes jealous and petulant when he learns that his family's Irish housekeeper is leaving to raise a family of her own.

The others are no less impressive. W. H. Macy gives us, among other characterizations, a sheepish teenager who must beg his self-made grandfather for money and a father who flies into a rage upon learning that his homosexual uncle has been insulted at the country club. Lois de Banzie, last seen as the dithering fiancée in *Morning's at Seven,* provides a wide range of retiring matriarchs. Pippa Pearthree is able both as a teenager sneaking an after-school drink and as a sweet, senile grandmother who doesn't recognize her own sons at Christmas dinner.

Of John Shea and Ann McDonough, one cannot speak too highly. Mr. Shea, who is currently to be seen in Costa-Gavras's film *Missing,* has proved time and again that he is one of our theater's most sensitive young actors. Here he is in outstanding form as a Deerfield student who falls apart upon suddenly discovering his mother's infidelities or another son who watches his remote, aged father suddenly reach out to him for love. Ms. McDonough, a pretty, bright-eyed comedienne with an affecting tremor in her crisp voice, is funny indeed when she's ordering her recalcitrant daughter to join the Junior Assembly. But she is also a sad figure of regret when, for a passing instant, she contemplates running out on her own child's birthday party with someone else's husband.

Fine as the actors are, they cannot, of course, give Mr. Gurney's anecdotes a dramatic spine. One also wishes this play had fewer forced, *Preppie Handbook*–style jokes and fewer theme-italicizing scenes, in which contemporary characters want to remodel or do away with the dining room and all the ghostly tradition it represents. Mr. Trainer, whose staging otherwise interweaves the vignettes with nonstop fluidity, tends to choke when the writing does: He punches some jokes too hard and puts portentous space around lines like "This room has such resonance" or "Nowadays people eat in kitchens."

The Dining Room is most resonant when the action speaks for itself. Nowhere is this truer than in a beautiful Act 2 encounter between Mr. Shea, as a proper, Wall Street father, and Ms. Pearthree, as his married daughter. Ms. Pearthree has come home because she wants "to start all over again." Her marriage is over, and neither her children, nor a new lover, nor a brief lesbian fling has arrested her fear that "I don't know where I am." But her father, while polite, doesn't want her back. Mr. Shea mixes a drink, offers a few useless words of distant, lawyerly advice, then turns away as if his anguished child had left the room. As in all of Mr. Gurney's most powerful scenes, we're reminded that even in the most privileged of homes, there's not always freedom from want.

≡ *No playwright was more prolific in the 1980s than A. R. (Pete) Gurney, who is probably best known for his omnipresent* Love Letters. *But I'm not sure he ever wrote anything as touching as this breakthrough work.*

COME BACK TO THE 5 & DIME, JIMMY DEAN, JIMMY DEAN

MARTIN BECK THEATRE, FEBRUARY 19, 1982

Forget about whether or not Mayor Koch is going to run for governor. The truly momentous question of the month is: Can Cher act? The answer, alas, is not to be found at the Martin Beck, where America's most beloved one-name entertainer made her Broadway debut last night. In Ed Graczyk's *Come Back to the 5 & Dime, Jimmy Dean, Jimmy Dean,* Cher does get to sling a few down-home epithets, to shake her torso, and to drink a few Lone Star beers—all of which she does with game bonhomie. But act? Cher has but one speech of any duration, and the director, Robert Altman, demands that she deliver most of it with her back to the audience.

But let's count our blessings. Next to the rest of this dreary amateur night, Cher's cheery, ingratiating nonperformance is almost a tonic. *Come Back to the 5 & Dime, Jimmy Dean, Jimmy Dean*—a comedy whose title does not belie its length—could do with a lot more Cher and a lot less of some of its other stars. It would also benefit from a new script, a total restaging, and a revamped set. The only thing it really can't do without is its amplification system, although even the miking doesn't succeed in making the cast audible at all times.

That's a blessing, too. Mr. Graczyk has written a memory play in which he isn't remembering life but half-remembering other plays, movies, and books. Intentionally or not, *Jimmy Dean* is a crude pastiche of *Vanities* and *The Last Picture Show,* with bows to William Inge and Rona Jaffe. The crudity can be found in both the work's craft and substance. Stripped of its endless repetitions, *Jimmy Dean* would shrink from two hours plus to roughly eight minutes. The author's thematic obsession seems to be his heroines' sexual organs, which he variously reveals to be disfigured, malfunctioning, or misplaced by evening's end.

Those heroines are rural Texas women who belong to a James Dean fan club that meets at the local Woolworth's. The action unfolds alternately in their halcyon, high-school days of 1955, when Dean himself was shooting *Giant* nearby, and in 1975, when the now disbanded club members gather for a reunion. Predictably enough, each character has some dark secret or false illusion from the past that must be burst open in the present. The playwright withholds these bombshells for an eternity, but anyone with more brains than his characters—which is to say anyone—will beat him to the punch.

Neither the gimmicky plot nor its clichéd participants are credible. Among other things, we must believe that the club's ringleader (Sandy Dennis) has successfully disguised the paternity of her illegitimate son, named after Jimmy Dean, for twenty years, and that Cher's character, the local good-time girl, has managed to hide the actual status of both her marriage and her health from her closest small-town pals. To buy other major plot twists, you must believe in a chance offstage meeting in Kansas City, the wonders of modern medicine, and just possibly the Easter Bunny.

Mr. Graczyk pads out these shenanigans with bosom jokes and canned nostalgic elegies to trains, sunsets, and old movie stars. Every line sounds familiar—from one heroine's cathartic "I just wanted to be noticed" to another's command that "you must face the truth about yourself." At least two characters sob out the line "I am so ashamed" when they at last reveal their secrets to one and all. It's only the author, apparently, who is shameless.

By staging this play at the pace of a dripping faucet, Mr. Altman has almost gleefully let Mr. Graczyk hang himself. It's hard to fathom that this is the same director who made such a promising theatrical debut with *Two by South* Off Broadway last fall. In *Jimmy Dean,* Mr. Altman rarely even bothers to separate the flashback scenes from the present-day ones. The characters don't change in age or appearance as they go back and forth between 1955 and 1975. Paul Gallo's lighting at first tries to indicate the time shifts, but finally lapses into incoherence when mere darkness would do.

The confusion is heightened further by the appearance of ill-defined extras and by David Gropman's very pretty, very wrongheaded set. This usually reliable designer has fastidiously re-created two Woolworth's—one in front for the present, one in the rear for the past. But when the actors retreat to the rear, they're cut off at mid-breast by the lunch counter and their voices enter an echo chamber. The set's putative mirror imagery is further blurred by the unnecessary addition of actual mirrors, which throw the whole jumble into prismatic chaos.

Mr. Altman doesn't seem to have directed his actors at all until the end, at which point each major player comes forward to deliver an exceedingly long good-bye that begs for applause. For much of Act 2, some of the women just stand along the sidelines in expressionless, frozen silence, even as their best friends have a cat fight center stage. Among the supporting cast, Sudie Bond and Kathy Bates acquit themselves with dignity, but Karen Black quickly descends into broadness. Marta Heflin, as the club dunce, doesn't seem to be among the living.

In the star spot, Ms. Dennis creates a non-Texan character indistinguishable from those she recently played in *The Supporting Cast* and *The Four Seasons.* She either runs on her sentences incoherently or scrambles them with false starts, jerky internal word repetitions, and teeth-baring snorts. Eventually she pauses long enough to explain that her peculiar behavior "comes from some place deep down inside." The gizzard, perhaps?

THE HOTHOUSE
TRINITY SQUARE REPERTORY COMPANY,
PROVIDENCE, R.I., MARCH 7, 1982

The Hothouse, the long-dormant 1958 Harold Pinter play now having its American premiere at the Trinity Square Repertory Company, is set in an oppressive, incompetent, government-run "rest home" where the incarcerated patients are all identified by numbers and where the staff spends full time engaged in vicious, Machiavellian infighting.

One could say that Mr. Pinter has written a parable about the fascist potential of all large bureaucracies, about the suffocating sickness of English society after Empire, about the sadomasochistic relationships that alienate us all. One could say all that—but let's talk about the duck.

The duck turns up in Act 2. The time is Christmas night, and the home's much beleaguered, middle-aged superintendent, Roote (George

Martin), is a bit around the bend. For one thing, he is being driven wild by an aide, appropriately named Lush, who keeps going to Roote's office window to observe the weather and keeps bringing back exactly the same report: "The snow has turned to slush." For another, Roote has received no cards or presents and is beginning to wax maudlin about his long-gone days as an army colonel. He also fears that someone is out to murder him.

At the height of his funk Roote switches on his intercom and finds himself eavesdropping on the home's annual Christmas raffle. The announcer reads out winning number after winning number, but all the prizes, from circus tickets to "a lovely crockery, cutlery, china, and cookery set," go unclaimed; it seems that no one has purchased a ticket.

What most rattles Roote, though, is that one of the unclaimed prizes is "a duck ready for the oven" that might go to waste. Lush tells his boss not to worry: All the unclaimed merchandise will be held until another raffle at Easter. But Roote finally loses his temper. "You can't keep a duck until Easter!" he shrieks. "It's just not sensible!" Lest Lush challenge his authority, he pauses and snaps, "There's not much I don't know about poultry."

It's a very funny scene—totally off-the-wall in the writing and wonderfully played by Mr. Martin, a pipe-smoking fussbudget of a small-potatoes martinet whose whiplash swings between pomposity and paranoia remind one of Terry-Thomas during his Ealing comedy days. And while the duck may not have much to do with the price of fish in a play that also features electroshock tortures and a full-scale massacre, it is typical of *The Hothouse* at its best. Mr. Pinter has always been the star-crossed child of Ionesco and Beckett, and in this early play it is the Ionesco genes that often dominate and always delight.

The Hothouse has had an odd history. Mr. Pinter wrote it between *The Birthday Party* and *The Caretaker* and put it aside until 1979, when he reread it and decided to stage it himself in London. The success of that 1980 production has led to this one, directed by the Trinity Square's major domo, Adrian Hall, with an early-rehearsal visit from Mr. Pinter.

The effort was worthwhile. Though *The Hothouse* is no neglected masterpiece, it offers a fascinating portrait of the playwright as a young man. Not only does it specifically prefigure other Pinter plays, right up to *No Man's Land* and *Betrayal*, but it also shows his still-developing vision in a frisky state of flux. There are some dramatic strategies in *The Hothouse* that Mr. Pinter had yet to perfect—and later would. But the unbridled comic riffs are more unpretentious and enjoyable than nearly any he has written since.

What Mr. Pinter did not accomplish in *The Hothouse* is his usual, elliptical evocation of an atmosphere of menace. Instead of a nameless, faceless dread, he gives us melodramatic villains whose wicked motives and methods are often out in the open—and therefore less frightening.

As if to suggest the mysteriousness he has failed to achieve, Mr. Pinter gives Roote lines like "Something's happening but I can't define it" and "Something's going on I haven't cottoned on to." Yet the audience, unlike the protagonist, does cotton on to the staff's various conspiracies and betrayals—and far too early.

This leads to a flatness in both the play's characterizations and anxiety level, at times reducing *The Hothouse* to a predictably plotted problem drama along the lines of *Shock Corridor.* But within its confines, Mr. Pinter has written circular dialogue that brilliantly parodies dithering bureaucratese: Almost every line is a question answered with another, and these exchanges often build to absurdist vaudeville routines.

No matter how many questions he asks, Roote finds it impossible to rectify the clerical confusion that has caused him to mix up patient 6457, who is dead, with patient 6459, who has been impregnated by an unidentified staff member. His relentless cross-examination about the fate of the unclaimed duck leads only to Lush's final revelation that "the duck is as dead as patient 6457."

The malevolent interrogations sometimes detonate, too—especially the Act 1 climax, in which two unseen interlocutors literally and figuratively grill a man strapped into a chair in a soundproof room. But Mr. Hall is smart to take care of the comedy first—through snappy, farcical pacing—and let everything else come tumbling after. At all times, the director receives solid support from Eugene Lee's set, a far-flung, elaborately realistic beehive of offices and corridors, from behind whose closed doors come the muffled screams and laughter of the unseen patients.

The bright staging bolsters a cast that is generally just adequate and rarely quite British enough. Mr. Martin is the constant exception, a prime nut in a play that is, for good and ill, every bit as cracked as the lunatics who run its hothouse asylum.

"MASTER HAROLD" . . . AND THE BOYS
YALE REPERTORY THEATRE, NEW HAVEN, MARCH 17, 1982

At the end of Athol Fugard's new play, two black men foxtrot to old-time jukebox music, gliding about a deserted South African restaurant, Astaire-Rogers style. The audience, meanwhile, is in emotional ruins. While some theatergoers struggle to stand and cheer, others cringe in their seats, their heads in their hands, so devastated that they can't even look at the stage. What has happened? What have they seen? It's not easy to put together the pieces. *"Master Harold" . . . and the Boys* is only an anecdote, really, and it's often as warm and musical as the men's dance. But somewhere along the way it rises up and breaks over the audience like a storm.

The audience is American, it must be remembered, not South African. *Master Harold,* now at the Yale Repertory Theatre, is the first Fugard play to have its premiere away from its author's native land. There seems to be a reason for that. While *Master Harold,* like the Fugard plays before it, dramatizes the stain of apartheid, the author has journeyed so deep into the psychosis of racism that all national boundaries quickly fall away, that no one is left unimplicated by his vision. *Master Harold* is ruthless in its pursuit of even an enlightened audience's conscience, and its tragic power stems from the playwright's great courage to be ruthless to himself.

Certainly Mr. Fugard's protagonist, a white South African teenager of 1950, must be somewhat autobiographical. Hally (Zeljko Ivanek) is an intelligent, witty prep-school student who questions the injustices of his society and already dreams about being an artist. On the day we meet him, he drops in from school to while away a rainy afternoon with the two black servants who work in the modest, failing Port Elizabeth restaurant owned by his parents. The servants, Sam (Zakes Mokae) and Willie (Danny Glover), are his lifelong second family: They dote on Hally, and he, in his way, on them.

The first half of this intermissionless, 100-minute play is almost idle chitchat. In between menial chores, the blacks twirl about the checker-clothed tables and lunch counter, practicing their steps for a coming dance contest. In a jocular way, Hally dismisses the dancing as simple-minded: He tells the servants that it's mere "entertainment," not "art"—for art, he explains, is "beyond beauty." Sam argues otherwise. Being on a dance floor, he says, is "like being in a dream about a world without collisions"—where rich and poor, black and white "don't bump into each other." And Hally begins to get the black man's point: If only everyone could "get the steps right," there might be "hope for mankind after all."

But the play switches its key when the men are interrupted by phone calls from Mr. Fugard's unseen yet fully realized secondary characters, Hally's troubled, actual family. The boy's father, it turns out, is an alcoholic and cripple who's about to be released from one of many hospital stays. For Hally, this is upsetting news. Erupting in tears as he talks to his mother on the phone, he begs her not to let the father return. "If the two of you start fighting again," he screams between sobs, "I'm leaving home."

Sam and Willie try to comfort their young companion, but Hally won't listen. Instead, he lashes out at the blacks, propelled by self-pity to release a torrent of ugliness he doesn't mean. He demands that Sam call him "Master Harold" and tells a racist joke about a black man's anatomy. He mocks a lifetime of shared intimacies with the men—an idyllic day when Sam taught him to fly a kite, a grueling long-ago night when the servant helped him rescue his father from a barroom floor. And, as the viciousness spews out, we see that Hally's torn feelings about his crippled father are psychologically inseparable from his feelings about Sam, the surrogate black father he attacks. "The one person who could teach you to be a man is the cause of your shame," says Sam—and that one person is equally Hally's dad and himself.

The operative word in that line is "teach." Though Sam has devoted a lifetime to teaching his "master" compassion—it's the one small clandestine political act even South Africa can't repress—the boy just isn't there yet. Are we? Mr. Fugard so successfully makes us empathize with the lonely, love-starved hero that we can't quite pull away when the boy loses his control. The author's seamless writing sweeps us up in the horrible logic of Hally's emotional violence, and in it we see our own potential for kicking life's underdogs if that's what it takes to make us feel better about ourselves.

More rending still, the force of that cruelty is heightened by the blacks' refusal to rise to the fight. "I want to hit him hard," says Willie, making a fist after Hally has spit at the men, "but maybe all I'll do is cry in the back." Sam responds to the boy's racist joke by slowly pulling down his pants—with great and harrowing dignity—to illustrate its punchline with his own flesh.

As with his last play, *A Lesson from Aloes,* Mr. Fugard has directed his new one himself—and perfectly. Mr. Ivanek—who doubled as a colonial Englishwoman and a homosexual hustler in *Cloud 9*—is a superb stand-in for the playwright and the audience: a likable, blue-blazered Christopher Robin who goes smash as his benevolent self-image is usurped by the shameful, innocence-ending recognition of who he really is. Mr. Mokae's Sam—an eloquent, patient man of almost Gandhi-like moral rectitude—is a towering presence. As his less-articulate, easygoing friend, Mr. Glover is touching when he, too, must learn some of Sam's lessons in dancing and life.

One might quarrel with the casualness of Mr. Fugard's setup—*Master Harold* needs some tightening and spells out its metaphors a few too many times. But no one can argue with Mr. Fugard's ability to hold a mirror up to the world—a mirror made totally clear and merciless by his unsparing honesty. And that's why the audience's response at the end of *Master Harold* is so divided. If some people are destroyed, it's because Mr. Fugard has forced us to face, point-blank, our capacity for hate. If others are cheering, it's because we're also left with the exultant hope that we may yet get Sam's "steps" right, we may yet practice compassion without stumbling.

The choice, of course, is ours. Mr. Fugard's wrenching play, which insists that we make it, is beyond beauty.

≡ **When** Master Harold *arrived on Broadway, it was minus Zeljko Ivanek—a big but not fatal loss. It remains, in my view, the best of Fugard's plays.*

CRITIC'S NOTEBOOK: IS THERE A SHOW— OR JUST AMBIANCE?
MARCH 28, 1982

At the beginning of *Pump Boys and Dinettes,* the popular country-rock revue on Broadway, the audience is asked to hold on to its ticket stubs for a post-intermission raffle. The prize is a packet of air freshener, and the winner gets to choose the scent of his choice, Christmas tree and skunk among them. The night I attended, the winner was a startled, maybe even mortified, middle-aged woman. Unlike television game-show contestants, she didn't whoop it up when she won, and she seemed less than thrilled to be dragged on stage to choose her scent. (She opted for Christmas, when surely the whole audience, eager for a laugh, was pining for skunk.) But she was a good sport: Before returning to the seat with her prize, she smiled gamely to pose with cast members for a Polaroid snapshot.

The snapshot is mounted in a lobby window case that proudly displays all the smiling past *Pump Boys* raffle winners. In the lobby you may also purchase beer and soft drinks—which, in a departure from usual Broadway practice, can be taken back to your seats. And, even without beer, there's a carnival aura in the auditorium. *Pump Boys and Dinettes* takes place in a gas station and adjoining diner on some Southern highway: The set is lovingly realistic, with bright billboards and neon beer signs extending into the audience. While one waits for the show to begin, ushers dressed as waitresses sashay about carrying fresh-baked pies.

It's all very homey, friendly, relaxed—but is there any show here to go with the ambience? I'm not convinced that there is, even by the very loose standards one might choose to apply to escapist-minded revues. But the success of *Pump Boys and Dinettes* is fascinating, even if the work itself isn't, as a symptom of the climate on Broadway right now. We may have reached the point where we're so grateful to enter a theater where we're greeted as guests at a family party, where we're not assaulted by pretensions and rude noise, that we're willing to accept less as more, to settle for relaxing in the theatrical equivalent of a warm bath.

This has, after all, been a sad season, especially for musicals: Many large and costly productions have gone thud in the night. Ticket prices are high, and when theatergoers pay them to see overblown, if well-intentioned, mishaps like *Merrily We Roll Along* or *The First,* they have every reason to feel ripped off. It's in this context that *Pump Boys* is an ideal antidote: It aspires only to be intimate and cheery, makes no demands or grand promises (no stars, no dancing), and operates at a lower-than-average ticket scale. Better to take a flyer on a down-home party at twenty dollars (plus beer) than to be affronted by thirty-five-dollars worth of slick, inflated mechanics pretending to be real theater about real people. Lowered expectations lower the risk of grave disappointment; unpretentiousness becomes its own reward.

But the pendulum may be swinging too far, for the raffle proves the only dramatic event in *Pump Boys.* The rest of the evening consists of watching six highly engaging singer-songwriters perform twenty numbers about the joys of the road, vacations, Dolly Parton, and waitresses' tips. A few sprightly turns of phrase and dashes of sentiment notwithstanding, there's none of the pain and little of the wit one finds in actual country music—qualities that were captured in the previous quasi-country-rock score on Broadway, Carol Hall's *The Best Little Whorehouse in Texas.* Nor are we hearing a revue songbook, like the one in *Sophisticated Ladies,* that stays with us for more than the length of the evening.

In *Pump Boys,* the songs, like the synthetic, Disneyland-esque atmosphere, merely purvey folksy, prefab Dixie atmosphere by the yard—they're as cute and happy and bland as "smile" buttons. The apparently all-white South they celebrate is so relentlessly congenial it makes Rodgers and Hammerstein's romanticized Oklahoma seem like Las Vegas by comparison. And, while it's unfair to demand that there be a libretto in a revue, one might ask for a bit more variety or feeling in the numbers, and for stylish, inventive staging to stitch them together. In *Pump Boys,* transitions are accomplished by a few lines of mock-libretto in which the gas jockeys jokingly talk about a Winnebago van that's been left in back for repairs. Choreography takes the form of a few intentionally amateurish tap steps. It's all over in ninety minutes, including intermission and a finale that reprises several of the earlier songs.

≣ *Little did I guess that environmental theater—theme-park theater, if you will—would soon dominate Broadway and Off Broadway alike. On Broadway, this would take the form of total-environment spectaculars, as perfected in London in such productions as* Cats (*in which the entire theater was turned into an artsy junk heap*), Starlight Express (*a roller derby*) *and* Five Guys Named Moe (*a nightclub, à la* Pump Boys). *Off Broadway would find its own bargain-priced, special-effects-free variation: simulated weddings* (Tony n' Tina's Wedding), *bar mitzvahs* (Cousin Bernie's Bar Mitzvah), *and even funerals* (Grandma Sylvia's Funeral), *in which, for the price of a ticket, you could converse with or be humiliated by an actor, help yourself to a buffet, drink at a cash bar, and become part of a "family" for a night.*

AGNES OF GOD
Music Box Theatre, March 31, 1982

When Elizabeth Ashley marches forward to give the opening speech in John Pielmeier's *Agnes of God*, you instantly feel that you're in good hands. Miss Ashley wears a professional woman's no-nonsense suit, and there's no-nonsense authority in everything she does. Her eyes are ablaze; her voice snakes through the Music Box as insistently as the smoke of her cigarette; her monologue lays out Mr. Pielmeier's premise with brisk, eloquent efficiency.

The stark set Ms. Ashley inhabits at the Music Box also promises a trajectory of pure, uncluttered theater: Eugene Lee has designed a curving expanse of blond wood that rises from the floor to the skies and contains only two chairs and one standing ashtray. And, once we meet the occupants of those chairs—no less than Amanda Plummer and Geraldine Page at full throttle—our expectations rise further still.

Equally alluring is Mr. Pielmeier's premise, which is designed to lock his gifted actresses into old-fashioned, to-the-mat conflict. Ms. Plummer, in the title role, is an angelic twenty-one-year-old nun facing a manslaughter charge: Although she fervently denies any knowledge of the crime, she is accused of giving birth to a baby in a convent, strangling the child with its umbilical cord, and stuffing the corpse into a wastebasket. Ms. Page is the nun's mother superior and chief defender. She wonders if there might not be another, supernatural explanation for the seemingly fatherless corpse—a miracle that would clear the devout, unworldly, and totally unlikely suspect. Ms. Ashley is Dr. Livingstone, the court-appointed psychiatrist determined to get to the bottom of Agnes's case.

So there you have it: a perfectly lurid triangle with a charged-up star at each corner and no extraneous furniture to get in the way. And need I tell you what predictably happens next? *Agnes of God* isn't a half-hour old before the playwright takes to shoveling verbal debris on the stage, until the triangle buckles and then breaks under the weight. The actors and the set, it can at least be said, remain sturdy to the end. Ms. Plummer, who literally climbs a wall at one point, even manages to take flight.

No playwright who quotes Robertson Davies in the *Playbill* can be all bad, and the author of *Agnes* does show promise. Mr. Pielmeier is capable of humorous digressions about such subjects as cigarette addiction and the possibility that some Hollywood vault contains an alternate, happy final reel to Garbo's *Camille*. He also knows how to write fiery scenes, even if they must be induced by a character entering hypnosis. But his play falls apart—ultimately to verge on the ridiculous—because he hasn't figured out how to meld its melodramatic and spiritual concerns. While *Agnes of God* aspires to be both a chilling thriller and a stirring reaffirmation of the power of faith, it fails on both counts.

Indeed, one concern cancels the other out. Mr. Pielmeier clearly sides with the mother superior in his play's central argument. He wants to believe that Agnes is "touched by God" and that her baby, like the inexplicable stigmata that bloodied the nun's hands before its arrival, was a divine phenomenon. Fair enough, but the audience wants its miracles and its whodunit, too. Mr. Pielmeier instead uses his message to throw a hocus-pocus smokescreen over the baby's paternity: The anticlimactic Act 2 of *Agnes of God* suggests what *Rosemary's Baby* or *The Exorcist* might be like if they had alternate, cheating final reels.

The philosophical debate that precedes the nonending is too tired to carry the play alone. As Dr. Livingstone and the mother superior plead their respective cases for the transcendent powers of rational medical science and primitive religious belief, the author replays *Equus*—even to the extent of drawing arch, explicit contrasts between the psychiatrist's sterile, lonely personal life and her patient's otherworldly, if murderous, religious passion. But this time the rhetoric is usually as pedantic as the sentiments it expresses, and there's not a horse in sight.

The sparring match really comes alive only when Mr. Pielmeier suddenly unveils unexpected, and unconvincing, revelations about his antagonists. Dr. Livingstone proves to be not only a lapsed Catholic—a neat coincidence for the author's dialectical purposes—but one whose sister also died in a convent under questionable circumstances. The mother superior proves not only Agnes's spiritual mother but a blood relative as well—a fact that is dishonestly withheld from the audience for too long. Though these and other bombshells keep us alert, they're too patently gimmicky—or textbook-dry Freudian—to add dimension to the play's characters, suspense, or theme. All they really do is stall for time while we wait for the scene in which Agnes finally reenacts her fateful night of childbirth and the hung jury can be adjourned.

While the actors can't overcome our ever-accelerating disappointment, they often stave off boredom. So does the director, Michael Lindsay-Hogg, who tirelessly molds arresting tableaux out of agonized bodies and empty space. If Ms. Ashley is sometimes mannered of posture, her force of personality is mesmerizing, as is her anguish once she inevitably discovers that, like all psychiatrists in fiction of this sort, she must heal her empty agnostic self. The apple-cheeked Ms. Page is blissful in defense of her God, bristling in defense of her young nun, and puckishly funny as she announces her ability "to smell an ex-Catholic a mile away."

Ms. Plummer doesn't have the role here she had in *A Taste of Honey*, but that doesn't throw her. With her ethereal smile, melodious voice, and creamy blank slate of a face, she's as close to an angel as we're ever likely to see on Broadway. Once Agnes must exorcise the grueling demons of both her troubled childhood and childbirth, she spills her mutilated guts with a volcanic abandon that moves us at a level the text never touches. A miracle? Not really. While the playwright waits around for divine intervention, Ms. Plummer and company simply use their heads and get down to serious work.

≣ *Shortly before* Agnes of God *opened, a minor scandal ensued when critics received a disparaging letter about the play allegedly signed by the press agent of another Broadway production opening the same week. Theater people routinely wrote me letters knifing their competitors—though they always did so anonymously or by hiding behind false names. A typical gambit was to knock a show in previews, in a letter signed "Insider," or some such. Like every other critic, I disregarded these missives even as I marveled at the level of backbiting in the business. The more successful the writer, star, producer, the larger the volume of anonymous mail attempting to blacken his or her reputation.*

PASTORALE
SECOND STAGE, APRIL 12, 1982

As befits a work titled *Pastorale,* Deborah Eisenberg's comedy at the Second Stage is a blast of fresh air. I don't know where Ms. Eisenberg comes from—it could be another planet—but she has the most original, not to mention the funniest, new comic voice to be heard in a New York theater since Beth Henley arrived with *Crimes of the Heart.* And while it's also true that *Pastorale* is slight and imperfect, why not laugh now and think later? Ms. Eisenberg's lapses are the forgivable ones of a first-time playwright, and you're going to want to say you knew her when.

Although the author is refreshingly derelict about exposition—there are no psychological or narrative announcements at all, in fact—*Pastorale* appears to be about a group of aging 1960s college pals who now live in drifting, semicommunal fashion in New England. In a series of blackout vignettes, we follow their disconnected lives through the early eighties. What happens? Not much. Ms. Eisenberg's characters fall in and out of bed (and, occasionally, love), take drugs, worry about money, eat every known variety of junk food, consider getting jobs, and sometimes actually get them. Toward the end, a sofa catches fire, and a character crashes into a tree at sixty miles an hour—but, have no fear, everyone is more startled than hurt.

What makes *Pastorale* so striking is Ms. Eisenberg's utterly lucid, yet off-center, view of her woolly-brained dropouts. The sparing, deadpan dialogue and action of the play aren't realistic or farcical, but in some magical, ditsy limbo in between—as if the sixties survivors one finds in the fiction of Ann Beattie or Laurie Colwin were twisted just a few degrees more askew. The tip-off to Ms. Eisenberg's special style comes right at the beginning. Heidi Landesman's set is a fairy-tale doll's house, brightly lighted by Frances Aronson, in which actual furniture intermingles with two-dimensional fixtures that are painted on the wall. The principal characters are first seen staring aimlessly into space, in little hurry to speak or move.

Chief among them is Melanie (Judith Ivey), a hard-drinking, casually sex-crazed woman, who always smiles and laughs in the best, crinkly-eyed hostess fashion, even after she's lost her job as a bar waitress for having slept with all the male employees. Melanie is fond of saying that her parents died when she was three and that she was adopted by "a transvestite who didn't speak English." But she's also a liar, who, it turns out, "grew up in New Canaan, like everybody else." Compulsively neat when we first meet her, she eventually embraces slovenliness to the point where she refuses to dispose of her house's dead mice and just covers the corpses with tea cups instead.

Her closest friend is the bespectacled and somewhat catatonic Rachel (Christine Estabrook), who comes to visit Melanie for a weekend and never leaves. Rachel is not assertive about her opinions or her emotions. She feels that it's impossible to judge the merits of a place "unless you're in another place at the same time," and she never leaves her perch on the sofa, even for lust. Though she fears that she isn't so much "leading" her life as "representing it to the public," she always has a rationalization for her inertia. Asked why she doesn't bother to read newspapers, she explains: "Basically, you either know what's going on, or you don't. And if you basically don't, reading the papers isn't going to help."

Melanie and Rachel's closest platonic male friend is Steve (Thomas Waites), an easygoing fellow who works in construction and has a younger girlfriend (Taylor Miller). We also meet an invading platoon of "great-looking humanoids from Colorado," who get drunk and pass out one night; various unidentified local rakes, and an obnoxious go-getting entrepreneur named Edie (Elizabeth Austin), who is always dressed in the latest fashions (devilishly designed by Nan Cibula). Edie is the kind of pest who dreams up party games built around questions like "What is the worst thing your parents ever did to you on Christmas?" Yet Steve claims that "she's basically OK, really—you just have to be sort of loose about what you think OK is."

Many scenes are small gems—especially one in which Rachel hallucinates while on LSD about false eyelashes shortly after Melanie starts to make out with a stranger on her lap. A few jokes fall flat, as does the sweet, but too facile ending. Even when the writing falters, the entire cast is in perfect harmony with the odd rhythms of Ms. Eisenberg's menagerie—as is the director, Carole Rothman (of *How I Got That Story*).

Mr. Waites, last seen in Al Pacino's *American Buffalo,* is quite endearing as well as funny as he concludes that if he's "always tired and sad," it must be because he likes it that way. Ms. Estabrook's Rachel is a still pond who ripples delightfully on, contemplating her worst recurrent nightmare—grabbing "the food off the plate of the person next to me in a restaurant." Ms. Ivey, always a first-rate actress, gets the chance to wear racy lingerie on her head and, in general, to show off her high style as a comedian. Carving up a lemon for her gin, she brings down the house by laughingly announcing, of all things, "Whenever I do this, I always picture the blade in my heart!"

The line, like the knife, cuts both ways. Underneath the comic doodlings of *Pastorale,* Ms. Eisenberg is writing about lost people who, as they put it, know "there's something real, but don't know what it is" and who can't even answer the question "What do you want to do?" when applied to half-hour time periods.

While theatergoers unfamiliar with this particular lost generation may find the affectless, rudderless lives of *Pastorale* a bit opaque, they do have their own wacky logic. "It may look like a sequence of empty gestures," says Steve, trying to justify his behavior, "but it may turn out to be real life." And so, thanks to the gifted Ms. Eisenberg, it most uproariously does.

≡ *This, as far as I know, was Ms. Eisenberg's only effort for the theater. She went on to become an acclaimed writer of fiction.*

THE CHALK GARDEN
ROUNDABOUT THEATRE COMPANY, APRIL 30, 1982

Whatever the drawbacks of the Roundabout's revival of *The Chalk Garden*—and they are serious—you still leave the theater full of admiration for three remarkable women. They are the evening's stars, Irene Worth and Constance Cummings, and the author, Enid Bagnold. The actresses need no introduction. The playwright, who died last year at the age of ninety-one, may be too keenly remembered these days for *National Velvet* or for her last play, Katharine Hepburn's unsatisfying Broadway vehicle, *A Matter of Gravity.* She shouldn't be. *The Chalk Garden* is in a whole other league—it just may be a classic of its kind.

But what kind? Writing on the occasion of the play's Broadway premiere in 1955, Bagnold's friend Cecil Beaton said that the work was "as whimsical as Sir James Barrie, as poetic as Giraudoux, sometimes as zany as the Marx Brothers, yet with all the elements of a detective story." And so it is—not that the play's undefinable quality ends there. Esthetically speaking, *The Chalk Garden* is extraordinarily modern for a high comedy set in the drawing room of a stuffy Sussex manor house: Its plot and structure are elliptical; its witty lines aren't brittle but are instead redolent with what the author calls "the shape and shadow of life."

The Chalk Garden is also quite moving—one aspect that is too often lost at the Roundabout. The loss is wasteful. Once this theater had snared two matchless stars for this infrequently revived gem, why didn't it go the rest of the way and ensure that the entire production would be at the same high level? Wonderful as Ms. Worth and Ms. Cummings are, it's impossible to ignore the stodgy staging, the weak casting of other principal roles, and the cheesy fixtures of the set. Be prepared to take the dreary with the sublime.

The sublimity is apparent from the opening, haunting image—the plain sight of Ms. Worth, in no-nonsense chocolate-brown suit and hat, seated in a chair. The actress is playing Miss Madrigal, an applicant for a nanny's job at the home of Mrs. St. Maugham (Ms. Cummings), a wealthy old widow. We don't know anything about Miss Madrigal yet, but Ms. Worth, simply by the way she sits, sets up the mystery of the play. Though she looks as proper and prim as any starchy governess, the actress creates dark, inexplicable tension by the sheer rigidity of her posture, the evasiveness of her baggy, downcast eyes, the almost magnetic field of silence with which she cloaks herself.

Once she's hired, it turns out that Miss Madrigal is in fact a mystery woman, "burnt out and lunar," who has "cut off her past like a fish's tail." Bagnold's play is in part a journey to the bottom of Miss Madrigal's identity; it is also about the effect the woman has on her employer's household. Mrs. St. Maugham is a selfish, eccentric paragon of privilege who spends her days gardening but can't make anything grow. She is raising her precocious, severely troubled fourteen-year-old granddaughter, Laurel (Sallyanne Tackus), with scarcely more fruitful results. By the end of the evening, Miss Madrigal will have taught both the dowager and child about "the astonishment of living," but not before she has taught them about death.

For reasons that won't be revealed here, Miss Madrigal has a special understanding of death. So does the playwright. The talk and action in *The Chalk Garden* are screwball-comedy light, but the shadow of mortality hovers over all, refracting the play's Shavian banter into unexpectedly rueful patterns.

And as Bagnold's characters are seen from the perspective of their finiteness, so is the declining society they inhabit. Mrs. St. Maugham is pointedly a relic of Regency England, stranded between her memories of the battle of the Marne and the debacle of Suez that's just around the corner. Her lifelong butler is dying upstairs; her dining room table is "laid with the fragments of forgotten ritual." The denizens of her heartbreak house—who also include a phlegmatic judge (I. M. Hobson) and a paranoid manservant (Donal Donnelly)—are all slightly mad and, each in his way, imprisoned by the past.

After a somewhat inhibited start, the petite Ms. Cummings makes funny, piquant poetry out of Mrs. St. Maugham's predicament. She sweeps about in pastel silk, strewing Bagnold's best lines around the room like diamonds. ("I never allowed myself to think," she explains early on. "I have another method.") It is hilarious to watch her make a grand show of checking a proffered wine bottle at dinner: She raises her eyebrows to the rafters but never bothers to focus on the label at hand.

There would be more laughs still if John Stix's direction minded the bubbly rhythm of Bagnold's language, and if the usually first-rate Messrs. Hobson and Donnelly were a shade sharper. There would be more heartbreak if the production's Laurel and her returning, long-lost mother (Elizabeth Owens) weren't such callow stick figures. Laurel is the one character who must escape this household—and here we don't care whether she does or not.

But we never do tire of watching her elders buzz about her, the governess ever prodding her employer to confront the buried truths that might yet "light up everything." Eventually the exasperated Mrs. St. Maugham is pushed so hard that she asks, "What have I let in here?" and Miss Madrigal snaps back, with utter finality, "The East Wind!" And so Ms. Worth is indeed that bracing wind, just as Ms. Cummings is the yellowing leaf that flutters so brightly, then so helplessly in her path.

MEDEA
Cort Theatre, May 3, 1982

Euripides has a strong ally in Zoe Caldwell, who brought her special flame to the otherwise routine revival of *Medea* that opened last night at the Cort. Possibly the most modern of Greek dramatists, Euripides demands an intense psychological realism from actors—and that is what Ms. Caldwell has bestowed on her marathon role. This actress makes us believe in the warped logic by which Medea murders her two sons to wreak vengeance on Jason, the ambitious husband who has betrayed her for a Greek princess. And because she does, we are, by evening's end, brought right into the thunderclap of Euripides' tragedy.

As befits a barbaric sorceress lost in exile, Ms. Caldwell is set off from the rest of the company by her swarthy complexion; her eyes are dark horizontal slashes that summon up an exotic East. There is a seething physicality to her every gesture; mercurial and sinuous, she is indeed, as Robinson Jeffers's adaptation has it, a mixture of "serpent and wolf." Yet she is a woman, too. Though Ms. Caldwell has many opportunities to chew up the scenery, she usually resists them by shading her portrayal with carefully considered nuances. This at times almost Hedda-like Medea makes the lineage from Euripides to Ibsen abundantly clear.

One of Ms. Caldwell's trump cards is wit. Her Medea gets genuine laughs when she sarcastically extols the virtues of "civilized" Greece and her "kind" Jason—neither of whom have treated her with anything like civility or kindness. The heroine's sexuality is also turned up full throttle. When Ms. Caldwell suddenly kisses Jason (Mitchell Ryan) in the midst of their debate, we see the hot-blooded lust that once made her sacrifice all for him—just as we later see the inverse of that passion in her orgasmic cries of hate and murder. And underneath the frenzy, there is a helplessness as well. Quietly asking how she has been "pulled down to the hell of vile thoughts," Ms. Caldwell becomes a blank; she's so adrift from reason that the answer is really lost forever.

From there, it's only a small leap to the unthinkable. In the crucial scene with the sadly childless Aegeus, Ms. Caldwell's sly smiles show us the idea of child murder taking root in Medea's crazed mind. When, at last, the crime is at hand, the actress fully dramatizes the struggle between her hunger for revenge and her love of her sons. One moment she is drawing the boys to her breasts in full maternal affection; then she is taking them behind closed doors to spill their blood. There is a relentless sweep to the extreme transition. Like the gods, we can understand, if not pardon, the primal impulse that drives her to the ultimate act of annihilation.

Well paced and shrewdly calculated as this performance is, it isn't quite perfect. In the early scenes, Ms. Caldwell's body language—the tremulous fingers, the shaking thighs, the slithering to the floor—can be stylized to the point of mannerism. Her voice, happily, never follows suit. It is a superb, supple instrument—husky yet feminine and full of longing. When she partakes of her "bottomless cup" of hate, she heaves with a primordial ooze that threatens to make the earth open up before us.

If Ms. Caldwell's performance often seems more a virtuosic acting exercise than an integral component in a play, that's because the production cuts too much ground out from under her. The director, Robert Whitehead, has fashioned a by-the-book, meat-and-potatoes *Medea*, and even Ms. Caldwell can't always break through its mustiness.

Mr. Whitehead's association with the play dates to 1947, when he produced the celebrated revival starring Judith Anderson, for whom Jeffers wrote his adaptation. Dame Judith is back again here, in the role of the nurse, and her presence gives this *Medea* the valuable resonance of theatrical tradition. While her delivery of the early speeches sounds a bit too patrician and occasionally matter-of-fact, she builds steadily. Her climactic attempts to thwart the heroine's mayhem—a chorus of "no's" that sends her off her tree-branch cane and up Medea's steps—are harrowing.

The rest of the acting is bland or bombastic, with the exceptions of Pauline Flanagan's direct, beautifully spoken chorus leader and Giulia Pagano as one of her seconds. While Mr. Ryan's Jason is fine in his final collapse—when he caves in to his nihilistic awareness that it no longer matters "who lives and who dies"—he's far too plodding a dissembler along the way. Because his overtly callow rationality is no match at all for Ms. Caldwell's savage force, the play's central argument is left unengaged.

No one, least of all Mr. Ryan, has been aided by Jane Greenwood's attic Attic costumes. But Ben Edwards's majestic set, reportedly a reworking of the one he did in 1947, has been lighted with an eerie glow of foreboding by Martin Aronstein, and there's music to match by David Amram. Mr. Whitehead's staging is friezelike in its rigidity, and awkward in its deployments of the chorus. True, *Medea* is a very hard play to stage, but that doesn't mean one must approach it as if it were a boulder to be pushed up a cliff.

But once Mr. Whitehead does get to the peak, in the last fifteen minutes, the payoff is considerable. At that point, Ms. Caldwell's volcanic eruption at last sets fire to this *Medea,* and even the dead wood around her must burn hellishly in her wake.

NINE

46TH STREET THEATRE, MAY 10, 1982

There are two unquestionable reasons to cheer *Nine,* the extravagantly uneven musical that opened at the 46th Street Theatre last night. Their names are Tommy Tune and Maury Yeston. In this, his most ambitious show, Mr. Tune provides the strongest evidence yet that he is one of our theater's most inventive directors—a man who could create rainbows in a desert. Mr. Yeston, a newcomer to Broadway, has an imagination that, at its best, is almost Mr. Tune's match. His score, giddily orchestrated by Jonathan Tunick, is a literate mixture of showbiz and operatic musical genres that contains some of the season's most novel and beautiful songs. Together Mr. Yeston and Mr. Tune give *Nine* more than a few sequences that are at once hallucinatory and entertaining—dreams that play like showstoppers.

In those numbers, *Nine* is remarkably faithful to the spirit of its problematic, unacknowledged source material, Federico Fellini's 8½, without being imprisoned by it. Though *Nine* tells the same story as 8½—that of a creatively and emotionally blocked film director in midlife crisis—it does not make the mistake of slavishly replicating the film's imagery. True, the setting is once again an Italian spa, where fantasy, reality, and flashback intermingle as the hero, Guido (Raul Julia), sorts out the many formative women in his life. But where Mr. Fellini dreamed of harems and traffic jams, Mr. Tune and Mr. Yeston fill the stage with glittering, tuneful reveries of the Folies-Bergère and rococo opera buffa.

There's so much rich icing on *Nine* that anyone who cares about the progress of the Broadway musical will have to see it. There is also a hollowness at the show's core that requires real patience. At the gut, emotional level, *Nine* never makes us understand or care about Guido or most of the women who gnaw at his soul. As drama, the show's structure seems static: Act 1 is overlong exposition that leads to sudden resolution in Act 2—climaxed by an abrupt, unmotivated happy ending that is even more dishonest than Mr. Fellini's. There are also severe lapses of taste: For all the brilliantly styled moments in *Nine*, there are others where stylization curdles into the vulgarity of kitsch and camp.

If the show is a complex mixture of ecstatic highs and crass lows, its staging concept is simplicity itself. With the exception of Mr. Julia and the boys who play the childhood Guido and his playmates, the entire cast of *Nine* is women—twenty-two of all shapes and sizes, each with her own pedestal on Lawrence Miller's expansive white-tiled spa set. Mr. Tune uses the women as a Greek chorus and, with the aid of William Ivey Long's spectacular costumes, as the show's real scenery. Placed against a void, they give *Nine* its colors, its characters, its voices, even its Venetian gondolas—and remind us that the musical, in fact, unfolds inside Guido's troubled head.

The conceit also allows Mr. Tune and company to create their own theatrical equivalent of Mr. Fellini's subliminal cinematic style. As a group the women can form a cacophonous mob that emblemizes the forty-year-old Guido's mental collapse—or a haunting, nun-filled Roman Catholic vision of his early youth. (Underemployed, the rows of black-clad figures at times can also become oppressive.) Meanwhile, individual chorus members glide about in specific roles, with no need for laborious set changes or conventional book scenes to affect the show's nonlinear, nonchronological transitions.

Some of those individuals—and their numbers—are stunning indeed. When Liliane Montevecchi, as Guido's producer, summons up her past as a Folies dancer, we get not a conventional Folies number but one as seen through the eyes of the impressionable young hero—in which the performer's runway dance routine and even her black feather boa are magically refracted into Freudian shapes. Ms. Montevecchi, herself a former Folies headliner, is a knockout—a glorious amalgam of music-hall feistiness and balletic grace, with Toulouse-Lautrec shadows about the eyes.

Karen Akers, as the hero's wife, brings a powerful cabaret singer's voice to two laments. As Guido's favorite movie star, Shelly Burch is a Modigliani goddess with another strong voice and an almost other-worldly presence. Impressive, too, are Kathi Moss, as Saraghina, the earthy fat lady who introduces the young Guido and his friends to sex by means of a tambourine-shaking tarantella, and Taina Elg, as Guido's pix-ieish mother, who sings a lullaby to her son from her grave even as she reenacts his birth.

Mr. Tune's most dazzling choreographic gem belongs to the brassy, redheaded Anita Morris, who plays Guido's mistress in a black-lace body stocking: She superbly executes a one-body simulation of two-body cop-ulation. But Ms. Morris is also saddled with one of the show's broadest characterizations. Her breast-shaking siren goes beyond even Fellini-esque exaggeration to become a caricature of female sexuality—and it sets the tone for the more grotesque shenanigans of other, anonymous chorus members. By Act 2, there are so many gags about female sexual organs and so little actual eroticism that one wouldn't blame Guido for abandoning both sex and cinema for a monastery.

But who cares what Guido wants? For all his musical inspiration, Mr. Yeston can write pedestrian lyrics—and the weakest are used to define the hero and his wife. Guido's introductory song tells us only that he's split between the immaturity of age nine and the maturity of age forty—and this clichéd definition is often repeated but never much deepened. Ms. Akers's soaring torch-song melodies come with standard-issue senti-ments about unhappiness in love ("No need to carry out this masquer-ade"); neither they nor the performer's affectless personality create a character. No matter how hard *Nine* tries to force Mr. Julia, Ms. Morris, and Ms. Akers into a magnetic love triangle, they often seem as isolated as residents of different planets.

Arthur Kopit's sometimes stylish book doesn't find the lines that might help bring the man at center stage into focus. And Mr. Julia's sometimes charming star performance—persuasively Italian but vocally weak—lacks the galvanizing charisma that might draw us to Guido in spite of the text's holes. As a result, the big set piece of Act 2—in which Guido's personal and creative crises resolve themselves in a surreal movie-opera-dream sequence about Casanova—is less a cathartic climax than an empty, if sumptuous, exercise in style. It breaks through the show's overly diagrammatic black-and-white color scheme but not through the hero's skin.

Yet it is still fun to watch, and Mr. Tune has more visions up his long sleeve, too. My favorite occurs before the start of Act 2 when the young Guido (Cameron Johann) walks through the audience, climbs up on the cakewalk surrounding the glowing orchestra pit and waits expectantly with the rest of us for the curtain to rise. What the image sums up is Mr. Tune's pure, childlike rapture for the theater, and while that's the only real emotion in *Nine,* it's so potent that it just may carry those who share it through the rest.

RED AND BLUE
PUBLIC THEATER, MAY 12, 1982

The only two visible performers in *Red and Blue,* the theater piece at the Public Theater's Other Stage, are a pair of lightbulbs. If you've seen the human acting on display in the Public's current production of *Antigone,* you can instantly appreciate that this is not necessarily a bad thing. Lightbulbs are bright. They are rarely hammy. And when they're red and blue, they can be kind of cute.

The lines they speak were written by Michael Hurson and are recited from offstage by Earl Hindman (Red) and Randy Danson (Blue), with occasional interruptions by a third voice (James Hurdle), organ chords, phone rings, "fierce typing," and the thunderstorms of old-time radio drama. Mr. Hurson, who describes himself as a visual and conceptual artist in the program, is no writer or thinker, but, intentionally or not, his scenario for *Red and Blue* at times sounds like an Americanized parody of *Last Year at Marienbad*—or maybe of the Public's current *Three Acts of Recognition.*

Mr. Hurson's hour-long script is a chic, fractionalized, sporadically funny, and often tedious study of anomie and alienation. Disembodied people (literally disembodied, in this case) traipse through vacant rooms asking questions like "Is the pain of birth a dream?" or "Do you know what ellipses are?"—believe me, we do—or that old reliable "What is the question?"

In addition to Red and Blue—who light up on either side of the stage as they "speak"—we hear of such phantoms as Simone, the author of a long poem titled "A History of No Place"; Mr. CinemaScope; Streep, a gym teacher who "comes into the city to overturn chairs in the apartments of people he knows"; Paul Stuart, who is either "rich or gay," and the ubiquitous, mysterious Thurman Buzzard. My favorite character is "a blonde dressed in a black cocktail dress" who is chewed out by a deli owner after she presumes to help herself to a paper bag.

There is much talk about the "ever contracting and expanding distance" between Red and Blue, the "concentrated madness" of people inside rooms, and about the dark void beyond those rooms. But the sensibility that informs this work is best summed up by the recurring image of a Gucci loafer. In keeping with the general scheme, the production's soundman and stage manager, both perched beside the audience, wear black tie and sip champagne.

Red and Blue has been directed by JoAnne Akalaitis, whose productions of *Request Concert* and *Dead End Kids* were among the outstanding Off Broadway offerings of last season. But with all due respect to her and her stars, it must be said that the most inventive collaborator in this exercise is the set and lighting designer, John Arnone. He has built a tall doll's house, in which we see nine miniature rooms—or are they the same room?—from various off-center perspectives, complete with peeling walls, fireplaces, and Streep's overturned chairs. The remarkably varied and precise lighting, abetted by Stephanie Rudolph's projections, at times creates sad and tense drama out of uninhabited space.

Mr. Arnone is a genuine artist. The playwright he serves is a General Electric stockholder's best friend.

SUNDAY ESSAY: THE LESSONS OF A LACKLUSTER SEASON
MAY 23, 1982

The perfect symbol for the now officially concluded 1981–82 theater season is not a performance or a play—or even a forty-dollar ticket stub—but a pile of rubble that sits on West Forty-fifth Street between Broadway and Eighth Avenue. That rubble, you may recall, was once the Morosco, which gave way for the Portman hotel. Unlike so many of the season's ostensible dramatic events, the razing of the Morosco and its neighbor, the Helen Hayes, truly did galvanize the entire theatrical community into fierce debate and high emotions. In part, the debate was totally rational: Two no doubt well-meaning camps had conflicting visions of a healthy future for the Times Square theater district.

But at the emotional level the fight to save the Morosco and the Hayes had a symbolic meaning—one that transcended the sheer desire to preserve two fine playhouses. The Morosco had been the first home of *Death of a Salesman,* the Helen Hayes of *Long Day's Journey into Night.* To cling to these two buildings was also to cling, desperately, to a glorious past in the American theater. And when the wrecking ball struck on a blustery late-winter morning, tears were shed not only because there would never be another Morosco or Hayes, but also because of the nagging, unspoken fear that there would never be another *Salesman* or *Long Day's Journey* as well.

I choose, in the end, not to take that pessimistic view—just as I choose to avoid walking by the debris on Forty-fifth Street whenever possible. But this was a season to challenge anyone's Pollyannaism. Something is terribly wrong when the Tony Award nominators, to come up with a full slate of contenders, must give a nomination to a performer from *Marlowe* (possibly the worst—definitely the most ludicrous—musical since *Portofino*). Or when one considers that the season's most persistent theatrical prop was a wheelchair. Or when one strolls by the TKTS booth at Duffy Square and finds that on many nights, nearly every show on and off Broadway has tickets available at half-price.

Nonetheless, the season was far from a total loss. One is most grateful, perhaps, for that extraordinary South African dramatist, Athol Fugard, whose *"Master Harold"* . . . *and the Boys* is the best play of this season, as his *A Lesson from Aloes* was of last. As always, one must bow to the contributions from British theatrical companies and playwrights—the Royal Shakespeare Company's *The Life and Adventures of Nicholas Nickleby,* Ronald Harwood's *The Dresser,* Harold Pinter's *The Hothouse.*

There were also, again as always, some good and better revivals—*Othello* on Broadway, as well as the Roundabout's *A Taste of Honey, Misalliance, The Chalk Garden,* and *The Browning Version.* These were sparked by the fire and ice of Christopher Plummer, Amanda Plummer, Philip Bosco, Irene Worth, Constance Cummings, and Lee Richardson.

More unusual, this was a season offering not one, but two flamboyantly original musicals—complete with new scores by gifted new songwriters. (By contrast, last season's Broadway musical hits had scores by Harry Warren and Duke Ellington.) Michael Bennett's *Dreamgirls,* with music and lyrics by Henry Krieger and Tom Eyen, is a heartbreaking, groundbreaking show about the triumphs and compromises of black people who struggle for success within white America. Because of its visually abstract, cinematic staging and its subtle, idiomatic rhythm-and-blues score, it probably divides audiences more violently, at times along generational lines, than any smash pop-culture extravaganza since *2001: A Space Odyssey.* Tommy Tune's *Nine,* with lovely music and so-so lyrics by Maury Yeston, is an imaginative exercise in showbiz style (forget about content) that also invites its audience to dream on a grand scale. Unofficially adapted from Federico Fellini's 8½, it proves to be Mr. Tune's camped-up answer to Bob Fosse's *All That Jazz.*

But what about American plays—those that might have once played the Morosco? Here's where the good news is hard to find. Indeed, Charles Fuller's Pulitzer Prize–winning *A Soldier's Play,* at the Negro Ensemble Company, was the sole high-powered, fully written new American drama to open in New York during the 1981–82 season. (It is also, as coincidence would have it, the perfect companion piece for *Dreamgirls*—for it deals with the same subject in the same unsparing manner.)

Yes, there were other American plays of quality this season, but they were all works that had originally been produced in New York or elsewhere in seasons past: Beth Henley's *Crimes of the Heart* (from Louisville's Actors Theatre and the Manhattan Theatre Club), Bill C. Davis's *Mass Appeal* (also from the Manhattan Theatre Club), and, best of all, Jules Feiffer's relentless journey into an assimilated American-Jewish family's dark heart, *Grown Ups* (from Harvard's American Repertory Theatre). Similarly, most of the bigger Off Broadway successes—Christopher Durang's *Sister Mary Ignatius Explains It All for You,* Harvey Fierstein's *Torch Song Trilogy,* and Amlin Gray's *How I Got That Story*—had previous, pre-1981 production histories Off Off Broadway or out-of-town.

This in itself is no cause for alarm at all. It's just smart producing. For many seasons now, the best commercially produced plays (and many of the best musicals) tend to be those previously seen in nonprofit Off Broadway companies, in regional theaters, and abroad. What made this season so unsettling is the fact that New York's institutional theaters generally failed to produce the new plays or musicals that might fill our fifty-odd commercial theaters, on and off Broadway, during the seasons to come. In the 1981–82 semester, much of the New York theater dried up at its roots.

Take, for instance, our usually most dependable source of fresh, innovative work, Joseph Papp's New York Shakespeare Festival. Last fall, the Public got off to a splendid start with its joint productions of two plays by the young Chinese American playwright David Henry Hwang, soon followed by James Lapine's uneven but ambitious Jungian drama,

Twelve Dreams. After that? Mr. Papp has announced that he wants to produce "abstract" plays—fair enough—but the ones he's done are largely frail imitations of the avant-garde prototypes of yesteryear. By May, the Public was offering four calamities on its various stages, ranging from an ill-conceived revival of *Antigone* to *Red and Blue,* a derivative theater piece starring two light bulbs.

The Manhattan Theatre Club fared little better, though it did cast some superb actors in second-best plays. But this is the organization that, in recent years, has offered the New York premieres of *Crimes of the Heart, Mass Appeal,* and *Ain't Misbehavin'.* The seasons at the Phoenix Theatre, the American Place, the Hudson Guild, and the WPA were mostly washouts. So, shockingly, was that of the Circle Repertory Company, first home of *Talley's Folly* and *Fifth of July.* Even as it hubristically expanded to two playhouses, this company fielded its weakest plays and productions in memory. Meanwhile, New York's ostensibly premiere nonprofit theater, the Lincoln Center Repertory Company, remained dark awaiting the Vivian Beaumont's refurbishment.

A handful of small institutional theaters did heroically buck the trend, including the young Second Stage (Deborah Eisenberg's *Pastorale,* Wendy Kesselman's *My Sister in This House*) and the Ensemble Studio Theatre. Playwrights Horizons may be the most remarkable success story in the New York theater right now. To follow last season's *March of the Falsettos,* this theater staged *Sister Mary Ignatius* (first seen at the Ensemble Studio Theater) and then A. R. Gurney Jr.'s poignant and beautifully acted canvas of upper-middle-class WASP life, *The Dining Room.* This month brought *Geniuses,* Jonathan Reynolds's savage satire of all things Hollywood, which my colleague Mel Gussow has described as a work of "comic genius." It's a judgment I share, although I must add that Mr. Reynolds is an old friend from days long before either of us ever imagined that we'd be working different sides of the same street.

But after one separates the few survivors from the many corpses, the enduring questions remain: Why was the season so poor, on Broadway and off? What can be learned from the failures and successes? Where do we go from here?

I have no insightful answers to the first question as far as Off Broadway is concerned. When two of our best playwrights falter twice in one season—as did Lanford Wilson (*A Tale Told, Thymus Vulgaris*) and John Guare (*Lydie Breeze, Gardenia*)—one begins to wonder if the gods haven't cursed our fates. When Joseph Papp makes so many poor choices, one wonders if he wasn't spending more time fighting for the Morosco than reading scripts. (In which case, his lapses are at least understandable.) And perhaps everyone should be wary of Canadian plays, as typified by the Public's *Zastrozzi* and the Phoenix's *Maggie and Pierre.*

On Broadway, the failures are far more explicable—and far less pardonable. Producers this season have made the same mistake over and over again: Too often they have decided that the star, not the play, is the thing—and have paid this miscalculation's high price, both artistic and financial, almost every time.

There's nothing wrong with stars per se: Usually stars are stars because they are top-flight actors. When the right ones are in the right roles in the right plays, the results can be exciting—as was the case this season with Milo O'Shea, Tom Courtenay, Zoe Caldwell, and, most emphatically, Mr. Plummer's Iago. But the season's other star vehicles included: *The West Side Waltz, A Talent for Murder, Come Back to the 5 & Dime, Jimmy Dean, Jimmy Dean, Einstein and the Polar Bear, Agnes of God, Curse of an Aching Heart, Special Occasions, Duet for One,* and *Little Johnny Jones.*

Would these plays have been produced without Katharine Hepburn, Claudette Colbert, Cher, Peter Strauss, Geraldine Page, Amanda Plummer, Faye Dunaway, Suzanne Pleshette, Anne Bancroft, Max von Sydow, and Donny Osmond? I doubt it. Yet did the presence of these star names mean anything to the creative or box-office life of these shows? Not enough. Some of the stars did give excellent performances—but if the plays are severely lacking, good acting won't paper over the holes.

Nor did most of these stars save their shows at the box office; two of the vehicles collapsed on opening night, and only one (*Agnes of God*) is still running. The sole hit in this group was *The West Side Waltz,* but Ms. Hepburn is no mere star: She is one of maybe two or three American acting legends who could recite the phone book and still pack audiences in. And this season that's almost what she did.

Conversely, it's worth noting that many of Broadway's bigger recent critical or popular hits—*Amadeus, Dreamgirls, Nicholas Nickleby, Master Harold, Annie, Crimes of the Heart*—made it with no marquee names at all. The moral, I think, is clear: If a play is worth doing, it doesn't matter whether it has a star or not. If there's a star and no play, chances are that talent, energy, and money are about to be poured directly into the gutter. We might be spared a lot of waste next season if only this simple axiom could at last be committed to memory.

The season's biggest phenomena—*Nicholas Nickleby, Dreamgirls,* and *Master Harold*—have other lessons to teach us as well. The lessons are not new, but they are given fresh urgency by these three works.

Although *Nicholas Nickleby* and *Dreamgirls* have little in common—besides their size and the cinematic bravura of their staging—they were both created in the same way: in slow, painstaking workshop sessions that took months. In the case of *Nicholas Nickleby,* those workshops were affordable because the company that nurtured it is partially subsidized by the British government. The workshops of *Dreamgirls* were privately financed by Michael Bennett—and were affordable because Mr. Bennett had previously struck gold with *A Chorus Line.*

What does this prove? It refuels the unassailable argument that, now more than ever, a private or governmental subsidy is essential to the continued growth of the theater. Just as plays like *Crimes of the Heart* or *Mass Appeal,* as well as avant-garde experiments, are now almost always developed in nonprofit institutional theaters before they are snapped up by commercial producers (if they are), so prohibitively costly, large-scale efforts—theatrical epics and big Broadway-bound musicals alike—must find their equivalent laboratories if they are to flourish.

One can only wonder if some of this season's saddest, most ambitious failures, from *Lydie Breeze* to *Merrily We Roll Along,* might have had happier endings had they had their own extended workshops, away from paying audiences and commercial pressures. To go frantically from rehearsals to public previews to opening night is not a path that serves anyone anymore. Yet, except for occasional sugar daddies like Mr. Bennett or the Public Theater (also made wealthy in part by *A Chorus Line*), few private producers or nonprofit theaters can foot the bills for lengthy, large-scale workshops.

But what is to be done? We live in a time of recession and governmental cutbacks: Even our existing institutional theaters are fighting to stay solvent. Still, the struggle must continue; the fight for a national theater—or for the survival and expansion of our existing mini-national theaters, whether in New York or Louisville—must be fought harder than ever before. It is our theater's best, maybe only, hope.

Master Harold, though also first produced in a nonprofit institution (the Yale Repertory Company), teaches another lesson—about esthetics, not producing. Here is a work that does so much of what the theater can do: It speaks profoundly about specific social issues and about the universal nature of hate and love; it makes us laugh and cry; it fills us with both pain and hope. But what happens in it? Three men while away an afternoon in a shabby tea room, dancing about and talking, for a scant 100 minutes.

Certainly not all plays—or most plays—should be written in imitation of *Master Harold.* Every writer must be his own man, innovate, take chances. But, in the most general way, there is so much to be learned from the simplicity of this work: By speaking honestly, economically, deeply, Athol Fugard achieves the exact effects that have eluded so many of this season's overelaborate, heavy-breathing theatrical efforts. He reminds us that basic, primal theater can still be as simple as three men in a bare room—that, if our theater can't afford its own *Nicholas Nickleby* right now, it is by no means the end of the world.

Mr. Fugard may be a South African writer, but who doubts that his play upholds the same tradition as those classic American plays symbolized by the Morosco? And, as it happens, *Master Harold* is playing only a block away from that rubble on Forty-fifth Street—where it stands as an inspiration to our own theater, imploring us to think clearly, to seize the future, to rebuild.

FOURTH
SEASON
1982—83

Elizabeth Taylor and Richard Burton in *Private Lives*

HENRY IV, PARTS I AND II
Royal Shakespeare Company, London, June 12, 1982

Before a single line was spoken, the audience broke into warm applause at Wednesday's all-day press premiere of the Royal Shakespeare Company's new *Henry IV, Parts I and II*. Some of the applause, no doubt, was for the theater itself. With this production, the company officially occupies its new London home at the Barbican Centre, and a splendid home it is. Tasteful, comfortable, and blessed with ideal sightlines, the Barbican Theatre seems a model of how to design a substantial (1,160 seats) yet intimate modern playhouse. It's so cozy that one can almost forget about the oppressive complex that contains it—a grim concrete jungle that makes Los Angeles's Century City or Washington's Kennedy Center look like Versailles by comparison.

But there may have been another reason for the anticipatory applause as well. Upon taking its seats to face the Barbican's huge thrust stage, the audience found a John Napier set—wooden constructs poised to slide diagonally across a planked floor—that resembles the designer's work for *Nicholas Nickleby*. And the heady promise of a new *Nickleby* didn't end there.

Henry IV is another marathon production—seven hours, plus dinner break, for those who choose to take in both parts in one day. It has been directed by Trevor Nunn, the company's artistic director, who codirected *Nickleby*. What's more, the two history plays at hand may be as Dickensian as any in the Shakespeare canon. In *Henry IV*, one finds the entire social spectrum of England on display, from royalty down to the lowliest Eastcheap tavern riffraff. In the play's matchless knight errant, Falstaff, one can see a prototype for all manner of glorious Dickens clowns.

Nonetheless, it would be hard to argue that this *Henry IV* comes anywhere near justifying its audience's first flush of high enthusiasm. From the King's opening speech, delivered with leaden pauses by Patrick Stewart, a sinking sensation sets in, and little happens to defray it during the long, long hours to come. While the Royal Shakespeare Company may be the greatest acting troupe in the English-speaking world, it often seems on this occasion to be fielding a second team. Nor does Mr. Nunn's staging much come to the rescue. Though the director keeps the scenic units moving about like mammoth chess pawns—and though he fills the stage with a *Nickleby*-like chorus of perpetual onlookers—he never creates the teeming visions or cinematically swirling action one expects from him. Indeed, much of this *Henry IV* takes the form of rigid, front-and-center declamatory bouts, with the cast posed like statuary against a gloomy void.

Because the company's actors are so well trained in speech and movement, the performance level never sinks to the catastrophic depths one encounters in too many classic productions in New York; instead, blandness generally rules the day. Yet Mr. Nunn may have found his equivalent to Philip Anglim's Macbeth in Gerard Murphy, the actor he has cast as Prince Hal. With his long, greasy blond locks, gaping smiles, and weightless, reedy voice, the slouching, slightly pudgy Mr. Murphy looks like a second-rate rock singer gone to seed. Even after he is finally crowned as Henry V at the end of Part II, he still remains an unreformed ninny. The stops along his ascent to power are all too cute, or, in the case of the reconciliation scene with his father, too syrupy.

As Falstaff, Joss Ackland looks and sounds right, and he never underestimates the knight's intelligence. But the actor fails to capture the character's Rabelaisian sense of fun and chaotic excess; one never quite believes that he is truly addicted to sack. As a result, his choicest comic bits tend to provoke at most titters from the real audience, even as the onstage onlookers whoop it up at his every turn. It comes as a considerable relief when some strong second bananas—Mike Gwilym's Pistol, Robert Eddison's Shallow, and Miriam Karlin's Mistress Quickly— emerge to prod him to somewhat friskier heights in Part II.

About the only thing to recommend Part I is Timothy Dalton's dashing, fast-talking Hotspur—at once ridiculous and heroic in his literally leapfrogging hurtle to self-immolation. The minor scene in which he receives a letter from a lord who backs off from the revolt is surprisingly touching: Mr. Dalton keeps refolding the letter aimlessly as he vainly tries to hide his panic from his wife (Harriet Walter). The actor also taps into a rich boyishly sarcastic vein of humor as he irrepressibly mocks the supernatural pretensions of his trying ally Glendower (Bernard Lloyd).

The staging has its scattered moments, too. Although Mr. Nunn tends to hit Shakespeare's father-son theme with a sledgehammer, there is an affecting bit on the eve of Shrewsbury in which Hal and his two putative fathers, Henry and Falstaff, form a still, triangular tableau in the fading light. The play's ever-quickening intimations of mortality are all well accounted for: Mr. Ackland delivers Falstaff's catechism on the bankruptcy of military "honor" while surrounded by the specter of steel-armored soldiers about to die in war. Later on, the king receives the news of Glendower's death with a shudder, not joy, for he knows too well that he'll soon join his adversary in the grave. There is also a superb opening for Part II: Rumour's speech is divided up among a candle-holding chorus, which then disperses to reveal that the victim of its rumors, Northumberland, had been hidden within its midst.

But such isolated bits are, as Shakespeare would have it, small beer, and they're certainly no substitute for the larger canvas that *Henry IV* should be. At least it's consolation to learn that American theatrical companies aren't the only ones who mark their entrance into shiny new quarters by slipping directly on a banana peel.

SEVEN BRIDES FOR SEVEN BROTHERS
ALVIN THEATRE, JULY 9, 1982

So how does one begin to describe *Seven Brides for Seven Brothers,* the threadbare touring package that mistakenly unpacked on Broadway last night? Perhaps it's fitting to start with the brothers themselves. There are indeed seven of them—all singing, all dancing—but what in heaven's name, one wonders, has happened to their hair? On close examination, it seems that someone decided to transform all the brothers into redheads—and then abandoned hope in mid–dye job. The result is an unmatched collection of strawberry-streaked chorus boys who, while purporting to be rugged farmers in 1850 Oregon, look for all the world like clowns.

Seven Brides for Seven Brothers, the fifth musical bomb to be planted in the Alvin in ten months, has its other lunacies, too. As directed by Lawrence Kasha, its scenes don't so much end as lurch into darkness. The sets, by the sometimes admirable Robert Randolph, are flimsy and dreary in a 1950s fashion that hasn't been seen since—well, since Mr. Randolph's last show at the Alvin, *Little Johnny Jones.* This musical also marks the Broadway debut of Debby Boone. To which one might well say, bring back Donny Osmond!

The inspiration for this enterprise is the 1954 Metro-Goldwyn-Mayer movie musical of the same title. In its original incarnation, *Seven Brides* was less than thrilling, yet let's be grateful that this show's collaborators didn't choose to monkey around with *The Band Wagon* or *Singin' in the Rain* instead. Nonetheless, the original *Seven Brides* did have one major strength: its galvanic Michael Kidd choreography, danced by an illustrious, high-flying team of brothers that included Russ Tamblyn, Jacques d'Amboise, Matt Mattox, Tommy Rall, and Marc Platt.

The movie also offered a few pleasant songs in its generally standard-issue Gene de Paul–Johnny Mercer score. Some of those songs (notably "Wonderful, Wonderful Day" and "Goin' Courtin' ") have been preserved here, outfitted in appealingly old-fashioned Broadway arrangements by Irwin Kostal. They are, however, overrun by eight new numbers from Al Kasha and Joel Hirschhorn, last known as the perpetrators of *Copperfield*. For this occasion, this team has come up with one tuneful cornball ballad ("Love Never Goes Away"), as well as a shameless, God-invoking inspirational piece that apparently aspires to repeat the success of Ms. Boone's legendary hit single, "You Light Up My Life." The rest of the score might benefit by being left unmiked.

The energetic choreography, attributed to Jerry Jackson, attempts, with fitful success, to simulate Mr. Kidd's style, but one waits in vain for a full rendition of the movie's famous barn-raising number. In fact, one waits through most of Act 1 for a full-fledged dance, period. The two hoedowns in Act 2 are pretty much variations on the first, though one of them, set in the spring, is framed by plastic flowers. For added ballast, the choreography is often accompanied by cartwheels, clapping jags, mock fisticuffs and cries of "ya-hoo!" and "yippee!"

The remainder of the time, which doesn't pass like lightning, is devoted to Lawrence Kasha's and David Landay's book. As in the film, the scant story is Stephen Vincent Benét's transplanted reworking of Plutarch's tale of the Sabine women. But it's not until after intermission that the brothers finally get a move on and kidnap their unwilling brides. Up until then, there are gags about the brothers' longjohns, about a bed that collapses on the hero and heroine's wedding night, about the etiquette of courting. Act 2's big kneeslapper is a line containing the word "outhouse."

The hero is played by David-James Carroll, whose sturdy singing voice and colorless personality valiantly uphold the Howard Keel tradition. In the Jane Powell role, Ms. Boone sings ably and smiles constantly—in the remote, rigidly ungiving manner of a veteran professional gladhander or beauty-pageant contestant. The star's acting skills are minimal, but when her hair is up and her forced good cheer is particularly frosty, one can picture her doing a rude impression of Nancy Reagan on *Saturday Night Live*.

≡ *The seven brothers and some other red-haired cohorts, saying that I was "killing family entertainment," picketed the* Times *to protest this review— an old-fashioned publicity stunt infinitely more charming (and entertaining) than their show.*

SUNDAY ESSAY: AUDACIOUS
GAMBLES WITH HIGH COMEDY
JULY 25, 1982

George C. Scott and Richard Foreman may both be creatures of the stage, but their artistic credos have about as much in common as, say, the political ideologies of General Patton and Che Guevara. Mr. Scott is a grand old veteran of the theatrical establishment; Mr. Foreman, an avant-gardist, likes to toss Ontological-Hysteric hand grenades. Yet they do share one trait not unknown among theater people—pure, unbridled egomania. And this summer they've each flexed their egos in the same way—by superimposing their own personalities over every pore of the vintage high comedies they've chosen to revive.

The comedies are Molière's *Don Juan,* which Mr. Foreman mounted in Central Park for the New York Shakespeare Festival, and Noël Coward's *Present Laughter,* which Mr. Scott has just brought to Broadway's Circle in the Square. The two productions, like the plays, couldn't be more different in terms of sensibility or achievement, yet the headstrong (one might say arrogant) modus operandi in each one is identical. Both directors have cut and somewhat rewritten the original texts, partially yanking them out of their social and esthetic contexts. They've also performed radical surgery on Molière and Coward's famous heroes. While Don Juan and the actor Garry Essendine are both written as debonair, hedonistic rakes, Mr. Foreman and Mr. Scott transform them into overweight, rumpled, even sexless clowns.

It's enough to make purists weep, and indeed Mr. Foreman's *Don Juan* induced enough tears that Central Park's Belvedere Lake by now should be an ocean. But wrongheaded as Mr. Foreman and Mr. Scott at times can be, they're not stupid, and there are real intellectual pleasures to be had in watching them dare to go one-on-one with the formidable ghosts of Molière and Coward. In Mr. Scott's case, the results are entertaining as well as fascinating: While his *Present Laughter* beats Coward to a bloody pulp, the audience still emerges as the winner.

This hasn't always been true of Mr. Scott's more egotistical artistic adventures. Two Broadway seasons ago, he apparently bemused himself into believing that his acting talent alone would be enough to bolster a dreary C.I.A. thriller, *Tricks of the Trade.* The play folded on opening night. A few years before that, he directed, produced, distributed, and starred in the ludicrous movie *The Savage Is Loose,* an overheated *Swiss Family Robinson* retread that looked as if it had been shot at Trader Vic's.

No wonder, then, that one approaches *Present Laughter* with the fear of stumbling onto another vanity production. Here again Mr. Scott is audaciously doubling as director and star. And when he makes his first entrance, the spectacle is disconcerting, to say the least. Garry Essendine, a role Coward wrote for himself, is an aging British matinee idol—elegant, svelte, to the grand manner born. Mr. Scott, his stocky body at sea in a silk dressing gown, glides through Garry's glittering Art Deco flat looking less like Coward than Buffalo Bill in drag. The actor's voice is stranger still. It's possible that Mr. Scott is actually attempting a British accent, but the gravelly snarl that emerges sounds as if it were stranded somewhere between Alabama and Transylvania.

Yet the actor's gamble pays off, because, by playing Garry Essendine totally against type, he's carrying the play's central comic conceit over into real life. Garry is a conceited, hammy, manipulative big-time Star of the old school—in other words, the kind of fellow, like Mr. Scott in *Present Laughter,* who insists on playing a role that doesn't expressly suit him. As a result, Mr. Scott's own egomania magnifies the comic egomania of the character. One of Coward's better jokes involves his hero's unrealized ambition to play Peer Gynt—an ambition constantly thwarted by his managers. It's doubly funny here because we realize that, but for the grace of God, Mr. Scott himself might well be doing Ibsen instead of *Present Laughter* at the Circle in the Square right now.

The other ace the actor has to play is his talent, which he's turned up to a high flame for the first time on stage since *Sly Fox.* Maybe his Garry is more Beverly Hills than Mayfair, but he comes equipped with a full, tightly disciplined arsenal of arched eyebrows, clenched-teeth rages, oleaginous grins, and self-pitying crocodile tears. The technique is so assured that it props up some of the lesser one-liners. When we laugh at Garry's insulting reference to an actress with "the sex appeal of a haddock," we realize that it's Mr. Scott's bristling delivery, not the author's mechanical wisecrack, that tickles us. In the same way, Mr. Scott's hellzapoppin' direction of the farcical scenes, his elisions in the text, and his almost epileptic leaps and pratfalls help levitate a play that even its author regarded as second-best.

Chances are that Mr. Scott's monkeying about wouldn't suit, say, *Private Lives.* But in *Present Laughter,* there's little to lose by taking liberties. Garry's various romantic entanglements, which form the plot, are too passionless and thinly contrived to be played for keeps: The Coward sensibility at work here isn't heterosexual or homosexual—it's nonsexual. This proves a liberating creative boon to Mr. Scott, who affects extravagantly campy arm gestures even as he barks like a drill sergeant: He thus

spoofs the epicene Coward persona and his own persona simultaneously—finding that high-comedy heaven where the narcissistic excesses
of all stars converge.

As Mr. Scott uses *Present Laughter* as his personal trampoline, so Mr.
Foreman tried to do the same with *Don Juan*, which concluded its run
yesterday. But in the end, the text rose up, like the statue of the commander in Molière's final act, to knock the director to the ground. Mr.
Foreman's esthetic personality is every bit as distinctive as Mr. Scott's,
and he, too, poured it over his entire production. *Don Juan* came
equipped with the same electronic noise, hallucinatory tableaux, crisscrossing wires, and blinding fluorescent lighting that Mr. Foreman has
applied to his own abstract Ontological-Hysteric pieces as well as to his
versions of contemporary plays. Mr. Foreman apparently can't abandon
these conceits any more easily than Mr. Scott can jettison his raspy lar-
ynx or extra pounds.

While few of the director's trademark devices pertain to *Don Juan,* some
of Mr. Foreman's other perverse ideas did make some thematic sense—in
a caricaturedly theatrical way. In order to exaggerate the point that the
play's hero is the one intellectually honest man in a seventeenth-century
society full of moral and religious hypocrites, the director turned that society into a madhouse—an avenging mob of crucifix-bearing, chalk-faced
grotesques who might have popped out of Peter Brook's *Marat/Sade* or
Woody Allen's *Stardust Memories.*

Mr. Foreman's Don Juan (played by John Seitz) seemed only a bit
more human. While the hero, unlike the surrounding chorus, projected
intelligence and sardonic wit, he was also a scowling, unattractive
gnome who walked like a crab. This uncharitable view of Don Juan also
fits the play, in principle anyway, for, if Molière's hedonistic seducer is
more enlightened than the pious gentlefolk he scandalizes, he is still
cruel and cold: His belief in pure reason, unalloyed with feeling, leads to
the destruction of others and, finally, himself. Mr. Foreman seemed to be
saying that Don Juan is better than his society only in the sense that a
one-eyed man can be king among the blind.

The trouble with Mr. Foreman's idiosyncratic visual embodiment of
the play's themes was that it sent him into a cul-de-sac when he had to
deal with the letter of the text. If all the supporting players are nearly
identical zombies, what happens to all of Molière's deliciously styled
scenes in which these characters individually encounter the hero? Audiences found out soon enough: Just as every performance was straitjacketed by Mr. Foreman's conception, every scene played the same as the
one before. While Mr. Foreman cut some of the text to try to solve the

problem, he couldn't cut all of it. So he decided to differentiate the scenes by grafting a single silly gag on to each of them: One character cracked a self-flagellating whip, others spoke with weird accents, and so on. Even if the gags were funny, they couldn't have borne the fifteen minutes of constant repetition that this one-gag-per-scene method required. Meanwhile, Molière's witty jokes were thrown away.

As Mr. Scott's assertion of ego might have failed if applied to a stronger play, so Mr. Foreman's might have worked if applied to a weaker one (or, better still, to one of his own, free-associative Ontological-Hysteric texts). Yet the real source of Mr. Foreman's failure is his inflexibility and lack of inventiveness. He applied his esthetic personality to *Don Juan* so rigidly that he was finally like a child trying to force round pegs by brute force into square holes; he didn't push himself to think of new, funny ideas, as Mr. Scott does, that might have met the author halfway. He settled instead for proving that he could give a four-century-old classic the Foreman stamp, no matter what—and if the operation was a success, the patient nonetheless died before intermission.

While Mr. Scott is certainly capable of such rigidity—he's played Patton in more movies than *Patton*—his ego has more give to it in *Present Laughter*. Maybe he isn't about to go so far as to adapt his voice or body to fit Garry Essendine. Maybe he isn't going to surround himself with too many actors who might upstage him. But, when we see him leap about the stage flapping his arms in a most undignified manner, it's quite clear that he'll risk a lot, even ridicule, to make sure that he and the audience, if not Noël Coward, get every last laugh.

CRITIC'S NOTEBOOK: A THEATRICAL MYSTERY—THE MISSING BALCONIES
SEPTEMBER 9, 1982

The summer's great theatrical mystery was posed in Peter Kerr's recent dispatch in this newspaper about the strange disappearance of balcony seats in Broadway theaters. It seems that some innocent theatergoers shelled out twenty-six dollars for "rear mezzanine" tickets to *Sophisticated Ladies* only to discover that their seats were situated against the back wall in the Lunt-Fontanne's highest reaches—an aerie that looked suspiciously like what used to be called the balcony. Complaints were lodged with the New York City Department of Consumer Affairs, but Camille Ranson, house manager of the Lunt-Fontanne, gave her own explanation to Mr. Kerr.

"It's really just a linguistic thing," she said. "Each theater designates their seats somewhat differently. At different theaters you will find thirty different terminologies for theater seats."

Ms. Ranson sounded quite logical, except that I distinctly recall sitting in the uppermost section of the Lunt-Fontanne once upon a time—and not for twenty-six dollars—to see the original production of *Little Me*. And I remember vividly that my tickets were designated with the terminology *balcony*. No longer having the stub to verify this, I turned to the *Times*'s microfilm, looked up the old theater ads, and discovered that in fact the theater did sell balcony seats in the early 1960s.

I also learned that the Broadhurst and the Imperial had both mezzanines and balconies when they were housing *Oh What a Lovely War* and *Fiddler on the Roof* during that period, yet these days the same theaters have mezzanines but no balconies for *Amadeus* and *Dreamgirls*.

Where did the balconies vanish over the last two decades, one might ask, and has their disappearance been cleared with the Landmarks Commission?

Well, wherever they went, they may be coming back—however gingerly. Snooping about recently in the theater district, I found that the Lunt-Fontanne now listed its least expensive seats as being in the balcony, not rear mezzanine, in its lobby posting of ticket prices. (Curiously enough, another sign indicates that "balcony" seats for *Sophisticated Ladies* will become "rear mezzanine" again when ticket prices are raised in October.)

While the Broadhurst and the Imperial have yet to make any stab in this direction, one can hope that consumer watchdogs might force their balconies to rematerialize sometime soon.

≡ *No such luck.*

A DOLL'S LIFE
MARK HELLINGER THEATER, SEPTEMBER 24, 1982

The season is still young, but it's not likely to produce a more perplexing curiosity than *A Doll's Life*, the dour musical that opened at the Mark Hellinger last night. On this occasion, three legendary Broadway hands—Harold Prince, Betty Comden, and Adolph Green—have inflated a spectacularly unpromising premise with loads of money, good intentions, and hard work, only to end up with a show that collapses in its prologue and then skids into a toboggan slide from which there is no return. These calamities happen, of course, but not usually to artists who've been leading lights in the musical theater for two generations. Call *A Doll's Life* a casual blunder, which, like Topsy, just grew and grew and grew.

It doesn't take long to see that things are wildly out of control. Confusion reigns once the curtain rises to reveal a bunch of actors and stagehands, dressed in 1982 street clothes, as they rehearse Act 3 of Ibsen's *A Doll's House*. (In what translation? It's the first time I've heard Nora trill "Good-bye" before her final exit.) The rehearsal is contentious, perhaps because the actor who plays Torvald, George Hearn, is also unaccountably the director; he keeps stopping Nora (Betsy Joslyn) in mid-scene to give her instruction. But once he shuts up, Ms. Joslyn is finally allowed to slam Ibsen's famous door.

What next? The scenery flies away, Ms. Joslyn disappears, and a chorus chants "Is she here or isn't she? Are we here or aren't we?" Good questions—but the precise answers never come. Through some undefined magic—maybe H. G. Wells's time machine lurks in the wings—the cast suddenly travels back to 1879 Norway. At that point, Ms. Comden and Mr. Green's libretto begins to speculate about what happened to Nora after she left her husband and children to make a new life alone. Yet we still don't always know where we are. Between the garbled Act 1 flashbacks to *A Doll's House* and Act 2's rushed, cryptic chronology (in three different time frames, no less), we expect at any moment to land in Act 5 of *Peer Gynt*.

If all this Pirandellian gimmickry is baffling and unnecessary, the main story is more so. The Nora of *A Doll's Life* isn't Ibsen's Nora, and she doesn't resemble the fizzy, independent heroines of delightful Comden-Green musicals past. She's merely a symbol: The Unliberated Female. In an episodic, didactic fashion—and in a psychobabble idiom that suggests a ten-year-old *Phil Donahue* show—she's propelled through a series of agitprop consciousness-raising crises. Among other things, Nora learns that sex can be fun, that women deserve equal rights and pay, that economic power is a political tool, that we're all "human beings" who can "make choices." At this late date, these revelations are facts of life, but even so, *A Doll's Life* can't muster what should be a foolproof case for them. The characters who teach the heroine these lessons are cut from the same threadbare, old-fashioned musical-comedy cloth that she is: The men she encounters are mostly abject cads (as Ibsen's Torvald was not), and the shackled women she tries to liberate are tarts or clowns.

Though Nora waltzes through many liaisons, into a sweatshop and jail, and finally into a relationship with a perfectly enlightened man (Kris

Kristofferson's great-grandfather, no doubt), the cartoon characterizations foreclose the possibility of drama. Worse still, *A Doll's Life* at times unintentionally parodies or trivializes feminism—and misreads Ibsen's play—by paradoxically arguing that most men are despicable and that a woman's goal should be to "act like a man."

Mr. Prince drapes this material in black crepe, lest we not recognize how heavy it is. The set, by Timothy O'Brien and Tazeena Firth, is dominated by dark Expressionist swirls: Edvard Munch dipped in mud. Ken Billington, that unequaled master of gloom, provides the shadowy lighting. The gifted Florence Klotz's costumes, when visible, recall the ones she did for Mr. Prince's last foray into period Scandinavia, *A Little Night Music,* but this time with all the pastels expunged.

As always, Mr. Prince's direction is fluid, but, remarkably, there isn't a single idea in the staging that he hasn't done before—and better. As in *Sweeney Todd* and *Evita,* there's a bridge from which the chorus constantly comments on or glowers at the action below. (One keeps expecting the assembled to cry out "Sweeney! Sweeney!") We also get a symbolic pair of ghostly ballroom dancers (*Follies*), an oversized bed of carnal passion (*Evita*), and a finale that returns us to the show's beginning (a Prince staple since *Cabaret*). If only the script actually showed us the parfumerie that Nora runs during her entrepreneurial phase, we might even have been transported back—and gladly—to *She Loves Me.*

The director's apparent exhaustion carries over to the choreographer, Larry Fuller, who also reprises a routine from *Evita* (wind-up-doll phalanxes of society folk). The casting is as erratic as in last season's *Merrily We Roll Along.* Ms. Joslyn, a would-be Barbara Cook whose voice wavers as her self-satisfied expression does not, is too inexperienced to create a character where there isn't one in the script. Her personality hardly changes from beginning to end, and we never understand why every man drops dead with lust before her. Nor is it remotely clear why Edmund Lyndeck, who still seems to be playing the villainous Judge of *Sweeney Todd,* is cast as her most sexually magnetic paramour.

Mr. Hearn acts and sings his roles with an unpretentious charm that is highly refreshing under the circumstances; one may choose to forget that his Torvald has a Nazi accent. The rest of the company is undistinguished, with the passing exception of the attractive, if tentative, Peter Gallagher, as a young bohemian who delivers a pretty ballad before vanishing into the blackness.

The one other participant who emerges with some minor distinction is the composer, Larry Grossman. His operetta-like score, feelingly orchestrated by Bill Byers, is frequently impaled by the prosaic lyrics, but it strives for subtle, thematically integrated effects rather than Broadway numbers. Despite a few thrown-in party songs, some Sondheimisms, and an opera parody as endless as the one in *Nine,* Mr. Grossman at least seems to know where he's going in *A Doll's Life.* Maybe his next collaborators will turn up the lights so he can find his way.

≡ *Perhaps not since Oscar Hammerstein II piled up a string of flops in his drought years prior to hitching up with Richard Rodgers has a major figure in the Broadway musical theater hit such a dry spell as Harold Prince did in the 1980s, beginning with* Merrily We Roll Along *and continuing through a half-dozen oddball projects like* A Doll's Life. *He would return to form with* The Phantom of the Opera.

CATS
WINTER GARDEN THEATRE, OCTOBER 8, 1982

There's a reason why *Cats,* the British musical which opened at the Winter Garden last night, is likely to lurk around Broadway for a long time—and it may not be the one you expect.

It's not that this collection of anthropomorphic variety turns is a brilliant musical or that it powerfully stirs the emotions or that it has an idea in its head. Nor is the probable appeal of *Cats* a function of the publicity that has accompanied the show's every purr since it first stalked London seventeen months ago. No, the reason why people will hunger to see *Cats* is far more simple and primal than that: It's a musical that transports the audience into a complete fantasy world that could only exist in the theater and yet, these days, only rarely does. Whatever the other failings and excesses, even banalities, of *Cats,* it believes in purely theatrical magic, and on that faith it unquestionably delivers.

The principal conjurers of the show's spell are the composer Andrew Lloyd Webber, the director Trevor Nunn, and the designer John Napier. Their source material is T. S. Eliot's one volume of light verse, *Old Possum's Book of Practical Cats.* If the spirit of the Eliot poems is highly reminiscent of Edward Lear, the playful spirit of *Cats* is Lewis Carroll, refracted through showbiz. Mr. Nunn and Mr. Napier in particular are determined to take us to a topsy-turvy foreign universe from the moment we enter the theater, and they are often more extravagantly successful at that here than they were in the West End *Cats* or in their collaboration on *Nicholas Nickleby.*

Certainly the Winter Garden is unrecognizable to those who knew it when. To transform this house into a huge nocturnal junkyard for Eliot's flighty Jellicle cats, Mr. Napier has obliterated the proscenium arch, lowered the ceiling and stage floor, and filled every cranny of the place with a Red Groomsesque collage of outsized rubbish (from old Red Seal records to squeezed-out toothpaste tubes) as seen from a cat's-eye perspective. Well before the lights go down, one feels as if one has entered a mysterious spaceship on a journey through the stars to a cloud-streaked moon. And once the show begins in earnest, Mr. Napier keeps his Disneyland set popping until finally he and his equally gifted lighting designer, David Hersey, seem to take us through both the roof and back wall of the theater into an infinity beyond.

The cast completes the illusion. Luxuriantly outfitted in whiskers, electronically glowing eyes, masklike makeup, and every variety of feline costume—all designed by Mr. Napier as well—a top-notch troupe of American singer-dancers quickly sends its fur flying in dozens of distinctive ways. It's the highest achievement of Mr. Nunn and his associate director-choreographer, Gillian Lynne, that they use movement to give each cat its own personality even as they knit the entire company into a cohesive animal kingdom. (At other, less-exalted times, Mr. Nunn shamelessly recycles *Nickleby* business, as when he has the cast construct a train—last time it was a coach—out of found objects.)

The songs—and *Cats* is all songs—give each cat his or her voice. If there is a point to Eliot's cat cycle, it is simply that "cats are much like you and me." As his verses (here sometimes garbled by amplification) personify all manner of cat, so do the tuneful melodies to which Mr. Lloyd Webber has set them. The songs are often pastiche, but cleverly and appropriately so, and, as always with this composer, they have been orchestrated to maximum effect. Among many others, the eclectic musical sources include swing (for the busy Gumbie cat), rock (the insolent Rum Tum Tugger), Richard Rodgers–style Orientalism (a pack of Siamese), and Henry Mancini's detective-movie themes (Macavity, the Napoleon of crime).

But while the songs are usually sweet and well sung, *Cats* as a whole sometimes curls up and takes a catnap, particularly in Act 1. The stasis is not attributable to the music or the energetic cast, but to the entire show's lack of spine. While a musical isn't obligated to tell a story, it must have another form of propulsion (usually dance) if it chooses to do without one. As it happens, *Cats* does vaguely attempt a story, and it also aspires to become the first British dance musical in the Broadway tradition. In neither effort does it succeed.

If you blink, you'll miss the plot, which was inspired by some unpublished Eliot material. At the beginning the deity-cat, Old Deuteronomy (an owlishly ethereal Ken Page), announces that one cat will be selected by night's end to go to cat heaven—"the heaviside layer"—and be reborn. Sure enough, the only obvious candidate for redemption is chosen at the climax, and while the audience goes wild when the lucky winner finally ascends, it's because of Mr. Napier's dazzling *Close Encounters* spaceship, not because we care about the outcome of the whodunit or about the accompanying comic-book spiritualism.

As for Ms. Lynne's profuse choreography, its quantity and exuberance do not add up to quality. Though all the cat clawings and slitherings are wonderfully conceived and executed, such gestures sit on top of a repetitive array of jazz and ballet clichés, rhythmically punctuated by somersaults and leaps.

It's impossible not to notice the draggy passages in a long number like "The Jellicle Ball," or the missed opportunities elsewhere. To a tinkling new music-hall melody that Mr. Lloyd Webber has written for Mungojerrie and Rumpleteazer, Ms. Lynne provides only standard strutting. The stealthy Macavity number looks like shopworn Bob Fosse, and the battle of the Pekes and the Pollicles in Act 1 could be an Ice Capades reject. For the conjuring cat, Mr. Mistoffolees, Ms. Lynne's acrobatics never match the superhuman promise of either the lyrics or the outstanding soloist, Timothy Scott.

It's fortunate for *Cats* that Ms. Lynne is often carried by the production design and, especially, by her New York cast. At the risk of neglecting a few worthy names, let me single out such additional kitties as Anna McNeely's jolly Jennyanydots, Donna King's sinuous Bombalurina, Bonnie Simmon's tart Griddlebone, Reed Jones's railroad-crazed Skimbleshanks, and Harry Groener's plaintive Munkustrap. Aside from the dubious intermingling of British and American accents—which is not justified by the uniformly English references in the lyrics—the only real flaw in this large company is Terrence V. Mann's Rum Tum Tugger, who tries to imitate Mick Jagger's outlaw sexuality and misses by a wide mark.

By virtue of their songs, as well as their talent, there are two other performers who lend *Cats* the emotional pull it otherwise lacks. Stephen Hanan, singing Gus the Theater Cat to the show's most lilting melody, is a quivering bundle of nostalgia and dormant hamminess who touchingly springs back to life in an elaborate flashback sequence. (He also contributes a jolly cat about town, Bustopher Jones, earlier on.) To Betty Buckley falls the role of Grizabella the Glamour Cat and the task of singing "Memory," the Puccini-scented ballad whose lyrics were devised by Mr. Nunn from great noncat Eliot poems, notably "Rhapsody on a Windy Night." Not only does Ms. Buckley's coursing delivery rattle the rafters, but in her ratty, prostitute-like furs and mane she is a poignant figure of down-and-out catwomanhood.

One wishes that *Cats* always had so much feeling to go with its most inventive stagecraft. One wishes, too, that we weren't sporadically jolted from Eliot's otherworldly catland to the vulgar precincts of the video-game arcade by the overdone lightning flashes and by the mezzanine-level television monitors that broadcast the image of the offstage orchestra conductor (the excellent Stanley Lebowsky). But maybe it's asking too much that this ambitious show lift the audience—or, for that matter, the modern musical—up to the sublime heaviside layer. What *Cats* does do is take us into a theater overflowing with wondrous spectacle—and that's an enchanting place to be.

≡ Cats *went on to outrun* A Chorus Line, *becoming in 1997 the longest-running show in Broadway's history. It was also in retrospect the most influential Broadway production of its era, proving that there was a bottomless tourist audience for a show that pushed spectacle over content and that indeed required virtually no knowledge of English to be appreciated, whether by young children or foreign visitors. With ticket prices rising into the stratosphere, the success of* Cats *made it difficult for less-lavish musicals to compete. Audiences wanted to see where all their money went: Why—some theatergoers reasoned—should anyone pay the same high ticket price for a musical that didn't have a spaceship or a falling chandelier or a helicopter but only, say, good songs or provocative drama? The fallout eventually affected the commercial fortunes of straight plays on Broadway as well, since they found it harder and harder to compete for Broadway's increasingly dominant tourist audience. It could also be argued that* Cats *eventually led to Disney's arrival on Broadway, since it implicitly showed Disney the potential for exploiting cartoon animals—and the animated movies containing them—as stage musicals.*

By the late 1990s, there were some signs that the audience was tiring of a steady diet of lavish, kids-oriented musicals and would once again embrace flintier, lower-budget musicals relying more on imagination than machinery (Rent, Bring in 'da Noise Bring in 'da Funk, *the revival of* Chicago). *But then Disney's second Broadway musical,* The Lion King (1997)—*following the 1994* Beauty and the Beast—*pushed the pendulum back again. Disney's cats took the theatrical premise of* Cats *to an even more extravagant level and were as big a commercial hit.*

ANGELS FALL

CIRCLE REPERTORY COMPANY, OCTOBER 18, 1982

Sometimes I am amazed at how human everyone is," says the Roman Catholic priest (Barnard Hughes) at the center of Lanford Wilson's new play, *Angels Fall*. He may be amazed, but we're not. By now we've come to depend on Mr. Wilson's talent for finding the humanity in everyone he places on a stage, whether the setting be the Hotel Baltimore or the Talley family's Missouri farm. With equal depth, this writer can draw young people and old, men and women, Jews and Christians (both faithful and lapsed), hetero- and homosexuals, idealists and cynics. Mr. Wilson is one of the few artists in our theater who can truly make America sing.

Though *Angels Fall*, which opened at the Circle Repertory Company on Saturday night, is not a successful play, its unmistakable flaws are often drowned out by the moving sound of its author's tender, democratic voice. There are six Wilson characters on view in this work—all different, all fully realized in the writing and by the exquisite cast assembled by the director, Marshall W. Mason. One is grateful to be among them even if they've been brought together by dubious means.

We meet them in a sunbaked mission in remote, northwest New Mexico, where the priest, named Father Doherty, does his good works with the sometime aid of his unofficial foster son, an Indian (Danton Stone) who's soon to pursue a brilliant medical career. On the day *Angels Fall* unfolds, this tranquil sanctuary is invaded by two September-May couples. A psychologically unraveled, middle-aged Ivy League art-history professor (Fritz Weaver) arrives with the young wife (Nancy Snyder) who is taking him to a plush sanitarium in Phoenix. They're soon joined by a wealthy local widow (Tanya Berezin) and her new "boy toy" of a lover (Brian Tarantina), an aspiring tennis star.

What these people have in common is that they are all spiritually confused. What keeps them together for the length of the play is a device: A nuclear accident occurs in the midst of New Mexico's nearby atomic complex, trapping everyone in the mission for its duration. This premise allows Mr. Wilson to stage what is called "a little rehearsal for the end of the world" and to raise a biblical question: If the apocalypse is really around the corner, "what manner of person" are we all to be? *Angels Fall* is a series of debates and crises that propels each troubled character into making that choice.

The play's ailments, a few cheap jokes aside, are built in. Mr. Wilson can't escape the contrived nature of his plot gimmick; it seems like double overkill that his lost souls find themselves in both a real-life apocalypse and a church as they grapple with their crises of faith. And along with the locked-room format come the creaky conventions of the well-made play. The path from exposition to catharsis to resolution is too predictable; it's implausible as well as sentimental that all six characters would neatly arrive at individual epiphanies by the final curtain.

Yet the human spirits bottled up in the play's artificial enclosure are real. Mr. Wilson is a master at confounding our expectations about characters who, at first glance, might appear to be stereotypes. Initially, one might mistake Father Doherty for a typical Barnard Hughes leprechaun: He's a jolly, liberal clergyman who enjoys Top 40 radio music, tolerates profanity, and serves his visitors both jokes and lemonade. ("I love a tirade!" he sings, vaudeville-style, as his visitors argue.) But there are unmistakable creases of pain at the corners of Mr. Hughes's dancing eyes, and the playwright ultimately explains them by showing that even the good Father is capable of unsaintly vanity.

The others are no less surprising. Ms. Berezin's tough-minded widow (her husband was a celebrated artist) is buoyed by unexpected gusts of warmth and generosity. Mr. Tarantina's tennis pro is no petulant gigolo, but a likable, even farcical hypochondriac. Mr. Stone's Indian, torn between a future spent helping his needy people or a glamorous job in cancer research, first appears to be a hostile, self-righteous prig, then breaks out of that shell to emerge, paradoxically, as the play's foremost hero and biggest child.

Mr. Wilson's supreme achievement in this play, though, is the academic couple. The sad old professor, whose thirty-year career ended when he had a breakdown in mid-lecture, is a volatile mixture of dissipation, terminal self-doubts, and lingering intellectual arrogance. Having renounced his own scholarly works and the ivory tower that fostered them, he is left with only one belief—that "teaching is harmful." As played with a broken patrician voice, a sunken insomniac's face, and idly floppy hands by Mr. Weaver, he seems to embody all the glories and tragedies inherent in the academic life. His beautiful wife, a former student who became his keeper, is a paragon of self-composure and strength, but not so much so that she doesn't crack, however delicately, when her panicked husband tries to shove her, too, into his abyss.

Ms. Snyder, who hasn't worked nearly enough since she memorably created the role of the flipped-out heiress in the original Circle Rep production of *Fifth of July,* is the perfect, counterbalancing force to the dynamic Mr. Weaver. But the whole production is above reproach. Mr. Mason's staging suffuses *Angels Fall* with a mood of repose that reinforces the setting's serenity and suggests the ecstasy of inner peace that the characters seek. John Lee Beatty has designed a Spartan adobe mission of dreamlike radiance, and Dennis Parichy floods it with Southwestern light worthy of Georgia O'Keeffe. Even the finest details in Jennifer von Mayrhauser's costumes help distract us from the evening's larger failings. If you examine Mr. Weaver's flamboyant breast pocket handkerchief, you'll find that it is soiled yet fastidiously folded—a white flag of surrender that, like Mr. Wilson's fallen but salvation-hungry angels, can't quite give up the fight.

PLENTY
Public Theater, October 22, 1982

It's not until late in Act 2 that the audience hears the noise of breaking glass in David Hare's *Plenty*, but long before then, we've become terribly familiar with the harrowing sound of things going smash. A partial list of the evening's casualties would include at least three lives, one empire (the British), the egalitarian ideals of a generation, and many of the conventions of the traditional narrative play.

But if this sounds reckless, Mr. Hare is no indiscriminate vandal. Out of the bloody shards of the ruins, this young British playwright has meticulously erected an explosive theatrical vision of a world that was won and lost during and after World War II.

Plenty, which was first produced by England's National Theatre in 1978, received its New York premiere last night at the Public's Newman Theater, where it brings this stillborn theatrical autumn to stunning life. Like the original production, the current one has been directed by the author and stars Kate Nelligan. It couldn't be any other way. Working with a largely American cast, Mr. Hare has staged his work with a precise and chilling lyricism that perfectly complements his disquieting writing. As for Ms. Nelligan, the Canadian-born actress known for her screen role in *The Eye of the Needle,* mere adjectives are beside the point. Only a fool would hold his breath waiting to see a better performance this season.

The star, who is onstage throughout, plays Susan Traherne, an Englishwoman who, at seventeen, served as a courier for the French Resistance behind German lines. *Plenty* is about what happens to Susan during the war and in the two disillusioning decades to come. Convinced that the heroic values of the Resistance would carry over to the "New Europe" of peacetime, Susan soon finds herself traipsing through mindless jobs and destructive relationships in a declining England that is choking on "plenty" but has lost its moral rudder. Intolerant of both her society and intimates, she drifts into madness and takes her innocent, loving husband, a Foreign Service officer played by Edward Herrmann, down with her.

Mr. Hare tells Susan's tale in a dozen scenes that are ripped out of chronological order. His play's structure, which can be slightly confusing, employs flashback, flashforward, and in medias res. While it's a jigsaw puzzle that only comes together at the end, it's no gimmick: Mr. Hare has found a visceral theatrical embodiment for the central tension in his heroine's soul. The France of the 1940s is always as much in focus as the modern England of Suez and rampant commercialization; we constantly see each setting refracted through the other.

The liberated chronology also allows the author to crystallize his highly selective story and character details; he strips away psychological, plot, and ideological exposition to achieve a concentrated naturalism. Susan, like the Hedda Gabler she sometimes resembles (gun included), is an incandescent, troubling force who doesn't have to be explained away: We see her in context and she just is. As Ms. Nelligan says to Mr. Herrmann in their first meeting, "I tell you nothing—I just say look at me and make a judgment." That complicated judgment, which is ultimately asked from all of us, is the incendiary crux of the play.

The writing's jagged fractionalization further gives *Plenty* a hallucinatory, nightmarish quality that makes it feel more like a disorienting Nicolas Roeg film than John Osborne's *Look Back in Anger*. The mood of mystery is heightened by Nick Bicat's subtly ominous music and the superb physical production.

John Gunter's sets float like haunted Magritte rooms within the stage's walls, which are papered with a ghostly black-and-gray mural of a bygone romantic England. Jane Greenwood's costumes, meanwhile, anchor the characters in vivid social reality. The lighting designer, Arden Fingerhut, gives the gloom of contemporary London a remarkable variety of dreamlike textures even as she creates the dangerous, pulse-quickening glow of a nocturnal war-torn France where parachutes plummet from the stars.

The dialogue within each scene is often a tour de force interweaving subliminal rage, ellipses, and caustic wit. Mr. Hare doesn't waste words, and the ones he uses are crackling, whether they deal with the dreary English climate (even "passion comes down at you through a blocked nose") or the internecine politics of a Foreign Service that requires six thousand officers to dismantle an empire that once only took six hundred men to run. In the play's most remarkable scene—a diplomatic party in the midst of the Suez debacle—a grueling marital fight is blended in with an anguished political debate, comical small talk about an Ingmar Bergman film, and the hilarious malapropisms of a sycophantic Burmese ambassador (Conrad Yama).

The mostly exemplary supporting cast begins with Mr. Herrmann, who may be giving the performance of his career as Susan's husband, a moneyed, generous, self-reproachful man who sadly pursues his diplomatic calling because, as he plaintively asks, "What other world do I have?" His sputtering collapse is preceded by one brave and rending effort to break through his cheery reserve and jolt Susan back into reality.

No less brilliant is George Martin, who provides a tragic yet funny, Graham Greene-esque version of the farcical, fussbudget British bureaucrat he performed in Harold Pinter's *The Hothouse* last season. There is also flawless work from Ellen Parker as Susan's best friend, a bohemian who survives her alienation as the heroine does not, and from Daniel Gerroll, as an amiable working-class fellow who is pitifully gored by Susan's sexual manipulations.

Ms. Nelligan's performance can be admired in a multitude of ways: for its unflagging intensity, for its lack of mannerisms in delineating a neurotic character, for the seamlessness with which it blends the clear-eyed, rosy-cheeked Susan of seventeen with the feverish, slow-burning firecracker of a woman who follows. In the play's middle stretches—when she's tossing out sardonic wisecracks about her advertising copywriter's job or calmly plotting to have a child by a man she "barely knows"—the actress manages to show us how a deeply disturbed woman could appear completely lucid, even dazzlingly self-possessed.

Later on Ms. Nelligan provides "a psychiatric cabaret"—first when she lashes out with unprovoked obscenities at Mr. Herrmann in public circumstances, then when she levitates into drugged hysteria while meeting a revered but now pathetic old Resistance comrade (Kelsey Grammer) for a nostalgic assignation in a seedy Blackpool hotel room. Yet, as magnetic and moving as Ms. Nelligan is, she never neglects the selfishness and cruelty of a woman who makes the wrong people pay for the failings of a civilization.

That's important, because, in Mr. Hare's view, Susan is perhaps more responsible for those failings than anyone around her. If the author believes that idealists have a right to "a kind of impatience" with a world that betrays their noble, hard-won victories, he also seems to feel that Susan should have struggled anew for those ideals rather than "lose control" by giving in to bitterness and cynicism. And, of course, his perspective applies not only to World War II Resistance fighters, but also to the endless waves of defeated idealists who came before and after.

That's why the sharp edges of this relentlessly gripping play reach beyond its specific milieu to puncture our conscience. It's also why *Plenty* pointedly ends not with its heroine's defeat, but with a blazing tableau in which the young, innocent Susan of 1944 climbs a bucolic hill to "get a better view" of the newly liberated France that once promised her a utopian future. In *Plenty*, Mr. Hare asks that we, too, climb up to reclaim a "better view"—but not before he has shaken us violently at the bottom of that hill, not before he's forced us to examine just how we choose to live in our own world of plenty right now.

≡ *Though I would later get in a public brawl with David Hare—as recounted in "Exit the Critic"—I was one of his most fervent cheerleaders among New York drama critics.* Plenty *had a mixed reception and only a modest run when it transferred to Broadway.*

FOXFIRE
ETHEL BARRYMORE THEATRE, NOVEMBER 12, 1982

Jessica Tandy is the only real reason to consider seeing *Foxfire*, the play that opened last night at the Ethel Barrymore, but that's a reason to be taken seriously. Everything this actress does is so pure and right that only poets, not theater critics, should be allowed to write about her.

Here is one legendary performer who doesn't use her advanced years as an excuse to settle into a ritualistic star turn. Instead, she keeps refining a talent that has never, in my experience, been less than brilliant. In her last Broadway appearance, as Glenda Jackson's mother in a dull piece called *Rose*, Ms. Tandy only appeared in a single, quiet scene, yet she found more drama in the simple act of sitting in a chair and gripping her purse than most actors do in whole plays. The image is indelible for those who saw it, even though the rest of *Rose* has long since evaporated completely.

Foxfire also evaporates, but it gives Ms. Tandy more, if by no means enough, to do. The actress plays Annie Nations, a seventy-nine-year-old Appalachian matriarch at the crossroads of her past and future. Dressed in a shapeless black dress, her white hair up in a bun, this beautiful woman has made herself look unglamorous and plain, as befits a widow in Rabun County, Ga. Yet we keep getting caught up in the homely, finely spun details that can make the ordinary spellbinding—the delicate, sparrowlike hand-flutters that appear only when words won't do, the slightly stooped walk that one only gradually recognizes as arthritic and the face that's as smooth and tranquil and kindly as a baby's but that can suddenly draw up into a death mask of grief and fear.

And, even so, one isn't prepared for what Ms. Tandy does in a transcendent moment that shakes *Foxfire* out of its lethargy early in Act 2. Asked to jump back sixty-two years in a flashback—to the time Annie first was courted by her husband—the actress leaps high into the air, as lithe and controlled as a ballerina, and in a few jig steps shakes off all the layers of time she has previously cloaked about herself. My guess is that you could watch this moment again and again and not figure out the magic—call it art—by which Ms. Tandy instantly transforms an aged woman into a dewy girl.

If you want to see that moment once—and any student of acting would—you'll have to stomach a hard bargain. Inspired by the popular folklore anthologies of the same title, *Foxfire* was not so much written as pasted together by Ms. Tandy's costar and husband, Hume Cronyn, in collaboration with Susan Cooper. It's a patchwork job that makes the actual patchwork quilts on stage look like whole cloth by comparison. The kind-spirited contents include a halfhearted story, some mildly amusing down-home anecdotes about vanished folkways, and several modest country songs written by Jonathan Holtzman and sung by the guitar-strumming Keith Carradine, in the role of Mr. Cronyn and Ms. Tandy's prodigal son.

The story is so predictable that you can guess most of it as soon as Mr. Carradine and Trey Wilson, as a real-estate entrepreneur, descend on Annie Nations in the play's opening minutes. The son, a successful singer, wants to convince his mother to leave her isolated Blue Ridge mountain homestead and live with him and her grandchildren in Florida; the salesman wants to buy the old log cabin and develop the property. Should Annie Nations turn her back on the land that her husband and his father before that worked their whole lives? Has her son already sold out his heritage by becoming a show-business hillbilly? The threadbare conflict between tradition and progress is joined in a flash, soon to be elaborated on ad infinitum in regional dialect.

There are other complications, too, including the son's marital problems, but the whole story never really does get going; midway in Act 2, it peters out entirely until a sudden surge at the final curtain. What slows the evening further, until it plays like *The Waltons* under water whenever Ms. Tandy isn't around, are the playwriting gimmicks that inhibit such action as there is.

While *Foxfire* is loaded with flashbacks to fill in the Nations family past, they are usually too snapshotlike to mean much; they mainly serve to halt the present-day plot each time it summons the courage to lurch forward. The other dubious device is that Hector Nations, the father played by Mr. Cronyn, has been dead for five years when the play opens. Except in the splintery memory sequences, he appears as a ghostly narrator—a cross between the *Our Town* stage manager and Topper.

What this means is that Mr. Cronyn and Ms. Tandy can rarely have sustained scenes together in the play's present; a few delightfully tart exchanges aside, they often pass like ships in the night. This is a grievous loss that cheats the audience and both actors, especially when one recalls the fiery Cronyn-Tandy interplay in their past vehicles. In the longest scene the couple shares here, a flashback, Ms. Tandy must address Mr. Cronyn as Hector's corpse, stretched out on a table.

Mr. Cronyn's upright solo turns, laced with cracker-barrel vignettes and Tevye-like biblical quotations, are well done. The role is a Pa Kettle cliché—the set-in-his-ways, emotionally reticent, backwoods family autocrat—but the actor delivers his spiels with dyspeptic comic relish reminiscent of his work in *The Gin Game*. Though he can't redeem the homiletic lectures about the virtues of the land and "plain hard work," perhaps not even Gabby Hayes could.

Mr. Carradine's forced hail-fellow-well-met routine is journeyman acting. In smaller roles, the talents of Mr. Wilson and James Greene are underused; Katherine Cortez does nothing with the cryptically defined character of a schoolteacher, and, like everyone except Ms. Tandy and Mr. Wilson, has the wrong Southern twang.

David Trainer's direction, which puts great stock in repeated tableaux and the hokey uses of rocking chairs, takes us clear back past Golden Pond to Tobacco Road. Happily, the overly posed pictures are framed within an elaborate, weatherbeaten David Mitchell set, backed by shimmering blue green peaks, that indeed makes us believe that we are seeing what *Foxfire* calls "the most beautiful place in America."

But let Ms. Tandy step in front of the mountains, and we totally forget that any scenery is there.

SUNDAY ESSAY: WHAT AILS TODAY'S BROADWAY MUSICALS?
NOVEMBER 14, 1982

It seems like only a faint memory now, but there actually was a time when it was a joyous experience to go to a Broadway musical. You'd dash down Shubert Alley with the cocky assurance that you were in for a lift. There was the ecstatic anticipation of hearing a rousing overture, of feeling that electric charge that comes when the house lights dim, of watching the curtain rise on performers who would sing and dance their hearts out. And if the show proved to be *Bajour* instead of *My Fair Lady,* you wouldn't feel heartbroken, just disappointed. A bad musical could be laughed off like a junky movie.

Those pleasures have pretty much vanished in recent years. The most durable of American theatrical commodities, the escapist musical, has lost so much fizz that we've lived to see the once unimaginable day when a British musical, *Cats,* can steal Broadway's thunder. The great promise of the serious musical has atrophied to the point where the only one to be produced this season, *A Doll's Life,* can fold in five performances. What has brought both types of musical to a state of creative depletion is a steady retreat from fresh inspiration into an endless regurgitation of Broadway's past. What has dampened the excitement of going to nearly all musicals is a radical change in the musical theater's ambiance.

It's no longer a casual thing to go to a show when orchestra seats can go as high as forty-five dollars (for *Cats*) and even the "cheap" seats in the upper balcony (now known as the "rear mezzanine") can cost the equivalent of five first-run movie tickets. Nor can there be much spontaneity—the spontaneity that should distinguish live theater—when most musicals are ridiculously overproduced and overamplified. No matter how hard the performers work, their efforts come to us through a numbing fog of noise and glitter; though a strong star (such as Jim Dale in *Barnum*) can sometimes cut through the blare by sheer force of personality, weaker ones (such as Raquel Welch in *Woman of the Year*) can be reduced to robots.

Even the orchestra often isn't present in the pit anymore, but is piped in from backstage; other shows seem piped in in their entirety, since they play in cavernous modern auditoriums (the Minskoff and the Uris) best suited for ice hockey. To go to a musical these days is an anxiety-inducing rather than a lighthearted outing: You fear that your senses are going to be assaulted by electronic overkill and that your bank account will be taken for a ride.

The mood has become so heavy in Broadway houses that it may forever kill off the satirical or purely farcical musical comedy that only aims to make us laugh and hum. If *Guys and Dolls* or *A Funny Thing Happened on the Way to the Forum* were produced in today's theatrical environment, their effervescence would be smothered by the miking and synthesizers, the high ticket prices, the physical extravagance—all of which are antithetical to laughter. *42nd Street,* the foremost current example of an old-fashioned light musical on Broadway, has its virtues, but does anyone really find it giddy and carefree? It's so overwhelming a contraption that it exhausts rather than lifts the spirit.

No wonder that few people even attempt to write such shows for Broadway anymore. The unpretentious joys of the comic musical are best discovered and savored Off Broadway, as is the case with the current *Little Shop of Horrors*, a show that spreads simple delight in the way a *Pajama Game* or *Bells Are Ringing* once did uptown. Escapist musicals still exist on Broadway, but, occasional exceptions like *Annie* notwithstanding, they're mostly repackagings of old material rather than new works with fresh books and scores. If they're not stage adaptations of movie musicals (from *42nd Street* down to *Seven Brides for Seven Brothers*), then they're revivals of past Broadway hits or vintage songbook anthologies. The assumption seems to be that because we already know the jokes and tunes going into the theater, we'll respond by Pavlovian habit. Appropriately enough, even the laughter and applause can sound canned as they waft through the electronic din.

It's in this context that *Cats* is different. Uneven as this Americanized British import may be, it does posit a new approach to the escapist musical. Rather than pretend that the old theatrical rules still apply in this time of big money and high-tech mechanics, the creators of *Cats* have gone ahead and conceded that the spectacle is the show. The effects aren't grafted on to otherwise conventional settings to create glitzy, decorative stage pictures, as they are in most other big-budget musicals—they're used instead to create a whole new theatrical environment.

The strategy works in *Cats* to the extent that it does because the spectacle is often wondrously conceived. John Napier's set is not just a huge expenditure of money—though it's certainly that—but it's also a transporting piece of artistic ingenuity. Rather than merely decorate the Winter Garden, the designer has turned a proscenium house into a disorienting fantasy world that keeps our eyes constantly on the move, that takes us into a feline universe that's reinforced by the costumes, performers, and T. S. Eliot verses. Perspectives are altered with a daring that makes Broadway's previous free-flowing musical spectacles (*Hair* or the 1973 *Candide*) seem timid; even the stage walls and auditorium ceiling seem to be obliterated. If only *Cats* had a dramatic shape and choreography as bold as the physical production and as buoyant as the cast and score, the whole show might have lifted off in an orbit new to the musical theater.

At the same time, it's possible that the techniques of *Cats* won't be refined in the future, but coarsened. When this show uses its special effects for their own vulgar sake, rather than to create its cat's-eye environment—as it does in the climactic appearance of a *Close Encounters* spaceship—one sees how this kind of entertainment could disintegrate into the theatrical answer to a videogame or the most soulless imitation Spielberg-Lucas movies.

The successors to *Cats* may cross that line more often, by fashioning special-effects musicals that squeeze out music, performers, and dance entirely. The recent, short-lived *Rock 'n' Roll! The First 5,000 Years* took a step down that path. In that revue, some extremely clever and well-executed multimedia spectacles dominated the stage to such an extent that they completely dwarfed the performers. You felt as if you were watching a projection television screen or an entirely automated Disneyland exhibit—not that you were at the theater. Only at the curtain call, when the slide shows stopped, did the cast come out from under the electronic shroud to make direct human contact with the audience; it was as if suddenly someone opened a door to let in a gust of fresh air.

Maybe the possible proliferation of such shows wouldn't be so troubling a prospect if the serious Broadway musical (or the concept musical, or whatever one chooses to call it) were in healthy shape. If we could believe that a new *West Side Story* or *Fiddler on the Roof* or *Company* were waiting in the wings, it might be easier to tolerate an onslaught of video-arcade extravaganzas: The two types would counterbalance each other just as Billy Rose's *Jumbo* might once have coexisted with *Porgy and Bess*. But as *Cats* has pointed a potentially dangerous direction for future escapist musicals, so the season's other lavish Broadway musical, the short-lived *A Doll's Life,* is a poignant dramatization of the bankruptcy that now threatens the serious musical theater.

A Doll's Life was a sincere effort, created primarily by three people—the director Harold Prince, the librettists Betty Comden and Adolph Green—who owe no apologies, for they have done more than most to enliven the Broadway musical since World War II. Their brave notion this time was to write an operetta-like sequel to *A Doll's House.*

Yet once again one immediately wondered why such a musical should have been so elaborately mounted. No one would produce a revival of the Ibsen play with huge, towering sets and amplification; to do that with a purported sequel seemed a decadent contradiction in terms. It was no surprise that the overproduction of *A Doll's Life* led only to overblown and counterproductive Pirandellian staging conceits that seemed more designed to keep the machinery busy than to enlighten or move an audience.

What was most distressing about *A Doll's Life,* though, was not its extravagance or even its failures of artistry. The real question raised by this musical—and by many other similarly ambitious recent musicals—is whether it was really serious, or merely pretentious. To write a show in 1982 that espouses a primerlike feminist credo—as if feminism had only entered the public mind yesterday—seems, in its own way, a form of escapism (and not even an entertaining form at that). Why should sophisticated theatergoers be hectored as if they'd never previously heard of such notions as equal pay for equal work or a woman's right to the same sexual satisfaction as men? However pure the intentions, such heavy-handed preaching of received ideas can strike an audience as condescension.

If this confusion of attitudinizing with weighty content seems familiar, it's because it has also muddied other latter-day Prince musicals, many of which were rich in theatrical merits. The 1976 *Pacific Overtures* was implicitly an attack on the United States involvement in Southeast Asia, but it was produced almost a decade too late—long after the Vietnam War had been rejected by most of the American public. The show's strident, accusatory finale ended an often adventurous work on an unjustified, holier-than-thou note. In *Evita*, the audience is angrily addressed by the narrator, Che Guevara, as if it were somehow responsible for the Perón regime's rise to power—or as if fascist Argentine history were a cautionary tale directly applicable to our own society. Since the librettist, Tim Rice, never successfully made this case—he just presented it as axiomatic—the supposedly important message of *Evita* became frivolous.

A similar kind of scattershot guilt-mongering also needlessly damaged *Sweeney Todd*, a musical whose Stephen Sondheim score is one of the great treasures of Broadway history. By inflating a Dickensian tale to cosmic proportions, the enormous production seemed to imply that the audience were guilty of the Victorian injustices that led to Sweeney's murderous acts of revenge. Might not the hero's tragedy have better stood simply and intimately on its own? The answer could be found last month on cable television, where *Sweeney Todd* proved far more moving and biting once the camera had stripped away the original production's elaborate, overpopulated Brechtian effects.

Mr. Prince is not the only one who indulges in superficial seriousness in the musical theater; he's merely left holding the bag because he's most strenuously set the fashion. In *Nine*, the highly inventive Tommy Tune staging and lovely Maury Yeston music sit on top of a libretto that purports to describe a film director's emotional breakdown but in fact does nothing of the kind. One would be hard-pressed to argue that any of this show's many female characters, who are ostensibly the dominant figures in its hero's troubled psyche, amounts to more than a camp cartoon.

In *Nine*, like nearly every musical on Broadway, we also find the other major form of déjà vu in the current musical theater: the incessant recycling of directorial ideas. Mr. Tune has come up with many original sequences for this show, but nonetheless the most Felliniesque pageant he offers, the *Casanova* opera parody, is strongly reminiscent of the surreal (and brilliant) "Loveland" sequence of Mr. Prince's 1971 *Follies*. (In both shows, a monochromatic set is suddenly filled with color, as a gaudy show-within-the-show drops down to resolve the story's emotional conflicts through fantasy.) In *Cats*, the English director Trevor Nunn harks back to Mr. Prince's 1973 *Candide*, just as his staging of *Nicholas Nickleby* owed something to both *Candide* and *Sweeney Todd*.

Since everyone else is cannibalizing Mr. Prince, it perhaps only follows that he would do the same: *Evita, Sweeney Todd,* and *A Doll's Life* are at times indistinguishable from one another in terms of staging. How one wishes that this director, who did so much to destroy the clichés of musical staging that existed on Broadway when he began his career, would once again leap ahead of the fray. His innovations of the 1960s and early 1970s have now become as calcified as the conventions he once helped overthrow.

There are some bright spots. One major director of Broadway musicals who has avoided most of his peers' traps is the Michael Bennett of *Dreamgirls*. (This wasn't always true of Mr. Bennett, whose *A Chorus Line* dipped back into *Follies*, on which he had collaborated with Mr. Prince.) Like it or hate it, *Dreamgirls* doesn't look like any other show. It doesn't use its mechanized production to create overelaborate, gilded versions of otherwise routine pictorial sets but instead to create an ever-changing abstract space that allows the staging the freedom of fast, innovative movement. *Dreamgirls* also avoids the potential pitfalls of its content, which deals with black singers who sell their souls to cross over into mainstream white American show business. Rather than glibly point a finger at the audience to blame it for all the mishaps that befall the characters, this show eschews knee-jerk rhetoric and suggests that the people on stage are at least partially responsible for their own anguish.

In addition to *Dreamgirls*, what also gives one some hope for the musical is that Mr. Prince and Mr. Tune, like Mr. Bennett, do try to work with new performers and new writers in their shows. *Dreamgirls, A Doll's Life,* and *Nine* all had relative unknowns in at least some of their principal roles; in each of their last three productions, Mr. Bennett and Mr. Tune have employed composers and librettists new to Broadway.

This is essential, because, without the push of superstar directors, producers are unlikely to gamble $4 million budgets on the young, untried talents who might help recharge the writing of musicals. One hopes, too, that these directors might try to restore dance to the serious musical—*Dreamgirls, A Doll's Life,* and *Nine* all have scant choreography—even as they search for truly meaty and contemporary themes to build their shows around.

Yet all such efforts will be for naught if the musical theater's artists don't take charge of the new Broadway technology before it takes charge of them. The impact of that technology has been so pervasive that it even has changed the way we listen to Broadway original cast albums. A show record used to be an adjunct to the show itself—a tool for re-creating an exciting theatrical night in the mind's eye. Today, one often finds oneself listening to an original cast album to get the theatrical experience that one missed in the first place: The scores and performances of many present-day musicals seem much more immediate and intimate when heard on a stereo at home than when encountered in the daunting, over-busy productions that encumber them in the flesh.

That equation must be reversed. If theatergoers are to dash to musicals with exuberance again, we'll have to be reconvinced that Broadway is a street of human dreams, and not just another conveyor belt ushering our culture into the no man's land of future shock.

84 CHARING CROSS ROAD
NEDERLANDER THEATRE, DECEMBER 8, 1982

After seeing *84 Charing Cross Road,* the tiny divertissement that opened at the Nederlander Theatre last night, you don't feel as if you've been to the theater, but to afternoon tea. For nearly two hours, two fine actors, Ellen Burstyn and Joseph Maher, stand at either side of the stage and recite good-natured, sporadically amusing, utterly innocuous letters that were once written between a struggling New York writer named Helene Hanff and a London antiquarian book dealer named Frank Doel. Although Ms. Burstyn does take the radical step of crossing from her side of the stage to Mr. Maher's at play's end, this is mostly an evening of sedentary gentility.

To put it another way, *84 Charing Cross Road* is a staged reading that's been tricked-up into a Broadway production by the casting of a star and by the erection of an imposing Oliver Smith set. Fans of its source material—Ms. Hanff's slight and breezy epistolary memoir of 1970—will probably delight in the faithfulness with which the adapter, James

Roose-Evans, has brought it to the stage. Audiences in search of a play offering genuine emotional or intellectual stimulation or even steady laughter are likely to find that this sketch fails to satisfy, and that its modest nontheatrical charms wear thin fast.

Being ungrateful for this trifle is, I realize, like being against Christmas. Its subject is the love of literature. The self-schooled Ms. Hanff, a would-be playwright turned television scenarist, wrote her letters to order second-hand books from Mr. Doel and his firm of Marks & Co. over a two-decade span ending in 1969. Those books were the best—from Plato to Woolf—and Ms. Hanff cherished their "soft vellum and heavy cream-colored pages." Mr. Doel responded to her requests with alacrity and would have a seizure if his demanding customer were mistakenly sent, say, an abridged Pepys diary instead of the complete text.

But, a few mild digressions about John Donne aside, the talk in this play is not literary; it's about the quaint, bygone rituals of personalized mail-order commerce. If its heroine were ordering duck shoes from L.L. Bean, *84 Charing Cross Road* would not be much different—though it might have to be retitled *Freeport, Maine 04033*. All that would be lost would be the Anglophilic and bibliophilic cachet, and that loss would bring a welcome gain in unpretentiousness. The vacuous lip service this play pays to the joys of England's literary heritage is no more than fancy name-dropping. *84 Charing Cross Road* is high-minded but resolutely nonintellectual—a play for those who get more pleasure out of owning handsome old books than reading them.

The superficial plot that strings together the book orders is a platonic version of Ms. Burstyn's last Broadway vehicle, *Same Time, Next Year*: A cross-cultural affection develops between the two correspondents over the years. Ms. Hanff is a sassy eccentric, eager to "puncture that proper British reserve" of her book dealer. She succeeds quickly, with situation-comedy results. Helene and Frank drop the formalities and use each other's first names; they share holiday presents and family news, happy occasions and sad ones; they take to using the colloquial expressions of each other's native form of English. But they never do meet and have a scene together.

With imagination, *84 Charing Cross Road* could have offered more than its saccharine hands-across-the-sea sentiments and leather-binding fetishism. Why couldn't Mr. Roose-Evans have dramatized the characters in his heroine's life, even if he had to fictionalize to do so? We never learn why Helene Hanff is presented as a near dipsomaniac, or why she calls her bookseller "the only soul alive who understands me." Does she have family, lovers, a psychiatrist? And why are Frank's much-talked-about wife and children kept offstage even as we watch six other actors traipse through Marks & Co. in forgettable walk-on roles? Though it may work on the printed page to see the two characters frozen at their respective desks, the method looks like a lazy contrivance in the theater.

About the most energetic change that Mr. Roose-Evans has made in Ms. Hanff's book is the removal of the comma that followed the street number in her title. He also emphasizes the calendar-marking historical events and adds a shamelessly tear-jerking final monologue, featuring a prized rubber duck, that may make your skin crawl. The adapter's staging is a lulling—some may call it civilized—game of theatrical Ping-Pong that sends us rhythmically back and forth between Marks & Co. and Ms. Hanff's various New York dwellings.

Because of the play's constricted form, both lead actors face the trap of sinking into cute stand-up routines. Ms. Burstyn, to this fan's amazement, falls into it. She is, as always, a forceful presence, even with a dangling cigarette, bohemian clothes, and ratty wigs. Her timing of her caustic one-liners is expert—maybe too expert. With excessive hand gestures and winks, she sometimes indicates just where she'd like us to laugh or applaud. It would help if she had better jokes—too much is made of her dental problems and mispronunciation of British names—and could play to another actor instead of some indeterminate point in the balcony.

Long a specialist at portraying fuddy-duddy Englishmen, Mr. Maher is in top form: Pink-faced and silver-haired, he is so stiff-upper-lipped that he seems to be sucking on a lemon in the early scenes. Later, he is a warm and wooly English clerk of a benign Dickensian sort—and, finally, a weary old man who ages more effectively without cosmetic aids than his costar does with them. You may well enjoy seeing what Mr. Maher is up to here, but the time will pass faster if you bring along a good book.

≡ *The back-to-back success of* Amadeus, Nicholas Nickleby, *and* Cats *led to a run of Broadway Anglophilia that knew few bounds. Any minor London success was imported, usually with dire results. Serious plays like Pam Gems's* Piaf *and C. P. Taylor's* Good *both failed, even with their well-received Royal Shakespeare Company lead actors (Jane Lapotaire and Alan Howard, respectively), and so did light comedies like* 84 Charing Cross Road, Stepping Out, *and* Steaming *with American stars. The most talented English playwrights—David Hare, Caryl Churchill, Tom Stoppard, Simon Gray—fared better, more often than not Off Broadway.*

ALICE IN WONDERLAND
VIRGINIA THEATRE, DECEMBER 24, 1982

If there's any philanthropist around who's still frantically shopping for a present to give New York City this Christmas, his worries are now over. At Broadway's Virginia Theatre, there is an exquisite collection of scenery and costumes that must be preserved for the delight of future generations of children—no matter what the cost.

This isn't a joke. In the otherwise flat revival of the Eva Le Gallienne *Alice in Wonderland* which opened last night, the set designer John Lee Beatty and the costume designer Patricia Zipprodt have done an extraordinary job of bringing to life the celebrated storybook illustrations of Lewis Carroll's collaborator, John Tenniel. Virtually every Tenniel drawing has been rendered to the stage perfectly intact—from the ugly Duchess's kitchen to the Mad Tea Party to the Queen of Hearts' croquet ground to the flock of fowl gathered for the caucus race.

As befits the demands of the theater, the images are now large, three-dimensional, and, with the help of the gifted lighting designer Jennifer Tipton, splashed with color. But the artisans at work have not vulgarized the originals: They've exercised tremendous care and good taste. Every detail is in place—even the curls of line on the sole of Humpty Dumpty's shoe—and all are lovely. For the Walrus and the Carpenter, we even get huge puppets (by a firm called The Puppet People), which are soon surrounded by lively smaller puppets taking the parts of dancing oysters. How wonderful it would be if this Victorian fantasy world were placed on permanent display in, say, the Cooper-Hewitt Museum.

As for the rest of the show at the newly refurbished Virginia, I'm sorry to say that there's nothing worth saving except Ms. Le Gallienne's very brief appearance as the White Queen in the second act. Something has gone terribly wrong with this sweet mission to restore the pageant that was first performed triumphantly by the Civic Repertory Company a half-century ago and that was successfully revived in 1947. Even the beautiful physical trappings can't long prevent us from noticing that the current incarnation of *Alice in Wonderland* is lifeless nearly from beginning to end.

The problem is not in the adaptation that Ms. Le Gallienne wrote with Florida Friebus way back when. It is a scrupulously faithful tour of the most cherished vignettes in the two Alice books. Like its source material, the text is episodic, indeed plotless, but even on stage that's a surmountable difficulty. One assumes it was surmounted on the previous occasions by a marshaling of all the theatrical energy that this version lacks.

The first deficiency presents itself as soon as the curtain rises—Alice herself. Kate Burton, who plays the part, is a well-spoken, hardworking young actress dressed to resemble her literary counterpart. But by no fantastical stretch of the imagination does she have the dazzling personal charm or even the warmth that might draw an audience closely to her or that might suggest a heroine with "pure unclouded brow and dreaming eyes of wonder." Nor does Ms. Burton as yet have the skills that might allow her to vary her performance from one scene to the next. She is earnest but boring—a deadly mix in the starring role of a big Broadway show, especially when that role is the only one to turn up in every single scene.

The other mishaps have to do with the staging and the supporting cast. Except for the puppets, a cameo appearance by a trained pig, and Ms. Le Gallienne's airborne arrival, there are no surprises the entire evening. Nearly every scene is identical: The lights come up to reveal Mr. Beatty's and Ms. Zipprodt's imaginative handiwork, and then the whole tableau remains frozen in place for a seeming eternity, like a department store window, until it's time for the next set to glide on.

The actors rarely move: They just model the costumes. And while they do indeed speak the famous Carroll words, they do so in a remote, disembodied way, as if the audience were not being invited to travel through the looking glass, but instead to look at Wonderland under the looking glass. The show isn't twenty minutes old before one is consulting the *Playbill* to count up how many scenes there are to go before it's time to go home. Children in the audience may well opt for sleep.

While there are some excellent comic actors in view—including John Heffernan, Mary Louise Wilson, and MacIntyre Dixon—none of them breaks through the torpor for more than ten seconds. They make the measliest attempt to create the topsy-turvy, caricatured human beings that their witty lines and outfits suggest. Ms. Le Gallienne, a vision in white and silver with clown makeup and chalky voice to match, fares better: The only real laugh comes when she tells Alice, "Never jam today!" It's almost but not quite enough to make us overlook the fact that this giant of the American theater shares responsibility for the direction with John Strasberg.

According to a letter the production's management sent to the press this week, various other unbilled hands have visited *Alice* during previews to add "flow" and choreography to the enterprise. It's hard to imagine what they contributed, since there's no flow and next to no dancing. On the brighter side, Richard Addinsell's slight but pretty score has been attractively "adapted" by Jonathan Tunick. This proves of little avail, however, when one discovers that not a single member of the company can sing.

Let's just call it a sad day in Wonderland. A white knight couldn't rescue the Gryphon and the Mock Turtle and all the other endangered species at the Virginia soon enough.

≡ *Eva Le Gallienne (1899–1991) was not just a great actress but one of the true heroes of the American theater, in essence inventing the whole idea of Off Broadway with her adventurous, high-minded Civic Repertory Company in the Greenwich Village of the late 1920s. In the early 1960s she barnstormed the country with her American Repertory Theatre, playing in modern classics like* The Sea Gull *and Jean Anouilh's* Ring Round the Moon. *The houses were small, but surely I wasn't the only young theatergoer who first saw such plays in Le Gallienne's productions.*

In 1981, two years before this ill-fated Alice, *she had appeared to great acclaim from me and Walter Kerr in the starring role of* To Grandmother's House We Go, *but the play was weak and the run was only two months. The poignant behind-the-scenes story of how* Alice *got away from Le Gallienne—who took on more than she could handle at age eighty-three and didn't trust her young collaborators—is told in Helen Sheehy's 1996 biography,* Eva Le Gallienne.

TOP GIRLS

PUBLIC THEATER, DECEMBER 29, 1982

In the long-running *Cloud 9,* her first play to be seen in New York, the English playwright Caryl Churchill turned our usually well-ordered theatrical universe topsy-turvy. She sent her cast leaping in and out of two centuries and continents, three genders, and even one another's roles. Whatever the effort's flaws, it was always the product of a strikingly original and supple imagination. You could feel the author's bracing determination to liberate both the theater and the audience from every esthetic and sexual shackle in sight.

Ms. Churchill's newest play, which journeyed intact from London to the Public's Newman Theater last night, is no match for its predecessor, but, happily, it is every bit as intent on breaking rules. The work's title is

Top Girls, and its protagonist, Marlene (Gwen Taylor), is the newly named managing director of the Top Girls Employment Agency in contemporary London. In an opening scene that is almost beyond daring, Marlene throws a dinner party to celebrate her promotion. The setting is a trendy Anglo-Italian restaurant called La Prima Donna. The guests, it could be said, are all dead.

The women joining Marlene for white wine and pasta are none other than real and fictional prima donnas of the past: Isabella Bird, a Victorian explorer; Lady Nijo, a medieval Oriental concubine turned pioneering Buddhist nun; Dull Gret, the armor-plated woman who led a female charge through hell in Brueghel's painting *Dulle Griet;* Pope Joan, who may have presided briefly over the Vatican in the ninth century; and Chaucer's Patient Griselda. Dressed in their appropriate historical outfits (amusingly designed by Pam Tait), these women chattily compare notes and laud their hostess on her new success. Such is Ms. Churchill's great gift for making the illogical both human and plausible that we quickly forget that we're in a time-warped cloud-cuckoo-land.

The wild tricks of *Top Girls* don't end there. Though we never see Marlene's party guests again, other surprises follow as Ms. Churchill gets to the main business of her play, which is primarily a realistic probing of Marlene's rise to the top at Top Girls. The actresses in the company keep popping up in new roles; the setting switches abruptly and at first inexplicably between London and a dreary working-class home in provincial Suffolk; the evening ends with a scene that predates the rest of the action by a year. Ms. Churchill also makes abundant use of overlapping, intentionally indecipherable dialogue, Robert Altman–style, as well as of lengthy pauses and stage waits that would make any Pinter play seem as frantic as a Marx Brothers sketch by comparison.

One cannot be too thankful for all these brave gambles, the strangely compelling and somehow moving silences included. Ms. Churchill sees the theater as an open frontier where lives can be burst apart and explored, rather than as a cage that flattens out experience and diminishes it. Because of the startling technique and several passages of dazzling writing, *Top Girls* is almost always fascinating, even when it is considerably less than involving.

Some of the play's slippage does occur, it's true, when Ms. Churchill's experiments run on self-indulgently. It seems unduly perverse that almost every scene must trail off before ending. The fantasy prologue, fun as it may be, is seriously overlong; later on, the author has trouble resisting the urge to lecture. Yet the major difficulty in *Top Girls* is a matter of content, not form. To these male American ears, Ms. Churchill's new statement about women and men seems far more simplistic and obvious than the fervent pansexuality of *Cloud 9*.

The message announces itself in that first scene, which proves an almost anthropological search for the ties that bind history's strongest sisters. Like Marlene, the famous icons at her table are "top girls"—courageous women who have "come a long way" by accomplishing "extraordinary achievements." But they've all paid a price for success: They've sacrificed their personal lives and children, been abused by men, and lost contact with women who did not become "top girls." And we soon learn that Marlene, the present-day inheritor of their hard struggles for independent womanhood, is worse off yet. In order to fight her way up from her backwater proletarian roots to the executive suite, she has become, figuratively speaking, a male oppressor.

When we watch Marlene's chillingly antiseptic agency in action, we quickly see that it is designed to coach its female clients into adopting the most odious male traits and values: the steely selfishness and aggression that ostensibly propel one forward in the Darwinist business world. Marlene's own emotional and sexual life is as barren as Lady Macbeth's—she pointedly recoils at the mere mention of the word "gynecology." She's even abandoned her illegitimate and dull-witted daughter (Carole Hayman), leaving her sister to raise the girl as her own child instead.

Marlene treats women of lower social status—from the waitress at La Prima Donna to her clients and family—as callously as any man might; she chastises the working class she's left behind as "lazy and stupid." Finally, she even consigns her tubby, misfit daughter to the social junk heap by coldly remarking, "She's a bit thick—a bit funny. She's not going to make it." To Marlene, the ability to make it by male success standards is the only criterion of female worth.

No one can deny that women like Marlene exist. As Ms. Churchill ultimately makes too clear, her heroine is partly a caricature of the ultimate British "top girl," Prime Minister Margaret Thatcher. But the playwright seems to beg her complicated issues by showing us only her monstrous heroine at one extreme, and, at the other, the victimized women that the Marlenes of this world exploit and betray. The absence of the middle range—of women who achieve without imitating power-crazed men and denying their own humanity—is an artificial polemical contrivance that cuts the play off at the heart. We're never quite convinced that women's choices are as limited and, in the play's final word, "frightening" as the stacked case of *Top Girls* suggests. Even in England, one assumes, not every woman must be either an iron maiden or a downtrodden serf.

Still, we're often carried along by the author's unpredictable stage-craft, her observant flashes of angry wit and pathos. Among the best moments are the brief and scabrously sketched interview sessions with the pathetic clients at Top Girls and the affecting final confrontation between Marlene and her nonachieving sister (Deborah Findlay). Under the sensitive direction of Max Stafford-Clark, the entire play is perfectly acted by the tight-knit ensemble, led by Ms. Taylor's vibrant and not wholly unsympathetic Marlene. Lindsay Duncan is particularly delightful as a blonde Lady Nijo. Selina Cadell is wry and sad as both Pope Joan and a present-day corporate middle-manager—both women who passed as men to advance their careers, then met with tragic ends.

The production at the Public has been transported from the adventurous Royal Court Theatre, under a laudable new exchange program. The run is limited to a month with this cast. However trying *Top Girls* can be, that doesn't alter the fact that New Yorkers have a rare but brief opportunity to see a brand-new work by an important English playwright in its original staging. Everything considered, it might well be wise to catch what Ms. Churchill is up to while you can and quarrel with her later.

QUARTERMAINE'S TERMS
Long Wharf Theatre, New Haven, January 7, 1983

If Humpty Dumpty were shaped like a cigar, he might look like Remak Ramsay in the Long Wharf Theatre's production of Simon Gray's *Quartermaine's Terms*. Mr. Ramsay—tall, rail-thin, a bit baldish—has the innocent, eggy smile of a baby and seems just as fragile. He tends to perch himself precariously on a soiled, green easy chair, and we keep worrying that someone will shove him to the floor. We know that once that push comes Mr. Ramsay is certain to break.

The actor is playing St. John Quartermaine, an instructor at a downtrodden but proud school that teaches English to foreigners in Cambridge, England. We never meet any of the students, but surely none of them could be as lost as Quartermaine. A bachelor of endless good cheer and limited brain power, he has a tendency to doze off in mid-conversation, to drift away early from his own classes, to miss the punch line of any joke. But he's one of those benign fellows who can be carried on indefinitely by arcane British institutions. Though professionally incompetent, Quartermaine is unfailingly polite, loyal, and undemanding. Except when he's needed to serve as a last-minute baby-sitter or dinner companion, no one even notices whether he's present in the school staff room, where the play is set.

The character is also a departure for both actor and author. Long a specialist at playing strong-willed, stiff-upper-lip protagonists—most recently in *The Winslow Boy* and *The Dining Room*—the extraordinarily precise Mr. Ramsay proves here that he can be just as effective as a retiring, ineffectual loser. For Mr. Gray, this teacher is quite a switch from the central figures of *Butley* and *Otherwise Engaged*. Though Quartermaine shares Butley's profession and is indeed otherwise engaged, he is as inarticulate and slow-witted as his predecessors were caustic and brilliant. But this hasn't prevented Mr. Gray from dramatizing him with his customary fine care.

As for *Quartermaine's Terms*, which was first seen in London under Harold Pinter's direction in 1981, it is a casual, minor-key Gray play that proves consistently entertaining. At the Long Wharf's intimate Stage II, the director Kenneth Frankel has given it an endearing and unusually well-cast production. If the script is a string of gentle anecdotes, a few of which are contrived, the wit and feeling of the writing and acting give *Quartermaine's Terms* the texture of a poignant, delicate novella.

The anecdotes unfold over a roughly three-year period in the early 1960s. Mr. Gray does not center the play on Quartermaine but devotes equal attention to all his colleagues. It's a sad group, because, as we're told, "teaching foreigners is a job for failures." One teacher (Kelsey Grammer) is a bitter, would-be novelist whose unrealized fantasies of fame have driven away his wife and son. Another (Dana Ivey) is a sexless matron chained to an invalid mother. The others must cope with sadnesses ranging from a troubled child to a philandering husband to financial disappointment. The school is run by a pair of elderly homosexuals, only one of whom is onstage and both of whom are in declining health.

Mr. Gray charts the emotional ups and downs of this unofficial family and their institution in lightly sketched strokes. By the end, a lot has happened—deaths, marriages, births, heated rows—but little has changed. For all his Waughian sideswipes, the author seems to have an affectionate regard for the school: It may be useless, but at least it provides a comfortable haven for lost souls. Yet Mr. Gray knows that even in England, progress must come, however slowly. In *Quartermaine's Terms,* the tiniest breeze of change may prove enough to propel Quartermaine into extinction.

The play is at its weakest when the playwright pulls at our heartstrings too tenaciously by piling up a large number of offstage, between-scenes tragedies. It's at its considerable best when the calamities are funny—

such as when a group of Japanese students runs amok in a local French restaurant, or when the police show up to investigate the case of a murdered swan, or when Quartermaine appears incongruously in evening clothes simply because he had come across them in an old suitcase. The actors have a field day throughout, not in the least because all the characters except Mr. Ramsay's gain in complexity as the play unfolds.

Ms. Ivey, so amusing as George C. Scott's brittle secretary in *Present Laughter* on Broadway, is wonderfully dotty as she slowly transforms herself from a dowdy middle-aged drudge into an eccentric religious hysteric. Anthony Heald is at his farcical best as an accident-prone new teacher who somehow lands on his feet after his every physical or personal mishap. But everyone does well, including Mr. Grammer, Caroline Lagerfelt as the insecure teacher with the roving husband, Roy Poole as the officious but not unsympathetic coheadmaster, and John Cunningham as a faculty boor who isn't entirely as silly as he first appears.

Next to these relatively strong personalities, Mr. Ramsay's Quartermaine could pass for a piece of furniture: He's a vacuum defined by the others. No matter how many lives fall apart in front of him or how much his supposed friends selfishly exploit his good nature, he remains oblivious to it all, choosing instead to hide behind the inane and ritualistic manners of the anachronistic English gentleman. But Mr. Gray and Mr. Ramsay convince us that nonentities are people, too. While Quartermaine may look and act like a fool, we never doubt that somewhere within that hollow-looking shell hides a lonely man, bleeding.

'NIGHT, MOTHER
AMERICAN REPERTORY THEATRE,
CAMBRIDGE, MASS., JANUARY 12, 1983

It seems like just an ordinary night in an ordinary house in some ordinary Middle American neighborhood. Jessie Cates (Kathy Bates) and Thelma (Anne Pitoniak), her widowed mother, are rattling around their living room, getting ready for another evening of dinner, crocheting, and idle talk. But only a few minutes into Marsha Norman's new play, *'night, Mother,* Jessie makes a calm but shattering announcement. "I'm going to kill myself, Mom," she says.

Though Thelma at first prefers to disbelieve her ears, her daughter isn't kidding. Jessie is all packed and ready to go. She's made a list of things to do before she shoots herself: She wants to teach her mother how to work the washing machine, to eat a last caramel apple, to get the real lowdown on her parents' marriage. The list isn't long, however, and in ninety minutes Jessie has taken care of every item. By the time the play reaches its inevitable climax, death itself is almost redundant. "You're already gone, aren't you?" asks the mother with horror some time after feeling her daughter's unnaturally cold hands. And so, we come to realize, Jessie almost is.

'night, Mother, which is having its premiere at Harvard's American Repertory Theatre, is one of the most disturbing American plays of recent seasons. You can pick at it and argue with it, but you can't hide from its bruising impact. Unlike so many latter-day plays that ask "Whose life is it, anyway?" this one is not a sentimental problem drama about suicide or a stirring paean to man's right to die with dignity. Ms. Norman, the author of the powerful *Getting Out,* is more concerned with honesty than preaching. She takes two barren lives and, a few small melodramatic contrivances aside, serves them up raw in a dramatic format that seems as inexorable as classic tragedy.

During the brief time that separates Jessie's announcement from the play's resolution, we learn everything about daughter and mother that we need to know—no more. Jessie is an overweight, shy loser whose husband has long ago left her and whose teenage son is a criminal on the lam. Her mother is a "plain country woman," gabby, selfish, and useless. Both their lives are defined by shopping lists, television shows, junk food, and small-town gossip.

Ms. Norman, a Louisville native, gives the Cateses a Southern twang, but her women don't belong to the eccentric Old South of Beth Henley and Flannery O'Connor; they're part of the flat, homogenized New South we find in the fiction of Bobbie Ann Mason or in Robert Altman's *Nashville.* As brilliantly designed by Heidi Landesman, their ticky-tacky home is a modern shrine of alienation—as sterile as a Kmart, as lonely as an Edward Hopper painting. Early on, Thelma says that she never fears thieves breaking into the house because "we don't have anything people would want." It isn't hard to see what she means.

Yet if these two women are inarticulate and their lives are without point, they are still mother and daughter. Much of the play is a relentless exploration of that blood tie, with all the guilt and hurt and misunderstanding and love that it entails. Thelma begs Jessie to stay "a few more years" so that she won't have to face her own death alone. "You are my child!" she cries, but her daughter replies sadly, "I am what became of your child." Ultimately, it is the mother who becomes the child, crying on the floor, throwing pots in a temper tantrum, trying anything to get her way. But Jessie will not be moved.

As the daughter sees it, her life is "all I really have that belongs to me" and she is entitled to end it. She never amounted to much and has no reason to believe things will change. "I'm somebody I waited for who never came and never will," she says dispassionately. "I'm not going to show up. There's no reason to stay." Even her own child brings her no solace, for she views her delinquent son as the eternally doomed product of his battling parents: "Ricky is the two of us together for all time, in too small a place, tearing each other apart."

'night, Mother is full of such plain, explosive dialogue. This spare play is not an inflated, abstract argument about life versus death, but an intimate eavesdropping on two people, who, in the mother's words, don't know what they're here for and, until this moment, have tried not to think about it. It is all so real that we're all the more conscious of those rare moments when the playwright intrudes. It seems excessive that Jessie, on top of all her other woes, would have a disease (epilepsy) that her mother has refused to acknowledge for many years. It also seems archly theatrical, even in a drama set in real time, for the set to have six clocks that count down to zero-hour.

The director, Tom Moore, has choreographed the action masterfully, with a forceful, uncluttered naturalism that recalls the New York production of Franz Xaver Kroetz's similar German work, *Request Concert,* two seasons ago. The actresses, both veterans of Louisville's Actors Theatre, are also excellent, though there are occasional moments of actorly artifice that could be stripped away.

Ms. Bates makes no bid for sympathy: She simply embodies the daughter's dull, anonymous personality. In her baggy clothes and sheenless, scraggly hair, she could be any of the many lumpy people we see every day but don't notice. We certainly understand why her husband ran out on her and why her most successful job has been as a saleswoman at a hospital gift shop.

As the mother, Ms. Pitoniak has more to do. This actress, the lady with the lamps in *Talking With* at the Manhattan Theatre Club earlier this season, must ride through fear, desperation, self-pity, rage, grief, and even forced good cheer. She is very funny when she talks about a friend "who burned down every house she ever had." She can be pathetic when announcing that "this is all my fault, but I don't know what to do about it now."

When the mother finally accepts her fate, Ms. Pitoniak is harrowing. Suddenly worrying about what she'll tell the neighbors about Jessie's suicide, she pulls her face into a grotesque mask of sociability and rehearses her line in front of her daughter: "It was something personal—that's what I'll say."

But what can anyone say, really? In *'night, Mother*, Ms. Norman sends us crashing into one of life's horrible, unpreventable accidents, then leaves us helplessly contemplating the casualty list.

≡ *Marsha Norman, who won the Pulitzer Prize for this play after it moved to Broadway, went on to write a novel, plays produced outside New York, and the book for the Broadway musical* The Secret Garden.

MERLIN
Mark Hellinger Theatre, January 31, 1983

If *Merlin*, the musical at the Mark Hellinger, devoted its entire length to the magic tricks of Doug Henning, it would be something to see. Mr. Henning is beyond compare as an illusionist, and the half-dozen or so major stunts he pulls off in this show are indeed spectacular. They involve levitation, leaping flames, dancing water, a floating bubble with a man inside, and, in the incredible pièce de résistance that opens Act 2, a live white horse and rider that vanish into thin air. Mr. Henning believes in magic, and he makes us true believers, too.

The trouble with *Merlin* is that its creators refuse to stick with their strong suit. Only about a third of their show—and this may be a very generous estimate—gives us the star doing what he can do best. The rest of *Merlin* is a sprawling Broadway musical with the consistency of glue. It's as if someone were to produce a show starring Barbra Streisand and let her sing only four or five songs so that the rest of the evening could be devoted to dog acts.

Merlin, it must be noted, has not yet officially opened. In contrast to most Broadway musicals, which tend to preview for a month or less in New York before an official premiere, this one is now in its eighth week of previews. Three "opening" dates have been announced for the show—the third of which was last night—and then canceled. The fourth, most recently announced opening date is February 13, and should changes made in *Merlin* by then justify a substantial reappraisal, it will be provided here.

This report is based on Thursday night's preview. While the producers of *Merlin* may consider the musical not yet ready to be seen by critics, they have allowed in more than 60,000 paying customers since December 10 at the full, forty-dollar top ticket scale. Open or not, *Merlin* is already, after *Cats*, the second-longest-running musical of the season.

The show I saw Thursday is by no means in chaos. It's slickly produced, with a well-oiled physical production by the same high-power design team responsible for *42nd Street, A Chorus Line,* and *Dreamgirls.* The choreography, by Christopher Chadman and Billy Wilson, is skillfully danced, even if it is mediocre. The performances are as polished as the caliber of the cast and the material will allow. The maladies that afflict this musical, I'm afraid, seem to be built into its very conception.

The book is by Richard Levinson and William Link, who are best known as the creators of television's Lieutenant Columbo. Their fairytale plot, which is paradoxically at once simple and confusing, involves the efforts of a wicked Queen (Chita Rivera) to install her idiot son (Nathan Lane) on the English throne. To achieve this Machiavellian coup, the Queen must sabotage the legendary wizard Merlin, who is determined to promote the royal ascendancy of another would-be future king named Arthur.

Certainly musicals can get by on a story as frail as this—remember *Barnum?*—and at times Mr. Levinson's and Mr. Link's script threatens to rekindle durable narrative devices from *Damn Yankees* and *Camelot.* But the writers struggle with a major esthetic problem that no magic wand can wave away. Because Mr. Henning, who plays Merlin, cannot act, dance, or sing, the authors must write their show around their title character and build it instead on the shoulders of the secondary players. No wonder the audience often feels, like Tom Stoppard's Rosencrantz and Guildenstern, that it is watching a series of digressionary subplots while the main story unfolds out of view.

The few lines and song lyrics that Mr. Henning does get to recite are mumbled. When he is not performing his illusions, he just smiles absently and seems to be an anonymous gatecrasher at his own party. Almost everything that surrounds him is filler. Ms. Rivera and Mr. Lane each have several villainous numbers that all sound alike. (Ms. Rivera works like a demon, by the way, and looks quite funny in red-and-copper-lamé insect wings.) Two good guys and one ingenue—Edmund Lyndeck, George Lee Andrews, and Michelle Nicastro—also pop up to lend their muscular voices to songs that make little point and no impression. The jokes in between are not at the level of *The Muppet Show.*

Perhaps an even more crucial failure of *Merlin* is its inability to transport us to its purported fantasy world of a mythical England. Except for the fact that Merlin cuts a woman "in twain" instead of "in two," the idiom of the dialogue and performances is less storybookland than Saturday-morning televisionland. The songs, with music by Elmer Bernstein and lyrics by Don Black, have no character, with the possible exception of a jolly opening number ("It's About Magic") that fleetingly recalls the opening number of *Pippin* ("Magic to Do"). Ivan Reitman's direction is sprightly only when compared with the recent *Alice in Wonderland*.

A romantic prologue sequence, set in a starry firmament seemingly stretching into infinity, is as close as *Merlin* gets to spinning a genuinely enchanting spell. After that, the fog machines, Tharon Musser's spooky lighting, and Theoni V. Aldredge's imaginative costumes provide what atmosphere there is. (Sometimes, however, Mrs. Aldredge too strenuously tries to evoke both *Cats* and *Star Wars*.) Robin Wagner's sets, elaborate as they are, prove more dark, steely, and austere than fun: They suggest what *Kismet* might have looked like if it had been designed by Albert Speer.

Children who are old enough to appreciate magic but not old enough to be bored by tirelessly prancing chorus boys—say, those from the ages of five to twelve—will undoubtedly enjoy *Merlin* on its own terms. Parents accompanying them may well wish that they knew the secret of Mr. Henning's truly remarkable vanishing act.

≡ *When producers don't feel like fighting with their actors or production personnel, they usually take on the critics, an even safer target and one sure to generate press coverage. One trick is to postpone a show's opening as many times as possible, with the hope that a miracle will cure the production's ills (which sometimes happens) or that "word of mouth" will create a public groundswell that poor reviews can't obliterate (which rarely happens if the show is no good). In the 1980s, the champion of this technique was* Merlin, *which began previewing December 7, 1982—was the choice of Pearl Harbor Day a coincidence?—and, in increments, gradually postponed its opening until February 13 of the following year.*

After two of the postponements, editors at the Times *and the* Daily News *got together by phone and decided that the time had come to serve our readers by evaluating the show at the end of January; throughout the metropolitan area kids were begging their parents to buy tickets for* Merlin, *which was heavily promoted in TV commercials during and past the holiday season. The Associated Press also decided to review the show, but Rupert Murdoch's New York Post, which was not about to offend a potential advertiser, strenuously supported a producer's right to preview undisturbed by press coverage indefinitely.*

When the rebellious critics showed up to review Merlin *on January 29, a friendly press agent was there to welcome us. So much for the cloak-and-dagger opportunities of drama reviewing on Broadway. All the reviews were of the same mind—and the initial judgments were seconded by most other critics when they reviewed the show two weeks later. (I went back, as promised, to see the finished version; the differences between it and the earlier* Merlin *were negligible.) Nonetheless, a hundred members of the Broadway trade organization, the League of American Theaters and Producers, met to protest our decision to review* Merlin *so "early." One producer, Elizabeth McCann, earned cheers from the assembled by expressing her resentment that I had gone so far as to mention the price of a ticket to the show in my review; to do so, she said, was "in effect [to accuse] us of charging more than we should for an inferior product." (You couldn't put anything over on her!)*

Though Doug Henning was little heard from again in New York, the actor cast as the villain of Merlin, *Nathan Lane, and the show's director, Ivan Reitman (later to direct Hollywood hit movies like* Ghostbusters *and* Kindergarten Cop), *were not impeded by this misadventure.*

PAINTING CHURCHES
SECOND STAGE, FEBRUARY 9, 1983

Margaret Church, known as Mags, is a young artist about to have her first one-woman show at a Fifty-seventh Street gallery. Her specialty is painting portraits in an impressionistic style that's been acclaimed as "a weird blend" of Bonnard, Cassatt, and Hockney. In Tina Howe's *Painting Churches*, Mags returns to her childhood Beacon Hill home to do just what the play's title promises—to paint a portrait of her elderly Brahmin parents, Gardner and Fanny Church.

The painting, though eventually completed, is never revealed to the audience. What we see instead is a play that provides a portrait of the Churches in the exact, ravishing style of Mags's art. *Painting Churches*, which opens the Second Stage's season at its temporary new home on Theatre Row, is in the dreamiest impressionistic spirit. It remakes reality with delicate, well-chosen brush strokes, finding beauty and truth in the abstract dance of light on a familiar landscape.

Were it rendered in an ordinary, flatly representational manner—the theatrical equivalent of, say, Norman Rockwell—this play's landscape would be unbearably familiar: It's another family drama in which the prodigal child returns home to resolve her relationship with her parents, even as the parents settle scores with each other. The accompanying themes—the indignities of old age and death, the misunderstandings between generations—summon up the dread specter of *On Golden Pond*. It's a high compliment to Ms. Howe, the author of *The Art of Dining* and *Museum*, that the old bones of her material rarely peek through her writing's high, lacy gloss.

The play is set at a time of transition for all three characters. As Mags (Frances Conroy) is about to start her career in New York, so her parents are winding one down in Boston: They're packing up their belongings to move permanently to their summer cottage on Cape Cod. Gardner (Donald Moffat), a revered poet who was once the peer of Pound and Frost, is increasingly "ga-ga" of mind and short of cash. "His last Pulitzer Prize didn't even cover the real-estate taxes on this place," explains Fanny (Marian Seldes), a grande dame who is angry at her husband for preceding her into senescence.

What makes *Painting Churches* surprising and involving is the playwright's Jamesian use of shifting points of view. In Act 1, our sympathies are with the daughter and doddering father. Both seem to be neglected by the domineering, selfish mother, who is more concerned with maintaining her wardrobe and patrician airs than her family's emotional needs. But Ms. Howe redeems Fanny in Act 2 by showing us the full severity of the lonely burden this proud woman now bears, as well as the frailties of her husband and child. "If you want to paint us," she says to her daughter late in the play, "paint us as we really are." In *Painting Churches*, both Mags and the audience are taught the same lesson in perception: Whether painting or observing a family portrait, it's essential to see beyond the surface reality.

A few lapses aside, Ms. Howe is both subtle and humorful as she deepens our perspective on the Churches. A monologue in which Fanny remembers the sexual thrill of sledding with the young Gardner becomes a fading but vibrant glimpse into a passionate marriage that time has disfigured. When Mags recalls how she once melted crayons on a radiator to get revenge on her parents for punishing her, the speech proves a telling account of how the girl first found her "own materials" and "abilities" as an artist. Yet, once Gardner and Fanny fill in their own selective memories of the same incident, the speech becomes an equally incisive paradigm of the missed connections that have haunted this family for a lifetime.

When the playwright occasionally extends a joke or scene too long, the pitch of Carole Rothman's direction strains in tandem. Otherwise, Ms. Rothman, whose previous Second Stage productions include *Pastorale* and *How I Got That Story*, is up to her usual high standard. In a crucial Act 2 climax, in which the parents rekindle their buried antagonisms by breaking out in a hurtful childish spat, the director achieves the perfectly balanced mixture of pathos and absurd farce that recalls Ring Lardner's classic account of an aged couple's final reckoning, "The Golden Honeymoon."

The performances are excellent. The buoyant Ms. Conroy keeps the somewhat thinly written daughter from becoming the pill that children usually are in fiction of this type. As her mother, Ms. Seldes strips away layers of overbred dottiness like paint, transforming herself from a figure of fun into the play's most mature character. (But not before she up-stages her daughter by unveiling her own hilarious artistic project—a lampshade she's decorated to represent "the Grand Canal at dusk.") Mr. Moffat's patriarch looks every bit the literary lion in winter—sweet and abstracted, then red with rage as he rails at his own unpreventable de-cline. In one cruel moment, the tuxedo-clad actor serenely recites a fa-vorite e. e. cummings verse while age's ravages make a mockery of his dignity.

As knowingly designed by Heidi Landesman and lighted by Frances Aronson, the Churches' living room could well be both Mags's and the author's blank canvas. It's been stripped of most furniture and shrouded with gray canvas in anticipation of the new tenants' paint job. A spring glow hangs in the air; the mural-like colonial wallpaper has faded into a nonrepresentational impressionistic swirl.

But this composition, like Mags's, can only be finished when Gardner and Fanny finally arrive at their most truly revealing pose. They find it on moving day, when they waltz around the room one last time, emulating the dancers in their favorite, half-remembered Renoir. As they do so, the portrait of the Churches on stage perfectly fits the judgment Gardner has rendered about his daughter's completed portrait a few moments earlier. "The whole thing shimmers," he says, in a line of art criticism that can also serve as an apt description of Ms. Howe's lovely play.

MOOSE MURDERS
Eugene O'Neill Theatre, February 23, 1983

From now on, there will always be two groups of theatergoers in this world: those who have seen *Moose Murders,* and those who have not. Those of us who have witnessed the play that opened at the Eugene O'Neill Theatre last night will undoubtedly hold periodic re-unions, in the noble tradition of survivors of the *Titanic.* Tears and booze will flow in equal measure, and there will be a prize awarded to the bearer of the most outstanding antlers. As for those theatergoers who miss *Moose Murders*—well, they just don't rate. A visit to *Moose Murders* is what will separate the connoisseurs of Broadway disaster from mere dilettantes for many moons to come.

The play begins in the exact manner of *Whodunnit*—itself one of the season's drearier offerings, though at the time of its opening we didn't realize how relatively civilized it was. There's a loud thunderclap, and the curtain rises to reveal an elaborate, two-level, dark wood set. Amusingly designed by Marjorie Bradley Kellogg, the set represents a lodge in the Adirondacks and is profusely decorated with the requisite stuffed moose heads. Though the heads may be hunting trophies, one cannot rule out the possibility that these particular moose committed suicide shortly after being shown the script that trades on their good name.

The first human characters we meet—if "human" is the right word—are "the singing Keenes." The scantily clad Snooks Keene bumps her backside in the audience's face and sings "Jeepers Creepers" in an aggressively off-key screech while her blind husband, Howie, pounds away on an electric hand organ. Howie's plug is soon mercifully pulled by the lodge's beefy middle-aged caretaker, Joe Buffalo Dance, who wears Indian war paint and braids but who speaks in an Irish brogue.

This loathsome trio is quickly joined by a whole crowd of unappetizing clowns. The wealthy Hedda Holloway, the lodge's new owner, arrives with her husband, Sidney, a heavily bandaged quadriplegic who is confined to a wheelchair and who is accurately described as "that fetid roll of gauze." Sidney's attendant, Nurse Dagmar, wears revealing black satin, barks in Nazi-ese, and likes to leave her patient out in the rain. The Holloway children include Stinky, a drug-crazed hippie who wants to sleep with his mother, and Gay, a little girl in a party dress. Told that her father will always be "a vegetable," Gay turns up her nose and replies, "Like a lima bean? Gross me out!" She then breaks into a tap dance.

For much of Act 1, this ensemble stumbles about mumbling dialogue that, as far as one can tell, is only improved by its inaudibility. Just before intermission, Stinky breaks out a deck of cards to give the actors, if not the audience, something to do. The lights go out in mid-game, and when they come up again, one of the characters has been murdered. Such is the comatose nature of the production that we're too busy trying to guess which stiff on stage is the victim to worry about guessing the culprit.

Even Act 1 of *Moose Murders* is inadequate preparation for the ludicrous depths of Act 2. I won't soon forget the spectacle of watching the mummified Sidney rise from his wheelchair to kick an intruder, unaccountably dressed in a moose costume, in the groin. This peculiar fracas is topped by the play's final twist, in which Hedda serves her daughter Gay a poison-laced vodka martini. As the young girl collapses to the floor and dies in the midst of another Shirley Temple–esque buck and wing, her mother breaks into laughter and applause.

The ten actors trapped in this enterprise, a minority of them of professional caliber, will not be singled out here. I'm tempted to upbraid the author, director, and producers of *Moose Murders,* but surely the American Society for the Prevention of Cruelty to Animals will be after them soon enough.

≡ *"Through most of the production, the audience simply sat and stared, open-mouthed," wrote June Gable, a distinguished member of the* Moose Murders *cast, in her diary of the experience, later published in* Esquire. *Of the critics' performance I attended, Gable wrote: "The audience also was very strange. I imagined that [the producer] had personally bussed in all the schizophrenics from mental hospitals around the city. They fought loudly over their seats after the curtain had gone up, they yelled to each other from different sections of the theater, there was a terrible odor emanating from somewhere in the orchestra, and the show never got a laugh, except one: when the actor wearing the moose head got socked in the groin."*

For my account of covering this epic fiasco, see "Exit the Critic" later in this volume.

ON YOUR TOES
Virginia Theatre, March 7, 1983

The biggest thrill offered by *On Your Toes,* the 1936 musical revived last night at the Virginia, is the poster outside the theater. There you will find three of the most illustrious names of Broadway history—Richard Rodgers, Lorenz Hart, and George Abbott—as well as a fourth name that transcends both Broadway and history, George Balanchine. It's sad that the show heralded by the poster has only a marginal relationship to the giant talents who share top billing.

On Your Toes is one of the weakest endeavors ever to engage the concentration of these men, together or separately. It is a mystery why Mr. Abbott and some dedicated new collaborators—among them such ballet royalty as Natalia Makarova and Peter Martins—have devoted so much loving care and expense to resuscitating it now. The last Broadway revival of this musical, in 1954, was a failure, and that clearly was no fluke. Though *On Your Toes* is an undeniable historic artifact—what work created by these artists would not be?—it is of footnote caliber. Its few assets as entertainment are scattered like sweet and frail rose petals on a stagnant pond.

In its original production, the show was cheered primarily because of its star, Ray Bolger, and because it contained the first ballet ever to be integrated into the plot of a musical, "Slaughter on 10th Avenue." Given its mirthless, lengthy book and (by Rodgers and Hart standards) middling, brief score, *On Your Toes* needs a dynamic leading man of Mr. Bolger's stature to have even a prayer of flying today: The musical's hero—a hoofer-turned-music professor caught up with a Russian ballet company and the underworld—is at the center of nearly everything.

At the Virginia, this role has unaccountably fallen to Lara Teeter, a standard Broadway chorus dancer with little discernible personality. He fails to carry the show and undermines its noble efforts to reproduce the past faithfully. Paired with Christine Andreas in two supreme duets, "There's a Small Hotel" and "It's Got to Be Love," he provides insipid crooning that sends the normally vibrant Ms. Andreas crashing to his level. Paired with Ms. Makarova in "Slaughter on 10th Avenue," he brings such leaden strain to its final passage that he deflates his partner's delightful contribution and mars the hard work done by Mr. Martins, who has fastidiously reconstructed the Balanchine choreography for this production.

Even if Mr. Teeter were an airy and antic Bolgeresque dancer, however, it's not clear that the climactic ballet would be a sufficient payoff to the dull subplots and hoary gags that precede it. Though "Slaughter" has aged far better than most of its surroundings, this splash of gangster-motif jazziness is but a doodle next to *Who Cares?*, the Balanchine classic set to Gershwin tunes of the same period. Nor does "Slaughter" seem the stunning theatrical innovation that audiences found it in 1936. While the dance may be worked into the show's plot, that plot is so arbitrary and silly that the exercise is a pointless technical feat. It was really the Rodgers and Hammerstein collaboration with Agnes de Mille in *Oklahoma!* seven years later that meaningfully wedded serious dance to the fabric of a Broadway musical.

The other Balanchine dance of the evening, the Act 1 finale, is a gag that has outlived its time: a parody of Fokine's ballet *Schéhérazade*. Because the satirical target is no longer a popular favorite, this extended cartoon plays to dead silence. Only Ms. Makarova and her expert partner, a fellow American Ballet Theatre alumnus, George de la Peña, get the joke. It says how much Mr. Balanchine has remade the face of dance in the decades since *On Your Toes* that he, not his Russian predecessors, is now a subject of parody in a current Broadway musical: "Slaughter on 10th Avenue" is ribbed mildly by Gower Champion in *42nd Street*.

On Your Toes also has a considerable amount of new, non-Balanchine choreography in the appropriate period vernacular, provided by Donald Saddler. The best of it can be found in the title number, which is rousingly conceived as a fantasy battle between ballet and tap dancers: It is graced by an all-too-brief appearance by another fine soloist, the lithe Starr Danias, but is also chilled by the all-black setting provided by the designer, Zack Brown.

Like the dancing, the music is generally presented with admirable authenticity. The score is heard in mostly the original Hans Spialek orchestrations; a large band (shimmering twin pianos included) plays it to soaring effect under the exceptional direction of John Mauceri. The miking is minimal—it's a pleasure to find no credit for "sound design" in the *Playbill.* Unfortunately, most of the solo singers have trouble projecting their lyrics past the pit. Though we hear the routine Hart sentiments to the lovely Rodgers tune for the choral number "Quiet Night," the more dexterous words to "Small Hotel" and "Too Good for the Average Man" tend to evaporate.

As for Mr. Abbott's staging, it's the patented article—straightforward, uncampy, all-American in its foursquare ingenuousness. How one wishes he had chosen to apply his firm hand to a revival of a subsequent Rodgers-Hart-Abbott musical such as *The Boys from Syracuse* or *Pal Joey* instead. One also wishes that Mr. Abbott had given the show's book major instead of cosmetic surgery and that he had gotten more out of his cast: From Mr. Teeter and Ms. Andreas through the ranks (which include George S. Irving and Dina Merrill), we get at most dogged professionalism.

The surprising exception is Ms. Makarova, all dolled up as a flirtatious blond ballerina. It's true that her comic displays of temperament are amateur, but it's equally true that great acting isn't required. What Ms. Makarova brings to *On Your Toes,* in addition to her leggy mock-stripper's turn in "Slaughter," is a sense of freshness and fun. She seems to be the only one who finds doing this show an invigorating novelty, rather than a rigorous academic exercise in historical preservation. And it's only when she's onstage that we feel we're at the theater, witnessing something alive and new, rather than at school, dutifully poring over the musty lesser sketches of the old masters.

≡ *Since I love Rodgers and Hart, I don't know why I was so sour about this revival. It was a lonely opinion—only Arthur Gelb declared that I had been "too kind" to* On Your Toes.

Variety ran a big article pronouncing me "an exceptionally hard-to-please critic" even as it noted that "most legit observers concede that his tenure has coincided with a creatively unsatisfying period in legit" and that *"Rich's notices in general haven't been much more downbeat than the overall critical consensus."* Here, though, I bucked the consensus, and so Variety *declared that the musical's fate would "provide further illustration of the degree of power wielded by legit reviews in* The New York Times, *widely acknowledged as the single most influential critical outlet."*

Had Variety *done a follow-up story, which it did not, it would have had to report that the degree of power was fairly small.* On Your Toes *was a long-running hit on Broadway and repeated its success in the West End.*

SUNDAY ESSAY: ON THE PARTICULAR PLEASURE OF SEEING A LEGENDARY FLOP
MARCH 20, 1983

Like everyone who caught the theater bug at an early age, I always made a point of saving *Playbills*. Not just my *Playbills*, mind you, but the entire world's: Between a matinee and evening performance during adolescence, I would skip dinner in order to tour Times Square garbage cans and scoop up the programs of all the plays I had not seen. People who share this affliction surely know how near and dear those *Playbills* become as the years pass by. That's why we weep unabashedly over the scene in Moss Hart's memoir *Act One* in which the author's angry father torments his elderly, theater-loving aunt into "dropping her beloved programs from trembling hands all over the floor." It's as if Hart's father had sacked a holy shrine.

But there comes a time in adulthood when one must either break this acquisitive habit entirely or rent a warehouse. I quit cold turkey, not to be overly exact about it, on September 14, 1967. Or almost. There are still rare occasions when the old urge takes over and a *Playbill* simply must be tucked away for posterity. These exceptions are not the ones you might expect. I now realize that there's no point in saving programs from great nights in the theater. Those nights become part of history and will be profusely documented forever; it's always possible to dig up a *Playbill* from *Who's Afraid of Virginia Woolf?*, after all, if really necessary. The *Playbills* that are truly worth saving are the rarest: those from the worst nights in the theater. And not just any worst night, either, but the very worst—those of the legendary bombs.

What makes certain bombs into legends? It's hard to say, precisely—they don't wear fur coats. Once it was a mark of distinction for a play to close in one night, but in these troubled times even that phenomenon is a sad commonplace. Some theater people define legendary bombs by the amount of money that went down the drain, or the high caliber of talent expended, or the extravagant foolhardiness of the esthetic mission. Others let Joe Allen, the theater district bistro, be the final arbiter: That restaurant has a whole wall bedecked with posters from a select group of famous turkeys. Whatever the definition, it can't be quantified—a flop just must have a certain je ne sais quoi to rise to legendary status. But what I do know is this: The only *Playbill* I've saved thus far in this decade is the one from *Moose Murders.*

Moose Murders, for those with short memories, was a catastrophe that reared its ugly stuffed head, complete with antlers, last month. Let's not review its contents here except to say that it was a comedy whose climax consisted of a gauze-wrapped quadriplegic rising from his wheelchair to kick a man wearing a moose costume in the groin.

In any case, I come not to bury *Moose Murders* again, but, in a fashion, to praise it. A legend it most certainly is. Those few of us who saw *Moose Murders* will always look back at it less with anger than with guilty pleasure. Indeed, since reviewing this show, I have received a near-flood of mail from *Moose Murders* audience members who, while detesting the play, were glad to have seen it, for reasons I'll explain. (You can bet that these correspondents are saving their *Playbill*s, too.) Other letters have arrived from jealous folk who sorely resent not having made it to *Moose Murders* just to experience for themselves how atrocious it was. (These correspondents, no doubt, were frantically searching through Broadway trashcans for the *Playbill* the morning after the opening/closing night.)

Why the regret about having missed a dreadful play? Why the guilty pleasure in having seen it? The crazy thing about a *Moose Murders* is that it does remind one, however backhandedly, of the particular excitement of witnessing live theater.

If a great play unites audience and actors alike into a transcendent emotional or intellectual journey, so a truly wretched one can band audience and actors together into a shared nightmare. As passengers will always remember an ecstatic transatlantic journey on the *France,* so will survivors always remember the camaraderie of their ill-starred crossing on the *Titanic.* A communal, we're-all-in-this-together feeling takes over, sink or swim.

It's not an experience available at run-of-the-mill flops, which are just boring and conventionally wasteful, or at the movies: While the audience at *Heaven's Gate* may draw tightly together, the actors making fools of themselves on the screen are not there to share in the collective embarrassment—they're already back sipping white wine and getting tan in Malibu. In my theatergoing years, the Broadway show that best illustrates the special allure of seeing a legendary flop—and diehard theatergoers' ravenous hunger for that adventure—is a musical called *Rachael Lily Rosenbloom and Don't You Ever Forget It!* Does anybody remember it? It never exactly opened. After a few preview performances at the Broadhurst in December 1973, a discreet announcement appeared in the Saturday papers that the show would close, prior to its premiere, that night. Happening to be in the vicinity of the Times Square half-price ticket booth that day, I bought a pair in the mezzanine for the musical's farewell performance. Arriving at the Broadhurst just before 8 p.m., I was startled to discover that the sold-out sign was up and that strangers were waving fifty-dollar bills in the air for any available ticket. Not for a second was I tempted to clear an eighty-dollar profit on my pair and miss out on this spectacle. Inside the theater, the atmosphere was so heady you'd think you were at a Tony Awards gala. There were celebrities from all the arts, ranks of standees in the back of the orchestra, paparazzi and autograph hounds pushing and shoving. When the lights dimmed, a voice came over the loudspeaker to announce that "Tonight *Rachael Lily Rosenbloom* will be played without an intermission." These words alone were enough to prompt the audience to break into a prolonged, punch-drunk ovation.

What followed was a musical fantasy of surpassing lavishness that made no sense, at any level, from beginning to end. The majority of the crowd fell into a sullen, open-mouthed stupor like that with which the audience greets the opening scenes of *Springtime for Hitler,* the fictitious Broadway flop within Mel Brooks's film *The Producers.* But no one walked out: *Rachael Lily Rosenbloom* became an existential test which everyone was determined to pass. The cast, many of whom were dressed in silver-lamé G-strings, attacked their tasks as if they were performing *Guys and Dolls.*

After the show, I ran into an acquaintance and asked him why the house was packed for the closing night of such a fiasco. He surveyed the lobby and said, "These are all the people who didn't see *Breakfast at Tiffany's.*" He was right. To this day, there are thousands of theatergoers, me included, who regret having missed that legendary 1960s bomb—a big-budget musical starring Richard Chamberlain and Mary Tyler Moore, adapted by Edward Albee from the Truman Capote story, that the producer David Merrick folded in previews at the Majestic. We weren't going to make the same mistake twice.

It was also at *Rachael Lily Rosenbloom* that I learned the answer to the eternal question that always follows in the wake of such theatrical disasters. That question, of course, is, "Why didn't anyone realize how hopeless this show was before risking all the trouble and expense and public ridicule of putting it on?" Some people speculate that the creators of a *Rachael Lily Rosenbloom* or *Breakfast at Tiffany's* or *Moose Murders* are suffering from temporary insanity. Others postulate that such shows are tax gimmicks or maybe clandestine pranks hatched by foreign agents out to undermine the American way of life. But the real answer is more benign and simple than that. Theater people, like all people, would always rather believe good news than bad news, especially about their own work—and someone is always willing to give them encouragement, no matter how ridiculous the project at hand may be.

If a musical on its way to Broadway gets terrible reviews and audience catcalls in Boston, it's often said, that musical's creators will ignore those omens entirely and instead choose to believe the opinion of the Ritz-Carlton waiter who confides, while waiting for a tip, that he found the show superior to *My Fair Lady*. At *Rachael Lily Rosenbloom*, one could see this process in action: In scattered pockets throughout the otherwise shell-shocked house were claques of theatergoers who sang along with the musical numbers and gave mini–standing ovations at the end of most of them.

These partisans had clearly seen earlier previews of the show and adored it; they were in tears when the final curtain rang down. No doubt there were other such *Rachael Lily Rosenbloom* fans at every stage of the show's development. There will always be somebody who loves a bomb, no matter how deadly, and there will always be at least one person connected with the production who will grab on to the straws of hope that these cheerleaders provide.

This myopia can afflict all theater artists, however mighty. It has happened to nearly everyone. But when the turkey finally rests in its grave, its perpetrators often bounce back. Pulling out my cherished *Playbill* for *Rachael Lily Rosenbloom*, I find that its coproducer went on to produce *Evita*; that its colibrettist went on to write *Dreamgirls*; that its female leads have recently found acclaim and stardom in *Nine* and *Little Shop of Horrors*; that three of its chorus people were later leads in *A Chorus Line* (one winning a Tony Award) and another was a star of *Ain't Misbehavin'*. They probably look back and laugh, too, by now.

I can't promise that all will end so happily for the cast and crew of *Moose Murders*. We'll wait ten years and see. In the meantime, I'm holding on tightly to my rare *Playbill*. It's a remembrance of a genuine theatrical occasion, and just possibly, given my correspondents who would kill for it, an annuity for my old age.

BRIGHTON BEACH MEMOIRS
ALVIN THEATRE, MARCH 23, 1983

After having seen *Brighton Beach Memoirs,* at the Alvin, one can only have positive feelings about its author, Neil Simon. In this flat-out autobiographical memory play, a portrait of the writer as a Brooklyn teenager in 1937, Mr. Simon makes real progress toward an elusive longtime goal: He mixes comedy and drama without, for the most part, either force-feeding the jokes or milking the tears. It's happy news that one of our theater's slickest playwrights is growing beyond the well-worn formulas of his past.

The other likable aspect of Mr. Simon's writing here is its openness and charity of spirit. Far more than most Simon plays, *Brighton Beach Memoirs* deals explicitly with the Jewishness of its people. While one might fear that this development could lead to caricature, it generally does not. Mr. Simon's characters—the seven members of the extended Jerome family of Brighton Beach—are, for all their archetypal manners, appealing. Even though Mr. Simon is trying to come to terms with his less-than-rosy Depression adolescence, he looks back not with anger but with an affection that is too warm to be fake.

Thanks to these attributes, *Brighton Beach Memoirs* offers more surprises than any Simon play since *The Sunshine Boys.* It is also, disappointingly, not nearly so good as one keeps expecting it to be. Oddly enough, Mr. Simon's kindness eventually extends so far that it has a boomerang effect: Even as it makes us like the man who wrote this play, it softens the play itself. *Brighton Beach Memoirs* boasts some big laughs (in Act 1) and some genuinely tender speeches, but it never quite stops being nice and starts being either consistently involving or entertaining. It's a pleasant evening, blessed with a handsome and highly energetic production, that lacks emotional and theatrical bite.

The makings of a more forceful play are certainly in evidence. Eugene, the fifteen-year-old hero played by Matthew Broderick, lives in crowded, lower-middle-class circumstances. His household not only contains his father (Peter Michael Goetz), mother (Elizabeth Franz), and older brother (Zeljko Ivanek), but also the mother's widowed sister (Joyce Van Patten) and her two daughters. "If you didn't have a problem, you wouldn't live in this house," says the father—and that's no joke. Two of the characters have heart disease, and one has asthma; two at least temporarily lose jobs needed to keep the straitened family afloat. There is an offstage car accident; two of the children contemplate running away from home.

Mr. Simon uses the family's miseries to raise such enduring issues as sibling resentments, guilt-ridden parent-child relationships, and the hunger for dignity in a poverty-stricken world. When the mother and her sister air a lifetime's pent-up angers or when the bone-weary father, a garment-district cutter, plods home from work as wearily as Willy Loman, we find real, eloquently stated pain.

But the author doesn't fully trust his material. He leans on Eugene's narration to spoon-feed us his messages and, eventually, he sweeps both the play's crises and promise of dramatic tension under the rug. In Act 2, most of the family's problems, moral dilemmas, and conflicts are neatly resolved; by the end, Mr. Simon even reaches over to Europe to rescue some unseen Polish cousins from the coming Holocaust. Perhaps life can be this benign, but these happy endings are paraded so patly that they push an affectionate play over the line into unconvincing Pollyannaism.

In this context, the author's handling of his onstage alter ego is highly revealing. No matter how miserable the goings-on around him, Eugene is usually ready with a wisecrack—and he records those gags in the composition book that is the repository of his first literary effort, his "memoirs." After a while, Eugene's good-natured brand of story-telling all too glaringly points up the deficiencies of Mr. Simon's own writing in *Brighton Beach Memoirs*. We feel that a brisk, superficial glibness is papering over the rough edges of the lives in view— especially the hero's.

Eugene, in the end, proves less a character than a master of cere-monies. Unlike the others, this boy has few personality flaws—some slight selfishness and a rampant lustfulness for his sixteen-year-old cousin ex-cepted. He is, as his brother says, "a terrific kid," and however preoccupied he may be with sex or the Yankees, he still gets nearly straight A's in school.

As in *Chapter Two,* Mr. Simon's autobiographical stand-in is finally so saintly and resilient he becomes elusive and opaque—a vacuum where the play's sensitive center should be. At one point Eugene asks, "How can I be a writer if I don't learn how to suffer?"—yet we never really see him suffer. Eugene has most of the jokes, and they're not the bleeding kind: They obscure rather than reveal his true feelings.

If the play's undercurrents don't run deep, its surface mostly gleams. Mr. Simon wittily captures the texture of the Jeromes' milieu—where all gentiles are malevolent "Cossacks" and where a contentious family din-ner can, in Eugene's words, begin like "a murder mystery in Blenheim Castle." Though some of the Jewish mother, puberty, and food gags are overdone, others are dead-on. Trust Mr. Simon to explain, hilariously, how Eugene's first wet dreams resemble *The 39 Steps* or to demonstrate how certain words must always be whispered in a Jewish home.

Gene Saks's staging is muscular, even when the round robin of somber Act 2 reconciliations plunges the play into overlength. The beautiful production design—by David Mitchell (scenery), Tharon Musser (lighting), and Patricia Zipprodt (costumes)—poetically re-creates the flavor of a bygone time and place while refracting that world through the glow of memory. The stage becomes a twilight-shaded sepia photograph suitable for the scrapbook of anyone's dreams.

The cast is full of top-flight actors, not all of whom are at their best. Mr. Goetz and Mr. Ivanek are: As the wise father and conscience-stricken brother, they give the play its most sustained interludes of gravity and weight. As the mother, Ms. Franz is a bit strident, despite some concerted stabs at sweetness in Act 2; there's a touch of last season's Sister Mary Ignatius in her yet. Ms. Van Patten is too stagy as the aunt, and so are the actresses playing her daughters.

As Eugene, Mr. Broderick possesses both the polished performing skills and the magnetism that are essential to keep *Brighton Beach Memoirs* rolling. But he sometimes has the too-calculated delivery of a stand-up comic, along with an odd, middle-aged posture that eerily resembles Walter Matthau's. Like the playwright he impersonates, this young star hasn't quite shaken the entertainer's habit of using charm as a mask. One hopes there will be a chapter two to *Brighton Beach Memoirs,* in which Mr. Simon and Mr. Broderick build on their often-endearing work by, paradoxically, trying a little less hard to please.

YOU CAN'T TAKE IT WITH YOU
PLYMOUTH THEATRE, APRIL 5, 1983

At the end of the new Broadway revival of *You Can't Take It with You,* the cast refuses to take a polite curtain call. Instead, the actors pair off, collapse into one another's arms and take to dancing about the stage. And it isn't polite dancing, either: As choreographed by Reed Jones, the couples leap about, still in character, with such rowdiness that you'd think they'd all been at a party rather than performing a play. Actually, the 1936 George S. Kaufman–Moss Hart screwball comedy at the Plymouth is more party than play—but, either way, you're glad to be part of the merriment.

You Can't Take It with You has probably been ruined by more high-school productions than anyone can count, and, let's face it, its confectionery charms are not foolproof: The writing is far too slipshod in design to be mistaken for classic farce, much too landlocked by its simple, best-things-in-life-are-free Depression escapism to speak to the ages. But the assets—sentimental warmth and giddy high spirits—are there, if only actors are willing to play them for keeps. Let's thank the director, Ellis Rabb, who also staged the hit 1965 revival of this work, for again assembling just such players and knitting them into a family that almost anyone would want to adopt for far longer than three acts.

As you no doubt know, Kaufman and Hart's characters are the Sycamore clan, an eccentric lot who have mostly retreated from the troublesome real world. Grandpa (Jason Robards) gave up business thirty-five years earlier to enjoy himself collecting snakes and attending Columbia University commencements. Daughter Penny (Elizabeth Wilson) writes steamy plays simply because someone delivered a typewriter to the house by mistake. Her husband (Jack Dodson) builds firecrackers in the basement with Mr. DePinna (Bill McCutcheon), who dropped by years earlier to deliver some ice and never left.

Yet what makes *You Can't Take It with You* so consistently appealing in this production—even as the toothless jokes about Roosevelt and Trotsky have faded—is that Mr. Rabb and company do not settle for defining the principal characters exclusively by the comic traits that the authors rather mechanically doled out to them. Whenever the script gives them room, the actors insist on portraying these zanies as real people whose behavior is not merely a setup for gags but a valiant response to hard times.

When Mr. Robards speaks of how much he hated the "jungle" of the business rat race—and how much he prefers a bohemian life that allows him "just to go along and be happy"—he is expressing sentiments that we've heard in dozens of 1930s comedies. But what usually sounds like idle fantasizing is given so much conviction by this actor that we're half-tempted to quit our jobs and seize happiness just like him. (Only later do we realize, unlike the authors, that it takes an independent income or maybe a redistribution of wealth to put the plan into effect.) Ms. Wilson's Penny, while a loon, is also a matriarch: When she speaks musically of planning a feast featuring Campbell's Soup, she gets the laugh but also finds poignancy in Penny's ability to cope no matter what.

Even the play's potentially drippiest passages become radiant under this approach. The romantic scenes between Penny's daughter, Alice (Maureen Anderman), and the well-bred boss's son, Tony (Nicolas Surovy), are sexy and touching because the young lovers are played as adults, not juveniles. Alice describes herself as "the Kay Francis" of her office, but the heavenly Ms. Anderman is more Margaret Sullavan: The only "sane" member of her family, she's bursting with so much intelligence and love that we forget she's written according to type. The same goes for the earnest, determined Mr. Surovy, who whirls Ms. Anderman around the darkened living room to "These Foolish Things" as if he can't wait to take her to bed (after a marriage ceremony, of course).

The better jokes are well served, too. Mr. Robards is, as always, a flinty wit, and when he explains the stubborn logic by which he refuses to pay income tax, he could be the patrician George Burns. Mr. McCutcheon, hound dog faced and dumpy, is quite droll posing in a Roman toga. Ms. Wilson, pure sunshine in her summer-print dresses, shows off her distinctively ditsy timing (of eyebrows and chin as well as of voice) when she none-too-innocently embarrasses Tony's stuffed-shirt parents by springing a free-association parlor game built around the words "sex" and "lust."

A few studied tableaux aside, Mr. Rabb rides the waves of chuckles and affection that flow through the homey set designed by James Tilton, and he usually has a secure hand on the farcical explosions that are sparked by unexpected firecracker displays and invasions from G-men.

In the large, powerhouse cast, there are only a few lesser lights. James Coco, as the Russian ballet teacher, is funnier than the balletomanes in Broadway's other current 1936 revival [*On Your Toes*], but he falls into shtick that this production otherwise avoids. Carol Androsky is routine as his principal student and a trifle mature for Christopher Foster, who is charming as her xylophone-playing husband.

But Rosetta Le Noire and Arthur French, as the black servants, and Richard Woods and Meg Mundy, as Tony's Wall Street–snooty parents, all succeed in stretching period stereotypes into people. And, as an Act 3 dessert, we get Colleen Dewhurst, dripping in velvet and braying of "blintzes," as the Russian Grand Duchess who "hasn't had a good meal since before the Revolution" and now works as a waitress at Child's. It's a cameo role, but Ms. Dewhurst, functioning as a cleanup hitter, knocks every laugh line clear out of the park.

Not long after her exit, the dancing begins, soon to be capped by a sing-along in which audience and actors join to croon "Good Night, Sweetheart." By then we're feeling, as Mr. Robards says, that "life is kind of beautiful," and it's no easy thing to leave the festivities at the Plymouth to face the ruder life that lies in wait outside.

THE MAN WHO HAD THREE ARMS
LYCEUM THEATRE, APRIL 6, 1983

Edward Albee's *The Man Who Had Three Arms*, at the Lyceum, isn't a play—it's a temper tantrum in two acts. A celebrated man known only as Himself—why is it always so hard for Mr. Albee to give people proper names?—stands at a lecture-hall podium, backed by potted plants and flags, and spends nearly two hours alternately insulting the audience and announcing how bitter he is.

This static premise is not, per se, a hopeless idea for theater: If Mr. Albee were inclined to be ruthlessly honest, he might have written a work as excoriating and funny as a Lenny Bruce routine. But the bitterness that pours out of Himself is a mixture of unearned self-pity and abject rancor. *The Man Who Had Three Arms* arouses roughly the same emotions as those *People* magazine cover stories in which movie stars grouse about how hard it is to escape grasping fans while shopping in Beverly Hills.

Himself, played by Robert Drivas, is mad because he was once "the most famous man in the world" and now he isn't so famous anymore. A standard-cut advertising man with a wife and three kids, he had one day awakened to discover that he was growing a third arm on his back. Suddenly Himself was sought after by royalty, cheered by ticker-tape parades, and toasted by talk-show hosts. He had become, one might say, a contemporary Elephant Man—complete with trunk.

But when we meet Himself, the parade has passed by. The third arm ultimately withered away, and so did the protagonist's celebrity and fortune. While he used to command $25,000 for a personal appearance, he now speaks for "half a grand and a toddle or two of gin." In the lecture we see, Himself is a last-minute replacement for a more famous speaker who has died. Drunk and in debt, he's now just another ordinary-looking man at the end of his rope.

One of the more shocking lapses of Mr. Albee's writing is that he makes almost no attempt even to pretend that Himself is anything other than a maudlin stand-in for himself, with the disappearing arm representing an atrophied talent. Though the speaker tells us about his family and advertising career, we never believe in these fictional biographical details for a second. They're thrown in without specificity or conviction, and, before long, they're forgotten as Himself lashes out against drama critics, speaks in the same overripe language as past Albee narrators, and starts wrapping himself in the cloaks of such literary men as Agee, Melville, and Nabokov.

But whoever Himself is—whether a one-time freak or a playwright in mid-career crisis—his beefs with the world are shrill and unmoving, no matter how much the author tries to inflate them into an indictment of "the American Dream." It's hard to feel much sympathy for a man who, by his own account, greedily helped himself to the perks of fame—unlimited publicity, power, money, and sex—and now complains that the adulation was "idiotic," that the power was short-lived, that the fortune was recklessly squandered, and that the sex was empty. Himself even gives us endless tirades about the food on the lecture circuit, as if his lucrative speaking engagements were a mandatory jail sentence rather than an easy, voluntary way to make lots of money for little work.

Thrown into this mix is a virulent and gratuitous misogyny that has little relevance to the character at hand but is totally of a piece with the last Albee play, *Lolita*: "Baggage" is easily the nicest term by which Himself refers to women. Indeed, the only person not treated contemptuously during the monologue is the speaker, who frequently likens his martyrdom to Christ's.

Whatever one thinks of the content of *The Man Who Had Three Arms*, the craftsmanship is rudimentary. Act 1 is all throat-clearing and padding. The sequences in which two other actors, William Prince and Patricia Kilgarriff, impersonate figures from the protagonist's past—doctors, parents, a Catholic priest—are so perfunctory they might as well be part of the crude slide show Himself sporadically uses to illustrate his lecture. The jokes include many wordplays on the hero's former appendage—"arm in arm in arm" and so on—and canned wisecracks about the press.

Under the author's direction, the tireless Mr. Drivas is reasonably successful at accomplishing the play's stated aim—to whip Himself and the audience "into mutual rage and revulsion." But only at the end does the anger come to a point. It's then that Mr. Albee at last begins to deal seriously with the issue his play wants to be about—an inability, as Himself puts it, "to distinguish between my self-disgust and my disgust with others." As the curtain falls, the sobbing Mr. Drivas falls to his knees, torn between asking the despised audience to leave and begging it to stay.

It's a painful, if embarrassing, spectacle, because it shows us the real and sad confusion that exists somewhere beneath the narcissistic arrogance and bile that the author uses as a dodge to avoid introspection the rest of the time. While *The Man Who Had Three Arms* is mostly an act of self-immolation, its final display of self-revelation holds out at least the slender hope that Mr. Albee might yet pick himself up from the floor.

ALL'S WELL THAT ENDS WELL
Martin Beck Theatre, April 14, 1983

Until the climactic scene, in which the gold of dawn at last peeks through, the light in the Royal Shakespeare Company's *All's Well That Ends Well* comes in shades of gray. That's how it should be. This comedy is indeed the problem play everyone has always said it is. Call *All's Well* what you will—a romance studded with nasty thorns, a cynical satire, a jumble—it is often cloudy. But gray, in Shakespeare's hands, becomes silver, and this play, stepchild of the canon though it may be, is still a mirror, however cracked, held up to the world. It reflects the intensity of life from the oddest of angles.

Or so it seems when *All's Well* is mounted with the high style, considered intelligence, and wit that are to be found in the production that has traveled from England to the Martin Beck. Trevor Nunn, the director, can't always overcome the author's slow exposition, passages of crabby poetry, and infelicities of structure and characterization. But he has created a shimmering, sophisticated evening that upholds the play's rich and long view of human nature, its dark music, its double-edged laughter. If *All's Well* lacks the crowd-pleasing attributes of the last two Nunn epics to play New York, *Nicholas Nickleby* and *Cats,* it's the most fascinating of the group and, when it hits its high points, the most rewarding.

The play is essentially about warfare—of sex, class, and the battlefield. Its principal plot, taken from Boccaccio, tells of Helena, a poor physician's daughter who is mad for Bertram, the Count of Rossillion. After magically curing the dying King of France, Helena is awarded Bertram's hand in marriage by the monarch. But the snotty Bertram refuses to have anything to do with his forced marriage to a lowborn woman and runs away to the Italian wars. The disguised heroine gives chase, finally to trap Bertram into a marital consummation by staging a fiendish mistaken-identity trick in bed.

Mr. Nunn's principal conceit for elevating this disagreeable and thin tale is to move the action to the late Edwardian era. As fabulously designed by John Gunter (who also did *Plenty* and London's current hit revival of *Guys and Dolls*), this *All's Well* unfolds in a glass pavilion that eventually encompasses a gymnasium, a gentlemanly officers' club, a belle epoque bistro, a gilt ballroom, a tent-and-smoke-filled war zone, and an autumnal, Chekhovian mansion belonging to the wise dowager Countess who is both Bertram's widowed mother and Helena's protective guardian. The stunning costumes (from the men's goggles and boots to the Italian nurses' Red Cross outfits) and the dying fall of Guy Woolfenden's Chopin-tinged music complete the period palette.

But the modernized setting is not just a fashionable sugarcoating. Mr. Nunn has taken seriously Shaw's famous observation that Helena was a precursor of Ibsen's New Woman. By leaping to the Ibsen-Shaw time frame, the director has brought a fresh and illuminating context to an implacably courageous heroine who will do anything and everything to get the man with whom she has a neurotic, even nymphomaniacal obsession. Harriet Walter fills out the conception by playing the role with a galvanizing mixture of intense feeling (too tremulously so early on) and flaming determination. She further takes the curse of foolishness off the role by making the ironic most of Helena's gradual, Ibsenesque realization that it is self-destructive for a smart woman to distort her life to a silly man's will.

The Edwardian ambience also achieves a resonance with the play's overriding theme that merit, not blood, determines human worth. While the historical details of the text don't accurately square with actual early-twentieth-century history, its spirit meshes remarkably with its new period. As World War I marked the last gasp of both the old European aristocracy and Victorian sexuality, so this *All's Well* is a fantasy about the shattering of those strictures. By the time the production's second half opens with a literal hole gaping through its elegant pavilion, one feels that Mr. Nunn has not only shown us the continuum that links Helena to Ibsen's Nora, but also the one that links Shakespeare's larger social critique to, say, Joan Littlewood's empire-smashing *Oh, What a Lovely War*.

This isn't to say that all of the director's good work stems from his setting. Many of the best moments in this *All's Well* are simply a marriage of good old-fashioned theatrical inventiveness and superb acting to a scrupulous reading of the text. The choice of period has nothing to do with the farcical delight that attends Helena's selection of a mate at the French court, which is here choreographed as a wicked game of musical husbands, or with the sisterly solidarity that binds Helena to her female coconspirators in Florence.

Perhaps the grandest scenes are those involving Bertram's dissolute crony, the braggart Parolles. Long considered a poor man's Falstaff or Pistol, this character achieves full Shakespearean depth in Stephen Moore's sensational performance. He's a scarf-betwined, cigarette-gesturing fop of surpassing asininity, and it is riotous to watch him squirm when his fellow officers snare him in their cruel humiliation plot. But once Parolles is undone, there is a heroic poignancy in this twit's stubborn conviction that he can go on—that "Simply the thing I am shall make me live." He exemplifies the compassionate spirit of a play that sees people as "a mingled yarn, good and ill together" and the world as containing a "place and means for every man alive."

There are many other strong, fully rounded performances. The play's exceptionally sensible and appealing elder characters are particularly brilliant: Robert Eddison's mellifluous but acerbic Lord Lafeu; John Franklyn-Robbins's circumspect King of France, who exercises power by sheer force of personality rather than by bombast; and Margaret Tyzack's elegant and maternal Countess, who is rendingly torn between love for her supercilious son and the ward he spurns. Only Ms. Tyzack's relative youth prevents her from completely equaling the transcendent Countess contributed by Peggy Ashcroft to this production at its inception.

Though the departure of Ms. Ashcroft hasn't harmed this *All's Well*, there's been some slippage since I saw it at London's Barbican Centre last year: The smaller stage space on Broadway has cramped some of the staging and the set, and the expository first act seems more raggedly paced. In addition, some of the play's problems, then and now, remain unsolved. The bland Philip Franks is a handsome Bertram, but neither he nor Mr. Nunn have found a way to make us believe that this opaquely written, petulant cad would be appealing to Helena or would undergo a sudden conversion in the final scene. Geoffrey Hutchings, with a crook-backed posture and twangy accent, finds charm and sadness but few laughs in the misbegotten clown Lavache.

Yet Mr. Nunn seems to recognize that he can't work all the miracles necessary to make all go well with *All's Well*. He asks us to accept this open-ended work, whose title is not to be taken at face value, as the ambiguous, imperfect creation that it is. While he opens the evening with a couple waltzing rhapsodically in the wintry light, the closing waltz for Bertram and Helena pointedly breaks that promise: The ostensibly reconciled lovers pull apart from each other in mid-step and walk side by side but separately into the dark. It's not the happy finale of a comedy— just the perfect ending for this rare production that captures the elusive glow of a play as melancholy and peculiarly radiant as a lunar eclipse.

≡ *Spoiled by the immediate Broadway success of his* Nicholas Nickleby *and* Cats, *the director Trevor Nunn was startled that good reviews didn't guarantee sell-out Broadway audiences for a play as thorny and unknown to Broadway (where it had never been produced) as* All's Well That Ends Well. *The day my review appeared, Nunn wrote me a letter in which he said that while he agreed with my review, tickets were moving slowly and the producers were threatening to close the show. His solution was that I supply some ad copy: "Will you add a paragraph to your remarks about* All's Well *and simply say that people should go and see it now that it's here in New York?"*

What Nunn had discovered, others soon enough would: A favorable Times *review could not in and of itself make a noncommercial drama succeed on Broadway. And if I had written ten pieces extolling* All's Well *in the hard-sell language suggested by Nunn, it still wouldn't have fared bet-*

ter than Grown Ups. *Could anything have made it—or any Shake-spearean production without a star—run on Broadway? Probably not. But if the producers—the Shuberts, also coproducers of* Cats*—had promoted the show as cleverly and expensively as they promoted musicals, maybe it would have had more of a shot. (Perhaps Nunn could have devoted some of his* Cats *profits to an* All's Well *push, too.) Instead of fighting for their plays, though, lazy producers of the eighties simply sat back and expected favorable reviews to do their work for them—no matter how many times the disastrous results of this approach suggested they were overestimating the critics' power.*

All's Well, *it's worth noting, had not run commercially in London, either, and probably would have failed if it had moved to the West End and had to compete with* Cats *there. It thrived only in repertory at the Royal Shake-speare Company, a national theater, where its run was subsidized by public funds. In a touching essay in the RSC's 1983–84 yearbook, Philip Franks, who played Bertram in* All's Well, *succinctly summed up the difference be-tween the two cities. "We opened [on Broadway] to a set of reviews stuffed with superlatives," he wrote. "However, shortly after opening, we nearly closed; advance bookings were not high enough. To most of us in the Com-pany, nurtured in the British subsidized theater, this sudden exposure to the commercial world of total success or total failure was a nasty shock . . . A salutary experience, though, seeing the horror as well as the hype of New York theater. The success ethic is alarmingly prevalent—if you're doing well there is nothing that people won't do for you. If not, your drink is snatched out of your hand. I'm not at all sure that this kind of pressure is conducive to good work in the theater, [but] for all that New York's theater world has a vast body of hardworking and talented people working in it."*

LE BOURGEOIS AVANT-GARDE
Ridiculous Theatrical Company, April 15, 1983

Charles Ludlam's new farce, *Le Bourgeois Avant-Garde*, bills itself as "a comedy after Molière," and that's about the only line of the evening that's not a joke. Mr. Ludlam—director, author-in-permanent-residence, and star of the Ridiculous Theatrical Company at One Sheridan Square—has indeed rewritten *Le Bourgeois Gentilhomme*, transposing it to the present day. By turns viciously funny, tasteless, slapdash, and rude, this play is Mr. Ludlam's brightest prank since he assaulted analysands in *Reverse Psychology* three seasons ago.

This time the satirical target is the New York art scene, downtown division. Mr. Ludlam plays Mr. Foufas, a bourgeois grocery-store magnate who lives only to be "the premier patron" of the arts. But no old-hat art will do: Mr. Foufas will support only artists who are so avant-garde they are "avant-derrière." The leeches who have attached themselves to the hero include the advocates of mixed-media theater "pieces" involving live turkeys, structuralists, and a graffiti artist named Moderna 83 who speaks exclusively in gibberish. It is Mr. Foufas's fondest wish that Moderna 83 will marry his daughter, Pru, who is hopelessly in love with Newton Entwhistle, the pinstriped bank officer next door.

With a glee that some might call philistine, Mr. Ludlam paints these esthetes as craven, absurd clowns. They fight among themselves by petulantly hurling such epithets as "Fauve!" and "Realist!" They explain that postmodernism can't be the same as futurism because "the future was over in the 1930s." They choose not to be called talent but "post-talent." They argue in favor of a new "convenient art substitute" called "artex"—"art without anguish."

But Mr. Foufas, like Molière's Monsieur Jourdain, worships at these charlatans' feet. And, however much the artists mock their vulgar patron in private, they bow down before him—thereby facilitating his ability to lean on their backs when writing checks. In partial exchange for the money, the artists arrange for Mr. Foufas to meet the woman of his dreams—Poland's foremost avant-garde film actress, Maia Panzaroff (say the name aloud for full effect).

As written and played by Mr. Ludlam, the pretentious grocer is a lovable lunatic. A man who is "ravenous for culture," he broods that his deprived middle-class upbringing prevented him from ever being "in love with a prostitute who got jealous and burned my manuscript." His pursuit of the latest fashions in high seriousness is crazed in its intensity. In one of the best bits—executed like an old Jackie Gleason–Art Carney *Honeymooners* routine—he refuses to send Maia Panzaroff a love letter until he has successfully deconstructed its text. Mr. Foufas also insists on wearing "avant-garde" clothes: In Act 1, he looks like a white octopus in heat, and in Act 2, he's dressed like an outsized pickle (with shoes to match).

The script's jokes, even when quoting or paraphrasing *Le Bourgeois Gentilhomme,* are often the last word in hip. Who but Mr. Ludlam would open a play with gags that assume an audience's familiarity with both the Comédie Française and Richard Foreman's treatments of Molière? If you're not up on the latest tides in theater and dance performance art, you may get lost. If you are in the know, you may be offended—which is, of course, part of the point. Probably everyone will agree, however, that the level of comic invention falls off considerably about fifteen minutes into Act 2.

Through thick and thin, the actors play in the familiar company style. Every role is a put-on to be carried out as amateurishly and outrageously as possible, in the manner of a bunk show at summer camp. Everett Quinton, in drag, is particularly funny as Mrs. Foufas, a proper platinum-haired matron who is out dining at Beefsteak Charlie's when her husband's putative mistress comes around. Mr. Quinton also designed the production's costumes, some of the zaniest of which he gets to wear himself.

Maia Panzaroff is played by the redoubtable Black-Eyed Susan, with an accent even the Gabor sisters might find a bit much. She offers a wicked explanation of why Poland is a "land of opportunity" and gets to tell a joke about how many Americans it takes to screw in a lightbulb. But if there's any performer to identify with, it's probably Zelda Patterson, in the role of Mr. Foufas's very properly uniformed maid. Even when Mr. Ludlam threatens to silence her with his fist, Ms. Patterson can't resist the urge to laugh hysterically into his ridiculous face.

≡ *Charles Ludlam's plays were often written to be disposable vehicles for his company—though they are collected in a fascinating posthumous anthology—and are hard to imagine without him and/or Everett Quinton. But in retrospect some of them—and* Le Bourgeois Avant-Garde *is an example—hold up both as farce and as social criticism. Certainly no one else, except perhaps Richard Greenberg in a series of plays typified by* Eastern Standard, *so well caught the excesses of hip and pseudo-hip moneyed Manhattan in the eighties.*

TEANECK TANZI: THE VENUS FLYTRAP
NEDERLANDER THEATRE, APRIL 21, 1983

There are two diversions to occupy theatergoers just before the start of Claire Luckham's play *Teaneck Tanzi: The Venus Flytrap*. The first is the refurbished Nederlander Theatre—a Broadway house that the designer Lawrence Miller has ingeniously transformed into a full-fledged wrestling arena. With a burst of gaudy lights above the ring and much architectural fiddling, Mr. Miller transports us well beyond Teaneck—all the way to Atlantic City.

The other source of amusement is one of the ushers. Slipped in among the bona fide employees of the Nederlander is a ringer—the comic Andy Kaufman. Mr. Kaufman's shtick, as his fans know, is hostility, and here he is, in the highest of dudgeon, a cigarette dangling from his lips, barking at seated customers. He demands to see our ticket stubs, and, should we not immediately locate them, he loudly threatens to eject us clear out to the street. As most of Mr. Kaufman's victims don't recognize him, there's sadistic fun to be had in watching the surly comedian provoke the uninitiated into angry screaming. A critic near me almost slugged him.

As it turned out, that may have been the high point of that critic's evening; it certainly was of mine. *Teaneck Tanzi* is an Americanized, retitled version of London's biggest comedy hit since *Steaming,* and its charm must have bailed out somewhere over the Atlantic. What we find at the Nederlander is a theatrical gimmick whose execution produces a pounding sensation in every part of one's head except the brain.

The gimmick—also employed ineffectually by John Sayles in his play *Turnbuckle* two seasons ago—is to stage a putative drama in the form of a wrestling match. Instead of scenes, there are ten "rounds" (you'll count them). Instead of dialogue, there are bouts in which the heroine settles emotional disputes with her family by means of flips, half nelsons, hairpulling, and body presses.

Because Tanzi and her antagonists are symbols devoid of flesh or blood, we don't care who vanquishes whom in the ring: They're all pop-up dolls. The wrestling, though noisy, is less convincing than an average Three Stooges melee. There are also songs, seemingly composed on a washboard. The instrumental accompaniment, led by an electric organ, isn't worthy of a seventh-inning stretch at Shea Stadium.

The author's metaphor cloaks a feminist message-play, set in some anachronistic land (surely not New Jersey) where women are so oppressed they are denied higher education and any career other than housewife. Tanzi's despotic husband, a professional wrestler, is dressed as a 1950s greaser and, in a typical sample of the evening's wit, is named Dean Rebel. (Another sample: Tanzi's lascivious school psychiatrist is named Dr. Grope.) After much tedious biographical exposition, which charts the heroine's progress "from potties to panty hose," we reach the "main event": Tanzi becomes a lady wrestler so she can finally challenge hubby to a do-or-die battle for her liberation from the kitchen. Anyone who can't guess the winner in advance deserves a lifetime pass to *Rocky III.*

With the aid of audience plants, the director, Chris Bond, tries to whip us into a frenzy of cheering and heckling. He has a particular fondness for sight gags involving the male crotch. The cast's mugging, Mr. Kaufman's fitfully amusing referee aside, is also well below the belt. Theatergoers can choose between two alternating pairs of performers in the roles of Tanzi and Dean—a choice that, under the circumstances, means about as much as being allowed to pick either coffee or tea at one's last supper.

I saw both casts, a feat that certainly earns me a mention in Ripley's. The better duo is Caitlin Clarke and Thomas G. Waites—legitimate actors who can't be blamed if they decide to fake injuries entitling them to insurance benefits as padded as their costumes. The other stars, the rock singer Deborah Harry and Scott Renderer, make a worthwhile contribution by slurring some of their lines.

≡ *Another misguided, Americanized London import but memorable for the unlikely Broadway appearance of the comedian Andy Kaufman—a strange, driven figure who died of lung cancer while still in his thirties. Though I remember little about the play, I still recall seeing one of my colleagues, drunk and disoriented by the reconfigured auditorium, leap out of his seat to bolt as soon as the show was over but end up instead among the actors backstage—who soon shoved him rudely back into the auditorium.*

SHOW BOAT
URIS THEATRE, APRIL 25, 1983

During the first twenty-five minutes or so of the new revival of *Show Boat*, you'll be nervous. This production, which originated at the Houston Grand Opera, has been traveling the country for months previous to its arrival at the Uris—and looks it. The sets are touring sets, flimsy and crudely lighted; the staging, by Michael Kahn, seems to be chiseled in stone. But it's amazing what glorious voices, in concert with beautiful theater songs, can do to make you forget about all that. My guess is that you, like me, will begin forgetting about all that from the moment Bruce Hubbard sits on a barrel to sing "Ol' Man River."

As sung and acted by Mr. Hubbard—with a voice at once chesty and light, booming and supple—"Ol' Man River" doesn't just roll along; it crests into a tidal wave. And that tidal wave sets off a flood. Whatever else is to be said about *Show Boat*, its Jerome Kern–Oscar Hammerstein II score is a treasure beyond estimation. Hardly has "Ol' Man River" passed than we are on to "Can't Help Lovin' Dat Man," "You Are Love,"

"Why Do I Love You?" and the show's single Kern–P. G. Wodehouse collaboration, "Bill." Every one of these standards—and let's not forget "Make Believe"—is sung for keeps by performers as uniformly gifted vocally as Mr. Hubbard.

If *Show Boat* isn't the best Broadway score on the boards right now, that's only because of *Porgy and Bess*, whose current revival also has roots at the Houston Grand Opera. If it must be said that Mr. Kahn's version of *Show Boat* sags when it isn't singing, be grateful that the singing only rarely subsides. Flaws and all, there is more than enough evidence at the Uris to justify this work's giant status in the American musical theater. If only *Oklahoma!* were running alongside *Porgy* and *Show Boat*, New York audiences would indeed be able to see the first half of the modern musical's history in one season.

Show Boat, originally produced by Florenz Ziegfeld in 1927, is chronologically the first of the trio, and perhaps the most startling. Hammerstein's book, adapted from Edna Ferber, was innovative in its time because its songs grew out of character and plot, because its themes (racism, marital strife, psychological self-destruction) were mature, because it did without silly chorus girls. Those assets are academic matters today, and yet other aspects of Hammerstein's libretto remain daring and fresh. Here is a book that, while still tied somewhat to the period conventions of melodrama and burlesque, moves freely from the post-Reconstruction Deep South to Theodore Dreiser's industrialized Chicago, all the way to the radio-and-movie-crazed jazz age of the 1920s. Here, too, is what may be the first modern Broadway "concept" musical, built around a metaphor. That old Mississippi River stands for time, which both opens and heals the characters' wounds.

Although the story's actual events are a bit too thin and contrived to support the grandeur of the conception and the music, there's pleasure in watching Hammerstein's pursuit of an epic, adult vision. One sees the groundwork for the musicals he'd write with Richard Rodgers later on. One can even argue that a subtle *Show Boat* motif, the appropriation of black music by white singers, foreshadows *Dreamgirls*—and that the double-edged use of vaudeville numbers, to indicate historical and character developments, anticipates *Gypsy* and *Follies*. (Stephen Sondheim, in fact, seems to pay specific homage to "Why Do I Love You?" in *Follies*.)

This is why Hammerstein's libretto, unlike so many others in vintage musicals, need not be swept under the rug; it's worthy of inventive thinking by a contemporary director. It's a waste that Mr. Kahn, working with a decent choreographer (Dorothy Danner) but with scenery that is old-fashioned and noisy as well as tacky, didn't stage the show with the cinematic flow that the writing invites. His uninspired tableaux—rhythmically punctuated by blackouts and the rising of scrims—try to push *Show Boat* back into the realm of operetta, which its creators were trying to escape.

But Mr. Kahn can be forgiven a lot because of the tender care given the score, down to Jack Everly's meticulous conducting of the authentic underscoring and orchestrations, and because of the casting. Lonette McKee, billed as the first black actress to play the mulatto Julie, is a great beauty with an openhearted, smoky voice and an incandescent presence. Wasted last season in *The First,* she should achieve stardom now: Her renditions of "Can't Help Lovin' Dat Man" (surely the best Gershwin blues not written by Gershwin) and "Bill" are heart-stopping. Sheryl Woods, as Magnolia, is another lovely singer and warm actress, and one only wishes that her equally mellifluous romantic partner, Ron Raines, brought more Rhett Butler–style sexual dash to the dissolute Gaylord Ravenal.

As Cap'n Andy, proprietor of the show boat *Cotton Blossom,* Donald O'Connor gives the show a special resonance: It's fun to watch an ace showman from one vanished era play an ace vaudevillian of an adjacent past. He gets his laughs, by hook and crook, and contributes a delightful (if brief) display of his old razzmatazz tap style in Act 2. The comic secondary lovers, precursors of Ado Annie and Will Parker in *Oklahoma!,* are handled in a conventional, if pleasing, manner by Paige O'Hara and Paul Keith.

There is standout work by Karla Burns in the Aunt Jemima role of Queenie. Ms. Burns has been handed a sizzling, rarely heard song, "Hey, Feller!," that's been restored to *Show Boat* for this production. Used at the show's climax to help catapult the action from 1905 to 1927, "Hey, Feller!" brings a vo-de-oh-do exclamation point, complete with a spiffy Charleston, to the end of a score whose opening number ("Cotton Blossom") harks back to Victor Herbert.

The evening's actual finale, of course, is the last reprise of "Ol' Man River"—a song so much a part of our cultural fabric, so pure in its perfect union of yearning lyrics and surging music, that it seems as indestructible as the flag. The misty-eyed audience can't be blamed for leaping to its feet to pay a proper salute.

≡ Show Boat *was a box-office failure despite good reviews. A dozen years later, a Harold Prince revival playing the same theater—and again with Lonette McKee as Julie—would become a hit, more a reflection of changing times (a growing curiosity in our musical-theater and racial heritage alike) than the difference between the two productions.*

MY ONE AND ONLY
St. James Theatre, May 2, 1983

Capt. Billy Buck Chandler (Tommy Tune), the derring-do 1920s hero of the musical *My One and Only*, dreams of being "the first man in history to fly nonstop to Paris." It's giving away nothing to say that Billy at last takes flight in Act 2, and, as he does, so does the entertainment that contains him. The second half of the handsome show at the St. James levitates with some of the most inspired choreography Broadway has seen in several seasons—all set to the celestial music of George Gershwin and danced to kill by a company glittering in Art Deco swank.

Until then, *My One and Only* is a smart and happy, if less than electrifying, spin down memory lane. Yet even at its most innocuous, this show receives a considerable boost from its Gershwin songs: The entire score, stitched together by a pastiche period book, derives from the Broadway trove created by the composer and his brother, Ira, a half-century ago. When Mr. Tune and his adorable leading lady, Twiggy, glide about in moonlight to "He Loves and She Loves" and "'S Wonderful," they may not make you forget Fred Astaire partnering Audrey Hepburn to the same standards in the film *Funny Face*. But the Gershwin tunes and lyrics are so potent you'll be transported all the same.

As has been widely publicized, the Gershwins are perhaps the only authors whose contributions to *My One and Only* are completely identifiable. During this production's troubled gestation period, seemingly half of show business pitched in to offer anonymous help—no doubt the half that wasn't toiling on the screenplay of *Tootsie*. The result of the effort is not the brilliant musical the theater desperately craves, but nonetheless a slick one, brimming with high-hat confidence.

My One and Only even has a coherent—and delightful—style. From its bright, cartoonish sets in shiny David Hockneyesque primary colors to the relaxed, debonair gait of the direction and choreography by Mr. Tune and Thommie Walsh, this musical achieves an airy, easygoing charm that runs happily counter to Broadway's current aggressive fashion. However much sweat went into *My One and Only*, the show doesn't feel like work.

Though the songs are familiar, the approach is often clever. In the opening number, "I Can't Be Bothered Now," the directors' cockeyed slant is established by a trio of tuxedo-clad scat singers who deliver the song with mischievous insouciance. "Sweet and Low-Down," soon to follow, is a black-tie-and-tails strut, in which the white canes and gloves glow in phosphorescent light. When "'S Wonderful" is danced by the stars on a deserted beach, the couple enter a pool of water to splash on beat.

At no time is the classic music compromised by contemporary tampering—even when "Funny Face" is sung by the show's most clownish performers, the able Denny Dillon and Bruce McGill, seated on the floor. The orchestrations (by Michael Gibson) and the dance arrangements (by Wally Harper, Peter Larson, and Peter Howard) are ever so delicately jazzed-up rethinkings of the past. The voices, while not sterling, are firm. Mr. Tune brings a forceful belt to "Strike Up the Band," which he delivers as a vehement, slow-tempo anthem in the manner of the early Barbra Streisand's "Happy Days Are Here Again." Twiggy has an odd catch in her throat that summons the bygone vocal idiom of the twenties.

Most of what Twiggy does is fetchingly odd. Not quite an accomplished actress, singer, or dancer, and not quite beautiful, she has a striking, slinky presence and vulnerable, little-lost-flapper look that is instantly winning. Cast as an Englishwoman famous for swimming the English Channel, she gets to appear in some smashing black-and-silver bathing costumes (exquisitely designed by Rita Ryack) with shimmering helmets to match. But whatever she's wearing, it's her plaintive, intimate renditions of "Boy Wanted" and "Nice Work If You Can Get It" that give *My One and Only* its essential warmth.

Mr. Tune—a far more polished performer and a fantastic dancer—could learn from his costar. If she holds back, he is much too eager to please: From his first entrance, he is making cute faces at us, asking for applause, and while his feet ultimately earn that approbation, his relentless aw-shucks pose is more obsequious than ingratiating. This excessive narcissism contributes to one of the show's failings, which is the lack of any credible sexual or romantic passion to spark the ostensible love story.

The other failing—minimized by the snappy staging, with its distracting parade of white umbrellas and steaming locomotives—is the book by Peter Stone and Timothy S. Mayer. It's a professional but mechanical retelling of the boy-meets-girl-loses-girl-finds-girl plots of the Astaire-Rodgers movies. The jokes, except for a silent-film parody set in Morocco, are either forced or propped up by four-letter words. The message—celebrity isn't everything—is repeated once too often and presumably holds deeper meaning for the authors than for the audience.

Because the lines and love scenes don't dazzle, it's up to the dancing to push *My One and Only* beyond pleasant whimsy and unvarnished camp into excitement. The first jolt of true lightning occurs shortly after intermission, when the dapper and immortal Charles (Honi) Coles, as the hero's fairy godfather, teaches the towering Mr. Tune a lesson about wooing by teaching him how to tap to the title song. An understated exercise in precise terpsichorean pointillism, this showstopper by two master hoofers is a rare reminder of how less can be more in a big musical.

The grandest prize to follow, "Kickin' the Clouds Away," is an extravagant ensemble piece set at a Harlem chapel, whose quack reverend is played by a bemused Roscoe Lee Browne. Again the mode is tap, but instead of the Busby Berkeley drill one expects, the choreographers create a disjointed, centrifugal whirlwind of movement that sends individual dancers twirling into separate, idiosyncratic variations on the overall twenties pattern. On a Broadway rife with vintage shows, here is one demonstration of how the clouds really can be kicked away—of how valuable old songs can be liberated from musty staging clichés. Though *My One and Only* isn't always so fresh or buoyant, it's the only new or old musical of the season that sends us home on air.

PRIVATE LIVES
Lunt-Fontanne Theatre, May 9, 1983

The tone of the Richard Burton–Elizabeth Taylor *Private Lives* is established right off. When Mr. Burton makes his first entrance on to the attractive Deauville hotel terrace designed by David Mitchell, he looks anything but happy. His face is a taut mask, frozen in an expression of less-than-exquisite pain, and there's no bounce as he walks about on his stacked boots. He's not Noël Coward's flippant hero Elyot Chase—he doesn't even seem to be an actor. In his immaculate Savile Row business suit, Mr. Burton mostly resembles a retired millionaire steeling himself for an obligatory annual visit to the accountant. He's bored out of his mind but grimly determined to clip the coupons and sign the papers that will allow him to maintain his cash flow for the next year.

Ms. Taylor, soon to follow, is scarcely more buoyant. She enters in the first of several Theoni V. Aldredge costumes that fail to further the illusion of what Coward described as his "quite exquisite" heroine. Her curly mop of hair is meant to suggest the fashion of the 1920s but instead recalls the matronly Toni permanents that were in vogue during the 1950s. Not that it matters—Ms. Taylor isn't trying to play Amanda

Prynne. When she looks at her costar, her glances betray neither rapture nor revulsion; she looks past him, not at him. It's only when she stares out into the vast reaches of the Lunt-Fontanne that her eyes reveal a hint of sparkle: What she sees then is a full house.

And so you have the complete picture. While this *Private Lives* does plod on—and on and on—for another two and a half hours (despite substantial pruning of the script), the first impression it leaves is the last. From the start, the production never even pretends to be anything other than a calculated business venture. Though the irresistible plot mechanics keep Act 1 sporadically afloat, the two acts to come have all the vitality of a Madame Tussaud's exhibit and all the gaiety of a tax audit. Nothing that happens at any time has any bearing on Coward's classic 1930 comedy.

That play, the seeming inconsequentiality of its dialogue notwithstanding, is a wise and painful statement about both the necessity and the impossibility of love. In this version, whose billed director is Milton Katselas, there's no attempt to mine the gold beneath the text—or to make the most of the on-the-surface dross. Instead we get an intermittent effort by the stars to create the fan-magazine fantasy that their own offstage private lives dovetail neatly with Coward's story of a divorced couple who rekindle their old passion after meeting by chance on their second honeymoons. Announcing that she's "scared of marriage," Ms. Taylor takes a disingenuous pause almost long enough to contain a whole one-act Coward play and then winks at the audience, lest we miss the purple irony.

But life doesn't imitate art in this *Private Lives*—it obliterates it. Early on, we see that, unlike Elyot and Amanda, Mr. Burton and Ms. Taylor have little lingering affection for each other—or none that they can either convey or fake on stage. When Mr. Burton finally crosses from his side of the terrace to embrace Ms. Taylor in Act 1, he approaches the task with the stealthy gait of Count Dracula stalking a victim. When, in the Paris flat of Act 2, he grabs his costar's (covered) breast from behind, he evinces the perfunctory, clinical detachment of a physician who's examined too many patients in one day—and Ms. Taylor responds as if under anesthesia. Even the slapstick battle to follow fails to light a fire—it's a ghost of a pillow fight that makes us wonder whether Amanda's address might be the Rue Morgue.

Between these vulgar displays, which are thrown to the voyeuristic multitudes like so many stale breadcrusts, we can do little but anticipate the intermissions (which must be among the longest in Broadway history), recoil at the overacting of John Cullum and Kathryn Walker as the discarded spouses, and dwell sadly on the dimming of the stars' luster since they last appeared in their respective revivals of *The Little Foxes* and *Camelot*.

Ms. Taylor lists about, her hands fluttering idly, like a windup doll in need of a new mainspring. Her voice—sometimes a Southern-accented falsetto, sometimes a campy screech—often mangles simple words (like "pompous") and occasionally defies the amplification system by evaporating entirely. The single line she speaks with conviction is a plaintive, "How long, oh Lord, how long?" Mr. Burton's voice, by contrast, remains a crisp, mellifluous instrument that snares a few legitimate laughs on some of Coward's more barbed lines. But the words could well be piped in, so robotic is the figure from which they emanate.

Perhaps if the stars acted as if they were enjoying themselves, this evening would have worked as a trashily amusing old-time burlesque stunt, redolent of that vanished era when tabloid celebrities exploited their fame by touring the vaudeville circuit. But Ms. Taylor and Mr. Burton look whipped and depressed as they go through the motions of *Private Lives*. Far from turning back the clock to a more glamorous past— whether Coward's, Elyot's and Amanda's, or their own—they succeed only in making the rest of us feel very, very old.

THE CRADLE WILL ROCK
AMERICAN PLACE THEATRE, MAY 10, 1983

Just before each performance of *The Cradle Will Rock* at the American Place Theatre, John Houseman walks to a podium to deliver a ten-minute lecture. We're used to watching Mr. Houseman lecture these days: With his bow tie, crusty demeanor, and authoritative voice, he has become, courtesy of television, our foremost unofficial university professor. But the speech he's giving this time is not manufactured rhetoric. What Mr. Houseman reads instead is his own account of how Marc Blitzstein's "labor opera" first faced a New York audience almost forty-six years ago.

Mr. Houseman was there back then—he coproduced the first *Cradle*. His associates included such illustrious theater people as Orson Welles, Jean Rosenthal, Howard da Silva, Hiram Sherman, and Lehman Engel, all employees of the WPA Federal Theatre Project. And the story of how this then-incendiary musical went on—despite attempts by both Congress and Actors Equity to shut it down—is surely one of the great adventure sagas of the American theater. As Mr. Houseman warms to the riveting tale, he suddenly ceases to be a grand old man of 1983. He seems transported right back to that legendary hot June night when, with Blitzstein at the piano, he and his troupe defied the authorities to perform *Cradle* without sets and costumes before a delirious throng.

Mr. Houseman concludes by promising that the performance to come—directed by him with a cast drawn from the alumni of The Acting Company—will re-create the style of the original. Only witnesses of the first *Cradle* can say how much he succeeds, but to this observer his production is remarkably effective at conveying the excitement not only of Blitzstein's music but also of the Depression ideology it enshrines. However dated and simplistic *Cradle* may now seem as proletarian political thought, it still breathes fire when sung, acted, and staged as fervently as it is in this revival.

The libretto tells of how the evil industrialist Mr. Mister and the heroic labor organizer Larry Foreman battle for control of the mythological Steeltown, U.S.A. If the characters are symbols and the moral issues black and white, the music has a force and sophistication that give permanent, heartfelt life to the sloganeering. What makes this version of *Cradle* particularly poignant is the youthfulness of the performers. Unlike Mr. Houseman, they are not remembering history: They project the piece's anger and idealism as if feeling them for the first time.

The cast contains a number of standouts. Patti LuPone—working, for a change, without miking or mannerisms—delivers a moving, beautifully sung performance as the downtrodden prostitute who snakes plaintively through the action. As Larry Foreman, Randle Mell leads the title song—a rallying cry for proletarian justice—with thunderous, charismatic bravado. Michele-Denise Woods turns "Joe Worker Gets Gypped" into a sustained wail of pure (but disciplined) rage, and David Schramm is perfect as the villainous magnate at whom the rage is aimed. As Gus Polock, an innocent young immigrant worker doomed to be killed by Mr. Mister's henchmen, Casey Biggs can induce tears with the simple, lullaby-flavored couplet, "I make a little bed from wood/So my son sleep good."

The comic roles—especially Tom Robbins's Editor Daily and Gerald Gutierrez's craven violinist, Yasha—are spicily handled. Though there's the occasional weak voice, we do hear the full range of the score—an eclectic mixture of operatic flights, Kurt Weillisms, and sassy period pop parodies (led by the witty "Spoon/Croon").

As Aaron Copland wrote years ago, Blitzstein, whose life was ended by murder in 1964, proved "the first American composer to invent a vernacular musical idiom that sounded convincing when heard from the lips of the man in the street." How one wishes this company would now go on to some of the rest of the composer's canon, starting with the neglected Sean O'Casey adaptation, *Juno,* which has been rarely seen since it failed on Broadway in 1959.

A few of the sillier didactic sequences aside, Mr. Houseman's staging courses smoothly along. As promised, the show is performed on a dark stage, decorated only with chairs and Dennis Parichy's poetic lighting. At dead center is the upright piano, whose expert player, Michael Barrett, delivers the Brechtian scene-setting announcements as Blitzstein once did. When, at the end, the entire company storms forward to cry out a final plea for justice, you'll feel those goosebumps that come when the past suddenly rises up and grabs you by the throat.

FOOL FOR LOVE
CIRCLE REPERTORY COMPANY, MAY 27, 1983

No one knows better than Sam Shepard that the true American West is gone forever, but there may be no writer alive more gifted at reinventing it out of pure literary air. Like so many Shepard plays, *Fool for Love,* at the Circle Repertory Company, is a western for our time. We watch a pair of figurative gunslingers fight to the finish—not with bullets, but with piercing words that give ballast to the weight of a nation's buried dreams.

As theater, *Fool for Love* could be called an indoor rodeo. The setting is a present-day motel room on the edge of the Mojave Desert, where, for ninety minutes, May (Kathy Baker) and Eddie (Ed Harris) constantly batter one another against the walls. May and Eddie have been lovers for fifteen years; they may even, like the fratricidal antagonists of *True West,* be siblings. But May has had it: She'd now like nothing more than to "buffalo" Eddie by stabbing him in the middle of a passionate kiss.

Eddie is some sort of rancher, complete with saddle, rifle, and lasso. Yet there's no more range—Marlboro men ride only in advertising—and he lives in a tin trailer. The motel room is May's most recent home. With its soiled green walls and a window facing black nothingness, it looks like a jail cell; its doors slam shut with a fierce metallic clang. When Eddie uses his rope, all he can snare is a bedpost. When the two lovers want to escape, they don't mount horses for a fast getaway—they merely run to the parking lot and back.

But if the West is now reduced to this—a blank empty room with an unmade bed—Mr. Shepard fills that space with reveries as big as all outdoors. When the play's fighting lets up, we hear monologues resembling crackling campfire tales. The characters—who also include May's new suitor (Dennis Ludlow) and a ghostly "old man" (Will Marchetti) sipping Jim Beam in a rocking chair—try to find who they are and where they are. Though the West has become but a figment of the movies, Eddie contends that "there's not a movie in this town that can match the story I can tell."

Laced with the floating images of cattle herds, old cars, and even a spectral Spencer Tracy looming in the dark, these hallucinatory stories chart the Shepard vision. His characters are "disconnected"; they fear being "erased"; they hope to be "completely whole." In *Fool for Love*, each story gives us a different "version" of who May, Eddie, and the old man are, and the stories rarely mesh in terms of facts. Yet they do cohere as an expression of the author's consciousness: As Shepard's people race verbally through the debris of the West, they search for the identities and familial roots that have disappeared with the landscape of legend.

Not finding what they seek, they use their dreams as weapons, to wipe each other out. The old man, a ghostly figure who may be May and Eddie's father, tells the couple that they could be "anybody's children"— "I don't recognize myself in either of you and never did." Eddie and May respond in kind, even as they obliterate their own shared past. "You got me confused with someone else," says May to her lover, vowing never again to be suckered into one of his "little fantasies." What remains of Eddie's fantastical West is ultimately destroyed, too: His few horses burn in the play's apocalyptic finale.

Mr. Shepard's conceits are arresting and funny. Eddie, in explaining his particular erotic fixation, tells May that her neck keeps "coming up for some reason." The old man contends he is married to Barbara Mandrell and announces, without much fear of contradiction, that the singer's picture is hanging on an empty wall. There is a strange poignancy to May's suitor, a gentle maintenance man too lost even to dream of a self. Like a much talked-about "countess" of Eddie's supposed acquaintance, this sweet gentleman caller, intentionally or not, provides *Fool for Love* with an odd, unlikely echo of Tennessee Williams.

The production at the Circle Rep allows New York audiences to see the play in its native staging. *Fool for Love* has been transported here from Mr. Shepard's home base, the Magic Theater of San Francisco, complete with the original cast under the author's direction. The actors are all excellent: With utter directness, they create their own elusive yet robust world—feisty, muscular, sexually charged—and we either enter it or not.

Fool for Love isn't the fullest Shepard creation one ever hopes to encounter, but, at this point in this writer's prolific twenty-year career, he almost demands we see his plays as a continuum: They bleed together. In the mode of his recent work, this play has a title and beat that's more redolent of country music than rock; the theatrical terms are somewhat more realistic than outright mythic (though reality is always in the eye of the beholder). The knockabout physical humor sometimes becomes excessive both in the writing and in the playing; there are also, as usual, some duller riffs that invite us to drift away.

It could be argued, perhaps, that both the glory and failing of Mr. Shepard's art is its extraordinary afterlife: His works often play more feverishly in the mind after they're over than they do while they're before us in the theater. But that's the way he is, and who would or could change him? Like the visionary pioneers who once ruled the open geography of the West, Mr. Shepard rules his vast imaginative frontier by making his own, ironclad laws.

FEN

Public Theater, May 31, 1983

Fen, the new Caryl Churchill play at the Public, could well be called *Bottom Girls.* As the author's *Top Girls* told of Marlene, a self-made businesswoman who sells out her provincial working-class roots and humanity for corporate success in London, so the new one examines the less-privileged sisters such top girls leave behind. The characters of *Fen* are downtrodden farmworkers in the Fens of East Anglia. Marlene would dismissively claim that these women deserve their fate because they're too "lazy and stupid" to claw their way up the economic ladder as she did. But in Ms. Churchill's view, it's the Marlenes of contemporary England who callously keep the benighted poor in their lowly place.

As befits the shift in focus, the new play contains little of its predecessor's laughter: Even as the audience enters the Public's LuEsther Hall, it is swept up in a gloomy mist that pours out from the stage. *Fen* is dour, difficult, and, unlike either *Top Girls* or *Cloud 9,* never coy about its rather stridently doctrinaire socialism: It's the most stylistically consistent of Ms. Churchill's plays and at times the most off-putting. It is also yet another confirmation that its author possesses one of the boldest theatrical imaginations to emerge in this decade.

Fen was created by Ms. Churchill with the Joint Stock Theatre Group, the communal London fringe company whose actors conduct their own documentary research into the characters they portray. As an impressionistic, class-conscious portrait of an agrarian community, the play recalls David Hare's Joint Stock piece about a similar village in nascent revolutionary China, *Fanshen*: A few actors—five women, one man—play more than twenty roles in a mosaic of Brechtian vignettes. But unlike *Fanshen*, which was seen here this year in a weak local staging, *Fen* has been brought intact from London as part of the Britain Salutes New York festival. It's a high-powered production, faultlessly directed by Les Waters with an acting ensemble as accomplished as the imported Royal Court cast of *Top Girls*.

The action unfolds on a stunning set designed by Annie Smart: The stage floor is carpeted with the dirt of the potato fields and surrealistically bordered by walls and furnishings suggesting the women's dreary homes. In Tom Donnellan's eerie lighting—all shades of Thomas Hardy dankness, no sunlight—the ninety minutes of scenes loom in the icy dark like fragmented nightmares. One minute the women are picking potatoes in a thunderstorm; then, through startlingly sharp transitions, that dominant image gives way to the sight of two illicit lovers dancing in moonlight or a Madonna-like portrait of mother and child or a forlorn Baptist revival meeting.

"We're all rubbish," says one of the suffering Baptists, "but Jesus still loves us, so it's all right." As in *Top Girls*, Ms. Churchill sees one and all as helpless, exploited victims of a dehumanizing capitalistic system. She further feels that women can only escape its clutches, as Marlene did, by adopting that system's most selfish, ruthless traits.

There are two top girls in *Fen*—an unfeeling workers' overlord and a slick real-estate entrepreneur—and even their power doesn't give them freedom from top guys. They must answer to the countryside's real barons—a faceless multinational conglomerate, which, as a prologue implies, is or will be owned by the Japanese.

Most of the women in *Fen*, however, are laborers, bound to the land by an age-old, oppressive tradition that enslaves them from birth to grave. As Ms. Churchill presents these sad serfs, they can only ameliorate their misery in self-destructive ways: by drinking in a pub or gossiping or taking Valium or betraying one another or going mad. Yet if the playwright's definition of these women's choices is rigidly deterministic, her concentrated dramatization of their lives has an open, poetic intensity that transcends the flat tendentiousness of mere agitprop.

Shadowy and spare as the brief scenes are, luminous individual characters gradually emerge. Chief among them is Val (Jennie Stoller), who leaves her daughters for a new lover (Bernard Strother)—only to discover, to her eternal torment, that she can't live either without her children or without her man. Angela (Amelda Brown) is a sexually frustrated woman who lets out her anger by torturing her stepdaughter Becky (Tricia Kelly), a teenage misfit not unlike the "dim" daughter Marlene disowns in *Top Girls*. In one grotesquely disturbing scene, Angela and Becky wound one another by composing limericks that are alternately sadistic and suicidal. The self-hating stepmother explains that only by hurting her ward can she "feel something."

Other characters waft in and out like plumes of smoke. We meet a male oligarch who sells off his estate, thereby becoming a tenant on his own grandfather's land; a spectral 150-year-old peasant woman stalking a despised landowner for eternity; a hermaphrodite taunted by neighborhood kids; a trio of schoolgirls singing a capella of their circumscribed futures as housewives, hairdressers, and nurses; a 32-year-old grandmother caring for a baby and a senescent 90-year-old grandmother lost in reveries of coffins and long-ago union strife.

Eventually, there is a tragic climax—a death as ritualized as an act of hara-kiri. Depending on whether or not you buy the author's position that her women have only no-win alternatives, you'll either be moved by this gruesome catharsis or left cold.

After that comes the evening's somewhat sentimental but striking coda, in which the characters all haunt the Fens as ghosts: They drift through the suffocating green mist, soliloquizing like Dylan Thomas phantoms radicalized by the [left-wing British] playwright Edward Bond. "The earth's awake!" says one of them—and it's Ms. Churchill who has awakened it. Here's a writer, amazingly enough, who is plowing new ground in the theater with every new play.

FIFTH SEASON
1983—84

Bernadette Peters and Mandy Patinkin in
Sunday in the Park with George

Michael Hordern doesn't wait for his first line to get his first laugh in the National Theatre's new revival of Richard Brinsley Sheridan's *The Rivals*. He sets the audience to giggling the moment he enters in the period costume and wig of Sir Anthony Absolute. And the giggle builds into a roar when the frazzled, gouty Mr. Hordern swivels on his cane to get a better view of the backside of the young maid who's just escorted him into Mrs. Malaprop's drawing room: The actor lets loose with a long, low, rumbling growl of unbridled lechery that is as close to poetry as an aural leer can be. Then the leer becomes a mournful sigh: This fellow is all too keenly aware that sex is behind him in his declining years.

Once the lines do come, Mr. Hordern continues to work hilarious variations on his theme of frustrated randiness. In the scene that requires the matchmaking Sir Anthony to sell his errant son, Jack, on the physical charms of young Lydia Languish, Mr. Hordern devours eggs as he talks, soon turning his breakfast into a frenzied eruption of vicarious lust for his son's intended bride. Indeed, Mr. Hordern's basset-hound face—tugged upward by raised eyebrows, downward by palpitating jowls—is itself something of a runny egg. It is surely the funniest sight in the English theater right now.

If Mr. Hordern looks as if he's having the time of his life, that may be because he is. A fifty-year veteran of the stage, he was knighted in January. His Anthony Absolute has been widely acclaimed as his richest star turn since his memorable creation of the addled philosopher in Tom Stoppard's *Jumpers* at the Old Vic more than a decade ago. But Mr. Hordern is in no danger of curbing his devilish comic attack and becoming a grand old man. If anything, his performance in *The Rivals* is an uninhibited expansion of the lascivious old coot he played in the film version of *A Funny Thing Happened on the Way to the Forum* in the 1960s.

The production surrounding him in the National's large thrust-stage house, the Olivier, has also received high local praise—much, if not all, of it deserved. John Gunter has designed an extraordinary set that seems to place all of Sheridan's eighteenth-century Bath in view, the four-story Georgian façades of the town's Royal Crescent included. Peter Wood, the director, devotes a lot of energy to choreographing the wondrous scenic changes, but he is less inclined to move his actors once the scenes begin. Next to Trevor Nunn's recent staging of *All's Well That Ends Well* on a similarly elaborate Gunter set, Mr. Wood's work in *The Rivals* looks old school.

The mostly exemplary cast usually props up the sags in the direction —even if it can't always redeem the endless plotting that comes with Sheridan's otherwise acute post-Restoration comedy of manners. Tim Curry, as the country bumpkin Bob Acres, transforms a buffoonish oaf into a touching loser. Wearing a sly, sheepish grin and a ridiculously baroque powdered wig, he is at once a vulnerable seeker of unobtainable romance and a clownish martyr to his society's empty, foppish fashions.

Mr. Hordern's prime foil, however, is Geraldine McEwan's Mrs. Malaprop. A bit too young and handsome for the role, the actress can't persuade us that she is, as the text has it, an "old weatherbeaten she-dragon." But that's a small price to pay, given the rest. Her outrageous turns of phrase are all somberly and bitingly delivered after intense deliberation, leaving no doubt that Mrs. Malaprop regards herself as an intellectual giant among pygmies. The gap between her lofty pretensions and her actual brainpower is so vast and pathetic that the others can only greet her bloopers with stunned silence. Mr. Hordern responds with a series of sly double takes that turn his encounters with Ms. McEwan into the classiest imaginable George Burns and Gracie Allen routines.

Such are the resources of the National Theatre that right across the lobby from *The Rivals*—at the company's proscenium house, the Lyttleton—one can find another knight on the boards. A frail-looking but mesmerizing Ralph Richardson is holding forth in *Inner Voices,* a fascinating dark comedy by Eduardo de Filippo, the octogenarian Neapolitan author of *Saturday, Sunday, Monday* and *Filumena.* Under the smart direction of Mike Ockrent, a large cast, which also includes Robert Stephens and Michael Bryant, taps right into the soul of a tricky, even bizarre script.

Set in 1948 Naples, the play places its star in the role of an elderly man who orders the police to arrest an entire neighboring family for murder. Yet we soon discover that the crime never took place—the accuser only dreamed it. Or did he? "I could have been awake when I thought I was dreaming," the hazy Mr. Richardson says.

More dreams follow until Mr. de Filippo creates a nightmarish parable about Italy's decline into "the law of the jungle" in the post–World War II era. He does so by mixing such seemingly antithetical theatrical modes as domestic farce, detective melodrama, and Luis Buñuelesque Surrealism. In Act 2, the action moves startlingly from a bustling kitchen to an eerie, cryptlike warehouse. We even meet a mad recluse (Daniel Thorndike), who only communicates with the world by setting off loud and at times blinding fireworks.

But the Roman candles eventually sputter out, leaving an enveloping gloom. Once the play grows darker and angrier, Mr. Richardson becomes more ethereal and retreats into the warehouse's shadows. In the evening's stunning final image, he sits quietly at a table, his face buried in his hands, the bald crown of his head glowing forlornly in a dim spotlight. As Mr. Hordern can crack us up without saying a single word, so a still and mute Mr. Richardson can make an entire audience break into an almost otherworldly shiver of grief.

≡ *Ralph Richardson died in October 1983, not long after he finished his run in* Inner Voices.

CRITIC'S NOTEBOOK: EDWARD HOPPER SETS THE STAGE
JULY 28, 1983

In a New York season that has seen sets echo the sculptor George Segal (*The Transfiguration of Benno Blimpie*) and the photorealist painter Robert Bechtle (*Winterplay* at Second Stage), one of the most impressive designs is Heidi Landesman's indirect evocation of Edward Hopper for *'night, Mother.*

Ms. Landesman's assignment was to create an entirely ordinary American middle-class home for a family that, in the spiritual sense, is homeless—and a theatrical arena for a play that deals in matters of life and death. Without ever quoting from a specific Hopper painting—as the photographic poster of *'night, Mother* does (from *Solitude*)—the designer dexterously uses the artist to reinforce a drama that shares his terseness and emotional tone. The home she designed—realistic but blanched of detail—is framed in black, to give us Hopper's perspective of looking through a window at night; the bright lighting (by James F. Ingalls) adds to the Hopper mood of loneliness and isolation that defines the two characters and their setting.

To see Hopper's influence on *'night, Mother* and other plays and movies (*Badlands, Pennies from Heaven*) is to watch a bit of art history come full circle. As the curator Gail Levin writes in the catalogue for the Hopper exhibition at the Whitney in 1980, the artist was an inveterate theatergoer: "He saved many ticket stubs and carefully recorded the name of the play on the reverse of each." We all know Hopper's paintings of theaters and movie houses, but Ms. Levin further suggests that a major cityscape, *Early Sunday Morning*, may have been inspired by Jo Mielziner's 1929 set for Elmer Rice's *Street Scene*—even to the extent that the painting's "elevated vantage point" reflects the fact that Hopper saw *Street Scene* from the second balcony.

Ms. Levin concludes her argument with a delightful passage that must be quoted. "Hopper's interest in both stage sets and lighting," she writes, "is confirmed by a comment he made upon seeing some foliage illuminated by light coming from a restaurant window at night: 'Notice how artificial trees look at night? Trees look like a theater at night.' "

LA CAGE AUX FOLLES
PALACE THEATRE, AUGUST 22, 1983

La Cage aux Folles is the first Broadway musical ever to give center stage to a homosexual love affair—but don't go expecting an earthquake. The show at the Palace is the schmaltziest, most old-fashioned major musical Broadway has seen since *Annie,* and it's likely to be just as popular with children of all ages. Were you hoping for a little more? I must confess that I was. The glitz, showmanship, good cheer, and almost unflagging tunefulness of *La Cage aux Folles* are all highly enjoyable and welcome, but, in its eagerness to please all comers, this musical is sometimes as shamelessly calculating as a candidate for public office.

Sometimes, but, happily, not always. There are more than a few startling occasions in this rapaciously busy extravaganza when the vast machinery comes to a halt—when David Mitchell's glorious pastel-hued scenic visions of Saint-Tropez stop flying, when the transvestite dancing girls vanish, when the running gags about whips and wigs limp away. Suddenly, we find ourselves alone with the evening's stars, George Hearn and Gene Barry, and they insist on providing the intimacy and candor that the evening otherwise avoids. You simply won't be able to get enough of these performers, or of the Jerry Herman songs that accompany their more tender self-expressions.

Mr. Hearn plays Albin, who, as Zaza, is the headline attraction at the nightclub that gives the musical its title. For twenty years, Albin has had a tranquil domestic life with Georges (Mr. Barry), the club's impresario. Albin is the more flamboyant of the pair. It is he who must dress up in drag every night to entertain the customers and who has the most to fear from growing old. What Mr. Hearn does with this role is stunning—a breakthrough, at last, for a fine, hardworking actor who last season alone paid his dues in two Broadway flops.

Whether in his female impersonations or in civilian guise, Mr. Hearn is neither campy nor macho here: He could be any run-of-the-mill night-club entertainer in midlife crisis. But it is precisely his ordinariness that makes him so moving. When Mr. Hearn sits in front of his dressing-room mirror to sing plaintively of how he applies "a little more mascara" to make himself feel beautiful, we care much more about what the illusion of feminine glamour means to the otherwise humdrum Albin than we do about the rather routine illusion itself.

That's how it should be. By making us see so clearly how precariously his self-esteem is maintained, Mr. Hearn makes it all the more upset-ting to watch what happens when that identity is attacked. And, as in the French film of *La Cage aux Folles* (which began life as a Jean Poiret play), that shock quickly arrives. Albin and Georges's "son"—fathered by Georges in a long-ago, one-night heterosexual fling—announces his intention to marry the daughter of a bigoted politician. To help the young man perpetuate the fiction that he had a standard upbringing, Georges cruelly asks Albin to disappear when the prospective in-laws come to call.

What follows, at the end of Act 1, is the evening's moment of triumph. Mr. Hearn rushes on the stage of La Cage to perform as Zaza—only to stop in midstride and let loose with his real feelings of rejection and be-trayal. In drag though he may be, the actor sings in a full-throttle baritone —with a pulsating force that induces shivers. The song, titled "I Am What I Am," is full of rage but, better still, of pride: Even as Albin defends his right to live as he wishes, he pointedly asks not for either "praise" or "pity." And Mr. Hearn acts the song as searingly as he sings it: Remaining still, he just lets the words cascade from the wide, black gash of a mouth that belies the cosmetic joyousness of his makeup and plumed hairdo.

The charming Mr. Barry has nothing as showy to do, but his contri-bution is invaluable. He gets two sweet ballads, "Song on the Sand" and "Look Over There," that are unvarnished declarations of Georges's long-time devotion to Albin; though the lyrics can be soupy, Mr. Barry sings them with such modest simplicity and warmth that we never question their sincerity. Nor do we question Georges's self-loathing when, in a quivering and falsely merry voice, he sells out his lover for the sake of middle-class propriety.

If you add up all of the high points by Mr. Barry and Mr. Hearn—including a soaring arm-in-arm duet called "With You on My Arm"—you have the winning half of *La Cage aux Folles*. And in Mr. Herman, there is always a third partner in that achievement. We expect snappy, old-style Broadway melodies from the author of *Hello, Dolly!* and *Mame*—as well as the thrown-in Hit Song sung in a restaurant (here it's a dandy, a "Those Were the Days"–style item titled "The Best of Times")—but we don't expect passion. This time we get that passion, and it is Mr. Herman's score, jauntily conducted by Donald Pippin, that gives the charge to every genuine sentiment in the show.

When the stars aren't delivering those songs, *La Cage aux Folles* can be as synthetic and padded as the transvestites' cleavage. In sharp contrast to Mr. Herman, Harvey Fierstein, writer of the book, has misplaced his craftsmanship and bite on this outing; he's exercised few of his options to bolster a property that was thin and coarse to begin with. The tiny plot of *La Cage* is dribbled out with painful lethargy in Act 1, then resolved chaotically (and confusingly) for the final curtain. Worse, there is a homogenized, sitcom tone to the script, which suggests that Mr. Fierstein is pandering to what he apparently regards as a squeamish Broadway-musical audience.

The ostensibly tart backstage wisecracks of Zaza's fellow transvestites are so tame and tired that they make the equivalent jokes of, say, *Victor/Victoria* or Mr. Fierstein's own *Torch Song Trilogy* sound like hardcore porn. (The lyrics of Mr. Herman's comic numbers, notably an ironic demonstration of "Masculinity," are equally short on sophisticated laughs.) In the book scenes, unlike the songs, Georges and Albin are so relentlessly square that they become homogenized homosexuals in the manner of the scrupulously genteel black people of Hollywood's *Guess Who's Coming to Dinner* era. The lovers' turncoat son (John Weiner) is too wanly characterized for us to understand his casual callousness; the parents of the bride are such caricatured villains that even the more zealous homophobes in the audience can feel morally superior to them—and thereby escape the reach of the show's plea for tolerance.

Perhaps reflecting the blank nature of the secondary characters (who also include some ersatz townsfolk), the casting of them is routine and worse. That lapse aside, Arthur Laurents's direction is fast-paced, stunt-laden, and knowing. (Sometimes what it knows is Jerome Robbins's immortal staging of *Gypsy*, for which Mr. Laurents wrote the book.) The physical production—Mr. Mitchell's sets, the lighting designer Jules Fisher's crystalline Mediterranean nights, Theoni V. Aldredge's unstoppable parade of ice-cream-color drag costumes—is exquisite and Gallic (as the accents, lyrics, and orchestrations most glaringly are not). While all the elements can seem messily jammed together, they can also merge in magical theatrical harmony—as when the living room of Georges and Albin breaks away for the son and his fiancée (Leslie Stevens) to glide through a fantasy duet in the shimmering style of a Cyd Charisse–vintage MGM musical.

In the nightclub numbers, Scott Salmon's choreography substitutes acrobatics and sheer length for imagination. Though we're promised that the routines for the *Cage* chorines will be "dangerous," they often look exactly like the by-the-book cancans and kicklines trotted out for Paris-by-night bus tours, rather than witty comments upon them. The men who perform the dances (in concert with two bona fide women) are skilled as drag artists, yet not to the point where they achieve that real androgynous sexiness which might challenge a heterosexual audience's received definitions of gender. It's easy to keep a safe distance and ignore the real point.

But even when the authors are cautiously watering down their material, their splashy entertainment usually hums along in its unabashedly conventional way. Wait for those privileged occasions when Mr. Hearn, Mr. Barry, and Mr. Herman summon up the full courage of the show's convictions, and you'll hear *La Cage aux Folles* stop humming and sing.

≡ *Writing in a Sunday essay after* La Cage *had opened, I noted that Fierstein's book tried to push the show's soul "back in the closet" and wondered: "Was everything else toned down in* La Cage *out of a desire to flatter the audience and avoid the slightest risk of offending a single member of it? It certainly looks that way—especially by the time we meet the bigoted heterosexual villains of the piece, who are so overdrawn that they seem calculated to make even the audience's homophobes go home congratulating themselves on how tolerant they are by comparison. One can't help wishing that the creators of* La Cage *had given enlightened theatergoers more credit, had challenged the prejudices of the less-enlightened—and had not assumed that the common denominator of the Broadway audience's sensibility (and sense of humor) is somewhere in the nether reaches of the Nielsen ratings." Then again, maybe the authors knew what they were doing.* La Cage *was a long-running hit in New York, but it collapsed on the road the moment the AIDS epidemic struck, as if the show itself were under quarantine from a wary public that still had much to learn about the plague.*

Yet years later La Cage *would resume its role of mainstreaming homosexuality for mass consumption when Mike Nichols (who had originally
wanted to do the Broadway version) did another, nonmusical adaptation of
the original French film, reset in Miami's South Beach, as* The Birdcage.
*It became something of a surprise hit in 1996, during an election year in
which the losing candidate, Bob Dole, stoked some of the homophobic fires
in his party.*

GALAS
RIDICULOUS THEATRICAL COMPANY, SEPTEMBER 16, 1983

Having spent the past few seasons impersonating neurotic middle-
aged men, Charles Ludlam has decided to jump into women's
clothes again. But not just any woman's clothes. In *Galas,* his new play
at the Ridiculous Theatrical Company, Mr. Ludlam has wrapped himself
in the extravagant gowns and furs of Maria Magdalena Galas—a larger-
than-life opera diva whose dramatic singing career is matched only by her
tumultuous offstage adventures with the rich and mighty Greek shipping
tycoon Aristotle Plato Socrates Odysseus (known to his friends as "Soc").

"I am music!" proclaims Galas shortly after we meet her. As portrayed
by Mr. Ludlam, Galas (rhymes with Callas) may not be music and she
may not always quite be womanly, but she surely is a comic creation of a
high order. All but tipping over from the weight of his wigs and eye
makeup, Mr. Ludlam gives us the regal Maria Callas of legend and gossip: a narcissistic superstar who orders her maid to adopt "a manner of
excessive politeness," who brings the impresarios of La Scala to their
knees, who dismisses Pope Pius XII (here called Pope Sixtus the Sev-
enth) as "just another bishop."

He even gives us the Callas of those final, bitter years—a sobbing,
lonely lady of leisure who rattles around in her Paris apartment bemoan-
ing the fact that all her friends are "either dead or in Monte Carlo" and
that there is "nothing particularly good on television" to distract her
from the demise of her career and love life. *Galas* is subtitled "A Modern
Tragedy," and while that's an overstatement, the evening does end with a
played-for-keeps whiff of *Madama Butterfly.*

What allows the star to pull off his stunt is the same comic skill that
informs all his performances. Though the Ridiculous troupe surrounding him can be campy, Mr. Ludlam is not interested in parodying femininity or doing a drag act but in getting honest laughs through precise
physical business and flawless, slow-burn timing worthy of Jack Benny.

When Galas has her audience with the Pontiff, Mr. Ludlam turns the act of kissing the Pope's ring into a prolonged, farcical game of one-upmanship that wickedly demonstrates the heroine's ability to upstage anyone under any circumstances. In the weepy final scene, in which Galas is otherwise lost in tears of self-pity, Mr. Ludlam knows just how to prick the mood with a perfectly lobbed, low-register non sequitur ("I really wanted to be a dentist!").

Is this what Callas was like? I don't know, but after a while, the star makes us suspend disbelief: We cease to watch a man playing a woman and instead see a comic heroine who is completely consistent on Mr. Ludlam's own terms. To do this takes total conviction as well as talent, and it is that fierce conviction that elevates the performance from the realm of caricature to that of inspired clowning.

As patrons of the Ridiculous know, Mr. Ludlam writes and directs his own shows—even at the cost of stretching himself thin. Still, by the scrappy lights of this company, *Galas* is more carefully staged than most. In collaboration with his set designer, Jack Kelly, Mr. Ludlam has even given a theatrical look to some scenes—notably one in which we watch the diva's famous mid-performance flight from *Norma* in Rome. The overweight Galas's opening entrance—into a train station in Verona, circa 1947—is staged with an effect that, however modest by most standards, may be more extravagant than some entire past Ridiculous productions.

The text itself has its limitations. "The characters in the play are real," writes Mr. Ludlam in a program note. "Only their names have been changed to protect the playwright." He speaks the truth. *Galas* actually is a fairly factual, if broad, account of some high points in Callas's life, starting with her first marriage to a brick tycoon. And Mr. Ludlam is not unsympathetic to his subject. "To have everything and lose it—now, that isn't funny," says Galas at the end. Ludlam the actor gets a laugh on the line, but Ludlam the playwright isn't entirely kidding.

To the extent that *Galas* tries to speak seriously about its heroine's suffering (especially in Act 2), the writing suffers, too. But if Mr. Ludlam's biting style and unsparing social observations are sometimes cramped by his biographical comprehensiveness, he just as often gives in to the urge to be rude. There are some very funny, not to mention tasteless, jokes scattered throughout, involving topics as varied as Galas's contempt for the public, Eva Perón's philosophy of government, the merits of Wagner, and the dietetic uses of tapeworms.

The supporting cast is mostly the usual gang of unbridled amateurs. But Everett Quinton, who also doubles as the play's witty costume designer, is at his bizarre best as the heroine's devoted maid, a one-time opera singer who can predict just how many times Galas will ever sing *Norma* (eighty-six) simply by looking into her throat. It is also Mr. Quinton's rueful duty to keep reminding his employer that the best artists are "acknowledged but never forgiven." The least the rest of us can do is acknowledge Mr. Ludlam's artistry and hope that somewhere Maria Callas is forgiving him.

CRITIC'S NOTEBOOK:

A CHORUS LINE *NO. 3,389*

SHUBERT THEATRE, OCTOBER 1, 1983

The only sad thing about a great night in the theater is its evanescence. When it's over, it's over. You can remember the performance forever, of course. But you can't re-create that virgin sensation—that almost numbing exhilaration—of witnessing something new and different and exciting in the theater for the very first time.

So there was a lot of reminiscing Thursday night, when 1,472 friends of *A Chorus Line* gathered in Shubert Alley for a reception preceding the musical's record-breaking 3,389th performance. Strolling about, I heard the same conversation over and over. People were trying to reconstruct that electric night eight years ago when they first saw this show at the Public Theater before anyone knew that *A Chorus Line* might move to Broadway, let alone become the longest-running production of all time.

And implicit in these conversations was that sadness. While everyone was looking forward to having grand fun at the gala, everyone was also conceding, in advance, that the past could not be recaptured. Whatever happened inside the Shubert Theatre, once the curtain went up at 10:30, would still be second-best to that first, revelatory performance of years ago. Worse, no one could escape the fact that, however advanced *A Chorus Line* was for its time, that time was already part of history. The revolutions this musical wrought—in the way musicals are staged, produced, and written—had long since been assimilated in hit musicals that followed. There were no surprises left, heaven knows, in the show's text. Pressed to the wall, some of the gathered might even have confessed a reluctance to hear yet another rendition of "What I Did for Love."

But two and a half hours later, as the same audience poured back into Shubert Alley, no one was jaded anymore, no one was talking about old memories. What people were saying, instead, is simply this: They had rarely, if ever, seen anything as exciting in a Broadway theater as the 3,389th performance of *A Chorus Line*.

It is perhaps impossible to explain or understand all the factors that transformed a promotional event into a theatrical experience that was even more poignant than it was thrilling.

Some of the charge can be attributed to the good will that ran like a red-hot current through the house. When Michael Bennett said, "I love you, Joseph Papp," and embraced Mr. Papp on stage at the evening's end, it wasn't just showbiz sentimentality. Mr. Bennett is the foremost director in the big-money commercial theater; Mr. Papp is the foremost producer in the innovative nonprofit theater; as lines in the American theater are drawn, these men work opposite sides of the street. Yet neither Mr. Bennett's Broadway career nor Mr. Papp's Public Theater might have thrived if Mr. Papp hadn't given Mr. Bennett a home to develop *A Chorus Line* a decade ago. When the men embraced, it was the most palpable imaginable reminder that the best people in the American theater, whatever theatrical tastes they represent, share a common bond and goal.

But surely the most crucial factor in the evening by far was Mr. Bennett himself. This director is always a step ahead of the audience—and that proved to be true even when the audience was as knowing as the one that gathered Thursday night. Mr. Bennett's plan for the evening was to work every *Chorus Line* alumnus he could find into the performance. But Mr. Bennett—even with only four days of rehearsals—did not settle for just throwing an extra three hundred bodies on stage. Rather, in a feat of artistry and logistics that boggles the mind, he gave us a new show that accomplished the seemingly impossible: He made us look at now overfamiliar material through fresh eyes.

Amazingly, this large new version did not jazz up *A Chorus Line*—it took the musical back to its intimate roots, to the emotions it aroused at the start. We were forced to remember that *A Chorus Line* is, simply, a show about those brave performers who insist on devoting their lives to the theater, even though the chances of fame, fortune, and recognition are terribly slim. They are talented people who care about their work more than about the rewards.

And they are performers who exist anywhere there is a stage. Among the ones at the Shubert were Chikae Ishikawa, who belted out "Nothing" in Japanese, and a whole group of international *Chorus Line* alumni who performed the penultimate scene in the show in eleven languages simultaneously. That's the scene in which the dancers explain why they stick with the theater until their bodies can't take it anymore—a scene that, as performed by this polyglot assemblage, gave the ensuing "What I Did for Love" a literal universality that blotted out every previous version of the song.

But perhaps the most extraordinary of Mr. Bennett's touches came at the show's outset. The introductory number, "I Hope I Get It," was at first performed by the current New York company. But at the climax, when the dancers retreat into the blackness to fetch their résumés and publicity photos, Mr. Bennett, in a lightning-fast cinematic dissolve, replaced them with another cast. As this identically costumed new cast marched forward to the white line downstage, photos in front of their faces, a white banner dropped bearing the legend "The Original Company." And, as the audience gasped, that company lowered the photos— revealing the performers we hadn't seen in eight years. Some looked as we remembered them, some looked older, and some, distressingly, we couldn't remember at all.

The effect was a reverse version of a legendary number in Mr. Bennett's 1971 musical *Follies,* in which a line of retired, middle-aged Ziegfeld Follies alumni were suddenly replaced by a mirror image phalanx of chorus girls representing their younger, vanished selves. On Thursday night, the effect was chilling because it reminded us that the anonymous backstage stories dramatized in *A Chorus Line* are echoed in real life: Though many of the show's original cast members have successful careers, none of them became Broadway stars. What most of them did for *A Chorus Line* in 1975—and before and since—they did for love.

In this light, Thursday's *Playbill* was an amazing document. Like a program for a class reunion, it contained biographies of everyone in the show. Reading through it, one discovered that those *Chorus Line* alumni who are still dancing are still in the chorus—whether in the drag chorus of *La Cage aux Folles* or the feline zoo of *Cats.* Others run dancing schools, or make commercials, or are looking for work. Yet, as each *Chorus Line* alumnus passed through, it was plain to see that the assemblage's depth of talent, dedication, and professionalism epitomize everything stirring that *A Chorus Line* and the theater that produced it stand for.

One could go on forever about individual performers. There were new faces like Kerry Casserly (who did a hilarious rendition of "Sing!") and Gordon Owens (whose dancing as Richie whipped up hysteria in "Hello Twelve, Hello Thirteen, Hello Love"). There was the familiar face of Donna McKechnie, whose lines as Cassie, the brilliant chorus dancer who can't graduate to stardom, took on greater resonance than ever. When Ms. McKechnie convulsively danced her mirror number, the ring of mirrors lifted away to reveal ten other Cassies mirroring her steps.

There was also Sammy Williams, who originated the role of Paul, the Puerto Rican homosexual. As staged by Mr. Bennett, his confessional monologue became a group recitation—with ten Pauls forming a phalanx of lost men, like the Sharks in *West Side Story,* all sharing their unhappy youthful memories with one another in a tableau of minority solidarity and mutual support.

A little later, after Paul injured himself, Mr. Bennett replaced one *Chorus Line* company with another before our eyes, with a choreographed walk that seemed to fill the entire theater with ghosts of Broadway dancers past. And not long after that came the grand finale, the full-regalia version of "One," in which ranks of kicking dancers kept pouring from the aisles onto the stage. Even this number was in part a new dance devised by Mr. Bennett for the occasion.

By then, the audience was on its feet. Surrounding us at every turn were the dancers in their gold top hats, all singing and crying and kicking clear up to our ears. The theater seemed to shake. The cast and audience had become one, united in the at least momentary conviction that *A Chorus Line* was the best thing that had ever happened to any of us. People were screaming and, when the lights slowly dimmed to black, they were sobbing. They were sobbing because they were moved, and perhaps even more so because the show was over. The stage with the white line was soon empty again, as if nothing had ever happened.

Like those first performances down at the Public, the 3,389th Broadway performance of *A Chorus Line* can never be recaptured. But that was the only crushing part of this event, and it's a price that just must be paid for a night in the theater that its witnesses will remember for the rest of their lives.

≡ *Who would have guessed that this one-night-only triumph, created by Bennett in a marathon four-day rehearsal period, would prove to be the last new work he would create for Broadway? He died in 1987; A Chorus Line closed in 1990 and, in 1997, its record-breaking run was surpassed by that of Cats.*

A RAISIN IN THE SUN
GOODMAN THEATRE, CHICAGO, OCTOBER 5, 1983

It was twenty-five years ago that a twenty-eight-year-old black woman from this city changed American theater forever with her first produced play. The woman was Lorraine Hansberry, and the play, of course, was *A Raisin in the Sun.*

Taking her title from Langston Hughes's poem "Harlem," Ms. Hansberry forced both blacks and whites to reexamine the deferred dreams of black America. She asked blacks to reconsider how those dreams might be defined; she demanded that whites not impede the fulfillment of those dreams for one more second. And she posed all her concerns in a work that portrayed a black family with a greater realism and complexity than had ever been previously seen on an American stage. A writer of unlimited compassion, Ms. Hansberry believed that all people must be measured, as she put it, by both their "hills and valleys."

To celebrate the anniversary of this seminal play—which sparked the growth of the black theater movement in the 1960s—the Goodman Theatre opened its season here Monday night with a full-scale revival, directed by Thomas Bullard. (Lloyd Richards, the original Broadway director of *Raisin*, will produce another major revival next month at the Yale Repertory Theatre.) It is poignant to see the play again in Chicago, which, besides being the author's hometown and the drama's setting, has also recently elected its first black mayor.

The Goodman's production, unfortunately, falls short, but it usually doesn't obscure the play's strengths. Ms. Hansberry, who died of cancer at the age of thirty-four in 1965, wrote *Raisin* well before the marches on Washington, the assassination of the Reverend Dr. Martin Luther King Jr., and the inner-city explosions. Yet, with remarkable prescience, she saw history whole: Her play encompasses everything from the rise of black nationalism in the United States and Africa to the advent of black militancy to the specific dimensions of the black woman's liberation movement. And she always saw the present and future in the light of the past—clear back to the slavery of the Old South and the new slavery that followed for black workers who migrated to the industrial ghettos of the North.

Ms. Hansberry works within the confines of what might be called a kitchen-sink drama, set in a cramped, trigenerational household on the South Side in the 1950s. At the plot level, *Raisin* is about how the Younger family will spend a $10,000 insurance payment it has received after its patriarch's death—and about whether the family will move into a now affordable new home in a hostile, lily-white neighborhood. But Ms. Hansberry's real drama is the battle for the soul and identity of Walter Lee Younger, the family's son. Walter, thirty-five, is a chauffeur who wants to get rich by opening a liquor store. Without quite realizing it, he oppresses his wife, Ruth, a domestic, and mocks the ambitions of his twenty-year-old sister, Beneatha, a fledgling activist and medical student. "I got me a dream," says Walter early in the play—but his dream is not to be confused with Dr. King's. What he wants is "things," and, as he tells his horrified mother, Lena, he no longer regards money merely as a passport to freedom but as the essence of life.

In this sense, Walter is not just a black victim of white racism but also a victim of a materialistic American dream that can enslave men or women of any race. Seeing *Raisin* again, one is struck by how much Ms. Hansberry's protagonist resembles those of other Chicago writers, from Dreiser's Sister Carrie to David Mamet's proletarian schemer Teach in *American Buffalo*. What makes *Raisin* so moving is that Walter finally does rise above his misplaced values to find a new dignity and moral courage—and that he does so with the support of his contentious but always loving family.

Ms. Hansberry said that it was *Juno and the Paycock* that first sparked her passion for theater, and the best of *Raisin* shares O'Casey's muscular poetry, robust humor, and faith in human perseverance. If there's anything dated about the work now, it is only its dependence on mechanical plotting and, notably in Act 2, its somewhat jerry-built structure.

The Goodman staging seems to remember too keenly the original Broadway production, most of which was preserved in the film version. Though arrestingly designed by Karen Schulz and lighted by Dennis Parichy, it contains performances that look like dogged, at times strangulated imitations of those by Sidney Poitier, Diana Sands, and Ruby Dee. The pacing is sluggish—the running time is three hours—and it would be hard to say that Brent Jennings digs much beneath the surface of the volcanic contradictions of Walter. To the extent that Mr. Jennings flattens out this pivotal role, *Raisin* becomes a simplified melodrama.

Yet some strong fresh thinking is provided by Melva Williams, as Walter's mother. In some ways this lovable matriarch is almost too good to be true, but Ms. Williams's flinty, intelligent underplaying keeps sentimentality at bay to give us a woman of commanding strength and pride. In her triumphant final moment—in which she takes a last look at her tenement home before leaving it forever—we can almost feel Lorraine Hansberry herself looking ahead to the future that she helped make but, tragically, never knew.

≡ *I had first seen this play as a kid in Washington when my mother took me to see it during its post-Broadway tour, around 1960. The effect it had on what must have been a largely white audience was palpable; Hansberry described de facto segregation that still pervaded the D.C. area.*

What I couldn't have imagined in 1983 is that a few years later a new, young black playwright of my own time—George C. Wolfe—would write a hilarious parody of Raisin, *a sketch called "The Last Mama-on-the-Couch Play" in* The Colored Museum, *the production that would start him on his way to becoming a major player in the New York theater.*

BABY WITH THE BATHWATER
PLAYWRIGHTS HORIZONS, NOVEMBER 9, 1983

Ijust don't want to make the child insane, that's all," says the mother, Helen, to her husband, John, as they contemplate their newborn baby in its shiny wicker bassinet. Given that these parents inhabit Christopher Durang's new comedy at Playwrights Horizons, *Baby with the Bathwater,* need I tell you that they soon drive their child absolutely bonkers?

Helen, a frustrated novelist who would rather have given birth to *Scruples* than a child, tries to quiet the baby's tears by singing "There's No Business Like Show Business." John, an alcoholic and unemployed, has sex with the baby's Nanny in the kitchen. Nanny—a warped Mary Poppins, as played by Dana Ivey—believes that cuddling children only spoils them. She gives the baby a rattle made of asbestos, lead, and Red Dye No. 2.

As you can see, Helen, John, and Nanny are secular versions of Mr. Durang's Sister Mary Ignatius: They're adults who sadistically chew up their young, then spit the remains onto a psychiatrist's couch. And, a few bright lines notwithstanding, we can't ignore that Act 1 of *Baby with the Bathwater* is a strained variation on past Durang riffs. We're so inured by now to this writer's angry view of parental authority figures that at intermission we feel like shaking him and shouting: "Enough already! Move on!"

Which is exactly, to our amazement, what he does. If Act 1 of *Baby* is a string of *Mommie Dearest* gags in which Mr. Durang's feelings of victimization are more pronounced than the freshness of his comic invention, the second gives us a different, more provocative range of feelings and far funnier lines in the bargain. The explanation for this is simple: The writer finally lets us see his play's victim, rather than just his tormentors.

That victim at first seems a typical Durang sick joke. Baby, we learn, spent his entire childhood as an inert lump—a condition his mother attributes to a lack of "joie de vivre." He would awaken only to attempt suicide by running in front of a moving bus, and his gender was indeterminate. Though his parents named him Daisy (as in the song containing the lyric "half-crazy"), the child would also assume names ranging from Ponchitta Pierce to Charles Kuralt. When we meet the college-age Baby, he is played by a man (Keith Reddin) wearing a dress.

But if Mr. Durang hasn't abandoned his hyperbolic style in defining his protagonist, Daisy proves a fuller creation than the outrageous facts suggest. Watching the character undergo therapy, we feel the pain that leads him to have more than seventeen hundred sexual partners, that makes it impossible for him to find an identity or a name. We also feel, as the unseen doctor says, that Daisy can't blame his parents forever—and, after several hundred sessions, Daisy actually does start to overcome his childhood.

Perhaps more revealingly, the therapist also breaks through his patient's writing block. For ten years Daisy has been trying to complete a freshman English composition that begins with an incomplete sentence: "*Gulliver's Travels* is a biting, bitter work that—" When Daisy at last becomes able to complete that sentence, Mr. Durang achieves an equivalent breakthrough. A playwright who shares Swift's bleak view of humanity, he conquers bitterness and finds a way to turn rage into comedy that is redemptive as well as funny. By the time Daisy has moved beyond therapy, Mr. Durang has moved well beyond his last play, *Beyond Therapy.* The somewhat hopeful ending of *Baby* is earned, not contrived.

This isn't to say that more work can't be done. If Daisy is the first Durang hero who works through his rage to become an adult—instead of just joking the anger away or pulling out a gun—he could bear further examination still. The author's compulsive gag-making might also be in tighter control. Only Mr. Durang could hit comic targets as varied as the Spence School, *The Brothers Karamazov,* CBS network executives, James Taylor, the *New York Post,* ASCAP royalty policies, Sylvia Plath, *A Doll's Life,* and Cliff's Notes. Some of the punch lines are indeed priceless, but not all of them are germane.

If *Baby with the Bathwater* is a big but not final step toward the definitive Durang play, it is nonetheless receiving a definitive production. Jerry Zaks's direction is in perfect harmony with the author's distinctive voice. Using jolly, inventive pop-out sets by Loren Sherman and bright lighting by Jennifer Tipton, Mr. Zaks summons up the flat look and slam-bang pace of *I Love Lucy,* turned up to a deranged absurdist pitch.

The exemplary cast includes Christine Estabrook, whose Helen radiates good humor even when threatening to "shake and bake" her child; W. H. Macy, who makes high farce out of the father's delirium tremens; and Leslie Geraci, as three women who actually show affection for

Daisy. Ms. Ivey, last seen as the evangelical teacher in *Quartermaine's Terms,* tops her Nanny with an additional role—a possibly bisexual school principal who gives the young Daisy an A for writing a suicidal essay combining the styles of Donald Barthelme and *Sesame Street.*

Last but not least is Mr. Reddin, as the baby who is not, after all, thrown out with the bathwater. When Daisy finally puts his parents behind him, recognizing that they aren't "evil" and may even have "meant well," this tender actor makes us feel something we've never felt in a Durang play before: the joy of being sane.

LA TRAGÉDIE DE CARMEN
Vivian Beaumont Theater, November 18, 1983

For his *Tragédie de Carmen,* Peter Brook has transformed the Vivian Beaumont's stage into a bullring carpeted with gravel and earth. It's an arena buffeted on every side by fate, and its round shape is echoed in every step of this production's relentless thrust.

When we first meet the gypsy temptress Carmen, she tosses tarot cards into a small circle of rope placed on the dirt. When we last see her eighty minutes later, she and her outcast soldier lover, Don José, make one final walk around the ring before meeting up with the destiny those cards have dealt. Many other circles come in between—drawn in sand and outlined in rope—but the largest of them all is not seen, only felt: It's the noose that Mr. Brook, through the astonishing power of his art, steadily tightens around the audience's throats.

The impact of this *Carmen* is so strong that even the evening's inevitable climax makes us gasp. The gasp is not motivated by surprise: As Mr. Brook's *Carmen* is an adaptation of Georges Bizet's opera, we know that José will ultimately rip a knife into the heroine's heart. We gasp because Mr. Brook has forced us to feel the fated denouement as if it were new again. In a world rife with esthetic overkill, this director has found the one way to put savagery back into tragedy: complete and utter simplicity.

Yet the evening is not just an emotional purging. There are other wonders of lighter effect—slapstick comedy played at silent-movie pace and gravely beautiful romantic tableaux cast in a Goyaesque glow. Magic is everywhere, and to appreciate it a theatergoer need only bring an open mind. You'll get the most from this *Carmen* if you focus on what it contains rather than what it leaves out.

What's been left out is much of the letter and some of the spirit of what may be the world's most popular piece of musical theater. Mr. Brook and his collaborators, the screenwriter Jean-Claude Carrière and the composer Marius Constant, have demolished their source: They've removed roughly half of Bizet's score and retained only four singing roles from the original Meilhac-Halévy libretto; they've stripped away the traditional settings; they've cut the orchestra down to fourteen pieces and shoved the surviving musicians into the wings.

And what, you ask, remains? Not Bizet's *Carmen,* that's for sure. This version is no substitute for the glorious original and can't be taken as such. Nor have we regained the whole of Prosper Mérimée's *Carmen,* the novella that inspired Bizet and to which the current collaborators have returned for some of their revisions. But neither do we have a pop *Carmen,* reduced to its greatest hits. If that were the creators' cynical intention, they wouldn't have excised one of the biggest hits, the Act 2 quintet, or reduced another, the "Cigarette Song," to an incidental musical joke. Even the music that remains has been rearranged and radically reordered: The overture turns up fifteen minutes before the end, in the sacrilegious form of a recording.

No, *La Tragédie de Carmen* must instead be seen as a new, pointedly retitled work that bends Bizet's score and themes, like found objects in a collage, to reflect the concerns of its creators. It's a modernist tragedy that opens with a Beckett image—Carmen emerges from what might be a dung heap—and continues to pile up sparsely populated stage pictures that ache with desolation and loneliness. The setting can hardly even pass for Spain anymore. The bullring is backed by a gray wall of wood that is nothing if not the void that Mr. Brook has been exploring at least as far back as his *Endgame*-inspired *King Lear* of two decades ago.

One can also hear the voice of Mr. Carrière, the scenarist of Luis Buñuel's late films, including *Belle du Jour.* The production's few props, mainly knives and cigars, are phallic. The action is charged with dirty, roughhouse sex and violence—twin passions that are interwoven with incendiary force. The once angelic Micaëla is now in full-fledged pursuit of José's affections; she and Carmen tumble into the dirt in a catfight. José's obsessive jealousy drives him to commit two murders unknown to the original opera. Escamillo, the matador, is now a preening whorehouse roué who delivers his "Toreador Song" as a narcissistic sexual proposition.

Heated up and stripped of its social context, *Carmen* is no longer a conflict between Carmen's liberated gypsy passions and José's imprisoning bourgeois values. Carmen and José are now equal partners in a raw, brutal tale of mutual self-destruction that's fueled by both lust and existential bloodlust—and is as deadly for others as it is for themselves. The writing and staging are pitched accordingly, from the repeated emphasis on Bizet's death-intoned card aria (the first music we hear) to the hallucinatory telescoping of the story. This *Carmen* is indeed written like a Buñuel screenplay: Fragments of the original libretto, sprinkled with new dialogue, have been reassembled to achieve the associative shape and force of an archetypal nightmare.

Mr. Brook's direction achieves its own dreamlike intensity through stark, fluent, exquisitely composed movement. His staging is of a piece with the other so-called "magic carpet" shows he's done with his Paris-based International Center of Theatre Research. In the past, however, Mr. Brook has at times tried to realize his goal of creating ritualistic, truly international theater by inventing sounds and language. How much better the director's strategy works when the universal language isn't gimmicky, nonsensical bird chatter but Bizet's sumptuous music and the French words wedded to it.

That music is effectively sung by performers who share several crucial virtues: They can act, they are sexy, and they are young. Liberated from the conductor, the proscenium arch, and any vestige of nineteenth-century pageantry, they achieve direct contact with one another and the audience, as well as balletic freedom of movement. The three rotating casts (out of five) I've seen in critics' previews at the Beaumont varied only marginally in collective impact. Each Carmen—Helene Delavault, Eva Saurova, and Patricia Schuman—achieved roughly the same order of lewd, mysterious voluptuousness (with Ms. Schuman perhaps proving first among near-equals). In other roles, I saw outstanding performances by Carl Johan Falkman as Escamillo, Veronique Dietschy and Beverly Morgan as Micaëla, Alain Maratrat as the saloon keeper Lillas Pastia, and, best of all, by Laurence Dale as a doleful, almost Chaplinesque José.

The only problem with Mr. Brook's *Carmen*, as with his landmark *Midsummer Night's Dream*, is that its lessons will undoubtedly be misapplied by faddist imitators for years to come. Other directors should not regard the production's radical surgery on a sacred text as either an end in itself or a manifesto calling for the demolition of all operas (or all *Carmen*s). But Mr. Brook has certainly taught a needed, durable lesson to the current, renovation-fixated management at the Beaumont. Through sheer ingenuity, not costly reconstruction, the director has made this house into an intimate, playable auditorium where one can see and hear as clearly as in Broadway theaters of equivalent size.

What one sees and hears can be mesmerizing. In one haunting interlude, Carmen and José find their brief and only peace by pledging their troths in a secluded gypsy campsite bathed in the flickering, rust-colored twilight of ritual bonfires. Later, when Escamillo makes his final entrance in full matador regalia, the evening's only bright costume is chillingly mocked by the premonitorily embalmed expression on the toreador's face.

But most memorable of all is that final image of Carmen and José—dressed in black, drained of blood, kneeling in the dirt to meet their fate while a mournful, kettle-drum echo of Carmen's first song, the "Habanera," plays in the distance. Though only eighty minutes have passed in Mr. Brook's bullring, we nonetheless feel we've shared the whole, cruel arc of the lovers' journey—a full circle that has led inexorably from dust to dust.

≣ *I didn't love everything Peter Brook did during the 1980s, but when he was flying, he had few equals. His* Carmen *and* Cherry Orchard *were almost in the league of his Royal Shakespeare Company stagings of* King Lear *(with Paul Scofield, in 1964) and* A Midsummer Night's Dream *(1970), of which I've never seen the equal.*

MARILYN
MINSKOFF THEATRE, NOVEMBER 21, 1983

If you read all the fine print in the *Playbill* for *Marilyn: An American Fable,* you'll discover that the new musical at the Minskoff has sixteen producers and ten songwriters. If you mistakenly look up from the *Playbill* to watch the show itself, you may wonder whether those twenty-six persons were ever in the same rehearsal room—or even the same city—at the same time. On top of its many other failings, *Marilyn* is incoherent to the point of being loony. I defy anyone to explain—just for starters—why ten chorus boys dressed in pink plumbers' costumes sing a song about bubble baths at the climax of Act 2.

The woman who summons the plumbers is supposed to be Marilyn Monroe, and it can be said without fear of contradiction that *Marilyn* is meant to be the story of the ill-starred actress's life. But even this fact is occasionally in doubt. Patricia Michaels's libretto makes only scant mention of Monroe's movies (no mention at all of *Some Like It Hot* or *The Misfits*) and vastly abridges the story of the actress's tempestuous personal life. If *Marilyn* is to be believed, Monroe's biggest problem was insomnia—an ailment soon rectified when she takes to tap dancing through the streets of New York with fellow classmates from the Actors Studio.

We do, however, hear about Marilyn's various husbands. Husband No. 1, Jim Dougherty, pops up in a high-school jitterbug number, then pops up again in a World War II soldiers' number, then disappears without a trace. Husband No. 2, Joe DiMaggio, is a moony juvenile who is first seen carrying a baseball bat and later discovered daintily clutching a red rose. He and Marilyn break up when she refuses to eat every meal at his restaurant on San Francisco's Fisherman's Wharf. Husband No. 3 is Arthur Miller, who lives in a New York penthouse and always speaks with a pipe in his mouth. Marilyn leaves him shortly after delivering the line "But you're Arthur Miller—how can you be so boring?"

Still, most of *Marilyn* is not about Marilyn or her famous husbands. This show has more symbolic figures and narrators than it does characters with recognizable proper names. A fey trio of singers known collectively as Destiny forever weaves in and out of the action, tossing glittery stardust on one and all. Two of Marilyn's fans periodically wander on to declare their devotion with lyrics like "My knees are weak / And I can't even speak." A pair of chorus girls campily outfitted as "Hedda" and "Louella" are dragged in at intervals to dish the "gossip" about Monroe—but their gossip is so bowdlerized that they might as well be describing the private life of Shirley Temple.

Alyson Reed, the professional and hard-working performer cast in the title role, has precious little to do under the circumstances. In Act 1, she must deliver most of her characterization with her chest and derriere. Monroe she's not, but, when she's stuffed into the famous costumes, you can squint your eyes and accept her as a Madame Tussaud's replica. Ms. Reed also mimics Monroe's voice effectively—until she takes to delivering her Act 2 songs in a standard Broadway belt.

The production surrounding the star looks as if it suffered a bombing raid during previews. Tom H. John's gloomy scenery, built around a soundstage motif, is a gutted retread of Robin Wagner's design for Jerry Herman's Hollywood musical, *Mack and Mabel*. Joseph G. Aulisi's costumes, Marilyn's excepted, look as if they were picked up at a fire sale. The dance numbers are often thinly populated, and the pit band sounds decimated. The disposable songs, some of them joltingly out of period, also seem to have been radically cut: a few mercifully give up the ghost in less than a minute.

The amateur direction and choreography are attributed to Kenny Ortega; the *Playbill* also thanks another director, Thommie Walsh. Perhaps someday one of these men or their several dozen collaborators will reveal what they had in mind. *Marilyn: An American Fable* is so confused that it never gets around to its heroine's death. If nothing else, it must be the first exploitation of the Monroe legend that even denies necrophiliacs a good time.

DOONESBURY

BILTMORE THEATRE, NOVEMBER 22, 1983

The qualities that have made Garry Trudeau's comic strip "Doonesbury" a national treasure are all present in the musical-comedy version at the Biltmore Theatre. You'll hear the offhand dialogue that snares the self-contradictions of college kids of the 1960s. You'll find some sly political jokes aimed at targets as ideologically diverse as William P. Clark and Jane Fonda. Best of all, you'll notice that the tone of Mr. Trudeau's work is intact: On stage, as in the strip, Mr. Trudeau speaks in a sweet voice that lifts him well above the madding crowd of diurnal satirists.

The more literal specifics of the newsprint "Doonesbury" have been preserved as well. Jacques Levy, the director, has engaged young performers who not only look exactly like the members of Mr. Trudeau's Walden Puddle commune but also sound just as we always imagined they would—even when they sing. Peter Larkin and Patricia McGourty, the set and costume designers, have done a clever, light-handed job of duplicating the spirit of Mr. Trudeau's airy funny-pages doodling.

No wonder, then, that *Doonesbury* is a pleasant show. The surprise is that it's dull. A few bright interludes notwithstanding, this musical never catches fire. Some of the shortfall can be traced to conventional failings of craft in Mr. Trudeau's book and a weak score by Elizabeth Swados. There is also a philosophical problem. Aren't we all, Mr. Trudeau included, getting a bit tired of watching sixties-style students as they beat a hasty retreat into the big chill of the middle-class mainstream?

Mr. Trudeau seemed to acknowledge as much when he suspended his comic strip early this year. After more than a decade, he and his many imitators (on and off the funny pages) had said all there was to be said about such archetypes as Zonker, the spaced-out tanning-fanatic from California, or Mark, the hipper-than-thou disk jockey. In his book for the musical, Mr. Trudeau wants to be done with these characters altogether: The show's premise places the Walden crowd on the eve of graduation, as they venture into the real world seeking jobs and mates.

Because the commencement exercises don't occur until the final scene, Mr. Trudeau must invent other story twists to fill up the evening. Zonker's Uncle Duke—a recreational drug enthusiast originally inspired by the journalist Hunter S. Thompson—conspires to bulldoze the students' off-off-campus house and replace it with condominiums. Mike Doonesbury awkwardly tries to court the feisty J.J., and J.J. tries to come to terms with her long-lost mother, Joanie Caucus. Yet the plotting seems perfunctory, as if the author is only killing time while waiting to bid everyone adieu. Many of the book scenes are enervated rehashes or continuations of old strips.

The show's flimsy structure only accentuates its warmed-over feel. Mr. Trudeau is torn between writing a standard musical-comedy narrative (complete with mawkish resolutions) and a series of sketches, with the result that neither form is realized. (For some reason the punch lines that precede the blackouts are the flattest in the script.) Only the straight political gags have bite. At various arbitrary times—but not enough times—a cartoon White House suddenly descends and we laugh heartily at the topical, piped-in lines that Mr. Trudeau has given to our incumbent president.

Oddly enough, Mr. Trudeau's song lyrics, his first ever, are far better than his book; perhaps the tight discipline of comic-strip writing has provided him with the miniaturist's skill required. In the funniest (if most irrelevant) song, a preppie chanteuse named Muffy declares, "I love Nancy Reagan / I love Ronnie, too / What a pity their money is so new." It's too bad that Ms. Swados accompanies such words with merrily intentioned but mostly flavorless music, wanly played by an onstage, synthesizer-laden four-man band. *Doonesbury* cries out for a score by Randy Newman—or, failing that, one with the zip of such Broadway progenitors as *Bye Bye Birdie, Grease,* or *Hair.*

Margo Sappington's choreography is as minimalist as the music. But Mr. Levy's efficient staging and lively cast keep the show moving, however vague its destination. With the exception of Gary Beach's vastly oversold Duke and the nondescript contributions of Lauren Tom (Duke's Chinese sidekick Honey) and Barbara Andres (Joanie), the performers could not be better. They include Ralph Bruneau and Kate Burton as the haltingly lovesick Mike and J.J., Keith Szarabajka as the football-crazed B.D., Albert Macklin as Zonker, and Reathel Bean as the most fatuous ABC-TV newsman ever to appear on "30/30." That fine actor Mark Linn-Baker does as well as possible by Mark, whose big song is especially lackluster.

In a class by herself is Laura Dean, as the blond cheerleader Boopsie. "I Can Have It All" is the title of her solo turn, and this performer does have it all: She is a charismatic singer, dancer, and comedienne who is good-naturedly sexy without ever becoming a stereotype. Watching her, we remember how sweetness and sharp humor came together to ignite "Doonesbury," the comic strip. *Doonesbury,* the musical, too often seems pale by contrast: The Walden gang has finally grown up, and, as Mr. Trudeau might pejoratively put it, mellowed out.

THE GLASS MENAGERIE
Eugene O'Neill Theatre, December 2, 1983

The new Broadway revival of *The Glass Menagerie* leaves much to be desired, but that fact doesn't diminish the largest aspect of the event. The spirits of Tennessee Williams and Jessica Tandy have been reunited for the first time in a generation, and their partnership, now as in legend, is one of the most fundamental in the history of the American theater. Perhaps some theatergoers will want to hold out for a better *Glass Menagerie* than the one at the O'Neill Theatre, and no doubt it will eventually arrive. But you pass up Ms. Tandy's Amanda Wingfield only at your own peril: You may turn around one day to discover that, in Mr. Williams's phrase, the past has turned into everlasting regret.

Along with *Long Day's Journey into Night, The Glass Menagerie* is in a class apart among autobiographical American plays. "The play is memory," says Tom, Mr. Williams's alter ego and narrator—and so it is. What lifts this work above so many other family living-room dramas is its author's insistence on refracting the past through a complex and vulnerable sensibility: A remembered reality is rearranged to express the music, both sweet and discordant, of a young poet's soul. It is Ms. Tandy's ability to ascend to that same realm—to give us not just the simple truth, but "truth in the pleasant disguise of illusion"—that makes her performance a piece of music that lingers in our minds as persistently as Amanda lingered in the author's.

The simple truth of Amanda is plain enough. A woman who has long since been deserted by both her husband and her genteel Southern youth, she lives in shabby circumstances in Depression-era St. Louis; she fights incessantly for her children's happiness even as she nearly smothers them to death. But if that were the sum of Amanda, Mr. Williams wouldn't have written about her. Within the exasperating nag, there is still the coquettish plantation belle. Within the woman battered on all sides by the painfulness of existence, there is still the indomitable fighter who clings to her faith in "the superior things of the mind and the spirit."

Ms. Tandy, trim and in blond curls, wraps all these Amandas together in a portrayal of prismatic translucence. One second she is hectoring her son for his selfishness in a raspy Southern drawl, then she is all maternal good will, quietly tightening a muffler around Tom's neck. A second after that, she is a calculating flirt, cajoling the young man into finding his sister, Laura, a gentleman caller. When Tom takes the bait, she skips buoyantly about her drab apartment, clapping her hands in childish delight.

As always with this actress, delicate precision is all. When Amanda tells her daughter to aspire to "charm" and then remembers that charm was also her husband's fatal attribute, the word descends from a cheery high note to a death rattle in the same sentence. When Amanda trudges home defeated by the discovery that Laura has abandoned business college, Ms. Tandy enters in a moth-eaten cloth coat, looking aged and weary; then, by the mere dignity with which she removes her gloves, she reasserts the pride and determination of a woman who perseveres in the face of any defeat. Later on, while reminiscing to her son about her marriage, the actress clasps her arms to her chest on the line "There are so many things in my heart I cannot describe to you." Her eyes tell us those indescribable things, and one of them is the unmistakable red-hot fever of sexual passion.

Ms. Tandy brings one other strong asset to this role—beauty. When she puts on her yellow-linen cotillion dress to greet Laura's gentleman caller, there is nothing campy or self-parodistic about the mother's retreat to her vanished past. Sashaying about the room with a bouquet of jonquils in her hand, the actress just turns back the clock as magically as she did in *Foxfire*. Yet when disappointment sets in afterward, the same woman in the same dress withers like a leaf: The glow is gone, and we're left with a ghost floating through the lurid red shadows cast by the Paradise dance hall next door.

Unlike so many Amandas, Ms. Tandy doesn't refrain from making the audience despise her—and that's how it must be, if we're to believe that she will ultimately drive her son, like her husband, out the door forever. This Amanda is tough, and even her most comic badgerings leave a bitter aftertaste. John Dexter, the British director of this production, follows the same severe tack in the rest of the revival—even to the point of using some of the distancing, slide-projected title cards that Mr. Williams calls for in the published text (but are rarely seen in performance).

Though the notion of fighting against a maudlin *Glass Menagerie* is laudable, the execution has gone astray. The exemplary designer Ming Cho Lee has created a set that appropriately serves the abstraction of memory rather than kitchen-sink reality, but it is too big, too contemporary, and too icy in its austere high-tech design. Even Andy Phillips's evocative, pointillist lighting can't always prevent it from combating the play's intimacy.

The supporting cast, though populated by accomplished actors, is frequently playing at a routine level. Though she works hard, Amanda Plummer is miscast as Laura: As you'd expect, she captures the pathological shyness of a young woman who lives in a fantasy world of glass figurines, but a gleaming smile alone can't convey the inner radiance that is waiting to be unlocked; we just don't believe that she would haunt her brother for the rest of his life. Bruce Davison's Tom has a Williamsesque accent that comes (in the narration) and goes (in the scenes proper)—and the performance is in and out, too. A cagey opponent for Ms. Tandy in their fights, the actor gives an exaggeratedly actorish delineation of a dreamy poet battling for salvation.

John Heard comes off much better as the Gentleman Caller: He mines the low-key generosity of the man, thereby keeping total disaster at bay in his long scene with the almost resolutely ungiving Ms. Plummer. But his flights of Dale Carnegie–style self-boosterism are accompanied by artificial and anachronistic gestures—as if he and Mr. Dexter were guessing blindly at the manners of a bygone American prototype.

That the play is often absorbing and affecting, if imbalanced, in spite of these considerable drawbacks is a testament to the enduring pull of the writing and to the flame of Ms. Tandy. The wrong notes are there to be heard, but so is the voice of our cherished, departed poet, pouring directly out of one of the few incandescent theater artists he has left behind.

BABY

ETHEL BARRYMORE THEATRE, DECEMBER 5, 1983

When you're pregnant, your emotions run all over the place," says a mother-to-be in *Baby*, the new musical at the Barrymore. *Baby* runs all over the place, too, but never so far afield that it forsakes those intimate emotions. At a time when nearly every Broadway musical, good and bad, aims for the big kill with gargantuan pyrotechnics, here is a modestly scaled entertainment that woos us with such basic commodities as warm feelings, an exuberant cast, and a lovely score. Perfect *Baby* is not, but it often makes up in buoyancy and charm what it lacks in forceful forward drive.

Should you wish to avail yourself of the evening's assets, be prepared for the drawbacks: You'll have to put up with a jerry-built book littered with sitcom jokes. *Baby* also requires a fondness for its subject. This show is indeed about making babies, and it's definitely not for anyone who believes that expectant parents should be seen and not heard.

Set in an unidentified college town, *Baby* focuses on three prototypical couples as they progress (or try to progress) through the nine longest months in any family's life. The youngest parents (Liz Callaway and Todd Graff) are undergraduates who find it easier to commit to parenthood than to marriage. The eldest (Beth Fowler and James Congdon) are middle-aged marrieds who have already raised three kids when the stork unexpectedly comes knocking again. (Mom is forty-three.) In between are Martin Vidnovic and Catherine Cox, as a couple whose hunger for a child is thwarted by the mathematics of infertility.

As you can see, the book's author, Sybille Pearson, has chosen her characters as if she were a pollster in search of a statistical cross section of modern (and uniformly model) parents. Worse, this writer—as in her play *Sally and Marsha*—values hit-and-miss one-liners over substance. Though the infertile couple is written with sensitivity, the college-age couple is defined by canned youth jargon (especially the word *punk*); the older parents hardly exist in the book at all. Ms. Pearson is also fond of such plot contrivances as mixed-up lab reports, and, in Act 2, the story runs out altogether. The last trimester for the mothers in *Baby* is as much of a waiting game as it can be in real life.

Yet David Shire, the composer, and Richard Maltby Jr., the lyricist, rush to the book's rescue by addressing the show's concerns with both humor and intelligence. Given the complexity of those issues—from genetic worries to the pain of delivery—it's surprising how airy the songs are: Even a topic as potentially didactic as a mother's choice between family and career is handled with a peppy tune and boomeranging lyric. A number called "Fatherhood Blues," delivered by the men's weekend baseball team, may be the last word about the countervailing forces of levitating exhilaration and crushing panic that induce whiplash in incipient fathers.

The more sober songs are equally impressive. One in which the most mature couple evaluate their marriage's shortcomings is so eloquent about the vagaries of marital love that it lifts the characters above the banalities of their dialogue. The Act 1 finale, in which a fetus's first kick prompts the youngest mother to sing about "the chain of life," is resolutely ungooey. "I was young/ I didn't know that some things outlive me," sings Ms. Callaway—and the simplicity of that universal discovery, wedded to cascading music, is what allows *Baby* to provide its share of goosebumps.

To keep up with the varied ages of the characters, Mr. Shire writes with sophistication over a range that embraces rock, jazz, and the best of Broadway schmaltz. His music receives its full due from Jonathan Tunick's lithe, endlessly varied orchestrations and from a sizable onstage band conducted by Peter Howard. Mr. Maltby's lyrics are not just smart and funny, but often ingenious—as befits a lyricist who has a sideline inventing intricate crossword puzzles for *Harper's* magazine.

Mr. Maltby also doubles as the show's director. With the aid of some brief but clever choreography by Wayne Cilento, he at times achieves the limber spontaneity he brought to his staging of *Ain't Misbehavin'*. He also does a dexterous job of interweaving projected film animation into the action: As the mothers push toward D day, we follow their intrauterine development to ultimately touching effect.

Even so, the production has its sloppy loose ends. The raspy sound system needs fixing, and so does the pleasant, pastel-colored fairy-tale set. The designer John Lee Beatty, who does so well by single-set plays, has once again run into trouble with moving scenery: *Baby* relies on a network of mobile circular curtains that, while eventually paying off in a shrewd final flourish, are otherwise too busy and noisy.

The cast, which includes a small band of chorus people, is led by the endearing Ms. Callaway, a ragamuffin out of a Koren cartoon. Possessing a clarion voice and an ingenuous smile, she glows with the sensuality of a pregnant woman; when she takes to boogeying about in her sixth month, we're treated to what may be the most unlikely instance of sexy dancing ever seen in a Broadway musical. As her boyish stringbean of a partner, Mr. Graff could use toning down, but he's a prodigious song-and-dance man. Mr. Vidnovic, last seen in the revival of *Brigadoon,* and Ms. Cox bring tenderness and old-time Broadway style to the nonexpectant couple. Ms. Fowler is amusingly sardonic as the eldest mother, though Mr. Congdon is a shade too bland as her husband.

If the virtues of *Baby* can't override all its hitches, so be it. In achievement, this show is a throwback to the early 1960s—the last era when Broadway regularly produced some casual-spirited musicals that were not instantly categorizable as blockbusters or fiascoes. Those musicals—like, say, *Do Re Mi* or *110 in the Shade*—weren't built for the ages but could brighten a theater season or two: They were ingratiatingly professional, had both lulls and peaks, and inspired you to run to the record store as soon as the original cast album came out. So it is with *Baby,* and wouldn't it be cheering if such a show could find a home on the do-or-die Broadway of today?

≡ *Maltby and Shire remain the great "almost" story of the Broadway musical, writing good songs for shows that don't quite make it. (Their next on Broadway, more than a decade later, would be the even less successful* Big, *though Maltby did work on the lyrics for* Miss Saigon *along the way.)*

NOISES OFF
Brooks Atkinson Theatre, December 12, 1983

Prod them a little, and congenital theatergoers will admit the dark and dirty truth: The most calamitous nights in the theater can be almost as memorable as the most successful. It's strangely involving to watch actors struggle heroically in a ludicrous play. When absolutely everything goes wrong on stage, as when everything goes right, we're treated to drama that is urgent, spontaneous, unmistakably alive.

Yet whoever heard of a play in which both extremes of theatergoing pleasure occupy the same stage at the same time? That's what happens at Michael Frayn's *Noises Off,* the double-whammy English farce newly arrived at the Atkinson. All three acts of this play recycle the same theatrical catastrophe: We watch a half-dozen has-been and never-were British actors, at different stops on a provincial tour, as they perform the first act of a puerile, door-slamming sex farce titled *Nothing On.* With a plot involving wayward plates of sardines, misplaced clothing, and an Arab sheik, *Nothing On* is the silliest and most ineptly acted play one could ever hope to encounter. But out of its lunacies, Mr. Frayn has constructed the larger prank of *Noises Off*—which is as cleverly conceived and adroitly performed a farce as Broadway has seen in an age.

The fun begins even before the curtain goes up. In the *Playbill,* we find a program-within-the-program, complete with cast biographies and advertisements, for the play-within-the-play. Among other things, we learn that the author of *Nothing On* is a former "unsuccessful gents hosiery wholesaler" whose previous farce *Socks Before Marriage* ran for nine years on London's West End. Once the curtain does rise, it reveals a hideous set (wittily designed by Michael Annals) that could well serve all those sex farces (*No Sex Please—We're British* and the like) that do run for nine years in the West End. Billed as the interior of a two-level country house, the set is outfitted with seven doors, soiled walls, and a blizzard of chintz.

The actors who stumble into view are scarcely more appetizing. The leading lady, cast as a jolly housemaid, is a broken-down television comedienne (Dorothy Loudon) who keeps misplacing those sardines. Her fellow players range from a drunk (Douglas Seale) who misses his every cue to a terminally vacant ingenue (Deborah Rush) who habitually loses her contact lenses in mid-speech. Guiding one and all is an addled director (Brian Murray) who interrupts the performance to offer his company the grave instruction that "doors and sardines" are what farce, theater, and life "are all about."

It happens that Act I of *Noises Off* is the frantic final run-through of *Nothing On,* on the eve of its premiere in the backwater of Weston-Super-Mare. As the run-through is mostly devoted to setting up what follows, it's also the only sporadically mirthless stretch of Mr. Frayn's play: We're asked to study every ridiculous line and awful performance in *Nothing On* to appreciate the varied replays yet to come. Still, the lags are justified by the payoff: Having painstakingly built his house of cards in Act 1, the author brings it crashing down with exponentially accelerating hilarity in Acts 2 and 3.

Indeed, Act 2 of *Noises Off,* both as written by Mr. Frayn and staged by Michael Blakemore, is one of the most sustained slapstick ballets I've ever seen. *Nothing On* is now a month into its tour, and we discover that its actors are carrying out a real-life sex farce that crudely parallels the fictional one they're appearing in. Mr. Frayn lets us see both farces at once, through the device of showing us a chaotic Wednesday matinee of *Nothing On* from the reverse angle of backstage. Every time an actor playing an illicit lover in *Nothing On* exits through a slamming door, he lands smack in the middle of the illicit love triangles that are destroying the company in private.

Besides being an ingeniously synchronized piece of writing and performing—with daredevil pratfalls and overlapping lines that interlock in midair—Act 2 of *Noises Off* is also a forceful argument for farce's value as human comedy. Perhaps nothing could top it, and Act 3 doesn't always succeed. Yet, if some loose ends remain, the third and final rendition of *Nothing On* has been sharpened since *Noises Off* opened in London. At last at the end of their tour—and in open revolt against each other and their production—the actors rewrite and sabotage every line of their script, wrestle their recalcitrant props to the ground, and even contend with an understudy who suddenly assumes his role in mid-performance.

By that point Miss Loudon has been reduced to a limping, snarling, quivering sack of raw nerves, her eyes bulging in agony: She gets every laugh, not the least of which is a terrified "Who are you?" delivered to the unexpected understudy. Watching the glee with which Ms. Loudon attacks her role, one imagines that she's recollecting every bomb that blighted her own theatrical career during those long years before *Annie* brought her in from the wilderness.

But *Noises Off* is an ensemble effort, and everyone works to a slaphappy hilt: Ms. Rush, who ultimately takes to delivering her lines as if she were a malfunctioning windup doll; Victor Garber, as a stalwart young leading man who veers steadily and subtly into nervous and physical collapse; Paxton Whitehead, as a sonorous-voiced dolt who uses Stanislavsky neither wisely nor well; Mr. Seale's sotted old ham; Linda Thorson as the company's most dutiful ad-libber in adversity ("How odd to find a telephone in the garden!"), and Jim Piddock and Amy Wright as the dim backstage staff. While Mr. Murray's director is at first too extravagantly frazzled, he finds his usual acidic tone once he starts blurring the distinctions between *Nothing On* and his other ongoing theatrical assignment, *Richard III*.

As the evening's real director, Mr. Blakemore has let only a few broadly embroidered fits mar his replication of his original London production. Rightly, the text hasn't been Americanized, and it's possible that some onlookers will be left cold by Mr. Frayn's satirical jabs at a genre of West End play that has no exact Broadway equivalent. But Broadway audiences, especially these days, are keenly familiar with theatrical disaster. A joyous and loving reminder that the theater really does go on even when the show falls apart, *Noises Off* couldn't have arrived in New York a moment too soon.

≡ *"What was* Moose Murders *like?" I wrote in a sum-up piece at the end of the year. "It was almost exactly like* Nothing On, *the intentionally catastrophic farce performed within* Noises Off."

Noises Off *was, is, perhaps always will be the funniest play written in my lifetime. Like so many theatrical works that take the theater as their subject—starting with* A Chorus Line—*it was adapted by Hollywood into one of the worst movies ever made.*

PEG
LUNT-FONTANNE THEATRE, DECEMBER 15, 1983

Dressed in a flowing gown of white and silver, her head crowned by a halo of glitter, Peggy Lee takes to the stage of the Lunt-Fontanne like a high priestess ascending an altar. And *Peg*, the "musical autobiography" that Ms. Lee has brought to Broadway, is nothing if not a religious rite.

In this evening of song and chat, one of our premier pop singers presents herself as a spiritual icon. There is some entertainment in *Peg*, not to mention some striking musicianship, but the show is most likely to excite those who are evangelistically devoted to both Peggy Lee and God—ideally in that order.

For those who respect Peggy Lee as a vocalist but who don't worship her as a public personality, *Peg* may seem bizarre. Though this one-woman career retrospective vaguely resembles Lena Horne's in format, its tone and impact are vastly different. Unlike the more spontaneous Ms. Horne, Ms. Lee recites the blow-by-blow story of her life with great solemnity and saves many of her famous songs for a final medley. Roughly half of the numbers in *Peg* are new, designed to enshrine the red-letter events in the star's life.

Those events are not happy. Ms. Lee has survived childhood whippings (musicalized in a song titled "One Beating a Day"), her beloved first husband's bout with alcoholism, and her own share of paralyzing (and unidentified) illnesses. All in all, it is remarkable that the singer has overcome so many hard knocks. But if the story Ms. Lee tells is often courageous, the way she tells it is something else. In addition to sacrificing introspection for inspirational homilies ("God has never let me down"), the star regards her personal history from an omniscient and self-deifying perspective.

Sometimes Ms. Lee speaks about herself in the third person, as when she breaks into self-authored verse to describe the birth of "a child who would sing." (Her late father, represented by an amplified chorus singer's voice, then chimes in to describe his daughter's birth with sepulchral reverence.) At other times, Ms. Lee's memory seems peculiarly selective: We hear more about her successful defense against a nuisance plagiarism suit than her career with Benny Goodman's band.

Many of the anecdotes sound as if they were long ago homogenized by press agents for mass dissemination through talk shows. Recalling her husband's death, the star focuses on the fact that she was toasting the jazz pianist George Shearing at a party when she heard the sad news.

Tom H. John's set could serve Merv Griffin: Ms. Lee often holds forth from one of two upholstered chairs that are backed by potted plants. Her manner can be just as blandly impersonal. Her speaking voice has few inflections, and her principal expression is a fixed, impassive smile. The gestures accompanying her singing are mechanical, as are her arm-raising acknowledgments of the audience's applause.

The new songs, in which Ms. Lee's lyrics are usually set to Paul Horner's music, are professional, but only one, "Daddy Was a Railroad Man," catches fire. The familiar numbers, from "Fever" to "Is That All

There Is?," are just as sparky as always. Though Ms. Lee's voice is a small instrument, it is usually sure in pitch. Her rhythmic attack can't be beat.

The musicians who serve the star—even to the embarrassing extent of recounting her past kindnesses to fans—are first-rate. The show's crack conductor, Larry Fallon, leads a hard-driving big band and small chorus. The quartet at center stage includes some frequent associates of such other top singers as Ms. Horne and Mel Tormé: Mike Renzi (piano), Grady Tate (drums), Jay Leonhart (bass), and Bucky Pizzarelli (guitar). The orchestrations, by such illustrious hands as Billy May and Larry Wilcox (among many others), and the sound system, credited to Jan Nebozenko and the record producer Phil Ramone, are way above usual Broadway standards.

Peg was directed by Robert Drivas, presumably with the assistance of the "creative consultant" Cy Coleman. The staging is efficient, but these experienced theater men can only take their star so far. The Lunt-Fontanne is a large house that requires a huge theatrical personality to dominate it. Lacking so sizable a presence, Ms. Lee has let her ego inflate to fill the gap.

THE REAL THING
PLYMOUTH THEATRE, JANUARY 6, 1984

Henry, the hero of Tom Stoppard's *The Real Thing*, is an English playwright of unbeatable intellectual prowess. He knows how to make words "go on replicating themselves like a spiral of DNA" and how to ad-lib a brilliant rejoinder to any question. Both in life and in the theater, he can always get the last word and the smartest laugh. But there's one question Henry can't so easily answer or write about or joke away: What is this thing called love?

In *The Real Thing*, we watch Henry (Jeremy Irons) find the answer— and we watch Mr. Stoppard do so, too. In the play at the Plymouth, the author of such high-flying neo-Shavian farces as *Jumpers* and *Travesties* turns his attention to private passion—and he does so without mortgaging an intellect that has few equals in the contemporary theater. The Broadway version of *The Real Thing*—a substantial revision of the original London production—is not only Mr. Stoppard's most moving play, but also the most bracing play that anyone has written about love and marriage in years.

Yet Mr. Stoppard, being Mr. Stoppard, hasn't settled only for that high achievement. If *The Real Thing* is about love, it is also about the literary coordinates of love. The story of Henry's awakening to passion is always linked to the story of how he learns to reconcile those messy emotions with his austere, high-minded credo of playwriting. *The Real Thing* is as much about how a writer learns to write *The Real Thing* as it is about how he learns to experience the real thing.

There is much more going on as well—debates about the moral imperatives (if any) of such other abstract "things" as politics and justice, running jokes that somersault into each other, Pirandellian theater games that illuminate the play's theme even as they give the evening its shape. *The Real Thing* is so densely and entertainingly packed with wit, ideas, and feelings that one visit just won't do. Given the sublime cast led by Mr. Irons and Glenn Close—and the bravura force of Mike Nichols's direction—any repeat viewings are likely to be as dazzling as the first.

The Real Thing begins with what might almost be a Nichols and May spoof of Nöel Coward. A terribly elegant Englishman, wearing a silk smoking robe, sits in a toney drawing room, waiting for his wife to return from a business trip. When the wife enters, the husband confronts her with evidence of adultery. But even as the couple surveys the ruins of their marriage, the badinage keeps flying. The husband even sings a Gershwin phrase from "Let's Call the Whole Thing Off."

This opening sketch, it soon turns out, is not *The Real Thing*, but a play-within-the-play—a scene from Henry's latest comedy, *House of Cards*. In real life, the leading lady, Charlotte (Christine Baranski), is Henry's wife, while her onstage husband, Max (Kenneth Welsh), is married to another actress, Annie (Ms. Close). As we meet these two couples at brunch on the play's day off, we learn that a real adulterous relationship is afoot—between Henry and Annie. But when Annie confesses her betrayal to Max at home a few scenes later, the actor doesn't behave at all as he does on stage in Henry's play. Now in a tattered cloth robe, Max has no quip to paper over his grief: He collapses like a house of cards into miserable sobs.

From that point on, Mr. Stoppard concentrates on the new marriage that Henry and Annie build after they discard Charlotte and Max. For the new marriage to work, however, Henry must change—and the psychological distance he must travel is the same that separates the synthetic Max he presents in *House of Cards* from the agonized Max presented by Mr. Stoppard. Though Henry may describe *House of Cards* as a play about a man who achieves "self-knowledge through pain," his seventeen-year-old daughter correctly dismisses it as fluff. *The Real*

Thing is essentially the play Henry really meant to write—and he finds the self-knowledge needed to write it, as well as to give himself in love, only after Annie inflicts the same pain on him that she inflicted on Max.

But if Annie's new infidelity is the plot mechanism by which Mr. Stoppard brings his cerebral hero in touch with his heart, it's far from the sum of the author's method. As Henry sorts out his own understanding of what love is, or should be, Mr. Stoppard dexterously quotes or alludes to other playwrights' views—from the seventeenth-century John Ford to Strindberg, Wilde, and Coward. As he does, he knocks down Henry's highbrow argument that love is an "unliterary" subject—"happiness expressed in banality and lust"—that's best left to the lowbrow pop singers (The Righteous Brothers, Herman's Hermits) that Henry guiltily reveres.

And as the protagonist grows as a man, so *The Real Thing* expands as a play. Early on, it's fast and funny, like Henry's comedy. According to Charlotte, the difference between a play like *House of Cards* and real life is that there's more thinking time between the lines in real life. But Henry's life, as Mr. Stoppard first reveals it, is just like his play: Henry is a "reflex joke machine" who finishes Annie's sentences for fear that any thinking time will make love "go wrong, change, spoil."

Once Henry begins to mature, Mr. Stoppard's writing flowers until it's more spiritually akin to Ford's open-throated blank verse than the brittle, sublimating cadences of *House of Cards*. Only then can Henry and Annie face each other with utter nakedness. Only then can Henry find the language that celebrates love as the bond between two people who fully know each other's private selves, no matter what other identities they present to the world.

Mr. Stoppard's championing of a man's private soul over his public posture does, alas, lead *The Real Thing* into one cul-de-sac. Throughout the play, Henry's ideals about art and language are set against those of a fledgling playwright—a militant antinuclear demonstrator named Brodie who writes poorly, but, unlike Henry, champions a social cause. Whatever the relative merits of polemical playwrights versus "pure" writers, no light is shed here. By painting Brodie as a moral fraud and loutish philistine, Mr. Stoppard lets Henry demolish him without contest—and reduces a complex debate to a smug, loaded dialectic.

In part because Annie is a radical-chic Brodie booster, she is not an equal with Henry in their love match. Charlotte, the hero's sardonic, tough-minded first wife, is at times more likable than her successor—which may not have been Mr. Stoppard's intention. Otherwise, the script changes since London (notably in Act 2) tighten and crystallize a play left incompletely fulfilled in the West End.

Mr. Nichols's all-new staging sews up the rest. With the aid of the inspired set designer Tony Walton, the director prevents the frequent, potentially cumbersome scene shifts from breaking the production's pace; Tharon Musser's poetic lighting and Anthea Sylbert's delicate, ever-changing costume modulations enhance the illusion of cinematic speed and style. Every supporting role is perfectly done—from Ms. Baranski and Mr. Welsh as the rejected spouses to the one-scene contributions of Cynthia Nixon (as Henry's rebellious daughter) and Vyto Ruginis (Brodie). In the smallish part of a young actor, the charismatic Peter Gallagher once again reveals an outsized talent that wins over an audience in a flash.

If Annie can be a thankless role, the frizzily redheaded Ms. Close concedes nothing: She's warm and persuasive even when her character's convictions and behavior are dubious. More important, she joins with her costar to give the play its essential sexual charge. Mr. Irons, meanwhile, has never been better: He captures Henry's magnetic public charm, then goes on to reveal the suffering and longing within.

This actor's first tour de force arrives early in Act 2—when he delivers a glorious speech likening the sacred power of a writer's words to convey ideas to a cricket bat propelling a ball. But Mr. Irons's Henry goes further later on, after love has hit hard and language has begun to fail him entirely. Collapsing in his chair under the weight of Annie's betrayal, the author of the glib *House of Cards* is finally left alone with only a primal, anguished cry—"Please, please, please don't!"—as a weapon against pain. Spare and "unliterary" as Henry's words have at last become, Mr. Stoppard, through his art, has made them sacred. He and Mr. Irons, as if wielding cricket bats, land every one of them right where it hurts.

≡ *I hadn't liked* The Real Thing *in London, where it was a considerable hit despite a fussy production and the sexless star coupling of Roger Rees and Felicity Kendal. The New York version was completely recast and restaged and significantly revised. It not only outshone the earlier version but became the biggest commercial hit Stoppard has had in America.*

OLD TIMES
Roundabout Theatre, January 13, 1984

There are some things one remembers even though they may never have happened," says a mysterious visitor in Harold Pinter's *Old Times,* now receiving a fine revival at the Roundabout. People are constantly remembering things past in this chilling 1971 play, but we never do learn which of those things really happened and which did not. It doesn't matter. Perception, in all its subjectivity, is the reality in the Proustian landscape of *Old Times*. What matters is not what happened but what people think happened. What people think defines who they are—or wish they were.

The three people of *Old Times* converge in a luxuriously converted English farmhouse. The house belongs to Deeley (Anthony Hopkins), a filmmaker, and his wife, Kate (Marsha Mason). It's an antiseptic place—a sparsely furnished, off-white temple of modernism that looks like an iceberg adrift in a primeval black wilderness. When the couple's visitor, Anna (Jane Alexander), arrives from her home in Sicily, she congratulates Kate and Deeley for electing to "stay permanently in such a silence." And then, like so many intruders in Pinter plays, Anna sets out to shatter that silence.

Anna first knew her hostess twenty years earlier. The two women were roommates and best friends, "poor and young" in London together. For most of *Old Times*—which runs a taut seventy-odd minutes (plus intermission)—Anna and Kate do what old friends do at a reunion: They reminisce about old times. But Anna does most of the talking and much of what she has to say is directed at her friend's husband. Deeley has his own memories of London twenty years ago, none of which jibe with Anna's.

As Kate's former and present roommates dredge up their respective versions of seemingly trivial events, we realize that they are at war. Deeley and Anna are fighting not only for possession of the past but also for ownership of Kate herself. Yet, as always with Mr. Pinter, the struggle for power is undeclared. Only gradually do we realize that an anecdote about stolen underwear might be about spiritual or sexual theft. Or that two different accounts of a long-ago visit to the movie *Odd Man Out* might ultimately determine whether it's Anna or Deeley who ends up as the odd person out of Kate's life.

Mr. Pinter's ability to load simple sentences with highly charged psychological freight is amazing. Even single words can become time bombs. In Act 1, Deeley offhandedly mocks Anna for using a word as stilted as "gaze"; in Act 2, he uses the word himself in another context, turning it into a stiletto-sharp weapon of verbal rape. Sometimes Mr. Pinter bends other writers' words to his esthetic will. When Deeley and Anna try to one-up each other by singing snippets of old songs to Kate, the innocent lyrics of "They Can't Take That Away from Me" and "These Foolish Things" lose their nostalgic meaning and become crackling, malevolent epithets.

Perhaps Mr. Pinter's method is best described by Anna, when she breaks into a flowery reverie about a river: "Ripples on the surface indicate a shimmering in depth down through every particle of water down to the riverbed." The ripples can be funny, too: One of Anna and Deeley's most pointed duels takes the form of an exchange about the performances given by Robert Newton and F. J. McCormick in *Odd Man Out*. There are also a few times—notably during some lumpy speeches in Act 2—when Mr. Pinter slips a bit and, in the interest of resolving the play, plunges us directly to the riverbed.

At the Roundabout, the director is Kenneth Frankel, who did the outstanding New York production of *Quartermaine's Terms* (a play originally directed by Mr. Pinter in London). Beginning with the opening word of *Old Times*—"dark," fittingly enough—Mr. Frankel precisely serves the author's elliptical chamber music, both in his staging and through his cast.

Mr. Hopkins, seedy in his leather carcoat, slowly transforms Deeley from a snappy terrier into an aroused bulldog—and, eventually, into a howling one. Ms. Alexander looks more elegant than ever and reveals a knack for comic timing I'd never previously noticed; she is as withering and frightening an Anna as can be. But the most difficult role is Kate, who must be enigmatic and implacable, yet so tantalizing that the others would almost kill to win her. Much to Ms. Mason's credit, she gives an uncharacteristically controlled performance—as befits an unknowable woman whose elusive presence is frequently likened to dreams and death. If the actress's manner and accent are still a shade too tentative to convey Kate's primal magnetic force, she's bound to close the gap soon enough.

In keeping with most of the production, Marjorie Bradley Kellogg's good set recalls the Royal Shakespeare Company's original rendition of *Old Times*. Judy Rasmuson's lighting delivers Mr. Pinter's bleak coda, in which the past finally surges and recedes over the present like a huge white wave—only to leave the characters forever alone, in the dark.

≡ *The great Anthony Hopkins stage performance of the decade—as a thinly disguised Rupert Murdoch in David Hare and Howard Brenton's* Pravda *at London's National Theater—was often promised for New York but never materialized.*

THE ARCHAEOLOGY OF SLEEP
JOYCE THEATRE, JANUARY 19, 1984

As is their wont, the nomadic members of the Living Theatre scamper through the aisles of their new temporary New York home, the Joyce Theatre. And, as is also their wont, they're not content to leave well enough alone. Suddenly, I found a performer poised above me, asking the question, "Are you afraid if I touch you like this?" And, even as the performer's final sibilant lingered in the air, I felt a sweaty kiss on my right ear. Before I could respond, another performer—Julian Beck, the Living Theatre's cofounder, no less—was by my side, asking the same question. The next thing I knew, Mr. Beck had reached his hand under my notebook and placed it between my legs.

Perhaps the only way to avoid such tactile encounters is to extend one leg and send Mr. Beck into a pratfall during one of his earlier journeys up the aisle. I'll never know. Perhaps Mr. Beck had singled me out for special treatment because he identified me as a journalist and was hoping I'd create a scene that would play into his penchant for self-promotion. But feeling more bemused than shocked, I just sat there—call me a pacifist or, if you will, a coward—and started counting the minutes until I could get home.

I also started thinking back to the Living Theatre's last American tour, in 1968. In those days, learned people actually engaged in heated, serious debates about whether the Living Theatre's Dionysian group rites might presage a revolution in world theater. There aren't likely to be any such debates this time. Though Mr. Beck and his partner, Judith Malina, are still turning their old tricks, their gimmicks look tacky now. In 1984, we can see the Living Theatre's sexual assaults for what they are: pathetic and impotent attempts to camouflage the troupe's far cruder assaults on our brains.

The Archaeology of Sleep, the first of four Living Theatre productions in repertory, is a quasi-Adlerian, quasi-Joycean meditation on the "millennium-old mysteries of sleep." We know this not because of what happens on stage but because Mr. Beck announces his intentions in one of the program's several turgid manifestos. (Ms. Malina's program note is a poem reminding us that "in sleep the linkage of images from the subconscious to the remembered is allowed.") The program further contains a complicated but useless explanatory list of over sixty scenes and subscenes—each with cute titles like "Dante's Circles" or "Terry and the Pirates."

The program also lists five sleepers whose dreams we are meant to follow—but you must add five to the theater's seating capacity to get an accurate total of the number of sleepers in the house. It's impossible to tell the official somnambulists apart in any case. The Living Theatre is now a scraggly collection of indistinguishable riffraff; the troupe could be a defrocked Moonie ashram, or maybe a seedy bus-and-truck company of *Godspell* at the end of a fifteen-year tour. (It's no treat when a half-dozen cast members expose themselves in the coy, living-statues finale.) Some of the performers have only a passing acquaintance with English, and, thank heaven, almost no one can project a line. The company's once-praised mass choreographic movement has degenerated into mass chaos; the slitherings and gyrations could pass for an adolescent game of Capture the Flag.

Mr. Beck and Ms. Malina have lately been in exile in France—where they are apparently objects of veneration second only to Jerry Lewis. Perhaps that's why they are so out of touch with the avant-garde New York theater. The hallucinatory theatrics attempted in *Sleep* have long since been perfected by Richard Foreman, Robert Wilson, and JoAnne Akalaitis. Next to these artists' most elegant effects, the Beck electronic soundtrack is tinny and their images are threadbare. The big visual conceit in *Sleep* is a shaky, moving platform referred to as "the train of thought."

What's more, the rigorously conceived associative links that give other dreamy theater pieces their surreal continuity are nonexistent in *Sleep*. The sloppy vignettes tumble forward incoherently under Ms. Malina's direction—and require periodic professorial monologues from Mr. Beck to acquire their banal significance. The orgiastic interludes are thrown in arbitrarily, like old songs in a campy nostalgia revue, in a vain attempt to break the boredom. The mystical religious rituals and lame invocations of high culture icons (Artaud, Shakespeare, Wagner) are bald attempts to intimidate the illiterate. A typical witticism is the line "The void is nothing." A typical chant goes "Slumber! Sandman! Soporific!"—and that's no joke.

And what has happened to the Living Theatre's anarchic cries for revolution? Aside from a pointless mention of Trident missiles, the only political concern of *Sleep* is a strong antivivisectionist stand against the use of cats in scientific sleep experiments. The point is illustrated by a bit in which one actor, playing a cat, simulates an act of necrophilia with an actor playing a cat corpse. With friends like the Living Theatre, the feline community might just as well go to the dogs.

≡ *This was a sad if somewhat comic postscript to what had once been the most admired radical American theater company of the 1960s. The Beck-Malina troupe had almost no resemblance to the company that electrified the theater with* Frankenstein *some fifteen years earlier. It now seemed instead like a demented cult that had lost its way after too many years abroad and too many drugs. This was, however, the only time that I was actually molested in the theater—an experience so weird I was more stunned than angry. But Doug Watt, my colleague on the* Daily News, *was so angry about what he witnessed that he offered to go slug Beck on my behalf. I took a pass.*

THE RINK

Martin Beck Theatre, February 10, 1984

When Chita Rivera steps down front to put over her first John Kander–Fred Ebb song in *The Rink,* you feel a surge of relief. Liberated from the draconian attire of *Merlin* and looking in every way terrific, Ms. Rivera is in command of a Broadway stage for the first time since her 1975 appearance in the Kander–Ebb *Chicago.* And if her song is more likable than inspired, Ms. Rivera raises it higher: Her voice is firm and sparky; her crinkly smile, often forced in recent years, is spontaneous; her taut dancer's body is in perfect concord with the music's beat.

Ms. Rivera has been a powerhouse performer for roughly three decades, and it's a pleasure to see that power unleashed again, its force undiminished by time. As *The Rink* lurches forward, the star continues to delight—whether she's leaping and high kicking in a jitterbug or brassily harmonizing with her costar, Liza Minnelli. Indeed, Ms. Rivera is a performer you could watch forever—but, in the end, even she's not enough to save *The Rink.* The show's running time is forever and a day.

The turgid, sour new musical at the Martin Beck is a curious affair. As staged by A. J. Antoon, much of it is as polished as Ms. Rivera's skills. The small supporting cast is capable, and Mr. Kander's melodies, orchestrated with panache by Michael Gibson, can linger in the ear. But no glossy Broadway professionalism can mask the work's phony, at times mean-spirited content—or give credence to its empty pretensions. It's impossible to care about anything on stage except Ms. Rivera—and we even lose some interest in her, once she passes through a gratuitous dance number simulating a gang rape.

The idea behind the show—which often seems a forced hybrid of *Follies,* John Guare's screenplay for *Atlantic City,* and a previous Kander-Ebb musical, *The Happy Time*—was to create a Proustian-flavored reunion between a long-estranged mother and her grown-up daughter. The acutely symbolic setting, designed with ingenuity and affection by Peter Larkin, is a decaying roller rink along the boardwalk of a tattered Eastern seaboard resort. Anna (Ms. Rivera), the rink's proprietor, has sold the old joint. But just as the wreckers arrive, her daughter, Angel (Ms. Minnelli), returns from a seven-year California exile to search for roots and settle old scores.

What ensues in Terrence McNally's book is a series of repetitious present-day squabbles, punctuated by flashbacks. Mr. McNally is a smart and witty playwright, but you'd never know it from this synthetic effort. His dialogue is banal, and his characters are ciphers. Anna is merely a spunky widow; Angel is a caricatured 1960s dropout defined by scruffy clothes. *The Rink* is static because nothing specific or compelling is at stake for the two women. Their only real conflict is a generalized, all-purpose logjam: They've never learned how to say "I love you."

To inflate the show, Mr. McNally pays lip service to sociological themes (such as urban decay) and loads the memory segments with lurid, melodramatic revelations that might well constitute a parody of William Inge. We learn that Anna's late husband was an alcoholic womanizer; we also hear of an illegitimate birth, Anna's postmarital promiscuity, and a fatal car crash. Though none of these soap-operatic incidents adds depth to Angel and Anna, they and that rape do reinforce the evening's distasteful tone. Almost every male character is a crude sexual adventurer, and both women are presented as reformed "tramps."

Mr. McNally resolves the mother-daughter relationship by fiat. Angel and Anna end up on terms of endearment thanks to another plot trick and several lines of "I'm OK–You're OK" psychobabble. Mr. McNally also attempts to pander to the audience in a climactic flashback: To free the daughter from her past, he presents antiwar protesters of Angel's generation as bubbleheads who didn't even know where Southeast Asia was. That cynical judgment is then embroidered in Ms. Minnelli's final song—in which Mr. Ebb's lyrics characterize the idealists of an entire decade as ineffectual Frisbee throwers and draft-card burners. Somehow this holier-than-thou indictment of the Vietnam War era lacks authority when couched in trivial terms befitting Mr. Ebb's last show, *Woman of the Year.*

Mr. Kander's discordant music for that final song sounds like *Sweeney Todd* played at the wrong speed, as does the music for an equally preposterous number in which Ms. Rivera angrily renounces her belief in God. When he sticks to nostalgic, upbeat, showbiz songs—most of which provide a heavily ironic counterpoint to the action—the composer writes with his usual flair. The best number, though formulaic, is the first: a hurdy-gurdy evocation of memory, well sung by Ms. Minnelli and dreamily enlivened by Marc B. Weiss's atmospheric lighting effects. The title song, though otherwise pointless, perks up Act 2 by allowing the six-man chorus to perform some enjoyable Graciela Daniele choreography on roller skates.

The talented chorus men play all the male roles in the show—and, for no valid reason, some of the women. Jason Alexander comes off best, as Anna's one well-meaning suitor. Until the end—when she opens up the floodgates of her tear ducts—Ms. Minnelli is convincing in the thankless role of the unkempt daughter. But in *The Rink*, it's only Ms. Rivera who spins.

≡ *In addition to Jason Alexander, the supporting cast included Scott Ellis, who went on to become a director of plays and musicals, including Kander and Ebb's* Steel Pier, *a near-double for* The Rink *that appeared on Broadway in 1997.*

ROCKABY
SAMUEL BECKETT THEATRE, FEBRUARY 17, 1984

It's possible that you haven't really lived until you've watched Billie Whitelaw die. The death occurs in *Rockaby*, the last of three brief Beckett pieces that have brought the English actress to the newly named Samuel Beckett Theatre. In *Rockaby*, she plays a woman in a rocking chair, rocking herself to the grave. The assignment looks simple. The only word Ms. Whitelaw speaks onstage is *more*, repeated four times. The "more"s are separated by a litany of other words—the tortured final thrashings of a consciousness, as recorded by the actress on tape. Then there is no more.

At that point, Ms. Whitelaw stops rocking. The lone light that picks her face out of the blackness starts to dim, and, in the longest of Beckett pauses, we watch the light within the face's hollow eyes and chalky cheeks dim, too. During the long silence, the actress doesn't so much as twitch an eyelash—and yet, by the time the darkness is total, we're left with an image different from the one we'd seen a half minute earlier. Somehow Ms. Whitelaw has banished life from her expression: What remains is a death mask, so devoid of blood it could be a faded, crumbling photograph. And somehow, even as the face disintegrates, we realize that it has curled into a faint baby's smile. We're left not only with the horror of death, but with the peace.

And there you have it. With no words, no movement, and no scenery, the world's greatest living playwright and one of his greatest living interpreters have created a drama as moving as any on a New York stage. Indeed, one might almost say that the entire Beckett canon is compressed into this short coda to a fifteen-minute play. In the long pause, we feel the weight of the solitary, agonizing, seemingly endless night of living. In Ms. Whitelaw's descent to extinction, we see the only escape there can be—and we feel the relief. Death becomes what it must be in a Beckett play: a happy ending.

Like the other works of this evening, *Rockaby* is late Beckett—as are the Beckett plays still running at the Harold Clurman Theatre next door. The author's dramatization of stasis has been distilled to its most austere, pitch-black quintessence; the writing is so minimalist that even the scant, incantatory language has been drained of color, vocabulary, and at times even of feeling. Yet if *Rockaby* (1980) and its predecessor on the bill, *Footfalls* (1976), make unusual demands on the audience, they are riveting theater. Or so they are as performed by Ms. Whitelaw, for whom Mr. Beckett wrote them, and as impeccably directed by Alan Schneider.

The evening opens with the actress reading a Beckett story, *Enough* (1966). Though not as forceful as the plays, the recital serves a valuable function. The narrator of *Enough* is someone of indeterminate sex, looking back—and trying to forget—a now severed relationship with a grotesque character known only as "he." In its use of interior monologue and in its depiction of the imprisoning nature of time, the story helps crystallize the plays that follow. But even more important is Ms. Whitelaw's tone. Chummy and in street clothes, the actress really does present herself as an unpretentious storyteller. She implies in advance that, despite the barren theatricality of *Footfalls* and *Rockaby*, they contain stories of sorts as well.

Footfalls is about a woman named May talking to her aged, infirm mother (the offstage voice of Sybil Lines). May is trapped—has long been trapped—in memory and in space. Her world is a small rectangle of light on the floor, through which she paces back and forth incessantly. (The superb lighting is by Rocky Greenberg.) The pacing, which gives off a sandpapery sound, could well be the rocking "to and fro" of *Rockaby*. It's what May does until she has finished "revolving it all" in her "poor mind." And "it all" are the play's two dominant words: Into such lonely syllables does Mr. Beckett pour all the anguish of a life.

Another line in *Footfalls* is the phrase "a faint tangle of pale gray tatters." It might describe Ms. Whitelaw's appearance as May. With her frayed, ghostly gown and silver wig, she is a skeletal, bent-over, red-eyed crone—a fossilized Miss Havisham denied even small expectations. As she courageously rakes through her addled subconscious, trying and failing to gain a foothold in the past, we feel that her last connection to existence is the sound of her feet "however faint they fall." But, apparitional as the woman may seem, the actress finds many gradations in the role. When she offers to help the unseen mother with her bedpan and sheets and pillows, the list of sickroom duties takes on an even-toned, otherworldly music. When "it all" is about to end, Ms. Whitelaw trails off into a silent scream and, soon after, a little girl's scream—both bloodcurdling.

In *Rockaby*, the actress continues to create variations within a tiny palette. Each of the four "more"s becomes more fearful; the speaker's "famished eyes" more and more dominate her face. Though the recorded speeches that follow the request for "more" tend to sound alike, subtle differences in both the writing and the performance gradually unfold the desolate tale of a woman's terrifying search for "another creature like herself"—for "one other living soul." An echoed phrase—"time she stopped"—serves as a refrain in each speech until we at last reach the "close of a long day." Then Mr. Beckett and Ms. Whitelaw make time stop, and it's a sensation that no theatergoer will soon forget.

SUNDAY ESSAY: TO MAKE SERIOUS THEATER, "SERIOUS" ISSUES AREN'T ENOUGH
FEBRUARY 19, 1984

Of all the ills that plague the American theater right now, none is more disturbing than the widespread perception that American plays simply do not matter anymore. There was a time when writers like O'Neill and Williams and Miller were at the center of this country's intellectual life—when a major play on Broadway was as fit a subject for universal comment and debate, pro or con, as the latest major novel or museum show or ballet. These days, theater is a special interest, occupying a ghetto on the cultural landscape. While the fluffiest Broadway entertainments are consumed by the masses (or at least the wealthiest masses), serious American theater is followed by a far smaller coterie—and is often either ignored or viewed with contempt by the general public and the arts-minded elite alike.

A theater critic discovers this when he encounters old friends, who are sure to boast that they haven't been to a play (the current hit musical or English import excepted) since *Who's Afraid of Virginia Woolf?* But one doesn't need such statistically skewed polling methods to discern what's going on. In most general-interest or literary periodicals, theater is written about, if it's written about at all, by theater critics only, in the parochial theater columns. One could scour the pages of some learned journals for months to find a reference to a living American playwright (the auteurs of movies fare far better); in collections of literary essays—such as John Updike's recent *Hugging the Shore*—the names of American playwrights never surface in discussions of American novelists who often share the same concerns as those playwrights. If Mr. Updike doesn't see or read American plays these days, it would be unfair to fault him for this oversight. Public evidence suggests that many American writers of his stature—playwrights excepted—are no different. Even essayists who once examined new American plays (or wrote them) —writers like Susan Sontag, Elizabeth Hardwick, Gore Vidal, or Mary McCarthy—have long since stopped caring. Perhaps the most extreme expression of this animus comes from the director and author Jonathan Miller, himself once a Broadway performer (in *Beyond the Fringe*), in a recently published interview. Asked "What importance does Broadway have to theater?" he replies: "I don't think Broadway matters at all. It's just a sewer. People don't go to Broadway to have serious theatrical experiences."

If the American theater no longer plays a central part in our cultural ferment, the reasons can only be damning. It must be assumed that we no longer have playwrights who write about issues that matter—or who connect with the rest of our literature, past and present—or who swim with the modernist and postmodernist currents of international art. But, as the theater's dwindling but hearty enthusiasts know well, this isn't the case at all.

Nonetheless, the perception persists, and, to a great extent, it has been created by the plays that have been overpraised, overattended, and overawarded—especially in the commercial theater and especially (though not exclusively) on Broadway. Much of what is most loudly acclaimed as serious theater in New York—and is then disseminated nationwide through regional and touring productions—isn't really serious at all.

In recent years, for instance, some of the most popular plays by American authors on Broadway have been works like *The Shadow Box*, *Children of a Lesser God*, and *The Elephant Man*. Entertaining, well-acted, theatrical, and (in the case of *Elephant Man*) well-written as these plays can be, they are, in the end, plays that tell theatergoers little that they didn't know upon arriving at the theater. *The Shadow Box*—a Tony Award winner for best play, no less—was a drama that took an uncompromising stand in favor of the humanity of the terminally ill. *Children of a Lesser God* and *The Elephant Man*—also Tony Award winners—did the same for the deaf and the physiologically deformed. (The English equivalent of this play, also a Broadway hit, was *Whose Life Is It, Anyway?*—which pleaded for the dignity of the paralyzed.) Who could disagree with the point of view of any of these dramas? Far from raising any kind of debate—or touching an audience at any level deeper than the sentimental—these plays mainly succeeded in congratulating audiences on their own self-righteous piety.

Another popular kind of play that has passed for serious over the past decade is the one that celebrates antisocial behavior as a form of primal passion. The genesis of this kind of escapist play can be found in fashionable sixties pop culture (Ken Kesey, R. D. Laing), and its continued appeal is as retrograde as it is baffling. The Broadway prototype is an English hit—*Equus*, in which a boy who blinds horses is held up as a paragon of spirituality in a world full of unfeeling rationalists. *Agnes of God*, which ran a season on Broadway and has since spawned two national road companies, made the same case for a nun who gave birth to and then murdered a baby, and *Extremities*, last year's commercial Off Broadway hit, came perilously close to making a similar claim for a rapist. The reductio ad absurdum of these dramas—and unaccountably a fast Broadway failure—was last season's *Total Abandon*, which asked us to cry for a father who fatally, if soulfully, bashed his young son against a wall.

It's not hard to see why most of these plays are produced or why they are popular. The commercial theater is in business to produce what sells, and what sells is what's most pleasing (and familiar) to the largest common denominator. That common denominator is now defined by television drama—and television drama can even be produced at the noncommercial, supposedly serious regional theaters that are supposed to be alternatives to Broadway. *Extremities* and *Agnes of God* originated at Louisville's Actors Theatre; *Children of a Lesser God* and *The Shadow Box* at the Mark Taper Forum in Los Angeles.

By television drama, I refer specifically to those socially conscious made-for-TV movies that now frequently dominate the Nielsen ratings. Plays like *The Shadow Box* and *Agnes of God* are serious in the same way that TV movies like *Something About Amelia* and *The Day After* are serious. They take big, headline issues (incest, nuclear war) and reduce them to simple, unassailable, uncontroversial messages. *The Day After* says that nuclear war is bad; *The Shadow Box* says that cancer is bad. Often this message is defined by a social worker, psychiatrist, or lawyer—and, indeed, these professions are prominently featured in most of these works, much as homily-spouting clergymen dominated middlebrow drama of other eras.

Aside from their open-and-shut intellectual simplicity, the great fallacy that underlies these dramas is the notion that the mere mention of a social issue gives a work of art a claim to importance. And this fallacy is not only shared by the producers who mount these plays, but sometimes by playwrights who know better. Lanford Wilson, one of the best American dramatists around—and one who might well be talked about by literary critics in the same breath as Anne Tyler or Ann Beattie—made nuclear poisoning an issue in two recent plays (*A Tale Told, Angels Fall*). Yet in both instances that concern, however pressing and passionately held, surfaced as a gratuitous plot device that was force-fed into the real tales Mr. Wilson wanted to tell. (By contrast, Mr. Wilson's masterwork about the Vietnam era, *Fifth of July,* made the war an organic aspect of the characters' shared lives.) Even an accomplished entertainer like Neil Simon has felt compelled to inject cancer, the Holocaust, and the Depression into such recent plays as *Chapter Two* and *Brighton Beach Memoirs.* Neither of those works seems as spontaneous or heartfelt as *The Odd Couple,* a flat-out comedy about poker and divorce.

The truly serious plays in the American theater now—many of which have minor runs on Broadway, if they make it to Broadway at all—may well deal with social issues, but the issues bubble to the surface instead of being plastered on top like posters. The best plays, as always, arise not from the agenda of journalism or politics, but from the private agenda of the writer's sensibility. If that writer's feelings are connected to the ideas and social currents of the world around him, his plays may ultimately tell us more about a society—and the anxiety-making public issues that riddle that society—than those plays that wear cancer or nuclear radiation on their sleeves. And, as often as not, these serious plays are funny. Rising out of the old, unpretentious Jewish family jokes in Wendy Wasserstein's *Isn't It Romantic* is an agonized dissection of the difficult choices made by two generations of American women (both Jewish and WASP); in Jules Feiffer's *Grown Ups,* the same jokes explode into a scathing assault on the American success ethic.

Tom Stoppard makes the case for such writers at the beginning of Act 2 of *The Real Thing,* when his playwright-hero, Henry, argues against polemical plays. Instead of writing plays that specifically address such matters as "politics" and "justice," Henry argues that writers should write personal plays that "perhaps alter people's perceptions so that they behave a little differently at that axis of behavior where we locate politics or justice." (It's unfortunate that Mr. Stoppard then undercuts his own argument by launching a stacked polemical attack against a polemical playwright who figures as a minor character in *The Real Thing*.) Mr. Stoppard's point is also made by Sam Shepard in his few published essays. Noting that he was affected strongly by the social currents of the Vietnam years, Mr. Shepard then adds that none of the specific detritus of that era now remains a part of his creative life except "the idea of consciousness." And it's that consciousness that is the wellspring of his work: "Ideas emerge from plays," he explains, "not the other way around."

It has never been any different, even in the plays of Brecht or Shaw. To believe otherwise is to think that Ibsen wrote *Ghosts* because he wanted to address the question of syphilis, or that Williams wrote *The Glass Menagerie* because he wanted to speak about poverty during the 1930s, or that Beckett's *Endgame* was motivated by rising anxiety about the H-bomb in Europe during the late 1950s. The best writers write what they are burning to write, not what they're told to write or what they think they should write. It's television writers, whether writing for the networks or the theater, who begin with the concrete "idea" (or, in Hollywood lingo, "concept")—whether that idea be "nuclear holocaust" or *Love Boat*—and then work from the outside in.

Serious American playwrights who let their ideas emerge from their plays are rarely celebrated at the Tony Awards or in the long-run record books. Marsha Norman's *'night, Mother,* which closes next weekend after a decent but unspectacular Broadway life, might have been a major hit if the author had turned it into a TV-style problem play. If only the heroine, Jessie, were a paraplegic or had been raped or wanted to be a martyr to a political cause, audiences would have immediately understood her intention to commit suicide.

In this sense, Jessie's mother represents the television audience's sensibility: She thinks she can talk Jessie out of suicide by solving all of the daughter's personal "problems" and by getting rid of the television and newspapers that trumpet the outside world's crises. But Ms. Norman—through Jessie—gives neither the audience nor the mother the easy way out. The daughter tells Mama: "It doesn't much matter what else happens in the world or in this house, even"—and persists in her intention to kill herself. At that point, theatergoers are either lost—or are forced to look at larger questions about both existence and American life that are not directly articulated by the playwright. Those who do stick with Jessie and Ms. Norman find themselves at the center of a conundrum no different from that found in the similarly compact stories of Bobbie Ann Mason or Raymond Carver.

Like Ms. Norman, David Mamet, Charles Fuller (*A Soldier's Play*), and Christopher Durang (among others) march to their own beat rather than address "problems" per se. Mr. Durang's *Sister Mary Ignatius* is written as a personal vendetta against an authoritarian nun teaching at a Catholic school and mentions such "issues" as cancer, rape, and homosexuality along its way. But these issues are just pebbles carried by the wave of the author's consciousness—which is most of all grappling with a fundamental question that underlies all those issues, the existence (or nonexistence) of God. That question is not resolved at the final curtain.

Needless to say, Mr. Durang, Mr. Feiffer, and Mr. Mamet have never had a hit on Broadway (though Mr. Mamet's *American Buffalo* made it in revival, when it was warped into a star vehicle for Al Pacino). If these writers weren't American, it would help: Non-American writers of their caliber, such as Mr. Stoppard, David Hare, or Athol Fugard, have fared somewhat better in the commercial theater, even if for the wrong reasons. What's more outrageous, however, is that Sam Shepard has never even been produced on Broadway at all.

One can see why: He's frightening. There are absolutely no easily legible, television-drama signposts for an audience at a play like *True West*. Two brothers, one an aspiring Hollywood screenwriter and the other a petty criminal, fight each other to a standoff for two raucous acts. Though no explicit social issue is grafted onto their battle—as the Depression is grafted onto the relationship of the two brothers in *Brighton Beach Memoirs*—the play concerns almost everything that plagues Americans: money, power, a search for identity in a world made of plastic, a search for self in the midst of spiritual chaos.

Mr. Shepard, as much as any contemporary American playwright, gives our theater its claim to seriousness and its connection to other art. *True West*—in which events don't necessarily symbolize anything and characters don't necessarily have logical motives or represent clear-cut points of view—is as modernist a work as anyone could wish. Mr. Shepard's writing is fragmented and at times beyond exegesis: Who can precisely explain why the brothers' mother arrives late in the play, insistent in her conviction that Picasso (though dead) is visiting Los Angeles? The author is so resistant to the notion of attaching easily explicable editorial labels on his people that he pointedly notes in his stage directions that "the costumes should be exactly representative of who the characters are and not added onto for the sake of making a point to the audience." (This language is echoed by Ms. Norman, whose published text of *'night, Mother* instructs, "Under no circumstances should the set and its dressing make a judgment about the intelligence or taste of Jessie and Mama.")

True West is also a decidedly American work—the brothers could almost be Tom and Huck, torn between freedom (the true West) and civilization as they straddle an eroding frontier. Even Mr. Shepard's language and structure fulfill William Dean Howells's admiring appraisal of Twain. "He was not enslaved to the consecutiveness in writing which the rest of us try to keep chained to," wrote Howells of his friend. "That is, he wrote as he thought, and as all men think, without sequence, without an eye to what went before or should come after."

It's quite possible that Mr. Shepard will never be produced on Broadway—and one had begun to fear that he might never come to the attention of audiences who had given up on Broadway and, with it, given up on the American theater. But the cause isn't lost yet. Mr. Shepard, again like Twain, has another career in addition to writing—as a performer. And, thanks to his emergence as a movie star, a wider audience is being lured to his plays. *The Right Stuff,* by indirection, may be the best thing to happen to the American theater in a while: It has no doubt lengthened the runs of *True West* and *Fool for Love* Off Broadway, just as it has made Mr. Shepard's published work fly off the shelves of bookstores.

The irony of this phenomenon, given Mr. Shepard's own withering attitude toward American stardom in his plays, is wicked. So be it. If it's Mr. Shepard's celebrity as much as his talent that starts to introduce a larger audience to the serious American theater—and leads that audience to discover Mr. Shepard's many gifted peers—let's not complain; such is often the bizarre way of our culture. Maybe there's already some cause for hope. Even as television dramas crowd serious plays out of the front lines of our theater, it's worth noting that *True West,* a play too serious for Broadway, reached its widest audience yet this month—on television.

≡ *With the major exception of Mamet, none of the serious playwrights cited in this essay (including the Pulitzer winners Shepard, Norman, and Fuller) would find a home on Broadway, and some drifted away from the theater altogether.*

CINDERS
PUBLIC THEATER, FEBRUARY 21, 1984

In *Cinders,* the new play at the Public Theater, words and phrases have funny definitions. "I understand" means "I don't understand." "We have nothing to hide" means "We have everything to hide." The adverb "gently" is used to modify the verb "to terrify," and "solitary confinement" is identified as a form of "humanitarianism." "Democracy" describes a plebiscite in which there are no secret ballots and no dissenting votes.

The setting of *Cinders*, I needn't tell you, is a totalitarian state—specifically, present-day Poland. Written by Janusz Glowacki, a dissident Polish writer now in exile in the West, this play urgently reminds us that Orwellian Newspeak is by no means a dead issue in 1984. And like so many of his Eastern European peers—including Vaclav Havel, whose *Private View* recently played the Public—Mr. Glowacki has a keen ability to mine the dark absurdist humor in the language of terror. *Cinders* may be diffuse and imperfect, but one can only admire the author's will to make elegant Kafkaesque comedy out of his nation's ongoing nightmare of repression.

Mr. Glowacki's title refers to *Cinderella*. Set in a girls' reform school near Warsaw, *Cinders* is about what happens when a documentary movie director (Christopher Walken) arrives to film the inmates as they perform a dramatization of the fairy tale. The authorities welcome the director's arrival: His film will show the world how enlightened the state can be in its institutions of social welfare. The director is excited by the project, too. By filling out the *Cinderella* performance with interviews detailing the girls' sad childhoods, he'll create a poignant tale of how innocent children have been rescued from "the web of society." It's just the documentary to win him acclaim at film festivals in the West.

Out of this premise, Mr. Glowacki creates a parable that reaches well beyond the reform school's walls. If topsy-turvy language is the comic currency of *Cinders*, the play's drama derives from the warping of souls as much as words. The documentary's director is a liberal, and so is the school's principal (George Guidall). Yet when the girl playing Cinderella (Lucinda Jenney) defies the official plan by refusing to participate in the phony, state-manipulated interviews, both men end up as collaborators in her subsequent punishment. In Mr. Glowacki's view, the men capitulate not because they're evil or conscienceless, but because they're self-absorbed and weak. Those flaws are all it takes for well-meaning citizens to become tools of a government's well-oiled machinery of propaganda and oppression.

As crisply translated by Christina Paul, the play is flecked throughout with some extremely clever and provocative writing—starting with the use of *Cinderella*. In a program note, the author explains that there are hundreds of known versions of the *Cinderella* story stretching back through history; though each of them is about "an ill-treated heroine" who is eventually recognized for her "truth and goodness," the surrounding details vary according to the society that is telling the tale. In *Cinders*, we find several indigenous variations of *Cinderella*—all casting harsh ironic light on contemporary Poland.

The *Cinderella* performed for the documentary, for instance, becomes an affectless, joyless acting out of the girls' imprisonment; it's reminiscent of the play-within-the-play of *Marat/Sade*. (The biting music, fittingly enough, is by the *Marat/Sade* composer, Richard Peaslee.) In a bittersweet dormitory bedtime scene, the girls delight in a contemporary *Cinderella* that expresses their fantasies of liberation: The prince is a Western millionaire with a silver Mercedes. Meanwhile, *Cinders* itself is a *Cinderella* tale—albeit one whose final revelation of its heroine's "truth and goodness" can only come in the form of a harrowing act of political martyrdom.

Mr. Glowacki is less successful at differentiating his characters or creating plot. It's hard to tell some of the schoolgirls apart or to believe the more convenient story twists of Act 2. The play's structure can be maddeningly loose, if not confusing, and some of the big scenes seem arbitrarily inserted. Usually, though, the set pieces are bracing in themselves. In the best, the Machiavellian deputy principal (Robin Gammell) congratulates the girls on writing a "genuinely moving" song about their despair—and then proceeds to suggest "improvements" that gradually transform an autobiographical dirge into a cheery nationalistic anthem. As subtly written and performed, this scene becomes a chilling paradigm of the process by which a state can muzzle all its dissenting artists.

The play's director, John Madden, and his designer, Andrew Jackness, use the Public's LuEsther Hall in an arena configuration: We look down onto the institution's grim expanse of linoleum-tiled floor. Aided by Paul Gallo's lighting, Mr. Madden fluidly choreographs the often brief and overlapping scenes, sweeping us into the school's desultory daily rhythms. Still, there could be a bit more menace in the atmosphere—and a bit less of an American tone to the acting.

Mr. Walken, though careless with diction, is amusing as the fatuous, self-important director—especially when expressing his disappointment that one particular thirteen-year-old murderer will not be available for use in his film's opening-credits sequence. Mr. Guidall's tormented but ineffectual do-gooder of a principal and Mr. Gammell's smiling thug of a deputy are both exemplary: In posture as well as manner they capture the obsequious demeanor of low-rung apparatchiks. As Cinderella, Ms. Jenney is convincing as both a tough street urchin and an embryonic princess. In a world in which all language is a lie, she asserts her nobility as she must—with silence so defiant that her wordlessness becomes a synonym for freedom.

The title of Eduardo Machado's new play, *Broken Eggs*, refers to that famous political proverb often attributed to Lenin: "You cannot make an omelet without breaking eggs." The play's characters are the broken eggs—a family of upper-middle-class Cubans who lost everything when Fidel Castro's revolution forced them to flee their homeland in the early 1960s. But in *Broken Eggs*, which is set in Los Angeles in 1979, the family isn't doing all that badly anymore. Mr. Machado's characters have more jewelry, Lincoln Continentals, swimming pools, and Valium than they know what to do with.

Broken Eggs, now at the Ensemble Studio Theatre, unfolds on a wedding day. The setting is the Woodland Hills Country Club, where Lizette Marquez (Ann Talman) is about to marry a nice Jewish boy in a ceremony costing $8,000. But while Lizette and her extended, three-generation family enjoy the fruits of material success in their adopted country, they're still haunted by memories of home. They worry that they are 3,000 miles away from their "real lives." They idly fantasize that Cuba might still be "liberated," and they cling to the memory of the old society that the revolution displaced. They "feel like choking," and yet they "don't know why."

Mr. Machado, himself a Cuban émigré in America, has a rich subject in *Broken Eggs*. What's more, he handles it—or tries to—in an offbeat way. Its grave underpinnings notwithstanding, his play is often written as a domestic comedy—as a *Father of the Bride* with weltschmerz. Even as his characters try to come to terms with exile and their Latin past, they engage in woolly husband-wife and parent-child squabbles or throw themselves into tizzies over a shortage of wedding cake. The author's method recalls that of David Henry Hwang's *Family Devotions*—in which a wealthy family of assimilated Chinese Americans, also living in contemporary Los Angeles, goes to absurd (and unsuccessful) lengths to sever its spiritual ties to pre-Communist China.

Mr. Machado isn't as yet as fully developed a writer as Mr. Hwang. In *Broken Eggs* he doesn't entirely integrate his themes into the comedy. When he takes to making his larger points—especially in Act 2—the jokes must stop so that each family member can state the themes point-blank, over and over again. The result is a scrambled evening, in which neither the play's farcical design nor sorrowful substance is fulfilled. Still, there are some tart lines and bright observations along the way—

most notably when Mr. Machado is dealing with the breakdown of the family's traditional verities and hierarchies under the pressure of such newfangled notions as divorce and open homosexuality.

James Hammerstein has directed *Broken Eggs* in an appropriately dizzy style and with an uneven cast. The superior performances come from Leonardo Cimino as the family's shrewd grandfather, Theresa Saldana as the secretly pregnant and cocaine-snorting sister of the bride, and, best of all, from Julie Garfield as a cynical aunt who wallows in American sexual freedom even as it leaves her alienated. Both Keith Gonzales's set and Deborah Shaw's costumes have their own witty comments to make about the family's nouveau-riche blandishments.

Even more important than the specifics of the production, however, is the Ensemble Studio's continuing support of Mr. Machado. Last winter, this company produced *The Modern Ladies of Guanabacoa*—in which the playwright examined the roots of the family of *Broken Eggs,* back in pre-Batista, 1928 Cuba. It, too, was a flawed effort, but, like the new play, it demonstrated that its young author has a strong comic voice and a passion to examine the meaning of a people's history. There is little question that Mr. Machado is going to create a first-rate play one day; in the meantime, the Ensemble Studio is performing a valuable service by nurturing him, step by step, toward that goal.

≡*A full decade later* Broken Eggs *and other thematically related Machado plays I'd covered over the course of the decade were presented by the Mark Taper Forum in Los Angeles in the marathon format with which it had also presented* Angels in America *and* The Kentucky Cycle.

GLENGARRY GLEN ROSS
JOHN GOLDEN THEATRE, MARCH 26, 1984

The only mellifluous words in David Mamet's new play are those of its title—*Glengarry Glen Ross*. In this scalding comedy about small-time, cutthroat real-estate salesmen, most of the language is abrasive—even by the standards of the author's *American Buffalo*. If the characters aren't barking out the harshest four-letter expletives, then they're speaking in the clammy jargon of a trade in which "leads," "closings," and "the board" (a sales chart) are the holiest of imperatives. There's only one speech in which we hear about such intimacies as sex and loneliness—and that speech, to our shock, proves to be a prefabricated sales pitch.

Yet the strange—and wonderful—thing about the play at the Golden is Mr. Mamet's ability to turn almost every word inside out. The playwright makes all-American music—hot jazz and wounding blues—out of his salesmen's scatological native lingo. In the jagged riffs of coarse, monosyllabic words, we hear and feel both the exhilaration and sweaty desperation of the huckster's calling. At the same time, Mr. Mamet makes his work's musical title into an ugly symbol of all that is hollow and vicious in the way of life his characters gallantly endure. The salesmen—middle-class blood-brothers of the penny-ante Chicago hustlers of *American Buffalo*—are trying to unload worthless tracts of Florida land to gullible victims. It's the cruelest cut of all that that real estate is packaged into developments with names like "Glengarry Highlands" and "Glen Ross Farms."

Mr. Mamet's talent for burying layers of meaning into simple, precisely distilled, idiomatic language—a talent that can only be compared to Harold Pinter's—is not the sum of *Glengarry Glen Ross*. This may well be the most accomplished play its author has yet given us. As Mr. Mamet's command of dialogue has now reached its most dazzling pitch, so has his mastery of theatrical form. Beneath the raucous, seemingly inane surface of *Glengarry,* one finds not only feelings but a detective story with a surprise ending. And there's another clandestine story, too, bubbling just underneath the main plot: Only as the curtain falls do we realize that one of the salesmen, brilliantly played by Robert Prosky, has traveled through an anguished personal history almost as complex as Willy Loman's.

So assured and uncompromising is Mr. Mamet's style that one must enter his play's hermetically sealed world completely—or risk getting lost. Taken at face value, the actual events, like the vocabulary, are minimal; the ferocious humor and drama are often to be found in the pauses or along the shadowy periphery of the center-stage action. But should this work fail to win the large public it deserves—a fate that has befallen other Mamet plays in their first Broadway outings—that won't be entirely because of its idiosyncratic form. *Glengarry,* which was initially produced at London's National Theatre last fall, is being seen here in a second production, from Chicago's Goodman Theater. Mr. Prosky's contribution aside, this solid but uninspired staging isn't always up to the crackling tension of the script.

In the half-hour-long first act, that tension is particularly Pinteresque. We watch three successive two-character confrontations that introduce the salesmen as they conduct business in the Chinese restaurant that serves as their hangout and unofficial office. The dialogue's unfinished sentences often sound like code; one whole scene turns on the colloquial distinction the characters draw between the phrases "speaking about" and "talking about."

But these duologues in fact dramatize primal duels for domination, power, and survival, and, as we penetrate the argot, we learn the Darwinian rules of the salesmen's game. Those who sell the most "units" receive a Cadillac as a bonus; those who hit "bad streaks" are denied access to management's list of "premiere leads" (appointments with likely customers). Worse, this entrepreneurial system is as corrupt as it is heartless. The losing salesmen can still get leads by offering kickbacks to the mercurial young manager (J. T. Walsh) who administers the business for its unseen owners.

When the characters leave the dark restaurant for the brighter setting of the firm's office in Act 2, Mr. Mamet's tone lightens somewhat as well. The office has been ransacked by burglars, and a detective (Jack Wallace) arrives to investigate. Even as the salesmen undergo questioning, they frantically settle fratricidal rivalries and attempt to bamboozle a pathetic, tearful customer (Lane Smith) who has arrived to demand a refund. As written (though not always as staged), Act 2 is farce in Chicago's *Front Page* tradition—albeit of a blacker contemporary sort. While we laugh at the comic cops-and-robbers hijinks, we also witness the unraveling of several lives.

The play's director is Gregory Mosher, Mr. Mamet's longtime Chicago collaborator. Mr. Mosher's work is often capable, but sometimes he italicizes Mr. Mamet's linguistic stylization: Whenever the actors self-consciously indicate the exact location of the text's hidden jokes and meanings, they cease being salesmen engaged in do-or-die warfare. This is not to say that the actors are inept—they're good. But, as we've seen with other Mamet works, it takes a special cast, not merely an adequate one, to deliver the full force of a play in which even the word *and* can set off a theatrical detonation.

The actors do succeed, as they must, at earning our sympathy. Mr. Mamet admires the courage of these salesmen, who are just as victimized as their clients; the only villain is Mr. Walsh's manager—a cool deskman who has never had to live by his wits on the front lines of selling. Among the others, there's particular heroism in Mike Nussbaum, whose frightened eyes convey a lifetime of blasted dreams, and in Joe Mantegna, as the company's youngest, most dapper go-getter. When Mr. Mantegna suffers a critical reversal, he bravely rises from defeat to retighten his tie, consult his appointments book, and march back to the Chinese restaurant in search of new prey.

Mr. Prosky, beefy and white-haired, is a discarded old-timer: In the opening scene, he is reduced to begging for leads from his impassive boss. Somewhat later, however, he scores a "great sale" and expands in countenance to rekindle his old confidence: Mr. Prosky becomes a regal, cigar-waving pontificator, recounting the crude ritual of a contract closing as if it were a grand religious rite.

Still, this rehabilitation is short-lived, and soon Mr. Prosky is trying to bribe his way back into his employer's favor. As we watch the bills spill from his pockets on to a desk, we at last see greenery that both befits and mocks the verdant words of the play's title. But there's no color in the salesman's pasty, dumbstruck face—just the abject terror of a life in which all words are finally nothing because it's only money that really talks.

DEATH OF A SALESMAN
BROADHURST THEATRE, MARCH 30, 1984

As Willy Loman in Arthur Miller's *Death of a Salesman*, Dustin Hoffman doesn't trudge heavily to the grave—he sprints. His fist is raised and his face is cocked defiantly upwards, so that his rimless spectacles glint in the Brooklyn moonlight. But how does one square that feisty image with what will come after his final exit—and with what has come before? Earlier, Mr. Hoffman's Willy has collapsed to the floor of a Broadway steakhouse, mewling and shrieking like an abandoned baby. That moment had led to the spectacle of the actor sitting in the straight-back chair of his kitchen, crying out in rage to his elder son, Biff. "I'm not a dime a dozen!" Mr. Hoffman rants, looking and sounding so small that we fear the price quoted by Biff may, if anything, be too high.

To reconcile these sides of Willy—the brave fighter and the whipped child—you really have no choice but to see what Mr. Hoffman is up to at the Broadhurst. In undertaking one of our theater's classic roles, this daring actor has pursued his own brilliant conception of the character. Mr. Hoffman is not playing a larger-than-life protagonist but the small man described in the script—the "little boat looking for a harbor," the eternally adolescent American male who goes to the grave without ever learning who he is. And by staking no claim to the stature of a tragic hero, Mr. Hoffman's Willy becomes a harrowing American everyman. His bouncy final exit is the death of a salesman, all right. Willy rides to suicide, as he rode through life, on the foolish, empty pride of "a smile and a shoeshine."

Even when Mr. Hoffman's follow-through falls short of his characterization—it takes a good while to accept him as sixty-three years old—

we're riveted by the wasted vitality of his small Willy, a man full of fight for all the wrong battles. What's more, the star has not turned *Death of a Salesman* into a vehicle. Under the balanced direction of Michael Rudman, this revival is an exceptional ensemble effort, strongly cast throughout. John Malkovich, who plays the lost Biff, gives a performance of such spellbinding effect that he becomes the evening's anchor. When Biff finally forgives Willy and nestles his head lovingly on his father's chest, the whole audience leans forward to be folded into the embrace: We know we're watching the salesman arrive, however temporarily, at the only safe harbor he'll ever know.

But as much as we marvel at the acting in this *Death of a Salesman*, we also marvel at the play. Mr. Miller's masterwork has been picked to death by critics over the last thirty-five years, and its reputation has been clouded by the author's subsequent career. We know its flaws by heart— the big secret withheld from the audience until Act 2, and the symbolic old brother Ben (Louis Zorich), forever championing the American Dream in literary prose. Yet how small and academic these quibbles look when set against the fact of the thunderous thing itself.

In *Death of Salesman,* Mr. Miller wrote with a fierce, liberating urgency. Even as his play marches steadily onward to its preordained conclusion, it roams about through time and space, connecting present miseries with past traumas and drawing blood almost everywhere it goes. Though the author's condemnation of the American success ethic is stated baldly, it is also woven, at times humorously, into the action. When Willy proudly speaks of owning a refrigerator that's promoted with the "biggest ads," we see that the pathological credo of being "well liked" requires that he consume products that have the aura of popularity, too.

Still, Mr. Rudman and his cast don't make the mistake of presenting the play as a monument of social thought: The author's themes can take care of themselves. Like most of Mr. Miller's work, *Death of a Salesman* is most of all about fathers and sons. There are many father-son relationships in the play—not just those of the Loman household, but those enmeshing Willy's neighbors and employer. The drama's tidal pull comes from the sons' tortured attempts to reconcile themselves to their fathers' dreams. It's not Willy's pointless death that moves us; it's Biff's decision to go on living. Biff, the princely high-school football hero turned drifter, must find the courage both to love his father and leave him forever behind.

Mr. Hoffman's Willy takes flight late in Act 1, when he first alludes to his relationship with his own father. Recalling how his father left when he was still a child, Willy says, "I never had a chance to talk to him, and I still feel—kind of temporary about myself." As Mr. Hoffman's voice breaks on the word "temporary," his spirit cracks into aged defeat. From then on, it's a merciless drop to the bottom of his "strange thoughts"— the hallucinatory memory sequences that send him careening in and out of a lifetime of anxiety. Mr. Rudman stages these apparitional flashbacks with bruising force; we see why Biff says that Willy is spewing out "vomit from his mind." As Mr. Hoffman stumbles through the shadowy recollections of his past, trying both to deny and transmute the awful truth of an impoverished existence, he lurches and bobs like a strand of broken straw tossed by a mean wind.

As we expect from this star, he has affected a new physical and vocal presence for Willy: a baldish, silver-maned head; a shuffling walk; a brash, Brooklyn-tinged voice that well serves the character's comic penchant for contradicting himself in nearly every sentence. But what's most poignant about the getup may be the costume (designed by Ruth Morley). Mr. Hoffman's Willy is a total break with the mountainous Lee J. Cobb image. He's a trim, immaculately outfitted go-getter in a three-piece suit—replete with bright matching tie and handkerchief. Is there anything sadder than a nobody dressed for success, or an old man masquerading as his younger self? The star seems to wilt within the self-parodistic costume throughout the evening. "You can't eat the orange and throw away the peel!" Willy pleads to the callow young boss (Jon Polito) who fires him—and, looking at the wizened and spent Mr. Hoffman, we realize that he is indeed the peel, tossed into the gutter.

Mr. Malkovich, hulking and unsmiling, is an inversion of Mr. Hoffman's father; he's what Willy might be if he'd ever stopped lying to himself. Anyone who saw this remarkable young actor as the rambunctious rascal of *True West* may find his transformation here as astonishing as the star's. His Biff is soft and tentative, with sullen eyes and a slow, distant voice that seems entombed with his aborted teenage promise; his big hands flop around diffidently as he tries to convey his anguish to his roguish brother Happy (Stephen Lang). Once Biff accepts who he is— and who his father is—the cathartic recognition seems to break through Mr. Malkovich (and the theater) like a raging fever. "Help him!" he yells as his father collapses at the restaurant—only to melt instantly into a blurry, tearful plea of "Help me! Help me!"

In the problematic role of the mother, Kate Reid is miraculously convincing: Whether she's professing her love for Willy or damning Happy as a "philandering bum," she somehow melds affection with pure steel. Mr. Lang captures the vulgarity and desperate narcissism of the younger brother, and David Chandler takes the goo out of the model boy next door. As Mr. Chandler's father—and Willy's only friend—David Huddleston radiates a quiet benevolence as expansive as his considerable girth. One must also applaud Thomas Skelton, whose lighting imaginatively meets every shift in time and mood, and the set designer Ben Edwards, who surrounds the shabby Loman house with malevolent apartment towers poised to swallow Willy up.

But it's Mr. Hoffman and Mr. Malkovich who demand that our attention be paid anew to *Death of a Salesman*. When their performances meet in a great, binding passion, we see the transcendent sum of two of the American theater's most lowly, yet enduring, parts.

≡ *This controversial new take on a Broadway classic was not popular within the industry; nor was the star's refusal to play a full eight-performance-a-week schedule. Neither Hoffman nor Malkovich received Tony nominations. The production survives on video, in its successful TV adaptation.*

THROUGH THE LEAVES
Public Theater, April 6, 1984

The radio is almost always on in *Through the Leaves*, the latest Franz Xaver Kroetz play to appear in New York. The dial is tuned to an easy-listening station that broadcasts lulling songs like "Moon River" and "Chances Are." Yet there are few other soothing sounds in this acidic account of a woman butcher and her abusive lover. When the heroine's yelping dog isn't drowning out the radio, we're likely to be assaulted by the cacophonous grunts of coarse sex—or the grinding of a butcher's saw cutting through a thick bone.

Through the Leaves is not pleasant, but it sticks like a splinter in the mind. Mr. Kroetz is a young West German dramatist who chronicles the alienated working class, and he practices kitchen-sink realism of the grimmest sort. (Let Mr. Kroetz's characters approach a kitchen sink, and they're likely to stick their hands into the disposal.) The playwright's abrasive style is so distinctive that he's fast becoming as cultishly popular in New York as his fellow Bavarian (and one-time collaborator), the late filmmaker Rainer Werner Fassbinder. *Through the Leaves*, which was written in 1976, is one of three Kroetz works to be staged Off Broadway this season alone.

The play that launched the boom in earnest was *Request Concert,* a monodrama about a woman's suicide that was staged by JoAnne Akalaitis at the Interart Theater two years ago. *Through the Leaves* has also been forcefully directed by Ms. Akalaitis at the Interart, and it resembles the other work in length (seventy-five minutes) and focus. The protagonist, Annette (Ruth Maleczech), not only listens to the radio as constantly as the office worker of *Request Concert* but she also suffers from the same abject (if less than terminal) loneliness.

In Mr. Kroetz's view, the butcher's plight begins with her job. Annette's butcher shop is a specialty operation that sells only the inferior "utility" cuts of meat—the entrails used primarily as animal feed. Annette herself might as well be a discarded animal organ. Though she delights in her status as an "independent" business woman, we see that she is chained to dehumanizing drudgery by day and to her adding machine at night.

Victor (Frederick Neumann), the man who suddenly invades Annette's constricted existence, is also a prisoner of economic circumstance: He's a brutish, beery laborer who regards "freedom" as the right to disappear on weeklong drunken binges. A slave to his own job, he likes to be "the boss about everything" with women during off hours. When he has sex with Annette, he mocks her frumpy middle-aged appearance and tells her not to waste his time by disrobing completely. "Just get rid of the underpants," he commands.

Annette obeys the oppressive Victor—not because she's a fool, but because she's desperate for any human contact. Throughout the play, we hear the butcher's diary entries, and while they often end with phrases like "everything is fine," it's clear that Annette knows better. Unlike her lover, she's introspective: She dreams of finer things like "imagination" and at one point composes a homely poem. What Annette doesn't know is the cause of her distress, or its cure. She believes that "being diplomatic" will arrest Victor's endless badgering, and she rationalizes her subjugation with tortured logic: "Maybe he'll kick me so far down that he'll pick me up again."

The action unfolds in stark fragments that are set both in the gleaming butcher shop and its squalid backroom parlor (designed with grotesque panache by Douglas Stein). The lighting scheme, by Frances Aronson, makes frightening use of a harsh white glare: After a while, the two characters begin to resemble the calf's head that's displayed behind plate glass in the butcher shop's refrigerated display case. But there's some gallows humor to lighten the chill. When Victor and Annette decide to partake of the leisure-time fun that is their reward for hard work, they dress up in incongruous costumes from *My Fair Lady* to go to a "Night in the Tropics" ball.

The actors—who, like the director, belong to the Mabou Mines troupe—are capable. At times, though, Ms. Maleczech affects a mannered, distracting laugh that recalls Thelma Ritter's. A greater distraction is the director's decision to take Roger Downey's pungent English translation, which retained the play's German setting, and relocate it in Queens. Ms. Akalaitis similarly transposed *Request Concert,* but the switch didn't seem too far-fetched in a piece that contained no dialogue. In *Through the Leaves,* the social texture remains Germanic (as typified by the specialty butcher shop)—and both lovers seem too unworldly to be inhabitants, however downtrodden, of an America in which everyone is exposed to *The Phil Donahue Show.*

As a result, the production unfolds in an abstract cultural limbo—and sometimes gives the unjust impression that the author is condescending to his characters. It says a lot about Mr. Kroetz that even this impediment can't mute the jarring strains of his genuinely disturbing theatrical voice.

SUNDAY IN THE PARK WITH GEORGE
BOOTH THEATRE, MAY 3, 1984

In his paintings of a century ago, Georges Seurat demanded that the world look at art in a shocking new way. In *Sunday in the Park with George,* their new show about Seurat, the songwriter Stephen Sondheim and the playwright-director James Lapine demand that an audience radically change its whole way of looking at the Broadway musical. Seurat, the authors remind us, never sold a painting; it's anyone's guess whether the public will be shocked or delighted by *Sunday in the Park.* What I do know is that Mr. Sondheim and Mr. Lapine have created an audacious, haunting, and, in its own intensely personal way, touching work. Even when it fails—as it does on occasion—*Sunday in the Park* is setting the stage for even more sustained theatrical innovations yet to come.

If anything, the show snugly fitted into the Booth owes more to the Off Broadway avant-garde than it does to past groundbreaking musicals, Mr. Sondheim's included. *Sunday* is not a bridge to opera, like *Sweeney Todd;* nor is it in the tradition of the dance musicals of Jerome Robbins and Michael Bennett. There is, in fact, no dancing in *Sunday,* and while there's a book, there's little story. In creating a work about a pioneer of modernist art, Mr. Lapine and Mr. Sondheim have made a contemplative modernist musical that, true to form, is as much about itself and its creators as it is about the universe beyond.

The show's inspiration is Seurat's most famous canvas, *A Sunday Afternoon on the Island of La Grande Jatte.* That huge painting shows a crowd of bourgeois nineteenth-century Parisians relaxing in a park on their day off. But *La Grande Jatte* was also a manifesto by an artist in revolt against Impressionism. Atomizing color into thousands of dots, Seurat applied scientific visual principles to art. Seen from a distance, his pointillist compositions reveal people and landscapes in natural harmony. Examined up close, the paintings become abstractions revealing the austerity and rigor of the artist's technique.

Seurat, here embodied commandingly by Mandy Patinkin, could well be a stand-in for Mr. Sondheim, who brings the same fierce, methodical intellectual precision to musical and verbal composition that the artist brought to his pictorial realm. In one number in *Sunday,* Seurat's work is dismissed by contemporaries as having "no passion, no life"—a critique frequently leveled at Mr. Sondheim. But unlike the last Sondheim show, *Merrily We Roll Along,* this one is usually not a whiny complaint about how hard it is to be a misunderstood, underappreciated genius. Instead of a showbiz figure's self-martyrdom, we get an artist's self-revelation.

In Act 1, this is achieved by a demonstration of how Seurat might have created *La Grande Jatte.* In a fantastic set by Tony Straiges—an animated toy box complete with pop-ups—Mr. Patinkin's George gradually assembles bits and pieces of the painting, amending and banishing lifesize portions of it before our eyes. In the process, Mr. Lapine and the congenitally puzzle-minded Mr. Sondheim provide their own ironic speculations about who the people in Seurat's picture might be. The most prominent among them is identified as the painter's mistress (named Dot, no less, and radiantly performed by Bernadette Peters). The others include such diverse types as boorish American tourists, a surly boatman, and a class-conscious German servant.

Yet most of these people are little more than fleeting cameos. As is often the case in Sondheim musicals, we don't care about the characters—and here, more than ever, it's clear we're not meant to care. To Seurat, these people are just models for a meditative composition that's not intended to tell any story: In his painting, the figures are silent and expressionless, and even Dot is but fodder for dots. Mr. Lapine and Mr. Sondheim tease us with their characters' various private lives—which are rife with betrayals—only to sever those stories abruptly the moment Seurat's painting has found its final shape. It's the authors' way of saying that they, too, regard their "characters" only as forms to be manipulated into a theatrical composition whose content is more visual and musical than dramatic.

As a result, when Seurat finishes *La Grande Jatte* at the end of Act 1, we're moved not because a plot has been resolved but because a harmonic work of art has been born. As achieved on stage—replete with pointillist lighting by Richard Nelson and costumes by Patricia Zipprodt and Ann Hould-Ward—the "fixing" of the picture is an electrifying coup de théâtre. Tellingly enough, the effect is accompanied by the first Sondheim song of the evening that allows the cast to sing in glorious harmony. The song's lyric, meanwhile, reminds us that the magical order of both the painting and this musical has transfigured—and transcended—the often ugly doings in "a small suburban park" on an "ordinary Sunday."

Act 2, though muddled, is equally daring: The show jumps a full century to focus on a present-day American artist also named George (and again played by Mr. Patinkin). This protagonist is possibly a double for Mr. Sondheim at his most self-doubting. George makes large, multimedia conceptual sculptures that, like Broadway musicals, require collaborators, large budgets, and compromises; his values are distorted by a trendy art world that, like show business, puts a premium on hype, fashion, and the tyranny of the marketplace.

The fanciful time-travel conceits that link this George to Seurat are charming. Rather less successful is the authors' reversion to a compressed, conventional story about how the modern George overcomes his crisis of confidence to regenerate himself as a man and artist. When George finally learns how to "connect" with other people and rekindles his esthetic vision, his breakthrough is ordained by two pretty songs, "Children and Art" and "Move On," which seem as inorganic as the equivalent inspirational number ("Being Alive") that redeems the born-again protagonist in Mr. Sondheim's *Company*.

The show's most moving song is "Finishing the Hat"—which, like many of Mr. Sondheim's best, is about being disconnected. Explaining his emotional aloofness to Dot, Seurat sings how he watches "the rest of the world from a window" while he's obsessively making art. And if the maintenance of that solitary emotional distance means that Seurat's art (and, by implication, Mr. Sondheim's) is "cold," even arrogant, so be it. *Sunday* argues that the esthetic passion in the cerebrally ordered classicism of modern artists is easily as potent as the sentimental passion of romantic paintings or conventional musicals.

In keeping with his setting, Mr. Sondheim has written a lovely, wildly inventive score that sometimes remakes the modern French composers whose revolution in music paralleled the Postimpressionists' in art. (A synthesizer is added for the modern second act.) The accompanying lyrics can be brilliantly funny. Mr. Sondheim exploits the homonyms "kneads" and "needs" to draw a razor-sharp boundary between sex and love; a song in which Seurat's painted figures break their immortal poses to complain about "sweating in a picture that was painted by a genius" is a tour de force. But there's often wisdom beneath the cleverness. When Seurat's aged mother laments a modern building that her son admires, the Eiffel Tower, Mr. Patinkin sings that "all things are beautiful" because "what the eye arranges is what is beautiful."

What Mr. Lapine, his designers, and the special-effects wizard Bran Ferren have arranged is simply gorgeous, and the fine supporting players add vibrant colors to their palette. Mr. Patinkin is a crucible of intellectual fire—"he burns you with his eyes," says Dot, with reason—and the wonderful Ms. Peters overflows with all the warmth and humor that George will never know.

Both at the show's beginning and end, the hero is embracing not a woman, but the empty white canvas that he really loves—for its "many possibilities." Look closely at that canvas—or at *Sunday in the Park* itself—and you'll get lost in a sea of floating dots. Stand back and you'll see that this evening's two theater artists, Mr. Sondheim and Mr. Lapine, have woven all those imaginative possibilities into a finished picture with a startling new glow.

≡ *For a full account of this minority opinion and its repercussions, see "Exit the Critic" near the end of this volume.*

THE MISS FIRECRACKER CONTEST
MANHATTAN THEATRE CLUB, MAY 28, 1984

When Beth Henley is really flying, her comic voice has the crazed yet liberating sound of a Rebel yell. In *The Miss Firecracker Contest,* her comedy at the Manhattan Theatre Club, this Mississippi-bred playwright reaches that high pitch for the first time since her celebrated debut, *Crimes of the Heart.* Who but Ms. Henley can describe one tragedy after another and send us home smiling? This time, we hear about midgets, orphans, and deformed kittens—and they're the fortunate ones. Other characters, whether on stage or off, are afflicted by cancer, tuberculosis, venereal disease, and, most of all, heartbreak. Even so, the evening's torrential downpour of humor—alternately Southern-Gothic absurdist, melancholy, and broad—almost never subsides.

Ms. Henley wrote this play after *Crimes*—but before *The Wake of Jamey Foster,* her Broadway misfire of two years ago. While *Miss Firecracker* at times seems a slighter, messier version of the author's first success—which also focused primarily on three troubled young women—it doesn't have the warmed-over feeling of *Jamey Foster. Miss Firecracker* also benefits from an unusually sympathetic production, directed by Stephen Tobolowsky. If you're going to do one of Ms. Henley's plays, you'd better have actors who are ready to bounce off the walls. Mr. Tobolowsky has them.

A wonderful actress named Holly Hunter opens the evening by bouncing quite literally about. Ms. Hunter plays Carnelle Scott of Brookhaven, Miss. Carnelle wants nothing more than to be crowned Miss Firecracker in the beauty pageant at the town's annual Independence Day celebration. To this end, she has whipped up a talent-show act in which she tap dances and somersaults to "The Star-Spangled Banner" while clenching a sparkler in her teeth. Watching Ms. Hunter rehearse this performance in her living room, we wonder what could possibly be dizzier.

We find out soon enough. Carnelle's costume seamstress is a bespectacled, awkward young woman named Popeye (Belita Moreno), who began her couturier's career at age four by making outfits for bullfrogs. (Her family couldn't afford dolls.) The orphaned Carnelle also has a pair of first cousins, Elain and Delmount, with whom she was raised as a sibling. Elain (Patricia Richardson), a prissy former Miss Firecracker, has just fled her boring wealthy husband in Natchez. Delmount (Mark Linn-Baker), lately a lunatic asylum inmate, has just quit his menial state job of "scraping up dead dogs from the road." Delmount now aspires to earn a philosophy degree in New Orleans so that he can "let everyone know why we're living." But first he must sell off the oppressive Victorian house that represents both the family's legacy and curse.

The Miss Firecracker Contest is about how all four principal characters try to escape their unhappy pasts and find out "what you can reasonably hope for in life." Yet Ms. Henley has neatly folded her own philosophical pursuits into a wild account of her heroine's pursuit of her prize. By Act 2, the action has moved from the family manse to the fairgrounds—where the ongoing contest is punctuated by a bloody fistfight and unexpected romantic crises for each character. "Wonders never do quite cease," says the carnival's balloon man (Budget Threlkeld), and, after a while, those wonders have more to do with the attainment of spiritual grace than beauty-pageant honors.

For all the play's hyperbolic comic shenanigans, Ms. Henley never loses sight of the sad, real people within. Carnelle isn't just trying to be Miss Firecracker; she's trying to overcome the low self-esteem engendered by her miserable childhood, as well as the unsavory reputation that has led the town's men to dub her "Miss Hot Tamale." Elain and Delmount are trying to flee the psychological grip of their late mother, a "mean" woman who, through bizarre medical circumstances, came to resemble an ape shortly before her death. While Popeye's past remains vague, she knows she must now escape to the Elysian Fields—once she can locate this paradise on a map.

Though Ms. Henley arranges her characters' Act 1 catastrophes and Act 2 comebacks a bit mechanically, almost every line is infused with revealing, vividly observed details. When Elain talks about running away from Natchez, she mourns the "beautiful clocks" she left behind, not her two sons. Delmount, a self-confessed "romantic," pursues women with "at least one classically beautiful characteristic"—only to be tortured by nightmares about mutilated "pieces of women's bodies."

Mr. Tobolowsky's staging, John Lee Beatty's Charles Addamsesque sets, and Jennifer von Mayrhauser's costumes are all faithful to Ms. Henley's stylistic amalgam of realism and 100-proof Southern consciousness. (But the Manhattan Theatre Club, however inadvertently, proves too faithful to the "blazing heat" of the play's setting; the auditorium is a sweatbox.) Ms. Moreno's unworldly Popeye and Mr. Linn-Baker's obsessive yet aristocratic Delmount are both memorably idiosyncratic characterizations; Ms. Richardson's Elain is a fine figure of an indolent, unreconstructed belle.

As Carnelle, Ms. Hunter has dyed crimson hair to match her patriotic tap-dancing costume, but somehow we always see the roots. This actress is at once an antic, sexy Miss Firecracker and a plain, vulnerable girl desperately trying to belong. "They say we're all going to be dying someday, and I believe it," she says in one of her more reflective moments—and, if anything, death is the specter haunting almost every joke and character in the play. What makes Beth Henley heroines like Carnelle both nutty and touching is that they struggle against that inevitability right up to the moment they go.

≡ *Henley wrote some interesting plays after* Miss Firecracker *but none yet to match either it or* Crimes of the Heart. *Holly Hunter moved West, permanently, to build a career as a movie star in films as various as* Broadcast News *and* The Piano.

SIXTH SEASON

1984—85

Theresa Merritt in August Wilson's
Ma Rainey's Black Bottom

CIRCLE REPERTORY COMPANY, JUNE 1, 1984

When Lanford Wilson wrote *Balm in Gilead,* his first full-length play, he was still in his twenties and the Off Off Broadway theater movement was young. The play—a naturalistic visit with twenty-nine low-life denizens of an all-night Upper Broadway coffee shop—caused a sensation at the Café La Mama in 1965; witnesses say that the doors had to be locked to keep out excess theatergoers. Mr. Wilson soon went on to cofound the Circle Repertory Company and to produce a body of work that only one other American playwright—a fellow Off Off Broadway renegade, Sam Shepard—has matched over the last twenty years.

Until one witnesses the stunning revival of *Balm in Gilead* at Circle Rep, it's hard to imagine how the excitement of two decades ago could be rekindled today. Later (and better) Wilson plays, from *The Hot l Baltimore* to *Fifth of July,* have made the writer virtually an establishment figure. *Balm in Gilead*—improvisational in style, awash in the rock-and-drug culture—is a patchy artifact of the sixties. Yet the electricity that must have swept through La Mama—that of discovering original theatrical talent—still courses through the new *Balm in Gilead* almost from start to finish.

We can't discover Mr. Wilson again, of course; we settle gladly instead for reacquainting ourselves with the youthful, naive brio he brought to this early play. What we do discover here is an imaginative young director out of Chicago's Steppenwolf Theatre Ensemble, which first staged *Gilead* in 1980, and the actors he's brought with him. The director is John Malkovich—himself an extraordinary actor who first came to Off Broadway with Steppenwolf's production of Mr. Shepard's *True West* and is now Biff in Broadway's *Death of a Salesman.* His cast includes such other Steppenwolf veterans as Gary Sinise, who directed *True West* and costarred in it; Terry Kinney, who was the exemplary director of

Steppenwolf's . . . *And a Nightingale Sang,* seen in New York earlier this year; and Laurie Metcalf, whose twenty-minute Act 2 monologue in *Balm in Gilead* should in itself prove one of the year's most memorable theatrical events.

In concert with the Circle Rep's own fine young actors—such as Danton Stone, Jonathan Hogan, and Brian Tarantina (here in full drag)—these Chicagoans have given Mr. Wilson's play a contemporary beat. The work's time frame has been advanced to 1972, and the evening rides on waves of Bruce Springsteen music that bleed into the here and now. Though Mr. Malkovich pays homage to sixties fashions—his actors circulate among the audience, hustling them into street-style encounters—he isn't recycling the past. As if to accentuate the roots that Mr. Wilson and Mr. Shepard once shared, this muscular production is closer in feel to *True West* than to *Talley's Folly.*

Mr. Malkovich and his designer, Kevin Rigdon, have transformed the entire theater into Mr. Wilson's forlorn café. The booths and horseshoe-shaped counter float in a sea of cigarette butts and crushed beer cans; on our way to our seats, we're confronted by the coffee shop's filthy, graffiti-splattered urinal. But it's Mr. Malkovich's choreography of his huge company that is crucial: We are completely locked into a seething nocturnal community with its own rituals, laws, loyalties, manners, and language.

That community consists of whores, pimps, junkies, and pushers of all races and sexual orientations. Mr. Wilson's play is an almost documentary slice of this netherworld's life, told in a constant, often chaotic flow of overlapping dialogue, scenes, and brawls. Somewhere in *Balm in Gilead,* there is also a plot—a predictable one about a newly arrived, good-hearted whore from Chicago (Ms. Metcalf) and the pusher (Mr. Stone) for whom she develops a passion.

Balm in Gilead is a young man's work. One feels that Mr. Wilson was dazzled by every odd soul he met in New York and couldn't wait to write everything down. The experiments in form—the repetition of scenes, the time-stopping devices—reveal a writer who's as charged up about the possibilities of theater as he is about the world around him. Mr. Wilson's enduring qualities are also apparent. There are beautiful, idiosyncratic speeches explaining the anthropology of cockroaches, the relationship of prostitutes to pimps, and the ability of heroin addicts to remain upright at their counter stools.

Mr. Wilson's most distinguishing characteristic is his overwhelming compassion—and he empathizes with his community of misfits as strongly as he does with the disparate communities of his later works. If a prostitute must have a pimp, it's because she needs "someone who won't leave"—and, as a character explains, that need is as "natural as anything." The derelicts on stage didn't begin life in the gutter, and Mr. Wilson's people, however deranged, still have the ruins of their previous existences about them. You never know when a prostitute will speak of "symbiosis" or an addict will sing a lyric making witty use of the word "nought."

While not every character is fully drawn, Mr. Malkovich never falters in creating the cyclical behavioral patterns of his unruly crew; we recognize that each night is the same in the coffee shop, that no passing tragedy can alter the tribal dynamics. There are also quiet, intimate images to go with the frequently comic atmospheric hubbub—most strikingly, that of two nude, reposeful bodies gleaming in postcoital sweat in the neighborhood's dank fleabag hotel.

Those bodies belong to Mr. Stone and Ms. Metcalf, who play the coffee shop's truest misfits—still-innocent hustlers who mistakenly believe they can triumph over their circumstances. And in a play full of sad people, Ms. Metcalf's prostitute, Darlene, is the most pathetic—stupid, sweet, and doomed. In her marathon stream-of-consciousness monologue, she reminisces to another whore (the excellent Glenne Headly) about her married past in Chicago—all the while wrapping tragic events within the most inane and trivial digressions. Ms. Metcalf's delivery of the speech, in which Darlene's good-natured gregariousness fights a losing battle against her unarticulated desperation, is a tour de force. But even as we're stirred by the performance, we're equally moved by the way a young team of inspired stage artists has linked arms with Mr. Wilson to make yesterday's new theater new once more.

≡ *Laurie Metcalf was also snapped up by Hollywood, notably by* Roseanne, *the long-running TV sitcom.*

HURLYBURLY
PROMENADE THEATRE, JUNE 22, 1984

It seems too good to be true to walk into an Off Broadway theater—during the summer, no less—and find a half-dozen of our best young actors performing a new David Rabe play under the direction of Mike Nichols. New plays by serious American writers are rare these days; new American plays that attract the likes of Mr. Nichols, William Hurt, and Sigourney Weaver even rarer. But the marquee for *Hurlyburly* at the Promenade is no idle come-on. Until it crash lands at midpoint—halfway through the second of three acts—*Hurlyburly* offers some of Mr. Rabe's most inventive and disturbing writing, in a production of any playwright's dreams. Since the better half alone runs ninety minutes, this is far from a raw deal.

Hurlyburly is set in the Hollywood Hills—seemingly a world apart from the Vietnam-era Army base of the last Rabe-Nichols collaboration, *Streamers*. But the tropical villa designed with seedy élan by Tony Walton might as well be a barracks, and the battles haven't entirely changed. Mr. Rabe remains a dynamic chronicler of the brutal games that eternally adolescent American men can play. When his buddies aren't assaulting one another, they're on search-and-destroy missions against the number one enemy—the women they invariably refer to as "broads," "ghouls," "bitches," or worse.

The house in *Hurlyburly* is shared by two casting directors, played by Mr. Hurt and Christopher Walken. Their cronies include a struggling tough-guy actor (Harvey Keitel) hoping to land a network series, and a hack screenwriter (Jerry Stiller) chasing development deals, and their various female prey.

The first of these victims is Donna (Cynthia Nixon), a Midwestern teenage drifter whom Mr. Stiller finds living in a hotel elevator and brings to the house as a willing "CARE package" for his pals. No less pathetic are Darlene (Ms. Weaver), a photojournalist fond of the word "weird," and Bonnie (Judith Ivey), an exotic dancer who doesn't mind performing fellatio on strangers in front of her six-year-child.

Most of the men have discarded wives and children; they're all nose-deep in the cocaine culture. At his impressive best, Mr. Rabe makes grim, ribald, and surprisingly compassionate comedy out of the lies and rationalizations that allow his alienated men to keep functioning (if not feeling) in the fogs of locustland. According to one character, television "cuts the truth out of stories and leaves only the surface." Mr. Rabe's people live in a similar manner, with dense, contorted language to match. They dismiss depravities as "whims," try to "maintain a viable relationship with reality," and hope to sell their "marketable human qualities." They work in an industry so corrupt that its only honest executives are those who openly admit that they lie.

Amid the ebb and flow of the drug-sotted bull sessions and requisite Hollywood gags are some inspired set pieces. At the outset, Mr. Keitel storms on to explain that he beat his wife because she made him lose his train of thought during a stoned rumination about "how to take Vegas and save the world." By the time he's finished telling the tale, the wife is the villain: She allowed her tooth to injure the hand that slugged her. A bit later, Ms. Nixon's bubble-headed waif delivers a Leslie Fiedler–like mythological exegesis of her only prized possession, Willie Nelson's *Stardust* album. We also get to hear Mr. Keitel's surreal description of how a vibrator functions after it's been smashed by bodybuilding weights in the trunk of a car.

Mr. Rabe's pièce de résistance is his first act curtain scene—in which Mr. Hurt and Ms. Weaver decide to have sex only moments after their "relationship" had seemed permanently kaput. As the lovers exchange new romantic vows, Mr. Nichols's staging ricochets off the lines to provide a classic bit of nasty carnal farce: The couple's ever-phonier declarations of sentiment are belied by ever lewder acts of disrobing.

The evening's collapse begins not long thereafter, once Mr. Rabe has finished diagnosing the anesthetized, unhinged, and unfocused lives in view. As in *Streamers,* one man is a psychotic waiting to detonate. When the explosion comes—in successive acts of automotive violence—*Hurlyburly* sputters out irrevocably. Suddenly, those characters in any remote touch with their anguish start to emote about "desperation"—and, as they do, the speeches buckle and the tears flow in the manner of a John Cassavetes male menopause film.

The ensuing revelations aren't terribly revealing—"I don't feel loved," cries Mr. Hurt—and the tributes to the tough guys' previously hidden vulnerability are banal. At the end of both Acts 2 and 3, it's sentimentally demonstrated that the men are at least capable of offering paternal, if not romantic, affection to the opposite sex.

This is a paltry, amorphous payoff to the strong buildup, and it's unaccountably larded with intimations of nuclear apocalypse. Mr. Hurt takes to ranting about the metaphysics of neutron bombs, as if he'd been handed spare pages from Arthur Kopit's *End of the World.* Perhaps a latent concern for the world's fate will at last allow this man to connect to other people—and to stop bouncing around the "vague hurlyburly" of his anomic existence. But we feel instead that the playwright is floundering and fudging. By imposing grand, crowd-pleasing significance on his characters, Mr. Rabe avoids the painful task of facing his own conclusions about them.

As a Mike Nichols project, *Hurlyburly* almost seems a hybrid of the film *Carnal Knowledge,* another acidic treatment of misogyny in a show-biz milieu, and *The Odd Couple,* a far merrier look at divorced bachelor roommates. Here, the director is highly sensitive to Mr. Rabe's languid L.A. comic rhythms; the staging is flawless, though the sordid West Los Angeles atmosphere seems several shades lighter than the real thing. The cast could not be better. It's beyond even Mr. Hurt's power to make us care about the most articulate of the men, but the actor's febrile intelligence and sensitivity are at high flame. Mr. Walken, as a self-protective cynic, offers what may be his least mannered, most fully ripened comic performance ever. Mr. Stiller, the sole representative of Hollywood's older, Jewish generation, is a frazzled amalgam of vulgarity and wounded vanity—loonily outfitted (by Ann Roth) in Western gear. In her smaller role, Ms. Weaver sports a cloudily vacant face that nods in affectless agreement with any degrading proposition set before her. The prodigious Ms. Nixon, the bright British daughter of *The Real Thing*, is just as persuasive as a mindless Hollywood Boulevard orphan.

Mr. Keitel and Ms. Ivey rise highest in this illustrious crowd. Mr. Keitel's down-and-out actor, feral in appearance and gravelly of voice, is a dim-witted, tightly knotted animal who arouses contempt, laughter, and pity. The dazzling Ms. Ivey—who's surely born to rehabilitate Mr. Rabe's *Boom Boom Room* someday—captures the boisterous manners and miraculous strength of a somewhat sentimentalized tart. In one of the evening's snappiest lines, she announces, "Doom and gloom have come to sit in my household like some permanent kind of electric appliance." Be grateful that only the second half of *Hurlyburly* illustrates exactly what she means.

SUNDAY ESSAY: THEATER'S GENDER GAP IS A CHASM
SEPTEMBER 30, 1984

No one doubts that many feminist battles have been fought and won over the past decade or two. There's never been a time in American life when men and women have tried so hard—and, with increasing frequency, succeeded so well—at dealing with one another on equal, enlightened terms. But enter a theater where a hit play by almost any male American dramatist is on the boards, and you may well come away with quite a different impression.

If art reflects the society that spawns it, what in the world are we to make of such prominent, popular, and largely acclaimed works as David Rabe's *Hurlyburly*, David Mamet's *Glengarry Glen Ross*, and Sam Shepard's *Fool for Love*? In these plays, women and men are so far apart that even the vogue term "gender gap" seems an inadequate description of the distance between the sexes. The gap is a chasm, bordered on either side by armed camps.

Hurlyburly, the latest of these plays, is perhaps the most shocking in its refusal to observe any recent cease-fires in the war between men and women. Though set in a with-it contemporary community—that of trendy, cocaine-infested Hollywood—it dramatizes a set of attitudes that might be considered retrogressive in a Marine barracks of forty years ago. Its principal characters are men who are all either separated or divorced from unseen wives. One of them, an out-of-work actor named Phil (Harvey Keitel), has beaten up his wife just before the play begins; his best friend, Eddie (William Hurt), rationalizes his pal's behavior on the grounds that Phil's wife must be "a whore" who "hates men."

Eddie, meanwhile, wants to have "a meaningful relationship" with a "dynamite lady"—"a very special lady." This special dynamite lady proves to be Darlene (Sigourney Weaver), a bubble-brained photojournalist who moves so frequently from bed to bed that she can't be sure of the paternity of a baby she aborts. Eddie can sustain this meaningful relationship primarily because Darlene is "out of town two out of every three weeks."

The other two women in *Hurlyburly* are, in the play's parlance, out-and-out "bimbos." Donna (Cynthia Nixon) is a teenage drifter whom Artie (Jerry Stiller), a hack screenwriter, picks up in an elevator and brings to Eddie and his friends as "a CARE package"—an utterly compliant, nearly mute sexual "pet" to be used by one and all "just to stay in practice." Later we meet Bonnie (Judith Ivey), a nude nightclub dancer whom Eddie describes as "a good bitch—with a heart of gold." Bonnie likes to sleep with many different men because it's "interesting," but she doesn't want to feel that she and her many lovers are just "things with clothes on." When she goes out with Phil, she tries to inject "humanity" into the sexual transaction by talking about the weather during their drive to her boudoir. Phil responds to her social niceties by pushing her out of the moving car and leaving her in a bruised heap on the side of the road.

The locker-room atmosphere in *Glengarry Glen Ross* is just as thick as in *Hurlyburly.* There are no women at all on stage in Mr. Mamet's play— which is only appropriate in a work whose characters, a group of cutthroat Chicago real-estate salesmen, regard women as beside the point (if they think about women at all). When one poor schnook of a customer visits the real-estate office to try to get his money back, he explains that he has been sent after the refund by his wife. The salesman Roma (Joe Mantegna) tries to browbeat the customer out of his refund by impugning his masculinity: Real men, Roma implies, don't let their wives tell them what to do. In the play's climax shortly thereafter, Roma blows up at his boss—a manager who is disliked by all the salesmen because he hides behind a desk instead of selling. Searching for the nastiest possible epithet to call the boss, Roma finally finds it—a four-letter word for the female sexual organ. *Glengarry Glen Ross* is laced with scatological insults from beginning to end, but it's the one that means "woman" which its characters regard as the ultimate calumny.

Fool for Love marks Mr. Shepard's first concerted effort to put a major female character on stage—but his heroine, May, and his hero, Eddie, find little common ground. Eddie and May—who are lovers or half-siblings or both—circle each other like wrestlers for most of the ninety minutes that they spend trying to "erase" one another in a seedy motel room. In May's words, Eddie believes that the only real men are those who "half kill themselves falling off horses or jumping on steers." Eddie wholeheartedly concurs. The consummate male-female relationship in *Fool for Love* is the romance between a spectral character, the Old Man, and a female icon he describes as "the woman of my dreams." The woman of the Old Man's dreams is the singer Barbara Mandrell, whom he apparently knows only as a pinup he's tacked to a wall.

The Old Man also has fond memories of May, who may be his daughter, as a little girl. In *Glengarry* and *Hurlyburly,* the only strong male-female bonds are also, curiously and sentimentally enough, between fathers and daughters. In Mr. Mamet's play, the eldest, washed-up salesman, Shelly Levene, refers tenderly on two occasions to "my daughter"— as if the mere mention of the fact that he has a daughter will somehow redeem his sense of self-worth. Mr. Rabe's play uses father-daughter relationships as a warm counterpoint to the hostile sexual couplings. When Eddie speaks to his despised ex-wife on the phone, he tells her, "If you hurt my little girl, I'll kill you." Eddie also confesses to retroactive guilt over having taken Bonnie's six-year-old daughter along to watch her mother perform oral sex in a car. Later, when Phil briefly kidnaps his own baby daughter from the home of his ex-wife, all the men in *Hurlyburly* coo over the swaddled infant. "This sweet little innocent thing is a broad of the future," says Artie. "Maybe if we kept her and raised her," Eddie says, "she could grow up and be a decent human being." The idea is dropped when another of the men suggests that it may be "biologically and genetically inevitable that at a certain age [girls] go nasty."

There is much more going on in all three of these plays, needless to say, than the severed connections between men and women. To judge or reject these works on the grounds of the archaic sexual attitudes of their characters would be to deny oneself entry into some of the more interesting writing—in the case of *Glengarry,* the most interesting writing— available in the American theater right now. Nor can any theatergoer believe that the attitudes expressed by the plays' men reflect the views of their creators. Just because Mr. Rabe and Mr. Shepard's respective Eddies treat women like chattels doesn't mean that the authors endorse such behavior. If anything, the reverse may be true. Perhaps these male playwrights—all of whom came of creative age during the social upheavals of the sixties—are warning the audience that it shouldn't congratulate itself too heartily on the postfeminist era supposedly at hand. Behind closed doors, these writers may be saying, men will still be boys—and there will always be women willing to go along with the game.

One could also argue a less charitable view. Is it possible that Mr. Rabe, Mr. Mamet, and Mr. Shepard, whatever their personal convictions, have not yet reached the point where they can dramatize men and women who can talk to one another as equals? Prior to *Fool for Love,* women have been at best symbolic or peripheral in Mr. Shepard's plays—and, at their fullest (in *Buried Child, True West, Curse of the Starving Class*), either mothers or siblings of the dominant male characters. Mr. Rabe's most ambitious attempt to write a female character prior to *Hurlyburly* was Chrissy in *In the Boom Boom Room*—a much abused, gold-hearted go-go dancer who bears more than a passing resemblance to the dancer Bonnie in the new play. (One wonders if Eddie's ex-wife in *Hurlyburly* phones instead of visits because Mr. Rabe wouldn't know how to portray her on stage.) In past Mamet plays such as *Sexual Perversity in Chicago* and *Edmond,* the women and men are as juvenile as those in *Hurlyburly.* Mr. Mamet's most tender male-female pairing to date has been between a father and a daughter (in *Reunion*); his most strenuous effort to portray a pair of equally matched lovers, *The Woods,* was a fiasco. Indeed, like Mr. Rabe (in *Streamers*) and, to a slightly lesser extent, Mr. Shepard, Mr. Mamet often is at his best (in *American Buffalo* as well as *Glengarry*) when he can keep women offstage altogether.

These men can take heart in the fact that they are part of a long chain of male American writers, whether playwrights or not, who have been flummoxed by the demands of creating adult male-female bonds. As Mr. Shepard would be the first to say, old myths die hard. Leslie Fiedler has long reminded us that American novelists from Cooper and Twain to Hemingway couldn't see much past male-male couples; we need only walk into the recent revivals of *Death of a Salesman* and *A Moon for the Misbegotten* to remember that Arthur Miller's best play contains a bevy of B-movie tarts and a wanly characterized wife who is more mother than spouse—or that the last great Eugene O'Neill heroine was an almost mystical amalgam of mother, daughter, and virgin whore. And it's conceivable, too, that our most resolutely masculine writers can expand their range in plays to come. No male American playwright of recent vintage has drawn more convincing male-female pairings than Lanford Wilson in *Talley's Folly* and *Serenading Louie*—but Mr. Wilson's first full-length play of twenty years ago, the currently revived *Balm in Gilead*, features an empty-headed prostitute who, like the "dynamite lady" in *Hurlyburly*, is a shade too predictably named Darlene.

Mr. Rabe, Mr. Mamet, and Mr. Shepard may never change, of course. Given their better work, one might well not want them to. Certainly none of their plays, the tedious second half of *Hurlyburly* excepted, is lacking for enthusiastic audiences—and it may not only be the skill of the writing and acting that is winning theatergoers over. There remains the heretical, not to mention distressing, possibility that these gifted writers reflect the real world of men and women in 1984 more accurately than most of us would care to think.

AFTER THE FALL
PLAYHOUSE 91, OCTOBER 5, 1984

If Arthur Miller's *After the Fall* was ever to be rescued from the oblivion where it's rested for two decades, the miracle would have to happen in the revival at the Playhouse 91. Working with two tireless and commanding stars, Frank Langella and Dianne Wiest, the director John Tillinger sets out to make the most forceful possible case for a play that was belittled as a gossipy, self-serving mea culpa in 1964, when it launched the equally ill-fated Lincoln Center Repertory Company.

So assured is the staging—and so absorbing is Mr. Langella's driving performance in the marathon role originated by Jason Robards—that some of the evening is entertaining and nearly all of it is energetic. Yet we still go home feeling more exhausted than enlightened. Even with a substantially revised and edited new text, *After the Fall* is never as moving or profound as it wants to be. The play remains a collection of sporadically arresting autobiographical fragments—all floating in a glutinous interior monologue that substitutes tortuous rhetoric for psychological or metaphysical insight.

The stream-of-consciousness narrator is Quentin (Mr. Langella), a successful Jewish lawyer in whose "mind, thought, and memory" the drama takes place. Much like Mr. Miller—and like characters in other Miller plays, before and after *Fall*—Quentin is a witness to alarming public and personal catastrophes: the stock market crash, the Holocaust, the McCarthy witchhunts, and the self-destruction of a show business idol to whom he is married. It's immaterial now, as ever, whether Quentin is actually a stand-in for Mr. Miller—or whether other characters represent Marilyn Monroe, Elia Kazan, and Lee Strasberg. The real issue is what, if anything, the playwright has created out of his recollected past.

At his best, Mr. Miller sets forth crackling vignettes. The scene in which a blacklist-era informer rationalizes his betrayal of an old colleague is a grisly microcosm of a national hysteria, ferociously limned by the actors Benjamin Hendrickson and Henderson Forsythe. The dissolution of Quentin's first marriage, to a self-possessed woman who bores him, is the most convincing male-female brawl Mr. Miller has ever written—and it gains essential balance from Mary-Joan Negro's hearty portrayal of Mr. Langella's domestic sparring partner.

The Act 2 centerpiece—the showdown between Quentin and his new celebrity wife, Maggie—also works in its odd fashion. Or at least it does if one can adjust to Mr. Tillinger's revisionist version of Mr. Miller's heroine. By casting the brunette Ms. Wiest as Maggie, a top-of-the-charts singing star, the director has gone out of his way to play down the character's resemblance to Monroe. The notion, while intriguing, seems misguided at first: Ms. Wiest just isn't persuasive as the national sex symbol the text claims her to be, and, when we meet her in Act 1, she's performing a calculatedly campy impersonation of a dumb starlet.

But once the storm arrives after intermission, the actress's bravura technique takes over. Maggie's decline from guileless naïf to self-hating monster to incipient suicide is a seamless dance of death—paying off with the image of a puffy-faced Ms. Wiest tumbling to the floor as weightlessly as a broken doll. Once the enraged and battered Mr. Langella is wrestling with her over bottles of sleeping pills and whiskey, *After the Fall* achieves real fire. It's not a Strindbergian fire, exactly—but, so uncannily does Ms. Wiest's singer resemble Judy Garland, that the spectacle suggests what *A Star Is Born* might have been like if Vicki Lester, rather than Norman Maine, were its alcoholic protagonist.

The reason that even the play's stronger scenes engage us only at the level of pulp fiction is Mr. Miller's conception of his hero. Quentin, who desperately wants to live in "good faith," is such a fount of guilt and atonement that *After the Fall* was perhaps destined to be revived on the eve of Yom Kippur. But it's not the guilt that makes Quentin sound so whiny—it's how he disposes of it. A Portnoy with a fatal lack of humor or irony, Quentin tours the debris of his life so sanctimoniously that he seems to be surveying the Stations of the Cross.

Though the hero admits to some flaws—lust, for instance—he is nearly always on a higher moral plane than the name namers, mercenary parents, and coquettish women who claw at him. Worse, his spiritual voyage is banal and preordained. Quentin wants to find out why he can still have hope for a world in which no one is an innocent. The solution to this dilemma doesn't spring out of the play's main events; it's handed down, deus ex machina, by Holga (Laurie Kennedy), an impossibly wise anti-Nazi German archeologist who is destined to be Quentin's third wife.

Holga explains early on that "one must finally take one's own life into one's own arms." Two and a half hours later, Quentin concurs: We must accept the fact that we don't live in Eden but in a dangerous world where life goes on in spite of everyone's capacity to inflict hatred and "many, many deaths." It might be easier to swallow this platitudinous pontification if Mr. Miller didn't so strenuously attempt to merge the history of civilization with that of his hero: The play concludes with an unseemly, not to mention preposterous, analogy between the deaths in concentration camps and the death of Quentin's love for Maggie. How seriously are we to take a man who equates a desire to throttle his wife with the Holocaust?

Even in slimmed-down form, Quentin's self-searching monologues are quite a mouthful—full of circumlocutions, portentous questions, and conundrums such as "Maybe it's not enough—to know yourself. Or maybe it's too much." (When Quentin says, "We are killing one another with abstractions," he could be describing a mass murder.) The intense Mr. Langella is a marvel at making such musings seem rational and provocative—at least until one stops to think. Though John Lee Beatty's gray, couch-laden set represents Quentin's mind as a high-tech furniture showroom, Mr. Tillinger, aided by Dennis Parichy's fluent lighting, swiftly dispatches the characters who constantly float in and out. It's hard to imagine a better—or, for that matter, another—production of *After the Fall* for some time to come.

≡ *Actually, it proved not so hard to imagine a better production. Six years later Michael Blakemore, Arthur Miller's most persistent interpreter in England, did an intimate* After the Fall *for the National Theatre; Blakemore banished the Monroe image entirely by casting a superb young black actress, Josette Simon, as Maggie.*

MA RAINEY'S BLACK BOTTOM
CORT THEATRE, OCTOBER 12, 1984

Late in Act 1 of *Ma Rainey's Black Bottom,* a somber, aging band trombonist (Joe Seneca) tilts his head heavenward to sing the blues. The setting is a dilapidated Chicago recording studio of 1927, and the song sounds as old as time. "If I had my way," goes the lyric, "I would tear this old building down."

Once the play has ended, that lyric has almost become a prophecy. In *Ma Rainey's Black Bottom*, the writer August Wilson sends the entire history of black America crashing down upon our heads. This play is a searing inside account of what white racism does to its victims—and it floats on the same authentic artistry as the blues music it celebrates. Harrowing as *Ma Rainey's* can be, it is also funny, salty, carnal, and lyrical. Like his real-life heroine, the legendary singer Gertrude (Ma) Rainey, Mr. Wilson articulates a legacy of unspeakable agony and rage in a spellbinding voice.

The play is Mr. Wilson's first to arrive in New York, and it reached here, via the Yale Repertory Theatre, under the sensitive hand of the man who was born to direct it, Lloyd Richards. On Broadway, Mr. Richards has honed *Ma Rainey's* to its finest form. What's more, the director brings us an exciting young actor—Charles S. Dutton—along with his extraordinary dramatist. One wonders if the electricity at the Cort is the same that audiences felt when Mr. Richards, Lorraine Hansberry, and Sidney Poitier stormed into Broadway with *A Raisin in the Sun* a quarter-century ago.

As *Ma Rainey's* shares its director and Chicago setting with *Raisin*, so it builds on Hansberry's themes: Mr. Wilson's characters want to make it in white America. And, to a degree, they have. Ma Rainey (1886–1939) was among the first black singers to get a recording contract—albeit with a white company's "race" division. Mr. Wilson gives us Ma (Theresa Merritt) at the height of her fame. A mountain of glitter and feathers, she has become a despotic, temperamental star, complete with a retinue of flunkies, a fancy car, and a kept young lesbian lover.

The evening's framework is a Paramount-label recording session that actually happened, but whose details and supporting players have been invented by the author. As the action swings between the studio and the band's warm-up room—designed by Charles Henry McClennahan as if they might be the festering last-chance saloon of *The Iceman Cometh*—Ma and her four accompanying musicians overcome various mishaps to record "Ma Rainey's Black Bottom" and other songs. During the delays, the band members smoke reefers, joke around, and reminisce about past gigs on a well-traveled road stretching through whorehouses and church socials from New Orleans to Fat Back, Ark.

The musicians' speeches are like improvised band solos—variously fizzy, haunting, and mournful. We hear how the bassist Slow Drag (Leonard Jackson) got his nickname at a dance contest, but also about how a black preacher was tortured by being forced to "dance" by a white vigilante's gun. Gradually, we come to know these men, from their elusive pipe dreams to their hidden scars, but so deftly are the verbal riffs orchestrated that we don't immediately notice the incendiary drama boiling underneath.

That drama is ignited by a conflict between Ma and her young trumpeter Levee, played by Mr. Dutton. An ambitious sport eager to form his own jazz band, Levee mocks his employer's old "jugband music" and champions the new dance music that has just begun to usurp the blues among black audiences in the urban North. Already Levee has challenged Ma by writing a swinging version of "Ma Rainey's Black Bottom" that he expects the record company to use in place of the singer's traditional arrangement.

Yet even as the battle is joined between emblematic representatives of two generations of black music, we're thrust into a more profound war about identity. The African nationalist among the musicians, the pianist Toledo (Robert Judd), argues that "We done sold ourselves to the white man in order to be like him." We soon realize that, while Ma's music is from the heart, her life has become a sad, ludicrous "imitation" of white stardom. Levee's music is soulful, too, but his ideal of success is having his "name in lights"; his pride is invested in the new shoes on which he's blown a week's pay.

Ma, at least, senses the limits of her success. Though she acts as if she owns the studio, she can't hail a cab in the white city beyond. She knows that her clout with the record company begins and ends with her viability as a commercial product: "When I've finished recording," she says, "it's just like I'd been some whore, and they roll over and put their pants on." Levee, by contrast, has yet to learn that a black man can't name his own terms if he's going to sell his music to a white world. As he plots his future career, he deceives himself into believing that a shoeshine and Uncle Tom smile will win white backers for his schemes.

Inevitably, the promised door of opportunity slams, quite literally, in Levee's face, and the sound has a violent ring that reverberates through the decades. Levee must confront not just the collapse of his hopes but the destruction of his dignity. Having played the white man's game and lost to its rigged rules, he is left with less than nothing: Even as he fails to sell himself to whites, Levee has sold out his own sense of self-worth.

Mr. Dutton's delineation of this tragic downfall is red-hot. A burly actor a year out of Yale, he is at first as jazzy as his music. With his boisterous wisecracks and jumpy sprinter's stance, he seems ready to leap into the stratosphere envisioned in his fantasies of glory. But once he crash lands, the poison of self-hatred ravages his massive body and distorts his thundering voice. No longer able to channel his anger into his music, he directs it to God, crying out that a black man's prayers are doomed to be tossed "into the garbage." As Mr. Dutton careens about with unchecked, ever-escalating turbulence, he transforms an anonymous Chicago bandroom into a burial ground for a race's aspirations.

Mr. Dutton's fellow band members are a miraculous double-threat ensemble: They play their instruments nearly as convincingly as they spin their juicy monologues. Aleta Mitchell and Lou Criscuolo, as Ma's gum-chewing lover and harried white manager, are just right, and so is Scott Davenport-Richards, as Ma's erstwhile Little Lord Fauntleroy of a young nephew. It's one of the evening's more grotesquely amusing gags that Ma imperiously insists on having the boy, a chronic stutterer, recite a spoken introduction on her record.

Ms. Merritt is Ma Rainey incarnate. A singing actress of both wit and power, she finds bitter humor in the character's distorted sense of self: When she barks her outrageous demands to her lackeys, we see a show business monster who's come a long way from her roots. Yet the roots can still be unearthed. In a rare reflective moment, she explains why she sings the blues. "You don't sing to feel better," Ms. Merritt says tenderly. "You sing because that's a way of understanding life."

The lines might also apply to the play's author. Mr. Wilson can't mend the broken lives he unravels in *Ma Rainey's Black Bottom*. But, like his heroine, he makes their suffering into art that forces us to understand and won't allow us to forget.

≡ *This was the third time I'd written about* Ma Rainey's Black Bottom *as it took its circuitous path to Broadway. I had never heard of August Wilson, whose career had pretty much been limited to his then home of St. Paul, Minn., when I first encountered this play as a staged reading—actors with scripts in hand, no set, no props, no musical instruments—at the Eugene O'Neill Playwrights Conference in Waterford, Conn. A sort of summer camp for theater people situated a short drive from the old O'Neill family home in New London, this institution develops new playwrights by awarding its well-cast professional readings annually to a lucky dozen or so (selected through script submissions). The press is allowed to visit but not to review. I bent the rule slightly when in a long essay about the O'Neill "process" I described my experience of seeing a raw* Ma Rainey's—*really raw, some four hours in length and performed in a sweltering unair-conditioned barn—during the summer of 1982. Noting that the play had "virtually no story [and] some speeches that run, I would guess, ten minutes," I added that "like most of the audience, I was electrified by the sound of this author's voice." I justified my breach to myself by saying I was simply reporting what I had seen. Despite the extreme heat and the late hour, no one in the barn walked out on* Ma Rainey's Black Bottom.

CYRANO DE BERGERAC
GERSHWIN THEATRE, OCTOBER 17, 1984

You're not going to spend the evening staring at Derek Jacobi's nose at the Royal Shakespeare Company's *Cyrano de Bergerac*. There's just too much else going on. In his beguiling presentation of Edmond Rostand's classic piece of hokum, the director Terry Hands fills the Gershwin's stage with teeming choruses of Parisian swells, smoky battlefield explosions, and all the picture-book moonlight required to send us flying back to a lost romantic age. This is a *Cyrano* as outsized as grand opera—and, in Mr. Jacobi, it has its virtuoso soloist, the very exemplar of panache.

As Cyrano explains, panache is not merely the white plume in his hat—it's his "visible soul." Mr. Jacobi is a slight man, and, even with his "strawberry Punchinello nose," he has an almost anonymous face. But as the story of Cyrano's life is a triumph of radiant inner resources over a grotesque exterior, so Mr. Jacobi's performance makes mind, voice, and heart soar over matter. The soul of his Cyrano—a noble amalgam of poetry and fire—floods every corner of the RSC's throbbing theatrical tapestry.

Cyrano, of course, is Rostand's nostalgic, late-nineteenth-century fantasy version of a mid-seventeenth-century paragon of honor and derring-do. "I decided to excel in everything!" the hero explains. Poet and philosopher, swashbuckling swordsman and razor-sharp wit, he thinks nothing of composing rhymed couplets aloud even as he fights a deadly duel. Yet Cyrano always stands a nose away from achieving the one conquest he most wants. Too ugly to win his beloved Roxane (Sinead Cusack) for himself, he must settle instead for wooing her by proxy—by selflessly writing the love letters that she receives from her handsome, dim-witted heartthrob, Christian (Tom Mannion).

The high point of Mr. Jacobi's performance comes in the balcony scene, when Cyrano has his one chance to express his passion to Roxane in his own voice. Hiding in the shadows so that his goddess won't suspect that Christian speaks through a surrogate, Cyrano lets loose with an aria of longing. His poetry makes its recipient tremble, and no wonder. The ecstatic lines erupt through Mr. Jacobi's trim frame in wave after rising wave, as if Cyrano's spirit were willing itself to leap to the window where his body can never go.

When the actor repeatedly incants the words "love" and "Roxane," his voice reaches a shuddering, erotic pitch—but with a dying fall. He's all too sadly aware that consummation is forever to be denied. As Christian climbs up to claim the kiss that Cyrano has won, Mr. Jacobi brings a black ironic chill to the line "It's my words she kisses, and not his lips— there is cause to be cheerful there."

It's no surprise that the actor handles the role's other aspects with flair. The withering sarcasm of his Benedick in the RSC's *Much Ado About Nothing* is turned up to bombastic force here—from his first entrance, when Cyrano contemptuously chases a ham actor off a Parisian stage. It is no less a treat to watch the swaggering star raise his sword to heaven to lead the Gascon cadets into battle at Arras.

Even more important is Mr. Jacobi's ability to make us believe that Cyrano is the purest truth-sayer who ever lived—a man of inviolate principle who, at the price of being an outcast, will challenge authority, received ideas, and fashion to preserve his integrity of thought and action. Though Cyrano can win a single-handed victory over a hundred antagonists in a sword fight, it's more stirring still that he fights "for far more than the hope of winning." When Mr. Jacobi announces that he tilts at windmills in order to reach "up to the stars," his chivalric fervor is both inspiring and a little mad.

Cyrano de Bergerac is sentimental and melodramatic, but those qualities don't infect its star performance. Mr. Jacobi's softness is never spineless. In his staging, Mr. Hands is no less mindful of the pitfalls that could derail a play in which almost every event is incredible, every scene a parade of dramatic hyperbole. A few wrong notes and *Cyrano de Bergerac* could become this year's Mel Brooks parody.

But Mr. Hands has perfect pitch. This director's virtuosity is as impressive as his star's. Though the actors and design team are the same, *Cyrano* has nothing in common with its repertory companion piece. Mr. Hands's reading of Rostand is as emphatic and muscular as his *Much Ado* is airy and delicate.

Whether he's choreographing the opening mob scene in a ghostly, garish Hotel de Bourgogne (in which even Dumas's D'Artagnan makes a cameo appearance) or making Roxane's gilded fairy-tale coach materialize in a tattered camp of starving soldiers, the director has a sure grip on the son-et-lumière spectacles that make *Cyrano* ascend. It's only in the intimate convent epilogue, where the final emotional crescendo should come, that the show loses its battle with the cavernous Gershwin. As partial compensation, there is a huge autumnal chestnut tree that, as designed by Ralph Koltai and lighted by Mr. Hands, seems to give us a glimpse of a burning eternity.

The director is aided throughout by Anthony Burgess's ingenious translation, which serves Rostand's wit while adding a few fillips of its own ("Oh that this too too solid nose would melt," goes one interpolation). Preserving rhyme but minimizing the heroic couplets, Mr. Burgess easily surpasses the *Cyrano* libretto he wrote a decade ago for a Broadway musical adaptation; at times his highly playable verse rivals Richard Wilbur's translations of Molière.

The large supporting cast doesn't squander a line. Ms. Cusack does all that can be done with Roxane, a silly, syrupy debutante who isn't worthy of anyone's love until the play's conclusion. Mr. Mannion finds humor and appealing honesty in the empty-headed pretty boy Christian, and Pete Postlethwaite conveys both the big heart and antic mind of Ragueneau, the pastry cook who would rather be a poet. John Carlisle, an uncommonly devilish villain in *Much Ado,* moves from high comedy to serene pathos as Cyrano's nemesis, the pompous, cowardly aristocrat de Guiche.

The evening is very long—well over three hours—and not all of it is priceless. Yet somehow the excessive length seems part of the point in a production that champions theatrical extravagance as its own reward. If Rostand's drama lacks ideas, psychological depth, or logic, Mr. Hands and Mr. Jacobi demonstrate that it has other qualities that could only flourish in the theater. At the RSC's *Cyrano,* we're reminded that plays need not replicate literature or the real world to thrill us. Plain old-fashioned stage magic can still have its own panache.

≡ *This RSC company contained in its supporting cast some actors who would go on to other triumphs, including the now ubiquitous film actor Pete Postlethwaite (who first reached prominence playing opposite Daniel Day-Lewis in* In the Name of the Father*) and John Carlisle (whose Dr. Rank was an integral part of the* Doll's House *in which Janet McTeer wowed Broadway in 1997). But Terry Hands, who directed this glittering show as well as many other RSC hits dating back to the late 1960s, would later become part of an unwanted Broadway legend, as director of the 1988 musical fiasco* Carrie.

Accrding to Broadway lore, the impresario Mike Todd walked out of a New Haven tryout performance of the first Richard Rodgers–Oscar Hammerstein II musical, pronouncing its doom: "No legs, no jokes, no chance!" The year was 1943, the show was *Away We Go!* A few weeks later, under the new title of *Oklahoma!*, Rodgers and Hammerstein's self-styled "musical play" arrived in New York and changed the course of American musical theater.

Oklahoma! indeed had no legs—in the form of a chorus-girl kick-line—and precious few jokes. But it had beautiful songs and Agnes de Mille ballets, all tightly integrated into a moody, bittersweet libretto that took little time out for the formulaic, vaudeville-and-operetta-spawned trivialities that marked most Broadway musical comedies of its time. Building on innovations previously introduced by Hammerstein and Rodgers with other collaborators—notably, in the Hammerstein–Jerome Kern *Show Boat* (1927) and the Rodgers–Lorenz Hart–John O'Hara *Pal Joey* (1940)—*Oklahoma!* ushered in the era of the "serious" musical.

The old-fashioned musical comedy would never go away, of course. Just as *Oklahoma!* shared its debut season with Cole Porter's *Something for the Boys,* so *Oklahoma!* descendants like *West Side Story* and *A Chorus Line* would later coexist with *The Music Man* and *Annie.* But there was no turning back once *Oklahoma!* had paved the way, commercially and artistically, for an American theatrical form in which script, song, and dance merged to create drama as well as escapist, fairy-tale entertainment. A revolution had begun—albeit a slow one. Broadway musicals are created in the rough-and-tumble world of big-money show business; experimentation is tempered by the perilous realities of the mass-entertainment marketplace.

Of all the artists who have tried to transform the Broadway musical since *Oklahoma!,* no one has been more persistent than the composer and lyricist Stephen Sondheim. Though working in a theatrical form that has usually straddled pop and middlebrow culture, Sondheim is as adventurous and as accomplished an author, playwrights included, as Broadway has produced over the last two decades. And this year, with *Sunday in the Park with George,* Sondheim has won his largest victory yet in his struggle to expand the Broadway musical theater to the size of his own artistic ambitions. *Sunday*—with a libretto by its director, James Lapine—may not be the most enjoyable or seamless show in the Sondheim canon. But like some other idiosyncratic musicals that faced mixed receptions initially—*Porgy and Bess, Pal Joey, Candide*—it is likely to leave a lasting imprint on the form.

Unlike those other shows, *Sunday* has, at least for now, found a sizable following; in spite of a divided press, it has played to full houses since opening last May. All things considered, this is an amazement. Who would have guessed that Sondheim would find what may prove his largest audience to date for his most daring musical? Here is a Broadway musical that lacks not only legs but dancing. Lapine's libretto is stronger on theme than on narrative or characters; Sondheim's score contains few numbers that fit traditional Broadway definitions of the term "song"; its second act opens with the company frozen in a silent tableau, held so long that it might give Pinter pause; the pit band contains only eleven musicians, and the instrumentation sets one to thinking of Ravel and Poulenc rather than the traditionally brassy, jazzy, or schmaltzy Broadway sound.

As befits a show whose subject is the creation of a landmark in modernist painting—Georges Seurat's *Sunday Afternoon on the Island of La Grande Jatte* (1886)—*Sunday* is itself a modernist creation, perhaps the first truly modernist work of musical theater that Broadway has produced. Instead of mimicking reality through a conventional, naturalistic story, the authors of *Sunday* deploy music and language in nonlinear patterns that, like Seurat's tiny brushstrokes, become meaningful only when refracted through a contemplative observer's mind. As the art critic Meyer Schapiro explained, Seurat let "solid masses emerge from an endless scattering of fine points"—the points being strokes of basic colors that seem abstract when viewed at the painting's surface but that converge into shimmering images of infinite chromatic variation when viewed from a distance. The Sondheim-Lapine colors are notes and words, often arranged with the same formal rigor as Seurat's pigments, that have an accretional esthetic, emotional, and thematic effect.

But *Sunday* is almost as unusual for what it is not as for what it is. It breaks with the history of the serious Broadway musical, much as Seurat broke with the history of art. It even breaks with the history of Sondheim's musicals—which have long been considered among the theater's most innovative. In a season when two Broadway musicals, George Gershwin's *Porgy and Bess* and Sondheim's *Sweeney Todd*, are receiving the ultimate high-culture imprimatur of entering the opera repertory— at the Metropolitan Opera and New York City Opera, respectively—

Sondheim and Lapine have rewritten the rules by creating a musical that is as far removed from opera as it is from *42nd Street*. *Sunday* is a watershed event that demands nothing less than a retrospective, even revisionist, look at the development of both the serious Broadway musical and of Sondheim's groundbreaking career.

Those two histories have been intertwined for four decades. Beginning in his preteen years—even as *Oklahoma!* was in its planning stages—Sondheim became a surrogate son and protégé to Oscar Hammerstein II. It was Hammerstein, the librettist of the breakthrough shows *Show Boat* and *Oklahoma!*, who instructed the young man in the craft of writing for the musical stage. Once Sondheim's professional career began in the 1950s, he collaborated on shows with many other innovators in the musical theater—among them, Rodgers, George Abbott, Jerome Robbins, Leonard Bernstein, Harold Prince, and Michael Bennett. Judging from *Sunday,* one might say that Sondheim lived through the entire history of the modern Broadway musical to reach the point where he could create "something of my own," as his latest hero George puts it. And so, *Sunday* is at once a culmination of past musical-theater innovations and a rejection of them.

The serious musicals that precede *Sunday in the Park* have come in several distinct forms—the musical play, in which libretto and score carry equal weight; the operatic musical, and the dance musical. Sondheim has been associated with them all. The musical play was pioneered by Hammerstein. Before *Show Boat* and *Oklahoma!*, musical numbers either didn't advance a script or advanced one that was at best jazz-age fluff. *Show Boat,* an adaptation of Edna Ferber's novel, dealt with unhappy marriages and miscegenation; *Oklahoma!,* from Lynn Riggs's play *Green Grow the Lilacs,* had a sexually threatening villain. In form, *Oklahoma!* went beyond its predecessor by accentuating songs in which the characters directly expressed their motivations and feelings; its ballets were not thrown in for divertissement but, like the score, either advanced the story or explored a character's psyche.

Musical plays, frequently adapted from sturdy plays and novels, reached their peak in the 1950s with shows such as Frank Loesser's *Guys and Dolls* (adapted from Damon Runyon) and the Alan Jay Lerner–Frederick Loewe *My Fair Lady* (adapted from Shaw). Just how important a libretto's architecture became to the musical can be seen by how few predecessors of *Show Boat* and *Oklahoma!* can hold the stage today—even when they contain a larger quotient of standard songs than the fluffy, libretto-poor musical comedies of the same period. Of all the Gershwin musicals, only *Porgy and Bess* is stageable now on its own terms instead of as a nostalgic, if not camp, artifact. Time has also eroded all Rodgers and Hart musicals, except those based on Shakespeare (*The Boys from Syracuse*) or on O'Hara (*Pal Joey*), all Cole Porter musicals except his Shakespeare adaptation (*Kiss Me, Kate*), and all Irving Berlin musicals except *Annie Get Your Gun* (which was produced by Rodgers and Hammerstein).

Yet even as the musical play ruled among Broadway's serious musicals, and helped streamline the shape of less-ambitious musical comedies, composers and choreographers were trying to stretch the musical away from the book and toward its other components—score and dance.

The operatic musicals—not to be confused with actual operas that were booked into Broadway theaters (such as Virgil Thomson and Gertrude Stein's *Four Saints in Three Acts*, Marc Blitzstein's *Regina*, or Gian Carlo Menotti's *The Consul*)—are few, because few composers working within the Broadway system had either the musicianship or ambition to attempt them. They have often resulted when serious composers decided to meet Broadway's showbiz demands halfway—as typified by Kurt Weill's *Street Scene*, Blitzstein's *The Cradle Will Rock,* and Bernstein's *Candide.* Aside from Sondheim and Gershwin, the only notable Broadway-bred composer to attempt an operatic musical was Frank Loesser, in *The Most Happy Fella.*

Dance musicals, meanwhile, grew out of de Mille's advances in *Oklahoma!* Though George Balanchine had staged the first ballet that served a musical's plot—"Slaughter on Tenth Avenue" for Rodgers and Hart's *On Your Toes* in 1936—it was de Mille's Freudian dream ballet for Rodgers and Hammerstein that integrated dance into the emotional fabric of a musical's story. De Mille soon became one of the first choreographers to stage an entire Broadway musical—the third Rodgers and Hammerstein show, *Allegro,* in 1947 (on which the teenager Sondheim served as a production assistant).

Ten years later, the dance musical's ascendancy began in earnest—with Sondheim's first Broadway show, *West Side Story,* for which he wrote the lyrics. To Arthur Laurents's adaptation of *Romeo and Juliet* and Bernstein's alternately Broadway ("Cool") and operatic (the "Tonight" quintet) score, the director-choreographer Jerome Robbins added not only dances but danced sequences: The whole show seemed choreographed.

In spite of Sondheim's important excursions into the operatic musical (*Sweeney Todd*), the musical play (*A Funny Thing Happened on the Way to the Forum,* 1962), and operetta (*A Little Night Music,* 1973), he made his reputation with the dance musical. After *West Side Story,* he wrote the lyrics to Jule Styne's score and Laurents's book for the next Robbins production and perhaps, to this day, the most perfectly achieved dance musical—*Gypsy* (1959). In 1964, Sondheim contributed a score to another, experimental dance musical, choreographed by Herbert Ross— the unsuccessful *Anyone Can Whistle.*

It was also in 1964 that Robbins staged what has thus far proved to be his last Broadway show, *Fiddler on the Roof.* In the two decades since *Fiddler* and Gower Champion's equally triumphant (if less hefty) dance musical of the same year, *Hello, Dolly!,* the dance musical has been furthered by only two men, the director Harold Prince and the choreographer Michael Bennett. Their theatrical careers reached a creative peak, as Robbins's had, when they intersected with Sondheim's. In back-to-back musicals, *Company* (1970) and *Follies* (1971), Prince, Bennett, and Sondheim gave new twists to the Robbins dance-musical tradition.

In a departure from both the Rodgers and Hammerstein and Robbins musicals, *Company* was a largely plotless show in a Brechtian format: It was a series of vignettes on the theme of marriage, and the songs often commented on the action instead of advancing a story. *Follies* took the danced dream sequences pioneered in *Oklahoma!* to their surrealistic apotheosis: A group of neurotic, retired Ziegfeld chorus girls hold a reunion in their old, soon-to-be-demolished theater and bury their pasts after a lengthy Felliniesque flashback transports them back to the fabled showbiz glory days of their youth.

Follies was at once the seminal Sondheim-Prince musical and a dead end. The show's climactic phantasmagoric flashback sequence was a rite of exorcism. Sondheim filled it with songs in the style of old-time musical comedy numbers by Kern and Hammerstein, and others; then, at the sequence's conclusion, he blended them all together in a nightmarish aural-visual spectacle of dissonance and chaos. Both in form and substance, *Follies* seemed to be saying that the musical theater's old traditions were as unsalvageable as the gutted, ghostly theater in which *Follies* was set. But, having made this statement, neither Sondheim, Bennett, nor Prince seemed to know how to move beyond those traditions.

The dance musical could not be further advanced under the Prince-Sondheim auspices—and for a simple reason: There was no longer the essential collaborator needed for the task, a first-class choreographer. After *Follies,* Michael Bennett parted with Prince to go out on his own (with *A Chorus Line,* which further refined staging techniques from *Follies*). Robbins was not about to leave his ballet career to return to Broadway, and neither, needless to say, were the only other master choreographers who had passed through the musical theater, Balanchine and de Mille.

Though Prince hired choreographers for his subsequent Sondheim musicals, they were neither major talents nor major factors in the productions. And even if Bennett had stayed with Sondheim and Prince—or had been succeeded by such roughly comparable (if less visionary) talents as Bob Fosse, Tommy Tune, or Gower Champion—it is far from clear if any of these choreographers could have staged musicals that required a dance vocabulary beyond that of show business. While Robbins, de Mille, and Balanchine were classically trained dance makers, their successors as Broadway director-choreographers were graduates, however brilliant, of the musical-comedy chorus line. If Robbins could choreograph vintage showbiz routines for *Gypsy,* street-gang warfare for *West Side Story,* and shtetl folk rituals for *Fiddler,* his descendants have thus far only mastered the *Gypsy* portion of this spectrum. The last Bennett, Champion, Tune, and Fosse musicals have been *Dreamgirls, 42nd Street, My One and Only,* and *Dancin'*—all either set in showbiz milieus or staged in a showbiz vernacular.

Having grand ambitions for the musical theater but no choreographer to further the dance musical line, Prince and Sondheim then turned to their operatic shows—the rehabilitating 1973 revival of *Candide* (for which Sondheim wrote some new lyrics), *Night Music,* and *Sweeney Todd.* But *Sweeney* was sandwiched between two strange, anomalous musicals, *Pacific Overtures* and *Merrily We Roll Along.* Both were neither dance nor operatic musicals but musical plays that retreated, in their fashion, to the Hammerstein tradition. In retrospect, these two neo-Hammerstein musicals, both failures, can be seen as essential way stations to *Sunday in the Park with George.*

Unsurprisingly, Sondheim and Prince didn't seem comfortable with the musical play form in *Pacific Overtures.* Aspiring to create a Rodgers and Hammerstein musical that in no way resembled a Rodgers and Hammerstein musical, they and the librettist John Weidman fractured the book's narrative to the point of confusing the audience. And as they floundered in dramatic limbo, they seemed to be scrambling for subject matter. How many times could they tell an audience that, to paraphrase a paradigmatic *Night Music* lyric, every day is a little death? In *Pacific Overtures* and then *Sweeney Todd,* they turned to political themes—cultural imperialism, class warfare—but dramatized them with pessimistic variations on Rodgers and Hammerstein's old liberal bromides.

There was passion in Sondheim's music, but it was inaccessible to some, for it seemed to spring from a source other than his identification with the oppressed proletariats of nineteenth-century Japan and England. In none of these musicals, however, did his invention ever flag.

His scores were imaginatively tailored to the needs of the dramatic material, and, unlike Rodgers and Hammerstein, he made no concessions to Broadway taste. As Rodgers had not done in *The King and I,* Sondheim embodied the theme of *Pacific Overtures* in his score by rigorously merging American and Oriental music (however unsettling the sound to Broadway ears). What is not clear is whether the books of *Pacific Overtures* or *Sweeney Todd* (by Hugh Wheeler) merited Sondheim's profligate expenditure of talent. One could argue that these scores sound better on their original cast albums, out of context, than when heard on stage in the shows that contained them.

Sondheim also found that no matter what he did, he was a target for attacks from all sides. A committed theater man, he never, not even in *Sweeney Todd,* took the full plunge into opera, nor would he give in to the conservative idea of show music. He was also outside the pop-music fold. With the rise of rock, songwriters roughly comparable to Sondheim in ambition (such as Laura Nyro or Paul Simon) worked in the pop-music arena, not the theater, and took their sympathetic listeners with them.

Sondheim, dismissed by serious music audiences, reviled by conservative Broadway theater audiences for failing to write "hummable" songs, and unknown to most hip young audiences, inevitably became a cult figure. Of his five musicals during the 1970s, only one, *A Little Night Music,* produced an old-fashioned Broadway standard—"Send in the Clowns"— and, perhaps inevitably, *Night Music* had the largest critical and most widespread popular success of the group. Most of the time, Sondheim was praised for the brilliance of his lyrics and decried for the coldness of his music. It was actually the Prince-Sondheim shows, not the music, that had become cold—they increasingly seemed to be willed into existence rather than deeply felt.

It took the fiasco of the 1981 *Merrily We Roll Along* to jolt Sondheim into *Sunday in the Park.* The analogous Rodgers and Hammerstein project to *Merrily* is *Allegro,* also a failure. Told in *Our Town* style with a contemporary Greek chorus, *Allegro* was about the first thirty-five years in the life of a doctor who is poisoned by big-city success and then redeems himself by returning to the simple values of small-town life. *Merrily* was about a successful Broadway songwriting team that is also spoiled by success—and it, too, was told with an arty, modernized Greek chorus. But, once again, Sondheim's show reversed the tone of the Rodgers and Hammerstein precursor. *Merrily* unfolded in reverse chronology, as did the George S. Kaufman–Moss Hart play that was its source, and ended not with redemption but with defeat. The good values that the characters trade away for success are imprisoned in the past at the musical's conclusion, never to be retrieved.

Miscast, sloppily written, and hideously designed, the production's vulgarity mitigated the feeling of the music. The ugly set, confused narrative transitions, and summer-stock choreography demonstrated that even the once-slick craftsmanship of the Sondheim-Prince musicals had collapsed. Given the sophisticated conceits of the score, *Merrily* has developed a following on the basis of its posthumously released cast album. But on Broadway, it came across as an overfed exercise in self-pity: Sweeney Todd's anger at the English class system was now replaced by the anger of a successful showbiz artist who has to suffer money, fools, and celebrity as if they were Job-like curses.

Merrily also cast a harsh light on the Sondheim-Prince artistic partnership—by ruthlessly exposing how their previous innovations in format and tone had hardened into clichés as rigid as those the two men had once fought. The disillusionment of the showpeople in *Follies* now devolved into contempt for both Broadway and its audience; the Prince-Sondheim musical's signature traits (the interweaving of present and past, the use of choral commentary, the cynical view of all male-female pairings) became as calcified and mechanical as Rodgers and Hammerstein's once-ingenuous optimism had become by the time they wrote their caramelized final shows, *Flower Drum Song* and *The Sound of Music*.

Even the pastiche musical gags had an unpleasant edge. In one *Merrily* song, "Opening Doors," the songwriter-hero is chastened by a vulgar producer for not writing a commercial score for a Broadway musical. Echoing many criticisms Sondheim has suffered over the years, the producer sings to the hero: "There's not a tune you can hum . . . / Why can't you throw 'em a crumb? / What's wrong with letting 'em tap their toes a bit? / I'll let you know when Stravinsky has a hit—Give me some melody!"

The lyric recalls that of a Rodgers and Hammerstein song for their backstage musical *Me and Juliet* in 1953. In that song, "Intermission Talk," an audience at a Broadway musical criticizes Rodgers and Hammerstein's innovations much as the producer in *Merrily* knocks Sondheim's: "They don't write music any more / Like the old Vienna valses! The guy today who writes a score / Doesn't know what schmaltz is."

But "Intermission Talk" is good-natured. In Sondheim's "Opening Doors," the vulgar producer hums his idea of a good Broadway show tune—and it turns out to be Rodgers and Hammerstein's "Some Enchanted Evening." One felt that Sondheim was mocking his mentor, even as *Merrily* itself was a decadent descendant of a Rodgers and Hammerstein show.

Merrily We Roll Along expired in three weeks, seemingly bringing the Sondheim age of the musical to an end. He had run through the dance musical, the operatic musical, and the musical play—only to end up, in *Merrily*, with an insular, self-martyring diatribe that blamed Broadway and possibly even Hammerstein for his own creative and commercial frustrations. Even the score of *Merrily*, which developed musical themes in the same reverse-chronology format as the libretto's plot, seemed a formal retreat. The producer's admonition to the hero notwithstanding, *Merrily* contained more traditional Broadway melodies than most Sondheim musicals.

Sunday in the Park with George grows directly out of the ashes of *Merrily*, and rebels against it. Catastrophe may have inspired Sondheim to revise his thinking about the Broadway musical. The first received notion to be jettisoned was the Broadway ethic itself. For the first time since a short-lived musical adaptation of Aristophanes' *The Frogs* at the Yale Repertory Theatre a decade ago, Sondheim initiated a musical outside the Broadway system: *Sunday* began its career at Playwrights Horizons, a nonprofit 150-seat theater Off Broadway. This allowed the piece a far longer gestation period than Broadway economics permit and also enabled Sondheim to have an uncharacteristically intimate involvement with the day-by-day production process.

Sunday also marked the first time in years that Sondheim did a musical without Prince or any other Broadway veterans as collaborators. The link to Playwrights Horizons was the thirty-five-year-old James Lapine, who had never previously worked in the commercial theater. At Playwrights, Lapine had directed the most talented new Off Broadway musical to emerge in the 1980s, William Finn's *March of the Falsettos*. He brought Sondheim the gifted young *Falsettos* orchestrator Michael Starobin and a new designer, Tony Straiges. But, more important, in his libretto and direction, Lapine gave *Sunday* the whiff of a sensibility unknown to the Broadway musical.

In his play *Twelve Dreams*, produced at the Public Theater in 1981, Lapine had written and staged a Carl Jung–inspired drama in which the associative, meditative "story" was told in terms more suggestive of the Sam Shepard school of dreamlike playwriting than either the well-made or Brechtian plays that had determined the shape of past Sondheim musicals. Lapine's characters were not so much people as figures in a theatrical composition drawn from the unconscious. The same is true in *Sunday*—whose foremost innovation may well be the redefining of plot and characters as they've been known in most Broadway musicals since *Show Boat*.

This radical step is not a whimsical one—or a gimmick—but a the-atrical response to the musical's subject. Seurat's painting, *La Grande Jatte*, may be inhabited by people strolling in a real park, but it tells no story and leaves its figures uncharacterized (indeed, expressionless). The subject of *La Grande Jatte* is art itself; it's a pictorial manifesto that melds pure form, color, and light into a pleasing, harmonic synthesis.

The subject of Act 1 of *Sunday* is the process by which such art is cre-ated. Accordingly, Sondheim and Lapine tell their story in a theatrical manner equivalent to Seurat's own esthetic method. The characters of the painting are on stage—as invented by the authors—but we see them through Seurat's impersonal eyes. ("I am not painting faces," he ex-plains.) They are mostly fodder for his composition—forms to be atom-ized into abstractly patterned "dots" of color. Seurat even seems largely oblivious to the two models to whom he is intimately related—his mother and his lover, Dot.

As the painter sketches his figures from his dispassionate point of view, so Sondheim and Lapine dramatize their characters just as sketch-ily. Once the various plots start to approach their Act 1 climax, they end abruptly. The act concludes with Seurat completing *La Grande Jatte*, and, as he does, the fractious, petty characters all freeze in the tranquil postures of the painting: Transformed into the painter's essentially non-narrative art, the characters are removed from their own narratives. In defiance of a Broadway musical audience's usual expectations, the sto-ries never do reach completion—and one also waits in vain to find any dancing. The most telling dab of choreography occurs when Dot, antic-ipating a night on the town with George, fantasizes about being a dancer in "the Follies." Her dance ends almost as soon as it's begun—as if to say Sondheim has himself moved beyond his own *Follies*, his last dance mu-sical. As Seurat valued stillness in art, so Lapine stages *Sunday* at a lan-guorous, contemplative pace that is the antithesis of the razzle-dazzle Broadway musical.

In keeping with this style, Sondheim has written a score that is a more austere experiment in form than even his unconventional past scores. Though the *Sunday* songs may sometimes express a character's feelings, the songs play off one another as the colors do on Seurat's canvas. As the separate specks of color mix, fuse, and intensify optically on a viewer's retina, so repeated musical and lyrical phrases in various songs merge in the theatergoer's ear to produce a cumulative, shimmering composition. This technique is dictated not by the musical's narrative but by George's artistic process, stated in the musical's opening lines: "White. A blank page or canvas. The challenge: Bring order to the whole. Through de-sign, composition, tension, balance, light, and harmony."

When Seurat first recites these lines, Lapine and the designers transform an initially all-white stage—the theater's blank canvas—into a rough draft of *La Grande Jatte*. As George progresses further on his canvas in subsequent scenes, Sondheim matches the musical's visual technique by remaking and reshaping his own phrases in imitation of the painter's constant refinement of colors and forms.

As Seurat used eleven basic colors, so Sondheim uses a core group of musical phrases and words recurrently in different contexts. And, like Seurat's colors, which appear to change in hue according to which colors surround them on the canvas, Sondheim's basic units of expression change in meaning with each appearance. "God, it's hot up here," sings Dot in the opening scene, as she chafes at posing for her lover. Later, while working at his canvas in his studio, Seurat expresses his frenzy and exhaustion in the phrase "Hot hot hot it's hot in here." But when the painting is at last finished at the end of Act 1, the cast sings in ensemble harmony for the first time, and the uncomfortable heat has been relieved by the harmonic order of Seurat's creation: The once-hotheaded bickerers in the park are now the serene forms of *La Grande Jatte*, singing of "pausing on a Sunday by the cool blue triangular water." Still another variation on the theme occurs at the outset of Act 2, in a song titled "It's Hot Up Here." One could just as soon follow other repeated words or phrases straight through the show—"connection," "move on," "Sunday," "tree," "color and light," "I'm not surprised"—as well as the variations on the recurrent musical phrases that accompany them.

This process continues in the second act, after *La Grande Jatte* is completed and George is dead. Leaping ahead to 1984, *Sunday* turns its attention to an American artist, also named George, who may be Seurat's great-grandson and who makes multimedia sculptures prized by the present-day art world. But the "dots" this George uses are not Seurat's: He must build up his public image "dot by dot"—with dabs of "hype"—to ensure the continued patronage of the curators and foundations needed to support his costly computer-run compositions. In other words, George is working in a commercial art world that resembles Broadway—and he is suffering a crisis akin to Sondheim's after *Merrily*. "Art isn't easy," he sings. "Overnight you're a trend / You're the right combination— / Then the trend's at an end, / You're suddenly last year's sensation."

Act 2 is about how George reawakens and stretches his artistic vision by leaving the mercantile art world and past collaborators behind to return to his roots. "If you want your work to reach fruition," he sings, "What you need's a link with your tradition." That voyage takes him back to Seurat's Parisian park of *La Grande Jatte*—the site of the modern George's artistic and possibly genealogical "family tree." Revivified, he decides to "move on" and make "things that will be new." In turn, *Sunday* is the product of a similar spiritual voyage and breakthrough for Sondheim. This musical is in one sense a return to Sondheim's own "family tree"—for, with its carefully crafted if untraditional libretto, it is a reconciliation with the musical-play heritage that Hammerstein willed him forty years ago. But it also moves on to something new, because Lapine's libretto reflects the revolutionary changes that have occurred in American drama since Hammerstein's day.

"Connect, George, connect," George tells himself—and that's what he and Sondheim finally do. *Sunday* allows Sondheim at last to channel his own passion into a musical that is not about marriage, class inequities, or other things he doesn't seem sincerely to care about, but is instead about what does matter to him—art itself, and his own predicament as a driven artist whose austere vision, like Seurat's, is often incorrectly judged as heartless.

This is why *Sunday,* albeit the most demanding of the Sondheim musicals, is the first of them to touch audiences as profoundly as the Rodgers and Hammerstein shows touched audiences of another era. Theatergoers always know when they're being addressed with burning passion: When *La Grande Jatte* snaps into its finished form on stage, the spectacle is more dramatic and emotionally transporting than any conventional story Sondheim has ever tried to tell. And if Sondheim sometimes seems to be answering his own critics, as he did in *Merrily,* he is elevating the tone and substance of the argument from the sour-grapes, showbiz gripes of the previous show to the impassioned arena of esthetic debate. When a salon painter dismisses Seurat's canvases as being "all mind, no heart" in an early song in *Sunday,* Sondheim doesn't respond with snide wisecracks. "I am not hiding behind my canvas," George insists later, "I am living in it."

The show's entire fabric argues, by example, that just as much heart can go into the making of cerebral modern art as into romantic art (whether that romantic art be representational paintings or conventional, sentimental musicals). The case is brought to its finest point in a moving song called "Beautiful," in which Seurat's aged mother, who decries the newly constructed Eiffel Tower as an ugly portent of a fast-arriving modern esthetic order, is sweetly instructed by her son: "All things are beautiful, Mother. . . . Pretty is what changes. What the eye arranges is what is beautiful."

In the same song, Seurat tells his mother, "You watch while I revise the world." Still, if Sondheim is revising Broadway, he isn't leaving it entirely behind. It's because *Sunday* does retain an elaborate text, with many considerable spells of spoken dialogue, that it is not a new-wave opera of the Robert Wilson–Philip Glass breed any more than it is a traditional opera. It is, quite clearly, a Broadway musical. But *Sunday,* not to mention its success with audiences, blurs old definitions—those that separate Broadway and Off Broadway, show music and serious music, commercial entertainment and art, the theater and the musical theater.

Whether *Sunday* will prove to be a glorious anomaly or a pathway to even more adventurous musicals is anyone's guess. Much will depend on what young artists follow Sondheim into the musical theater—and on what Sondheim himself does next. Reportedly, Sondheim is already at work on new projects with Lapine—a sign that he is stepping up the pace at which he has written new musicals in the past.

Having broken through to genuine autobiographical concerns in *Sunday,* Sondheim may be ready to launch a sophisticated attack on passions (starting with death and sex) that have been superficially toyed with in *Company, Follies,* and *Sweeney Todd.* Much depends on his continued collaboration with librettists, whether Lapine or others, who open up such subjects in part by liberating them from conventional plots.

The commercial success of *Sunday,* meanwhile, may prompt other producers to take a chance on more ambitious shows. Operatic musicals and dance musicals could yet return to Broadway in new, contemporary incarnations, should *Sunday* pave the way for iconoclastic composers, choreographers, and performance artists to experiment in the commercial theater.

Why should anyone care about the esthetic upheavals caused by a Broadway musical? A few years ago, in a published reminiscence about Oscar Hammerstein, Sondheim offered his own view. Hammerstein was a "giant," Sondheim wrote, because he "changed the texture of the American musical theater forever, first with Kern, then with Rodgers. And to change that means not only to change musical theater all over the world, but to change all American theater as well, because musical theater has affected playwriting profoundly and permanently."

It's debatable whether Hammerstein changed all American theater, but that has been the great hope for Broadway's one original theatrical form throughout its history. In *Sunday in the Park with George,* Sondheim, the inheritor of that history, has changed the texture of the musical as radically as Hammerstein once did in *Show Boat* and *Oklahoma!*—but, even more than Hammerstein did, he has built a bridge between the musical and the more daring playwriting of his time. Should Sondheim keep moving on and moving others with him, he may yet become the giant he saw his teacher to be—one who leaves our theater profoundly and permanently changed.

WHOOPI GOLDBERG
LYCEUM THEATRE, OCTOBER 25, 1984

Certain facts are not in doubt about Whoopi Goldberg, the comic actress and monologist who has brought her one-woman show to Broadway. Ms. Goldberg is a warm, almost childlike performer with a sweet clown's face, an elastic body, a sensitive social conscience, and a joyous stage name. What is in question is whether she yet has the range of material and talent to sustain a night of theater. Don't be surprised if you leave the Lyceum feeling more enthusiastic about Whoopi Goldberg, the personality, than *Whoopi Goldberg,* the show.

During the course of her sporadically entertaining ninety-minute presentation (plus intermission), the actress creates six principal characters, all social misfits. With only a simple pants-and-shirt costume, a few props, and an empty stage (superbly lighted by Jennifer Tipton), Ms. Goldberg can instantly transform herself from a jivey, feral black male drug addict to a whiter-than-white twelve-year-old Los Angeles Valley Girl.

Impersonating a deformed, disabled woman later on—"This is not a disco body," she explains—the actress suddenly untangles her crippled physique and voice to act out the character's touching, balletic fantasy of being "normal." It is also endearing to watch Ms. Goldberg don a hat and puff up her cheeks to play a proud, aged, gummy-mouthed bum lost in fading memories of tap dancing with the Nicholas Brothers.

Such high points notwithstanding, the suspicion persists—at least to a first-time Goldberg watcher—that a still-developing fringe-theater act has been padded and stretched to meet the supposed demands of a Broadway occasion. Ms. Goldberg, much like Lily Tomlin, wants to make us laugh, cry, and think. Yet her jokes, however scatological in language, can be mild and overextended, and her moments of pathos are often too mechanically ironic and maudlin to provoke. At least twice, Ms. Goldberg announces that she doesn't intend for her putatively threatening outcast characters to make the audience "nervous." How one wishes that such disclaimers were actually necessary.

Take, for instance, the opening routine about the junkie. Ms. Goldberg imagines that the character would fly from New York to Amsterdam and end up paying a solemn visit to the Anne Frank museum. This is an inventive premise, but the overstuffed execution runs nearly a half hour. Part of the excess is wholly gratuitous. When Ms. Goldberg strings together wisecracks about cold airline food or sends up the television series *Bonanza* as dubbed into German, she's reviving Bob Newhart and Shelley Berman stand-up shtick of twenty years ago. A more exasperating form of self-indulgence tames the sketch's potentially startling dénouement. The spiritual communion that the stoned black man achieves with a Nazi victim loses its impact once Ms. Goldberg allows her previously inarticulate character to hammer in the message—even to the point of explicating Anne Frank's most famous diary entry.

Though the other segments are briefer, they all go on too long—and they nearly all follow the same primitive dramatic formula. The sketches usually start out friskily and then lurch toward a sentimental trick ending. Sometimes the sentimental conclusion is downbeat—the dippy Valley Girl is heading toward an abortion—but more often it is uplifting: The deformed woman finds love, and the old dancer invites the audience to hold hands in brotherhood.

The epiphanies that soon result—"Normal is in the eye of the beholder" or "Take somebody by the hand and you are free"—are no less platitudinous for being declared in earnest. Ms. Goldberg breaks through the homilies only in the ingenuous and compact final sketch, in which she portrays a nine-year-old black girl facing the realization that she'll never be white, blue-eyed, and blond.

Like many young writers and performers, Ms. Goldberg hasn't mastered the art of letting the content of her material emerge elliptically from its specific details. By repeatedly shifting from diffuse clowning to omniscient preaching, she vitiates her characters' spontaneity and manages to make even her deepest feelings sound contrived. One need only examine the work of Ms. Tomlin and Richard Pryor—or, to be less invidious, that of such Off Broadway–spawned quick-change performers as Charles Ludlam and Eric Bogosian—to see that the most stinging comic cameos wrap any message seamlessly (and subversively) within the laughter.

Ms. Goldberg's show has been "supervised" by a master of comedy, Mike Nichols. The supervision doesn't seem to have been particularly tough-minded. Besides failing to edit and shape the sketches, Mr. Nichols permits his star to step out of character with long, coy takes acknowledging the audience's response to the better punch lines. Perhaps the director was so taken by the actress's charm—as who wouldn't be—that he feared any tampering might blunt it. Whatever the explanation, Whoopi Goldberg's liberating spirit fills up the theater, even as her considerable comic promise is left waiting to be fully unlocked.

ROMANCE LANGUAGE
PLAYWRIGHTS HORIZONS, NOVEMBER 15, 1984

To write a play about the history and meaning of the American imagination, one must have dreams as big as the territory. For all that's sloppy, juvenile, and exasperating in *Romance Language,* the new Peter Parnell play receiving an exquisite production at Playwrights Horizons, it is the creation of a bold writer with an abundant vision.

It takes guts to concoct a comedy whose principal characters include Walt Whitman, Emily Dickinson, Henry David Thoreau, and Ralph Waldo Emerson. But Mr. Parnell aims higher still: He's not just portraying these culture heroes on stage, but trying to pick up where they left off. *Romance Language* is its young author's cheeky attempt to write his own, up-to-date *Walden, Leaves of Grass,* and *Adventures of Huckleberry Finn.* He can't deliver on such grand aspirations, but it's amazing how often he stakes original claim to this hallowed ground.

Set in 1876, *Romance Language* starts off as an irreverent reverie in the revisionist vein of the critic Leslie Fiedler. Mr. Parnell imagines that Whitman (Al Carmines) and Huck Finn (Jon Matthews) would go West together, arriving in Montana just in time for Little Bighorn. We also witness a previously unrecorded sexual liaison between Louisa May Alcott (Frances Conroy) and General Custer (William Converse-Roberts), not to mention a tumultuous lesbian union of Dickinson (Valerie Mahaffey) and the barnstorming actress Charlotte Cushman (Cynthia Harris). Such is Mr. Parnell's antic bent of mind that Dickinson not only leaves Amherst but ends up touring as Juliet opposite her lover's Romeo.

Some of the gags are funny, others flat. When Mr. Parnell goes out on the highest limbs, he can fall with a thud. Yet, however up-and-down the quality of the jokes, the substance of *Romance Language* keeps blossoming. Like Whitman, this playwright wants to embrace and give voice to an entire nation. With ever-increasing urgency and passion, Mr. Parnell asks: What happened to our writers' ideal of a democratic America and how can it be reclaimed today?

To dramatize that question, the playwright brings two conflicting nineteenth-century ideologies—one literary, one militaristic—into explosive fusion. It's not happenstance that he sends all his writers out West with the cavalry. If the frontier was the repository of our writers' best hopes for an egalitarian society, it was also the land where those hopes were buried by genocide and greed. Once Mr. Parnell's characters reach Montana after intermission, their transcendental fantasies are washed away in an apocalyptic flood of bloodletting.

Even so, as Huck says, the ghosts of the country's past don't "have to bog us down." Out of the ashes of Custer's last stand, Mr. Parnell reawakens the spiritual legacy symbolically defeated there. "If the country's a dream," says Whitman to Huck in a posthumous epilogue, "let us dream it right here." To which Mr. Parnell seems to add: Let us dream it now. Were we to listen to the men and women who most eloquently envisioned our country's soul, we might yet create a society where "one person," however isolated from the crowd, can feel at home in "a nation of persons."

The solitary individuals championed by Mr. Parnell belong to sexual minorities as well as racial and intellectual ones: At his Little Bighorn, there are nearly as many new women and homosexuals among the casualties as there are Indians. And, as the author slaps a twentieth-century social framework onto the past, he does the same with the play's language. The words of the legendary writers are freely intermingled with contemporary vernacular—much as the composer Jack Eric Williams remakes traditional period music in his lush incidental score.

The play's picaresque structure has its own literary tenor. From the opening, *Peter Pan*–like scene, in which Whitman dreams up Huck's visitation to his Brooklyn flat, *Romance Language* is a spiraling series of interlocking dreams—erotic, fantastic, and patriotic. Figuratively, and sometimes literally, the play is a raft ride down Mark Twain's hallucinatory river—a stream, as it's said, "going in the direction of our thoughts."

How one wishes that Mr. Parnell had better edited those thoughts: At least a third of his sixteen scenes are repetitious, inessential, or excessively cute. Thanks to Sheldon Larry's staging, however, *Romance Language* only occasionally stands completely still. Working with glorious sets, costumes, and lighting—by Loren Sherman, Sheila McLamb, and Jeff Davis—the director sweeps us buoyantly through Walden Pond, old-time theaters, a Sioux camp, a gruesome battlefield (with battles staged by B. H. Barry), and, finally, a heaven that might have been painted by Jasper Johns. The front curtain depicts an American map, and eventually we feel that we've crossed that landscape, as the characters have, on a crystalline, star-filled night when anything can happen.

Mr. Larry's cast is uniformly fine, but special note must be made of Mr. Carmines, whose frisky yet paternal Whitman provides an essential center of wisdom and gravity, and of Ms. Mahaffey, whose dizzy belle of Amherst is a new comic high point in the actress's already lofty young career. One could just as soon talk about Ms. Conroy (whose Alcott is anything but a "little woman"), Ms. Harris, Mr. Converse-Roberts, and, among many others, Marc Castle as a poignant, uncelebrated sexual pioneer.

At evening's end, the entire company at last reaches the same destination, where everyone babbles at once in language as varied as the land they inhabit. It's the sound of Whitman's America singing, of course. And, while Mr. Parnell doesn't always keep the song going, he does leave us with an inspiring sense of how beautiful both its cacophonies and harmonies were meant to be.

≡ *Peter Parnell was one of a number of talented playwrights championed by Playwrights Horizons—along with Harry Kondoleon, Ted Tally, Jonathan Reynolds (a friend, whose very funny Hollywood sendup,* Geniuses, *I didn't review), Mark O'Donnell, and Keith Reddin—who wrote consistently interesting plays that never quite broke through to the general public in the way those of fellow Playwrights Horizons writers Wendy Wasserstein, Alfred Uhry, and A. R. Gurney did. Reynolds and Tally turned increasingly to screenwriting (Tally won an Oscar for* The Silence of the Lambs*); O'Donnell became better known for his fiction than his theatrical work; Kondoleon died. Reddin and Parnell remain devoted to the theater—Parnell most recently as the author of a widely produced marathon adaptation of John Irving's novel* The Cider House Rules.

ACCIDENTAL DEATH OF AN ANARCHIST
BELASCO THEATRE, NOVEMBER 16, 1984

Until the State Department at last lifted its ban and granted him a visa this month, the leftist Italian playwright Dario Fo was deemed too incendiary to be admitted into the United States. Theatergoers who now visit the first Broadway production of a Fo work, *Accidental Death of an Anarchist,* can't be blamed if they wonder what all the fuss was about. The farce at the Belasco is considerably less biting than the average David Letterman monologue and not nearly as funny.

This is an evening of strained silliness that defies even the Herculean, high-flying efforts of its star, the gifted English actor Jonathan Pryce, to galvanize it. Mr. Pryce, a perfect-pitch mimic, often seems to be playing all the Marx Brothers at once: Every time there's a lull in the proceedings—which is to say during all of Act 1 and most of Act 2—he will instantaneously try on a new wig, accent, costume, and nutty personality.

Mr. Pryce's talent and ingenuity are boundless, yet his performance, like everything else, leaves us more exhausted than amused. You have to be a comic genius, not merely a terrific actor, to get laughs without material.

Mr. Fo's play was inspired by an unsavory incident that actually happened in Milan in 1969. An anarchist train worker, charged in a terrorist bombing, mysteriously fell to his death from a window at the police headquarters where he was in custody. The anarchist's defenestration may have been an accident or a suicide—or, just possibly, an officially sanctioned murder designed to cover up the government's own malevolent role in the bombing.

Mr. Pryce plays a lunatic confidence man, known only as "The Fool," who visits the site of the anarchist's fall. Described as a "histrio-maniac," this Fool is a brilliant quick-change impostor: By impersonating a variety of characters, including a high-level judicial authority and a bishop, he tricks the addled police into reopening the anarchist's case and revealing all the doctored transcripts, false alibis, and undercover schemes that attended it.

Because the real truth is apparent early on—the civil servants on view are all power-greedy fascists—it's hard to get too excited about the Fool's painfully slow-starting investigation. *Accidental Death* rises or falls on the jokes that attend Mr. Pryce's various ruses. Many of the gags are leaden Monty Python knockoffs of an apolitical nature. The bigger knee-slappers include a line about "nitroglycerine suppositories," references to the menstrual cycle, and a long sequence featuring a misplaced glass eye.

It's possible that not all of these comic inventions are Mr. Fo's own—and that his native, populist theatrical style has been sanitized for New York consumption. The Broadway *Accidental Death* isn't a strict translation of Mr. Fo's script or a transplant of the hit 1979 London version (which I didn't see), but a new adaptation written by the American playwright Richard Nelson last season for Washington's Arena Stage.

Whatever else he may have done, Mr. Nelson is surely responsible for the many American jokes that are inserted willy-nilly throughout. While the play's improvisational style can certainly accommodate such interjections, Mr. Nelson's contributions are unsophisticated and out-of-date. The butts of his topical one-liners include television game shows, money-market accounts, Mobil Oil Corporation grants, and, I kid you not, "Whip Inflation Now" buttons. There are also so many obsolete digs at Ronald Reagan's campaign gaffes that one wonders if Mr. Nelson is aware that the election has already been held.

The innocuous American jokes don't blend into the play's Italian context—or illustrate any trenchant connections between American and

Italian political nefariousness. What they mainly do is wreck the play's farcical structure and jolt both audience and cast out of its intended grip. Nor does either the author or the adapter use satire to shake up the audience. Mr. Fo takes a strong stand against political corruption and hypocrisy—and who is going to disagree with him? Mr. Nelson pulls punches, picks safe targets, and never risks offending anyone. Even his wisecracks about the president are rarely tougher than those Mr. Reagan has made about himself.

The frantic, often inelegantly executed slapstick bits were presumably devised by the director, Douglas C. Wager. The characters repeatedly stamp on one another's feet, and, when all else fails, don women's wigs and march around singing, "Look for the union label." Yet, for all these shenanigans, the director never figures out how to use the clown Bill Irwin, who plays one of the Milanese policemen. Why cast Mr. Irwin, the most accomplished physical comic our theater has produced in years, and then give him virtually nothing to do?

The other officials are competently played by Gerry Bamman, Joe Grifasi, and Raymond Serra. For reasons that seem as baffling to her as they are to us, Patti LuPone drops by for a thankless cameo appearance after intermission. *Accidental Death* is always Mr. Pryce's show, and from his charming opening monologue to his climactic appearance in an array of prosthetic devices, he never stops working to make us merry. Were anyone to try to revoke his visa, I'd make a federal case of it.

≡ *Four misused talents—Jonathan Pryce, Patti LuPone, Bill Irwin, and Dario Fo—went down in this classic example of why (toothless) satire closes on Saturday night on Broadway. But the last sentence of my review proved unwittingly prophetic (see "Jonathan Pryce vs. Actors' Equity," August 10, 1990, page 755). Fo later did perform in New York in authentic, un-Americanized recitals of his work. In 1997, he won the Nobel Prize for Literature.*

A PLAY OF GIANTS
YALE REPERTORY THEATRE, NEW HAVEN, DECEMBER 11, 1984

Political satire hardly exists in the American theater anymore, and when it does, it's so mild that audiences need never run for cover. That's why it's uncommonly bracing to encounter *A Play of Giants*, the lethal Wole Soyinka comedy now having its world premiere at the Yale

Repertory Theatre. Mr. Soyinka, the Nigerian playwright, poet, novelist, and essayist, spares no one in this farcical fantasy about African dictators at loose in New York. The first, second, and third worlds, eastern and western divisions, are all mowed down in the relentless comic barrage.

Before anyone grabs the next train to New Haven, however, an important caveat must be added. If Mr. Soyinka is arguably Africa's foremost literary renaissance man, he does not seem particularly gifted as a director of comedy. He has staged *A Play of Giants* himself, with little flair and a mostly lackluster cast; the production, unlike the text, can appear inert. One leaves the Yale Rep feeling that the play is a time bomb that, while alive and ticking, has yet to be detonated.

The evening's premise is as wicked as can be. Mr. Soyinka has imagined that four power-crazed "life presidents" have gathered at the Bugara Embassy to the United Nations to sit for a statuary group portrait being crafted by a sculptor imported from Madame Tussaud's London waxworks. The host of this absurd conclave is the Bugaran dictator, Field Marshal Kamini—with Bugara and Kamini proving transparent stand-ins for Uganda and its former strongman, Idi Amin. The remaining three "giants" on display are similarly undisguised caricatures of past and present real-life tyrants who have variously terrorized and looted the Central African Republic (Jean-Bedel Bokassa), Zaire (Mobutu Sese Seko), and Equatorial Guinea (Nguema Masie Biyoto).

But it is "big daddy" Kamini, played by Roger Robinson, who dominates. At once a mischievous child and a brutal psychopath, Kamini is Amin down to his bizarre declarations of love for other world leaders ("If Fidel Castro is a woman, I will marry him") and his weird paranoiac explosions. Told by Bugara's chief banker that his country's indiscriminately minted currency is as worthless as "toilet paper," Kamini accuses the man of being in conspiratorial cahoots with the World Bank and has his head smashed into a toilet in full view of the embassy retinue (and the audience). Kamini also whimsically insists that the United Nations give permanent display to the forthcoming statues—a request that ultimately sparks a violent international contretemps that is the fulcrum of the play's plot.

This work could only have been written by an African such as Mr. Soyinka, who spent nearly two years in solitary confinement on trumped-up charges during the Nigerian Civil War of the 1960s. The anger in *A Play of Giants* is bottomless—yet the author miraculously transmutes it into gallows humor. One of the play's "giants" rationalizes a massacre of his country's supposedly subversive schoolchildren by calmly arguing, "Better the loss of a few children than the poisoning of their growth by the horror of rebellion." This logic is grotesquely funny in itself, but it is then topped by Kamini's loony, nonsensical response: "All great men love children, like Hitler. I see photographs of him kissing children, like me." One doesn't know whether to laugh or scream.

Even more impressive is Mr. Soyinka's evenhanded political analysis. Kamini travels with a homegrown academic and speechwriter who constantly explains away "aberrations in African leadership" as being the product of colonialism's "economic and historical conditions." The playwright will have none of such apologist sentiments, and neither will he allow Kamini to get away with branding his critics as "racists." To Mr. Soyinka, megalomania is a psychosis, sexual and narcotic in its symptoms, that transcends race, political creed, or historical circumstances; Kamini and his cohorts may exploit the rhetoric of black liberation and anti-imperialism to justify their mass murders and tortures, but there is no mistaking these leaders for anything other than deranged thugs.

Just the same, the author demands that the rest of the world accept responsibility for complicity in what has happened—and what still happens. In the play's published introduction, Mr. Soyinka reminds us that Amin was "sustained in power at various periods" by nations as varied as the United States and the Soviet Union, Great Britain and Libya—as well as by "the cheerleaders among the intelligentsia of the African continent and the Black Caucuses of the United States." The playwright accordingly provides an ecumenical, clownish parade of such Kamini sympathizers on stage—among them, American and Soviet diplomats, a leftist Scandinavian journalist, and a black American mayor.

In Mr. Soyinka's view, these representative power brokers are all guilty of ignoring the dictator's human-rights abuses when it suits their geopolitical or ideological ends. Not until Kamini's excesses threaten to undermine or embarrass his patrons' self-interests is he at last shunned by the left and right, blacks and whites. The only character of integrity on stage is the sculptor, who might well represent the playwright: In the evening's final image, the artist, severely wounded but undaunted, continues to work as bullets and explosions rock the embassy.

Fans of Mr. Soyinka's best-known work in the United States—his bucolic 1981 memoir, *Ake: The Years of Childhood*—may be stunned by this work's savage tone. But with the principal and essential exception of Mr. Robinson's alternately buffoonish and blood-curdling Kamini, that tone is perfunctorily served here. Of the nineteen supporting players, only Ray Aranha's professor and Christopher Noth's sculptor leave firm impressions; the staging, which should have the manic intensity of *Dr. Strangelove,* too often proves sedentary and static. *A Play of Giants* is a sleeping giant of satirical theater that another production could—and, in good conscience, must—wake up.

≡*Alas,* A Play of Giants *was never realized in New York; the one Soyinka play that did make it,* Death and the King's Horseman, *was a failure at Lincoln Center in 1987—again because the author insisted on directing his own work, this time in an even larger, more highly populated production in which he was totally at sea. Presumably it's hard for producers to say no to Nobel laureates who fashion themselves as directors.*

A DAY IN THE DEATH OF JOE EGG
HAFT THEATRE, JANUARY 7, 1985

Theatergoers are not likely to think about Jim Dale and Stockard Channing in quite the same way ever again after *A Day in the Death of Joe Egg,* the Peter Nichols play that has brought them into perfect harmony at the Haft Theatre.

Mr. Dale is best known in New York for his high-flying acrobatics in the entertainments *Scapino* and *Barnum.* Ms. Channing, whose talents were submerged in three flop plays last year, is most widely remembered for her ditsy appearances in trivial movies and television series. We can forget about all that now. In this Roundabout Theatre Company revival directed by Arvin Brown, Ms. Channing and Mr. Dale may make us laugh, but the humor is a form of protective coloring. *Joe Egg* tells of the most painful kind of marital breakup—one that even love can't prevent—and the stars tear through it with a naked intimacy that is as compelling as any acting we've seen this season.

The subject of *Joe Egg* is often thought to be infirmity, not marriage—which may explain why this disturbing, funny play, the breakthrough work by the author of *Privates on Parade* and *Passion,* lingered only a few months in its original West End and Broadway productions of 1967 and 1968. The confusion is understandable: Mr. Nichols's title refers not to Bri and Sheila, the middle-class English couple at center stage, but to their twelve-year-old child Josephine, eponymously nicknamed Joe Egg.

The daughter is an incurably brain-damaged spastic who spends much of the evening in a wheelchair, lolling about in the blind, wordless, incontinent state she has always known. Yet even so, *Joe Egg* is not a precursor of the many sentimental whose-life-is-it-anyway plays that have followed it. Mr. Nichols puts Joe Egg (Tenney Walsh) on stage simply as a fact of life—only one of the many horrifying, inexplicable facts of life in a world supposedly governed by a divine plan. Given such unalterable facts, the playwright then asks, how do we go on?

Sheila and Bri don't sit around crying; they usually tell jokes. Nor do they debate any possible "solutions" to Joe Egg's plight; they've long ago decided against institutionalization and euthanasia, in favor of keeping the girl at home. Sometimes they pick through the past: Sheila guiltily wonders if her premarital promiscuity somehow produced Joe Egg, and both parents wonder if their child was maimed by incompetent doctors. But mostly, Bri and Sheila just cling tightly to their own respective ways of coping with the present.

Those methods are antithetical. Bri, a schoolteacher who once dreamed of being an artist, makes endless wisecracks about the "vegetable" whose diapers he constantly changes. He has stopped looking for parables and explanations that might rationalize Joe Egg's suffering; he'd rather believe in nothing than "a lot of lies." Sheila still has faith. As Bri explains—with awe, not cynicism—his wife is a "truly integrated person" who "embraces every living thing."

Contrary as the couple's philosophies may be, they are also complementary. Mr. Nichols has written Act 1 of *Joe Egg*, as he has some of his subsequent plays, as a quasi-Brechtian music-hall routine: Bri and Sheila chattily confide in us from the downstage edge of their living room, as if they were a Midlands George Burns and Gracie Allen exchanging well-practiced shtick on their front porch. As Mr. Dale recalls the nightmare of the child's birth, he does jolly burlesque impersonations, firm in accents and postures, of a German pediatrician and a hip, patronizingly supportive clergyman. Ms. Channing responds with a straight man's knowing, encouraging smiles and, occasionally, a bit of her own: To explain how Joe Egg's brain malfunctions, she mimics a harassed telephone switchboard operator at a company appropriately named Universal Shafting.

These two actors have never worked together before, but they seem lifelong partners. The strong bond between them, both of sympathy and sexuality, suggests that Sheila and Bri have the ideal marriage, if not the ideal family. The couple's disagreements are loving conflicts which neither spouse tries to win; if Sheila can't stop enjoying even Bri's sickest, Thalidomide-tinged gags, Bri can't stop adoring Sheila's simple candor and utter lack of self-pity.

No wonder it's devastating when the relationship starts to fall apart. What makes our sorrow even greater is Mr. Nichols's refusal to pin the couple's rupture directly on Joe Egg. "Everyone is damaged in some way," Bri tells us—and it is the husband's infirmity, not his daughter's, that wrecks the fabric of a marriage. Like his child, the boyishly middle-aged Bri can never grow up: He wants to be the only "spoiled, coddled baby" in the household, and he's jealous of Joe's claims on Sheila's affections.

"Our marriage might have worked as well as most if Joe hadn't happened," Bri says. We're not so sure. If the marriage in *Joe Egg* is put to the cruelest imaginable test, Mr. Nichols is asking tough questions about the nature of emotional responsibility, of giving and loving, of faith and defeat, that challenge and trouble us no matter what kind of children we may or may not have at home.

Mr. Brown has directed many Nichols plays at New Haven's Long Wharf Theatre and in New York, but this one is the first, in my experience, that he's gotten exactly right. His production is different from, but no less valid than, Michael Blakemore's Broadway staging, which starred Albert Finney and Zena Walker. The onstage band, which punctuated the jokes, has been removed; the tone is more reflective than harsh. The sporadic Act 2 lulls are bolstered by the amusing yet human performances of Gary Waldhorn and Joanna Gleason as posh, hypocritical neighbors who try to appropriate Joe Egg as a cause.

As Mr. Brown has knit his stars into a team, so he has also elicited powerful solo turns in which Bri and Sheila give full vent to the two differing visions of existence that make and break their marriage. Mr. Dale's big moment is a harrowing fantasy of infanticide—a ghoulish practical joke that only a master comic actor could prevent from curdling. When it's over, the actor has done what Bri intends—forced us to feel the relief that might arrive were Joe Egg to disappear.

Ms. Channing makes us feel something else. At the end of Act 1, she sits alone in fading winter light to tell us of the one, long-ago time when Joe Egg showed a short-lived sign of improvement. As she pours maternal joy into a description of how her child seemed to master the simple task of moving an arm, the actress makes us share Sheila's belief in miracles as fully as we do Bri's bleak realism. And though Joe's miracle ended almost as soon as it began, the mother won't give up. Speaking in sweet, working-class intonations and looking completely defenseless, Ms. Channing goes on to deliver Sheila's clichéd declaration of faith as if it were a revelation: "I believe, where there's life, there's hope," she says. Then the actress takes a long pause, looks directly at us with brimming, begging eyes, and, in a whisper, asks, "Do you?"

≡ *Stockard Channing and Jim Dale were actors who'd made big impressions on me early in their careers. Channing, then known as Susan, dazzled in college and resident-theater productions in the Boston area when I was at Harvard. Dale I'd first seen at the Old Vic in London in 1971, as the touching lead of another Peter Nichols play,* The National Health, *directed by Michael Blakemore for the National Theatre. In the years before* Joe Egg, *Channing had largely been seen in forgettable movies and as a replacement star in musicals (she had even taken over for Liza Minnelli during the final gasps of* The Rink) *while Dale had become a musical-comedy star (in* Barnum). *After* Joe Egg, *Channing moved from one serious acting challenge to another; Dale returned to musicals, last appearing in* Candide *on Broadway in 1997.*

THE KING AND I
BROADWAY THEATRE, JANUARY 8, 1985

The longest-running theatrical star turn of our time can no longer be regarded as a feat of acting or even endurance. After thirty-odd years of on-and-off barnstorming in the Richard Rodgers–Oscar Hammerstein II classic, Yul Brynner is, quite simply, The King. Man and role have long since merged into a fixed image that is as much a part of our collective consciousness as the Statue of Liberty. One doesn't go to Mr. Brynner's "farewell engagement" at the Broadway to search for any fresh interpretive angles—heaven forbid! One goes to bow.

In its current rendition, Mr. Brynner's King cannot, in any case, be called mechanical. The performance is ritualistic, all right, but the high stylization the actor brings to every regal stance, arrogant hoot, and snarling declaration of "etcetera" has the timelessness of Kabuki, not the self-parody of camp. Even his flaring eyebrows suggest exaggerated Japanese stage paint: Mr. Brynner is the only performer around whose photograph might be indistinguishable from his Al Hirschfeld caricature.

At Friday's critics' preview, the star, according to the show's press representative, had a cold. This prompted some hoarse diction, as well as the deflating omission of Mr. Brynner's only solo song, "A Puzzlement." Far be it from me to dispute the King's royal prerogative to remove that number on occasion—even if it reduces him to something of a functionary in Act 1—but the gap might be less of a puzzlement for the audience if an announcement were made in advance.

Even without his solo, Mr. Brynner still dominated the production, and, even with his cold, he looked extremely fit. His high points included his fond, paternalistic joshing with his brood in "The March of the Siamese Children," his dumb-show antics while attempting to force the

English schoolteacher Anna to bow, and, of course, the death scene. It's not the passing of the King of Siam that makes the end of *The King and I* so moving; what we mourn is the inevitable passing of an archaic but entirely lovable tradition of Broadway showmanship.

The star aside, such showmanship is too often lacking in this *King and I*. The production has declined steeply since its last, elegant New York outing in 1977. As perfunctorily staged by Mitch Leigh, Act 1 seems almost painfully sluggish, and, if Act 2 picks up, that's mainly because Mr. Brynner has more to do in it.

The trouble with Mr. Leigh's direction is that he treats *The King and I* as a period piece far more geriatric than it actually is. To be sure, the book is dated now. The subplot for the star-crossed young lovers is creakily managed; the show's theme, the civilizing influence of the West on the barbaric East, is presented from a patronizing perspective equally redolent of old-time English colonialism and 1950s Broadway liberalism. But in this work, as in their previous shows, the authors were attempting to bring a new realism to the Broadway musical; they wanted their story played for keeps. Mr. Leigh's staging and casting are throwbacks to the soupy, artificial operettas that Rodgers and Hammerstein had rebelled against.

While most of the supporting players can sing, almost none of them can act. Impassioned ballads like "We Kiss in a Shadow" and "I Have Dreamed" are robbed of all meaning and spontaneity when sung by standard-cut ingenues who don't even pretend to have any romantic interest in one another. The book scenes fare worse: The lines are treated as inconveniences that must be disposed of as expeditiously as possible.

The evening's crucial role—far larger than Mr. Brynner's—is Anna. Mary Beth Peil, who plays it here, is a handsome woman with the right accent and a big voice. Hers is a respectable performance, but it has no glow: The heroine's schoolmarmishness takes on an excessive, almost Margaret Thatcher–like chill. We don't really feel this Anna melt in "Getting to Know You" and "Hello, Young Lovers," and we don't really feel her anger in "Shall I Tell You What I Think of You?"

Still, some of the evening's components continue to click along. Peter Wolf's gilt-edged sets, well lighted by Ruth Roberts, retain their hokey picture-book charm. Stanley Simmons's re-creations of Irene Sharaff's bright, silken costumes are gorgeous. Jerome Robbins's Act 2 ballet, "The Small House of Uncle Thomas," lacks a witty edge in Rebecca West's restaging, but it is still the most sophisticated embodiment of the show's cultural clash: Look closely at Mr. Robbins's Oriental burlesque of *Uncle Tom's Cabin*, and one sees the genesis of *Pacific Overtures*.

The pit band, conducted by Richard Parrinello, does splendidly by Robert Russell Bennett's orchestrations (uncredited in the *Playbill*) and makes important contributions to the show's more stirring moments. Nowhere is this more true than in the unbeatable climax, "Shall We Dance?"—in which the band so famously swells as the King at last takes Anna in his arms for a whirling polka. Even if this turgid *King and I* weren't so easy to halt, this number, as performed by Mr. Brynner, would still be the most authentic show stopper in town.

≡ *Brynner was very ill and died nine months later, but, as Ted Chapin of the Rodgers and Hammerstein office would later inform me, the star had routinely cut the "Puzzlement" number when it suited him even during the show's original Broadway run in 1951. Brynner was not an easy guy. During the run of the show, we appeared together on* Nightline *to discuss the theater season, and the* Nightline *producer told me that no guest, not even Henry Kissinger, had demanded as regal treatment as Brynner did—including a motorcade from the stage door of the Broadway Theatre to the studio a dozen or so blocks away. Once on the air, the star was imperious and disdained the notion that young people couldn't afford the high price of theater tickets: "I look into my audience and see children there every night."*

The King and I *would finally be liberated from Brynner's autocratic grip—much like the people of Siam—by Lou Diamond Phillips, whose fresh performance as the King revitalized the show and introduced it to a new generation in the 1996–97 Broadway season.*

TRACERS
PUBLIC THEATER, JANUARY 22, 1985

A t the beginning of *Tracers*, the new arrival at the Public Theater, a snaking line of Vietnam veterans gyrates about the stage to a driving rock beat. It's an unexpectedly energizing sight. *Tracers* is a play about a grim war, written and performed by men who were there, and yet this opening sequence provides the electric lift of the Jets' song in *West Side Story*. The pride, fellowship, and shared tribal codes of these men—expressed only in kinetic body language and fraternal glances, not in words—fuse into a palpable spiritual force. It doesn't make any difference what ideological side we chose during the war—we're on the side of these veterans as soon as we meet them.

Those initial feelings compound steadily throughout the evening. There is, one could say, nothing new in *Tracers*. It's a blunt, free-flowing documentary collage in which a platoon of all-American "grunts" once again stumbles ritualistically through the terrors of free-fire zones, trip wires, body bags, "subterranean rat-infested bunkers," and search-and-destroy missions—only to return home, if they return at all, to a country that would rather forget. Even the accompanying period rock songs ("Sympathy for the Devil," "Higher," "Fixin' to Die Rag") are exactly the ones we would expect. But the piece is no less powerful for that. When a nation's horror tale is told by its actual witnesses—and told with an abundance of theatricality, a minimum of self-pity—it can still bring an audience to grief.

Tracers, whose title is a metaphorical reference to tracer bullets, was devised in 1980, in workshops at the Odyssey Theater in Los Angeles. Its authors are the eight veterans who initially appeared in it—two of whom, Richard Chaves and Vincent Caristi, are still with the show at the Public. The original director, John DiFusco, has guided the current production, and, under the auspices of New York's Vietnam Veterans Ensemble Theater Company, has enlisted six new actors, also veterans, to replace the departed original cast members.

Many of the play's segments are straightforward oral history, but such was the nature of Vietnam that its oral history will always have an arresting ring. When the soldiers describe their adventures in the jungle or in Saigon bordellos, they do so in a jivey, at times funny, language that combines timeless military lingo with rock-'n'-roll cadences, drug jargon, pidgin Vietnamese and English, and an almost surreal litany of profanity. It's an authentic form of stylized diction, ideal for the theater, that few playwrights could invent from scratch.

Yet *Tracers* doesn't settle for just its vital language, or for enacting its now-familiar anecdotes. Mr. DiFusco and his dramaturge, the playwright David Berry (author of the Vietnam drama *G. R. Point*), have artfully stirred the fragments into a hallucinatory dramatic whole. In one typical sequence, a boot-camp drill instructor (J. Kenneth Campbell) terrorizes his raw recruits by barking sadistic orders; it's an archetypal scene, but when it's over the sergeant surprises us by suddenly stepping out of character. No longer a blowhard but a withered harbinger of doom, the sergeant softly reminds us that, of his young charges, "eighty percent are targets, ten percent are fighters, and one in a hundred may become a warrior."

Once we're in the war itself, the inventive Mr. DiFusco uses sound effects, skillful lighting (by Terry Wuthrich), and balletic movement—but little scenery—to make us smell the stench of death. In one scene, the actors mime a "blanket detail"—in which they try to solve the macabre "jigsaw puzzle" of reuniting their dead comrades' torsos with their severed fingers and arms. While the gore is left to our imaginations, we can't help sharing one soldier's urge to vomit. Even crueler, perhaps, is the play's double-whammy ending—during which two alternative destinies for the platoon, both faithful to history, merge into a single, bleeding mural commemorating the war's legacy.

One war that is not refought in *Tracers* is the battle over the conflict's origins and validity. The few explicit political statements flow naturally from the action—as when one veteran, now an Army lifer, sardonically describes recent American casualties in Lebanon as another example of "the unwilling" being "led by the uneducated to do the impossible for the ungrateful." In general, the concerns in *Tracers* are more primal than polemical. "How does it feel to kill somebody?" is the unsettling question that ricochets like an incantation throughout the play.

As good as the entire cast is, the two original players are exceptional. Mr. Caristi, as a scrawny recruit from Brooklyn, starts off as a naive figure of fun, then is transfigured by battle into a survivor who rationalizes his absurd wartime experience as "a party." But it's a party, Mr. Caristi's increasingly glassy eyes tell us, whose revelers are mostly ghosts. The open-faced Mr. Chaves has many disturbing solo turns. Aghast to find himself overwhelmed by his first trigger-happy "frenzy of killing," he soon loses another kind of innocence when a first shot of "skag" reduces his fit body to that of a crablike rodent scuttling about mindlessly on the barracks floor.

At the play's conclusion, Mr. Chaves and his colleagues revivify themselves for a musical finale that, like the opening, is a prideful anthem of solidarity. "In my dream, we've all come home together," explains one of the men. That dream of peace is long dead, but the survivors of *Tracers* heroically honor its memory and demand its renewal by keeping the Vietnam nightmare alive.

JACQUES AND HIS MASTER
AMERICAN REPERTORY THEATRE,
CAMBRIDGE, MASS., JANUARY 24, 1985

If ever there was a Cultural Event, it is *Jacques and His Master*, the Milan Kundera play now at Harvard's American Repertory Theatre. Not only is this production the American premiere of the Czechoslovak writer's sole stage work, but it also marks the American debut of Susan Sontag as a theater director. Leafing through the program, one half expects to discover Irving Howe and Philip Roth in the cast list. They're not, alas—although one is pleased to find such sturdy theatrical hands as Robert Drivas and Priscilla Smith.

There's nothing wrong with a Cultural Event, of course, provided that its perpetrators don't let the event upstage the culture. I'm not convinced that this trap has been avoided in Cambridge. Mr. Kundera's play, as translated by Michael Henry Heim, is a liberating folly—a playful "homage" to Denis Diderot and his protomodernist, late-eighteenth-century novel, *Jacques the Fatalist*. Ms. Sontag has staged it with fastidious care, but also with a pomposity that can drain away the fun. It's all too characteristic of the production that the director advertises the play's pedigree by gratuitously dragging a bust of Diderot on stage.

Mr. Kundera wrote *Jacques and His Master* in 1971—after his literary banishment in Czechoslovakia, before his emigration to France. Like its source—and like much of Mr. Kundera's own fiction—the play is an ironic construct of philosophical paradoxes; its meaning is to be found as much in its prismatic form as in the anecdotes filtered through that form. In one beguiling digression, a character laments those plays that proclaim "unnecessary truths," such as "The world is rotten!" Rather than ply us with unnecessary truths, Mr. Kundera asks us if—and how—we can ever know what the truth is.

During the work's three acts (played without intermission), the servant Jacques (Thomas Derrah) and his aristocratic Master (Mr. Drivas) trudge rudderlessly through a void inhabited only by an innkeeper (Ms. Smith). Along their way to nowhere, the men swap tales of their past romantic misadventures. But Jacques and his Master keep interrupting and amending their stories—and are themselves interrupted by the innkeeper, who recounts still another tale of sexual betrayal.

Each of the narratives is a variation on the others—as the playwright didactically explains near the end. By interweaving their disjointed anecdotes, Diderot and Mr. Kundera throw the nature of existence into flux. The fatalistic Jacques would have us believe that man's fortunes are "written on high," while his Master often holds out for the potency of free will and fortuity. Both positions are affirmed and contradicted in the play—as are the differing ethical systems they foster—but what remains inviolate is the creative spirit. Whether or not a divine master has written man's history on high, Jacques and his Master both see themselves as inventions of the literary masters—Diderot and Mr. Kundera—who dreamed them up. As the playwright's own experience in Czechoslovakia exemplifies, the man who chooses to imagine can still, to a point, know freedom.

Mr. Kundera has long championed Diderot—and Diderot's esthetic forebear, Laurence Sterne—as influences on his fiction. In *Jacques,* we're reminded of how strong that influence has been. The play's techniques— the contrapuntal use of multiple narrators, the variational structure, the interjected metaphysical debates—take us from Mr. Kundera's first novel, *The Joke,* through *The Book of Laughter and Forgetting* and *The Unbearable Lightness of Being.* Onstage, these devices often play as Pirandellian—even as the symbiotic servant-master pairing pointedly evokes a literary continuum stretching from Cervantes to Molière to Beckett.

Yet, for all that baggage, *Jacques* usually achieves its disquieting effects through ribald comedy. Ms. Sontag's staging lacks the requisite velocity and fizz, and the performances, especially those of the seven actors populating the internal narratives, are mostly flat and sexless. While Mr. Drivas summons up the appropriate dandified style of the Master, Mr. Derrah's nondescript Jacques denies him a foil. Only Ms. Smith brings the play fully alive. As the lowly innkeeper acts out the cautionary tale of the high-born Marquise de La Pommeraye, the actress leaps between wildly disparate social and theatrical roles with perfect timing and sly humor. Her performance alone unlocks the explosive laughter in existential anxiety.

Even if the other actors rose to Ms. Smith's level, the production would still be hobbled by its set and score. In both his stage directions and dialogue, Mr. Kundera demands an empty stage; he writes in his published introduction that Diderot's contribution to the antinaturalistic novel was "a stage without scenery." So why has Ms. Sontag asked her talented designer, Douglas Stein, to provide an eggshell-colored Roman ruin abstractly patterned after a Piranesi engraving? For no reason I can tell, except to add intellectual window dressing and accompanying documentation in the program. Worse, the actors enter through sets of sliding doors that, as crowned with recessed lights, resemble an elevator bank in a convention hotel.

The music is by Elizabeth Swados, who punctuates every sexual reference with distracting percussion noises that are arty equivalents of the drumrolls that fleck a Johnny Carson monologue. The evening's conclusion—in which master and servant march forward—is frozen into an ominous tableau, with still more portentous underscoring. While such theatricality may befit a Cultural Event, it doesn't fulfill *Jacques and His Master.* The ART hasn't so much staged Mr. Kundera's play as annotated it with unnecessary truths.

LIFE AND LIMB
PLAYWRIGHTS HORIZONS, JANUARY 25, 1985

For a brief while, one might mistake Keith Reddin's *Life and Limb,* the new play at Playwrights Horizons' Studio Theater, for another straight-faced account of an alienated veteran's homecoming. The evening's hero is a Korean War enlistee, Franklin Roosevelt Clagg (Robert Joy), who returns home to bucolic Morristown, N.J., after having lost an arm at Pork Chop Hill. Once an optimist, Franklin is now depressed. He can't find a job, and he can no longer talk to his sweet wife, Effie (Elizabeth Perkins). Pretty soon, Effie is spending afternoons away from home, seeking out movies and another man.

But even as Mr. Reddin sets up this standard tale, there are signs that he has no intention of abiding by its usual rules. A realistic opening scene on the Atlantic City Boardwalk suddenly gives way to a lecture, in which Effie stands before a map to explain the military dimensions of the Korean conflict. Yet the lecture also comes to an abrupt halt: Effie digresses into an effusive description of her favorite movie, *It's a Wonderful Life.* Not long after that, we find Franklin at home, reading his wife the funny papers. In Franklin's recitation of *Blondie,* Dagwood bludgeons Blondie with a ball peen hammer.

Life and Limb grows far more surprising thereafter. This is the first full-length play by Mr. Reddin, who has been previously known to Off Broadway audiences as a promising young actor. He shows even more promise as a playwright. Far from being a maudlin account of a veteran's reassimilation into the American mainstream, *Life and Limb* is a macabre journey through that mainstream, told in a deadpan, cold-bloodedly ghoulish, comic style. The values that arouse Mr. Reddin's ire—the conformity, materialism, and cultural kitsch fostered by the Eisenhower era—are hardly fresh targets for attack, and, because of that, *Life and Limb* does leave one unsatisfied. So inventive is Mr. Reddin's imagination, however, that his perversely funny vignettes have an inflammatory afterlife that his overriding message does not.

It's only fitting that the author's last prominent acting role, also at Playwrights Horizons, was as the lead in Christopher Durang's *Baby with the Bathwater.* Mr. Reddin, like some other young playwrights championed by this theater, shares some of the Durang sensibility. In *Life and Limb,* rude jokes, narrative daring, and Roman Catholic guilt know few bounds—and neither does the author's obsession with the camp detritus of pop culture.

The play opens with the sound of the Twentieth Century–Fox fanfare and a CinemaScope projection of the famous *Life* magazine photograph showing a rapt 3-D movie audience in cardboard eyeglasses. The ensuing scene changes are accompanied by seemingly every hit-parade song recorded by Nat (King) Cole, Perry Como, and Doris Day.

The script itself is often written in pastiche movie vernacular; its story proves a nasty inversion of the post–World War II Frank Capra tearjerker that Effie so admires. The Claggs could be James Stewart and Donna Reed, living in a small-town America that promises a boundless, wonderful life. But here it's a life defined by advertising and movies—a consumer's paradise stuffed with such products as televisions, chrome-finned cars, and dinette sets. When a villain disrupts this nirvana, he's far more malignant than the banker played by Lionel Barrymore in the Capra picture. The most powerful tycoon in Morristown (Patrick Breen) is a sadistic, go-getting artificial-limb manufacturer who will give Franklin a job only if he agrees to perform a degrading sexual act.

Nor does Mr. Reddin follow Capra by including heaven as part of his universe. When characters die in *Life and Limb*—as they do when a movie-palace balcony collapses during a showing of *Cattle Queen of Montana*—they go straight to hell. To this playwright, hell is a place where starry-eyed film fans are told the disillusioning truth about Montgomery Clift's private life—and where the damned are punished by being forced to make potholders or shop in supermarkets for eternity. It is one of Mr. Reddin's points that hell doesn't look so different from all-American Morristown—and that both realms resemble the antiseptically sunny images of domesticity propagated by Hollywood and glossy magazines.

This look is fully realized by Stephen Strawbridge's lighting, David C. Woolard's costumes, and John Arnone's ingenious sets. Mr. Arnone provides a riot of tacky fifties furnishings (from pole lamps to oppressive Venetian blinds) and makes florid use of such favored period colors as peach and Formica-green. As directed by the playwright Thomas Babe, with just the right tone of curdled good cheer, the show unfurls like a retrospective of vintage advertisements for Westinghouse appliances and Pabst Blue Ribbon beer.

In addition to the three leads—who are perfect revisionist stand-ins for their screen progenitors—the other lively cast members include Robin Bartlett as an eccentric Rumanian neighbor, Benjamin Hendrickson as hell's superintendent, and Tom Toner as an aged invalid who receives anonymous phone calls announcing his imminent death. The younger generation is represented by J. David Rozsa, as a meanspirited

Davy Crockett fan whom the merciless Mr. Reddin gleefully sends to hell by a particularly grisly route.

THE COMMON PURSUIT

LONG WHARF THEATRE, NEW HAVEN, FEBRUARY 2, 1985

Picture *The Big Chill* populated by wildly fictionalized caricatures of Kenneth Tynan, Ian Hamilton, and Clive James—or *Merrily We Roll Along* transplanted to London's toniest literary warrens—and you'll have an idea of the indecent pleasures to be had in Simon Gray's new play, *The Common Pursuit*.

In this acidic comedy, the author's first since *Quartermaine's Terms*, we follow five of Cambridge University's best and brightest young literary stars from their halcyon common-room days in the mid-1960s through a decade and a half's worth of personal and professional travails. Mr. Gray's characters aspire to the high intellectual ideals exemplified by the F. R. Leavis book from which the play borrows its title; they settle quickly instead for petty adulteries, BBC talk-show gigs, and flip journalistic assignments from *Vogue*. The play's only semblance of a hero is the one man who doesn't destroy any lives "except his own."

When I first saw *The Common Pursuit* in its London premiere last summer, it seemed a formulaic effort from a playwright whose past works include *Butley* and *Otherwise Engaged*. In its American premiere at the Long Wharf Theatre, the play is still superficial—but highly entertaining in its superficiality. Since the summer, Mr. Gray has polished the script—not to the extent of deepening it, but certainly to the point of sharpening its cleverness. And the Long Wharf's director, Kenneth Frankel (who also did *Quartermaine*), has helped out mightily by fielding a looser-limbed production than Harold Pinter's London version. Mr. Pinter tended to stage *The Common Pursuit* as if it could carry the weight of his own *Betrayal*. Mr. Frankel, working with an exemplary American cast, lets Mr. Gray's chronicle of dissipated lives roll along merrily indeed.

What makes the play enjoyable is its piquant erudition and bountiful supply of upscale soap-opera plot twists. After the introductory Trinity College sequence, each scene leaps forward a few years, and each comes equipped with a juicy new development or two: a marriage or divorce, a birth or abortion, a publishing triumph or fiasco, a hetero- or homosexual debauch. Though some of the narrative variations are mechanical—notably those involving two celebrated poets kept offstage—others are ingenious: A casual opening bit of farcical business, in which one of the young men inadvertently walks in on a pal's sexual escapade, reverberates through somber crises to come. With no shame whatsoever, Mr. Gray piles on ironic events that, as one line acknowledges, are "of the kind that only happen in literature."

That the characters' steady degeneration never seems melodramatic is a tribute to the buoyancy of both the dialogue and the cast. Playing a rumpled critic who prostitutes both his writing and love life, Nathan Lane is such a puckish satyr that his most self-destructive binges are charming; he can make us laugh at a witty defense of cigarette smoking even as he's dying of emphysema. Peter Friedman, as a brilliant Scottish philosopher-poet who can't "perform his worldly tasks to his own satisfaction," makes us chuckle, not sigh, when he decides to abandon his career-long effort to write a masterwork on Wagner: "Everything I've written about him reduces him to my own sort of size," he explains. "Which makes him too small to be interesting to me."

No less delightful are Mark Arnott, as a once-promising historian who devotes his energies to coffee-table tomes and compulsive philandering, and Michael Countryman, as a self-confessed no-talent who lives vicariously through his friends. They're both far too ingenuous to be pitied. If anything, Mr. Arnott, the most unabashed of Lotharios, and Mr. Countryman, the most generous-spirited of nerds, make moral weakness seem an appealing spiritual calling.

The one strained performance comes from William Converse-Roberts in the lead role of Stuart, a high-minded esthete who can't balance his devotion to his wife (a spirited Ellen Parker) with his dedication to his elitist literary journal (named *The Common Pursuit*). It's not the actor's fault that he seems ill at ease. His part, like the others, is sketched, not fully written—but, because it is the largest role, Mr. Converse-Roberts can't hide behind bon mots and is instead sacrificed to the sketchiness.

When the uncompromising Stuart suddenly relinquishes his deeply held private and professional goals at center stage, we realize that Mr. Gray has not made us understand why—and it's beyond any actor's power to fill in the blanks. While the other characters' betrayals, sell-outs, and lies are not subjected to the same audience scrutiny as Stuart's —they are often announced briskly, after the fact—they seem just as arbitrarily motivated in retrospect. Such is the toll taken when a plot decrees its characters' behavior rather than the other way around.

With such authorial determinism at play, *The Common Pursuit* can't be as moving as the similarly structured *Quartermaine*—or as resonant as the work it most closely resembles, Frederic Raphael's *Glittering*

Prizes. But we don't ask too many questions while the evening rushes self-assuredly on. Even David Jenkins's inventive set—which propels the young men clear across the stage to rendezvous with destiny—adds just the right gloss of sweep and depth to an evening of shallow but captivating fun.

≡ *The talent of Nathan Lane, whose career began in such musical bombs as* The Wind in the Willows, Love, *and* Merlin, *was a revelation of the decade. The touching note in his acting—later to be mined by the playwright Terrence McNally in* The Lisbon Traviata, Lips Together, Teeth Apart, *and* Love! Valour! Compassion!*—has been dormant more recently as he's found a mass audience for his clowning through Broadway's* Guys and Dolls *and* A Funny Thing Happened on the Way to the Forum *and in Hollywood projects typified by* The Birdcage.

STRANGE INTERLUDE

NEDERLANDER THEATRE, FEBRUARY 22, 1985

When Eugene O'Neill's *Strange Interlude* opened on Broadway in 1928, it was widely hailed as a revolutionary experiment—a thunderous psychodrama that ushered Joycean modernism and Freudian theory into the American theater. The play won its author his third Pulitzer Prize, had a smash run, and spawned two road companies. But thirty-five years later—as seen in the Actors Studio revival of 1963—*Strange Interlude* had been eclipsed by the O'Neill masterworks that followed it. Not only did many cease to find this work profound or powerful; *Strange Interlude* looked so dated that some relegated it to the oblivion of kitsch.

Now, two decades have passed, and a further reappraisal could be at hand. Whatever else this five-hour play has been called by its adherents and detractors since 1928, no one has ever claimed it was fun. Yet that's exactly what *Strange Interlude* proves to be in the inspired English revival that has arrived at the Nederlander. Two awesome actors—Glenda Jackson and Edward Petherbridge—and a courageously impudent director, Keith Hack, have given this work a fresh and unexpected life. While *Strange Interlude* hardly emerges as the cosmic statement that O'Neill intended—and while some of it is, indeed, pretentious pulp—it often seems the most enjoyable, not to mention deranged, comedy of sexual anxiety that Noël Coward or Philip Barry never wrote.

In outline, *Strange Interlude* sounds less like comedy than a dime-novel parody of Strindberg or Ibsen. Over nine acts stretching through twenty-five years, O'Neill unfolds the saga of Nina Leeds (Ms. Jackson), an angry, strong-willed woman determined to love, mother, and, if need be, destroy the many men who intersect her orbit. The plot is pure—and, in its later stages, laughable—soap opera. As Nina toys with the dashing doctor Edmund Darrell (Brian Cox), the jovial advertising man Sam Evans (James Hazeldine), and the asexual novelist Charles Marsden (Mr. Petherbridge), we're treated to a many-course feast of lurid doings: nervous breakdowns, promiscuity and adultery, an abortion, cases of congenital insanity and disguised paternity, as well as enough sudden deaths to stock a season of *Dynasty*.

O'Neill hoped that this story would turn the manipulative, ever-changing Nina into a vessel for all his addled, conflicted thoughts about womanhood. While that theme dies aborning, another survives—and it is the key to Mr. Hack's radical reinterpretation. In *Strange Interlude*, the characters are constantly trying to create happiness by controlling and ordering life; even a baby is eugenically conceived. Yet such schemes are always undone by unruly emotions. No matter how much Nina meddles and calculates to get what she wants, she ultimately finds that "our lives are merely strange dark interludes in the electrical display of God the Father."

Looked at somberly—as O'Neill apparently wished—such futile thrashings against destiny could be considered tragic. But couldn't they also be seen as absurdly funny? Ms. Jackson delivers that line with a mad chuckle—just as she has laughed earlier while decrying the God who makes life "a lie" and "a joke." What Mr. Hack and his cast discover throughout the text is that O'Neill's language, while often too purple to support breast-beating, can sustain a sardonic tone with no loss of meaning. Far from mocking the script, this company—at amazing risk—has unearthed what still seems genuine and vital in it.

In the process, Mr. Hack has made a startling virtue of what most would consider the play's dead weight—its so-called "thought asides." These are the lengthy soliloquies in which the characters pause in mid-scene to confess their inner feelings directly to the audience. Even in the twenties, Groucho Marx mocked these stream-of-consciousness confessionals (in *Animal Crackers*), and certainly they can be rhetoric-infested or redundant. But unlike past directors of the play, Mr. Hack doesn't portentously arrest the action for the asides. Colloquially spoken—and often indicated only by a slight shift of a speaker's head or vocal key—they become the crux of an evening in which characters hide behind "the sounds called words."

This is particularly true when they're delivered by Mr. Petherbridge's Marsden. A timid, high-minded mother's boy who writes popular genteel novels about "dear old ladies and devilish bachelors," Marsden emerges here as a witty, bitchy chorus—a detached Jamesian observer who is always the first to spot everyone's hypocrisies, including his own. With his prissy whine, fragile bearing, and gloomy, shadowy eyes, Mr. Petherbridge always looks like the "old maid" he's claimed to be; he twists like a weathervane when buffeted by others' passions and forever seems to be fastidiously picking at stray lint. But whether he's passing judgment on fellow characters or the adolescent materialism of the Jazz Age, his asides are undiluted acid—and hilariously expressive of a fatalistic vision that O'Neill put to loftier uses elsewhere in his career.

Mr. Petherbridge, last seen as Newman Noggs in *Nicholas Nickleby*, is simply priceless in this role; by the time he reaches his delicate drunk scene, the audience is eating up his every word. Though their characters aren't as juicy, Mr. Cox, as the dashing doctor who turns rancid, and Mr. Hazeldine, as the innocent dope who evolves into a brash exemplar of twenties Babbitry, are also first-rate. Their asides contain more spelled-out Freudian motivations than slashing observations, but the actors still create a comic tension between the characters' secret yearnings and public masks, between their highest ideals and tawdriest actions. So springy are the constant, Ping-Pong–like shifts between word and deed that the cathartic Act 6 closing, in which Nina claims psychic dominance over her three men, almost plays like Tracy Lord's champagne-fueled nocturnal roundelay with her trio of suitors in *The Philadelphia Story*.

Ms. Jackson even sounds a bit like Katharine Hepburn—but, with her helmet of hair and gashed features, she looks like a cubist portrait of Louise Brooks. Her role has breadth, not stature: Nina is but a conceit designed to represent successively every breed of woman O'Neill could imagine (from wanton to predatory mother), and the motivation for her maniacal behavior (the death of her betrothed in World War I) is ludicrously thin. The actress nonetheless jumps through each hoop with grace and conviction: She's equally mesmerizing as a Zelda Fitzgeraldesque neurotic, a rotting and spiteful middle-aged matron, and, finally, a spent, sphinxlike widow happily embracing extinction.

When Ms. Jackson's young Nina sobs over her inability to mourn her dead father—or when Mr. Cox's decrepit middle-aged Edmund is rejected by his own son—there's also sorrow to go with the mean, ironic laughter. Some other affecting passages arrive when the asides meld and spiral into free-floating, anxiety-ridden verbal chamber music (with Ms.

Jackson always serving as the resonant cello). By liberating the script from naturalism—Voytek's towering clapboard-box set, spookily lighted by Allen Lee Hughes, often disregards O'Neill's scene settings—Mr. Hack rethinks nearly every moment he can. He hasn't, however, done the impossible: From the hopelessly melodramatic Act 3 (in which a dirty family secret thumps about like a hooked fish) to the frail (and sometimes inadequately cast) supporting roles, *Strange Interlude* still has plenty of cracks.

Just the same, we return eagerly from the two intermissions; only in the final stretch does restlessness set in. Foolishly overreaching and yet theatrically gripping, *Strange Interlude* cannot be ranked with O'Neill's major works but can at least be catalogued with, if beneath, such other one-of-a-kind American cultural artifacts of its age as *Intolerance, U.S.A.,* and *Porgy and Bess*. There's something endearingly crackpot about this play—it speaks to us from the century's boom time, when our culture, like the author, was at once naive and inordinately ambitious. While it's remotely possible that others might uncover more in *Strange Interlude* than Mr. Hack's troupe has, do figure that another century will be here before we find out.

AS IS

CIRCLE REPERTORY COMPANY, MARCH 11, 1985

There are some subjects audiences would just as soon not hear about in the theater, and surely one of them is AIDS, the lethal illness dramatized by William M. Hoffman in his play, *As Is*. But it would be a mistake for any theatergoer to reject this work out of squeamishness. Strange as it may sound, Mr. Hoffman has turned a tale of the dead and the dying into the liveliest new work to be seen at the Circle Repertory Company in several seasons. Far from leaving us drained, *As Is* is one of the few theatrical evenings in town that may, if anything, seem too brief.

This isn't to say that this ninety-minute play is painless. A free-flowing journal of the recent plague years for New York's homosexuals, *As Is* rarely spares us the clinical facts of acquired immune deficiency syndrome; only at the end is the audience shielded from the physiological and psychological torments. Yet Mr. Hoffman has written more than a documentary account of an AIDS victim's grotesque medical history. As we follow the tailspin of a promising fiction writer named Rich

(Jonathan Hogan), the playwright reaches out to examine the impact of AIDS on hetero- and homosexual consciences as well as to ask the larger questions (starting with, "Why me?") that impale any victims of terminal illness.

It's a feat that Mr. Hoffman accomplishes with both charity and humor. When Rich is hit by AIDS, he is breaking up with Saul (Jonathan Hadary), a photographer who has been his longtime lover. Saul has been badly hurt by Rich, but not so much so that he will turn his back at a time of grave need. Even as the two men bitterly split up their household possessions—from copper pots to "the world's largest collection of Magic Marker hustler portraits"—Saul decides to stick by Rich come what may, to accept him "as is."

Others behave just as compassionately. Although suffering cruel social ostracism, Rich eventually receives support from his married brother (Ken Kliban), from fellow AIDS victims (one of them female), from a maternal hospice worker (Claris Erickson). But such kindnesses are not so easy for the protagonist to accept. Rich swings between denial and anger, lashing out at both friends and strangers. He at first rejects Saul's affections with torrents of abuse and, at one point, vows to spread his infection indiscriminately through New York's demimonde of sex bars. "I'm going to die and take as many as I can with me," cries Mr. Hogan, his voice coursing with rage.

Among other pointed digressions, *As Is* offers a satirical tour of that demimonde. We travel to a sadomasochistic haunt whose identically costumed clientele go by the names of Chip, Chuck, and Chad; Rich and Saul recall fond memories of past anonymous liaisons in leather bars and Marrakech graveyards. Mr. Hoffman doesn't deny his characters' enjoyment of what they euphemistically refer to as "noncommitted, nondirected" sex (or laughingly refer to as sleaze). But, in mocking obsessive promiscuity with light wit, the playwright can gracefully bid such behavior a permanent farewell without adopting a hectoring moralistic tone.

Mr. Hoffman devotes more attention to exploring both the present panic and solidarity of a group that has found itself rightly "terrified of every pimple." For the play's homosexuals, the discovery of AIDS was an epoch-altering event: In a group recitation, they each remember where they were when they first heard of the mysterious epidemic. In another chilling scene, Rich is bombarded by a chorus of doctors' voices incantatorily repeating a single sentence: "The simple fact is that we know little about acquired immune deficiency syndrome." The moment is counterbalanced by a vignette in which two men answering phones at an

"AIDS hot line" dispense as much solace as they can without pretending to omnipotence or saintliness.

Sometimes the characters of *As Is* seem a bit too saintly: Mr. Hoffman eventually resolves Rich's conflicts with others in the neat, upbeat manner of *Terms of Endearment*. But so fluent is Marshall W. Mason's direction of the overlapping scenes that we don't notice the play's begged questions or superficial examinations of character until we're out of the theater. Mr. Mason may arrange the cast's choral configurations too pretentiously, yet his staging is mostly inventive: When Saul discovers a lesion on Rich's back, his reassuring words ("I'm sure it's nothing") are ferociously contradicted by the anxiety-heightening sound of a hospital curtain yanking shut.

The acting could not be better. Mr. Hogan gives the breakout performance of his career as Rich: When he's not loudly venting terror, he also reveals a sensitive writer who had just found his way when the disease struck. In what may be his most affecting speech, he recounts Rich's ability to overcome a lonely childhood in which, as he says, "I was so desperate to find people like myself I would look for them in the indexes of books, under H."

Mr. Hadary's conflicted, at times comically whiny Saul is just as compelling, as are the performances of Mr. Kliban and Lou Liberatore in multiple roles. Ms. Erickson's generous-spirited hospice worker, whose epiphany-laden monologues open and close the evening, may be more of a sentimental conceit than a character, but the actress makes her moving even so. "My job is not to bring enlightenment, only comfort" is how she describes her mission to the dying and their loved ones. Mr. Hoffman's play, as much as is possible under the grim circumstances, brings a stirring measure of both.

≡ *In retrospect a dated play perhaps, but an important one for a moment when the disease was still a mystery to most audiences. (Moved from the Circle Repertory Company in the Village to Broadway, it all too predictably flopped, however.) If there's a theatrical legacy to AIDS, it is several-fold. The disease forced the theater (and eventually the rest of the culture) to portray homosexuals (or at least male homosexuals) as real people on stage rather than as just figures of either camp farce or bathos. (Though the bathos would return as the plague dragged on.) AIDS also brought the American theater back into the social-protest arena it had previously entered in other national crises such as the Depression, the racial upheavals of the sixties, and the Vietnam war. Finally AIDS was in part responsible for provoking the great American play of the era, Tony Kushner's* Angels in America.

BILOXI BLUES

Although the laughter rarely stops in *Biloxi Blues,* Neil Simon's joyous and unexpectedly rewarding new comedy, the most surprising line of the evening by far is not a joke, but a reprimand. The reprimand is delivered to the young hero, Eugene Jerome (Matthew Broderick)—who has now graduated from the Depression adolescence of Mr. Simon's previous autobiographical play, *Brighton Beach Memoirs,* to basic training in the wartime Army of 1943.

Eugene is still an aspiring writer, fond of scribbling his every private observation into a composition book. But at this moment in *Biloxi Blues,* he censors those observations: He rips a completed page out of the journal and throws it away. It's then that Eugene's best friend in the platoon, a high-minded Jewish intellectual named Arnold Epstein (Barry Miller), lets him have it. "Once you start compromising your thoughts," Arnold tells Eugene, "you're a candidate for mediocrity."

What makes the line so startling is that it applies not only to the apprentice Neil Simon, as represented by Eugene, but also to the latter-day Neil Simon, as represented by his recent unfulfilled plays and mechanical screenplays. And as Arnold's sharp warning makes a strong impression on the hero, so the playwright seems finally to be heeding the same warning in the new play at his namesake theater. Gone from *Biloxi Blues* is the self-congratulatory air of *Brighton Beach Memoirs* and *Chapter Two*—works in which Mr. Simon presented himself as a near-saint and invoked death and disease to prove he was writing with a new seriousness. This time, the writer at last begins to examine himself honestly, without compromises, and the result is his most persuasively serious effort to date—not to mention his funniest play since the golden age bordered by *Barefoot in the Park* (1963) and *The Sunshine Boys* (1972).

There is no contradiction in that assessment: When a playwright is writing honestly, he writes in his own voice—and Mr. Simon's honest voice is not the official, middlebrow tone he's adopted over the last decade but the comic vernacular of his first hits. In *Biloxi Blues,* we can feel Mr. Simon's exhilaration at giving that voice full vent again, and we can be doubly grateful that Mr. Broderick is the instrument of its expression. Not since François Truffaut and Jean-Pierre Léaud have a popular storyteller and his public alter ego been so ideally matched.

Mr. Broderick is even more appealing here than in his last appearance as Eugene. Now that the character has aged six years, the performer no longer seems a practiced stand-up comic masquerading in little boy's clothing but an assured actor at one with a full-bodied role. His comic timing, now as much physical as verbal, has attained a textbook perfection. He can bring down the house and Act 1 curtain with merely a simple, precisely calibrated turn of his head. Given a chance to smoke his first swaggering precoital cigarette in Act 2, he whips up pandemonium.

But heaven knows the star has lines to play with, too. Act 1, in which Eugene and his fellow "dogfaces" get acclimated to Army discipline at their Mississippi training post, is service comedy as Broadway probably hasn't seen since *No Time for Sergeants*. Eugene, leaving Brooklyn for the first time, must contend not only with a sergeant (Bill Sadler) who in no way resembles the kindly taskmasters he's anticipated from James Stewart movies, but also with an entire new gentile world: hick bunkmates with low IQs and high incidences of tooth decay, parochial-school girls, and goyishe mess-hall foods with exotic names like creamed chipped beef.

Eugene has a sharp riposte for every new jolt. Listening to his lines in Act 1 of *Biloxi Blues* is like watching a graceful basketball player sink shot after shot. Every joke hits its exact mark, none are wasted. As befits the setting, many of the gags are of the locker-room-and-latrine variety, but others dramatize the hero's predicament as a Jew in an alien land: Hard-pressed, Eugene will invent a new High Holiday to escape the chow line. While Mr. Simon's brand of Jewish humor has often occupied a safe, bland middle ground between the poles occupied by his fellow one-time Sid Caesar writers Mel Brooks and Woody Allen, here he merrily embraces both low Brooks and neurotic Allen.

For once the playwright also lets his plot develop from character rather than the other way around. When we first meet Eugene, he explains that he has three goals in the war—to become a writer, stay alive, and lose his virginity. The second of these goals is reached by one of the evening's final jokes, the last by a priceless variation on the standard boy-meets-prostitute scene. But the story of how Eugene becomes a writer is Mr. Simon's true passion, and it's what gives *Biloxi Blues* its affecting bite.

The playwright unfolds the tale by really giving his hero something to write about in his journal. Eugene witnesses the anti-Semitic and anti-homosexual humiliations of fellow recruits. Yet Mr. Simon's plan is not, as one might fear from past efforts, to write a gratuitous problem play about prejudice in the World War II armed forces. Quite the contrary: The author unearths some human qualities in the play's ignorant bigots and reserves his harshest judgments for his hero, who stays meekly on the sidelines of the conflicts around him.

Mr. Simon's real subject is not prejudice, but how Eugene perceives prejudice. As the ever-instructive Arnold explains, Eugene is too much an ingratiating, naive observer, neatly reducing other people's dramas to clever diary entries. If he is to become a real writer, he cannot forever remain "neutral, like Switzerland." He will have to stop making peace and jokes and start entering the battles worth fighting, whether for principle or love. It's a lesson that Mr. Simon seems to be learning along with his protagonist, and we soon watch Eugene grow up as no other Simon character has.

Mr. Miller's Arnold is always the invaluable catalyst for the hero's education in life and literature. A New York Jew from a far different background than Eugene's, Arnold seems an incipient McCarthy-era martyr; he's an outspokenly principled idealist, Talmudic philosophizer, and snob who boasts of having read *War and Peace* five times and who challenges orders by threatening baffled officers with postwar congressional investigations. In Mr. Miller's exemplary performance, Arnold never becomes an unctuous or cartoonish caricature, with the result that he and Eugene form an odd couple that is emotionally bound.

Under Gene Saks's exceptionally fine direction, the other Biloxi soldiers are equally well rounded—from Mr. Sadler's quixotic sergeant to the platoon's dreamer (Alan Ruck), bully (Matt Mulhern), and prize dunce (Brian Tarantina). Randall Edwards and Penelope Ann Miller are no less delightful as the women who respectively introduce Eugene to sex and love. The only actor left out of the fun is Geoffrey Sharp, a recruit whose role is left deliberately ill-defined in order to spring a calculatedly melodramatic guessing game in Act 2.

That externally imposed plot contrivance is one of Mr. Simon's few reversions to bad habits. The play's other flaws are two expendable scenes and one overextended romantic tryst that add roughly fifteen minutes of flab to the second half. Even then, Mr. Saks keeps the action spinning quickly and amusingly through David Mitchell's airy, mobile sets, which the lighting designer Tharon Musser fills at first with bright Southern torpor and then with ever-heavier clouds of war.

By evening's end, the buddies of "Biloxi Beach" are on the first leg of the journey from Mississippi to that war. Eugene is worried about his uncertain future on the front, but no less so about the prospect of having to decide "what kind of writer" he will be. But as he clutches a going-away present—a brand-new journal—we sense that neither the wised-up hero nor his recharged creator will again be filling up pages with the often glib writings of their past. Surely Mr. Broderick is speaking as much for the Neil Simon of 1985 as of 1943 when he peers out of the darkened train and, with a pride that even silences laughter, announces how liberating it feels to be a writer who's at last "heading for places and events unknown."

LEADER OF THE PACK

Ambassador Theatre, April 9, 1985

Although there are as yet no candidates in the competition for best musical of the Broadway season, the race for most calamitous musical has gained a strong new contender with *Leader of the Pack,* a purported tribute to golden rock and roll oldies at the Ambassador. While not as pointless as *The Three Musketeers* or as lengthy as *Harrigan 'n Hart* or as becalmed as *Quilters,* this show does lead the pack in such key areas as incoherence (total), vulgarity (boundless), and decibel level (stratospheric, with piercing electronic feedback).

What makes *Leader of the Pack* a particularly impressive fiasco, however, is that it, unlike its competitors, didn't have the advantage of starting off with a humdrum score. There are some fun songs in this show, and one can only wonder at the ingenuity and strenuous effort required to stamp the life out of nearly all of them.

Most of those songs were written by Ellie Greenwich and her then husband, Jeff Barry, in the early 1960s. Like Tin Pan Alley songsmiths of an earlier day, the team toiled in the Brill Building on Broadway, churning out material for immediate sale in the pop marketplace. The Greenwich-Barry specialty was so-called girl-group music, fashioned for such female trios or quartets as the Shangri-Las, the Ronettes, and the Crystals. Their archetypal efforts—"Chapel of Love," "Hanky Panky," "Maybe I Know"—can still evoke an innocent era of teen romance. Among the many undying Greenwich-Barry fans are not only nostalgic American children of the sixties but also even so unlikely an enthusiast as the high-minded hero of Tom Stoppard's play *The Real Thing*.

In *Leader of the Pack,* the songs meld into one long screech. They're delivered by mostly charmless performers whose primary responsibility is to model an extravagant assortment of hideous costumes and grotesquely campy beehive wigs. Even the band arrangements are garish: If the legendary sixties rock-record producer Phil Spector erected a "wall of sound," this show drops a shroud of sheer noise. Of two dozen numbers, only one captures the spirit of Greenwich-Barry pop. The appealing Darlene Love, an actual veteran of the girl-group era, provides a tumultuous, gospel-flavored rendition of Tina Turner's one-time signature anthem, "River Deep, Mountain High."

Between the songs, there is a book such as Broadway has not encountered since the dumbfounding Marilyn Monroe musical biography, *Marilyn,* of 1983. While the intention appears to be to chronicle the backstage story of Greenwich (Dinah Manoff) and Barry (Patrick Cassidy), the splintery scenes all seem to begin and end offstage and frequently feature characters whose identities are known only to the authors.

Then again, the identities of the authors are also unclear. The *Playbill* lists no book credit for *Leader of the Pack,* although it does hold a trio of writers responsible for the musical's "liner notes" (Anne Beatts), "additional material" (Jack Heifner), and "original concept" (Melanie Mintz). One only hopes that future theater historians will determine who devised the Jewish-mother and knock-knock jokes that are the show's most sophisticated stabs at humor—or who came up with the undeniably original concept of beginning a musical set in the sixties with an underpopulated Las Vegas–style conga line that, we're told, represents "the eighties."

The production's director-choreographer is Michael Peters—a cocreator of such high-style rock entertainments as the Motown girl-group musical *Dreamgirls* and Michael Jackson's music videos. *Leader of the Pack* looks nothing like *Dreamgirls* or an MTV extravaganza, though it might pass for a banana republic's revival of *Your Hit Parade.* A lengthy prom sequence is so sparsely decorated that the prom might well be taking place in a reform school. In the title song, motorcycles are represented by prancing chorus men holding bicycle handlebars—and, even so, they soon disappear into a smoke effect that leaves the closest spectators gasping for breath. While every number also comes equipped with choreography, the repetitive boogie routines are less reminiscent of dance crazes of the sixties or eighties than of production numbers in Academy Awards telecasts and flop John Travolta movies.

Unlike the dancing, the script at least has the good grace to call it quits twenty minutes before the show does—with an abrupt, post-divorce nervous breakdown for a heroine who had previously seemed to possess a nervous system somewhat less developed than that of a Barbie doll. At that point, Tony Walton's uncharacteristically tacky set (rotating platforms painted to suggest 45 rpm records) also gives up the ghost, so the audience can enjoy an unimpeded view of the stage's pipe-covered rear wall.

But *Leader of the Pack* is determined to stretch itself to ninety-five minutes, and, to that end, the matronly real-life Ellie Greenwich soon wanders uneasily on stage to lead the adoring troops in a finger-snapping medley. Then comes the pièce de résistance—a brand-new song with inspirational lyrics like "We're going to make it after all" and "Say goodbye to all the tears and sorrow." It's not much of a finale, but it does send us home with renewed appreciation for the relative profundity of such vintage Greenwich compositions as "Do Wah Diddy" and "Da Doo Ron Ron."

≡ *The producers of this embarrassment topped it by battling each other in a noisy melodrama of acrimonious litigation that entertained Broadway denizens far more successfully than their show had—and that ran longer, too.*

GRIND
MARK HELLINGER THEATRE, APRIL 17, 1985

For most of Act 1, it is nearly impossible to figure out the real ambitions of *Grind*, the new musical that the director Harold Prince has brought to the Mark Hellinger. But as we discover when *Grind* grinds to its halt just before intermission, ignorance at this show is bliss. An enormous amount of showbiz expertise, some of it striking and inventive, has been lavished on this gargantuan enterprise, and, as long as its creators' intentions remain cloudy, the sheer rush of imaginative activity churns up a strange air of mystery. We don't really know what's happening, but, for a while, there's so much to watch that we don't really care.

That mysterious aura is most splendidly established by the setting, which, as designed by Clarke Dunham and lighted by Ken Billington, is as eerie as the House of Usher before the fall. The time is 1933, and the place is a Chicago burlesque house whose black and white performers are kept rigidly segregated onstage and off. Mr. Dunham's towering set can twirl to reveal the theater's gaudy marquee and façade, its stage, its wings, and its several flights of gloomy, clutter-filled dressing rooms. The labyrinthian backstage area suggests a teeming slum—as if Catfish Row had been plunked down in a Reginald Marsh painting of a Depression movie palace.

Soon we're watching the performers who slave at this theater, and their acts also have a bleak, intriguing edge. When the lovely Leilani Jones steps out on a light-ringed runway for a striptease, there's no joy in her routine; her face is as blank as a prostitute's, and the nasty gait of her Larry Grossman–Ellen Fitzhugh song forecloses any eroticism. Ben Vereen, as a song-and-dance headliner, suddenly breaks out of a standard chorus-line number for a private psychological soliloquy. The show's baggy-pants clown, Stubby Kaye, performs a vintage doctor-patient sketch that seems to lose its nerve at every punch line.

Mr. Prince knits these arresting incidents together with more assurance than he's mustered in any of his musicals since *Sweeney Todd*. As was also true of *Sweeney Todd*, an undertow of anger ripples beneath every song, scene, and performance. But why? For the first hour or so, almost nothing happens in Fay Kanin's book. Ms. Jones rejects Mr. Vereen's invitation for a date. Mr. Kaye, having lost his act's straight man, recruits a new one—a down-and-out Irish immigrant played by Timothy Nolen. This is hardly the stuff to justify the musical's urgent tone of barely suppressed rage.

But the supposed justification comes abruptly and retroactively with the Act 1 finale—and, as the wave of anger finally crests, the show's insinuating atmosphere turns torpid, its mystery evaporates into banality. At last forced to reveal its hand, *Grind* brings on a gang of anonymous white toughs to assault the black characters on a street corner. The intermission arrives as Mr. Vereen returns to the burlesque stage to go on, bitterly, with his show.

The ironic juxtaposition of the entertainer's escapist act with the racial violence beyond the theater's walls is all too heavily didactic—and all too familiar. Substitute 1930s Berlin for 1930s Chicago, Jewish victims for black ones, and Joel Grey for Mr. Vereen, and you have a replay of Mr. Prince's *Cabaret*. This time, however, the cataclysm seems thrown in for easy theatrical effect, rather than arrived at dramatically, and the accompanying moral seems gratuitous, not to mention self-righteous. Surely it's overkill to erect as huge an edifice as *Grind* to tell us that life wasn't all a cabaret in the urban America of 1933.

From then on, the show disintegrates into similarly contrived and disjointed melodramatic events, accompanied by similarly tired messages. Act 2 offers a violent interracial love triangle, a suicide, an account of a terrorist bombing overseas, and, for a finale, a large-scale race riot engulfing the auditorium. Ms. Kanin's aspirations are honorable: She apparently sees the show's setting as a metaphor large enough to contain a compressed history of American racial conflicts, with both the civil rights and black separatist movements thrown in along the way. But a burlesque house built exclusively on metaphor cannot stand. By failing to give her characters much definition in Act 1, the writer robs their various tragedies of all impact in Act 2. If the people of *Grind* don't engage each other or the audience, how can we care about either them or the larger themes they represent?

As the musical leans on history to lend significance to soap-opera developments, so it increasingly leans on other musicals to find a style. Broadway's previous quasi-Brechtian treatments of vaudeville and burlesque (*Gypsy, Follies, Chicago*) are all accounted for—and, eventually, Mr. Nolen, who played Sweeney Todd at the City Opera this season, sings a grim autobiographical epiphany, preposterous in this context, that could well belong to that demon barber of Fleet Street. By the time Mr. Vereen performs a tucked-elbow solo strut reminiscent of his last Broadway turn in Bob Fosse's *Pippin,* the show has become a desperate barrage of arbitrary musical numbers, portentous staging devices, extravagant costumes (gloriously designed by Florence Klotz), confused plot twists, and sociological bromides. In form and content alike, *Grind* flattens out to become Broadway's answer to Francis Ford Coppola's *The Cotton Club.*

One could weep for the talent that is expended to so little cumulative effect. Mr. Prince and his choreographer, Lester Wilson, open Act 2 with a haunting dressing-room sequence in which a half-dozen strippers slowly warm up in the dim light, sadly don their costumes, and segue into their nightly dance routine. Like Ms. Fitzhugh's lyric for the title song earlier on, the interlude gives rueful life—but only brief life— to the show's subsidiary point that grind-show performers are never free of the brutal daily grind that they allow their Depression audiences to escape.

Ms. Fitzhugh's lyrics are usually accomplished, but they can't plug the holes in Mrs. Kanin's characters. Mr. Grossman's music, if never remotely matching its John Kander and Stephen Sondheim prototypes, is far superior to his work for Mr. Prince's *A Doll's Life.* Though the score is often carried by Bill Byers's rip-roaring orchestrations and Paul Gemignani's crack band, there is an affecting pastiche Harold Arlen torch song for Ms. Jones, a lively Sophie Tucker–style comic number for the belter Sharon Murray, and a rousing gospel funeral peroration gorgeously sung by Carol Woods. (Never mind that a character is killed off gratuitously to justify that funeral.)

The stars work hard, with mixed results. Mr. Vereen rarely persuades us that he's the callow rake or, later, the fist-raising firebrand that he's claimed to be, but he's tireless in his attempts to provide ingratiating showmanship. Ms. Jones, in her Broadway debut, is a find—a gifted young performer lacking only a little flash. Although Mr. Nolen has a beautiful voice, his acting skills are too rudimentary to bring off the musical's one truly demanding role—that of a mystery man who changes identity in almost every scene.

Mr. Kaye, still hardy thirty-five years after he made his name in *Guys and Dolls,* is the very embodiment of the old-time trouper he plays. In an early number, he touchingly describes that noble professionalism that propels entertainers to go out and do a show, no matter what goes wrong onstage or off. "I Get Myself Out" is the song's title, and its spirit bleeds through the entire evening. For all that's gone wrong with *Grind,* one never stops admiring the valor with which Mr. Prince and company get themselves out there and give it all they've got.

≣ *This was one of the most elaborate follies ever done on Broadway—a huge, hulking musical about racial violence. Harold Prince would examine many of these themes in a somewhat more subtle manner in his hit revival of* Show Boat *almost a decade later.*

PENN & TELLER
WESTSIDE ARTS THEATRE, APRIL 19, 1985

Penn Jillette is a tall, bespectacled fellow who looks and sounds like an untenured English instructor driven slightly goofy by too many nights spent grading student term papers. His much shorter partner, known only as Teller, is a gloomy-faced imp who never speaks. In their gray, Brooks Brothers–style suits, neither man is particularly prepossessing, and neither much fits the conventional image of an entertainer. But entertainers they are, and the little show they've brought to the Westside Arts Theatre is one of the season's most original infusions of fun.

Penn & Teller is in the same spirit as such New Wave vaudeville turns as the Flying Karamazov Brothers and Avner the Eccentric. The performers are master magicians and jugglers who fold their tricks into hip comic riffs. Yet Penn and Teller, unlike their peers, will be enjoyed even more by adults than by children. This pair's jokes are often as witty as their stunts are amazing. What's more, their humor and sleights-of-hand merge into a theatrical statement that runs deeper than the act's individual ingredients might suggest.

The comic tone of *Penn & Teller* often recalls the wry cynicism of David Letterman—with some Pinteresque sadomasochism thrown in as well. Penn humiliates Teller for doing a card trick—card tricks are "intrinsically wimpy," he explains—and is, in general, fond of deconstructing the whole notion of showmanship. Even as he juggles knives and an apple (taking bites out of the apple each time it reaches his mouth), Penn announces that the routine is a self-destructive and exhibitionistic form of psychological "overcompensation." He is equally quick to point out which parts of the show are filler and which gestures are contrived to milk an audience's laughter or applause. The "cheap histrionics" of other performers are also savaged: Penn's running spiel is punctuated by witheringly funny asides about Marcel Marceau, Doug Henning, Bruce Springsteen, and avant-garde performance artists.

But as much as Penn and Teller burst the balloons of their own trade, they paradoxically continue to reassert its wonder. Such illusions as levitation and needle-swallowing are brought off with a skill worthy of Mr. Henning. The show's double-edged method is perhaps best illustrated by the finale. Penn sits on the empty stage, his face illuminated only by a campfire torch he's holding, and sweetly recounts his lifelong admiration for the "self-made freaks" of the circus. Then he explains in detail how he mastered the technique of fire swallowing, even to the point of describing how the tongue burns feel. Yet when the time finally comes for Penn to swallow the torch's flame, the stunt seems more magical, not less, for all the explication—and more engagingly personal a feat than such circus pyrotechnics usually are.

Penn & Teller has been "supervised" (and stylishly) by Art Wolff, the director best known for his staging of the similarly quirky comedy of Shel Silverstein. Mr. Wolff might yet demand a few trims in Act 2, when a few routines go on too long and one strange interlude, a dark and precious playlet involving handcuffs, falls completely flat. In that sketch and at a few other moments, the team's excursions into the ghoulish curdle into the ponderous.

Still, such is the show's overall buoyancy that the audience volunteers drafted throughout the evening are not used merely as props, but are transformed, through Penn's ad-libbing, into a pick-up cast of supporting players. The performers evolve into characters, too. Mute as Teller remains, he conveys a full clown's personality with his repertory of generally sour but occasionally demented deadpan takes. While Penn may bully his partner, he wins us over with his nonstop comic erudition and with his contagious affection for "the American sideshow." Lest anyone in the audience stubbornly resist his charms, he circulates in the lobby at intermission and after the final curtain—to spring a few more jokes and hawk souvenir T-shirts.

What we don't learn about these self-described "eccentric guys," however, is exactly where they've come from. The *Showbill* is reticent on the subject, and, by evening's end, all we really know for sure is that the team has been playing gigs around the country for a decade or so. It's even more certain that those travels will now have to be curtailed. Once New Yorkers get a whiff of this delightful show, they're not likely to let Penn and Teller take off for the road again anytime too soon.

THE NORMAL HEART
PUBLIC THEATER, APRIL 22, 1985

The blood that's coursing through *The Normal Heart*, the new play by Larry Kramer at the Public Theater, is boiling hot. In this fiercely polemical drama about the private and public fallout of the AIDS epidemic, the playwright starts off angry, soon gets furious, and then sky-rockets into sheer rage. Although Mr. Kramer's theatrical talents are not always as highly developed as his conscience, there can be little doubt that *The Normal Heart* is the most outspoken play around—or that it speaks up about a subject that justifies its author's unflagging, at times even hysterical, sense of urgency.

What gets Mr. Kramer mad is his conviction that neither the hetero- nor homosexual community has fully met the ever-expanding crisis posed by acquired immune deficiency syndrome. He accuses the gov-ernmental, medical, and press establishments of foot-dragging in com-bating the disease—especially in the early days of its outbreak, when much of the play is set—and he is even tougher on homosexual leaders who, in his view, were either too cowardly or too mesmerized by the ide-ology of sexual liberation to get the story out. "There's not a good word to be said about anyone's behavior in this whole mess," claims one char-acter—and certainly Mr. Kramer has few good words to say about Mayor Koch, various prominent medical organizations, *The New York Times,* or, for that matter, most of the leadership of an unnamed organization ap-parently patterned after the Gay Men's Health Crisis.

Some of the author's specific accusations are questionable, and, needless to say, we often hear only one side of inflammatory debates. But there are also occasions when the stage seethes with the conflict of im-passioned, literally life-and-death argument. When the play's hero, a writer and activist named Ned Weeks (Brad Davis), implores his peers to curtail sexual activity rather than risk contracting AIDS, another equally righteous activist vehemently counters that such sweeping measures will negate years of brave, painfully hard-fought battles for the freedom to practice homosexual love "openly" and "without guilt." While the logic may be with Ned—"AIDS is not a civil rights issue but a contagion issue," he says—Mr. Kramer allows the antagonist, woundingly played by Robert Dorfman, to give full ideological and emotional vent to an op-posing point-of-view.

Such issues constantly arise in *The Normal Heart,* giving it a profile quite distinct from that of *As Is,* William Hoffman's more intimately focused play about the AIDS plague. Mr. Kramer was a founder of the Gay Men's Health Crisis who parted with his colleagues after fraternal disputes about political tactics. The history of the protagonist in *The Normal Heart* is similar. Ned is a loud, tireless firebrand who favors confrontational strategies in dramatizing the AIDS threat; the mostly timid men who join him in founding an AIDS-awareness organization are often afraid either to risk public exposure of their sexuality or to take on the heterosexual power structure forthrightly. To thicken the conflict further, Mr. Kramer has Ned fall in love with such a weakling—a fictional *New York Times* reporter named Felix (D. W. Moffett) who can't decide how completely to step out of the closet.

The constant squabbles between the radical Ned and his cautiously liberal friends—which often sound like replays of those that divided the antiwar movement of the sixties—can become tiresome. The trouble is not that the arguments are uninteresting, but that Mr. Kramer is not always diligent about portraying Ned's opponents, including the organization's frightened president (David Allen Brooks), in credible detail. Worse, there's a galloping egocentricity that overruns and upstages the play's most pressing issues. The more the author delves into the minutiae of the organization's internecine politics, the more *The Normal Heart* moves away from the larger imperatives of the AIDS crisis and becomes a parochial legal brief designed to defend its protagonist against his political critics.

The writing's pamphleteering tone is accentuated by Mr. Kramer's insistence on repetition—nearly every scene seems to end twice—and on regurgitating facts and figures in lengthy tirades. Some of the supporting players, notably Ned's heterosexual brother (Phillip Richard Allen) and a heroic doctor (Concetta Tomei), are too flatly written to emerge as more than thematic or narrative pawns. The characters often speak in the same bland journalistic voice—so much so that lines could be reassigned from one to another without the audience detecting the difference.

If these drawbacks, as well as the somewhat formulaic presentation of the Ned-Felix love affair, blunt the play's effectiveness, there are still many powerful vignettes sprinkled throughout. Much to his credit, Mr. Kramer makes no attempt to sanitize AIDS; the scenes featuring the disease's suffering victims are harrowing. The playwright is equally forceful—and at his most eloquent—when he passionately champions a prideful homosexual identity "that isn't just sexual."

The production does not always pump up the writing's flaccid passages. The director, Michael Lindsay-Hogg, tends to freeze Ned and his opponents in place to declaim, as if they were members of a college debating society. The performances can also go slack. Mr. Davis has the unenviable assignment of playing a shrill public scold—who, like the author, can be his own worst enemy—and one admires the actor's refusal to sentimentalize him. But Mr. Davis does seem vacant in his reposeful romantic scenes with Mr. Moffett, whose characterization of the honestly conflicted Felix is the most complex and moving of the evening. In the lesser roles, only Mr. Dorfman and William DeAcutis, as another organization member, make sharp impressions.

The set, designed by Eugene Lee and Keith Raywood, encloses the audience in a whitewashed box, on which are emblazoned the names and state-by-state death tolls of AIDS victims. While one wishes that the play's outrage had been channeled into drama as fully compelling as its cause, the writing on the theater's walls alone could drive anyone with a normal heart to abandon what Mr. Kramer calls the "million excuses for not getting involved."

≣ *I thought some of* The Normal Heart *was already dated when it opened— so closely did Kramer follow actual events and fading controversies of the earliest days of the AIDS crisis, already ancient history by 1985. I was completely wrong.* The Normal Heart, *far from being a transitory exercise in topical theater, turned out to have the longest run of any play at Joseph Papp's Public Theater; it has been a hit all over the world and continues to be produced widely, even as the specific circumstances it describes in the early days of the AIDS crisis have faded into history. (A movie version is also perennially rumored to be on its way.) As it happened, the play's lead actor, Brad Davis, would die of AIDS, but Larry Kramer, despite his own HIV-related health travails, proved the most outspoken gay political leader of the AIDS era. Somehow he also found time to continue writing for the theater.*

His outspokenness threw the Times *into a panic on the eve of the play's opening. Word had filtered to management from previews that* The Normal Heart *was unsparing in its criticism of the paper's early AIDS coverage—criticism, sadly, that, however overstated, was far from undeserved. And so on the day I was filing my review, I was stunned to discover that my piece would be followed by a little news brief in which the paper and another Kramer nemesis, Mayor Koch, would refute his play. The squib, titled "The Times and Koch Comment," read:*

A spokesman for The New York Times *said yesterday that charges in* The Normal Heart *that the* Times *suppressed news about AIDS are untrue. As soon as the* Times *was informed about the existence of the disease, a member of the science staff was assigned to cover the story, and an article appeared on July 3, 1981, making the* Times *one of the first—if not the first—national news media to alert the public to the* scientific recognition and spread of the disease. After that, scores of articles, including a full-length report in The New York Times Magazine, were published as researchers reported their findings about the danger and spread of AIDS.

"I haven't seen the play," Mayor Koch said through a spokesman, Leland Jones. "But I hope it's as good as As Is, which is superb."

After I left the drama critic's job, I became friends with Larry Kramer, truly one of the most interesting and exasperating people I've ever met. The various angry letters he'd written me on the job about one thing or another were forgotten, but he continues to pick new fights with me, the Times, *and the world almost daily. Larry's outrage is a natural force and, on those occasions when it's focused on the right targets, a national resource.*

BIG RIVER
EUGENE O'NEILL THEATRE, APRIL 26, 1985

Big River: The Adventures of Huckleberry Finn is the last Broadway musical of the season—but, more important, it is the first that audiences can attend without fear of suffering either profound embarrassment or terminal boredom. This show has a lot going for it: a tuneful score by the country-music songsmith Roger Miller; exuberant performers; and a gifted young director, Des McAnuff, who is full of clever ideas about how to bring Mark Twain's masterpiece to the stage.

If all of Big River were up to its high-water marks, the season might even have found the exciting new musical it desperately craves: The raw ingredients for such an achievement are on display at the Eugene O'Neill. But there are too many times, especially in the second act, when the imaginative flow of Big River slows to a trickle, and the show loses its promising way. While young theatergoers may well enjoy the entire bustling enterprise, adults can't be faulted for finding the evening a mixture of the modestly engaging and the tolerably bland.

At its best, Big River is much more faithful to its source than one might expect. The musical's creators understand that Twain's bottomless novel, in which a river journey limns the dark soul of a nation, is not merely a boy's adventure tale. When Huck and Jim board their raft to a rousing song called "Muddy Water," Mr. McAnuff and his designer, Heidi Landesman, magically convey the characters' exhilaration at fleeing home; the moonlit river rises up on stage like a silver ribbon, tugging the audience and heroes alike into a mysterious, uncharted wilderness of the American spirit. In the similarly impressive opening scene, the whole social fabric of Twain's Missouri unfurls before us: As genteel townsfolk, browbeaten slaves, and boisterous boys spill across the stage and into the auditorium, we see both the idyllic pleasures and unacknowledged injustices of the civilization from which Huck (Daniel H. Jenkins) and Jim (Ron Richardson) must escape.

If the makers of *Big River* can send us floating dreamily down the Mississippi or can summon up a vanished nineteenth-century world in a flash, it should be simple for them to accomplish such relatively easy tasks as telling the novel's plot, repeating its jokes, and dramatizing its resonant love story between an outcast boy and a runaway slave. But, as it happens, *Big River* does the hard things well and the easy things sloppily. William Hauptman's script is as formulaic as Mr. McAnuff's staging is daring. Even as the production promises us the visionary sweep of Twain, the libretto provides a lengthy but comic-book–style digest of the novel that flattens out an American *Ulysses* into *The Hardy Boys*.

Mr. Hauptman has made several dubious decisions. He attempts to include too many of the novel's anecdotes and, in so doing, must often truncate or rush them to the point where their comic payoff (and, at times, narrative thrust) is lost. Yet the few incidents he does leave out— the Grangerford-Shepherdson feud, the vigilante lynching—are precisely those that are most essential to preserving the novel's bite. Worse, the libretto is so haphazardly structured that Jim and Huck sometimes seem to disappear: By the Act 1 finale, the show has shifted its focus away from its heroes to center instead on those vagrant con men, the Duke (René Auberjonois) and the King (Bob Gunton). Once that happens, not even a climactic Act 2 embrace can recharge the tidal thematic and emotional pull of the Huck-Jim bond.

The music and lyrics, often riding on giddy banjo-and-fiddle-flecked hoedown arrangements, at first rise well above the text. Mr. Miller writes in indigenous Southern and Western American idioms that are ideally expressive of Twain's characters and their salty vernacular. Act 1 contains one lively song after another, including a talking-blues diatribe against "Guv'ment" (flintily delivered by John Goodman as Pap Finn), a sweet spiritual for anonymous slaves, and a haunting anthem ("River in the Rain") in which Huck and Jim apotheosize the wonders of the mythic Mississippi.

But once the book bogs down irrevocably in Act 2, Mr. Miller turns to clichés. Some irrelevant and arbitrarily inserted numbers, notably a puppy-love ballad for Huck and a passing female acquaintance (Patti Cohenour), seem to have been written for the pop charts rather than *Big River*. When Huck and Jim sing of how they are "worlds apart" or when

Jim delivers a canned paean to freedom ("I wish I could spread my wings and fly!"), we've left Twain country behind for platitudinous musical-comedy land.

By Act 2, even Ms. Landesman's wondrous set, which conjures up both sunlit settlements and foggy nights downriver, runs out of surprises. But the cast by and large remains endearing. The powerful-voiced Mr. Richardson makes for a majestic Jim—although the slave is timidly and anachronistically bowdlerized here as an incipient twentieth-century civil rights activist. Mr. Auberjonois, looking like a Dr. Seuss drawing, and Mr. Gunton, resembling a dyspeptic Gabby Hayes, bring a devilish edge to their bunkum artists—most delightfully so when they perform their hammy burlesque renditions of Shakespeare for Arkansas rubes. There are also spiky cameo contributions from Carol Dennis, Jennifer Leigh Warren, Gordon Connell, William Youmans, and, most crucially, John Short as a brash and cunning Tom Sawyer.

Mr. Jenkins's Huck is more problematic. While the performer has a nice voice and the right twang, he is too old to play a boy in his early teens—and too domesticated to convey a corrosive, conscience-stricken outsider who would rather light out for territory than be "sivilized." But he's always charming company and, in that sense, he's the perfect Huck Finn for an ingratiating musical that can't quite bring itself to raise hell.

≡ *With little help from me,* Big River *was a Tony-winning hit. I've been arguing about this review ever since with Rocco Landesman, the producer who would eventually take over one of the three Broadway theater chains, Jujamcyn, and become a major force for Broadway's good in the 1990s. One of the happier aspects of leaving the drama critic's job was that it freed me to become a friend of Rocco, himself a lapsed drama critic who once taught drama criticism at the Yale School of Drama. He's still sore that I didn't love* Big River *but is more upset by far that Roger Miller, whom he idolized, didn't live to write another musical.*

ORPHANS

WESTSIDE ARTS THEATRE, MAY 8, 1985

In recent seasons, Chicago's Steppenwolf Theatre Company has introduced New Yorkers to a sizzling, idiosyncratic performance style as brawny, all-American, and blunt as the windy city that spawned it. Steppenwolf's specialty is not the development of new plays, but the galvanic staging of existing ones—as exemplified by its productions of *True West* and *Balm in Gilead.* To that impressive pair can now be added *Orphans,* the company's newest offering. It is riveting to watch this evening's three stunning actors—Kevin Anderson, Terry Kinney, and John Mahoney—rip themselves apart with a raw ferocity that is Steppenwolf's theatrical answer to the esthetics of rock 'n' roll.

Orphans is theater for the senses and emotions, not the mind. The play itself, by Lyle Kessler, is best regarded as a taut trampoline for its levitating performers. What Mr. Kessler has devised is a pastiche—a hybrid of the Sam Shepard of *True West* and the Harold Pinter of *The Caretaker.* While it's a shrewd pastiche that gains steadily in passion and tension, it won't stand up to any detailed exegesis. Examine *Orphans* too carefully, and one is less likely to learn about the savage and solitary nature of man (which is, I fear, the theme) than to uncover synthetically re-created gestures from other plays.

But there's little time for such close scrutiny while *Orphans* unfolds. The director, Gary Sinise (who also staged and costarred in *True West*), grabs us from his first image—that of Mr. Anderson curled up on a window ledge, blowing bubbles in an icy blue light. Typically, the eerie calm of that tableau ends abruptly. When Mr. Kinney arrives, Mr. Anderson leaps up, as if shot out of a cannon, and gyrates around a barren, darkened living room with the kinetic energy of a child playing a life-or-death game of hide and seek.

The two actors are cast as brothers who share a North Philadelphia home as rubbish-strewn as that of the fraternal slobs of *True West.* The older brother, Treat (Mr. Kinney), is a petty thief who has looked after the younger Phillip (Mr. Anderson) since childhood. Treat spends his days holding up victims at switchblade-point downtown, and he has connived to imprison his sibling at home. An overgrown wild child in torn sweat clothes, the innocent Phillip cannot read and does not know the identity of common objects like loafers and maps. His worldly experience is limited to television viewing; even his diet (exclusively Star Kist tuna and Hellman's mayonnaise) is dictated by the brand names hawked on the tube.

Orphans gains a plot with the arrival of a mysterious older character— a well-spoken, natty, silver-haired Chicago mobster named Harold (Mr. Mahoney). Like his hosts, this intruder is also an orphan—but he wouldn't mind being a civilizing father figure to young men he likens romantically to Hollywood's "dead end kids." In Pinter fashion, Harold sets off a chain reaction of role reversals and power struggles that lead all three men to find the familial connections that their literally and metaphorically orphaned existences have always denied them.

Flecked with biblical allegory, bondage motifs, enigmatic symbols, and malevolent allusions to "the free-enterprise system," *Orphans* is part absurdist black comedy and part metaphysical melodrama. Mr. Sinise transforms it into a creepy, hermetically sealed environment where every weird event seems realer than real. The men trapped within this spooky world beat their heads against its walls. Rather than walk down the stairs, the actors fall down them; they don't cross the room, but crash violently around it, sometimes slamming face-first into shut doors. Meanwhile, the spectral lighting (by the set designer, Kevin Rigdon) and edgy jazz score (by Pat Metheny and Lyle Mays) heighten the rippling undercurrents of incipient apocalypse.

The showiest of the roles belongs to Mr. Anderson, who may well create the stir John Malkovich did in *True West*. Staring at life only through windows, Phillip expertly mimics everyone he sees or hears about—a fast-talking game-show announcer, a strolling woman and her pet, and, most amazingly for a slight white actor, a heavyset black man. But Mr. Anderson always refracts these comic contortionist turns through Phillip's own feral identity. Looking not unlike a forlorn mongrel puppy, the actor creates a sweet, lost naïf desperately searching for a parental shoulder to nestle against.

Mr. Kinney, who directed Steppenwolf's . . . *And a Nightingale Sang* and appeared memorably in *Balm in Gilead,* counterpunches with his volatile, brutal Treat; he not only smacks his kid brother but at one point even beats himself up (and to a pulp). But the character is witty in his offhandedly vicious way ("I tried to work in a department store once and burned it down"), and he's not merely a teeth-baring wolf. When at last forced to confront his own wounds instead of wounding others, Mr. Kinney expectorates the repressed terrors of his childhood in primordial sobs far more bloodcurdling than the actual bloodletting of the play's dénouement.

No less commanding is Mr. Mahoney, whose dry, insinuatingly nasty performance as the cooler, middle-aged visitor makes one hunger to see him tackle Pinter and Mamet. He brings an unsettling, sepulchral tone to his repeated mythological reveries (part Horatio Alger, part Dreiser) about the romance of his Chicago orphanage upbringing. When rendered comatose by bourbon, he becomes a strangely pitiable figure, crying out for his unknown mommy in a wheezy, muffled bleat of longing.

Mr. Mahoney also has several lines expressing Harold's macabre fascination with Harry Houdini—an interest he coincidentally shares with Penn and Teller, the mischievous entertainers situated downstairs from *Orphans* at the small, double-decker Westside Arts Theatre. It may take

Houdini himself to cram in all the starved theatergoers who will want to see these neighboring shows—both of which bring startling high-wire theatrical stuntmanship to this season of mostly low blows.

THE MARRIAGE OF BETTE AND BOO
PUBLIC THEATER, MAY 17, 1985

Christopher Durang's comedy *The Marriage of Bette and Boo* is so speedy and chipper that it could almost be mistaken for a Bob Fosse musical. The large cast is always on the run, scurrying frantically among the fast-sliding crimson panels of Loren Sherman's sleek set to perform thirty-three scenes in two hours. Most of those scenes contain jokes; a few contain songs; all of them, as impeccably directed by Jerry Zaks, boast a choreographic pizzazz. Throw in the bright lighting (by Paul Gallo) and the high comic sheen of the performances, and *Bette and Boo* looks like pure cheer.

Yet here is what happens in this new family play by the author of *Sister Mary Ignatius Explains It All for You:* A woman gives birth to four successive stillborn babies, each of whom is unceremoniously dumped onto the hospital floor by the obstetrician. There are onstage deaths by stroke and by cancer. One character is an alcoholic, another a psychotic, another senile. And heaven help those who seek solace from the neighborhood priest. As Father Donnally (Richard B. Shull) explains, he is powerless to do anything except "mumble platitudes" to the "stupid people" who come to him with "insoluble problems."

How can one reconcile the tragic goings-on in *Bette and Boo* with its buoyant style? For Mr. Durang, that's no problem—it's an esthetic and moral calling. Once more he is demonstrating his special knack for wrapping life's horrors in the primary colors of absurdist comedy. In Mr. Durang's world, there is no explanation for misery: Even if one sifts through "the endless details of everyday life" hoping to "order reality," nothing will make sense. In *Bette and Boo*, as in his previous *Baby with the Bathwater*, the playwright lays out the loony facts of a boy's grotesque childhood, hoping the utter comic insanity of it all will somehow ease the pain.

What remains unclear this time is whether Mr. Durang is easing the pain or merely papering it over. *Bette and Boo*, now at the Public Theater, is sporadically funny and has been conceived with a structural inventiveness new to the writer's work: As the story progresses, its chronology pointedly becomes more scrambled and its connections with any literal reality increasingly severed. But at the same time, Mr. Durang's jokemaking is becoming more mannered and repetitive—an automatic, almost compulsive reflex. *Bette and Boo* has a strangely airless atmosphere, and it says little the author hasn't said with greater wit and emotional ferocity before.

In a sense, this play is Mr. Durang's version of *The Glass Menagerie*—with the playwright himself cast in the role of the narrator-son, here named Matt. The tale begins with the marriage of Matt's parents, the title characters played by Joan Allen and Graham Beckel, and ends over two decades later with the family's dissolution. By then, Matt is making his way in the world and has begun to accept the lessons of his upbringing. "I don't believe that God punishes people for specific things," says Mr. Durang at evening's end. "He punishes people in general for no reason."

Certainly there is evidence to support this view. Matt's fraternal grandfather, Karl (Bill Moor), is a sadistic businessman who rarely looks up from his work, unless it's to crack a joke about "an albino humpback with a harelip." Karl openly refers to his wife (Olympia Dukakis) as an "idiot" who has "never said one sensible thing in thirty years of marriage." Matt's aunts on his mother's side include a frequent sanatorium patient (Kathryn Grody) who wanders about with a cello and is constantly writing notes of apology for her real or imagined transgressions. "Is the phrase 'my own stupidity' hyphenated?" she asks while composing one such missive.

Bette and Boo are scarcely healthier. When Matt's mom isn't giving birth to the stillborn babies she dreams of naming after A. A. Milne characters, she is compiling a calendar that records which days her husband is "half drunk" or "dead drunk." Yet Matt marches gamely on, stepping forward to address the audience about his favorite movies (from 8½ to *The Nun Also Rises*), as well as about the relevant works of Joseph Conrad, Virginia Woolf, Robert Benchley, and his collegiate academic specialty, Thomas Hardy.

While too many of the evening's gags are regurgitated endlessly, the cast makes the most of the best. Ms. Allen, a member of Chicago's Steppenwolf Company, is as convincing as a cartoonishly suffocating American mother as she was as the vulnerable English daughter she memorably played in . . . *And a Nightingale Sang*. Mr. Moor, all dour nastiness, and Ms. Dukakis, forever laughing as hideously as a carnival lady, seem like refugees from a Charles Addams cartoon.

Mr. Shull, in the evening's outstanding set piece, provides a priest who could be Sister Mary's brother: In the midst of a family-counseling session, he falls on the floor to impersonate a strip of frying bacon. The others, notably Mercedes Ruehl as a terminally bitter aunt and Bill McCutcheon as Matt's speech-impaired maternal grandfather, are just as tart.

Although the victim of all these monsters, the author performs his downstage monologues with an ingratiating air. But his cherubic smile fades in the affecting episodes that impale Matt at the end of each act. Forced to participate in horrifying parental scenes—rather than merely to joke about them—Mr. Durang, both as playwright and actor, ceases to be an entertainer and becomes a crippled boy, shivering in the shadows. It says a lot about the increasingly visible limitations of the author's style that these two brief spells of real darkness are more biting than all the terribly bright dark comedy that is the dazzlement of *Bette and Boo.*

≣ *I was often a fan of Chris Durang's, not just as a playwright* (Sister Mary Ignatius Explains It All for You, Baby with the Bathwater) *but as a revue performer with Sigourney Weaver in the riotous* Das Lusitania Songspiel. *But much like Robert Brustein and Jules Feiffer, his colleagues at Cambridge's American Repertory Theatre, he turned into a bitter critic of mine when I proved less than an automatic enthusiast for his work. He told* The Wall Street Journal *that this review "discouraged investors from bringing this play to Broadway" and told interviewers that it stopped him from writing plays, period, driving him to a career as a supporting comic actor in Hollywood movies. In fact, though, he wrote other plays (and screenplays), including* Laughing Wild, *which, alas, I also didn't love.*

Perhaps Bette and Boo *could have made it commercially on Broadway, no matter what my review. But no Durang play has lasted more than a few weeks in that arena either before* (A History of the American Film), *during* (Beyond Therapy), *or after* (Sex and Longing) *my tenure as* Times *drama critic. This may say at least as much about Broadway as it does about Durang. His English comic antecedent, Joe Orton, has never made it on Broadway, either.*

THE COUNT OF MONTE CRISTO
KENNEDY CENTER, WASHINGTON, D.C., MAY 20, 1985

The hero of *The Count of Monte Cristo*, the innocent sailor Edmond Dantes, spends eighteen years locked away unjustly in the dungeons of the Chateau d'If. After watching the director Peter Sellars's stage version of Alexandre Dumas's 1844 warhorse, an audience will know just how Dantes felt. While the production at the Kennedy Center's Eisenhower Theatre runs only three and a half hours (plus intermission), it does provide more than a glimpse of eternity.

This inflated enterprise, which opened Saturday night, is the second offering of Mr. Sellars's new, self-proclaimed American National Theatre. It was preceded by Timothy Mayer's staging of *Henry IV, Part I*, which closed prematurely after a disappointing critical and box-office reception. Like *Henry IV, Monte Cristo* isn't exactly an American play, although it does figure in American theater lore: This is the ramshackle, hand-me-down adaptation of Dumas that James O'Neill, father to Eugene, performed for roughly thirty years in barnstorming cross-country tours. As *Long Day's Journey into Night* most famously tells us, *Monte Cristo* was a golden trap for the elder O'Neill. Unable or unwilling to escape the lucrative vehicle, he never fulfilled his promise of becoming a tragedian to rival Edwin Booth.

In the Kennedy Center's exhumation, Dantes is played by Richard Thomas—a sensitive, forceful actor who also has the potential to reach classic stature. His passionate performance is above reproach, but Mr. Sellars's conception keeps reining him in. Rather than stage *Monte Cristo* as the entertaining slice of romantic claptrap that it is, the director uses it as an excuse for an eclectic tour of modern theatrical history.

The modus operandi is outlined in Mr. Sellars's own review of his production, which is provided as a program insert. "The evening contains at least five different plays, each with its own method and tone," the director writes, before tossing around references to "the impulse toward pure expressionism," "constructivist narrative," and "the Brechtian ideal." He's not joking. Watching this *Monte Cristo* is like leafing through a book of production photographs that begins with the Russian avant-garde of Meyerhold and his heirs, moves on to Weimar Berlin, and ends up with such recent phenomena as the Mabou Mines's stagings of Beckett, Harold Prince's *Sweeney Todd,* Trevor Nunn's modernist Royal Shakespeare Company productions, and the deconstructionist exercises of the Wooster Group.

Working on a deep stage emptied of all but a few pieces of all-purpose scenery (high-tech bridges and towers, three mobile neo-Deco armoires), Mr. Sellars does re-create some of his sources well and, on occasion, summons up arresting tableaux. In the Chateau d'If sequences, Mr. Thomas's head peeks out of a trapdoor in the vast, darkened space—his face a tiny flame of humanity flickering in a sooty void of infinite solitude. The director also makes amusing use of the exposed theatrical machinery, especially the elevator and catwalks along the stage's rear wall.

But many of the overfamiliar devices, like the anachronistic costumes and props, could be superimposed arbitrarily on any text to the same clashing effect. (Indeed, Mr. Sellars does recycle gimmicks from *Hang On to Me,* his adaptation of Gorky's *Summerfolk* at Minneapolis's Guthrie Theater.) Rather than bring out new values in Dumas's saga, the staging vitiates its old-fashioned virtues. The melodramatic plot twists and exclamatory asides, often fractionalized by busy lighting cues and echo-chamber amplification, are played as pure camp, in a manner that does not recall the cinema of D. W. Griffith (as the program note suggests) but that of Douglas Sirk. The bond between Dantes and his beloved Mercedes (Patti LuPone) is sexless; the final duels unfold in near-darkness, with whispered dialogue and slow motion action. When the hero escapes his dungeon by sea, the ocean's waves are stylized by undulating silver-foil banners in the increasingly overworked Asian tradition.

In lieu of fun or even coherence, Mr. Sellars pounds in didactic themes. He makes much of Dumas's tortured father-son relationships—inviting us, perhaps, to see the characters of *Monte Cristo* as prototypically tragic (or as stand-ins for the O'Neills). That's fair enough, but how seriously can we take the injections of black-white racial divisions or the attempts to trump up Napoleonic history into a paradigm of modern fascism? By the time totemic eagles start appearing, we seem to have landed in imperial Germany—but not, alas, in Robert Wilson's theater piece, *the CIVIL warS,* which makes such brilliant use of some of the same history and iconography.

For added diversion, there are interpolations from Lord Byron and the Bible, as well as an onstage string ensemble, which at one point performs a partial recital of Alfred Schnittke's Second Quartet. (The program describes this interjected concert as "a relentless, harrowing interlude" that's "dedicated to the memory of the Soviet filmmaker Larissa Schepitko." Relentless it is.) Although the cast boasts some excellent actors, they are often encouraged to caricature their past work. The sonorous, apparitional presence of that fine Beckett interpreter David Warrilow is milked for near-parodistic Beckett pastiche. Tony Azito's hysterical clowning, Roscoe Lee Browne's stentorian voice, and Ms. LuPone's tart sexuality are similarly ill-used. Both Michael O'Keefe and Zakes Mokae seem lost.

Still, the entire company, like the audience, can be applauded for its stamina. Let those who disinter this play the next time around remember that by the end of his career James O'Neill was performing it in vaudeville, in a tabloid version cut to forty-five minutes.

≡ *Boston, Washington, Los Angeles—Peter Sellars, Harvard wunderkind, undertook lavish, heavily promoted theatrical ventures in any town that would put up the cash, then let others pick up the pieces when something better tempted him to split. Most of his productions were fascinating in their audacity (if not always their achievement). The national theater Sellars planned to create at the Kennedy Center went nowhere; for all the various efforts to start a permanent theater company there, the center remains a Broadway-road booking house. But Sellars finally found his home and artistic balance in opera.*

RAT IN THE SKULL
PUBLIC THEATER, MAY 22, 1985

Audiences who have sampled the Public Theater's recent English plays—*Tom and Viv, Virginia,* and *Salonika*—might well believe that London dramatists are a hopelessly nostalgic lot, lost in the mists of Bloomsbury and the trenches of World War I. But the United Kingdom has a tempestuous present as well, and it has playwrights who are willing to bring the raging battles to the stage. Ron Hutchinson is such a writer, and his *Rat in the Skull,* the latest import at the Public, is a raw descent into the morass of Northern Ireland. An authentic and savage political play, it provides a most welcome antidote to its genteel English predecessors of the season.

Rat in the Skull, like *Tom and Viv,* has been transported intact from London's Royal Court Theatre, under the direction of Max Stafford-Clark. Be warned that the evening can be as demanding of American ears as *Glengarry Glen Ross* might be of English ones. The accents are thick. The text contains so much English and Irish slang that one would have to memorize the program's four-page glossary to have a prayer of understanding every line. Yet such is the force of the acting and staging—and the one-act play's corrosive overall shape—that patient theatergoers will find the two hours rewarding, even as some individual passages drift out of reach.

The setting is a cell in a London police station, where a suspected IRA bomber, Roche (Colum Convey), has been detained for questioning. To help them in the interrogation, the London coppers have summoned Nelson (Brian Cox), a detective from Northern Ireland's predominantly Protestant police force, the Royal Ulster Constabulary. As we learn early on, Nelson ultimately beats up his prisoner—an act that, under the law, will allow the bomber to escape punishment. Most of *Rat in the Skull* is a flashback, in which the interrogation is reenacted so that we might learn why Nelson would so lose control of himself, at the self-defeating price of letting the IRA bomber go free.

Mr. Hutchinson uses this central question to telescope the whole sorry story of the Irish troubles. And he does so without resorting to agitprop. Although the battle lines between Nelson and Roche at first seem clearly drawn, they gradually blur until we finally have equal sympathy for both sides of an unstoppable blood feud—even as we see that neither side can claim the moral high ground and that neither side can win.

For much of the interrogation, the young IRA man remains a mute martyr, chafing under a hot lamp while the older Protestant inquisitor lambastes him with torrents of abuse. Trying to "break" his prey, Nelson mocks legendary IRA heroes and screams anti-Catholic epithets (each of which, as he eloquently puts it, is "a particular conjugation in the grammar of hate"). But once Roche speaks back, the playwright deftly demonstrates that the antagonists, while homicidally despising each other, are also suicidal blood brothers—each of them martyrs to the same history.

Both men, after all, have "followed coffins down the street a thousand times." Both live in constant fear not only of murder but of that "rat in the skull"—the gnawing, unspoken doubts about the rightness of their respective causes. It is the tragedy of both men—and the constituencies they represent—that the repression of those doubts forecloses any possibility of a peacefully achieved truce.

In Mr. Hutchinson's view, the English are no more likely to forge a solution. The play's London police officers (Philip Jackson and Gerard Horan) prove to be nearly as patronizing to their Ulster colleague as they are to the prisoner; they speak in a flat bureaucratese which contrasts sharply with the rich language of the Irish pair. By stating that the gulf between English and Irish is even wider than that which separates Irish Catholics and Protestants, the playwright drops the full panorama of an eternal, triangular stalemate into place.

It is impressive that Mr. Hutchinson can dramatize so much so fairly with four characters and a simple anecdote. The intimacy of his approach is further heightened by the fine performances. Mr. Cox, last seen in the much different role of Darrell in *Strange Interlude,* has most of the lines and provides the evening's tour de force. His Nelson may be a violent battering ram of an inquisitor, stopping at nothing to get "behind the eyeballs" of his victim, but he's also an intelligent, self-aware, tragic protagonist, irresistibly drawn to his fate.

Mr. Stafford-Clark's staging, which unfolds on a spare and bleakly lighted set, has the slam-bang vitality of police melodrama; it reaches a still higher plateau in a dreamlike finale which raises the play's conflict to a metaphor for decades of fratricide. For all the impenetrable interludes of *Rat in the Skull*, we just can't escape the horrifying central image it distills from Northern Ireland—that of "two fellows in a ditch, clubbing each other, till the one dropped dead."

THE ROAD TO THE GRAVEYARD
Ensemble Studio Theatre, May 27, 1985

At the end of *The Road to the Graveyard*, Horton Foote's new one-act play at the Ensemble Studio Theatre, a small-town Texas family sits in its homey parlor, each member lost in silent contemplation. The year is 1939, and the air is warm and still. The only sound is that of distant waltz music drifting in from a party of Mexican laborers enjoying a night off.

The music is sweet, as is the reposeful final tableau. But the effect of *The Road to the Graveyard* is something else. While Mr. Foote may have simulated a vintage *Saturday Evening Post* cover, there is an unbearable turbulence beneath that tranquil surface. The only peace in this play is indeed the discordant peace of the graveyard. A family is dying, and so is a social order soon to be upended by World War II.

These themes are not new to Mr. Foote, who has been writing about a changing Texas for decades, most recently in the films *Tender Mercies* and *1918*. This work, the last of four offerings in Series B of the EST's one-act-play marathon, may be among the finest distillations of his concerns. In roughly a half-hour, he surveys the tragic ruins of a household—even as he looks back, with more anger than nostalgia, at a world whose idyllic glow belies all manner of unacknowledged neuroses and sexual and economic injustices.

All of this is accomplished with a subtlety that suggests a collaboration between Faulkner and Chekhov. Not much happens in *The Road to the Graveyard*. A middle-aged spinster, India (Roberta Maxwell), goes about the daily business of nursing her elderly, failing parents (Margaret Thomson and Emmett O'Sullivan Moore). India's brother, Sonny (Frank Girardeau), who has spent eighteen years working as a menial at the local "picture show," contemplates getting married. A neighbor (Carolyn Coates) drops by for tea and gossip.

But pain keeps seeping through. In Ms. Maxwell's extraordinarily unnerving portrayal, India seems grotesquely disfigured by sexual repression and by the dread fear of her parents' and brother's imminent desertions. Sonny, a mild-mannered and overgrown mamma's boy, politely excuses himself to tend to the violently nervous stomach where his unexpressed bitterness resides. The nearly senile matriarch, though often dreamily plucking imaginary "bunny rabbits" out of the air, can still inflict guilt on her adult children and on the husband who failed to buy cheap land before Texas was carved up by speculators. The prattling neighbor is revealed to be an insomniac who spends most nights driving her car aimlessly on empty roads.

As deftly directed by Curt Dempster, the play's five perfect actors seamlessly thicken the initially airy atmosphere into a suffocating, magnetic field of anxiety.

≡ *This one-act play ended up restarting Horton Foote's New York theater career—which had been dormant, really, since the 1950s as he left Broadway to win two Oscars as a screenwriter* (To Kill a Mockingbird, Tender Mercies). *Now in his eighties, Foote remains a prolific writer of plays, screenplays, and memoirs. He won the Pulitzer Prize for his play* The Young Man from Atlanta *in 1995.*

SEVENTH
SEASON

1985—86

Lily Tomlin in *The Search for Signs of*
Intelligent Life in the Universe

No one can accuse Herb Gardner of betraying his convictions to keep up with changing times. Almost twenty-five years after his first Broadway success, *A Thousand Clowns,* he is still writing roughly the same play—the comedy about the cranky but endearing New York eccentric who refuses to capitulate peacefully to the crass workaday world. Mr. Gardner's new variation on the theme, now available in an attractive production at the American Place Theatre, is titled *I'm Not Rappaport,* and there's a valor to it. During much of this playwright's career, nonconformity has been fashionable, but these days, it's not. Mr. Gardner, like his onstage heroes, stubbornly continues to say what he thinks.

One only wishes that he did so with more dramatic verve and less preaching. In spite of its occasionally funny, flavorsome lines and pervasive sweetness, *I'm Not Rappaport* often seems didactic and repetitive. Mr. Gardner's characters tend to be either lovable lunatics or uptight pills, and the outcomes of their unambiguous confrontations are always predictable. While the author wants the audience to wake up and question the humdrum patterns of bourgeois life, his stacked theatrical technique achieves the reverse effect: We're lulled into tranquillity, rather than stimulated into self-examination, by the easy moral victories that the hero achieves over his antagonists.

That hero is Nat (Judd Hirsch), a cantankerous octogenarian who remains an unregenerate, Gompers-bred socialist of the old *Daily Worker* school. Though slowed by the infirmities of age, Nat still keeps the rabble-rousing faith—whether by obstreperously protesting the meat prices at Gristede's or by hectoring his adult daughter (Cheryl Giannini), a onetime antiwar firebrand who has now sold out to the mercenary splendors of Great Neck. Nat is such a consummate humanitarian that he not only champions the rights of the elderly and the poor but even defends his own mugger as a fellow victim of the city's dog-eat-dog Social Darwinism.

Nat's daughter, I needn't tell you, would like him to settle safely in a senior citizens' enclave. But Nat stubbornly holds his ground, the ground being the Central Park bench where he spends every afternoon kibitzing with another aged man, an ailing, black, apartment-house superintendent nicknamed Midge (Cleavon Little). For much of the play, which unfolds entirely in the park, the two old geezers perform a series of mild, cross-cultural *Sunshine Boys* routines. Some of the bits are canned—"I was smoking dope when you were eating matzoh balls," says Midge—but a few are amusing: Nat reenacts the comic Willie Howard's most famous vaudeville sketch (the source of Mr. Gardner's title), and Midge pays vocal tribute to his own idol, Joe Turner. While the pals' other conversations are often treacly reveries about long-lost loves or urban decline, Mr. Gardner's writing rises to an affecting pitch when Midge describes the sad deterioration of his eyesight or when Nat mourns Stalin's betrayal of his lifelong ideals.

These exchanges are periodically interrupted by the callow, meddling young folks whom Nat must outwit. In addition to the daughter, the interlopers include a neighborhood tough (Jace Alexander), a cocaine dealer (Ray Baker), and an apartment-house tenants' committee representative (Michael Tucker) who wants to fire Midge. The plotting is clumsy—and, in Act 2, preposterously melodramatic—but it does allow Mr. Hirsch to perform some set comic turns. To disarm intruders, Nat spins the tallest of imaginary tales and variously impersonates an undercover agent, a hotheaded litigator, and even a Mafia Godfather.

While Mr. Hirsch's voice often seems more youthful than his credibly geriatric makeup, his brash, ineffable New York Jewishness is well suited to Nat. The actor is utterly persuasive as a man who will angrily shout "Strike!" or "Cossacks!" at the slightest provocation, out of an undying belief that "the proper response to outrages is still to be outraged." If Mr. Hirsch's burlesque guises have an excessively cute sameness about them, it's nonetheless fun to watch him sing "Puttin' on the Ritz" while playfully tapping out the rhythm with his walker. When the reality of old age sinks in later on, Mr. Hirsch briefly shrinks into a moving embodiment of defeat and decrepitude.

Mr. Little is a winning foil as Midge, but Mr. Gardner, perhaps less assured at portraying a black man, shortchanges the character. Mr. Tucker and Ms. Giannini humanize the spoilsports, and the other actors capably delineate roles that amount to little more than plot cogs. The florid incidents of violence aside, the director Daniel Sullivan smartly underplays scenes that threaten to curdle completely into abject sentimentality or bombast.

The staging benefits further from the designer Tony Walton's elaborate and loving evocation of the nook below a Central Park bridge, as well as from the autumnal palette of Pat Collins's lighting. But these and the evening's other passing pleasures still leave us more soothed than involved. While the iconoclastic Nat tirelessly insists on "shaking things up," his free spirit is domesticated by Mr. Gardner's refusal to shake up the formula that tames his independent-minded play.

≣ *When Herb Gardner accepted the Tony Award for Best Play for* I'm Not Rappaport *(after its move to Broadway), he exulted in the show's commercial success, declaring it proof that "there's life after Frank Rich." Indeed,* Rappaport *lived on to become an even more treacly movie in the 1990s.*

SINGIN' IN THE RAIN
GERSHWIN THEATRE, JULY 3, 1985

When we think of MGM's *Singin' in the Rain*, the happiest movie musical ever made, we think first of Gene Kelly, madly in love with his girl and his life and even his umbrella, as he dances about exultantly on a fantasy Hollywood street in the midst of a rainstorm. It says much about what's amiss with Broadway's new stage version of the film that it doesn't send us home with the image of a joyous man singing and dancing. What is most likely to be remembered about this *Singin' in the Rain* is the rain.

The rain is wonderful. It descends from the flies of the Gershwin Theatre in sheets at the end of Act 1, drenching a Santo Loquasto courtyard set that floats beneath a distant, twinkling HOLLYWOODLAND sign and is lighted (by Jennifer Tipton) with that starry, seductive darkness that can only be found in the western precincts of Los Angeles at 2 a.m. Even the sound of the rain is right, summery and cleansing and revivifying. It makes us feel that anything is possible—which is exactly how the hero, the matinee idol Don Lockwood, feels on a night when he has not only solidified his romance with his beloved Kathy Selden but has also discovered an ingenious way to salvage his first talking picture, which had bombed in a sneak preview only hours before.

But the rain can only take us so far. The spirit of the title song is as much in the fusion of performer and dance as it is in the setting. At the Gershwin, the choreographer Twyla Tharp has skillfully re-created much of the movie's immortal choreography by Mr. Kelly and Stanley

Donen. In Don Correia, who is the evening's Don Lockwood, Ms. Tharp has a gifted hoofer who can dance the steps. Yet Mr. Correia never succeeds in making us stop thinking about the rain and start thinking about him.

Can the trouble be that the star, for all his acrobatic prowess, is a charmless actor? Partly. But there's a graver difficulty that even a more ingratiating performer couldn't solve. *Singin' in the Rain* was a fantasy movie about the dream factory of the movies. Once transposed to the stage in realistic terms, the fantasy evaporates even as the rain pours down. No matter how much Ms. Tharp re-creates specific gestures from the film, they play differently in the theater. Watching her Don Lockwood splash about, we aren't carried away into never-never Hollywood-land, transported like Mia Farrow in *The Purple Rose of Cairo*. We're still in the humdrum everyday world, wondering how stage technicians achieve the effect and watching an actor get very, very wet.

Because Ms. Tharp has failed to meet—indeed, even to consider—the central challenge of transposing a quintessentially cinematic work to the theater, her show usually flattens out in exactly this way. Her *Singin' in the Rain* is a pleasant but innocuous matinee spectacle. It is exuberantly danced throughout and has been attractively and sumptuously mounted in a style equally suggestive of 1920s glitz and the contemporary artist Ed Ruscha's hard-edged Hollywood vistas. The songs by Nacio Herb Brown and Arthur Freed are irresistible (although the voices and pit band can sound thin), and, until intermission, the large enterprise unfurls professionally. If the leading players had more pizzazz—and if the love story of the classic Betty Comden–Adolph Green screenplay had not been shredded—the musical might even have had some of the sexiness and exhilarating lift it lacks.

Given Ms. Tharp's enormous talent and keen affection for pop culture, however, it's amazing how little she has made of her first Broadway musical. To be sure, she faced a demanding task—the inverse of that required of those who must adapt the stagebound *Chorus Line* to the screen. But both as director and choreographer, she seems to be condescending to the show. Surely this artist must know that such numbers as the soundstage duet for Don and Kathy or the comedy turns "Make 'Em Laugh" and "Moses Supposes" will lose a great deal once deprived of camera movements, cuts, and close-ups that are integral to their punch. But Ms. Tharp makes no attempt to find theatrical equivalents to film techniques—throwing in extra chorus men for "Make 'Em Laugh" is no solution—and the dances often look lost in the frame, as if viewed through the wrong end of a telescope.

Still more surprising is the director's inability to invest the show with any sense of cinematic continuity and mobility. While Mr. Loquasto's scenery may lift or slide (notably in "Good Morning") in approximation of the movie's camera gyrations, Ms. Tharp frequently halts her scenes with blackouts. The retrograde staging is a throwback to the pageant style of mid-1950s stage musicals, as if Jerome Robbins and Michael Bennett had never figured out how to create montage and crosscutting effects in the theater. This is particularly apparent in the Act 2 opening—a sampler of pastiche Warner Brothers musical numbers. While the sequence contains some lovely toyland dancing, its brief takes are not knitted into the intended, kaleidoscopic whole.

Ms. Tharp's other major choreographic contribution is a lengthy, Act 2 comic spoof of a production number in Lockwood's film, *The Dancing Cavalier*. A crazy-quilt mixture of period French costumes (hilariously designed by Ann Roth), Hollywood camp, and roller-skating, it's wittier in principle than in practice. (Perversely enough, it replaces the one number in the film with a Broadway setting, the "Broadway Melody" ballet.) Only in the show's final moments, when the entire cast dons yellow rain slickers to perform a wacky, windblown retooling of the movie's opening credits sequence, do we find the Tharp imagination aflame.

The script fares less well than the numbers. Along with the Kaufman-Hart *Once in a Lifetime,* the screenplay for *Singin' in the Rain* is the funniest treatment ever of Hollywood at the panicked dawn of talkies. Ms. Tharp muffs (or omits) the jokes in such bits as Lockwood's dissembling account of his early days in show business or his angry acting of a silent love scene with a despised costar. The prototypical Hollywood characters—from the gossip columnist at the Grauman's Chinese Theater premiere to the mogul and director at Monumental Pictures—are all too broadly played. The interpolated, parodistic film sequences—shot by the cinematographer Gordon Willis and reminiscent of his vintage newsreel simulations in *Zelig*—preserve at least some of the Comden-Green satirical edge. So, in its way, does Faye Grant's over-the-top caricature of the vulgar silent-film queen Lina Lamont.

It would be invidious to compare the show's principal players with their Hollywood predecessors; suffice it to say that the trio at hand is less than ideal. Mr. Correia has so much grace and vitality as a dancer that one is constantly disappointed when his Lockwood otherwise proves too plebeian a Hollywood heartthrob. Mary D'Arcy, as Kathy, has a beautiful voice and, once she relaxes, a sweet presence. But there are no romantic sparks between her and her leading man, and there's little camaraderie between the couple and their clownish sidekick, cloyingly played by

Peter Slutsker. What this proves, I guess, is that it's easier to manufacture the rain made in heaven than the stars who are born there. Ms. Tharp and company have turned a celestial entertainment into a mild diversion that remains resolutely earthbound.

THE MYSTERY OF EDWIN DROOD
DELACORTE THEATER, AUGUST 23, 1985

While it may be possible to imagine a more exciting show than *The Mystery of Edwin Drood*, the jolly new musical at Central Park's Delacorte Theater, it's hard to picture a more democratic one. The audience not only gets to see this New York Shakespeare Festival extravaganza for free, but it also gets to help write the script's ending. *Edwin Drood* is a very loose adaptation of the half-finished novel Dickens left at his death in 1870. When Dickens's plot runs out in mid–Act 2 of the musical version, the audience "solves, resolves, and concludes the mystery" by voting by voice and hand to a series of multiple-choice propositions.

This rollicking plebiscite, which shapes the musical's final half hour, is both delightful and ingenious. Much of the delight comes from watching the evening's waspish emcee, the convivial George Rose, lead the voting with a tongue so far up his cheek that one half-expects it to emerge from his ear. The ingenuity belongs to Rupert Holmes, the author of the show's book, music, and lyrics. Mr. Holmes has written an ending, songs included, that can flexibly accommodate any balloting results. Since there are seven suspects who might have murdered Drood— not to mention two other plot questions adding more variables to the mix—Mr. Holmes's all-purpose conclusion must cope with nearly as many statistical possibilities as a Lotto contestant.

The voting is such a tonic that one sometimes wishes the procedure might be extended throughout *Edwin Drood*. This is a charming, attractively cast musical that allows both veteran musical performers (Mr. Rose, Betty Buckley, Cleo Laine) and relative newcomers (Howard McGillin, Patti Cohenour) the opportunities to shine in some fetching moonlight. It is also a diffuse show that would benefit from being a shade tighter, zippier, wittier, and more melodic than it is. If only its creators had made firmer choices in editing and focusing their material, *Edwin Drood* might offer as much pizzazz as it does sweet spirits and cheering interludes. Too bad the audience can't vote along the way to decide which extraneous songs, scenes, and gags might be weeded out.

The roots of the show's big promise and uneven follow-through all stem from its imaginative premise. Mr. Holmes has not merely written a straightforward musical version of the Dickens novel, but has instead made *Edwin Drood* a play-within-the-play. The musical is set in a provincial town, Greater Dorping-on-Sea, where a motley London music-hall troupe is performing its own hammy *Drood* adaptation—"a musicale with dramatic interludes," as the company's impresario, Mr. Rose, puts it. In other words, we are watching a parody—a Dickens dramatization as it might be done by the Victorian acting troupe satirized by Dickens in *Nicholas Nickleby*.

If executed to the fullest, this conceit would be wickedly funny. Dickens's unfinished novel is a dark tale boasting a Jekyll-and-Hyde villain, sleazy opium dens, haunted cathedral crypts, and grave intimations of warped sexuality. Once refracted through the addled sensibility of Mr. Holmes's fictive period actors, *Edwin Drood* might suggest *Sweeney Todd* as performed by an antecedent of the third-rate touring company of *Noises Off*. But if Mr. Holmes's book has its amusing moments—often in the form of Mr. Rose's asides about backstage calamities—its broad jokes about anachronistic theatrical conventions and Dickensian melodrama run out too soon. The humor isn't sharp enough to propel the evening on its own, and yet it's persistent enough to defang Dickens's thrilling plot and soften its eerie psychosexual atmosphere.

The score, which seems to unfurl by the yard at every conceivable and inconceivable cue, is similarly and sometimes pleasurably stranded between comedy and horror. Mr. Holmes, a pop composer, has written pretty ballads as well as boisterous vaudeville numbers, many of them in sophisticated re-creation of vintage styles. But, as augmented by metallic amplification and pseudo–Kurt Weill orchestrations, some of the plot songs are far harsher than the libretto's light tone can support.

The happier numbers, meanwhile, swing between clever Gilbert and Sullivan pastiche and syrupy sentimentality. The flat generic opening song ("An English Music Hall") recalls Broadway's Victorian musical-murder mystery of the 1950s, *Redhead*, while such more tuneful ensemble ditties as "Don't Quit While You're Ahead" and "The Writing on the Wall" are burdened with lyrics as determinedly uplifting as anything Lionel Bart wrote for *Oliver!* When the company implores us "to live forever and give up never" in the finale, one wishes that the author had ignored his own advice and indeed quit while he was ahead.

The production team collaborating with Mr. Holmes on *Edwin Drood* is largely the one that brought *The Pirates of Penzance* to the park five summers ago. That triumph seems to weigh on everyone's mind. Coincidentally or not, the show is set in the same year (1880) in which *Pirates* had its London debut; it also contains a kickline number in which the choreographer Graciela Daniele reprises her own dance steps from the previous show's thunderous "With cat-like tread." While Ms. Daniele's other music-hall routines in *Edwin Drood* all look alike, they do offer a welcome springiness that Wilford Leach's staging lacks. The director and his set designer, Bob Shaw, make a fetish of mocking the flat, posed look and exaggerated posturing of Victorian theater. What begins as lively summer camp eventually congeals into a static academic exercise.

Mr. Leach's cast and their best musical turns are the evening's happiest and most consistent assets. Mr. McGillin and Ms. Cohenour, standout leads in the director's pop *Bohème* of last fall, bring impressive voices and fetching personalities to the roles of the villainous choirmaster John Jasper and the china-doll heroine Rosa Bud. Ms. Buckley, billed as a foremost male impersonator, provides an endearing Edwin Drood who is part English schoolboy, part Broadway belter, and part old-school prima donna. Ms. Laine's smoky voice, if not her benign countenance, is ideal for the opium den mother; the young Don Kehr, as a sprightly street urchin, has a voice we'd gladly hear more of.

In addition to Mr. Rose, whose mischievous kibitzing sets the show's entire tone, the choice clowns include Jerome Dempsey as the drunken stonemason Durdles, Larry Shue as the kindly Reverend Crisparkle, Jana Schneider as a voluptuous Ceylonese orphan, and, particularly, Joe Grifasi as a bit player whose dreams of greater theatrical glory inspire some of Mr. Holmes's smartest lyrics. It will be up to you and your conscience to decide which one of this crew deserves to be voted the murderer of Edwin Drood. The entire cast can be found guilty of infusing an erratic musical with an indecent sense of fun.

≣ *Not a great show, but Papp got a decent run out of it after moving it to Broadway—at one nonsensical point promoting it by changing its title to the simple, if ambiguous,* Drood. *Alas, the producer's continuous quest for another* Chorus Line—*i.e., another gold mine that could support the rest of the New York Shakespeare Festival—led to a number of costly, ill-fated Broadway transfers, including a pleasant musical by Galt MacDermot adapted from Saroyan's* The Human Comedy, The Secret Rapture, Serious Money, *and* Café Crown. *None of them lasted more than a few weeks.*

FOLLIES

AVERY FISHER HALL, LINCOLN CENTER, SEPTEMBER 15, 1985

What does a Broadway hit sound like? According to a Stephen Sondheim song titled "It's a Hit!," it's "the sound of an audience losing its mind." That's not a sound that has been largely associated with Mr. Sondheim's commercially problematic career—even "It's a Hit!" was written for a Broadway flop, *Merrily We Roll Along*—but the joyful noise could be heard last weekend at Lincoln Center, where the composer's *Follies* was revived for two nights in a concert performance. As played by the New York Philharmonic, conducted by Paul Gemignani, and sung and acted by an illustrious cast of past and present Broadway hands, *Follies* filled Avery Fisher Hall with the sound of an audience losing its mind long before Barbara Cook got around to delivering the show's torch song, "Losing My Mind." New York's theatrical community, which shared the hall with civilian ticketholders, found itself enjoying its first uninhibited hoot since the gala, record-breaking performance of *A Chorus Line* two Septembers ago.

The celebration is sure to spread after RCA Red Seal releases a recording of the concert late this fall. Yet *Follies,* a downbeat show and a commercial failure on Broadway in its first, 1971 production, might well seem a surprising catalyst for such pandemonium. As *A Chorus Line* enshrines Broadway's myths by dramatizing the romantic dreams of aspiring young chorus performers, *Follies* debunks those myths by unmasking the wasted lives of middle-aged song-and-dance has-beens. Its characters are retired Follies performers whose bodies and psyches are as much in ruins as the crumbling theater where they gather for an all-night reunion.

Even seven Tony Awards didn't prevent *Follies* from antagonizing the public and proving a complete fiscal washout in its initial airing. I saw the show a number of times back then, starting with its pre-Broadway opening night at Boston's Colonial Theatre, but only on one occasion— its closing night at the Winter Garden in August 1972—did it churn up continuous excitement among my fellow spectators. (Broadway loves funerals, especially when they're costly.) On a bootleg tape of *Follies* recorded midway in its New York run, one can hear song after song and line after line fall flat before a coughing, feet-shuffling audience. When the lavish production tried to recoup its losses in a post-Broadway tour, it folded for good in the very first city (Los Angeles) it played.

There has been no major production of *Follies* since. Only this summer was the show staged in England—and not in London's West End, but in Manchester. While some of the musical's songs have been repeatedly recorded on Sondheim anthologies through the years, the complete *Follies* score has survived mainly in the memories of its first fans. The record that should have preserved the entire score, the Capitol original cast album, was a hastily assembled calamity, on which some songs are missing and others are abridged. Although the steadily rising stock of Mr. Sondheim's reputation has prompted increased interest in everything he's written, *Follies* seemed likely to remain as much of a cult item as his *Anyone Can Whistle, The Frogs,* and *Merrily.*

The Philharmonic concert, which was put together as a belated antidote to the Capitol recording, has now changed all that—perhaps more so than anyone might have imagined. The prime mover in the event was the record producer Thomas Z. Shepard, who, not for the first time, felt an obligation to give an important Broadway score its due on disk. Mr. Shepard has recorded many previous Sondheim shows, including the unlucrative failures, and he has been responsible for the most complete recordings of *Porgy and Bess* (the 1976 Houston Grand Opera production), *Oklahoma!* (the 1979 Broadway revival), and *Candide* (the 1973 Broadway revival).

But this time, Mr. Shepard was taking more of a risk than before: There being no existing or contemplated revival of *Follies* to record, the album could be made only if Mr. Shepard created his own transitory revival, from scratch. To produce the recording, in other words, he first had to produce the show. Implicit in the effort was the possibility that such an elaborate public recording session would be a bust. If *Follies* failed to find a large audience on Broadway the first time around, what reason was there to believe that a reconstituted version would win over crowds fourteen years later?

That Mr. Shepard's longshot bet paid off last weekend—and should pay off further with the dissemination of the record and, next year, a television documentary of the concert—is attributable to several factors, starting, of course, with Mr. Sondheim's score. In 1971, *Follies* was thought of as a series of oppressively clever period pastiche numbers (in which the author re-creates the songwriting styles of vintage Broadway) and excessively brittle contemporary arias (in which the characters sing of their present-day bitterness). As performed at Avery Fisher Hall, the score emerged as an original whole, in which the "modern" music and mock vintage tunes constantly comment on each other, much as the script's action unfolds simultaneously in 1971 (the year of the reunion) and 1941 (the year the Follies disbanded).

The same is true of the lyrics, in which every invocation of a rosy Tin Pan Alley greeting-card homily ("Love Will See Us Through") contains a jarring, often Freudian linguistic thorn ("ego bolstering"). Heard complete and with scant interruption, Mr. Sondheim's merging of past and present in *Follies* creates a searing dramatic conflict. We're always aware of the pathetic gap that separates the optimistic, showbiz-spawned illusions of the characters' innocent, between-the-wars youth from the grim contemporary reality that is their middle age.

In the original production of *Follies,* as staged by Harold Prince and Michael Bennett, this juxtaposition of glamour and decay was apparent in every aspect of the show. In James Goldman's book and Mr. Prince's direction, each principal player was shadowed by an onstage alter ego—a ghost representing the character's younger self. Boris Aronson's set, the haunted, rubble-strewn remains of a half-demolished theatrical palace, could return in a brilliant flash to the opulent splendor of its vanished heyday. Mr. Bennett's choreography, which anticipated and at times surpassed his work on *A Chorus Line,* set a chorus line of middle-aged Follies girls against a mirror-image chorus line representing the same women in their prime.

The explosive impact of that number, "Who's That Woman?," could hardly be suggested in the concert version, yet such is the power of Mr. Sondheim's score that it could carry *Follies* on its own, independent of the first production's other inspired elements. From the cacophonous musical lead-in, one could even get a rough sense of the full scale of "Loveland," the climactic sequence in which the characters' past and present finally merge into a nightmarishly surreal Follies show. Indeed, if the Prince, Bennett, and Aronson contributions to *Follies* had been added to the performances last weekend, an already excitable crowd might well have required the ministrations of a riot-control squad.

It's a further testament to Mr. Sondheim's music, as orchestrated by Jonathan Tunick, that it stood up so easily to the Philharmonic. Not all show music, Mr. Sondheim's included, can survive such concert-hall inflation. On an otherwise superb Sondheim anthology released by Book-of-the-Month-Club Records this summer, themes from *Pacific Overtures* are stretched past the breaking point in symphonic arrangements. The same phenomenon can be heard during the more pompous passages of Leonard Bernstein's lush new "operatic" recording of *West Side Story.*

But the emotions that *Follies* touched in its audience last weekend may say as much about how Broadway has changed since 1971 as it does about the merits of the piece. While in no way nostalgic, *Follies* has the tone of a valedictory. Not for nothing is it set in a ghostly Broadway theater soon to be razed for a parking lot: As the show tells the story of its characters' punctured dreams, so it indirectly mourns the death of the world that created those dreams. It's not merely a theater that's being torn down but what that theater represented—the classic Broadway musical and the values it propagated to a faithful public during the glory years of Gershwin and Porter and Rodgers and Hammerstein. "New York's all changed," says one of the Follies girls when she arrives at the reunion, "I couldn't even find the theater tonight." In 1971, such sentiments may have seemed hyperbolic. They don't now.

Since *Follies* was first produced, more Broadway theaters have been demolished. The house where *Follies* played fourteen years ago is now occupied by Broadway's only smash hit, an English musical (*Cats*). The production of new American musicals has slowed to a trickle—*Follies* would probably cost at least $5 million to mount at today's prohibitive rates. And talent has fled. The stunning cast in the concert *Follies* seemed chosen in part to dramatize that fact. Among the more glittering performers were Barbara Cook, Carol Burnett, Lee Remick, and Elaine Stritch—all stars of musicals during the last fertile period for the Broadway musical, the 1950s and early sixties, and all long gone from the New York theater. It took a two-night-only event, staged twenty blocks north of Shubert Alley by a record producer, to bring them back to town in a major Broadway show.

The theater people at Avery Fisher Hall last weekend were not unaware of how time and history had at last caught up to the perceptions of *Follies*. The cheering went on and on—in part to honor a restored musical treasure, in part to postpone that painful moment when the visiting ghosts of a glamorous old Broadway would once again disperse.

≡ Follies *did not immediately get a full-fledged revival. The British impresario Cameron Mackintosh, who had never seen the show in its original incarnation, did a lavish production in London three years later with Daniel Massey, Diana Rigg, Julia McKenzie, and Dolores Gray, some new (and weak) Sondheim songs, and a revised script. English critics raved over it, pronouncing it superior to the Broadway original (which few of them, judging from their reviews, had seen). But it was a dull desecration of the original, and the British public rejected it, despite the reviews. Broadway managements that might have tried to revive* Follies *with the skill of Shepard's one-night concert version had a good excuse not to try. Not until thirteen years after the Lincoln Center concert was* Follies *rediscovered by critics and audiences in a lavish new production at the Paper Mill Playhouse in suburban New Jersey.*

SONG & DANCE
ROYALE THEATRE, SEPTEMBER 19, 1985

In *Song & Dance,* the new Andrew Lloyd Webber show at the Royale, the star, Bernadette Peters, and the choreographer, Peter Martins, all but break their necks trying to entertain us. In the first act, Ms. Peters belts and sobs and shimmies her way through a solo song cycle that runs for a full hour. After intermission, Mr. Martins takes over, sending nine admirable dancers, led by Christopher d'Amboise, into a nonstop, forty-minute exhibition of pyrotechnics. So why is *Song & Dance* grating (Act 1) and monotonous (Act 2)? The mystery isn't hard to solve. No one has given Ms. Peters anything to sing about or Mr. Martins's dancers any reason to leap. Empty material remains empty, no matter how talented those who perform it.

Ms. Peters is more than talented: As an actress, singer, comedienne, and all-around warming presence, she has no peer in the musical theater right now. In her half of *Song & Dance,* she works so hard you'd think she were pleading for mercy before a firing squad. Yet for all the vocal virtuosity, tempestuous fits, and husky-toned charm she brings to her one-woman musical marathon, we never care if her character lives or dies (as long as she's brief about it). That heroine, an English hat maker named Emma who settles in New York, is a completely synthetic, not to mention insulting, creation whom no performer could redeem.

Describing herself as "a girl who lets men take advantage," Emma devotes most of her twenty-odd songs to sulking about her misadventures with various, unseen men who take her to bed and then kick her into the street. The authors treat her almost as shabbily. They don't bother to examine Emma—they merely exploit her. For all the time we spend with this woman, we learn little about her beyond her sexual activities. She is an empty-headed tramp with a heart of gold, exhumed from the graveyard of sexist stereotypes, and her mechanically told story might as well be the song delivered by Perón's discarded mistress in Mr. Lloyd Webber's *Evita* ("Another Suitcase, Another Hall") played over and over, as if on a maddening film loop.

The men who created Emma are Don Black, who wrote the lyrics used in the even drearier 1982 London version of *Song & Dance,* and Richard Maltby Jr., the gifted lyricist and director (*Baby*) who receives credit for providing the show's Broadway edition with "additional lyrics" and its "American adaptation." A few howlers aside—"Loneliness must be the worst feeling of all" or "Show me a dream and I'll show you a nightmare!"—Mr. Maltby has injected his customary professionalism into the inept London text. But he must share the blame for perpetuating, if not accentuating, the patronizing characterization of the heroine. And why didn't he give Ms. Peters any material to capitalize on her sense of humor? The one comic song, a London holdover titled "Capped Teeth and Caesar Salad," recycles Beverly Hills jokes that had seen better days when Joan Rivers was still in college.

It's a tribute to the star, who's incapable of a dishonest moment, that Act 1 of *Song & Dance* doesn't earn unintentional laughs even in a scene in which Emma's receipt of a green card is treated with a dramatic intensity worthy of *Saint Joan*. While much of Mr. Lloyd Webber's impersonal and bombastically orchestrated music sounds like the stuff that's piped into a 747 just before takeoff, Ms. Peters does get to sing a few sprightly tunes. As is this composer's wont, the better songs are reprised so often that one can never be quite sure whether they are here to stay or are simply refusing to leave.

In Act 2, Mr. Lloyd Webber provides no original music—this show is as miserly as his *Cats* is profligate—but instead offers his own variations on Paganini's A-minor Caprice. Rachmaninoff need not worry. Mr. Lloyd Webber's main contributions to Paganini, conducted by John Mauceri, are electronic gimcracks and a rock beat. Certainly his variations have failed to inspire Mr. Martins, whose labored vision of nocturnal Manhattan fleetingly recalls *Fancy Free* and *Slaughter on Tenth Avenue* but is unlikely to join them in repertory at the New York City Ballet.

Most of the choreography is a cynical, acrobatic approximation of vintage Broadway dancing, without the repose, pacing, and conviction that make the prototypes electric. To forge a shotgun marriage between the song and dance halves of the evening, Mr. d'Amboise is costumed as one of Emma's Act 1 lovers—a cad named Joe whose only known characteristics are his place of birth (Nebraska) and favorite color (red). A fine young dancer who as yet lacks the stage presence to drive a Broadway show, Mr. d'Amboise raises his fist joyously when it's time to applaud.

Among his uniformly good supporting dancers, Cynthia Onrubia, Charlotte d'Amboise, and Gregg Burge offer the least cutesy impersonations of the oppressively funky street people who inhabit Mr. Martins's Day-Glo fantasy world of subways and discos. Mr. Burge, last seen memorably in *Sophisticated Ladies,* has the standout bit, in which he instructs Mr. d'Amboise in tap dancing much as Charles "Honi" Coles did Tommy Tune (to more exciting effect) in *My One and Only.*

None of the designers—Robin Wagner (sets), Jules Fisher (lighting), Willa Kim (costumes)—gives Mr. Martins a break. Their glitzy work is far too busy, with the ludicrously incessant costume changes, scenic gy-rations, and lighting cues often fighting one another and upstaging the choreography. During Mr. Maltby's static staging of Act 1, when such frenzied activity would be welcome, the design is subdued (and, in the case of some already smudged purple panels, tacky). But Ms. Kim has designed one imaginative set of costumes with a Chrysler Building motif for Act 2, and Mr. Wagner unveils a Manhattan skyline that looks as deep and mystically hazy as the Grand Canyon. There is also a starry fir-mament at evening's end, when Ms. Peters reemerges and *Song & Dance* becomes so desperate for inspiration that it actually deigns (for about a minute) to give us song and dance at the same time.

≡ *Bernadette Peters is, without question, the most talented Broadway mu-sical actress of her generation—with credits dating back to the role of one of Rose's young daughters in a road company of* Gypsy *in the early 1960s. Why she only found one assignment worthy of her talents—Dot in* Sunday in the Park with George—*over the two decades following* Mack and Mabel *(1974) is not so much a mystery as an indictment of the state of Broadway musical theater (and the imagination of its producers). When not engaged in dumb shows like* Song & Dance *and the subsequent* Good-bye Girl, *Peters bided her time taking her singing act on the road, with time out for occasional roles in Hollywood and a smallish but beloved turn in Sondheim's* Into the Woods.

THE SEARCH FOR SIGNS OF
INTELLIGENT LIFE IN THE UNIVERSE
PLYMOUTH THEATRE, SEPTEMBER 27, 1985

In *Nashville*, the Robert Altman film that marked her graduation from television-sketch comedienne to actress, Lily Tomlin was just one of many vivid characters in a throbbing panorama of contemporary American life. To say that this artist has continued to grow in the decade since then is to abridge the story drastically. In Act 2 of *The Search for Signs of Intelligent Life in the Universe*, her new show at the Plymouth, we find that Ms. Tomlin and her longtime collaborator, the writer and di-rector Jane Wagner, are attempting what might well be considered their own theatrical update to Mr. Altman's epic. They treat the audience to an idiosyncratic, rude, blood-stained comedy about American democracy and its discontents—and, this time around, Ms. Tomlin plays all the parts herself.

The results are something to see. While Ms. Tomlin's chameleon-like ability to inhabit a wide range of personalities is not news to those who saw her previous Broadway recital, the 1977 *Appearing Nitely,* this time she knits her creations (almost all of them new) into what can rightly be called a play. What's more, the script is nearly as daring as Ms. Tomlin's single-handed assault on it. As the star trails like a comet through a galaxy of characters—with no props, costume changes, or scenery for artificial propulsion—so Ms. Wagner attempts to sum up a generation of social history in a tightly compressed saga of a few representative lives. Even the occasional blurring of Ms. Tomlin's characterizations and the fitful melodramatics of Ms. Wagner's writing can't diminish the fact that Act 2 of *The Search for Signs* is original, not to mention absorbing, theater.

This postintermission segment, which follows a relatively benign Act 1 assortment of vignettes, is also the most genuinely subversive comedy to be produced on Broadway in years. It's a radical critique not only of the national status quo but also of some activists who have fought (ineffectually, in the author's view) for change. In telling the story of a California feminist named Lynn over a period that begins with the birth of *Ms.* magazine and ends with Geraldine Ferraro's ascension to the Democratic ticket, Ms. Tomlin and Ms. Wagner make equal sport of men and women (hetero- and homosexual), liberals and reactionaries, rebellious multimedia performance artists and middle-management corporate pawns. True, the bourgeois fashions of West Los Angeles and Marin County get hit particularly hard: Lynn and her husband live in a geodesic dome (built from a kit advertised in *Mother Jones* magazine) and enlist in every est-inspired training program going. But only the self-deceiving will fail to recognize Ms. Wagner's play as an indictment of everyone who has spent the last decade either standing still or attempting "to be politically conscious and upwardly mobile at the same time."

For all the anger that underlies the piece, it is more seductive than abrasive in the watching. Ms. Tomlin makes us care about the well-meaning Lynn, who discovers too late that it is impossible to "change the system" and be a "total woman" (replete with children, money, power, cosmic consciousness) while constantly doing all the cooking and produce shopping required to maintain a gourmet health-food kitchen. We also grow to like Lynn's best friends—Edie, a radical lesbian journalist whose newspaper is purchased by Rupert Murdoch, and Marge, who eventually discovers a most macabre outlet for her skill at macramé. Even Lynn's hypocritical husband, Bob, isn't a total loss. Like the title of Edie's forthcoming book, *What's Left of the Left,* the slogan on his favorite T-shirt—"Whales save us"—could well be the plaintive epitaph for an age.

Ms. Tomlin shifts among the female personae so fast—with alterations of voice, posture, and facial muscles—that Lynn's tale almost takes on the hallucinatory flow of consciousness as it spills about the black stage. Ms. Wagner's lines rarely miss a witty trick, whether they're describing Lynn's preferred marijuana ("paraquat-free Panama Red") or the products sold by Bob's raised-consciousness catalogue business ("New Age chatchkes"). Some of the dialogue has a shapeliness that circumscribes character while making us laugh: "If I had known what it would be like to have it all," says a beleaguered Lynn, "I might have settled for less."

Lynn's Act 2 drama aside, *The Search for Signs* sometimes does settle for less. Although Ms. Tomlin's energy never flags, Ms. Wagner's writing is variable. Some of the show's many other characters go on too long. In Act 1, the laughs and insights are outnumbered by preachy pronouncements ("God has Alzheimer's disease and forgot that we exist") and maudlin sketches (an alienated teenage punk rocker turns to her grandparents for solace). The woman who serves as the evening's unofficial narrator—Trudy, a nutty Manhattan bag lady who is conducting the metaphysical search of the title—is a treacly Ken Kesey–era cliché, stuffed with cute, curmudgeonly aphorisms that reek of Humanity and idiot-savant wisdom. Ms. Tomlin, whose eyes squint into shifty half-moons when playing Trudy, is a little cloying in the role, too.

Much more convincing are such characters as Chrissy, a health-club devotee in doomed search of self-esteem and good-looking men ("If it weren't for false hopes, the economy would just collapse," she concludes); Brandy and Tina, a pair of prostitutes (one white, one black) living "the life" at Forty-ninth and Broadway; and, most hilariously, Kate, a trendy, jaded socialite who is bored by everything from "uplifting theater" to slick magazine articles about boredom. What Ms. Tomlin and Ms. Wagner don't do to differentiate among these and the others, their inventive lighting designer, Neil Peter Jampolis, does: The punk rocker is embalmed with the sallow fluorescent light of an all-night fast-food joint, while the drugged-out streetwalker is aglow with the reflected glare of Times Square's own nocturnal spectrum.

At the end of the show, after Lynn's story has been told, almost all the characters converge on stage at once, brought together by Ms. Tomlin's masterful acting and a series of rapid-fire Dickensian coincidences. As they do, the tone turns abruptly sentimental. No longer are we being told that life is meaningless, that the contents of Middle American homes are "garbage," that G. Gordon Liddy's *Will* is the self-help bible of our time, or that "evolution works on the Peter Principle." Instead, Trudy the bag lady offers comforting talk about life's awesome "mysteries"—among them "the goose-bump experience" of attending a play at which "a group of strangers sitting together in the dark are laughing and crying about the same thing."

Perhaps these final-curtain declarations of optimism are what the other characters—and their heretofore tough-minded creators—might cynically dismiss as "false hopes" or, worse, "uplifting theater." But by then, Ms. Tomlin has drawn her audience completely into the goose-bump experience, and who can stop tingling long enough to resist?

≡ *This show ran and toured forever. After it, Tomlin never returned to the theater.*

THE ICEMAN COMETH
Lunt-Fontanne Theatre, September 30, 1985

Nothing glows when the lights rise on Harry Hope's waterfront gin-mill and flophouse in José Quintero's new production of *The Iceman Cometh*. What comes dimly into view is a moldering, black-and-brown cave, barely discernible in a smudged gray green haze. The derelicts who populate Eugene O'Neill's play describe this squalid setting as "a morgue" and "a tomb," as "The End of the Line Café" and "The Bottom of the Sea Rathskeller." As designed by Ben Edwards and lighted by Thomas R. Skelton at the Lunt-Fontanne, Hope's saloon of 1912 looks as ghostly as those glimpses of the submerged *Titanic*. But in *The Iceman Cometh* the bodies of the inhabitants are still visible—still terrifyingly alive, twitching in the silt. To see O'Neill's bums sprawled comatose across their sooty dive is to know one of the most harrowing images ever produced by the American theater.

For most plays, that image would be an ending. In *Iceman*, it's only a beginning. O'Neill begins with a vision of existence at rock bottom and then, for nearly five hours (three intermissions included), just keeps plunging down, taking us and his characters past despair to utter hopelessness: We can't go home until we understand that the only truth that exists in life is the truth that kills. The guide for this pitiless journey is a hardware salesman named Hickey—a role that brought Jason Robards fame when he first played it, under Mr. Quintero's direction, in the 1956

Circle in the Square revival that helped restore O'Neill's then-tarnished reputation. In the current staging, which originated at Washington's American National Theatre, Mr. Robards has reunited with Mr. Quintero, and both men are in brilliant form. Along with some other outstanding actors, led by the superlative Donald Moffat, they give us as stirring a production of O'Neill's masterwork as one might hope to see.

The word "masterwork" is not invoked lightly. *The Iceman Cometh,* which was written in 1939 and first produced in 1946, is equal to and perhaps more influential than *Long Day's Journey into Night* and *A Moon for the Misbegotten,* the two other towering plays at the end of O'Neill's career. *Iceman* occupies a secure position on the continuum of twentieth-century drama that runs from *The Lower Depths* to *Waiting for Godot;* seeing it now, one finds the seeds of contemporary American plays as diverse as *Who's Afraid of Virginia Woolf?* and *Glengarry Glen Ross* within its rat-infested corners. If O'Neill's theatrical architecture can be ham-fisted and his language repetitious, his tragic vision remains undiminished by time. In *Iceman,* we see man's desperate need for sustaining illusions, even as the hollowness of those illusions, God included, is cruelly exposed.

The illusions are referred to as "pipe dreams" in the play's argot. During the seventy-odd minutes that precede Hickey's arrival at Harry Hope's, we learn that the bar's alcohol-sotted inmates, a "Who's Who in Dipsomania" ranging from a defrocked Harvard-educated lawyer to prostitutes who think of themselves as "tarts," all cling to some such pathetic self-delusion: They are all masters at rationalizing yesterday's defeats and perpetuating tomorrow's false hopes. When the newly sobered-up Hickey appears, he vows to bring his old cronies peace and salvation from guilt by forcing them to put aside those lies for good—to face the fact that they never will graduate from the social ash heap. "Honesty is the best policy," Hickey proselytizes—not realizing that he, too, continues to cling to a pipe dream and that the destruction of that last illusion will bring no peace except that of the grave.

Like the characters in *Moon* and *Long Day's Journey* who share a bloodline to O'Neill's brother James, Hickey could have been written for Mr. Robards. In his three-piece suit and straw boater, with his flashing teeth and whorehouse bonhomie, the actor is the consummate salesman—a hard-selling, evangelical drummer whose all-American vulgarity becomes a kind of charisma. After that go-getting, finger-snapping self-assurance is shaken, Mr. Robards seems to be pouring decades of preparation (as indeed he is) into delineating Hickey's collapse. His chuckles (invariably punctuating the word "happy") hang ghoulishly in the septic air; his eyes recede into deep, coal-black sockets; his feet shuffle under the weight of dread; his bray slurs and slides into an ashen croak. Once Mr. Robards reaches his marathon, self-immolating confessional of Act 4, he is the majordomo of the charnel house. As he sweatily expatiates his unspeakable, guilty secret—his hatred for his murdered wife—his Hickey seems to be repeatedly confronting his own pasty face in the mirror and recoiling in nauseated disgust at the sight.

It's hard to fathom how this performance could have been better in 1956—or how Mr. Robards could ever have a better foil than Mr. Moffat, who plays Larry Slade. A onetime anarchist who has now taken "a seat in the grandstand of philosophical detachment," Larry is Hickey's most formidable antagonist among the pipe dreamers; he clings to the illusion of believing in nothing. But the atheist proves little match for the nihilist. "Be God, there's no hope!" Mr. Moffat cries out, writhing in his chair as he finally realizes that he is Hickey's "only real convert to death." From then on, Mr. Moffat's dignified body stiffens and his grizzled face drains of color, as if Larry were realizing Hickey's own wish of frying in the electric chair.

There are some other beautiful performances, too. Barnard Hughes brings a bleaker brew of his pixieish Irish whimsy and a wee, defeated voice to Hope, the proprietor who's been too frightened to leave his bar for twenty years. James Greene, with gloom-swollen eyes and knocking knees, is the saddest imaginable Jimmy Tomorrow, a has-been Boer War correspondent foolishly awaiting a comeback. The play's sporadic gallows humor is well served by John Pankow, as the insolent, bartending pimp, and Allen Swift, as a onetime circus bunko artist whose happiest reminiscence is of flimflamming his own late sister.

Roger Robinson, as the black gambler Joe Mott, and John Christopher Jones, as the father-hating lawyer Willie Oban, need only to edit out some excess staginess to sharpen their adept characterizations. While the others are merely adequate—and generally account for the flabbier interludes—the only seriously damaging performance comes from Paul McCrane, who doesn't capture the haunted or hunted qualities of the young stool pigeon (and Hickey alter ego) Parritt.

Although a bit at sea in such a cavernous house, Mr. Quintero's staging is meticulous down to the frayed shoelaces in Jane Greenwood's shabby costumes. As we tour the depths in Act 1, the director seems to be choreographing to his own sepulchral water music. When Hickey presides over Hope's midnight birthday party in Act 2, we get a macabre Antichrist's Last Supper. When Hickey forces the nocturnal pipe dreamers outdoors into the chaos of reality in Act 3, the men scurry from the sunlight like cockroaches fleeing poison.

By the time Hickey gets to his last-act monologue, Hope's tenants are as comatose as they were at the beginning—only now, having temporarily lost their pipe dreams, they can't even find solace in anesthetizing themselves with booze anymore. As Mr. Robards waltzes dementedly about, we look into rows of shuddering eyes that, like ours, have seen O'Neill smash through the bedrock of life's lies to expose the bottomless, beckoning pit underneath.

≣ *Like the original Broadway production of* The Iceman Cometh, *this revival failed to find an audience on Broadway.*

LET THE ARTISTS DIE
CAFÉ LA MAMA, OCTOBER 15, 1985

In *Let the Artists Die,* the new theater piece from the Cricot 2 company of Cracow, a half-dozen ragtag traveling players trudge in a circle in a black void, clutching their threadbare props as if they had been touring Europe since the beginning of time. Suddenly a gray wooden door opens in the darkness behind them to admit a regiment of generals wearing rubbery silver uniforms. The men's faces are caked with slime; their limbs move jerkily to booming martial music. They seem to have tottered, half-awakened, from their graves, much as a hero among their ranks rides a horse whose flesh has rotted away to reveal the yellowed skeleton within.

As the soldiers relentlessly advance and the music rises to an excruciating pitch, the traveling players and their own hurdy-gurdy music are swept away—forced to scatter into the abyss, perhaps to graves of their own. And the audience is overwhelmed by two or three minutes of drama as intense as any New York has seen since Cricot 2's last visit to the La Mama Annex, with *Wielopole, Wielopole,* in 1982. With the simple, hallucinatory images that rise before us in *Let the Artists Die,* the director Tadeusz Kantor and his company seem to circumscribe the vicious circle of twentieth-century Polish history: the destruction of ceaseless wars, the ashes of Auschwitz, the crushing of those who resist then and now. Yet this powerful achievement is accomplished with only the most elliptical references to real-life events. Mr. Kantor is one of those rare artists—like Buñuel in film or De Chirico in painting—whose private dreams, once summoned onto a larger canvas, tap right into the unconscious terror of a civilization.

Those familiar with Mr. Kantor's work will recognize part of the artistic landscape here. Some of the devices—the soldiers, the iconographic use of crosses and twin-image characters, the pounding waves of music, the ritualistic repetitions of suicides and murders—could be found in *Wielopole* and its predecessor, *The Dead Class* (1979). But the continuity of Cricot 2's work is best emblemized by the physical presence of Mr. Kantor himself. Wearing a black suit and open-collared white shirt, the slight, seventy-year-old director again serves as his own onstage stage manager—a doleful Prospero hovering in the shadows, nervously signaling a lighting cue or snapping his fingers to direct an actor into place. Given that at least three of the characters in the piece also represent Mr. Kantor (at various ages, as both fictional and "real"), we feel adrift in the continuum of his consciousness. We also look at the piece through his eyes: We, too, sit on the periphery of the stage, peering with Mr. Kantor into a dark chamber that variously seems to be his memory, a metaphysical prison, a mass cemetery, a circus tent, and the hell of an apocalyptic great beyond.

In this psychically ordered space, all kinds of unexpected collisions and metamorphoses occur. The troupe of traveling comedians not only shares the stage with an invading army but with splintery apparitions from Mr. Kantor's childhood—a garrulous old mother, a young boy riding a militaristic hobby horse. Two symbols of resistance—the twentieth-century patriot Marshal Jozef Pilsudski and the fifteenth-century sculptor Viet Stoss—also appear. But, as can often happen in dreams, they enter in distorted form: Stoss wears the clothes of a nineteenth-century Montmartre esthete from *La Bohème* and dances a tango with a cabaret prostitute who is among the traveling players.

What may be the evening's most extraordinary sequence soon follows: A representation of Stoss's most famous achievement, his high altar at St. Mary's Church in Cracow, disintegrates into a collection of tall, Dadaesque art objects, which are then attached to the backs of actors as instruments of hideous torture. Religious mythology is quickly consumed by the horror of the death camp—which then dissolves into a demonic dance of the corpses and a strange tableau of peace, in which the torture machinery is placed in a pile suggestive of human remains. Along the way, *The Blue Angel* merges with Delacroix—the black-lingerie-clad prostitute becomes a black-flag-waving angel of death. The audience is left with a crazed panorama of man's capacity for self-destruction.

Even if one can translate the few lines of Polish dialogue (I can't)—and even with the aid of a helpful "Guide to the Performance" sold in the lobby—some of Mr. Kantor's dreams are destined to defy explication; nor can the emotions aroused always be labeled with precise names. It doesn't matter, for this work is no more about literal meaning, let alone narrative, than any surrealist painting is. We are asked to experience *Let the Artists Die* as metaphor—and, absorbed without an excess of intellectualization, it has a direct impact that stage illustrations of reality can't aspire to. As we are bombarded by the recurrent sight of a man hanging himself in a lavatory—or of a panicked woman kneeling with her rosary—we retrieve individual associations of our own that are probably as mysterious and nightmarish as their creator's.

Mr. Kantor brings this off not merely by digging into himself but by honing all the elements of theater (except dialogue) into a juggernaut of sensory experience: Music, recorded sounds, props, lighting, and movement are all precisely in sync. The actors, who range from a small boy to the director's wife, have the faces that Fellini cherishes; we variously regard the cast as the Cricot 2 company, as the eternal traveling troupe of Mr. Kantor's imagination, and as the ever dislocated Polish people. A pair of dextrous male clowns even allows the author to make a bleak, Harpo Marx–like cartoon out of the specter of his own mortality.

So much happens in this densely packed work that it's hard to believe that it really does pass like a dream—in only seventy minutes or so. Do figure that it will take another five or ten minutes to scrape yourself out of your seat.

AUNT DAN AND LEMON
PUBLIC THEATER, OCTOBER 29, 1985

It's the running gag of Wallace Shawn's comedies—*Our Late Night, Marie and Bruce, The Hotel Play*—that polite, literate, seemingly well-mannered people say and do the most outrageous things. The most civilized discourse can, without warning, turn into a beastly description of bodily functions (both sexual and alimentary), frequently punctuated by the word "pig." Mr. Shawn's brave new play at the Public Theater, *Aunt Dan and Lemon,* is no exception, but this time the people are more refined than ever, their pronouncements the most piggish of all. And the running gag, at long last, reaches its explosive, horrifying punch line— for Mr. Shawn has harnessed it to nothing less than a central moral question of our age.

Simply put, this is a play about how literate, civilized societies can drift en masse into beastliness and commit the most obscene acts of history. The evening opens and closes with monologues in which a creamy-toned young Englishwoman, named Leonora and known as Lemon

(Kathryn Pogson), very sweetly tells us why she rather admires the Nazis for their "refreshing" lack of hypocrisy. The rest of the play explains, in flashbacks, how Lemon came to hold these pro-Nazi views, and it does so in a most insinuating way. The single-minded Mr. Shawn never supplies a character to challenge Lemon's articulate arguments. Instead, the audience is left to think up its own rebuttal—forcing us to wonder whether we could and would counter the spurious polemics of a clever fascist like Lemon in real life. I can't remember the last time I saw a play make an audience so uncomfortable, and I mean that as high praise.

Along with the discomfort, there is a lot of mordant laughter. Much of it is provided by the character known as Aunt Dan (Linda Hunt), a friend of Lemon's parents who, during the Vietnam sixties, was the principal influence on the youthful heroine. A brilliant, American-born Oxford don, Dan (for Danielle) is obsessed with defending the honor of Henry Kissinger. As she explains to Lemon at bedtime each night, Mr. Kissinger was a "prayerful" man offering "the entire world the hope of a safe and decent future" even as he was thwarted by "filthy, slimy" journalists and "young intellectuals who studied economics at the Sorbonne or Berkeley." Dan's rabid tirades—in which she defends her idol's dates with starlets as strenuously as the bombing of North Vietnam—often backfire hilariously, but she does score some points. Like its companion play at the Public, David Hare's *A Map of the World* (whose published text cites Mr. Shawn in its dedication), *Aunt Dan and Lemon* has its own nefarious reasons for giving the right wing its say.

In this play's case, Dan's pro-Kissinger arguments are warped and expanded in her acolyte's subsequent rationalizations of Nazi Germany. But Mr. Shawn goes further still, refusing to settle for blaming Lemon's callous convictions entirely on the political ideology she inherits from Aunt Dan. As we gradually learn, Dan instructed the young Lemon not just in public policy but also in private morality, regaling her with reminiscences of her wild salad days as an Oxford student. Most of these reminiscences center on Mindy—a high-priced prostitute who gleefully murders a client and whom Dan regarded as "the most exciting person" she ever met.

Mindy's amoral escapades—approvingly recounted by Dan and presented voyeuristically on stage in sexually graphic, hallucinatory fragments—are the ultimate dramatizations of what Mr. Shawn regards as the rot eating away at a supposedly civilized world. Throughout *Aunt Dan and Lemon,* we are reminded that tabloid headlines like MOTHER EATS INFANT BABY WHILE FATHER LAUGHS lower our resistance to cruelty, that even an obsessive interest in morbid crime fiction can desensitize us (as it does Lemon) to the crimes of Treblinka. Dan and Lemon stand accused not for the political views they hold but for the compassion they have lost—a point brought home in a climactic scene at the older woman's death bed, when even the friends' compassion for each other goes unexpressed. And it is only compassion that can allow anyone, in prewar Germany or elsewhere, to puncture the smooth but specious analogies with which the shrewdest leaders may argue that the preservation of a privileged "way of life" is worth any moral price.

All of Mr. Shawn's own arguments, including his implicit view of Mr. Kissinger, are open to debate, of course—which, along with his refusal to tell the audience what to think and his omission of any "sympathetic" characters, helps make *Aunt Dan and Lemon* the most stimulating, not to mention demanding, American play to emerge this year. The most artful it is not. One may well want to resist the dramaturgy, which is plotless, all but structureless, and almost entirely dependent on lengthy monologues. The crazed language with which the characters plead their obsessions usually, though not unfailingly, carries the speechifying. Only Mr. Shawn could turn even a description of Arnold Schoenberg's music into a memorable riff of Lenny Bruce-ese.

The production, which has been imported from London's Royal Court Theatre under Max Stafford-Clark's direction, is good enough, but hardly definitive. Some of the staging, especially of the lurid Mindy scenes, lacks an edge, and I'm not convinced that the lively Ms. Hunt, who seems at times to be impersonating Dr. Jeane Kirkpatrick, is the dazzling don who could permeate a girl's entire existence. The rest of the Anglo-American cast seems perfect. Ms. Pogson's Lemon remains as elegant as Princess Di no matter what poisonous sentiments emerge from her pert mouth, and there are crisp supporting cameos from Lynsey Baxter as Mindy and Larry Pine as a roué who finds the most unsavory forms of hedonism a cause for only genteel giggles.

The most ferocious comic turn, however, comes from Mr. Shawn himself, who appears in three roles. The first and best of them is that of Lemon's American-born father, a proper auto-parts executive who suddenly flies into a digressionary rage about the dog-eat-dog Darwinism of the business world. Described by his daughter as "kind of a caged animal," the character is typical of those proper-looking monsters who have exploded before us from a safe distance in past Shawn plays. A couple of hours later we're rather startled to discover that, as playwright, Mr. Shawn has finally succeeded in unlocking the beasts within ourselves.

≣ *Another minority opinion. This play offended many, but Papp kept it running (downtown—for once he didn't make the mistake of what would have been a disastrous Broadway move) and ultimately recast it with Pamela Reed when Hunt had to leave to make a movie.*

THE NEWS
HELEN HAYES THEATRE, NOVEMBER 8, 1985

When the house lights go down at *The News*, the new musical at Broadway's Helen Hayes Theatre, an announcer informs us that the show will run ninety-nine minutes, with no intermission. As it's impossible to predict the running time of any live performance so precisely—there might be unexpected ovations, after all—we are immediately suspicious. And why are we being told the running time in any case?

Well, the answer arrives soon enough.

Every minute of *The News*, as it happens, is agony—and, even without ovations, there are more minutes than the number claimed. But by planting that two-digit figure of 99 in the audience's mind, the management clearly hopes to keep it patiently captive until the end, secure in the knowledge that relief is only the merest moments away. This is easily the cleverest stroke of the evening, and it worked at the critics' preview. Everyone stayed seated through the amplification system's final burp, though whether they were absorbed in the show or counting the seconds in ninety-nine minutes (5,940), I couldn't say.

A would-be Brechtian rock opera with music and lyrics by Paul Schierhorn, *The News* is about a large metropolitan tabloid, *The Mirror*, which inflates its circulation with screamer headlines (POPE AND PARTY GIRLS UNDRESSED) and a promotional game called "Super Singo." While *The Mirror*'s logo resembles that of the *New York Post*, any similarities are surely coincidental. Indeed, it's not clear whether *The News* is set in New York. The paper's editor (Jeff Conaway) lives in an apartment overlooking snowcapped mountains reminiscent of suburban Zurich. *The Mirror*'s newsroom—a littered, gloomy jumble containing more microphones and punk-styled band members than desks and reporters—has been inexplicably designed to resemble a sushi bar.

The show's often nonsensical plot concerns a psychopathic killer who, for some reason, is never pursued by the police. The editor is so busy exploiting the story on his front page that he doesn't notice that his own, neglected, teenage daughter is soliciting a date with the murderer through the paper's personals columns. I won't tell you what happens, except to say that it's one of Mr. Schierhorn's themes that beauty can still disarm a beast.

The News also wishes to lecture us about the role played by sensationalist journalism and salacious pop culture in promoting violence.

Unfortunately, this musical is part of the problem, not the solution. Mr. Schierhorn's aggressively screechy songs could teach yellow journalism a thing or two about bad taste. A typically sardonic lyric describes an ordinary urban day as one in which there's "Just a paper bag on Broadway / With seven hands and seven feet." For comic relief, Mr. Schierhorn sets various newspaper features, including the stock quotations, to numbing rock chords.

The cast members model a wide array of loud sunglasses and hideous costumes. Mr. Conaway, a pleasant performer in other circumstances, plays the first newspaper editor in history who bumps and grinds (choreography by Wesley Fata) while shouting "Get me rewrite!" Lisa Michaelis, who might be more persuasive as his older sister than his daughter, acts like a soft-core porno movie's idea of a ponytail-bobbing schoolgirl. As the killer, the overwrought Anthony Crivello doesn't so much recall Robert DeNiro's taxi driver as Jerry Lewis in mid-telethon.

David Rotenberg, the director, tries to whip up excitement by having the killer incessantly raise and lower his window's Venetian blinds. Lest we miss a murder, *The News* is broadcast in video close-up on four television monitors flanking the stage. Walk forward to change the channel, and you may find yourself with a theater full of newfound friends.

SUNDAY ESSAY: AUTEUR DIRECTORS BRING NEW LIFE TO THEATER
NOVEMBER 24, 1985

When people talk about memorable evenings in the theater, they usually tend to cite indelible plays, performances, scenes, and lines. But, with ever-increasing frequency in recent seasons, one could just as easily compile a list of highly charged theatrical moments that have little or nothing to do with playwriting or even acting in the conventional sense. They are directors' moments—often visual or gestural rather than verbal—and, at their best, they carry a weight that can rival a dramatist's highest achievements. While such stage pictures may not create characters or tell stories, they invade or provoke an audience's consciousness, producing what Artaud once called "the truthful precipitates of dreams."

From the past few months of theatergoing alone, in and outside of New York, one could cite several prime productions in which the director, as a film critic would say, serves as auteur. In Tadeusz Kantor's *Let the Artists Die,* a production of Poland's Cricot 2 company seen at La Mama last month, a single recurrent image—that of a phalanx of generals marching on and dispersing a ragtag troupe of traveling players—created a tragic ritual out of the dislocations, repressions, and genocide that are the history of twentieth-century Poland. In *the CIVIL warS,* a Robert Wilson epic performed in excerpt at the American Repertory Theatre in Cambridge last spring, a tranquil opening image plucked from a Matthew Brady photograph—that of soldiers dressing for battle at camp in a steely gray dawn—slowly evolved into a historical presentiment of mass annihilation.

More intimate directors' moments can be found in *Orphans,* as produced by Chicago's Steppenwolf Theatre Company Off Broadway and directed by Gary Sinise: Two feral brothers, lost in urban America, exorcise their private demons not by articulating them in words but by repeatedly bouncing into walls, tumbling down stairs, and, in general, behaving like crazed circus acrobats. In Act 1 of *The Iceman Cometh,* as directed by José Quintero on Broadway, the dead-drunk denizens of Harry Hope's saloon are often frozen in place, as if they really had, to paraphrase Eugene O'Neill, sunk down to the bottom of the sea. Rather than give the actors bits of barroom business to amuse us, Mr. Quintero holds his still tableau as long as Mr. Wilson does his Brady image: The setting and its occupants seem caked with a brackish mold, as if physically corroded by the passing of time and the death of hope.

Because the directors of these four productions come from widely different cultural backgrounds, one might think that their work couldn't possibly share esthetic similarities. But each exemplifies the auteurist stage director—from the extreme case of Mr. Kantor, who actually appears on stage and directs traffic in Cricot 2 productions, to the more modest example of Mr. Quintero, whose deliberate stage pictures are intended to serve his firm reading of O'Neill. The directors' devices sometimes overlap as well. The visions they offer, however elaborate, are not decorative or illustrative—they transport the audience into states of mind rather than real places. (The ostensibly realistic bar of *Iceman* or living room of *Orphans* are stripped down to hallucinatory essentials.) These directors tend to call attention to the artifice of the stage instead of camouflaging it, and often emphasize music as well as movement and imagery over text. One is more likely to recall the Pat Metheny–Lyle Mays jazz score than the author Lyle Kessler's lines in *Orphans,* to remember the Hans Peter Kuhn, David Byrne, or Philip Glass music than the East German playwright Heiner Muller's aural collage in *the CIVIL warS.* While one does remember the words in *Iceman,* Mr. Quintero uses O'Neill's rhetorical repetitions much as Mr. Wilson used Mr.

Glass's repeated musical phrases in *Einstein on the Beach*: The wavelike, ebbing-and-flowing cadences invite a meditative reflectiveness from audiences that is closer to the languorous rhythms of the metaphysical Oriental theater than the jazzed-up cadences that so often typify the psychological naturalism of the American stage.

Although such naturalism shows no signs of losing its potency with American theatergoers, the director's theater has now gained its most pronounced stronghold in this country since visits by Peter Brook's *Marat/Sade* and Jerzy Grotowski's Polish Laboratory Theatre ignited a flock of imitators in the 1960s. The list of prominent practitioners of this theater has grown continuously since the mid-1970s, as has the list of terms used to describe it: *postmodern theater, theater of images, theater of visions* (Stefan Brecht's term for Mr. Wilson's work), *theater of essence* (Jan Kott's term for the work of Mr. Kantor and Mr. Brook), and so on. The best-known auteur-directors—sometimes as varied in style as they are unequal in talent—include JoAnne Akalaitis, Ping Chong, Martha Clarke, Richard Foreman, James Lapine, Elizabeth LeCompte of the Wooster Group, Des McAnuff, and Peter Sellars, as well as the Rumanian émigrés Liviu Ciulei, Lucian Pintilie, and Andrei Serban. Many of these directors work constantly in New York—Off Broadway (Mr. Ciulei will stage *Hamlet* at the Public Theater later this season), at the Brooklyn Academy of Music's Next Wave Festival, occasionally at opera houses, and even on Broadway (Mr. Serban's current *Marriage of Figaro*).

Perhaps even more significant is the extent to which the director's theater has become a truly national phenomenon. In addition to Chicago's Steppenwolf and Cambridge's American Repertory, there are other resident theaters that champion such directors' work—geographically ranging from the La Jolla (Calif.) Playhouse (where Des McAnuff is artistic director and Mr. Sellars is often in residence) to Washington's American National Theatre at the Kennedy Center for the Performing Arts (where Mr. Sellars is artistic director and where Mr. Quintero's *Iceman* originated). Given the reasonably frequent American visits of Mr. Kantor, Mr. Brook, and the dance-theater choreographer Pina Bausch, some of the prime European director-auteurs are also becoming American fixtures—although some other important figures have passed through the New York area only briefly (Giorgio Strehler, of Milan's Piccolo Teatro) or not at all (West Germany's Peter Stein, France's Ariane Mnouchkine, Sweden's Ingmar Bergman, and Scotland's Philip Prowse).

Although often referred to as avant-garde, today's visionary directors are each, to some extent, reinventing the wheel. They draw on philosophies and practices that have been formulated by this century's earlier theatrical innovators, who themselves frequently fused modernist experiments with ideas drawn from Japanese, Chinese, and Balinese theater. When Mr. Wilson says, in an interview in the *CIVIL warS* program, that he wishes to counter a theater in which "everything is subservient to the text," he could be paraphrasing Artaud's second *Theater of Cruelty* manifesto demanding the renunciation of "the theatrical superstition of the text and the dictatorship of the writer." Mr. Wilson's and Mr. Kantor's marionette-like deployment of performers sets one thinking of Meyerhold's biomechanics in postrevolutionary Moscow. Mr. Wilson's merging of music and painterly lighting capitalizes on the theories of the Swiss visionary Adolphe Appia; Mr. Sinise's use of acrobatic movement in *Orphans*, or fellow Steppenwolf director John Malkovich's choreographed friezes in *Balm in Gilead*, could be Alexander Tairov's "synthetic theater" of the 1920s adapted to the sensibility of rock and roll. What is often called mixed-media theater or performance art—in which an authorial director combines film, dance, and music with text—was the "total theater" so often dreamed about in the Soviet Union's heyday of esthetic ferment.

This theatrical program remains valuable. At a time when our stage desperately needs to win back audiences lost to movies and television, it can only gain by being more theatrical—by giving theatergoers experiences that can only be had in the theater. "If people are out of the habit of going to the theater," wrote Artaud between the wars, "it is because we have been accustomed . . . to a purely descriptive and narrative theater-story-telling psychology." Such narrative now having been permanently appropriated by the screen, the theater has much to gain by varying the usual diet.

But there is a down side, too. Like some of their prototypes, a few of our current auteur-directors form cults and practice unchecked self-indulgence. The hype that attends the current art scene has spilled over into the nonprofit theater and some of its booster publications, where experimental directors are sometimes publicized as insistently and indiscriminately as any entertainment sold on Broadway. Not every imagist director is an artist, any more than every nonrepresentational painter is: They can't all be celebrated by saying, as a character in *Sunday in the Park with George* reflexively does when confronting a mixed-media artwork, "I like the images." Even the more imaginative auteur-directors produce variable work—as those who saw the gorgeous but empty Magritte-and-Delvaux tableaux of Mr. Wilson's *Golden Windows* at the Next Wave Festival can attest. Others, such as Martha Clarke in *The Garden of Earthly Delights*, stage choreographed picture-book illustrations in the theater that they might think twice about offering to serious dance audiences. And when some of these directors attempt to make existing theatrical texts bend to their wills, they end up mutilating them.

This fall it is Mr. Kantor who has made the best case for a directors' theater, demonstrating what it can do that a playwrights' theater sometimes can't. Within the same week that his *Let the Artists Die* turned up at La Mama, two other productions opened Off Broadway, both of which also aspired to convey the horror of wartime carnage. And unlike *Let the Artists Die*, these other works, *Not About Heroes* and *Yours, Anne,* had access to some of the most poignant firsthand literature available on the subject: respectively the life and writings of the World War I soldier-poet Wilfred Owen, and the diary of Anne Frank. Yet neither work was remotely as powerful as Mr. Kantor's seventy-minute vision, which contained only a few lines of untranslated Polish. *Let the Artists Die* had an incantatory power that rendered words or even literal wartime images (such as a bleak no-man's-land diorama used in *Not About Heroes*) superfluous. History's horror found an expression in a private, metaphorical visual vocabulary more Jungian than literary or journalistic.

The directors' theater at its worst, by contrast, can currently be found at the Circle in the Square, where Mr. Serban has staged Beaumarchais's *Figaro* on roller skates, swings, and skateboards. As the director's gimmicks distract us even from the title character's famous Act 5 political tirade, we wonder why he bothered to stage this play at all. One might ask similar questions about Mr. Serban's several Chekhov productions (some of his Lincoln Center *Cherry Orchard* excepted), and such large-scale Peter Sellars endeavors as *Hang On to Me* (for Minneapolis's Guthrie Theater in 1984) and *The Count of Monte Cristo* (at Kennedy Center last spring). In these two productions, Mr. Sellars applied the same parade of Constructivist, Expressionist, and Brechtian mannerisms to his retitled adaptation of Gorky's *Summerfolk* and to James O'Neill's acting version of the Dumas warhorse—texts that have nothing in common except their inability to survive the ornamental application of such disparate styles. In the process, much as Mr. Serban does in *Figaro*, Mr. Sellars humiliated the good actors whom his staging emasculated.

It is nothing new for such directors to alter texts, of course. Meyerhold's most celebrated productions included revampings of Molière's *Don Juan* and Gogol's *The Inspector General*—plays that have also attracted Richard Foreman and Mr. Sellars. But not every imagist director is Meyerhold, or, for that matter, the Peter Brook of *A Midsummer Night's Dream* and *Carmen.* It was pitiful to watch Lee Breuer of the

Mabou Mines turn *The Tempest* into a garbled comic strip in Central Park in 1982—especially for anyone who saw Liviu Ciulei's and Giorgio Strehler's far more daring visions of the same play before and after that fiasco. Indeed, it could be argued that some of the auteur-directors function best when working with texts of their own commission or with no text at all. Mr. Foreman's imaginative, if solipsistic, Ontological-Hysteric pieces are far preferable to his *Don Juan,* much as James Lapine's direction of his own script for *Sunday in the Park* had a theatrical force lacking in his muddy Central Park staging of *A Midsummer Night's Dream.* With Mr. Wilson staging Euripides' *Alcestis* and Ms. Akalaitis doing Genet's *The Balcony* in Cambridge this season—and Mr. Sellars staging *The Sea Gull* in Washington—the debate over the value of strong-willed directors applying their distinctive personalities to classics is likely to continue.

When Mr. Wilson and Ms. Akalaitis stage their plays in Cambridge, they will do so with hot musical collaborators, Laurie Anderson and Ruben Blades respectively. It may well be in the musical theater that many of the current American auteur-directors will make their major contributions—as some, such as Mr. Wilson, already have. Like the Steppenwolf directors, Mr. Lapine, Mr. Breuer (*The Gospel at Colonus*), and Mr. McAnuff (*Gimme Shelter, The Death of Von Richthofen, Big River*) have been attempting to harness varied forms of music to imagist theater. So has Mr. Sellars, who, in addition to his operatic experiments, has now made two theatrical attempts to bridge Constructivism with Gershwin songs (in *Hang On to Me* and *My One and Only,* from which he was dismissed). In interviews, the director has likened Mayakovsky verses to Ira Gershwin lyrics and Meyerhold's lengthy production process to that of Fred and Adele Astaire—observations that have thus far been more successfully explored in Michael Bennett's painstakingly developed *Dreamgirls,* whose technologically abstract staging was more Constructivist than that of Mr. Sellars's Gershwin projects. The principles are not as far-fetched as they sound. The musical theater—whether based in contemporary pop music, Glass repetition, Broadway show tunes, Weill or Bizet or Wagner—does allow the extravagant room for a director's total theater that the best plays often deny.

The best playwrights may themselves deny experiments which place their texts at a director's mercy. Samuel Beckett and Arthur Miller have already protested the alterations made on *Endgame* and *The Crucible* in productions directed by JoAnne Akalaitis and Elizabeth LeCompte. Even Ms. Akalaitis's stunning versions of the hard-edged plays of the West German playwright Franz Xaver Kroetz (*Request Concert, Through the*

Leaves) tamper significantly with the original scripts. "I always tried to remove the author as far as possible from the theater, since the playwright always interferes with the true director-artist," said Meyerhold, in a statement that seems to reflect the views of many of our current auteur directors. While Beaumarchais and Molière may now have no choice in the matter, it's hard to imagine David Mamet or Sam Shepard going gently into the night.

They don't have to, needless to say. We have room enough for stages where writers dominate—and for those where directors do. As Meyerhold said of Stanislavsky, "We are two systems, each of which completes the other." It's a sign of a thriving theater that a director's actions can speak as loudly as, if not louder than, a writer's words.

A LIE OF THE MIND
PROMENADE THEATRE, DECEMBER 6, 1985

Late in Act 1 in Sam Shepard's new three-act, four-hour play, *A Lie of the Mind,* a man named Jake (Harvey Keitel) stands at the edge of the California bedroom he grew up in, peering into an inky night. Behind Jake, picked out by a spotlight on his bed, is a small leather box containing the ashes of his father, an alcoholic Air Force pilot who had deserted his family. Ahead of Jake, far off in the mysterious distance and illuminated only by a high green moon, is a woman whose nude back beckons with the mesmerizing lure of a distant, flickering neon sign along a desolate Western highway. The woman is Jake's wife, Beth (Amanda Plummer), and she is literally a highway away, back at her own childhood home in Montana.

The sight of Jake poised in the blackness between these two primordial magnetic poles—the father he can't escape and the woman he can't stop loving—is only one of many astonishing images in the altogether transporting play at the Promenade. And it may be the one that best envelops the sweep of the whole. By the time *A Lie of the Mind* is over, Jake will have to achieve a symbolic reconciliation with the old man, and he will have to cross the gulf (both literal and figurative in Andy Stacklin's set) that separates his bedroom from Beth's. The journey is far more difficult than it sounds. Not only did Jake help incite his father's drunken death long ago, but he has also just tried to kill Beth.

This being a Shepard play—even if in his recent, relatively realistic mode—the story of how Jake gets from where he is to where he ends up is not about one man's travels between two geographical or even psychological points. Indeed, after Act 1, Jake's pivotal position in the play is usurped by his younger, milder brother (Aidan Quinn). Once the author reaches his final curtain—a domestic tableau of familial and romantic love lost and found, as eternal as a homecoming in a John Ford western—our vision has widened beyond both brothers, their phantom father, and Beth to take in a larger landscape. Mr. Shepard has illuminated those archetypal genetic fates we all share, finally to transcend them to find that urge for salvation, that hunger for love, that allows us, like Jake, to go on.

A Lie of the Mind may be its author's most romantic play. However bleak and chilly its terrain—some of it unfolds, in more ways than one, in a blizzard—no character, alive or dead, is beyond redemption: There is always hope, as Mr. Shepard's closing metaphor has it, for a miraculous "fire in the snow." And the work's buoyancy doesn't end there. By turns aching and hilarious—and always as lyrical as its accompanying country music—*A Lie of the Mind* is the unmistakable expression of a major writer nearing the height of his powers. Mr. Shepard has written more innovative, let alone tidier, plays, as well as those that achieve a firmer sense of closure. But these four hours pass like a dream, with scene after scene creating a reverberant effect.

Sometimes the play echoes through Mr. Shepard's recent work. Jake and Beth could be Eddie and May, the combustible fools for love; their parents and siblings are amalgams of those in the family trilogy of *Curse of the Starving Class, Buried Child,* and *True West.* This play also seems to ricochet through American dramatic literature: As it shares O'Neill's vision of mirror-image fathers and sons locked in mutually destructive combat, so it contains flaky Williams mothers (Geraldine Page as Jake's, Ann Wedgeworth as Beth's) and, once it moves surprisingly from darkness to light, a pop-art domestic absurdity reminiscent of Albee's *The American Dream.* Mr. Shepard's inheritance from Mark Twain remains apparent, too: Men are forever taking off to the lonely road, hoping, as one Huck-sounding character explains, to escape the "feebleminded women in civilization." Only now the frontier has vanished: As Jake's mother ruefully notes, the West is no longer big enough for every loner to start a new town of his own.

The play's most powerful reverberations, however, are prompted by those pure Shepard inventions that deliver the evening's inseparable poetry, action, and content. It's the one, shimmering constant in this work that characters are mistaking the living for the dead, one brother for another brother, sons for fathers, sisters for wives—even, at one loony point, a man for a deer. Sometimes the people can't remember their own identities: Beth and her mother both mistake themselves for a lobotomized family matriarch.

Such repeated confusions—some of which are acted out through the author's signature scenes of metamorphosis, in which "a whole life turns upside down in a flash"—create a cumulative dramatic sensation not quite like that produced by any other American playwright. We feel we are passing through the turbulent magnetic fields of the play's two interlocked families, almost palpably experiencing the knotted blood ties that keep tugging at the characters on stage.

These ties, as immutable as a tribal code, also seem to be the lies of the title. It is the roles the characters play in their eternal family scenarios, the mythic stories that are reenacted ritualistically in generation after generation, that dog Mr. Shepard's people. Even Jake's runaway father, in his final years alone in Mexico, can't stop himself from sustaining an illusion of family by posting snapshots of his children among pinups of his favored pop culture heroes (Bing Crosby, Ginger Rogers). Jake's mother is fueled only by her desire to seek revenge on her husband, however long he's been dead. Beth can't resist being drawn to her own abusive husband, either: Not even the brain injury she suffered from Jake's beating can wipe out the thought of him.

Jake's mother keeps hoping in vain that she'll be released from her tie to the past by "winds that wipe everything clean." Mr. Shepard's characters burn down their homes, run away, lose their memories, try out their new roles (Beth actually is, to delicious comic effect, an actress)—and yet fail to escape the family pull. But if, as Jake's mother says, "love is a disease," it still "makes you feel good while it lasts." Mr. Shepard seems to believe in the saving possibilities of love between men and women, if not between parents and children. Love is the play's only "plain truth." It's the characters who drive away a lover who end up in exile; they are spoken of as "lost" or "dead," even if they're alive.

A Lie of the Mind eventually bleeds its personal story into a larger cultural mythos: The final reconciliations are played out in counterpoint to both Hollywood clichés and the tradition-bound folding of a flag. As both writer and director, Mr. Shepard has filled the play, past the brim at times, with virtuosic sequences mixing the colloquial and the fantasist. The evocative music of the live band, the Red Clay Ramblers, and Anne E. Militello's hallucinatory lighting help regulate the imaginative flow.

One could—and, alas, someone will—write a dissertation about the thematic wordplays (mummy-mommy, custom-costume) that attend Beth's brain damage, or about speeches pursuing the metaphysics of the mind to a surreal end. Mr. Shepard has also written his best scene yet for women—galvanically acted by Ms. Page and, as the scorned daughter who relentlessly circles her in rage, Karen Young. In the unexpected farcical nightcap of Act 3, a neurotic Ms. Wedgeworth and craggy James Gammon form a comic pair suggesting a tragic union of Barbara Stanwyck and Gabby Hayes. The couple's domestic war simultaneously lampoons and reinforces Mr. Shepard's notions about the biological identities of the sexes.

Ms. Plummer's sporadic mannerisms notwithstanding, the cast, which also includes Will Patton as another son helplessly emulating his father's rabid brutality, is near perfection. Mr. Quinn, the appealing young hero of the films *Desperately Seeking Susan* and *An Early Frost,* and Mr. Keitel, our foremost interpreter of wife beaters, are a particularly good team as the quintessential good brother–bad brother Shepard alter egos. Mr. Quinn proves a master of deadpan while coping with the indignities, starting with a gunshot wound, that turn his innocent's life into a slapstick hell. Mr. Keitel, meanwhile, may be forever linked with the play's most overpowering theatrical moment: When Jake tries to achieve communion with his father by gently blowing a plume of his ashes into the moonlight, it's as if Mr. Shepard had emblazoned a man's timeless destiny like a star shower across a Western sky.

≡ *As far as I can tell, only critics loved this play. It won the New York Drama Critics Circle Award and has rarely been seen since.*

BENEFACTORS
Brooks Atkinson Theatre, December 23, 1985

When last heard from, in the uproarious *Noises Off,* the English playwright Michael Frayn was demonstrating how the clockwork machinery of farce falls crazily apart when careless actors lose their props, drink too much, and tumble down stairs. *Benefactors,* Mr. Frayn's equally dazzling new play at the Atkinson, would seem a complete departure: It's a comedy only in the darkest sense.

Yet the two works are connected—and not only by the huge talent of their author or by the superbly acted productions, both under the unerring direction of Michael Blakemore, that have brought them to New York. As *Noises Off* was set within the perfect order of theatrical farce, so *Benefactors* unfolds within the idealized order of modern liberal society: The setting is a late-1960s London community of happy families, good neighbors, and utopian political credos. But in this world—the real world, not the theater—it's a matter for heartbreak, not laughter, when people get careless. It is, as one character explains, "like one of those bad dreams when you suddenly realize something has gone wrong." What comes crashing down in *Benefactors* are marriages, principles, and, most unsettling of all, man's plaintive and often sustaining faith in personal and social change.

"People—that's what wrecks all our plans," says Mr. Frayn's protagonist, David (Sam Waterston), a well-meaning architect who dreams of "building the new world we're all going to be living in." *Benefactors* tells of how David designs a redevelopment project for a South London slum neighborhood known as Basuto Road—only to discover that practicalities breed compromise ("In the end, it's not art, it's mathematics") and that the beneficiaries of his scheme don't even want the "New York–style skyscrapers" he envisions for them.

The play's story also concerns David's marriage to Jane (Glenn Close), a cool and capable anthropologist, and the couple's relationship to their neighbors and presumed best friends, Colin (Simon Jones) and Sheila (Mary Beth Hurt). Colin, a hack journalist who joins with the Basuto Road protesters, may want to destroy his old pal David; Sheila, a former nurse, loves David from a lonely, unacknowledged distance.

Such is Mr. Frayn's prowess as a theatrical architect that *Benefactors* has as many levels as David's projected housing towers. This is not a problem play about urban planning, and neither is it a domestic drama about a would-be extramarital love triangle. Told in flashback ten or fifteen years after the events it describes—and narrated, in turn, by each of the four characters—this prismatic work circumscribes the disillusionment of an era, no less American than English, in which grandiose dreams of a universally benevolent democracy died. "Basuto Road. There's the whole history of human ideas in that one name," says David. Basuto Road—which dates back to the nineteenth-century, when England still had its African empire—eventually stands as a comic graveyard not merely for the vanished imperial West but also for the dashed hopes of the enlightened welfare state that replaced it.

Mr. Frayn dramatizes his dour view of civilization in both public and private configurations. As the title indicates, everyone in *Benefactors* wants to help other people. Although on opposite sides of the skyscraper debate, both David and Colin see themselves as helping the city and the poor. As nearly inseparable neighbors, each couple presumes to be propping up the rocky marriage of the other. But Mr. Frayn upholds the principle, as Colin states it, "that other people's lives are at least as complicated as your own." Is David really trying to build a better world in Basuto Road, or is he merely erecting (pun intended by the playwright) a monument to his own ego? In protesting David's plans, is Colin fighting for social good or venting his jealousy at a more successful friend? Which marriage, if either, is really unhappy? Which characters are really the do-gooders, which the destroyers?

The answers to these and other questions keep changing, never to be firmly resolved. The evening's final image—of David overhearing a poor Basuto Road woman laughing, but having no idea of "what she was laughing about"—is emblematic of the entire work. Just as the schemes of social reformers can fail because the reformers don't understand the people they want to help, so Mr. Frayn's two couples constantly misjudge each other, naively mistaking evil for good, selfishness for charity. The characters kill with kindness as often as they help, and, for all their daily intimacies, remain strangers. In separate incidents, Sheila and Jane each get a chance to sneak around and examine the private nooks of the other's house; both find their best friends' dwellings as mysterious as if the families had never met.

In favor of benefaction but despairing of its attainment, Mr. Frayn aches for all four characters and for the unseen inhabitants of Basuto Road. The engineering term "progressive collapse"—a potential calamity in high-rise structures—carries a sad double meaning throughout the evening. Mr. Frayn doesn't see society or his characters progressing. At the end we do hear much talk about rehabilitation and change—and, indeed, in the plot sense, all four lives (as well as "public opinion" about urban development) have been dramatically altered. But the people haven't so much changed as adjusted (with or without psychiatric help).

"Life goes around like a wheel," says Colin. "People don't know what they want until they've got it," says Sheila. According to David, even "new and amazing" architecture leaves a site looking "the same as before." Its allusions to *The Master Builder* notwithstanding, *Benefactors* is particularly reminiscent of Chekhov (of whom Mr. Frayn is a foremost translator). The evening's chipper ending, in which survival and wisdom prove to be life's pyrrhic victories, is about as happy as that of *The Sea Gull*.

The writing in *Benefactors* is as meticulously conceived in a witty, poetic vein as the farcical mechanics were in *Noises Off*. The imagery of the opening monologue—with its delicate play of clouds and sunlight, present and past—establishes the kaleidoscopic method used throughout. Further enhancement is provided by Martin Aronstein's quicksilver lighting, which conducts its own precise drama of light and dark on the stylized Michael Annals set depicting the two interlocking households. And Mr. Blakemore, as always, brings amazingly modest ingenuity to the text. Although Act 1 still feels a bit attenuated, the recast New York *Benefactors* seems to exceed the London version in speed and warmth.

Ms. Close is at her most commanding as the strongest of the four characters, the feet-on-the-ground wife of a head-in-the-clouds archi- tect. Striking just the right balance of heartiness and chill, the actress makes us see the "blackness" she shares with the destructive neighbor Colin, whom Mr. Jones plays with immaculately sinister wit. As seem- ingly the most fragile of the quartet, the lovesick and loveless Sheila, Ms. Hurt gives what may be the performance of her stage career: Her mousy, awkward Englishwoman, poised constantly between airy fits of giggles and wrenching sobs, is as wounding a comic creation as the antithetical Southern siren the actress memorably played in *Crimes of the Heart*.

Mr. Waterston is at first woolly in his Englishness, but his perfor- mance reaches a brilliant pitch in Act 2 as David ceases to be a "bemused neutral observer" of the conflicts around him and starts to become their victim. By the end, he is the embodiment of a devastating play: Once a bright-eyed young man fired by magical visions of saving humanity, Mr. Waterston's architect gradually slouches with age and disappointment, his spirit spent by the exhaustion of saving no one but himself.

IT'S ONLY A PLAY
MANHATTAN THEATRE CLUB, JANUARY 13, 1986

It's Only a Play* is both the title and the most persistent refrain of the frequently uproarious Terrence McNally comedy now to be found at the Manhattan Theatre Club. "Whatever happens tonight, it's only a play," the revelers at an opening-night party keep reminding themselves as they wait for the reviews of Broadway's newest arrival, *The Golden Egg*. But Mr. McNally knows well that his characters protest far too much. For the fictional show people in *It's Only a Play*, the play's the thing, the only thing—at least until an offer from Hollywood comes along.

Only a writer who loves the theater and has survived its bloodiest wars could have written a comedy like this one, in which naughty showbiz in- jokes coexist with genuine tributes to the theatrical calling. Mr. McNally, the author of some pricelessly funny hits (*Bad Habits, The Ritz*) and the occasional bomb (*The Rink*), is the ideal playwright for the task. Indeed, *It's Only a Play* is itself an example of the perilous vicissitudes that attend a career in the American theater. Under the title *Broadway, Broadway,* this play folded during its 1978 pre-Broadway tryout in Philadelphia. Mr. McNally revised the script and instituted the current title for a well-received 1982 Off Off Broadway production (at the Manhattan Punch Line) that almost no one saw.

The Manhattan Theatre Club's additionally revised edition, directed by John Tillinger, is no doubt definitive. Its cast contains the original star of *Broadway, Broadway,* James Coco (in funniest form), as well as the director of the 1982 *It's Only a Play,* Paul Benedict. Now, as before, Mr. McNally's comedy is more a cascade of jokes than a play. But, except for roughly fifteen minutes of scattered dead spots in Act 2, the jokes are so well made that one doesn't dwell on the playwright's disinclination to provide the fully drawn characters of *All About Eve* or the farcical structure of *Noises Off.* Casual theatergoers should be warned, however, that a knowledge of theatrical ephemera is required to appreciate most of the punch lines. If you cannot identify the likes of Bernard Jacobs, Robert Patrick, and *The Man Who Had Three Arms,* this may not be your hoot.

Among the other butts of Mr. McNally's cleverest gags are Rita Moreno, Lanford Wilson, Charles Nelson Reilly, Linda Hunt, "Betty" Bacall, and Tovah Feldshuh, not to mention regional theater, preview audiences, and certain real-life drama critics (only some of whom work for *The New York Times*). The forum for the wisecracks is the pink upstairs bedroom (designed by John Lee Beatty) in the moneyed town house where the producer of *The Golden Egg* is giving "the party of the year" for "all Broadway—or what's left of it." The only real event in Mr. McNally's comedy, aside from a reported attack on Arlene Francis by the producer's pet dog, is the arrival of the *Times's* review of the play-within-the-play. The press agent has predicted "an out-and-out rave."

While waiting for the newspaper, those who are associated with the play pray for success, even as their best friends secretly wish them failure. Chief among the smiling backbiters is Mr. Coco, cast as James Wicker, a television sitcom star ("I'll even do *Love Boats!*") who began his career Off Off Broadway with the author of *The Golden Egg.* Surely Mr. McNally, whose 1969 Off Broadway play *Next* gave Mr. Coco a career boost, tailored James Wicker for his star. A dyspeptic Humpty Dumpty in a crimson-trimmed tuxedo, Mr. Coco is both hilarious and lovable in his two-faced, egomaniacal bitchery. No sooner do we laugh at his bad-mouthing of the lead actor in *The Golden Egg* ("He has all of my mannerisms and none of my warmth"), than we are unexpectedly touched by a speech recalling the now-jaded Wicker's romantic old dreams of playing Falstaff or Willy Loman in stock.

The evening's other outstanding performance comes from Joanna Gleason, last seen as the chilly neighbor in *Joe Egg* and here playing a Tony-winning actress returning to Broadway after several movie flops and more than a few cocaine "hits." Christine Baranski, while occasionally too exaggerated in pitch, also earns many chuckles as the neophyte producer, a wealthy dilettante who insists on telling her theatrical associates the meaning of the expression "break a leg." In smaller roles, there are sharp contributions by Mr. Benedict, Florence Stanley, and Jihmi Kennedy, who respectively impersonate an acerbic magazine drama critic friendly with Lina Wertmuller, a philosophical cabdriver, and an aspiring actor who delivers an exceptionally appalling rendition of "Raindrops Keep Falling on My Head." Only Mark Blum's playwright and David Garrison's director, a Yale prodigy known for his all-male *Wild Duck,* are at times shrilly acted and written.

Mr. Tillinger's staging doesn't miss an opportunity for mirth—down to the last of Rita Ryack's many witty costumes. But Mr. McNally deserves full credit for the evening's warmth. The theater people in *It's Only a Play* are, to be sure, ridiculously myopic: They know more about the history of the Ethel Barrymore Theatre than current events and would rather listen to the barroom philosophy of a former chorus girl from *Panama Hattie* than read a book. Yet the author's affection for his self-absorbed characters—and his concern for the survival of their "noble profession" and even their endangered Broadway—keeps peeking through. "New York without a theater district might as well be Newark," says the cabbie, in one of many lines calculated to remind us that the theater is too precious and too precarious for the audience to think of any play as only a play.

LILLIAN

ETHEL BARRYMORE THEATRE, JANUARY 17, 1986

There are few, if any, more startling sights in a New York theater right now than the one that opens *Lillian,* the new one-woman play at the Barrymore. As the curtain rises, we are confronted by an eerie reincarnation of the writer Lillian Hellman—complete with wavy blondish hair, elegant gray suit, pearl necklace, mountainous nose, lighted cigarette, and, most unsettling of all, a fierce smile that seems more an invitation to hostilities than an offering of warmth. Makeup, of course, can do wonders, but so can a fine actress. Zoe Caldwell, one of the more estimable actresses around, has surely captured the seething physical presence of Hellman, a woman whose volatile political and personal battles were inseparable from her careers as playwright, screen writer, and memoirist.

The trouble with *Lillian* is that Ms. Caldwell, having presented us at the start with that incredible image, is not always given the means to explore and enhance it. Intense as her energy and concentration are, the star is chained to a sanitized Hellman portrait that, like all bowdlerized official biographies, lacks the conflict and depth essential to create a dramatic or psychologically gripping character. Ms. Caldwell describes some highly charged events—she addresses us from the hospital where Lillian's off-and-on lover of thirty years, Dashiell Hammett, is dying in 1961—but we usually observe her impressive solo turn from a slight emotional remove.

The script's author is William Luce, who has fashioned *Lillian* from the three major Hellman memoirs—*An Unfinished Woman, Pentimento,* and *Scoundrel Time.* If Hellman's own accounts of her life sometimes glossed over crucial areas, Mr. Luce's adaptation has gone the original texts one better. Hellman's controversial attacks on fellow liberals with whom she parted ways have been eliminated here, as have her scathing portraits of friendly witnesses before the House Un-American Activities Committee. Even her catty nonideological remarks about Tallulah Bankhead are judiciously toned down in *Lillian.* The result is a play that casts its subject in an even more roseate glow than the film *Julia* (which was adapted from a chapter of *Pentimento*). While Mr. Luce's Lillian admits to flaws, her flaws are never as grave as those of her antagonists and her anger is always in the cause of right.

Hellman partisans will enjoy this opportunity to worship at the shrine. Hellman's detractors will probably be reduced to apoplexy. (Were her most vociferous literary opponents to see *Lillian* en masse, Broadway might have its first riot in years.) Nonpartisan theatergoers will find a moderately engaging tour of the Hellman saga that, in the free-associative style of its heroine's books, covers her upper-middle-class upbringing in New Orleans and New York, the development of her social conscience, her encounters with Hollywood vulgarity, and her life with "Dash." As in the memoirs, her Broadway career is only cursorily recalled.

Easily the evening's high point, which arrives late in Act 2, is the greatest scene of Hellman's career, in real life or the theater. This is her appearance before HUAC, accompanied by the reading of her defiant letter in which she refuses to cut her conscience "to fit this year's fashions." Ms. Caldwell faces her unseen inquisitors from a tense, seated position, with tape-recorded voices creating the ghosts of the 1952 Washington hearing room. Her words remain a stirring expression of bravery and integrity during a time of witch hunts.

Some of the other livelier interludes in *Lillian* include the accounts of both the young and middle-aged Hellman's symbiotic relationships with black female servants, and, more frivolously, anecdotes involving Lee Shubert, Irving Thalberg, Norma Shearer, and Dorothy Parker. Rather harder to take are the lengthy tributes to Dash, who, for all his cited drinking and womanizing, still emerges as an impossibly saintly paragon of artistic and moral rectitude.

Although the play's hospital framing device is hokey, Mr. Luce has deftly stitched together the fragments from his already elliptical source material. In the process, we're reminded that Hellman's best prose attained an eloquence and lilt often lacking in her theatrical melodramas. The fluency of Mr. Luce's anthology is matched by Robert Whitehead's staging, which unfolds on a sparsely furnished black-and-white set (by Ben Edwards) suitable for a late Beckett play. The only real lapses in the direction are the incidental music and lighting, which occasionally hammer in the monologue's shifts of mood or time frame.

Even when she is turning into mush over bucolic rural domesticity with Dash or laying on the one-of-the-guys braggadocio a bit thickly, Ms. Caldwell is invigorating to watch. Her voice, however, is not always on pitch. The actress's rendition of Hellman's deep, wheezy vocal register has an Anglican tinge, reminiscent of Tammy Grimes. The disparate characters that Lillian briefly impersonates—whether her father or wet nurse, Dash or Joseph McCarthy—often sound roughly alike. One also feels that some of Ms. Caldwell's poses, particularly those revealing her in profile with crooked arm and tilted cigarette, suggest an icon posing for a book jacket rather than a person drawn from life.

But the star's achievement is still considerable. If her performance only rarely ascends from a first-rate impersonation to a compelling characterization, that's because too many pieces are missing from the story to allow the role to add up. It's hard to reconcile the rather sugary, only slightly curmudgeonly figure presented here with the vinegary rebel who stirred up tempests for almost five decades on the public stage. In *Lillian,* the unfinished woman who was Lillian Hellman has been given the polished finish that obscures as much as it glows.

There are few theatrical experiences more exhilarating than watching a talented young artist fulfill his promise. That experience is now to be had at the American Place Theatre, where the performer Eric Bogosian, a downtown fixture for almost a decade, has put together an airtight eighty-minute show in which his gifts for acting and social satire collide to their most incendiary effect yet. *Drinking in America* is the evening's title, and, like such past Bogosian efforts as *FunHouse* and *Men Inside,* it is a breakneck, hair-raising comic tour of the contemporary American male psyche, with its creator playing all the roles. But if this is the funniest and most shapely of Mr. Bogosian's shows, the edges of his humor have not been smoothed out: *Drinking in America* leaves a hangover of outrage that a theatergoer can't easily shake.

The demographically diverse men on view include, among others, a grasping showbiz hustler, a latter-day Willy Loman on the road, a ghetto junkie, and a gyrating heavy-metal rock star. While many of the characters are indeed intoxicated—on cocaine, quaaludes, or heroin as well as alcohol—*Drinking in America* charts a more pervasive spiritual malady. The men we meet are gluttons for power, money, and sex as well as for chemical stimulants; they have pigged out on the American way. Although Mr. Bogosian hardly approves of a neo-Nazi television evangelist who appears late in the show, he does seem to share the preacher's conviction that "the Devil seduced us with a life of plenty and invited us into hell."

Such is the ecumenical nature of Mr. Bogosian's harsh indictment that he mocks not only the self-satisfied affluent but also the self-indulgent have-nots. The narcotized derelicts of *Drinking in America* proselytize for "having it all" as ferociously as those characters who do live the good life: From the gutter, the addicts gleefully endorse the virtues of big cars, compliant women, and other supposed rewards of the success ethic. Nor does Mr. Bogosian spare himself from attack. In one bit, a performer named Eric records a voice-over for a smarmy commercial hawking an imported beer to the upwardly mobile.

As an actor, Mr. Bogosian has now reached a level of expertise that approaches Lily Tomlin's. Dressed in jeans and a white shirt, he uses his balletic physicality and perfect-pitch vocal mimicry to inhabit each of his men completely. (Marc Malamud's excellent lighting assists when Mr. Bogosian plays a black man.) The metamorphoses can be amazing.

Early on, like a butterfly bursting out of a cocoon, he transforms himself from a fetal-postured, near-comatose bum to a wired Hollywood agent trying to sell a "major American talent," Lee Marvin, for "a little pocket change" ($40,000 for a television miniseries cameo). Not long after that, Mr. Bogosian becomes a fat, middle-aged, slow-drawling conventioneer—the country's number one "industrial ceramic tile salesman." With a poignancy recalling David Mamet's self-deluded dog-eat-dog salesmen, this sad Sun Belt drummer tries to convince himself and an unseen hundred-dollar-a-night "escort" that he is a "success" because he "cares about people."

Mr. Bogosian's writing also reveals his uncommonly sharp ear for all kinds of American voices. He is equally adept at capturing the language of an ethnic coffee-shop owner, a slickly hypocritical rock disk jockey, and a young urbanite employed in a "semicreative job with very little pressure to perform." Yet the writing is not merely jokey, and at times it can lift off into extravagantly surreal flights. In what may be the tour de force of *Drinking in America,* a blue-collar hood regales a buddy with an account of an all-night booze-and-acid binge of "partying" that escalated into a violent crime spree. The events are described in vivid subliterate vernacular, and, like a car pileup on a highway, they are grotesquely slap-stick. But even as we laugh, we are terrified by the cruelty of a hooligan whose manic giggles and cracker-barrel storytelling style cannot hide a complete absence of conscience.

If there are several such high points in *Drinking in America,* there are no real valleys. Whether due to experience or to the added presence of the director Wynn Handman, Mr. Bogosian has for the first time edited his material and his performance to the quick. *Drinking in America* rarely slows down, and it has been cohesively assembled to achieve a cumulative effect.

The show even has a beginning and an end. At the outset, Mr. Bogosian reads from a composition book containing a journal he purports to have written while attending Boston University in 1971. A hilariously accurate parody of the period's LSD-induced, messianic flower-child rhetoric, the diary contains such entries as "There's no point to a liberal-arts degree now" and "I want to change the world, and I know I can do it." At the end of *Drinking in America* Mr. Bogosian indicates how little progress he thinks the world has made: He appears as a heavy-lidded, slurred-voiced panhandler, hustling the audience for quarters from the stage edge.

Striving to be obsequious, the bum reassures his potential donors by saying, "You should just get rid of me, forget about me." But even though this threatening, feral apparition weaves away into the dark night soon after, Mr. Bogosian, still eager to change the world, has seen to it that we cannot forget.

LOOT

Manhattan Theatre Club, February 19, 1986

"We must keep up appearances," says a young English nurse named Fay at the final curtain of Joe Orton's *Loot*. Fay has already murdered at least eight people—seven of them former husbands—but, as she says, the appearances of middle-class propriety must be upheld. In Orton's lethal farce, one of the funniest and meanest in the contemporary theater, the characters often act like prim, well-mannered, God-fearing representatives of the bourgeoisie, even as their every private deed and thought reek of greed, blasphemy, sadism, and lust. As the curtain descends on *Loot*, Fay may be contemplating a new homicide, but first she must bow her head in silent prayer.

Loot, now at the Manhattan Theatre Club, was initially produced in the West End in 1966 and flopped in three weeks on Broadway in 1968. It was the second of three major works that its author wrote before his own life was ended by murder, at age thirty-four, in 1967. Largely through the championship of his biographer, the critic John Lahr (*Prick Up Your Ears*), Orton's reputation has risen steadily in recent years, at least in England. New Yorkers had to wait until John Tillinger's 1981 Off Broadway staging of *Entertaining Mr. Sloane* to see an Orton play enjoy an extended run in a genuinely first-class production.

Now, it is Mr. Tillinger again—once more in league with the star of *Sloane*, Joseph Maher—who has given this playwright the New York airing he has long deserved. This altogether brilliantly acted *Loot* reveals that, two decades after its controversial inception, Orton's play has lost none of its furious wit or capacity to shock.

The setting for the mayhem is an English household (a font of dowdy bad taste, as designed by John Lee Beatty) where the middle-aged McLeavy (Charles Keating) prepares for his wife's funeral. Mrs. McLeavy's corpse, newly embalmed, resides in a coffin awaiting burial—or so it does some of the time. The family's teenage son, Hal (Zeljko Ivanek), has just robbed a bank with his bisexual companion, the undertaker Dennis (Kevin Bacon). To escape the prying detective Truscott (Mr. Maher), the boys and the equally predatory Fay (Zoë Wanamaker) play an elaborate shell game in which they periodically empty the coffin of the bandaged cadaver in order to hide their loot.

The method of the play's madness is highly sophisticated, far more so than in the work of the many Orton-influenced playwrights (among them, such Americans as Christopher Durang and Harry Kondoleon). *Loot* is timeless because its author's rage against hypocrisy is conveyed not by preaching or idle wisecracks but by the outrageous farcical conception and by pungent, stylized dialogue in the tradition of Wilde and Shaw. In making a house of mourning and a corpse the stuff of humor, Orton goes beyond mere black comedy to exploit the tragic implications of farce. The subversive structure of *Loot*, in which money replaces death as the ostensibly bereaved characters' gravest preoccupation, turns the world upside down for both polemical and mirth-making effect.

The comic inversions soon multiply at a riotous pace. Hal expresses his oedipal horror of seeing his late mother in the nude ("It would be a Freudian nightmare") even as he dances about using her false teeth as castanets. Fay vows that she will never marry a man who isn't a Roman Catholic, although she has yet to marry a man she doesn't murder. The corrupt snoop Truscott, who has his own designs on the loot, browbeats a suspect by shouting, "Under any other political system I'd have you on the floor in tears!" As he yells, his bullied victim lies on the floor in tears.

For *Loot* to realize its full hilarity, it is essential that these and the many other double-edged jokes be played straight. Only if the characters believe in their own sanctimonious poses does the gap between their proper self-image and disgusting activities become funny—and deliver Orton's scabrous judgment of the world. Mr. Tillinger's production is scrupulous on this score. While one might wish his staging had provided more inventive slapstick juggling of the mummified mom, every performance is impeccably conceived, every line exquisitely timed.

Ms. Wanamaker, a Royal Shakespeare Company actress last seen in New York as the sidekick in *Piaf*, is wonderful as Fay; her starchy Catholicity remains intact no matter how many cardinal sins she gleefully commits. The nurse could be speaking for herself when she places a copy of the Ten Commandments on Mrs. McLeavy's casket and, without a trace of irony, announces, "She was a great believer in some of them." Later on, the actress tops even that laugh when, having been figuratively caught with her hand in the coffin, she does a series of double takes that protest her innocence too much, and then some.

Just as masterly is Mr. Keating, as the widower whose slavish worship of civic and spiritual authorities is rewarded by his continuous humiliation at the hands of those authorities. (Goodness has nothing to do with justice in *Loot*.) Left dazed and whimpering by such indignities as an unexpected dog attack and a household plumbing failure, he comes to regard his wife's funeral as, relatively speaking, an occasion for "high spirits." As the indolent son, Mr. Ivanek follows his portrait of the intellectual journalist in David Hare's *A Map of the World* with an impressively antithetical comic creation: The sullen Hal is so stupid that even he is left shuddering by the extent of his own idiocy. Mr. Bacon, as his cheeky partner in larceny and lasciviousness, finds amorality a joke and makes us see the humor in his antisocial activities as well.

In the dominant role of Truscott, a would-be Hercule Poirot ineptly masquerading as a Metropolitan Water Board fact finder, Mr. Maher conveys the character's megalomania with mid-sentence bursts of anger, usually preceded and followed by mad streams of stiff-upper-lip bureaucratese. It is surely the most unglued—and uproarious—performance of the actor's career. By the time this detective reaches an Act 1 gag in which he must identify (in part by licking) the corpse's stray glass eye, we certainly realize just why *Loot* was, in its author's own words, "vulgar and offensive in the extreme to middle-class susceptibilities." Those who are liberated rather than offended by Joe Orton's anarchic vision may be laughing so hard that they join Mr. Maher's victims on the floor in tears.

≡ *David Merrick, of all people, came back from his seeming, stroke-induced oblivion to move* Loot *to Broadway, where it was just as wonderful—with another up-and-coming actor, Alec Baldwin, replacing Kevin Bacon in a supporting role—but just as short-lived as it had been on Broadway in 1968. The revival of John Guare's play of the same period,* The House of Blue Leaves, *fared much better, enjoying a long Broadway run when it transferred from Lincoln Center (see below).*

THE HOUSE OF BLUE LEAVES
Mitzi E. Newhouse Theater, March 20, 1986

Returning to *The House of Blue Leaves* fifteen years after its Off Broadway premiere, one expects to find a musty, archetypal artifact of late 1960s black comedy. Set in Sunnyside, Queens, on that 1965 day when Pope Paul VI visited New York, John Guare's early, breakthrough play features mockingly observed nuns, a lethal (but farcical) political bombing, a GI earmarked for Vietnam, and, as a protagonist, a zookeeper who dreams in vain of making it big in Hollywood as a songwriter. As if that weren't enough countercultural loopiness, the zookeeper, Artie Shaughnessy, has a wife named Bananas who really is bananas. In the period's R. D. Laing–Ken Kesey tradition, Bananas, a schizophrenic destined for a cuckoo's nest (the house of Mr. Guare's title), is the sanest character in the work.

Yet a funny thing has happened to *Blue Leaves* in the loving revival, flawlessly directed by Jerry Zaks, that's been mounted at the Newhouse Theater by Lincoln Center's fledgling theater company. The play no longer seems all that funny, and it's none the worse for the shift in tone. While some of Mr. Guare's jokes are indeed dated remnants of the sixties, his characters and themes have gained the weight and gravity so lacking in his more pretentious recent plays. Time hasn't healed the wounds described in *Blue Leaves*—it's deepened them. One still leaves the theater howling at Mr. Guare's vision of losers at sea in a materialistic culture, but the howls are less of laughter than of pain.

Much of that pain derives from an extraordinary performance by Swoosie Kurtz, as Bananas. If Mr. Guare's zaniness is muted here, so is this actress's characteristically daffy comic assault. All but unrecognizable, Ms. Kurtz wears a ragged, misbuttoned cardigan over a faded nightgown; her hair is a dark, silver-tinged mop, framing a pallid face with bulging, swimming eyes. Making her first entrance in silence, she stands in the gloomy fringes of her threadbare cage of a living room, watching her husband, Artie (John Mahoney), and his mistress, a platinum-haired downstairs neighbor named Bunny (Stockard Channing), plot their elopement to California. Powerless to do anything to halt the plan— which will place her in the loony bin—the spectral Ms. Kurtz exits as quietly as she entered, a catatonic ghost. And without a single line, she casts the entire play in tragic shadows.

Blue Leaves can accommodate that darkness. Mr. Guare has found the terror as well as the absurdity in working-class Queens nobodies who aspire to be somebodies; at its best, his play often seems like *The Day of the Locust* as rewritten by Tennessee Williams. Certainly Ms. Kurtz seems as lost as Blanche DuBois in her climactic Act 2 speech, in which Bananas madly recalls having been at Forty-second Street and Broadway, "the crossroads of the world," on a day when Jacqueline Kennedy, Cardinal Spellman, Bob Hope, and President Johnson were all at that intersection hailing cabs. Bananas explains that she gave the celebrities a lift—only to discover later that night that the disastrous results were recounted as comic anecdotes on the Johnny Carson show. Recalling her humiliation before thirty million television viewers, Bananas wonders why stars can't "love" fans like herself. As crushingly delivered by Ms.

Kurtz, the monologue is not just a surreal shaggy joke: Bananas's pathological relationship to glamorous American myths becomes grotesquely
symbolic of a national psychosis.

This isn't to say there is no humor left in *Blue Leaves*. When those
wayward nuns appear in Act 2, they fly like bats into the iron window
bars of the Shaughnessy living room. We meet a deaf Hollywood starlet,
deliciously acted by Julie Hagerty, whose hilarious confusions include
what must be the single funniest gag ever sparked by the word *Unitarian*.
There are also Artie's many failed Tin Pan Alley songs—would-be Hoagy
Carmichael ditties with titles like "Where Is the Devil in Evelyn?" Mr.
Mahoney delivers them raspily at a piano with the not-quite-slick showbiz moves of every benighted fool who ever regarded Ted Mack's amateur
hour as the pinnacle of artistic aspiration.

What makes these comic twists closer in spirit to Nathanael West
than the 1960s is Mr. Guare's refusal to condescend. The playwright
sees his characters sympathetically, as helpless victims of a society in
which movie stars and the Pope are indistinguishable media gods, in
which television is a shrine, in which assassins are glorified in headlines.
In such an icon-ridden landscape, the best hope is the pathetic one
stated by the brash Bunny: "When famous people go to sleep at night,"
she wistfully posits, "it's us they dream of."

Bunny also claims, apropos of the Pope's visit, that "there's miracles in
the air." But the miracles she and the others long for are either spiritually bankrupt or unobtainable. Mr. Guare's Sunnyside denizens believe
that a neighborhood boy turned filmland big shot (Christopher Walken)
will bring them instant fame and fortune; they even believe that the
Pope, by addressing the United Nations, can end the war in Vietnam.
Such starry-eyed fantasies do little but drive everyone bananas. The blue
spotlight of stardom craved by the songwriting Artie may be as much of
a nuthouse as the blue-leaf-shaded asylum where he would dispose of
his wife. When the Shaughnessys' son (Ben Stiller) auditions for the role
of Huckleberry Finn in a Hollywood movie, his various stunts (all
learned from the *Ed Sullivan* show) are pointedly mistaken for the behavior of a "mental defective."

Mr. Zaks's direction always illuminates that frontier where Mr.
Guare's absurdism blazes into nightmare. The care extends to the production design: Ann Roth's tacky sixties costumes are at once satirical
and sadly shabby, while Tony Walton's set (apocalyptically lighted by
Paul Gallo) is a Stuart Davis–like collage in which the Shaughnessys'
vulgar domestic squalor is hemmed in by the urbanscape's oppressive
brand-name signs. With the exception of Mr. Walken's clichéd cameo

appearance, the acting is of high quality throughout. Mr. Mahoney, last seen as the mysterious mobster in *Orphans,* and Ms. Channing are exceptionally impressive as they find decency and humor in the often clownish and cruel Artie and Bunny.

Still, it's Ms. Kurtz whom audiences will be talking about for the rest of the season, and then some. By evening's end, Bananas has actually become one of her husband's animals. Bananas likes animals, she has explained, because they're not famous and because they represent to her the buried feelings that her fit-regulating pills usually restrain. Ms. Kurtz's metamorphosis brings the theater to a shocked hush. Her slender hands become paws dancing in the air, her voice trails off into a maimed puppy's whimper. As Bananas nuzzles helplessly against her husband, Mr. Guare's inspired image of the all-American loser acquires a metaphorical force as timeless as West's locusts. Where once there was a woman with stars in her eyes, we see a battered mutt, the forgotten underdog that the bright lights of our national fairy tales always pass by.

SUNDAY ESSAY: KEVIN KLINE'S HAMLET
MARCH 30, 1986

Kevin Kline is the pride of the American theater—a homegrown actor who might yet be our Olivier (and a singing and dancing Olivier at that), a show business star who has never misplaced either his devotion to the stage or his integrity. One can safely speculate that commercial theatrical managements offer Mr. Kline nearly every starring role for which he might be remotely suited. Yet, since making his Broadway debut in a supporting part in the musical *On the Twentieth Century,* the actor has limited his Broadway appearances to classics (*The Pirates of Penzance, Arms and the Man*) and a superior contemporary play (Michael Weller's *Loose Ends*)—all under the aegis of nonprofit theatrical institutions. Mr. Kline's choice of Hollywood film projects (*The Big Chill, Sophie's Choice, Silverado*) has been similarly schlock-free. Without making a public case of it, this actor is one of the very few of his generation and gifts who has made no discernible effort to sell out.

The most impressive aspect of Mr. Kline's professional deportment is his continued pursuit of Shakespeare. For an actor of his prominence, there is no particular career advantage—and, heaven knows, no mercenary reward—in wrestling diligently with the classics. In the showbiz whirl of New York and Hollywood of the 1980s, as opposed to that of, say, John Barrymore's day, few prospective employers care whether an actor has proved himself in Shakespeare; *Hurlyburly* is more likely to boost an actor's reputation than *Hamlet*. If anything, a star risks derailing his career, should his performance in a Shakespearean role prove notoriously embarrassing. (A rising young actor [Philip Anglim], fresh from winning a Tony Award in his first Broadway role, faded into oblivion after his disastrous Macbeth at Lincoln Center several seasons ago.) Presumably motivated by a desire for esthetic growth, Mr. Kline has nonetheless maintained his impassioned investigation of the canon. Under the sponsorship of Joseph Papp's New York Shakespeare Festival, he has created a *Richard III* (1983) and *Henry V* (1984)—both in Central Park—and now, at the Public Theater, his much-awaited Hamlet.

Each of these appearances has been distinguished by Mr. Kline's restless, pungent wit, not to mention his balletic grace of body and speech. Even when the performances have been inconsistent, they've been spellbinding. And, in each case, Mr. Kline has been in some degree hobbled by the productions surrounding him. Jane Howell, the English director of *Richard III*, never gave Mr. Kline the guidance needed to help prune the comic excesses—possibly left over from the *Penzance* Pirate King—that prevented his intellectually charged Crookback from sounding the blackest chords of evil. In *Henry V,* much more capably directed by Wilford Leach, Mr. Kline seemed stymied by the production's inability to reconcile itself to the play's jingoism: Persuasive as his king was when circumspectly debating war's merits with his common soldiers—or when merrily courting his lovely Katherine (Mary Elizabeth Mastrantonio)—he fell into hollow cadences when storming Harfleur.

The Public's *Hamlet,* directed by Liviu Ciulei, is more erratic still. It's easily the most handsome of the three productions—one can see that the Rumanian-born Mr. Ciulei was trained as an architect. But was Mr. Ciulei so preoccupied with the stunning look of his staging that he forgot about the figures in the landscape? His supporting cast is too often inept.

That Mr. Kline has what it takes to be a great Hamlet is beyond question—but that is not the question that this production raises. One must instead ask why this star, having decided to pour himself unsparingly into the most demanding role in our literature, should be repaid for his efforts by having his performance thrown to the wolves of Mr. Ciulei's bizarrely populated Elsinore. It seems incredibly wasteful to cripple what might have been an outstanding Hamlet of our generation.

To understand the extent of the waste, one must first appreciate how substantial a contribution Mr. Kline has tried to make. His training in

Richard III and *Henry V* has paid off here. His voice seems wider in range than one recalls, his grasp of the poetry ever more secure. And if sometimes Mr. Kline thinks too much, as his character does, one must admire a performance in which every single moment has been duly considered. The actor has made precise artistic choices throughout this *Hamlet*. Some of them may be mistaken—too many speeches build to a histrionic rant—but they are intelligent and, on occasion, inspired.

This is a scholarly Hamlet, who, in his first appearance in a long nineteenth-century coat, suggests a garret philosopher out of *La Bohème*. This is also a Hamlet who feigns his madness; Mr. Kline leaves no doubt that he really does know "a hawk from a handsaw" when it suits his purposes. But what is most stirring about Mr. Kline's performance is its conversance with the metaphysical despair of the role. The actor opens his palms as if to weigh life's nothingness when declaring that "the time is out of joint"; his ensuing lament that he "was born to set it right" is delivered with a sinking, fatalistic shudder of foregone defeat. Contemplating man as the "quintessence of dust" or, indeed, deciding whether "to be or not to be," this Hamlet is more than a little in love with death. Mr. Kline conveys his condition with an androgynously beatific facial pallor (his "sullied flesh" does seem about to melt) and with grave notes of nullity in his voice (the "weary, stale, flat, and unprofitable" uses of the world are catalogued in a bone-rattling timbre).

But if this Hamlet's spiritual relationship to mortality is clear, what's he to Gertrude or Ophelia to him? It's impossible to tell. For all the abstract ontological sorrow of Mr. Kline's Hamlet, the specific psychological torment of a betrayed son is missing. Given the supporting cast, the results could not be otherwise. When a Hamlet must attempt to strike sparks from damp wooden pawns in crucial roles, any scene dramatizing the play's complex web of domestic entanglements is doomed to collapse.

Hamlet's anguished confrontation with his mother is etiolated when the Gertrude (Priscilla Smith) seems under heavy sedation, unable to match her son's volley with anything more than a dry whine. By the time Hamlet would banish this production's shrill Ophelia (Harriet Harris) to a nunnery, the audience has long since wondered what self-respecting nunnery would take her; we also wonder if her madness, like Hamlet's, might be feigned. The Polonius, Leonardo Cimino, is too bland to be worthy of angry mockery; when Hamlet calls him a "fishmonger," the insult sounds like overkill. Claudius—as played by Harris Yulin, an actor who knows better—never convinces us that he has any passion for Gertrude or hunger for power. When Mr. Yulin speaks of his "heavy burden," he hardly seems to have a consciousness, let alone a conscience; he might be describing a mild cold. Even at the play's climax, he stares indifferently ahead, refusing to raise so much as an eyebrow at the carnage engulfing him.

Some of the minor players are even more incompetent: We know something's rotten in *Hamlet* when the Marcellus declares the rottenness of the state of Denmark as if he were announcing a race at Hialeah. Such wholesale slippage unhinges the play. In *Hamlet,* the hero must contend with the erosion or corruption of every order. As the boundary between life and death becomes increasingly blurred and meaningless, so does that between the real and the spectral. The state, the family, religion, sex, and love all warp out of stable shape. No Hamlet can convey the horror of tumbling into a distorted universe if that universe isn't populated, for him and us to see. This is why Mr. Kline's performance, through little fault of his own, goes nowhere in the second half, never fully descending into a nightmarish personal maelstrom. One can palpably feel the audience's disappointment when, after nearly four hours, *Hamlet* fails to arouse more than a tepid emotional response.

What might have been can be seen on those few occasions when Mr. Kline actually does have an actor to play against. His terrified initial confrontation with the ghost, his puckish instructions on acting to the Player King, and his sarcastic exchange with the courtier Osric are among the production's liveliest encounters. As it happens, the star's partners in these scenes are each played, with impressive variety, by the same actor—Jeff Weiss, the Off Off Broadway maverick who is the one memorable member of a supporting cast numbering twenty-six. This may be the first *Hamlet* in history in which Hamlet's relationship with Osric is more compelling than his bond with either Ophelia or Gertrude—and in which Yorick's skull seems a more supple acting partner for the hero than most of the characters who still retain their flesh and blood.

If Mr. Ciulei were a hack director—or if the New York Shakespeare Festival were a second-rate organization—the shocking casting lapses of *Hamlet* might be comprehensible. But Mr. Ciulei is a gifted theater man whose *Tempest,* produced at the Guthrie Theater in Minneapolis, is one of the most imaginative Shakespearean productions to be seen in this country in this decade. With other performances, this *Hamlet* might also have been a creditable, if imperfect, outing. Bob Shaw's set, in which mobile brass columns constantly change the stage's spatial configurations (much like the towers in Robin Wagner's visionary set for *Dreamgirls*), offers unusually striking playing areas. The tilted neutral backdrop

allows the lighting designer, Jennifer Tipton, to create an o'erhanging firmament awash in constantly shifting colors and clouds.

Rather more problematic are William Ivey Long's costumes, which set
the play in some sort of Bismarckian nineteenth-century empire. The
chronological alteration is harmless enough (as are the few textual cuts
and transpositions)—until the Laertes-Hamlet duel is unaccountably set
against a *Brideshead Revisited* assemblage of straw-hatted swells sitting
on white wicker furniture. Another lapse in taste occurs when Ophelia's
mad scene is set at a dinner table, with her insanity reduced to a mere
matter of having left her manners at home. Still, Mr. Ciulei's vision of
the play, however weakly executed by his performers, is often lucid in
theory, and there is at least one inventive sequence: Using Mr. Shaw's
pillars to divide the stage at center, the director presents the court's
denizens dressing for the evening as a mirror image of the players
preparing for their performance of *The Murder of Gonzago*.

As Mr. Ciulei is capable of better than this *Hamlet*, so, certainly, is the
New York Shakespeare Festival. Only a few summers ago, it presented a
Henry IV, Part I, directed by Des McAnuff, that put to shame Trevor
Nunn's staging of the same play at the Royal Shakespeare Company the
following year. Casting, of late, also tends to be of high caliber in Papp
productions. One could even begin to recast *Hamlet* out of the ranks of
The Mystery of Edwin Drood: George Rose as Polonius, Patti Cohenour
as Ophelia, Howard McGillin as Laertes, Joe Grifasi as Horatio.

It's a tribute to Mr. Kline's talent that the audience sticks with this
Hamlet anyway, with respect if not rapture: He is one of those rare performers whose next entrance is always awaited eagerly. Yet as the evening
falls off to its so-what conclusion, we're left with an actor's tragedy, not
Shakespeare's. Kevin Kline has given more to our theater than most of
its artists. He is owed the *Hamlet* that might allow his heroically conceived Hamlet to scale the classic heights.

≡ *Much to his credit, Kline undertook Hamlet again four years later, this
time directing himself, again for Joseph Papp. It was, unfortunately, more
bloodless than the first attempt. A great Hamlet is hard to find, and I'm not
sure I've ever seen one. The most vivid during my* Times *years was at the
National Theatre in London—a feverish Daniel Day-Lewis, directed by
Richard Eyre, with a memorable Gertrude from Judi Dench. The most
neurotic was William Hurt's for the Circle Repertory Company in New
York (runner-up, Peter Stormare, in the Ingmar Bergman Hamlet), the
most forgettable was Roger Rees's for the Royal Shakespeare Company in
London, the most constipated was Kenneth Branagh's for the RSC (though*

Branagh had been a startling Laertes, at the dawn of his career, in the Rees Hamlet). Perhaps the most memorable image of Hamlet was Nicol Williamson playing the ghost of a drunk Jack Barrymore in full Elsinore regalia in Paul Rudnick's Broadway comedy I Hate Hamlet.

BIG DEAL
BROADWAY THEATRE, APRIL 11, 1986

For a generation, one of the few durable thrills of the constantly eroding Broadway musical has been the choreography of Bob Fosse. With the death of Gower Champion, Mr. Fosse may now be the last active theater choreographer who knows how to assemble an old-fashioned, roof-raising showstopper in which every step bears the un-mistakable signature of its creator. *Big Deal,* the new Fosse musical at the Broadway, contains exactly one of those showstoppers, and attention must be paid. If only for ten minutes or so just before the end of Act 1, Mr. Fosse makes an audience remember what is (and has been) missing from virtually every other musical in town.

The number is set to the old song "Beat Me Daddy (Eight to the Bar)," and it unfolds in a Chicago ballroom of the 1930s called (need I tell you?) Paradise. There's a big band on a platform, and somewhere in the blackness below are two song-and-dance men (the frisky Bruce Anthony Davis and Wayne Cilento) slithering in flickering silver light. The men's shoulders start to roll, their elbows sharpen, their hands hang limp even as the rest of their bodies gyrate at hard angles. And, just as these gentlemen seem to have merged with the high notes blared by the raucous horns above them, they are joined by a large chorus of bubbly revelers, who, by crossing the stage on a jagged diagonal, somehow manage to liberate both the show and the audience from conventional burdens of time, space, and care.

The dizzying sense of levitation that Mr. Fosse achieves in this dance is one of those unquantifiable elements—like the house lights dimming during the final stretch of an exciting overture—that defined the Broadway musical when it really was a going concern. The disappointment of *Big Deal* is that even Mr. Fosse, one of the form's last magicians, can conjure up that joy so rarely. There are some other pleasurable passages in this musical—period songs (or snatches of them) agreeably sung or danced by talented performers—but this is a mostly lackluster effort that often seems to be lumbering clumsily about. By the plot-heavy shank of

Act 2, *Big Deal* has congealed to the point where not even the second-best full-company number, a gospel version of "I'm Sitting on Top of the World" led by the ebullient Cleavant Derricks, can shake the blues away.

Much, though far from all, of what's gone wrong is that old bugaboo of old-fashioned book musicals—the book. Mr. Fosse, who manfully takes credit for writing this one, began with a not unpromising idea. *Big Deal* is *Big Deal on Madonna Street*, the 1958 comic caper film, transposed to South Side Chicago of the Depression and equipped with vintage songs largely of that pop heyday. In place of Marcello Mastroianni, Vittorio Gassman, and the rest of their Italian gang that couldn't shoot straight is a quintet of unemployed black men (led by Mr. Derricks, as a failed boxer) who hope to find happy days by cracking a safe.

Given that Mr. Fosse has staged some of Broadway's funniest musicals, such as *How to Succeed in Business Without Really Trying* and *Little Me,* it's hard to understand how the book of *Big Deal* grew to be ponderous and cheerless. A tiny farcical anecdote is dragged out to such convoluted lengths that the hapless robbery scheme begins to rival the Normandy invasion in heavy logistic detail.

The dull preliminaries that precede the actual crime—among them, the theft of a camera, the securing of a safecracker and some keys—are endless, only to be exceeded in tedium by the attenuated enactment of the heist itself. Along the way, there's a pro forma comic love story for Mr. Derricks and Loretta Devine (playing a domestic who's the keeper of the keys), as well as a maudlin one for a star-crossed young couple who inexplicably seem to have wandered in from *West Side Story.* The crude, lame jokes, some of which are as discomfortingly patronizing as *Amos 'n' Andy,* include sight gags featuring baby pacifiers and urinals.

Although Mr. Fosse keeps the show on the move, and, for the robbery, exploits a *Cats*-style catwalk along the mezzanine, the cinematic staging techniques are of little use when the story being told is static and mirthless. The set, designed by Peter Larkin, spreads more gloom. While *Big Deal* wants to be an airy period pastiche musical of the frolicsome *My One and Only* sort, it unfolds in a somber modernist black box decorated with some forbidding scaffolding, a halfhearted sliding platform (under which the dancers are often pointlessly caged in), and a few neon signs. This Chicago is a variation on Tony Walton's design for Mr. Fosse's twenties *Chicago,* but with all the glamour and style removed. As fussily but grimly lighted by Jules Fisher, the gaping dark space looks more suitable for a hanging than a comedy.

Such humor as there is comes in the dancing. Mr. Fosse has conceived "Ain't We Got Fun" as a shuffling chorus line for a prison chain gang. "Me and My Shadow" gives us the dancers Gary Chapman, Valarie Pettiford, and Barbara Yeager in the choreographer's latest replica of his undying *Pajama Game* showstopper, "Steam Heat." Alde Lewis Jr., the pipsqueak of the men, joins four of the sexiest female dancers for a tap fantasy of wealth ("Hold Tight") set in a seafood restaurant where lobsters can be ordered by the tank.

Other numbers—including such potentially rousing songs as "Pick Yourself Up," "Chicago," and "Love Is Just Around the Corner"—seem truncated, lest they impinge on the deathless book. Still others are distorted by either the coarse amplification or the synthesizer-laden rap-and-disco arrangements that self-destructively sabotage the thirties idiom of the dancing, the snazzy Patricia Zipprodt costumes, and the choices of songs themselves. (If a musical is going to use old standards— a second-class substitute for an exciting new score to start with—why mutilate them?) The best singing is the least electronically adorned— that of Alan Weeks, Larry Marshall, Bernard J. Marsh, Mel Johnson, and, most notably, the petite Desiree Coleman, whose huge voice flies into the gospel stratosphere.

Mr. Derricks and Ms. Devine, a wonderful pair in *Dreamgirls*, are less captivating here—not in the least because they are asked to mug and, in the leading lady's case, to shriek some lines and lyrics in a manner perilously reminiscent of Butterfly McQueen. But Ms. Devine's comic sense eventually shines through her oversold "I'm Just Wild About Harry," and Mr. Derricks's talent and spectacular charm win many more rounds than the down-and-out boxer he plays. These are performers of the breed who used to be transformed into stars by the best Bob Fosse musicals. At *Big Deal*, we can very dimly recall what those glorious shows felt like, even as we must contemplate yet again how subsequent Broadway musical history has been so unkind.

≡ *Bob Fosse choreographed the first two Broadway musicals I saw on the road as a child in the 1950s,* Damn Yankees *and* The Pajama Game—*and cochoreographed the first musical I saw on Broadway,* Bells Are Ringing. *By the 1970s he had become a top film director—*Lenny, All That Jazz— *but following the failure of the movie* Star 80, *he returned to Broadway for the first time in nearly a decade. According to the account of his biographer, Martin Gottfried,* Big Deal *was a disaster from the first day of rehearsal and Fosse was in no physical condition to rework it. Certainly this was not the Fosse of the fifties, sixties, and seventies.*

Only two weeks after Big Deal *began its brief run, a two-decade-old Fosse hit,* Sweet Charity, *was revived to great reviews. Fosse died the fol-*

lowing year of a heart attack—joining Gower Champion and Michael Bennett as the third of the greatest Broadway director-choreographers to die too young in the 1980s.

SOCIAL SECURITY

ETHEL BARRYMORE THEATRE, APRIL 18, 1986

Any crackpot can risk writing a play, but it takes a genuine madman to try to concoct two acts' worth of jokes. When a play falters for a spell, the audience can always contemplate the plot or characters or themes while waiting for things to get moving again. In a potpourri of gags like *Social Security,* the new offering at the Barrymore, there is far less margin for sloughing off. By opting for a sitcom premise instead of a story, stock figures instead of characters, and fortune-cookie messages instead of feelings, this entertainment bets all on its jokes: Like a stand-up comedy act, *Social Security* either gets its laughs or drops dead.

The evening's talented creators, the writer Andrew Bergman and the director Mike Nichols, know the stakes, and, not surprisingly, do have their very funny innings. Mr. Bergman, the screenwriter of *Blazing Saddles* and *The In-Laws,* is one of those shrewd jokesmiths, like Mel Brooks or Larry Gelbart, who knows just what brand name of car can detonate an otherwise negligible punch line or just what a Jewish mother might remember most about the cuisine at Lutèce. At his best in *Social Security,* Mr. Bergman also imagines how a nebbishy accountant would garble his college-age daughter's slang terminology for oral sex, or how the accountant's wife might sanction the same child's sexual proclivities when performed with a rabbinical student. For his part, Mr. Nichols shows off a previously undisclosed flair for slapstick sequences in which arthritic octo- and nonagenarians struggle to negotiate steps or sit down on a couch.

There are some other deliciously low gags, too, but the real question is whether they are generated in sufficient quantity to sustain two brief acts. Theatergoers with a Pavlovian relish for lines mentioning "bazooms," Long Island, Macy's White Sale, and gefilte fish may ignore the big duds (including one utterly irrelevant wisecrack about Twentieth Century–Fox) and decide that *Social Security* narrowly squeaks by. Those who feel that man cannot live by gefilte fish, let alone bazooms, alone, may share my conclusion that this effort is far closer to the spotty, domesticated

Bergman screenplays for *Fletch* and *So Fine* than the continuously up-roarious *In-Laws*. Mr. Nichols isn't at top form, either: By miscasting one major role, he has arguably robbed the writer of some of his rightful laughs.

The miscast performer is Marlo Thomas, who may have taken Act 2's gratuitously sober encomiums to sexual fulfillment even more seriously than the author; she seems to be laboring under the misimpression she's appearing in *Hedda Gabler*. Her actual role is that of Barbara Kahn, who, with her husband (Ron Silver), runs a Fifty-seventh Street art gallery of dubious sophistication. As propelled by shopworn situations reminiscent of *Where's Poppa?* (in Act 1) and *Barefoot in the Park* (in Act 2), the Kahns fly into panic when Barbara's aged mother (Olympia Dukakis) threatens to move into their fancy East Side apartment for an extended stay. Ms. Thomas, who behaves as if pouting and crisp vocal projection were the sum of comic acting, rarely looks at others or lets a smile cross her impassive mask of a face. We never even believe that she's Mr. Silver's wife or Ms. Dukakis's daughter. Her fits of nutty despair—among them, a masticatory encounter with the living room drapes—come off as abject depression rather than, as seemingly intended, maniacal farce.

The shortfall in the star's performance is brought into acute relief by the sharp professionals around her. The always reliable Mr. Silver not only has the evening's dirtiest lines, but he also knows how to turn every one of them into a perfectly timed sneak attack on an audience's pretensions to good taste. The remarkable Joanna Gleason, as Barbara's prudish and eternally disapproving sister from Mineola, once again demonstrates her ability to turn every gesture into a funny statement of character—and every character into a distinct theatrical creation. In the past year, this actress's varied repertory has already included the snotty English neighbor in *Joe Egg*, the has-been Broadway star in *It's Only a Play*, and the startled wife of a potential artificial inseminator in the film *Hannah and Her Sisters*.

Armed with a walker and a running gag involving sourballs, Ms. Dukakis is a formidable paragon of guilt-inflicting piety as the mother, even when she must contentiously deliver an unimpeachable sermon (on loan from *I'm Not Rappaport?*) about a senior citizen's right to be "alive." Stefan Schnabel is also charming as a still older character, a painter we are meant to confuse with Chagall. While Kenneth Welsh is not used to full advantage as Barbara's milquetoast brother-in-law the accountant, he's still amusing when rejecting a lime for his Tab as if it were an invitation to hell.

In keeping with the usual panache of Mike Nichols productions, the set designer Tony Walton has provided a terminally trendy East Side living room that, like Ann Roth's costumes, cracks its own jokes. (Not the least of Mr. Walton's witty contributions is a painting that parodies Chagall and Alex Katz in a single blow.) But just as one wonders why Mr. Bergman has too often tamed his outrageous instincts in his theatrical debut, so it's unclear why Mr. Nichols suddenly aspires to the sledgehammer directorial style of Broadway entries like *Doubles* and the female *Odd Couple*. This evening contains two scenes in which characters are caught in their underwear, and yet such are the lax standards that neither Mr. Bergman nor Mr. Nichols can be bothered to top the first with an inspired variation of writing or staging in the second. In *Social Security*, two experts at comedy, like their embarrassed characters, are to be found at half-mast.

VIENNA: LUSTHAUS
St. Clement's Theatre, April 21, 1986

The pre–World War I Vienna of *Vienna: Lusthaus*, the new theater piece conceived and directed by Martha Clarke, is the place where civilization had the nervous breakdown from which it has never recovered. In *Vienna: Lusthaus*, now at St. Clement's, Ms. Clarke seeks to evoke that cataclysmic historical and cultural turning point in a mere sixty minutes of hallucinations sculpted with dance, words, music, and light. She has succeeded beyond one's wildest dreams—perhaps because she has tapped into everyone's wildest dreams. As Vienna was where Freud intersected with Hitler, so the visions of *Vienna: Lusthaus* keep pulling us, with a delicacy so light as to be nearly subliminal, from sex to death.

Ms. Clarke, a former member of Pilobolus Dance Theater, was last represented as a director by *The Garden of Earthly Delights*, a resourceful but literal-minded enactment of Bosch's painting that allowed the viewer's imagination little room to roam. While *Earthly Delights* featured flying performers, it's *Vienna: Lusthaus* that really flies. Ms. Clarke again re-creates some painterly images—notably the nudes of Gustav Klimt—and yet the overall canvas is an original creation occupying in its own distinctive esthetic territory. Like Balanchine and Ravel in *La Valse* and Schnitzler in *La Ronde*, Ms. Clarke captures what the historian Carl Schorske calls the "acutely felt tremors of social and political disintegration" in fin-de-siècle Vienna. But *Vienna: Lusthaus* isn't pure dance and isn't a play; it sporadically recalls (without exactly resembling) the imagist experiments of such varied theater artists as Tadeusz Kantor, Robert Wilson, and Peter Brook.

The setting (by Robert Israel, who also designed the sumptuous costumes) is a room with tall, blank, unsettlingly tilted walls. Metaphorically at least, it's the Lusthaus of the title—a pleasure pavilion such as the one built in the Prater in the sixteenth century. Ms. Clarke's performers—women in either period petticoats or gowns, men in gray military tunics and red britches—tumble about in a wide spectrum of sexual activities. In one of several extraordinarily erotic sequences, a woman and a half-nude man roll across the stage, their tangled arms a sensuous Art-Nouveau design made pointedly flesh. Somewhat later the stunning dancer Robert Besserer brings off a tour de force in which he mimics both of the partners in an athletic sexual marathon.

Mr. Besserer's incredible simulation of boudoir gymnastics concludes on a sadomasochistic note, and, indeed, the progress of *Vienna: Lusthaus* on every front is from innocence to bestiality, harmony to discord, civility to violence. The piece's inevitable chorus of deathly waltzers becomes more and more frenzied throughout, even as Richard Peaslee's lovely pastiche score threatens to bleed from the gaiety of Johann Strauss into the dissonance of Schoenberg. In a way that suggests Ms. Clarke's previous theatrical excursion into Kafka (*A Metamorphosis in Miniature*), we watch one soldier (Gianfranco Paoluzi) transform himself into a horse— and the equine imagery later recurs in other couplings, including one featuring a riding crop.

The gradual coarsening of the initially lyrical sexual imagery is matched by the subtle shifts of the text. The author is Charles Mee Jr., a playwright and historian (*Meeting at Potsdam*), and what he has written is a plotless, occasionally cryptic collage of speeches and dialogue fragments. We hear dreamlike descriptions of suicide and of tentative sexual exploration (incestuous and homosexual)—both prominent phenomena of imperial Vienna. We hear a liaison-fixated diary that might have been Schnitzler's and are told surreal anecdotes (notably one set at a performance of *Fidelio*) that could be nightmares destined for analysis by Freud. Ambiguous or absurdist as much of the script is, there's no mistaking that characters start to invoke the word *Jew* in an incipiently anti-Semitic manner, and that Mr. Mee's text, combined with the escalating militarism of the visual imagery and music, prefigures the death wish and death camps of twentieth-century history. Not for nothing does the final line of *Vienna: Lusthaus* answer the question "What colors does a body pass through after death?"

By then, snow has been falling on stage for some time, and the waltzers' feet have begun to sound like soldiers marching. What's amazing is how seamlessly Ms. Clarke and all her collaborators have achieved the seismic shift of mood. While this work is described in the program as "in progress," little progress needs to be made. Every performance, including those of the musicians who occasionally wander (with harp or French horn) into the action, is impeccably choreographed into the whole. Paul Gallo's lighting, at one with the director's cinematic dissolves and superimpositions, is so detailed that it could be a show in itself: His spectrum runs from a mystical Danube ("a shade of emerald green almost painful in its brilliance and depth") to the tall Expressionist shadows that apocalyptically overwhelm the snowy final minutes.

For all the intelligence and talent that's been poured into *Vienna: Lusthaus,* however, we're never really conscious of the effort while watching it. The piece hits us at a pre-intellectual level, because Ms. Clarke has distilled both the beauty and the ominous chaos of a vanished Vienna into a shape that seems completely contiguous with the modern world it has bequeathed us. That's why, although we look at this work through a gauzy scrim, that veil seems to have dissolved by evening's end. That's also why we needn't consult a history book or *The Interpretation of Dreams* to figure out what rats are lurking within the shattered civilization with which *Vienna: Lusthaus* finally engulfs us. To our horror, we discover that the headlines of today's newspapers will do.

≡ Vienna: Lusthaus *opened by chance just as fresh revelations of Kurt Waldheim's Nazi past became an issue during his campaign for the Austrian presidency.*

SWEET CHARITY
MINSKOFF THEATRE, APRIL 28, 1986

Can six or seven knockout song-and-dance turns transform an also-ran Broadway musical into a classic? Of course not, but just try telling that to the audiences who are about to have some indecent fun at the revival of *Sweet Charity.* As choreographed by Bob Fosse and performed by the dynamic Debbie Allen and company, the numbers in this 1966 musical adaptation of Federico Fellini's *Nights of Cabiria* tear away from its dreary book with centrifugal force. By the late hour when the star leads a crack battalion of red-and-gold troops through the torrential kicks and leaps of "I'm a Brass Band," hard-core addicts of old-time Broadway might be tempted to parade in the aisles, if only the Minskoff weren't a modern Broadway house without any aisles.

The preceding numbers, though separated by listless scenes, are often as electric, showing off Mr. Fosse's range of choreographic razzle-dazzlement with encyclopedic ardor. "If My Friends Could See Me Now," winningly set forth by Ms. Allen, is the archetypal top-hat-and-cane solo, refurbished in cleverness by the delayed introduction of each of the dancer's props. "There's Gotta Be Something Better Than This" is a lovingly vulgar variation on Jerome Robbins's torrid "America" in *West Side Story*, and "I Love to Cry at Weddings," which begins as a Frank Loesser–style comic chorale, breaks into the sprightliest of soft shoes. Mr. Fosse's fondness for sending his dancers to the edge of the proscenium is exploited in "Rhythm of Life," his eye for elegantly stylized parody in the snooty, white-gloved calisthenics of "Rich Man's Frug."

The signature dance of *Sweet Charity*, famously heralded by the raunchy downbeat provided by the composer Cy Coleman, is "Big Spender"—in which the painted hostesses of a New York tango palace joylessly entice their customers to a "good time" from behind the long railing that borders their nightly encampment. The bleak yet affectionate deadpan humor of the staging is worthy of Reginald Marsh drawings of Depression honky-tonks. Even more impressive is that moment when the women suddenly come together to move as a single, finger-snapping organism through the blue nocturnal light: The various bodies form a syncopated Rube Goldberg contraption, a pulsating sculpture of human neon advertising soulless sex. This is a glimpse of hell—lewd, fleshy, funny—as only an inspired student of burlesque like Mr. Fosse could imagine it.

None of these routines would deliver if they weren't outfitted with galvanizing dancers and music. Mr. Fosse's corps is first-rate, and the choreography has been drilled to that precise point where skyrocketing limbs seem to melt into the ice-cream-colored skies of Robert Randolph's sets and lighting. No less attention has been paid to the cinematic staging transitions, in which the dancers, often seen in silhouette and crowned by flashing title cards, assume characteristic Fosse postures (knees turned in, fingers spread out) to give *Sweet Charity* the look of silent-film comedy. Mr. Coleman's accompanying, rousing show tunes are trumpeted by the belting voices, percussion-minded orchestrations (by Ralph Burns), and swinging band (led by Fred Werner) that this kind of musical requires.

Be warned that the kind of musical in question is the tired-businessman's entertainment, mid-1960s subdivision. With its mildly off-color jokes, laughably spurious song cues, jolly subway straphangers, and rolling cartfuls of living-room scenery, the form seems as dated as the miniskirts and hoop earrings of Patricia Zipprodt's tongue-in-cheek period costumes. Yet it says a lot about how the Broadway musical has deteriorated—as gloomily exemplified by Mr. Fosse's own current *Big Deal*—that *Sweet Charity*, an average musical in its day, seems to have appreciated in value now. This is attributable to the decline of the competition, not to an improvement in the show's quality.

While Mr. Coleman has modestly modernized the sound of a couple of songs, Neil Simon's hapless script could still use major surgery. Maybe the author himself might choose to forget this book, which starts off flat and reaches oblivion by the fumbled bittersweet conclusion. In remaking Fellini's Roman prostitute into a Manhattan taxi dancer, Mr. Simon created a love-starved heroine (named Charity Hope Valentine, no less) of such sentimentalized masochism that she makes a doormat seem like the Rock of Gibraltar. Only Dorothy Fields's delightful lyrics lavish some humor and compassion on the stereotyped "girls and chicks" of the evening. The lyricist, who died in 1974, sardonically imagined that dance-hall hostesses would aspire to a bourgeois respectability in which they eat "frozen peaches and cream" and wear "a copy of a copy of a copy of a Dior."

Neither Ms. Fields's nor Mr. Simon's words benefit much from the acting, which is mostly broad. Bebe Neuwirth and Allison Williams, as the heroine's hardened sidekicks, are better seen dancing than heard wisecracking; Mark Jacoby brings a robust voice but little else to the role of an Italian film star. Far superior is Michael Rupert, whose kindly charm redeems Charity's Mr. Right, a milquetoast in a gray-flannel suit whom she meets in a stalled elevator at the Ninety-second Street Y. Lee Wilkof is another happy exception to the general comic pushiness, summoning up the Runyonesque spirit of Stubby Kaye as the brash but good-hearted Fan-Dango Ballroom proprietor.

Ms. Allen may have spent a bit too much time in television since her memorable Anita in the 1980 *West Side Story;* her joking, too, can be overstated, and she doesn't find the pathos in the Fields lyric for "Where Am I Going." But if she somewhat lacks the vulnerability of the original Charity, Gwen Verdon (who assisted on this production), Ms. Allen is almost eerie in her re-creation of her predecessor's Chaplinesque gait and sparkling gymnastics. Let Mr. Fosse place his sizzling star before his phalanx of dancers, and a vastly imperfect musical ignites, as if by spontaneous combustion, into a rollicking show.

LONG DAY'S JOURNEY INTO NIGHT
Broadhurst Theatre, April 29, 1986

If there's one word said more often than any other in Eugene O'Neill's *Long Day's Journey into Night*, it must be *fog*. The fog in this play doesn't come on little cat feet; its arrival is predicted incessantly in the Connecticut summer home where the author's surrogate family, the four haunted Tyrones, will settle the scores of a lifetime during a single day in 1912. And once the fog has swallowed up the household, as with nightfall it must, it brings both sadness and peace to O'Neill's pitiful brood. The alcohol-fueled journey into the fog in *Long Day's Journey* is a journey back through time. When the Tyrones finally accept that "the past is the present," they can begin to forgive, if not forget, the betrayals of which their tragic history is made.

As the fog of *Long Day's Journey* has a swirling movement, so does its dramatic structure. The play repeats its cycles of recriminations, confessions, and apologies, gathering more force with each round. But in the director Jonathan Miller's startling new production, now at the Broadhurst, the author's rhythms are deliberately broken. There's little fog-bound about this fast-paced *Long Day's Journey*, which clocks in at three hours (one intermission included). A diligent cast led by Jack Lemmon as the Tyrone father, James, gives us a family prone to flash floods of bickering in which the loudest antagonist drowns out the others. We're not slowly enveloped by the Tyrones' past so much as yanked there in fits and starts.

After David Leveaux (*A Moon for the Misbegotten*) and Keith Hack (*Strange Interlude*), Mr. Miller is the third and most daring English director to rethink O'Neill in as many Broadway seasons. In his *Long Day's Journey*, some lines are shouted down, others are trimmed, and still others are rattled off so quickly that the mother, Mary, persuades us that her morphine addiction produces symptoms often associated with amphetamines. There's a case to be made for Mr. Miller's experiment. The greatest play in our dramatic literature has become an icon that theatergoers can't always visit innocently anymore. This director wants us to see the work fresh, as if it and its autobiographical characters had no history, and, to an extent, he succeeds. This is an engrossing evening for those who want to think about *Long Day's Journey*, although not, I'm afraid, for those who want to feel it.

Indeed, the Robert Altman–style bursts of overlapping dialogue are so cleverly done that we're at first more conscious of the theatrical technique than of the characters. After the novelty wears off, we realize that Mr. Miller is forcing us to listen to the lines as a family's animated conversation rather than as portentous signals of impending doom in a Great American Tragedy. This is how relatives might converse if, as the youngest son, Edmund, puts it, they're regurgitating old grievances they've all heard "a million times" before. A burden is lifted from some of the trivial exchanges, at times with the dividend of found laughter. But when the major monologues and confrontations arrive, Mr. Miller is no fool; he puts on the brakes.

This is particularly true after intermission, when the production achieves its instances of raw power. Mr. Lemmon—his voice fading into a low rumble as his body sinks defeatedly into a couch—is affecting as he bitterly rues the financially lucrative role that sapped Tyrone's promise as an actor. Bethel Leslie, as Mary, retrieves the mad mother's girlish naïveté in her long soliloquy, recalling how the young James wooed her away from convent propriety. Peter Gallagher's Edmund gives us the poet as well as the consumptive; his intelligence and sensitivity flare so dangerously in his big dark eyes that, in his nihilistic reveries of the sea, we see the birth of O'Neill as an artist. Kevin Spacey's Jamie, his body contorted by booze, finally transcends his cynical Broadway sport's bitchery to reach out tenderly to the younger sibling he wants both to love and to destroy.

Yet even these individual achievements can't fill in the missing pieces in O'Neill's painful exorcism of the Tyrones' ghosts. Some crucial scenes, including the father's angriest battles with his sons and the mother's final descent into insanity, leave scant impact. We wonder whether Mr. Miller's novel approach to the text is responsible for the shortfall—even Mary's last scene is slightly revised—or whether the generally good acting in this *Long Day's Journey* isn't quite good enough.

There's a little blame for everyone. It's a pleasure to report that Mr. Lemmon, a wonderful comic actor who turned to mush in the serious roles that followed the lachrymose 1973 film *Save the Tiger*, is highly disciplined here. He creates Tyrone, the old ham, without being hammy himself. His mane of silver hair, whiskey voice, and slightly stooped walk—not to mention his sense of humor—all serve the faded matinee idol well. But this star still can't quite bring himself to let an audience hate him, however transitorily. Although Mr. Lemmon illuminates the redemptive aspects of the father that O'Neill finally forgave in this penultimate play, he neglects the balancing black side—the poisonous, "stinking old miser" whose pathological behavior helped prompt the rage and self-destruction the others now exhibit before us.

Ms. Leslie, whose ravaged Mary is exceptionally beautiful, is most effective when her eyes retreat in a junkie's fear of self-disclosure, when her nervous hands clutch the cross around her neck, or when she is mothering the favored Edmund (even as she tries to torture him with guilt). Her failure to sound the deepest notes of despair in the loneliest of matriarchs may in part be a function of her voice, which is thin and narrowly nasal in range. Mr. Spacey's technically impressive Jamie can also lack depth, but Mr. Gallagher is, as usual, above reproach: Edmund has rarely seemed a fuller or, when acting out a fast-action precis of *Macbeth*, funnier character.

Perhaps if Mr. Miller hadn't devoted so much energy to the tricky verbal logistics of his concept, he might have induced a more consistent pitch of passion from the entire cast. It's also possible that the concept could be more uniformly executed—Tony Straiges's well-designed but somewhat abstract set is an arty obstacle to the plain naturalism of the cross talk—or that the concept is faulty. *Long Day's Journey*, unlike the earlier *Mourning Becomes Electra* or *Strange Interlude*, does not carry the excess baggage of a writer straining for poetic grandeur. The circular repetitions and loquacity of the mature O'Neill masterpieces may be as integral to their inexorable grip as pauses and reticence are to Beckett's.

The director seems to recognize that something is missing. Presumably to add emotional kick, there's some strategically placed table pounding in Acts 1 and 2; each of the final two acts ends with Mr. Lemmon's providing melodramatic vocal effusions not in the text. These retrograde interjections don't detract from the fascination of a provocative staging that genuinely wipes the dust off a theatrical monument. But in his desire to give us O'Neill without tears, Mr. Miller has muted a work "written in tears and blood." When this *Long Day's Journey* ends, the night seems young not just because a long play runs shorter but because we're still waiting for that dark, cathartic fog to roll in.

THE BOYS IN AUTUMN

CIRCLE IN THE SQUARE, MAY 1, 1986

With the arrival of *The Boys in Autumn*, Bernard Sabath's new play at the Circle in the Square, the 1985–86 Broadway season has reached its official close. While this season never did produce any cutthroat competition for the honor of best play, the worst play sweepstakes is being bitterly contested right up to the final hour. *The Boys in Autumn*, a terminally innocuous speculation about Huckleberry Finn and Tom Sawyer in middle age, almost makes one long for *The Boys of Winter,* a Vietnam war drama that had been the prize 1985–86 turkey until this point. Let's be grateful that the season has ended before anyone could write *The Boys of Spring* or turn Roger Kahn's good book *The Boys of Summer* into a flop musical.

What would Huck (George C. Scott) and Tom (John Cullum) be up to when they have a surprise reunion in 1920s Hannibal? It would be cruel to divulge the evening's bombshells, although I will end obvious speculation by reporting that, *pace* Leslie Fiedler, the men have not opened a Missouri branch of La Cage aux Folles. Mr. Sabath has instead given the men lurid secrets that reduce two of the most beloved characters in our cultural heritage to extras in a Harold Robbins novel.

Those who wish to learn those secrets are hereby forewarned that Tom's confession doesn't begin until late in Act 1, while Huck's must await late Act 2. The rest is padding. Mr. Sabath opens the evening with a tedious cat-and-mouse game in which the two men must laboriously determine that they are indeed the Huck and Tom who knew each other when. (They use different names now.) Other stalling comes in the form of Mr. Cullum's demonstration of a vaudeville routine long performed by Tom on the whistle-stop two-a-day circuit. ("Get the hook!" shouts the annoyed Mr. Scott, and not a moment too soon.) The men also get to complete one of those newfangled crossword puzzles, and, at the start of Act 2, Mr. Cullum tinkers at some considerable length with a recalcitrant hand-cranked automobile.

Other Twain characters are accounted for along the way, with Becky Thatcher proving, in absentia, a Freudian fall woman to rival Mrs. Bates in *Psycho.* The rambling exchanges are linked by lines like "Well, let's talk about something else." The name-dropping and occasional quotations of actual Twain passages aside, there's not a trace of the great man's voice or wit in Mr. Sabath's dialogue. The Huck and Tom of the playwright's dreams have rolled off contemporary Hollywood's male-menopause assembly line. They are soppy, boozy buddies who mourn their lost youth while hoping that somehow they "could help each other" get past adulthood's humbling blows. This being the roaring twenties and all, Huck and Tom are as likely to find redemption by going into real-estate speculation as by riding a raft, but the Mississippi still exerts its tidal pull. As Mr. Scott says wistfully at the final curtain, the river "goes on forever"—which makes it sound somewhat shorter than this play.

It's hard to know what attracted either star to *The Boys in Autumn.* They'd find more challenge playing the Duke and the King in a bus-and-truck tour of *Big River.* Under the direction of Theodore Mann, Mr. Cullum pours on the corn pone rather heavily, but Mr. Scott, with a raised eyebrow here and a froggy belch there, finds a few laughs as the latently civilized Huck. How one wishes that this actor could be channeling his festering energy into a part like Hickey or James Tyrone.

As for the playwright, he warns us in a *Playbill* essay that he is also busy speculating about the futures of other fictional characters—from Holden Caulfield to Blanche DuBois. "I feel I know what Biff and Happy Loman are doing today," he writes, "and what Eve Harrington is up to." Unlike Mr. Sabath, I have no idea what those characters are up to, but if their creators have any sense, they're busy renewing their copyrights.

EIGHTH
SEASON

1986–87

Alan Rickman and Lindsay Duncan in
Les Liaisons Dangereuses

The first thing that a theatergoer notices at the London theater this season is the empty seats.

Although I've sat with my share of sparse audiences over years of London theatergoing, I don't recall ever having previously seen the best-received Royal Shakespeare Company productions play to less than half-occupied houses. This plunge in attendance, attributed to the absence of American visitors, baffles the English. On a local replica of the *Today* program one May morning, Albert Finney, the star of the West End *Orphans,* rued the fact that "the cream" of his play's audience had fled. One could only pity his fellow guest, the American actress Jane Curtin, whose routine promotional interview was soon ambushed by questions asking her to account for the entire falloff in American tourism.

But if the "cream" of the warm-weather ticket-buying crowds has evaporated in London for now, an English audience does remain. According to *The Economist,* an astounding one third of Great Britain's adults see a play or more a year. For both better and worse, that audience seems to be getting a theater that reflects its tastes and self-doubts. The current London season, at least as this observer sampled it night and day for two weeks, reveals a theatrical culture at one with Mrs. Thatcher's majority middle-class constituency.

The most representative example—and perhaps the most entertaining play in town—is the RSC's *Merry Wives of Windsor.* The director, Bill Alexander, has transported Shakespeare's most trivial comedy—a play that demands invention to ward off rigor mortis—to the late 1950s. This is the materialistic, fast-changing progenitor of today's England: It's the booming society of which then Prime Minister Harold Macmillan said, "Most of our people have never had it so good." Even the production's program comes in the form of a yellowed back issue of a home-furnishings magazine, complete with ads for ugly television consoles and dinette sets.

In the staging itself, giddy nostalgic humor reigns. Falstaff is a tweedy golf-club boor, and the merry wives plot against him while sitting under hair dryers in the local beauty salon. (When the knight lands in a laundry basket, the escapade could be a Lucy and Ethel stunt from *I Love Lucy*.) The ingenues, Anne Page and Fenton, are an aspiring Annette Funicello and black-leather-jacketed Jack Kerouac; the Dr. Caius sounds like Peter Sellers's Inspector Clouseau. The mock Henry Mancini score recalls the period's Hollywood and Ealing film comedies, and the curtain call is a joyous sock hop.

Just the same, there's an unsettling edge to the merriment of this *Merry Wives*. The Technicolor hues of William Dudley's inspired set seem to curdle; a once-quaint village landscape is overrun by consumer products and crowned by a logo for Shell Oil. The play is too slight to support much polemical weight, but the staging is implicitly skeptical, rather than purely celebratory, of the self-satisfied bourgeoisie of the second Elizabethan England. Are these people really having it so good, or are they bored and glutted?

That skepticism is also to be found in the best new play I saw in London, *A Chorus of Disapproval*. The author is the prolific Alan Ayckbourn, whose comedies of English middle-class life keep growing in depth. In *Chorus,* we watch a provincial operatic society's calamity-ridden rehearsals of John Gay's *The Beggar's Opera*. While the amateur theatrics are hilarious—"I've seen rougher trade on a health food counter," says the exasperated director (Colin Blakely) of his production's "prissy little madam"—Mr. Ayckbourn also takes us backstage in the company's disappointed private lives. The contemporary England he uncovers is populated by middle-aged couples stuck in lonely marriages and tedious white-collar jobs, drifting and alienated young adults, and the discarded elderly. One aged man wanders around listening through a Walkman to a BBC tape emblematically titled *Vanishing Sounds of Great Britain*.

Mr. Ayckbourn's play has just moved from the National Theater to the West End, where the most popular revival is J. B. Priestley's 1938 comedy about pre–World War I middle-class provincials, *When We Are Married*. The prosperous, smug, but emotionally straitened characters—English Babbitts all—are the ancestors of Mr. Ayckbourn's sad present-day villagers. The modern urban middle-class, meanwhile, is represented in Anthony Minghella's *Made in Bangkok,* a West End comedy about English entrepreneurs who exploit cheap labor and sex in the Third World. Still, the steamy *Bangkok*—like *Merry Wives, Chorus,* and *Married*—is as much a slick entertainment for its bourgeois audience as an attack on it.

What's missing from the new-play scene in London right now are the more provocative theatrical voices, a Shepard or Mamet or Shawn, that, as John Lahr titled his Joe Orton biography, "prick up your ears." To be sure, some intelligent current plays are of a thematic piece with the more piercing English dramas of recent seasons. Following David Hare's *Plenty,* Michael Frayn's *Benefactors,* and Doug Lucie's *Progress,* such works as Dusty Hughes's *Futurists* and Trevor Griffiths's *Real Dreams* investigate the failure or betrayal of idealistic programs of social change. But *Futurists,* which dramatizes writers such as Gorky and Mayakovsky (the mesmerizing Daniel Day-Lewis) in the Petrograd of 1921, and *Real Dreams,* which tells of collegiate radicals in the United States of 1969, seem blunted in passion. Is it because the authors dramatize their issues from a geographical and chronological remove? In this becalmed context, a modest but immediate American play like Larry Kramer's *The Normal Heart,* now in the West End, strikes the English as an incendiary novelty.

The falloff in new English plays this season may be a cyclical aberration. Some of the big guns have been silent of late. Harold Pinter has been directing American stars (Lauren Bacall, Faye Dunaway) in scripts by others; there's been no new Tom Stoppard play since *The Real Thing* (1982), although he's now represented at the National with *Dalliance,* a precious but affecting version of Arthur Schnitzler's *Liebelei.* Mr. Frayn has also devoted himself to adaptation (*Wild Honey*) and, like Mr. Pinter (*Turtle Diary*) and Mr. Stoppard (*Brazil*), has worked on a screenplay (*Clockwise,* with John Cleese). While Peter Shaffer has produced his first new work since *Amadeus,* a strained Old Testament parable titled *Yonadab,* he has already declared that he'll rewrite it for any subsequent productions.

If the shortage of new plays is uncharacteristic of London, the proliferation of new English musicals is even more unexpected. The West End, perhaps determined not to lose its hold on its bedrock audience as Broadway has, now surpasses Broadway as a manufacturer of musical extravaganzas. What's more, a distinctive London musical-theater style has emerged—one that consolidates and coarsens the Disneyland-ride format of *Cats.* As with that commercial smash, English musicals now tend to be deafening soft-rock operettas, in which lavish environmental sets (often designed by John Napier, of *Cats,* and usually replicated in an elaborate line of merchandised knickknacks) take precedence over story, dancing, or characters. Thus does the sci-fi musical *Time* rely on a firmament of floating planets, *Starlight Express* on roller-skating tracks, and the latest arrival, *Chess,* on an enormous tilting chess board.

There will always be an English theater, but the current season reveals that missing playwrights, if not missing Americans, take a toll on that theater's vitality. Perhaps it was my imagination, but I thought I detected a note of longing when a character in one of the few new London plays (*Futurists*) delivered the line "I'm told the theater is very, very good in New York."

ME AND MY GIRL
MARQUIS THEATRE, AUGUST 11, 1986

There is nothing more primal in the lexicon of musical comedy than the number in which the young hero declares his undying love for the woman of his dreams. About a half hour into *Me and My Girl,* the restored 1937 English musical now on Broadway, that number is to be found in its most clichéd form: Every word, note, and gesture collides with a civilization's collective memory of vintage stage and movie musicals.

Yet, astoundingly enough, one finds oneself wishing that the title song of *Me and My Girl* would never end. When the leading man, Robert Lindsay, croons and twirls his way through his romantic declaration, the audience is as enraptured as Maryann Plunkett, the fresh-faced heroine who eventually joins him for a delirious tap pas de deux on top of a banquet table. *Me and My Girl*—both the number and the show—has uncorked the innocence of the old-fashioned musical comedy so ingenuously that for once a theatergoer is actually sucked directly into that sunny past rather than merely suckered into nostalgia for it.

The sheer happiness at hand is less a tribute to the quality of the material—which is variously charming and inane between-the-wars fluff—than to the winning way in which it is unfurled. Better musicals than *Me and My Girl* have been revived in New York and London in recent years, but few have been as free of contemporary cynicism or camp in their staging. And few musicals of any kind on either side of the Atlantic have had a star to match Robert Lindsay. Known primarily as a serious actor before opening in the West End *Me and My Girl* revival eighteen months ago—he was Edmund in the televised Olivier *Lear*—this slightly built performer at times recalls Kelly and Cagney. But there's nothing imitative in his virtuoso performance. Mr. Lindsay doesn't recreate the great song-and-dance clowns of this musical's era—he's the genuine item in his own right, miraculously discovered among the mere mortals of today.

His role is that of Bill Snibson, a Cockney cutup from Lambeth who is belatedly identified as the long-lost Earl of Hareford (family motto: "Noblesse oblige") and who must learn posh manners if he is to inherit his title and estate. Much of *Me and My Girl* is low-burlesque *Pygmalion:* The vulgar, insolent Bill is forever affronting the snobbish swells who congregate at the Hampshire mansion that is his newfound family's country seat. Wearing a busker's checked suit and a brown bowler, with a cigarette or two stashed behind his ears, Mr. Lindsay enters Hareford Hall swaggering, leering, and sneering: He's willing to grab any gold pocket watch or large female breast left untended by its owner. When he isn't scandalizing the stiff butlers and triple-chinned dowagers, Bill likes to mock the household's deaf octogenarian in an obscene, improvised sign-language that, like Mr. Lindsay's entire performance, adds just the proper dash of vinegar to what might have been a vat of unadulterated mush.

Some actors keep audiences hanging on every word. Mr. Lindsay, who makes a nonstop charade of intricate vocal and physical details look relaxed, compels us to cherish his every syllable, wink, and step. His subversive timing snares the laugh on each hoary pun, double entendre, and malapropism. (Asked if he likes Kipling, Bill typically replies, "I don't know—I've never kippled.") The slapstick sequences—which require the star to play leapfrog with a seductress on a couch and to wrestle a royal robe and tiger rug to the floor—are full of surprising, daredevil pratfalls. As a singer, Mr. Lindsay captures the reedy vocal style of the thirties without falling into stylized parody; as a dancer, he's just as graceful gliding about a lamppost in debonair evening clothes as he is tapping up a vaudeville storm. Nor can one overlook this onetime Hamlet's acting: While his performance boasts more funny walks and quicksilver flashes of mimicry than some whole farces, it's never marred by star mannerisms or showiness and is always informed by an astringent wit.

In the West End, Mr. Lindsay seemed the only reason for visiting *Me and My Girl*—or such was the case at the performance I attended well into the run. That's not true of the New York staging, which inaugurates the new and, for a modern musical house, surprisingly commodious Marquis Theatre. The Broadway *Me and My Girl,* while roughly a duplicate of the continuing West End production, has exchanged a mechanical English supporting cast for a freshly minted American one, jettisoned a deadly number, and added a jazzy Act 1 Charleston. Mike Ockrent's lovingly archaic direction, as well as Stanley Lebowsky's pit band, have been drilled to Broadway's higher standard, even as Martin Johns's Edwardian sets and Ann Curtis's bright "Tennis anyone?" costumes remain amusing reminders of the latter-day West End's tatty notions of lavish production values. Gillian Gregory's expanded pastiche choreography, which exuberantly reprises the loony thirties dance craze "The Lambeth Walk" and alludes to at least two numbers from the film *Singin' in the Rain*, benefits enormously from American performance expertise. The production's only ill-advised revision for New York is a brief and patronizing nod to Hasidic Jews.

The musical's larger faults, however well masked, have hardly disappeared. For all the pruning and polishing done to the original L. Arthur Rose–Douglas Furber book and lyrics, every scene still seems five minutes too long (especially in the far windier Act 2); the unfunny corny punch lines still outnumber the funny ones (also corny). Noel Gay's tuneful score, abetted by interpolated songs from his other shows and by Chris Walker's quintessentially Mayfair dance-band orchestrations, has its dreary interludes—particularly when chained to the more prosaic plot-advancing lyrics. One must also note that the musical's unreconstructed caricatures of social classes remain rooted in 1937, even as the original period is disregarded for anachronistic allusions to *My Fair Lady* and Richard Nixon.

With the exceptions of Timothy Jerome's excessively cute Gilbert and Sullivan model of a comic solicitor and Jane Summerhays's overdone vamp, the large company brings welcome precision to the preposterous goings-on, down to the bit roles filled by the spirited likes of Thomas Toner and Elizabeth Larner. George S. Irving and Jane Connell are the ideal pros to play the farcical elders in charge of the hero's tutelage in the Hareford manner. Nick Ullett finds new comic life in the stock aristocratic twit who regards the prospect of a job as "disgusting" and who is always finding new ways to wear argyle.

By far the most beguiling—and crucial—member of the supporting cast, however, is Ms. Plunkett, as the spunky Cockney girlfriend whom the Hareford set would have Bill dump on his way up the economic ladder. Adorable but not glamorous, this American actress, last seen as Bernadette Peters's successor in *Sunday in the Park with George,* is convincing as a working-class Englishwoman, convincing as she belts out syrupy lyrics like "You've got to follow your heart," and convincing as a strong partner for a star whose magnetic grip on the audience is never relinquished. From their duet on the title song through their fog-swept dream reunion, Ms. Plunkett and Mr. Lindsay persuade us that they're intimately connected by a generous, unsentimental affection—both as characters and as performers sharing a stage. Strange as it may sound in this modern musical era, *Me and My Girl* enchants by making us believe once again that there's no more wonderful reason to sing and dance than the love between a guy and his girl.

≡ *Robert Lindsay's career hasn't lived up to this triumph. The same cannot be said of his charming leading lady in the West End, where I first saw this production—Emma Thompson.*

RAGS

MARK HELLINGER THEATRE, AUGUST 22, 1986

Teresa Stratas is one of those performers whose giant talent makes audiences forget just how tiny she is. That talent is to be found not only in her voice, which has entranced opera audiences for a quarter-century now, but also in her stage personality, which, like her looks, can sometimes recall the unstable mixture of street-tough sexuality and pathetic vulnerability that was Piaf. This quality has served Ms. Stratas famously in her opera-house appearances as Berg's Lulu and Weill's Jenny, and it's just as well suited to her first starring role on Broadway. Rebecca, the heroine of the new musical *Rags*, is a Jewish immigrant determined to rise above the sweatshop squalor of the Lower East Side, circa 1910. Who better than Ms. Stratas to make us believe that a frail wisp of a European woman might conquer the nasty, broad-shouldered new world?

It was a smart idea to cast this diva as Rebecca, all right—but, as the evidence at the Mark Hellinger suggests, a risky one, too. When the star's voice and spiritual fire blast out of her frame, the show must be ready to match her, eruption for eruption. The failure of *Rags* can be found in the simple fact that, for once, Ms. Stratas seems as small as life from curtain-rise to finale. Rebecca may be able to rise above poverty, anti-Semitism, and male scoundrels in *Rags*, but the star's performance, even when riding the crests of some soaring Charles Strouse music, usually remains planted in earth.

The evening's author, Joseph Stein, also wrote *Fiddler on the Roof*—a musical whose equivalent central figure, Tevye, was so richly conceived that the lesser actors who followed Zero Mostel into the role seemed to gain in magnitude merely by putting on the milkman's costume. Rebecca, who might well have been a refugee from the same Russian pogrom as Tevye, shackles Ms. Stratas because she's not really a character at all. This heroine is instead a symbol of Indomitable Immigranthood—as opaque as the

Statue of Liberty, that congenital scene-stealer who inevitably pops up in the musical's opening and closing sequences. While the plot gives Rebecca a husband (Larry Kert) and would-be lover (Terrence Mann) to bounce between, we never get a compelling sense of what she feels for them or they for her. A plaster saint, even when played by Ms. Stratas, is sexless.

The men are bland symbols as well. Mr. Kert stands for the opportunist, assimilationist immigrant (he's Sammy Glick as a party hack) while Mr. Mann is the idealist (a union organizer). Nearly every character is similarly archetypal, and no wonder: *Rags* wants to cover so much ground that there isn't time for people who don't pull their thematic weight. The show recklessly tries to encapsulate the concerns of Henry Roth's *Call It Sleep*, Abraham Cahan's *The Rise of David Levinsky*, and Jerome Weidman's *I Can Get It for You Wholesale*. It earnestly attempts to touch on everything from the heyday of the Yiddish theater to the birth of the garment workers' union, the origins of ethnic machine politics, the conflicts between first- and second-wave immigrants, the advent of feminism, and the virtues of both Marxism and capitalism. The milieu may be melting-pot America, but the show itself is a stewpot in which the multitudinous ingredients either cancel or drown each other out.

The only way so many major topics can be packed into a conventional Broadway musical is superficially. In the case of *Rags*, the potentially moving content is abridged into triviality by archaic romantic subplots (some of them hand-me-downs from Tevye's daughters), theater-party-targeted jokes (with which Ms. Stratas seems ill at ease), and fudged melodramatic jolts (preposterous reunions, ill-explained vigilante episodes, a death). So lax and, at times, chaotic is the structure that the placement of songs seems arbitrary. Why, for instance, does Rebecca stop to sing of her traumatic past ("Children of the Wind") just at the moment when the book belatedly gathers its first present-tense force?

The *Rags* that might have been is best heard in Mr. Strouse's score, galvanically orchestrated by Michael Starobin. It's no secret that the composer of *Bye Bye Birdie* and *Annie* knows how to concoct first-rate show tunes, and this musical has its share of those. Yet, perhaps inspired by his subject or by the presence of Ms. Stratas, Mr. Strouse has really stretched himself here. Evoking composers as diverse as Joplin, Sousa, Weill, and Gershwin, he uses his music to dramatize the evolution of a vernacular American pop music, much of it fostered by immigrant Jews during the period in which *Rags* is set. Sometimes Mr. Strouse's ambitions run away with him, and sometimes he retreats from his own scheme to Broadway basics (as in a pandering Act 2 comic duet for a flirtatious middle-aged couple). Still, this music is worthy of further hearing—doubly so when the star is expressing the churning excitement of heady new urban experience in fragrant songs like "Brand New World" and "Blame It on the Summer Night."

By contrast, Stephen Schwartz's lyrics, however professional, contain few surprises; like much of the plot, they can be heard coming a clunky beat or two away. (Jews didn't emigrate to America "to be hurt again" or "to be dirt again," we're told.) The supporting cast is in the same vein—competent and predictable. Mr. Kert, Mr. Mann, Lonny Price (as a putative William Paley), Marcia Lewis (a yenta), Dick Latessa (a stern peddler), and Rex Everhart (an Irish pol) are cast so exactly to type that one begins to think they're re-creating roles in a revival. Judy Kuhn's angry solo in the title song transcends the general level, while Josh Blake's self-absorbed portrayal of Ms. Stratas's son falls below it.

Gene Saks, the director, joined the production after it was cast and designed (unimaginatively by Beni Montresor, with apt Florence Klotz costumes and buckets of red lighting by Jules Fisher). While Mr. Saks keeps the show coming at the audience—disconcertingly so when transitions are missing—he can't give it drive or cohesion. Indeed, in the nearly static second act, the director rhythmically alternates often unrelated scenes and songs as if he were dispassionately adjudicating equal-time demands of the book and score. The choreographer, Ron Field, seems hardly to have gotten a word in edgewise: There's scant dancing, and the one attempt to force-feed a Cohan-like hat-and-cane number for Mr. Kert peters out just as it begins.

Ms. Stratas, however, does launch a brief hora later on. As she bounces nervously about, a tentative smile curling up to her spectacularly red hair, one sees the ghost of another Weill champion, Lotte Lenya, whose Broadway turn in *Cabaret* twenty autumns ago was marked by another charming party dance choreographed by Mr. Field. Ms. Stratas, like her predecessor, is an unexpected and highly welcome immigrant to the popular stage. But life on Broadway, unfortunately, is not always a cabaret.

≡ *Stratas never came back to Broadway. But Strouse's score survives in a cast recording in which Julia Migenes substitutes for the original star.*

CUBA AND HIS TEDDY BEAR
LONGACRE THEATRE, AUGUST 28, 1986

Most aspiring playwrights would probably kill to be Reinaldo Povod. As if it weren't enough that Joseph Papp decided to mount Mr. Povod's very first play, *Cuba and His Teddy Bear*, at the Public Theater, the producer recruited Robert De Niro, Ralph Macchio, and Burt Young as stars. Then Mr. Papp moved the production to Broadway, where theatergoers are clamoring for tickets as they haven't for any serious new American play in this decade. Not a bad boost for a writer who's all of twenty-six years old.

Yet Mr. Papp's favor to Mr. Povod isn't without its price. The presence of Mr. De Niro's name on the marquee arouses impossibly high expectations from audiences. These days top-rank film stars usually return to Broadway only in dramas of the magnitude of *Death of a Salesman* (Dustin Hoffman) or *American Buffalo* (Al Pacino). Mr. Povod isn't yet at the point—nor should he be—when he can deliver that sort of dramatic miracle. *Cuba* is, most persistently, a messy, wildly overlong, sometimes soppy autobiographical work. As such, it may well be as talented as Arthur Miller's and David Mamet's early efforts: Whatever his infelicities of dramaturgy, Mr. Povod has an ear, a heart, and a sense of humor. But under the starry circumstances, the audience at *Cuba* half expects a Second Coming, and, once the play descends to monotony in its second act, restlessness and disappointment set in. While one needn't shed any tears for Mr. Povod, the glitz surrounding *Cuba* makes it difficult for audiences to see his work as the modest, promising first play it is. Instead, it's "the De Niro show," with all the burden the phrase implies.

Mr. Povod will now have to bounce back from this early "success." We'll learn more about his gifts when he writes a play that doesn't hit so close to his own kitchen sink, and when that play is cast with regular Joes. In the meantime, theatergoers have every right to be puzzled by the curious lapse in Mr. De Niro's otherwise compelling performance as Cuba, a good-hearted, old-fashioned Lower East Side dope peddler (so old-fashioned he may be the only person in New York who never mentions crack). For some reason, Mr. De Niro makes no attempt to fill in the Hispanic background of this character—even though ethnic identity is a pressing, generational issue dividing him and his son (Mr. Macchio). In Martin Scorsese movies, Mr. De Niro has shaved his head (*Taxi Driver*), put on weight (*Raging Bull*), and learned to play the sax (*New York, New York*). So why does he stint on so important a detail as an accent in *Cuba*?

Mr. Macchio also has his drawbacks, but he's definitely an actor to watch. When *Cuba* first opened at the Public, his performance was a graphic demonstration of what can happen when an untrained actor, however experienced in film, is thrown on the stage. Mr. Macchio didn't know how to walk, stand, or use his voice. Yet even then, he achieved an affecting account of Teddy, a sensitive teenager at sea in his father's hostile urban jungle. As those who have endured Mr. Macchio's *Karate Kid* movies know, this actor does have presence, even in puerile material. Given a good role in *Cuba,* he has clearly been inspired to work hard: The performance I saw Mr. Macchio give at the Longacre last week showed far more technical skill than before, although he still acts too much with his hands for a karate-less assignment. While we must wait to see how this Broadway venture affects Mr. Povod's development, the equally young Mr. Macchio already has artistic growth to show for the experience.

≣ *Reinaldo Povod did a second work under Papp's aegis* (La Puta Vida Trilogy) *a year later. He died of tuberculosis, at age thirty-four, in 1994.*

THE COLORED MUSEUM
PUBLIC THEATER, NOVEMBER 3, 1986

There comes a time when a satirical writer, if he's really out for blood, must stop clowning around and move in for the kill. That unmistakable moment of truth arrives about halfway through *The Colored Museum,* the wild new evening of black black humor at the Public Theater. In a sketch titled "The Last Mama-on-the-Couch Play," the author, George C. Wolfe, says the unthinkable, says it with uncompromising wit, and leaves the audience, as well as a sacred target, in ruins. The devastated audience, one should note, includes both blacks and whites. Mr. Wolfe is the kind of satirist, almost unheard of in today's timid theater, who takes no prisoners.

The target in this particular sketch, the longest of the ninety-minute entertainment's eleven playlets, is nothing less than *A Raisin in the Sun,* Lorraine Hansberry's breakthrough play of 1959 and a model for much black American drama that came later. Mr. Wolfe's new version of it is introduced by an elegant *Masterpiece Theater*–type announcer (Tommy Hollis) in black tie, who promises us "a searing, domestic drama that tears at the very fabric of racist America." The principal inhabitants of the tenement setting are a "well-worn mama" (Vickilyn Reynolds), forever sitting with her Bible on her "well-worn couch," and her son Walter-Lee-Beau-Willy (Reggie Montgomery), whose "brow is heavy with three hundred years of oppression."

Ms. Reynolds and Mr. Montgomery provide stinging parodies of both the lines and performances of Claudia McNeil and Sidney Poitier in

Raisin—with Mama forever instructing the angry son to let God settle his grievances with "the Man." But if Mr. Wolfe is merciless in mocking the well-made plays, "shattering" acting, and generational conflicts of a 1950s black American drama preoccupied with "middle-class aspirations," he doesn't stop there. "The Last Mama-on-the-Couch Play" eventually satirizes a more pretentious, latter-day form of black theater (blamed on Juilliard in this case)—and finally turns into an all-black Broadway musical that spirals into a nightmarish indictment of the white audience's patronizing relationship to black performers. By then, Mr. Wolfe, too, has torn "at the very fabric of racist America"—but not before he has revealed the cultural blind spots of blacks and whites alike. Although the letter of Ms. Hansberry's work has been demolished, the spirit of its political punch is upheld.

Not all of *The Colored Museum* is as funny as "The Last Mama-on-the-Couch Play," but even the lesser bits are written at the same high level of sophistication. The evening as a whole amounts to more than its uneven, revuelike parts. The director L. Kenneth Richardson, working with an exceptional cast and elegant designers, has given *The Colored Museum* the pacing and unity of a sustained play in the pop-art absurdist mode. Mr. Wolfe's themes are also sustained. The issue raised by his Hansberry parody percolates in every sketch: How do American black men and women at once honor and escape the legacy of suffering that is the baggage of their past?

This dilemma is drawn before the first sketch begins. Brian Martin's sleek all-purpose set, of an antiseptic modern museum displaying exhibits of "colored" history, is a civilized repository of black America's ancestral baggage. But the past can't be so neatly stored away. There is nothing civilized about the gruesome slide show, depicting the horrors of slavery, that overwhelms the museum's impersonal walls in the prologue. The opening sketch sharpens Mr. Wolfe's conflict. The actress Danitra Vance, wearing a hot-pink stewardess outfit and a hideously perky grin, welcomes us to a "celebrity slaveship" whose Savannah-bound passengers are forced to obey a FASTEN SHACKLES sign and are warned that they will have to "suffer for a few hundred years" in exchange for receiving a "complex culture" that will ultimately embrace the Watusi, "Miss Diahann Carroll in *Julia*," and such white hangers-on as Gershwin and Faulkner.

The other "exhibits" in Mr. Wolfe's museum are contemporary blacks torn between the cultural legacy of oppression and revolt and the exigencies of living in the present. Perhaps the prototypical Wolfe character is a pinstripe-suited businessman who tries to throw away his past ("Free Huey" buttons, Sly Stone records, his first dashiki) only to discover that his rebellious younger self refuses to be trashed without a fight. A Josephine Baker–like chanteuse named LaLa (Loretta Devine) similarly finds that her carefully created, Gallicized showbiz image is haunted by the "little girl" she thought she'd left for dead in backwoods Mississippi. A woman dressing for a date is traumatized when her two wigs—one a 1960s Afro, the other that of "a Barbie doll dipped in chocolate"—come alive to debate the ideological identity conflicts they have represented in their owner's life for twenty years.

Mr. Wolfe's characters "can't live inside yesterday's pain," and yet they can't bury it, either. When two *Ebony* magazine fashion models try to retreat from their past into a world of narcissistic glamour, they find only "the kind of pain that comes from feeling no pain at all." Another would-be escapee, a campy homosexual nightclub denizen known as Miss ROJ (Mr. Montgomery), looks beneath the surface of his glittery nocturnal existence to find maggot-laced visions of "a whole race trashed and debased."

While *The Colored Museum* may sound depressing, it's not. Mr. Wolfe is always lobbing in wisecracks about Michael Jackson's nose or *The Color Purple*. Mr. Richardson's staging, which uses a turntable to bring exhibits of black experience past and present into chilling juxtapositions, adds energy even to the more lugubrious sketches. Although the whole cast deserves credit for injecting still more vitality, one is especially pleased to see Ms. Devine and Ms. Vance used to such fine effect after having watched them suffer last season in, respectively, the musical *Big Deal* and television's *Saturday Night Live*. Ms. Vance is not only funny but also noble in a monologue in which Mr. Wolfe retrieves the dignity of a very innocent, very pregnant teenager.

It's left to Ms. Reynolds, though, to resolve the playwright's themes in a lyrical final monologue. The speech belongs to a woman named Topsy Washington who imagines a big blowout of a party, "somewhere between One Hundred Twenty-fifth Street and infinity," where "Nat Turner sips champagne out of Eartha Kitt's slipper" and Angela Davis and Aunt Jemima sit around talking about South Africa. As this fantasy merging of present and past grows and grows, "defying logic and limitations," Topsy decides to put her rage about the past behind her so she can "go about the business of being me" and celebrate her own "madness and colored contradictions." Given that history soon rises up around Topsy in the form of music, other characters, and projected images, it's clear that the baggage of slavery cannot really be banished from *The Colored Museum*. But the shackles of the past have at the very least been defied by Mr. Wolfe's fearless humor, and it's a most liberating revolt.

≡ *This was an auspicious debut. George Wolfe would later take over the leadership of Joseph Papp's New York Shakespeare Festival, stage two daring Broadway musicals (* Jelly's Last Jam, Bring in 'da Noise Bring in 'da Funk), *and collaborate with Tony Kushner on the Broadway production of* Angels in America.

COASTAL DISTURBANCES
SECOND STAGE, NOVEMBER 20, 1986

In his ingenious lighting for Tina Howe's new play, *Coastal Disturbances*, the designer Dennis Parichy has captured the entire spectrum of weather known to habitues of New England beaches in August. Mr. Parichy graces the horizon of Tony Straiges's sand-carpeted set not merely with the blinding sunniness of midday but also with the frail pink cumulus clouds of dusk, the chilly mica silver of a lost rainy afternoon, and the pale, smoky blue of a foggy dawn. Not that a catalogue of colors tells the whole story. What lifts Mr. Parichy's work beyond decoration and into poetry is his ability to unfurl the transitory sky that hasn't yet determined what's going to be. It's that blank canvas of heaven, pregnant with the volatile possibilities of precipitous change, that gives the beach its true romance.

Mr. Parichy's art is worth talking about in its own right, but also because it so aptly reflects the quality of Ms. Howe's play, her first since *Painting Churches*. In *Coastal Disturbances,* now at the Second Stage, the weather above is inevitably a metaphor for human frissons below. And, some Act 2 erosion aside, Ms. Howe has kept up her end of the bargain with the same watercolor delicacy of Mr. Parichy's lighting. The people in *Coastal Disturbances,* four generations' worth of vacationers on a private Massachusetts beach, are always welling up with exhilaration or lust or love or anger whenever one least expects. As written by Ms. Howe and acted by one of the finer casts in New York, the emotional cloudbursts, no less than the meteorological, can take the breath away.

A modern play about love that is, for once, actually about love—as opposed to sexual, social, or marital politics—*Coastal Disturbances* usually just lets its disturbances happen. A heretofore chipper divorced woman named Ariel (Joanne Camp) starts to chew out her young son and suddenly loses self-control, flying past boiling point to violent rage. Ariel's old Wellesley roommate, the pregnant Faith (Heather MacRae), gossips merrily once too often about the beach's "well-endowed" lifeguard, Leo

(Timothy Daly), and finds herself breaking into uncontrollable, sidesplitting laughter. The play's heroine, a photographer named Holly Dancer (Annette Bening), tells the lifeguard a phantasmagoric fantasy about an orgiastic all-night party of well-heeled, anthropomorphized dolphins, and, as she does so, Leo can't resist the frantic urge to bury the dream-dizzied Holly in the sand.

These incidents are, respectively, aching, hilarious, and erotic. In each of them Ms. Howe takes a specific character's concern—the battle-scarred Ariel's hatred of men, Faith's ecstatic anticipation of motherhood, Holly's and Leo's growing sexual attraction—and distills it into a concentrate of intoxicating feeling. Yet, like Holly, who is seeking a "wider focus" in her photographs and life, the playwright wants to examine love from all the additional points of view she can find.

An older couple, played by Rosemary Murphy and Addison Powell, provide the perspective of age: Having survived nine children, decades of marriage, and infidelities, they now can see that younger people are "always losing things" that they at last have found. At the other end of the cycle are Ariel's son, Winston (Jonas Abry), and Faith's adopted daughter, Miranda (Rachel Mathieu)—kids already parroting both the "kissy" and tragically self-destructive behavior of adults. Ms. Howe even takes into account generations to come. Transcendentally obsessed with the "biological chain," Faith reminds us that a girl is "born with all her eggs" and tells of how she used to shake Miranda to hear them rolling about.

Ms. Howe's vignettes are brief and pointedly impressionistic—in the style of the young painter who kept trying to find the right angle on her parents' portrait in *Painting Churches*. In *Coastal Disturbances*, Ms. Murphy, who could be the Brahmin mother in the previous play, paints tightly composed, realistic beachscapes. "Hold still!," she complains as the scene before her shifts. "Why does everything have to keep moving?" Ms. Howe understands that everything must keep moving, that there is no "right" angle, that love and its responsibilities are something to "figure out as you go along." Not for nothing is Ms. Murphy reading Quentin Bell's biography of Virginia Woolf on the beach. Ms. Howe, who shares with Woolf what one character calls "the transforming eye of the artist," sees all her people, the men included, in the funny, sexy, and finally forgiving round.

Carole Rothman, who also directed *Painting Churches*, is unfailingly sensitive to Ms. Howe's airy technique, which could be mutilated by either too light or heavy an application of theatrical brush strokes. In league with Mr. Straiges, the director creates the illusion that a small stage is a vast stretch of coast, seen from an ever-rotating vantage point and rippling with overlapping waves, action, and conversation. Though the heightened colors of *Coastal Disturbances* recall Joel Meyerowitz's lush Cape Cod photographs, the director begins or ends most scenes with a theatrical equivalent of candid Polaroid snapshots: A glimpse of private behavior is fixed and emblazoned on memory, then fades quickly, as if to reinforce the small, distant presentiment of death with which Act 1 begins.

In a cast that even boasts an exceptionally charming child actor (Mr. Abry), special praise belongs to the leads. Ms. Bening, an actress new to New York, provides a quicksilver Holly whose psychological and physical swoons into tears, laughter, and lust all convey the mystery of a woman floating ambiguously but passionately between love and nervous collapse. As the drifting lifeguard with whom she tumbles, the extremely likable Mr. Daly burrows to the real meat of his role. With shy humor and ingenuously articulated longing, he makes us believe that his universally admired physique really does cloak the "very sweet," unsophisticated, and defenseless young man he claims to be.

Compelling as these performances are, *Coastal Disturbances* nonetheless subsides in Act 2, when Ms. Howe settles for working Mr. Daly and Ms. Bening into a conventionally bittersweet summertime triangle, completed by an unexpected visit from Holly's big-city roué (Ronald Guttman) and capped by a *Tempest*-flecked reconciliatory ending that is schematic and sentimental.

Other characters, especially the contrasting young mothers, leave well before one wants to bid them farewell. But if Ms. Howe is hardly the most able maker of finished plays in our theater, she must be one of the most perceptive and, line by line, most graceful writers. *Coastal Disturbances* is distinctly the creation of a female sensibility, but its beautiful, isolated private beach generously illuminates the intimate landscape that is shared by women and men.

≡ *Both Annette Bening and Timothy Daly quickly decamped for Hollywood.*

THE FRONT PAGE
VIVIAN BEAUMONT THEATER, NOVEMBER 24, 1986

As everyone who's seen *The Front Page* knows—and is there anyone who hasn't seen *The Front Page*?—it's one play that will never receive a negative review in a newspaper. That's because Ben

Hecht and Charles MacArthur wrote about newspaper people as newspaper people liked to think of themselves and still do, no matter that humming computer terminals have replaced rattling typewriters, that the discovery of a "love nest" rarely merits an extra anymore, or that cities like Chicago no longer have eight dailies engaged in cutthroat competition for the big scoop. *The Front Page,* to borrow from Shea Stadium parlance, is newspapering like it oughta be. Not even a critic as uncompromising as Joseph Cotten's Jed Leland in *Citizen Kane* would be so foolish as to question the work—part farce, part melodrama, all cartoon—that is the Rosetta stone of his and his colleagues' romantic self-image.

To see Hecht's and MacArthur's 1928 valentine to the press now, in Jerry Zaks's attractively cast and appropriately slam-bang revival at the Vivian Beaumont, is also to appreciate it as a play. Well, not as a play exactly—but as an efficient machine (once cranked up) for manufacturing mirth. As Walter Kerr memorably wrote on the occasion of the last Broadway appearance of *The Front Page,* in 1969, plays of this American vintage were meant to be machines: "A play was like a watch that laughed." As recent revivals have demonstrated, *The Front Page* still ticks louder and faster and funnier than equivalent Broadway contraptions manufactured a decade (*You Can't Take It with You*) or two decades (*Arsenic and Old Lace*) after it.

One knows that the old thing is going to work at Lincoln Center early on, when Jeff Weiss, the Off Off Broadway maverick who went legit last season in the Kevin Kline *Hamlet,* appears as Bensinger, the man from the *Tribune.* Bensinger is the fussbudget of the newsroom at the Chicago Criminal Courts Building—that dread animal, a neat reporter who thinks of himself as a poet, no less. Mr. Weiss, his mouth razorblade-thin, simply can't wait to pull out his bottle of disinfectant and zap any offending germ in the vicinity of his roll-top desk. He does so with a snap of the wrist so wicked it could induce whiplash. When subsequently mocked by colleagues for his prissiness, he responds with an "Oh shut up!"—withering and yet defensive—that Jack Benny might have admired.

Arriving minutes later, but no less welcome, is Richard Thomas, the Hildy Johnson of this outing. Mr. Thomas, a benign presence, is not the obvious choice for the role of a brash star reporter who enters "stinko" and soon thinks nothing of trading his prospective mother-in-law (the formidable Beverly May) for the story of a condemned anarchist's jailbreak. But as he's proved several times on stages in several cities in recent seasons, Mr. Thomas isn't the juvenile he's mistaken for—he seeks out acting challenges and rises to them.

Affecting a mustache and an all-purpose Windy City ethnic accent, he soon becomes the swaggering mug required, far more desperate to please the managing editor he's supposedly just quit forever, Walter Burns, than the fiancée whom he's promised to meet at the 11:18 p.m. train for New York. (The usually thankless role of the fiancée is played by Julie Hagerty, whose determined appeals to reason in the face of chaos make humorlessness a howl.) Once John Lithgow's Burns joins Mr. Thomas in Act 2, the real marriage of the evening is complete. Whether the tall Mr. Lithgow is trying to detain the deserting Hildy by tossing him on the floor ("At a time of war, you could be shot for what you're doing!"), or sadistically plotting Bensinger's humiliation, or feigning sentimental enthusiasm for Hildy's marital plans ("I was in love once, with my third wife"), he provides comic ruthlessness of a high style. Be assured, too, that Mr. Lithgow delivers the play's immortal curtain line with such bravura finality that one can easily forgive the Beaumont's lack of a curtain.

Like many good newspapermen, Burns regards politicians as his sworn enemy, and this *Front Page* is especially acerbic in its portraits of the bumbling, platitudinous Chicago officials who cross him. Richard B. Shull, forever wincing as if life were one long embarrassing encounter with a whoopee cushion, plays the incompetent sheriff "Pinky" as the exact kind of backroom "moron" that he's called—moronic enough to permit a jailbreak but not so stupid that he neglects to hire his relatives at city expense for the search party. The scene in which he and Jerome Dempsey's windbag Mayor try to bribe Bill McCutcheon's slow-witted, reprieve-bearing gubernatorial messenger is as clownish as any scenario on the Watergate tapes.

Indeed, dated as the Hecht-MacArthur portrayal of newspapering may sometimes seem—one does hear rumors these days of reporters who have actually bettered the play's going pay scale of seventy dollars a week—its cynical view of the political circus remains pertinent. The ward heelers of *The Front Page* lie and pander to voters as shamelessly as contemporary pols and are as adept at exploiting capital punishment and radical conspiracies to self-aggrandizing ends. Nearly every scene bristles with the still-extant realities of politics in an urban society of racial and class divisions.

Mr. Zaks properly maintains a frisky tone, even so. *The Front Page* is not foolproof—witness the logy 1974 Billy Wilder film version—and it really must move. Mr. Zaks keeps everyone running, although one might question whether he needs a set deep enough to accommodate a marathon. Tony Walton has designed a cigar-hued newsroom set against a mammoth gray courthouse—a handsome edifice whose imposing size and gloom smack a bit of Marienbad. Both the designer and Mr. Zaks conquered the Beaumont's problematic stage more resourcefully when their *House of Blue Leaves* passed through last spring in transit to Broadway.

Aside from the usual lulls during the by-now ritualistic plot exposition and resolution, the evening's only other significant blemishes are both anachronisms: The opening invocation of a Frank Sinatra recording of "Chicago" is more redolent of 1960s Las Vegas than of the 1920s Chicago found in Willa Kim's nostalgic costumes, and, worse, only wimpy amounts of tobacco smoke becloud the poker-playing reporters of the Lucky Strike era. Not the least of the romantic newsroom notions propagated by *The Front Page*, after all, is that one becomes a newspaperman precisely because it's hazardous to one's health.

≡ *This was the production—under the new Lincoln Center Theater regime of Bernard Gersten and Gregory Mosher—that finally broke the Vivian Beaumont jinx. More specifically, the director Jerry Zaks and the designer Tony Walton, unlike so many before them, found a way to conquer the awkward thrust stage that they would perfect in such subsequent productions as* Anything Goes *and* Six Degrees of Separation.

The Beaumont was hardly the only American playhouse to confront the ghosts of ill-considered theater design in the 1980s. During the 1950s and sixties "thrust" and arena stages had been the rage, but by now the fashion had long since run out. In Washington, the pioneering Arena Stage has been upstaged by proscenium houses elsewhere in town (including Arena's own second, proscenium theater, the Kreeger); in New York both the Broadway and downtown incarnations of the once-popular Circle in the Square fell into artistic disfavor, eventually plunging the company itself into bankruptcy. The Guthrie Theater in Minneapolis, built in the same era as the Beaumont in a similar "thrust" style (an amphibious hybrid of proscenium and arena), also retooled itself at this time to make itself more inviting (and intimate) to directors, actors, and audiences. So did others in America and abroad.

For all the theatrical innovations of the post–World War II era, there's still much demand for the "old-fashioned" houses built on Broadway and in the downtowns of many major American cities, largely by the Shuberts and their then-rival, the so-called Syndicate, from the end of the nineteenth century until the Depression. Their sightlines, acoustics, and atmosphere remain unmatched, even though patrons note that the seats seem to have become narrower and narrower through successive refurbishings over the years—thereby increasing the number of tickets that can be sold.

BROADWAY BOUND
BROADHURST THEATRE, DECEMBER 5, 1986

In an Act 2 monologue that's the indisputable peak of Neil Simon's *Broadway Bound,* a middle-aged Jewish mother named Kate Jerome tells her younger son, Eugene, about the most glamorous incident of her life—a night at the Primrose Ballroom, thirty-five years earlier, when George Raft asked her to dance. Both as written by Mr. Simon and acted by Linda Lavin, Kate's reminiscence spirals upward like the opening clarinet glissando in Gershwin's *Rhapsody in Blue.* It's a mesmerizing journey to a bygone working-class Brooklyn where first-generation American Jews discovered the opportunities and guilt that came with the secular temptations of a brash new world.

Bernard Malamud couldn't have bettered the perfect pitch of this speech, yet young Eugene, the aspiring writer previously seen in Mr. Simon's *Brighton Beach Memoirs* and *Biloxi Blues,* is already imagining how his mother's past might be reshaped into a movie that will keep the audience "at the edge of its seats." Kate doesn't seem to notice her son's editorial interjections, however, until Eugene announces that his movie will have "a happy ending." It's then that Ms. Lavin suddenly stiffens her posture, as if throwing off the dreaminess of memory to reassume the weight of present-day reality, and closes the scene with an abrupt admonition: "The movie isn't over yet."

That moment crystallizes both the meaning of the play at the Broadhurst and the wonderment of following its author's recent career. *Broadway Bound* shows us its hero as he prepares to break into comedy writing on radio in the late 1940s, but not before he learns that life, unlike the movies, doesn't always come to a clear-cut, let alone happy, finale. Throughout the evening Eugene is tempted to draw neat conclusions about the troubled relatives in his fractious Brighton Beach household only to discover that their "whole story" is far more complicated, ambiguous, and eternal than he ever imagined. And, of course, the story of Mr. Simon's development as a playwright isn't over yet, either. In *Broadway Bound,* Broadway's most successful practitioner of tidy dramaturgy continues to enhance the complexity that has brought him artistic rebirth in his cycle of alliteratively titled autobiographical plays.

The result, a transitional work, is messy, in both the positive and negative senses of the word. *Broadway Bound* contains some of its author's most accomplished writing to date—passages that dramatize the timeless, unresolvable bloodlettings of familial existence as well as the humorous conflicts one expects. But the merging of laughter, character, and emotion that ignited *Biloxi Blues* is only intermittently achieved here. There are stretches, especially in Act 1, when *Broadway Bound* isn't funny or moving but just reportorial and expository, with plot twists and thematic invocations piling up undigested, like the heavier courses at an attenuated Passover seder. "Every writer needs an editor," says Eugene, and one must wonder if a great play has been left unextracted from the rich but bulky material at hand.

What's most impressive about *Broadway Bound* is Mr. Simon's expanded generosity toward characters who are not himself. Eugene, a role that the talented Jonathan Silverman has now inherited from Matthew Broderick, is not the protagonist of this play. That position falls instead to Ms. Lavin's Kate—a woman who must contend not only with the impending departure of Eugene and his brother, Stanley (Jason Alexander), but also with the probable desertion of her wandering husband of thirty-three years (Philip Sterling) and the growing frailty of her elderly live-in father (John Randolph). While Kate has lived for the single goal of raising a family, the post–World War II *Broadway Bound* finds her at a personal and historical moment when both her single-minded purpose and the Old World values that instilled that maternal mission are fast becoming obsolete.

Though Mr. Simon has either sentimentalized or caricatured his past heroines, he sees Kate whole, refusing to sanctify or mock her. Kate is a remarkable achievement—a Jewish mother who redefines the genre even as she gets the requisite laughs while fretting over her children's health or an unattended pot roast. She's a woman who takes "her own quiet pleasure" in a world that goes no farther than her subway line, and if her life is over once her dinner table is deserted, she greets her fate with stoical silence, not self-martyrdom. One only wishes that Ms. Lavin, whose touching performance is of the same high integrity as the writing, could stay in the role forever. It's all too easy to imagine the coarse interpretations that could follow this actress's meticulously, deeply etched portrait of a woman who is a survivor, not a victim, of an immigrant family's hard path to assimilation.

Almost as stirring, in both conception and performance, is the character of Kate's father, the unreconstructed, if sometimes hypocritical Trotskyite played with a matchless mixture of buried affection and shrewd comic timing by Mr. Randolph. This crotchety old man is a fresh take on the archetype the actor previously played in Arthur Miller's *The American Clock*—no matter whether he's suffering the humiliations of age, or humorlessly applying socialist utilitarianism to his grandson's frivolous jokes, or confusing paternal anger for political ideals in an early joust with Kate's well-off sister Blanche (an empathic one-scene appearance by Phyllis Newman). Another product of tough circumstance, Mr. Randolph's grandfather, too, helps us see why Eugene pines so strongly for the luxury of intimacy that previous generations of Jeromes have been denied.

Oddly enough, Eugene's most intimate current companion, the older but more juvenile brother who is his mentor and writing partner, is less fully drawn. Stanley and Eugene aren't as hilariously fused as Mr. Simon's past male odd couples, nor do they achieve the Cain-and-Abel bonding of the equivalent brothers in Miller and Shepard plays. Perhaps to make up the difference, the usually witty Mr. Alexander starts Stanley off at a shrill pitch and stays there: The anger Stanley expresses in a fit of writer's pique is undifferentiated from the far more primal rage with which he confronts his father later on. Then again, the father, competently performed by Mr. Sterling, also fails to carry the dramatic weight attached to him: Mr. Simon seems to be expecting us to think back to *Brighton Beach Memoirs* to find a vestige of the principled, lovable patriarch that Kate and her sons keep claiming once existed within the spent, drab figure before us now.

The lengthier squabbles featuring the father or Stanley defy even the efforts of Ms. Lavin or of the impeccable director, Gene Saks, to animate them. Far livelier are the interludes in which Mr. Simon, with a nostalgic gusto reminiscent of Moss Hart's *Act One,* dissects the ambitions and craft of aspiring showbiz comedy writers. When Eugene and Stanley finally get their break on CBS, their silly, period radio sketch is interpreted or misinterpreted differently by everyone who hears it—leading to a masterly delineation of how even writing intended for a mass audience begins with specific details, and before that, in the unexplored subconscious.

Mr. Silverman presides over these interludes with appealing brio. It takes a while to forget Mr. Broderick's Eugene, but once one does, it's clear that his successor has captured both the "nice, likable, funny" shell of the young man and the "angry, hostile" writer-on-the-make within. By the time Eugene coaxes his mother to dance with him, in oedipal emulation of that long-ago invitation from George Raft, we also see the compassion of a fledgling playwright who may someday come to terms with his childhood.

In *Broadway Bound,* Eugene's grown-up creator hasn't always come to those terms. One must endure those scenes in which the author, still bound by Broadway realism, settles for a smoothly crafted chronicle of his Brighton Beach memoirs, finite details instead of subconscious truth. But the compensating rewards are there when Mr. Simon, like mother and son in their imaginary ballroom, uncovers the family history that's never over, and, mature artist that he is, makes it spin.

THE WIDOW CLAIRE
CIRCLE IN THE SQUARE (DOWNTOWN), DECEMBER 18, 1986

Of course, almost nothing happens in *The Widow Claire*, the latest Horton Foote play to reach a New York stage. In keeping with his writing habits of four decades, the author of *The Trip to Bountiful* and *Tender Mercies* whisks us into the fictional small Texas town of Harrison and sets his characters about their diurnal business. *The Widow Claire*, a ninety-five-minute anecdote in one act, describes only a single long summer night of 1911. Horace Robedaux (Matthew Broderick), a poor but ambitious twenty-one-year-old about to enroll in a six-week business course in Houston, spends the eve of his departure courting the title character (Hallie Foote), a twenty-seven-year-old widow with several suitors and two rambunctious kids. Daybreak brings Horace's leave-taking and an exchange of farewells so formal one might wonder whether the couple had in fact stolen a few chaste kisses under the new moon of the night before.

Those attuned to Mr. Foote's style, however, may find another, more moving drama percolating beneath the placid surface of *The Widow Claire*. During the poker games of the whiskey-swilling men back at Horace's boarding house—interludes that could be mistaken for atmospheric filler—fragments of thwarted lives spill out with the gossip. We hear fleetingly of an insomniac walking around town all night in desperate search of peace, of alcoholic drifters and their fifty-cent prostitutes, of a gambler wiped out by two rogues from Galveston, of the penniless itinerant laborers of the pre-industrial South. The couple at center stage reveal more than they intend, too. When Horace sits on the steps of his date's front porch and matter-of-factly recounts his autobiography, the genteel, uninflected cadences and perfectly formed sentences can't entirely obscure the terrors of an adolescence marked by parental abandonments, rejections, and deaths.

The work of an artist who knows just what he wants to do and how he wants to do it, *The Widow Claire* has the lucid details and buried poignancy of a naturalistic American short story from the era in which it is set. At the Circle in the Square Downtown, the director Michael Lindsay-Hogg and his company bring the script the precise intensity required. But even after all these years, Horton Foote may still strike some as an acquired taste. Among observers of small-town existence, he lacks the exotic Gothic humors of Eudora Welty and Beth Henley, or the debunker's anger of a Sinclair Lewis or Edgar Lee Masters. Nor are his plain characters to be confused with the more extravagant and tragic souls of Faulkner and Williams. Mr. Foote is a chronicler of the quotidian. His Texans often survive and sometimes prosper, though not until they've cracked open just enough for attentive onlookers to discover the hard compromises, devastating losses, and unshakable faith in familial love that have forged their spirit.

The Widow Claire belongs to the nine-play cycle known as *The Orphans' Home,* which has already spawned two films (*On Valentine's Day* and *1918,* both featuring Mr. Broderick and Ms. Foote in other roles) and another current Off Broadway play (*Lily Dale,* in which Don Bloomfield plays the Horace Robedaux of 1909). If there's a specific theme to this particular episode of Mr. Foote's family saga, it has as much to do with the love between parents and children as that between women and men. Claire's ten-year-old son (John Daman) and younger daughter (Sarah Michelle Gellar) are consumed by nightmarish, if unarticulated, terror of the gentlemen callers campaigning to be their stepfather. Horace is a long-shot contender for Claire's hand, yet he's also a victim of his own father's death nine years earlier and his mother's remarriage. Drawn to Claire's children as strongly as he is to Claire herself, Horace finds the possible roles of son, parent, and lover all arrayed confusingly before him. One suspects his choices cannot be made until he puts his past to rest, at once literally and symbolically, by fulfilling his goal of earning the money needed to place a tombstone on his father's grave.

In a gray suit and straw boater, Mr. Broderick is as impressive an inarticulate, sensitive young Texan as he was Neil Simon's loquacious Eugene Jerome. Horace's feelings and energy are belied by his solemnly fastidious manners and polite drawl; his hurt and drive alike flicker in his dark, penetrating eyes. The character's few dramatic actions—among them a short-lived fistfight—are of minor moment next to what he doesn't do and doesn't say. One of the evening's saddest passages occurs when Mr. Broderick stands at a shadowy distance, paralyzed with fear and incomprehension, as a town bully uses violence to intimidate and arouse Claire in ways Horace has never witnessed in the prim sexual arena of the ballroom floor.

Ms. Foote, the author's daughter, is perfect as Mr. Broderick's older nocturnal partner. Her red-haired, quick-tongued Claire, first seen dancing and smoking in erotic abandon around her Victrola, is the kind of sensuous, independent-minded beauty that one can picture whole towns gossiping about. But as she chooses frantically among what she sees as her only options—marriage for either financial security or sexual excitement—Ms. Foote's widow seems to relinquish her youth and radiance in anticipation of domestic incarceration.

In a good supporting cast that prominently features Victor Slezak, Patrick James Clarke, and William Youmans, the most memorable appearance is by Dan Butler, as a vulgar, mangy yokel in whom the compassionate playwright eventually finds dignity, generosity, and romance. "Do you prefer the light or the dark meat of chicken?" Mr. Butler asks apropos of nothing, trying as best he can to strike up a friendship with Horace. The production's other assets include Van Broughton Ramsey's costumes, the set designer Eugene Lee's old-time wooden porch, and a Natasha Katz lighting scheme that gradually takes *The Widow Claire* from a golden midnight to a pitch-black 4 a.m. to a glaring new day. The earth turns slowly in Horton Foote's small-town Texas, all the better for us to get to know the brave inhabitants who cling to it for dear life.

CRIME AND PUNISHMENT
ARENA STAGE, WASHINGTON, D.C., JANUARY 9, 1987

When Raskolnikov, the lapsed student turned ax murderer, is consumed by delirium in the director Yuri Lyubimov's adaptation of *Crime and Punishment*, he doesn't merely sulk or weep—he becomes almost literally unhinged. Raskolnikov (Randle Mell) stands against the blood-smeared white door of the scene of his crime and writhes in pain as if crucified. A slender vertical bar of light seems to pin him there, and just as the agony reaches breaking point, the door tears away from its frame and sends the still-squirming Raskolnikov hurtling with it across the blackened stage. Like a passenger on a grotesque amusement-park ride, Raskolnikov finds other terrors awaiting—eerie echoes, more swinging doors, anonymous phantoms of the psychic underground. But for him, there's no sunlight at the end of the tunnel, no exit from the nightmare of guilt.

Mr. Lyubimov, the leader of Moscow's famed Taganka Theater until the Soviet government stripped him of his job and citizenship in 1984, has long been considered one of the world's great directors. Visitors to Washington's Arena Stage, where *Crime and Punishment* marks his American debut, will find out why. This free-floating approach to Dostoyevsky, which originated in Moscow and was last replicated in London in 1983, offers a freshly hallucinated vision of a novel that has never lacked for stage and screen interpreters. That the Arena Stage's acting company is woefully ill-equipped to handle Mr. Lyubimov's artistic demands adds more fascination to the occasion. Conceived by its director to condemn Soviet attempts to justify Raskolnikov's crime as a revolutionary strike against capitalism, *Crime and Punishment* in Washington also becomes an inadvertent condemnation of practices in the American theater.

Even as inadequately acted at Arena, Mr. Lyubimov's meditation on Dostoyevsky is an urgent cry of faith. Beginning and ending with a display of sacramental candles—and haunted throughout by the corpses of Raskolnikov's two murder victims—this is *Crime and Punishment* as pure Christian morality tale. The line delivered loudest all evening is the police investigator Porfiry's "Pity the criminal all you like, but don't call evil good." Mr. Lyubimov rejects a moral "arithmetic," whether propagated by Raskolnikov or Stalinist regimes, that would balance one expeditious murder with a hundred subsequent good deeds. Raskolnikov's regeneration cannot come with the overthrow of Czarist repression but only through confession, hard labor in Siberia, and a love of God.

If there is little that is philosophically startling about Mr. Lyubimov's reading of the book, his theatrical presentation of his case is full of surprises. With his co-adaptor Yuri Karyakin, the director has splintered and shuffled the novel's scenes, as if he were dreaming about Dostoyevsky's own dream-laden narrative. Although some episodes and characters are eviscerated, most of the novel is preserved, albeit in radically reimagined form.

In place of much of Dostoyevsky's text is a distillation of sound and metaphorical images. Most characters possess a musical leitmotif (by Adison Denisov); each major event leaves a distinctive trail of phantasmagoric noise. Blinding, mobile klieg and strobe lights (and their accompanying shadows) dramatize the fear of a police inquisition, or the swirl of St. Petersburg's lower nineteenth-century depths, or even the velocity of a pistol's bullet. And in a production modest in scenery and props, doors count for everything. As the door of the murdered pawnbroker and her sister becomes the iconographic emblem of Raskolnikov's conscience, so there are doors that metamorphose into death beds and coffins and still other doors that open into all manner of psychic hells.

To label Mr. Lyubimov's techniques "avant-garde" would be mistaken. His *Crime and Punishment* speaks to us of the Russian avant-garde of six decades ago, the heady futurist theater that blossomed in the brief corridor of freedom between the respective orthodoxies of Stanislavski and Stalin. Many of Mr. Lyubimov's devices are familiar to American audiences. The tradition he mines is the same that has been popularized in recent years by Western directors as various as Robert Wilson and Trevor Nunn, JoAnne Akalaitis and Richard Foreman, Harold Prince and Peter Sellars (among many others). In *Crime and Punishment,* Mr. Lyubimov reminds us how simple such theater can be.

Almost as if to contrast his Russian heritage of rigorous experimentation with passing, less fruitful American theatrical fashions, the director has staged his piece not in Arena Stage's main, namesake theater but in its second, proscenium house, the Kreeger. Just as damningly—if unintentionally—does he expose the weaknesses in the training of his actors. What's required by Mr. Lyubimov is the kind of performance one sees in productions like Peter Brook's *Carmen* or Steppenwolf's *Balm in Gilead,* or the Polish director Tadeusz Kantor's *Let the Artists Die*—a go-for-broke emotional intensity, combined with dynamic physical and vocal agility, that could exorcise the extravagant, overheated Dostoyevskian passions and sweaty, teeming slum life of nineteenth-century Russia. With the important exception of Mr. Mell, whose intelligent, energetic performance has the makings (if not yet the depth) of a harrowing Raskolnikov, most of the cast behaves as if it were appearing in a Stanislavskian realistic play set in the Virginia suburbs.

The protagonist's best friend, Razumikhin, seems a Big Ten frat-house buddy, his sister Dunya an efficient airline purser, his mother a sitcom boob. As Raskolnikov's relentless official pursuer Porfiry, Richard Bauer is such a fount of jokey vocal and physical tics that his performance is better watched (and far scarier) in shadow than in the flesh. Thanks to Arena's precise execution of the director's audio and visual stagecraft, *Crime and Punishment* still remains vivid to the ears, eyes, and intellect—but without the spectrum of feeling that the proper performances would provide, it is emotionally dead.

The fault isn't necessarily with the individual actors. It's not for nothing that Moscow's legendary state-supported theaters have lengthy rehearsal schedules that budgets don't allow in the United States. Perhaps with more time in Washington, Mr. Lyubimov might have found or created the ensemble his work demands: He might have shaped a vital company to his own esthetic personality instead of having just dropped in and out of an existing, clashing company for a single production. Now

Mr. Lyubimov is scheduled to move on to projects in Cambridge and Chicago, following the freelance career required of most directors in the American theater. While one is grateful that this brilliant Soviet exile is opening new doors on our stages, his work is no less susceptible to mutilation than our own artists' when the doors revolve too fast.

≡ *Reviewing this play thrust me into an idiotic brouhaha with politics that might baffle even Washington.*

Crime and Punishment *was opening the same night as the Broadway debut of* Sweet Sue, *a romantic comedy starring Mary Tyler Moore and written by A. R. Gurney, and I argued to my editors that Lyubimov's American debut was the more newsworthy opening, however good* Sweet Sue *might turn out to be. (Not very, I would later learn.) The editors agreed— as did those of the* Times's *rival papers,* The Wall Street Journal *and* The Washington Post, *both of which were giving major opening-night coverage to the Lyubimov—and so I reviewed* Crime and Punishment *while another* Times *critic, Mel Gussow, reviewed* Sweet Sue. *This was a change in policy because the* Times *was for the first time saying that a Broadway opening did not automatically get dibs on the paper's first-string critic over any other play that was opening the same night. This prompted the Dramatists Guild to protest angrily that the* Times *was slighting American playwrights in favor of dead Russians. But there was no turning back, and the* Times's *first-string critics now routinely delegate Broadway openings to others if there are more newsworthy openings Off Broadway or out of town.*

Meanwhile, Lyubimov's uneasy Washington debut would subsequently be echoed by other Russian directors who came to America. Both Boris Morozov's production of Zoya's Apartment *at Circle in the Square in New York and Oleg Yefremov's staging of* Ivanov *with William Hurt at the Yale Repertory Theatre were in part done in by the visitors' unfamiliarity with American actors.*

HUNTING COCKROACHES
Manhattan Theatre Club, March 4, 1987

Hunting *Cockroaches,* the new Janusz Glowacki comedy at the Manhattan Theatre Club, is a Polish reverie about the American dream—but it begins with the funniest Shakespearean nightmare since Jack Benny played Poland's foremost Hamlet in *To Be or Not to Be.* Dianne Wiest, dressed in white nightgown and socks, emerges from the shadows of a Lower East Side flat to deliver Lady Macbeth's sleepwalking soliloquy in a thick Eastern European accent. Ms. Wiest is cast as a Polish émigré actress named Anka, and she wants us to see why her performance won awards in Warsaw. She also wants to demonstrate why there are no roles for her in New York. "They say I have an awful accent," she says. Then she looks into the audience, curls her face into an imploring smile, and inquires, "Do I?"

She does, of course, but who would hurt her feelings by saying so? It's typical of Ms. Wiest's priceless star turn that Anka's fractured English, hilarious as it is, never descends into burlesque; Anka is too warm and genuine to invite mockery. Long a valued stage performer, Ms. Wiest seems to have come into her own in her recent film assignments in Woody Allen's *Hannah and Her Sisters* and *Radio Days*. Under Arthur Penn's direction in *Hunting Cockroaches,* she lets go as she never has in the theater. Forever flying about in her nightgown, her arms in Isadora Duncan–like extensions, Ms. Wiest's uninhibited, unabashedly actressy Anka is a far more galvanizing exemplar of freedom than the ubiquitous Statue of Liberty souvenirs in her tenement apartment. If she can't wow New York with her Lady Macbeth, then she'll model herself on the city's wheeler-dealers or street people or even its predatory park pigeons—any role she can find that might help teach her and her husband Jan (Ron Silver) how to survive in the "strange country" they have called home for three impoverished years.

Like Mr. Glowacki, whose *Cinders* was produced at the Public Theater in 1984, Jan is a writer who was driven West during Poland's post-Solidarity crackdown. *Hunting Cockroaches* takes the form of a sleepless night in which Jan and Anka pop frantically in and out of bed, worrying about the friends they left behind and their prospects in the city outside. In addition to the eternal search for literary contacts and rent money, Jan's current frustrations include his inability to find anything to write about in his adopted country. It isn't a problem that Mr. Glowacki shares; in *Hunting Cockroaches,* the playwright has not only found a fertile subject but also wedded it to an inventive yet unpretentious theatrical form.

Indeed, the evening's form is its content. When Anka and Jan aren't complaining about their past indignations, present insomnia, or future options, they are interrupted by dream sequences that erupt full-blown from their large, Oblomovian bed. Some of the dreams are memories of repression in Poland, others are of such lesser New York indignities as a neighborhood wino or a showbiz agent. While Mr. Glowacki uses these sketches to make some glancing analogies—an American immigration officer's "interview" is likened to a secret-police interrogation—he's too imaginative a writer to settle for simplistic political equations. In the very style of the play's hallucinations, we find a complex contrast between Eastern European and American literary esthetics—and that revealing disparity comes to represent the huge, if not insurmountable, cultural gulf that Jan and Anka must now learn to span.

No wonder Mr. Glowacki invokes cockroaches in his title. In Eastern Europe, a cockroach can express the nightmarish anxieties of writers like Kafka. In New York, cockroaches are not surreal metaphors—they're real insects who must be hunted down and stamped out. The dream sequences of *Hunting Cockroaches* swing accordingly in tone between the Kafkaesque and the naturalistic, just as the characters must adjust from the Kafkaesque state they left behind to the more pragmatic, materialistic mores of middle-class Manhattan. To succeed in America, Anka and Jan may have to exchange their hard-won, historically rooted, fabulist view of existence (and art) for the new world's more practical imperatives of self-promotion, pest control, and the creation of salable work.

Mr. Glowacki never stops searching for clever ways to weave this conflict into his comedy's fabric. His playful display of clashing cultures extends even to a comparison of Old and New World maps: After observing that the national boundaries of Europe "twist and turn and twitch like worms in a can," Jan looks at the bricklike configuration of the western United States and concludes, "That's what you call a neat job." Perhaps more surprisingly, Mr. Glowacki and his translator, Jadwiga Kosicka, also have a sharp ear for the uptown fast track to which their immigrants aspire. Whether the Polish characters are speculating about what might constitute a commercial Broadway play about immigration (it sounds like *Rags*) or fending off the self-serving compassion of Park Avenue liberals (perfectly embodied by Joan Copeland and Paul Sparer), the lines hit our homes as well as theirs.

Not every scene is equal: A few minor roles (though not those played by Reathel Bean and Larry Block) are colorlessly acted. Mr. Silver's performance, always charming and eventually full-blown in its farcical despair, sometimes suffers from accent slippage. But these are minor lapses in Mr. Penn's lithe staging—which, like Heidi Landesman's set, seems to float as the dreamy characters do between vastly different states of civilization and mind. Eventually, author and director alike merge the two worlds into an original, unified one. Ms. Wiest's Anka, her accent still unassimilated, finally shelves her identity as Warsaw's foremost Shakespearean actress to try and make it in the all-American profession of stand-up comedian. *Hunting Cockroaches*, without repressing any of its author's Polish nightmares, follows suit by metamorphosing into a quintessentially brash, not to mention delightful, New York play.

THE KNIFE
PUBLIC THEATER, MARCH II, 1987

With the possible exception of the Public Theater audience that's watching him, there's no one gloomier in town right now than Mandy Patinkin in *The Knife*. From the opening number of this new, all-sung English musical, the actor is in a funk so thick one could cut it with a hacksaw. As a lyric has it, Mr. Patinkin is "lost at sea," and the question is why. Perhaps he is down because the lighting is. Or maybe he's defeated by the phalanxes of performers that keep marching to and fro with a solemnity that makes a Greek chorus seem as frivolous as a conga line. Or is it the confusion of locale? While the program states that *The Knife* is set in Winchester, England, no one on stage speaks with an English accent. It can't be easy pretending to be "lost at sea" when you're not sure which hemisphere the sea is in.

Yet eventually David Hare, the author of the evening's book, and Tim Rose Price, the lyricist, do get around to providing a motive for their protagonist's melancholia. The motive proves to be unusual, at least by musical-theater standards, but odder still is its delayed revelation. Mr. Patinkin—whose character, Peter, has not been identified as a waiter—is suddenly found delivering a room-service order to an airline hostess in a hotel room. "From the way you looked at me," sings the stewardess (Mary Elizabeth Mastrantonio), "you could be a woman." Peter is so taken with this suggestion that he decides then and there to seek a sex-change operation—and never mind waiting around for a tip.

One would like to report that the clouds of depression and confusion lift thereafter, but the only thing that rises in *The Knife* is the pitch of Nick Bicat's attractive music for the hero-cum-heroine. Mr. Hare, the fine English playwright who has brought wit to subjects as serious as Britain's postwar disillusionment (*Plenty*) and the aspirations of the third world (*A Map of the World*), seems to be stymied when confronting the equally fascinating (if less impersonal) topic of transsexuality. He and Mr. Rose Price—with Mr. Patinkin following suit—substitute intellectualizing for thought, murkiness of characterization for the mysteries of behavior. How can a musical dramatize a man's choice of sexual identity if its creators can't bring themselves to make such mundane choices as the identity of his profession and the location of his home?

In lieu of the specific details that might illuminate Peter and draw us into his rending predicament, the writers indulge in remote, highfalutin metaphors. When Mr. Patinkin tells us what he feels, he doesn't sing of masculinity or femininity or sexuality or family but of textbook Freudian water imagery—oceans and swimming pools. The surgeon who performs the operation puts aside matters of medical practice and ethics to contemplate the apparently symbolic "colored patterns" of windows. Couples falling in and out of love speak less of romance and anger than of seedlings and dancing shadows. (The shadows, by the way, are the only dancers in this musical.)

When the libretto does eschew its fuzzy abstractions for concrete drama, it either embraces clichés or strains credulity. For all the authors' condemnations of sexist men, they patronizingly present Peter's deserted wife (Cass Morgan) as a stereotyped matron, complete with buttoned-up cardigan sweaters and windup tots out of *The Sound of Music*. The stewardess, through no fault of the exquisite Ms. Mastrantonio, makes no sense whatsoever. Her alternately affectionate and antagonistic relationship with Peter has less to do with her emotions—or with Peter's gender at any given moment—than with the mechanical plot formulas of old-time woman-meets-unavailable-man musicals.

By using characters to illustrate conceits rather than examining its people from within, *The Knife* inevitably becomes as chilly and clinical as its title. At times, Mr. Hare and company also invite damaging comparisons between Stephen Sondheim musicals and this pretentious derivative—not only with the casting of Mr. Patinkin (lately of *Sunday in the Park with George* and the concert *Follies*) but also with songs that wanly recall the barber's erotic aria about his knife in *Sweeney Todd* and a trio for manhandled stewardesses in *Company*. The similarly imitative finale of *The Knife*, a reconciliation duet for son and female father, has none of the emotional heft of its prototype in the breakthrough musical about a son and homosexual father, William Finn's *March of the Falsettos*.

Such is the smug, right-minded tone of *The Knife* that its few instances of originality—notably, paired comic songs contrasting homosexual and heterosexual chauvinism—come off flatter than they might in a friskier context. Mr. Hare, who can be an inspired director of his own work, harms his cause this time by staging a large-cast musical as if it were a three-character play with extras. The static production's most animated fixture is a wedge-shaped platform, right out of London's current musical *Chess*, that arbitrarily elevates and sinks during the glaringly extraneous interludes (among them a lengthy Act 1 choir recital contrived mainly to introduce a secondary Act 2 character).

Although most of the high-caliber supporting players are wasted, Ms. Morgan adds welcome conviction to the drab wife's one extended musical turn. Ms. Mastrantonio is such a truthful actress and powerful singer that she makes her big Act 2 ballad ignite in spite of its baffling, crypto-poetic sentiments. Mr. Bicat's accomplished score—which falters only when it panders to conventional pop and Broadway tastes—is expertly served as well by the strings and woodwinds of Chris Walker's lush orchestrations and by the star's remarkably wide-ranging voice. But those looking for Mr. Patinkin's range as an actor—let alone for the tour de force Vanessa Redgrave brought to the television fictionalization of Renée Richards's story—will be disappointed. In Mr. Patinkin's Peter, as in the rest of the musical, the only dramatic difference between being a man and a woman is a costume. By dulling the sharp human distinctions it intended to explode, *The Knife* draws etiolated literary analogies instead of blood.

LES MISÉRABLES
Broadway Theatre, March 13, 1987

If anyone doubts that the contemporary musical theater can flex its atrophied muscles and yank an audience right out of its seats, he need look no further than the Act 1 finale of *Les Misérables*.

At that point in the gripping pop opera at the Broadway, the strands of narrative culled from Victor Hugo's novel of early-nineteenth-century France intertwine in a huge undulating tapestry. The unjustly hounded fugitive Jean Valjean (Colm Wilkinson) is once more packing his bags for exile on the "never-ending road to Calvary," even as his eternal pursuer, the police inspector Javert (Terrence Mann), plots new malevolent schemes. The young lovers Marius and Cosette are exchanging tearful farewells while Marius's unrequited admirer, Eponine, mourns her own abandonment. And everywhere in the Paris of 1832 is the whisper of insurrection, as revolutionary students prepare to mount the barricade.

Were *Les Misérables* unfolding as a novel—or in one of its many film adaptations—these events would be relayed sequentially, or through literary or cinematic crosscutting. But in the musical theater at its most resourceful, every action can occur on stage at once. Such is the thunderous coup that brings down the Act 1 curtain. The opera-minded composer Claude-Michel Schönberg, having earlier handed each character a gorgeous theme, now brings them all into an accelerating burst of counterpoint titled "One Day More." The set designer John Napier and lighting designer David Hersey peel back layer after layer of shadow—and a layer of the floor as well—to create the illusion of a sprawling, multilayered Paris on the brink of upheaval. Most crucially, the directors Trevor Nunn and John Caird choreograph the paces of their players on a revolving stage so that spatial relationships mirror both human relationships and the pressing march of history.

The ensuing fusion of drama, music, character, design, and movement is what links this English adaptation of a French show to the highest tradition of modern Broadway musical production. One can hardly watch the Act 1 finale without thinking of the star-crossed lovers and rival gangs preparing for the rumble in the "Tonight" quintet of *West Side Story*—or of the revolving-stage dispersal of Tevye's shtetl following the pogrom in *Fiddler on the Roof*. In *Les Misérables*, Mr. Nunn and Mr. Caird have wedded the sociohistorical bent, unashamed schmaltz, and Jerome Robbins staging techniques from those two American classics with the distinctive directorial style they've developed on their own at the Royal Shakespeare Company. This production is the Nunn-Caird *Nicholas Nickleby* gone gloriously showbiz—which is to say, with conviction, inspiration, and taste.

The evening may not appeal to those enraptured by the 1,300-page edition of Hugo. The musical thinks nothing of condensing chapters of exposition or philosophical debate into a single quatrain or unambiguous confrontation; encyclopedic digressions and whole episodes are thrown out. Unlike *Nicholas Nickleby,* which slavishly attempted to regurgitate its entire source, *Les Misérables* chooses sweeping and hurtling motion over the savoring of minute details. That artistic decision, however arguable, is in keeping with the difference between Hugo and Dickens as writers, not to mention the distinction between musicals and plays as theatrical forms.

While facts and psychological nuances are lost and even the plot is often relegated to a program synopsis, the thematic spirit of the original is preserved. Sequence after sequence speaks of Hugo's compassion for society's outcasts and his faith in God's offer of redemption. When the poor Fantine is reduced to "making money in her sleep," her downtrodden fellow prostitutes are apotheosized in golden light as their predatory clients circle in menacing shadows. When the story's action moves from the provinces to Paris, two hulking wooden piles of domestic bric-a-brac converge to form an abstract representation of a mean slum, bordered on every side by the shuttered windows of a city coldly shunning its poor.

In a subsequent and dazzling transition, the towers tilt to form an enormous barricade. Later still, the barricade twirls in mournful silence to become a charnel house—*Guernica* reimagined as a Dada sculpture—crammed with the splayed corpses of a revolution that failed.

Except for that uprising's red flag, Mr. Napier's designs, all encased in a dark, beclouded prison of a proscenium, are drained of color. *Les Misérables* may be lavish, but its palette, like its noblest characters, is down-to-earth—dirty browns and cobblestone grays, streaked by Mr. Hersey with the smoky light that filters down to the bottom of the economic heap. The proletarian simplicity of the design's style masks an incredible amount of theatrical sophistication. In one three-dimensional zoom-lens effect, Valjean's resolution of a crisis of conscience is accompanied by the sudden materialization of the courtroom where the moral question raised in his song ("Who Am I?") must be answered in deed. *Les Misérables* eventually takes us from the stars where Inspector Javert sets his metaphysical perorations to the gurgling sewers inhabited by the parasitic innkeeper, Thenardier—and in one instance even simulates a character's suicidal fall through much of that height.

Mr. Schönberg's profligately melodious score, sumptuously orchestrated by John Cameron to straddle the eras of harpsichord and synthesizer, mixes madrigals with rock and evokes composers as diverse as Bizet (for the laborers) and Weill (for their exploiters). Motifs are recycled for ironic effect throughout, allowing the story's casualties to haunt the grief-stricken survivors long after their deaths. The resourceful lyrics—written by the onetime London drama critics Herbert Kretzmer and James Fenton, from the French of Alain Boublil and Jean-Marc Natel—can be as sentimental as Hugo in translation. Yet the libretto has been sharpened since London, and it is the edginess of the cleverest verses that prevents the Thenardiers' oompah-pah number, "Master of the House," from sliding into *Oliver!*

It's New York's good fortune that Mr. Wilkinson has traveled here with his commanding London performance as Valjean intact. An actor of pugilistic figure and dynamic voice, he is the heroic everyman the show demands at its heart—convincingly brawny, Christ-like without being cloying, enraged by injustice, paternal with children. Mr. Wilkinson anchors the show from his first solo, in which he runs away from his identity as paroled prisoner 20601 with a vengeance that burns his will into the inky void around him. He is symbiotically matched by Mr. Mann's forceful Javert, who at first acts with his sneering lower lip but soon gains shading in the soliloquy that passionately describes the authoritarian moral code driving him to stalk the hero obsessively for seventeen years.

Though uniformly gifted as singers, the American supporting cast does not act with the consistency of its West End predecessors. Randy Graff delivers Fantine's go-for-the-throat "I Dreamed a Dream" like a Broadway belter handed a showstopper rather than a pathetic woman in ruins. David Bryant, as Marius, brings fervor to a touching hymn to dead comrades ("Empty Chairs at Empty Tables"), but not before he's proved a narcissistic romantic lead. Jennifer Butt plays the funny but cruel Mme. Thenardier as if she were the toothlessly clownish orphanage matron of *Annie*.

Other roles fare better. Frances Ruffelle, the production's second London émigrée, is stunning as the bedraggled Eponine: She's an angel with a dirty face and an unrelenting rock balladeer's voice. Leo Burmester's moldy-looking Thenardier really metamorphoses into the vicious, dog-eat-dog social carnivore his lyrics claim him to be. Judy Kuhn's lovely Cosette and Michael Maguire's noble rebel, Enjolras, are also first-rate. Donna Vivino, the young Cosette, and Braden Danner, the urchin Gavroche, tower over most child actors, however diminutively.

That *Les Misérables* easily overrides its lesser performers, candied romantic tableaux, and early Act 2 languors is a testament to the ingenuity of the entire construction. This show isn't about individuals, or even the ensemble, so much as about how actors and music and staging meld with each other and with the soul of its source. The transfiguration is so complete that by evening's end, the company need simply march forward from the stage's black depths into a hazy orange dawn to summon up Hugo's unflagging faith in tomorrow's better world. The stirring sentiments belong to hallowed nineteenth-century literature, to be sure, but the fresh charge generated by this *Misérables* has everything to do with the electrifying showmanship of the twentieth-century musical.

≡ *This show—still thriving in London and on Broadway in 1998—even survived a public-relations fiasco a decade into its Broadway run when its management conceded that the production was tired and replaced most of its cast.*

STARLIGHT EXPRESS
GERSHWIN THEATRE, MARCH 16, 1987

In a full-page program note, the composer Andrew Lloyd Webber modestly explains that he conceived his new musical, *Starlight Express,* as an entertainment "event" for children who love trains. Over two numbing hours later, you may find yourself wondering exactly whose children he has in mind. A confusing jamboree of piercing noise, routine roller-skating, misogyny, and Orwellian special effects, *Starlight Express* is the perfect gift for the kid who has everything except parents.

The high-tech scenic environment, designed by John Napier, is something to see, if only at intermission. A three-level Erector set of simulated train tracks, the design recalls a previous Gershwin Theatre occupant, *Sweeney Todd*—had that production been dipped in pink and purple bubble gum. The principal feature of Mr. Napier's hydraulic construction is a huge steel-and-Plexiglas suspension bridge that twirls and lowers, flashing like a large disco chandelier. Beware of that bridge. Its descent usually indicates that it's time for the cast to skate around in circles until theatergoers of all ages surrender their appetite for a post-performance snack.

According to Richard Stilgoe's libretto, these bouts of skating are "heats" in a "great race" to determine "the fastest locomotive in the world." The prize is the least costly prop on stage—a silver dollar. But who are the competitors? At first, the audience is introduced to rival trains from various nations (each presented according to ethnic stereotype)—and yet those elaborate identifications are soon forgotten as we're asked to concentrate on Rusty (a steam train), Electra (an electric train), and Greaseball (a diesel). The rules of the race are equally baffling, and so are the arbitrary, anticlimactic results. As chaotically choreographed by Arlene Phillips, the heats of *Starlight Express* make television's old roller derbies seem as orderly as a Rockettes kick line.

In the London production of *Starlight,* there is at least the novelty of being surrounded by the skaters, who circle the entire auditorium. In New York, the tracks extend only a few rows in front of the proscenium; for most of the audience, the experience is about as involving as standing on the sidelines while other people take one of the lesser rides at Disneyland. There have been other counterproductive alterations in *Starlight Express* for Broadway as well. The show has been "Americanized" by the plastering of signs like KALAMAZOO and CINCINNATI on Mr. Napier's set. There are some new musical arrangements, which, along with the amplification, succeed in making a theatrical extravaganza sound as if it were piped in from a Far Rockaway junior prom.

As in Mr. Lloyd Webber's *Cats,* the songs are intended to personify the different breeds of train. To this end, Mr. Stilgoe, who is not to be confused with T. S. Eliot, has written sporadically audible lyrics like "Freight is great" and "Woo-woo, nobody does it like a steam train!" The score is sadder still. Instead of aspiring to his usual Puccini variations, Mr. Lloyd Webber has gone "funky," English style, by writing pastiche versions of

American pop music—with an emphasis on blues, gospel, and rap. Short of a Lennon Sisters medley of the Supremes' greatest hits, soul music couldn't get much more soulless than this.

The show's patronizing attitude toward black pop is matched by its view of women. Grizabella, the top female cat of *Cats,* is a prostitute, and so *Starlight Express* features Belle, "a sleeping car with a heart of gold." But all the women are subservient carriages vying for the favors of mostly abusive male locomotives—with only an androgynous male caboose occupying lower social status. This hierarchical scheme is reinforced by Ms. Phillips's muscle-flexing choreography, seemingly inspired by male physical-culture magazines, and by the robotic costumes, which emphasize codpieces for the men and tight corsets and miniskirts for their groupies.

Like other Lloyd Webber projects, from *Joseph and the Amazing Technicolor Dreamcoat* to *Cats* and *Requiem,* this one tries to mitigate such vulgarity by wrapping itself in the deity. In fact, the title of *Starlight Express* alludes to God, and when His spirit appears in Act 2, Mr. Napier and the lighting designer David Hersey are inspired to achieve the one effect worthy of their work in *Les Misérables.* A nocturnal celestial blur suddenly obliterates the dehumanizing metallic harshness of the set and, for that brief instant, renders the show transporting.

Otherwise, this is an evening about the prevention of traffic accidents, and it has been directed accordingly by Trevor Nunn. No outstanding skaters, dancers, or actors surface in his cast, but the stronger pop voices belong to Greg Mowry, Reva Rice, Jane Krakowski, and Steve Fowler. The company's youngest and most vocal performer is Braden Danner, playing a little boy who tries to impose order and drum up suspense by reciting a continuous play-by-play commentary through the public-address system. The narration, however, has been recorded on tape. As the *Playbill* explains, Braden "is currently appearing live as Gavroche in *Les Misérables*"—the living proof that kids are not as gullible as the adults behind *Starlight Express* seem to think.

≣ *Trevor Nunn was apparently happy with the ticket sales of* Cats *and* Les Misérables, *since he didn't contact me, as he did after* All's Well That Ends Well, *to suggest how I might include more promotional copy in my review. But I did hear from him several weeks after the opening of* Starlight Express. *He pointed out to me that the London press embraced* Starlight *with superlatives, adding that the London critics were in his view part of the British theater's collaborative process. This was, if nothing else, an accurate statement of the difference between two journalistic cultures; Lon-*

*don critics are often chummy with their subjects whereas American jour-
nalists in any field tend to keep at arm's length from those they cover, believing that the reader comes first.*

Noting that Starlight Express *received standing ovations every night, he
expressed further happiness about hearing the perennial rumor that I was
leaving my job. No such luck—for me or for him. I would still have to review his dreadful productions of two other Broadway megamusicals,* Chess
and Aspects of Love, *though this would be mitigated somewhat by his fine
stagings of* Heartbreak House *and* Arcadia, *which I covered in England.*

*What offended me about Nunn's letter, however, was his denigration of
the New York theater—"a desolate patch [as he put it] where very little
grows except hardy annuals and whatever is fertilized by money." Coming
from the director of* Cats, Starlight Express, *and* Les Mis, *all of which
were fertilized by much money, quite a bit of it ending up in his own
pocket, his denigration of big-budget musicals in the same letter that he
defended them struck me as hypocritical and cynical even by show-
business standards. His dismissal of the rest of New York theater was outrageous, and I urged him to see* Fences, The Colored Museum, Coastal
Disturbances, *and* The Widow Claire, *among other recent openings. I
doubt he did, and I never heard from him again.*

Starlight Express *eventually found its ideal home—as a long-term tenant at the Las Vegas Hilton.*

FENCES
46TH STREET THEATRE, MARCH 27, 1987

To hear his wife tell it, Troy Maxson, the middle-aged Pittsburgh
sanitation worker at the center of *Fences,* is "so big" that he fills up
his tenement house just by walking through it. Needless to say, that description could also apply to James Earl Jones, the actor who has found
what may be the best role of his career in August Wilson's new play, at the
46th Street Theatre. But the remarkable stature of the character—and of
the performance—is not a matter of sheer size. If Mr. Jones's Troy is a
mountainous man prone to tyrannical eruptions of rage, he is also a dignified, delicate figure capable of cradling a tiny baby, of pleading gravely
to his wife for understanding, of standing still to stare death unflinchingly
in the eye. A black man, a free man, a descendant of slaves, a menial laborer, a father, a husband, a lover—Mr. Jones's Troy embraces all the contradictions of being black and male and American in his time.

That time is 1957—three decades after the period of Mr. Wilson's previous and extraordinary *Ma Rainey's Black Bottom*. For blacks like Troy in the industrial North of *Fences*, social and economic equality is more a legal principle than a reality: The Maxsons' slum neighborhood, a panorama of grimy brick and smokestack-blighted sky in James D. Sandefur's eloquent design, is a cauldron of busted promises, waiting to boil over. The conflagration is still a decade away—the streetlights burn like the first sparks of distant insurrection—so Mr. Wilson writes about the pain of an extended family lost in the wilderness of de facto segregation and barren hope.

It speaks of the power of the play—and of the cast assembled by the director, Lloyd Richards—that Mr. Jones's patriarch doesn't devour the rest of *Fences* so much as become the life force that at once nurtures and stunts the characters who share his blood. The strongest countervailing player is his wife, Rose, luminously acted by Mary Alice. Rose is a quiet woman who, as she says, "planted herself" in the "hard and rocky" soil of her husband. But she never bloomed: Marriage brought frustration and betrayal in equal measure with affection.

Even so, Ms. Alice's performance emphasizes strength over self-pity, open anger over festering bitterness. The actress finds the spiritual quotient in the acceptance that accompanies Rose's love for a scarred, profoundly complicated man. It's rare to find a marriage of any sort presented on stage with such balance—let alone one in which the husband has fathered children by three different women. Mr. Wilson grants both partners the right to want to escape the responsibilities of their domestic drudgery while affirming their respective claims to forgiveness.

The other primary relationship of *Fences* is that of Troy to his son Cory (Courtney B. Vance)—a promising seventeen-year-old football player being courted by a college recruiter. Troy himself was once a baseball player in the Negro Leagues—early enough to hit homers off Satchel Paige, too early to benefit from Jackie Robinson's breakthrough—and his bitter, long-ago disappointment leads him to decree a different future for his son. But while Troy wants Cory to settle for a workhorse trade guaranteeing a weekly paycheck, the boy resists. The younger Maxson is somehow convinced that the dreams of his black generation need not end in the city's mean alleys with the carting of white men's garbage.

The struggle between father and son over conflicting visions of black identity, aspirations, and values is the play's narrative fulcrum, and a paradigm of violent divisions that would later tear apart a society. As written, the conflict is also a didactic one, reminiscent of old-fashioned plays, black and white, about disputes between first-generation American parents and their rebellious children.

In *Ma Rainey*—set at a blues recording session—Mr. Wilson's characters were firecrackers exploding in a bottle, pursuing jagged theatrical riffs reflective of their music and of their intimacy with the African American experience that gave birth to that music. The relative tameness of *Fences*—with its laboriously worked-out titular metaphor, its slow-fused Act 1 exposition—is as much an expression of its period as its predecessor was of the hotter twenties. Intentionally or not—and perhaps to the satisfaction of those who found the more esthetically daring *Ma Rainey* too "plotless"—Mr. Wilson invokes the clunkier dramaturgy of Odets, Miller, and Hansberry on this occasion.

Such formulaic theatrical tidiness, while exasperating at times, proves a minor price for the gripping second act (strengthened since the play's Yale debut in 1985) and for the scattered virtuoso passages throughout. Like *Ma Rainey* and the latest Wilson work seen at Yale (*Joe Turner's Come and Gone*, also promised for New York), *Fences* leaves no doubt that Mr. Wilson is a major writer, combining a poet's ear for vernacular with a robust sense of humor (political and sexual), a sure instinct for crackling dramatic incident, and a passionate commitment to a great subject.

Mr. Wilson continues to see history as fully as he sees his characters. In one scene, Troy and his oldest friend (played with brimming warmth by Ray Aranha) weave an autobiographical "talking blues"—a front-porch storytelling jaunt from the antebellum plantation through the preindustrial urban South, jail, and northward migration. *Fences* is pointedly bracketed by two disparate wars that swallowed up black manhood, and, as always with Mr. Wilson, is as keenly cognizant of its characters' bonds to Africa, however muted here, as their bondage to white America. One hears the cadences of a centuries-old heritage in Mr. Jones's efforts to shout down the devil. It is a frayed scrap of timeless blues singing, unpretty but unquenchable, that proves the overpowering cathartic link among the disparate branches of the Maxson family tree.

Under the exemplary guidance of Mr. Richards—whose staging falters only in the awkward scene transitions—the entire cast is impressive, including Frankie R. Faison in the problematic (but finally devastating) role of a brain-damaged, horn-playing uncle named Gabriel, and Charles Brown, as a Maxson son who falls into the sociological crack separating the play's two principal generations. As Cory, Courtney B. Vance is not only formidable in challenging Mr. Jones to a psychological (and sometimes physical) kill-or-be-killed battle for supremacy but also seems to grow into Troy's vocal timbre and visage by the final scene. Like most sons, Mr. Vance just can't elude "the shadow" of his father, no matter how hard he tries. Such is the long shadow Mr. Jones's father casts in

Fences that theatergoers from all kinds of families may find him impossible to escape.

SUNDAY ESSAY: THE EMPIRE STRIKES BACK
MARCH 29, 1987

A New York theatergoer stricken by an inferiority complex in London could perennially take solace in the one American beachhead along the West End—the musical. For all its classical glories, London has long been dependent on New York for that levitating synthesis of song, dance, drama, and performance that is Broadway's one undisputed contribution to world theater. Let Yankee tourists queue up for the Royal Shakespeare Company or National Theatre; the hungry locals packed the Drury Lane in Covent Garden to see replicas of Broadway entertainments stretching chronologically from *Oklahoma!,* which spread the Rodgers and Hammerstein esthetic revolution immediately after World War II, to the current *42nd Street,* now in its third West End year.

The replicas weren't and aren't always of the highest New York quality—particularly after the imported American leads were succeeded by less fleet British performers in mid-run—but they still tended to tower above most English competition. Given the choice, who wouldn't prefer to see an approximate London facsimile of *A Funny Thing Happened on the Way to the Forum* over some contemporaneous English musical clodhopper like *Charlie Girl?* The English understood snazzy Broadway showmanship about as well as Margaret Dumont got Groucho Marx's jokes.

Now, however, the world seems to be turning upside down. New York has not produced a single hit musical of its own this season, and no further American musicals are even contemplated for production by summer. The transatlantic jet stream of talent has dramatically reversed direction. Instead of creating musicals that might be exported to the West End, Broadway is frantically mounting duplicates of London hits— some of which star dancing or singing English actors, such as Robert Lindsay and Colm Wilkinson, of the highest caliber. *Les Misérables,* an English adaptation of a French spectacle, and *Me and My Girl,* a retooled revival of a 1937 London favorite previously unknown to New York, are among the season's most popular productions with both the critics and the public.

According to the trade paper *Variety,* one of every three Broadway ticket-buyers in mid-March was attending one of those two shows or two other London musical imports, Andrew Lloyd Webber's *Cats* and *Starlight Express.* Of twenty-two attractions on Broadway, these four musicals were the only productions not reduced to dumping unsold tickets at the half-price booth. The phenomenon has spread to Off Broadway's nonprofit theaters as well: On the eve of the openings of *Les Misérables* and *Starlight,* Joseph Papp's New York Shakespeare Festival, long a bastion of American theatrical chauvinism, staged the premiere of an elaborate English musical, *The Knife.*

For the New York theater, the rise of London as a musical-theater capital is as sobering a specter as the awakening of the Japanese automobile industry was for Detroit. Whether it is a real cultural phenomenon or merely a passing series of coincidences is another question. One could argue that the new London musical is a triumph of merchandising and of a handful of English artists, frequently abetted by Americans, rather than a significant and lasting artistic breakthrough. Of the four London musicals currently on Broadway—and the two scheduled for next season, *The Phantom of the Opera* and *Chess*—all but one (*Me and My Girl*) rely on the composer Andrew Lloyd Webber, the director Trevor Nunn, or both. It can also be argued that when Broadway lost the independent producers who once nurtured and assembled its major musicals—starting with David Merrick—it was inevitable that shrewd English impresarios would fill the vacuum by default.

But a case can be made that English musicals have improved, in part by expanding upon the brightest Broadway innovations (as in the staging of *Les Misérables*) but also by pursuing original, homegrown theatrical notions, some of which tap into (or pander to) the taste of a younger generation with which the New York commercial theater, to its own peril, has long since lost touch. To appreciate just how much English musicals have—and have not—changed on their way to their new status, one must see today's developments in the context of the last period when London shows were the Broadway rage. That was from roughly 1958 until 1965, when a rapid succession of West End musicals arrived in New York, usually under the Merrick aegis. Two of them, *La Plume de Ma Tante* and *Irma la Douce,* were, like *Les Misérables,* anglicized Parisian works. The others included literary adaptations in the reigning American style of *My Fair Lady* (*Oliver!, Pickwick*) and the more Brechtian experiments of Joan Littlewood (*Oh, What a Lovely War*) and Anthony Newley and Leslie Bricusse (*Stop the World—I Want to Get Off*).

The all-English musicals of this period were often revised, cut, or strenuously polished for New York, and only *Oliver!* ran as long as two seasons. The 1965 *Half a Sixpence*—a fluffy romantic vehicle for Tommy Steele remarkably similar to *Me and My Girl*—had to be completely revamped by the American director Gene Saks and choreographer Onna White to satisfy the standards of a Broadway audience by then attuned to the high-flying dance-musical standards of the 1964 blockbusters *Hello, Dolly!* and *Fiddler on the Roof*.

Since then, the once-amateurish rank and file of West End musical-theater performers has grown more professional: London now has a much larger supply of competent singers, dancers, and pit musicians than it did only five years ago. But one need merely compare the London and New York editions of *Cats* or *Me and My Girl* to see how inferior West End standards can still be in Broadway song-and-dance skills, once one looks beyond the principal performers.

Nor has the London theater yet produced any choreographers remotely approaching the sophistication of a Jerome Robbins, Gower Champion, Michael Bennett, or Bob Fosse. Gillian Lynne, who provided the routine choreography for *Cats*, was also responsible for the routine choreography of *Pickwick* two decades earlier. *Song & Dance* and *Me and My Girl*, the most dance-oriented of recent English musical imports, had to spruce up their West End songs, direction, and choreography for New York, much as *Half a Sixpence* did so long ago.

Even in the crucial matter of songwriting talent, the West End lags behind. The Broadway scene, however depleted, still boasts many active composers—Stephen Sondheim, Cy Coleman, Jerry Herman, Charles Strouse, John Kander, and Marvin Hamlisch, among others—while the London roster ends with only a couple of fairly obscure names following that of the ubiquitous Mr. Lloyd Webber. Successful as Mr. Lloyd Webber is, his work can't yet be compared seriously with Broadway's best of any period. He's primarily a canny, melodic pastiche artist, and his music has declined sharply since he lost the lyrics of his original collaborator Tim Rice (who parted ways after *Evita*) and T. S. Eliot (the unwitting lyricist of *Cats*).

But it is still Mr. Lloyd Webber, more than anyone, who is responsible for the resurgence of the English musical. This may have less to do with his talent than with his ability to assimilate contemporary, mainstream pop music into his work. While Broadway's mild flirtation with rock petered out soon after the run of *Hair*, Mr. Lloyd Webber kept his eye on the bullets on *Billboard*'s charts. His through-composed scores don't reflect the operetta tradition of Gilbert and Sullivan as much as a watering down of the rock "concept albums" inspired by the Beatles' watershed *Sgt. Pepper's Lonely Hearts Club Band.*

And, beginning with *Jesus Christ Superstar* in 1971, Mr. Lloyd Webber has been mindful of how that music is sold. His musicals are often born as record-industry products—as albums fabricated in the recording studio to promote individual songs before the shows themselves exist. Although Mr. Lloyd Webber's homogenized music may be too lacking in distinctive personality to attract the serious rock fans of David Byrne or Bruce Springsteen or the Broadway-minded admirers of Richard Rodgers or Stephen Sondheim, it has cornered the international marketplace where the middle-of-the-road majority resides between those two camps.

The form is so commercially viable, at least until fashions change again, that it doesn't require Mr. Lloyd Webber to execute it. Any competent purveyor of Europop will do, and so the Swedish rock group Abba's musical wallpaper for *Chess* (with lyrics by Mr. Rice) is indistinguishable from Mr. Lloyd Webber's output.

While Broadway has composers of larger talent, it has yet to attract any who can write in this hugely marketable rock vein. Even the recent pop-music industry recruits to the writing of Broadway songs, Roger Miller (*Big River*) and Rupert Holmes (*Drood*), have styles closer to the less commercial, traditional Broadway sound than that of lowest-common-denominator rock.

Along with Mr. Lloyd Webber's ability to connect with mass taste, the other key to the English musical's new success is its shift in emphasis in musical staging. Unable to compete with Broadway's high-powered choreography, the English musical had to turn elsewhere for kinetic energy. The option chosen was spectacle: If the performers can't dance, why not let the scenery do so instead?

The modern pioneer in this technique was the late English set designer Sean Kenny, who re-created Victorian London in *Oliver!* with mobile constructs of suggestive wooden scaffolding, crowned by a bridge flown in from above. So influential was this inspired Kenny design of a quarter-century ago that it has surfaced with variations in many English and American productions ever since—most notably in the Trevor Nunn–John Caird nonmusical Dickens adaptation for the Royal Shakespeare Company, *Nicholas Nickleby,* and now in that production's offspring, *Les Misérables.*

In retrospect, an even more influential Kenny design may be the one he did for *Blitz,* a subsequent, 1962 collaboration with the author of *Oliver!,* Lionel Bart. In *Blitz*—so costly that not even Mr. Merrick risked transferring it to Broadway—the designer attempted to re-create the Nazi blitzkrieg of London in the West End's Adelphi Theatre. Along with the simulated explosions, the set included a realistic replica of an underground station, with moving subway train.

As Kenny's restrained *Oliver!* design persists in the designer John Napier's imaginative sets for *Nickleby* and *Les Misérables,* so the Disneyland extravaganzas of Kenny's *Blitz* surface in the environmental scenery Mr. Napier has designed for *Cats* and *Starlight Express.* Like *Blitz,* these spectacles are top-heavy with smoke-filled special effects, simulated trains, and all the other toys that a big budget can buy.

As visitors to *Starlight Express* soon discover, hardware, money, and noise are no substitute for inspiration. With its dehumanized look and equally metallic canned sound, *Starlight* is as heavy and remote an evening in its way as pre-electronic English musicals were in theirs. Should *Starlight* fail to draw the audiences needed to turn a profit in New York—it's too early to tell—producers will think twice before spending millions of dollars on transporting similarly heartless high-tech displays from London to Broadway, with or without Lloyd Webber scores and no matter how popular they are with London audiences and critics. (*Starlight* received better reviews than *Les Misérables* in London.) The best hope for the English musical remains the same as that of the American musical—productions in which the showmanship is at the service of emotions, drama, or ideas, not just sensory bombast. What's impressive about *Les Misérables* is how its creators—many of them contributors to the antithetical *Starlight*—use the modern arsenal of musical-theater techniques to convey the very heart of Victor Hugo's novel. Unlike the Lloyd Webber spectacles, *Les Misérables* employs a proscenium set, not an amusement-park "environment," and is stripped of decorative frills (including most colors except for those of ash, dirt, blood, and impoverished, sunless streets).

In one typically stunning transition late in Act 1, the hero Jean Valjean waltzes lovingly with Cosette, the young child he has rescued from abusive foster parents, only to be swept aside by a thunderous burst of music and movement that advances the story's chronology by ten years and fills the stage with the shrieking beggars and grinding horror of nineteenth-century Paris slums. The codirectors, Mr. Nunn and Mr. Caird, may lose the letter of Hugo, but not the writer's intimate perspective on his characters, his narrative drive, or his rage at social injustice.

Still, is *Les Misérables* an indigenously English musical? Hardly. It originated in a much different form in Paris, and its principal authors, Claude-Michel Schönberg (music) and Alain Boublil (book), are Frenchmen, influenced as much by Bizet as by Kurt Weill, the Frank Loesser of

The Most Happy Fella, and, in their use of pop-opera conventions, Mr. Lloyd Webber. The show's dark, early industrial-age *Bleak House* look—from a bridge above to a trapdoor entrance to the sewers below—absorbs not only *Oliver!* and the codirectors' own previous *Nickleby* but also Harold Prince productions of musicals in New York and London, including those of Mr. Sondheim's *Sweeney Todd,* with its similar nineteenth-century characters and themes, and Mr. Lloyd Webber's *Evita.*

Behind the Prince influences, one inevitably finds the staging ideas of Jerome Robbins, with whom Mr. Prince was associated as a producer before his own directorial career began. The electrifying Act 1 finale of *Les Misérables*—in which the full depth of the stage is used to bleed together the contrasting motivations and actions of the individual characters—recalls the staging of the "Tonight" quintet in Mr. Robbins's *West Side Story,* as well as the "Hello Twelve, Hello Thirteen, Hello Love" sequence of Michael Bennett's Robbins-influenced *A Chorus Line.* The central image of *Les Misérables*—that of a paternal, middle-aged peasant talking to God and fleeing from an oppressive society on a revolving turntable—is that of Tevye in Mr. Robbins's *Fiddler on the Roof.*

Such cinematic staging, shiver-inducing in the theater, can only be achieved by a catalytic fusion of all the musical's elements, from orchestration to lighting cues. It has nothing to do with the slavishly "American" showbiz dancing (largely tap) of most English musicals—and, until *Les Misérables,* it has been well beyond London's reach. There must, of course, be more productions of this quality (and more composers, directors, and choreographers to create them) if the West End is to seize the franchise that Broadway has let lapse. But in *Les Misérables* the English have for once beaten the Americans at their own game by mastering the lessons taught by Broadway directors and choreographers from de Mille through Bennett in the decades since *Oklahoma!* Watching the new English hit at the Broadway Theatre, an American theatergoer feels the unmistakable sensation that much more than a turntable is coming full circle.

SAFE SEX
LYCEUM THEATRE, APRIL 6, 1987

Harvey Fierstein, playwright and actor, wants an audience to adore him. In *Torch Song Trilogy,* his breakthrough plays about a professional drag queen, and now in *Safe Sex,* a lumpy trilogy of one-act plays about the AIDS crisis, Mr. Fierstein pushes love—love for himself and, of course, love for all humanity. As a writer, he dreams of a world where everyone gets along: homosexuals and heterosexuals, women and men, adults and children. As a performer, he dreams of holding forth at center stage, getting every laugh with his bullfrog's voice, milking every tear with his wounded, over-the-hill torch singer's gaze.

By writing his own scripts, Mr. Fierstein can guarantee that at least the second of these dreams comes true. In *Safe Sex*, he appears in all but the opening segment, dominating the stage with an alacrity recalling the similarly voluminous and boisterous Zero Mostel. Like Mostel, he gets results. Dressed in a billowing nightshirt, Mr. Fierstein ignites roars of laughter by proclaiming his volatile erotic disposition—"I've got two faucets, hot and cold!"—with a self-mocking bravado worthy of Mae West. He induces tears later on, when, as the bereaved lover of an AIDS casualty, he shares a familial hug with the former wife and son that the dead man also left behind. Structured like *Torch Song Trilogy*—each successive play extends its protagonist's family—*Safe Sex* again hopes to leave us feeling that any character played by the author is the most humorous and generous friend, lover, mother, father, or child that any sensitive person could ever hope to find.

If you found Mr. Fierstein adorable last time around, chances are you'll like him here, too. But one must still ask if this gifted artist's desire for approval—each of this bill's last two plays culminates in a sentimental embrace—really does serve him, the audience, and his devastating subject. *Safe Sex*, which began as a modest workshop production at La Mama this winter, has arrived at Broadway's Lyceum Theatre as a throne-like showcase for its star, burdened with a mostly amateurish supporting cast to keep histrionic competition at bay and a soppy, overblown staging to match the more treacly and self-indulgent excesses of the text. While it would be absurd to suggest that a dramatic treatment of AIDS need be as grim as a clinic, the immediacy of *Safe Sex* is often diffused by Mr. Fierstein's hugging and mugging, both as actor and playwright.

The evening is at its most forceful when its creator's anger burns through his other personas of saint and class clown. The bill's second (and titular) play, a literally seesawing comic squabble between two on-and-off-again lovers, suddenly drops its compulsive joke-making for a monologue describing what the homosexual community has lost and gained from the new heterosexual awareness (and fear) of AIDS. "At last we have safe sex—safe for them," declares Mr. Fierstein at the end of an extraordinary speech describing two decades of American sociosexual history. As he does so, he looks into the audience, his voice and face quivering with rage.

In the closing play, *On Tidy Endings*, Mr. Fierstein is equally powerful when defending his "intangible place" in the history of the partner he had nursed until death. "He died in my arms, not yours!" he screams at his lover's patronizing "first" wife, who, though played with decency by Anne De Salvo, just can't stop herself from appropriating grief that is not primarily her own. Mr. Fierstein forgives her a little later in another beautifully written speech cataloguing his forlorn mementos from the international circuit of clinics and quacks for desperate victims of terminal disease.

The plays' funnier moments also seem to arrive when Mr. Fierstein forsakes his desire to please and lets off steam. The "do's and don'ts" of "safe sex," though serious business, spawn a comic, nostalgic riff about the days when a "broken heart" and "crabs" were among the harsher penalties for lovemaking. Yet for every joke that's to the point there are a half-dozen extraneous one-liners. As the middle play in *Torch Song* sometimes recalled Neil Simon's *Chapter Two,* so the second play this time offers a prefabricated insult duel between a sloppy jock and a prissy homemaker out of *The Odd Couple.* Even the mournful final play takes time out for irrelevant, formulaic jokes about Mr. Fierstein's excess weight ("Even my stretch socks have stretch marks!") and urban gentrification.

Perhaps a tougher director than Eric Concklin could have convinced the author to strip away the evening's theatrical flab. The opening skit—in which Mr. Fierstein elects not to appear, presumably not without reason—is an entirely arch attempt to dramatize the plight of an AIDS-virus carrier in precious poetic incantations that might have been written by a high school personal-hygiene instructor. In the better efforts that follow, Mr. Concklin accentuates the writing's failings with a production that sometimes seems a parody of the mishaps that can befall a play that spares no tasteless expense in "going Broadway."

Not the least of the evening's misguided accoutrements is a cloud-streaked set, designed by John Falabella and bathed in scarlet sunsets by Craig Miller, that seems to place all three plays in the curdled Technicolor heaven of a second-rung MGM musical. In league with Ada Janik's pushily elegiac incidental music, this florid atmosphere sanitizes and perfumes the entire evening—as if the stage had been sprayed with a tank of air freshener. At his most courageous, Mr. Fierstein doesn't need these or any of the evening's other artificial sweeteners. *Safe Sex* finds its life when it lashes out with a ferocity to match the plague.

≡ *I was one of the few left cold by Fierstein's* Torch Song Trilogy, *and I was no fan of his book for* La Cage aux Folles. *This ill-fated venture, another Off (actually Off Off) Broadway show inflated and distorted for Broadway, seemingly propelled him to Hollywood, where he has animated gay stereotypes in entertainments as diverse as* The Simpsons *and* Independence Day.

PYGMALION
PLYMOUTH THEATRE, APRIL 27, 1987

The erratic amusements offered by Broadway's new revival of *Pygmalion* may have only a glancing connection to Shaw's wonderful play, but it would be folly to pretend that they don't exist. Not every day do New Yorkers get to see a precise replica of a London "all star" mounting of a classic—the sort of package that draws busloads of international tourists and British provincials to the Haymarket.

A production like this is not to be confused with the rarefied imports from the Royal Shakespeare Company and National Theatre or, at the other end of the esthetic spectrum, with Broadway's own star assemblages, such as the current *Blithe Spirit*. The entertainment at the Plymouth—from its crazy-quilt assortment of titled and plebian marquee names to its elaborate yet slightly tatty scenery—defines the West End midweek matinee. This is theater to sip Earl Grey tea by.

Those who attend with the proper expectations will be diverted by at least half—the first half—of the unhurried, nearly three-hour-long proceedings. Much of that enjoyment is provided by Peter O'Toole, whose display of star attitude is often commanding even when out of sync with the character of Henry Higgins. Modeling an ever-changing array of bespoke Edwardian tailoring, the tall, reedy actor rules this *Pygmalion* on the grounds of elegance and talent, if not always concentration. Mr. O'Toole has no qualms about making goo-goo eyes directly at the audience, if that's what it takes to keep its attention—and, given that the eyes retain the iridescent blue of *Lawrence of Arabia,* who will complain?

His is a funny, if odd, performance. The intelligence, arrogance, and ill-mannered bullying of Wimpole Street's master phonetician are all accounted for: Mr. O'Toole relishes those moments when Higgins can bark an "Oh, shut up!" at his "deliciously low" pupil, Eliza Doolittle (Amanda Plummer). One also feels the emotional detachment of a man Shaw described as "a confirmed bachelor with a mother fixation." The solitary, almost cadaverous laughter with which Mr. O'Toole brings down the final curtain is not the sentimental chuckling of a secret romantic but the braying triumph of a chilly, cynical intellect.

Such achievements coexist with interludes in which the star seems to drift away. Mr. O'Toole has a habit of tilting a bit from side to side when standing. When he sinks in an armchair to listen to Alfred Doolittle's marital plans during the final act, the actor allows his face to register boredom as well: His glazed-over look is that of a first-class ocean-liner passenger who has grown sick of his card partners three days into a transatlantic crossing. The star's vocal pyrotechnics can also be weird. If Rex Harrison famously "talked" the songs when playing Henry Higgins in *My Fair Lady,* Mr. O'Toole has a tendency to sing the talk. Some of his longer speeches rattle by at considerable speed, all the while running up and down a scale ranging from sonorous baritone to near-falsetto.

The most damaging handicap afflicting this Higgins, however, has nothing to do with Mr. O'Toole's own acting. Ms. Plummer, an impassioned performer in other circumstances, proves to be every bit as miscast in this Shaw comedy as she was in *You Never Can Tell* earlier this season. Her Liza is unbelievable whether spunky or weepy, whether in her Cockney flower-girl guise or in her later Cinderella turn as a well-spoken, ersatz duchess. Only after the heroine achieves her last and most significant metamorphosis—by ceasing to be a "slave" to gentility and seizing her real independence as a woman—does some uncontrived passion seep through. "I only want to be natural," says Liza then, and that's the single occasion when Ms. Plummer is.

Without a credible leading lady prior to that very late point, *Pygmalion* inevitably must collapse during the Higgins-Liza conflicts of Shaw's fourth and fifth acts (divided between Acts 2 and 3 here). But it would be wrong to blame Ms. Plummer's performance alone for the flatter stretches. Joyce Redman, whose regal maternal appearance as Mrs. Higgins is defeated by a spineless characterization, denies Mr. O'Toole another crucial foil. As Liza's father, Sir John Mills gives impeccably spoken yet completely unfunny readings of Doolittle's diatribes about "middle-class morality." There's nothing Falstaffian about Sir John's dustman, and his subsequent leap to respectability proves as undynamic a transformation as the one Ms. Plummer provides in dialectical contrast.

The other performances are all over the map, sometimes pleasingly so. As Higgins's housekeeper, Mrs. Pearce, the diminutive, handsome Dora Bryan reveals her roots as a sparky, longtime English music-hall artist. Lionel Jeffries's quintessential Colonel Pickering is reassuring to a fault; only the color of the tweeds draped over his geniality varies from act to act. The Eynsford Hill mother and daughter (Mary Peach and Kirstie Pooley) are much too willing to prove Higgins's contention that all women "might as well be blocks of wood," while brother Freddy (Osmund Bullock) is a society twit from the rear ranks of the *Me and My Girl* chorus. Even so, neither they nor Ms. Plummer's perfunctory comic delivery can mar the foolproof tea-party scene in which Liza first tries to pass as posh.

Aside from choreographing that farcical apex and taking liberties with Shaw's text, the director, Val May, has principally concerned himself with placating any theatergoers who would rather be at *My Fair Lady*. The curtain rises to trashy recorded music seemingly chosen to mimic the first bars of the musical's overture, and two scenes in succession end with the actors raising their arms in glee as if they had just sung "The Rain in Spain." The intended parallels falter in the physical production. The hideous female costumes of this *Pygmalion* owe nothing to Cecil Beaton, and Douglas Heap's otherwise decent scenic design is marred by Mrs. Higgins's drawing room, a riot of chartreuse that puts the chintzy back into chintz. But such eccentricities, too, are part of the frayed charm of a show that is as authentically English as a Harrod's display window and, at its liveliest, somewhat more animate.

≡ *Living in a small hotel, the Wyndham, for a few weeks while waiting to move into a new apartment, I suddenly discovered that all the principals of* Pygmalion *were staying there, too. As if directing a farce by Feydeau, not Shaw, the astute theater-buff owner kept us separated by several floors.*

LES LIAISONS DANGEREUSES
Music Box Theatre, May 1, 1987

For the Royal Shakespeare Company production of *Les Liaisons Dangereuses*, the stage at the Music Box Theatre has been remodeled into a sex-drenched boudoir of late eighteenth-century France. Signs of reckless carnal abandon are everywhere. Huge linen sheets, rumpled from hectic use, drape the proscenium and boxes. Lacy silk underthings tumble in messy profusion from the hastily slammed drawers of a towering chiffonnier. Tall slatted screens, the better for servants to peep through, cast distorted shadows. All that's missing is a proper regal bed. Instead, there's a constellation of settees and chaise longues: This is an arena for men and women who copulate on the run.

The setting, at once in period and nightmarishly abstracted in Bob Crowley's inspired design, does not belie the action. As readers of

Choderlos de Laclos's 1782 novel know, *Les Liaisons Dangereuses* is an epistolary daisy chain of mostly furtive couplings—arranged for vicious sport by two scheming, vengeful aristocrats, the Marquise de Merteuil and the Vicomte de Valmont. In the ingenious stage version, written by Christopher Hampton and directed by Howard Davies, the lubricious narrative is telescoped and preserved, but so, to the audience's discomfort, is the anxiety-inducing atmosphere of moral disorientation. Laclos, a tactics-minded military man, was writing about sex and power, not romance, about the strategies of seduction, not the joys of sensuality. The stage of the Music Box is not a love nest but a battlefield—soon to be strewn with the mutilated casualties of a pointless, never-ending war.

This is a compelling and, one must add, thoroughly nasty evening, its malicious wit fueled further by a pair of brilliant lead players, Lindsay Duncan and Alan Rickman. Far more savage than the archetypal contemporary English play about infidelity usually seen on Broadway, *Les Liaisons Dangereuses* also eschews the gentility of the middlebrow literary adaptations of *Masterpiece Theater.* The astringent Mr. Hampton, whose variable previous works have rethought Molière (*The Philanthropist*) and Verlaine and Rimbaud (*Total Eclipse*), merges a misanthropic modern sensibility with Laclos's equally icy, if poker-faced, perspective on the decadent ancien régime. Every time one tries to relax and enjoy *Les Liaisons* as a spicy, distanced period piece about rich villains in fancy costumes victimizing innocent fools, Mr. Hampton and company shift the perspective just enough to sow doubts as to which side we are really on.

To this unsettling end, the acting fills in the delicate, often ambiguous tonal nuances conveyed by the letters in the novel. Mr. Rickman, with his leonine matinee idol's mane, heavy-lidded eyes, and insinuatingly intimate vocal delivery, uses the whole notion of actorliness to define the dissolute Vicomte: He's a man who brazenly impersonates the role of languid lover so he can rape a mindless convent-educated girl of fifteen, Cecile Volanges (Beatie Edney), and then ruin Mme. de Tourvel (Suzanne Burden), "a woman famous for her strict morals, religious fervor, and the happiness of her marriage." As his partner in evil (and long-ago partner in bed), the spellbinding Ms. Duncan presents the unscrupulous Marquise as a poisonous fount of bitchy epigrams in private yet becomes a porcelain replica of a refined lady in public. The audience sees who she and the Vicomte really are when their lips part in quick, tightly drawn smiles that reveal a carnivore's mouthful of glittering teeth.

Both characters are handsome yet asexual—which is just as intended. They don't pursue their prey with "hope for any actual pleasure," for they know that pleasure unmixed with love "must lead directly to disgust." They get their kicks instead from the sinister exercise of brute ego and the piling up of "victories." Because the Vicomte and the Marquise are also the cleverest people in view—and, in their exploitative way, the most astute critics of their hypocritically "polite" society—they can't be summarily dismissed. Some of the world they selfishly smash is eminently deserving of dismantlement.

In the well-worn manner of present-day English playwrights, Mr. Hampton makes this political point explicit, perhaps overexplicit, by tying the play's latter scenes directly to the coming revolution, which had not happened when Laclos was writing, and by heightening the novel's incipient feminism. In an eloquent Act 1 monologue, Ms. Duncan reminds us that women of her time had no choice but to find any escape they could from the subservient role a society of double standards condemned them to play. "I was born to dominate your sex and avenge my own," the Marquise tells the Vicomte, chillingly indifferent to the fact that by reinventing herself as a "virtuoso of deceit" she is as monstrous to women as to men.

Although his character lacks any such rationale for his behavior, Mr. Rickman helps keep our snap moral judgments at bay by making it impossible for us to tell when his faked infatuation for the prudish Mme. de Tourvel ends and a real and selfless passion, a sensation he only half-remembers, might be struggling to begin. By Act 2 it's clear that the Vicomte himself no longer knows what he believes. Mr. Rickman, now reeling and sweaty, presents the harrowing spectacle of a man whose conscience awakens in time for him to recognize his lethal behavior but too late for him to control it.

As the Vicomte's prime target of destruction, the excellent Ms. Burden makes piety human—all the better to leave us horrified when forces beyond her imagination attack her catechism of existence. Once Mme. de Tourvel must choose between her convictions and her illicit passion, the countervailing forces of self-hatred and self-gratification prove so powerful that she can only come crashing to the floor, suffocating and shattered. The Vicomte's other victim, Cecile, proves a more comic figure in Ms. Edney's shrewd performance, though not when she emits a frightened little squeal that signifies her sad, perfunctory deflowering.

With the exception of Hilton McRae, who is too mature for Cecile's "mawkish schoolboy" suitor, Danceny, the supporting cast is fine. New York theatergoers who haven't seen Mr. Davies's work since his slick Brechtian stagings of *Piaf* and *Good* will be startled by how highly imaginative a director he has become. The transitions that keep the geographically dispersed scenes flowing on the single all-purpose set have a progressively more demented choreography, matched by Ilona Sekacz's increasingly macabre harpsichord music, which distorts and then strips away the sham minuet of eighteenth-century manners with which the characters camouflage their ruthlessness. The lighting by Chris Parry and Beverly Emmons takes its cues from wintry Bois de Vincennes sunlight outdoors and silver candelabra within; eventually the stage is suffused with a doom-laden Georges de la Tour glow that, like much of the production, recalls Stanley Kubrick's related dissection of late-eighteenth-century European civilization in his Thackeray adaptation, *Barry Lyndon.*

The image that begins and ends the evening is also out of de la Tour—women playing cards. That suits a work whose principal characters substitute social gamesmanship for emotion and liken themselves to cardsharps. Yet it's not just because Mr. Davies employs an echo-chamber effect that the closing game seems so much more resounding than the first—or that one of Mr. Hampton's final lines, "We're more than halfway through the eighties already," leaves us wondering which eighties the characters are talking about. By then, our sensitivity has been reawakened to the eternal way of a world in which aggression and narcissism almost invariably rout compassion and idealism. Two centuries after Laclos first dramatized these heartless liaisons, it's still a shock to realize how easily the deck of men and women can be stacked so that everyone is dealt a cruel hand.

NINTH SEASON

1987—88

Ron Silver, Joe Mantegna, and Madonna in
David Mamet's *Speed-the-Plow*

CRITIC'S NOTEBOOK: MICHAEL BENNETT DIES
JULY 3, 1987

It was one of those rare occasions when the theater seemed to have gathered its past, present, and future into one house on one night. The night was September 29, 1983, when Michael Bennett celebrated the record-breaking performance of *A Chorus Line* by restaging the entire show so that over three hundred of its alumni could join the regular company of thirty-two for a special gala edition. The audience was a who's who of the theatrical community. The enormous cast consisted of those legions of unsung performers who make shows go on year after year. And the director was a man who could make the whole extravaganza tick—and make it beautiful—in four days' rehearsal time. The feeling in the crowd was that the artist who could make *A Chorus Line* even better—3,389 performances into its run—was an artist who could do anything. An evening that began as a celebration of past glory became a promise of grander glories to come. Michael Bennett was barely forty.

At their news conference announcing Mr. Bennett's death yesterday, the two most powerful producers in New York, Joseph Papp and Bernard B. Jacobs, had to answer some tough questions. The stumpers were not, as one might expect, about the intimate details of Mr. Bennett's illness, but about his work. How do you describe his contribution to the musical stage without resorting to empty adjectives? Mr. Bennett was not an author, and, though he had been a performer, he wasn't a star. His career can't be looked up in a library or watched on videotape or pieced together from old photographs. A stage director's art lives only in the memory of its witnesses. In its evanescence, it is pure theater.

It is precisely that theatricality that sets *A Chorus Line* apart from most landmark Broadway musicals—from *Show Boat* to *Oklahoma!* to *My Fair Lady*. Unlike its predecessors, *A Chorus Line* did not boast songs, performances, or dances for the ages. When one recalls the show, one thinks of the exhilarating movement of performers through the depth of an empty stage. Mr. Bennett's chorus line was less inclined to dance than to splinter and reconstitute itself constantly. It was a giant, undulating organism forever torn between the theater's lonely backstage shadows and the fickle promise of the glamorous lights up front.

The staging of *A Chorus Line*—at once a celebration of Broadway mythology and a full exploitation of the stage's indigenous magic—was the essence of Michael Bennett. A former Broadway chorus performer, he never professed to be a brilliant dance maker, like Agnes de Mille or Bob Fosse, and he never aspired to be an intellectual. He had instead an innate genius for sculpting the plastic essentials of the stage—bodies, lighting, space—to overwhelming dramatic effect. Among Broadway directors and choreographers, he alone had the vision and talent to pick up where Jerome Robbins, whose last Broadway musical was *Fiddler on the Roof* in 1964, left off.

Mr. Bennett's coups de théâtre, though cinematic, could never be duplicated on film. In the opening number of *Company* (1970), a dozen or so performers darting about a two-level jungle-gym set simulated the anxiety, isolation, and frenzy of life in teeming contemporary Manhattan. In "Who's That Woman?" midway through *Follies* (1971), a chorus line of dumpy, middle-aged, retired showgirls was suddenly ambushed by a second, glittering chorus line in mirror image—a heartbreaking apparition of the women's and their crumbling old theater's vanished youths. In *Dreamgirls* (1981), the corrupt rise of a pop song up the Top 40 charts was dramatized by the literal rise of a hellish tableau to the proscenium arch.

With their sophisticated but often skeletal scenery (designed by Boris Aronson and, later, Robin Wagner) and intricate lighting (usually by Tharon Musser), Mr. Bennett's major shows, the early ones in collaboration with Harold Prince, were closer in style to the avant-garde experimental theater of constructivist, postrevolutionary Russia than the decorative, ego-charged spectacles that still constitute most Broadway big-budget entertainments. Yet even when working on a tiny scale—as in his staging of a three-character playlet for the Young Playwrights Festival or in the road-company *Dreamgirls* now on Broadway—Mr. Bennett brought breathtaking visual punctuation to a scene. His failures, too, had their treasurable moments: No one who saw the ill-fated *Ballroom* (1978) will forget the silver-haired couples casting off their diurnal working-class dreariness to twirl through the kaleidoscopic light of their urban dance palace.

As befits someone who grew up on the stage and loved it, Mr. Bennett wanted to be a benefactor to the art as a whole. He was generous to other talents and productions. He had ambitious plans, abandoned during his illness, for his own permanent workshop and theater.

But if Mr. Bennett's colleagues will miss his friendship, everyone will miss his gifts. To think of *A Chorus Line* now is not to remember the hundreds of dancers filling the stage at the gala record-breaking performance in 1983 but to think of the empty space that is left in the musical's chorus line late in the show every night, when a dancer injures himself and must leave the audition. Michael Bennett's death, at what might have been merely the midpoint of his career, leaves its own gaping void in the theater, and into that black hole vanish some of the American musical's brightest hopes.

≣ *The morning of Bennett's death on July 2, I had been awakened with the news by his lawyer and close friend, John Breglio; I passed it on to the* Times. *The nature of Bennett's disease had been kept secret until almost the end, reflecting the fear and stigma of AIDS. That night, after I wrote this piece, John, his wife, Nan, and I walked back and forth in the rain between the Shubert Theatre, where* A Chorus Line *was still running, and the Ambassador, where a stripped-down road company of* Dreamgirls *starring Lillias White had just opened four nights earlier to more acclaim than the original version. We stood in the back and watched a few numbers of each musical with the audiences, who'd been told of Bennett's death by stage manager announcements before the lights dimmed.*

BURN THIS
PLYMOUTH THEATRE, OCTOBER 15, 1987

From his first New York appearance—as the mangy outlaw brother in Sam Shepard's *True West*—John Malkovich has been a combustive figure on stage, threatening to incinerate everyone and everything around him with his throbbing vocal riffs, bruiser's posture, and savage, unfocused eyes. If you're going to write a play called *Burn This*, as Lanford Wilson now has, Mr. Malkovich is surely the man to fan its flames.

The actor's performance at the Plymouth delivers the firepower, all right. Playing a hopped-up interloper known as Pale, Mr. Malkovich enters a downtown loft by nearly beating down the door, then shouts out a free-associative tirade cursing the ills of urban life, then pounds the walls and furniture in a scatological fit of rage. All the while he is equally busy tossing a mane of long dark hair, hoping to arouse the carnal interest of the very pretty young woman who finds herself the surprise recipient of Pale's middle-of-the-night invasion.

The woman, a modern dancer named Anna (Joan Allen), is terrified and titillated. The audience, by contrast, is more inclined to laugh. If there's a difference between the performer who rode to Off Broadway from Chicago in *True West* and the one who now stars uptown, it's a small but significant degree of self-consciousness. In *Burn This*, Mr. Malkovich makes a show of his dangerousness—an extended freak show that splits off from the play proper and is aimed as much at the balcony as it is at Ms. Allen.

He is still riveting and frequently funny: Let someone ask Pale to explain his bandaged hand and a crazed bark of "No!" silences that question and a half dozen to come. Yet the harrowing rage that tore up the apartment in *True West* and mauled the pious self-image of Dustin Hoffman's Willy Loman in *Death of a Salesman* seems sweetened here. With his dems-and-dose accent, unexpected bursts of sensitivity, and slightly adrogynous sexuality, Mr. Malkovich's Pale is a latter-day Stanley Kowalski, a blue-collar animal out to claw through the genteel veneer of the downtown esthete Anna. But he's a domesticated Stanley: He goes for the gag before he goes for Anna's throat, and the gun he carries is only for dramatic effect.

Even so, his performance yanks us through this always intriguing, finally undernourishing three-hour play. A tamed Stanley may in fact be just what Mr. Wilson wants. Though often more muddled than pointed, *Burn This* really does suggest a cuter, softened *Streetcar Named Desire* for the yuppie 1980s, down to its Windham Hill–style jazz-fusion score and its upbeat ending. Despite much onstage brawling and crying and precoital theatrics, Anna and Pale don't fight to the death, as Stanley and Blanche did, so much as slowly settle down to make the choices facing those New York couples who inhabit the slick magazines. What begins as a go-for-broke sexual struggle trails off into sentimental conflicts between love and career, unbridled passion and intellectual detachment, a loft lifestyle and the biological clock.

Although the payoff of *Burn This* is perilously slight, the play initially promises the abundance one anticipates from Mr. Wilson, as wise and accomplished a playwright as we have. The evening opens within the shadows of a sudden, accidental death: Robbie, a brilliant young dancer who was one of Anna's roommates and her artistic inspiration, has died with his lover in a boating accident. Anna mourns Robbie, a homosexual, as if he had been her own lover. The mysterious arrival of Pale, Robbie's heterosexual and somewhat homophobic brother, as a sexually fulfilling substitute for the dead man promises to explode that fascinating choreography of love, gender, and sex.

Those issues are largely ignored as Mr. Wilson propels the Anna-Pale relationship mechanically, according to the predictable conventions of breezy romantic comedies. Anna bounces didactically back and forth between the feral, brutish, erotically charged Pale, an uninhibited force of nature who incongruously turns out to be a Montclair, N.J., restaurant manager, and her all too antithetical suitor—a wealthy, tony screenwriter named Burton. (Jonathan Hogan finds charm in Burton, the eternal Ralph Bellamy role, in spite of a Laura Crow sportswear wardrobe that has Bourgeois Jerk plastered all over it.) In Act 2, Anna and Pale spat and reconcile for no reason other than the requirements of sustaining a love triangle plot. One yearns for the depth of Mr. Wilson's *Talley's Folly,* in which another romantic odd couple had to sit tight for ninety minutes to have everything out.

As one expects from this writer, *Burn This* has a sociopolitical component, too: Both Pale (in Act 1) and Anna (in Act 2) deliver speeches lamenting an alienating modern civilization in which people must fight to preserve their humanity in the face of daily indignities, from battling for parking spaces to real or figurative rapes. But this apocalyptic urban backdrop doesn't unfurl naturally, as it did in Mr. Wilson's *Balm in Gilead* (as directed by Mr. Malkovich); instead, the message seems superimposed, much like the nuclear disaster in *Angels Fall,* to lend weight to the thinner characters. Anna is particularly emaciated. However frequently she may sob out of grief or anger, she defies even the talented Ms. Allen's efforts to convey some emotional rationale for her whimsical shifts between Pale and Burton. Perhaps if there were a hot sexual charge between her and Mr. Malkovich, which there is not, such logic wouldn't matter.

Arguably the play's most telling character is the one least integral to its story: an unattached homosexual advertising man named Larry who is Anna's remaining roommate. Winningly played by Lou Liberatore with a warmth and wry intelligence that keep bitchiness at bay, Larry fields Mr. Wilson's funniest lines, on subjects as varied as Detroit, gay New Year's Eve parties, and corporate Christmas cards. Larry is a third wheel, perennial bachelor, and latent cupid—the Tony Randall role—and yet there seems much more to him than just that. In a play in which no pair of lovers—whether homosexual or heterosexual—has ever lived together,

Larry's voyeurism and disconnectedness seem to say more about the playwright's feelings of loss and longing than the showier romance at center stage.

Burn This was directed by Mr. Wilson's longtime creative partner, Marshall W. Mason. As usual, Mr. Mason's staging is fluid and the John Lee Beatty set (diaphanously lighted by Dennis Parichy) is handsome, but one wonders why the director didn't exert a stronger editorial hand. The play's length seems to advertise its self-indulgent, excisable blind alleys; one is constantly struck by small details that are fudged for plot contrivance's sake, from the inconsistent use of the loft's front-door buzzer to Larry's convenient firsthand familiarity with Pale's Montclair restaurant.

Mr. Mason has been much more attentive to the considerable "burn" imagery in the text: Both acts open with the striking of matches, and the final curtain rings down on the dying embers of a torched confidential note. Yet the promised illumination of torrid intimacies and larger-than-life passions never quite emerges, either in the text or the performance. One feels so much invigorating heat at *Burn This* that it's all the more frustrating to be left with so little light.

THE MAHABHARATA
MAJESTIC THEATER, BROOKLYN, OCTOBER 19, 1987

More than nine hours after it begins, Peter Brook's production of *The Mahabharata* is still not over—but at least the world is coming to an end.

The apocalypse before us is the long-awaited climax of an epic struggle between two opposing sets of cousins in an ancient Indian dynasty. It is the cue for Mr. Brook, one of the great theater minds of our age, to unleash his full imaginative arsenal. The battles of multitudes are conveyed by acrobatic displays of Eastern martial arts, by dozens of white arrows flying through the air, by horizontal ladders spinning violently on a vast stage carpeted with dirt. A mud-caked warrior sucks the bloody guts out of an eternal enemy; a god creates a solar eclipse with the merest flutter of a hand. For an instant we can imagine that we may be witnessing what one character calls "the last night of the world," a conflagration that leaves eighteen million dead and that threatens to shrivel the earth itself.

The stylization of this war—achieved almost entirely by ritualistic visual poetry rather than modern backstage technology—is characteristic of Mr. Brook's esthetics and ideally suited to his source. *The Maha-bharata*, the voluminous Sanskrit poem dating from 400 B.C., is an all-encompassing compendium of Hindu history, mythology, and thought—a work whose primeval roots demand a stage adaptation of timeless theatrical simplicity. Whether the rest of Mr. Brook's production achieves this simplicity, as opposed to merely simulating it, is a matter that audiences at the Brooklyn Academy of Music's Next Wave Festival will strenuously debate for the rest of this marathon work's run. For this viewer, eleven consecutive hours of *The Mahabharata* (including two breaks) never gathered the cumulative power that Mr. Brook's previous New York offering, *La Tragédie de Carmen*, harnessed in a mere eighty minutes.

Is it possible that something has been lost since this theatrical endeavor began its life to ecstatic acclaim at the Avignon Festival in 1985? There *The Mahabharata* was performed from sunset to sunrise in natural surroundings (a limestone quarry), and was spoken in the French in which Mr. Brook's longtime collaborator, Jean-Claude Carrière, had written his adaptation. In Brooklyn, where the production's three parts can be seen either in one day (starting at 1 p.m.) or over three nights, the setting is an old downtown movie-and-vaudeville palace, the Majestic, that the Academy has admirably reclaimed from oblivion. To simulate the conditions of Mr. Brook's working-class base of operations in Paris, Les Bouffes du Nord, the theater has been artfully restored to a semidilapidated state, with chipped plaster, exposed brick, mottled paint, and, for seating, punishingly hard benches. For this production, such chic, postmodern asceticism seems contrived—an environment for a Beverly Hills ashram rather than for a genuine rendition of a Hindu epic.

The delivery of Mr. Carrière's text is even more problematic in New York than its setting. Mr. Brook has translated the script into mostly prosaic, sometimes unidiomatic English, which is then spoken by an international company for whom English is, in too many cases, an awkward second language. Given the several linguistic and verbal layers through which it has been filtered and refracted, the dialogue of *The Maha-bharata* almost inevitably must sound distanced, as if we were listening to a dubbed foreign film.

This wouldn't matter so much if Mr. Brook's show were primarily a visual experience. But if there are indeed a number of glorious sequences for the eyes—and if every scene is handsomely set forth—there is also an avalanche of tedious talk. In his script, Mr. Carrière has heroically attempted to pack in much of the plot and nearly all the major characters of a poem that runs over a hundred thousand verses in eighteen volumes. As a daredevil screenplay-writing stunt—and Mr. Carrière has been a brilliant scenarist for such directors as Buñuel and Wajda—this abridgement of *The Mahabharata* is ingenious. Yet the writer chooses to cover so much ground—generations of familial rivalries, complex genealogies, interlocking fairy tales, tortured conflicts between choice and destiny—that the narrative by necessity is more often recited than dramatized.

Those raised on *The Mahabharata* may enjoy sampling the rush of familiar high points in this way, much as Westerners can get a kick out of Cecil B. DeMille's depiction of *The Ten Commandments*. But just as one wouldn't look to that movie to learn the meaning of the Bible, so the spiritual import of this *Mahabharata* remains elusive, crowded out rather than expressed by the plot. Much of the work's moral substance, including the lengthy debate of the Bhagavad-Gita, is reduced to easily digestible sermons and homilies that only superficially explore the enigmatic Hindu concept of self-fulfillment ("dharma"). The exhortations to self-knowledge are so broad they are virtually indistinguishable from the messages of Mr. Brook's past cosmic excursions, such as *The Conference of the Birds* (from a twelfth-century Persian poem) and the film *Meetings with Remarkable Men* (from Gurdjieff).

When the talk and theology give way to action, the director takes complete charge of a stage space whose depth, height, and burned-clay colors evoke a huge archeological excavation site. In addition to making spectacular use of fire and two permanent bodies of water (a downstage pool and upstage river), the director provides a veritable tour of Oriental theater techniques—Balinese and Japanese as well as Indian. Brightly patterned carpets and fabrics of red and gold are constantly spread and swirled before us. Actors playing characters that are often half animal or half divine achieve their hybrid status with mime and masks. Billowing cloth can represent newborn children while a single large wooden wheel can stand for Krishna's chariot.

Like the expensively weather-beaten Majestic, however, Mr. Brook's smorgasbord of Oriental stagecraft also can appear a bit synthetic: A puppet sequence is perfunctory, and the relentless Eastern music (played by onstage musicians who come and go with distracting frequency) sounds as if it were purchased by the yard, along with the rugs. For all the Eastern exotica, the staging and the script still end up accentuating the common ground shared by *The Mahabharata* and the West. In the wanderings of the blind prince Dhritarashtra and the forest exile of the Pandavas, we are encouraged to make associations with Oedipus, the Old Testament, Shakespeare. Though the similarities are there to be found, one can't help wondering if the idiosyncratically Eastern character of *The Mahabharata* has been watered down to knock international audiences over the head with the universality of mankind's essential myths.

In keeping with this approach, Mr. Brook has assembled a multinational cast of highly variable quality. Some of the acting, especially of the comic and villainous roles, is quite broad. It's not until well into the production's third part, when Miriam Goldschmidt's Kunti reveals she is the mother of Jeffrey Kissoon's anguished Karna, that there is a powerfully acted scene. Among the other superior performers in the large cast are Mallika Sarabhai (the princess Draupadi), Robert Langdon Lloyd (the storyteller Vyasa), and Andrzej Seweryn (Yudishthira, a heroic prince with a tragic weakness for gambling). Perhaps the least helpful major performance is by Bruce Myers, whose Krishna (a Ralph Richardson role if ever there was one) substitutes showy British vocal resonance for the ethereal intangible of soul.

However unequal in achievement, everyone on stage and off works so hard and seriously in *The Mahabharata* that a theatergoer only wishes it were possible to join the company at their final, deserved destination—a golden, torch-lighted vision of Hindu paradise. But the hard work, paradoxically, may be exactly what keeps us from reaching the heavenly plane to which this work wishes us to ascend. In his landmark productions of sacred Western texts, from the similarly dirt-and-fate-fixated *Carmen* back to the Beckett-inspired *King Lear*, Mr. Brook has stripped down to essentials, to a metaphorical if not actual empty space, to take us on a journey to the ends of the world. *The Mahabharata*, by contrast, seems less a distillation of its source than a busy condensation; it often makes the simple look hard. One applauds the most magical pieces of the tapestry even while recognizing that the disappointing whole is too heavy to fly.

ANYTHING GOES
Vivian Beaumont Theater, October 20, 1987

Forget about the Coliseum, the Louvre museum, a melody from a symphony by Strauss—Patti LuPone is the top. As Reno Sweeney, the sassy nightclub singer in the Lincoln Center revival of *Anything Goes*, Ms. LuPone has her first sensational New York role since *Evita* in 1979, and, given that Cole Porter is the evening's buoyant guiding spirit, you don't have to fear that she'll succumb to death scenes in the second act.

With her burst of Lucille Ball red hair, a trumpet's blare in her voice, and lips so insinuatingly protruded they could make the Pledge of Allegiance sound lewd, Ms. LuPone's Reno is a mature, uninhibited jazz dame: loose, trashy, funny, sexy. Ethel Merman she's not—the difference in belting power is mainly apparent in "Blow, Gabriel, Blow"—but who is? Ms. LuPone has her own brash American style and, most of all, a blazing spontaneity: With this Reno, everything goes. At the end of Act 1, which should by all rights conclude with the full-throttle dance number accompanying the title song, she has the audacity to upstage the entire company and bring down the act with a broad wink into the Vivian Beaumont's auditorium. By then, most of the crowd is ready to take Ms. LuPone home, and not necessarily to mother.

Although the star and her share of unbeatable Porter standards (did I fail to mention "I Get a Kick Out of You"?) are the essential sparks for this *Anything Goes,* the production, directed by Jerry Zaks and choreographed by Michael Smuin, has its other lightheaded though inconsistent virtues. Indeed, yesterday's performance by the stock market may allow the show to serve the same escapist mission in 1987 that it did in 1934, when it tickled those Depression audiences who could still laugh at jokes about suicide leaps on Wall Street.

In *Anything Goes,* nearly everyone has money and love to burn. The setting is a ship of foolishness en route from New York to London, the S.S. *American,* whose passenger list includes a stowaway swain named Billy Crocker (Howard McGillin), the debutante he adores from afar (Kathleen Mahony-Bennett), the debutante's foolish but wealthy English fiancé (Anthony Heald), and Moonface Martin, a gangster disguised as a parson. Moonface, who is Public Enemy No. 13 and aiming higher, is played by Bill McCutcheon, most recently of *The Front Page,* and to say he has a moonface is to do the performer's priceless mug a disservice. His is a moonface that might have been carved out of pink, quivering Jell-O, with a bite taken out where the chin should be. Throw in a slow-burn comic delivery that harks back to the vanished traditions of burlesque—not even a dog's invasion of his trousers can excite Mr. McCutcheon—and you have to wonder if even the fabled Victor Moore got more laughs in the role.

The evening can use all the low humor at Mr. McCutcheon's disposal, because *Anything Goes* does tend to list when the singing subsides. Timothy Crouse and John Weidman have good-naturedly but perhaps too earnestly rejiggered the original book (a Guy Bolton–P. G. Wodehouse and Howard Lindsay–Russel Crouse affair). There's an excess of routine farcical exposition to get the right romantic partners together and to provide cues for songs that are too famous to require any windy introduction. The corny, sporadically amusing one-liners, many of them at the expense of Porter's alma mater of Yale, give the script the collegiate air of a Harvard Hasty Pudding show.

In keeping with contemporary practice, Mr. Crouse and Mr. Weidman have interpolated Porter songs not originally written for *Anything Goes*— some of them welcome ("It's De-lovely," "Friendship"), some of them dead weight ("I Want to Row on the Crew," "Good-bye, Little Dream, Good-bye"). Mr. Zaks, the superb director of *The House of Blue Leaves* and other plays, reveals real promise as a stager of big-time musical comedies, but he as yet lacks the eye, or maybe the ruthlessness, required to trim those numbers or scenes that break the show's momentum. There are extended, avoidable sags in the shanks of both acts.

Mr. Zaks's casting also frays a bit around the edges. Though Mr. McGillin is an ideal clean-cut leading man—his full voice and Brooks Brothers looks are perfection without being saccharine—we never understand why his Billy prefers Ms. Mahony-Bennett's insipid ingenue to Reno Sweeney. There's far more eroticism in "You're the Top," an early showstopping duet for Mr. McGillin and Ms. LuPone, than there is in the subsequent pairings of Mr. McGillin and his sweetheart on "It's De-lovely" and "All Through the Night." In the secondary comic roles, the happy contributions of Mr. Heald's malaprop-prone, tango-dancing English twit and Linda Hart's brassy good-time girl are somewhat counterbalanced by mugging fellow passengers who look ready to ship out in a stock tour of *No, No, Nanette.*

Nearly everything else has gone right. Mr. Smuin, inexplicably absent from Broadway as a choreographer since *Sophisticated Ladies,* does a clever job of finessing the limited dancing abilities of his leads even as he lets his chorus loose in beguine, tap, soft-shoe, and ballroom routines that lovingly evoke the Hollywood of Astaire and Hermes Pan. That gifted lighting designer Paul Gallo bathes the dances in radiant hues that somehow reproduce the exact quality of moonshine in black-and-white movies while splashing the stage in the widest imaginable spectrum of Technicolor.

In this feat, Mr. Gallo is aided by Tony Walton, whose sets and costumes are a mad yet always tasteful fantasy of Art Deco glitz. The Beaumont stage becomes a two-level ocean liner, with Edward Strauss's swinging band holding forth on the top deck, that recalls the topography of Mr. Walton's design for Bob Fosse's *Chicago* yet also evokes Donald Oenslager's celebrated set for the original *Anything Goes.* The costumes, from the starched sailors' whites to the translucent red top hats of the most statuesque chorus women, are afizz. At one point Ms. LuPone is poured into a slinky white gown embroidered with a strategically placed silver highball glass. Reno Sweeney may get no kick from champagne, but the audience can't be blamed for drinking it all up.

CABARET
IMPERIAL THEATRE, OCTOBER 23, 1987

There can't be a creepier sight on Broadway right now than Joel Grey. Back in the role of the sleazy emcee in the musical *Cabaret*, the actor is made up just as he was in 1966—with patent-leather hair, rouged cheeks, purple lips, and drag-queen eyelashes. He darts about like an overwound windup doll, twirling his cane with a spastic jerkiness. As his eyes bulge, so his tongue has a most appalling way of flopping out of his mouth. And when Mr. Grey sings, his voice is a piercing siren that doesn't so much welcome revelers to his cabaret, the Kit Kat Klub, as lure them into the hell lurking just out of view—Berlin, 1929.

Mr. Grey's alarming stunt—if anything, rendered more grotesque by the facial lines and showbiz bruises of two added decades—allows us to see some of the excitement that attended *Cabaret* in its initial Harold Prince production. It was Mr. Prince's masterstroke, following Jerome Robbins's symbolic use of a Chagall fiddler in *Fiddler on the Roof* two seasons earlier, to make Mr. Grey's nameless character and his seedy cabaret a metaphor for a decadent Germany splintering fast into fascism. The emcee was a cadaverous George Grosz caricature brought to life, the embodiment of a morally and economically spent society ripe for Hitler. Though the actual plot of *Cabaret* concerns other characters, the emcee's ironic cabaret turns gave the musical its unifying, Brechtian style—a shocking Broadway novelty at the time—and charted the pulse of a civilization going mad.

The new *Cabaret* at the Imperial, again directed by Mr. Prince, doesn't merely ask Mr. Grey to embody the evening's themes; this time the performer must carry the entire show as if it were a star vehicle. That demand is preposterously unfair to Mr. Grey. In the original production, he received fifth, not first, billing, and that billing was more or less commensurate with his part. To have a *Cabaret* reliant on its emcee is almost like reviving *Oklahoma!* as a star vehicle for the actor playing Jud. While Mr. Grey does his job as expertly as ever, he needs help during the long stretches when he's not at center stage.

He frequently fails to get it. This *Cabaret* is not, as its heroine Sally Bowles would say, "perfectly marvelous," but it does approach the perfectly mediocre. Of the four principal performers surrounding Mr. Grey, only one (the opera singer Regina Resnik) is adequate. The David Chapman sets—"based on original set design by Boris Aronson," says the *Playbill*—are tacky, stripped-down cannibalizations of the influential originals, and this, mind you, in the first musical to arrive on Broadway with a fifty-dollar top ticket price. Even the original costume designer, Patricia Zipprodt, is at less than her best: How could chorus girls wear transparent plastic aprons in 1929?

The effect of this cheesiness is to soften Mr. Prince's hard-edged conception and to reveal just how old-fashioned and plodding *Cabaret* was when dealing in musical-comedy specifics rather than in directorial metaphor. As inadequately acted, Joe Masteroff's talky script, an adaptation of John Van Druten's stage version of Christopher Isherwood's *Berlin Stories*, seems tame now in its treatment of Nazism, especially in light of some of the franker Prince musicals (*Evita*, *Sweeney Todd*) that came later. Fresh alterations in the book and score notwithstanding, *Cabaret* still follows the double-romance formula of Broadway confections long past. Sally (Alyson Reed), an English cabaret singer, carries on with an expatriate American novelist, Cliff (Gregg Edelman), in counterpoint to a theater-party-pitched romance between a world-weary, middle-aged landlady (Ms. Resnik) and a kindly Jewish fruit peddler (Werner Klemperer).

In the current version, Mr. Masteroff has nudged Cliff closer to Isherwood and to Bob Fosse's 1972 film version of *Cabaret* by making him explicitly bisexual. But even a double sex-change operation might not redeem the blandness of the central, passionless couple. Ms. Reed, a capable singer and dancer, never remotely suggests the "mysterious and fascinating" Sally; she doesn't even wield her long cigarette holder authoritatively. Mr. Edelman's writer, though also of pleasant voice, is so mild that one is constantly taken aback to discover he is the toast of two sexes in at least that many nations. With his corduroy suit and hayseed accent, he seems less likely to write a novel than a homeowner's insurance policy.

Cabaret got away with only slightly flashier casting of the young couple the first time around. The show's not-so-secret weapon in 1966 was Lotte Lenya as the landlady—for Lenya, an indomitable representative of all things Brecht-Weill, added priceless authenticity to the production's evocation of the Weimar period and lent throaty credibility to the pointed echoes of *The Threepenny Opera* and *Mahagonny* in the extremely clever John Kander–Fred Ebb songs. While Ms. Resnik acts and sings the role nearly as well as Lenya, she can never—through no fault of her own—flood her audience with the eerie associations that her predecessor did. As her suitor, the competent Mr. Klemperer lacks the essential warmth of his character's originator, Jack Gilford.

Under these circumstances, many of the better numbers, including Sally's title declaration of defiance and the older couple's charming seduction duet ("It Couldn't Please Me More"), lose their oomph. The songs that fare best are fielded by Mr. Grey and by the witty choreographer, Ron Field, who has impeccably re-created his imaginative parodies of jazz-age social dancing and frenzied before-the-deluge nightclub routines.

Mr. Prince's staging is also pretty much as one remembers it—to the extent one can ignore the weak performances and the missing colors and images of the original sets. The chilling sequences are those that open and close each act and that feature the distorting mirror and blinding white lights that do survive the first production. At the end of Act 1, when an innocuous beer-drinking polka ("Tomorrow Belongs to Me") evolves into a Nazi anthem, Mr. Prince abruptly freezes the mob in place, lifts the set up into the darkness, and then sends out Mr. Grey to point his face toward the audience in a hideous, mocking grin. As the white lights jolt us into intermission, we feel just how timely a consistently tough *Cabaret* could have been, especially for those partying in a boom world at the brink of a crash.

≡ Cabaret *would receive the jolting Broadway revival it deserved in 1998, in a staging by the British director Sam Mendes starring Natasha Richardson and Alan Cumming (as the emcee) that escaped the long shadows of Harold Prince and Joel Grey.*

FRANKIE AND JOHNNY IN THE CLAIR DE LUNE
Manhattan Theatre Club, October 28, 1987

When we first meet the title characters of Terrence McNally's provocative new play, *Frankie and Johnny in the Clair de Lune,* they are grunting through an orgasm on a Murphy bed in a dreary Hell's Kitchen walk-up. But Frankie (Kathy Bates) and Johnny (Kenneth Welsh) are hardly sweethearts. They are fellow employees of a greasy spoon—she a waitress, he a recently hired short-order cook—and this is their first and quite possibly their last date. They've been to a movie. They've made small talk. Now they've had sex. What else can they give one another? As the couple's panting subsides, Frankie hopes only that Johnny will get dressed and get out so she can resume her usual nightly ritual of watching television and eating ice cream in peace.

Yet Johnny refuses to leave. A nonstop talker and meddler, he repeatedly proclaims his undying love for the dumpy, sarcastic waitress even as she rudely mocks his ludicrously overblown compliments and points him toward the door. The exasperated Frankie thinks Johnny is "too needy" and worries he may be a creep. "You just don't decide to fall in love with people out of the blue," she says. Johnny argues back that Frankie, much wounded by other men, is simply too fearful of rejection to accept true affection when it comes her way. "Pretend we're the only two people in the world," he says, insisting that he and Frankie, both middle-aged and "not beautiful," have only this one last chance "to connect." Should they fail to seize the moment, they'll never know more than the isolation and loneliness that already is their lot—a life of merely "bumping into bodies."

Frankie and Johnny in the Clair de Lune, which opens the main-stage season of the Manhattan Theatre Club, has the timeless structure of romantic comedies: Will there be a second night to this odd couple's problematic one-night stand? As one expects from Mr. McNally, the author of *Bad Habits* and *It's Only a Play,* the evening often floats by on bright and funny conversation, some of it dotted, however parenthetically, with jaundiced references to show business (*The Sound of Music, Looking for Mr. Goodbar,* Kathleen Turner). But there has always been another side to Mr. McNally's highly lacquered sophistication: Even his raucous gay-bath sex farce, *The Ritz,* had something poignant to say about transitory romantic attachments. In *Frankie and Johnny in the Clair de Lune,* the playwright examines his characters' connections with a new forthrightness and maturity, and it's just possible that, in the process, he's written the most serious play yet about intimacy in the age of AIDS.

To be sure, *Frankie and Johnny* is not about AIDS per se. There is only one vague reference to the disease, and its characters do not belong to high-risk groups. Still, there's a pointed end-of-the-world feel to James Noone's drab tenement set and to the blank, Edward Hopperesque solitude of the couple's existence. Mr. McNally seems to be taking stock of what's really important in a society where life can be "cheap and short," where sexual marauding can no longer pass as its own reward, where emotional defenses are so well fortified that human contact is harder to achieve than ever.

The persistent, nosy Johnny is as obnoxious a suitor as Frankie says he is—he's the kind of guy who picks at any visible scab—but his relentless battering does make her and us think about how much of love is fleeting chemistry and how much is merely a willingness to overcome the inertia of detachment and engage in hard work. Perhaps Johnny is right when he says his and Frankie's only hope is that they somehow forget "the million reasons they don't love each other" and build instead on the few reasons that did bring them together, if only for an hour and by chance, on one desperate moonlit night. Perhaps, too, the durability of their bond will have less to do with their various similarities and differences of personality than with their ability to remember the "music" of their first, hungry romantic passion. Music—from that alluded to in the title to bits of Bach, Wagner, and Frederick Loewe—figures throughout *Frankie and Johnny*. The play's offstage third character is a pretentious FM disk jockey who would "still like to believe in love."

Mr. McNally may or may not still believe in love himself, but he has dexterously managed to avoid the tragic dénouement of folklore's Frankie and Johnny (and of his last and thematically related play, *The Lisbon Traviata*) as well as the guaranteed happy endings of boulevard comedies. In *Frankie and Johnny*, it's enough of a victory for the hero and heroine to share unselfconsciously the intimate domestic activity of brushing their teeth. But if the playwright avoids the trap of reaching for a definitive final curtain, he sometimes exerts too firm a controlling hand along the way. The hash-slinging characters both seem like second-hand William Inge–style Middle Americans—as if they were archetypal figures contrived to enact a parable rather than people drawn freely from life. Sometimes their credibility is further compromised by their slips into knowing badinage reminiscent of Mr. McNally's upscale Manhattanites.

Under the fine direction of Paul Benedict, two excellent actors supply the spontaneity and conviction needed to override the moments of contrivance in their roles. Mr. Welsh keeps us guessing as to whether Johnny is merely sickeningly sincere or a weirdo, finally allowing us to see and understand all the pieces of a complex, damaged man. While Ms. Bates's Frankie superficially resembles the suicidal daughter she played in *'night, Mother*, the actress creates a wholly new character—a tough waitress whose wisecracks mask not a sentimental heart but an unsparing vision of the world. When Johnny tells her that he's a romantic who likes seeing things in a shadowy light, she typically snaps back that his idea of romance is her idea of "hiding something." As it happens, we can understand both points of view in a play that brings fresh illumination to the latest phases of that old lovers' moon.

INTO THE WOODS
MARTIN BECK THEATRE, NOVEMBER 6, 1987

When Cinderella, Little Red Ridinghood, and their fairy-tale friends venture into the woods in the new Stephen Sondheim–James Lapine musical, you can be sure that they won't miss the subconscious forest for the picturesque trees. The characters of *Into the Woods* may be figures from children's literature, but their journey is the same painful, existential one taken by so many adults in Sondheim musicals past.

Like the middle-aged showbiz cynics who return to their haunted youths in *Follies* and *Merrily We Roll Along,* or the contemporary descendant who revisits Georges Seurat's hallowed park in *Sunday in the Park with George,* or the lovers who court in a nocturnal Scandinavian birch forest in *A Little Night Music,* Cinderella and company travel into a dark, enchanted wilderness to discover who they are and how they might grow up and overcome the eternal, terrifying plight of being alone. To hear "No One Is Alone," the cathartic and beautiful final song of *Into the Woods,* is to be overwhelmed once more by the continuity of one of the American theater's most extraordinary songwriting careers. The lyric's terrifying opening admonition—"Mother cannot guide you"— sends one reeling back three decades to the volcanic finale of *Gypsy,* in which the mother played by Ethel Merman at last cast her children into the woods of adulthood with the angry outburst, "Mama's got to let go!"

The material of *Into the Woods* is potent stuff—as old as time, or at least as old as fairy tales. One needn't necessarily have read Bruno Bettelheim's classic Freudian analysis to realize that, in remaking Grimm stories, Mr. Sondheim's lyrics and Mr. Lapine's book tap into the psychological mother lode from which so much of life and literature spring. What is harder to explain is why the show at the Martin Beck, though touching both of its authors' past themes at their primal source, is less harrowing than, say, *Sweeney Todd,* which incorporated its own Sondheim variations on "Rapunzel" and "Hansel and Gretel," and less moving than *Sunday in the Park,* which made related points about children and art and gnarled family trees through similarly Pirandellian means.

To understand how much *Into the Woods* disappoints, one must first appreciate its considerable ambitions and pleasures. The authors have not just tried to match the Grimms but to top them. In Mr. Lapine's book for Act 1, Cinderella (Kim Crosby), Little Red Ridinghood (Danielle Ferland), and the giant-killing Jack (Ben Wright) join two newly invented characters reminiscent of *Sunday in the Park,* a childless baker (Chip Zien) and his wife (Joanna Gleason), in an intricate tripartite plot also yanking together one witch (Bernadette Peters), one wolf (Robert Westenberg), two princes (Mr. Westenberg and Chuck Wagner), and countless parents and stepparents. Although the principal characters, true to their Grimm prototypes, gain new wisdom in the woods, their pre-intermission happy endings hardly deliver the promised eternal "tenderness and laughter." In Act 2, everyone is jolted into the woods again—this time not to cope with the pubescent traumas symbolized by beanstalks and carnivorous wolves but with such adult catastrophes as unrequited passion, moral cowardice, smashed marriages, and the deaths of loved ones.

The conception is brilliant, and sometimes the execution lives up to it. Mr. Sondheim has as much fun as one expects with his wicked airing of the subtext of the old tales: Mr. Westenberg's rakishly sexual wolf sings, "There's no possible way / To describe what you feel / When you're talking to your meal." Mr. Lapine's script has its own bright jokes, many of them belonging to the production's two performing finds—the sassy Ms. Ferland, whose Lolita-like Red Ridinghood evolves into a ferocious little fox in a wolf stole, and the tender Ms. Crosby, whose insecure, weak-kneed Cinderella has a lovely, comic fragility that recalls the young Paula Prentiss. Only when Barbara Bryne is mugging campily as Jack's mother does the humor compromise the production's fundamental belief in grave, ontological fairy-tale magic. The designer, Tony Straiges, transports us from a mock-proscenium set redolent of nineteenth-century picturebook illustration into a thick, asymmetrical, Sendakesque woods whose Rorschach patterns, eerily lighted by Richard Nelson, keep shifting to reveal hidden spirits and demons.

Unfortunately, the book is as wildly overgrown as the forest. Though the structure of *Into the Woods* leans on Sondheim trademarks—puzzles and scavenger hunts—its architecture has not been ingeniously worked out in Mr. Lapine's script. Perhaps the enterprise could use less art and more craft. The interlocking stories, coincidences, surprise reunions, and close calls do not fall gracefully into farcical place as they did in the theatrically equivalent books for *A Little Night Music* and *A Funny Thing Happened on the Way to the Forum.* Instead, the various narrative jigsaw pieces often prove either cryptic or absent, and, with the aid of a sort of postmodernist antinarrator (Tom Aldredge), they must finally be patched together to achieve a measure of coherence.

The confusion breeds stasis; the show stands still during the huffing and puffing of voluminous plot information. Worse, the convoluted story has a strangulating effect on the musical's two essential sources of emotional power, its people and its score. The characters are at such frantic mercy of the plot that they never gather the substance required to make us care, as we must, about their Act 2 dilemmas of conscience, connectedness, and loss. This is often true even of the musical's real leads, the baker and his wife, in spite of a good performance by Mr. Zien, who is funnier than his wimpy Chico Marx costume promises, and a wonderful one by Ms. Gleason, whose intentionally anachronistic suburban matron blossoms in fairy-tale land.

Mr. Sondheim's numerous songs, though often outfitted with incomparably clever lyrics, sometimes seem as truncated as the characters, as if they were chopped off just when they got going to make way for the latest perambulations of the book. With the exception of "No One Is Alone," the most effective songs are directly tied to the plot (as in the extended title number, a gloss on "A Weekend in the Country" in *Night Music*) or are their own self-contained jokes (as in "Agony," a duet for philandering princes).

Too many of the other songs bring the action to a halt, announcing the characters' dawning self-knowledge didactically ("You've learned . . . something you never knew") rather than dramatizing it. And sometimes the soliloquies describing psychological change are written in interchangeable language, as if the characters were as vaguely generic to Mr. Sondheim as they are to the audience. Time and second hearings always tell with a Sondheim score, but this one, its atypically muted Jonathan Tunick orchestrations included, makes the mildest first impression of them all.

The work's weaknesses and strengths alike are emblemized by the predicament of Ms. Peters, who is very funny as a cronish, crooked-finger witch but whose connection to the many plots is so tenuously gerrymandered that she is assigned a sermonizing song in Act 2 for no apparent reason other than her billing. Without this star, who delivers her numbers with enough force to bring down houses (whether theaters or little pigs'), *Into the Woods* would be a lesser evening, but the paradoxical price for her appearance is a deflatingly literal-minded explication of the musical's message (and of the witch's character), not to mention overlength.

There is enough to look at and think about, however, that the overlength rarely induces tedium. As director, Mr. Lapine may make little call on the services of his musical stager, Lar Lubovitch, but the tales keep sprinting on stage and into the auditorium. The result is unique to its composer's canon—the first Sondheim musical whose dark thematic underside is as accessible as its jolly storytelling surface. *Into the Woods* may be just the tempting, unthreatening show to lead new audiences to an artist who usually lures theatergoers far deeper, and far more dangerously, into the woods.

BREAKING THE CODE

NEIL SIMON THEATRE, NOVEMBER 16, 1987

Breaking the Code, the new London import at the Neil Simon Theatre, is yet another English drama about a sensitive genius whose homosexuality leads to his crucifixion by the hypocritical establishment. But if Hugh Whitemore's flawed, discursive play shares many of the symptoms of its well-worn genre, it finally pulls away from the sentimentality of *Another Country* and *Prick Up Your Ears* and all the recent rest. *Breaking the Code* is a work about a gay martyr that moves the audience precisely because its protagonist, as presented by Mr. Whitemore and as beautifully acted by Derek Jacobi, never thinks of himself as a martyr. When the story of a badgered nonconformist is told as a tale of proud self-assertion rather than maudlin self-pity, one finds not a saintly victim, but a stirring hero, at center stage.

The hero, Alan Turing, is drawn from life (and from a biography by Andrew Hodges). A mathematician who pioneered in computer theory, Turing (1912–1954) was recruited by Churchill's government to help crack the Nazis' Enigma code during the war. When we meet Turing in *Breaking the Code*, the war is over and his arrest for "gross indecency" is imminent. In the person of Mr. Jacobi, the mathematician looks, as he later describes himself, like "an old poof." A man of about forty, Turing retains a King's College wardrobe, a boyish cut to his sandy hair, and a strained, Peter Pan youthfulness about his large, dewy eyes. When he speaks, he stammers and chews absently on his nails.

The stammer is a Jacobi trademark dating back to *I, Claudius*, but before one can condemn the actor for dipping into a typically British bag of histrionic tricks (or tics), the pertinence of the performance to the role becomes gripping. This is not a pathetic "old poof." Turing stutters because he is an intellectual whose words can never keep up with his ideas; his racing mind drags around the body and arrested social graces of an eternal student. When speaking about math, Mr. Jacobi's accelerating voice makes Turing's academic calling into a consuming erotic passion: The statement that "Gödel's theorem is the most beautiful thing I know" arrives like an orgasm at the climax of a lengthy disquisition. Sex, by contrast, makes Turing sound like a detached theorist. Confessing his sexual preference to a female colleague (Jenny Agutter) who has fallen in love with him, Mr. Jacobi forthrightly, almost placidly, states, "I am a homosexual." This matter-of-fact honesty makes the character honorable even as it leads to his doom in a bigoted era.

The crossed circuits of mind and body is one of many themes that waft through Mr. Whitemore's script. As the evening moves back and forth over a roughly thirty-year period bracketed by the protagonist's public-school youth and his death, we see that Turing's obsession with the mind's ability to exist apart from a body dominates both his personal and scientific concerns. When he takes a lover in Greece, he would rather putter around with the inner workings of a radio than dance with his friend to the music played on the radio. In his postulation of a "universal" computing machine, Turing dreams of an electronic brain unencumbered by the needs and pains of the heart and the flesh.

As one expects from the author of the spy play *Pack of Lies* and the Alger Hiss television drama *Concealed Enemies,* Mr. Whitemore is also preoccupied by the state's ability to crush citizens for expedient ends: Turing's wartime code-breaking counts for nothing when he violates society's antediluvian social code. *Breaking the Code* further desires to explore the connections between science and morality. Is there a link between Turing's unabashed, unapologetic homosexual behavior and his courageous championing of a pure, abstract mathematics that does away with simple concepts of right and wrong?

To raise these fascinating questions, one must say, is not the same as delving into them. Mr. Whitemore remains a middlebrow, if upscale, television writer in that he sends an audience home with debating points to consider but with little substantive ammunition for deepening the discussion. He would rather quote or summarize relevant passages in Wittgenstein, Tolstoy, and Bertrand Russell than take a striking stand of his own and follow it through to a challenging end. Such intellectual timidity, in turn, can lead to dramatic inertia. The supporting characters—whether Turing's angelic first public-school crush, or a no-nonsense detective or a proletarian hustler—are stereotypes who wander in and out (usually a niggardly one at a time) to serve as springboards for Mr. Jacobi's monologues. When Mr. Whitemore wishes to impart his themes, he clears the stage entirely so Turing can deliver an undisguised classroom lecture.

Though the play's talkiness, glibness, and stubborn resistance to the grand dramatic gesture are readily apparent, they are sometimes countered by Clifford Williams's fluid, imaginative production. Liz da Costa's all-purpose set—a huge, cloud-backed hangar that might also be the imprisoning computer of Turing's worst nightmares—is more theatrical than the play. The mostly new and impeccable supporting cast is far superior to the one I saw in the West End last summer.

It is amazing to see how much the variously sunny and ashen Rachel Gurney makes of the clichéd role of Turing's distant yet vivacious mother—seemingly the same woman who gave birth to every gay Cambridge University student seen on stage or screen for the past decade or so. (Dad, needless to say, is absent.) Even more impressive is Michael Gough as Dillwyn Knox, Turing's silver-haired, bespectacled, by-the-book wartime superior. Mr. Gough, like Michael Bryant and Michael Gambon, is one of those remarkable English character actors who should be much better known to American audiences. There is fine, supple Chekhovian detail to his every small gesture, from his slow-dawning owlish smiles to the buttoning of his ill-fitting tweed jacket to the revealing tentativeness with which he fingers through a personnel file.

With meatier roles, Mr. Gough, Ms. Gurney, and Ms. Agutter, the putative female love interest, might well be as touching as the star. But there is plenty of Mr. Jacobi to fill the vacuum: He virtually never leaves the stage. Even when Turing's biography trails off into public ostracism, the hideous punishment of estrogen treatments, and the contemplation of suicide, the actor continues to emphasize the mathematician's breathtaking explorer's vision over his cruel humiliation. The honest, restless bravery of Mr. Jacobi's performance seems the born artistic expression of a code breaker's iconoclastic soul.

SUNDAY ESSAY: SONDHEIM'S WINDING PATHS
NOVEMBER 29, 1987

There's Something About a War" goes the title of a song that was written for, but never used, in Stephen Sondheim's first musical as a Broadway composer, the 1962 *A Funny Thing Happened on the Way to the Forum.* There's something about a Stephen Sondheim musical that's something like a war—and, until the arrival of his latest and perhaps most tranquil show, *Into the Woods,* that war had threatened to rival the Thirty Years' War in duration. People have never been neutral about the work of Stephen Sondheim. He leaves some theatergoers elated and others enraged. At the theaters where his musicals are playing, the heat and tension of battle seem to charge the air.

I was baptized into this phenomenon a quarter-century ago, when *Forum* played its pre-Broadway tryout engagement at the National Theatre in Washington. As soon as I spotted a newspaper ad heralding the new musical, I had sent off a hard-earned $4.80 mail order, and was overjoyed to receive a fourth-row center orchestra ticket in response. (A pasteboard marked D101 is any stagestruck teenager's dream come true.) But I was somewhat chagrined to read the Washington reviews of *Forum* once the show hit town. The musical was dismissed as a certain Broadway fiasco, and, given its scantily clad courtesans, a morally subversive entertainment for the young.

I was undeterred. My ticket was for the final Saturday matinee of the three-week run—the penultimate performance before *Forum* shipped on to take its chances with New Yorkers at the Alvin Theatre on Broadway. With great pride, I allowed the usher to escort me to my fourth-row seat in the vast house. My feelings of privilege were short-lived, however, because as the lights dimmed for the overture, I turned around to discover that there was no one seated in the twenty-odd rows and two balconies behind me. In the 1,700-seat theater, at most fifty tickets had been sold.

But the ensuing show dispelled the gloom of loneliness. Though the production still lacked the opening number ("Comedy Tonight") that would famously reverse its fortunes during New York previews a week later, *Forum* was (and is) about the funniest musical comedy ever written. To see masterful clowns like Zero Mostel, Jack Gilford, and David Burns perform "Everybody Ought to Have a Maid"—even to a deserted house—was to enter the burlesque heaven otherwise unattainable to theatergoers too young for the heyday of Ed Wynn and Bert Lahr and Bobby Clark. Yet my joy was tempered by rage—not about the empty seats but about those few theatergoers who did occupy the seats around me. They shared the view of the critics. They were antagonized by the bawdiness. In Act 2, those who returned stubbornly refused to laugh, and, at the curtain call, barely deigned to applaud. At that moment, *Forum* became my cause—I've since learned that every Sondheim musical is somebody or other's cause—and, when I subsequently saw the show on Broadway, this time by buying standing room, I gloated over the fact that New Yorkers were embracing the same musical Washingtonians had shunned.

In other years, other cities, and other lives, my experience with Sondheim musicals—and I expect that of most Sondheim enthusiasts—has inevitably been the same.

One sits in a theater where people are cheering or sneering; the pitch and conflict of battle drift into intermission, where heated arguments ensue. At the packed closing performance of *Follies* at the Winter Garden in 1972, people threw flowers at the stage in the same theater where, only a week or so earlier, audiences had greeted the same production with indifference and coughing. At an early preview of *Sweeney Todd* (1979), dozens of unprepared theatergoers ran for the exits once it became apparent that cannibalism was on the evening's menu. At a final-week performance of the short-lived *Merrily We Roll Along* (1982), scattered clumps of theatergoers rose to give every song an ovation while the majority of the house looked on in perplexed, dumbfounded silence. I never saw a performance of *Sunday in the Park with George* (1984) at which some members of the audience didn't walk out early—often not even waiting until intermission to do so—while others, sobbing in their seats, refused to budge until well after the house lights were up.

Into the Woods is another—and, I think, tellingly anomalous—story. What makes this Sondheim musical fascinating is that it's the first of his darker shows to reach a truce with the audience. Lavishly produced, charmingly cast, and familiar in subject (Brothers Grimm fairy tales), it has been better received than most Sondheim works, and it may well have a longer run than most. This has been accomplished without cynicism on the authors' part; *Into the Woods* is hardly a sellout to commercial pressures. All the usual Sondheim sourness is on display—betrayals, disillusionments, and deaths. No one will mistake the music for that of Andrew Lloyd Webber or Jerry Herman. The show is even structured like the groundbreaking *Sunday,* in that its second act is a postscript designed to fracture and then reconstitute the personal and esthetic harmony that the characters and narrative achieve in the Act 1 finale. But the results don't arouse the hysterical passions of other Sondheim musicals; it's hard to imagine anyone turning *Into the Woods* into Exhibit A for either the pro- or anti-Sondheim cause. While one can respect the effort and enjoy it—or respect it and be mildly bored by it—*Into the Woods* is an unlikely candidate to make anyone vote with his feet, whether by rising for a standing ovation or storming out early.

The evening's mild effect may reflect that *Into the Woods* is as much a thematic culmination, a resolution, for Mr. Sondheim as *Sunday in the Park,* which he also cowrote with the playwright and director James Lapine, was a stylistic breakthrough. Fairy tales are not a new subject for Mr. Sondheim, but until now, he's tended to shy away from pursuing them directly. The elaborate song "Two Fairy Tales" (which included the lyric "Fairy tales are foolish") was cut in preproduction from *A Little Night Music* (1973). The Act 1 finale of *Into the Woods*—"Ever After"— is prefigured in other discarded lyrics sung by jaded lovers in two previous Sondheim musicals: the 1965 *Do I Hear a Waltz?* ("Happy endings can spring a leak / Ever after can mean one week") and the 1970 *Company* (whose original finale, later replaced by "Being Alive," was sardonically titled "Happily Ever After").

This time Mr. Sondheim, presumably prodded by Mr. Lapine, wades right into the material he previously approached glancingly. *Into the Woods* dramatizes the adventures of Little Red Ridinghood, Cinderella, the beanstalk-climbing Jack, and a childless baker and his wife as they all venture into a mysterious Brothers Grimm forest. What inevitably happens, as the psychoanalyst Bruno Bettelheim tells us in his classic study of fairy tales, *The Uses of Enchantment,* is that the characters grow up. Adrift in the darkest wilderness of their consciousness, they learn to overcome childhood traumas and to form adult bonds.

"The path is straight / I know it well," sings Little Red Ridinghood as she heads for her grandmother's house in the new musical's opening and title song. As it happens, Mr. Sondheim has written about exactly the same path to self-development in similar language throughout his career—including in those shows written well before *The Uses of Enchantment* was published (in 1977). Little Red Ridinghood's lyrics about her path into the woods could be those of the protagonist, Ben, in *Follies.* A middle-aged man who still hasn't figured out what he wants from life, Ben expresses his dilemma in a song called "The Road You Didn't Take"; he finally takes a detour into a figurative, enchanted woods by entering a dream sequence called "Loveland" that snakes though the goblin-strewn follies (and showbiz Follies) of his youth before finally delivering him into maturity.

In *Merrily We Roll Along,* the characters also sing constantly of "soft" and "bumpy" roads as they journey to self-knowledge. For the revised version of *Merrily,* staged in La Jolla, California, by Mr. Lapine in 1985, Mr. Sondheim wrote a new song, appropriately titled "Growing Up," whose lyric could belong to the title song of *Into the Woods:* "Every road has a turning / That's the way you keep learning." The same introspective journey is taken by Fredrik Egerman, the unhappily married protagonist of *Night Music,* and George, the stalled contemporary artist in Act 2 of *Sunday in the Park:* They respectively travel into a Scandinavian birch forest and the tree-filled park of the island of La Grande Jatte so that they might grow up, learn how to "connect," and then "move on" to live as adults.

If Cinderella, Little Red Ridinghood, and Jack—whether in *Into the Woods,* the original Grimm tales, or Bettelheim's analysis—all achieve their rebirth in part by separating from their parents, so, as well, do the inhabitants of past Sondheim musicals dating back to *Gypsy* in 1959. In Act 2 of *Into the Woods,* several characters are liberated, psychologically speaking, by the deaths or disappearances of their mothers. Two of those mothers, Jack's and Rapunzel's, are played by the same actresses (Barbara Bryne and Bernadette Peters) who played the mother of Georges Seurat and the grandmother of his twentieth-century American descendant George in *Sunday in the Park*—and those matriarchs died as well when their sons approached a new artistic and personal awakening. The heroine of *Sweeney Todd*, Johanna, was a Rapunzel figure (tresses included) whose salvation was preceded by the death of her mother (disguised as a witchlike beggar woman); the elderly matriarch played by Hermione Gingold in *Night Music* released that musical's heroine from middle-aged disappointment by presiding, fairy-queen-like, over forest revels. *Night Music* not only shares the enchanted woods of *Into the Woods*; its magical action is marked by three "smiles" of the summer night's moon much as *Into the Woods* marks time by the passing of three fairy-tale midnights.

But the new musical lacks the intensity of feeling of its overlapping predecessors. By making his usual themes overexplicit, Mr. Sondheim has written a show that is at once his most accessible and least dramatic. An audience that had to work—to either its excitement or annoyance—to unearth the meaning of a song like "Lesson No. 8" in *Sunday* is now presented with songs that deliver their lessons didactically. "I know things now . . . that I hadn't known before," sings Little Red Ridinghood after her adventures with the wolf; "You know things now that you never knew before," sings Jack after climbing the beanstalk. The "things" are soon enumerated, thereby robbing *Into the Woods* of its dramatic tension much as fairy tales are stripped of their imaginative force and therapeutic power for children (as Dr. Bettelheim notes) when parents spell out their significance.

Obscurity for its own sake, of course, is no asset in art, but Mr. Sondheim has never been as willfully opaque as his unsympathetic critics maintain. The passion and excitement of his work is to be found in his elliptical dramatization of his themes: The tension between his meaning and his expression of that meaning is what gives a Sondheim musical its biting theatricality. Without that tension, the electricity dissipates. This is why the mother played by Ethel Merman in *Gypsy* is a more terrifying witch than the actual witch who is Rapunzel's mother in *Woods*, and why the lyric for "Everything's Coming Up Roses" (with music by Jule Styne) is a more harrowing expression of maternal possessiveness than Bernadette Peters's equivalent, straightforward admonitions to her daughter in the new musical. We care more about George reaching out to his "family tree" through the abstract art of painting in *Sunday* than about a baker literally finding his father among the trees in *Woods*. Similarly, the murders conducted by the vengeful barber of *Sweeney Todd* traumatize the audience as the equally numerous killings and bloody mutilations in *Woods* do not. *Sweeney Todd*, a minefield of shadowy characters and ambiguous motivations, retains the anxiety and mystery—which is to say the drama—of violent familial emotions denied the homily-spouting fairy-tale figures of *Woods*.

As a piece of theater, the new musical has its other, purely technical failings. The interwoven tales of *Woods* never fall into place with the order and harmony of the equally splintered stories of *Forum, Night Music,* and *Sunday*. The musical numbers often cry out for firmer final punctuation in the staging, and the Act 2 plot developments are often arbitrary or confusing. But these flaws are all "fixable," as they say on Broadway. What can't be fixed in *Into the Woods* is the prosaic way in which its authors explicate once-hot material: The personal traumas that seemed like open wounds in past Sondheim musicals are all presented as open-and-shut cases in *Into the Woods,* as if the authors had fought and won their own battles in the woods well before they sent their characters to explore there. The elusive, neurotic subtext of the composer's past work becomes the obvious, conventionally uplifting text this time.

The softened, predigested conflicts in the book and lyrics take their toll on the score—almost every song in *Woods* has an edgier, more combative analogue in a previous Sondheim musical—and even the Act 2 evocations of a fiery apocalypse fail to release the composer's usual depths of melancholy and anger. Accordingly, *Into the Woods* is, to borrow Cinderella's description of her Prince, a "very nice" show. But, as Little Red Ridinghood learns from the wolf, "nice is different than good." Much as one respects Mr. Sondheim's maturity—and, as always, his enormous talent and integrity—his new, placid musical leaves the unmistakable impression that his art is spoiling for a fresh fight.

SERIOUS MONEY
PUBLIC THEATER, DECEMBER 4, 1987

When the antiquated London stock market finally cast off tradition and plugged into the deregulated frenzy of modern Wall Street in 1986, the phenomenon was heralded as the Big Bang. In *Serious Money,* a ferocious new satire about the financial wheeler-dealers born in the ensuing boom, Caryl Churchill takes the term literally.

The play at the Public Theater travels to the trading pits and board rooms of London's financial district, the City, to find the precise pitch of the arena of arbitrage, inside trading, greenmail, corporate raiding, and leveraged buyouts. *Serious Money* wants us to hear the very sound of megascale greed as it is practiced on that circuit of telephone wires and computer screens blinking twenty-four hours a day from Tokyo to New York.

That sound is not the sound of music. It is not the polite ringing of a cash register. It is not even the insistent chatter of a ticker tape. The noise emanating from the brokers and bankers and dealers in *Serious Money* is a cacophonous, feverish screech of numbers and obscenities that builds into a mad roar. It is, indeed, a big bang, and it rivals other apocalyptic explosions of our nuclear age in its potential for devastation. As Ms. Churchill and the recent crash both demonstrate, the bursting financial bubble can leave small investors, large corporations, third-world countries, and Western economies shattered in its wake.

Yet in the theater, the noise creates a strange, if chilling, exhilaration. If *Serious Money* is an angry, leftist political work about ruthlessness and venality, about plundering and piggishness, it is also vivid entertainment. The fun comes in part from the vicarious pleasure always to be had in watching the flimflams of others. Ms. Churchill opens her play with an excerpt from a 1692 Thomas Shadwell comedy about stock jobbers— and a bit of *The Solid Gold Cadillac* could have made the same plus ça change point. But even more of the evening's lift can be attributed to Ms. Churchill's own inventive approach to her enduring subject. As her characters have rewritten the rules of the marketplace to create a new order of Darwinist capitalism, so she rewrites the rules of the theater expressly to capture that bizarre world on stage.

Such daring is typical of this playwright, who in her previous *Cloud 9* and *Top Girls* has sent characters floating between historical periods and genders to make trenchant points about sexual and economic oppression. While *Serious Money* is well aware of Ben Jonson, Restoration comedy, and Brecht, it has been written in its own outrageous style. The script is almost entirely composed of rhymed couplets, many of them juvenile and scatological, some of them clever ("If it was just inside dealing / It's not a proper crime like stealing"). The action is fast and confusing—intentionally so, given all the overlapping dialogue—and the people are no more than cartoons. The closest thing *Serious Money* has to a plot—the mysterious death of a commercial paper dealer—is never even resolved.

The overall result, repetitive and unruly as it sometimes may be, is wholly theatrical. Though based on up-to-the-minute research and clearly inspired in part by the actual Guinness and Boesky scandals in London and New York, *Serious Money* is not a *Nightline*-style documentary. Nor is it a work of satirical narrative fiction, like *The Bonfire of the Vanities,* Tom Wolfe's thematically related novel about a high-rolling Wall Street bond trader. Ms. Churchill valiantly makes the case, as so very few playwrights do these days, that the stage can still play its own unique role, distinct from that of journalism or television or movies, in dramatizing the big, immediate stories of our day.

Only in a theater could we watch a Peruvian businesswoman (Meera Syal) deliver a long, rhymed soliloquy that captures the fashions, ethos, and economic basis of a cocaine-fueled branch of the OPEC jet set. Or watch the traders on the floor of Liffe—the London International Financial Futures Exchange, and pronounced like "life"—transform their hand signals and brokerage jargon into a rap number (with lyrics by Ian Dury) that really makes their business seem, as one character describes it, "a cross between roulette and Space Invaders." While Ms. Churchill does periodically send her players forward to explain terminology and history, one need not be able to define "junk bonds" or know the real-life basis of a scene inspired by the fall of Lehman Brothers to grasp her polemical drift. Visceral theater, not didactic sermonizing, is the medium of her message.

Nor is that message as simplistic as one might think. To be sure, Ms. Churchill is tough on red-suspendered, champagne-guzzling hustlers who speed down the fast lane in BMW's and Lamborghinis on their way to the scrap heap at age thirty-five. She is also tough on the paternalistic, old-style businessmen overturned (and often taken over) by the new deal-makers and on African and black American entrepreneurs who sell out their own for a share of the spoils. But *Serious Money* is more an indictment of a system than of specific sharks and crooks. When money—not even land or widgets or pork bellies—is the main commodity traded on the floor of Liffe, the game loses all connection to life. Real lives are soon cold-bloodedly crunched along with the fast-flying abstract numbers.

When *Serious Money* falters—and it does, notably after intermission—the problem is only partly Ms. Churchill's refusal to engineer her story as niftily as Mr. Wolfe or a Restoration playwright might. The principal actors, all English but only some of them from the first Royal Court Theatre cast, too frequently fail to etch firmly the writer's caricatures. In addition to laughable American accents, we get a corporate raider (Daniel Webb, in a role originated in London by Gary Oldman) who rants like a George Raft impersonator, and a narrating banker (Paul Moriarty) of no discernible personality whatsoever. Much better are Ms. Syal's smooth Peruvian cutthroat, Joanne Pearce as the yuppiest of fe-

male traders, Allan Corduner as several impressively different representatives of a dying old-boy establishment, and especially Linda Bassett as
three of those hatefully hard Thatcher-era "top girls" Ms. Churchill loves
to skewer. Among Ms. Bassett's roles is a public-relations expert who ad-
vises the Boesky-like raider to sweeten his image by sponsoring London's
National Theatre—a particularly rude joke, given the real Mr. Boesky's
onetime service on the board of the theater in which the New York audience of *Serious Money* sits.

Working on a smart Peter Hartwell set that vandalizes London's
classical architectural past with the flickering electronic hardware of the
financial bullring, Max Stafford-Clark stages the play at a fittingly breakneck pace. "Sexy greed is the late eighties," says Ms. Bassett's PR
woman, and the director does not ignore the racy pull of "massive sums
of money being passed around the world." In concert with the slangy,
punchy script, he gives the show the overheated tone of the raunchy
London gutter press. But on the one occasion when two of the characters actually try to arrange a romantic tryst, they fail to find a free hour
in common in their Filofax diaries. The Big Bang leaves no time for that
kind of orgasm; Ms. Churchill's traders regard even AIDS as just another
"great market opportunity." In *Serious Money,* the heartlessness of the
late eighties finds its raucous voice in comedy that is, as it must be, hilariously, gravely sick.

≡ Serious Money *was not a popular play, except with drama critics. I met
few who liked it, and many who found the language so fast and thick that
they couldn't understand what anyone on stage was saying. Despite this—
and despite the fact that Equity decreed that the original British cast
would have to return to England after the agreed-upon limited engagement—Joseph Papp and the Shuberts decided to move it to Broadway. I
was in London reviewing plays when the move occurred and though the
transferred version got a good review in the* Times *in my absence, the almost immediate failure of* Serious Money *in its uptown digs was blamed
on me by Papp. Sounding notes familiar from the Dramatists Guild's
protest of my not reviewing* Sweet Sue, *Papp declared in a letter that it was
unpatriotic of me to be reviewing London theater rather than remaining in
New York to cheerlead with a second review an American theater's efforts
to move a serious play to Broadway. (Never mind that the play being moved
was British.) I got back from London just in time to see the new Broadway
version. Recast and underrehearsed, it was awful—if anything, Papp got a
lucky break that I was away—and it made me feel I had overrated* Serious
Money *in the first place.*

THE CHERRY ORCHARD
MAJESTIC THEATER, BROOKLYN, JANUARY 25, 1988

It is not until the final act of *The Cherry Orchard* that the malevolent thud of an ax signals the destruction of a family's ancestral estate and, with it, the traumatic uprooting of a dozen late-nineteenth-century Russian lives. But in Peter Brook's production of Chekhov's play, the landscape seems to have been cleared before Act 1 begins. Mr. Brook has stripped *The Cherry Orchard* of its scenery, its front curtain, its intermissions. Even the house in which the play unfolds—the Brooklyn Academy of Music's semirestored Majestic Theater—looks half-demolished, a once-genteel palace of gilt and plush now a naked, faded shell of crumbling brick, chipped paint, and forgotten hopes.

What little decorative elegance remains can be found on the vast stage floor, which Mr. Brook has covered, as is his wont, with dark Oriental rugs. And that—plus an exceptional international cast, using a crystalline new translation by Elisaveta Lavrova—proves to be all that's needed. On this director's magic carpets, *The Cherry Orchard* flies. By banishing all forms of theatrical realism except the only one that really matters—emotional truth—Mr. Brook has found the pulse of a play that its author called "not a drama but a comedy, in places almost a farce." That pulse isn't to be confused with the somber metronomic beat of the Act 4 ax—the Stanislavskian gloom that Chekhov so despised—and it isn't the kinetic, too frequently farcical gait of Andrei Serban's fascinating 1977 production at Lincoln Center. The real tone of *The Cherry Orchard* is that of a breaking string—that mysterious, unidentifiable off-stage sound that twice interrupts the action, unnerving the characters and audience alike with the sensation that unfathomable life is inexorably rushing by.

We feel that strange tingle, an exquisite pang of joy and suffering, again and again. When the beautiful Natasha Parry, as the bankrupt landowner Lyubov, returns to her estate from Paris, her brimming eyes take in the vast reaches of the auditorium in a single sweeping glance of nostalgic longing. But when she says, "I feel like a little girl again," the husky darkness of her voice fills in the scarred decades since childhood, relinquishing the girlishness even as it is reclaimed. Later, Ms. Parry will simply sit in a chair, quietly crying, as Brian Dennehy, in the role of the merchant Lopakhin, announces that he has purchased her estate at auction. Lopakhin, whose ancestors were serfs on the land he now owns, can't help celebrating his purchase, but his half-jig of victory is slowly tempered by the realization that he has forfeited any chance of affection from the aristocratic woman he has just bought out. Mr. Dennehy ends up prostrate on the floor behind Ms. Parry's chair, tugging ineffectually at her hem. We're left with an indelible portrait of not one but two well-meaning souls who have lost what they most loved by recognizing their own desires too late.

That Lopakhin is as sympathetic and complex a figure as Lyubov, rather than a malicious arriviste, is a tribute not just to Mr. Dennehy's performance but also to Mr. Brook's entire approach to the play. When Trofimov (Zeljko Ivanek), the eternal student, angrily tells Ms. Parry to "face the truth" for once in her life, she responds rhetorically, "What truth?" The director, like Chekhov, recognizes that there is no one truth. Each character must be allowed his own truth—a mixture of attributes and convictions that can't easily be typed or judged. Mr. Dennehy gives us both sides (and more) of the man whom Trofimov variously calls a "beast of prey" and "a fine, sensitive soul." Mr. Ivanek does the same with Trofimov, providing a rounded view of the sometimes foolish but fundamentally idealistic young man whose opinions swing so wildly. Though the student may look immature telling off Lyubov or Lopakhin, his vision of a happier future is so stirring that Mr. Ivanek quite rightly prompts the moon to rise while proclaiming it ("I can feel my happiness coming—I can see it!") at the end of Act 2.

Ms. Parry, Mr. Dennehy, and Mr. Ivanek are all brilliant under Mr. Brook's guidance, and they're not alone. As Lyubov's brother, Gaev—a forlorn representative of czarist Russia's obsolete, decaying nobility—the Swedish actor Erland Josephson embodies the fossilized remains of a civilization. Elegant of bearing yet fuzzy of expression, his voice mellifluous yet childlike, he snaps into focus only when drifting into imaginary billiard games. One of the evening's comic high points is his absurdly gratuitous tribute to a century-old family bookcase, but the hilarity of his futility is matched by the poignancy of his Act 3 entrance, in which his exhausted posture and sad, dangling bundle of anchovy and herring tins announce the estate's sale to his sister well before Lopakhin does.

As Firs, the octogenarian family retainer, Roberts Blossom is a tall, impish, bearded figure in formal black, stooping over his cane—a spindly, timeless ghost from the past, as rooted to the soil as the trees we never see. Stephanie Roth is a revelation as Varya, whose fruitless religious piety is balanced by a bravery that saves her from despair when her last prayer for happiness, a marriage proposal from Lopakhin, flickers and then dies in Mr. Dennehy's eyes. Linda Hunt (Charlotta), Jan Triska

(Yepikhodov), and Mike Nussbaum (Pishchik) find the melancholy humor of true Old World clowns in their subsidiary, more broadly conceived roles. If the play's younger generation—Rebecca Miller (Anya), Kate Mailer (Dunyasha), and David Pierce (Yasha)—is not of the same class, holding one's own with a company of this stature is no small achievement in itself.

In keeping with his work with the actors, Mr. Brook's staging has a supple, airy flow that avoids cheap laughs or sentimentality yet is always strikingly theatrical. In Act 3, the reveling dancers twirl around velvet screens in choreographic emulation of the ricocheting rumors of the estate's sale. Throughout the evening, the transitions of mood are lightning fast. In an instant, Ms. Parry's reminiscence of her son's drowning can be dispelled by the jaunty strains of a nearby band. Neither Lyubov nor anyone else is allowed the self-pity that would plunge *The Cherry Orchard* from the flickering tearfulness of regret into the maudlin sobs of phony high drama.

The mood that is achieved instead, though not tragic, recalls Mr. Brook's *Endgame*-inspired *King Lear* of the 1960s. Beckett is definitely on the director's mind, as is evident not just from the void in which he sets the play but also by his explicit evocation of the Beckett humor in several scenes. When Ms. Hunt's governess gives her monologue describing her utter lack of identity—she doesn't know who she is or where she came from—it's a cheeky, center stage effusion of existential verbal slapstick, with a vegetable for a prop, right out of *Waiting for Godot* or *Happy Days*. When, at evening's end, old Firs is locked by accident in the mansion, we're keenly aware of the repetition of the word "nothing" in his final speech. As Mr. Blossom falls asleep in his easy chair, illuminated by a bare shaft of light and accompanied by the far-off sound of the ax, one can't be blamed for thinking of Krapp reviewing his last tape.

But the delicate connections Mr. Brook draws between Beckett and Chekhov are inevitable and to the point, not arch and pretentious, and they help explain why this *Cherry Orchard* is so right. Though Chekhov was dying when he wrote this play, he didn't lose his perspective on existence and the people who endure it. Horrible, inexplicable things happen to the characters in *The Cherry Orchard*—the shadow of death is always cloaking their shoulders, as it does Beckett's lost souls—but, as Mr. Brook writes in the program, "they have not given up." They simply trudge on, sometimes with their senses of humor intact, sometimes with a dogged faith in the prospects for happiness.

That's the human comedy, and, if it isn't riotously funny, one feels less alone in the solitary plight, indeed exhilarated, watching it unfold on stage as honestly and buoyantly and poetically as a dream. This is a *Cherry Orchard* that pauses for breath only when life does, for people to recoup after dying a little. I think Mr. Brook has given us the Chekhov production that every theatergoer fantasizes about but, in my experience, almost never finds.

THE PHANTOM OF THE OPERA
MAJESTIC THEATRE, JANUARY 27, 1988

It may be possible to have a terrible time at *The Phantom of the Opera*, but you'll have to work at it. Only a terminal prig would let the avalanche of preopening publicity poison his enjoyment of this show, which usually wants nothing more than to shower the audience with fantasy and fun, and which often succeeds, at any price.

It would be equally ludicrous, however—and an invitation to severe disappointment—to let the hype kindle the hope that *Phantom* is a credible heir to the Rodgers and Hammerstein musicals that haunt both Andrew Lloyd Webber's creative aspirations and the Majestic Theatre as persistently as the evening's title character does. What one finds instead is a characteristic Lloyd Webber project—long on pop professionalism and melody, impoverished of artistic personality and passion—that the director Harold Prince, the designer Maria Bjornson, and the mesmerizing actor Michael Crawford have elevated quite literally to the roof. *The Phantom of the Opera* is as much a victory of dynamic stagecraft over musical kitsch as it is a triumph of merchandising über alles.

As you've no doubt heard, *Phantom* is Mr. Lloyd Webber's first sustained effort at writing an old-fashioned romance between people instead of cats or trains. The putative lovers are the Paris Opera House phantom (Mr. Crawford) and a chorus singer named Christine Daaé (Sarah Brightman). But Mr. Crawford's moving portrayal of the hero notwithstanding, the show's most persuasive love story is Mr. Prince's and Ms. Bjornson's unabashed crush on the theater itself, from footlights to dressing rooms, from flies to trap doors.

A gothic backstage melodrama, *Phantom* taps right into the obsessions of the designer and the director. At the Royal Shakespeare Company, Ms. Bjornson was a wizard of darkness, monochromatic palettes, and mysterious grand staircases. Mr. Prince, a prince of darkness in his own right, is the master of the towering bridge (*Evita*), the labyrinthine inferno (*Sweeney Todd*), and the musical-within-the-musical (*Follies*). In

Phantom, the creative personalities of these two artists merge with a literal lightning flash at the opening coup de théâtre, in which the auditorium is transformed from gray decrepitude to the gold-and-crystal Second Empire glory of the Paris Opera House. Though the sequence retreads the famous Ziegfeld palace metamorphosis in *Follies,* Ms. Bjornson's magical eye has allowed Mr. Prince to reinvent it, with electrifying showmanship.

The physical production, Andrew Bridge's velvety lighting included, is a tour de force throughout—as extravagant of imagination as of budget. Ms. Bjornson drapes the stage with layers of Victorian theatrical curtains—heavily tasseled front curtains, fire curtains, backdrops of all antiquated styles—and then constantly shuffles their configurations so we may view the opera house's stage from the perspective of its audience, the performers, or the wings. For an added lift, we visit the operahouse roof, with its cloud-swept view of a twinkling late-night Paris, and the subterranean lake where the Phantom travels by gondola to a baroque secret lair that could pass for the lobby of Grauman's Chinese Theater. The lake, awash in dry-ice fog and illuminated by dozens of candelabra, is a masterpiece of campy phallic Hollywood iconography—it's Liberace's vision of hell.

There are horror-movie special effects, too, each elegantly staged and unerringly paced by Mr. Prince. The imagery is so voluptuous that one can happily overlook the fact that the book (by the composer and Richard Stilgoe) contains only slightly more plot than *Cats,* with scant tension or suspense. This *Phantom,* more skeletal but not briefer than other adaptations of the 1911 Gaston Leroux novel, is simply a beast-meets-beauty, loses-beauty story, attenuated by the digressions of disposable secondary characters (the liveliest being Judy Kaye's oft-humiliated diva) and by Mr. Lloyd Webber's unchecked penchant for forcing the show to cool its heels while he hawks his wares.

In Act 2, the heroine travels to her father's grave for no reason other than to sell an extraneous ballad whose tepid greeting-card sentiments ("Wishing You Were Somehow Here Again") dispel the evening's smoldering mood. The musical's dramatic thrust is further slowed by three self-indulgently windy opera parodies—in which the sophisticated tongue-in-cheek wit of Ms. Bjornson's sumptuous period sets and costumes is in no way matched by Gillian Lynne's repetitive, presumably satirical ballet choreography or by Mr. Lloyd Webber's tiresome collegiate jokes at the expense of such less than riotous targets as Meyerbeer.

Aside from the stunts and set changes, the evening's histrionic peaks are Mr. Crawford's entrances—one of which is the slender excuse for Ms.

Bjornson's most dazzling display of Technicolor splendor, the masked ball ("Masquerade") that opens Act 2. Mr. Crawford's appearances are eagerly anticipated, not because he's really scary but because his acting gives *Phantom* most of what emotional heat it has. His face obscured by a half-mask—no minor impediment—Mr. Crawford uses a booming, expressive voice and sensuous hands to convey his desire for Christine. His Act 1 declaration of love, "The Music of the Night"—in which the Phantom calls on his musical prowess to bewitch the heroine—proves as much a rape as a seduction. Stripped of the mask an act later to wither into a crestfallen, sweaty, cadaverous misfit, he makes a pitiful sight while clutching his beloved's discarded wedding veil. Those who visit the Majestic expecting only to applaud a chandelier—or who have twenty-year-old impressions of Mr. Crawford as the lightweight screen juvenile of *The Knack* and *Hello, Dolly!*—will be stunned by the force of his Phantom.

It's deflating that the other constituents of the story's love triangle don't reciprocate his romantic or sexual energy. The icily attractive Ms. Brightman possesses a lush soprano by Broadway standards (at least as amplified), but reveals little competence as an actress. After months of playing *Phantom* in London, she still simulates fear and affection alike by screwing her face into bug-eyed, chipmunk-cheeked poses more appropriate to the Lon Chaney film version. Steve Barton, as the Vicomte who lures her from the beast, is an affable professional escort with unconvincingly bright hair.

Thanks to the uniform strength of the voices—and the soaring, Robert Russell Bennett–style orchestrations—Mr. Lloyd Webber's music is given every chance to impress. There are some lovely tunes, arguably his best yet, and, as always, they are recycled endlessly: If you don't leave the theater humming the songs, you've got a hearing disability. But the banal lyrics, by Charles Hart and Mr. Stilgoe, prevent the score's prettiest music from taking wing. The melodies don't find shape as theater songs that might touch us by giving voice to the feelings or actions of specific characters.

Instead, we get numbing, interchangeable pseudo-Hammersteinisms like "Say you'll love me every waking moment" or "Think of me, think of me fondly, when we say good-bye." With the exception of "Music of the Night"—which seems to express from its author's gut a desperate longing for acceptance—Mr. Lloyd Webber has again written a score so generic that most of the songs could be reordered and redistributed among the characters (indeed, among other Lloyd Webber musicals) without altering the show's story or meaning. The one attempt at highbrow composing, a noisy and gratuitous septet called "Prima Donna," is unlikely to take a place beside the similar Broadway operatics of Bernstein, Sondheim, or Loesser.

Yet for now, if not forever, Mr. Lloyd Webber is a genuine phenomenon—not an invention of the press or ticket scalpers—and *Phantom* is worth seeing not only for its punch as high-gloss entertainment but also as a fascinating key to what the phenomenon is about. Mr. Lloyd Webber's esthetic has never been more baldly stated than in this show, which favors the decorative trappings of art over the troublesome substance of culture and finds more eroticism in rococo opulence and conspicuous consumption than in love or sex. Mr. Lloyd Webber is a creature, perhaps even a prisoner, of his time; with *The Phantom of the Opera*, he remakes La Belle Epoque in the image of our own Gilded Age. If by any chance this musical doesn't prove Mr. Lloyd Webber's most popular, it won't be his fault, but another sign that times are changing and that our boom era, like the opera house's chandelier, is poised to go bust.

≡ *My qualms not withstanding,* Phantom of the Opera *is well on its way to becoming the longest-running and most lucrative production in the history of the American theater. This review, however, thrust me into a farcical international sparring match with Lloyd Webber, who has made a second career out of crying all the way to the bank. (For more details, see* "Exit the Critic" *at the end of this volume.) My favorite account of Lloyd Webber's anger about my review appeared in the London tabloid* Today, *under the headline:* WEBBER SAVAGES BUTCHER OF BROADWAY: WHAT DOES HE KNOW ABOUT LOVE AND ROMANCE?" *In it, Lloyd Webber was quoted as asking,* "Why doesn't he look after his own life and divorce and stop writing about normal theater?" *Before long, he had divorced Sarah Brightman, though he continued to employ her in provincial tours and replacement casts of his long-running productions.*

WOMAN IN MIND
MANHATTAN THEATRE CLUB, FEBRUARY 18, 1988

The true test of an artist, whatever the art form, is often to be found in the half-tones, not the primary colors. Stockard Channing, an actress whose indelible recent performances in *Joe Egg* and *The House of Blue Leaves* leave her with little need to prove anything, subjects herself to this rough test and triumphs in *Woman in Mind,* the modest but watchable Alan Ayckbourn play at the Manhattan Theatre Club.

As Susan, a middle-aged hausfrau of the English suburbs, Ms. Channing is in every way a smudged figure. Even her appearance blends into the scenery: minimal makeup, matronly print dress, sensible shoes, half-streaked and half-combed hair. But in Ms. Channing's muted spectrum of feelings—as often to be found in her distracted or bemused or anguished reactions to others as in her own mild lines and actions—there is ceaseless illumination of an ordinary woman's first, shell-shocking encounter with her own despair.

When we initially meet Susan in her garden, she is regaining consciousness after knocking herself out by stepping on a rake. For the next forty-eight hours, she takes the audience into the stilled heart of her long marriage to a pompous vicar (Remak Ramsay), but she does so from the point of view of a victim of a concussion or a nervous breakdown or both. Susan vacillates between madness and sanity, between fainting and waking, between pungent eloquence and verbal dysfunction, between erotic arousal and menopausal exhaustion. How Ms. Channing retains her fragile balance between such poles, never tilting to any one behavioral extreme until the devastating (and yet still understated) final curtain, is a mystery too haunting to be explained away by technique. Indeed, as was not the case with her London predecessor in the role, Julia McKenzie, the technique is invisible. When Susan experiences rage, Ms. Channing is less likely to raise her voice than dilate a single distressed eye.

Grand gestures would be inappropriate. Susan isn't Hedda Gabler or Sylvia Plath. Her sorrows are banal—an adult son (John David Cullum) who has rejected her for a Moonie-like sect, a whiny and omnipresent sister-in-law (Patricia Conolly), a husband who has subsumed his entire existence into the preparation of a dreary sixty-page history of his parish. It's the theatrical conceit of *Woman in Mind* that Susan retreats from this humdrum household not by contemplating revolt or suicide but by conjuring up a second, fantasy family—a devoted husband (Daniel Gerroll), daughter (Tracy Pollan), and brother (Michael Countryman). Dressed in tennis whites and forever sipping champagne, the imagined relatives are preposterous Noël Coward sophisticates who step into Susan's suburban garden much as the glamorous Jeff Daniels stepped out of the movie screen into Mia Farrow's drab life in Woody Allen's *The Purple Rose of Cairo.*

Like Mr. Allen, Mr. Ayckbourn soon reveals that his heroine's fantasy companions are no closer to perfection than the real-life characters they threaten to usurp. But *Woman in Mind* sets forth this point and others too schematically. The play doesn't run very deep in its view of Susan's psychology or her alternatives for liberation. The complex issues of marriage and family are ignored or tightly circumscribed as Mr. Ayckbourn asks his protagonist to choose between good and bad husbands and children rather than to question her own enslavement to the roles of wife and mother.

The superficiality of Susan's predicament is compounded by Mr. Ramsay's and Ms. Conolly's buffoonish portrayals of the family she would leave behind: They're so grotesquely idiotic that one wonders how Susan ever tolerated them. Mr. Cullum's sullen, insolent son is far more persuasive, however—an ashen specter of parental neglect past—and Lynne Meadow's production is in general sharper than Mr. Ayckbourn's own West End staging of 1986. Mr. Gerroll, Ms. Pollan, and Mr. Countryman bring the right sinister edge to Susan's dazzling second family. The set designer, John Lee Beatty, jazzes up the surreal denouement in which the author, in a typical upending of conventional dramatic form, shuffles reality and hallucination to vertigo-inducing effect.

Though *Woman in Mind* isn't remotely as funny or chilling as its prolific author's more ambitious and savage recent works (*A Chorus of Disapproval, A Small Family Business*), one can see Ayckbourn at his best peeking through here and there. Of the supporting characters, the most fully realized by far is a family physician, superbly played by Simon Jones. A tweedy, awkward, congenitally apologetic sort, the doctor does little but tend to Susan's ailment with toothy smiles and innocuous chatter. Yet, without ever losing his jolly bedside manner or announcing an emotion, Mr. Jones delicately reveals the man as a lonely misfit with a bankrupt marriage of his own. In one of the playwright's characteristic coups de grace, the pathetic man's one attempt to reach out to Susan, by good-naturedly participating in her fantasy life, leads only to a cruel, farcical humiliation.

Bottomless suffering and cruelty presented in the deceptively sunny guise of middle-class domestic farce—such is the substance of the bitter latter-day Ayckbourn deserving of much wider circulation in New York. *Woman in Mind* is too slight to fill that vacuum, but Ms. Channing, on stage virtually throughout, fills an evening with her diaphanous account of one woman's free fall through her own inner space.

M. BUTTERFLY
EUGENE O'NEILL THEATRE, MARCH 21, 1988

It didn't require genius for David Henry Hwang to see that there were the makings of a compelling play in the 1986 newspaper story that prompted him to write *M. Butterfly.* Here was the incredible true-life tale of a career French foreign service officer brought to ruin—conviction for espionage—by a bizarre twenty-year affair with a Beijing Opera diva. Not only had the French diplomat failed to recognize that his lover was a spy; he'd also failed to figure out that "she" was a he in drag. "It was dark, and she was very modest," says Gallimard (John Lithgow), Mr. Hwang's fictionalized protagonist, by half-joking way of explanation. When we meet him in the prison cell where he reviews his life, Gallimard has become, according to his own understatement, "the patron saint of the socially inept."

But if this story is a corker, what is it about, exactly? That's where Mr. Hwang's imagination, one of the most striking to emerge in the American theater in this decade, comes in, and his answer has nothing to do with journalism. This playwright, the author of *The Dance and the Railroad* and *Family Devotions,* does not tease us with obvious questions such as is she or isn't she?, or does he know or doesn't he? Mr. Hwang isn't overly concerned with how the opera singer, named Song Liling (B. D. Wong), pulled his hocus-pocus in the boudoir, and he refuses to explain away Gallimard by making him a closeted, self-denying homosexual. An inversion of Puccini's *Madama Butterfly, M. Butterfly* is also the inverse of most American plays. Instead of reducing the world to an easily digested cluster of sexual or familial relationships, Mr. Hwang cracks open a liaison to reveal a sweeping, universal meditation on two of the most heated conflicts—men versus women, East versus West—of this or any other time.

As a piece of playwriting that manages to encompass phenomena as diverse as the origins of the Vietnam War and the socioeconomic code embedded in Giorgio Armani fashions, *M. Butterfly* is so singular that one hates to report that a visitor to the Eugene O'Neill Theatre must overcome a number of obstacles to savor it. Because of some crucial and avoidable lapses—a winning yet emotionally bland performance from Mr. Lithgow and inept acting in some supporting roles—the experience of seeing the play isn't nearly as exciting as thinking about it after the curtain has gone down. The production only rises to full power in its final act, when the evening's triumphant performance, Mr. Wong's mesmerizing account of the transvestite diva, hits its own tragic high notes. Until then, one must settle for being grateful that a play of this ambition has made it to Broadway, and that the director, John Dexter, has realized as much of Mr. Hwang's far-ranging theatricality as he has.

As usual, Mr. Hwang demands a lot from directors, actors, and theatergoers. A thirty-year-old Chinese American writer from Los Angeles, he has always blended Oriental and Western theater in his work, and *M. Butterfly* does so on an epic scale beyond his previous plays, let alone such similarly minded Western hybrids as *Pacific Overtures* or *Nixon in China*. While ostensibly constructed as a series of Peter Shafferesque flashbacks narrated by Gallimard from prison, the play is as intricate as an infinity of Chinese boxes. Even as we follow the narrative of the lovers' affair, it is being refracted through both overt and disguised burlesque deconstructions of *Madama Butterfly*. As Puccini's music collides throughout with a percussive Eastern score by Lucia Hwong, so Western storytelling and sassy humor intermingle with flourishes of martial-arts ritual, Chinese opera (Cultural Revolution Maoist agitprop included), and Kabuki. Now and then, the entire mix is turned inside out, Genet and Pirandello style, to remind us that fantasy isn't always distinguishable from reality and that actors are not to be confused with their roles.

The play's form—whether the clashing and blending of Western and Eastern cultures or of male and female characters—is wedded to its content. It's Mr. Hwang's starting-off point that a cultural icon like *Madama Butterfly* bequeaths the sexist and racist roles that burden Western men: Gallimard believes he can become "a real man" only if he can exercise power over a beautiful and submissive woman, which is why he's so ripe to be duped by Song Liling's impersonation of a shrinking butterfly. Mr. Hwang broadens his message by making Gallimard an architect of the Western foreign policy in Vietnam. The diplomat disastrously reasons that a manly display of American might can bring the Vietcong to submission as easily as he or Puccini's Pinkerton can overpower a Madama Butterfly.

Lest that ideological leap seem too didactic, the playwright shuffles the deck still more, suggesting that the roles played by Gallimard and Song Liling run so deep that they cross the boundaries of nations, cultures, revolutions, and sexual orientations. That Gallimard was fated to love "a woman created by a man" proves to be figuratively as well as literally true: We see that the male culture that inspired his "perfect woman" is so entrenched that the attitudes of *Madama Butterfly* survive in his cherished present-day porno magazines. Nor is the third world, in Mr. Hwang's view, immune from adopting the roles it condemns in foreign devils. We're sarcastically told that men continue to play women in Chinese opera because "only a man knows how a woman is supposed to act." When Song Liling reassumes his male "true self," he still must play a submissive Butterfly to Gallimard—whatever his or Gallimard's actual sexual persuasions—unless he chooses to play the role of aggressor to a Butterfly of his own.

Mr. Hwang's play is not without its repetitions and its overly explicit bouts of thesis mongering. When the playwright stops trusting his own instinct for the mysterious, the staging often helps out. Using Eiko Ishioka's towering, blood-red Oriental variant on the abstract sets Mr. Dexter has employed in *Equus* and the Metropolitan Opera *Dialogues of the Carmelites,* the director stirs together Mr. Hwang's dramatic modes and settings until one floats to a purely theatrical imaginative space suspended in time and place. That same disorienting quality can be found in Mr. Wong's Song Liling—a performance that, like John Lone's in the early Hwang plays, finds even more surprises in the straddling of cultures than in the blurring of genders.

But Mr. Dexter's erratic handling of actors, also apparent in his Broadway *Glass Menagerie* revival, inflicts a serious toll. John Getz and Rose Gregorio, as Gallimard's oldest pal and wife, are wildly off-key, wrecking the intended high-style comedy of the all-Western scenes. Mr. Lithgow, onstage virtually throughout, projects intelligence and wit, and his unflagging energy drives and helps unify the evening. Yet this engaging, ironic Gallimard never seems completely consumed by passion, whether the eroticism of imperialism or of the flesh, and the performance seems to deepen more in pitch than despair from beginning to end. Though *M. Butterfly* presents us with a visionary work that bridges the history and culture of two worlds, the production stops crushingly short of finding the gripping human drama that merges Mr. Hwang's story with his brilliant play of ideas.

≡ M. Butterfly *was not only a confirmation of David Henry Hwang's long-apparent promise as a writer but a surprise commercial hit and Tony Award winner for Best Play.*

JULIUS CAESAR
PUBLIC THEATER, MARCH 23, 1988

The worst thing that ever happened to *Julius Caesar* was its adoption by teachers nationwide as the ninth-grade student's ideal introduction to Shakespeare. In countless classrooms, *Julius Caesar* became the play that was Good for You—a sodden launching pad for earnest discussions about the perils of democracy, despotism, mob rule, and . . . Are you dozing yet?

The second worst thing that can happen to *Julius Caesar* is for it to be staged as if Shakespeare had written the play as a pedantic civics lesson rather than as a stormy tragedy about practical politics and ambivalent morality in the volatile Western world we still inhabit. Such is the case with Stuart Vaughan's production at the Public Theater, the second offering in the New York Shakespeare Festival's Shakespeare Marathon. Mr. Vaughan's *Caesar*—stately, bereft of passion, indifferently acted—is safely removed not only from the chaotic Rome of 44 B.C. but also from its audience's present-day political environment. One leaves the theater not thinking about how *Julius Caesar* might relate to the news from Israel or Panama, but with the great relief that school is out.

Mr. Vaughan took a similarly neutral approach to Shakespeare in his fizzy *Two Gentlemen of Verona* in Central Park last summer. But while *Two Gentlemen* is a light comedy that can levitate in a straightforward staging with a sexy cast, *Julius Caesar* demands urgency and a point of view. That point of view shouldn't be reductively partisan—Caesar need hardly be outfitted in the fascist jackboots of trendier productions—but the audience must develop some strong feelings, however conflicted, about the complex politicians at center stage. Instead of giving us figures who might arouse the violent emotions prompted by a John Kennedy or Richard Nixon, this *Caesar* suggests that republican Rome had all the polemical drama of a preprimary debate among the Democratic Party's current field of hairsplitters.

The liveliest of the leads by far is Edward Herrmann, who boasts a patrician air of rectitude, an affinity for speaking verse, and a gift for conveying the conflicts of conscience. Although he tends to burst into yelling to indicate moral outrage—and though he greets death through peculiarly crossed eyes—Mr. Herrmann has the makings of an excellent Brutus. Unfortunately, he has been cast as Cassius, a part to which he brings a lean yet scarcely hungry look.

The actual Brutus is Martin Sheen, whose performance here recalls not the dynamic actor of *Badlands* and *Apocalypse Now* but his becalmed appearances as an intensive-care patient in the film *Wall Street*. With his perfectly curly Roman coiffure (mussed up for the battle scenes) and narrow vocal range, Mr. Sheen ambles through the night, the assassination included, with the mechanical good cheer of a television game-show host. The occasional furrowing of his brow aside, he gives no evidence that Brutus is tormented by guilt and "hideous" dreams, and even bids farewell to his dead wife, Portia, as if he were discarding an old toga. So low key is Mr. Sheen's climactic confrontation with Mr. Herrmann in the camp at Sardis that the men could well be fighting over a check at Sardi's.

Though Al Pacino's Marc Antony is also a one-note affair—and possesses not even an anachronistically Brandoesque hint of noble bearing—at least the note is forceful. It is, however, off pitch. Mr. Pacino delivers the play's apex, Antony's funeral oration, as a diatribe—seemingly unaware that some charm and ironic wit might be required to win over the crowd that has come to bury Caesar. If Antony is revealed as an opportunistic demagogue from the outset, there's nowhere for the performance (or the play) to go. Mr. Pacino's handling of the language also leaves much to be desired—not so much because he talks in New Yorkese, but because the New Yorkese seems to have been subjected to quick-fix elocution training. The staccato pauses following Mr. Pacino's strenuous enunciation of final consonants obliterate the meaning of his lines.

Some of the other performances, led by the silver-haired John Mc-Martin's plausible if unsurprising Caesar, are better. The young actors in the cast worth tracking, some of them *Verona* stalwarts, include James M. Goodwin (Marullus), Richard Ziman (Casca), John Fitzgibbon (doubling as Cinna the conspirator and Cinna the poet), and Robert Curtis-Brown (Octavius Caesar). Bob Shaw's sliding sets, which make effective use of the Newman Theater's brick decor, and Arden Fingerhut's lighting are also solid, though they cannot alone supply the terrifying atmosphere of social disintegration absent from the staging. Mr. Vaughan's idea of civil strife is stylized and antiseptic violence, Roman mobs nearly as placid (though not nearly as numerous) as the extras in a Franco Zeffirelli opera, and war scenes less thunderous than the lightning storm that prefigures them. While the month may be almost over, this *Julius Caesar* makes the case that it is never too late for theatergoers to beware the ides of March.

JOE TURNER'S COME AND GONE
Ethel Barrymore Theatre, March 28, 1988

August Wilson continues to rewrite the history of the American theater by bringing the history of black America—and with it the history of white America—to the stage. In *Joe Turner's Come and Gone,* Mr. Wilson's third play to reach New York, that history unfolds with the same panoramic sweep that marked *Ma Rainey's Black Bottom* and *Fences.* As the new play's characters hang out in the kitchen and parlor of a black boardinghouse in the Pittsburgh of 1911, they retrace their long hard roads of migration from the sharecropping South to the industrialized North, and those tales again hum with the spellbinding verbal poetry of the blues. Whether a lost young woman is remembering how her mother died laboring in the peach orchards or a bitter man named Herald Loomis (Delroy Lindo) is recounting his seven years of illegal bondage to the Mississippi bounty hunter Joe Turner, Mr. Wilson gives haunting voice to the souls of the American dispossessed.

But to understand just why the play at the Barrymore may be Mr. Wilson's most profound and theatrically adventurous telling of his story to date, it is essential to grasp what the characters do not say—to decipher the history that is dramatized in images and actions beyond the reach of logical narrative. In *Joe Turner,* there are moments when otherwise voluble men reach a complete impasse with language, finding themselves struck dumb by traumatizing thoughts and memories that they simply "ain't got the words to tell." And there are times when the play's events also leap wildly off the track of identifiable reality. Late in Act 1, Herald Loomis becomes so possessed by a fantastic vision—of bones walking across an ocean—that he collapses to the ground in a cyclonic paroxysm of spiritual torment and, to the horror of his fellow boarders, scuttles epileptically across the floor on his back, unable to recover his footing and stand up.

These are occasions of true mystery and high drama, and they take Mr. Wilson's characters and writing to a dizzying place they haven't been before. That place is both literally and figuratively Africa. Though on its surface a familiar American tale about new arrivals in the big city searching for jobs, lost relatives, adventure, and love, *Joe Turner's Come and Gone* is most of all about a search for identity into a dark and distant past. That search leads the black characters back across the ocean where so many of their ancestors died in passage to slavery—and it sends Mr. Wilson's own writing in search of its cultural roots. As the occupants of the Pittsburgh boardinghouse are partly assimilated into white America and partly in thrall to a collective African unconscious, so Mr. Wilson's play is a mixture of the well-made naturalistic boardinghouse drama and the mystical, non-Western theater of ritual and metaphor. In *Joe Turner,* the clash between the American and the African shakes white and black theatergoers as violently as it has shaken the history we've all shared.

To achieve his sophisticated end, Mr. Wilson has constructed an irresistible premise. *Joe Turner* begins when the bizarre Loomis, imposing and intense in Mr. Lindo's riveting performance, comes knocking fiercely at the boardinghouse door with his delicate eleven-year-old daughter (Jamila Perry) incongruously in tow. With his years of servitude to Joe Turner at last behind him, Loomis is searching for the wife who deserted him at the start of his captivity a decade earlier. But Loomis is a "wild-eyed, mean-looking" man who looks as if he "killed somebody gambling over a quarter"; he's so pitch-black in mood and dress that there must be more to his story. Bynum Walker (Ed Hall), an eccentric fellow boarder with a penchant for clairvoyance and other forms of old-country voodoo, becomes obsessed with the strange intruder, intent on linking Loomis somehow to the supernatural "shining man" who haunts his own search for the "secret of life."

Yet the metaphysical cat-and-mouse game played by Bynum and Loomis is only the spine of *Joe Turner*. Everyone in the boardinghouse is looking, each according to his own experience, for either a lost relative or a secret of life, or both. The proprietor (Mel Winkler), the son of a free man, seeks salvation by becoming a typical American entrepreneur; he has no sympathy for a new young tenant (Bo Rucker) who arrives in Pittsburgh with rustic cotton-picking manners and crazy dreams of escaping menial labor with his guitar music. The women of the house also range across a wide spectrum—from a worldly cynic (Kimberly Scott) to a naive romantic searching for a man (Kimberleigh Aarn) to the good-hearted proprietress (L. Scott Caldwell) who believes that laughter is the best way "to know you're alive."

By throwing such varied individuals together, Mr. Wilson creates a web of emotional relationships, including some tender, funny, and sexy courtships sparked by the endearingly boisterous Mr. Rucker. But each character also has a distinct relationship to the black past, just as each has a different perspective on the white urban present. It's only when all the boardinghouse residents spontaneously break into an African "juba," singing and dancing at a Sunday fried-chicken dinner, that the extended family of *Joe Turner* finds a degree of unity and peace. As Bynum says to anyone who will listen, each man must find his own song if he is to be free. Loomis, the sole character who fails to join in the juba, must find his song if he is to reconnect to life and overthrow the psychic burden of his years of slavery. Only then will Joe Turner—the play's symbol of white oppression as well as the subject of the W. C. Handy blues song that gave it its title—be truly gone.

As usual with Mr. Wilson, the play overstates its thematic exposition in an overlong first act. There are some other infelicities, too, most notably the thin characterization of a pair of children. While one wishes that the director, Lloyd Richards, had addressed these flaws with more tough-mindedness during the two years of refinement that followed the play's premiere at the Yale Repertory Theatre, the production is in every other way a tribute to its extended development process in resident theaters around the country. The first-rate cast, which also includes Raynor Scheine as a benign white river rat and Angela Bassett as a fervent convert to the white god that failed her ancestors, forms a supple, harmonic ensemble. Mr. Richards's staging is equally conversant with scenes of romantic flirtation, rending tableaux of divided families, and galvanic climaxes in which the past erupts in a frenzy of exorcism.

The oblique, symbiotic relationship between Mr. Hall's otherworldly Bynum and Mr. Lindo's Loomis is particularly impressive. The two men's subliminal, often unspoken connection emerges like a magnetic force whenever they are onstage together. Loomis, we're told, was in happier days the deacon of the "Abundant Light" church. Under Mr. Hall's subtle psychological prodding and healing, Mr. Lindo gradually metamorphoses from a man whose opaque, defeated blackness signals the extinction of that light into a truly luminous "shining man," bathing the entire theater in the abundant ecstasy of his liberation. The sight is indescribably moving. An American writer in the deepest sense, August Wilson has once again shown us how in another man's freedom we find our own.

THE ROAD TO MECCA
PROMENADE THEATRE, APRIL 13, 1988

The artist at the center of Athol Fugard's new play, *The Road to Mecca,* does not want to change the world. Miss Helen, as she is known, is a reclusive old widow in a dusty, isolated village in the South African wilderness. Her art is an oddball collection of concrete sculptures exhibited in her garden—wise men, mermaids, and animals that she calls her "Mecca." Her sparse audience is her neighbors, most of whom regard her not as an artist but as the town madwoman, a laughingstock.

Since Mr. Fugard is an artist who does want to change the world—and arguably has—one might wonder why he is telling us the story of Miss Helen. The author of such indelible tragedies of apartheid as *Blood Knot* and *"Master Harold" . . . and the Boys* would seem to have scant connection with an eccentric whose art is obsessively, idiosyncratically private and devoid of political content. But the connection is made, and, once it is, the play at the Promenade becomes a career summation, its author's own "Mecca." The stage is flooded with light—literally and figuratively—as Mr. Fugard finds in Miss Helen's homely artistic credo a cathartic statement of what it means to be a true artist in any place, at any time.

The revelation is overwhelming. In a living room glittering in candlelight, Yvonne Bryceland, as Miss Helen, is trying to explain her mission to Mr. Fugard, who plays the role of Marius, the village's hidebound minister. With her matted silver hair, sandals, and bulky clothing, Ms. Bryceland looks almost like a bag lady. Mr. Fugard, dark and stern, is a narrow puritan who would like to usher his rebellious old friend into the Sunshine Home for the Aged. But when Ms. Bryceland, her eyes blazing and her voice rising, waves her fists in exaltation to describe her initial vision of her "Mecca" as "a city of light and color more splendid than anything I ever imagined," she forces us and Marius to see that wondrous spectacle, too. And as she recounts what it took to realize that vision—the hard work of grinding beer bottles and mixing cement with her arthritic hands, the courage to survive the ostracism of her community—we see even more about the will that drove her on.

What we don't see is Miss Helen's sculptures—and with good reason. Their content doesn't matter. To be an artist, Mr. Fugard is saying, is to be what Miss Helen is, not what she makes. Artists are driven to forge their version of the truth even when they have no hope of an audience, even when they must work with the most humble of materials in the middle of nowhere. Artists are dangerous because they won't deviate from that truth, no matter what pressure to conform is applied by the society around them. Artists are frightening to those who would suppress freedom because to be an artist is to exemplify freedom.

Miss Helen, however apolitical, can stand in for Mr. Fugard, all right. Yet she touches a universal chord by reminding us that the artistic conscience is inseparable from the moral conscience. Not for nothing does the play's third character, a radical Cape Town schoolteacher played by Amy Irving, invoke the spirit of Camus. As the soul of a Government-defying South African playwright is reflected in Miss Helen, so too is the spirit of anyone who persists in the often lonely struggle for what is right.

While as seemingly slender in polemical effect as its heroine's sculptures, *The Road to Mecca* is its author's most personal play, an essential Rosetta stone for the entire canon. The production, impeccably staged by the playwright, beautifully designed (by John Lee Beatty and Dennis Parichy) and, for the most part, superbly acted, is a huge improvement over the work's botched premiere at the Yale Repertory Theatre in 1984. But one cannot pretend that *The Road to Mecca* is all easy going. The play's powerful climax is preceded by a long, tedious first act that advertises Mr. Fugard's playwriting deficiencies as assertively as the second act does his strengths.

Act 1 is a repetitive conversation between Helen and Elsa, the schoolteacher who has traveled eight hundred miles to rescue her friend at a time of crisis. Mr. Fugard's plays have often had slow fuses, but the expository dialogue he hands Ms. Bryceland and Ms. Irving is embarrassingly hamfisted—a question-and-answer session for the audience's benefit rather than a credible conversation between two loving friends. The lines are littered with explications of the play's metaphors (led by darkness and light) and ominous references to melodramatically withheld facts (the contents of a letter, the genesis of a fire). As if to accentuate the falseness of the writing, Ms. Bryceland, so affecting later, plays Helen with a beatific, mannered dottiness of grating artificiality.

Mr. Fugard's minister arrives at the Act 1 curtain, and it is his efforts to get Helen to sign away her life to the old-age home over Elsa's objections that give the play its drama and meaty debates. While the overwriting does not vanish after intermission—let Ms. Bryceland look radiant, and someone will spoil our discovery by announcing it and explaining it—the ambiguities of character and meaning increase. Mr. Fugard's own role of Marius is crucial. Far from being an abject villain, the Afrikaner minister proves honestly concerned about Helen's welfare. Thanks equally to Mr. Fugard's compassionate writing and acting, one aches for the man at that moment when he belatedly sees the import of Helen's "Mecca" and, in the same instant, realizes that such an ecstatic spiritual plane is forever beyond his reach.

Ms. Irving gives her most forceful stage performance to date. Though Elsa's personal crises seem authorial contrivances for the sake of thematic symmetry, the actress whips up a cataclysm of pain. Even more disturbing is her account of having given a ride to a homeless black woman who is hiking eighty miles with her baby on her back and only a plastic shopping bag's worth of possessions to sustain her. With ruthless self-incrimination, Ms. Irving explains that her offer of a lift was only a sop to the conscience and not "a real contribution" to an apartheid victim's life. No doubt the author, like his characters, also questions what "real contribution" he makes to ease the suffering he chronicles. But his play, profiting from Miss Helen's courageous example, renders defeatism irrelevant with its compelling insistence that one must take one's own solitary road to Mecca before the world's journey there can at last begin.

CHESS

IMPERIAL THEATRE, APRIL 29, 1988

Anyone who associates the game of chess with quiet contemplation is in for a jolt at *Chess*, the new musical that does for board games what another Trevor Nunn production, *Starlight Express*, did for the roller derby. For over three hours, the characters onstage at the Imperial yell at one another to rock music. The show is a suite of temper tantrums, all amplified to a piercing pitch that would not be out of place in a musical about one of chess's somewhat noisier fellow sports, like stock-car racing.

Many of the fights pertain to the evening's ostensible story, an extended struggle between a Soviet chess master, Anatoly (David Carroll), and an American challenger, Freddie (Philip Casnoff), for the world championship. Freddie is an ugly American, John McEnroe–style, who will throw a drink in a reporter's face or upend a chess board if he doesn't get his way. When Freddie is tired of fighting with Anatoly, he brawls with his chess second and former lover, Florence (Judy Kuhn), or with his CIA keeper (Dennis Parlato), who then argues with his KGB counterpart (Harry Goz). As the action moves from Bangkok to Budapest at the start of Act 2, even the neutral arbiter of the chess match (Paul Harman) jumps fully into the fray. In an unintelligible but ineffably loony solo, the official starts barking indiscriminately at anyone who will listen, including one poor lady who wishes only to collect her luggage at the airport.

If contentiousness were drama, *Chess* would be at least as riveting as *The Bickersons*. That the evening has the theatrical consistency of quicksand—and the drab color scheme to match—can be attributed to the fact that the show's book, by the American playwright Richard Nelson, and lyrics, by Andrew Lloyd Webber's former and cleverest collaborator, Tim Rice, are about nothing except the authors' own pompous pretensions. *Chess* tells us over and over again that all the world is a chess game, that all the men and women are merely pawns, that everything from global conflicts to love to détente is subject to the same strategies and moves. "They see chess as a war / playing with pawns just like Poland," sings Freddie of the Russians. So what else is new?

The metaphor could grab an audience only if Mr. Nelson and Mr. Rice dramatized it in specific, compelling terms. They haven't. Their tale of international intrigue, with its nefarious spies and headline-making defection, is incoherent and jerry-built, John le Carré boiled down to a sketchy paragraph. Even more ridiculous (and windier) is the parallel love story—which sends Florence, a Hungarian refugee to the United States, ricocheting arbitrarily between the American and the Soviet players as if she had no self-respect or political convictions. By the time the love triangle turns into a rectangle, with the sudden addition of Anatoly's estranged but impossibly noble wife (Marcia Mitzman), *Chess* starts to resemble Chinese checkers.

Rather than condescend to throwing the audience a bone of genuinely romantic or melodramatic entertainment—or even providing a tense chess game—the authors pass the time pontificating about politics in sweeping generalities reminiscent of Mr. Rice's *Evita*. The show's mindless point of view, carefully fashioned to avoid offending any paying customer and therefore bereft of bite, has it that the Soviet and American governments are equally duplicitous in pursuit of nearly identical goals, no matter what the changes in administrations or the fate of glasnost.

The sole time *Chess* takes a strong stand on anything, and tries (without success) to muster a sense of humor, is in an early song mocking companies that merchandise and exploit chess with cheesy products. But the musical's moral stance proves hypocritical minutes later, when, for no reasons other than to plug a catchy song ("One Night in Bangkok") and give the production its one iota of dancing, *Chess* takes us on an exploitative tour of Bangkok's sleazy flesh palaces. As choreographed by Lynne Taylor-Corbett, the number looks like a hermaphroditic burlesque of the "Uncle Tom's Cabin" ballet in *The King and I*.

The studied ideological neutrality of the script is matched by the music—composed in a sometimes tuneful but always characterless smorgasbord of mainstream pop styles by Benny Andersson and Bjorn Ulvaeus of the Swedish rock combine Abba. Robin Wagner's set, fussily lighted by David Hersey, has even less personality. It's a presumably Kafkaesque configuration of oppressive, mobile towers in cinder-block gray. Though Mr. Wagner has given the Broadway *Chess* a different design than he did in London, where the production was initiated by Michael Bennett and completed by Mr. Nunn, one still finds the ghost of the Bennett-Wagner partnership on *Dreamgirls* in the towers at the Imperial.

For all the redesigning, rewriting, and recasting that have followed the West End premiere, it's amazing how little success Mr. Nunn has had in levitating *Chess*. He doesn't seem to be injecting passion into a play so much as adding a branch store to an international conglomerate. His main achievements have been to add running time, to remove the glitzy video and hydraulic special effects, and to tack on a prologue, replete with smoke and tattered flags, that makes the 1956 Hungarian revolution look like the Parisian barricades sequences of his far superior *Les Misérables*. His work is so mechanical here that he can't even whip up feeling in a shamelessly sentimental reunion between the heroine and a man she believes is her long-lost father—in spite of putting the man in a wheelchair and having him lead his daughter in a Hungarian lullaby.

The casting is also quixotic, with either broad or inept performances in every supporting role. The leads, all powerful singers, are much better. The most impressive acting comes from Mr. Carroll's Anatoly, who brings real fire to a generic patriotic anthem that ends Act 1 and who also evinces a sweetness reminiscent of the Russian created by Robin Williams in *Moscow on the Hudson*. Mr. Casnoff does everything humanly possible to bring shading to the spoiled, one-note American, even while shrieking a last-minute aria in which Freddie demands that we forgive his obnoxious arrogance because he comes from a broken home.

The largest role by far belongs to Ms. Kuhn. This talented but misused young actress spends almost the entire second act belting out unmotivated and often self-contradictory songs of love, defiance, and moral indignation, sobbing unconvincingly through most of them. While Ms. Kuhn may acquire the magic necessary to carry a big musical some day, she needs more experience—and more help from everyone, from the authors to the costume designer—to do so. But her efforts are not entirely in vain. Watching Ms. Kuhn's brave struggles against impossible odds, we do at last find some substance to the musical's metaphorical equation of chess and war. War is hell, and, for this trapped performer and the audience, *Chess* sometimes comes remarkably close.

≡ *The checkered history of* Chess *began in London, where Michael Bennett started directing it—then withdrew from the job in mid-production for cloudy reasons attributed to a heart ailment. (Only near the end of his life did it begin to become known that the real reason was that he had learned of his AIDS diagnosis while in London.) In the West End version, it was possible to see a few Bennett touches—Trevor Nunn had inherited the set and costumes—especially in the opening number.*

The New York version, by now totally revamped by Nunn for the worse, expired in a matter of weeks; the producers starting making further cuts and changes in it after it opened, once Nunn was out of town. But the score retains its devoted fans. There have been other stagings of Chess *around the country by other directors, though none of them has returned to Broadway.*

SPEED-THE-PLOW
ROYALE THEATRE, MAY 4, 1988

Hell hath no fury like a screenwriter scorned, and American culture is all the livelier for it. Out of the rage of embittered novelists and playwrights in studio backlots has come an enduring literature, nearly all of it practicing the same scorched-earth policy toward Hollywood that Nathanael West first apotheosized in *The Day of the Locust*.

While the theater has made many contributions of its own to the genre in the six decades since Kaufman and Hart mocked the early talking-picture industry in *Once in a Lifetime,* David Mamet's new play, *Speed-the-Plow,* may be the most cynical and exciting yet.

What we have at the Royale is not merely another screenwriter's bitchy settling of scores. Even as Mr. Mamet savages the Hollywood he calls a "sinkhole of slime and depravity," he pitilessly implicates the society whose own fantasies about power and money keep the dream factory in business. *Speed-the-Plow* refuses to hold out the sentimental hope that art might someday triumph over commerce. Mr. Mamet takes the darker view that show business titans know all too well whereof they speak when they claim to make "the stories people need to see."

By turns hilarious and chilling—and, under Gregory Mosher's exhilarated direction, wire-taut from start to finish—*Speed-the-Plow* is the culmination of this playwright's work to date. Bobby Gould (Joe Mantegna) and Charlie Fox (Ron Silver), the movie-industry sharpies at center stage, are tribal hustlers in the prize tradition of the penny-ante thieves of *American Buffalo,* the lowlife real-estate salesmen of *Glengarry Glen Ross,* and the poker-playing con men of Mr. Mamet's film *House of Games.* This time the scam is "entertainment." Charlie, a producer, is asking Bobby, a newly anointed head of production, to get approval for a "package": A big star will do a prison melodrama sure to make a zillion, provided that within twenty-four hours the studio gives the project the green light.

No one, of course, actually cares what this commodity is. The movie's plot, outlined in buzz words, is a riotous morass of action—and message-picture clichés that finally must be boiled down to the single phrase needed to sell it to the studio chief: "buddy film." But Mr. Mamet, like his moguls, is not concerned with the substance of the movie so much as the games that attend the making of the deal. As Charlie and Bobby, longtime pals who started out in the mail room together, fantasize about how much money they can make ("The operative concept is lots and lots"), they engage in a sub-rosa power struggle—a warped, Pinteresque buddy movie of their own. The supplicant Charlie literally as well as figuratively kisses Bobby's behind to enlist his support with higher-ups at the other end of the phone. Though the men frequently and proudly label themselves whores, they are sentimental whores who boast of their brotherly loyalty and describe Hollywood as a "people business" even as they stab anyone handy in the back.

If *Speed-the-Plow* were only the story of these two men scheming to get a movie made, it would still be a worthwhile, funny evening. Exhaustively mined as the territory is, Mr. Mamet has come up with fresh Hollywood gags and newly minted Goldwynisms ("It's only words unless they're true"). His pungent, scatological dialogue skyrockets with the addition of such industry locutions as *net* and *coverage*. Yet *Speed-the-Plow* contains a third character and a second film project—forces that collide to push Mr. Mamet's drama and themes well beyond parochial showbiz satire.

The catalytic character is a temporary secretary named Karen (Madonna), a naive young woman who is so unused to thinking in "a business fashion" that she can hardly fetch coffee, let alone adopt the proper phone attitude required to secure a lunch reservation for her boss at a trendy industry restaurant. The play's second, much-discussed potential film property is *The Bridge, or Radiation and the Halflife of Society,* a book by an "Eastern sissy writer" that an agent has submitted to Bobby's boss. *The Bridge* is the sort of artsy tome anathema to Hollywood—an allegorical tale of apocalypse rife with allusions to grace, the fear of death, and the decay of Western civilization. Bobby has promised to give the book "a courtesy read" before rejecting it, and he also wouldn't mind taking his temporary secretary to bed. To accomplish both missions as expeditiously as possible, he gives Karen the task of preparing a reader's report on *The Bridge,* with the hint that the assignment might advance her career to "the big table."

Mr. Mamet has developed into a more inventive storyteller than most people working in the movies, and his new play is full of the unexpected twists that have distinguished *Glengarry Glen Ross* and *House of Games* from much of his earlier work. In *Speed-the-Plow,* the spiraling plot not only pays off in a violent catharsis reminiscent of *American Buffalo,* but also gives the drama the hallucinatory mood of *The Water Engine,* Mr. Mamet's spectral radio play about an idealistic inventor who is silenced and destroyed by nightmarish forces of industry during the 1930s.

As *The Water Engine* was haunted by the recital of a mysterious chain letter, so the frequently cited preachments by the anonymous author of *The Bridge* percolate elliptically through *Speed-the-Plow.* The more fun is poked at *The Bridge* and its lofty warnings about the end of the world, the more it seems that a religious vision of salvation may be presenting itself to one of the hardened moguls, prompting him to change the world and maybe even to make better movies. Or is God himself just another exploitable concept—or con—in the greedy machinations of American commerce? Mr. Mamet certainly gives full sway to the consideration that religion might be the last refuge of whores.

Although her role is the smallest, Madonna is the axis on which the play turns—an enigma within an enigma, in the manner of the Lindsay

Crouse heroine in *House of Games*. It's a relief to report that this rock star's performance is safely removed from her own Hollywood persona. Madonna serves Mr. Mamet's play much as she did the Susan Seidelman film *Desperately Seeking Susan,* with intelligent, scrupulously disciplined comic acting. She delivers the shocking transitions essential to the action and needs only more confidence to relax a bit and fully command her speaking voice.

The men could not be better. Mr. Silver gives the performance of his career as the producer who has waited too long for his big break and will now stop at nothing to keep it from eluding his grasp. While one expects this actor to capture Charlie's cigar-chomping vulgarity, Mr. Silver's frightening eruptions of snarling anger and crumpled demeanor in the face of defeat make what could be another Beverly Hills caricature into a figure of pathos. Just as brilliant is Mr. Mantegna, whose reptilian head of production is a distinct creation from his past Mamet lowlifes. The actor is very funny when he demonstrates Bobby's delight in his new decision-making authority by barking "Decide! Decide! Decide!" into a phone. But when unforeseen circumstances suddenly force this self-assured Machiavelli to declare "I'm lost," Mr. Mantegna evinces just the ashen, glassy-eyed pallor needed to convey the vertigo-inducing moral void that Mr. Mamet has opened up before him and the audience.

Speed-the-Plow, not so incidentally, cannot be opened up by the movies. A two-set, three-person play that leaves no room for expansion, it would probably make terrible cinema. Perhaps that's another part of Mr. Mamet's revenge on Hollywood—to torture the studios to death with a script that is this entertaining and yet so far out of their reach. In *Speed-the-Plow,* Mr. Mamet has created riveting theater by mastering the big picture that has nothing to do with making films.

≡ *Most people hated Madonna. I'll stick by my judgment, though just three minutes of watching her emote in the trailer for the film version of* Evita *in 1996 did make me wonder if I had been suffering from temporary insanity during* Speed-the-Plow.

CARRIE
Virginia Theatre, May 13, 1988

Those who have the time and money to waste on only one Anglo-American musical wreck on Broadway this year might well choose *Carrie,* the new Royal Shakespeare Company coproduction at the Virginia Theatre. If *Chess* slides to its final scene as solemnly and pompously as the *Titanic*, then *Carrie* expires with fireworks like the Hindenberg. True, the fireworks aren't the greatest; the intended Stephen King pyrotechnics wouldn't frighten the mai-tai drinkers at a Polynesian restaurant. But when was the last time you saw a Broadway song and dance about the slaughtering of a pig? They've got one to open Act 2 of *Carrie*, and no expense has been spared in bringing the audience some of the loudest oinking this side of Old McDonald's Farm.

Fans of this musical's source material, Mr. King's Gothic novel of the same title, will remember why a horde of mean-spirited high-school students ends up at a pig sty. They want to pull a blood-splattering practical joke on Carrie, the class loser, at the senior prom. But why would the kids perform an exuberant number titled "Out for Blood"—leaping over the trough under flashing red disco lights—while carrying out the butchery? Presumably there are still some mysteries that mankind is not meant to unravel. Only the absence of antlers separates the pig murders of *Carrie* from the *Moose Murders* of Broadway lore.

Were the rest of the evening as consistent in its uninhibited tastelessness, *Carrie* would be a camp masterpiece—a big-budget excursion into the Theater of the Ridiculous. Even so, one is grateful for the other second-half pockets of delirium, including a song in which the telekinetically empowered Carrie (Linzi Hateley) cutely serenades her ambulatory powder puff, hairbrush, and prom shoes. As Carrie's stern mom, a religious fanatic dressed up in dominatrix black from wig to boots, even the exemplary Betty Buckley earns one of the show's bigger unwanted laughs. "Baby, don't cry," she gently tells her daughter after stabbing her with a dagger.

Most of *Carrie* is just a typical musical-theater botch, albeit in the echt West End style (lots of smoke, laser and hydraulic effects). The disaster was not inevitable, since *Carrie* was a workable idea for a musical, and because the director Terry Hands, whose Royal Shakespeare repertory of *Cyrano de Bergerac* and *Much Ado About Nothing* enchanted New York, is a gifted theater man. As the film director Brian DePalma demonstrated in his screen adaptation, *Carrie* can make for scary, funny, and sexy pulp entertainment—provided the thrills, wit, and post-pubescent sensuality are as sharp as that knife.

The musical *Carrie* fails in all these areas. It's no surprise that the visual scare tactics concocted by Mr. Hands and the set designer Ralph Koltai can't compete with those on film, but surely someone might have found stage blood (porcine or human) that doesn't look like strawberry ice-cream topping. Though the author of the musical's book, Lawrence D. Cohen, also wrote the film script, his work here is just a plodding series of song-and-scenery cues. The only laughs in the text of this *Carrie* are the whopping clichés in Dean Pitchford's lax, pseudo–*Bye Bye Birdie* lyrics. "Was it his voice? Was it his smile? I haven't felt so wonderful in quite a while," sings the lovesick heroine.

What is most fatal to *Carrie* is its inability to deliver its Cinderella story and the encompassing hothouse high-school atmosphere. Oppressed by her Bible-toting mom, Carrie is a naive, awkward shut-in—so unworldly that she has a near-breakdown during her first (and perhaps a Broadway musical's first) menstrual period. When Carrie later blossoms into womanhood under the loving ministrations of a kindly gym teacher (the warm-voiced Darlene Love) and her class's foremost prince charming (Todd Graff), the transformation should be real and moving—thereby making Carrie's eventual sadistic humiliation all the more horrifying. But if Ms. Hateley has a belter's voice in the reigning (and amplified) English rock-musical manner, she has none of the vulnerability of Sissy Spacek's film Carrie. Love and acceptance do not transform Ms. Hateley into a romantic prom queen; she still begs cloyingly for our sympathy, as one might expect from an actress whose primary previous stage experience was as an orphan in *Annie*.

Carrie's classmates are even less convincing. In the opening gym sequence, the high-school "girls" are dressed like suburban aerobics instructors and look old enough to be guidance counselors. Carrie's immediate friends and enemies—roles vibrantly played in the movie by Amy Irving, Nancy Allen, William Katt, and John Travolta—are amateurishly caricatured on stage (by the hideously misused dancer Charlotte d'Amboise, among others). When the casting errors are compounded by uncertain American accents, Mr. Koltai's abstract black-and-white Mondrian box of a set, and Alexander Reid's grotesque sub–Atlantic City costumes, one often isn't sure where or when *Carrie* is taking place. Though one scene is set in a *Grease*-era drive-in, we also visit a teenage "night spot" where the boys and girls dress in black leather and studs suitable for *Cruising*. As choreographed by Debbie Allen, who shouldn't wait another moment to return to her performing career, Carrie's senior prom looks like the sort of cheesy foreign-language floor show one flips past in the nether reaches of cable television.

What burning passion is to be found in this *Carrie* has little to do with teenage eroticism or Gothic horror and everything to do with a more traditional Broadway subject—settling scores with a domineering mom. The only surge in Michael Gore's otherwise faceless bubblegum music is in those songs in which Carrie and her mother do battle. Though the matriarch remains a misogynic cartoon, the fiercely concentrated Ms. Buckley brings theatrical heat to every slaphappy bout of corporal punishment, every masturbatory hand gesture indicating her sexual repression, and every aria invoking Jesus and Satan. After a theatrical decade that has taken her from *Cats* to pigs, the time has come for Betty Buckley to receive a human musical as her heavenly reward.

≡ *Not quite* Moose Murders, *but it would do until the real thing came along.* Carrie *inspired a hilarious book,* Not Since Carrie, *in which the theater historian Ken Mandelbaum sifts the ashes of every major musical disaster in Broadway history.*

TENTH SEASON

1888—89

Waiting for Godot: Robin Williams, Steve Martin,
F. Murray Abraham, and Bill Irwin

ZERO POSITIVE
PUBLIC THEATER, JUNE 2, 1988

If the time has come for a second wave of AIDS plays, Harry Kondoleon's striking though exasperatingly inconsistent new comedy at the Public Theater, *Zero Positive*, may lead the way. Although two of its characters test seropositive—positive for the AIDS virus, if not necessarily for the disease—*Zero Positive* contains no facts and figures about the epidemic, no debates about public health, no pleas for tolerance. Mr. Kondoleon's play is about as far away from journalism as the theater of social concern can get. Act 1 ends with a striptease by a philanthropically minded heiress emulating a porno novel about the erotic mythology of nurses. In Act 2, a hospital solarium becomes an amphitheater for Greek mythology so the characters can perform a classical play-within-the-play titled *The Ruins of Athens*.

Mr. Kondoleon, a prolific young writer whose other works include *Anteroom* and *Christmas on Mars*, has never played by the rules. *Zero Positive* is full of his signature surprises—flights into fantasy and ritual, anarchic sexual couplings redolent of Joe Orton, neo–Oscar Wildean tea parties in which the conversation is far more piquant than the food. In the past, Mr. Kondoleon's theatrical playfulness has too often been its own insufficient reward, with dexterous word-spinning substituting for sustained wit and a hip attitude straining to blossom into meaning. While the writer's capacity for self-indulgence and pretension hasn't disappeared in *Zero Positive*— the play tends to preach and to mistake structural laxity for crazy-quilt experimentation—there is a new gravity rooting its many diverse elements to earth. Without ever mimicking the real world outside the theater, Mr. Kondoleon has found a way to dramatize its suffering while remaining inside his own hermetically sealed esthetic universe.

That universe is a place where tragedy keeps buckling into farce. When Mr. Kondoleon's cynical protagonist, Himmer (David Pierce), learns of his seropositive test result, he doesn't get gloomier but instead gives himself up to an ecstatic outpouring of artistic fervor: If modern man is still as much at the mercy of "the fate machine" as the ancient Greeks, he reasons, why not make art out of chaos, as the Greeks did, by making a play? Himmer's loony father, an elderly poet named Jacob Blank (Edward Atienza), has his own creative riposte to mortality. He recovers from the "deep, punishing loss" of his wife by retreating into the time warp of second childhood, taking a younger lover (Beth Austin) and, at one antic point, dancing a demented jig to the accompaniment of Benny Goodman's "Sing, Sing, Sing" and the roar of his elaborate set of toy electric trains.

Mr. Kondoleon is in favor of such defiance. At a time when it's easy to "fall prey to despair," this playwright looks for salvation and beauty in acts of art and of kindness. Though *Zero Positive* contains an offstage double suicide, an onstage suicide attempt, and a plan by Himmer to drink actual poison (out of a plastic Tom Collins tumbler) in the hemlock scene of *The Ruins of Athens,* hope survives. It's the hope of personal rather than medical miracles. Himmer is sustained by his friendships with Samantha (Frances Conroy), a compulsive lover of married men and a fellow virus carrier, and with Prentice (Richard McMillan), a sad-eyed homosexual with scant self-esteem and a generous spirit. Himmer and his theater, in turn, sustain his friends. As the play's funniest character, a congenitally out-of-work actor (Tony Shalhoub), comes to realize, everyone must play one's role in a tragedy to the fullest, however brief the part. It may be less painful to make a final exit if one can believe it made sense to enter in the first place.

In trying to make his own sense of "a world crashing down"—the setting is New York City, 1987—Mr. Kondoleon pays full heed to the nonsensical. As the unemployed actor is simultaneously up for roles in plays by writers as incongruously antithetical as Clifford Odets and Jean Genet—and as *The Ruins of Athens* purports to mix Plato and Feydeau—so *Zero Positive* can leap from a comic digression about Ronald Reagan to Samantha's complaints about the "stupid, queer songs written for straight women" like Edith Piaf and Judy Garland. Yet even the funnier lines can't paper over the arbitrariness with which the characters, situations, and explanatory monologues are sometimes tossed together. Anarchy demands its own internal logic in the theater, and, when Mr. Kondoleon fails to provide it, the result is a deadly inertia.

The flattest (and longest) punch line of all turns out to be the evening's would-be payoff—the Act 2 "burlesque of tragedy." An excursion into Charles Ludlam ridiculousness, the pastiche *Ruins of Athens* isn't funny enough or cathartic enough to give *Zero Positive* its deus ex machina. Except for that flat sketch, which could also use a sharper edge in performance, the play's lapses cannot be blamed on the production, which, for all its well-publicized travails during previews, has opened in credible shape.

Following the example of Broadway's *Macbeth,* the *Playbill* names the play's departed "original" director (Mark Linn-Baker) along with Kenneth Elliott, its final one. Mr. Elliott reveals more of a range than his collaborations with Charles Busch on *Vampire Lesbians of Sodom* and *Psycho Beach Party* might suggest. In happy contrast to many past Kondoleon productions, the entire company, whether the nominally conventional leads or the more peripheral zanies, joins Adrianne Lobel's set in straddling the recognizable and the bizarre. That helps deliver an off-center evening in keeping with the play's punning, paradoxical title. Where an earlier AIDS play might have offered documentary portraits of its individual seropositive cases, *Zero Positive* forsakes the clinical to take the spiritual temperature of a society torn between blank despair and positive valor as it struggles to emerge from a viral eclipse.

≡ *It seems I wrote the same review of a half-dozen or so Harry Kondoleon full-length plays that came my way over a decade: striking voice, unfinished play. (The one-act plays—Slacks and Tops was my favorite—fared much better.) He was a young writer with an exciting talent worth attending to, so producers and critics alike kept boosting him. He died of AIDS in 1993, leaving behind some published fiction as well as his theatrical work.*

LONG DAY'S JOURNEY INTO NIGHT
Neil Simon Theatre, June 15, 1988

When people see a ghost, they are anticipating death, and that is unmistakably what Jason Robards feels as the thick fog of despair rolls into the Tyrone household for keeps in Eugene O'Neill's *Long Day's Journey into Night.*

Mr. Robards, in the role of the family patriarch, James, is sharing midnight whiskey, recriminations, and confessions with his son Edmund when he hears the dreaded sound of his wife, Mary, thrashing about offstage in a morphine stupor. James had hoped against hope that Mary would be well again. In the moment, he must recognize that the hope, like the young convent girl he married so long ago, has vanished—and that Mary is, as Edmund has warned, "nothing but a ghost haunting the past." Once the recognition arrives, Mr. Robards's eyes seem to retreat into their sockets, the wind seems to leave his body, his physique seems to shrivel within his regal but frayed smoking jacket. We don't yet see the ghost he sees—the final spectral visit of his wife is still minutes away—but such is the apparitional reach of Colleen Dewhurst's Mary and the horror in Mr. Robards's expression that we experience the alarming, involuntary shudder of a glimpse into the grave.

Mary Tyrone is not the only ghost to be seen in *Long Day's Journey*, as revived in repertory with *Ah, Wilderness!* as part of the First New York International Festival of the Arts. O'Neill's autobiographical play gives us a quartet of haunted Tyrones—each character haunted by O'Neill's own family, which was itself haunted by failed promises and blasted dreams and all the rest of what Mary calls "the things that life has done to us." The production at the Neil Simon Theatre is shadowed by theater history as well. Mr. Robards and the director, José Quintero, restored O'Neill's reputation three decades ago with their legendary Circle in the Square revival of *The Iceman Cometh*. Their partnership continued with the triumphant 1956 American premiere of *Long Day's Journey*, then crested again, with the luminous addition of Ms. Dewhurst, in the 1973 Broadway restoration of *A Moon for the Misbegotten*.

Given the rare constellation of talent—and the further astrological constellation of the O'Neill centenary—one almost inevitably arrives at this *Long Day's Journey* expecting to find salvation in the guise of what is nearly everyone's first or second favorite American play. The rewarding, if imperfect, production actually at hand is best approached with more rational expectations. Like other renditions of this work, Mr. Quintero's staging illuminates one parent-child axis—Mary and Edmund—more strikingly than the other. But the evening is never less than essential theatergoing. One cannot assume that there will be another chance to watch these three great theater artists explore the writer who has been their consuming passion for virtually their entire professional careers.

A somewhat subdued first act aside, an exploration is what this *Journey* proves to be. As life does more things to all of us, O'Neill's play takes on new colorations and meanings with repeated encounters; it's unlikely that Mr. Quintero has the same view of the text now that he did over thirty seasons ago. The current version has the bare-bones simplicity and sepulchral darkness of the director's 1985 *Iceman Cometh* on Broadway—as befits the abstract, dreamlike, classically unified quality of the nominally realistic late O'Neill masterworks. The production's acting revelation is Ms. Dewhurst's extraordinary, almost shockingly unsentimentalized Mary. One sees just how little the author forgave his mother and understands just what Kenneth Tynan meant when he said that Mary, while "on the surface a pathetic victim," was "at heart an emotional vampire."

Ms. Dewhurst has a rending tragic dimension, to be sure. When she is left alone in her shabby summer home to contemplate her loneliness, the panic and longing on her pained face seem so lacking in focus that we see the internal chaos that drives her to drugs. Yet this Mary, for all her ethereal beauty and maternal silver hair, is no Dewhurst earth mother—she's a killer, forever twisting the knife in old familial wounds. The actress makes us constantly aware of how Mary repeatedly plays one son against the other and follows her strangled pleas for help with manipulative denials that she needs any help at all. Her declarations of love come with a nasty sting ("I know you didn't mean to humiliate me," she tells James by way of thanks for her second-hand car) or with a cruel infliction of guilt ("I never knew what rheumatism was until after you were born," she tells Edmund so he can take the blame for her addiction to the painkiller).

Campbell Scott, the impressive Edmund, is her born victim. With his pasty face, jet-black hair, and long, delicate fingers, the soft-spoken Mr. Scott is the image of the Irish-American artist as a consumptive young man, absorbing each shock into his burdened soul until he just can't take it anymore. His belated, angry lashings out at his mother, brother, and father drive the final act. It is when Mr. Scott rises over his seated father, berating him for the miserliness that will send the son to a state sanitorium, that Mr. Robards's eyes and phlegmy voice take their final plunge into his lifetime's reservoir of shame.

Explaining the sources of that shame—the bitter childhood poverty at the hands of "the Yanks," the sacrifice of his Shakespearean acting ambitions to "money success"—Mr. Robards, as always, gives resonant, ruefully comic voice to every barroom pipe dreamer in the O'Neill canon. Before the illusion-stripping final act, however, the actor, like the unreconstructed matinee idol he plays, relies a bit too easily on his trademark vocal and facial gestures; the performance wants for shading. As Jamie, the profligate son Mr. Robards created in 1956, the talented Jamey Sheridan lacks his theatrical father's air of Broadway dissipation. Mr. Sheridan is still the earnest, self-righteous Arthur Miller son he was in the last revival of *All My Sons*—an injured straight arrow taking to drink rather than a sneering cynic greasing his own skids into hell.

Such a Jamie can't quite provide the histrionic bridge to Mary's final mad scene, but Ms. Dewhurst, her skin now as parchment-pale as the old wedding dress she clutches, completes the journey into night nonetheless. We see what Edmund meant when he talked about being "a ghost within a ghost." Breaking through Ms. Dewhurst's drug-ravaged face is the skeletal image of the demure, innocent girl she once was. "The past is the present—it's the future, too" is how Mary earlier explains the affliction of living every day with the painful awareness of who one is. While death can disperse the ghosts of the Tyrones, their agony, accessible to any family, will eternally claw at us from the play O'Neill wrote in tears and blood.

JUNO AND THE PAYCOCK

John Golden Theatre, June 22, 1988

The curtain rises very slowly on the Gate Theatre Dublin's thrilling production of Sean O'Casey's *Juno and the Paycock,* now at Broadway's Golden Theatre. Even so, our eyes must struggle to adjust to the dim light and to take in a panorama of poverty so grim that one might think the rear wall of the playhouse had been torn away to expose the innards of a Hell's Kitchen tenement just outside.

The tenement in O'Casey's play belongs to the Boyle family of Dublin, during the Civil War days of 1922. The home's crumbling walls are caked with slime, as if sewage had been flushed through the living room. The windowpanes, cracked and sooty, are framed by the cobweb remains of lace curtains, while the meager furniture has long since spilled its guts.

What family could live in such squalid decay? Only a doomed family, says O'Casey: In *Juno and the Paycock,* we watch the steady destruction of the household headed by the indomitable mother Juno and her drunken, strutting paycock of a husband, "Captain" Jack Boyle. But crippling poverty and social disintegration are not exclusively Irish troubles, and *Juno,* to many the quintessential Irish play, is not parochial. The slum in this work does bleed into the impoverished war zones of our own city and time. A remarkable Irish company, visiting under the auspices of the First New York International Festival of the Arts, is out to prove to a new generation that O'Casey's tragicomedy belongs to the world.

That case is made by a director, Joe Dowling, who has a deep vision of the play and the perfect cast to execute it. His *Juno* is alive at every level—as boisterous comedy, as wrenching tragedy, as blistering social commentary. O'Casey isn't Shakespeare or Beckett, but that Shakespearean brew of taproom farce and high drama materializes here, as do the bleak shadows of a distinctly modern Irish landscape. In Mr. Dowling's staging, a fizzy party scene awash in song can expire in an instant as a passing funeral procession, carrying another unnecessary victim of community fratricide, throws its gloomy pall from the street. The alcoholic buddy act of Boyle (Donal McCann) and his faithful pub-crawling sidekick Joxer Daly (John Kavanagh) can instantly veer from grotesque tableaux of degradation to burlesque routines worthy of legendary music-hall clowns.

Mr. Kavanagh's indelible portrait of Joxer is the key to Mr. Dowling's conception. A hypocritical sycophant, Joxer will do anything to cadge a drink or a crust of bread. Whenever Boyle is telling fictitious tales of his nonexistent career at sea or pontificating about politics and the church, Joxer is always there to flatter, often by tossing around the all-purpose compliment "darlin'." But from the moment we see Mr. Kavanagh, we sense the evil beneath the blarney, the potential betrayer masked within the ostensibly loyal friend.

A twisted and cadaverous tramp with rotting teeth and a long moth-eaten coat, Mr. Kavanagh rocks his hunched shoulders in and out of his haze of booze and cigarette smoke, his beady sewer rat's eyes forever searching for the next vulturous score. "It's better to be a coward than a corpse," Joxer says. A thief and a parasite but no idiot, he is the kind of rootless, selfish exploiter who always comes out on top in a human hell—even as he pretends to decry "man's inhumanity to man." Yet Mr. Kavanagh still cuts a comic image: He earns laughs up to the terrifying climactic moment when, in a symbolic gesture not in O'Casey's stage directions, he performs an act akin to robbing his best friend's grave.

As Joxer's collaborator in dereliction, Mr. McCann is equally brilliant at blending robust humor with brute nastiness. This performance won't be confused with twinkling Irish rogues of stage lore—or with Mr. McCann's poetic Gabriel Conroy in John Huston's film of *The Dead*. Certainly, the actor is hilarious early on when Boyle fakes leg pains to evade work. And the comedy continues when the Boyles become convinced that an inheritance will bring them prosperity: Mr. McCann makes a vain bourgeois show of signing important documents and is soon pompously preaching the same pieties he had ridiculed in an earlier tirade. The blotchy-faced liar and bully never disappears entirely, however, and finally rises up with frightening force just at that moment when his wife and pregnant daughter need compassion most.

With such men about, O'Casey's empathic appreciation of his heroine is all the more striking and moving. Geraldine Plunkett's Juno, desperately trying to keep a family together under impossible circumstances, is not a plaster saint but a mortal woman whose moral strength cannot camouflage her physical and emotional weariness. When the mother finally stands alone, her last few possessions in a bundle at her feet, and demands that God "take away our hearts o' stone and give us hearts o' flesh," Ms. Plunkett strips the sentimentality from the line to offer a plain plea from a woman who has reached a serene acceptance of her tragic losses. Juno also makes her own use of the word "darlin' "—to describe a boy "riddled with bullets"—and the love in Ms. Plunkett's inflection brings the hollowness of the "darlin' " constantly spewed by her husband's most constant companion into bitter relief.

Almost as impressive are the supporting players: Rosemary Fine as the Ibsenesque daughter Mary, Stella McCusker as another grieving mother, and Joe Savino as the Boyle son whose crippled state stands for Ireland's past bloodbaths and whose half-mad demeanor prefigures horrors yet to come. Of particular note is Maureen Potter, a longtime Irish variety performer, who brings a priceless authenticity to the role of the gabby neighbor Maisie Madigan. Though Maisie is delightful when tippling and singing, it's not coincidence that she is Joxer's dancing partner in the party scene. When she later decides to collect a debt by walking off with the Boyles' gramophone, Ms. Potter rids her previously hearty characterization of its own merry music to reveal a predatory soul.

Such is the staging's keen attention to detail that the props, set (by Frank Hallinan Flood), costumes (by Consolata Boyle), and lighting (by Rupert Murray) also play important roles in animating the Boyles' Dublin. When money is briefly plentiful in Act 2, the new, bright-red furnishings and Boyle's spiffier nautical costume become mocking emblems of the affluence kept tantalizingly out of the poor's reach. By the time the furniture has been repossessed—and the Boyles' last hopes along with it—the tenement is a cave with only the eerie glow from a distant streetlamp to illuminate the blackness.

"Th' whole worl's in a terrible state o' chassis!" is Boyle's famous line as he stumbles around that bare room, his stupor anesthetizing him from the chaos and his own role in it. Then Mr. McCann passes out on the floor, a grimy sack of a man tossed into the night, an unnerving double for the men we'll step around in the street as we make our way from Sean O'Casey's play to the safety of home.

≡ *This is the best production that no one ever saw. As part of a New York summer arts festival,* Juno *could not extend beyond its one-week run; people rioted to get the few seats available.*

RECKLESS
CIRCLE REPERTORY COMPANY, SEPTEMBER 26, 1988

I'll be home for Christmas," sings Bing Crosby, "if only in my dreams."

With that soothing lyric lingering in our ears, the lights go up on Craig Lucas's anything-but-comforting *Reckless,* the play that opens the Circle Repertory Company's twentieth-anniversary season on an exhilarating note. It's Christmas, all right—in more ways than one. With *Reckless,* a revision of a play briefly seen Off Off Broadway in 1983, Mr. Lucas has given us a bittersweet Christmas fable for our time: *It's a Wonderful Life* as it might be reimagined for a bruising contemporary America in which homelessness may be a pervasive spiritual condition rather than a sociological crisis.

What's more, the playwright, whose other works include *Blue Window* and *Three Postcards,* possesses a theatrical imagination that levels the rigid walls of the Circle Rep's habitual naturalism. While *Reckless* finally has a simple emotional pull akin to that of a Crosby ballad born of the lonely World War II home front, it yanks us through every conceivable absurdist hoop, fracturing narrative, language, and characterization on the way to its rending destination.

Reckless begins as a cheerful contemporary fairy tale. Rachel (Robin Bartlett), a contented mother of two young boys, sits up in bed with her husband (Michael E. Piontek) and counts her Yuletide blessings. Rachel is having a "euphoria attack"; she's convinced she is "going to be terminally happy." Even the snowstorm swirling outside the bedroom window is benign—a "monster" perhaps, but a sweet one that will "carry us away into a dream."

Only moments later, however, a panic-stricken Rachel finds herself leaping through her window in her housecoat and slippers, beginning a bizarre odyssey that may or may not be a dream. Among other adventures, she becomes the unofficial adoptive child of a physical therapist (John Dossett) and his deaf paraplegic wife (Welker White), serves as a contestant on the game show *Your Mother or Your Wife?,* and witnesses a double murder engineered by an embezzling employee of a nonprofit humanitarian foundation called Hands Across the Sea. As Rachel leaves her own children farther and farther behind, Christmas follows Christmas, and town follows town, each of them named Springfield. "I don't even know what state we're in," says the heroine by the middle of Act 2.

Neither do we. Rachel's fantastic journey induces a state of dreamy disorientation in the audience, as if it, too, were tumbling through existence in a perpetual free fall. But Mr. Lucas isn't idly spinning out a shaggy dog story; a pattern emerges from the screwball riffs. Like Rachel, almost everyone she meets proves to be using an assumed name and running guiltily away from a past life. We learn that the play's most selfless characters have accidental manslaughters in their past, that the most paternal men and maternal women have deserted their children. "Do you think we ever really know people?" asks Rachel early on. Mr. Lucas's implicit answer is no. The only hope for the people in *Reckless* is that they truly know themselves.

Although the process by which Rachel and the others achieve that self-knowledge is sometimes spelled out in clinical terms (especially in the stridently oedipal game show), Mr. Lucas at his best dramatizes his characters' breakthroughs with striking originality. After intermission, the comic dreaminess of *Reckless* curdles and darkens until finally we realize that clichéd Freudian landmarks (from the journey through the birth canal to the loss of parents) have been reenacted elliptically in the crazy-quilt narrative, to traumatic effect. "The past is irrelevant; it's something we wake up from" is Rachel's Pollyanna view of life in the first act. By Act 2, she and we come to appreciate, as other lines have it, that "things happen for a reason" and that "the past is the nightmare you wake up to every day."

While this realization dawns, Mr. Lucas ingeniously merges his characters' pasts and presents, their real lives and their dream lives. It's not incidental that this playwright and his director, Norman René, once collaborated on a Stephen Sondheim revue, *Marry Me a Little,* which emulated Mr. Sondheim's lyrical wordplay by stitching together unrelated trunk songs as if fitting them into a Double-Crostic. As a psychiatrist (Joyce Reehling) in *Reckless* reminds us, dreams are also anagrams—of our wishes and fears. Mr. Lucas's play is an anagram in which all the quirky character and plot details of Act 1 are rearranged into a new and revealing pattern in Act 2. Eventually that pattern takes shape as a hallucinatory maze of transference: The evening's haunting final scene can be read—with equal validity and equal pathos—as a first session between a therapist and a new patient or as an unexpected Dickensian reunion between a mother and a long-lost son. Either way, loving hands reach across the sea: The characters have at last come home for Christmas, if only in their dreams.

Reckless is not flawless. Mr. Lucas can be carried away by his own cleverness; there are cloying gags and self-indulgent repetitions. But the writer's compassion, so redolent at times of Anne Tyler's novel *Dinner at the Homesick Restaurant,* usually rescues his play from its precious excesses. "Life's been reckless with these people," we're told of the homeless people inhabiting a shelter. Mr. Lucas feels for all victims of life's recklessness—from those psychotic homeless who "carry no identification whatsoever" to the ordinary rest of us whose own intimations of homelessness and death must arrive sooner or later with one hurtful form or another of parental abandonment.

In his lyrical staging, Mr. René is keenly responsive to Mr. Lucas's every mood. Starting with the quicksilver Ms. Bartlett, who passes from Dorothy-in-Oz girlishness to celestial maturity in two hours, the cast is uniformly superb at meeting constant changes in tone and character. Loy Arcenas's imaginative sets and Debra J. Kletter's lighting depict a snowy American landscape of silent cobalt-blue nights and mysterious Edward Hopper domestic spaces, where either Santa Claus or a reckless if not homicidal parent might come down the chimney at any moment. There have been merrier Christmases than Mr. Lucas's, but how many of them have been so true?

THE COCKTAIL HOUR
PROMENADE THEATRE, OCTOBER 21, 1988

Nobody goes to the theater anymore," says Bradley, the well-off seventy-five-year-old WASP father who presides over *The Cocktail Hour,* the new A. R. Gurney comedy at the Promenade. As far as Bradley (Keene Curtis) and his wife, Ann (Nancy Marchand), are concerned, modern plays contain too much screaming and disrobing to lure them to Manhattan from their home in upstate New York. But this couple can still remember a distant time when "wonderful plays" regularly visited their local Erlanger Theatre. A wonderful play was one featuring an attractive, "very sophisticated" couple—invariably the Lunts—a "minor indiscretion," and a happy ending. A wonderful play gave the audience something "to celebrate at the end of the day."

What Ann and Bradley fear is that their very own son, a full-time publisher and sometime dramatist named John (Bruce Davison), has written a brutal autobiographical diatribe in the post–Lunt-Fontanne theatrical style. John's play, described as hitting "pretty close to home," is called *The Cocktail Hour,* and he has traveled to his parents' house at cocktail hour to ask their permission to proceed with it. The audience watching Mr. Gurney's *Cocktail Hour* never finds out exactly how inflammatory John's *Cocktail Hour* is, but if the two plays are at all alike—which, of course, they must be—the parents needn't worry. The author of *The Dining Room* and *The Perfect Party* is not the sort to turn an evening of martini-fueled drawing-room banter into a truly drunken *Long Day's Journey into Night*. *The Cocktail Hour* is a play its own characters would find pretty wonderful, if not entirely so.

From its genteel set and tweedy costumes, which could serve any S. N. Behrman comedy or bygone Best & Company display window, to its vibrant, high-gloss acting, the entire production might well be a replica of a fizzy, between-the-wars star vehicle. While the author does have his darker aspirations—which remain unfulfilled and prove a serious drag on the second act—he is at the top of his form when being unapologetically anachronistic and letting the zingers fly. Even at this late date, Mr. Gurney still has new and witty observations to make about a nearly extinct patrician class that regards psychiatry as an affront to good manners, underpaid hired help as a birthright, and the selling of blue-chip stocks as a first step toward Marxism.

The laughter in Act 1 is almost continuous, and much of it is prompted by Ms. Marchand's irresistible suburban grande dame. Ms. Marchand has created memorable WASP matrons before, in *Morning's at Seven* and in television's *Lou Grant*, but never one more hilarious and more real than Ann. Just to hear the actress order a refill of her martini—a frequent occurrence—is to get a lesson in comic timing and inflection. Yet the performance doesn't settle merely for a blunt, gin-dry astringency. While the mother has narrow notions of domestic decorum and little use for intimacy, she somehow emerges as generous and vulnerable in Ms. Marchand's portrayal. What might have been a *New Yorker* caricature is instead a complex illustration of how both nurturing affection and punishing neglect can coexist in reticent parents of the breed Mr. Gurney describes.

As directed by Jack O'Brien, the other actors also seem to have materialized from a Broadway boulevard comedy of the *Radio Days* era. Mr. Curtis's stiff patriarch, a snobby clubman whose mustache seems to do the bristling that his bald pate cannot, is a made-to-order foil for his loopier costar. Funny as Mr. Curtis is when decrying Roosevelt or apotheosizing golf, he is also touching at that one moment when remembered pain briefly causes his austere façade to crack. As his offspring, Mr. Davison and Holland Taylor are attractive as only middle-aged malcontents to the Philip Barry–manner born can be. Though Ms. Taylor's role is billed as minor—to her frustration, both in her family's priorities and in her brother's play—she still captures both the resilience and anguish of a perfect daughter, wife, and mother who sublimates life's disappointments into a curious obsession with seeing-eye dogs.

If Mr. Davison's John makes less of an impression, it's not the actor's fault, but that of Mr. Gurney's play. Ms. Taylor describes John as "a mess" and presumably he is a troubled man, driven to write his autobiographical *Cocktail Hour* to try to come to terms with his unhappiness. But except for a stirring moment at the end of Act 1 in which Mr. Davison can fleetingly let us see one source of his sorrow, the character, as written, remains opaque: a blank journalistic interlocutor gathering research on his parents rather than a playwright urgently sifting through his past to achieve an emotional or artistic reckoning.

After intermission, when John takes over center stage for a series of one-on-one confrontations, he becomes the vacuum that saps the play's vitality. We don't know him well enough to care about his plight; the deficiencies he cites in his play become signposts that point to the shortfalls in the play before us. Once John tries to nail down the family secrets, big scenes, and final curtain that might bring his *Cocktail Hour* closer to the truth, Mr. Gurney leaves pure froth behind to try to provide those elements in his own *Cocktail Hour*. He doesn't succeed. Every surprise seems contrived and hollow, including a long, supposedly revelatory monologue for Ms. Marchand and the reconciliation that provides the unconvincing, albeit happy, ending. The canned familial insights don't compensate for the punch lines they supplant. By the time the family leaves behind the cocktail hour for the dining room, one is still waiting for Mr. Gurney to push his characters beyond the circumscribed limits of *The Dining Room*.

As if to head off his own critics, the playwright gives Ms. Marchand a speech in which she accuses her son's reviewers of panning his plays because they resent his WASP characters. "They think we're all Republicans and all superficial and all alcoholics," she says. Though it's a funny line, it begs the issue. It isn't Mr. Gurney's characters who are superficial but, in the final clutch, his presentation of them. Not that audiences should mind. Until it turns sober, *The Cocktail Hour* is about as entertaining as superficiality in a theater without the Lunts can get.

THE WARRIOR ANT
MAJESTIC THEATER, BROOKLYN, OCTOBER 24, 1988

If the Brooklyn Academy of Music's Next Wave Festival is a serious portent of cultural things to come, the term *avant-garde* can finally be retired from New York's vocabulary. The festival's opening attraction for 1988, *The Warrior Ant,* is nothing if not a throwback to the smorgasbord esthetics of that totemic artistic happening of the 1950s, the *Ed Sullivan Show.*

For this extravaganza, which can be viewed from the hard benches of the Majestic Theater, the author and director Lee Breuer and the composer Bob Telson have recruited Brazilian and Trinidadian musical ensembles, a classical string trio, a master Japanese Bunraku puppeteer, a bevy of break dancers, a circus aerialist, and one bona fide belly dancer. There is narration read by high-toned actors outfitted in glitzy eighteenth-century garb suitable for a Las Vegas rendering of *Les Liaisons Dangereuses,* and there are enough singers equipped with hand mikes to stock a Jerry Lewis telethon. There's even an eighteen-foot-high toy ant, built from found objects in the style of *Cats,* that could eat Sullivan's favorite performing mouse, Topo Gigio, for breakfast. All that's missing is Alan King—which is not to say that the evening is short of laughs.

The ostensible point of *The Warrior Ant* is to tell a "mock epic poem" about a samurai ant whose metaphysical search for identity combines echoes of Genesis, Virgil, Dante, Cervantes, Bruce Lee, and, just possibly, *Charlotte's Web.* The first and most musical of the three chapters, "An Ant Conceived," takes place during an Afro-Caribbean Carnivale after a "day of days known as funky Tuesday" in "the Age of Considerable Boredom." As the warrior ant is born, the various bands ride about the stage on trucks decorated like the tackier cannoli stands in a Little Italy street festival. After intermission, the age of considerable boredom dawns in earnest: A Bunraku puppet show depicts the ant's descent into hell, where he meets up with the great worm Maeterlinck and with his long-lost father, a closet termite. In the final chapter, our hero proves to have a fatal attraction to a death moth.

Mr. Breuer's many literary references do not lend his fable any weight; they merely illustrate Pope's adage that a little learning is a dangerous thing. The real agenda of *The Warrior Ant* is far from cosmic. "There is a certain message here, or at least a certain metaphor," Mr. Breuer writes of the ant world, "for the queens live and multiply, and the drones love and die." As one listens to the alternately pretentious and facetious script, whose undisciplined asides extend to excretory and baseball jokes, one wonders if there has ever been so much droning in the service of one man's castration fantasies. As for poetry, we're told that "death melts the sun with love" and that "there is no upper limit to a tower of euphoria." There is also no upper limit to the amplification, which renders some lines and all song lyrics blessedly unintelligible.

In the last Breuer-Telson collaboration, *The Gospel at Colonus,* there was always the score, thrilling gospel music rousingly sung, to carry the audience past the text. Mr. Telson remains a musician of impressive sophistication, capable of composing with equal verve for a steel band or his own rock band (Little Village) or his frequent interpreter, the gospel belter Jevetta Steele. But the *Ant* numbers, however individually vibrant, don't gather the cumulative effect of the *Gospel* score, perhaps because they are not prompted by a clear (and spiritual) thematic impulse this time, or perhaps because the eclectic musical idioms simply cancel one another out.

Certainly Mr. Breuer's sloppy staging fails to fuse the international theatrical idioms gathered together in *The Warrior Ant.* The cultural imperialism on view here is not to be confused with the practice of revolutionary Western artists, whether in the theater or dance or painting, who have raided other cultures to reinvent old forms. Mr. Breuer simply throws everything at us at once, intellectually unsynthesized, thereby relegating foreign performance arts to the status of sideshows and assuring that confusion reigns.

When all the bands and conga-line ant dancers and puppets are going at full funky tilt in the first act, one could be at a nightclub in pre-Castro Cuba or perhaps in a nightmare set at the international pavilions of the 1964 World's Fair. Later, it is depressing to watch the dignified Yoshida Tamamatsu, a master puppeteer from the Osaka Kokuritsu Bunraku Theater, execute his delicate art in flickering lighting (by Julie Archer) against busy, aggressively ugly scenery (by Alison Yerxa), while competing for our attention with the belly dancer in gold lamé. Just as patronizing is Mr. Breuer's notion that his narrators in any way evoke the art of the West African storyteller, the griot.

The story, in any case, is far from over. This nearly three-hour helping of *The Warrior Ant* is only a third of the projected full version, which, as the present macho theatrical fashion requires, is promised to reach the length of Robert Wilson's *the CIVIL warS* and Peter Brook's *The Mahabharata.* Given that it took four years to create this segment alone, *The Warrior Ant* may still be with us long after most other entomological infestations— plagues of locusts, for instance—would have run their course.

≡ *Lee Breuer is an acquired taste I never acquired. Neither his impressively angry letters nor his best production,* The Gospel at Colonus—*best because the music was so good he couldn't ruin it—made me a convert. But his serious fans include the MacArthur Foundation, which awarded him a "genius" grant in 1997.*

CAFÉ CROWN
PUBLIC THEATER, OCTOBER 26, 1988

The audience—and it may not be the youngest audience you'll ever meet at the Public Theater—oohs and ahs in unison twice at the revival of *Café Crown,* a 1942 Broadway play by Hy Kraft. The first peal of delight is prompted by Santo Loquasto's stunning set: a plush, sconce-lighted replica of an old Second Avenue café, with pickles at every table and autographed photographs on every wall. The second round of cooing occurs at the start of Act 2, when we discover the set filled to capacity with the production's large cast. Not every night do we find almost twenty actors on stage in a nonmusical comedy, the entire company rewarded with real, speaking roles.

Those two moments encapsulate the broad nostalgic pleasures of the entire, elaborately catered affair. *Café Crown* is a sentimental journey back through time, into the warm glow of two nearly extinct forms of theatrical endeavor. The play's setting and characters are drawn from the Lower East Side's once-thriving Yiddish theater. The Café Crown is a stand-in for the old Café Royale, which served as a Second Avenue schmoozing and kibitzing ground, a Sardi's with schnapps, to the legendary likes of Maurice Schwartz and Jacob Ben Ami. The second vanished theatrical world on stage is the one now represented by Kraft's play itself. Though *Café Crown* was utterly typical of the Broadway theater of its era, today a light comedy with its costly cast and modest aspirations would not even be considered for uptown production.

That Joseph Papp has exhumed it—and done so with a loving fidelity the New York Shakespeare Festival rarely bestows upon Shakespeare—says a lot about the producer's own relation to the past that Kraft has chronicled. Mr. Papp belongs to the genealogy of larger-than-life Yiddish theater impresarios: showmen of high and often adventurous artistic ambitions, infinite cunning, and towering egos. In *Café Crown,* the type is represented by David Cole—a thinly disguised Jacob Adler—a flamboyant actor-manager and director who hopes to improve upon *King Lear* by giving Shakespeare's protagonist a wife and a palatial apartment on Riverside Drive. Surely it's no coincidence that Cole, marvelously played by Eli Wallach, has been outfitted to resemble the public image of Mr. Papp.

Don't expect to care whether Cole scrapes together the money and cast needed for his *Lear,* or about the rest of the *Café Crown* plot, either, with its trivial, most un-*Lear*-like family feuds. No one should go to *Café Crown* hoping to see a good play. No one did so in 1942, when it ran four months at the Cort. As Elia Kazan, whose first modest success as a Broadway director came with the original production, wrote in his memoirs this year: "Hy Kraft, a Hollywood screenplay writer, had the thinnest talent of any playwright I've worked with—but he did have a talent. It was for the Jewish anecdote." In other words, *Café Crown* is a feast of Jewish waiter jokes and Jewish theater jokes, heavily laced with schmaltz.

And such waiters! They are Bob Dishy, his expression so dill-sour that even his tufts of hair seem exasperated, and Fyvush Finkel, tall and slightly stooped and sure to say "You'll love it!" to any irritating customer who alights upon one of the less palatable daily specials. Mr. Dishy's role is a classic Jewish comic type: a conniver and sometime theatrical investor with a secret soft heart. (No wonder Kraft would later write a musical for Phil Silvers, *Top Banana*.) Mr. Finkel, a longtime Yiddish theater performer, is priceless, the soul of meticulous clowning whose every contemptuous glare and shambling step reflects decades of comic practice.

As extravagantly led by Mr. Wallach—who turns every entrance and exit into a cane-waving, stentorian-toned megillah—the theater crowd, all self-anointed "geniuses," is just as amusing. Particularly funny are Marilyn Cooper as an actress reduced to Cleveland engagements in *The Kosher Wife*, Harry Goz as a prolific hack dramatist whose idea of a "very short" play is seven acts long, and Felix Fibich as a bit actor hysterically torn between a standing pinochle game and his *Lear* role of Kent. Joseph Leon, as a critic who writes his *Jewish Daily Forward* reviews in advance of opening night, and Anne Jackson, cast true-to-life as Mr. Wallach's actress wife, are also good, though Ms. Jackson could part with some of her modern comic restraint.

The director, Martin Charnin, has recruited pleasant young actors (David Carroll among them) as the old timers' straight men. Although the pacing could use some George Abbott drive, his staging smartly follows Mr. Kazan's advice for this play. Writing that it would "be a bad mistake" to pump up *Café Crown* into "anything better" than the "small folk piece" that it is, Mr. Kazan made sure, as Mr. Charnin does, that the jokes stayed front and center.

While one indeed shouldn't make *Café Crown* into anything more than it is, the play inevitably carries rueful history now that it didn't in 1942. When Kraft was writing, he could not have known that the Yiddish theater would soon be exterminated entirely in Europe, or that the

American Yiddish theater, like American Yiddish culture in general, would shrink of natural causes to the point where both the Café Royale and Maurice Schwartz's Yiddish Art Theatre across the street would be defunct by 1950. In *Café Crown*, the assimilationist second-generation Americans (one of them presumably based on Stella Adler) are already following Second Avenue defectors like Paul Muni to the glamorous English-speaking show business of Broadway and Hollywood. But the depletion of the ranks is still treated mostly as a joke; the Yiddish theater's woes seem grave but hardly terminal.

Café Crown remains what Mr. Kazan labels it: "slight stuff." Yet to see the play in 1988, performed with such authenticity at a theater in the same neighborhood as its demolished setting, proves an occasion not just for laughter but for paying a grand, departed theatrical universe affectionate final respects.

≡ *This play and production were so out of character for Joseph Papp that I probably should have guessed that he was sick.* Café Crown *was suffused with nostalgia for the producer's youthful encounters with the theater. As he compulsively did with so many plays that couldn't survive the journey to Broadway during this period, he moved it uptown and watched it close within weeks after the transfer.*

EASTERN STANDARD
MANHATTAN THEATRE CLUB, OCTOBER 28, 1988

In *Eastern Standard*, his new play at the Manhattan Theatre Club, Richard Greenberg captures the romantic sophistication of the most sublime comedies ever made in this country: those produced by Hollywood from the middle of the Depression until the waning days of World War II.

Mr. Greenberg's characters have youth, brains, money, and classy professions. Their last names—Wheeler, Paley, Kidde—are redolent of Philip Barry's Park Avenue; their fresh good looks and bubbly voices recall Katharine Hepburn and Henry Fonda. And like Carole Lombard, the heiress who adopts a tramp in *My Man Godfrey*, or Joel McCrea, the Hollywood director who goes underground as a hobo in *Sullivan's Travels*, they are driven by conscience to see how the other half lives. The bright young things of *Eastern Standard* invite a bag lady to stay with them in the Hamptons.

If Mr. Greenberg's only achievement were to re-create the joy of screwball comedies, from their elegant structure to their endlessly quotable dialogue, *Eastern Standard* would be merely dazzling good fun. But what gives this play its unexpected weight and subversive punch is its author's ability to fold the traumas of his own time into vintage comedy without sacrificing the integrity of either his troubling content or his effervescent theatrical form. *Eastern Standard* opens with its characters meeting cute in a Manhattan restaurant; it ends with them toasting their future happiness on a Long Island beach. Yet in between, both Mr. Greenberg's people and his audience have been rocked by the plight of a city in the midst of "a nervous breakdown." It's a city where developers rob the poor of their homes and the entire citizenry of its sunlight. It's a city where people constantly wake up with hot sweats—whether they are guilty perpetrators of financial corruption or innocent victims of AIDS.

When we first meet the four incipient lovers of *Eastern Standard* at a restaurant serving such dishes as grouper tortellini, they are too selfish and complacent to worry much about all that. Drew (Peter Frechette) is a downtown painter whose épater le bourgeois pose and haughty verbal "reflex of belittlement" are at hypocritical odds with his decadent existence. His best friend from Dartmouth days, Stephen (Dylan Baker), is an architect just awakening to his own complicity in Manhattan's urban blight. At the neighboring table are Phoebe (Patricia Clarkson), a Wall Street investment counselor caught up in an insider trading scandal, and her brother, Peter (Kevin Conroy), a television producer who spends "days at a time defending nearly invisible principles" while pounding socially conscious scripts into fluff at CBS.

Since Drew and Peter are both gay, and Stephen and Phoebe are not, it's only minutes before the college chums and brother and sister can mix and match in a way Preston Sturges never could have imagined in *The Palm Beach Story*. In his ingenious first act, Mr. Greenberg achieves the couplings with three overlapping scenes, Alan Ayckbourn–style, that replay the same action from the varying perspectives of different tables in the restaurant. Even then, a disturbing counterpoint accompanies the heavy-breathing flirtations. As the sexual repartee reaches its crescendo, so do the disquieting obscenities of an unseen woman trying to storm the barricades of Upper East Side trendiness.

That woman is the homeless May (Anne Meara), a casualty of welfare bureaucracy who just wants "to sit like everyone else and drink some Perrier water." When her wish comes true in screwball fashion at Stephen's beach home after intermission, Mr. Greenberg manages to uphold the escapist tone of his classic Hollywood models while refusing to permit his characters to escape. Act 2 of *Eastern Standard,* set on a beautiful beachfront designed by Philipp Jung and lighted by Dennis Parichy, retains the champagne-informed dizziness of the poolside wedding eve in *The Philadelphia Story.* Freed from inhibition as if by magic, the characters switch partners, quit their jobs, and vow to be reborn. But May isn't a cuddly homeless doll; she refuses to disappear in what another character calls "the wonderful solvent of a politically correct project." When the pretty lovers of *Eastern Standard* finally sober up, it is not merely because they've figured out who they really love but because they at last see their true roles, hardly attractive ones, in the urban nightmare they've tried to flee.

Under the swift and buoyant direction of Michael Engler, *Eastern Standard* goes by so blithely that not until after it's over can one dip beneath the play's brilliant surface to explore its depths. Mr. Greenberg, a thirty-year-old writer whose previous work includes a one-act play of great promise (*Life Under Water*) as well as the arch full-length *The Maderati,* is maturing at an accelerating rate. *Eastern Standard* itself has been enriched considerably since its May premiere at the Seattle Repertory Theatre.

As always, this playwright is a fount of epigrammatic lines and bright jokes. Julian Schnabel (among others) is described as being on "the cutting edge of the passé," and one offstage mother is deemed so conservative that "there's not a revolution in history that would have failed to execute her." The laughs never depart from a human foundation. Here is that uncommon writer who can make heterosexual and homosexual romances equally credible and erotic. The play's close sibling relationship is also gripping, and so, most impressively, is the college-spawned fraternity between Drew and Stephen. Whether engaging in juvenile locker-room humor or propping each other up in tearful sorrow, these two friends achieve a fluent intimacy that, in my experience, has never previously been allotted to male stage characters of opposite sexual preference.

With the occasional exception of the gifted Mr. Frechette, who caricatures Drew's facetiousness in Act 1 before hitting an affecting stride, the acting is as full-bodied as the play. Mr. Baker and Ms. Clarkson, who have floated about Off Broadway in supporting roles for a few seasons now, are transformed into radiant leading players by *Eastern Standard.* Like Stewart and Hepburn, they convey appealing but muddled moral rectitude that can flare into either intoxicating giddiness or bitter self-recrimination as the champagne flows on.

In an extremely tough assignment, Ms. Meara is scrupulous in refusing to conform to the sentimentalized role that her bleeding-heart benefactors wish her to play. Her bag lady strikes the perfect balance between Lily Tomlin–like curmudgeonliness and frightening psychosis. Barbara Garrick, the one Seattle cast holdover, is similarly unclichéd as a struggling actress representing the hard-put Manhattan economic class just above the homeless, and Mr. Conroy is touching as the producer determined to resist self-pity despite having AIDS. "No one ever looked at me without thinking I'd live forever," he says, and, indeed, he looks like a Bruce Weber model in an advertisement for Ralph Lauren beachwear. Later, when Mr. Conroy breaks the tranquillity of the pose and its setting by crying out a simple, terrifying line—"I'm sick!"—the effect is devastating. As his rage tears through the Hamptons landscape, it seems to lower the curtain on a Bloomingdale's diorama of a decade in which easy money and easy pleasure were unlimited for the privileged few.

Just the same, and perhaps to the distress of ideologues, the author refuses to condemn outright his once-charmed and always charming characters. Mr. Greenberg has no better utopian schemes for conquering social inequities than they do. Like Drew, who is a middle-class artist because "no other class is open to me," Mr. Greenberg must write about what he knows: people who got fat from the ethos of the 1980s but may finally begin to examine the connection between their own behavior and the sick city left in the wake of the spree.

True to form, *Eastern Standard* holds out hope for its people and their post-crash society much as Hollywood's Depression comedies did. It will be up to history to determine whether Mr. Greenberg's faith in the fundamental decency of his characters is as justified as Frank Capra's was. But that's our problem, not the author's. For anyone who has been waiting for a play that tells what it is like to be more or less middle-class, more or less young, and more or less well-intentioned in a frightening city at this moment in this time zone, *Eastern Standard* at long last is it.

≡ *Only a few critics shared my enthusiasm for* Eastern Standard, *which also died soon after it moved to Broadway. (Where is this power of the* Times?, *I kept wondering.) Richard Greenberg had impressed me with a number of offbeat plays Off Broadway before I saw this one (initially) at the Seattle Repertory Company (where it starred the excellent Tom Hulce). Greenberg went on to write some other interesting plays—notably* The American Plan, The Extra Man, *and* Three Days of Rain. *Still young, he will write better plays yet.*

ITALIAN AMERICAN RECONCILIATION
Manhattan Theatre Club, October 31, 1988

When the moon hits your eye like a big pizza pie, that's amore. But these days it may also be a new script by John Patrick Shanley, who has followed his Oscar-winning screenplay for *Moonstruck* with another slice of sometimes gooey, sometimes piquant, always moonlit romanticism, Italian American–style. Mr. Shanley's new work, a play set in Little Italy, is baldly titled *Italian American Reconciliation*. It can be found at the Manhattan Theatre Club Stage 2, a few steps and several cultural eons away from Richard Greenberg's *Eastern Standard,* which brought a younger, designer-pizza generation's love stories to the company's main stage only last week.

Not at all unpleasantly, Mr. Shanley's writing recalls Paddy Chayefsky's *Marty* gone loopily punch-drunk. Through his career he has refined his sentimental vision of ethnic urban romance, from the inane bromides of *Welcome to the Moon* (at the Ensemble Studio Theatre in 1982) to the fierce but still saccharine *Danny and the Deep Blue Sea* to *Moonstruck* itself, which achieved the best balance yet between the writer's zesty comic voice and his weakness for breast-beating bathos. *Italian American Reconciliation* is a small-scale gloss on the smash film, and it proves enjoyable until Act 2, when it could sorely use Cher's pretension-deflating comic attack.

Once again Mr. Shanley has provided two contrasting men—brothers in *Moonstruck,* best friends here—who are stuck in the orbit of a powerful, man-agitating heroine. Huey Maximilian Bonfigliano, played by John Pankow, is the Nicolas Cage figure: a slightly mad, obsessive, Puccini-sotted soul prone equally to fits of eccentric animalistic behavior and flights of beery poetry. What was the Danny Aiello character in *Moonstruck*—the overage momma's boy—is now named Aldo Scalicki and played by John Turturro. The woman tormenting both men is Huey's former wife, Janice (Jayne Haynes), a sharp-tongued loner who facilitated her marriage's disintegration by shooting her husband's dog.

Italian American Reconciliation is charmingly presented as a tall folk tale, narrated by Mr. Turturro, who chats up the audience before the play proper begins. The tale is essentially an anecdote about a farcical scheme to reconcile Huey and Janice, if only for a night. Three years after his divorce, Huey still feels that he cannot go on with his life—and regain his strength "as a man"—unless he can put his broken marriage

behind him. He enlists Aldo in his plan, but Aldo, too, is in need of a reconciliation with the past. A confirmed bachelor, he must cut his mother's
apron strings if he is to lose his "fear of women as a race" and begin his
own adult love life.

In the easygoing first act, Mr. Shanley has fun not only with Aldo's digressionary narration and the men's buddy relationship but also with a
pair of female characters at a neighborhood luncheonette. Huey's current girlfriend, the waitress Teresa (Laura San Giacomo), and a middle-
aged widow, Aunt May (Helene Hanft), dispense minestrone and home
truths with colloquial verve. As they ease us into the playwright's fantasy
idealization of his New York setting, so we warm up to his old-fashioned
storytelling. When Aunt May closes Act 1 by saying she'd give anything
to be a fly on the wall of the events of Act 2, her curiosity about the narrative's outcome is contagious.

The follow-through is a letdown. Act 2 opens, hilariously, with a satirical deployment of the bombastic opening bars of *Turandot,* but is the
ensuing balcony scene a mock-operatic put-on or simply genuine, inflated corn? Either way—whether humor or pathos—it fails to satisfy.
Worse, as the play descends into yelling and tears, we hear the tautolog-
ical morals promised us by the narrator at the outset. After constantly re-
iterating Freudian banalities—children must overcome dead or distant
fathers, for instance—Mr. Shanley lets loose with the epiphany he wants
us to take home: "The greatest—the only—success is to be able to love."
As with *Moonstruck,* one wonders if the author really believes in his
greeting-card sentiments and accompanying happy endings or is merely
(and cynically) trying to market what audiences most want to hear.

As a director of his own script, Mr. Shanley is assured in everything
but his handling of actors. While Mr. Turturro, at his most restrained
and ingratiating, provides a sympathetic portrait of a self-deluded loser
who belatedly recognizes his own sad clownishness, Ms. Haynes's Janice
crosses the line from comic neuroticism into psychosis. Her eyes are so
wild she seems capable of ax murders as well as dog slayings. By contrast, the reliable Mr. Pankow is a shade blander than required as the
overwrought Huey. Ms. San Giacomo and Ms. Hanft, the latter in what
can only be described as the Olympia Dukakis role, get their laughs, not
the least of which is a candid reassessment of Oedipus' tragic flaw.

For the second time in a week—the first being *Café Crown*—the designer Santo Loquasto has lovingly evoked a downtown ethnic enclave.
In *Italian American Reconciliation* he does so in a fairy-tale storybook
style precisely setting the boundaries on the intimate scale and folkloric
aspirations of the play. In keeping with the Oscar-winning formula, the

atmosphere is further heightened by the intermingling of Puccini with 1950s pop-music kitsch, "Papa Loves Mambo" instead of "That's Amore," throughout the action. As for Peter Kaczorowski's lighting, it is so ceaselessly moonstruck that you may leave Mr. Shanley's romantic nocturnal New York pining at least a little for the cold, harsh light of day.

WAITING FOR GODOT
MITZI E. NEWHOUSE THEATER, NOVEMBER 7, 1988

Late in Act 1 of the new Mike Nichols production of *Waiting for Godot*, one wait is over. Not the eternal wait for Godot, of course, but the wait to see how, if ever, Mr. Nichols and his all-star company might connect to the Samuel Beckett play that brought the theater into the terrifying limbo of the nuclear age.

The scene is set in the middle of nowhere, at the end of another long day, indistinguishable from any other day. Vladimir, the tramp played by Steve Martin, has been passing the time with his companion, Estragon, played by Robin Williams. There is nothing to be done except wait in vain for some justification to live until tomorrow. And now, as burlesque parlance has it, comes the final kick in the pants: A boy (Lukas Haas) walks on to announce that Godot, who may be that justification, will not be coming tonight.

Disappointing as this news is, Mr. Martin relaxes his face into a child-like smile and instructs the messenger, "Tell him you saw us." As he delivers the line, Mr. Martin's countenance takes on the radiant orange glow of sunset, as if the simplest imaginable proof of his own existence— being visible to another—were somehow a glimpse of salvation. In this quiet moment, as acted with plaintive wistfulness and cloaked in wintry dusk (by the lighting designer Jennifer Tipton), Mr. Nichols's *Godot* at last achieves the pathos of Beckett's fundamental image of man, born of the charnel house of World War II. Stripped of absolutely everything, including any external sign of a rationally or divinely ordered civilization, a Beckett hobo will still reach within himself to find some tiny shred of human dignity that will allow him, bravely, to go on.

One wishes that the rest of this evening were as pure as that haunting tableau. For all that has been written about *Godot* since it began remaking the world's theater, no play could be more elemental in either form or content. *Godot* speaks equally to prison inmates and university students because it reduces the task of existence to its humblest essentials:

eating, excretion, sleeping, companionship, waiting anxiously for life to reach some point (whatever that point may be). That simplicity, expressed in theatrical terms of matching spareness, too often eludes Mr. Nichols and his company. While ostensibly working in the unpretentious circumstances of Lincoln Center's smallest theater, the Mitzi E. Newhouse, Mr. Nichols has at times turned *Godot* into exactly the sort of production that Beckett's theater rebels against.

Given the talent of everyone involved—the cast also includes F. Murray Abraham and Bill Irwin as its excellent Pozzo and Lucky—the production is sometimes entertaining and never boring. The evening begins on a high note as Mr. Williams and Mr. Martin, each an adept physical comedian, make the most of funny business involving ill-fitting boots and unchecked body odor. From then on, the stars come across as comfortable, disciplined stage performers, seemingly eager to serve Beckett's play rather than to use it as a trampoline for their own egos.

That's not quite the case with Mr. Nichols. The naked realism of *Godot,* which belongs to no specific place or time but to all places and all time, does not suit a director whose gift is for comedy strongly rooted in contemporary social detail. Rather than expanding his artistic reach to meet Beckett's, he contracts the play to fit his own chilly esthetic. The efficient, emotionally remote approach Mr. Nichols takes to *Godot* is not all that different from the one he took to his last Broadway production, that rat-a-tat barrage of Jewish mother-in-law jokes titled *Social Security.*

The director tightens his leash the second the houselights dim: The first scene is heralded by an apocalyptic rumble (lest anyone doubt that Beckett wrote in the shadow of the bomb) followed by a vaudeville-theater drum roll (so we can remember that Vladimir and Estragon are in the baggy-pants-and-bowler-hat comic tradition of Laurel and Hardy). Then we get a good look at Tony Walton's set. While this *Godot* takes place in a circle of dirt rather than by the country road indicated in Beckett's text, Mike Nichols is no Peter Brook. The sandbox at the Newhouse isn't the abstract setting of a Brook rethinking of a classic but is instead a realistic rendering of a rubble-strewn, present-day American desert, complete with a rusted Nevada license plate.

Philistine and reductive as it may be, there's nothing intrinsically malevolent about applying a glaze of Sam Shepard–David Hockney chic to *Godot*—even if Beckett dialogue mentioning the Macon country now refers to the Napa. (Why hasn't a reference to the Eiffel Tower been changed to the Trans-America pyramid?) But once Mr. Williams starts availing himself of the cowboy-movie accents and jokey props (a coyote skull, novelty-shop eyeglasses) afforded by the setting, it's clear that the switch in locale exists in part to prompt more comic business than the ample music-hall routines Beckett already provides. Mr. Nichols abhors the pauses where feeling might enter *Godot,* so he fills most of them up with shtick. Even the set's tree is given more business: The joke in which Vladimir refers to the nearly bare tree as being "covered with leaves" is inflated by reducing the number of leaves on its branch from Beckett's specified "four or five" to a lonely one.

The most frenetic horseplay belongs to Mr. Williams, who at one point regurgitates the theme music of television's *Twilight Zone* as if he were still playing his old sitcom character of Mork. A brilliant mimic, the actor never runs out of wacky voices, but where is his own voice? As *Good Morning, Vietnam* seemed to evaporate whenever Mr. Williams had to forsake comedy routines for love scenes, so his Estragon vanishes whenever he has to convey genuine panic or loneliness or despair. There's more humor (and heartfelt agony) in the famous Richard Avedon photographic portrait of Bert Lahr's Estragon than there is in a whole night of Mr. Williams's sweaty efforts to keep us in stitches.

Mr. Nichols's relentless pacing of the verbal volleys no doubt dictates some of Mr. Williams's performance, but Mr. Martin's Vladimir rises above it with the sweet innocence that made his latter-day Cyrano so sympathetic in *Roxanne.* To be sure, Mr. Martin invokes his own comic style (and sometimes hilariously so); he provides one of his quintessentially crazed, open-mouthed double takes after Estragon insultingly calls him a "critic." Still, Beckett's character usually comes first, and it seems a waste that Mr. Williams rarely stands still long enough to permit his partner to engage him in an intimate exchange. Without repose and rapport, Vladimir and Estragon cannot become a classic comedy team, let alone an affecting representation of two interdependent souls who haven't been able to live with or without each other for fifty years.

Perhaps because Pozzo and Lucky's partnership follows the master and servant hierarchy of an older world—and the theatrical artifice of old-fashioned drama—Mr. Abraham and Mr. Irwin achieve the symbiosis that the stars do not. The flamboyant Mr. Abraham plays Pozzo as part Mafioso, part anachronistic ham actor, while Mr. Irwin offers a Buster Keaton–like mournfulness as his quaking slave. When this couple reappears in Act 2, Pozzo now blind and Lucky now dumb, the actors and Mr. Nichols go further, creating what amounts to an affecting, if sentimental, encapsulation of the tethered relationship of Lear to his fool.

At such moments, one feels privileged to be at this *Godot.* But those denied that privilege should not feel that the loss is a tragedy—or even a theatrical deprivation comparable to missing the other Beckett work at the Newhouse this year, the stunning Gate Theater of Dublin production of *I'll Go On*. Though Mr. Nichols's *Godot*, by dint of its fleeting run, is a box-office phenomenon, the play remains the permanent phenomenon. Audiences will still be waiting for a transcendent *Godot* long after the clowns at Lincoln Center, like so many others passing through Beckett's eternal universe before them, have come and gone.

SPOILS OF WAR

Music Box Theatre, November 11, 1988

"Why can't things be different?" pleads Martin (Christopher Collet), the troubled sixteen-year-old caught in the crossfire of Michael Weller's *Spoils of War*. Martin is asking the question of his parents, whose divorce a decade earlier he still refuses to accept and whose reconciliation he still hopes to accomplish. The question is rhetorical, of course; things can't be different for Martin's parents now or ever. But what child of divorce ever stops asking? In Mr. Weller's climactic scene, it is harrowing to watch the cold truth at last sink in: Martin, his eyes glazed and his thin body taut with panic, stands frozen midway between his warring mother and father, paralyzed by the recognition that his lifelong pipe dream is never to be.

That moment alone would make the play at the Music Box wrenching, but Mr. Weller, whose previous works include the Vietnam-era lamentations *Moonchildren* and *Loose Ends,* has never been a writer to settle for unalloyed domestic drama. When Martin asks his parents his crucial question, his words spill well beyond his family's walls. In *Spoils of War,* Mr. Weller wonders if things could have been different not only for his young protagonist but also for the American generation represented by the boy's parents. Elise (Kate Nelligan) and Andrew (Jeffrey DeMunn) are more than battle-scarred veterans of a marital war of silence, they are also survivors of national conflagrations: the radical movements of the Great Depression, World War II, the Cold War that spawned the McCarthy witch hunts. Setting his play in New York during the materialistic and complacent Eisenhower 1950s, Mr. Weller finds in one family's disintegration a paradigm of the postwar collapse of liberal idealism.

First seen at Off Broadway's Second Stage last winter, *Spoils of War* arrives on Broadway with Ms. Nelligan's bravura performance intact but with substantial alterations in its text, supporting cast, and physical production. Revisions were called for. Mr. Weller, always a fine writer, seemed on the verge of a major breakthrough with this work: His script had the potential to merge the lyricism of a classic memory play in the *Glass Menagerie* tradition with the pungent social thought that has marked all his writing, including his screenplays for Milos Forman's *Hair* and *Ragtime*.

The results of the retooling are mixed. For all the changes in *Spoils of War,* some of them quite constructive, the overall effect remains disappointingly the same. This is without question Mr. Weller's most absorbing play, always intelligent and at times moving, but it is still too lumpy, both in the writing and in Austin Pendleton's erratic direction, to achieve the lofty theatrical stature promised by its characters and ideas.

Now, as before, *Spoils of War* is compulsively watchable whenever Ms. Nelligan is on stage. A voluptuous figure in scarlet—from her Rita Hayworth pile of hair to her full lips to her drop-dead high-heel shoes—this mother is clearly the kind of powerful woman whom "people don't get over." She's also an original personality whose contradictory traits can't be folded into any standard characterization. Hard-drinking, much-married, and sexually voracious, Elise nonetheless works selflessly at a menial job to keep Martin in a progressive boarding school. She is a romantic who yearns to write poetry and to live for "something better than rent and the price of hamburger," but she is also prey to passionate excesses and irresponsible fantasies that destroy her best personal and ideological intentions.

Elise has principles in common with the disappointed fifties renegade Ms. Nelligan played in David Hare's *Plenty*—especially when she chastises her conformist decade for its selfishness and triviality. But Mr. Weller's play allows the actress to display far more resilience, warmth, and humor. Even at her most incestuously flirtatious, Ms. Nelligan's Elise is convincingly a nurturing, self-sacrificing mother. Her generous friendship with a less glamorous comrade from the movement's salad days—played with a lovely fragility by Alice Playten—is just as credible as her childish sexual teasing of a male drifter (an affable Kevin O'Rourke). Ms. Nelligan has the role of her career here—not for nothing does Elise liken herself to Tallulah—and she is never less than riveting.

The star has also gained a true partner to play against, at least in Act 2. Mr. Weller has bolstered the previously sketchy role of Martin's father. Andrew is a self-righteously lapsed leftist and delinquent parent but by no means a villain; Mr. De Munn's impressively layered performance allows us to see both how he got tangled up with Elise and why he ultimately had to leave her. Unlike so many writers of coming-of-age plays,

Mr. Weller has the maturity to portray the strengths and frailties of each parent—with generosity but never to a sentimental fault.

What the playwright does not see so penetratingly is his own onstage alter ego. Though Martin finally proves a somewhat articulate spokesman for his resentments and anger, he is still too much of a cipher for too long. It's no reflection on Mr. Collet's able acting that his cute Act 1 scheming to reunite his parents seems juvenile, more appropriate to Hollywood-style comedies of the fifties like *The Courtship of Eddie's Father* or *A Hole in the Head* than a play of these ambitions. While we wait and wait for Martin's plan to take effect, the play lacks a center of gravity that neither parent can provide.

If Martin remains underwritten, occasional passages of *Spoils of War,* particularly the flourishes for Ms. Nelligan in the final scene, seem overwritten, as if the playwright were trying to inflate his generally eloquent and pointed dialogue to serve some anachronistic definition of Broadway grandeur. A greater calamity, no fault of Mr. Weller's, is the recasting of the role of the father's girlfriend, a zoo worker not much older than Martin. As played last year by Annette Bening, the character was a disarmingly direct oddball who further compounded the familial and sexual tensions of the play. In the synthetic performance of Marita Geraghty, she comes across as irritatingly intrusive, and her once-provocative scenes with Martin bog down both acts.

In addition to that unfortunate blot on his otherwise sensitive work with his cast, Mr. Pendleton again demonstrates, albeit on a larger scale and with a different designer than at the Second Stage, that he pays scant attention to the visual aspects of directing. Andrew Jackness's settings, a stylistically unfocused mishmash of campy period furniture and abstract urbanscapes, are gloomy and cluttered. A turntable notwithstanding, Mr. Pendleton stages every scene with the same static symmetry, as if the play's every incident deserved the same theatrical weight.

That stasis, thankfully, is often overcome by Mr. Weller, Ms. Nelligan, and Mr. DeMunn. The reunion in which Elise and Andrew briefly resurrect the laughter and affection of their dead bond, then abruptly erupt once more in the rage that smashed it, is an exceptionally truthful, compact, and upsetting scene from a marriage. As his young protagonist must learn, Mr. Weller entertains few illusions that domestic history, private or public, can be rewritten or that its truces can be more than shortlived. While *Spoils of War* might have brought home its wars more fully, the wounds it rips open are too many, too real, and too bloody not to hurt.

CORIOLANUS
PUBLIC THEATER, NOVEMBER 23, 1988

Politics is a dirty business, yet, in a democracy, someone has got to do it. But who? To many Americans, the answer was hardly satisfactory in 1988, a year in which the handlers, the pollsters, and the advertising men often seemed to have more say than either the candidates or the voters. The national disenchantment that was registered on November 8, when a low turnout produced a mandate of dubious import, could hardly find more articulate or sorrowing expression than it does in *Coriolanus*, Shakespeare's corrosive view of Roman democracy in the fifth century B.C. *Coriolanus* is a tragedy in which the political process proves every bit as chaotic and poisonous as war.

The point is brought home with blazing, bitter irony in Steven Berkoff's striking production at the Public Theater, the sixth and easily the most provocative offering of the New York Shakespeare Festival's Shakespeare Marathon. Mr. Berkoff is an idiosyncratic English playwright, director, and actor (he's Hitler in television's *War and Remembrance*) whose view of Shakespeare will infuriate purists. His *Coriolanus* is performed in more-or-less-modern dress, nearly all of it black, with the star, Christopher Walken, outfitted in the hip, double-breasted jackets worn by aging pop royalty. The play's pulse has been quickened to a rock beat by textual slashing and fiddling, sharply choreographed movement (alternately martial and MTV), and an inventive all-percussion score (by Larry Spivak) that echoes Shakespeare's own percussive imagery even as it recalls Philip Glass's thematically related music for the film *Mishima*.

Those who have seen Mr. Berkoff's stage work—most specifically, *West*, a neo–*West Side Story* about London's disaffected working-class young—will recognize his blueprint for *Coriolanus*. One would hate to see the high-pitched Berkoff brand of stylization imposed upon most classics, but *Coriolanus* is one (*Arturo Ui* might be another) that is enriched by his colloquial approach. Mr. Berkoff also deserves credit for his work with actors. In addition to presiding over Mr. Walken's most impressive classical performance to date, the director has fielded an excellent, tightly drilled company that does not often succumb to the usual Shakespeare Festival malaise in its lower ranks.

Neither Mr. Berkoff nor his actors make a fetish of the modern touches. Though the *Playbill* specifies Rome, the staging techniques sometimes suggest the Oriental theater, the accents are variously American and British, and the exact place and time of this *Coriolanus* remain vague; it's the intellectual point of view that's firm. Usually in concert with the author, Mr. Berkoff takes a cynical stand on nearly everyone in the play. The Roman plebeians are black-shirted rabble, virtually indistinguishable from their enemy, the fascistic Volscian army commanded by a vulgar Aufidius (Keith David). The people's tribunes (Larry Bryggman and André Braugher) are conniving, street-corner gangsters in pinstripes, while the generals (Thomas Kopache and Moses Gunn) are steely bureaucrats. Menenius Agrippa, the garrulous patrician sometimes portrayed as a well-meaning liberal, is revealed in Paul Hecht's witty, meticulous characterization as a patronizing hypocrite. Coriolanus's hard-driving mother, Volumnia, is the quintessential political manipulator, always masking her lust for power as maternal affection in Irene Worth's sonorous, highly cunning performance.

It's no wonder that Mr. Walken's Caius Marcius, who is awarded the surname Coriolanus after conquering the Volscian city of Corioli, detests being a candidate for the consulship. Given the populace and its leaders, the campaign can only soil a brave military man of his patrician standing and egotistical pride. When Mr. Walken refuses to surrender his "own truth" to electoral expediency—choosing to be an enemy of the people rather than a toady to them—our sympathies are with him. In this production, Coriolanus's arrogant refusal to pander to the popular will, though ultimately carried to destructive extremes, is clearly the principled response of an honest man to a system that would warp him into an instrument of demagoguery.

Except when he slips self-indulgently into jokey Brandoese more appropriate to his showbiz roles in *Hurlyburly* and *The House of Blue Leaves,* Mr. Walken fulfills the protagonist's tragic stature. He is a majestic hero on the battlefield and a vain but undeniably magnetic autocrat when confronting the mob at home. In exile later, his face a shadowy terrain of exhaustion and despair, Mr. Walken becomes a vulnerable "boy of tears" who must save Rome and destroy himself by capitulating to his mother's wishes. In acting their last, hush-inducing scene together, he and Ms. Worth seem to pick up and gravely deepen the neurotic intimacy—part child-mother, part sexual—that they created over a decade ago when costarring in a revival of Tennessee Williams's *Sweet Bird of Youth.*

When Mr. Walken meets his inevitable extinction soon after, the scene earns more pity than it usually does in contemporary productions of *Coriolanus,* including Peter Hall's celebrated 1985 quasi-modern-dress version, in which Ms. Worth's Volumnia was partnered by Ian

McKellen at the National Theatre. This is attributable in part to Mr. Walken's ability to humanize the off-putting hero, but also to Mr. Berkoff's spare and highly theatrical staging. Aside from a dozen straight-back chairs that are deployed in seeming emulation of Harold Prince's junta tableaus in *Evita,* Mr. Berkoff and his imaginative designer, Loren Sherman, use a minimum of scenic clutter in *Coriolanus.* The stabbing of Mr. Walken, like the battle sequences earlier on, is mimed without swords but with such conviction that the scene leaves far more room than conventional outpourings of stage gore for an audience's grotesque imaginings.

It can't be happenstance that while Mr. Berkoff dispenses with all actual weapons in his *Coriolanus,* he pointedly does emphasize one realistic prop: a gray diplomatic envelope containing a peace treaty. The evening ends with a chilling sequence in which that document, so frail a symbol of a citizenry's best hopes, is abruptly doomed to the oblivion of a government briefcase. The brutal political caravan, meanwhile, inexorably marches on.

OUR TOWN
LYCEUM THEATRE, DECEMBER 5, 1988

Thornton Wilder wasn't bashful about revealing his own high opinion of *Our Town.* Late in Act 1, the play's narrator, the ubiquitous Stage Manager, tells the audience that he will leave the script in the cornerstone of a new bank, so that people "a thousand years from now" can see "the way we were: in our growing up and in our marrying and in our living and in our dying." Let other writers worry about whether their work will survive the season; Wilder had his eye on a millennium.

That millennium still has 950 years to go, but, a half century after its premiere, *Our Town* remains a most stageworthy and sometimes touching American play. Does it tell us "the way we were"? One wonders. As prettied up by Wilder, the sleepy Republican town of Grover's Corners, N.H., from 1901 to 1913, seems to say less about the country we live in now than does the earlier New England of eighteenth- and nineteenth-century literature. As an example of American playwriting of the 1930s, *Our Town* is closer in weight to Kaufman and Hart than to O'Neill.

Yet if Wilder is at his most treacly when celebrating diurnal living—and advertising just how universal his observations are—he is completely at home with the finality of dying. When the author briefly interrupts his idyllic opening narrative to announce that the nice Grover's Corners paperboy will die in World War I or that a husband will long outlive his seemingly healthy wife, the casual obituaries are rending. The Act 3 cemetery scene, a masterly feat of reticence in which the living and dead share the stage, really does achieve the timelessness that the rest of *Our Town* tries to fabricate with poetic rhetoric.

Gregory Mosher, the director of the play's new Lincoln Center Theater production at Broadway's Lyceum Theatre, is attuned to Wilder's melancholy. His *Our Town* is dark, with a Beckett-like grayness to the physical production—yes, the scenery and props are still minimal, but the costumes, tables, chairs, and stage walls are all gray—and with an urban edginess to some of the acting. With such stylization, Mr. Mosher seems to be attempting to justify his unadventurous saunter into *Our Town* by linking it to such other Lincoln Center productions of the year as *Waiting for Godot* and *Speed-the-Plow*. This esthetic statement is made at a price, because it has led to one major casting miscalculation, Spalding Gray's flip Stage Manager, that constantly disrupts the fragile text, the firm staging, and the otherwise well-chosen cast.

Mr. Gray notwithstanding, the virtues of this production are there to be savored. In Penelope Ann Miller and Eric Stoltz, two occasional stage actors with growing film careers, Mr. Mosher has a most attractive George and Emily. Ms. Miller, in particular, takes the goo out of the Andy Hardy–like sequences of courtship and marriage; she's a beauty, all right, but just enough stuck-up about her prowess as a star high-school student that we still resent her ability to bring the affable, red-haired Mr. Stoltz prematurely to heel. The couple's parents are also decent without being cloying: Peter Maloney's generous-spirited newspaper editor, James Rebhorn's stern doctor, and Roberta Maxwell and Frances Conroy as their constricted wives.

In Ms. Conroy's Mrs. Gibbs, at once loving and astringent, we can sense some discontent in Grover's Corners. The speech in which she pines in vain to travel to France—"a country where they don't talk in English and don't even want to"—reveals an undertow of bitterness about the provincialism of her community. In Mr. Mosher's reading, the passage in which the Stage Manager is questioned from the audience about the town's drinking, social inequities, and lack of culture also has unusual bite. Jeff Weiss, cast as the alcoholic church organist, sounds discordant notes of his own. Though the character has few lines, Mr. Weiss, a hollow-eyed and spindly figure in black, haunts Grover's Corners as if he were the repository of its citizens' smashed hopes and the lifelong victim of its mean, unspoken bigotry.

But Wilder was primarily a celebrant of the small town and the American century; he was not a debunker to be confused with Sinclair Lewis or Edgar Lee Masters. The attempt, through Mr. Gray, to turn the play-wright into something he's not derails Mr. Mosher's *Our Town*. While it would no doubt be sickening to see a Stage Manager resembling the lov-able old codgers in wine-cooler commercials, Mr. Gray swings too far the other way, presenting the narrator as if he were a narcissistic new-wave raconteur exactly matching the storyteller in his own autobiographical performance pieces. Much as one may have enjoyed Mr. Gray's *Terrors of Pleasure* and *Swimming to Cambodia,* their blasé TriBeCa hipness be-longs to another planet than that of *Our Town*.

Mr. Gray's silver hair and New England accent do serve the role. His smart-aleck attitude and lapsed preppie outfit do not. "Nice town, y'know what I mean?" says the Stage Manager early in the play; in Mr. Gray's de-livery, the second clause of the line is punched with a snide cynicism, as if to imply that Grover's Corners is less a nice town than a precursor of the setting of *Blue Velvet*. One can't really fault the performer; he's just doing his star turn out of context, following the Lincoln Center com-pany's indulgent example of Robin Williams's Estragon in *Godot*. Mr. Mosher should have realized, however, that *Our Town* becomes merely unpleasant, rather than revisionist, when our guide through Grover's Corners seems to be condescending to his fellow performers, the audi-ence, and the play.

The more emotional scenes in *Our Town*—notably the Act 2 wedding—suffer from the lack of a warm Stage Manager. But perhaps nothing can or ever will dismantle Wilder's finale, in which black, rain-splattered um-brellas emblematize the mourners at a burial while serene actors sitting in straight-backed chairs speak to us as the graveyard's dead. "It goes so fast," cries out Ms. Miller, the scene's one radiant figure in white, as she looks back on her evanescent existence from the other side. If *Our Town* is still a prototypical slice of Americana, it is because Wilder's almost jin-goistic certitude in the mission of our nation is ceaselessly undermined by his terror of the dark, unknowable wilderness beyond.

SINGLE SPIES
Royal National Theatre, London, December 20, 1988

Rarely does a single scene in a one-act play become the talk of the town, but such is the phenomenon created by *Single Spies,* the newly arrived Alan Bennett double bill attracting turn-away crowds to the National Theatre. It's not hard to see why; the scene is one the En-glish public literally has never seen before. Revue-sketch writers aside,

Mr. Bennett is the first dramatist to present a reigning British monarch—Queen Elizabeth II—as a character in a play.

The audience all but gasps when the comic actress Prunella Scales, nearly the spitting image of the Queen, appears during the second of the evening's offerings, *A Question of Attribution*. The setting is Buckingham Palace, where Sir Anthony Blunt, the royal family's curator of art, is fussing over a Titian. The time is apparently the early 1960s, when Blunt (played by Mr. Bennett) was under quiet investigation but had not yet confessed to being the "fourth man" in the Soviet spy ring that included Guy Burgess, Kim Philby, and Donald Maclean. The impromptu conversation that ensues between the Queen and Sir Anthony is ostensibly small talk about the nature of art history, the exposure of art forgeries, and the function of portrait painting. "Portraits are supposed to reveal a secret self," says Her Majesty, who allows that she refused to sit for Francis Bacon lest she be portrayed as a "screaming Queen."

But Mr. Bennett, returning to themes familiar from his early play *The Old Country* through his recent screenplay for *Prick Up Your Ears,* is after far more than polite and learned chat, however amusing. (Asked if she takes any pleasure in acquisitions, the Queen admits that "one more Fabergé egg isn't going to make my day.") While the dialogue's surface is often in the third-person diction of the British Establishment, its subtext is aflame with subversive innuendo. Each time the cold, donnish Blunt tentatively patronizes his employer about esthetics, she returns the volley with a smiling but vaguely prickly remark that leaves the audience and Blunt wondering whether she might already be onto his treacherous game.

"If something's not what it's supposed to be, what do you call it?" asks the Queen of a painting. "An enigma," answers Blunt. In *A Question of Attribution*, Mr. Bennett intermingles all kinds of enigmatic codes: those embedded in art, in the English class system, in Blunt's shadow lives as a spy and as a homosexual. The parallels are brought home explosively during the play's incidental slide shows, in which the criminal evidence against Blunt, snapshots of his Marxist coterie from Cambridge in the 1930s, alternate with X rays revealing heretofore obscured third and fourth men in a sixteenth-century canvas of questionable attribution.

Without ever indulging in caricature, Ms. Scales makes a completely persuasive Queen: shrewd without being intellectual, convivial without being intimate, charming without being warm. The mixture of the regal and the human is so successful that the rapt audience applauds the actress's mid-scene exit—a rarity in London—as if the actual Queen were leaving the theater. Mr. Bennett, whom I haven't seen on stage since *Beyond the Fringe* a quarter-century ago, is just as impressive. Always hiding behind impeccably snobby capitalist manners, he is as aloof a mystery man as the late, real-life Blunt, "the cleric of treason" in George Steiner's memorable phrase.

A Question of Attribution has been directed by Simon Callow, who, like Mr. Bennett, has a distinguished triple career as writer, actor, and director. In the curtain-raising half of *Single Spies,* titled *An Englishman Abroad,* Mr. Callow acts the star part under Mr. Bennett's direction. The role is that of Blunt's comrade: the aging, alcoholic Burgess living in Moscow exile in 1958. Ms. Scales plays Coral Browne, the actress who encountered Burgess while on Soviet tour with the Old Vic's *Hamlet* and ended up filling the homesick spy's orders for Savile Row suits.

With its loopy juxtapositions of Stalinist repression and Etonian nostalgia, *An Englishman Abroad* suffers only by comparison with Mr. Bennett's original dramatization of Coral Browne's true story, the widely seen television movie of the same title, in which Alan Bates played Burgess and Ms. Browne played herself. Even so, both halves of *Single Spies* are essential to Mr. Bennett's unusually deep perspective on the juiciest and most voluminously chronicled of modern espionage tales.

SUNDAY ESSAY: CUTTING TO THE HEART OF THE WAY WE LIVE NOW
December 25, 1988

The theater year of 1988 opened with the falling of a chandelier and closed with the dropping of Robin Williams's pants.

In between came a lot of other, more worthwhile, drama, but the productions epitomized by these two images—Andrew Lloyd Webber's *The Phantom of the Opera* and Mike Nichols's *Waiting for Godot,* respectively—were, in 1988's political jargon, the year's defining events. *Phantom* and *Godot* both rode into town on tidal waves of hype. No one could get in to see them, so, of course, everyone wanted to see them. And for those who actually did get tickets—which is to say, those with money, connections, or luck—the experience may have been just as disquieting as being turned away at the box office.

Whatever else these shows were, and they did have their virtues, they were utterly impersonal. For all the perambulations of the *Phantom* chandelier and the conviction of Michael Crawford's performance, it was difficult to feel the passions of the beauty-and-the-beast romance that nominally prompted the vast outpouring of imaginative scenic opulence. For all the baggy-pants comic talent of Mr. Williams and his *Godot* costar Steve Martin, the two actors, each in his own separate orbit, failed to display any of the fraternal rapport that binds Beckett's tramps together in affection and agony. In both productions, glitter—whether the gilt of rococo decoration or the stardust of Hollywood celebrity—was its own reward.

Elitism at the door of admission. Money and conspicuous consumption substituting for passion. Every man for himself. If *The Phantom of the Opera* and *Waiting for Godot* did not capture the empty ostentation and narcissistic culture of the late 1980s, what theatrical spectacle would? Perhaps only our sole true national theater, the presidential campaign, in which hype and scenic backdrops also took precedence over content and precluded human contact between the performers (the candidates) and the audience (the voters). A pretty escapist slogan like "a thousand points of light" is the political equivalent of the superfluous *Phantom* scene in which a gondola glides past what seems like a thousand flickering candelabra.

While *Phantom* and *Godot* were the productions most symptomatic of 1988, the best plays often helped diagnose the malaise triggering the symptoms. To see David Mamet's *Speed-the-Plow* (ideally with the original cast of Ron Silver, Joe Mantegna, and Madonna) was to get a hilarious worm's-eye view of the jungle that produces our disposable pop culture. The cynical process by which Mr. Mamet's Hollywood producers put together a salable "buddy" film, all the while engaging simultaneously in vicious back-stabbing and sanctimonious self-congratulation, is surely analogous to the one by which *Waiting for Godot* was turned into the stage equivalent of a buddy film. (Did Lincoln Center Theater, which produced both *Godot* and *Speed-the-Plow*, take Mr. Mamet's hustlers too much to heart?) David Henry Hwang's *M. Butterfly* is as much preoccupied with nineteenth-century opera as is *Phantom*, but where Mr. Lloyd Webber represses the threatening sexual fires of his milieu, Mr. Hwang fans the flames. His protagonist, a French diplomat whose distorted erotic obsessions rival those of the masked phantom, can't even see that the frail female "butterfly" of his fantasies, a Beijing Opera diva, is actually a "masked" man. As currently acted by David Dukes and B. D. Wong, *M. Butterfly* searingly dramatizes the tragic havoc wreaked by sexual stereotypes—the male aggressor, the female victim—that the creators of *Phantom* are too busy exploiting to question.

The season's other best new plays—also American, as it happens—cut to the heart of how we live now, without forsaking the theater's capacity to transport us to a world of wonder far removed from the literal realities of the morning's headlines. A truly timely play does not necessarily take the form of civics lessons like *A Walk in the Woods* and *Chess*, this year's short-lived and already dated attempts to reduce American-Soviet confrontations to lighthearted pedagogical entertainment. In a play that really matters, one often finds one's own moment in distant settings and times. Is it coincidence that many of this year's best new works, as well as its two spectacular revivals (Peter Brook's *The Cherry Orchard,* the Gate Theater Dublin's *Juno and the Paycock*), speak about homelessness as a spiritual condition? This was certainly the year of the homeless in new American plays. In August Wilson's *Joe Turner's Come and Gone,* a homeless black man of 1911 named Herald Loomis (Delroy Lindo) travels from the South to a Pittsburgh boarding house to search for his long-missing wife. Herald's search for his family is really a quest for identity: To seize his life as a free man, he must confront and liberate himself from the oppressive heritage of slavery. *Joe Turner* never leaves its Pittsburgh setting, and yet, with the spiritual aid of a mysterious stranger (Ed Hall), its protagonist finally ends returning to the home, Africa, from which the white man uprooted him. Mr. Wilson's writing makes the same pilgrimage. *Joe Turner* starts out as a naturalistic American play, in tune with the author's *Fences,* and ends up an African one, bathed in ritual and metaphor.

"I'll be home for Christmas, if only in my dreams," goes the Bing Crosby song used as a theme for Craig Lucas's hallucinatory comic fable, *Reckless.* The play, given a beautiful production by the director Norman René at the Circle Repertory Company, tells the story of a wife and mother, Rachel (Robin Bartlett), who runs away from home only to find an America full of homeless parents and children, all on the run, all living in superficially homey towns named Springfield. "Life has been reckless with these people," we're told when Rachel ends up in a shelter populated by those who "carry no identification whatsoever." But *Reckless* doesn't limit its scope to one sociological caste of outcasts. The recklessness Mr. Lucas finds in contemporary American life (or, more specifically, in the modern American family) is all-pervasive. When *Reckless* ends, as *Joe Turner* does, with a regenerative parent-child reunion, the family reconciliation seems the hardest-won miracle imaginable in a congenitally bruising country—a genuine, snow-dusted Christmas fantasy come true, even if it's only in Mr. Lucas's dreams.

The homeless woman (Anne Meara) in Richard Greenberg's neoscrewball comedy *Eastern Standard* is transported to the Hamptons by a crowd of attractive young New Yorkers who have fueled the excesses of the *Bonfire of the Vanities* decade: a tower-building architect, a less-than-uncompromising television producer, an ethically tainted Wall Street analyst, a trendy downtown artist. Still, the latent pangs of conscience felt by Mr. Greenberg's characters cannot be eradicated by their "politically correct project" of adopting a neediest case; the bag lady won't let the yuppies turn her into an unpaid domestic for long. *Eastern Standard* proposes no glib election-year panaceas for a society's ills—nor will it take the other easy way out, by presenting bleeding-heart liberals as laughable fools—but it does demand that its characters make connections between lives spent "dancing on the rim of a champagne glass" and an urban landscape suffering a "nervous breakdown" marked by poverty, rampaging development, and AIDS. That Mr. Greenberg makes his points without self-righteous preaching but with acerbic wit and youthful romance makes *Eastern Standard* both highly entertaining and highly controversial. The unapologetic, one might say post-liberal, insouciance of the play gives voice to a new generation—the generation turning thirty, not thirtysomething.

With new plays like these about, it would be hard to bemoan the state of theater art (as opposed to the dismal state of theater business) in 1988. The year produced other notable works, too, by writers familiar and not: Athol Fugard's attenuated but powerful statement of the artist's mission, *The Road to Mecca,* in which the playwright acted with Yvonne Bryceland and Amy Irving; Michael Weller's absorbing though incompletely realized *Spoils of War,* with its galvanizing performance by Kate Nelligan; Howard Korder's sharp, Mametesque sketches of overgrown boys being boys, *Boys' Life*; A. R. Gurney's highly entertaining exercise in skin-deep drawing-room comedy, *The Cocktail Hour,* with Nancy Marchand as the doyenne of dry martinis; and *Woman in Mind,* minor Alan Ayckbourn that was the occasion for a major performance by Stockard Channing.

This was also a vintage year for the patriarch of the modern American theater, Eugene O'Neill, whose centenary was celebrated with a first-rate revival of *Long Day's Journey into Night* under the loving auspices of the O'Neill hands José Quintero, Colleen Dewhurst, and Jason Robards. Thanks to Joseph Papp's marathon presentation of the canon, Shakespeare was in unusual currency as well in 1988. Steven Berkoff's idiosyncratic staging of *Coriolanus,* starring Christopher Walken, was the most stimulating of six productions that also included the happy pairing of Kevin Kline and Blythe Danner for a Central Park *Much Ado About Nothing.*

As a year for musicals, 1988 is best, if not already, forgotten. It's indicative of the American musical theater's current state that the most enjoyable number of the year was the parody of *Les Misérables,* a hit Anglo-French musical from last year, in Gerard Alessandrini's latest edition of *Forbidden Broadway.* The most elaborate stabs at groundbreaking American musical theater were Martha Clarke's overintellectualized *Miracolo d'Amore* and the Lee Breuer–Bob Telson *Warrior Ant,* a chaotic, multicultural castration fantasy that opened the Next Wave Festival at the Brooklyn Academy of Music. Egomaniacal spectaculars like *The Warrior Ant*—which devour hundreds of thousands of donated dollars while moving, apparently unchecked, from one would-be with-it arts institution to another—are as representative of the waning gilded-age ethic as bloated English musicals.

Occupying a special category in 1988—and perhaps for all time—was the team of Donal McCann and John Kavanagh as Sean O'Casey's pub-crawling buddies, Captain Boyle and Joxer Daly, in Joe Dowling's visiting production of *Juno and the Paycock.* These two performances alone justified the First New York International Festival of the Arts that brought them here. It's hard to imagine that anyone who saw Mr. McCann and Mr. Kavanagh will ever forget the sight of them stumbling about in the near-dark in the final scene—a pair of bums, clear antecedents of Beckett's, barely clinging to life in a deserted, slime-encrusted tenement in the civil war–torn Dublin of 1922. When Mr. McCann's Boyle, bereft of his family and any dignity, finally collapsed to the floor in a stupor, and Mr. Kavanagh's Joxer, a feral scavenger with rat's eyes and a cadaverous grin, responded to his pal's plight by robbing him of his last coin, the audience at the Golden Theatre fell into shocked laughter. Here were the extremes of human degradation and human survival in the same theatrical image, and the image leaped out with such fury that it was as if someone had lifted a curtain to reveal a crack house in the shadowy netherworld just outside.

"The whole world's in a terrible state o' chassis!" is how Boyle sums up his divided Dublin of 1922. No wonder the line rang true to New Yorkers in 1988. As *Juno* was contiguous with the drug demimonde of Eighth Avenue during its visit, so it was also adjacent to the plush theater housing *The Phantom of the Opera.* Such juxtapositions—call them farcical or call them tragic—were typical of the year. In 1988, two antithetical New Yorks, one of boom and one of suffering, shared our stages no less than they shared our streets.

MASTERGATE

AMERICAN REPERTORY THEATRE, CAMBRIDGE, MASS., FEBRUARY 14, 1989

Maybe it was foolish to hope that Congress, the press, or the courts could ever explain the Iran-Contra scandal to anyone's satisfaction. From Fawn Hall's shredder to Robert McFarlane's planned birthday cake for the Ayatollah, this Washington escapade was a farce whose lunatic logic only Hollywood could understand—and only a Hollywood-trained president could have presided over.

Perhaps this is also why a Hollywood writer, Larry Gelbart, has written what may be the most penetrating, and is surely the funniest, exegesis of the fiasco to date. *Mastergate,* as Mr. Gelbart calls his satirical comedy at Harvard's American Repertory Theatre, takes the form of a Capitol Hill hearing in which self-aggrandizing congressmen windily seek to answer such questions as "What does the president know, and does he have any idea that he knew it?" The nominally fictionalized conspiracy under investigation—the latest incident of "governmental self-abuse," appropriately known as "Mastergate"—puts a film studio, Master Pictures, in cahoots with the White House. This time the CIA has illicitly armed Central American guerrillas by laundering $800 million through the budget of the forthcoming epic *Tet: The Movie.*

Mr. Gelbart was born for this endeavor. In its scornful attitude toward official bureaucracy, *Mastergate* overlaps with his television series *M*A*S*H;* in its cynical view of showbiz chicanery, it recalls *Tootsie,* which he cowrote. Running ninety mostly breathless minutes, *Mastergate* has the frenzied tone and topical perishability of old-time Sid Caesar sketches (some of which Mr. Gelbart also wrote) as well as the heartlessness essential to nasty satire (as one expects from a writer who adapted *Volpone* into Broadway's *Sly Fox*).

Just as crucial to *Mastergate* as the author's comic bent, however, is his moral outrage. Mr. Gelbart is furious, and not just at wrongdoers in public life. Even as he ridicules his Oliver North stand-in, the excessively decorated Maj. Manley Battle (played with the perfect mix of Boy Scout earnestness and sanctimonious arrogance by Daniel Von Bargen), the playwright mocks camera-hogging congressmen of both the smug left and the "gung-holier than thou" right (each acted, in an impressive about-face, by Alvin Epstein). Nor does Mr. Gelbart spare the medium that shaped his career. *Mastergate* is flanked by television monitors and narrated with surpassing fatuousness by Merry Chase (Cherry Jones) of the Total News Network. As has been true at least since Tet (the battle, not the movie), the distorted televised images of news events often matter more than the events themselves.

To Mr. Gelbart, language is a principal casualty in the post-Vietnam era of government by press conference and photo opportunity. And when language is corrupted, so is what the play's George Bush figure (Joseph Daly) genially dismisses as the "so-called truth." The oxymoronic officials of *Mastergate* follow the tradition of those who coined phrases like "pacification program" and "modified limited hangout" for obfuscating ends. Mr. Gelbart's politicos can invert the meaning of nearly any word.

One witness protects the national interest by being "steadfastly evasive and selectively honest." Another defends his administration's dreadful mistakes by pleading "they were honest mistakes, honestly made—honestly dreadful." The pro-American country "San Elvador" is described as having "a democratic form of government that has been run by its army for the past forty years." We learn where clandestine meetings that did not take place took place; we hear what was discussed in "non-discussions." A congressman delivers the lesson of Watergate: "Those that forget the past are certain to be subpoenaed."

The play's priceless doublespeak is more reminiscent of *Catch-22* than of *M*A*S*H*. (Mr. Gelbart's Major Battle is surely a descendant of Joseph Heller's Major Major.) Sometimes *Mastergate* buckles under its linguistic weight, but even when the fictive witnesses become as tiresome as their real-life counterparts, the inventive director Michael Engler puts on a bustling show.

The gifts that Mr. Engler brought to *Eastern Standard* are irrelevant here. Mr. Gelbart doesn't require character development or any emotion other than malice. He demands—and is given—the vivid strokes of an editorial cartoon. Philipp Jung's environmental set, with mannequins for extras and the painting of the signing of the Declaration of Independence as an ironic backdrop, is a three-ring Washington circus buffeted by flashbulb firestorms. Among the most delightful clowns are Jerome Kilty, as a committee chairman whose patrician elegance is matched only by his stupidity, and Jeremy Geidt as a schedule-pressed secretary of state who brusquely informs his inquisitors that "the truth will have to wait until after I finish testifying."

Mastergate leaves its audience wondering how much longer the truth can wait and how many more coinages using the syllable "gate" the nation can absorb. Mr. Gelbart brings down the curtain with the chilling specter of more clandestine plans being hatched by yet another crew of fanatical nobodies passing through the government on their way to either jail or higher office. Though it's natural to wish that a play of this quality might travel to New York, the national interest in this case should dictate a detour. *Mastergate* could be the most valuable contribution to public policy that Harvard has sent to Washington in years.

JEROME ROBBINS' BROADWAY

IMPERIAL THEATRE, FEBRUARY 27, 1989

For any child who ever fell in love with the Broadway musical, there was always that incredible moment of looking up to see the bright marquees of Times Square for the first time. I had always assumed it was an unrepeatable thrill until I saw the show that Jerome Robbins officially unveiled at the Imperial Theatre last night.

In *Jerome Robbins' Broadway*, the American musical theater's greatest director and choreographer doesn't merely bring back the thunderous excitement of songs and dances from classic musicals like *West Side Story* and *Peter Pan* and *Gypsy*. For an encore, he pulls off the miracle of re-creating that ecstatic baptism, that first glimpse of Broadway lights, of every Broadway theatergoer's youth.

The moment occurs as Mr. Robbins's show ends. The three World War II sailors of *On the Town*, winding down from their dizzy twenty-four-hour pass through the pleasures of New York, New York, come upon a dazzling, crowded skyscape of twinkling signs heralding the smash musicals Mr. Robbins staged between 1944 and his withdrawal from Broadway in 1964. Some of the theaters (the Adelphi, the New Century) are gone now; some of the shows are forgotten. But the awe that seizes those innocent young sailors of 1944 overwhelms the jaded Broadway audience of 1989, too—and not because of the simple scenic effect. While *Jerome Robbins' Broadway* may celebrate a vanished musical theater, it does so with such youthful exuberance that nostalgia finally gives way to a giddy, perhaps not even foolish, dream that a new generation of Broadway babies may yet be born.

Most certainly a new generation is visible on the Imperial's stage. For this fifteen-number anthology, Mr. Robbins has recruited sixty-two remarkable performers: most from the Broadway ranks, a few from ballet, and all too young to have seen their predecessors in these roles. They perform with a skill, sexiness, and zest that sometimes eclipses the originals, throwing off the cobwebs and camp that almost always attend Broadway revivals.

When the sailors Robert La Fosse, Scott Wise, and Michael Kubala go girl-chasing in their helluva town—and the girls include beauties like Mary Ellen Stuart and Alexia Hess—one doesn't think of every other cast to play *On the Town* (or its ballet precursor, *Fancy Free*). One instead feels the charge of fresh talent cockily strutting its stuff. What comes through is not an imitation of the original production but presumably an equivalent to the electricity with which the upstart creative team of Mr. Robbins, Leonard Bernstein, Betty Comden, and Adolph Green first took Broadway by storm.

Jerome Robbins' Broadway even succeeds in reclaiming legendary star roles for its young company. Jason Alexander, the evening's delightful narrator, accomplishes the seemingly impossible: He banishes the memory of Zero Mostel from the role of Pseudolus in *A Funny Thing Happened on the Way to the Forum*. Charlotte d'Amboise brings her own insouciant pixiness to *Peter Pan*. Debbie Shapiro, the production's lead singer, at once recalls and reinvents the jazzy comic vocal attack once owned by Nancy Walker.

As Mr. Robbins demonstrates that young performers can hold their own with Broadway's past, so he proves that his way of doing musicals has gone into hiding but not out of style. Audiences inured to the hydraulic scenic gizmos, formless acrobatics, deafening amplification, and emotional vacuity of this decade's Broadway spectaculars will find Mr. Robbins's musical theater a revelation. Many of the numbers in *Jerome Robbins' Broadway* are performed before simple or blank backdrops, and most of them prompt laughter or tears. While the show is undeniably lavish—the sumptuous costume reproductions are of museum-exhibition quality—it is the extravagance of taste, not money, that generates the joy.

That taste belongs to the arena of theater, not to the serious dance world to which Mr. Robbins turned permanently after *Fiddler on the Roof*. Nowhere is this more apparent than in the twenty-five-minute suite of dances from *West Side Story* that rocks the audience at the conclusion of the first act. It is not the steps of the dances—least of all the classic lifts of the "Somewhere" ballet—that get to us so much as Mr. Robbins's ability to propel a story, mood, and characters over music and space. The self-destructiveness of the warring Jets and Sharks is all the more poignant because the gangs' violent movements evolve out of the benign, timeless playground antics of urban teenagers. A born showman's brilliant theatrical lighting effect, even more than the choreography and lush Bernstein melody, boosts the "Somewhere" fantasy to a heavenly paradise.

"Hold my hand, and I'll take you there," goes a Stephen Sondheim lyric in that song. In "Tradition" (from *Fiddler*) and "I'm Flying" (from *Peter Pan*), as in the "Somewhere" ballet, characters take hands, often forming a circle as they do so, to suggest an idealized sense of family that will eventually be ripped apart. Yet the touching—some might say sentimental—side of Mr. Robbins is always balanced by a hearty affection for the knockabout showbiz traditions of unalloyed burlesque.

"Comedy Tonight" (the incomparable opening number of *Forum*), the "Charleston" from *Billion Dollar Baby*, and the Keystone Kops ballet from *High Button Shoes* are riotous, self-contained, swinging-door farces rendered entirely as nonstop dance. On a smaller scale, but no less witty, are Mr. Robbins's evocations of the lost vaudeville worlds of the soft-shoe (Mr. Alexander and Faith Prince's duet to "I Still Get Jealous" from *High Button Shoes*) and the striptease ("You Gotta Have a Gimmick" from *Gypsy*). It's only when Mr. Robbins's choreography reaches self-consciously from the theater into highfalutin dance that it seems more arty than artistic. "The Small House of Uncle Thomas" ballet from *The King and I* and "Mr. Monotony," a jazz ballet cut from two Irving Berlin musicals during their out-of-town tryouts, look like period curiosities now—though they are so beautifully performed that it's hardly torture to wait them out.

A more inherent limitation of *Jerome Robbins' Broadway* is its anthology form. However wonderful Mr. Robbins's showstoppers were, his most influential legacy to the musical theater was his gradual blurring of the halts between musical numbers and scenes. The last Robbins musicals were steamrollers in which script, movement, scenery, song, and dance all surged forward at once to create a seamless dramatic adventure.

In *Jerome Robbins' Broadway,* that gift for relentless theatrical flow comes through in the *West Side Story* suite and "Comedy Tonight," as well as in "I'm Flying" at that moment when the Darling house pulls away so Peter Pan and his recruits can soar above London to Never-Never Land. But the constant movement that was *Gypsy*—perhaps the quintessentially cinematic Robbins production—cannot be captured here, and, for some reason, the *Fiddler* suite in Act 2 is precise in its self-contained dances (the comic nightmare, the wedding bottle-dance) but warped in overall shape. The communal fight that breaks out in the middle of "Tradition" and the pogrom that flows out of the wedding dance have both been eliminated—which is tantamount to removing the rumbles from *West Side Story.* The sanitization leaves *Fiddler* looking more conventional and saccharine than it was when it first played the Imperial.

At no other time does *Jerome Robbins' Broadway,* to my knowledge, violate the spirit of the original works. So faithful is the production to Broadway's past that it becomes a one-evening tour of an entire era, highlighting not just composing giants like Jule Styne but also such bright asterisks to Broadway music as Moose Charlap. With the exception of a synthetic overture, the sound of the pit band, conducted by Paul Gemignani and orchestrated by Sid Ramin and William D. Brohn, is exhilaratingly authentic, down to the contributions made by the dance arrangers Betty Walberg and Trude Rittman.

Through the lyrics and snippets of dialogue, one rediscovers an era's wiseguy Broadway comic style, which united writers as disparate as Arthur Laurents and Sammy Cahn. Thanks to the efforts of the overall designers Robin Wagner (scenery), Joseph G. Aulisi (costumes), and Jennifer Tipton (lighting), *Jerome Robbins' Broadway* also offers what will probably remain a once-in-a-lifetime survey of Broadway theater design, from early Tony Walton to middle Jo Mielziner and late Boris Aronson. The dominant designer is Oliver Smith, whose glorious palette can encompass New Yorks as antithetical as those of *On the Town* and *West Side*

Story, and whose collaborations with the costume designers Irene Sharaff, Miles White, and Alvin Colt have no present-day match in Technicolor Fauvist verve.

If *Jerome Robbins' Broadway* is history, it is history that pulses and reverberates. The *West Side Story* suite alone harks back to Agnes de Mille's Broadway dream ballets even while anticipating the gyrating phalanxes of Michael Bennett's *Company* and *A Chorus Line*. No doubt Mr. Robbins's anthology won't mean the same thing to theatergoers who didn't grow up with his shows, but it may well attract new converts to traditions whose hold on the musical theater are as shaky as that fiddler on the roof. After seeing *Jerome Robbins' Broadway* at Thursday's press preview, I hurried back to the Saturday matinee with two young boys roughly the same age I was when I saw my first Robbins musical, *Peter Pan*. Long after Peter told them "to think lovely, wonderful thoughts," they were still flying.

METAMORPHOSIS
ETHEL BARRYMORE THEATRE, MARCH 7, 1989

It's hard to guess who will suffer most at Steven Berkoff's theatrical version of "The Metamorphosis": devotees of Franz Kafka, whose story is distorted into Marxist kitsch by this adaptation, or fans of Mikhail Baryshnikov, whose stage debut as a dramatic actor, however dignified, amounts to little more than a sideshow to the loud circus surrounding him. But at least one constituency, albeit a smaller one, should be happy—the Berkoff cult. The director doesn't even have to appear in the flesh to upstage Kafka and Mr. Baryshnikov throughout this piece's interminable (and intermissionless) hundred minutes.

Actually, Mr. Berkoff does have a surrogate on stage at the Barrymore, in the form of the show's true leading man, the actor René Auberjonois. With his greased-back hair and grizzly, scowling mien, Mr. Auberjonois barks out the role of Gregor Samsa's father as if he were doing an impersonation of Mr. Berkoff's impersonation of Hitler on the recent television miniseries *War and Remembrance*. And in that performance lies the message of this *Metamorphosis*. In Mr. Berkoff's retelling, Gregor Samsa, the commercial traveler who awakens one morning to find himself transformed into a gigantic dung beetle, is no longer a lost, alienated soul consumed by the terror of living. He is instead the martyred victim of a greedy, parasitic bourgeois society symbolized by his father. Let

Kafka worry about man's eternal, complex private war with himself and his family; Mr. Berkoff reduces *Metamorphosis* to a class struggle between the bug and the pigs.

Both in its ideology and in its once avant-garde Expressionist theatrical style, this *Metamorphosis* is very much a product of the late 1960s (when it was first produced in London, with Mr. Berkoff as Gregor). The stark setting is a gray void on which has been erected a spare, skeletal jungle gym that fans out like a spider's legs. While delivering a condensed choral recitation of Kafka's text, Gregor's father, mother (Laura Esterman), and sister (Madeleine Potter) perform mimed routines front and center, most of which reveal them to be grotesquely materialistic vulgarians. "Cash! . . . Cigars! . . . Shoes!" they yell at the prospect of any new income. At mealtime, they chomp away with a slobbering relish that might offend the residents of *Animal Farm*.

Mr. Baryshnikov, always wearing the workaday suit and rimless spectacles of the pre-metamorphosed Gregor, is never allowed to leave the stage, but neither is he often given the opportunity to dominate the action. He is usually sequestered in the shadowy background, on the cagelike platform that represents Gregor's room. There he performs contortionist stunts, all executed with exquisite grace and precision, that simulate the beetle's perambulations: hanging upside down from the ceiling, whirring his legs in helpless panic, masticating his food, scuttling across the floor. When Mr. Baryshnikov must speak, his accent gives *Metamorphosis* one of its few connections to the frayed Old World that spawned Kafka, but the emotional tone of his acting is no less facetious than that of his fellow players.

There is nothing embarrassing about Mr. Baryshnikov's work here. The real question is why he picked a stage assignment that, for all its High Culture trappings, makes no more demands on his great talent than would the title role of *Legs Diamond* [a short-lived vanity musical that starred the lounge singer Peter Allen]. Only once does *Metamorphosis* allow Mr. Baryshnikov to reveal the deep artistic soul that informs his gestural poetry. When Mr. Auberjonois throws the apple that penetrates Gregor's carapace, we not only see a dancer's delicate rendition of an insect's slow, crumpled fall to the ground but we also find, in the innocence of Mr. Baryshnikov's baffled expression, a man's far steeper descent into the clutches of mortality.

The rest of the evening's acting is so consistently clownish that the performers cannot be held accountable. Outrageous caricature is what Mr. Berkoff needs to make his polemical point, and, since that point requires that representatives of commerce be still more disgusting than the Samsa family, the crude portrayals of the chief clerk and the single, porky lodger (in lieu of the three in Kafka) are unwatchably gross. His strident ideological scheme notwithstanding, however, Mr. Berkoff can waffle for sentimental effect. Gregor's mother and sister, though previously presented as interchangeably heartless, weep their way through the beetle's death rattles.

In Mr. Berkoff's vibrant staging of *Coriolanus*, seen at the New York Shakespeare Festival this season, his martial theatrical techniques were well matched to a play dealing with politics, war, and civic behavior. Those same techniques are like jackboots when stamped upon Kafka's intimate journey into one man's soul. Larry Spivak, who provided the tingling electronic score for *Coriolanus*, fills *Metamorphosis* with percussion and piano poundings suitable for a silent horror movie. Mr. Berkoff's typically hyperbolic lighting scheme emerges as more florid than Brechtian: When the Samsa family imagines happier times (in slow motion, no less), grays and blacks give way to gooey floods of blue and yellow.

Such grand theatrical gestures are anathema to fiction whose power derives precisely from its author's ability to cloak terror within the dry, homely details of humdrum daily life. As written by Kafka, "The Metamorphosis" is "realism pure and simple, so realistic as to be hard to bear," writes his biographer Ernst Pawel in a wise program essay whose nearly every sentence rebukes the production on stage. Mr. Berkoff's bombastic *Metamorphosis* is hard to bear not because it locks us into Gregor Samsa's nightmare, but because it cavalierly crushes two sensitive artists, like so many insects, underfoot.

LEND ME A TENOR
ROYALE THEATRE, MARCH 3, 1989

A farce should be cleverly built, energetically directed, and buoyantly acted, but there is one thing it absolutely must be: consistently funny. As staged by Jerry Zaks and performed by a cast led by Philip Bosco and Victor Garber, *Lend Me a Tenor*, the jolly play by Ken Ludwig at the Royale, is an impeccable example of how to construct and mount a farce—up to a point. *Lend Me a Tenor* is all things farcical except hilarious.

There are some scattered big laughs, certainly, though one must wait through most of Act 1 for the first of them to arrive. The prime buffoon is Mr. Bosco, attired in the white tie, top hat, and tails of a Cleveland opera impresario in 1934. Mr. Bosco has just learned that his imported star for the night's sold-out performance of Verdi's *Otello,* the legendary Italian tenor Tito Merelli (Ron Holgate), is too ill to go on. The news that $50,000 worth of tickets may have to be refunded does not sit well. Mr. Bosco turns comatose from the shock, then reddens with apoplexy, then flies into a shrieking, violent rage, and finally subsides into an openmouthed stupor, looking like a bloated marlin just after the fisherman has removed the hook. It's the second priceless display of technique this season—the first, also partnered by Mr. Garber, was in *The Devil's Disciple*—by one of the best comic actors we have.

Nearly as splendid are both Mr. Holgate, who gets Mr. Bosco into this jam, and Mr. Garber, who must get him out of it. More than twenty-five years after he played Miles Gloriosus in A *Funny Thing Happened on the Way to the Forum,* Mr. Holgate still makes a fine comic specialty of vain ladies' men; his Tito, known to his adoring fans as "Il Stupendo," is a paragon of temperamental matinee-idol hamminess from his silver mane to his preposterously thick Italian accent.

Mr. Garber is his charming antithesis: Max, the nerdy, bespectacled Cleveland Grand Opera Company gofer who harbors Walter Mitty fantasies of being a great tenor himself. When he is drafted by Mr. Bosco to impersonate the ailing star in *Otello,* Mr. Garber carries out the hoax in high style, mimicking Mr. Holgate's personality (and singing voice) as effortlessly as Clark Kent turns into Superman.

Such is Mr. Ludwig's unabashedly silly, highly workable premise. In *Lend Me a Tenor,* two Otellos (in identical costumes and chocolate makeup) pop in and out of six slamming doors in a two-room hotel suite, all the while pursued by a bevy of understandably confused Desdemonas that includes Tito's long-suffering Italian wife (an insufferably mannered Tovah Feldshuh), Max's would-be fiancée (J. Smith-Cameron), and an ambitious soprano determined to sleep her way to the Met (Caroline Lagerfelt). What's more, Mr. Ludwig, who is a lawyer as well as a playwright, has done the hard work of crafting the machinery of farce. Unlike the lackadaisical Neil Simon of *Rumors,* he carefully maps out his mistaken identities and close shaves, even to the extent of making certain that each Otello clocks the same time at lovemaking (fifteen minutes, if you must know).

So why does *Lend Me a Tenor* fail to rise into comic pandemonium? The trouble is not Mr. Zaks's timing or slapstick choreography, which are as fast and stylish as one expects from the director of *Anything Goes* and *The Front Page.* Nor should one look too critically at the credibility of Mr. Ludwig's plot or characters. As is demonstrated in the evening's breathless coda—a silent-movie frenzy—farcical clowning has little to do with reality and a lot to do with the illogical lunacy of windup toys.

The play's real comic shortfall is in its details rather than in its master plan. The lines are almost never witty, settling instead for the hoary double entendres that so titillate the West End (where *Tenor* was a hit in another production). Worse, too many of the farcical situations seem like pale echoes of those in similar works from the play's period (notably Broadway's *Room Service* and Hollywood's *A Night at the Opera,* both of 1935). While farces always trade in stock elements, and while the author's homage to a Marx Brothers past is intentional, the old tricks must be augmented by new inventions if the audience is to be ambushed into riotous laughter. A final scene—or third act—that might have topped the traditional setups with fresh, hysterical surprises never arrives.

One must also ask whether Mr. Zaks is too kind to direct killer farce fueled by the basest human traits. The warmth that the director brings to comedies like *The House of Blue Leaves* and *Wenceslas Square* is misplaced in a piece in which every character will stop at nothing to get what he wants. Jane Connell (in the Margaret Dumont role of the Opera Guild dowager who might fire Mr. Bosco), Ms. Lagerfelt, and at times Mr. Garber seem benign rather than ruthless as they pursue their selfish ends. The softening of the characters' malice deflates the cartoonishness of a farce much as a Looney Tune might crumble if Tweety weren't placed in real jeopardy by Sylvester the cat.

With its speedy gait, gleaming lighting (by Paul Gallo), and wildly luxurious Art Deco sets and costumes (by Tony Walton and by William Ivey Long), the play looks so much like a prime example of its genre that one is all the more frustrated by the shortage of belly laughs. But the evening provides professional, painless fluff even so. If, as *Lend Me a Tenor* would have us believe, a Cleveland audience of 1934 can mistake a rank impostor for the world's most celebrated opera star, it would be foolish to underestimate the prospects of a simulated farce on Broadway in 1989.

≡ *Philip Bosco was an actor I'd grown up watching at Arena Stage in Washington, but he seemed to rise to a whole new level of achievement in the 1980s, becoming almost an American answer to Ralph Richardson—especially, though not exclusively, in classic farce. His encounters with Shaw and Molière were among the most reliable joys of the decade, finally bringing him to Broadway stardom in productions like* Lend Me a Tenor.

THE WINTER'S TALE
PUBLIC THEATER, MARCH 22, 1989

When Mandy Patinkin is on stage emoting—or, these days, on record crooning—there is always a second suspenseful drama percolating just beneath the official script. Will the actor keep his volatile emotions within the bounds of the character he's playing, or will he fly over the rainbow into an unedited orgy of tears and strangled tenor sobs that call more attention to his own overwrought sensitivity than to his role? The tension between the two Patinkins—the one in control, the other not—is the main reason he divides audiences as violently as any star around.

As Leontes, King of Sicilia, in James Lapine's inspired production of *The Winter's Tale* at the Public Theater, the actor is handed his greatest opportunities yet for self-indulgence. More irrationally than Othello, Leontes rises to a jealous rage in the opening scene, imagining without cause that his pregnant wife, Hermione (Diane Venora), is carrying a child fathered by his own lifelong best friend, the Bohemian King, Polixenes (Christopher Reeve). And at first Mr. Patinkin does let his feelings run away with him. Perhaps to avoid lachrymose hysteria, he beats out the neurotically short-circuited verse with a professorial waving of his hands and clamps his eyes shut to convey his paranoid consternation.

When the stakes are at their highest, however, Mr. Patinkin comes through with his most mature work yet, never to retreat thereafter. The leap occurs at the moment Leontes, having refused to heed Hermione's pleas of innocence, suffers an abrupt double punishment: His young son dies, and so, or so he is told, does Hermione. As Mr. Patinkin hears the wails of mournful news from a balcony above, he reels in grief by merely leaning a delicate step backward. And then he stands utterly still, his eyes wide open. His suffering is regal in its imposing aura of silence, not in histrionics. When he speaks again, it is in a new, broken, sweet voice; the arrogant ruler has become the humblest penitent.

Any successful production of *The Winter's Tale* must make that metamorphosis deeply moving—though few do—because Leontes's transformation is the play's fulcrum and its essence. In this late romance, Shakespeare takes his characters into the winter of destructiveness and death, then allows them to redeem themselves in a spring of both figurative and actual resurrection. It takes sixteen years for Leontes to pay penance for his needless transgressions. Only then can Hermione, disguised as a statue, miraculously be reborn as well. *The Winter's Tale* is an incredible play in every way—from Shakespeare's magical, affirmative dénouement to his awesome interweaving of high tragedy, low pastoral clowning, and the mistaken identities and familial reunions of classic farce.

If Mr. Lapine has been a helpful influence on Mr. Patinkin—they also collaborated on *Sunday in the Park with George*—he is even more impressive in his ability to knit Shakespeare's many moods into elegant unity. While one wouldn't have predicted this happy result from Mr. Lapine's muddy Central Park *Midsummer Night's Dream,* much of his other work, one realizes now, could have been preparation for *The Winter's Tale.*

The director's fascination with archetypal images of death and rebirth has been apparent since *Twelve Dreams,* his play about Carl Jung. He pursued the theme further when writing *Sunday in the Park* and *Into the Woods* with Stephen Sondheim. To achieve their characters' renewal, both musicals take a post-intermission flash-forward comparable to the sixteen-year jump in *The Winter's Tale.* As Leontes is redeemed only after embracing a living statue of his "dead" wife, so George in *Sunday* can move on only after embracing a beloved woman who is "reborn" by stepping out of a painting.

There are echoes of the Sondheim-Lapine musicals in this *Winter's Tale,* from the accentuation of parent-child bonds to the injection of a storybook motif (a Harlequin, played by the graceful dancer Rob Besserer, sets the fairy-tale tone) to the tingling music-box score by Michael Starobin, the Sondheim orchestrator, and William Finn. But it is the director's keen eye for every detail, a rarity in the New York Shakespeare Festival marathon, that really tells the tale.

Using handsome late-eighteenth-century sets (by John Arnone) and costumes (by Franne Lee), Mr. Lapine piles up the action on platforms, allowing for the highly dramatic vertical choreography of pivotal scenes of eavesdropping, trial, and flight. Beverly Emmons's lighting completes the poetic transition from the wintry candlelight of a mournful Sicilia to the vernal greenery of a festive Bohemia, with a chilling stop along the way for the coastal storm that leads a courtier to his grisly death and a changeling baby to her adoptive home.

Mr. Lapine's precision extends to his casting. Though Ms. Venora's Hermione starts by mothering the audience as much as her child, this fine actress's intelligence eventually burns away the saccharine excesses. The play's problematic, second-half comic antics are in hilarious hands. Rocco Sisto, as the irrepressible, ballad-singing rogue Autolycus, is a sneering yet likable cynic; his quick wit is the perfect foil for the slow burns of his most easily bamboozled victims, the bumpkin shepherd and son played with Laurel and Hardy vaudeville verve by MacIntyre Dixon and Tom McGowan. Mr. Reeve, though mirthless in comic disguise, is a surprisingly vulnerable Polixenes. Alfre Woodard's feisty Paulina, the play's conscience, and Graham Winton's Florizel and Jennifer Dundas's Perdita, its fairy-tale prince and princess, are the other standouts in a company that only occasionally sinks to the merely competent.

By the time he reaches the statue scene, Mr. Lapine has everything he needs to put the evening's complexities together. Mr. Patinkin, now serene and silver-templed, buries his head in Ms. Venora's neck, consummating a reconciliation that is the more rending for its simple stillness and its formal, indeed statuary, beauty. Perched above the idyllic embrace is a dark dream tableau invented by the director but consistent with a dream-fixated text: The dead characters stand in a flurry of snow, as if frozen within a child's crystalline paperweight. With this gesture, the cycles of life and of seasons merge in Mr. Lapine's staging as they so hauntingly do in Shakespeare's play. And the audience is left with just enough of winter's cruel chill to be intoxicated anew by the discovery that spring is here.

AMULETS AGAINST THE DRAGON FORCES
CIRCLE REPERTORY COMPANY, APRIL 6, 1989

While most of François Truffaut's *Small Change* has receded in memory, I can't imagine forgetting the scene in which a baby tumbles from a high apartment-house window and survives. Truffaut made an indelible image out of profound questions that had defined his career from *The 400 Blows* and that never leave most of us: By what miracle do some children survive? What happens to those victims of cruel, lonely, loveless childhoods who do grow up but don't bounce back?

These questions also animate the far different work of Paul Zindel, whose breakthrough play of 1970, *The Effect of Gamma Rays on Man-in-the-Moon Marigolds,* told of two sisters trying to escape the suffocating grip of their bitter mother. Mr. Zindel's new play at the Circle Repertory Company, *Amulets Against the Dragon Forces,* returns to the same themes, a similar mother, another Staten Island household (of 1955), and, as the title indicates, some of the same overwriting. It's easy to mock Mr. Zindel's unshapely hothouse drama, whose occupants are var-

iously afflicted by cancer, dipsomania, kleptomania, bisexual nympho-
mania, and poetic excess. Then we see the child at center stage trying to
ward off the horrors, the child too genuine to dismiss as fiction, and
Amulets becomes gripping and disturbing despite its Gothic overkill.

The child is the teenage Chris (Matt McGrath), who travels with his
mother (Deborah Hedwall), an itinerant practical nurse, from house to
house as she takes on live-in assignments with terminal patients. Chris
was long ago abandoned by his father, who fled to St. Augustine, Fla.
("near the Ripley's Believe It or Not Museum"). Now the boy finds himself carrying his suitcase and shopping bags into a dingy household populated entirely by abandoned souls. The dying widow (Ruby Holbrook)
in the care of Chris's mother is ignored by her son, a brutish, alcoholic
longshoreman named Floyd (John Spencer). The middle-aged Floyd reserves most of his love and abuse for the young Harold (Loren Dean), a
sweet hustler who had been abandoned by his own parents before finding his way into Floyd's bed.

Though they have not all been created with equal depth by Mr. Zindel,
the characters are invariably fascinating—even the ravaged, nearly comatose patient who bites anyone who comes near her. But *Amulets* is primarily a Tennessee Williams–like standoff between the sensitive Chris
and the bellicose Floyd, who will not rest until he has brutalized the vul-
nerabilities of everyone around him. Floyd not only hates women—his
mother, Chris's mother, his discarded wife—but he also likes to fire up
the local male roughnecks by inviting them over for booze and whores.

The struggle between the frail Chris and the destructive Floyd would
seem no contest. Chris has no defenses—only a collection of carved figures, his amulets, that provides him with a fantasy world of escapist storytelling. Floyd has ready fists and an abusive tongue poised to spill
anyone's most shameful secrets. But as the compassionate Mr. Zindel
avoided simple moral judgments with the mother in *Marigolds,* so he
does with Floyd: We can still find the abused child who was father to the
vicious man. In Mr. Spencer's volatile performance, the longshoreman is
alternately a "slobbering, horrendous freak" and an articulate student of
human nature, with equally devastating results.

As nakedly acted by the brave and talented Mr. McGrath, Chris is an
open wound, almost painful to watch. A gawky, delicate misfit with an
epicene voice, he tries to head off rejection by chattily advertising his
own precociousness. The only teacher who ever thought the boy anything but "completely deranged" had decided that he was a writer. Chris
clings to this diagnosis even though the teacher, a Shakespeare scholar,
herself suffered a nervous breakdown after being ridiculed by students.

In this teacher's class, Chris learned that "everyone loved action and suspense." Mr. Zindel, a popular author of fiction for adolescents, knows the same lesson, but he piles on too much florid action in *Amulets:* Do we need a smashed chandelier, a gay love triangle, a sudden financial windfall, and an orgy? None of these events are underplayed by the director, B. Rodney Marriott, or are left unaccompanied by Norman L. Berman's creepy incidental score. One must also quarrel with the overworked mythology of Chris's amulets, with the psychoanalytical symmetry of the parent-child relationships and with the unlikely Act 2 exchange of confessional monologues (however well written) between Floyd and Chris's mom, who otherwise hate each other.

Ms. Hedwall, despite some uneasiness with her lines, becomes rending in that scene, the starchy mother's one chance to reveal how she went from being one women's-magazine cliché (the model 1950s housewife) to another ("the desperate divorcée") without ever finding the woman she might have been. Mr. Dean's lost boy of the streets also commands attention—with his ethereal ingenuousness, if not with his mumbling.

But Chris is the child crashing toward earth in Mr. Zindel's play, and it is for him that the playwright holds out the blind hope denied the others. As the pitiful Mr. McGrath cries into a phone, begging his dismissive father in vain for love, it's hard to imagine how he can possibly grow up intact. "It's all in the timing" is Floyd's explanation of how Chris might yet survive the same dragon forces that maimed him, and who knows? It's not without wisdom that Mr. Zindel situates the searing drama of childhood, like Chris's absent father, in the mysterious, macabre neighborhood of Ripley's Believe It or Not.

ARISTOCRATS
Theatre Four, April 26, 1989

Audiences arriving at Brian Friel's *Aristocrats* are all but enfolded within a panorama of lush Irish greenery. The setting, a heaven-sent assignment for the designer John Lee Beatty, is a Georgian mansion in provincial County Donegal. Moss and ivy crawl over every wall; a towering tree spills leaves from above; an expanse of bright lawn flows from the house's exposed parlor to the stage's edge. It is summer, the mid-1970s, and the sun is out.

What we see is Ireland at its most ravishing, but Ireland being Ireland, and Mr. Friel being arguably the most penetrating Irish playwright of his generation, the skies cannot remain cloudless for long. *Aristocrats,* a Manhattan Theatre Club presentation at Theatre Four, is Mr. Friel's Chopin-flecked *Cherry Orchard* or *Three Sisters,* in which the ache of one family becomes a microcosm for the ache of a society. While Mr. Friel's touch in this 1979 work isn't always as subtle as Chekhov's, *Aristocrats* is a lovely play, funny and harrowing. Though the abrupt juxtapositions of the beautiful and the tragic may be any Irish writer's birthright, Mr. Friel makes the Irish condition synonymous with the human one.

To be sure, the house on stage, which belongs to a once-powerful district judge, is haunted by the country's troubles, as well as by the literary ghosts of Yeats and O'Casey, who, we're told, may have visited the mansion in its salad days. But if *Aristocrats* expresses the national political concerns hinted at by its ironic title, the politics follow rather than dictate what is largely the intimate drama of a family reunion prompted by an impending wedding and overtaken by illness. Judge O'Donnell has suffered a stroke, and four of his five adult children have gathered at his deathbed.

The O'Donnells are not a happy clan. The engaged daughter, Claire (Haviland Morris), is to marry a drab greengrocer twice her age. Her sister Alice (Margaret Colin) is an alcoholic who lives discontentedly in London with her embittered, lapsed activist of a husband, Eamon (John Pankow). Another sister, Judith (Kaiulani Lee), has given up an illegitimate child to an orphanage even as she is forced to cope with the second, incontinent childhood of her father. Though the lone brother, Casimir (Niall Buggy), purports to have a wife and three children in Hamburg, no one in the family has seen them. "It has the authentic ring of phony fiction," Eamon says of Casimir's obsessive boasts of domestic bliss.

What went wrong? We learn of a mother, long dead, who committed suicide. We sense the tyranny of the Lear-like father, who even now, in near delirium, bellows humiliating commands through his sickroom intercom. And in the isolation of each character we see a reflection of the entire household's alienation from Ireland. Even at home, this family is in exile. The judge, a Roman Catholic aristocrat with "a greed for survival," never bothered himself with the civil-rights concerns of his plebeian fellow Catholics in the village below, and yet could never be a part of the Protestant Establishment either. He sent his children abroad to school. He administered the law for whoever happened to be in power.

Aristocrats has the ring of phony fiction only when Mr. Friel pounds his Chekhovian notes of decay, notably in the neat final-act resolutions and particularly when he brings on a visiting American academic (Peter

Crombie) who is studying the local folkways. The rest of the evening offers the blend of psychological ambiguity and crackling theatrical instinct that has been Mr. Friel's signature since *Philadelphia, Here I
Come!* more than twenty years ago. Leave it to this writer to inject the esthetics of Beckett into a heartbreak house by creating an elderly uncle in
an elegant white-linen suit (Thomas Barbour) who remains mute as a
matter of principle. Mr. Friel's feel for absurdist black comedy is given
even fuller vent when the characters sit obediently in lawn chairs before
a boom box to listen to a taped, unwittingly callous message from the
one absent sister, an insufferably pious nun who fled to Africa seventeen
years earlier.

This writer's plays must be a joy for actors, and those assembled by the
director, Robin Lefevre (a visitor from London's Hampstead Theatre),
blossom in impressive tandem with roles that keep turning inside out.
It's typical of Mr. Friel's paradoxical way that he would make his most
antiestablishment character—the cynical, working-class Eamon—the
most nostalgic upholder of Irish cultural tradition by the final curtain.
It's typical of Mr. Lefevre's superb production that Mr. Pankow, an amazingly versatile American actor, is so sensitive to every nuance that the
metamorphosis is entirely credible.

All three sisters, also first-rate, undergo similar transformations. The
initially sunny Ms. Morris, though too gorgeous to pass for the brood's
ugly duckling, gradually comes to resemble her departed, depressive
mother. Ms. Colin swings between alcoholic hostility and sweetness, at
last to reach an affecting middle ground when she describes how she
could reach accommodation with her fearful father only when he could
no longer recognize her. Ms. Lee's moment to dazzle comes when she
suddenly tightens her voice and jaw, forsaking her previous maternal lilt,
to describe her crippled diurnal existence caring for the dying.

But it is Casimir, the son, most stifled by the father, who is indelible.
The role was originated at the Abbey Theater by John Kavanagh, the brilliant Joxer of the Gate Theater's *Juno and the Paycock* seen in New York.
Mr. Buggy, the onetime Abbey actor imported from London for the role
here, is another true original. Bald, round, and often boasting a child's
moony grin, he gives us an excitable, overgrown mother's boy who in
middle age retains vast illusions about his heritage (he plays an imaginary croquet game on the lawn) but none about himself.

Casimir knows he has always been a figure of fun, ridiculed by others
as either the village idiot or a homosexual. But with his factory job and
presumed family in Germany, he has found a way to feel and give happiness without risking "exposure to too much hurt." His hands frequently

flying about, his boisterous laughter just one note below hysteria, Mr. Buggy becomes the most fragile Humpty Dumpty; Casimir is a jolly life of the party clinging to that role because his own life depends on it. Only his father, of course, still has the power to send him tumbling back into the terrors of childhood. When the fall comes, as it must, we, too, experience terror, as a grown man collapses into pieces on that beautiful Irish sod and waters it with his tears.

ELEEMOSYNARY
Manhattan Theatre Club, May 10, 1989

There are some absent friends you don't realize how much you've been missing until they suddenly pop up again. Eileen Heckart, who has been away from the New York stage throughout this decade, is definitely one of them.

One of the first times I saw Ms. Heckart, about twenty-five years ago, she was good-naturedly choosing to ignore a chorus of boos from a disgruntled Broadway audience at Terrence McNally's memorably disastrous *And Things That Go Bump in the Night.* In *Eleemosynary,* the Lee Blessing play prompting her current Off Broadway appearance at the tiny Manhattan Theatre Club Stage II, she looks and sounds exactly the same as she did way back then. Ms. Heckart is what one might describe as a long actress—long of face, of torso, of tongue. There is mischief in her big glistening eyes. And when she speaks, it is in the low, crystalline, merry rasp of a wise aunt who has seen and understood everything (perhaps with cigarette in hand), relished most of it, and can't wait for the next adventure.

Ms. Heckart's role in *Eleemosynary* fits her profile. She plays Dorothea Westbrook, flintiness personified, an independent-minded matriarch who believes that women have the inalienable right to be extraordinary and who lives by the credo "There isn't anything the mind can't do." Dorothea chooses to be eccentric because the choice allows her to be a wife and mother and "still talk to animals." She also tries to invent a new way of flying and takes to conversing with the dead with an alacrity that might impress Shirley MacLaine. Happening upon James Monroe ("the last President to wear short pants"), Dorothea asks him if the Era of Good Feelings was really "as good as all that." His response? "He said it was fair," says Ms. Heckart, as matter-of-factly as if she were describing the weather.

Eleemosynary is a three-woman, three-generation family play about the havoc someone like the well-meaning but fundamentally selfish Dorothea can inflict on those closest to her. Her daughter, Artie (Joanna Gleason), is a perpetual malcontent, unable to be intimate with anyone, including her own daughter, Echo (Jennie Moreau). Dorothea raises Echo devotedly after Artie abandons her, only to discover that Echo, too, has become as brainy but difficult as the Westbrook women before her. Telling the story on a bare, platformed stage, Mr. Blessing takes us back and forth in time, through the characters' various childhoods and marriages and illnesses and rages, until his trio can find some common ground.

As is the case with such other recent Blessing plays as *A Walk in the Woods,* seen on Broadway last season, and *Cobb,* at the Yale Repertory Theatre earlier this spring, *Eleemosynary* is distinguished by its brevity (seventy-five minutes or so), its clever dialogue, its unassailable ideology (this play is as vehemently in favor of feminism as its predecessors were for disarmament and against racism), and its reconciliatory conclusion. Mr. Blessing can make familial relationships seem as uncomplicated as he does East-West arms negotiations. For the sake of psychological tidiness and theatrical compactness, he keeps the men in the women's lives not just offstage but virtually uncharacterized, and withholds his one dramatic confrontation until the waning minutes.

What we get in place of emotional or intellectual depth are words, lots of them. The play's title refers to the charity and forgiveness that ultimately overtake the Westbrooks, but it is also a crucial word for Echo, who overcompensates for her mother's inattention by devoting herself to winning spelling bees. Echo is forever showing off by reciting her favorite arcane dictionary entries. Those in the audience who recognize the words and know the spellings are given ample opportunity to join her orgy of self-congratulation.

The cast, under the fluid direction of Lynne Meadow, makes the most of its own opportunities. Ms. Gleason, another of our most distinctive comic actresses, makes a congenitally sour character funny and finally sympathetic; Ms. Moreau achieves the same feat for a brat. When *Eleemosynary* induces restlessness, as it does at least half the time, it's because the writing, not the acting, lacks the human reality that might root the play in the theater or in the audience's psyche. As the friend who attended a press preview with me said on the phone a day later, "I can't remember what that play was about or even the one thing I thought I had learned from it—how to pronounce 'eleemosynary.' "

Eileen Heckart, however, is just too dear to forget.

ELEVENTH SEASON

1989—90

Charles Durning in *Cat on a Hot Tin Roof*

THE REVENGERS' COMEDIES

STEPHEN JOSEPH THEATRE,
SCARBOROUGH, ENGLAND, JUNE 15, 1989

In this Yorkshire seaside resort, where pensioners practice ballroom dancing at the Victorian Grand Hotel while teenagers hang out at a shiny Pizza Hut, one can see the contradictions of England today. Pressing hard on the cozy English landscape that Americans still romanticize is the hard-edged environment of economic expansion, the Thatcher England of progress, or soullessness, depending on one's point of view. There is nothing unique about Scarborough, and that's why it is a fitting home for Alan Ayckbourn. The most extraordinary career in contemporary English playwriting is built entirely of the stuff of ordinary lives.

At a time when England boasts very few dramatists as vital as the dominant American playwrights of this decade, Mr. Ayckbourn is a one-man renaissance. As the artistic director of the three-hundred-seat Stephen Joseph Theatre in the Round in Scarborough, he spends most of each year directing other writers' scripts, then directs a new play of his own. This summer's production, *The Revengers' Comedies,* an epic achievement that opened here this week and runs until September 23, coincides with his fiftieth birthday and his thirtieth year in Scarborough. It is, incredibly, his thirty-seventh play—an output, English commentators fondly point out, that equals Shakespeare's.

Mr. Ayckbourn's plays eventually make their way south to London, whether to the West End or the National Theatre, sometimes recast with stars, again under the author's direction. *Henceforward . . . ,* seen in Scarborough in 1987, is now in its second West End cast, and *Man of the Moment,* last year's Scarborough premiere, is scheduled for London production next winter, with Michael Gambon in the lead. Mr. Gambon, the actor known primarily to American audiences for *The Singing Detective,* has appeared in two Ayckbourn triumphs in London in recent seasons, *A Chorus of Disapproval* and *A Small Family Business,* as well as in Mr. Ayckbourn's stunning revival of Arthur Miller's *A View from the Bridge.* Yet the Ayckbourn-Gambon collaboration has yet to be seen in the United States.

Were it not for the fine Manhattan Theatre Club production of *Woman in Mind,* a relatively minor work of 1985, New York audiences would have no idea of this writer's remarkable growth through the 1980s. Mr. Ayckbourn's American reputation largely rests instead on the Broadway productions of *Absurd Person Singular, The Norman Conquests,* and *Bedroom Farce*—none written later than 1976, all but the last erratically performed in New York and all still showing the author's boulevard-comedy roots. Mr. Ayckbourn's later, most ambitious writing scares away many American commercial producers and resident theaters with rare exceptions like the Alley Theatre in Houston, Arena Stage in Washington, and A Contemporary Theatre in Seattle. These plays demand large, versatile casts—John Gay's *Beggar's Opera* is folded within *A Chorus of Disapproval*—and also audiences who can stomach middle-class characters miserably lonely in marriage and consumed by greed.

For his fiftieth-birthday play, Mr. Ayckbourn decreed by press release that "something rather ambitious was in order." But what could he do to top his previous experiments in theatrical form and character? Mr. Ayckbourn's earlier works include a two-actor play cycle whose sixteen variants require eight different scripts (*Intimate Exchanges*), a trilogy about the same people in different locations of the same house over a single weekend (*The Norman Conquests*), a comedy in which two couples occupy different settings but the same stage space (*How the Other Half Loves*), and a play occurring in one of four different versions as determined at each performance by a coin toss (*Sisterly Feelings*).

Now Mr. Ayckbourn has outdone himself, making *The Revengers' Comedies* a work in two parts—one riotously funny, one chilling—that can be seen, *Nicholas Nickleby* style, in either two nights or in a six-hour marathon with a dinner break. At the marathon performance I attended, the playwright never lost the rapt attention of an audience widely heterogeneous in age and class. *The Revengers' Comedies* begins at a heavily plotted, hugely entertaining pitch that recalls the old movies to which it frequently pays homage—*Strangers on a Train, Rebecca, Kind Hearts and Coronets*—then expands after intermission to reveal an immensely disturbing vision of contemporary middle-class England poisoned by the rise of economic ruthlessness and the collapse of ethics.

Though there are two dozen characters, all indelibly portrayed by the Scarborough cast, *The Revengers' Comedies* is primarily about two strangers who meet by chance on a fogbound London bridge late one night while each attempts suicide. Karen Knightly (Christine Kavanagh) is a young, attractive, rapacious heiress who has been jilted by her lover. Henry Bell (Jon Strickland) is her social opposite: a "piddling" forty-two-year-old clerk who has lost his job in a multinational corporation by refusing to play office politics. Abandoning suicide, Karen and Henry make a pact to get revenge on each other's nemeses. Karen, impersonating a temporary secretary, goes to work for Henry's former employer while Henry goes undercover among Karen's horsey set in Dorset.

As these two characters burrow into their hilarious Machiavellian schemes, Mr. Ayckbourn's portrait of urban and rural England grows darker. The multinational corporation in London is a nightmare out of Caryl Churchill's *Top Girls*—a cesspool of sexism and careerism, epitomized by a boorish, burping, and leering executive with the memorable name of Bruce Tick (Jeff Shankley). In the country, where the landed gentry have names like Imogen Staxton-Billing (Elizabeth Bell), we meet the spookily daft Knightly servants and hear about a "mysterious accident," perhaps pyromaniacal, of long ago. Poor, nebbishy Henry finds himself dragged into a shotgun duel tacitly sanctioned by the local police. "This is the twentieth century, not the Dark Ages!" he cries.

Or is it? By the end of part one, in which Bruce Tick is driven to a heart attack in a London wine bar, the fun of justifiable revenge has been replaced by the excruciating spectacle of watching lives, some of them innocent, being cruelly destroyed. One begins to feel compassion even for the loathsome Tick. Yet Karen cannot let go of the game, and, in part two of *The Revengers' Comedies*, the game has become synonymous with the national sport of hostile corporate takeovers, wholesale job "redundancies," and industrial destruction of the countryside. "Being good is never enough in itself," says Karen by way of rationalization for her expedient behavior. With a subtlety beyond the reach of many polemical English playwrights, Mr. Ayckbourn does not shy away from presenting the alternative to good as pure evil.

While *The Revengers' Comedies* has a few false endings before arriving at its devastating, though not hopeless, conclusion, it is hard to speak highly enough of a work whose elegant writing and staging is accompanied by an utter lack of pretension. Mr. Ayckbourn would as soon make reference to the Everly Brothers' song "Cathy's Clown" as to Cyril Tourneur's Jacobean *Revenger's Tragedy*. That's in keeping with a writer who chooses to work on a small stage in a small town but whose talent and theatrical ambitions increasingly seem without limit.

TWELFTH NIGHT
DELACORTE THEATER, JULY 10, 1989

Not all movie stars are created equal. Some are born great, some achieve greatness, and some have greatness thrust upon them, to paraphrase William Shakespeare's *Twelfth Night,* the play serving as a Central Park summer camp for some visitors from Hollywood. Some stars, one might add, are not so great at all. But as visitors to the Delacorte Theater can discover, every variety of star, however dim, is welcome in the New York Shakespeare Festival production of a comedy that has rarely lived up so well to its full title, *Twelfth Night, or What You Will.*

This is a crazy-quilt evening that tells us more about show business— public relations, career advancement, egomania—than it does about the lovesick passions of Illyria. Given that the personalities involved include Michelle Pfeiffer, Jeff Goldblum, and Gregory Hines—not to mention the impresario who recruited them, Joseph Papp—the production is not without interest of an extratheatrical sort. As a night of Shakespeare, however, this *Twelfth Night* may most please audiences whose expectations have been sunk by exposure to the most star-laden of the previous Shakespeare Marathon productions, *Julius Caesar.* The idylls of July have it by a nose or two over the ides of March.

For that, we can mainly thank Mary Elizabeth Mastrantonio, whose Viola would be a treasure in any *Twelfth Night.* Central Park regulars may recall that as Katherine of France she was a dazzling sparring partner for Kevin Kline in the 1984 *Henry V* and that as the conscience-torn Isabella she was the sole life in the *Measure for Measure* of a summer later. As Viola, the shipwrecked young woman driven to disguise her true feelings and gender, Ms. Mastrantonio is given far wider territory and conquers it all.

Equally agile of tongue and limb, the actress is at home in the verse, heightening its most lyrical passages ("Make me a willow cabin at your gate. . . .") without adding artificial sweetener. In Edwardian cap, jacket, trousers, and bow tie as the page Cesario, she conveys boyishness without burying her own sexuality in androgyny; we never doubt how women and men alike might fall for her. And when the time comes for Viola to try to untangle the knot of mistaken identities that place her in the excruciating center of several interlocking, unrequited love affairs, Ms. Mastrantonio turns what might be a moment of whining histrionics into human high comedy. She tumbles to the ground and madly tries to draw a chart of all the confusions before finally turning her predicament over to a more effective arbiter, Time.

While Ms. Mastrantonio does not quite have to perform solo in *Twelfth Night,* she receives solid partnering only from Stephen Collins as Orsino, a duke who knows when the time has come to forsake his fatuous mooniness and turn on the charm, and from Graham Winton as her dashing twin brother, Sebastian. In the more important role of Olivia, the countess who pines in vain for the disguised Viola, Ms. Pfeiffer offers an object lesson in how gifted stars with young careers can be misused by those more interested in exploiting their celebrity status than in furthering their artistic development.

Did anyone connected with *Twelfth Night* see Ms. Pfeiffer's delightful Carole Lombard turn in Jonathan Demme's screwball comedy *Married to the Mob*? It's unfortunate that the actress has been asked to make both her stage and Shakespearean comic debut in a role chained to melancholy and mourning. It's also unclear why the director, Harold Guskin, a prominent acting coach, failed to come to the rescue of Ms. Pfeiffer's vocal delivery, shaky and wan even when miked. Only when the actress gives out an uninhibited yelp of lust in Sebastian's arms does she seem comfortably herself onstage.

Mr. Guskin's direction isn't entirely laissez-faire. The contradictory spirit of *Twelfth Night* lives in Peter Golub's rain-flecked score and in John Lee Beatty's set, an imaginative evocation of both the cliffside villas and beachfront pleasure domes of the fin-de-siècle Riviera. But as an acting coach, Mr. Guskin seems more of a cheerleader, allowing seasoned performers to reach heights of self-indulgence that would make an Oscar presenter blush.

Easily the most shocking offender is Mr. Goldblum, who gets no laughs in the heretofore foolproof scene in which Olivia's puritanical steward, Malvolio, is duped into romantic lightheadedness by a forged letter. Fracturing every line into unintelligibility with eye and tongue poppings, racing his voice up and down the octave, Mr. Goldblum fails to define Malvolio's pomposity in the first place, thereby rendering his subsequent fall and cruel humiliation meaningless. Malvolio may be "sick of self love," as Olivia says, but Mr. Goldblum's egotism is of another order entirely. This is a star appearance at the esthetic level of an autograph signing.

With the exception of Charlaine Woodard's sprightly Maria, the other comic players are just as mirthless. John Amos has none of the carousing Sir Toby's aura of ruined nobility, and Fisher Stevens, a little too young to be impersonating the "What me worry?" deadpan of Joey Bishop, misses the vulnerability that makes Olivia's hapless suitor, Sir Andrew Aguecheek, funny and pathetic. As the clown, Feste, the joyous Mr. Hines has his sweet moments but is often used as patronizingly as Ms. Pfeiffer. Mr. Hines's great talents as a dancer are constantly mocked— not for real laughs but to advertise his showbiz identity—and his bittersweet role is flattened into an obsequious and incessantly smiling jester, as if to dismiss his acting prowess. True, the clown's final lyric says that "we'll strive to please you every day," but pleasure is one thing, pandering another. Mr. Hines is at one point asked to bare his rump.

Though it would be pretentious to talk about Shakespeare in considering a *Twelfth Night* in which such discussions were probably kept to a minimum, the author does peek through here and there. This is palpably true when Ms. Mastrantonio, her tears of longing still gleaming in her wide eyes, leaps on Mr. Collins's back to celebrate the long-delayed reciprocation of her affections. Love, the gesture reminds us, requires a brave, selfless, potentially foolish leap beyond one's narcissistic romantic fantasies and into the unknown. In Illyria as elsewhere, it's only that lesser and passing thing, infatuation, that is written in the stars.

THE LADY IN QUESTION
ORPHEUM THEATRE, JULY 26, 1989

Selfish is too kind a word for Gertrude Garnet, "the leading concert pianist of the international stage" and the all-American heroine of *The Lady in Question,* Charles Busch's latest celebration of Hollywood kitsch. Hitler may be on the march, but Gertrude, on tour in Bavaria, can't worry her pretty head about politics. She finds the Germans "so warm, so friendly" and reassures the Nazis' victims that patience will reward them with an afterlife of "Champagne and caviar." For Gertrude, art comes first, then her wardrobe, then her cosmetics bag (Suzette, the maid, has stolen it), and then, of course, love. To paraphrase Lorenz Hart, the lady in question is a tramp.

As both written and acted by Mr. Busch, she is also hilarious company. This performer's Theater-in-Limbo company, best known for the long-running *Vampire Lesbians of Sodom,* has found its most assured style and, I suspect, its biggest hit in the new play at the Orpheum Theatre. Not that *The Lady in Question* can precisely be called a new play. A saga of war-torn romance and intrigue set in 1940, the piece has been distilled from such patriotic Hollywood potboilers of the period as *Es-*

cape, Reunion in France, and *Above Suspicion.* These were movies in which determined American women wearing Adrian gowns (Joan Crawford, Norma Shearer) joined with square-jawed Joes (Robert Taylor, Fred MacMurray) to beat suave Nazi swine (Conrad Veidt, Basil Rathbone) in a perilous midnight dash to the Swiss border.

As always, Mr. Busch knows his MGM schlock, but never previously has he or his director, Kenneth Elliott, dished it out with such sustained, well-paced discipline. Along with its double-entendre groaners, *The Lady in Question* actually offers some melodramatic chills and, thanks to the witty production design, the backlot shock effects allotted movies with B budgets. It's all here: the overblown soundtrack score, in which Wagner and Strauss enjoy a shotgun collaboration with Max Steiner; the propagandistic asides identifying the American cause with both God and Joe Stalin; the fake snow powdering the Alpine ski slopes; the stern, omniscient narrator who warns the audience that "yes, human life is cheap in the fatherland."

While Mr. Busch's plays are often linked with Charles Ludlam's lighter efforts, such generalizing distorts the artistry of both. Mr. Ludlam, a theatrical classicist and a political iconoclast, usually had a second agenda, ideological or esthetic, percolating within his gender-flipped sendups. Mr. Busch's attitude is the simpler one of "Hooray for Hollywood!" The man revels in trash. *The Lady in Question* mimics its source material so accurately and affectionately that it is as much homage as parody; the tone is closer to *Dames at Sea* or a Mel Brooks film than it is to the Ridiculous Theatrical Company. I'm not sure the show would play much differently if Mr. Busch took the radical step of casting a woman as Gertrude Garnet.

But what actor of either gender could top Mr. Busch? Last seen as Chicklet, a teenage girl with a multiple-personality disorder in the lesser *Psycho Beach Party,* he continues to be the Sybil of camp. With red Rita Hayworth hair and a low voice that variously recalls Bankhead, Bacall, Stanwyck, Davis, and Russell, Mr. Busch is a walking anthology of feminine Hollywood legends. Yet the performance is not another cabaret drag act in which the breathless quick changes are the oppressively showy point. His Gertrude is a subtle characterization, ready to meet any challenge, including the Greer Garson–like inspirational speeches that transform the heroine from a Stork Club hedonist into a selfless patriot by the final clinch. So complex is the illusion created by Mr. Busch that when Gertrude appears in Dietrichesque blazer and pants to go riding at Baron von Elsner's schloss, we don't even stop to think that we are watching a man impersonate a woman impersonating a man.

Mr. Busch's fellow clowns easily exceed their past Theater-in-Limbo turns. In the other cross-gender performance, Andy Halliday offers a vicious blond Nazi youth in braids and bows—a psychotic hybrid of a Trapp Family Singer and Patty McCormack in *The Bad Seed*. Julie Halston, as Gertrude's sidekick since vaudeville days in Sandusky, Ohio, is the apotheosis of wisecracking second bananas of the Joan Blondell–Eve Arden era. In the evening's most amusing double act, Meghan Robinson plays two disparate mothers, a Führer-worshipping Baroness and a high-minded anti-Nazi actress so self-dramatizing that one often feels she would rather win an Oscar than get out of Germany alive. "I must walk to freedom!" is Ms. Robinson's histrionic vow, and how she does so, her wheelchair and a steep staircase notwithstanding, gives *The Lady in Question* its funniest excursion into physical comedy.

It's a tribute to Mr. Busch that, without raising his voice, he is never upstaged by this riotous crew. Like the actresses he emulates, he rules by force of personality, often proving the cool, elegant, just slightly off-center eye of the farcical storm around him. That the lady in question is a man soon becomes beside the point. What matters here is that the performer in question is a star.

CRITIC'S NOTEBOOK: THE ASTERISKS OF OH! CALCUTTA!
AUGUST 8, 1989

On a sweltering August night when the entire population was looking for any excuse to take off its clothes, *Oh! Calcutta!* threw in the towel at last.

Sunday night was the 5,959th and final Broadway performance of "the world's longest running erotic stage musical"—the show that began its career in 1969 as a chic, notorious avatar of what was once called "the sexual revolution" but that in recent years settled into the anonymity of those New York tourist spots patronized mainly by visitors who don't speak English too well. *Oh! Calcutta!* has been running a very, very long time. As I took my seat in the Edison Theatre on Sunday, the armrest came off in my hand. Then the entertainment began with a striptease dance baring a truly hard-core anatomical fact: Even *Oh! Calcutta!* is not immune to cellulite.

As Broadway closings go, this one was hardly a sentimental occasion. The house was not packed to overflowing; as the ads used to say, there were good seats available at all prices. A desultory television camera crew loitered about, attracting little curiosity as it went through the motions of recording a slow night's News Event. Most of the audience— respectable-looking couples of all ages and non–New York points of origin—didn't realize it was a witness to history until the producer informed the crowd of the fact in preperformance remarks from the stage.

Yet history of what import, exactly? In theater history, *Oh! Calcutta!* is an asterisk. For the moment, it is the longest-running production to appear on Broadway, outstripping *A Chorus Line* by 127 performances. But *Oh! Calcutta!* achieved this temporary record in a theater with only one third as many seats to fill as its competitor, and it stacked the deck by frequently jamming two or three extra performances into the standard eight-performance Broadway week. What's more, the Edison *Oh! Calcutta!*, which opened in 1976, is actually a revival. The original *Oh! Calcutta!* ran roughly 1,300 performances from 1969 to 1972, first at the Eden Theatre (lately the Second Avenue Theatre) Off Broadway, then at the Belasco Theatre uptown. So thorny are the statistics that even *Variety* misplaced about 700 of the pre-Edison performances in its front-page farewell.

In the careers of its distinguished authors, *Oh! Calcutta!* is an asterisk as well. The show was conceived as a jape—"an entertainment in the erotic area in the best possible taste"—by the critic Kenneth Tynan, who rounded up such tony friends as Samuel Beckett, Sam Shepard, John Lennon, and Jules Feiffer to contribute sketches, songs, and poetry. (Kathleen Tynan says in her invaluable 1987 biography of her husband, *The Life of Kenneth Tynan*, that other participants he considered were Peter Brook, Edna O'Brien, Jean-Luc Godard, Federico Fellini, Michael Bennett, Elaine May, Joe Orton, Harold Pinter, and Tennessee Williams.) It was part of the revue's tongue-in-cheek tone that the *Playbill* did not identify who wrote what. It's a measure of the writing's slight quality that the authors never made a move of their own to divvy up credit.

"We are not trying to make a revolution," Tynan told reporters before the opening. He wanted to make mischief, fun, and money. But 1969 was a time of social upheaval in the United States on all fronts, and *Oh! Calcutta!*, with its full nudity and simulated sexual activity, was inevitably seen in the context of such contemporaneous stage and film breakthroughs in erotic frankness as *Hair, I Am Curious (Yellow), Dionysus in 69*, and the briefly censored *Che!* Caught in the ideological crossfire, Tynan's show was labeled too mild and schoolboyish silly by serious critics and yet reviled as "hard-core pornography" by the *Daily News*. Only the public loved it.

Oh! Calcutta! must have done something right. A theatrical production doesn't run off and on for twenty years at Broadway ticket prices, well into the era of video porn, simply by exposing a few breasts, buttocks, and penises. At the closing, the show looked shabby and was performed with the aggressive gaiety one normally encounters only in West End sex farces approaching their tenth anniversaries. Anachronistic dialogue references to Pee-wee Herman, Smurfs, and Famous Amos cookies made it clear that strict textual fidelity was not a pressing concern of the management. But the shell of the original, at least, remained, and to see *Oh! Calcutta!* in 1989 was to have an inkling of what once captivated so many theatergoers.

What I saw was a throwback to the *Bob & Carol & Ted & Alice* America of two decades ago—a land of would-be "swinging" couples, newfangled sex therapy, and the Playboy Philosophy. It was a place where women were erotic appendages to men, where the mere mention of euphemisms for sexual organs or acts caused blushing and eye-popping, and where masturbation was viewed not as a form of safe sex but as a naughty embarrassment. Two sketches are built around the second and third oldest jokes in creation—lecherous doctors and a farmer's randy son. Male homosexuality, explicitly forbidden from the show by Tynan, is alluded to once, with the word "weirdo." The evening's erotic ballets, accompanied by disco lighting, soft-rock music (some of it by Peter Schickele), and confessional Lenore Kandel poetry, could be a Feiffer parody of a Greenwich Village interpretive dance recital, circa 1964.

Is this an America where many of us would want to live now? Perhaps not, which explains why the native audience of *Oh! Calcutta!* was long ago supplanted by visitors from the Far East. Not only is the show less erotically daring than the advertising spreads in a typical present-day fashion magazine, but *Oh! Calcutta!* also subscribes to social attitudes, whether juvenile or sexist or unknowingly bigoted, that many, the original authors likely included, would now consider antediluvian. It is appropriate that the revue would have finished its New York run in a worn Art Deco building, the Edison Hotel, that is the largest relic of old New York left standing in its typically half-demolished Times Square block. At Sunday's performance, I felt I had stepped back into the past like the hero of Jack Finney's time-travel novel *Time and Again.*

Of course, one doesn't want to be carried away by nostalgia. Following the Mapplethorpe uproar and the erosion of *Roe* v. *Wade,* there is reason to wonder whether the clock may yet be turned back until the social climate is hospitable again for *Oh! Calcutta!,* with its celebration of strict erotic orthodoxy and unchallenged male supremacy. Should that time arrive, there will no doubt be another revival to chalk up still more asterisked performances. For now, however, *Oh! Calcutta!* is closed, and perhaps only its newly unemployed actors have real cause to mourn.

SWEENEY TODD
CIRCLE IN THE SQUARE, SEPTEMBER 15, 1989

Of all the powerful moments in the American musical theater, there may be none more perverse than the Act 1 apex of *Sweeney Todd*. That moment has never seemed either more moving or more sick than as played by Bob Gunton, the Demon Barber of Fleet Street, in the revival of Stephen Sondheim's musical that has arrived at the Circle in the Square.

Let others move us with tales of love among men and women. Mr. Sondheim in this scene writes of the passion of a man for murder. Having spent fifteen years in exile on a trumped-up prison charge, Sweeney has just returned to Victorian London to plot revenge on the judge who destroyed him and his family. The chalky-faced Mr. Gunton, his evenly parted hair shot with silver and his raccoon eyes rattling around their red-rimmed sockets, knows that the instruments of that revenge will be his old "friends"—the razors with which he has been reunited at long last. Sweeney sings affectionately to his razors, then stands up to raise one to the sky. "At last my right arm is complete again!" Mr. Gunton cries in surging, ecstatic voice as his long silver blade glints high in a spotlight, poised to slash through the night.

Homicidal rage may not be a pretty emotion, but who can deny that it is deeply felt? In *Sweeney Todd,* Mr. Gunton's soaring anger, the crowning feature of a blazing characterization, seizes us as surely as his razor will have at the throats of his many victims; this actor earns our sympathy even as he threatens to welcome us to the grave. One of the canards about Mr. Sondheim has always been that his musicals are longer on intellect than feeling. In keeping with the performance at its heart, Susan H. Schulman's production of *Sweeney Todd,* a remounting of her searing York Theatre Company staging of last spring, reveals the nonsense of that assumption. No one writes more passionately for the musical theater than Stephen Sondheim. It's the nature of those passions that makes frightened audiences want to shunt them aside by dismissing them as "intellectual." Mr. Sondheim fearlessly explores psychic caverns where civilized people are not dying to go.

Unlike Harold Prince's original 1979 Broadway production of *Sweeney Todd*—which inhabited the huge Gershwin Theatre (then the Uris) upstairs from Circle in the Square—Ms. Schulman's won't keep an audience at a safe remove from Sweeney's bloodthirstiness. The director eliminates the physical distance from the executioner's scalding soul by obliterating the proscenium arch and locking us in a gloomy arena set (by James Morgan) that surrounds us with the characters' sooty, squalid nocturnal London. But greater proximity does not alone explain why this *Sweeney Todd* is more upsetting than the first. Ms. Schulman's new take on Mr. Sondheim's musical has less to do with her staging—some of which owes a debt to Mr. Prince's in any case—than with her distinctive reading of what the show is about.

Mr. Prince's *Sweeney Todd,* amply supported by the Hugh Wheeler–Christopher Bond book as well as by the Sondheim lyrics, emphasized the dehumanizing horror of the Industrial Age. The first thing the audience saw was a front curtain depicting the oppressive British beehive, or social pecking order; the hulking set included part of an actual iron foundry. Sweeney was the victim of Darwinian class struggle; he was a wronged representative of "the lower zoo" rising up against "the privileged few." While such sentiments remain in the text, Ms. Schulman has played down the simplistically stated ideology of *Sweeney Todd* by removing Mr. Prince's Brechtian theatrical trappings and with them any trace of Brechtian alienation. We are instead asked to identify point-blank with Sweeney and his partner in crime, the pie-baking Mrs. Lovett (Beth Fowler), as tragic figures caught in conundrums of sex and death. The characters' universal internal demons, rather than the remote demons of their Dickensian London, are center stage.

While the original production had some of the tone of *The Three-penny Opera,* Ms. Schulman's is more like a penny-dreadful *Macbeth.* One misses the savage comic attack of Mr. Prince's version (and of Angela Lansbury's Mrs. Lovett) but receives in exchange a played-for-keeps tale of love and innocence thwarted and twisted into hate and destruction, of cannibalism with a shockingly human face.

Ms. Schulman's route into *Sweeney* begins with her superb cast, then blossoms through Mr. Sondheim's score. Ms. Fowler makes us believe in Mrs. Lovett's maternal heart, even as she grinds up Sweeney's victims for meat-pie filling, because we see a lonely woman hopelessly in love with the barber she first met years ago. If Mr. Gunton loves his razors more than the deluded Mrs. Lovett, his longing for his lost wife and his daughter is an overwhelming obsession, finally to reach a rending catharsis in his sobbing embrace of his wife's corpse.

The heated acting, if not always the authenticity of accents, extends to the key supporting players: SuEllen Estey as a feral beggar woman with a secret, David Barron's sadomasochistic Judge Turpin, Michael McCarty's mercurial Beadle, and especially Eddie Korbich's forlorn pie-shop assistant. They not only sing well (without amplification) but also infuse the stereotypes of nineteenth-century melodrama with pathos and madness. Though the strong-voiced young lovers, Jim Walton and Gretchen Kingsley, remain mannequins, they are somewhat shackled by the writing. Mr. Sondheim's forte is not dewy-eyed Romeo-and-Juliet couples (unless he's mocking them, as in *A Funny Thing Happened on the Way to the Forum*).

Thanks to the performances, the larger quarters at Circle in the Square do not entirely dismantle the cheek-by-jowl relationship the show enjoyed with its audience in the York's tiny quarters last spring. The ghostly atmosphere is inevitably dissipated, however, and some of it might have been reclaimed by stronger musical accompaniment. David Crane's clever synthesizer arrangements, effective at the York, lack the presence essential to deliver the score's Bernard Herrmann-like horror effects in the larger house.

Yet the beauty and drama of Mr. Sondheim's songs remain, and Ms. Schulman and company make us listen to them anew. Like his protagonist, Mr. Sondheim hears "the music that nobody hears": the music by which people act out their basest grand passions. We're increasingly aware that the plot's ugliest incidents inspire Mr. Sondheim's most gorgeous melodies. Rape comes with a minuet and murder with a rhapsodic ode to "Pretty Women." When Ms. Fowler fantasizes about domestic bliss with Sweeney—in a cozy resort hideaway equally suitable for lovemaking and throat-slitting—she expresses her deranged hopes in a cheery mock–Beatrice Lillie ditty, "By the Sea."

By forcing us to face Mr. Sondheim's music and the feelings it contains so intensely, Ms. Schulman doesn't obliterate the Prince production; she creates an alternative. Such is the depth of Mr. Sondheim's achievement that *Sweeney Todd* can support radically different interpretations (not to mention intervening assaults by opera companies) and easily hold its own without elaborate stage machinery. Stripped of its giant set, its politics, its orchestra, much of its chorus, and its dazzling original stars, this troubling musical still refuses to leave us alone and, if anything, insinuates its way further into the audience's own private darkness. A naked *Sweeney Todd* stands revealed as a musical of naked rage, chewing up everyone in its path as it spits out blood and tears.

ORPHEUS DESCENDING
NEIL SIMON THEATRE, SEPTEMBER 25, 1989

The fusion of Vanessa Redgrave and Tennessee Williams is an artistic explosion that was bound to happen, and the wonder is that we had to wait until Peter Hall's revival of *Orpheus Descending*. Williams and Ms. Redgrave were made for each other because they are brilliant theater artists in the same way. They run at life bravely, openly, without defenses and without fear of their inevitable destruction, like great, beautiful deer bounding across a highway after dark.

You don't go to Williams and Redgrave for an elegant intellectual evening or for a show of classical technique. You go to watch what the playwright once called a world lit by lightning. At the Neil Simon Theatre, where Mr. Hall's production has arrived on Broadway via the West End, the flashes of gut-deep humor and pain sear the night as Ms. Redgrave takes complete, perhaps eternal possession of the role of Lady Torrance, the middle-aged proprietor of a dry-goods store somewhere in a fetid Deep South.

Lady Torrance is an archetypal Williams outcast. The lonely daughter of an immigrant Sicilian bootlegger murdered long ago by the Ku Klux Klan, she has been married unhappily for twenty years to a bigoted tyrant now riddled by cancer. The Orpheus who descends to rescue her is Val Xavier (Kevin Anderson), a guitar-toting drifter of thirty whom Williams wrote with Elvis Presley in mind. That Val and Lady will end up sharing a bed is never in question. It's how Ms. Redgrave gets there, how she melts from a barren, rigid businesswoman to a radiant celebrator of the "life in my body," that astonishes.

What Ms. Redgrave does is fill out each moment, however tiny, with the dramatic (if sometimes funny) conflict of emotions, taking any risk she can that might allow her character to seep into every crevice of the play. Early on, when hypocritical neighbors tell Lady that they pray for her doomed husband, she responds not with stoic silence but with a mocking, spiraling laugh that establishes her contempt for her spouse even as it reveals the buried humanity that her marriage could not snuff out. Once Val appears seeking work, Ms. Redgrave greets him with a barking inquisition in her guttural Italian accent, and yet again she subtly reveals the countervailing forces tugging within. As Val empties his pockets trying to find a former employer's letter of reference, Ms. Redgrave's eyes scour the floor desperately, as if the stranger's each discarded scrap of paper might be a harbinger of hope.

By Act 2, Lady is sitting rigidly in a chair, trying to ward off Val's sexual pull by keeping her back to him. But Ms. Redgrave's glowing eyes and nervously grinning mouth are yanked as if by gravity in his direction anyway. Mr. Anderson helps bring Lady's body in line with her spirit by means of a neck massage that loosens her hair, voice, and torso until finally this tall woman seems to have merged with the play's central image of liberation—a floating, legless bird that lives "all its life on its wings in the sky." When Ms. Redgrave then takes off her silk robe to join Val in his itinerant's bed under the shop's staircase, the nudity seems completely natural. This Lady has long since been stripped of everything, including at least twenty years of age.

The grotesque fate that Williams holds in store for his lovers thereafter, and that brings Ms. Redgrave's performance to its devastating, tragic peak, is the substance not only of *Orpheus Descending* but of the playwright's life work as well. Lady and Val are sensitive nonconformists who, like that sweet bird and like most Williams protagonists, must be destroyed by the bullying real world as soon as they come down to earth. A two-month flop when staged by Harold Clurman on Broadway in 1957, *Orpheus Descending* can now be seen as a pivotal chapter in the author's canon, reverberating throughout his career. Under the title *Battle of Angels*, an early version of the play was Williams's first, unsuccessful attempt to storm New York in 1940. (It closed during its Boston tryout.) In 1957, *Orpheus* was the boundary between Williams's biggest successes and saddest theatrical travails.

That Mr. Hall and Ms. Redgrave would choose to revive this sprawling, problematic piece rather than one of the preceding, established Williams classics is heroic. What's more, the director has brought his full wide-ranging imagination to bear on the text. Abandoning any pretense of realism, Mr. Hall stages the play in a hallucinatory set (by Alison Chitty) that floats against a spooky, cloud-streaked azure sky. The lighting, by Paul Pyant with Neil Peter Jampolis, mixes theatrical expressionism with Hollywood film noir; blinding car headlights frequently sweep through the general store's rain-streaked windows. Stephen Edwards's electronic score, punctuated by the upstairs cane bangings of Lady's dying husband and the howling of flesh-hungry dogs, provides ominous underscoring to expository speeches delivered directly to the audience by the town's quasi-Greek chorus of ghoulish, gossipy harpies.

The hothouse imagery fits a play set in a Southern Gothic Hades belonging to a corrupt America "sick with neon." In *Orpheus*, characters are burned alive, babies are killed in the womb, and racist mob violence always threatens to erupt. Like Ms. Redgrave, Mr. Hall has the guts to embrace and explore the contradictions in Williams's play rather than to attempt to reconcile them in one rigid style or another. *Orpheus* is an un-wieldy mix of myth, ritual (a conjure man included), social realism, and bluesy poetry. Why not revel in the author's imagination instead of try-ing, as the original production apparently did, to domesticate it?

To pull off his balancing act, however, Mr. Hall needs a consistent level of acting that is left unfulfilled by his new New York supporting cast. One would expect American actors to do better by Williams than their London counterparts, but whether through miscasting or under-rehearsing, that's not the case here. Anne Twomey, as a ghostly drug-and-sex-eviscerated Cassandra of plantations past, and Tammy Grimes, as a sheriff's wife pathetically lost in spiritual visions, bring actressy technique rather than Ms. Redgrave's transparency of emotion to roles that should be affecting, not campy. Though Mr. Anderson, a much more honest actor, is a tender Val, he never emits the animalistic erotic charge of a character Williams likened to "a fox in a chicken coop." With the ex-ception of Sloane Shelton as one of the town scolds, the many evil Delta denizens are comic-book rednecks, most crucially Lady's husband (Brad Sullivan) and her former lover (Lewis Arlt).

As a result, this *Orpheus* is more of a triumph for Ms. Redgrave than for Williams, whose script reveals its seams when in the other actors' hands. But since everything the star does is in the playwright's service, his spirit always comes through, even when passages of his play do not. Nowhere is that spirit more powerfully conveyed than when Ms. Red-grave twirls about in a red and gold party dress in Act 2, defiantly savor-ing her hard-won freedom by imitating the monkey that long ago danced to her beloved father's hand organ.

Such happiness is at most transitory in a Williams play—notably one that takes as its credo "We're all sentenced to solitary confinement for life"—and Ms. Redgrave knows it. The intensity of her joy is so over-whelming that when the dance abruptly ends, as it must, the void in its wake is all the more unexpectedly shocking. It's as if the lights are blown out on stage, and our fellow theatergoers notwithstanding, we are plunged into Williams's solitary confinement, grief-stricken and alone.

THE SECRET RAPTURE
ETHEL BARRYMORE THEATRE, OCTOBER 27, 1989

In the one moving scene in David Hare's new play, *The Secret Rap-ture*—the last—the audience is suddenly overwhelmed by pity for a young woman it has hated all night long. The woman is Marion French, a Tory junior cabinet minister whose faith in dog-eat-dog capitalism is so unshakable and whose contempt for her adversaries is so patronizing that she makes Margaret Thatcher seem like Mary Poppins. But Marion has been shaken now. The home of her recently deceased father, a provincial bookseller, is being dismantled. Someone she loves has been murdered in a crime of passion. And so Frances Conroy, the actress who plays Marion in a progression of starchy yuppie business suits, cracks apart, her once stony face streaked by tears.

What consumes Marion, and what touches even those who despise her, is not her specific losses so much as her feeling of utter helplessness. She has been engulfed by the chaos that comes when people's passions spin out of control, and she realizes that there is nothing in her philosophy to save her. In *The Secret Rapture,* Mr. Hare uses the tragic story of Marion and her very different sister, Isobel (Blair Brown), as an ecumenical parable of the failure of all religions, temporal and spiritual, to offer salvation in the world we have made. The saintly Isobel, a free-spirited graphics artist who is as selfless as Marion is materialistic, is also crushed by the uncontrollable passions around her. So is the play's one true believer in old-time faith, Marion's sad-eyed husband, Tom (Stephen Vinovich), a born-again Christian entrepreneur who cannot find Jesus at the moment when he needs Him most.

Mr. Hare, the author of *Plenty* and *A Map of the World,* is not merely the flip socialist ideologue that he is so often taken for, and in *The Secret Rapture* he has gone further than before in marrying political thought to the compelling drama of lives that refuse to conform to any ideology's utopian plan. Framing his play with a pair of funerals, he tells a story of a warring family and obsessive love even as he folds in a polemical *Other People's Money*–style case history of corporate cannibalism and greed in the Thatcher-Reagan era. But Mr. Hare, serving as his play's director for its Broadway premiere at the Barrymore, is his own worst enemy. The passion and wit that reside in his script—and that are essential to engage an audience and lead it to his ideas—are left unrealized in this production.

Those who did not see last season's London staging of *The Secret Rapture,* directed by Howard Davies (*Les Liaisons Dangereuses*), are blameless if they find Mr. Hare's New York version baffling right up to that final scene. The textual tinkering since London may be minor, but the wholesale changes of casting and design have flattened the play's subtleties into coarse agitprop and tossed its overall intentions into confusion. It's a measure of how poorly *The Secret Rapture* has been mounted here that a designer as gifted as Santo Loquasto has provided a dingy black-and-tan set that makes England, as much a character in the play as its people, indistinguishable from, say, metropolitan Cleveland. Between the drab set and the leaden staging that often reduces people to poseurs standing around at a cocktail party, we might as well be home listening to Mr. Hare's words on radio or reading them in a book.

The colorless presentation is of a piece with most of the acting. One of the delights of Mr. Hare's best writing is his ability to offer fully rounded views of characters of either political pole. He gives his ideological devils their due as magnetic leaders (the V. S. Naipaul figure in *A Map of the World*, the Rupert Murdoch stand-in of *Pravda*) and is not afraid to mock the self-indulgence of would-be martyrs sharing his own leftist credo (Susan Traherne in *Plenty*). Such ambiguities are ignored by both lead actresses in *The Secret Rapture*, who instead perform a dull, diagrammatic bad sister versus good sister act. Until her final scene, the talented Ms. Conroy is a desexed martinet—a humorless heavy. (Penelope Wilton, the Marion in London, was feminine and funny as well as forbidding.) In Ms. Brown's bland reading, Isobel's purity is a matter of lofty smiles and holier-than-thou vocal posturing; the inner fire of deep conviction is replaced by a skin-deep air of self-satisfaction.

It's no secret that Mr. Hare created Isobel for Ms. Brown; the published text of *The Secret Rapture* is dedicated to her. But judging from this production and Mr. Hare's new movie, *Strapless*, in which Ms. Brown also stars as a good sister, it is clear that another director will have to help the actress realize the dream performances that remain locked in the playwright's imagination. Mr. Hare has undermined his leading lady further by assigning the role of her lover to an idiosyncratic character actor, Michael Wincott, who is never convincing either as her love object or, later, as a romantic obsessive whose behavior drives the play's entire second act. When Mr. Wincott and Ms. Brown come to emotional blows at the pivotal opening of that act, the display of yelling and hand-waving is so embarrassingly empty that it earns unwanted laughter.

Under these underinhabited circumstances, *The Secret Rapture* is up for grabs, and Mary Beth Hurt runs away with the show in the secondary role of Katherine, an abusive, foul-mouthed alcoholic who was the much younger second wife of Isobel's and Marion's father. As she accomplished in Michael Frayn's thematically related play, *Benefactors*, Ms. Hurt inexorably exposes the buried violence of the eccentric Englishwoman-next-door who also happens to be insane. It's part of Mr. Hare's point that people like Katherine, one of two characters in the play who brandish lethal weapons, practice an evil that is eternally beyond the reach of both a virtuous do-gooder like Isobel and a public scold like Marion. The world has become a place where no good deed, let alone bad one, goes unpunished.

"I hate all this human stuff!" says Marion at one point, frustrated by the way people with their "endless complications" insist on gumming up the best-laid plans by which she and all other right-thinking citizens would have society run smoothly. The beauty of *The Secret Rapture*, whose title refers to a nun's ecstatic unity with Christ at death, is that Mr. Hare embraces the human, messy though it may be. To do otherwise is to forestall rapture until death—or to settle for a soulless existence that one character calls a "perfect imitation of life." What I don't understand is how a dramatist so deep in human stuff could allow so pallid an imitation of life to represent his play on a Broadway stage.

≡ *This was a review that launched a thousand articles—as I describe in more detail in "Exit the Critic" at the end of this volume.*

No American critic had done more to promote David Hare than I had, but I had joined the anti-Hare majority of critics by panning The Knife, *his musical, and was stunned (as this review indicates) by how badly* The Secret Rapture *was produced in New York. Hare, who had never written me in the past, decided to write an angry open letter attacking me and my New York review of* The Secret Rapture—*to which I responded with an angry letter of my own.*

Would The Secret Rapture *have run longer than five weeks (three at the Public Theater, two on Broadway) if it had been done as well as it was in London (and reviewed by me accordingly)? I doubt it, given the recent poor runs of well-reviewed serious plays on Broadway. As with other Hare plays, a favorable review by me would probably have been a minority opinion once again:* The Daily News, *the New York Post,* The New Yorker, *and New York magazine all panned* The Secret Rapture.

*As it happened, I gave another favorable review in London to a subsequent Hare play—*Racing Demon. *It, too, was produced in New York with a replacement American cast—at Lincoln Center, after I'd left the drama critic's seat—and, like* Secret Rapture, *was greeted by a mixed critical response and mediocre attendance. It ran only six weeks.*

For those who are curious, here's what I had written in the Times *about the original production of* The Secret Rapture *in December 1988, in London:*

David Hare's new play, *The Secret Rapture,* alternates with *Single Spies* on the National's Lyttelton stage, and, as if to show off the virtues of repertory, picks up English history a generation later by examining the new Tory England that has risen in the old, discredited Establishment's wake. In a Thatcherite society marked, in Mr. Hare's view, by "loathsome materialism" and an "awful sanctification of greed," we watch the progress of two very different sisters who are brought together by the funeral of their father, an idealistic village bookseller. Isobel (Jill Baker) is a graphic artist who wants only to do "the right thing." Marion (Penelope Wilton) is a junior cabinet minister who ruthlessly promotes Mrs. Thatcher's Social Darwinist economic ideology. Their battle is joined when Marion's husband, a born-again Christian entrepreneur (Paul Shelley), generously capitalizes a takeover of Isobel's company that makes everyone wealthy at a high moral price.

The Secret Rapture will be seen in a new production directed by the author and starring Blair Brown as Isobel at the Public Theater next fall. What is clear from the largely excellent National production staged by Howard Davies (the director of *Les Liaisons Dangereuses*) is that Mr. Hare has produced at least the rough outlines of his most disturbing play since *Plenty.* Contrary to one's expectations, Isobel's saintliness is not a panacea for what ails a modern world, and Marion's self-righteousness is not without its saving graces. Neither woman can cope with their father's youngish, voluptuous, and alcoholic second wife (Clare Higgins), who proves to be a destroyer on an epic scale. Rather than settle for a rehearsal of didactic ideology, Mr. Hare addresses the larger, more troubling matter of how people's "out of control" passions refuse to conform to any rational utopian scheme of the left or the right.

As it stands, the contradictory currents in both sisters are sustained more by the moving, complex performances of Ms. Baker and Ms. Wilton than by the sudden reversals of character written into Act 2. The play's major male figure and crucial catalyst, Isobel's obsessive lover (Mick Ford), is underdeveloped, and that failing undermines the violent act of martyrdom that gives rise to Mr. Hare's title (an allusion to a nun's reunion with Christ in death). Yet much of the writing is an unsettling mixture of the witty and the sorrowful, as befits a play that doesn't pretend to have any more answers than its characters do. Whether unfulfilled by plenty or unfulfilled by opposition to it, both sisters of *The Secret Rapture* are in the end consumed by a memory, beautifully visualized in John Gunter's set design, of their father's vanished idyllic England. In that remembered past, they find a meager salvation that Mr. Hare, in a chilling closing line, calls "a perfect imitation of life."

THE THREEPENNY OPERA
LUNT-FONTANNE THEATRE, NOVEMBER 6, 1989

After emerging from the inert gray mass that is Broadway's *Three-penny Opera*, the first thing you want to do—assuming you don't drink—is run home and listen to any available recording of its score. The reason is not to revisit the evening's high points—there are none—but to make sure you are still among the living. How could these scathing songs, forged in the crucible of the century's apocalypse, sound as numbing as they do from the stage? One would have to be lobotomized not to respond to the blasted fusion of jazz, classicism, and political rage with which Kurt Weill and Bertolt Brecht first rocked Berlin in 1928.

As it happens, nearly any *Threepenny Opera* recording (Bobby Darin's possibly excepted) will resuscitate the spirit absent at the Lunt-Fontanne. One album of particularly relevant note is the 1985 anthology *Lost in the Stars,* in which contemporary musicians of many idioms take on the Weill canon. Among the recording's participants is Sting, Broadway's new Macheath. On record, he sings a monotonous "Ballad of Mack the Knife"—not his number now, but all too consistent with his current performance.

Yet a few cuts away on the same record, Tom Waits performs a nasty, pulsating "What Keeps Mankind Alive?"—a number Sting does puncture at the Lunt—and the incendiary Brecht-Weill spirit comes at you like a slap in the face. Mr. Waits even helps one understand the promising notion behind the mating of a serious pop icon and *The Threepenny Opera*: The raw aggression of Brecht can indeed overlap with the outlaw pose in contemporary rock.

But this idea, like the evening's other sincere intentions, is fumbled in the execution. A plausible actor in the films *Plenty* and *Stormy Monday,* Sting is a stiff onstage. He seems to hope that a large cane and a smug, insistent pout will somehow convey the menace of a character who is a murderer, rapist, thief, and arsonist—Brecht's idea of a ruthless capitalist. Not that the star's Macheath should be put on the gallows as the scapegoat for all the production's ills. So tepid is the level of performance throughout the company that one must wonder if another director might have coaxed more out of Sting and everyone else.

The director at hand is John Dexter, whose past forays into epic theater (*M. Butterfly*) and Brecht-Weill (the Metropolitan Opera's *Mahagonny*) would seem to make him ideal for *The Threepenny Opera*. Like

Richard Foreman, who staged the blistering 1976 revival with Raul Julia, he would rather be faithful to original Brechtian practice than to the 1954 Marc Blitzstein *Threepenny* adaptation that ran Off Broadway for seven years.

Mr. Dexter uses an unbowdlerized (if not uncut) translation by Michael Feingold that restores Brecht's scatology and the complete, correctly ordered score. Jocelyn Herbert's scenic rendition of lowlife Victorian London—a few scraps of wood that might have been left out in the rain—leaves acres of room to expose the stage's machinery. The lighting is harsh and white, the projected scene titles all in place. Far from trying to tart up *The Threepenny Opera* for Broadway, Mr. Dexter makes the show look so Spartan that by contrast *Our Town* might seem decadent.

Even so, the outward faithfulness to Brechtian alienation does not pay off, because the trappings are never harnessed to the theatrical energy that might animate Brecht's lacerating view of a bourgeois hell in which hypocrisy is the daily bread. The scalding style and passion required in the acting and music are absent. There's no visual focus to the staging, no Hogarthian imaginative verve to enliven the drab palette of Ms. Herbert's sets and costumes. Foolproof sequences pass without the bite of black humor: the Peachums' entrepreneurial display of the five pitiful beggars' costumes their employees use for cadging money from the guilty rich; Macheath and Polly's wedding amid posh stolen furnishings; the tango reunion of Macheath and the prostitute Jenny. Julius Rudel's onstage band, sitting on top of the squat and cluttered playing area, renders the familiar orchestrations with a lassitude more appropriate to a hotel-lobby tea service than a Weimar cabaret.

It says much about this production that the neighboring *Sweeney Todd,* a musical influenced by Weill and Brecht that shares the setting of *The Threepenny Opera* but not its rigorous banishment of sentimentality, comes across as a more vitriolic assault on capitalism's inequities. Lacking any clear line of attack or variations in pace, Mr. Dexter's staging often seems to leave his cast milling about aimlessly waiting for the next cue.

One never has the sense of a company unified in its effort to put across a show and its acidic ideology. Each performer occupies a different, yet equally inappropriate, theatrical universe, from Kim Criswell's campy Lucy to Larry Marshall's deadly earnest Tiger Brown to Suzanne Douglas's saccharine Jenny, who elocutes the nihilistic "Solomon Song" as if she were instructing the audience in "Getting to Know You."

At least some drama is provided by the predicament of Nancy Ringham, an understudy abruptly asked to fill in for Maureen McGovern, whose vocal ailments required her to vacate the role of Polly for several weeks. But here, as when she was similarly elevated to stardom on the opening-night eve of the last Rex Harrison revival of *My Fair Lady*, Ms. Ringham proves simply a competent ingenue.

Not that a Stratas or a Lenya might have made a difference. The company's experienced Brecht-Weill hands, Alvin Epstein and Georgia Brown as the Peachums, seem as tired and mechanical as the others, as if this *Threepenny* had been running for seven years. (They might at least bother to look at each other.) Though Ethyl Eichelberger's bald head and wicked scowl do make the Ballad Singer an arresting George Grosz caricature, he, too, wears out his early welcome by pursuing his shtick to unchecked, self-indulgent excess in the hours to come.

It is when Mr. Eichelberger first greets the audience that Mr. Dexter's production makes its one stab at a statement: He announces that we are to see a "new American version" of the piece "played by the poorest of the poor for an audience of their own." In the English-accented staging that follows, this conceit is more or less forgotten until a post-curtain-call coda, in which chorus members, apparently representing the homeless of New York, bed down for the night in cardboard boxes.

These "homeless" look more like hippies from *Hair* than the battered souls visible just outside the theater; they might well have received their ersatz beggars' costumes from the hypocritical Peachums. And who exactly are the hypocrites here? The creators of this *Threepenny Opera* aren't helping the poor by dragging them on clownishly to provide a boffo finale to a torpid show; like the Peachums, they are merely exploiting the poor to serve their own commercial enterprise. Not for the first time does Brecht get the last—and, in this production, the only—laugh.

THE PRINCE OF CENTRAL PARK

BELASCO THEATRE, NOVEMBER 10, 1989

The Prince of Central Park, the new musical at the Belasco, is a numbing evening of such guileless amateurism that it will probably have a future as a Harvard Business School case study, whatever its fate in the annals of drama. Even modest Broadway shows like this cost more money than the gross national product of some third-world nations. People put up this money. As long as there are people as gullible as the sponsors of *The Prince of Central Park*, the theater need never fear for its survival.

The author of the book is Evan H. Rhodes, whose novel of the same title also served as the basis for a Ruth Gordon made-for-television movie. He tells the *Harold and Maude*–ish story of Jay-Jay (Richard H. Blake), a twelve-year-old foster-home runaway who lives by his wits in a tree house in Central Park until he encounters Margie Miller (Jo Anne Worley), a jogger of late middle-age who has just lost her husband to a younger woman and her adult daughter to the career track.

Since Jay-Jay and Margie must meet cute—through chalk messages left on a pristine park bench—Act 1 is all exposition. In Act 2, Jay-Jay and Margie bravely overcome outmoded legal obstacles and moral attitudes to get married. They adopt five children, two of whom become the first sibling astronauts and together head a successful manned space mission to Pluto.

Actually, I'm lying. Something else entirely happens in Act 2. But I assure you that my version is more interesting.

The soft rock score, by Don Sebesky, is insistently cheery even when muggers are singing about ripping off little old ladies; the tunes don't so much linger in the mind as pound it senseless. Though in one number ("Zap") Gloria Nissenson's lyrics make nearly as much use of a four-letter synonym for excrement as does *The Threepenny Opera,* her more typical phrases deal with "turning a new leaf," "setting myself free," "growing my dreams," and discovering that "here's where I belong."

Tony Tanner's choreography doesn't just resemble aerobics. It is aerobics.

And the jokes? On her first entrance, Ms. Worley cups both breasts and says, "Gravity, gravity, what did I ever do to you?" Shortly after that she wishes to a star that her estranged husband's penis will "fall off in bed tonight." And to think that family entertainment had begun to appear a lost cause in the American musical.

The performances are nothing if not strenuous. The young Mr. Blake belts out every song mechanically and interchangeably, seeming less like a refugee of the streets than an aging Mouseketeer. Wearing a series of colored jogger headbands and novelty T-shirts, Ms. Worley plunges through the show like a Mack truck, mowing down everything before her with a personality undiminished in bulk or pitch since the halcyon days of *Laugh-In*. Among the supporting players, a dancer named Alice Yearsley proves to be the production's entire store of grace and style. Though her roles are several and small, she never fails to carve out her own delicate space from the crass spectacle around her.

Much of that spectacle has to do with celebrating the city of New York. This would be swell if one actually believed that anyone connected with *The Prince of Central Park* had spent much time in the city lately. (The show originated in south Florida, and there are a few gratuitous but knowing jokes about "retirement villages.") Among the Manhattanites on stage are a friendly park ranger out of a Smokey the Bear promotional campaign, an adorably cuckoo bag lady, and, for a dash of malevolence, a gang of well-scrubbed crack dealers whose ethnic makeup is so demographically balanced that they might have first convened at the United Nations. But the biggest unintentional laugh for a New York audience arrives when Ms. Worley ventures into Bloomingdale's and is immediately welcomed by a kindly silver-haired saleswoman who offers her complete undivided attention.

The Prince of Central Park also has a serious obsession with Tavern on the Green, whose name is dragged into nearly every scene before and after serving as a setting for a dance number. Given the vehicle for these insistent plugs, it's hard to know whether the restaurant should consider itself the beneficiary of free advertising or the victim of a dissatisfied customer's personal vendetta.

≡ *Variety, the trade publication that had once been famous for its skepticism about Broadway but in these lean years was the industry's principal apologist, complained of this review that "Rich tricked readers by supplying his own, ostensibly superior, libretto for the show."*

Variety notwithstanding, The Prince of Central Park was laughed off by all the critics and disappeared quickly, but not before its producer, Abe Hirschfeld, and some of his employees got embroiled in business disputes that would prove to be typical of Hirschfeld's strange career in the New York spotlight. A parking-lot magnate and sometime deputy mayor of Miami Beach, Hirschfeld soon made a further name for himself by running for various state and city offices in New York at the cost of millions, by briefly owning and nearly destroying the New York Post, and by battling numerous counts of tax fraud. In retrospect, The Prince of Central Park may have been one of the finer achievements of his career.

GRAND HOTEL
Martin Beck Theatre, November 13, 1989

The director and choreographer Tommy Tune may have the most extravagant imagination in the American musical theater right now, and there isn't a moment, or a square inch of stage space, that escapes its reach in *Grand Hotel*. The musical at the Martin Beck Theatre is an uninterrupted two hours of continuous movement, all dedicated to creating the tumultuous atmosphere of the setting: an opulent way station at a distant crossroads of history in Berlin—that of 1928. Think of a three-dimensional collage—or a giant Joseph Cornell box two tall stories high—filled with the smoky light, faded gilt fixtures, dirty secrets, lost mementos, and ghostly people of its time and place. Then imagine someone shaking the whole thing up as if waves were tossing around the *Titanic*. That's Mr. Tune's *Grand Hotel*.

Is that enough to make a musical? Not really, as it happens, but *Grand Hotel* should satisfy those with a boundless appetite for showmanship untethered to content. Visual craftsmanship doesn't get much more accomplished than this on Broadway. In a departure from the current fashion in theatrical spectaculars, Mr. Tune creates a world on stage without resorting to rococo naturalism or substituting money for creativity. Tony Walton's stunning set, in which an orchestra occupies the lofty second tier, is but a deep, dilapidated shell in which dreamy abstract imagery (strings of pearls floating inside transparent structural pillars) stands in for a literal hotel floor plan. Santo Loquasto's costumes and Jules Fisher's lighting—equally brilliant evocations of expressionism—don't try to wow the audience with Technicolor eruptions but instead hold to a dark crimson-to-sepia palette that suggests the vanished luxury pictured on frayed antique postcards and the fever dreams of a world on the brink of depression and war.

Mr. Tune's restless manipulation of these resources is often inspired. In the opening number—a directorial tour de force to match the equivalent prologue, "Wilkommen," in Harold Prince's Weimar Berlin musical *Cabaret*—phalanxes of performers crisscross the stage in ever-changing configurations, the characters individually singing of their lots, until finally the audience sees the panorama of lives, upstairs and down, intersecting throughout the vast hotel.

Though the effect is that of cinematic crosscutting, there's never an intrusion of scenic machinery to yank the characters about. *Grand Hotel* finds its kaleidoscopic activity and churning pace in the constant rearrangement of the dozens of straight-backed chairs that are the set's dominant furnishing, or in the sudden appearance of a quartet of desperate phone callers in a cacophonous downstage tableau, or in the hallucinatory fragments of period dance steps along the shadowy periphery of main events. As in Mr. Tune's *Nine*, the large cast is omnipresent and usually on the run. So dense is the atmosphere that finally it can be stilled only by eradication—an effect Mr. Tune accomplishes in the coup de théâtre that brings the evening to a close.

Even then, one remains haunted by this show's imagery. One does, however, forget nearly everything else. *Grand Hotel* never delivers those other, conventional elements one might want in a musical—attractive songs, characters to care about, an exciting cast. Nor does it work up the good cry achieved by the all-star 1932 MGM film. This *Grand Hotel* impresses the audience without engaging it, and, when the titillating dramatic promises of the opening sequence lead nowhere, monotony and impatience set in. One would have to go back past *Nine* to Michael Bennett's *Ballroom* to find a Broadway musical with so large a discrepancy between the mediocre quality of the material and the flair of its presentation.

The first instinct might be to blame the book, which in this case is not an adaptation of the Hollywood *Grand Hotel*, but of the Vicki Baum novel that was its source. Yet the author, Luther Davis, and the unbilled book doctor, Peter Stone, have done an efficient, clever job of compressing a complicated narrative into a scenario that recalls the movie's solid structure while altering some of its details. What's missing is the flesh that, in a musical, must be filled in by songs and performances.

Mr. Tune is presumably responsible for the evening's central failing, the miscasting of the doomed lovers at its center. Liliane Montevecchi, as a "dying swan" of a ballerina facing the end of her career, is unconvincing in or out of a tutu as a "great artist" of transparent vulnerability; her thin physique and Russian character name do not camouflage the temperament of a brassy French cabaret chanteuse. While David Carroll, as a count reduced to cat burglary, has a beautiful voice, his silver cigarette case seems more aristocratic and Continental than its owner. One doesn't have to make invidious comparisons to Greta Garbo and John Barrymore to see that the romantic and sexual chemistry between their stage heirs is nil.

Most of the other principals are only adequate: Jane Krakowski as a secretary who fantasizes about sleeping her way to Hollywood stardom, Timothy Jerome as a business tycoon in crisis, John Wylie as a bitter World War I veteran. As Ms. Montevecchi's devoted confidante, Karen Akers could pass as a dark-haired impersonator of Carol Channing's Lorelei Lee—with height, kewpie-doll makeup, and bangs to match. But when Ms. Akers sings it's as if Lorelei Lee were on Quaaludes: Taking her catch-in-the-throat vocal style to a fetishistic extreme, Ms. Akers slurs every lyric into unintelligibility. Were she not dressed as a man, even the love she feels for the ballerina would dare not speak its name.

Perhaps a stronger score would have buoyed the acting. One can see what might have been when Michael Jeter, as the dying clerk Otto Kringelein on a last fling, is given a musical number that expresses a character's emotion. Celebrating his liberation from clerkdom into high living by stepping out, Mr. Jeter lets loose like a human top gyrating out of control—literally breaking out of his past into a new existence. Fine as the performer is, it is because a song and choreography for once dramatize a character dynamically that this number is touching as the evening's others are not.

Though emphatically arranged (by Peter Matz and Wally Harper) and conducted (by Jack Lee), the rest of the score leaves the characters stranded in banalities. The only catchy melody is a cabaret number, "le jazz hot" style, for a dance team (David Jackson and Danny Strayhorn), and it doesn't build, even choreographically, as similar turns did in Mr. Tune's *My One and Only*. While that number is by Robert Wright and George Forrest (*Kismet*), many others are by Maury Yeston (*Nine*). Mr. Yeston could not resist writing a solo for Ms. Montevecchi titled "Bonjour Amour," and his big love ballad may give Andrew Lloyd Webber his first opportunity to accuse another songwriter of being derivative.

Mr. Tune also has his odd derivative moments. When he uses a pair of ballroom bolero dancers as metaphors for love and death or a chorus of advancing scullery workers to symbolize proletarian rage, he skirts the conceits of the Prince stagings of *Follies* and *Sweeney Todd*. Like the book's allusions to growing anti-Semitism or ponderous stabs at moralizing ("We're all dying, Otto"), such pretentious themes seem out of place in Mr. Tune's show and hardly substitute for the more basic ingredients that are missing. But even such lapses fail to obscure the director's own original gifts. Mr. Tune has built the grandest hotel imaginable in *Grand Hotel*. It would be a happier occasion if so many of its rooms weren't vacant.

GYPSY
ST. JAMES THEATRE, NOVEMBER 17, 1989

If someone asked me to name the best Broadway musical, I'd gladly equivocate on any side of a debate embracing *Guys and Dolls, My Fair Lady, Carousel, Porgy and Bess,* and—well, you know the rest. But I've always had only one choice in the category of favorite musical. It is *Gypsy,* and as I sat at its scorching new revival starring Tyne Daly, once again swept up in its goosebump-raising torrents of laughter and tears, I realized why, if anything, this thirty-year-old show actually keeps improving with age.

Gypsy may be the only great Broadway musical that follows its audience through life's rough familial passages. A wrenching fable about a tyrannical stage mother and the daughters she both champions and cripples—yet also a showcase for one classic Jule Styne–Stephen Sondheim song and rousing Jerome Robbins vaudeville routine after another—*Gypsy* is nothing if not Broadway's own brassy, unlikely answer to *King Lear*. It speaks to you one way when you are a child, then chases after you to say something else when you've grown up.

Like *Lear,* it cannot be done without a powerhouse performance in its marathon parental role. Ms. Daly, a television actress who might seem inappropriate to the task, follows Angela Lansbury in proving that not even Ethel Merman can own a character forever. Ms. Daly is not Merman, and she is not Ms. Lansbury. Her vocal expressiveness and attack have their limits (most noticeably in "Mr. Goldstone"), and warmth is pointedly not her forté. But this fiercely committed actress tears into— at times claws into—Mama Rose, that "pioneer woman without a frontier," with a vengeance that exposes the darkness at the heart of *Gypsy* as it hasn't been since Merman.

"Why did I do it? What did it get me?" Ms. Daly shouts as she accelerates into her final number, an aria of nervous breakdown titled "Rose's Turn." Rose is standing on an empty stage, at last deserted by everyone: June, the prized daughter she tried and failed to make into a star; Louise, the unfavored daughter who became Gypsy Rose Lee, queen of burlesque, in spite of years of maternal neglect; Herbie, the gentle agent who wanted only to become Rose's fourth husband.

Why did Rose pursue her dream? Why did she push everyone so hard that she drove them all away? Ms. Daly doesn't soften the news that Rose did it for herself. "Just wanted to be noticed," she says a little later. And as Ms. Daly stands there, crying her lungs out, demanding that a phantom audience give her a turn of her own in the spotlight—"Everything's coming up roses this time for me!"—one is confronted by a plea for recognition and love so raw and naked that Rose becomes a child again herself, begging as Louise and June once had for "Momma."

Ms. Daly's impressive turn reflects a staging that, as directed by Arthur Laurents, the author of the musical's book, is intent on exposing the primal family drama that always resides just beneath the bygone vaudeville veneer. Not that Mr. Laurents stints on that colorful surface. With the assistance of Bonnie Walker, who reproduced Mr. Robbins's choreography, and the designers Kenneth Foy (scenery) and Theoni V. Aldredge (costumes), he turns the apt St. James Theatre into a credible stop on the battered two-a-day road that reaches its dead end in burlesque during the era of talkies and the Depression. From the first rendition of "Let Me Entertain You," led by Christen Tassin's truly hilarious young Baby June, to that recurrent number's last reprise, in which Crista Moore, as the adult Louise, strips her way to the top at Minsky's, Mr. Laurents is in complete command of his show's running parodistic commentary on a vanished pop-culture past.

The thrills really begin with the overture, which, as orchestrated by Sid Ramin and Robert Ginzler, is an invitation to showbiz exhilaration second to none and is played accordingly by Eric Stern's roaring pit band. Mr. Laurents and the three actresses he cast as burned-out strippers (Barbara Erwin, Jana Robbins, Anna McNeely) also pull off the tougher job of making "You Gotta Have a Gimmick" funny and fresh all over again, despite its months of repetition in the neighboring *Jerome Robbins' Broadway*. But even in the glitzier numbers, Mr. Laurents burrows into the emotional undertow beneath the turn. When the delightful Robert Lambert—as a hayseed chorus boy with cocky dreams of glory—shows Louise his fantasy dance-team act, "All I Need Is the Girl," it is heartbreaking to watch the forlorn Ms. Moore act out her own doomed romantic fantasy in the shadows of an alleyway stage door.

In the meatiest dramatic numbers, Mr. Laurents pays Mr. Styne and Mr. Sondheim the compliment of reminding an audience that songs long assimilated into Broadway lore have a depth of character extending far beyond their unforgettable melodies and effortless verbal wit. "If Momma Was Married"—a comic lament for the grown-up Louise and June (Tracy Venner)—is not only two children's wish for a father but also a pathetic revelation of the sole common bond the very different siblings have enjoyed in their fractured, isolated childhoods. More harrowing still is "Everything's Coming Up Roses," the Act 1 railroad-platform finale in which Rose finally must switch her allegiance from the vanished June to the ugly-duckling Louise. As Ms. Daly approaches the lyric "We can do it / Momma is gonna see to it," she hugs the cowering daughter only to toss her instantly and violently aside.

Mr. Styne and Mr. Sondheim are both giants on their own, but in this onetime collaboration they brought out something in each other's talent that cannot quite be found in their extraordinary separate careers. If there's no song as angry as "Some People" in the rest of the Styne canon, neither is there one quite as fragile and vulnerable as "Little Lamb" in the rest of Mr. Sondheim's.

Mr. Laurents's book carries its own weight. In this production, one of the most moving moments occurs when Jonathan Hadary, giving his most abundantly shaded performance as the warm but weak Herbie, finally summons up the guts to walk out on Rose. When Mr. Hadary leaves Ms. Daly behind in a shabby burlesque dressing room, he does so with the weariness of Willy Loman but with the serenity of a man who has finally found himself after a lifetime of searching.

Though much about this staging will be familiar to those who saw the 1974 Lansbury revival, also directed by Mr. Laurents, there is no question that the new Rose radically alters the tone of the result. In a way, it works for *Gypsy* that Ms. Daly is not a glamorous, sexy, or sympathetic star—that she could not care less if anyone likes her or not. Rose is a monster, after all, and Ms. Daly is true to the fundamental statement of the piece, which is not a pleasant one.

It's the title character, not Rose, that *Gypsy* asks the audience to root for, and the lovely Ms. Moore, who steadily blossoms from a forgotten child to a self-possessed star, makes it easy to do so. By keeping both mother and daughter in tight and unsentimental focus, the entire production reveals why a musical that might seem so parochially about the small world of show business makes its red-hot connection with the real world beyond. There's never any doubt that the much-married Rose and her lonely, bruised children are driven to perform before an audience, to be gypsies, because that's their only hope of being noticed—of getting the love and acceptance they have been denied in life.

And might not the audience have its own deep needs in that respect? If *Gypsy* is the musical most beloved by theater fanatics, that may be because it forces those on both sides of the footlights to remember exactly why they turned to the theater as a home away from home.

CITY OF ANGELS
VIRGINIA THEATRE, DECEMBER 12, 1989

There's nothing novel about showstopping songs and performances in Broadway musicals, but how long has it been since a musical was brought to a halt by riotous jokes? If you ask me, one would have to travel back to the 1960s—to *Bye Bye Birdie, A Funny Thing Happened on the Way to the Forum, How to Succeed in Business Without Really Trying,* and *Little Me*—to find a musical as flat-out funny as *City of Angels,* the new show about old Hollywood that arrived last night at the Virginia Theatre.

This is an evening in which even a throwaway wisecrack spreads laughter like wildfire through the house, until finally the roars from the balcony merge with those from the orchestra and the pandemonium takes on a life of its own. Only the fear of missing the next gag quiets the audience down. To make matters sweeter, the jokes sometimes subside just long enough to permit a showstopping song or performance or two to make their own ruckus at center stage.

Since the musical's principal creators are the writer Larry Gelbart and the composer Cy Coleman—pros who worked separately on *Forum* and *Little Me* early in their careers—the exhilarating result cannot really be called a surprise. Yet Mr. Gelbart and Mr. Coleman, invigorated with the try-anything brio of first-time collaborators half their age, bring the audience one unexpected twist after another. Only the territory of *City of Angels* is familiar: the late 1940s Hollywood romanticized in hard-boiled detective fiction and ruled by tyrannical studio moguls who seemed to give nearly every movie a title like *Three Guys Named Joe.*

To take comic possession of the entire sprawling cultural landscape— to mock not just the period's movies but also the men behind the movies—Mr. Gelbart stages a two-pronged satirical attack. His hero, Stine (Gregg Edelman), is a novelist trying against considerable odds to turn his own book, *City of Angels,* into a screenplay that will not be an embarrassing sellout. But as Mr. Gelbart tracks Stine's travails in the film industry—where the "envy is so thick you can cut it with a knife lodged in every other back"—he also presents the hard-knock adventures of Stone, the Philip Marlowe–Sam Spade–like private eye of Stine's screenplay in progress and, in James Naughton's wonderfully wry performance, a comic shamus who is the stuff that dreams are made of.

There is no end to the cleverness with which the creators of *City of Angels* carry out their stunt of double vision, starting with a twin cast list (a Hollywood Cast and a Movie Cast) in the *Playbill.* Robin Wagner's highly imaginative set design—maybe the most eloquent argument yet against colorizing old movies—uses the lush black-and-white of a pristine Warner Bros. print for the Stone sequences and candied Technicolor for Stine's off-camera adventures. Because the Stine and Stone narratives have their ironic parallels—fiction's thugs and temptresses often resemble Hollywood's movers and shakers—the *City of Angels* actors frequently play dual roles, shifting continually between color and black-and-white settings and characters. In one spectacular turn that rocks the second act, the winning Randy Graff, as a loyal secretary to both Stone and Stine, leaps across the color barrier to belt out her blues as the other woman in two male lives.

Such tricks are brilliantly abetted not just by Mr. Wagner and his fellow designers Florence Klotz and Paul Gallo but also by the director Michael Blakemore, who juggles the farcical collisions between reality and soundstage as deftly as he did the on- and offstage shenanigans of *Noises Off*. With occasional injections of stock period film, *City of Angels* re-creates the swirling flashbacks, portentous tracking shots, and swift dissolves of movies like *The Maltese Falcon* and *The Big Sleep* even as it wallows in the kitschy glamour of nouveau-riche Bel Air mansions where the conversation is "never at a loss for numbers."

Mr. Gelbart's jokes come in their own variety of colors. As in his screenplay for *Movie Movie,* he is a master at parodying vintage film genres—in this case finding remarkably fresh ways to skewer the sardonic voice-over narration, tough-guy talk, and heavy-breathing imagery ("It's as though I was hit by a wrecking ball wearing a pinky ring") of the Chandler-Hammett film noir. But the funniest lines in *City of Angels* may well be those that assault the movie business—as personified by Buddy Fidler (René Auberjonois), an egomaniacal producer and director at Master Pictures, the same fictional studio that Mr. Gelbart accused of money-laundering in his Iran-Contra satire, *Mastergate*.

There are no angels in this show's Hollywood. Next to Fidler's self-serving Goldwynisms—"You can tell a writer every time: words, words, words!" he complains—the mixed metaphors of Stone's narration and the obfuscating double talk of the *Mastergate* politicians almost make sense. In Mr. Auberjonois's gleefully smarmy performance, Fidler congratulates himself on his philanthropic largess while destroying Stine's script in the interests of commerce or blacklist-era political cowardice. As he revises, the rewrites are carried out in the black-and-white flesh on stage, complete with mimed rewinding of the footage bound for the cutting-room floor. "You're Nothing Without Me" goes the title of the high-flying duet for Stine and Stone, but, in Mr. Gelbart's jaundiced view, the writer and his fictional alter ego are both nothing next to the greedy bully with casting approval, screenplay-credit envy, and final cut.

As the jokes leaven the book's rage until the bitter final number, so does Mr. Coleman's score—a delirious celebration of jazz and pop styles sumptuously orchestrated by Billy Byers and blared out by a swinging pit band led by Gordon Lowry Harrell. Mr. Coleman uses a scat-singing vocal quartet reminiscent of the Modernaires as a roving chorus; he freely mixes bebop with wild Count Basie blasts, sentimental radio crooning (well done by Scott Waara), and smoky soundtrack music reminiscent of David Raksin's score for *Laura*. The effect is like listening to *Your Hit Parade* of 1946, except that the composer's own Broadway personality remakes the past in his own effervescent, melodic style.

Though the young and talented lyricist David Zippel keeps up with Mr. Coleman's often intricate music, he only occasionally catches up with Mr. Gelbart's endlessly witty wordplay. His biggest success is Ms. Graff's song "You Can Always Count on Me," which recalls the sophisticated sass of the female solos Mr. Coleman once wrote with the lyricists Carolyn Leigh and Dorothy Fields. By contrast, Mr. Zippel's double-entendre duet for Stone and his femme-fatale client (Dee Hoty) is collegiate, and Mr. Auberjonois's big Act 1 solo isn't as biting about Hollywood as the dialogue surrounding it.

For all that's right about *City of Angels,* one must also question the casting of Mr. Edelman, a powerful singer whose affable boyishness seems inappropriate and anachronistic for a hard-edged forties novelist like Stine. It's hard to believe he could have created a character as worldly as Mr. Naughton's Stone, a Bogart incarnation that, for once, is not an impersonation. The show could also use much more dancing, a less arbitrarily plotted and more musical second act, and a livelier heroine than the lost love (for Stone) and temporarily lost wife (for Stine) decently played by Kay McClelland.

In the large supporting cast, special attention must be paid—and will be, since she first appears wearing only a sheet—to Rachel York, who sings a torrid seduction number ("Lost and Found") in Act 1 before serving as a self-promoting starlet in Act 2. As Stone says in somber voice-over when describing another Hollywood siren, "Only the floor kept her legs from going on forever." With lines like that, I, for one, would have been happy if *City of Angels* had gone on just as long.

≡ *I later learned that this show had been marked as a sure failure by virtually everyone in the New York theater. The night I reviewed it the theater was so cold, due to a heating failure, that I watched it bundled up in my winter coat. It just goes to show that good theater can warm and transport an audience even if it's feeling blue—literally so in this instance.*

TRU

BOOTH THEATRE, DECEMBER 15, 1989

When the curtain rises on the bloated, jowly bubble of flesh that is the title character of *Tru,* Jay Presson Allen's monodrama about Truman Capote, a sentimental theatergoer is not so much startled by the resurrection of Capote, who died in 1984, as shocked by the obliteration of Robert Morse, last seen on Broadway in the mid-1970s. Buried somewhere in that skin-colored tub of Jell-O—the work of makeup man Kevin Haney, whose credits include the movies *Altered States* and *Wolfen*—is the sprite whose grin of impetuous youth charmed a nation in *How to Succeed in Business Without Really Trying* a good quarter-century ago.

Somewhere, but where? As the present Mr. Morse warms to his task at the Booth, dangling his wrists and slurring his words while puttering about the designer David Mitchell's handsome replica of Capote's final home at United Nations Plaza, it's hard to find the performer one remembers. With his mad shopping-bag woman's cackle and darting lounge lizard's tongue, Mr. Morse so eerily simulates the public Capote of the pathetic waning years that he could be a Capote robot, an Audio Animatronic figure in a macabre theme park, Xenonland perhaps, envisioned by Andy Warhol.

As Tru rambles on, however, the actor inside the flab does eventually emerge, and engagingly so. Mr. Morse can still look at an audience as if it were a mirror reflecting his own smiling face back at him. The mischievous twinkle in his eyes is as bright as ever; the rasp in his throat still makes him sound not just like Capote but also like the director Harold Prince (whom he once spoofed in the musical *Say, Darling*). And when, late in Act 2, Tru takes to tapping and strutting to a Louis Armstrong recording of "The Sunny Side of the Street," Mr. Morse kicks a loose-limbed leg as high and friskily as he did when joining Bob Fosse's hoedown for the "Brotherhood of Man" finale in *How to Succeed.*

By then one is glad to have met up with this actor again, is impressed by his command of his technique and his audience, and is moved by the courage that has allowed him to return to a Broadway stage in so unlikely a vehicle. But even then, his two-hour solo flight of celebrity impersonation makes for a very weird night out.

A reunion with Capote—or at least Mrs. Allen's representation of him—may not be everyone's idea of theater. Intentionally or not, *Tru* is a creep show: a hybrid of necrophilia and tame fan-magazine journalism that doesn't so much rekindle fascination with a troubled writer as reawaken the willies prompted by those disoriented talk-show appearances (remember *The Stanley Siegel Show?*) that were the desperate final act of his career.

Mrs. Allen sets her discursive monologue in the nights before Christmas 1975, when Tru is reeling from the social ostracism that followed *Esquire* magazine's publication of "La Côte Basque, 1965," the gossipy excerpt from his never-to-be-finished roman à clef, *Answered Prayers.* Tru can no longer get his dearest friends, Babe (Paley) and Slim (Keith), on his heavily trafficked two-line speakerphone and instead must tag along with Ava Gardner to Quo Vadis. His last lover is nowhere in sight. Pills, vodka, cocaine, and chocolate truffles all tempt him to oblivion.

There is, heaven knows, a prospective drama here. Why did the author of such precocious fiction as *Other Voices, Other Rooms* and such adventurous new journalism as *In Cold Blood* betray his muse for the silly full-time job of being famous? Why did he turn on the super rich after two decades as their lap dog? Why did *Answered Prayers* mortally offend the *Women's Wear Daily* crowd? Speculative answers exist—most prominently in Gerald Clarke's biography *Capote*—but Mrs. Allen rarely explores them.

Tru's defense of *Answered Prayers*—spunky credos about the outlaw role of the writer—is too retroactive and pat to explain his literary death wish. His asides about mortality and suicide are not compelling enough to explain away his self-destruction. Even factual information essential to understanding Capote's current plight is missing, including any description of the actual contents of *Answered Prayers*.

While Tru announces that everyone loves stories that tell "something horrendous about someone impeccable," Mrs. Allen never does dish much dirt. Perhaps she, unlike Capote, is afraid to offend the living. Nothing truly bitchy is said about the many famous names titillatingly dropped in *Tru;* some major Capote antagonists (most conspicuously Gore Vidal) are not mentioned at all.

Nor does the audience get the measure of the man Capote used to be. It's typical of *Tru* that it offers references to his Christmas shopping at Tiffany's but no recollections about *Breakfast at Tiffany's*. A few childhood memories are recounted—complete with a hokey echo-chamber voice from the past—and, for schematic contrast with his grim 1975 holiday season, Capote's memoir *A Christmas Memory* is recited in excerpt. Yet Mrs. Allen's script is unable to evoke the ghost of the driving, eccentric writer who was still flourishing as late as when Mr. Morse was in *How to Succeed*.

In place of a life portrait with depth, *Tru* settles for its windup Mme. Tussaud's caricature of the wrecked 1975 model Capote. This Tru is sporadically funny—if one shares Ms. Allen's taste for the campiest of anecdotes and one-liners—and rarely boring. But since the soul of the younger Capote doesn't shine through as Mr. Morse's youthful spirit does, the potentially touching drama of decay is lost. The complex, possibly tragic figure of a wasted artist is replaced by a maudlin, some might say antediluvian, stereotype of *Boys in the Band* vintage: the alcoholic moneyed homosexual who, having lost his youth and beauty, is left all alone with his telephone and record collection in his penthouse on Christmas Eve.

A few manufactured tears notwithstanding, the evening's histrionic level is so uniform that any half-hour of *Tru* will probably be enough for most onlookers. True Tru fanatics, of course, will devour it all. Everyone will agree that the star's energy never flags. While Mr. Morse may not succeed in drawing the audience to Truman Capote, he does leave one eager to see a born-again actor inhabit other voices, other rooms.

THE MERCHANT OF VENICE
46TH STREET THEATRE, DECEMBER 20, 1989

Contrary to Broadway gospel, Dustin Hoffman does not have star billing in the new *Merchant of Venice* at the 46th Street Theatre. That honor is reserved instead for the Peter Hall Company—or, to put a finer point on it, for Peter Hall. Once you've seen the production, in many ways an unexpected one, you'll understand that Mr. Hall isn't being pretentious and that Mr. Hoffman hasn't suddenly been struck by false modesty. This really is the director's *Merchant*—at times Shakespeare's, too—and Mr. Hoffman plays a supporting role.

It's the modern practice that Shylock dominate any version of *Merchant,* whatever the interpretation, despite the fact that he appears in only five of twenty scenes. Mr. Hoffman's Shylock—meticulous, restlessly intelligent, emotionally and physically lightweight—does not. His performance is a character actor's polished gem rather than a tragedian's stab at the jugular; it is reminiscent of his fine work in *Death of a Salesman,* in which the outsize Willy Loman forged by Lee J. Cobb was whittled down to the humble proportions of a schlemiel. Whether Shakespeare's moneylender can weather the reduction of scale as well as Arthur Miller's salesman did is another question.

Wearing a beard, a ponytail, a long gabardine, a yarmulke, and sometimes a hat emblazoned with a yellow star, Mr. Hoffman presents a proud but long-suffering Jew who has almost become inured to the commonplace bigotry of the Christians around him. When the Venetians spit in his face, as they literally and frequently do in Mr. Hall's staging, Mr. Hoffman thinly masks his rage with a fixed, stoic grin. Shylock knows his gentile antagonists are bullies, but like the brilliant student trying to protect himself in a classroom of hoodlums, he makes deals to survive and doesn't advertise his intelligence. Only when driven to revenge does he fully reveal the sharp wit and sharper knife with which he intends to extract his pound of flesh.

Although Mr. Hoffman has not lost the strange accent (a Bronxish rasp) that, like Vanessa Redgrave's in *Orpheus Descending,* is apparently de rigueur for stars in a Hall production, his performance is less tentative than it was early in his London run last summer. Mr. Hoffman is always working, always thinking, always interesting to observe.

Leave it to this actor to make neurotic hay of Shylock's clipped repetitions—the punctuating use of the word "well" through his early lines and the incantatory rhetorical obsession with the size and span of his loan to Antonio (3,000 ducats, three months). Mr. Hoffman's loving but suffocating farewell to Jessica, the daughter who will soon desert him, has the paternal possessiveness of a melancholy Tevye, and his rendition of the "Hath not a Jew eyes?" soliloquy is dignified and searching, more Talmud than Old Testament.

But one wants more, and the role's deep notes of blind, distorting rage and vengeance are never sounded. Like it or not, Shylock in the end becomes a man driven to collect a debt in blood—whether because he is an anti-Semitic caricature or because, as Mr. Hall properly chooses to stress, his revenge has been provoked by the vicious anti-Semites of Venice. Yet Mr. Hoffman does not rise to the occasion. In his one cheap touch, the actor nudges the audience to milk a laugh in the trial scene—with a Henny Youngman shrug on "These be the Christian husbands!"—and kills any chance that his Shylock will tap into the dark passions of one of the most dramatic scenes in the canon. Even without the lapse into stand-up shtick, Mr. Hoffman looks unprepared to take the dangerous leap of risking an audience's revulsion or condemnation.

The avoidance of risk is uncharacteristic of this imaginative actor; it's the rare Hoffman performance that fails to arouse violent debates pro and con, but this may be one of them. The same may be true of Mr. Hall's impeccable staging, which seems to have been conceived with his star's limited characterization in mind. What does a Shakespearean director do with a cautious Shylock? If he's smart, and few are as smart as Mr. Hall, he stages *Merchant* as the comedy it was once meant to be.

Or so Mr. Hall does up to a tasteful point—to go all the way, to mock Shylock along the lines of Malvolio in *Twelfth Night,* would be to give license to the textual anti-Semitism that he and Mr. Hoffman must and do avoid. What the director has done instead is devote full attention to the other elements of Shakespearean comedy in the play. With luminous casting and design (by Chris Dyer), the director gives the sky-crowned Belmont scenes more weight than those in mercantile, copper-hued Venice. The real star of the evening becomes Geraldine James's Portia—the only character to figure prominently in both realms—and her pursuit of pastoral romance is presented as vividly as her prosecution of the urban trial scene.

Ms. James is well up to Mr. Hall's demands. Her Portia, who combines the tart intelligence of a Beatrice with the golden glow of a fairy-tale princess, is a delight who drives the production. Mr. Hall has cast her coconspirators in love vibrantly, too—including Nathaniel Parker's unusually effervescent Bassanio, Richard Garnett's Lorenzo, and Francesca Buller's Jessica. Michael Siberry, who previously visited New York as the hero in the Royal Shakespeare Company's return engagement of *Nicholas Nickleby*, is an exceptional Gratiano—both a merry jester and a lout. With these actors and others—most notably Leigh Lawson's excellent Antonio, who does not minimize the merchant's grave crush on Bassanio—Mr. Hall can stress the musical poetry of the various lovers' Act 5 reconciliations, so often trimmed in other productions.

Not all the comic aspects of *Merchant* reward Mr. Hall's tender care. Despite a game cockney turn by Peter-Hugo Daly, Lancelot Gobbo is a lesser buffoon, and the cruelty he inflicts on his pathetic father is not redeemed by dressing Old Gobbo (Leo Leyden) in the dark spectacles and moth-eaten coat of a Beckett clown. The pageantry that Mr. Hall has poured upon the casket scenes—those interludes in which Portia's suitors must play the Shakespearean equivalent of *Let's Make a Deal*—does not add to their thematic importance or humor, let alone accelerate them.

This *Merchant* is also likely to prove a big target for American theater people who routinely deplore British Shakespearean acting and staging. Though the production has gained some American actors since its London inception, its classical look and blander, if well-spoken, secondary performances are ripe for Anglophobic attack. But to criticize Mr. Hall's production as an exercise in fuddy-duddy Shakespeare is beside the point. The results may look conservative, but in this century it is almost a novel idea—even if born of necessity—to restore romance and comedy to *The Merchant of Venice*. Which isn't to say that Mr. Hall's novel idea is necessarily the whole idea. His solid, highly watchable production, like Mr. Hoffman's performance, leaves one thinking about this endlessly debated play without for a second being challenged or moved by it.

CRITIC'S NOTEBOOK: HOW SET DESIGN
CAN BOLSTER OR SABOTAGE
JANUARY 18, 1990

In a newsletter published recently by the League of New York Theatres and Producers, Aldo Scrofani, an executive with Jujamcyn Theatres, tells an archetypal theatrical anecdote. "When Anne Bancroft previewed in *Golda* at the Wilbur Theatre in Boston, an early morning fire destroyed the set and just about everything on stage," he reminisces. "We quickly arranged to move the show across the street to the Shubert and presented it on a bare stage with a desk from the carpenters' room, some chairs, lights, and black backdrop. Guess what happened? Yes, magic—theater—at least the Boston audiences thought so."

Everyone in the theater can tell a variation on this tale. A play is performed with no scenery—whether in a dingy rehearsal hall or because of a calamity like the one that struck *Golda*—and the result is moving, exciting theater such as one almost never sees. Then the same play opens on Broadway in full dress a bit later, and it is so stupefying that no audience, not even the audience that loved the stripped-down version, can understand what anyone ever saw in it. *Golda* was a case in point: It was rejected by New York audiences in a matter of weeks when it came in from Boston, scenery rebuilt, in 1977. The magic of that bare stage had fled.

What's the moral of such anecdotes? That every play would be better off performed with merely a desk, some chairs, lights, and a black backdrop? Try telling that to an audience. Theatergoers want scenery—sometimes for the wrong reason ("I paid sixty bucks for this ticket, so let's see where the money went!") but usually for the right one. If the theater is to be more than a literary experience, the visual elements of a production must help make it so.

Though the current season is only at its halfway point, it has already proved an exceptional one for stage design. Yet the role of design in the theater is still frequently misunderstood. While a designer cannot turn a poor script into a masterpiece, or vice versa, a set often plays a disproportionately large part in establishing an audience's first impression and lingering expectations about a play. The same visual elements that can strengthen a production can also grease the skids for its destruction.

So far this season, at least two shows (*Meet Me in St. Louis* and *Tru*) have been bolstered by their scenery while at least three far more substantial works (*The Secret Rapture, Artist Descending a Staircase,* and *The Threepenny Opera*), all now closed, were in varying degrees sabotaged by visual confusion. Two other productions, *Grand Hotel* and *City of Angels,* are design triumphs.

With so much at stake, the responsibilities of a designer in the theater—responsibilities that are or should be shared with the director—are enormous. Even a bare stage has to be designed, whether by set or lighting designers or both, to evoke the atmosphere of the dramatic event it contains. Samuel Beckett's *Rockaby,* Peter Brook's *Carmen,* Gregory Mosher's *Our Town,* and Michael Bennett's *A Chorus Line*—to take four productions of recent memory—all call for some form of an "empty stage," but none of these plays would look right in the empty stage created for any of the others. The inky quality of the blackness on a Beckett stage has little in common with the Iberian glow of *Carmen* or the diurnal grayness of Grover's Corners or the sparkle of a Broadway theater during a dancers' audition.

Once a designer's assignment requires more than an empty stage, every stick of furniture and prop, every actor's placement in the set, becomes an esthetic issue of potentially momentous consequence. A great design not only accommodates such primary matters of composition and logistics with ease and visual grace but also makes a larger statement of theme or mood. But that statement must be at one with the playwright's, or the designer, however much an artist, will smother the work instead of serving it.

The difference between designs that enhance a play and those that fight it can be seen even in the extravagant, rococo scenery that became so popular during New York's *Bonfire of the Vanities* decade of conspicuous consumption. While Maria Bjornson's sets for Broadway's *The Phantom of the Opera* and Franco Zeffirelli's for the Metropolitan Opera's *Turandot* both shimmer with gold-leaf opulence, the singers of *Phantom* always stand in sharp visual relief while those of *Turandot* often fade right into the gilt.

A great design does not require the large sums of money at Ms. Bjornson's disposal nor does it require a great play. Many of the most innovative visual feats—like Julie Taymor's *Juan Darien* or any dance-theater piece by Martha Clarke—depend more on imagination than money. Many sophisticated designs serve conventional, even ordinary, plays and musicals.

The two heroes of New York stage design at this moment are Tony Walton and Robin Wagner, whose long careers have gained new momentum in the last two seasons. Mr. Walton's set for *Grand Hotel*, which merges seamlessly with Tommy Tune's staging of that musical, is as interesting for what it leaves out as for what it includes. There are no drops, no heavy scenery, no realistic bedrooms. Instead, Mr. Walton creates the ambiance of nearly every public and private room of a grand hotel in Weimar Berlin by relying simply on three chandeliers, a proscenium-wide band platform, several dozen straight-backed chairs, a skeletal revolving door, and four ghostly, translucent pillars in which evocative period bric-a-brac floats like the cultural detritus in a Joseph Cornell box. The constantly changing configurations of these simple fixtures are all that is needed to take the action from a bar to a bedroom to the lobby and back again. The audience's eyes fill in what Mr. Walton leaves out.

Such artistry is nothing new for this designer, whose earliest American work, an exuberant Fauvist-like set for *A Funny Thing Happened on the Way to the Forum* (1962), has been happily resurrected for *Jerome Robbins' Broadway*. Mr. Walton's design for *Grand Hotel* echoes the Jazz Age environment he created for Bob Fosse's *Chicago* (which also had an elevated bandstand and a gloomy worldview) more than a decade ago. Yet his range is broader than ever, and his past tendency to overdesign has resurfaced only once lately—in his Technicolor set for Mike Nichols's Hollywoodized *Waiting for Godot*. Otherwise Mr. Walton's touch is so assured that even broad scripts are rewarded with subtlety.

For Jerry Zaks's staging of *Lend Me a Tenor*, his design at first seems a realistic rendering of a 1930s art deco hotel suite. But on closer examination, the glossy set's border is jagged and unfinished—as if the suite had been ripped out of the past. Like the comic-book bright colors Mr. Walton used for *Forum*, his jagged border for *Tenor* is a subliminal cue to the audience that the play at hand is not realistic at all but a frantic, hair-tearing farce.

It is also Mr. Walton, again in collaboration with Mr. Zaks, who has licked the most problematic theater space in town, the Vivian Beaumont—with his consecutive designs for *The House of Blue Leaves* (once it transferred from the Newhouse), *The Front Page,* and *Anything Goes.* To appreciate the difficulty of this accomplishment, one need only see how the gifted designer Santo Loquasto came to grief on the same stage this season with *The Tenth Man.* Though Mr. Loquasto's realistic rendering of a Long Island storefront synagogue was of a stylistic piece with the Second Avenue slice of American Judaica that brought him a deserved Tony Award last season for *Café Crown,* he didn't take proper account of the proportions of the Beaumont. A small, homely synagogue was stretched into an oppressive hulk at Lincoln Center, and it helped crush Paddy Chayefsky's already fragile play.

Robin Wagner's career is nearly as long as Mr. Walton's and just as impressive. As Mr. Walton did in his second-best designs for *Woman of the Year* and *Social Security,* Mr. Wagner sometimes turns out impersonal Broadway glitz (*42nd Street, Song & Dance*). But no Broadway musical set of the 1980s was as inspired, and antiglitz, as the one he created with the director Michael Bennett for *Dreamgirls.* While that showbiz saga was ostensibly set in glamorous, realistic locales, from recording studios to Las Vegas showrooms, Mr. Wagner and the lighting designer, Tharon Musser, used only austere, mobile towers of aluminum scaffolding to suggest the many settings. It was an almost completely abstract design—at once an extension of ideas practiced by the designer Boris Aronson in Harold Prince–Michael Bennett musicals of the 1970s (*Company, Follies*) and a prelude to the Walton-Tune conceits of *Grand Hotel*.

In *City of Angels*, Mr. Wagner not only shows off the logistical genius he brought to *Dreamgirls* and *Jerome Robbins' Broadway* (in which he had the daunting job of melding the classic sets of dozens of designers); he also offers a vivid palette and wit he hasn't before revealed. It's no small achievement to engineer a complex show that is half in black-and-white (for its 1940s detective-film-within-the-musical) and half in color. An even higher achievement is the quality of the black-and-white scenery, which has the silken halftones of a pristine Warner Brothers print screened at the Museum of Modern Art.

True man of the theater that he is, however, Mr. Wagner concludes *City of Angels* not with a cinematic illusion but with a soundstage set that is in truth little more than a deep theatrical stage from which most scenery has been removed. As that Boston audience at *Golda* discovered, a nearly bare stage is magic. But as Mr. Wagner proves in *A Chorus Line* and in the final coup de théâtre of *City of Angels*, a brilliant designer can make that magic happen every night.

SEX, DRUGS, ROCK & ROLL
ORPHEUM THEATRE, FEBRUARY 9, 1990

It's not news that Eric Bogosian is a great talent, a chameleon actor and penetrating social observer whose one-man shows have staked out their own mean streets in the crowded 1980s theatrical territory inhabited by Lily Tomlin, Spalding Gray, Whoopi Goldberg, and so many others, from stand-up comedians to sit-down performance artists. Nor will it be news that *Sex, Drugs, Rock & Roll*, Mr. Bogosian's new show at the Orpheum, follows the format of such preceding recitals as *Fun House* and *Drinking in America*. Once again the actor appears in black jeans, sneakers, and white shirt to take the audience on a nonstop ninety-minute tour through the mental states of men who live in these United States.

But there is news at *Sex, Drugs, Rock & Roll*, and it is this: With this show, his funniest and scariest yet, Mr. Bogosian has crossed the line that separates an exciting artist from a culture hero. What Lenny Bruce was to the 1950s, Bob Dylan to the 1960s, Woody Allen to the 1970s—

that's what Eric Bogosian is to this frightening moment of drift in our history. With the possible exception of Spike Lee, I know of no one else like him in pop culture right now. He knows which way the wind is blowing, and in *Sex, Drugs, Rock & Roll*, those icy currents smack you right in the face.

The show opens just as the day does for so many in the audience. A gimpy, insistent subway panhandler "just released from Rikers Island" announces to the captive straphangers: "This is the situation—I need your money." What follows is a riotous amalgam of the familiar spiels, and Mr. Bogosian, his large green eyes glazed, leaves little doubt that the reformed junkie pleading for spare change is still on drugs. But should the beggar's needs be dismissed because he's lying? Not necessarily. As the man drones on, attempting to flatter his potential benefactors by recycling the jargon he's picked up in a lifetime of contact with the city's social and penal bureaucracies, Mr. Bogosian subtly but even more corrosively indicts the system that greases the skids and blights hope for those who need help. "Underneath it all," says the subway beggar, "we're exactly the same."

Mr. Bogosian's next character—a fatuous, aging English rock star plugging his wares on a talk show—would seem to belie that statement. The musician is an anti-drug crusader who has joined forces with such other public moralists as Dan and Marilyn Quayle. ("She's hot—she's very hot!" the rocker assures his skeptical young fans about the Second Lady.) But as he takes deep drags on his cigarette and glamorizes his own drug past in every showbiz reminiscence, it's clear that the rock star is as much of a con artist as the subway hustler; only the size of the stakes has changed.

By the time he gets around to pitching his favorite cause, the Amazonian Indians—a charity that seems to be inspired more by the rock star's egomania and unacknowledged racism than by the needs of the third-world poor—Mr. Bogosian has come full circle. With only two characters, he has mapped out the entire international cycle of drug dependency, official hypocrisy, and economic exploitation that leaves the homeless locked in subterranean hell and the coked-up rich in Hollywood heaven, with everyone else, especially the young, battling the fallout in between.

In the roughly one dozen bits that follow, Mr. Bogosian fills in more and more of the bleak Western landscape of 1990. A raving, phlegm-spewing old man delivers an obsessive but persuasive exegesis of the industrial age's death cycle, the pollution patterns that turn cities into "human septic tanks" and oceans into "giant vats of oil and garbage and dead animals." Yet the monologue is not an environmentalist's boilerplate but rather a baroque fantasy, part Twain and part Ben Jonson, in which the narrative sweep takes in everyone from urinating outdoorsmen to well-heeled passengers vomiting caviar and pâté on an ocean cruise.

Just as far-reaching is the chilling soliloquy that concludes the evening. An unreconstructed 1960s dropout sits cross-legged at stage edge to make the case that the United States is already an "occupied country" run by computers, whether fax machines or supermarket checkout stations, that plot against people all night by jabbering to one another in indecipherable languages. With the aid of television's power to deliver subliminal messages, the machines may already be in charge. How else, the man reasonably asks, can one explain the proliferation of microwave ovens—a superfluous, television-hawked appliance whose only logical use may be to fry the nation's households en masse when the computers stage their coup?

This is paranoia, of course, but like the paranoia in a Hitchcock movie, it's a little too close for comfort. And by inhabiting his characters instead of condescending to them, Mr. Bogosian doesn't allow anyone a safe distance from his less philosophical men, like the Mametesque entrepreneur who uses each of four phone lines (and an intercom) to betray a different business associate or loved one, or the self-made exponent of "the good life" showing off his new Olympic-size swimming pool with a pride inextricably bound to a fear of death.

Mr. Bogosian's unflaggingly intense impersonations, directed by Jo Bonney on a simple but evocative set designed by John Arnone, are flawless; he doesn't need costume or makeup changes to give each character a distinct face, voice, and posture. And as always, Mr. Bogosian is a hilarious wit: There is one line after another, not too many repeatable here, that you will quote to friends. He is also a born storyteller with perfect pitch for the voices of various ethnic, racial, and economic backgrounds. A monologue in which an Italian American hoodlum describes "the best night I ever had in my life"—a pornographic tale of urban mayhem in which he and his drugged pals lay waste to a McDonald's as well as to themselves—is too riveting to dismiss as revolting.

Yet Mr. Bogosian isn't a documentarian, an X-rated Studs Terkel running a tape recorder. And he isn't a public scold of either the left or right, setting political agendas. His sketches don't end with neat moral codas but trail off, like distant radio stations vanishing into the night on a dark highway. The highly original writing in *Sex, Drugs, Rock & Roll* is realer than journalism—and more frightening—and its depth helps boost Mr. Bogosian to a new plateau.

This show is much more of a piece than *Talk Radio*, his first attempt to collaborate with other actors in a more conventional play. Though the characters don't share scenes, they do share a coherently depicted (if incoherent) civilization (if that's the word for it) where homelessness, guilt, and an addictive desire to feel "wonderful" (a state attained with drugs, power, money, or sex) are ubiquitous. The characters we don't see—the abused secretary, the obsequious talk-show host, the tense subway passengers—are often as vivid as the men who do parade across the stage.

The canvas is far broader than the title and quirky cast of characters suggest. Leaving the show, one is struck not so much by the uncanny resemblance between the real-life beggars outside the theater and the fictional ones of Mr. Bogosian's impersonations as by the way *Sex, Drugs, Rock & Roll* as a whole forces the audience to examine its own roles in the larger drama that, however unwillingly, it shares daily with the dispossessed.

The last of Mr. Bogosian's characters argues that the homeless are threatening not just because they evoke suffering and guilt but also because they represent revolt and freedom. They are the people who have been "thrown out of their cages," he says, because they refused to do "what they're supposed to do." At this remarkable historical moment, people all over the world are being thrown out of their cages, and among American writers for the theater, Mr. Bogosian is the first to see his own society as part of the big picture. Using every powerful means available to a theater artist, he shakes the cages of a complacent country engulfed by homelessness to ask just exactly who, if anyone, is at home.

MERRILY WE ROLL ALONG
ARENA STAGE, WASHINGTON, D.C., FEBRUARY 27, 1990

At the end of *Merrily We Roll Along,* three young people of 1957, all with dreams of theatrical or literary glory, stand on a roof in New York City to spot Sputnik, a symbol of their high hopes, as it streaks across a starry sky. Nine years after its failure on Broadway, *Merrily* continues to follow its own alluring, elusive trajectory through the musical theater.

In various revised versions, this Stephen Sondheim–George Furth adaptation of the 1934 play by George S. Kaufman and Moss Hart has been sighted at small companies from Los Angeles to London in recent seasons. Each production raises the hopes of partisans that a resurrected *Merrily* will soon redeem their faith in the show by splashing down triumphantly in New York.

Arena Stage's rendition of the musical at its proscenium house, the Kreeger Theatre, is the closest the reworked *Merrily* has gotten to Broadway—geographically, at least. One hopes the authors will not let up now. As it stands in Washington, the much improved *Merrily* still falls short of its exceptional score, whose haunting melodies and dramatic ingenuity were preserved by RCA in a posthumous Broadway-cast recording that has spread the musical's potential to a large audience that never saw the 1981 debacle. While part of the disappointment of the Arena *Merrily* can be attributed to Douglas C. Wager's prosaic production, that is not the whole problem. There's still some work for Mr. Sondheim and Mr. Furth to do.

Many of the major flaws of the 1981 *Merrily*, starting with its notorious gymnasium setting, have long since been jettisoned or rectified in intervening versions produced in La Jolla, California, and in Seattle. It is no longer difficult to follow the show's inverted time scheme, which follows three old friends in reverse chronology, from the pinnacle of jaded showbiz success in 1980 back through their climb to fame and disillusionment during the two preceding decades. The original production's confusing framing device, a high-school graduation, has been dropped (though a new and counterproductive prologue has been added). Most important, the characters in *Merrily* are now played by adults who appear to get younger as the evening progresses. In 1981, Harold Prince cast too many teenagers who looked silly impersonating worldly grown-ups.

In Washington, the most crucial role, that of the composer Franklin Shepard, has been given to Victor Garber. It's not an enviable assignment. Franklin has always been the most problematic figure in *Merrily*; he is one of the most unsympathetic leading men in a musical since *Pal Joey*. A successful Hollywood film producer when introduced in Act 1, he is in every way portrayed as a scoundrel. The audience rapidly learns that Franklin abandoned his musical talent to make schlock movies, that he betrayed two wives, that his closest friend and his son no longer speak to him. Mr. Furth and Mr. Sondheim then ask the audience to spend the next two hours caring about how and why this privileged, callous sellout went wrong.

Mr. Garber is a terrific choice for Franklin, not only because he is a first-rate comic actor who can sing but also because he is so appealing: He always projects intelligence and honesty. If anyone could keep an audience intrigued by Franklin, however expedient his choices in love and art, it is this performer. Mr. Garber's inability to do so in Act 1 of the Arena's *Merrily* should be a clear indication to the musical's creators that something is still amiss in their conception of the role.

The trouble with Franklin, Mr. Garber's performance makes clear, is not that he is a heel but that he is a passive, clichéd heel until *Merrily* is an hour old. People keep saying terrible things about him at Hollywood parties, and Mr. Garber, lacking a big scene or song of his own for too long, is left to stand around looking battered and forlorn. He doesn't have anything to act. Instead of the drama of character, Mr. Furth provides the noise of melodramatic events: Hyperbolic fisticuffs, not intimate moments of anguish or passion, punctuate both of the long Hollywood scenes that establish Franklin.

Nor does Mr. Sondheim come to those scenes' rescue. Act 1's early ensemble number, "That Frank," like the 1981 song it replaces ("Rich and Happy"), has Hollywood cynics describe Franklin's spiritual collapse without often letting the man speak for himself. Since the protagonist doesn't fully reveal his own feelings (or even his voice) at the start, it's impossible for the audience to be engaged by his predicament. While it would be disingenuous to soften Franklin's emptiness, is there any reason why he must be so remote?

Once *Merrily* has rolled back into Franklin's more animated past, the score and much of the book catch up with its ambitions. But Mr. Wager's production often lags behind. The emotional apex of Act 1, "Franklin Shepard Inc.," in which Franklin's collaborator and best friend, the playwright Charley Kringas, tells him off on a television talk show, is muted by David Garrison's low-key, naturalistic delivery of the song's hysterical emotions. Becky Ann Baker's promising performance as Mary Flynn, the platonic (and underwritten) woman in both men's lives, isn't as touching as it should be in lonely laments like "Old Friends/Like It Was" and the reprise of "Not a Day Goes By."

For all its typical Sondheim patina of regret, however, *Merrily We Roll Along* is not Chekhov. While Mr. Wager's production has bright sets (by Douglas Stein) and a Michael Bennett touch or two (choral phalanxes from *Company*, a bridge from *Dreamgirls*), it sags under the burdens of a muffled band and ponderous pacing. Act 2 opens with a new Sondheim gag—the song "Good Thing Going" is expanded into a mock Broadway turn of 1964, a double parody of *Hello, Dolly!* and *Funny Girl*—yet Mr. Wager and his choreographer, Marcia Milgrom Dodge, ask only that its able singer, Mary Gordon Murray, plod through it upstage.

"It's our time, coming through" Franklin and Charley sing later, as they stand on the New York rooftop of 1957, their futures still spread before them as infinitely as the night sky above. The time is surely coming for *Merrily,* too, but like the ambitious composer and playwright onstage, Mr. Sondheim and Mr. Furth should not be in too much of a hurry while deciding what that future will be.

CRITIC'S NOTEBOOK: SOME AMERICANS ABROAD/
CROWBAR/ WALTER KERR THEATRE OPENS
MARCH 14, 1990

I think this is the Pizza Hut where he wrote *Troilus and Cressida*," said my theater-fanatic friend during a pre-matinee stroll in Stratford-on-Avon, England, a few summers ago. We had already passed the McDonald's where, we imagined, Shakespeare had written *Twelfth Night*. (Or was it *As You Like It* at Burger King?) As we later wolfed down curry just in time to make the curtain at the Royal Shakespeare Company's evening performance of *The Merchant of Venice*, we concluded that we had finally found a Stratford restaurant the Bard might have missed. Neither of us could recall a single mention of mango chutney in the banquet scene of *Macbeth*.

Such fond memories of being a culturally high-minded American abroad are inevitably revived by *Some Americans Abroad,* Richard Nelson's very funny comedy at the Mitzi E. Newhouse Theater about Yankee tourists on an obsessive-compulsive playgoing tour of England. One of Mr. Nelson's scenes, in fact, is set in the Stratford Pizza Hut. By then, his characters are overdosing on the classics—"I think two Shakespeares in one day is asking for trouble," says an exasperated faculty wife, Kate Burton—and they can no longer recall the names of the plays they have seen (*Les Mis* always excepted).

It's Mr. Nelson's despairing point that these tourists, college professors and students on a tight budget, don't remember the content of the plays either. They are culture vultures who devour everything and digest nothing. The somewhat overheated plot of *Some Americans Abroad* pushes the characters into ethical and sexual conflicts that classic theater, or perhaps even *Les Liaisons Dangereuses* or the latest faculty common-room comedy by Simon Gray, might help illuminate. But to these consumers of literature, plays are valuable only as trophies for one-upmanship at sherry-sipping department socials or as springboards for publishable theses that grease the tenure track. The sole character in *Some Americans Abroad* with a clear conscience and an ability to act decisively in the arena of life—a rebellious student, incandescently played by Elisabeth Shue—is the one who goes AWOL during the plays to romp with a new boyfriend.

Taken to its depressing extreme, Mr. Nelson's play is a sequel to *The Innocents Abroad,* Mark Twain's caustic view of pretentious Americans abroad in the last century: Both works indict the well-educated American middle class for its supine and superficial relationship to Old World culture in general. Mr. Nelson's characters are particularly marked by a late-twentieth-century affliction, the *Masterpiece Theater* syndrome: They find it easier to worship all things British than to investigate the intellectual life of their own immediate surroundings.

Not once in *Some Americans Abroad* does any character refer to a play seen back home or to any American writer (except, of course, the expatriate Henry James, an honorary Briton). One feels that these theaterlovers would only go to the theater in New York to see a visiting English troupe, just as they favor any book that has been published in paperback by Penguin and purchased on Charing Cross Road. When the time comes for the Anglophilic academics of *Some Americans Abroad* to return to the United States, they gather together on the Westminster Bridge to sing "God Save the Queen."

But the British theater doesn't have a monopoly on history. The American theater has a past, too. Even if Mr. Nelson's characters knew that past existed, however, they would probably turn up their noses at it. It's a relatively short past, and, prior to World War I and Eugene O'Neill, a not infrequently trashy one. Premodern American theater history usually has more to do with show people (impresarios, actors, actor-managers) than with great native dramatists and enduring plays. Since showmen were more inclined to erect palaces to celebrate their own egos than to build a permanent dramatic literature for the general good, the legacy of American theatrical pioneers can be ephemeral. The productions and performances languish in specialized history books; the theaters have often vanished. American theatergoers don't have a quaint historical theater shrine like Stratford to visit. They have what remains of Times Square.

That being so, why not make the most of it? A new and eccentric theatrical event on the gaudiest and bawdiest block of West Forty-second Street, the En Garde Arts production of Mac Wellman's play *Crowbar*, attempts to do exactly that. It offers an intimate guided tour of a bona fide corner of the American theatrical past. Without waiting for the cloudy Times Square redevelopment scheme to fall into place, En Garde, an itinerant company specializing in site-specific performances, has gone ahead and liberated the oldest surviving theater on the street: the Victory, which was built in 1900 by Oscar Hammerstein as the Theatre Republic and was soon leased to David Belasco, who lent the theater his own name for seven years until he built another theater, the beautiful Belasco that now sits mostly dark on West Forty-fourth Street.

The Swan or the Globe the Victory is not. Christened with its current name in a quixotic burst of patriotism during World War II, the house has been a home to pornographic movies in recent years. The auditorium has been cleaned up, not renovated, for the limited engagement of *Crowbar*. There are holes in the partitions in the men's room. The audience sits on the stage, shrouded by the musty wing and fly space. Though plaster cherubs still ring the domed ceiling, they seem to float in a miasma of mold-colored decay. As imaginatively directed by Richard Caliban, the cast seems to float, too, performing Mr. Wellman's play throughout the house, from the dim second balcony with its red exit signs to the faded boxes to the creepy no man's land beneath the stage's trap doors.

The idea of *Crowbar* is exciting. The play's action unfolds during the intermission of the theater's first attraction, James A. Hearn's *Sag Harbor*, which a well-heeled matron in its audience describes as being about the "humble lives" of "simple fisher folk." Mr. Wellman's characters are ghosts—those of the playhouse and those of ordinary New Yorkers whose obituaries were culled from the same September 1900 newspapers that reported on the opening of *Sag Harbor*. It's too bad that the execution of this promising premise is often self-indulgent. While Mr. Wellman quotes Djuna Barnes and spins some pretty metaphors—the red-walled theater is like "the inside of a human heart, only bigger and not as empty"—his writing is too solipsistic to allow most of his characters to break loose from his voice and speak in their own.

Yet the theater itself is such a mesmerizing presence that it literally upstages *Crowbar*. The evening opens with a slide show, set to spine-tingling music by David Van Tieghem, of photographs of the Victory in its salad days, when its accouterments included a Paradise Roof Garden with a miniature farm village of livestock, cottages, a barn, a pond, and watermills. The photographic images bleed into all that follows, allowing the audience's imagination to run riot through the theater's past even as the characters are straitjacketed by tedious verbal arias in an arch contemporary mode. Patience is rewarded at play's end, when Belasco's ghost (Yusef Bulos) delivers a manifesto in favor of "good entertainment" and "good art" that reconnects *Crowbar* with the theater history that shares its stage.

"All theaters are haunted," goes a recurring line in the script. One wishes Mr. Wellman's play made more extravagant use of the many ghosts who haunt the Victory. Belasco's mistress, the actress Mrs. Leslie Carter, once occupied the impresario's studio apartment high above the stage. Blanche Bates performed at the Victory in Belasco's *The Girl of the Golden West*—soon to inspire Puccini—and not long after that Mary Pickford and Cecil B. DeMille teamed up on *The Warrens of Virginia* before going Hollywood.

Later still, *Abie's Irish Rose*, Broadway's most unexpectedly popular tearjerker, stayed five years at the theater, and, in the 1930s, Minsky's one and only burlesque arrived, trailed by frequent police raids. So haunted is this house that it seems instantly suitable, without the addition of scenery, for a staging of Jack Finney's time-travel novel of Old New York, *Time and Again*, or for the Stephen Sondheim–James Goldman musical of a half-demolished, ghost-swept Ziegfeld palace, *Follies*.

A few blocks up from the Victory, on the marginally more demure Forty-eighth Street, stands another old theater that has been reclaimed: the Ritz, built in 1921, lost to radio and television from 1943 to 1970, and restored over the past year by Jujamcyn, the theater owners who will present August Wilson's new play, *The Piano Lesson*, there next month. Last week the theater was officially opened with its new name, the Walter Kerr, before an audience that was dazzled by the renovation. Though the Kerr had the same architect, Herbert J. Krapp, as most other handsome Broadway theaters of its period, few, if any, of the others have been restored with such scrupulous fidelity to the original decorative details, from carpet pattern to pressed-copper marquee.

When the time came for Walter Kerr to take the stage to speak on his namesake theater's opening night, he first paused to luxuriate in the full vista of the glowing house, with its grandiose murals and gold-leaf trim. Then he spoke in a low, awestruck voice that reflected the audience's wonder at finding itself in a time machine: "Welcome to 1921," he said. In the hushed few seconds that followed, you could feel the theater people in the crowd communing with the ghosts who walk the Kerr's boards: Alfred Lunt and Lynn Fontanne, Ina Claire, Katharine Cornell, Leslie Howard, Bette Davis.

Let Americans abroad worship the Elizabethans of Stratford and London. Americans at home can rendezvous with their own exotic theatrical past at the Victory and the Kerr.

≡ *In 1990, no one had yet imagined that the Victory would be stunningly restored to its turn-of-the-century splendor and reopened as a young people's theater, the New Victory, only five years later, leading the way for a Forty-second Street revival that would bring about the similar restoration in 1997 of the old Ziegfeld palace, the New Amsterdam, by Disney across the street and the producer Garth Drabinsky's construction of a new theater, The Ford Center, out of the remains of two old ones to house* Ragtime *next door to the New Victory.*

PRELUDE TO A KISS
CIRCLE REPERTORY COMPANY, MARCH 15, 1990

Peter, the ingenuous hero played by Alec Baldwin in *Prelude to a Kiss,* loves the sign at the roller coaster: RIDE AT YOUR OWN RISK. It promises a journey into "the wild blue" in which anything can happen. The same sign could be posted at *Prelude to a Kiss,* for Craig Lucas, the author of *Reckless* and *Blue Window,* has again written a play that propels the audience through hairpin emotional turns, some soaring heavenward and others plummeting toward earth, until one is deposited at the final curtain in a winded and teary yet exhilarating state of disorientation.

I loved this play and the dreamy, perfectly cast Circle Repertory Company production, directed by Norman René, that is inseparable from it. But as the man says, ride at your own risk. *Prelude to a Kiss* takes a most familiar genre, romantic comedy, in directions that are idiosyncratic and challenging. The play's title comes from the Duke Ellington song sung by Ella Fitzgerald that perfumes the evening, and Mr. Lucas follows its prescription that "just a simple melody with nothing fancy, nothing much" can blossom into "a symphony, a Schubert tune with a Gershwin touch." The playwright also takes a cue from his characters' favorite book, *The White Hotel,* because *Prelude to a Kiss,* though only a prelude compared with D. M. Thomas's novel, is also a psychoanalytic fairy tale that rises from a maze of transference into a cathartic conflict between sex and death.

Mr. Lucas is not pretentious, and his play is as airily composed and, at first, as funny as the old-time Hollywood confections it sometimes paraphrases. Peter, a microfiche specialist at a scientific publishing concern, and Rita (Mary-Louise Parker), a bartender aspiring to be a graphic designer, meet at a Manhattan party, fall under the spell of love, and are married at the bride's family home in Englewood Cliffs, N.J. It is a fine romance, with lots of storybook kisses—most of them executed by Mr. Baldwin and Ms. Parker, an enchanting young stage couple made for each other as well as for audiences.

The romance consummated, the trouble begins. During a honeymoon in Jamaica, Peter finds himself increasingly at odds with the wonderful woman he thought he had married. Once he returns to New York, he is convinced that Rita isn't Rita at all. Through a magical plot device that could happen only in a movie—and frequently does—Rita's soul seems to have migrated to another body. The body is that of an old, bespectacled, potbellied man, played by Barnard Hughes, who is dying of lung cancer.

"I'm not equipped for this!" Peter cries. While he had sworn to Rita that he would love her even more in old age, when her teeth had yellowed and her breasts had sagged, he had not expected to be put to so blunt a test so soon. Can he love a woman who now looks like an old, decrepit man? What makes *Prelude to a Kiss* a powerful, genuine fairy tale rather than merely a farcical exploitation of the form's narrative devices is that Mr. Lucas insists on playing out Peter's outrageous predicament for keeps. The scenes in which the souls of Peter and Rita merge despite the impediment of Mr. Hughes's undesirable body are as tender and moving as those in which Mr. Baldwin and Ms. Parker strike erotic sparks.

It is not difficult to figure out the genesis of *Prelude to a Kiss*. Mr. Lucas is also the author of *Longtime Companion,* a much more conventionally written feature film about AIDS that is to open in May, and this play can be taken as an indirect treatment of the same subject. The epidemic is to Mr. Lucas what Babi Yar was to D. M. Thomas, and Peter's fidelity to his true love's soul, even as that soul is trapped in a dying male body, is a transparent metaphor. Yet Mr. Lucas never betrays his play's fantastical tone or sense of humor; its setting is an unspecifically "precarious" New York, and AIDS is never mentioned. The result is a work whose anguish excludes no one. The questions that Mr. Lucas addresses are timeless ones about the powers of compassion and empathy in a brutal universe where everyone is inevitably abandoned by parents, children, and lovers and where the only reward for that suffering is to disappear to "no one knows where."

The script's lyrical alchemy of bright comedy and deep feeling is matched by the staging of Mr. René, whose nearly decade-long collaboration with Mr. Lucas and a poetically minded design team has grown into one of the true joys of the American theater. All the performances are excellent, including those of Larry Bryggman and Debra Monk as slightly off-center suburban in-laws and Joyce Reehling as a sad-eyed middle-aged daughter who helps shift the entire play's emotional key in her own confrontation with mortality. Mr. Hughes, repressing a bit of his customary Irish twinkle, turns a role that is not that large into an indelible specter of love lost and found.

For Mr. Baldwin, Peter is a complete, and completely successful, switch on the scurvy contemporary men he has played so amusingly on stage (*Loot, Serious Money*) and screen (*Married to the Mob, Working*

Girl). It is no easy achievement, I'm sure, for an actor with such slick good looks to convey generosity of spirit rather than narcissism. Mr. Baldwin, whose character also serves as the evening's witty narrator, does so with natural ease, never resorting to charming tricks of the leading man's trade. Ms. Parker, recently seen as Jane Hogarth in *The Art of Success,* is going places as surely as her costar is. An uninhibited (but not undisciplined) comic actress whose pouty mouth and big eyes break into unexpectedly radiant smiles, she transcends her own attractive looks to imbue Rita with a soul for which a man might well sacrifice everything.

Such is Mr. Lucas's gift that he makes life's sacrifices seem its affirmation, not its burden, even as he by no means underestimates the courage required to make the leap. The leap is not merely figurative. Like *Blue Window* and *Reckless, Prelude to a Kiss* is dominated by the image of a window. Mr. Lucas often demands that his characters jump through it, leaving home for the unknown of a starry night and the arduous prospect of selfless love, just as he demands that audiences take the leap out of a literal reality and into the imaginative realm of an adult fable.

The amazing part is that if you can go the esthetic distance with this playwright, you may find yourself inspired to take the other, more intimate, much more dangerous leap, too. Though *Prelude to a Kiss* is never more than a heartbeat away from the fearful nightmare of death that inspired it, the experience of seeing it is anything but defeating. Mr. Lucas opens the window on love—true love, not fairy-tale love—so wide that, even in this cynical time, it seems a redemptive act of faith to take a free fall into the wild blue.

≡ *In another less-than-felicitous move to Broadway,* Prelude to a Kiss *traveled uptown without Alec Baldwin, who returned to his burgeoning movie career. His successor was Timothy Hutton, who was both less of a draw and less effective in the role. Nonetheless,* Prelude *ran a year uptown with a succession of leading men.*

CAT ON A HOT TIN ROOF
Eugene O'Neill Theatre, March 22, 1990

It takes nothing away from Kathleen Turner's radiant Maggie in *Cat on a Hot Tin Roof* to say that Broadway's gripping new production of Tennessee Williams's 1955 play will be most remembered for Charles

Durning's Big Daddy. The actor's portrayal of a sixty-five-year-old Mississippi plantation owner in festering extremis is an indelible hybrid of redneck cutup and aristocratic tragedian, of grasping capitalist and loving patriarch. While *Cat* is not the American *King Lear* its author hoped, this character in this performance is a cracker-barrel Lear and Falstaff in one.

Just try to get the image of Mr. Durning—a dying volcano in final, sputtering eruption under a Delta moon—out of your mind. I can't. *Cat* is a curiously constructed work in which the central but sullen character of Brick, the all-American jock turned booze hound, clings to the action's periphery while Act 1 belongs to his wife, Maggie, Act 2 to his Big Daddy, and the anticlimactic Act 3 (of which the author left several variants) to no one. Such is Mr. Durning's force in the second act at the O'Neill that he obliterates all that comes after, despite the emergence of Polly Holliday's poignant Big Mama in the final stretch.

Mr. Durning's Act 2 tour de force begins with low comedy: The portly, silver-haired actor, dressed in a sagging white suit and wielding a vaudeville comedian's stogie, angrily dismisses his despised, nattering wife and his bratty grandchildren, those cap-gun-toting "no-neck monsters" who would attempt to lure him into a saccharine birthday party. From that hilarious display of W. C. Fields dyspepsia, it is quite a leap to the act's conclusion. By then, Mr. Durning is white with fear, clutching the back of a chair for support, for he has just learned what the audience has long known: Big Daddy is being eaten away by cancer that "has gone past the knife."

In between comes a father-son confrontation that is not only the crux of Mr. Durning's performance but also the troubling heart of a play that is essential, if not first-rank, Williams. Big Daddy loves Brick (Daniel Hugh Kelly) and would like to favor him when dividing his estate of $10 million and "twenty-eight thousand acres of the richest land this side of the valley Nile." But there are mysteries to be solved before the writing of the will. Why are Brick and Maggie childless? Why is Brick, once a football hero and later a television sports announcer, now, at twenty-seven, intent on throwing away his life as if it were "something disgusting you picked up on the street"? How did Brick break his ankle in the wee hours of the night before?

Mr. Durning will have his answers, even if he has to knock Brick off his crutch to get them. But his Big Daddy, while tough as a billy goat, is not a cartoon tyrant. He wants to talk to his son, not to badger him. He offers Brick understanding and tolerance in exchange for the truth, even if that truth might be Brick's closeted homosexual passion for his best friend and football buddy, Skipper, now dead of drink. All Big Daddy wants is freedom from the lies and hypocrisy of life that have so long disgusted him. Yet Brick, while sharing that disgust, won't surrender his illusions without a fight.

"Mendacity is the system we live in," the son announces. "Liquor is one way out and death's the other." When the truth finally does emerge—and for both men it is more devastating than any sexual revelation—liquor and death do remain the only exits. Life without the crutch of pipe dreams or anesthesia is too much to take. As the lights dim on Act 2, Mr. Kelly is isolated in a stupor and Mr. Durning, his jaw distorted by revulsion and rage, is howling like Lear on the heath. Advancing relentlessly into the bowels of his mansion, the old man bellows an epic incantation of "Lying! Dying! Liars!" into the tall shadows of the Southern Gothic night.

Along with the high drama and fine acting—Mr. Kelly's pickled Adonis included—what makes the scene so moving is Williams's raw sensitivity to what he called (in his next play, *Orpheus Descending*) man's eternal sentence to solitary confinement. In *Cat*, Maggie probably does love Brick, Big Mama probably does love Big Daddy, and Brick loves Skipper and Big Daddy as surely as they have loved him. Yet the lies separating those who would love are not easily vanquished. In this web of familial, fraternal, and marital relationships, Williams finds only psychic ruin, as terminal as Big Daddy's cancer and as inexorable as the greed that is devouring the romantic Old South.

In his revival, Howard Davies, the English director last represented in New York by *Les Liaisons Dangereuses,* keeps his eye on that bigger picture: Williams's compassion for all his trapped characters and his desire to make his play "not the solution of one man's psychological problem" but a "snare for the truth of human experience." With the exception of Mae (Debra Jo Rupp), Brick's conniving sister-in-law, everyone on stage is human. The playwright doesn't blame people for what existence does to them. He has empathy for the defeated and admiration for those like Maggie who continue the fight for life and cling to the hot tin roof "even after the dream of life is all over."

From her salt-cured accent to her unabashed (and entirely warranted) delight in her own body heat, Ms. Turner is an accomplished Maggie, mesmerizing to watch, comfortable on stage, and robustly good-humored. Merely to see this actress put on her nylons, a ritual of exquisitely prolonged complexity, is a textbook lesson in what makes a star. Ms. Turner is so good as far as she goes that one wishes she'd expose her emotions a shade more—without compromising her admirable avoidance of a campy star turn. Her Maggie is almost too stubbornly a survivor of marital wars; she lacks the vulnerability of a woman "eaten up with longing" for the man who shuns her bed.

Though somewhat more can be made of Brick—and was by Ian Charleson, in Mr. Davies's previous staging of *Cat* in London—Mr. Kelly captures the detachment of defeat, and later the rage, of a man who buried hope in his best friend's grave. When Brick is finally provoked to stand up for the "one great good true thing" in his life, the actor gives an impassioned hint of the noble figure who inspired worship from all who knew him. But it's a major flaw of *Cat* that this character is underwritten. Williams defines the physique of his golden boy—and Mr. Kelly fleshes that out, too—but leaves the soul opaque.

Since Brick doesn't pull his weight in any of the playwright's third acts for *Cat,* it hardly matters which one is used. Mr. Davies reverts to the unsentimental original draft, which never made it to the stage in Elia Kazan's initial Broadway production. Ms. Holliday's Big Mama, an unstrung Amanda Wingfield brought to her own grief by others' mendacity, is a rending figure within the thunderstorm of the dénouement. Along with the supporting cast, the designers' vision of a decaying South—from the fading veranda to the intrusion of the latest American inoculation against intimacy, a 1950s console television—thickens the rancid mood of a household where, in Big Mama's words, "such a black thing has come . . . without invitation."

But even in Act 3, even offstage, Mr. Durning continues to dominate, and, in a way, he gets the big scene with the star that the script denies him. As Maggie tenaciously clings to her tin roof, Big Daddy can be heard from somewhere deep within, his terrifying screams of pain rattling that roof, threatening even at death's doorstep to blow the lid off life's cruel, incarcerating house of lies.

THE GRAPES OF WRATH
CORT THEATRE, MARCH 23, 1990

It's not just because audiences must step around homeless people to get to the theater that the time is right for the Steppenwolf Theatre Company's majestic adaptation of *The Grapes of Wrath.*

When John Steinbeck wrote his novel about dispossessed Okies heading west in search of the promised land of California, he was also writing about a nation in search of itself. After a decade of dog-eat-dog boom and another of depression, Steinbeck wondered what credo the survivors could still believe in. Fifty years later—after another 1920s-style orgy of greed and with many bills yet to be paid—Americans are once more uncertain in their faith. While an all-night party celebrating democracy is being uncorked around the world, the vast inequities of our own democracy leave some Americans wondering whether they deserve to be invited.

The production at the Cort, an epic achievement for the director, Frank Galati, and the Chicago theater ensemble at his disposal, makes Steinbeck live for a new generation not by updating his book but by digging into its timeless heart. On the surface, *The Grapes of Wrath* is one of the worst great novels ever written. The characters are perishable WPA-mural archetypes incapable of introspection, the dialogue is at times cloyingly folksy, and the drama is scant. In any ordinary sense, there's no "play" here (and without Henry Fonda's presence, a sweetened screenplay, and Gregg Toland's spectacular on-site cinematography, there wouldn't have been a movie, either). But Steinbeck wasn't trying to be Dickens or Hugo or Dreiser. Without embracing either a jingoist's flag or a Marxist's ideology, he was simply trying to unearth and replenish the soul holding a country together. That's the simple, important drama that Steppenwolf, with incredibly sophisticated theatrical technique, brings to the stage.

To be sure, Mr. Galati, as adapter, takes the audience through the narrative of the Joad family's travails by Hudson Super Six truck—a winding trail on Route 66 blighted by abject poverty, deaths, desertions, labor violence, natural disasters. But the evening's dialogue scenes are few and brief: The lines are reduced to a laconic minimum and the many people are defined by their faces and tones of voice rather than by psychological revelations.

What one finds in place of conventional dramatic elements—and in place of the documentary photography possible only on film—is pure theater as executed by a company and director that could not be more temperamentally suited to their task. As Steppenwolf demonstrated in *True West, Orphans,* and *Balm in Gilead*—all titles that could serve for *The Grapes of Wrath*—it is an ensemble that believes in what Steinbeck does: the power of brawny, visceral art, the importance of community, the existence of an indigenous American spirit that resides in inarticulate ordinary people, the spiritual resonance of American music, and the heroism of the righteous outlaw. As played by Gary Sinise and Terry Kinney, Tom Joad and the lapsed preacher Jim Casy—the Steinbeck characters who leave civilization to battle against injustice—are the forefathers of the rock-and-roll rebels in Steppenwolf productions by Sam Shepard and Lanford Wilson just as they are heirs to Huck and Jim. They get their hands dirty in the fight for right.

The audience meets Tom and Casy in the parched dust bowl, where they are introduced by the evening's first haunting mating of sight and sound: A fiddler in a lonely spotlight runs a bow across a handsaw, filling the antique Broadway house with the thin, plaintive wail of the barren plains. When the lights come up, the audience finds a set—a deep, barn-like shell of weathered wood, brilliantly designed and lighted by Kevin Rigdon—that will contain the entire event. Aside from the occasional descending wall or sign, the only major piece of scenery is the Joads' mobile truck, piled high with kitchen utensils, bundles of clothes, and plucky humanity.

What follows is a stream of tableaux whose mythic power lies in their distillation to vibrant essentials. One's worst fear about a *Grapes of Wrath* adaptation—that it will be a patchwork quilt of sugarcoated Americana—is never realized. Mr. Galati, a director of exquisite taste, strips away sentimentality and cheap optimism. If he has an esthetic model, it is Peter Brook, not *The Waltons*. His *Grapes* looks a lot like the Brook *Carmen,* for its atmosphere is created with the basic elements of earth, water, fire, and air. Even so, Mr. Galati and Mr. Rigdon do not re-gard homespun simplicity as a license for improvisatory amateurism. El-egance may seem an odd word to apply to *The Grapes of Wrath,* but it fits this one. While a stage production cannot compete with the photogra-phy of Walker Evans or Pare Lorentz, it can emulate the rigorous, more abstract painterly imagery of Edward Hopper or Thomas Hart Benton or Georgia O'Keeffe.

Mr. Galati conveys the loneliness of the open road with headlights burning into an inky night, or with the rotating of the truck under a starry sky to reveal each isolated conversation of its inhabitants. Camp-fires frequently dot the stage—the ravaged face of Mr. Kinney's itinerant preacher is made to be illuminated by lantern glow—and a sharp duel of flashlights dramatizes the violence of strikebreaking thugs. Equally as-tringent and evocative is Michael Smith's score, which echoes Woody Guthrie and heartland musical forms and is played by a migrant band on such instruments as harmonica, Jew's harp, and banjo. Sometimes salted with descriptive lyrics from Steinbeck, the music becomes the thread that loosely binds a scattered society.

Though trimmed since its premiere in Chicago in 1988, Act 1 of *The Grapes of Wrath* still requires perseverance. Mr. Galati, like Steinbeck, demands that the audience sink into a jerky, episodic journey rather than be propelled by the momentum of character or story. Act 2 pays off with the flood sequence—spectacularly realized here with a curtain of rain pouring down on men shoveling for their lives—and in remarkably fresh realizations of some of the novel's most familiar scenes. When Ma Joad—in the transcendent form of the flinty, silver-haired Lois Smith— delivers her paean to the people's ability to "go on," it isn't the inspirational epilogue that won Jane Darwell an Oscar but a no-nonsense, conversational reiteration of unshakable pragmatism. When Mr. Sinise leaves his already disintegrated family to join a radical underground, his "I'll be all around in the dark" soliloquy is not Fonda's Lincolnesque address but a plainspoken statement of bedrock conviction.

Like the superb Ms. Smith, Mr. Sinise, and Mr. Kinney, the other good actors in this large cast never raise their voices. Such performers as Jeff Perry (Noah Joad) and Robert Breuler (Pa Joad) slip naturally into folkloric roles that are permanent fixtures in our landscape. They become what Steinbeck believed his people to be—part of a communal soul that will save America from cruelty and selfishness when other gods, secular and religious, have failed.

Can they make us believe, too? The evening concludes with the coda the movie omitted, in which the Joad daughter, Rose of Sharon (Sally Murphy), her husband gone and her baby just born dead, offers to breast-feed a starving black man (Lex Monson) in a deserted barn. As acted and staged, in a near-hush and visually adrift on the full, lonely expanse of the wooden stage, the tableau is religious theater in the simplest sense. There is no pious sermon—just a humble, selfless act of charity crystallized into a biblical image, executed by living-and-breathing actors, streaked with nocturnal shadows and scented by the gentle weeping of a fiddle string.

Some of the audience seemed to be weeping, too, and not out of sadness, I think. The Steppenwolf *Grapes of Wrath* is true to Steinbeck because it leaves one feeling that the generosity of spirit that he saw in a brutal country is not so much lost as waiting once more to be found.

LETTICE AND LOVAGE
ETHEL BARRYMORE THEATRE, MARCH 26, 1990

There is only one Maggie Smith, but audiences get at least three of her in *Lettice and Lovage*, the Peter Shaffer comedy that has brought this spellbinding actress back to Broadway after an indecently long absence and that has the shrewd sense to keep her glued to center stage.

As Lettice Douffet, the most eccentric tour guide ever to lead bored American and Japanese visitors through one of England's dullest stately homes, Ms. Smith is, for much of Act 1, the dazzling revue comedienne she once was, dashing up and down a dark Tudor staircase while dispensing historical arcana and restroom directions with equally mad aplomb. Well, Ms. Smith is not running, actually—she just seems to be. Her long arms are in windmill motion, as if she were directing traffic at a rush-hour intersection. Her voice, the only good argument yet advanced for the existence of sinus passages, tucks an extra syllable or two into words already as chewy as "escutcheon." Her moon-shaped eyes, framed by cascading red curls, are as mischievous and wide and darting as those of Lettice's beloved pet cat.

The other Maggie Smiths on view at the Barrymore are no less extravagant, no less endearing. Eventually asked to share the stage, or at least cohabit it, with another actress, the estimable Margaret Tyzack, the star becomes the stylized classicist who can italicize a line as prosaic as "Have you no marmalade?" until it sounds like a freshly minted epigram by Coward or Wilde. Later still, Ms. Smith is permitted a moment as a tragedian: She stands in the shadows of Lettice's basement flat—a lonely woman for an instant deserted by her usual ebullience—and reveals her age and isolation through a veil of very small tears.

But that is about the only instance when Ms. Smith comes to parade rest in *Lettice and Lovage*; at times this inexhaustible entertainer even switches outrageous costumes in mid-scene. The exertion is needed. Mr. Shaffer's play, his first out-and-out comedy since *Black Comedy* in 1964, is a slight if harmless confection that at first matches Ms. Smith's bracing energy but by Act 3 must be bolstered by it. The jig would be up far earlier in the evening if anyone were so stupid as to ask the star to sit still.

Lettice and Lovage is essentially a high camp, female version of the archetypal Shaffer play, most recently exemplified by *Equus* and *Amadeus*, in which two men, one representing creativity and ecstatic passion and the other mediocrity and sterility, battle for dominance. In this case, the free spirit is Lettice, a lover of history and theater and a sworn enemy of all in life that is "mere." Lettice, who is inevitably referred to as incorrigible, loses her tour-guide job because she embellishes the official history of Fustian House in Wiltshire with outlandish Elizabethan fantasies (which are repeated in four riotous variations in Mr. Shaffer's bravura opening scene). The stick-in-the-mud who sacks her, played by Ms. Tyzack, is Lotte Schoen, a gray personnel bureaucrat who worships fact as much as Lettice reveres romantic fancy.

What makes this variation on the Shaffer formula less compelling than its predecessors is not so much its comic tone—there are, rest assured, no horses blinded here—as its lackadaisical dramatic structure and its shallow characterizations. The conflict between Lettice and Lotte is resolved fairly early, for it only takes a little lovage, an herb Lettice uses to brew an Elizabethan cordial, to turn them into bosom buddies.

Once these apparently asexual spinsters warm to each other, the author elects to arrest their development. Lotte is stripped of her wig but not down to her soul, thereby robbing Ms. Tyzack's flawless performance of the opportunity for a touching metamorphosis. Lettice's relationship to her former adversary remains jokey rather than intimate. The jokes, though written by Mr. Shaffer with a sure sense of the virtuoso instruments at his disposal, deliver more nostalgic tickles than laughter. They're largely impersonal gibes at the dehumanizing modern London the women discover they both deplore: a city full of automated teller machines and the sterile office towers that so nettle the Prince of Wales.

For all of his detestation of automation, Mr. Shaffer is not above using an intercom to keep his play going when all else fails. And too often he provides only a mere pastiche of civilized wit—the kind that impresses American Anglophiles on trust-house tours—by packing in references to Latin etymologies and the Shakespearean antics of Lettice's actress-mother or by having his characters deliver crowd-pleasing endorsements of yesteryear's values. The zingers promised by the actresses' sharp diction only occasionally materialize, and they're closer in tone to *Auntie Mame* than *The Madwoman of Chaillot*. In place of Mame's motto of "Live! Live! Live!" is Lettice's of "Enlarge! Enliven! Enlighten!" and, like Patrick Dennis's heroine, Mr. Shaffer's is dismissed from temporary employment at a department store and must win over a mousy secretary (Bette Henritze) and a stuffy lawyer (Paxton Whitehead) with her bohemian ways.

The staging, by Michael Blakemore, is as airtight as one expects from the director of *City of Angels* and *Noises Off*. Or so it is until Act 3, which, though given a new and pandering final curtain since the London premiere, still becomes mired in a complex narrative of preposterous offstage events that turn out not to matter anyway. While Alan Tagg's scenic design and Ken Billington's lighting practice an excess of dowdy realism in depicting the gloom of Lettice's Earl's Court flat, Ms. Smith's personality so saturates everything around her that, like the character she plays, she instantly floods a world of gray with color. This is idiosyncratic theater acting of a high and endangered order, not to be confused with the actress's tightly minimalistic film work. If *Lettice and Lovage* is but a modest excuse for it, what theaterlover needs any excuse whatsoever to have a rare reunion with Maggie Smith?

ASPECTS OF LOVE
BROADHURST THEATRE, APRIL 9, 1990

Andrew Lloyd Webber, the composer who is second to none when writing musicals about cats, roller-skating trains, and falling chandeliers, has made an earnest but bizarre career decision in *Aspects of Love,* his new show at the Broadhurst. He has written a musical about people.

Whether *Aspects of Love* is a musical for people is another matter. Mr. Lloyd Webber continues to compose in the official style that has made him an international favorite, sacrificing any personality of his own to the merchandisable common denominator of easy-listening pop music. Though *Aspects of Love* purports to deal with romance in many naughty guises—from rampant promiscuity to cradle-snatching, lesbianism, and incest—it generates about as much heated passion as a visit to the bank. Even when women strip to lacy undergarments, the lingerie doesn't suggest the erotic fantasies of Frederick's of Hollywood so much as the no-nonsense austerity of Margaret Thatcher's Britain.

The inspiration for the production's dour game of musical beds is a 1955 novella by David Garnett, a secondary Bloomsbury figure and the son of the great Russian translator Constance Garnett. The tone of the adaptation is more Barbara Cartland than Virginia Woolf. For two acts sprawling over seventeen bewildering years, the audience tries to track a young Englishman named Alex (Michael Ball) and his much older Uncle George (Kevin Colson) as they bounce between a French actress (Ann Crumb) and an Italian sculptor (Kathleen Rowe McAllen). The women, named Rose and Giulietta, have a quickie affair of their own along the way, to the extent that anything in *Aspects of Love* can be described as quick.

To find out why everyone is forever taking tumbles in the hay—literally so in a laughable hayloft scene—one must turn to the philosophical lyrics, which were written by the previous Lloyd Webber collaborators Don Black (*Song & Dance*) and Charles Hart (*The Phantom of the Opera*) and seem to have been translated, though not by Constance Garnett, from the original Hallmark. "Love changes everything, hands and faces, earth and sky," sings Alex. "Life goes on, love goes free," adds Uncle

George a little later. "There is more to love than simply making love," concludes Giulietta. But perhaps Alex is most to the evening's point when he sings at the outset that love can make "a night seem like a lifetime."

Every sentiment in *Aspects of Love,* as well as an ever-changing à la carte menu of food and aperitifs, is sung. And sung again and again. Mr. Lloyd Webber, as is his wont, rotates a few tunes throughout his show, some of them catchy and many of them left stranded in musical foreplay. But this time the composer's usual Puccini-isms have been supplanted by a naked Sondheim envy. The first song for the two young lovers, "Seeing Is Believing," echoes "Tonight" in *West Side Story,* and a later duet for dueling male rivals recalls *A Little Night Music* (as does much of *Aspects of Love,* its staging included). One also encounters the ghosts of Lerner and Loewe's *Gigi* in Uncle George, who is the avuncular, champagne-sipping Maurice Chevalier boulevardier reincarnated as a truly dirty old man. When men thank heaven for little girls in *Aspects of Love,* chances are the girls will turn out to be jail bait.

What neither Mr. Lloyd Webber nor his collaborators can provide is a semblance of the humanity that is also, to some, an aspect of love. The misogyny in this show is more transparent than in other Lloyd Webber musicals where the general rule is to present principal female characters as either prostitutes (*Evita, Cats, Starlight Express*) or sainted virgins (*Jesus Christ Superstar, The Phantom of the Opera*). Both heroines of *Aspects of Love* frequently behave like bitches and whores, to use the epithets of the male characters. Their men, meanwhile, are overgrown English schoolboys who have no idea that women can be anything other than girls they pick up at Harry's Bar or the nearest stage door.

The sexless casting of the principal roles by the director, Trevor Nunn, only adds to the musical's icy emotional infantilism. From her very first line—a line from *The Master Builder,* no less—Ms. Crumb's Rose is a tough cookie, unconvincing as a tempestuous star known for her performances of the classics or as a femme fatale who, in her words, "could have a thousand lovers." With her piercing singing voice and loud, fake laughter, this actress could shatter glass more easily than hearts.

Like Ms. Crumb, Ms. McAllen is an American performer who originated her role last year in the West End. She, too, is a brassy belter who makes no attempt to convey her character's European background and artistic temperament and who is further handicapped by unflattering costumes (by Maria Bjornson) that, in Giulietta's case, announce her Lesbian Tendencies with every pantsuit. While Mr. Colson's silver-maned Uncle George is an amiably drawn cliché—the cultured, mon-eyed old roué with a "lust for living"—Mr. Ball's Alex cuts a preposterous figure as a libertine. A beefy juvenile who would fit right in with the Trapp Family Singers, Mr. Ball bares his chest for no worthwhile esthetic or prurient reason, but not to the point of dismantling the chest mike from which emanates his entire personality.

With the exception of Andrew Bridge's lighting of mountain vistas, almost nothing in Mr. Nunn's production is appropriate to a work that aspires to romantic Continental finesse. Ms. Bjornson, an inspired scenic artist for dark material like *Phantom,* fails to lighten up. Her oppressive floor-to-ceiling design of concrete-colored brick and cobblestones suggests two more somber Nunn productions, *Chess* and *Les Misérables,* on an enforced holiday in Ceauşescu-era Romania. Even at its most bucolic, Uncle George's villa in the Pyrénées looks less like a pleasure dome than a forlorn provincial inn the season after being stripped of its Michelin Guide stars.

As much as its subject invites the spectacle of men and women dancing, *Aspects of Love* offers little, preferring instead to pay a gratuitous, static visit to a shooting gallery at a fairground. Gillian Lynne's scant choreography makes a superfluous circus number seem as grim as a subsequent *Zorba*-like funeral rite. The only steady semblance of movement in the staging is provided by a treadmill that sends people and furniture trundling across the stage with lugubrious monotony. While *Aspects of Love,* with its references to Huxley and Turgenev, may be the most high-minded of Lloyd Webber musicals, isn't it also the one in most desperate need of roller skates?

THE PIANO LESSON
WALTER KERR THEATRE, APRIL 17, 1990

The piano is the first thing the audience hears in *The Piano Lesson,* the new August Wilson play at the Walter Kerr Theatre. Three hours later, it seems as if the music, by turns bubbling and thunderous, has never stopped.

Though Mr. Wilson won a Pulitzer Prize last week for this work, no one need worry that he is marching to an establishment beat. *The Piano Lesson* is joyously an African American play: It has its own spacious poetry, its own sharp angle on a nation's history, its own metaphorical idea of drama, and its own palpable ghosts that roar right through the upstairs window of the household where the action unfolds. Like other Wilson plays, *The Piano Lesson* seems to sing even when it is talking. But it isn't all of America that is singing. The central fact of black American life—the long shadow of slavery—transposes the voices of Mr. Wilson's characters, and of the indelible actors who inhabit them, to a key that rattles history and shakes the audience on both sides of the racial divide.

Set in the Pittsburgh of 1936, just midway in time between *Joe Turner's Come and Gone* and *Fences,* Mr. Wilson's new play echoes his others by reaching back toward Africa and looking ahead to modern urban America even as it remains focused on the intimate domestic canvas of a precise bygone year. Though *The Piano Lesson* is about a fight over the meaning of a long span of history, its concerns are dramatized within a simple battle between a sister and a brother over the possession of a musical instrument. The keeper of the piano, a family heirloom, is a young widow named Berniece (S. Epatha Merkerson), who lets it languish unused in the parlor of the house she shares with her uncle and daughter. Her brother, Boy Willie (Charles S. Dutton), barges in unannounced from Mississippi, intending to sell the antique to buy a farm on the land his family worked as slaves and sharecroppers.

One need only look at the majestic upright piano itself to feel its power as a symbolic repository of a people's soul. Sculptured into its rich wood are totemic human figures whose knife-drawn features suggest both the pride of African culture and the grotesque scars of slavery. As it happens, both the pride and scars run deep in the genealogy of the siblings at center stage. Their great-grandfather, who carved the images, lost his wife and young son when they were traded away for the piano. Years later, Berniece and Boy Willie's father was killed after he took the heirloom from a new generation of white owners.

In *The Piano Lesson,* the disposition of the piano becomes synonymous with the use to which the characters put their ancestral legacy. For Berniece, the instrument must remain a somber shrine to a tragic past. For Boy Willie, the piano is a stake to the freedom his father wanted him to have. To Mr. Wilson, both characters are right—and wrong. Just as Berniece is too enslaved by history to get on with her life, so Boy Willie is too cavalier about his family's heritage to realize that money alone cannot buy him independence and equality in a white man's world. Like all Wilson protagonists, both the brother and sister must take a journey, at times a supernatural one, to the past if they are to seize the future. They cannot be reconciled with each other until they have had a reconciliation with the identity that is etched in their family tree, as in the piano, with blood.

Mr. Dutton and Ms. Merkerson prove to be extraordinary adversaries through every twist of their no-holds-barred dispute. They command equal respect and affection through antithetical acting styles. As he first revealed as Levee, the discordant trumpet player in Mr. Wilson's *Ma Rainey's Black Bottom,* the burly, broadly smiling Mr. Dutton is a force of nature on stage: a human cyclone who, as Berniece says, sows noise, confusion, and trouble wherever he goes. Here is that rare actor who can announce that he's on fire and make an audience believe he might actually burn down the theater. Yet the impressive Ms. Merkerson remains quiet and dignified holding her ground against him—at least up to a point. In the evening's most devastating scene, she slugs her brother in impotent fury, as if her small fists and incantatory wails might somehow halt the revenge-fueled cycle of violence that killed her father and her husband and their fathers before them.

Although the second act contains its dead ends, repetitions, and excessive authorial announcements—an O'Neill-like excess in most of this writer's plays—Mr. Wilson prevents the central conflict in *The Piano Lesson* from becoming too nakedly didactic by enclosing it within an extended household of memorable characters. The ebb and flow of diurnal activity in Berniece's home thickens the main theme while offering a naturalistic picture of a transitional black America in an era when movies, skyscrapers, and airplanes were fresh wonders of the world. A Wilson play feels truly lived in—so much so in Lloyd Richards's supple production that activities like the cooking of eggs, the washing of dishes, and the comings and goings from an audibly flushed toilet never seem like stage events, but become subliminal beats in the rhythm of a self-contained universe.

Still, the play's real music is in the language, all of which is gloriously served by the ensemble company that Mr. Richards has assembled and honed during the more than two years that *The Piano Lesson* has traveled to New York by way of the country's resident theaters. Carl Gordon, as an uncle who has spent twenty-seven years working for the railroad, and Lou Myers, as another uncle who has hit his own long road as a traveling musician, trade tall and small tales of hard-won practical philosophy, political wisdom, women, and whiskey—some of them boisterously funny, others unexpectedly touching. At other moments, their colloquial verbal cadences trail off into riffs of actual song, whether piano blues or roof-raising vocal harmonies, that express their autobiographies of pride, defiance, and suffering as eloquently as their words.

A younger generation of dispossessed black men with a different set of experiences and aspirations is just as vividly represented by Tommy Hollis, as a Bible-toting elevator man with dreams of leading his own Christian flock, and Rocky Carroll, as a wide-eyed rural drifter dazzled by his first exposure to the big city. A scene in which Mr. Carroll briefly courts Ms. Merkerson by presenting her with a dollar bottle of "French perfume" is, in writing, staging, and performance, a masterly romantic duet of crossed signals and unacknowledged longings that seems to float up from a distant, innocent time like a hallucination.

While there are no white characters in *The Piano Lesson,* the presence of white America is felt throughout—and not just by dint of past history. Boy Willie repeatedly and pointedly announces that he will sell the piano to a white man who he's heard is roaming through black neighborhoods "looking to buy musical instruments." Whatever happens to the piano, however, the playwright makes it clear that the music in *The Piano Lesson* is not up for sale. That haunting music belongs to the people who have lived it, and it has once again found miraculous voice in a play that August Wilson has given to the American stage.

SPUNK
PUBLIC THEATER, APRIL 19, 1990

When writers with clashing personalities share the stage, the result can often be a tug of war. But in *Spunk,* the exuberant show at the Public Theater celebrating the fiction of Zora Neale Hurston, George C. Wolfe, the author of *The Colored Museum,* submerges his own irreverent sensibility to serve, and serve ingeniously, the spirit of a far different literary voice. When one recalls how much satirical devastation Mr. Wolfe inflicted on Lorraine Hansberry and Ntozake Shange in *The Colored Museum,* his selfless devotion to Hurston is all the more impressive.

Mr. Wolfe is not, of course, the first in the theater or anywhere else to pick up the banner for Hurston, the Florida-born novelist, folklorist, and anthropologist who was a legendary figure in the Harlem Renaissance, a national literary star, and a thorny political ideologue before fading into obscurity and poverty at the end of her life. (She died in 1960.) In recent years there has been a steady procession of books, essays, plays, and television programs about her life and art. Most of Hurston's major works are now back in print and the unproduced play she wrote with Langston Hughes during the Depression, *Mule Bone,* is scheduled for production at Lincoln Center in August.

Spunk, in which three short stories have been adapted for the stage and folded into a bluesy musical framework, reveals how time has finally caught up with Hurston's view of the African American experience. Once attacked by Richard Wright, among other social realists, as having perpetuated minstrel stereotypes, she is now seen clearly as an astute observer of a hyphenated black culture merging the African and the American. A connoisseur and zealous reporter of indigenous speech, Hurston lovingly preserved the extravagant black English of the urban and rural America of her time. Yet the people doing the talking were dignified, fully realized characters—in no way minstrels—and the stories containing their verbal improvisations were often narrated in formal, omniscient prose that could swing seamlessly from the caustic to the tragic.

Serving as both writer and director, Mr. Wolfe makes sure that every precious, spiky Hurston word counts. With a company of six performers, two of them singers, he is not only faithful to the dialogue in the stories (and even, at one point, to a comic authorial footnote redefining the word "pimp"), but he also retains the narration, assigning it at will to those members of the free-floating ensemble serving as a chorus or to the characters themselves in mid-scene. The technique rarely seems stagy, because the entire evening, enhanced by the choreography of Hope Clarke and the Noh-like masks and puppets of Barbara Pollitt, has a folklorish gait. The style could anachronistically be likened to magic realism, but whatever one calls it, Mr. Wolfe has created a stage atmosphere in which the rules of conventional realism are suspended in favor of fabulist invention.

If there's a subject uniting the stories in *Spunk*, it is that of men and women. And the point of view is ideologically balanced. The first tale, *Sweat*, is about a physically and spiritually exhausted washerwoman abused and betrayed by her husband; the third, *The Gilded Six-Bits*, is about an adoring husband betrayed by his wife. In between the two marital fables comes a small comic masterpiece, *Story in Harlem Slang*, in which two sharp male idlers, seeking "wealth and splendor in Harlem without working," try to hustle a meal from a domestic enjoying a payday afternoon off. Along the way to meeting their comeuppance, the men treat the audience to a jamboree of 1940s uptown slang that is perfectly echoed by their burlesque zoot suits and the struts with which they percolate down Lenox Avenue.

The production's elegant stylization extends to the sets, costumes, and lighting—handsomely designed by Loy Arcenas, Toni-Leslie James, and Don Holder—and to the persistent guitar accompaniment provided by Chic Street Man, who also composed the music for the full-bodied blues interludes gutsily sung by Ann Duquesnay. The cast functions as such a closely knit ensemble that it's almost unjust to single out Danitra Vance's exceptional range in playing a trio of women who are in turn worn to the bone, full of sass, and aglow with innocence. (Ms. Vance can sing, too, and does a hilarious impersonation of a "pretty white woman" squealing.) Reggie Montgomery, as an assortment of con artists, and K. Todd Freeman, in broader bits, also make lively contributions. Kevin Jackson, the ingenuous, lovesick husband of *The Gilded Six-Bits*, is a young actor of unusual charm and talent.

While the theatrical trimmings that Mr. Wolfe's production pours on Hurston's prose can sometimes be too thick—it takes a while to untangle the narrative thread in *Sweat*, for instance—the show seems false to its source only in its repetition of an over-explanatory theme song that champions the characters' grit in corny terms seemingly intended to spoonfeed the stories to white audiences. The show's title is also questionable, for while Hurston did write a story called *Spunk*, it isn't dramatized here and its title is hardly the theme of this anthology's unsentimental vignettes, one of which ends with a grisly death.

The fallible people of *Spunk* in fact have no more or less spunk than anyone else, which is one reason that they seem so real and engaging. The true spunk in *Spunk* belongs to Mr. Wolfe, who has gallantly met Zora Neale Hurston in the theater on her own uncompromising terms and, better still, has found the imaginative means to make good on his half of so challenging a collaboration.

ACCOMPLICE

RICHARD RODGERS THEATRE, APRIL 27, 1990

In Rupert Holmes's last Broadway whodunit, *The Mystery of Edwin Drood,* the audience was invited to vote on the murderer at the end of the second act. In *Accomplice,* Mr. Holmes's new whodunit at the Richard Rodgers Theatre, the audience should be allowed to vote on the beginning, middle, and end of the second act. The winner, in a landslide, would surely be None of the Above.

Accomplice is one of those plays—like *Sleuth, Deathtrap,* and *Moose Murders,* to name beloved past examples—at which the patrons must be sworn to secrecy lest the author's surprises be ruined for future customers. Those secrets are safe with me because I found *Accomplice* incomprehensible after intermission, even though much of Act 2 is given over to extended round-table discussions among the characters as to what has happened or might happen or won't happen or can't happen. These verbose yet unilluminating explanations extend right through the curtain call, which itself is somewhat gabbier than any dénouement in Agatha Christie. Theater historians should note that the curtain call of *Accomplice* is additionally distinguished by the appearance of the playwright, who is given his very own bow and takes it with due modesty.

What the sepulchral Mr. Holmes, clad in a business suit, is doing onstage is one of those secrets indeed best left undivulged. Suffice it to say that the man is apparently prepared to travel the country with his play for eternity, as his script makes mandatory, should *Accomplice* find favor on the dinner-theater circuit. Some of the evening's other secrets are so poorly kept by the loose-lipped management that one doesn't even have to see the play to guess them: The *Playbill* gives no character names for its four cast members and includes more biographies for understudies than there ostensibly are roles.

It is also giving away nothing to say that the biggest shocks in *Accomplice* include some special effects unlikely to startle any theatergoer who has been within fifty yards of a Fourth of July sparkler. Further fireworks of a fashion are provided by a demographically balanced pair of homosexual kisses (one each for male and female couples) that may be becoming de rigueur on Broadway in the season of *Aspects of Love*.

The kissers, none of them in top form under the overemphatic direction of Art Wolff, include two accomplished clowns, Jason Alexander, late of *Jerome Robbins' Broadway,* and Michael McKean, most fondly remembered from *This Is Spinal Tap,* and their routine foils, Natalia Nogulich and Pamela Brull. In Act 1, the company dons fake-looking wigs and even faker accents to enact a reasonable though witless facsimile of the sort of West End thriller in which gin-sipping, cigarette-smoking Mayfair twits loll about an isolated weekend cottage (satirically designed by David Jenkins) and plot the murder of their own spouses or someone else's. The brittle repartee includes lines like "Medwick may give me insomnia, but I'm not going to lose any sleep over it" and, somewhat funnier in this context, "You should go to the theater more often— there's life in it yet." In Act 2, the wisecracks are largely about Broadway show business, with the inevitable butts being Los Angeles actors, backstage unions, and Mandy Patinkin.

It's in Act 2 as well that Ms. Brull finds herself at the center of a dispute as to whether she will bare her breasts on stage. This pressing issue is tabled rather than resolved, but not before it has engendered more tedious debate than a resolution about fishing rights before the United Nations Security Council. For her part, Ms. Nogulich is required to writhe on the floor with Mr. McKean in an exceptionally noisy carnal romp. It's enough to make one long for those predictable old whodunits in which the butlers always did it but at least had the common courtesy to do it quickly with their clothes and mouths both firmly zippered shut.

≡ *Jason Alexander soon scooted right back to* Seinfeld.

ONCE ON THIS ISLAND
PLAYWRIGHTS HORIZONS, MAY 7, 1990

In *Once on This Island,* the stage has found its own sugar-and-cartoon-free answer to *The Little Mermaid.* A ninety-minute Caribbean fairy tale told in rousing song and dance, this show is a joyous marriage of the slick and the folkloric, of the hard-nosed sophistication of Broadway musical theater and the indigenous culture of a tropical isle. No doubt the evening will nettle purists who insist that all American musicals be urbane or that all foreign entertainments exhibited in New York be homegrown. Most everyone else is likely to emerge from Playwrights Horizons ready to dance down Forty-second Street.

The parallel between *The Little Mermaid* and *Once on This Island* is not invoked flippantly. As the songs for the Disney film were provided by Alan Menken and Howard Ashman, who wrote the tongue-in-cheek Off Broadway musical *Little Shop of Horrors,* so the authors of this musical are Lynn Ahrens (book and lyrics) and Stephen Flaherty (music), a similarly smart Off Broadway team who made a promising debut with a comic musical, the unsuccessful *Lucky Stiff,* at Playwrights Horizons a year ago. What's more, *Once on This Island,* which has been adapted from a novel by the Trinidad-born novelist Rosa Guy, owes its own debt to Hans Christian Andersen. Set in the French Antilles, Ms. Guy's deeply felt tale of the romance between a black peasant girl, Ti Moune (La Chanze), and a worldly mulatto aristocrat, Daniel Beauxhomme (Jerry Dixon), is a revisionist *Little Mermaid* in which class and racial differences, rather than the sea, pull the star-crossed lovers asunder.

The musical's director and choreographer is Graciela Daniele, who opened this theater season with the short-lived *Dangerous Games* on Broadway and now ends it, showbiz-fairy-tale fashion, with her most effervescent achievement to date. *Once on This Island* is wall-to-wall dancing, movement, and mime. From the mood-setting first number, titled "We Dance" and reminiscent in spirit of Bob Fosse's "Magic to

Do" in *Pippin,* the audience is drawn into the evening's once-upon-a-time storytelling style and fantastical atmosphere. Yet to come are high-stepping, swivel-hipped calypso routines, ecstatic ritual dances to demanding gods, a rollicking Caribbean counterpart to "Follow the Yellow Brick Road," and even a delicate European waltz in the elegant hotel that serves as Daniel's princely palace.

In a show in which everything is of a piece, the staging is inseparable from the work of three superlative designers: Loy Arcenas (sets), Judy Dearing (costumes), and Allen Lee Hughes (lighting). What the Disney Studios can do with animation or Julie Taymor does with puppets in *Juan Darien,* these artists achieve with flesh-and-blood actors. When Daniel races his sports car around the island, Mr. Dixon serves as both vehicle and driver, running about the stage in a white linen suit and sneakers, twin flashlights illuminating his winding road. Rainstorms arrive as a parade of dancers crowned by magical umbrellas dripping silver. Jungle wildlife materializes through costumes, masks, and headdresses of hallucinatory design.

Mr. Arcenas, whose flair for fantasy has also been seen this season in *Spunk* and *Prelude to a Kiss,* encloses *Once on This Island* within a floor-to-ceiling mural emblazoned with faux-primitive flora and fauna, a tropical setting imagined in the Tahitian idiom of Gauguin, with the palette expanded to the cobalt blues and iridescent fuchsias of Matisse and Bonnard. When a large, lacy white patchwork quilt descends to become a lovers' bed, or when Mr. Hughes dims the sky to twinkling starlight or orange sunsets, *Once on This Island* almost makes one feel its orchid-scented breezes.

That Mr. Arcenas would present the tropics as Postimpressionists might have imagined them is in keeping with the songs of Mr. Flaherty and Ms. Ahrens. Though they have borrowed freely from the musical culture of their setting, the composer and lyricist do not pretend to authenticity, choosing instead to filter the story's environment through their own sensibility. Mr. Flaherty's lush, melodic music goes native in the way Richard Rodgers went "Oriental" when writing "Bali Ha'i" and "The March of the Siamese Children." The score is arranged with an apt transcultural lilt, for flute and bongo drum alike, by Michael Starobin, the orchestrator known for his associations with Stephen Sondheim, Charles Strouse, and William Finn.

In her lyrics and very spare dialogue, Ms. Ahrens doesn't make the mistake of writing cutesy mock-dialect, and, except in one rueful song ("Some Girls") about the hero's choosing of a bride, she forsakes the sharp wit apparent in *Lucky Stiff*. Her words are simple, direct, and poignant. Papa Ge, the Demon of Death played with sinuous Sportin' Life bravura by Eric Riley, declares himself "the secret of life nobody wants to learn . . . the car racing toward distant shores." When Ti Moune leaves home to pursue her love, her heartbroken parents (Sheila Gibbs and Ellis E. Williams) sing a tender yet guilt-inducing farewell: "What you are, we made you / What we gave, you took."

Before the show ends, nearly each performer in the lithe, full-voiced ensemble of eleven breaks out of the chorus to shine. The most golden throats and ethereal presences belong to La Chanze and Nikki Rene as the two very different women with claims to Daniel's love. Kecia Lewis-Evans brings down the house as the gospel-belting earth mother who helps ease Ti Moune into the woods and out again on the path to the fulfillment of her romantic dreams.

That path, of course, does not always run smooth. *Once on This Island* has the integrity of genuine fairy tales, in that it doesn't lead to a saccharine ending but to a catharsis, a transcendent acceptance of the dust-to-dust continuity of life and death. "Why We Tell the Story" is the concluding song for the evening's storytellers, and one of those reasons is that "our lives become the stories that we weave." As the story and its tellers at last come full circle in *Once on This Island,* the audience feels the otherworldly thrill of discovering the fabric of its own lives in an enchanted tapestry from a distant shore.

≡ *The songwriting team of Ahrens and Flaherty followed this musical with an overproduced fiasco at Lincoln Center,* My Favorite Year, *before collaborating with the playwright Terrence McNally and the director Frank Galati* (The Grapes of Wrath) *on the musical version of E. L. Doctorow's* Ragtime.

THE MERRY WIVES OF WINDSOR
FOLGER SHAKESPEARE THEATRE, WASHINGTON, D.C., MAY 30, 1990

Not even the metamorphosis of Robert Morse into Truman Capote can match that of the comic actress Pat Carroll into Sir John Falstaff for *The Merry Wives of Windsor.* When Ms. Carroll makes her first entrance, a nervous silence falls over the audience at the Shakespeare Theatre at the Folger here, as hundreds of eyes search for some trace of the woman they've seen in a thousand television reruns. What they find instead is a Falstaff who could have stepped out of a formal painted portrait: a balding, aged knight with scattered tufts of silver hair and whiskers, an enormous belly, pink cheeks, and squinting, froggy eyes that peer out through boozy mists. The sight is so eerie you grab on to your seat.

Then comes the walk. The first business Ms. Carroll must carry out in Michael Kahn's staging of Shakespeare's comedy is the simple descent of a staircase. As the actress negotiates her bulk down the steps, waddling and gasping all the way, one realizes that it is Shakespeare's character, not a camp parody, that is being served. Here is a weary, cynical clown, out of resources and near death, a shadow in every way but girth of the witty royal sidekick of *Henry IV, Parts I and II.* Legend has it that Shakespeare brought Falstaff back in *Merry Wives* at Queen Elizabeth's request. Whatever the truth, the obligatory Falstaff of this play is a pathetic buffoon, the butt of its most extravagant jokes. And that's the person, "a man of continual dissolution and thaw," that Ms. Carroll creates as she wheezes down those stairs: a hot-air balloon waiting to be burst, a pickled Humpty Dumpty riding for a fall.

The fall will come—the Falstaff of *Merry Wives* has "a kind of alacrity in sinking," whether into a laundry basket or the Thames—and Ms. Carroll will handle that, too, with the comic aplomb she has honed through a long career. Her performance is a triumph from start to finish, and, I think, a particularly brave and moving one, with implications that go beyond this one production. Ms. Carroll and Mr. Kahn help revivify the argument that the right actresses can perform some of the great classic roles traditionally denied to women and make them their own. It's not a new argument, to be sure; female Hamlets stretch back into history. But what separates Ms. Carroll's Falstaff from some other similar casting experiments of late is that her performance exists to investigate a character rather than merely as ideological window dressing for a gimmicky production.

As it happens, Mr. Kahn's production, though not gimmicky, leaves much to be desired itself. Ms. Carroll aside, his *Merry Wives* simply isn't as funny as it has to be. Unlike *Twelfth Night,* which Mr. Kahn staged so buoyantly with Kelly McGillis to open the Folger season, this Shakespeare text is not bolstered by feeling, ideas, and poetry. Everything rides on a series of farcical pranks in which Falstaff and some lesser fools are humiliated as they attempt to seduce either the merry wives Page and Ford or the Page daughter, Anne. In the funniest *Merry Wives* I've seen, directed by Bill Alexander for the Royal Shakespeare Company in 1986, the setting was advanced to prosperous 1950s suburbia, and no wonder: The pratfalls of this play are a perfect stylistic fit with the *Carry On* movies and *I Love Lucy.*

Mr. Kahn knows this. Though he keeps the setting firmly Elizabethan, his staging is as knockabout, and as mindful of the bourgeois complacency of the Windsor community, as was Mr. Alexander's. It's the execution, not the interpretation, that fails: Mr. Kahn's Windsor isn't populated by natural clowns but by straining actors simulating clowning with stock vocal and facial exaggerations, augmented by jokey props (a skeleton, a breakaway hat). The more energetic performers, led by Marilyn Sokol (Mistress Quickly), Edward Gero (Master Ford), and Floyd King (Doctor Caius), generally offer three broad gestures when a single sharp one would do, while the others, with the exceptions of Franchelle Stewart Dorn (Mistress Page) and Emery Battis (Justice Shallow), are too bland to register at all.

Perhaps the director put most of his energy into his collaboration with his star, and, for once, that may be achievement enough. Falstaff is played so convincingly as a man (yet without any phony lowering of the actress's voice) that he still seems masculine when the plot requires him to adopt the drag outfit of a witch. Ms. Carroll's unambiguous manliness is appropriate, because *Merry Wives,* in contrast to *Twelfth Night* or *As You Like It,* does not take sexual identity as a subject. Falstaff's designs on the Mistresses Page and Ford have mainly to do with money, not flesh.

But Ms. Carroll invests her performance with an extra dimension anyway. The success of her male camouflage makes the decrepit knight's isolation from the conventional folk of Windsor seem doubly pronounced. When this Falstaff receives his final comeuppance, in the Act 5 forest masquerade that requires him to don a deer's head and be "made an ass," the ridicule he suffers carries an unusually cruel aftertaste.

As befits a comedy, of course, the knight is soon forgiven for his misdeeds and is invited to join the townsfolk to "laugh this sport o'er by a country fire." But not before Ms. Carroll, still cowering in antlers, has stood alone and abandoned at the forest's shadowy edge, her eyes revealing just how lonely and humiliating it has been for her particular Falstaff to be dismissed as a freak. And not before the audience has seen a fearless comic actress hit a tragic note that promises to extend her Shakespearean range even further than this remarkable embodiment of the opposite sex.

TWELFTH
SEASON

1990—91

Jonathan Pryce, Lea Salonga, and
Willy Falk in *Miss Saigon*

Almost twenty-five years ago, the director Harold Prince pushed Broadway a significant step forward with *Cabaret,* a show that folded Brechtian storytelling, abstract theatrical metaphors, and the history of Nazism into the sophisticated glitter of a mainstream Broadway musical. In *Kiss of the Spider Woman,* his first musical since *The Phantom of the Opera,* Mr. Prince reunites with John Kander and Fred Ebb, the composer and lyricist of *Cabaret,* with far more radical ideas in mind.

Spider Woman, an adaptation of the 1978 Manuel Puig novel that also inspired the 1985 film with William Hurt and Raul Julia, is the first large-scale American musical told from an unapologetic and unsentimental gay point of view. In Terrence McNally's script, the entire narrative is seen through the eyes of Molina (John Rubinstein), a homosexual window dresser incarcerated in a Latin American prison, while the perspective of his cellmate, a political prisoner named Valentin (Kevin Gray), is reduced to the barest essentials. *Spider Woman* isn't shy about taking chances. It depicts torture with the grueling ferocity missing from Mr. Prince's *Evita,* has a morphine-fueled dream sequence of dancing hypodermic needles, and simulates an involuntary act of defecation. The evening culminates with the image of its title, a blood-spattering kiss of death.

The show is the first offering of New Musicals, a production company that has announced a season of four new American musicals at the State University College here. New Musicals informed the press that its attractions are works in progress and asked that drama critics not review them. *Spider Woman,* however, is presented to the audience as a full-dress commercial production rather than a workshop.

If anything, the tragedy of *Spider Woman* is that New Musicals, which describes itself as a "new Broadway" in its promotional literature, has not allowed the work to develop slowly in a laboratory staging, as non-profit, Off Broadway companies have helped develop adventurous musicals like *A Chorus Line* or *Sunday in the Park with George*. Instead, *Spider Woman* arrives already burdened with the full, and in this case crushing, weight of Broadway extravagance. It is as overproduced as other seriously intentioned Prince musicals of the past decade like *Grind* and *A Doll's Life*. But unlike those failures, *Spider Woman* has the kernel of an exciting idea, and it also has, in Mr. Kander and Mr. Ebb, superb, if often underrated, songwriters who are clearly hungering to rise to a challenge.

The show's potential virtues are being held hostage by a staging so overgrown that major esthetic reconsiderations, as opposed to cosmetic nips and tucks, are already foreclosed in this production. Though the musical's story is fundamentally an intimate one about two people—men of opposite sensibilities who teach each other about self-respect and self-sacrifice while in captivity—it is often difficult to find Molina and Valentin within the bloated trappings. As in its other incarnations, this *Spider Woman* intersperses its grim prison scenes with Molina's campy recounting of an old, fondly embroidered Hollywood movie that is his imaginary escape from present despair. But in this case, the fantasy film—here fittingly changed to an old movie musical—overwhelms the reality so completely that the compelling story of Molina and Valentin seems a mild, often incoherent intrusion.

Part of the problem may be endemic to Prince musicals that follow the *Cabaret* format of alternating realistic scenes with showbiz production numbers that comment thematically upon them. As recent revivals of *Cabaret* and *Follies* have demonstrated, those musicals' ironic cabaret and vaudeville turns hold up far better than the realistic scenes they are meant to annotate, and *Spider Woman* shares that shortcoming. Yet the new show has a graver defect: The lengthy movie-musical sequences of Molina's fantasies have only a nominal and repetitive relationship to his jail-cell reality. In contrast with the Joel Grey numbers in *Cabaret,* the glitzy routines of *Spider Woman* detract from, rather than enhance, the work's dramatization of fascist repression.

Though Mr. Kander and Mr. Ebb have written some typically amusing parodies for their movie musical, even their better numbers are defeated by the routine choreography of Susan Stroman and by the performance of Lauren Mitchell as the star of Molina's celluloid visions. What is needed in this role is not, perhaps, a mysterious reincarnation of Rita Hayworth (which is what Sonia Braga brought to the film version) but a dazzling musical-comedy presence of the Chita Rivera sort who has always ignited the flashiest Kander and Ebb songs. Ms. Mitchell has neither the personality nor the vocal authority for the task.

The casting of Molina and Valentin is even more damaging. The window dresser now sounds remarkably like the opera fanatic played by Nathan Lane in Mr. McNally's *The Lisbon Traviata,* and Mr. Rubinstein, not a natural comedian, pushes himself so hard that he crosses the line into retrograde gay caricature. Worse, his singing range is so narrow that he cannot be given the big emotional arias that his character must have, and that Mr. Kander and Mr. Ebb are prepared to write, as they demonstrate in a haunting early quartet. Without those songs, Molina becomes an outsider in his own story. While Mr. Gray's Valentin has a stronger voice, his character remains, in writing and performance, too vague to fill the vacuum, a poster-flat radical who looks like Che in *Evita* and sings an anthem, "The Day After That," as generic as "One Day More" in *Les Misérables.*

By evening's end, when Molina and Valentin are supposed to be achieving a redemptive symbiosis, the male stars hardly seem to have met each other. Instead of concentrating on the performances crucial to this psychodrama, Mr. Prince seems fixated on the big production numbers and scenic effects, as if he felt obligated to warp his show to placate Broadway audiences' presumed insistence on spectacle even when he is ostensibly working away from the commercial dictates of Broadway. And the spectacle falls short. The jailhouse choruses, though as grimly conceived as *Fidelio,* still have an antiseptic musical-comedy sheen. Thomas Lynch's scenic design, an inversion of the Hollywood-versus-reality color scheme of Robin Wagner's sets for *City of Angels,* is more busy than ingenious.

It's all frustrating because somewhere in *Kiss of the Spider Woman* is the compelling story its creators want to tell, which is nothing less than an investigation of what it means to be a man, in the highest moral sense, whatever one's sexual orientation. That story begins with two men in a tiny room, and if the creators of *Kiss of the Spider Woman* are to retrieve the intimate heart of their show, they may have to rescue it from the voluminous web in which it has so wastefully become ensnared.

≡*Another controversy. The producers of* Kiss of the Spider Woman, *apparently hoping to bring the show into New York proper from this suburban venue, tried to keep critics from covering it—even though it was a for-profit venture with Broadway prices that did not advertise itself as a work in progress. When the show finally arrived on Broadway three years later, it did much better than it would have had it appeared in anything like this form; it had clearly benefited from the unwanted criticism it had received in Purchase. A completely new cast included Chita Rivera as the Spider Woman—a notion ventured in this review. Even with the many improvements, my own feelings remained mixed, but* Spider Woman *won the Tony and had a long New York run.*

SIX DEGREES OF SEPARATION
Mitzi E. Newhouse Theater, June 15, 1990

Luisa Kittredge, the Upper East Side hostess at the center of John Guare's *Six Degrees of Separation*, delights in the fact that it only takes a chain of six people to connect anyone on the planet with anyone else. But what about those who are eternally separated from others because they cannot find the right six people? Chances are that they, like Ouisa, live in chaotic contemporary New York, which is the setting for this extraordinary high comedy in which broken connections, mistaken identities, and tragic social, familial, and cultural schisms take the stage to create a hilarious and finally searing panorama of urban America in precisely our time.

For those who have been waiting for a masterwork from the writer who bracketed the 1970s with the play *The House of Blue Leaves* and the film *Atlantic City*, this is it. For those who have been waiting for the American theater to produce a play that captures New York as Tom Wolfe did in *Bonfire of the Vanities*, this is also it. And, with all due respect to Mr. Wolfe, *Six Degrees of Separation* expands on that novel's canvas and updates it. Mr. Guare gives as much voice to his black and female characters as to his upper-crust white men, and he transports the audience beyond the dailiness of journalistic storytelling to the magical reaches of the imagination.

Though the play grew out of a 1983 newspaper account of a confidence scheme, it is as at home with the esthetics of Wassily Kandinsky as it is with the realities of Rikers Island. The full sweep of the writing—ninety nonstop minutes of cyclonic action, ranging from knockabout farce to hallucinatory dreams—is matched by Jerry Zaks's ceaselessly inventive production at Lincoln Center's Mitzi E. Newhouse Theater. A brilliant ensemble of seventeen actors led by Stockard Channing, John Cunningham, and James McDaniel is equally adept at fielding riotous gags about Andrew Lloyd Webber musicals and the shattering aftermath of a suicide leap. As elegantly choreographed by Mr. Zaks, the action extends into the auditorium and rises through a mysterious two-level Tony Walton set that is a fittingly abstract variation on the designer's *Grand Hotel*.

The news story that sparked *Six Degrees of Separation* told of a young black man who talked his way into wealthy white Upper East Side households by purporting to be both Sidney Poitier's son and the Ivy League college friend of his unwitting hosts' children. In Mr. Guare's variation, the young man (Mr. McDaniel), who calls himself Paul Poitier, lands in the Fifth Avenue apartment of Ouisa (Ms. Channing) and her husband, Flan (Mr. Cunningham), a high-rolling art dealer. Paul is a charming, articulate dissembler on all subjects who has the Kittredges in thrall. He is also a petty thief who invites a male hustler into the guest room he occupies while waiting for his "father" to take up residence at the Sherry Netherland Hotel.

Much as this situation, a rude twist on *Guess Who's Coming to Dinner,* lends itself to the satirical mayhem Mr. Wolfe inflicted on white liberals in *Radical Chic,* Mr. Guare has not written a satire about race relations. Paul, the black man whose real identity the Kittredges never learn, becomes the fuse that ignites a larger investigation of the many degrees of separation that prevent all the people in the play from knowing one another and from knowing themselves.

It is not only blacks and whites who are estranged in Mr. Guare's New York. As the action accelerates and the cast of characters expands, the audience discovers that the Kittredges and their privileged friends don't know their alienated children, that heterosexuals don't know homosexuals, that husbands don't know their wives, that art dealers don't know the art they trade for millions. The only thing that everyone in this play's Manhattan has in common is the same American malady that afflicted the working-class Queens inhabitants of *The House of Blue Leaves*—a desire to bask in the glow of the rich and famous. Here that hunger takes the delirious form of a maniacal desire to appear as extras in Sidney Poitier's purported film version of *Cats,* a prospect Paul dangles in front of his prey. Yet these people hunger for more as well, for a human connection and perhaps a spiritual one.

It is Paul, of all people, who points the way, by his words and his deeds. In a virtuoso monologue about *The Catcher in the Rye,* he decries a world in which assassins like Mark David Chapman and John W. Hinckley Jr. can take Holden Caulfield as a role model—a world in which imagination has ceased to be a means of self-examination and has become instead "something outside ourselves," whether a handy excuse for murderous behavior or a merchandisable commodity like van

Gogh's *Irises* or an escapist fashion promoted by *The Warhol Diaries*. Intentionally or not, Paul helps bring Ouisa into a reunion with her imagination, with her authentic self. His trail of fraud, which ultimately brushes against death, jolts his hostess out of her own fraudulent life among what Holden Caulfield calls phonies so that she might at last break through the ontological paralysis separating her from what really matters.

Among the many remarkable aspects of Mr. Guare's writing is the seamlessness of his imagery, characters, and themes, as if this play had just erupted from his own imagination in one perfect piece. "There are two sides to every story," says a comic character, a duped New York Hospital obstetrician (Stephen Pearlman), and every aspect of *Six Degrees of Separation,* its own story included, literally or figuratively shares this duality, from Paul's identity to a Kandinsky painting that twirls above the Kittredge living room to the meaning of a phrase like "striking coal miners." The double vision gives the play an airy, Cubist dramatic structure even as it reflects the class divisions of its setting and the Jungian splits of its characters' souls.

Mr. Guare is just as much in control of the brush strokes that shift his play's disparate moods: In minutes, he can take the audience from a college student who is a screamingly funny personification of upper-middle-class New York Jewish rage (Evan Handler) to a would-be actor from Utah (Paul McCrane) of the same generation and opposite temperament. Though Mr. Guare quotes Donald Barthelme's observation that "collage is the art form of the twentieth century," his play does not feel like a collage. As conversant with Cézanne and the Sistine Chapel as it is with Sotheby's and *Starlight Express,* this work aspires to the classical esthetics and commensurate unity of spirit that are missing in the pasted-together, fragmented twentieth-century lives it illuminates.

That spirit shines through. Great as the intellectual pleasures of the evening may be, it is Mr. Guare's compassion that allows his play to make the human connections that elude his characters. The people who walk in and out of the picture frames of Mr. Walton's set are not satirical cartoons but ambiguous, full-blooded creations. There's a Gatsby-like poignancy to the studied glossy-magazine aspirations of Mr. McDaniel's Paul, a Willy Loman–ish sadness to the soiled idealism of Mr. Cunningham's art dealer. As the one character who may finally see the big picture and begin to understand the art of living, the wonderful Ms. Channing steadily gains gravity as she journeys flawlessly from the daffy comedy of a fatuous dinner party to the harrowing internal drama of her own rebirth.

"It was an experience," she says with wonder of her contact with the impostor she never really knew. For the author and his heroine, the challenge is to hold on to true experience in a world in which most human encounters are bogus and nearly all are instantly converted into the disposable anecdotes, the floating collage scraps that are the glib currency of urban intercourse. In *Six Degrees of Separation,* one of those passing anecdotes has been ripped from the daily paper and elevated into a transcendent theatrical experience that is itself a lasting vision of the humane new world of which Mr. Guare and his New Yorkers so hungrily dream.

THE TAMING OF THE SHREW
DELACORTE THEATER, JULY 13, 1990

If Cole Porter and company could transplant *The Taming of the Shrew* to sedate, late 1940s Baltimore, why can't the New York Shakespeare Festival let Kate and Petruchio have their standoff in the wild, late-nineteenth-century West? A. J. Antoon's rambunctious production of Shakespeare's comedy, at the Delacorte Theater in Central Park, turns out to be its own best argument. With Morgan Freeman and Tracey Ullman, a theoretically unlikely yet entirely winning couple, at center stage, the entertainment is consistently more engaging than it may sound on paper. Were Mr. Antoon's *Shrew* a musical, it would be too broad to be *Kiss Me Kate* perhaps, but it could happily pass for *Annie Get Your Gun.*

As he proved in the 1970s with his radiant Teddy Roosevelt–era *Much Ado About Nothing,* also in Central Park, and more recently with his Bahia *Midsummer Night's Dream,* the inaugural show of Joseph Papp's Shakespeare Marathon, Mr. Antoon does not settle for merely dreaming up new settings for Shakespeare's comedies; he carries out his schemes to the finest details. Even before an actor appears in *Shrew,* the audience takes in John Lee Beatty's high-spirited Main Street set, a Hollywood-backlot façade decorated with a mock-Remington mural of stampeding horses, and watches some tumbleweeds dance about to a musical score (by Claude White) reeking of manifest destiny in the *Bonanza* key.

For all the chaps, buckskins, and spurs of Lindsay W. Davis's costumes and cumulus clouds of Peter Kaczorowski's lighting scheme, Mr. Antoon's staging soon proves more than a matter of fine decorative touches. While the director has rewritten and cut some of Shakespeare's text (most disappointingly the *Arabian Nights*–inspired prologue), he has also inventively coupled its action to his own merry purposes. When Kate plays a prank on her better behaved and more marriageable younger sister, Bianca (Helen Hunt), in this *Shrew,* she uses the poor girl as the centerpiece of a balloon-popping marksmanship exhibition. Bianca's rival suitors draw guns at the saloon, and, to be sure in a work that invites slapstick, at least one Paduan gets a good dunking at the town water trough. In one lovely, wintry nocturnal scene, Petruchio's servant, Grumio (José Perez), recounts his master's and mistress's misadventures while his audience of cowpokes thaws out by a warm stove.

Mr. Antoon's inspiration seems to be the airiest of Hollywood westerns. His *Shrew* never quite becomes a parody like, say, *Cat Ballou* or *Blazing Saddles,* but it does evoke the bucolic interludes of John Ford movies, which themselves had a bawdy Elizabethan sense of rustic comedy. For the *Shrew* subplot, in which Bianca's many suitors, led by Lucentio (Graham Winton), all but trip over one another in a maze of disguised identities, Mr. Antoon has recruited comic actors who recall such grizzled, idiosyncratic Ford stock players as Strother Martin, Andy Devine, and Woody Strode. Tom Mardirosian's deadpan Hortensio (who doubles as the town sheriff) and Robert Joy's cigar-chomping Tranio stand out among the younger generation of Paduan clowns, though even they are upstaged by a delightful pair of older pros: Mark Hammer as the creaky, unreconstructed skirt-chaser Gremio, and William Duff-Griffin as a tipsy, itinerant ham actor made up to resemble W. C. Fields at his most pink-cheeked and Dickensian.

Given the large number of slammable doors in Mr. Beatty's set, there are times when Mr. Antoon might have gone further with his farcical choreography. Some of the staging is static and some of the ludicrous vocal twangs wear out their welcome. But every time the whole stunt seems about to pall, Mr. Freeman and Ms. Ullman ride to the rescue, tongues and pistols ablazing. They not only fit in handily with the western scheme but they also help Mr. Antoon finesse the problematic sexual politics of a play that humorless contemporary audiences might regard as an endorsement of male supremacy and female submissiveness.

Mr. Freeman does everything brilliantly, whether he is falling on the floor in knockabout comic emulation of one of Ms. Ullman's temper tantrums or standing quietly in a soft spotlight to savor a reflective passage of verse or modeling an outlandish wedding costume that makes him look like a hybrid of Davy Crockett, Pancho Villa, and Sitting Bull. He is one of those rare actors whose easeful command of his art seems to inspire a higher level of performance from everyone around him. His highest achievement here, though, is to rescue Petruchio from piggishness without any sacrifice of masculine strength or wit. His proud, intelligent shrew-tamer is genial and firm, not vindictive and cruel, even when roping in his bonny Kate with a lasso or, in one hilarious bit of business, good-naturedly countering her well-aimed volley of spit. One always believes that this Petruchio is out to "kill a wife with kindness" and "curb her mad and headstrong humor" rather than to brutalize and subjugate her.

While Ms. Ullman's Kate could use a few more notes, especially in the ill-tempered brawls preceding her wedding, her fierce presence and sardonic comic attack usually rivet the attention. Once Kate's transformation from swaggering malcontent to affectionate spouse does occur, the actress rises to the occasion. Her climactic speech championing wifely duties is delivered with just the right twinkle of irony and is capped by an ingeniously managed physical gag that allows Kate to have her man and her feminist independence, too.

The real point of the production, however, is stated earlier by Petruchio, who notes that "where two raging fires meet together, they do consume the thing that feeds their fury." By the time Ms. Ullman ends up in Mr. Freeman's arms—in a romantic embrace both passionate and erotic—Mr. Antoon's *Shrew* hardly seems a war between the sexes, a shootout between heroes and villains. Kate and Petruchio are instead laughing together as equals, a true couple at last, excited to consummate their marriage ("Come, Kate, we'll to bed," says the text) and euphoric to share private jokes at an intimate remove from the rest of the world. If this *Taming of the Shrew* imparts the same lift as old-fashioned westerns, that's because Mr. Freeman and Ms. Ullman leave the audience with the unambiguous feeling that the good guys, man and woman alike, have won.

RICHARD III

ROYAL NATIONAL THEATRE, LONDON, AUGUST 8, 1990

The difference between a Shakespearean production that is committed to ideas about the world as opposed to one committed simply to ideas about the theater is brought into dramatic relief by the companion piece presented in alternating repertory with Deborah Warner's *King Lear* on the National's Lyttelton stage, Richard Eyre's *Richard III* with Ian McKellen.

Certainly there's nothing startling about the basic notion of Mr. Eyre's *Richard III*, which transplants the despot's tale to the fascist realms of the 1930s. Yet Mr. McKellen's dictator is not a distanced Hitler or Mussolini: He's unambiguously an Englishman. Regal in posture rather than humpbacked, with a paralyzed left arm whose deformity is matched by the unnaturally white left temple of his hair, this patrician, cigarette-smoking blackshirt vaguely recalls the Duke of Windsor. And not for nothing is the British fascist Oswald Mosley quoted along with Stalin and Göring in the program. With the aid of the designer Bob Crowley, who tops his Albert Speer–minded vistas with rows of inquisition lamps, Mr. Eyre ushers the audience into a creepy official England all too ready to collaborate with a strongman.

The atmosphere, thick with behind-closed-doors intrigue along corrupt corridors of power, recalls both Alfred Hitchcock movies and Graham Greene novels from the eve of World War II. The elegant, chalky-voiced Mr. McKellen, whose other dark recent Shakespearean roles have included Coriolanus and Iago, is chilling in a manner not quite like any Richard I've seen. Kinkily obsessed with horses long before he would exchange his kingdom for one, his Richard conveys evil with a bloodless equine hauteur, an intellectual aggressiveness that runs roughshod over the foolish and the weak. He easily out-argues and out-maneuvers everyone in his court, revealing the satanic madness beneath the façade only at the first-half climax, when his spine and sickly grin twist for an instant into the distorted figure of a grotesque George Grosz caricature marshaling a neo-Nazi salute.

What makes Mr. Eyre's direction of *Richard III* so impressive are his striking stage pictures, in which brutal executions sometimes share the stage with shadowy background tableaux of ineffectual Westminster political conferences, and his supple orchestration of the supporting company, which is led by Brian Cox's Buckingham. What makes this *Richard III* alarming are the plausibility and urgency with which it charts totalitarianism's easy, inky spread through a genteel world close to home. While Mr. Eyre's staging is scarcely Brechtian, his fiercely cautionary tone is of a piece with *The Resistible Rise of Arturo Ui*.

In the months ahead, the National will be touring in Europe and Asia, with stops contemplated for cities like Prague and Bucharest, where Richards have only recently been toppled. Mr. Eyre's *Richard III* has the terrifying march of history on its side.

≡ *Somewhat recast in supporting roles, this* Richard III *eventually toured the United States, stopping at the Brooklyn Academy of Music in New York.*

CRITIC'S NOTEBOOK: JONATHAN
PRYCE VS. ACTORS' EQUITY
LONDON, AUGUST 10, 1990

Only a few hours after Actors' Equity in New York announced its decision to bar Jonathan Pryce from acting in a Broadway production of *Miss Saigon,* Mr. Pryce was back on stage here, doing his job in the theater, giving an electrifying performance in the role of his career.

The scene was a packed Wednesday matinee at the Theatre Royal, Drury Lane, the enormous, legendary house that has long played home to visiting American actors in the musical theater, from Mary Martin, who opened *South Pacific* in London forty years ago, to the imported New York company that introduced the English to *A Chorus Line.* London is not known for producing exciting musical-theater performers, and in nearly thirty years of watching musicals here, I have seen only two singing and dancing stars who could be mentioned in the same breath as the Broadway greats the West End has so frequently had to airlift from New York. One is Robert Lindsay of *Me and My Girl.* The other is Mr. Pryce.

The occasion for Mr. Pryce's triumph, of course, is the new musical by the French authors of *Les Misérables,* Alain Boublil and Claude-Michel Schönberg, who, with the collaboration of the American lyricist Richard Maltby Jr., relocate the tragic tale of *Madama Butterfly* to Saigon in 1975. But Mr. Pryce's character in *Miss Saigon,* known as the Engineer, has no antecedent in the Puccini opera; it is instead a variant on the German nightclub emcee played by Joel Grey in *Cabaret,* another musical about modern civilization sliding into the charnel house of racism and war in the name of patriotism.

With his elongated death's head, perpetually swiveling pelvis, and sleazy leer, Mr. Pryce can effortlessly carry all the metaphorical weight *Miss Saigon* shovels upon him. This is a dangerous performance as well as a brilliant one, and it is as essential to *Miss Saigon* as Mr. Grey's was to *Cabaret.* Maybe even more so. As emotionally and at times musically powerful as the main drama of this pop opera is, the evening trails off into vague characterizations and musical monotony for large chunks of its postwar second half. By then, the ragged staging (by Nicholas Hytner) and design (by John Napier) must depend for levitation on the celebrated onstage helicopter, which proves only a special-effect stunt of the Universal Tours variety.

Given the rest of *Miss Saigon*—even were there not a principle involved—the producer Cameron Mackintosh had no choice but to cancel the Broadway production if he could not employ Mr. Pryce. A producer's job is to present the best show he can, and Mr. Pryce's performance is both the artistic crux of this musical and the best antidote to its more bloated excesses. It's hard to imagine another actor, white or Asian, topping the originator of this quirky role. Why open on Broadway with second best, regardless of race or creed? But there are principles at stake, too, and even if Mr. Pryce's performance were easily replicated by another actor, Mr. Mackintosh would still be right to cancel *Miss Saigon* rather than surrender his and his creative team's artistic rights on the grounds Equity has advanced.

The barring of Mr. Pryce is insupportable on every level. By refusing to permit a white actor to play a Eurasian role, Equity makes a mockery of the hard-won principles of nontraditional casting and practices a hypocritical reverse racism. This is a policy that if applied with an even hand would bar Laurence Olivier's Othello, Pearl Bailey's Dolly Levi, and the appearances of Morgan Freeman in *The Taming of the Shrew* and Denzel Washington in *Richard III* in Central Park this summer. Right now in London, to take only one of hundreds of examples that could be cited to puncture Equity's position, a black English actress, Josette Simon, is playing the character modeled on Marilyn Monroe in a National Theatre production of Arthur Miller's *After the Fall.*

Even if there were some credible intellectual rationale (and formula) for an Equity policy calling for single-race exclusivity in the casting of some roles and complete racial freedom in the casting of others, Equity could hardly have picked a worse example to argue the case than the Engineer in *Miss Saigon.* The Engineer is Eurasian in the first place (half French, half Vietnamese, according to a song lyric) only because of a plot twist that requires the character to have Vietnamese citizenship papers. The role is in reality a theatrical device, a chorus, an eternal camp follower—alternately American and Satanic in personality, a character without a proper name and without an ethnic or national identity of any recognizable sort in the text or on stage. Mr. Pryce now plays him without any Asian makeup, and the Engineer could be acted without any textual revision or ethnic makeup by black and Hispanic actors as well as by whites and Asians. If anything, the Engineer is a character that could have been invented as a textbook example to promote the idea of nontraditional casting. When Colleen Dewhurst, the president of Equity, likens *Miss Saigon* to a "minstrel show," she is demagogically misrepresenting the role and Mr. Pryce's performance. Or, worse, is it possible that she has not even bothered to go see the fellow actor whose work she has branded as perpetuating a racial stereotype?

The one unassailable point in the Equity argument about *Miss Saigon*—that Asian actors must have the acting opportunities racism has denied them in the past—is also poorly served by the union's behavior. By inviting the cancellation of *Miss Saigon*, Equity has denied its minority members the thirty-four Asian, black, and Hispanic roles in this musical—and not merely minor ones, as the union rhetoric would have the innocent believe. The show's title part of Kim, for starters, has far more stage time and many more songs than the Engineer; because of the vocal demands, this one role alone requires the hiring of two Asian actresses with star billing in London.

But as Mr. Mackintosh said in his statement canceling the Broadway production of *Miss Saigon,* this one musical and the art, money, and jobs it represents are really beside the point now. Much more is at stake. At a time when many people in the American arts community are rightly worried about grave threats against the freedom of artistic expression in the United States, a major organization of American artists has poisoned the atmosphere further by seeking to repress that freedom. And it has done so by distorting the artist's work under attack and by confusing the political issues, as mischievously as some conservatives have made sport of the work of Karen Finley and Robert Mapplethorpe.

Watching Jonathan Pryce create riveting drama on stage in *Miss Saigon* this week, I felt transported by the actor's art, as practiced by a master operating with the uninhibited liberty that must be any artist's birthright. By barring that art for American audiences under the disingenuous guise of promoting democratic principles, Actors' Equity has, I fear, stumbled into its very own Vietnam.

≡ *Equity backed off, Pryce came to Broadway, and* Miss Saigon *joined the pantheon of long-running West End musical hits in New York.*

RACING DEMON
Royal National Theatre
SINGER
Royal Shakespeare Company
London, August 29, 1990

What will the left-wing playwrights of England do when they don't have Prime Minister Margaret Thatcher to kick around anymore? While Mrs. Thatcher is still very much on the scene, the possibility of her political exit in a year or two, as predicted by public opinion polls, may already be sapping the energy from a theater whose most inventive recent writing has often been in red-hot opposition to her policies and values. In postwar Britain, at least, Conservative governments seem to raise the creative fevers of British playwrights, while Labor leadership tends to still the waters. Should the blandly liberal Laborite Neil Kinnock come to power, one could more easily imagine his ascendancy inspiring a nostalgic Terence Rattigan revival than inciting a new generation's antiestablishment *Look Back in Anger* or *Top Girls.*

David Hare's *Racing Demon* and Peter Flannery's *Singer,* the two most critically celebrated plays in London right now, and certainly the most fascinating, are both the work of leftist dramatists who seem to be wrestling with the anticipated transition to a new political era. Each writer tries to shift the focus of his ideological ire away from Thatcherism per se, if not always with success. At their impressive best, Mr. Hare and Mr. Flannery even leave the vicissitudes of present-day Britain behind entirely and go after God, an authority figure whose tenure even Mrs. Thatcher cannot outlast.

Racing Demon is in repertory at the National Theatre with *The Crucible,* and, like Arthur Miller's play, it dramatizes a violent spiritual division within a parish. In Mr. Hare's case, the parish is a poor Anglican one in contemporary South London where the presiding vicar, a theological doubter and political liberal, finds his leadership under challenge from a young evangelical curate. The vicar, Lionel (Oliver Ford Davies), believes that the Church of England's mission among inner-city blacks and immigrants begins with the practical good deeds of social work. The curate, Tony (Adam Kotz), insists that Lionel's "fiddle-faddle" only sows confusion and that people instead need a firm faith in redemption, as achieved by the rituals and rules set down in The Book.

Sometimes *Racing Demon* can be funny about its clerics, most notably when they are having one tequila sunrise too many at the Savoy. Sometimes the battle between Lionel and Tony sounds like a disguised replay of the secular debates in Mr. Hare's other plays, including the recent *Secret Rapture,* in which the equivalent antagonists, two sisters, were an idealistic artist and an evangelically capitalist Thatcher minister. As always, Mr. Hare balances his dueling partners. For all of Lionel's enlightened humanism, he is often as paralyzed and befuddled by doubt as his adversaries paint him to be, an ineffectual liberal of the type who earned Mr. Hare's disdain in *Plenty* and *Pravda.* Tony, in contrast, delivers his extreme fundamentalist views with a boyish vigor that makes him the sexiest figure on stage and the one natural leader among the many clergymen in view.

What finally makes the play deeply upsetting is Mr. Hare's ruthless demolition of the sincere spiritual credos of both men. When Tony becomes so eager to sell religious miracles that he asserts an AIDS patient has been cured by the power of prayer, his exploitation of human suffering for his polemical cause seems obscene. But the kindly Lionel becomes just as appalling. He is so infatuated with his own humble conscience that he fails to notice the tragedies of two intimates, his lonely, neglected wife (Barbara Leigh-Hunt) and a loyal gay minister (Michael Bryant) who is being hounded out of England by the gutter press. "God, where are you?" Lionel asks in the play's very first line, and the question hangs in the air throughout the evening. As impeccably directed by Richard Eyre on a stark crucifix-shaped set floating in the vast space of the National's Olivier stage, *Racing Demon* usually seems suffused with God's troubling silence, no matter who the worshiper.

It's only when Mr. Hare drags on a superfluous character to fill that silence that he betrays his play's Shavian eloquence for tedious didacticism. An attractive advertising woman keeps popping up unconvincingly in both Lionel and Tony's lives, whenever the playwright needs a convenient mouthpiece for either his plot exposition or his own stand on the issues ("I like the idea of justice better than God"). But even this role is well acted (by Stella Gonet), and the rest of the cast is superb, with Ms. Leigh-Hunt and Mr. Bryant proving especially touching as mere mortals trapped innocently in an earthly web of domestic injustices.

· · ·

The existence of a divine plan is under equally fierce attack in *Singer*, in which Mr. Flannery charts the postwar adventures of his title character, an Auschwitz survivor played with an incandescent mixture of malignant energy and feral charm by the great actor Antony Sher. "When someone builds a machine the size of half a continent, employing a cast of thousands, just to make you into soap, it's hard to take entirely seriously the idea of progress," says Mr. Sher's Peter Singer, voicing the play's particular agnosticism. "But it's necessary to go on trying."

Actually, the playwright doesn't try that hard. This epic drama, which evokes Jacobean tragicomedy and sends four decades of English life sprawling over the Royal Shakespeare Company's main stage at the Barbican Center, reveals history not as progress but as a vicious circle, endlessly repeating itself. As an immigrant in London, Singer tries to obliterate his Auschwitz memories by restlessly remaking himself into an amoral slumlord exploiting the poor and helpless; "Singerism" soon becomes a notorious national synonym for "wickedness, greed, evil." After faking suicide in 1960, an atoning Singer reemerges in "sackcloth and ashes" in 1968 as a do-gooder among the homeless, succumbing to a survivor's guilt as fervently as he once tried to deny it. Either way, his life is imprisoned in the shadow of the Holocaust.

Though diffuse and repetitive and no more convincing at creating female characters than Mr. Hare's play, *Singer* is admirable for its daring ambitions and extravagant theatricality. Mr. Flannery manages to mix such diverse historical and cultural phenomena as a Shakespearean Chorus (played by the excellent Joe Melia), a parody of a 1960s hippie musical, and fictionalized biographies of both Primo Levi (another good performance, by Mick Ford) and the infamous real-life Harold Macmillan–era scoundrels Peter Rachman and John Profumo. The issues at the play's core include, most pressingly, the question of how history's past atrocities can be remembered by a world "where people can't remember what they had for breakfast." Even so, Mr. Flannery has been accused by a critical minority of two separate but related offenses in *Singer*—of practicing anti-Semitism and of trivializing the Holocaust. The charge of anti-Semitism seems absurd unless one believes that any portrayal of a greedy Jewish character is anti-Semitic; besides, Mr. Sher's animalistic magnetism makes Singer, however grasping, not a caricature but a sympathetic and irresistible man with a "talent for life," trying to defy a Nazi-ordained fate any way a hostile society will allow. But the second charge is harder to deflect, largely because the writer has been unable to resist the temptation to inject the Great Housekeeper, as he scathingly refers to Mrs. Thatcher, into the politics of *Singer*.

The problem develops late in the production when the play's nightmarish opening tableau, a smoky evocation of Auschwitz hell brilliantly staged and lighted by Terry Hands, is repeated almost identically. In its Act 2 replay, however, the sequence is no longer set in World War II but in present-day London, with the walking cadavers now representing homeless people reduced to camping out by the South Bank. Is Mr. Flannery likening the plight of the neglected poor in Mrs. Thatcher's Britain to that of victims of Nazism? It would seem so, especially when Singer is soon after recruited by the present power elite to help build disciplinary internment camps in the British countryside for the homeless and "social misfits."

In response to his critics, Mr. Flannery has denied that he is equating today's Britain with Hitler's Germany, but whom should the theatergoer believe, the playwright or his own eyes? *Singer* is finally so distorted by its author's passionate but inappropriately superimposed political agenda that Nazi crimes are robbed of their specificity and the play ends up contributing to the very process of historical amnesia it previously condemned. After watching a writer as gifted as Mr. Flannery completely lose control of *Singer,* even one who shares the anti-Thatcherism of the English theater may wonder if the Great Housekeeper might yet drive her opponents mad before they can sweep her out.

THE ICEMAN COMETH
GOODMAN THEATRE, CHICAGO, OCTOBER 3, 1990

Brian Dennehy, most visible these days on film as Harrison Ford's treacherous boss in *Presumed Innocent,* is one of those indelible character actors who could very profitably spend the rest of his career in the movies playing crusty Irish pols and cops. But not unlike his most gifted predecessors in the same Hollywood niche, Charles Durning and the late Kenneth McMillan, Mr. Dennehy cannot keep away from the stage. A few seasons back he earned acclaim at the Goodman Theatre here for his title performance in Brecht's *Galileo.* Later he proved an exceptionally sensitive Lopakhin in the Peter Brook *Cherry Orchard* that visited Brooklyn. Now Mr. Dennehy has returned to the Goodman in a Eugene O'Neill role that is made for him—Hickey, in *The Iceman Cometh*—and his shattering turn leaves one hungry to see his Falstaff, his Macbeth, and, when the time is ripe, his Lear and his James Tyrone.

Mr. Dennehy is a big bear of a man, but sometimes more of a teddy bear than a grizzly. There's a buried, dainty tenderness in his burly frame as well as a hint of festering violence. As Hickey, a hardware salesman who comes to Harry Hope's end-of-the-line gin mill and flophouse on a deranged evangelical mission, the actor shows off a spectrum of passions that runs from love to hate, from a drummer's forced optimism to a condemned man's sweaty vertigo. His Hickey seems to encapsulate all the salesmen in American theatrical literature, from Meredith Willson's ebullient Harold Hill to Arthur Miller's weary Willy Loman. At the same time, O'Neill's four-and-a-half-hour play, written in 1939 and first presented on Broadway in 1946, bridges the illusion-stripping theatrics of early moderns like Ibsen and Strindberg and the bleak, godless terrain of postwar Beckett dramas that were still to come.

In *The Iceman Cometh,* Hickey is the man who, for guilty reasons of his own, elects to show the soused bums of Hope's sad establishment that there is no hope for the long-held pipe dreams that allow them to fantasize about someday redeeming their misbegotten lives. When Mr. Dennehy, in chalk-stripe suit and vest, first enters the dank saloon, he practices a soft sell, working the room with the wide, well-practiced grin and extravagant handclasps of a gregarious party hack. (He's big enough to embrace three giggling prostitutes at once.) Hickey assures his old drinking cronies that his only ambition now is to offer them the peace and salvation that comes from shaking off the haze of booze and the lies of self-delusion to face one's true self in the mirror. But for all his warm effusions, there is, as one skeptical observer puts it, "the touch of death" about this would-be angel of mercy. Mr. Dennehy's curtain line in Act 1—"All I want is to see you happy"—is delivered in an exhausted, broken cadence, with a quizzical half-smile that curls into a demonic grin just as the lights go down.

The meaning of that grin and the truly Herculean test in this role arrive much later, in the Act 4 soliloquy that made a star of Jason Robards in the landmark José Quintero *Iceman Cometh* revival of 1956. Neither fighting the Robards characterization nor imitating it, Mr. Dennehy gives his own riveting account of the marathon speech in which Hickey's sales pitch for personal salvation becomes intertwined with cruel autobiography and, finally, a confession of murder. The actor's mood swings are shocking. As Hickey describes how his wife, Evelyn, loved him, and his self-revulsion at betraying that love with whoring and drinking, Mr. Dennehy's voice becomes plaintive, his expression almost baby-faced; he recalls his marital bond facing forward from a center-stage seat, hat in hand, with a tender intimacy that brings him and the audience near tears. In the circumspect account of Evelyn's murder that follows, he stands and raises his voice just slightly, to acknowledge Hickey's light-headed feelings of relief in the immediate aftermath of the crime.

But dark laughter quickly dissolves into sheer blackness. Mr. Dennehy bellows to the rafters and smashes a chair into the floor when he reaches the moment of truth in which Hickey suddenly refers to the dead Evelyn as a "damned bitch." The full power of the actor's physique and voice, summoned at last after four hours of restraint, reveal a killer—and symbolically reenact a killing—on the spot where only moments earlier had stood a sympathetic O'Neill braggart with a touch of the poet.

By that point the surrounding production, directed by Robert Falls, is ready to meet Mr. Dennehy's Hickey in that O'Neill abyss from which the only deliverance is death. Earlier, especially in the hour or so of ham-fisted exposition that precedes the star's first entrance, this *Iceman Cometh* tries the patience somewhat. The younger derelicts in Hope's living morgue, the father-obsessed Harvard Law alumnus Willie Oban and the informer Don Parritt, are given stock renderings here, as are most of the elder inmates (with Larry McCauley's somnambulant Jimmy Tomorrow being a notable exception). In the final act, however, Mr. Falls and his two best supporting players, Jerome Kilty as the pickled Hope and James Cromwell as the terminally detached and lapsed anarchist Larry Slade, join with the set designer John Conklin and the lighting designer James F. Ingalls to give this staging its own corrosive identity.

The design plays a crucial role, with Mr. Conklin varying the standard set in each act to help push *The Iceman Cometh* out of kitchen-sink realism and into the timeless, trancelike realm it must finally inhabit. The third act, in which the barflies don their Sunday best in a doomed effort to return to the outside world, unfolds in a spooky, tilted barroom whose gates open into a Magritte sky. For Act 4, the full depth of the large stage is revealed for the first time, filled with gloomy row upon row of tables. The isolated patrons, no longer able to find the kick in their booze, stare straight ahead like mannequins and, in a surrealistic touch, are stripped of some clothes along with all their illusions.

When Hickey's final departure allows the bar's denizens to emerge from that stupor and retrieve their sustaining pipe dreams once more, they return to demented life by slamming all the tables together and drinking, stomping, singing, and dancing their way back to oblivion. The stage picture could be from Daumier, and the din accompanying it builds to such an obscene crescendo that not even the sound and sight of a suicide leap can upstage the ruckus. Mr. Falls can only extinguish the grotesque spectacle with an abrupt blackout that, like Mr. Dennehy's performance, puts the kick into a ferocious American classic that has lost none of its power to send one shaking into the middle of the night.

MACHINAL
PUBLIC THEATER, OCTOBER 16, 1990

When the American theater dusts off forgotten Broadway hits from the 1920s and thirties, it is usually with the hope of finding a charming period piece, like Paul Osborn's *Morning's at Seven* or the Ben Hecht–Charles MacArthur *Johnny on a Spot*, that might give hardy perennials like *The Front Page* and *You Can't Take It with You* a run for the box-office gold. A young director named Michael Greif, making a sensational debut at the New York Shakespeare Festival, has quite another idea in mind in his resuscitation of *Machinal*, a 1928 Broadway success by Sophie Treadwell that has languished in oblivion except for one fleeting Off Broadway revival thirty years ago.

Mr. Greif has no interest in nostalgia. He has taken a tough work about an ordinary woman who is destroyed by a world of men, money, and machines—"a tragedy in ten episodes," in its author's conception—and given it an imaginative, unpatronizing production that would befit a play written only yesterday. The result is a startling collision of past and present. Like an archeological treasure preserved in a subterranean air pocket, *Machinal* (pronounced mock-en-AHL) is both an authentic artifact of a distant civilization and a piece of living art that seems timeless.

The civilization to which the play belongs is that of the late twenties, on the eve of the crash, when the overweening business of America was business. Treadwell (1885–1970) loosely adapted her play from the scandalous Snyder-Gray murder trial, a suburban love-triangle case that led to the first execution of a woman in an electric chair. *Machinal* charts that woman, played by Jodie Markell and known simply as "young woman," as she progresses from anonymous secretary to wife of the boss to young mother, adulterer, and, finally, murder defendant. From the first scene, in which office life is presented as a dehumanizing clatter of number-crunching machines and clerks, to the last, in which the power of industry is harnessed to the task of electrocution, *Machinal* dramatizes urban America as an unrelenting assembly line, carrying the blank but thrashing heroine from one cruel way station to the next as if she were a lost lamb being led to slaughter.

As the critic Brooks Atkinson noted in *The New York Times* after attending the 1928 opening at the Plymouth Theatre, both the style and content of *Machinal* owe something to *The Adding Machine*, Elmer Rice's play of 1923, and to Dreiser's *An American Tragedy* (1925) as well as to "the whole mad tumble of Expressionist drama." One can also see the influences of Henry Adams (in *The Virgin and the Dynamo*), of early O'Neill, earlier Dreiser (starting with *Sister Carrie*), and the Sacco-Vanzetti case. Yet even as Atkinson pointed out the play's "resemblances" to other works, he found it "a triumph of individual distinction, gleaming with intangible beauty." For once, at least, a drama critic was right.

What makes *Machinal* individual and distinct from some similarly themed fiction written by men in the same period is simple enough: Treadwell sees her stifled female protagonist from the inside. More fascinating still, she writes in a deadpan tone that keeps both sentimentality and ideological boilerplate at bay. Her spiky use of language and stylized theatrical technique and her refusal to preach, even when challenging the masculine hierarchies of obstetrics and Christianity, make

Machinal seem far more contemporary than the social-protest plays that would soon be ushered in by the Depression. Treadwell strips everything bare, from dialogue to characterization to narrative, as she pours out her fable in the streamlined cadences of a modernist hallucination. When the nameless people talk about business in *Machinal,* it is in the repetitive, staccato shorthand of Babbitt-era salesmanship—"he signed on the dotted line" or "I put it over"—that today would be labeled Mametese. The characters preying on the heroine are boiled down to their essential animal drives. The boorish vice president who becomes the young woman's husband (John Seitz) is summed up by his repeated, mercantile ambition to one day buy a Swiss watch in Switzerland; her sour working-class mother (Marge Redmond) is interested only in the handouts her new son-in-law might provide. The murder that drives the plot is presented unmelodramatically offstage, within the blackouts separating the play's "episodes," as simply a naturalistic matter of fact.

Yet there is terror everywhere in this evening. In keeping with Treadwell's original intentions, Mr. Greif folds each scene within the "purgatory of noise" that marks the urban jungle: jackhammers and subway trains and grinding manufacturing machinery. With the collaboration of a gifted design team—David Gallo (sets), Sharon Lynch (costumes), and Kenneth Posner (lighting)—he places the entire action within a skeletal factory that is constantly and subtly reconfigured to serve such settings as a speakeasy, a furnished room, a resort hotel, a maternity ward, and a courtroom. The tall green window shades, the chiaroscuro of stark lamplight and shadows, the spooky silhouettes that rise in the smoky glass panel of an office door all conspire to re-create the lonely, sometimes surreal, often macabre American cityscapes found in the contemporaneous paintings of Sheeler, Shahn, and Hopper. The stage pictures are completed by the director's shimmering use of extras to suggest a Jazz Age ballroom or the buzzing domestic hive of a tenement apartment house.

Mr. Greif's relentless theatricality, which rightly leads him to eliminate an intermission, carries *Machinal* even when the acting is merely competent or an occasional scene (notably the trial) goes into overdrive. William Fichtner, who plays the heroine's illicit lover (a role originated by the young Clark Gable), does not reveal much personality, for instance, but it hardly matters, given the sweaty darkness, relieved only by a cigarette's solitary glow, with which Mr. Greif evocatively shrouds his mechanical bedroom technique. When the acting is distinguished—as it is in the key roles played by Ms. Markell, Mr. Seitz, and Ms. Redmond, and in ghoulish cameos contributed by Rocco Sisto—*Machinal* becomes nightmarish. Particularly chilling is the honeymoon night in which the sinister Mr. Seitz, a smiling pig with fat hands and a traveling salesman's crude bonhomie, bounces the flinching Ms. Markell on his knee while trying to coax her to a grotesquely pink bed. His bride ends up shivering and sobbing on the floor, begging in vain for "somebody" to rescue her.

That scene notably excepted, Ms. Markell sometimes could be a shade less tentative in her portrayal of an Everywoman, however ordinary, swept up in forces beyond her control. Even so, her anguished cries for peace and freedom are so affecting that they never fail to overwhelm the churning mechanical sounds of the hellish city engulfing her. What the audience hears, of course, is not just the passion of a young actress, but the piercing voice of a forgotten writer who, in an act of justice unknown to her tragic heroine, has been miraculously reborn.

OH, KAY!

RICHARD RODGERS THEATRE, NOVEMBER 2, 1990

If there is any serious doubt that David Merrick is one of the greatest showmen in Broadway history, it can be dispelled by the fact that his flops are as fabled as his hits. Nearly as much theatrical lore attends the ill-fated *Mata Hari, Breakfast at Tiffany's, Mack and Mabel,* and *Subways Are for Sleeping* as it does *Hello, Dolly!, Gypsy,* and *42nd Street.* Mr. Merrick, like most other high-rolling, larger-than-life impresarios, was rarely one to mess with the in-between, which is why *Oh, Kay!,* his new show at the Richard Rodgers Theatre and his first since *42nd Street* a decade ago, is an anomaly. This loose adaptation of the Gershwins' 1926 musical is a chintzy, innocuous slab of stock that is likely to leave more than a few theatergoers shrugging their shoulders and asking, "Didn't I doze through that a couple of summers ago in a barn?"

Actually, *Oh, Kay!* bills itself as "inspired by" a well-received production mounted at the Goodspeed Opera House in Connecticut last year with a mostly different cast. I didn't see the Goodspeed *Oh, Kay!*, but Mr. Merrick has undoubtedly had his way with the project since then: Faint quotations from his happier past achievements filter like ghosts through the evening's haze.

Dan Siretta's opening and closing dance routines (and surely the word *routine* was coined to describe them) are would-be clones of the Gower Champion numbers that bracketed *42nd Street,* though this time the size of both the chorus and the choreographer's imagination seem about half that of the originals. The Merrick legacy also figures in this production's "concept," credited in the program to Mr. Siretta. Just as the producer brought Pearl Bailey, Cab Calloway, and company into the long-running *Hello, Dolly!* a quarter-century ago, so he fields an all-black cast in *Oh, Kay!*, first written by Guy Bolton and P. G. Wodehouse for the English star Gertrude Lawrence.

Even in its time, Mr. Merrick's black *Dolly* was attacked in some churlish quarters as a minstrel show, but history should more kindly regard it as an exhilarating example of what current parlance calls nontraditional casting. *Hello, Dolly!* was not rewritten for its black performers, and Ms. Bailey and Mr. Calloway were given the same free rein to play Dolly Gallagher Levi and Horace Vandergelder as Carol Channing and David Burns, among others, had been before them. *Oh, Kay!*, by contrast, does seem like a minstrel show. An adapter, James Racheff, has clumsily transported the libretto to an ersatz Jazz Age Harlem, with eye-popping gags and stereotypes that are less redolent of the Cotton Club than of *Amos 'n' Andy*.

But *Oh, Kay!* is so deficient in more mundane theatrical areas that debating its curious racial politics is a critical luxury. Little in this show makes sense, starting with a vertigo-inducing opening scene in which a cry of "Raid!" sends chorus performers at the Paradise Club running around in circles while various curtains rise and fall to beat the band. Shortly after that, the entire company delivers cases of bootleg booze to a millionaire's town house while performing a song ("When Our Ship Comes Sailing In") that, as staged, might be mistaken for the hurricane sequence in *Porgy and Bess*.

When the town house's millionaire (Brian Mitchell) returns home soon after, he almost marries a preacher's daughter only to find himself falling instead for an intruder who must be the real love interest since her name is Kay (Angela Teek). This romantic triangle is then rehashed almost verbatim during the long opening scene of Act 2 before being abruptly resolved. The end of the plot is not the end of *Oh, Kay!*, however, for the show loiters in the Paradise Club for three gratuitous scenes more, among them a three-man comedy act of the sort that didn't so much kill vaudeville as drive it to suicide.

For punctuation along the way, there are hoary jokes masquerading as campy wisecracks ("If brains was a boulevard, you wouldn't even make an alley") and, more occasionally, such lovely Gershwin tunes as "Maybe," "Do, Do, Do," and "Dear Little Girl." Certainly it's not necessary for anyone to sing Gershwin's praises at this late date, but it says much about his music's durability that "Someone to Watch Over Me" still exerts a pull here, despite the fact that the muffled-sounding orchestration (by Arnold Goland) is trashy and the singer (Ms. Teek) is strident of voice and mechanical of gesture.

Most of the other songs are excuses for Mr. Siretta's dances, in which noisy tapping, frantic arm waving, and constantly accelerating speed exhaust an audience's spirits in the name of raising them. This choreographer seems to impose the same style on every show—even one as different from *Oh, Kay!* as *Pal Joey,* last summer at Goodspeed—and one can fully expect to find tap dancers having a go at the "Ascot Gavotte" some day when *My Fair Lady* rolls off his assembly line.

As director, Mr. Siretta does not show off his company to good advantage. There is no romantic rapport between the ice-cold Ms. Teek and Mr. Mitchell, the robotic leading man. The rest of the acting is outrageously broad by any measure this side of the circus. Only the dancer Gregg Burge's sharply defined, time-stopping leaps and turns in "You've Got What Gets Me" elevate *Oh, Kay!* to an elegant Broadway standard.

That standard was more or less defined by Mr. Merrick for a couple of decades. Who could have imagined then that he would later produce a musical in which most of the first act is imprisoned in a gloomy Victorian parlor (muddily designed by Kenneth Foy) suitable for *Arsenic and Old Lace?* *Oh, Kay!* can be labeled a Merrick enterprise only because of the size of his billing and the ubiquitousness of a shade of red that has been standard issue in all his productions since *Hello, Dolly!*

Romantically or not, I would like to believe that this legendary showman, notoriously the toughest of audiences, is seeing another kind of red as he surveys the pallid entertainment to which he has unaccountably lent his name.

≡ *For tales of my final duels with David Merrick, see "Exit the Critic" at the end of this volume.*

SHADOWLANDS
Brooks Atkinson Theatre, November 12, 1990

Jack is a crusty, remote middle-aged Oxford don, a devout Anglican who is more comfortable chatting to God than to the opposite sex. Joy is a fortyish New Yorker, a Jewish convert to Christianity with a big mouth and a failing marriage. Jack and Joy strike up an unlikely epistolary friendship, rendezvous in Oxford and, overcoming all obstacles, fall in love. No sooner do these opposites attract, however, than tragedy, in the form of terminal illness, tears them asunder.

Thus in rough outline goes *Shadowlands,* and who could imagine a tidier recipe for a television movie? The audience gets to have an odd-couple comic romance—a sort of May-September, transatlantic *Bridget Loves Bernie*—and a disease of the week, too. *Shadowlands* in fact began its life as a television drama, but because Jack is the nickname for C. S. Lewis (1898–1963), the scholarly proselytizer for Christianity and the author of the evergreen Narnia fantasies for children, and because Joy was Joy Davidman, the American poet he married near the end of both their lives, it was produced by the tony British television, not the usual Hollywood suspects. Starring Joss Ackland and Claire Bloom, the fifty-two-minute film was broadcast in the United States on public television in 1986.

Now *Shadowlands* is a play of considerably more than twice that length that has arrived on Broadway at the Brooks Atkinson Theatre via the West End. The stars are Nigel Hawthorne, a rightly beloved fixture on the British comedy series *Yes Minister,* and Jane Alexander, whose spunky Joy may remind many of her appearance as another strong-willed wife in another nonfiction TV romance, *Eleanor and Franklin.*

How you will feel about *Shadowlands* depends a great deal on your degree of Anglophilia. The play, by William Nicholson, has little more intellectual or emotional depth than a tearjerker set in two-car-garage suburbia, but it does boast a certain rarefied British atmosphere. This is the kind of work that is often described as "literate," especially by non-readers, because its characters frequently mention works of literature. As at *84 Charing Cross Road,* its London theatrical prototype, no visitor to *Shadowlands* need worry that anyone on stage will be so boorish as to discuss the actual substance of the books and authors whose names are bandied about.

Even those who find *Masterpiece Theater* as resistible as I do are likely to be charmed by the endearing Englishness of Mr. Hawthorne, who happens to be South African. With a rumpled, well-worn face and gingersnap voice to match his tweed jacket, Marks & Spencer sweater, and corduroy pants, his C. S. Lewis is Mr. Chips, Dr. Doolittle, and the shaggy professor once played by Michael Hordern in Tom Stoppard's *Jumpers* all in one.

Never pretending that Jack is anything other than an old softie at heart, Mr. Hawthorne is a joy to watch as *Shadowlands* lumbers toward the inevitable scenes in which Ms. Alexander's Joy penetrates his confirmed bachelorhood. In the play as in life, Jack first marries Joy "techni-cally"—so she can settle in England with her young son after her divorce—and then marries her in earnest, as she lies in a hospital bed, a victim of bone cancer. In between these two benchmarks, Mr. Hawthorne migrates from absentmindedness to passion. His performance reaches an exquisite peak of comic turmoil when he finds himself torn between the gesture he always uses to put off Joy's affection—a random, reflexive search of his many pockets for some unspecified object—and his raven-ous hunger for a kiss.

When suffering overwhelms his spirit, Mr. Hawthorne goes further still, spitting out his grief in pink-faced rage. The actor makes one see how *Shadowlands* might have been as moving as Lewis's own memoir, *A Grief Observed*. But Mr. Nicholson and Ms. Alexander undercut the actor by refusing to bring his romantic partner to life. As written, Joy is a generic, wisecracking literary broad, a Dorothy Parker windup doll.

While Ms. Alexander's comic timing is expert, notably during a Greek honeymoon that is the play's funniest interlude, she is never given a chance to act the rest of this woman, whose renunciations of Judaism and leftism were central to her character. (Can one imagine an American playwright reducing Joy Davidman's discarded Judaism to a gag, as Mr. Nicholson does?) The heroine's deeper feelings are usually sidestepped entirely, often by having the actress turn away from the audience or dart offstage at emotional climaxes. When Joy succumbs to love, Ms. Alexan-der lets down her hair, not her guard; her descent toward death is delin-eated most persuasively by her makeup and declining posture.

Perhaps to compensate for the absence of any real psychological intimacy—the couple's sex life, or lack of same, is never mentioned—*Shadowlands* turns to Lewis's Narnia books for mystical scenic tableaux that, in the most literal-minded fashion, periodically equate Jack's new domestic ecstasy with the world of wonder discovered by children in *The Lion, the Witch, and the Wardrobe* and its sequels. In lieu of fleshing out his characters, Mr. Nicholson also piles on touristic local color, padding the evening with repetitive anecdotes about the high-table clubbiness of Jack's masculine academic circle at Oxford. The weak American sup-porting cast, typified by Paul Sparer's buffoonish caricature of a misogy-nistic don, compromises what wit these scenes offer and also vitiates the authenticity of Mark Thompson's handsome scenery and the lighting de-signer John Michael Deegan's wonderfully exact wintry Oxbridge gloom.

Unlike most of his casting, Elijah Moshinsky's staging is graceful, ex-cept when he and the designers are playing with the set's front scrim or hammering in the Narnia-inspired metaphor of the title. The director has elicited one excellent supporting performance, too, from Michael Allinson, as Jack's devoted older brother and housemate. But the Lewises' fraternal bond, like the play's other important secondary relationship, between Joy's son and Jack, is so sketchily drawn that it cannot carry the dramatic weight it must in the evening's waning scenes.

The same superficiality attends the play's potentially fascinating philosophical conflict: How can Lewis reconcile his belief in a benevolent God's Heaven with the pain and suffering he experiences on earth? Mr. Nicholson raises such questions only to resolve them happily and instantaneously, before anyone might be tempted to turn the channel. In *Shadowlands*, even death becomes the stuff of genteel entertainment, no more troubling or surprising than a patch of gray during an otherwise sunny West End afternoon.

MONSTER IN A BOX

MITZI E. NEWHOUSE THEATER, NOVEMBER 15, 1990

To hear him tell it—and we do, for ninety delicious minutes— Spalding Gray was starting to worry that he might be pandering to the audience with his autobiographical monologues. *Swimming to Cambodia,* his soliloquy about his adventures as an actor in the movie *The Killing Fields,* was so successful on stage that Jonathan Demme adapted it into a hit film. Mr. Gray's answering machine was soon clogged with showbiz offers, with everyone from the Mark Taper Forum to HBO to Creative Artists Agency ("the Mafia of talent agencies") on the prowl. Maybe it was time to escape. Should he get away from his "self-deprecating, ironic voice" and look for a Jimmy Stewart role "with heart"? Should he stop performing altogether and write a book?

Monster in a Box, Mr. Gray's thirteenth and latest stage monologue, tells of how he sort of found that role and sort of wrote that book while enduring countless interruptions. The "monster"—one of the few props he requires on the bare stage of the Mitzi E. Newhouse Theater at Lincoln Center—is his manuscript, a novel called *Impossible Vacation* about "a New England puritan" named Brewster North who has trouble enjoying vacations. The "box" is the corrugated cardboard box that contains the monster, which was "due to be published by Knopf two years ago." Mr. Gray explains that he was inspired to write by the example of Thomas Wolfe, and judging from the imposing size of his manuscript, which makes even the Manhattan phone directory look wimpy, one assumes that Knopf will have to unearth Maxwell Perkins to edit it. In the meantime, Mr. Gray performs the airtight *Monster in a Box,* which he describes in the program as a piece "about the dizziness that comes from too much possibility" and which he describes from the stage as a "monologue about a man who can't write a book about a man who can't take a vacation."

Whatever happens with Mr. Gray's book, or, for that matter, with his vacations, there can be no doubt that *Monster in a Box* is a triumph for him as both writer and performer. Despite the addition of a director— Renée Shafransky, the companion who frequently turns up in his tales— he still addresses us informally from behind a table, on which sit a spiral notebook, a glass of water, and a microphone. As always, his talk is a mixture of personal confession, journalistic observation, sermon, and digression. There are stories within stories, anecdotes within anecdotes, and jokes within jokes, yet the whole sprawling narrative eventually comes full circle to fall into the same effortless unity that distinguished *Swimming to Cambodia* from its predecessors. *Monster in a Box* is a play, not a comedian's routine or improvisation, though it is a play probably best performed by its author, a silver-haired master of deadpan with a WASP's Rhode Island accent.

Not every actor can accomplish what Mr. Gray does here, which is to whip an audience abruptly yet gently from offhand reflections about his mother's suicide (a perennial Gray subject, at least as far back as *Rumstick Road*) to hilarious memories of his life in the theater. Such juxtapositions are central to Mr. Gray's particular humor and vision of the world; only in *Monster in a Box* could one hope to find links between the MacDowell Colony and *Psycho,* between *The World of Sholom Aleichem* and flatulence, between Pilot pens and a Soviet film festival attended by Richard Gere and Daryl Hannah. Little is off-limits. *Monster in a Box* may be the first play to make fun of low-risk heterosexual men whipping themselves into a frenzy of self-indulgent hypochondria about AIDS.

Though a few of Mr. Gray's observations about well-worn subjects (psychoanalysis and sun-dried Hollywood lunch menus) are tired, even they are redeemed by the freshness of their context. In the several years covered by this installment of Mr. Gray's perpetual Bildungsroman, our hero encounters everyone from a Nicaraguan nun to Charles Manson's lawyer to the anonymous Cambodian refugees and elderly shut-ins he tracks down while conducting a search for those citizens of Los Angeles who have yet to write a screenplay. Mr. Gray's most unforgettable character, however, is still himself, though the identity of that self remains open to question.

Within the funny autobiographical tales lies a poignant drama, and just the one that Mr. Gray promises at the evening's outset. Here is a man who is trying "to relate" to others in a "nonperformance mode," to discover what is authentic beneath the armor of his role as a theatricalized commodity known as Spalding Gray. The search for the man under the pose leads him not only into therapy and fiction writing but also to accepting the part of the Stage Manager in the recent Broadway revival of Thornton Wilder's *Our Town*, directed by Gregory Mosher. After first resisting the offer and suggesting Garrison Keillor for the assignment, Mr. Gray comes to see the play as his own *Tibetan Book of the Dead*, as a touchstone for getting back to his own roots as a child of New England and the son of a troubled mother. (Surely Brewster North, the hero of Mr. Gray's suspended novel, is as much an allusion to a Wilder character name as it is to a railroad station.) In *Our Town*, Mr. Gray decides, "I could speak from the heart if I could memorize those lines."

He did memorize the lines, and the payoff for his hard work was terrible reviews. In *Monster in a Box*, Mr. Gray recounts the experience of his Broadway opening and its aftermath with a Twain-like sense of absurdity that made even the author of one of those unflattering reviews laugh until he cried. To refute his critics, Mr. Gray finally slips back into Wilder again, reciting once more the lines he proudly memorized. And once more he seems too boxed into the role of Spalding Gray, too much of an edgy, contemporary urban ironist, to pass for an inhabitant of Grover's Corners.

So maybe the more homespun Garrison Keillor would have been a better casting choice after all for the Stage Manager for *Our Town*. As a stage manager for our town, Mr. Gray is right now without peer.

SHOGUN: THE MUSICAL
MARQUIS THEATRE, NOVEMBER 21, 1990

Had the actor Philip Casnoff not been beaned by a falling slab of scenery at a press preview last week, *Shogun: The Musical* might have been best remembered as the first Broadway musical extravaganza to beguile an audience with a song about a dildo. But Mr. Casnoff's accident and his speedy recovery upstaged all else in the show—and justly so. Mr. Casnoff is something. *Shogun*, with or without sexual toys, is something else.

I was at the fateful preview in which the actor was abruptly knocked flat, bringing screams from the audience and causing the immediate suspension of the show, which delayed its opening until last night.

When I returned to the Marquis Theatre a few days later to see the complete second act, I was struck not only by Mr. Casnoff's physical resilience but also by a remarkable change in his performance. Before he was injured, Mr. Casnoff, a gifted young New York actor little known outside the profession, was giving a dutiful but hardly stellar performance—well sung, agile, bland—in the role of John Blackthorne, the English sea captain who finds himself marooned in the civil-war-torn Japan of 1598. After his recovery, Mr. Casnoff had the swaggering self-assurance of a star in complete command of a vast production. He was enjoying himself as he had not been before, and, of course, the audience was adoring him in return.

Had the actor's brush with a possibly career-ending injury inspired him to take a gutsier stance on stage? Had all the publicity attending the incident pumped up his ego, forcing him to behave like a big deal rather than like just another unsung New York actor who happened to land a large part in a forgettable show? Whatever the explanation, Mr. Casnoff's accident, painful and terrifying as it must have been, can be seen from the vantage point of its happy ending as the biggest break of his career. And if that's not showbiz, what is?

As for the rest of *Shogun: The Musical,* I suspect it is best appreciated by fans of its James Clavell source, *Shogun: The Novel,* or perhaps by viewers of *Shogun: The Miniseries* or even wearers of *Shogun: The T-shirt. Shogun* aficionados will presumably experience the stage version as a progression of recognizable tableaux inspired by a sacred text. For those unfamiliar with the Clavell tale, the musical's book, by John Driver, is mostly incomprehensible, and the synopsis in the *Playbill* is itself in need of synopsis. ("Ishido schemes with the three Catholic Daimyos and passes a resolution demanding that Toranaga remain as a 'guest' in Osaka Castle, thus making Toranaga a virtual prisoner," goes one typical passage.) The *Playbill* is also equipped with a glossary of Japanese expressions, such as *kampai,* which means "bottoms up," and *seppuku,* which refers to the "ritual suicide" one samurai or shogun or another is threatening to commit in every other scene.

Curiously, the glossary does not list *pillowing,* which is the term *Shogun* gives its medieval Japanese characters as a synonym for copulation. It is in Mr. Driver's lyrics for the song "Pillowing" that female characters describe the joys of a portable phallus ("It never tires of women like a lazy, jaded man") with a gleeful prurience that almost makes one nostalgic for the relatively benign sexism of "I Enjoy Being a Girl" in Rodgers and Hammerstein's *Flower Drum Song.* Of the thirty-odd other musical numbers composed by Paul Chihara for *Shogun,* few are memorable except "Karma," this show's inevitable if ludicrous opening number, and a ballad titled "Born to Be Together" that, between its constant repetition and its orchestration by the Andrew Lloyd Webber arranger David Cullen, might as well be piped in from *Aspects of Love* around the corner.

Given its poverty in other departments, *Shogun* is the kind of show at which it is de rigueur to praise the physical production—if only because that's where the big budget was most conspicuously spent. Patricia Zipprodt, a costume designer second to none, has indeed done beautiful work here, turning out enough kimonos and other more extravagant ceremonial robes to make the silkworm an endangered species. Loren Sherman, a witty miniaturist in his scenic assignments Off Broadway, has not made the leap to Broadway overproduction too gracefully. The black-and-gold folding screens used as a front curtain look like the sort of heavy, ersatz chinoiserie that was popular in middle-class American homes in the 1950s, and a big earthquake effect is less redolent of Kabuki or Kurosawa than of *Godzilla.* The delicacy of Japanese esthetics is apparent only in a late-evening "Winter Battle" sequence, hauntingly lighted by Natasha Katz, in which warriors on silver horses advance from within a cloud of fog and snow.

By then, *Shogun* is almost three hours old, and it has not exactly flown by under the direction of Michael Smuin. A snazzy choreographer of period American dancing (*Sophisticated Ladies, Anything Goes*), Mr. Smuin seems to have little luck with actors. June Angela, the leading lady, who pillows with Mr. Casnoff in various Kama Sutra positions near the end of Act 1, has a squeaky soprano, a professional smile, and scant presence. Francis Ruivivar's jolly, rotund Shogun, John Herrera's shifty-eyed priest, and Joseph Foronda's monotoned villain all seem to be refugees from a Gilbert and Sullivan tour of the provinces, and not necessarily the Japanese provinces.

Mr. Smuin's choreography includes a stormy opening shipwreck sequence that, with its spangled, gyrating furies and fabric waves, looks like the Trump casino edition of Jerome Robbins's "Small House of Uncle Thomas" ballet from *The King and I.* The postintermission dance treat is an utterly gratuitous "Festival of the Fireflies" that is best applauded not for its Crazy Horse Saloon onslaught of scantily clad "insects" but for its temporary forestalling of Act 2's turgid scenes of exposition. After that, *Shogun* may leave all except its most fiercely committed partisans longing for a pillow of the old-fashioned, G-rated kind.

THE FEVER

PUBLIC THEATER, NOVEMBER 29, 1990

T his is a piece I've been doing mostly in people's apartments since January," says the actor and playwright Wallace Shawn by way of introducing *The Fever,* the one-hour-forty-five-minute monologue he is now reciting at the Public Theater. But which people, which apartments and, for that matter, which January?

Perhaps out of fear that an aspiring Tom Wolfe, reporter's pad in hand, might record one of these private performances for public sport, Mr. Shawn isn't saying. And no wonder. *The Fever* is nothing if not a musty radical-chic stunt destined to be parodied: a brave, sincere, and almost entirely humorless assault on the privileged class by one of its card-carrying members. In an orgy of self-flagellation that even Woody Allen might find a bit rich, Mr. Shawn naively tells the audience of his guilt about enjoying ice cream and good hotel rooms while peasants make do with beans; he didactically deplores the injustice of a capitalist economy that rewards an actor more extravagantly than a chambermaid or a beggar. All of which leaves one wondering: Were there any beggars and chambermaids in the apartments where Mr. Shawn honed *The Fever*—aside from those serving drinks and emptying ashtrays—or did he merely preach to other devotees of Häagen-Dazs?

Don't get me wrong: I admire Mr. Shawn's idiosyncratic comic gifts as both a writer and a performer. *Aunt Dan and Lemon,* a play so scabrous it managed to offend the ideologically antithetical drama critics of *The New Republic* and *The New Criterion* alike, was one of the most daring political comedies produced by the American theater in the 1980s, a work in which a civilized, well-educated heroine "defended" Hitler so that Mr. Shawn might argue how fascism could happen here and now. But while *The Fever* aspires to be similarly outrageous—it unfashionably defends Marxism during communism's lowest ebb—it has less in common with the mordantly funny *Aunt Dan and Lemon* than with the obvious, if intensely argued, essay about morality that Mr. Shawn appended to that play's published text. *The Fever* arrives at unassailable conclusions—"There's no piece of paper that justifies what the beggar has and what I have"—by a circuitous route that passes through dense thickets of syllogism unrelieved by vivid characters, dramatic anecdotes, arresting language, or even wisecracks.

Mr. Shawn delivers his earnest, scripted speech while remaining seated in a plain chair on an empty stage. In keeping with the new proletarian austerity he espouses, there are no *Playbill*s, no stagehands, no lighting cues, no curtain call, no intermission, only drab colors in his wardrobe, and a low ticket price (ten dollars). Next to *The Fever,* Spalding Gray's *Monster in a Box* and Eric Bogosian's *Sex, Drugs, Rock & Roll* look like Ziegfeld extravaganzas.

Presumably these Spartan conditions will prevail when *The Fever* moves on from the Public to other scheduled engagements at the Royal Court Theatre in London and at the Second Stage, La Mama, and Lincoln Center Theater in New York. Yet the studied informality does not recreate the casual experience of sitting in someone's living room. Mr. Shawn, his voice at an unvaried high pitch and his face sweating under the bright overhead lights, looks uncomfortable, like a Feiffer cartoon figure squirming before an inquisitor.

That's partly the point. The title of *The Fever* refers to the condition in which Mr. Shawn finds himself at the beginning of his talk. He has awakened "shaking and shivering" in "a strange hotel room in a poor country where my language isn't spoken." In between fever dreams and bouts of vomiting, he alternately offers selective accounts of his life to date, describes incidents of torture in "revolutionary" nations, and, at his most amusing, provides Marxist critiques of *The Cherry Orchard,* pornographic magazines, and "commodity fetishism." Along the way he marshals arguments both for and against leaving his own comfortable, selfish world "to fight on the other side" of the class struggle. With an honesty that is more admirable than intellectually compelling, he is still sitting on the fence, and in his chair, at evening's end.

What makes *The Fever* lulling rather than a challenging or inspiring act of social protest is not so much its unexceptional ideological content as its flat, unspecific mode of expression. Though an occasional phrase pricks the ear—an upper-middle-class childhood is emblemized by "orange juice on a table in a glass pitcher"—too much of the writing painstakingly attempts to imitate the archetypal diction of Kafka, as if any unnamed trial could pass for *The Trial* or any heavily symbolic waterbug might turn out to be Gregor Samsa. Just as the audience never learns the identity of those "people's apartments" where *The Fever* was first performed, so the specifics of the speaker's family, career, and friends—and those of the unnamed poor countries he visits—remain vague and generic. For a piece that presents itself as a self-critical, autobiographical confession, the monologue seems resolutely unrevealing and risk free. It's socialist art of the official, instructional kind.

Perhaps, like Eric Bogosian or, say, the well-heeled, conscience-ridden movie director in Preston Sturges's *Sullivan's Travels,* Mr. Shawn would retrieve his fanatical comic voice by gaining a more intimate knowledge of the downtrodden he wishes to apotheosize but fails to bring to life on stage. *The Fever* is a strangely insular event, charged with intelligence and a desire to do good, yet rendered nearly inert by its author's solipsism. For a play that condemns decadence, it is itself a luxurious exercise in escapism: Whether the arena is the theater or an apartment, Mr. Shawn's replay of old battles is a safe refuge from a real world poised at the brink of war.

ASSASSINS

PLAYWRIGHTS HORIZONS, JANUARY 28, 1991

No one in the American musical theater but Stephen Sondheim could have created the chorus line that greets—or should one say affronts?—the audience at the beginning and end of *Assassins,* the new revue at Playwrights Horizons.

Dressed in motley garb ranging from Victorian finery (John Wilkes Booth) to worker's rags (Leon Czolgosz) to shopping-mall leisure wear (John Hinckley), this chorus line is entirely populated by that not-so-exclusive club of men and women who have tried, with and without success, to kill the President of the United States. While their song may echo the sentiments in dozens of other Broadway musicals—"Everybody's got the right to their dreams" goes a lyric—the singers' expressions are variously glassy-eyed and vacant, demented and smiling, angry and psychopathic. Everyone strutting in this procession packs, and eventually points, a gun.

The effect of this recurrent chorus line, a striking image in a diffuse evening, is totally disorienting, as if someone had removed a huge boulder from the picturesque landscape of American history to reveal all the mutant creatures that had been hiding in the dankness underneath. In *Assassins,* a daring work even by his lights, Mr. Sondheim and his collaborator, the writer John Weidman, say the unthinkable, though they sometimes do so in a deceptively peppy musical-comedy tone. Without exactly asking that the audience sympathize with some of the nation's most notorious criminals, this show insists on reclaiming them as products, however defective, of the same values and traditions as the men they tried to murder.

To Mr. Sondheim, the dreams of presidential assassins seem not so much different from those empty all-American dreams of stardom he enshrined in *Gypsy:* These killers want to grab headlines, get the girl, or see their names in lights. In keeping with his past musicals animating the passions of the certifiably insane (*Anyone Can Whistle*) and mass murderers (*Sweeney Todd*), this songwriter gives genuine, not mocking, voice to the hopes, fears, and rages of two centuries' worth of American losers, misfits, nuts, zombies, and freaks. These are the people who have "Another National Anthem" because they are too far back in line to get into the ball park where the official one is sung. These are the lost and underprivileged souls who, having been denied every American's dream of growing up to be president, try to achieve a warped, nightmarish inversion of that dream instead.

One need not agree with Mr. Sondheim's cynical view of history and humanity to feel that *Assassins* has the potential to be an extraordinarily original piece of theater. In its Off Broadway premiere, unfortunately, that potential is unfulfilled. For a show that takes on so much, mixing and matching historical periods and characters with E. L. Doctorow's abandon, this work often seems slender and sketchy, and not just because it runs only ninety minutes and has only eight songs.

The gap that separates Mr. Sondheim's most acute contributions from Mr. Weidman's jokey book and Jerry Zaks's strangely confused production is often glaringly apparent. While *Assassins* can be applauded for intellectual ambitions unknown to most American musicals, such high intentions, intermittently realized, hardly seem like achievement enough. Given the subject and the talent at hand, shouldn't the artistic yardstick for the content of *Assassins* be Don DeLillo's novel *Libra* or Martin Scorsese's film *Taxi Driver* rather than, say, *42nd Street*?

Mr. Sondheim's better numbers in *Assassins* do aspire to the highest standard and not infrequently meet it. As the show as a whole attempts to rewrite American history, so the composer audaciously attempts to rewrite the history of American music. This is an antimusical about antiheroes. Every song upends a traditional native form: folk music, spirituals, and John Philip Sousa are all rethought along with Broadway idioms and the official national musical oratory of Irving Berlin and Francis Scott Key.

Some of the music is pretty in a manner that recalls the revisionist theatrical folk music of Frederick Loewe (in *Paint Your Wagon*) and Kurt Weill (*Johnny Johnson*). As in *Sweeney Todd*, the sweetest sounds are often heard when the singers' thoughts are most homicidal. In "Gun Song," Booth (Victor Garber), the Garfield assassin Charles Guiteau (Jonathan Hadary), and the McKinley assassin Czolgosz (Terrence Mann) achieve an eerie yet lovely harmony while singing "All you have to do is move your little finger, and you can change the world." In "Unworthy of Your Love," Hinckley (Greg Germann) and Lynette (Squeaky) Fromme (Annie Golden) sing of their warped devotion to Jodie Foster and Charles Manson in a sumptuous ballad that both parodies and exploits the soft-rock hits of their American generation. Guiteau and the would-be killer of Franklin Roosevelt, Giuseppe Zangara (Eddie Korbich), each belt out long end notes as they reach their spastic literal ends in, respectively, a hangman's noose and an electric chair.

Brilliant as these songs can be individually, they never cohere into a fully realized score that builds in cumulative effect the way most of the later Sondheim scores do. Perhaps that shortfall can be blamed on the show's revue format, or on the three-piece band necessitated by the small playhouse. (Though the three musicians are the august musical-theater hands Paul Ford, Paul Gemignani, and Michael Starobin, the synthesizer-laden arrangements sound tinny.) Harder to explain away are a prosaic "Ballad of Booth" that repeats a lame gag about the assassin's bad reviews as an actor three times, or a comic ditty ("How I Saved Roosevelt") that flatly burlesques the eyewitness-to-history theme of "Someone in a Tree," the wisest song in the previous Sondheim-Weidman historical musical, *Pacific Overtures*.

The flaws of the *Assassins* score—its stop-and-go gait and sometimes collegiate humor—become major failings when magnified in the show's book and staging. To his credit, Mr. Weidman does have some clever ideas for scenes: He brings together the two very different American women who took shots at Gerald Ford, Fromme and the junk-food-addicted housewife Sara Jane Moore (Debra Monk), and he lavishes attention on the fascinating Samuel Byck (Lee Wilkof), an articulate lunatic in a Santa Claus suit who was obsessed with Leonard Bernstein and wanted to crash a hijacked jet into the Nixon White House. But the sketches are neither funny enough nor serious enough, despite allusions to Thoreau, Shakespeare, and Arthur Miller. Too often Mr. Weidman regurgitates history without dramatizing it or, worse, settles for tired gags, whether about Mr. Ford's clumsiness or Mr. Sondheim's lyrics for *West Side Story*. The show's putative payoff, a Rod Serlingesque encounter between Booth and Lee Harvey Oswald (Jace Alexander) in the Texas School Book Depository, never delivers the promised chills.

Mr. Zaks, a masterly director of warm, funny plays (*Six Degrees of Separation* most recently), seems to have lost control of this nasty musical rather than to have found a style for it. The show looks handsome, but it has been far too busily designed by the gifted Loren Sherman, as if Mr. Zaks were throwing scenery at the evening's internal esthetic conflicts rather than trying to resolve them. *Assassins* does not flow like a musical, but seems to start anew with each scene, and the scenes sit like clumps in isolation from the songs. The order of the numbers often seems arbitrary, and the attempts to impose unity, whether with a fairground motif or a strolling folk balladeer (Patrick Cassidy), are at best haphazard.

As is to be expected with Mr. Zaks, the acting is generally excellent. (A grating exception is the strained camp of Ms. Monk's Sara Jane Moore.) If Mr. Korbich's burning Zangara, a Sweeney Todd–like avenger of the proletariat, and Ms. Golden's fanatical Manson acolyte are the most touching figures, that may be because, as realized in the writing, their characters most demonically demonstrate Mr. Sondheim's conviction that there is a shadow America, a poisoned, have-not America, that must be recognized by the prosperous majority if the violence in our history is to be understood and overcome.

This is not a message that audiences necessarily want to hear at any time, and during the relatively jingoistic time of war in which this production happens to find itself, some may regard such sentiments as incendiary. But Mr. Sondheim has real guts. He isn't ashamed to identify with his assassins to the extreme point where he will wave a gun in a crowded theater, artistically speaking, if that's what is needed to hit the target of American complacency. While that target is a valuable one, especially at this historical moment, *Assassins* will have to fire with sharper aim and fewer blanks if it is to shoot to kill.

LA BÊTE

EUGENE O'NEILL THEATRE, FEBRUARY II, 1991

La Bête, the new play by David Hirson at the Eugene O'Neill Theater, begins with a bang that can make even a jaded New York audience abruptly spring to attention. The lights come up on a chorus of babbling seventeenth-century French swells who are figuratively guillotined by a progression of elegant, falling front curtains, each more disfigured than the last by blotted, calligraphic graffiti. Not long after that, the same curtains rise on a new shock for the eye: a towering period anteroom in nearly unrelieved white, as seen from a skewed, fisheye-lens perspective. And then comes the pièce de résistance: A corpulent buffoon—the beast of the title, known as Valère and played by Tom McGowan—delivers a marathon soliloquy that runs some four hundred lines and, like the entire play, has been composed in rhymed verse!

No, one won't soon forget the first half-hour or so of *La Bête,* which takes the brave chances so rare in new American plays. The flip side of such daring, however, is the high expectations it raises. Mr. Hirson promises nothing less than a mock Molière comedy of manners and ideas as refracted through (or deconstructed by) a postmodern sensibility. His theme is equally expansive: the decline and fall of culture in a West where "mediocrity is bound to thrive / while excellence must struggle to survive." Yet the follow-through is almost nonexistent. By the time *La Bête* dwindles down to a coda as embarrassingly mawkish as its prologue was startling, one is still waiting for the promised laughter, ideas, and dramatic conflict to possess center stage.

The evening's premise certainly is capable of shouldering high ambitions. Mr. Hirson has amusingly imagined that Elomire (Michael Cumpsty), an austere theatrical genius whose name is an anagram of Molière, is forced by his royal patron, Prince Conti (Dylan Baker), to add Valère, a common street clown, to his company of actors. Valère is the bull in the china shop of art: a vulgar, self-infatuated, facilely talented self-promoter who will pander to any audience, whether a prince or the masses, to win applause. Elomire is his sworn enemy: an esthete holding out for the highest standards in a civilization where the lowest common denominator is increasingly prized.

Of course the world of *La Bête* is a double for our own. The Prince who tries to affect a shotgun artistic marriage between the disparate Valère and Elomire might as well be a cynical Broadway producer attempting to shoehorn this year's Hollywood sensation into a revival of *Peer Gynt.* Fair enough, but do we need to go to the theater to be instructed that the heathens are at the gates of high culture? After laying out his unexceptional moral, Mr. Hirson misses opportunity after opportunity to make something entertaining or challenging out of it. *La Bête* has no dramatic surprises, and the author never offers any intellectual corollaries or counterarguments to his initial, unassailable ideological position. The play instead runs in place, repeating itself over and over, louder and louder each time.

Valère's big soliloquy in Act 1, for instance, merely illustrates with countless, interchangeable examples what a self-congratulatory fraud the clown is. Much of the rest of that act and the beginning of the second is devoted to regurgitating Elomire's well-worn objections to the proposed partnership, with the end of Act 2 trailing off into another lengthy monologue in which Elomire reiterates the playwright's message several more times. The one actual theatrical event in *La Bête*—the Act 2 play-within-the-play in which Valère parades his emptiness—is a fizzle both as a satirical example of the beast's fake art and as a farcical collision between the two antagonists. For that matter, Mr. Hirson never provides a fiery, Peter Shafferesque duel of words between the genius Elomire and the mediocrity Valère; this is a play in which everyone talks at rather than to one another.

The dramatic inertia, often accentuated by the declamatory staging provided by the English opera director Richard Jones, might not matter so much if the couplets and star performance were consistently funny. Though Mr. Hirson's sustained versifying is impressive as a technical achievement and though his rhymes can be cute ("caterwaul" with "warts and all"), he never comes remotely near the standard of wit for simulated French couplets in English set by Richard Wilbur in his Molière translations and in his lyrics for the Leonard Bernstein *Candide*. Mr. Hirson provokes smiles when he needs howls.

So it goes as well with Mr. McGowan, a burly young actor who was a good incidental clown in the James Lapine *Winter's Tale* at the Public Theater two seasons ago. The steep demands of *La Bête*, which require that Valère make vulgarity both funny and chillingly evil, exceed his skills. While Mr. McGowan flounces through his lengthy Act 1 monologue with every syllable and low-comic gesture professionally intact, he offers the letter of burlesque clowning without the instinctual spirit that might make such antics hilarious and unsettling. The dangerous comic bravura of a Zero Mostel, Charles Ludlam, John Belushi—or, to descend to mere mortals, a Tim Curry or John Candy—is desperately needed to create a tour de force out of a role too laboriously written to soar on an industrious actor's energy alone.

Revealingly Mr. McGowan reaches his one outrageous peak not when he is speaking Mr. Hirson's lines but when he defaces the set with a marker, one of several striking visual gags in a production that has been brilliantly designed by Richard Hudson (sets and costumes) and Jennifer Tipton (lighting). In a supporting cast that includes underused talents (James Greene) and overstretched ones (Johann Carlo), the outstanding comic turn comes from Mr. Baker, who is almost unrecognizable under the wig, lengthy train, and pancake makeup of the campy, Cyril Ritchard–like Prince. ("I'm hardly king," he says, sounding every bit like a man who would be queen.) Mr. Cumpsty's impassioned Elomire is also very fine, given the limits of a bombastic role that is less a character than a one-note authorial stand-in.

That note is grating. Elomire eventually sounds less like Molière, or one of that playwright's puritanically rigid comic targets, than like a neoconservative scold. In his final, crowd-pleasing tirade, he rages at a culture that values form over content, highfalutin words over ideas, pretension over truth, and he attacks charlatans like Valère for appropriating the vocabulary of real art to justify their transgressions. But isn't *La Bête* pandering just as much as its villain? There is not a single idea or debate in this play aside from its cost-free endorsement of excellence over trash, and even that one conviction is conveyed not through theatrical excellence but by a sermon that implicitly flatters the audience for its own elevated taste and for its cultural superiority to the riffraff presumably watching those Broadway shows written in lowly prose.

Thus does an exceptionally promising work intended to shake up a complacent audience deteriorate into an almost insufferably smug example of the exact middlebrow fluff it wants to attack. Offering verse without poetry and the gilded rhetoric of culture as if it were the content, *La Bête* is not so much a play on Molière's *Bourgeois Gentilhomme* as a play for today's bourgeois gentilhomme, or for anyone who confuses high-mindedness with high art.

≡ *This play got wildly mixed reviews—raves and some pans more devastating than mine—a response that was later duplicated in London, with another cast.*

ABSENT FRIENDS
MANHATTAN THEATRE CLUB, FEBRUARY 13, 1991

Alan Ayckbourn has written more plays than William Shakespeare and perhaps as many good plays, of all shapes and sizes, as any other English dramatist of his generation. But if you wanted to define the Ayckbourn sensibility with a single incident in a single play, you could do it by turning to a passage in Act 2 of *Absent Friends*, the early comedy (1974) that is receiving its belated New York premiere in an exquisitely orchestrated production directed by Lynne Meadow at the Manhattan Theatre Club.

The incident involves a perfectly conventional suburban English housewife, Diana, who is sitting on her living room couch presiding over a Saturday afternoon tea party. Diana—played by the sublime English actress Brenda Blethyn, in her New York debut—is a cheery sort, with button eyes, rosy cheeks, and a jolly word for nearly anyone who will look benignly in her direction. But things have not gone well at her tea party, and suddenly Diana cracks at the realization that she long ago took a wrong turn in life and has ever since been stuck "doing all the wrong things." Her arms folded and her posture still erect, Ms. Blethyn starts crying and shrieking uncontrollably, inconsolably, plunging from chattery contentment to rage and nervous collapse.

It's an upsetting spectacle, and it will not quit. Diana just keeps sobbing from her perch on the couch. But what makes the scene quintessential Ayckbourn is what happens next: The poor woman's friends must restore order by somehow maneuvering her to her bedroom, where she can be put to rest. The trouble is that Diana won't go easily or quietly, and she is too heavy to be carried to the second floor. As her neighbors clumsily and at first ineffectually try to push her up the stairs, a tragic spectacle becomes a farcical one without relinquishing any of the gravity of Diana's despair. Mr. Ayckbourn, abetted by Ms. Blethyn's admixture of fragility and luminosity, really has carried off the trick of making an audience laugh and cry at the same time.

Absent Friends does not always reach this level of achievement, but it is a gem that succeeds at everything it wants to do in two brisk hours. Mr. Ayckbourn has described the play as being "about death and the death of love" and has decreed from hard experience (after its West End failure) that it is best performed in "a small intimate theater where one can hear the actors breathing and the silences ticking away." Ms. Meadow, who did such a good job with Mr. Ayckbourn's *Woman in Mind* a few seasons ago, is completely in sync with these intentions, as are her cast (all American except for Ms. Blethyn) and her set designer, John Lee Beatty.

Diana's living room, ostensibly a model of affluent interior decoration as decreed by glossy magazines, is just antiseptic enough to suggest a mausoleum. The death that briefly visits it is that of a woman who was engaged to be married to Colin (Peter Frechette), an amiable young man who moved to another town three years earlier. *Absent Friends* is a minute-by-minute account of the casual reunion Diana holds for the long-absent Colin when he returns to his old neighborhood for a visit. In truth, the hostess, her husband, and their guests didn't know and don't remember Colin that well—and never met his fiancée, who died in a drowning accident—but they feel obliged to make a show of sharing his grief.

Mr. Frechette, last seen at the Manhattan Theater Club as the trendy artist in *Eastern Standard,* is equally incisive here as a provincial Ayckbourn nerd, all kindly smiles and sentimental homilies. He isn't bitter about the loss of his beloved—he still has dozens, if not hundreds, of snapshots of her, which he pushes on anyone in sight—and he tells his old companions that he is not envious of their freedom from his nightmare. Yet Colin's good cheer has an inverse effect on everyone else. The more he natters away, complimenting his friends on their marriages, children, and careers, and recounting idyllic shared memories that they but dimly recall, the more his hosts are forced to confront the gap that separates Colin's fantasy of their contentment from the suffering and disappointment that are their actual lot.

Though the obtuse Colin cannot recognize the truth, his friends are all either parasites or losers, from a philandering, selfish businessman (Diana's husband, played by David Purdham), to a sad-sack salesman (John Curless) with a boundless repertory of irritating nervous tics, to an unconvincingly perky wife (Ellen Parker) martyred to a frequently bedridden, grotesquely overweight spouse. It is the way of the world in Mr. Ayckbourn's suburbia that the men tend to be either malevolent or helpless infants while the women are their lonely, unappreciated, and often abused nannies.

The only exception to this general rule is the youngest woman on stage, and the only one who is mothering an actual baby: Evelyn, a sullen malcontent with what one antagonist calls a "really mean little face" and a penchant for speaking solely in contemptuous words of one syllable (usually "no"). Gillian Anderson, the Chicago actress cast in the part, turns Evelyn into a dark void, a glowering presence as devoid of humanity as Mr. Frechette's Colin is overflowing with it. She is a hilarious, if frightening, representative of abject evil, yet it is Mr. Ayckbourn's grimmest joke that Colin's fatuous goodwill proves just as destructive as Evelyn's undisguised cynicism and malice.

As always, this playwright makes the mundane middle class theatrical by tucking the casual cruelty, deep sorrow, and occasional bravery of his characters into the humble, often funny calamities of diurnal domesticity—the ill-fated shopping expedition, the inopportune phone call, the baby carriage left out in the rain. If Mr. Ayckbourn were American, the underside of his plays' antics might be likened to the suburban tales of John Cheever: Terror always lurks just beneath the surface of ostentatiously comfortable homes where real comfort is nowhere to be found. By the final curtain, as the first shadows of evening fall across Diana's living room, nearly everyone in *Absent Friends* is more or less sedated. Though Colin calls sleep "the great healer," the fugue of deep breathing filling the twilight air is heavy with defeat and regret.

A couple of the pathetic revelers—those played by Mr. Curless and Ms. Parker—could be profitably explored for more depth. Some of the writing lacks depth, too. In later plays—and there have been more than two dozen since *Absent Friends,* most unseen in New York—Mr. Ayckbourn has camouflaged the machinery of his dramaturgy more expertly than he sometimes does here, and he has expanded his canvas beyond the living room to spread his darkness over an entire town (*A Chorus of Disapproval*), an entire nation (*A Small Family Business*), and an entire era (the epic *Revengers' Comedies*). But if *Absent Friends* is a chamber piece by the current Ayckbourn standard, it still takes the audience to the fractured heart of a comic universe where only the pratfalls don't hurt.

≡ *The two fine actresses in this play were discovered by mass audiences soon enough—Brenda Blethyn in Mike Leigh's film* Secrets & Lies, *and Gillian Anderson in the TV megahit* The X-Files.

LOST IN YONKERS
Richard Rodgers Theatre, February 22, 1991

Of all the odd couples created by Neil Simon in his thirty-year career in the theater, none has been less funny or more passionately acted than the battling mother and daughter indelibly embodied by Irene Worth and Mercedes Ruehl in *Lost in Yonkers,* the writer's new memory piece at the Richard Rodgers Theatre.

Ms. Worth, her usual elegance obliterated by a silver bun of steel-wool hair, rimless spectacles, and a limping stride, is an elderly widow known only as Grandma Kurnitz. A childhood immigrant from Germany to the United States, she has devoted her adulthood to the Yonkers candy store over which she makes her home. Bella, played by Ms. Ruehl, is the thirty-five-year-old child who never moved out and has paid with her life. A gawky woman with an eager smile and a confused, bubbly manner, Bella is, as one line has it, "closed for repairs." Her mind isn't quite right, her existence is bounded by the soda counter, and her development is arrested in early adolescence.

There's some humor in this, but, as one character remarks of Ms. Worth's Grandma, "I never said she was a lot of laughs." One doesn't have to be of German Jewish descent to recognize this ice-cold woman who yanks her face away from anyone who tries to plant a kiss on it and who belittles any relative who attempts to puncture her scowling reserve. She is terrifying, and not primarily because she wields a mean cane. As acted with matchless precision by Ms. Worth, Grandma is a nearly silent killer whose steely monstrousness can be found in the emotions she withholds rather than in whatever faint feelings she might grudgingly express.

As nature dictates, Bella is her opposite, and Ms. Ruehl imbues her with a vulnerability as electric in its way as the comic ferocity she so memorably brought to the role of a hell-bent Mafia wife in Jonathan Demme's film *Married to the Mob*. All elbows and knees, Ms. Ruehl seems to jitterbug constantly about the parlor, thirsting for any experience or human contact, however small and humdrum, that might come her way before her mother snuffs it out.

Grandma and Bella are on a collision course, and when the blowout arrives, it not only brings *Lost in Yonkers* to a wrenching catharsis, but it also wipes out much of the nostalgically sentimental family portrait that Mr. Simon presented to Broadway audiences in his autobiographical trilogy of the 1980s. Whatever the virtues of the author's Brighton Beach plays, they always seemed a little too roseate to be true. The relatives on stage were guilty of peccadilloes and frailties, never major crimes. That's not the case here, where the only lines referring to the family as a safe haven are bitterly ironic. Grandma has a crushed foot—from her Berlin childhood—and she is out to get revenge on the world by crushing anyone or anything in her path. While Mr. Simon's autobiographical cycle officially ended with *Broadway Bound*, it is in *Lost in Yonkers* that he seems at last to be baring the most fundamental scar of all, that of a child rejected by a parent.

I don't see how anyone can fail to be moved by the sight of Ms. Ruehl, the lonely repository of this grief, when she stands center stage in Act 2 of *Lost in Yonkers*, crying and begging for the intimacy, physical and otherwise, she has always been so cruelly denied. If this play kept its focus on Bella and Grandma throughout, one might even be able to mention it in the same paragraph, if not necessarily the same breath, as *The Glass Menagerie*, *The Effect of Gamma Rays on Man-in-the-Moon Marigolds*, and *Gypsy*, among other American classics about lethal mothers and oppressed daughters. But Mr. Simon, whether by sloppiness or design, falls considerably short of this hallowed territory. If he is no longer camouflaging human brutality, he is still packaging it within a lot of fluff, and not always his best fluff at that. While the gripping Grandma-Bella drama is never quite lost in *Lost in Yonkers*, it is too frequently crowded out by domestic comedy of a most ordinary sort.

As it happens, the dramatic axis of this play is not usually Bella but Grandma's teenage grandchildren, a pair of Hollywood-wise boys who share virtually all traits except their names with the brothers in the

Brighton Beach plays. They are reluctantly dumped at Grandma's for a period of months by their father, Bella's widowed and broken brother (a vivid Mark Blum), who must take to the road as a salesman to pay off his late wife's hospital bills.

The boys are well enough played by youngsters (Jamie Marsh and Danny Gerard) whose only sin is that they are not Matthew Broderick, but their characters often are as secondary as the Pigeon sisters in *The Odd Couple*: The brothers usually seem like wisecracking observers of the play rather than fully realized, fully engaged participants in it. For all their stage time, and all the talk about how much they may or may not be damaged by their own extended exposure to Grandma, their actual conflicts with her are bite-sized sitcom anecdotes, unsullied by the complexities of puberty or much visible fallout from the loss of their mother.

The other characters who pass through the Kurnitz apartment are two more of Grandma's damaged adult children, a daughter (Lauren Klein) who is reduced to a single scene and a single running gag and a mysterious gangster son who, as acted with a commanding mixture of malevolence and avuncularity by Kevin Spacey, presides over some of the play's fresher comic interludes. (Mr. Spacey also makes high drama out of a dazzling curtain line revealing the identity of his true partner in crime.) Like the boys, these supporting players seem to come and go arbitrarily, as if Mr. Simon wanted everyone to hang around to entertain the troops as a way of forestalling the main, troublesome events involving his principal antagonists.

Given this dramatist's recent command of his craft—let's forget *Rumors*—the flaccid structure and automatic-pilot jokeyness of *Lost in Yonkers* are unexpected. Among the clumsier lapses are an opening scene of exposition that repeats itself incessantly for no reason other than the hokey, artificial delay of the formidable Grandma's star entrance, and two subsequent scenes that amount to little more than blackout sketches with thudding payoffs. Nearly every joke, theme, or plot turn in *Lost in Yonkers* is laboriously telegraphed, to the point where even a playful conversation about a Bette Davis movie is drenched in pregnant meaning and virtually every character's guilty secret is transparent well before anyone onstage wises up. The only real narrative surprise all evening is an abrupt, supposedly shocking Act 2 sexual confession that seems pulled, unedited, from a Psych 101 textbook.

The passages that surround the confrontations between Ms. Worth and Ms. Ruehl are nothing if not painless, and they have been staged by the estimable Gene Saks with a bravura that sometimes is impressive (a family dinner in Act 2) and sometimes overcompensates for the weaker writing and for the expansive confines of the Rodgers, not the coziest of Broadway theaters for nonmusical plays.

Ms. Worth excepted, everyone in *Lost in Yonkers* is "on" in the show-biz sense most of the time, which may explain why at the press preview I attended a mood-shattering ovation could break out in the middle of Ms. Ruehl's big soliloquy, as if the actress were belting a medley of show-stopping songs. The whole production could use more of the delicacy to be found in Santo Loquasto's set, which, as affectionately lighted by Tharon Musser, recalls the designer's sepia Coney Island interiors of the same period for Woody Allen's *Radio Days* and, in a richly textured front curtain, the New York chiaroscuro of Reginald Marsh.

If such lightness of touch is otherwise rare, its absence is balanced by the presence of something new in the playwright's canon: a raw anguish that not even the usual (and forced) upbeat final curtain can wish away. *Lost in Yonkers* is hardly Mr. Simon's most accomplished work, but when the riveting Ms. Worth and Ms. Ruehl take center stage to tear at each other and the audience, the wounds run so deep that one feels it just may be his most honest.

THE SPEED OF DARKNESS
BELASCO THEATRE, MARCH 1, 1991

The *Speed of Darkness,* Steve Tesich's new play, is only a few minutes old when a character announces that blood will eventually be spilled on the living-room carpet of the all-American home where it takes place. By the time the final curtain falls more than two hours later, blood has indeed been spilled, and so have guts, shameful secrets, and a heap of dirt that stands for the stain on a family and a nation. That's the kind of play Mr. Tesich has written: one that tells you what it is going to do and then does it, messily perhaps, but with a vengeance and, once it finally gets going, with an inexorable grip.

It is also the kind of defiantly old-fashioned drama, big-boned, un-subtle, and aflame with passion, that few writers as high-minded as Mr. Tesich, best known as the author of the film *Breaking Away,* would be caught dead writing anymore. There could be no more perfect setting for it than the Belasco Theatre, a glorious old Broadway house that has known its own darkness more often than not in recent decades. David Belasco, the impresario and dramatist who built the place in 1907, believed in thunderous emotions, and his theater, an almost ecclesiastical cavern glinting with mosaics of colored glass, seems designed to showcase them. In *The Speed of Darkness,* Mr. Tesich's best scenes mesh with some thrilling acting to turn back the Belasco's clock.

The evening's cast is headed by Len Cariou and Stephen Lang, as Vietnam soulmates whose paths cross again twenty years after they left the service. Mr. Cariou is Joe—war hero Joe, self-made Joe, Middle American Joe, the archetypal father who runs a construction business and presides over the Naugahyde-upholstered South Dakota household at hand. Mr. Lang is Lou, the buddy he long ago rescued, and these days a homeless man with moth-eaten clothing, lice-infested hair, and a gift for street-corner philosophizing. Lou devotes his energies to following a copy of the Vietnam Veterans Memorial—a traveling "son of wall"—that has found its way to Sioux Falls as part of a cross-country tour. He soon settles in with Joe, Joe's wife (Lisa Eichhorn), and their high-school senior daughter (Kathryn Erbe) as an uninvited if not entirely unwelcome guest.

To say more about the story of *The Speed of Darkness* would be to spoil one of its prime assets, for Mr. Tesich unabashedly believes in narrative. He also has faith in other familiar verities of traditional American dramaturgy. The fifth member of the cast, that sensitive young actor Robert Sean Leonard, plays a neighborhood boy who doubles as an unofficial Greek chorus, promising the audience a tragedy and sometimes sounding like the lawyer who portentously narrates Arthur Miller's *A View from the Bridge.* Mr. Tesich also gives *The Speed of Darkness* a buried crime out of Mr. Miller's *All My Sons* and a symbolic baby out of Edward Albee's *Who's Afraid of Virginia Woolf?* or more recently Sam Shepard's *Buried Child.* Joe's family sometimes behaves like the Vietnam-era brood of David Rabe's *Sticks and Bones,* and is it my imagination that Mr. Cariou is starting to look like Lee J. Cobb?

Sure, there's a paint-by-numbers quality to some of this, and no, Mr. Tesich does not deliver a Great American Tragedy by the final scene—just a very chewy climactic soliloquy for Mr. Cariou that substitutes an excess of melodramatic revelations for the one deep truth that might raise characters and audience alike to higher ground. But speaking as someone who has found Mr. Tesich's more recent plays (*Division Street, Square One*) and screenplays (*The World According to Garp, Four Friends*) either precious or pretentious, I was almost always captivated by his heartfelt writing here, despite his sometimes open manipulation of his character's strings and the slow-motion exposition that cripples the first half or so of the first act.

Many of the best lines belong to Mr. Lang, a fascinating actor who specializes in psychos (*A Few Good Men,* the coming film *The Hard Way*) but here keeps us guessing whether Lou is the craziest or wisest person on stage, or both. With his military stature, feral eyes, and weathered face, he is, as always, a mesmerizing figure, and his diction, as classically polished as his body and clothes are filthy, adds to his unsettling presence. He could not have a better opportunity to show off his range than *The Speed of Darkness*. Mr. Lang is brilliant in his delivery of Mr. Tesich's funniest speech—a Robin Williamsesque spiel about the relative merits of pre- and postmodern public statuary to the urban homeless—and he gives a searing account of the play's most moving monologue, in which Lou recounts his arrest for trying to scratch his name with a can opener into the Washington wall of the dead.

Lou's point is that the survivors of the Vietnam War deserve a memorial, too, because many of them, like him, survived in name only and are still what he calls MIA, or Missing in America. ("We weren't saved. We were rescued" is how Joe puts his own emergence alive from battle.) Mr. Tesich's larger theme is that the entire country must break through the wall it has erected around an unhappy chapter in its history if it is to be free of its guilt. Along with the wall, the evening's other principal metaphor is garbage, for it is in garbage removal that Joe got his postwar start in civilian life, taking his neighbors' "trash and filth and waste" and burying it "somewhere, anywhere, out of sight." In the playwright's view, that waste, however ugly and poisonous, must be brought from the darkness into the light if it is at last to be understood and overcome.

Mr. Tesich has not so successfully worked out his play at the marital level, and Joe's wife, well played by Ms. Eichhorn in apparent emulation of Dianne Wiest, never adds up. Though it still lacks a wholly satisfying ending, *The Speed of Darkness* has otherwise been profitably shorn of much, if not all, of its overwriting since its premiere almost two years ago at the Goodman Theatre in Chicago. Then as now the firm director is the Goodman's artistic leader, Robert Falls, and if he shares responsibility for the evening's early leaden gait (and the unfortunate *Twilight Zone* music accompanying it), he also presumably deserves credit for the inspired recasting. (Only Mr. Lang is a holdover from the Chicago company.) In Ms. Erbe, a beautiful and poised young actress who makes Joe's daughter an intelligent girl-woman with a rapidly evolving, transparently exposed psyche, he may have made a major discovery.

For Mr. Cariou, *The Speed of Darkness* may be the most challenging assignment since *Sweeney Todd*, and he acts his heart out in a role that variously calls for Chamber of Commerce boorishness, belligerent drunkenness, paternal tenderness, and finally the promised self-exorcism in which he spews out Joe's own garbage of a lifetime. By then, the V-shaped back wall of Thomas Lynch's domestic set seems to have blackened into another, hellish image of the war memorial, a jolting go-for-broke gesture that typifies a drama intent on retrieving the theater's past no less than the trauma of Vietnam.

THE SUBSTANCE OF FIRE
PLAYWRIGHTS HORIZONS, MARCH 18, 1991

One need not be a jaded constituent of New York's literati to recognize Isaac Geldhart, the esteemed publisher and embattled Jewish father who stands at the center of *The Substance of Fire,* the new play by Jon Robin Baitz at Playwrights Horizons. A childhood refugee from the "wrecked world" of the Holocaust, Isaac came to New York an orphan, reinvented himself as a bon vivant, married well, and found a measure of fame and fortune as a rigorously independent champion of literary books that wouldn't be caught dead on a best-seller list. By the late 1980s, when Mr. Baitz's play unfolds, Isaac has long since been a brand name in the culture industry. He is one of those survivors, of postwar American intellectual firestorms no less than Old Europe's bloodbaths, who run Manhattan with an iron tongue.

Isaac is such a familiar type that one could draft an extensive list of actual literary power brokers—no names will be named here—who share some or most of his childhood background, professional resume, neoconservative politics, and cosmopolitan accent. But to recognize a Manhattan archetype is not the same thing as knowing one, and it is the searing achievement of *The Substance of Fire* that it keeps chipping and chipping away at its well-worn, well-defended protagonist until finally he and the century that shaped him and then reshaped him are exposed to the tragic quick. As written with both scrupulous investigative zeal and bottomless sympathy by Mr. Baitz and as acted in a career-transforming performance by Ron Rifkin, Isaac Geldhart is one of the most memorable and troubling characters to appear onstage this season.

He is also the harbinger of what is likely to be a major playwriting career for a dramatist who is only twenty-nine years old. Mr. Baitz, who has previously been represented in New York by the highly promising *Film Society,* is going to write better plays than *The Substance of Fire,* but line by line, insight by insight, scene by scene, his writing is already so articulate, witty, and true that it's only a matter of time before his theatrical know-how, some of which must come with experience, catches up with his talent. Mr. Baitz seems to understand so much—about people, language, society—and to be so eager to say what he knows that the naturalistic conventions of a work like *The Substance of Fire* simply cannot contain him.

Though this play wanders all over the place during its two enthralling hours, as if the young author were trying out different dramatic strategies for size, nearly every place it visits is of interest, not in the least because Mr. Rifkin's congenitally combative Isaac is always center stage. In Act 1, the publisher is placed in a typical family-business conflict: To save his increasingly insolvent firm from Japanese takeover sharks, he must browbeat his three adult children, all principal stockholders, into philosophical and financial submission. In Act 2, set a few years later, what seemed to be a potentially high-charged boardroom drama is all but forgotten (as are some of its players) while Mr. Baitz forces Isaac to confront the demons that would destroy him from within.

All of Isaac's struggles, of course, date back to the war in which his parents and grandparents died in the camps while he escaped incarceration. If Isaac has his share of survivor's guilt, compounded by the death of his wife six years before the play opens, he also has a survivor's arrogant omnipotence. With his natty, custom-made, double-breasted suits, verbal elegance, and chilling charm, Mr. Rifkin presents the publisher as a figure of dazzling intellectual authority who long ago realized that he was the smartest person in any book-lined New York room. He never hesitates to remind all listeners that in an America where so many people dispose of their history and convictions for expediency's sake, he has kept the "fire" ignited by his youth, the spirit that keeps him sticking up for the highest standards in morality and literature alike.

Even his attractive and accomplished children do not escape his bullying condescension. Isaac refers to his Wharton-educated son (Jon Tenney), a partner in the publishing business, as an accountant and to his other son (Patrick Breen), a Rhodes scholar who teaches landscape architecture at Vassar, as an "assistant gardener." He dismisses his sensitive daughter (Sarah Jessica Parker), an actress in children's television, as "a hired clown." When all three suggest that a commercial novel of the brat pack school might bail out his bottom line, Isaac sticks to his plan of publishing a six-volume scholarly work on Nazi medical experiments and delivers a hilarious discourse on "slicko hipster" fiction that surpasses any diatribe yet published about *American Psycho*.

For all his nastiness, it is hard to dislike Isaac, even as one is grateful that he is not one's own father or cocktail-party acquaintance. He is just too smart and funny and, on occasion, too right to be dismissed. Once Mr. Baitz ruthlessly challenges the premises by which Isaac has lived—

examining the real meaning of his survival, the substance of his "fire"—the audience is caught up in the sad reckoning facing him in late middle age. Is Isaac's proud insistence on holding on to his past the choice that allowed him to survive, or is it a burden that robbed him of any hope for happiness?

"I thought that if I published Hazlitt and Svevo, I'd be spared," says a frayed and clinically depressed Isaac in Act 2. But he has not been spared: If the Nazis destroyed his family in Europe, he has "trashed" his own family, effectively if not as definitively, in New York. Not for nothing does he pore over some illustrated letters among his prized possessions—"gestures of love" by other witnesses to the "bloodthirsty century" like Osip Mandelstam and George Grosz—with a teary intimacy he cannot achieve with his own children. Just as pointedly does Mr. Baitz indicate that the "most crucial part" of Isaac's collection of ephemera is a water-color postcard painted by the young Hitler in Vienna at a time when he "fancied himself a serious artist." Does Hitler's painting make a mockery of all humane connections between life and art? If so, is it possible that the life of literature that Isaac has invented in New York is an escape from life rather than life itself, just as the love of books is a flight from love?

To yank Isaac into these conundrums—and the audience into the timeless drama of how any adult succeeds or fails in replaying a traumatic childhood—Mr. Baitz must bring on a psychiatric social worker (a hardworking Maria Tucci) who has a few too many crosses of her own (and New York City's) for the evening to bear. To dramatize the harm Isaac has inflicted on his children, the playwright schematically gives each of them a casebook infirmity, psychological or physical, to serve as a literal parental scar. The dénouement of *The Substance of Fire* is also too pat, though it is so beautifully understated in Daniel Sullivan's staging that it is touching anyway.

Then again, Mr. Sullivan's entire production is flawless, from the snowy Gramercy Park light that the designer Arden Fingerhut visits on John Lee Beatty's elegant set to the perfect-pitch orchestration of dialogue that ranges from bitchy, sophisticated publishing-industry gossip to painful excavations of horrors civilization can never shake. Every performance is finely shaded in texture. Ms. Parker, an actress whose development has been a joy to watch since her childhood appearance in *Annie,* is both impassioned and comic as a weightier counterpart to the Los Angeles woman-child she plays just as winningly in the Steve Martin film *L.A. Story.* Mr. Breen and Mr. Tenney portray both the outward, hard-won maturity and buried, infantile hurts of Isaac's sons with equal conviction.

It says much about all three actors playing the Geldhart children that they can, when need be, stand up to Mr. Rifkin, whose caustic humor and infernal anger seem to be forces of nature. It says much about *The Substance of Fire* that when it is Isaac's turn to be flattened by life's blows, Mr. Baitz does not provide the satisfaction of a bully getting his comeuppance, just the ineffable melancholy of a flame flickering out. This is a deeply compassionate play, as imperfect as it is youthful, by a writer who with one play or another is bound to be embraced by the wrecked world.

I HATE HAMLET
Walter Kerr Theatre, April 9, 1991

"I love this apartment because it's like a stage set, it's like the theater," says Andy Rally, a young bicoastal actor who has taken up new digs in Greenwich Village after the cancellation of his television series *L.A. Medical.* And no wonder. Andy's new flat is the extravagantly Gothic apartment long ago occupied by John Barrymore, and even in 1991 it remains a suitably regal throne room for any show-business prince, past, present, or still aspiring. Since Andy (Evan Handler) is about to assume Barrymore's most celebrated Shakespearean role in a Joseph Papp production in Central Park, what is to stand in the way of his complete artistic fulfillment? Only one thing. Much as Andy loves his apartment, loves the theater, and loves stardom, he hates Hamlet.

I Hate Hamlet, the new comedy by Paul Rudnick at the Walter Kerr Theatre, is the unapologetically silly and at times hilarious tale of how Andy rises above his fear and loathing of the role people ritualistically refer to as "the greatest in the English-speaking world." To do so, he must seek the help of Barrymore himself, who comes back from the grave to give his young would-be successor instructions in Shakespearean acting, not to mention life and love. Don't ask how and why Barrymore rises from the dead—Mr. Rudnick's séance takes far too long as it is—but do be cheered by the news that the ghost is played by Nicol Williamson. A first-class Hamlet in his own right once upon a time, and on occasion as flamboyant an offstage figure as Barrymore was, Mr. Williamson offers a riotous incarnation of a legendary actor, lecher, and lush (not necessarily in that order) whom even death has failed to slow down.

Mr. Williamson gets the audience laughing from the moment he enters in full Hamlet regalia and makes a beeline, as if yanked by a magnet, to the nearest uncorked champagne bottle. Mr. Rudnick, a wisecrack artist whose other works include the play *Poor Little Lambs* and the novel *Social Disease,* quickly gives his star some high-flying bouts of drunken hamming worthy of Sid Caesar on *Your Show of Shows,* or Peter O'Toole in *My Favorite Year.* When Barrymore instructs his young protégé on the art of the curtain call, Mr. Williamson demonstrates how to milk the crowd with a cynical yet rousing bravura that might have impressed the real-life Barrymore clan. His woozy swoons, bombastic braggadocio, and swashbuckling sexual antics are so eerily reminiscent of John Barrymore himself in his self-parodistic decline that Mr. Williamson creates the illusion of bearing much more of a physical resemblance to his celebrated prototype than he actually does.

Charmingly enough, Mr. Rudnick's play tries, albeit with scarce success, to recall the screwy comic style of Barrymore's Hollywood and Broadway day: The spirit of *Here Comes Mr. Jordan, Topper,* and *Blithe Spirit* can be found in the supernatural pranks of *I Hate Hamlet,* and the director, Michael Engler, has added to that nostalgic mood with a fabulously glossy set by Tony Straiges, silver-screen moonlight by Paul Gallo, and hokey old-time background music by Kim Sherman. For a further whiff of period flavor, Celeste Holm, an actress whose own career dates back to the tail end of the Barrymore period, appears in *I Hate Hamlet* as a onetime Barrymore flame, and her reunion with her deceased paramour in Mr. Rudnick's play gives the evening an all-too-brief injection of rueful Lubitsch romantic fantasy.

That scene excepted, the tone of *I Hate Hamlet* tends to be more contemporary and collegiate, and the writing is highly variable, taking a noticeable plunge every time Mr. Williamson fades into the set's acres of Gothic woodwork. Mr. Rudnick is witty on such subjects as Method acting ("We must never confuse truth with asthma"), the resistance of modern audiences to Shakespeare ("It's algebra on stage!"), and Hollywood's patronizing attitude toward the New York theater. The humor becomes mechanical, however, when the playwright tosses in one-liners on such well-worn topics as television programming, real-estate brokers, and trendy courses of study at the New School.

The duller volleys of dialogue would not be so noticeable if the playwright had devised an airtight comic structure to keep the play moving forward no matter what. But *I Hate Hamlet* is too often content to be an extended two-hour sketch and never musters the theatrical ambitions of Michael Frayn's *Noises Off* and Terrence McNally's *It's Only a Play,* the better-made backstage comedies it occasionally echoes. Mr. Rudnick's oddest lapses are his inability to make consistently riotous farcical hay out of Barrymore's spells of ghostly invisibility and his decision to keep his play's promised climax, Andy's opening night, offstage. The most elaborate subplot in *I Hate Hamlet*—Andy's attempts to bed his virginal, Opheliaesque girlfriend—piles up far more stage time than laughs.

In his direction, Mr. Engler seems less secure here than he did in *Eastern Standard* and *Mastergate.* Snappily choreographed scenes intermingle with those in which Mr. Williamson seems to be lolling idly about like standby equipment. The production's biggest failure is the performance of Mr. Handler, who was so good this season as the enraged doctor's son in *Six Degrees of Separation.* As Andy Rally, he lacks what Mr. Rudnick calls the "right twinkle" required of a television star, and his comic range rarely extends much beyond that memorable note of hysteria he brought to his temper tantrum in *Six Degrees.* Jane Adams and Caroline Aaron, as Andy's pretentious love interest and pushy broker, are also adequate rather than inspired, though Adam Arkin is remarkably fresh as a Hollywood huckster who explains that television is artistically superior to theater, not in the least because the audience need not pay any attention to it.

Throughout the evening's running debate about the merits of the stage and the small screen, there is never any doubt which side Mr. Rudnick is on. It is even possible that the playwright does not hate *Hamlet,* all the jokes at its voluminously gloomy expense notwithstanding, for he permits Mr. Williamson to act Hamlet's advice to the players and act it movingly, after which the actor delivers an equally fervent soliloquy in which Barrymore regrets how he squandered his art and soul in Hollywood following his Shakespearean stage triumph in New York. That Act 2 speech seems to touch something deep, almost tragic, in Mr. Williamson, and so it does in us. But mostly *I Hate Hamlet* is light and ramshackle, affectionately amusing about the theater when at its sharpest, and, one must say, still a little funnier than *Hamlet* when not.

≣ *This show later became famous for the peculiar behavior of its star— whose history of acting up goes way back, to when he slugged David Merrick backstage during the original production of* Inadmissible Evidence *a quarter-century earlier. In this instance, Williamson started behaving erratically early in the run, sometimes wandering offstage. Eventually he struck his fellow actor, Evan Handler, in the back with the flat part of his sword during an Act 1 dueling scene, prompting Handler to flee the theater, never to return to* I Hate Hamlet.

MISS SAIGON
BROADWAY THEATRE, APRIL 12, 1991

There may never have been a musical that made more people angry before its Broadway debut than *Miss Saigon*.

Here is a show with something for everyone to resent—in principle, at least. Its imported stars, the English actor Jonathan Pryce and the Filipino actress Lea Salonga, are playing roles that neglected Asian American performers feel are rightfully theirs. Its top ticket price of a hundred dollars is a new Broadway high, sprung by an English producer, if you please, on a recession-straitened American public. More incendiary still is the musical's content. A loose adaptation of *Madama Butterfly* transplanted to the Vietnam War by French authors, the *Les Misérables* team of Alain Boublil and Claude-Michel Schönberg, *Miss Saigon* insists on revisiting the most calamitous and morally dubious military adventure in American history and, through an unfortunate accident of timing, arrives in New York even as the jingoistic celebrations of a successful American war are going full blast.

So take your rage with you to the Broadway Theatre, where *Miss Saigon* opened last night, and hold on tight. Then see just how long you can cling to the anger when confronted by the work itself. For all that seems galling about *Miss Saigon*—and for all that is indeed simplistic, derivative, and, at odd instances, laughable about it—this musical is a gripping entertainment of the old school (specifically, the Rodgers and Hammerstein East-meets-West school of *South Pacific* and *The King and I*). Among other pleasures, it offers lush melodies, spectacular performances by Mr. Pryce, Ms. Salonga, and the American actor Hinton Battle, and a good cry. Nor are its achievements divorced from its traumatic subject, as cynics might suspect. Without imparting one fresh or daring thought about the Vietnam War, the show still manages to plunge the audience back into the quagmire of a generation ago, stirring up feelings of anguish and rage that run even deeper than the controversies that attended *Miss Saigon* before its curtain went up.

Challenged perhaps by the ill will that greeted their every move, the evening's creators, led by the director Nicholas Hytner, have given New York a far sharper version of *Miss Saigon* than the one originally staged in London. The much publicized (and inane) helicopter effect notwithstanding, this is the least spectacular and most intimate of the West End musicals. The most stirring interludes feature two or three characters on an empty stage or in a bar girl's dingy hovel, and for once the production has been made leaner rather than fattened up for American consumption. (Though the Broadway Theatre is among the largest Broadway houses, it seems cozy next to the cavernous Drury Lane, where the show plays in London.) If *Miss Saigon* is the most exciting of the so-called English musicals—and I feel it is, easily—that may be because it is the most American. It freely echoes Broadway classics, and some of its crucial personnel are Broadway hands: the colyricist Richard Maltby Jr., the choreographer Bob Avian, the orchestrator William D. Brohn.

Without two legendary American theatrical impresarios, David Belasco and Harold Prince, there would in fact be no *Miss Saigon*. It was Belasco's turn-of-the-century dramatization of the Madame Butterfly story that inspired Puccini's opera, and it was Mr. Prince who, inspired by Brecht and the actor Joel Grey twenty-five years ago, created the demonic, symbolic Emcee of *Cabaret*, a character that is unofficially recycled on this occasion in a role called the Engineer and played by Mr. Pryce. These two influences are brilliantly fused here. Altered substantially but not beyond recognition, the basic *Butterfly* premise of an Asian woman who is seduced and abandoned by an American military man is affectingly rekindled in *Miss Saigon* by Mr. Schönberg's score and Ms. Salonga's clarion, emotionally naked delivery of it. Whenever that tale flirts with bathos, along comes the leering, creepy Mr. Pryce to jolt the evening back into the hellish, last-night-of-the-world atmosphere that is as fitting for the fall of Saigon as it was for the Weimar Berlin of *Cabaret*.

The theatrical poles of *Miss Saigon* represented by its two stars are equally powerful. Ms. Salonga, whose performance has grown enormously since crossing the Atlantic, has the audience all but worshiping her from her first appearance as Kim, an open-faced seventeen-year-old waif from the blasted Vietnamese countryside who is reduced to working as a prostitute in Saigon. As her romance with an American marine, Chris (Willy Falk), blossoms *South Pacific*–style in a progression of haunting saxophone-flecked ballads in Act 1, the actress keeps sentimentality at bay by slowly revealing the steely determination beneath the gorgeous voice, radiant girlish features, and virginal white gown. Once Chris and his fellow Americans have fled her and her country, the determination transmutes into courage, and the passages in which Kim sacrifices herself for the welfare of her tiny child, no matter how hokey, are irresistibly moving because Ms. Salonga's purity of expression, backed up by the most elemental music and lyrics, simply won't let them be otherwise.

Mr. Pryce, a great character actor whose nasty streak has been apparent since his memorable Broadway debut in Trevor Griffiths's *Comedi-*

ans fifteen years ago, makes disingenuousness as electrifying as Ms. Salonga's ingenuousness. The Engineer is a fixer, profiteer, and survivor who can outlast Uncle Sam and Uncle Ho: a pimp, a sewer rat, a hustler of no fixed morality, sexuality, race, nationality, or language. Wearing wide-lapelled jackets and bell bottoms of garish color, he is the epitome of sleaze, forever swiveling his hips, flashing a sloppy tongue, and fluttering his grasping fingers in the direction of someone's dollar bills or sex organs. With his high-domed forehead and ghoulish eyes, Mr. Pryce is also a specter of doom, and he manages to turn a knee-jerk number indicting the greedy "American Dream" into a showstopper with the sheer force of his own witty malice.

As choreographed by Mr. Avian in demented parody of an old-fashioned Broadway song-and-dance turn, "The American Dream" looks like the Felliniesque "Loveland" sequence in the 1971 Stephen Sondheim musical *Follies,* and no wonder, given the song's imitation Sondheim lyrics and the fact that Mr. Avian was Michael Bennett's associate choreographer on *Follies.* Among the other old favorites in *Miss Saigon* are a balcony scene out of *West Side Story,* a departing refugees scene out of *Fiddler on the Roof,* an Act 2 song for Mr. Pryce that recalls Fagin's equivalent solo in *Oliver!,* and some dancing North Vietnamese who seem a cross between the Perónists in *Evita* and the ritualistic Japanese dancers of *Pacific Overtures.* It is only when *Miss Saigon* imitates West End musicals of the 1980s, however, that it goes seriously astray. The helicopter stunt, which will most impress devotees of sub-Disney theme parks, is presented out of historical sequence in an Act 2 flashback, for no good reason other than to throw Andrew Lloyd Webber fans a pseudo-chandelier or levitating tire. A neon-drenched Bangkok nightlife spectacle in the same act is a grim reminder of the ill-fated *Chess.*

Of all the failings of modern British musicals, the most severe has been their creators' utter bewilderment about what happens between men and women emotionally, psychologically, and sexually. *Miss Saigon* is not immune to this syndrome, either, and it shows up most embarrassingly in the lyrics characterizing Chris's stateside wife, who, despite a game portrayal by Liz Callaway, induces audience snickers and giggles in her big Act 2 solo. Chris himself is nearly as faceless, and Mr. Falk, a performer with a strong pop voice and a Ken doll's personality, does nothing to turn up the hero's heat.

If anything, *Miss Saigon* would be stronger if Mr. Battle, who plays Chris's best friend, had been cast instead as Kim's lover. Mr. Battle's grit and passion are far more redolent of the marines who fought in Vietnam than Mr. Falk's blandness, and his one brief encounter with Ms. Salonga has more bite than any of her scenes with her paramour. Mr. Battle, who has heretofore been better known as a dancer than a singer, also rescues the sanctimonious opening anthem of Act 2—a canned plea for homeless Amerasian children—with a gospel delivery so blistering and committed that he overpowers an onslaught of clichéd lyrics, film clips, and a large backup choir.

With the aid of his designers, especially the lighting designer David Hersey, who uses John Napier's fabric-dominated sets as a floating canvas, Mr. Hytner usually keeps the staging simple. An opening *Apocalypse Now* sunrise that bleeds into a hazy panorama of a Saigon morning is as delicate as an Oriental print, and the Act 1 climax, in which boat people set off for points unknown, is stunning because it relies on such primal elements as an outstretched helping hand and the slow exit by the characters to the rear of a deep, darkened stage stripped of most scenery.

To be sure, the hallucinatory view of Vietnam familiar from the films of Oliver Stone, the journalism of Michael Herr, and the fiction of Robert Stone, among many others, is beyond Mr. Hytner's mission, if not his considerable abilities, just as any thoughtful analysis of the war is beyond the libretto. The text of *Miss Saigon*, second in naïveté only to the Peter Sellars/John Adams *Nixon in China,* says merely that the North Vietnamese were villains and that the Americans were misguided, bungling do-gooders. Facts and haircuts are fudged, the corrupt South Vietnamese regime is invisible, and any references to war atrocities are generalized into meaninglessness.

Yet the text is not the sum of a theatrical experience, and however sanitizing the words and corny the drama of *Miss Saigon*, the real impact of the musical goes well beyond any literal reading. America's abandonment of its own ideals and finally of Vietnam itself is there to be found in the wrenching story of a marine's desertion of a Vietnamese woman and her son. The evening's far-from-happy closing tableau—of spilled Vietnamese blood and an American soldier who bears at least some responsibility for the carnage—hardly whitewashes the United States involvement in Southeast Asia. *Miss Saigon* is escapist entertainment in style and in the sense that finally it even makes one forget about all the hype and protests that greeted its arrival. But this musical is more than that, too, because the one thing it will not allow an American audience to escape is the lost war that, like its tragic heroine, even now defiantly refuses to be left behind.

≡ *This may have been the last of the blockbuster West End musicals to repeat its London success in New York. The only subsequent import of its scale, Andrew Lloyd Webber's* Sunset Boulevard, *was a commercial disas-*

ter. The next collaboration between the producer Cameron Mackintosh and the Les Mis/Saigon *songwriting team of Boublil-Schönberg,* Martin Guerre, *was not well received in London and did not venture to Broadway. Nicholas Hytner, the director of* Miss Saigon, *went on to stage the visionary* Carousel *revival seen in London and then in New York. He's since made a name as a movie director:* The Madness of King George, The Crucible, *and* The Object of My Affection.

THE SECRET GARDEN
St. James Theatre, April 26, 1991

In *The Secret Garden*, the new musical at the St. James, a devoted team of theater artists applies a heap of talent and intelligence to the task of bringing Frances Hodgson Burnett's beloved children's novel of 1911 to the stage. They have accomplished that basic mission, all right, but whether *The Secret Garden* is a compelling dramatic adaptation of its source or merely a beautiful, stately shrine to it is certain to be a subject of intense audience debate. I, for one, often had trouble locating the show's pulse.

The musical's principal creators—the playwright Marsha Norman, the composer Lucy Simon, the director Susan H. Schulman, the designer Heidi Landesman—are nothing if not thorough. With flashbacks, dream sequences, and a strolling chorus of ghosts, they explore the meaning of the novel's every metaphor, the Freudian underpinning of every character and event, the spiritual hagiography of its Victorian milieu. From the rococo set, a pop-up period toy-theater that greets the audience upon arrival, to the Act 2 introspective soliloquies given even to characters who receive only scattered mentions in the novel, this musical leaves no stone unturned in *The Secret Garden*. Yet where, to use Burnett's own language, are the Magic and the Mystery that have made the work endure?

At its heart, after all, *The Secret Garden* tells a simple story that is endemic not only to children's literature, but also to such Broadway staples as *The Sound of Music* and *Annie*. A ten-year-old orphan, Mary Lennox (Daisy Eagan), must win the love of her distant, widowed guardian, her uncle Archibald Craven (Mandy Patinkin), even as she must find her own soul and self-worth by communing with nature in the locked garden of the uncle's vast Yorkshire estate. In the musical version, this tale's primal pull is often severed at its roots. Burnett had the cunning to keep the uncle a remote, mysterious figure for a third of the book, but since he is played by a star, the show must bring him on (and deflate the suspense) by the second scene. Worse, Burnett's exciting recounting of the obstacles Mary must overcome to enter the locked garden is shortchanged in Ms. Norman's script, and so, eventually, is the garden itself. The actual stage time devoted to this show's equivalent of Oz is brief, and the climactic, moving song about the garden's transforming powers—the equivalent to the "garden" songs of Leonard Bernstein's *Candide* and *Trouble in Tahiti,* for instance—never arrives.

Where Burnett practiced the instincts of a born storyteller, the creators of the musical prefer to intellectualize. Mary's dead parents and Uncle Archie's dead wife haunt almost every scene, lest anyone forget that death and rebirth are themes of *The Secret Garden,* and because these ghosts' appearances necessitate echo-chamber sound, supernatural lighting cues, and a totemic replay (sometimes in song and dance) of the past, the musical seems to take two clumsy steps backward for each one forward. Only once does this scheme advance the show instead of halting it: In a lovely, early trio, "I Heard Someone Crying," Mary, her uncle, and her dead aunt (Rebecca Luker) sleepwalk through the haunted mansion, projecting their own deepest familial longings on the sound of a child's crying deep within the night.

Otherwise, the musical's emphasis on subtext overwhelms the text. Much more so than *Into the Woods,* which was as much about Bruno Bettelheim's interpretation of Grimm tales as about the tales themselves, *The Secret Garden* favors theme over story, as if it were a learned essay about the book instead of a new version that might speak for itself. That would not be a problem if the characters were as clearly seen in the foreground of the musical as they are during the symbolic pageantry. But the leading players often seem upstaged by loudmouthed secondary figures—a chambermaid (Alison Fraser), an old gardener (Tom Toner)—who pop up at arbitrary intervals to sing cheery, on occasion inspirational musical-comedy ditties of the *Mary Poppins* variety and then disappear until another jolt of enforced ear-to-ear grinning is required.

Though performed with spirit by the young Ms. Eagan, Mary never really gets a chance to blossom as a girl in tandem with the garden that stimulates her emotional growth, and her sickly young cousin, Colin (John Babcock), never amounts to more than just another smiling Broadway tyke. Mr. Patinkin, by contrast, is given every opportunity to display the tortured psyche of the lonely, hunchbacked uncle, but by using the same contorted posture (loping walk, dangled left hand) he displayed in his excruciating Broadway concert recital of last season and by excusing himself from the rest of the company's efforts to maintain British accents, he turns *The Secret Garden* into a show about his own contemporary, New York showbiz persona whenever he is at center stage. I'm saddened to report that his trademark gestures—the squinting of the eyes, the cranking of the voice up an octave in mid-song—are calcifying into shtick, and they seem to dramatize Mandy Patinkin's notions of ambivalence, not Archibald Craven's guilt and grief. The finale, in which he reunites with the ghost of his lost love in the garden, is as synthetic here as it was heartfelt when Mr. Patinkin performed virtually the same reconciliation with a dead woman in the greenery of *Sunday in the Park with George.*

The star's voice is as lilting as ever, at least, and there is other powerful singing by Ms. Luker (who seems too talented to be filtered through sonic effects), the redoubtable Ms. Fraser, and that fine actor Robert Westenberg, whose incidental role of a doctor is ludicrously inflated into a quasivillain to vamp for time during Mr. Patinkin's long absence in Act 2. Ms. Simon's music, accompanied by the solid lyrics Ms. Norman often draws from Burnett's own dialogue, is fetching when limning the deep feelings locked within the story's family constellations. But when Ms. Simon descends to a conventional musical-comedy mode, the score falls apart, most notably in some songs for Dickon, the elfish boy who is Mary's unofficial guide to the garden. As sung by the charming, if opaquely accented, John Cameron Mitchell—unrecognizable after his turn as a wormy student con man in *Six Degrees of Separation*—the boy's dialect-laden odes to nature sound like Neil Diamond ballads as they might be delivered by Ringo Starr and orchestrated for *Brigadoon.*

The cluttered, scattershot approach of *The Secret Garden* to its drama and musical numbers extends to its every element, from the book's insistence on talky clumps of redundant exposition to Ms. Schulman's staging, which regurgitates the nightmare party sequence but not the dramatic urgency of her superb revival last year of *Sweeney Todd.* The gifted Ms. Landesman's collagelike scenic design, which embraces sources as varied as Victorian line drawings, Joseph Cornell boxes, and the spooky imagery of the director Robert Wilson, is fabulous to look at but not hospitable to actors, who have to fight to be in focus despite the exceptionally busy efforts of the brilliant lighting designer Tharon Musser. Since the choreography (by Michael Lichtefeld) is scant and amateurish, *The Secret Garden* has no theatrical means for achieving that graceful, seemingly effortless falling into place that levitates fairy-tale musicals (among others) into enchantment. In this show, the hard work is always apparent; one is constantly aware that the authors are thinking hard—too hard.

Fanatical devotees of the Burnett novel, young and old, are likely to enjoy the evening anyway, while those who have never heard of *The Secret Garden* or those who don't quite hold it in the same high regard as, say, the *Iliad* or *Charlotte's Web,* may be either baffled or bored by it. At its best, this show may not be a transporting entertainment like the MGM *Wizard of Oz* or Broadway *Peter Pan,* but it can certainly be considered a musical-theater equivalent to a profusely illustrated, and perhaps even more profusely annotated, edition of a children's classic.

Is it too churlish to wish that they turned the pages a little faster?

THE WILL ROGERS FOLLIES
PALACE THEATRE, MAY 2, 1991

Will Rogers never met a man he didn't like. Tommy Tune never met a costume he didn't like. Just how these two great but antithetical American archetypes—the humble cowboy philosopher, the top-hatted impresario of glitz—came to be roped together in a multimillion-dollar Broadway extravaganza is the real drama of *The Will Rogers Follies,* the most disjointed musical of this or any other season.

When Will Rogers—in the utterly beguiling form of Keith Carradine—is at center stage in the huge mock-Ziegfeld pageant at the Palace, *The Will Rogers Follies* is a drippingly pious testimonial to a somewhat remote American legend, written in a style known to anyone who does not doze during the presentation of the Jean Hersholt Humanitarian Award on Oscar night. But when Mr. Tune gets his chance to grab the production's reins, school is out! Suddenly Will is shunted aside so the high-flying director and choreographer, who has a theatrical eye second to none, can bring on the girls, the boys, the dog tricks, and a Technicolor parade of Willa Kim costumes and Tony Walton sets that not only exceed these designers' remarkable past achievements but in all likelihood top the living tableaux that Joseph Urban once concocted for Florenz Ziegfeld himself.

What the inspirational Rogers story and the blissfully campy Tune numbers are doing on the same stage is hard to explain and harder to justify, for they fight each other all evening, until finally the book wins and *The Will Rogers Follies* crash-lands with a whopping thud a good half act or so before Rogers has his fatal airplane crash in Alaska. Apparently, the show's authors—the playwright Peter Stone, the composer Cy Coleman, and the lyricists Betty Comden and Adolph Green—were overimpressed by the fact that Rogers was a headline performer in the *Ziegfeld Follies* of the 1920s, twirling his rope and taking humorous potshots at Congress while sharing the stage with chorines, Eddie Cantor, Fanny Brice, and Ed Wynn. This slender happenstance has led them to shoehorn the Rogers biography into their synthetic *Follies* show—a revue written in the style that dazzled audiences in the days before the modern musical and *The Ed Sullivan Show* were invented.

The concept, which is repeatedly explained in fussy, almost deconstructivist interruptions by an invisible Ziegfeld (a taped Gregory Peck), must have sounded better at a story conference than it plays in the theater. Rogers had many talents—joke-making, newspaper writing, political punditry, public speaking, rope twirling—but he was not a musical comedy song-and-dance man. It is impossible to build a showbiz musical around a character who isn't a singer (Mr. Carradine can sing, but not in the *Follies* style) or dancer—which is presumably why the real Rogers usually shared top billing with equally celebrated singers, dancers, and clowns in the Ziegfeld shows. It is also difficult to build a musical around a famous character whose private life was a bore, or seems so in Mr. Stone's retelling. For no discernible reason other than to follow the *Follies* format—which required an Act 1 wedding finale and torch songs—this show endlessly chronicles the courtship, marriage, and mild spats between Will and his wife, Betty (Dee Hoty), whose only character trait is a whiny insistence that her husband spend less time at work and more time back at the ranch.

When dealing with the substance of Rogers's career, Mr. Stone's book is longer on exposition than humor. Hardly has Mr. Carradine arrived than he is gratuitously explaining that Will Rogers was more than a name given to the hospital that perennially passes the hat at the nation's movie theaters. Yet the ensuing attempts to rekindle Rogers's topical wisecracks are toothless, and despite a promise that Will will draw gags from today's newspaper, the evening's most persistent comic target is the fateful pilot Wiley Post. More confusingly, *The Will Rogers Follies* never decides for sure what period it wants to make jokes about. Though the *Playbill* says the musical is set in "the present" and though there is much tedious explanation that Rogers has risen from the dead for our amusement, the evening's only dramatic event occurs when, abruptly in mid-Act 2, the legend *1931* is emblazoned on the stage, the scenery lifts away and a platoon of stagehands marches on to repossess the colorful costumes of the showgirls.

Is this the Twilight Zone, or what? Though the stagehands wear contemporary jeans and T-shirts, a grim-faced Mr. Carradine enters to deliver a long radio sermon championing the poor and homeless of the Great Depression. Yet as he does so, the theater's house lights come on, as if to embarrass the present-day audience into examining its own conscience in preparation for confronting the panhandlers lying in wait on Broadway after the final curtain.

Whatever decade we're in, the holier-than-thou tone of this lavishly expensive production's pitch for the downtrodden seems every bit as hypocritical as the similarly shameless Act 2 plea for Amerasian orphans in *Miss Saigon,* and it goes on even longer. One fully expects ushers to pass through the aisles soliciting for the Will Rogers Hospital. And those collection bottles are not all that is conspicuously missing: This show, which so strenuously wraps itself in Will Rogers's democratic values, does not have a single black performer. The WPA-style "We the People" finale that follows—in which a heavenly choir recites Rogers's famous achievements from behind slide projections of the great unwashed American masses—seems more than a little hollow in context.

It is a tribute to Mr. Carradine—his air of unpretentious conviction, humility, warmth, and good humor—that he keeps *The Will Rogers Follies* from riding off the rails into ridiculousness in its pompous waning scenes. He doesn't really resemble Rogers, and he's at best a passable lariat twirler, but he surely captures the man's engaging spirit even when the show is making every effort to embalm it.

The evening's second bananas—Ms. Hoty, Dick Latessa (as Rogers's dad), Cady Huffman (a leggy Ziegfeld emcee)—are all able, but their material is routine. Mr. Coleman's music, orchestrated to a brassy fare-thee-well by Billy Byers, recalls but never equals the period showbiz songs the composer wrote for *City of Angels, Little Me,* and *Barnum* (the Coleman show this one most resembles). The Comden-Green lyrics, faithful to the musical's misguided conception, are professional regurgitations of Ziegfeld-era specialties. The exceptions include a Woody Guthrie–style ecological lament sung by a guitar-strumming Mr. Carradine in Act 2, and the inevitable "Never Met a Man I Didn't Like," in which Will seems to be going through the Yellow Pages to list every single such man, from politician to mortician, from Napa Valley to Shubert Alley.

There would have been more fun if the songwriters had come up with the hilarious or sardonic numbers of such other Ziegfeld-inspired latter-day musicals as *Funny Girl* and *Follies.* Mr. Tune must lean for wit instead on the production's visual riches, immaculately lighted by Jules Fisher. The scenic design succeeds because of its cleverness, not its budget: Mr. Walton daringly builds his set around a material as humble if pertinent as rope. The props alone—rope phones, suitcases, doors—are more worthy of museum exhibition than the actual Rogers artifacts exhibited in the Palace's lobby, but even more spectacular is the vast proscenium arch that extends the Western motif into the upper reaches of the vast old two-a-day house. The bygone whimsy of a vaudeville past missing elsewhere in these *Follies* can always be found in Mr. Walton's fantasies, among them backdrops that render the totems of Rogers's career (sagebrush, Hollywood greenbacks) in iconography true to both Ziegfeld overkill and the abstract tenets of modern theatrical art.

Ms. Kim's costumes, which are more cognizant of Busby Berkeley and Vargas than the higher sexual consciousness of "the present," are just as breathtaking, with such minor details as the lining of a ten-gallon hat and the intricately stitched pattern of a pair of suspenders capturing the designer's full imaginative attention. In the show's first and best number ("Will-a-Mania"), the musical's chorus just keeps coming and coming at the audience over the horizon of the movable Follies staircase that dominates the set, each time with new chaps, new colors, new headdresses. Even though the heavily amplified lyrics are indecipherable, the text is anything but the point.

Not all of Mr. Tune's numbers are so thrilling, and some of them recycle his own routines from *The Best Little Whorehouse in Texas* and *A Day in Hollywood*, not to mention bits of Gower Champion (a ramp procession from *Hello, Dolly!*) and Bob Fosse (an ultraviolet gimmick from *Dancin'*). But this director is always a master of his particular art, which makes it all the more frustrating that, after exercising total control over every inch of *Nine* and *Grand Hotel*, he seems to be hog-tied for so much of this show. If *The Will Rogers Follies* could only be whittled down to the Tommy Tune Follies, grateful audiences would find a musical twice as buoyant and less than half as long.

THE MOST HAPPY FELLA
GOODSPEED OPERA HOUSE,
EAST HADDAM, CONN., MAY 30, 1991

Though *The Most Happy Fella,* the haunting and spectacularly ambitious show Frank Loesser wrote after *Guys and Dolls,* is receiving two major stagings this year—one at the Goodspeed Opera House here through July 12, the other to open at the New York City Opera in September—it has always been the most unlucky musical.

The original production, while well received, had the misfortune to be overshadowed by *My Fair Lady,* which beat it to Broadway by two months in 1956. Since then, this musical about the May-September union between an aging immigrant grape grower and his young mail-order bride in the Napa Valley of the 1920s has proved too problematic for frequent revival. With more than forty musical numbers—some in a mock-Puccini idiom and others, like "Standing on the Corner" and "Big D," in the Tin Pan Alley style of the author's "Once in Love with Amy" and "Luck Be a Lady"—*The Most Happy Fella* requires operatic and musical-comedy voices without landing firmly in either camp. The one previous major resuscitation—on Broadway in 1979 by people who had triumphed a few seasons earlier with *Porgy and Bess*—was a fine, loving effort but it revealed the seams in the piece and proved short-lived. The show went back to being a cult cause, kept alive mainly by the complete original cast recording (three LP's worth) that Goddard Lieberson produced for Columbia Records.

The Goodspeed production may change all that, for it justifies the minority view that Loesser created some sort of cracked American classic with this show, which took him four years to write and whose like he would not attempt again before his death in 1969. A serious rethinking of the musical rather than a museum restoration of it, this revival is an achievement of rare beauty. The audience arrives at the intimate, antique Goodspeed expecting the house's signature evening of nostalgia, laughter, and tap dancing and is soon swept away instead by an unfamiliar show whose calling cards are gorgeous music and unadulterated romance.

The director is Gerald Gutierrez, who has worked at Goodspeed before, but is best known to New York audiences for his highly polished stagings of bright contemporary comedies by playwrights like Wendy Wasserstein and Jonathan Reynolds. For *The Most Happy Fella,* Mr. Gutierrez has made a number of smart, gutsy decisions. His biggest gamble—really unthinkable to any *Fella* purist—is to remove the orchestra and, with it, the grand orchestrations by Don Walker, who arranged this score with the same feeling he brought to such stylistically related musicals as *Carousel* and *She Loves Me.* The Goodspeed pit is occupied by two pianos instead—playing a Loesser-approved arrangement by Robert Page—and much as one may miss the Walker underscoring and act preludes, the ear soon adjusts and the compensating pleasures soon outweigh the losses. By jettisoning the orchestra, Mr. Gutierrez liberates the show from both its operatic pretensions and its showbiz slickness—and frees the audience from its parallel expectations—with the result that the characters and their drama, pushed forward on a thrust stage, take over.

To further sharpen the focus, there has been some very subtle editing of the text, particularly the book but occasionally the score, with an eye toward eliminating digression and melodrama. (Nothing major is missing, and one musical passage cut during the original production's pre-Broadway tryout is restored.) Most important, Mr. Gutierrez has cast singers who can really act in every role, including such relatively minor ones as the three neighborhood chefs, who, as played by Mark Lotito, Buddy Crutchfield, and Bill Nabel and as delightfully choreographed by Liza Gennaro, prove that it is possible to sing an Italianate operatic trio (in Italian, yet) while juggling like the Flying Karamazov Brothers.

The lead performers offer perfect-pitch emotions to go with their voluptuous singing. The title character of Tony Esposito is completely stripped of buffoonish cliché by Spiro Malas, who, like his more illustrious predecessors in the part (Robert Weede in 1956, Giorgio Tozzi in 1979), is primarily an opera performer. Tony, the audience is told, is not good-looking, not young, and not smart, which is why he dishonestly sends a photograph of his handsome young foreman Joe (a robust-voiced Charles Pistone) rather than one of himself to Rosabella, the San Francisco waitress he woos by mail. The scrupulously truthful Mr. Malas, indeed neither good-looking nor young, makes Tony enormously appealing without shortchanging the character's obtuseness during the courtship or his severe depression after his young wife betrays him. Mr. Malas surely fulfills Loesser's highest intentions when, in his final aria, he seems to be thinking in song while sorting out what remains of his life. The intimacy with which the audience can view his passage from despair to reconciliation makes the show's happy finale inexorable and cathartic rather than glibly sentimental.

As his beloved, Sophie Hayden is no less wonderful. With a Barbara Cook–like emotional tremor lurking just beneath her clarion soprano, her Rosabella is desperate and battered enough to bet her life on an epistolary romance and reckless and angry enough to resort to infidelity when she discovers Tony's ruse. Ms. Hayden arouses compassion from her very first solo, "Somebody Somewhere," in which she comes far forward, wearing the institutional plaid cotton uniform, ratty cloth coat, and heavy-duty shoes of her dreary labors, to sing hungrily, not cloyingly, of how she "wants to be wanted, needs to be needed." When she and the crippled Tony fall in love for keeps much, much later—in the duet "My Heart Is So Full of You"—her world-weary cynicism and Mr. Malas's pathetic lack of self-esteem both melt away in what feels like a thunderclap of warmth, desire, and regeneration.

The song is big enough to contain its singers' highly charged feelings. In the years since Loesser wrote *The Most Happy Fella,* Puccini-isms and pop near-opera have become commonplace on the Broadway stage, but this songwriter's music and lyrics, unlike those of his successors, speak from an open heart and a witty, articulate mind. In this production, even Rosabella's wisecracking best friend, Cleo, proves to have a savage emotional undertow in Liz Larsen's bracing, belting performance, and the trio ("Happy to Make Your Acquaintance") she shares with the two leads, a song of newfound intimacy disguised as a farcical English lesson for Tony, has never been so funny and so touching all at once.

Mr. Gutierrez's faith in simple dramatic conviction is shared by the production designers—John Lee Beatty (scenery), Jess Goldstein (costumes), and Craig Miller (lighting)—who do not shy away from the autumnal moods and cold, threatening skies that sometimes darken the bucolic Northern California vineyards and barns where the love story unfolds. When Tony and Rosabella sing the tender "How Beautiful the Days," the golden glow of sunset becomes a bittersweet counterpoint to their contentment, as if to foretell the sorrow that will soon derail their happiness. That sorrow must come, of course, and when it does, it hurts. But this is one of those extraordinary nights when an audience cannot separate its tears for the characters from its own tears of sheer musical-theater joy.

≡ *This production later transferred to Broadway, where it had a mostly warm reception and a modest run.*

SUNDAY ESSAY: SLOWLY, THE LIGHTS ARE DIMMING ON BROADWAY
JUNE 2, 1991

How does one begin to dramatize the alarm that is spreading over the Broadway community as it stuffs itself into evening clothes to present the Tony Awards tonight? Well, for starters, consider the fact that the nominees, who will be honored on CBS starting at 9 p.m., do not represent the best of the 1990–91 season—they represent all of the 1990–91 season. Nearly every production seen on Broadway since this time last year has been nominated for something. The question raised by this award ceremony is not "How good do you have to be to get a nomination?" but "How bad do you have to be not to get a nomination?"

The answer to that question for musicals is: Hit rock bottom, and keep going. Every musical of the season, from a bus-and-truck *Peter Pan* to *Shogun: The Musical* to *Oh, Kay!* is in contention somewhere on the ballot. Among the season's plays, only *Zoya's Apartment, Stand-Up Tragedy, The Big Love, Taking Steps,* and *Mule Bone* failed to be cited for so much as best sound design. (Actually, best sound design is not a category, but it should be, if only to encourage producers to make their shows audible rather than merely loud.)

Given the bleak terrain, it's amazing that there are so many gifted nominees; some of those associated with short-lived productions, such as Jennifer Tipton (a lighting design nominee for *La Bête*) and Kathryn Erbe (best supporting actress for *The Speed of Darkness*), might merit their slots even if the competition were stiffer. It is not the fault of artists in the theater that the Tony field is such a sparse one this year. I do fault the Tony nominators, however, for spoiling tonight's fun by shunning one putative nominee, Nicol Williamson, whose erratic performance as John Barrymore's ghost in *I Hate Hamlet* became the stuff of newspaper headlines once he took to verbally and physically harassing a fellow actor in mid-performance. Had this star been nominated and then won, his words of thanks might have been the most anticipated televised oration since the Checkers speech.

A graver omission than Mr. Williamson from the Tony nominees this year is, like every year, the entirety of Off Broadway. This is why the most exciting play by a young writer this season, the Playwrights Horizons' production of *The Substance of Fire* by Jon Robin Baitz, and its brilliant star, Ron Rifkin, will go unacknowledged tonight, even though this wit-infused drama about the Holocaust's oblique fallout on a New York book publisher, his family, and his city seems to give many who see it new hope about the theater as a forum for adult emotions and ideas.

Also absent tonight will be such riveting Off Broadway performers as Eileen Atkins (*A Room of One's Own*), Spalding Gray (*Monster in a Box*), and Richard Venture and Tony Goldwyn (*The Sum of Us*).

The most fascinating revivals of the season—Michael Greif's production of Sophie Treadwell's 1928 *Machinal*, Richard Sabellico's revivification of the 1962 Jerome Weidman–Harold Rome musical *I Can Get It for You Wholesale*—won't be mentioned tonight. Nor will two of the best new musicals, the William Finn–James Lapine *Falsettoland* and John Kander and Fred Ebb's *And the World Goes 'Round,* or such vital plays as *The Good Times Are Killing Me* by Lynda Barry, *The American Plan* by Richard Greenberg, and *Absent Friends* by Alan Ayckbourn, not to mention the actors and production teams that made them sing. Had the most dazzling play of the season, John Guare's *Six Degrees of Separation,* not capitalized on the Tony Awards' one sleight of gerrymandering by moving from the ineligible Mitzi E. Newhouse Theater at Lincoln Center to the eligible Vivian Beaumont Theater upstairs in the same building, it, too, would be off the ballot tonight.

Perhaps it's silly to expect justice from the Broadway establishment, which regards the Tonys as a two-hour network television commercial for its own products and is not about to give up two minutes of air time to competing attractions. (There is a magnanimous Tony for the outstanding regional theater, which, by definition, is safely out of town.) But if Broadway producers had any instinct for public relations—or at least for self-preservation, let alone survival—they would realize that the inclusion of Off Broadway productions would bolster the national image of the entire New York theater, Broadway included, by presenting the city's theatrical world as a hive of creativity serving many tastes and pocketbooks. By restricting its focus to Broadway, the Tony Awards show instead sends a dreadful message that keeps new audiences, particularly young audiences, away. The Tonys this year will confirm the impression, not always accurate, that New York is exclusively the province of overproduced, overpriced musicals and boulevard plays that are aimed at wealthy tourists of limited attention span and advancing age.

Broadway is still capable of better fare: Last season at this time, for instance, the best-play nominees (all transfers from Off Broadway or resident theaters) included *The Piano Lesson, Prelude to a Kiss,* and the winner, *The Grapes of Wrath.* The best musical, *City of Angels,* was a satire that gave the audience credit for verbal and visual imagination.

This season's ceremony, by contrast, may well be dominated by Neil Simon's *Lost in Yonkers* and the musical *The Will Rogers Follies,* which, whatever their virtues (and they both have some), are escapist fare pitched at theatergoers nostalgic for the 1930s and 1940s. *Lost in Yonkers* contains several confrontations that passionately dramatize the pain of a miserable childhood, then takes it all back with an upbeat ending that tells the audience that all wounds do heal. *The Will Rogers Follies* goes a step further by bringing its title character (beguilingly reincarnated as Keith Carradine) back from the dead to give a speech that miraculously brings the Depression to an end. How fleeting on Broadway was the spirit of *The Grapes of Wrath*!

Maybe the dominance of fluff this season was inevitable, given that the recession has deepened during the last year. The fallout can be felt on Broadway, where tickets for most, if not all, of the Tony nominees are readily available and frequently discounted, and Off Broadway, where the crunch in public and private financial support for the arts is having a devastating impact. In such hard times, Off Broadway remembers its artistic mission—no one can accuse such artistic directors as Joseph Papp (the Public Theater), Lynne Meadow (the Manhattan Theatre Club), or André Bishop (Playwrights Horizons) of coddling their subscribers this season—but Broadway loses its head. By Labor Day, if not before, *Lost in Yonkers* may be the sole dramatic attraction on a Broadway stage, period, and there are few prospects in sight to keep it company next season.

The economic downturn has not only depleted the ranks of producers, investors, and ticket buyers who make the commercial theater a going concern, but it has also brought Broadway's leadership vacuum into sharp relief. There cannot be a healthy Broadway without the full involvement of the Shubert Organization, for it has the deepest pockets and owns nearly half the theaters. Yet the Shuberts, who kept Broadway afloat during the Depression and have in recent seasons underwritten the commercial transfers of many important Off Broadway productions, have ceased for the time being to be an active sponsor of Broadway plays. None of the Tony best-play nominees this season was a Shubert production or appeared in a Shubert house, and the flagship nonmusical playhouses of the Shubert empire on Forty-fifth Street were mostly dark all season. The rival Nederlanders, though serving as landlords to three of the best-play nominees, have not done much more for Broadway than they have done so far for the New York Yankees. The third and smallest theater owner, Jujamcyn, has more actively promoted new American playwriting, but with only five of the thirty-eight Tony-eligible Broadway theaters, two of them occupied by holdover musicals from last season, it could have at most an incidental impact on the larger scene.

To pick up some of the slack in play production, the League of American Theatres and Producers, the same Broadway trade organization that administers the Tony Awards, joined with the unions this season to activate the Broadway Alliance, a special arrangement by which dark Broadway dramatic houses are turned over to serious plays produced at discount budgets for a discount ticket price. The two plays to appear under this plan, Steve Tesich's *The Speed of Darkness*, now closed, and Timberlake Wertenbaker's *Our Country's Good*, a Tony nominee for best play, are solid works, but audiences have not been large, as if theatergoers feared that the bargain tickets signaled a rum deal.

In this depression atmosphere, it may not help the Broadway Alliance that its first two offerings deal with subjects (the Vietnam War, the early history of Australia as a penal colony) that sound worthy and depressing (even if the plays are not necessarily grim). It hasn't helped, either, that the productions of both plays, each of which originated in resident theaters beyond New York, did not have the consistency of acting and staging necessary to meet the high standards of audiences who have also seen *Six Degrees of Separation* and *The Substance of Fire.*

Musicals, being potential cash cows, do continue to engage the interest of Broadway theater owners and producers, and if none of the four nominees tonight is likely to prove a classic of the genre, the four added together would make one completely satisfying show: *Once on This Island* has the freshest score, *Miss Saigon* the most stirring performances (by Jonathan Pryce and Lea Salonga), *Will Rogers* the most eye-filling stagecraft (by Tommy Tune and his designers), and *The Secret Garden* the most literate intentions. But all four productions may be more interesting as symptoms of Broadway's current state and harbingers of its future than they are as examples of musical theater.

Miss Saigon, the show that aroused the season's most violent opinions pro and con well before it opened—and continues to, especially among those who have not seen it—may prove to be the last British musical of the *Cats* era, if it can be called British in the first place. (Its producer is British, but its authors are French and American, and its models are *South Pacific* and *West Side Story.*) Though it is a hit so far, its immediate predecessor among West End imports, Andrew Lloyd Webber's *Aspects of Love,* was the most costly flop in Broadway history, and there is no new English megamusical in London to follow *Miss Saigon* to Broadway.

There is not likely to be one anytime soon. The West End has its own recession drying up the pipeline, and American public opinion may have finally begun to turn on these imported extravaganzas. (Certainly New York opinion has: The running gag about *Cats* in *Six Degrees* was the most widely quoted of the season.) While *Miss Saigon* is easily the most intimate and the most gripping of its English peers—or so it is to someone like myself, who still is baffled by the general enthusiasm for *The Phantom of the Opera*—it has angered many for reasons generally extrinsic to the show itself. The repeated threats by its producer, Cameron Mackintosh, to cancel the New York opening, the record-breaking hundred-dollar top ticket price, the much hyped advance sale, and onstage helicopter effect (the show's most gratuitous and unconvincing concession to Lloyd Webberism) have made *Miss Saigon* a symbol of decadence and buccaneering foreign wealth at a time of American patriotism, belt-tightening, and economic xenophobia.

Curiously enough, the intense early controversy about *Miss Saigon,* prompted last summer by the Actors' Equity attempt to deny Mr. Pryce, a white Welshman, the right to repeat his London performance in a nominally Eurasian role, was forgotten by much of the theater community by the time the show actually opened, some pickets notwithstanding. *The Will Rogers Follies,* a musical that wraps itself in the flag and lectures the audience about its responsibilities to the homeless, opened without a single black face in its cast, but so far not a discouraging word has been heard from Actors' Equity or anyone else.

Like *Miss Saigon, Will Rogers* seems the end of a line, albeit an American one. It has the feel of a last hurrah by a showbiz old guard that is contemporaneous in age and taste with the benefit-and-theater-party crowd to which the show presumably means to cater. At the production's sporadic best, Mr. Tune's staging recalls the vaudeville sequences one associates with the classic MGM movies (*Singin' in the Rain* and *The Band Wagon*) written by the musical's distinguished lyricists, Betty Comden and Adolph Green. At its worst, this show is a ponderous mixture of synthetic corn and old-fashioned sexism of a sort that has passed out of the pop culture mainstream everywhere except Broadway, television included.

Miss Saigon and *The Will Rogers Follies* are thought to be the two chief contenders for the best musical Tony. While they could be regarded as political opposites—one resurrects a war the United States lost, the other embraces the boosterism that followed an American military victory in Iraq—they both represent the Broadway commercial powers that be. *Miss Saigon* stands for Mr. Mackintosh and the Shuberts, in whose theater the show plays. *Will Rogers* is at a Nederlander house, and its creators are the remnants of the American musical-comedy aristocracy that the Brits shoved aside in the *Cats* era. Is it cynical to wonder if the victor may be the production with the fewest enemies?

Should either *Once on This Island* or *The Secret Garden* win the best-musical Tony, consider it a palace revolution. Though *Once on This Island* was presented on Broadway by the Shuberts, it was produced by Playwrights Horizons, whose artistic leader, André Bishop, will succeed Gregory Mosher as artistic director at Lincoln Center Theater next year. The authors of *Once on This Island,* Lynn Ahrens and Stephen Flaherty, are relative newcomers to the theater, and hugely promising ones, though their show, with its simple appeal to the emotions and its slick repackaging of ethnic culture, is, like *Miss Saigon,* in the mode of Rodgers and Hammerstein's "Oriental" period.

The Secret Garden, an adaptation of Frances Hodgson Burnett's book, represents the small Jujamcyn chain, and it is in the style of the other Broadway musicals, *Big River* (from Mark Twain) and *Into the Woods* (from the Grimms), in which the Jujamcyn chief executive, Rocco Landesman, and the designer and producer Heidi Landesman have been involved: It is an adult treatment of classic and weighty children's literature. Indeed, *The Secret Garden,* a dark and introspective show, sometimes suggests a Stephen Sondheim musical without Sondheim; its structure, cast, and songs recall both *Into the Woods* and *Sunday in the Park with George.*

The trouble with *The Secret Garden* is its busyness, as if everyone connected with it was thinking too hard—it is overdirected, overwritten, overpopulated, and overdesigned. But since its opening, the show's creators have been stripping away some of the clutter and, like the other Jujamcyn musicals, it could find a sustaining audience, smaller but perhaps broader and younger, than those at the usual Broadway musicals.

What these Tony nominees have in common is that they are all greeted with partial or full standing ovations virtually every night. I did not see a musical on Broadway this season, the flops included, that failed to receive a standing ovation, whether at a press preview or a regular performance, and the same was true of most of the plays. Does this phenomenon mean that the Broadway audience is desperate to convince itself that its ticket money was well spent? Or does it mean that all the shows were fabulous? The truth is probably somewhere in between, but it is the business of the Tony Awards to uphold the latter point of view. There can be no ovations in dark houses, however, and the Tony Awards seem almost beside the point at a time when no one on Broadway seems to have a clue as to what will fill its vacant stages after tonight's cheering has stopped.

THIRTEENTH
SEASON

1991—92

Gregory Hines (center) in *Jelly's Last Jam*

Ithink these are terrible times to be a parent in," says Christine Baranski, as one of the two wives trying to enjoy a Fourth of July Fire Island weekend with their husbands in Terrence McNally's fine new play, *Lips Together, Teeth Apart*. Her sister-in-law, Swoosie Kurtz, counters: "I think these are terrible times to be anything in."

The times, of course, are our own, but on the surface they don't seem so terrible. In *Lips Together,* a comedy that hurts, two affluent couples laze about a newly inherited beachhouse that they liken to paradise—and whose market value they estimate at $800,000. As designed by John Lee Beatty at the Manhattan Theatre Club, the house floats on a breeze-swept landscape of dunes and is equipped with a glorious expanse of blond-wood deck, a kitchen bespeaking the tyranny of shelter magazines, and, reaching toward the audience's lap, a swimming pool whose crystalline blue is pure Hockney. "I can see right to the bottom," says Nathan Lane, as Ms. Kurtz's husband, a New Jersey building contractor, when he first goes near the water.

But the wives are right. There is terror in paradise. No one ever goes swimming in that pool—out of an unspoken if irrational fear that its previous owner, Ms. Kurtz's deceased brother, might have tainted it with AIDS. One of Mr. McNally's four fortyish characters is battling an invisible but terminal biological "malevolence" of a more traditional kind, while another is struck with random psychological dreads that reduce him to forgetting how to knot his tie and shoelaces. One couple is tormented by repeated miscarriages, and both are blighted by a love triangle that eventually sends the two brothers-in-law—Mr. Lane and Anthony Heald, a prep-school admissions officer—into a violent altercation at poolside. Terrible times for Mr. McNally's characters in *Lips Together* are the same as they were for those in *Frankie and Johnny in the*

Clair de Lune, his previous play about a couple skirmishing into the moonlit hours. Life is "cheap and short," and there are "a million reasons" for men and women not to love each other.

The playwright has no solution to this quandary beyond the prescription that gives his play its title—a bedtime litany that will allow one to fall asleep without grinding one's teeth. But because Mr. McNally can see right to the bottom of both his world and the people who inhabit it, most of his recent works, *The Lisbon Traviata* and the film *André's Mother* as well as *Frankie and Johnny,* offer unsentimental hope about the possibilities for intimacy at a time when fear and death rule even beachfront land. *Lips Together* is his most ambitious survey of this territory yet, and though not flawless, his most accomplished. The bright wit that has always marked Mr. McNally's writing and the wrenching sorrow that has lately invaded it are blended deftly throughout three concurrently funny and melancholy acts. The evening's moods are as far-ranging as its allusions to *A Star Is Born* and Virginia Woolf and as changeable as its incidental score, which runs from the showbiz cacophony of *Gypsy* to the serenity of *Così fan tutte.*

Mr. McNally's premise for *Lips Together* reaches back to *The Ritz,* his early bathhouse farce, for its fundamental fish-out-of-water gag is to inject heterosexual characters into a gay milieu. But how times have changed in two decades! The heterosexuals of *Lips Together* are enlightened—in varying degrees, up to a point—about homosexuality, and they coexist at a cordial distance with the occupants of the houses on either side of their own. Mr. McNally's perspective has changed, too. *Lips Together* is as much about what the hetero- and homosexual communities—or at least those of the white middle class—have in common in an infected, diminished civilization as it is about what sets them apart. The play's great generosity can be found in its insistence on letting the audience see each camp through the eyes of the other without distorting either point of view, and, as it happens, without bringing a gay character on stage.

Nowhere is the author's depth of understanding more visible than in the role of Sam Truman, the contractor played by Mr. Lane. Sam is the play's least sophisticated, most homophobic figure, an unpretentious suburban Joe. But both as written by Mr. McNally and as beautifully acted by the incomparable Mr. Lane, Sam is not unsympathetic. The "least defended" of the weekenders, he is a sloppy fount of humanity whose emotions cannot be predicted or typed. Sam may dismiss the gay neighbors as "the boys from Ipanema"—"What do these people have against Tony Bennett?" he howls after one musical selection too many from across the dunes—but by Act 3 and without pretending to reform his prejudices, he has found some vague, sustaining epiphany in the lovemaking of two men he spies in nearby bushes. For all his babyishness, Sam is desperate to connect to his straying wife, and Mr. Lane, that rare comic actor who is not afraid to expose himself completely (a riotously sudsy onstage shower included), makes the audience share that aching hunger.

Under the exquisitely modulated direction of John Tillinger, all the actors in *Lips Together* are first-rate, but, like Mr. Lane, Ms. Baranski is a little more equal than the rest. Her role of Chloe is an indelible and finally touching comic turn—a self-described "walking nerve end" and "overbearing" suburban matron who is constantly jabbering about inanities (sometimes in French) while serving hamburgers and Bloody Marys and bursting into songs (especially Miss Adelaide's from *Guys and Dolls*) that she performs in community-theater musicals back home. Ms. Baranski has played similar neurotics before (including Mr. McNally's), but in keeping with her brother Sam, Chloe has another dimension and a firmer, more valiant grip on her troubled life than her comic ditsiness might at first suggest. By the time she baldly concedes to her patronizing sister-in-law that "just about everyone is superior to me," the audience has stopped feeling superior to her—and is being touched by lines that earlier provoked laughs.

It's not the actors' fault that the spouses of these star siblings are less compelling. It's to the credit of the author that Chloe's preppy, selfish husband is not ennobled by illness—"With or without cancer, I'm still the same person," as he puts it—and Mr. Heald plays him with that pinched, insidious malice he first revealed in *The Lisbon Traviata* and perfected as the bureaucratic villain in *The Silence of the Lambs*. Ms. Kurtz brings her transparent honesty to the only dishonest writing in the play: Her most brooding speeches strain for the poetic—as does a symbolic, phantom swimmer she sees on the horizon—and Mr. McNally never makes it clear how her character, a painter of fragile sensibilities, became the wife of the plebeian Sam.

Otherwise, this is an evening in which people forever assail truth as unattainable and "too formless to grasp"—in life and art alike—yet inexorably zero in on it. The playwright's candor includes a willingness to let the play flow and ebb naturally rather than crest in false theatrical climaxes; no secrets are artificially withheld from the audience, and both the medical and marital crises of the plot are delivered in asides to the audience in the opening minutes. For the characters, truthfulness takes the form of an acute self-awareness that allows them to see their own limitations and those of their spouses and fight for love anyway, in a valiant effort to believe that they are not as alone and unprotected and doomed as the nattering insects whose electrocution by a nearby bug lamp punctuates the night.

"I wanted to see what death looks like and not be afraid of it," says Ms. Kurtz, as the character whose brother died of AIDS before the play begins. *Lips Together, Teeth Apart,* a work with real teeth and equally penetrating compassion, cannot take away that fear of death. But it does something that the theater must do now more than ever, by leaving an audience exiled from paradise feeling considerably less alone.

SUNDAY ESSAY: JOSEPH PAPP, THE LAST OF THE ONE-MAN SHOWS
SEPTEMBER 22, 1991

When Joseph Papp announced last month that he was appointing JoAnne Akalaitis to succeed him as artistic director of the New York Shakespeare Festival, he also announced, almost incidentally, that he would retain the title of "producer." It remains to be seen whether the post will prove honorary or real, but there has been nothing symbolic about Mr. Papp's identification with the role of producer until now. Joseph Papp has been the most important producer in the New York theater, period, for most of his thirty-five-year-long career. In recent seasons, as the other most significant producers of his generation stopped producing altogether (Harold Prince), left New York (Roger Stevens), died (Richard Barr), or reduced their output to a trickle (David Merrick), Mr. Papp has been the only giant left on the field.

This is why his illness-induced departure at age seventy has thrown the already reeling New York theater community into a deeper funk. There is much love for the man himself, a famously impossible character whose stormy, larger-than-life personality is the very essence of theater. There is much uncertainty about the future of the New York Shakespeare Festival, the institution Mr. Papp created in his own image and built into the most influential theatrical organization in the United States. But Mr. Papp's semiretirement also baldly dramatizes the increasing decline and possible extinction of the theatrical tradition, that of the impresario, which he represents.

Without producers like Mr. Papp, the theater cannot thrive in New York, on or off Broadway. Rather than a lack of theatrical talent, it is the dwindling of the producers' ranks that is most responsible for the New York theater's current state of depletion and disarray. On Broadway, where most independent producers have long since been driven away by skyrocketing costs, the concomitant decline in production is by now an old story. As Mr. Papp demonstrated, nonprofit companies Off Broadway need producers, too—whether they call themselves artistic directors or not—to create activity and excitement. But nonprofit companies are not geared to creating producers, either—Mr. Papp had no in-house heir apparent—and much of a generation of young producing talent has been lost to the film, television, and music industries. Ms. Akalaitis, fifty-four, whose primary theatrical experience has been as a director, must rise to the role of producer if the Shakespeare Festival is not to become another casualty of the New York theatrical malaise.

What is a producer? It is almost easier to say what a producer is not. A producer is not a playwright or, most of the time, a particularly gifted director. (Mr. Papp did direct on occasion, but often out of necessity and never, in my experience, memorably.) A producer does not have to be an intellectual, a businessman, or a manager. No specific training is required. Magic is, even if it is only pulled off with mirrors and smoke. What a producer does, usually out of view, is cause plays to be produced and induce people into attending those plays. A producer is not an artist but makes it possible for artists to do their best work and find an audience. To accomplish this, a producer must have the cunning of a master politician, the wiliness of a snake-oil salesman, the fanatical drive of a megalomaniac, and, given the eternal precariousness of the New York theater, nerves of steel. It doesn't hurt, either, to have some taste and a consuming passion for the stage.

Mr. Papp is the most spectacular case in point. He has all these attributes and then some, including an idealism that led him to fight for freedom of expression throughout his career, from his refusal to cooperate with the House Un-American Activities Committee through his earliest struggles with Robert Moses to pursue Shakespeare in Central Park, his 1973 altercation with CBS over the broadcast of the anti–Vietnam War play *Sticks and Bones,* and his recent battles against the National Endowment for the Arts. To appreciate fully how great a producer Mr. Papp has been, however, one cannot merely note the familiar laundry list of landmark shows and fervent causes associated with his name but must understand that he leaves the New York theater an almost completely different place than he found it.

In 1956, when Mr. Papp, still supporting himself by working as a stage manager at CBS, presented his first free Shakespeare production at the

East River Park Amphitheater, Broadway was the be-all and end-all of American theater. It was a vintage time for Broadway, too—since arguably the greatest American musical, *My Fair Lady,* the greatest American play, *Long Day's Journey into Night,* and the most revolutionary modern play from abroad, *Waiting for Godot,* all opened in Broadway houses in 1956. But a decade later, Mr. Papp, having turned Shakespeare in the Park into an institution, opened his indoor theater complex on Lafayette Street, the Public, and with his very first production, *Hair,* started a complete reversal of the power equation of the New York theater.

When *Hair* moved to Broadway, it helped prove that a nonprofit company's theatrical experiments could be the commercial theater's lifeblood, especially at a time when the Broadway theater had fewer and fewer ideas of its own and was increasingly out of touch with the new audience that *Hair* representatively tapped into. By the time *A Chorus Line* moved to Broadway from the Public in 1975, less than a decade after *Hair,* it had become standard practice for Broadway theater owners to turn to nonprofit theater companies, whether Off Broadway or beyond New York, for the plays and musicals that could fill their houses. That *A Chorus Line,* the quintessential Broadway musical, had originated Off Broadway was the final blow to Broadway's once unchallenged position of supremacy. Today, virtually all Broadway plays and musicals are transfers from nonprofit theaters like the Public, the only perennial exceptions being Neil Simon plays and London imports.

While Mr. Papp was hardly the first and certainly not the sole author of this revolution, he was the most visible and successful of its firebrands. He did not invent either Off Broadway or the nonprofit theater movement, both of which predated his arrival, but he consolidated the new system and made it flourish. He not only gave Broadway the hit musicals to which it is addicted—a role never contemplated by the early Off Broadway movement—but he also supplied it with prickly yet crowd-drawing plays like *That Championship Season, For Colored Girls,* and *Plenty.*

Paradoxically enough, he beat Broadway at its own game by reviving the lost arts of high-stakes artistic gambling and nonstop promotion that had once made the Great White Way an electrifying venue. His motives, to be sure, were different than those of most commercial producers. He was not out to make money for himself (though he was not always above searching for patently commercial projects to shore up institutional deficits, especially with his post–*Chorus Line* musicals). He believed in a truly public theater—one that, ideally, would not only have free admission (achieved in the park, not at the Public) but would also cater to many tastes, including those excluded from Broadway by high ticket prices and middlebrow, middle-class values. He wanted a racially and ethnically diverse theater on both sides of the footlights, one that might change, or at least nudge, the world.

Even so, he practiced many of the same skills that had once defined razzle-dazzle Broadway entrepreneurship. Though he did not need to hunt down investors eager for glamour and profit, he did have to solicit contributions from public and private sponsors looking for civic prestige. Though he did not have to fill seats to meet his payroll, he did have to fill seats to keep the Shakespeare Festival in the public eye—for without prominence, his theater could not attract exciting artists and its essential philanthropic subsidies. Most important, Mr. Papp, like any prolific commercial producer, had to gain the loyalty of writers, directors, and actors of all sorts, unknown and famous alike, and he had to do it by the sheer force of his personality and that of his theater, not by financial inducements that could hope to match Broadway's, let alone Hollywood's.

When Mr. Papp had been in the service in World War II, he was called "Mr. Show Biz" for the variety entertainments he produced (and sometimes emceed) for the stateside United States Naval Reserve. And Mr. Show Biz he remained. Just as he broke Broadway's rules, so he broke Off Broadway's, refusing to strike the notes of pious altruism and cultural high-mindedness that have inflated too many of the pioneers and apostles of the nonprofit theater movement (and some of their theaters) into pompous bores.

Mr. Papp wrote his own ticket. Like an egomaniacal showman out of the Ziegfeld era, he chomped a cigar in television commercials, plastered his name (and sometimes his picture) over advertisements and marquees, gave outrageous interviews, and announced grandiose projects that never materialized. He actually put together a nightclub act, performed with top hat and tails and drenched in schmaltz, in the late 1970s.

Nor did Mr. Papp shy from public squabbles with city officials and journalists when he wanted publicity or felt his theater or others, including Broadway's, were threatened. If there is a critic Mr. Papp did not yell at in the Public lobby—certainly I was not exempt—chances are Mr. Papp did not read him. Probably few playwrights or directors, no matter how sacrosanct, were exempt from the Papp fury, either.

Make no mistake about it: Mr. Papp sold his shows to the hilt, even if the goal was not to line his own pockets. Not the least of his achievements was to sell the public on Shakespeare, for without Mr. Papp's Shakespeare productions, as wildly variable as they are and always have been, it is hard to see what would have kept the canon a continuous presence in the New York theater, as opposed to the classroom, over thirty-five years.

Like most great producers in any branch of show business, Mr. Papp was an autocrat; there were no committee decisions at the Shakespeare Festival, as there had been at the fractious, short-lived Group Theater of the 1930s, whose goals Mr. Papp's company sometimes shared. And he had his own strong tastes, which were esthetically conservative and politically progressive, not unlike the activist theater, at the Group and elsewhere, of the Depression he grew up in.

The plays closest to Mr. Papp's heart, Shakespeare's always excepted, were those that challenged the establishment about issues like the Vietnam War, race relations, and the AIDS crisis and revealed the lives of the underclass. Yet his curiosity compelled him to reach out in other, seemingly contradictory directions. For all his preoccupation with the theater of current events, Mr. Papp was sentimental enough about the past to revive the likes of *The Pirates of Penzance* and *Café Crown*. For all his championing of American writers (and distinctly American productions of Shakespeare), he embraced English and European playwrights whose social activism echoed his own (notably Vaclav Havel, David Hare, and Caryl Churchill). For all his apparent affection for naturalistic agitprop, he encouraged theater that experimented in form, including that of the Mabou Mines, the troupe that introduced him to his successor, JoAnne Akalaitis.

What other producer right now, in the nonprofit or commercial theater, could attract (and work with) talents as varied as Michael Bennett and Richard Foreman, Miguel Piñero and John Guare, Linda Ronstadt and James Earl Jones, David Henry Hwang and Wallace Shawn, Meryl Streep and Eric Bogosian? The mix served Mr. Papp and the New York theater audience equally well because the Shakespeare Festival's more commercial work inevitably helped underwrite its more daring experiments, just as those hits would also lure some of their mainstream audiences into becoming subscribers who would then sample the offbeat productions on the Papp schedule.

This was smart producing of the old school updated for a new age. However inadvertently, the Papp program at the Public echoed the Theatre Guild's between-the-wars seasons in which groundbreaking premieres of Shaw and O'Neill would mix with an unconventional, unexpected musical hit like *Oklahoma!* In both his flair for publicity stunts and his eclectic producing schedule, Mr. Papp was not even so far removed from a Broadway archetype like David Merrick, who would use some of the cash generated by a *Hello, Dolly!* (and, in his case, the tax advantage of a nonprofit foundation) to bring New York an angry John Osborne play or the shocking Peter Brook *Marat/Sade*.

Who will fill the leadership role of producer in the New York theater now? On Broadway, where producing today is mostly the province of theater owners who book and bankroll shows without creating them, the last attention-grabbing showman, Cameron Mackintosh, is British and only interested in musicals. The other New York producers able to muster more than one show a season are, like Mr. Papp, the artistic directors of nonprofit Off Broadway companies, many of which were founded in emulation of the Public. While none of these producers has yet operated at Mr. Papp's epic scale, Lynne Meadow, at the burgeoning Manhattan Theatre Club, and André Bishop, soon to move from Playwrights Horizons to Lincoln Center, are poised to expand their already important roles in a brighter economy.

As for Ms. Akalaitis, she is in an impossible position under the best of circumstances, given the act she must follow, and the circumstances are awful, given the Shakespeare Festival's financial crisis. An ambitious, if uneven, stage director with a knack for stirring up controversy but scant record of collaborating with living American playwrights, Ms. Akalaitis is smart enough to know that she cannot imitate Joseph Papp and must follow her own instincts. But are her instincts those of a producer?

The answer will have little or nothing to do with her talents as a director. If she's doing her job to the fullest, she probably will be directing infrequently anyway. Nor will her producing prowess have much to do with her abilities as an administrator, or her nose for possible Broadway transfers, or her public positions about the Palestinians.

The proposition is simpler than that. Ms. Akalaitis has six theaters at her disposal, five in the Public Theater complex on Lafayette Street and one in Central Park, and her success or failure will ride on her ability, in a highly competitive environment, to attract the broad spectrum of artists and audiences required to make life happen in them. Working in the nonprofit arena, she should not be under any obligation to find the next *Chorus Line*, which cannot be divined in any case. But Ms. Akalaitis does live in the real, all-too-American theatrical world; she is not working in a basement performance space or, conversely, in a utopian state-supported theater.

One need look at the season schedule of any company of similar size to the Public, from Arena Stage in Washington to the Goodman Theatre in Chicago to the Guthrie in Minneapolis, to see that artistic directors, however different their own creative personalities, follow the Papp example of reaching out to many tastes, many artists.

Ms. Akalaitis will soon be buffeted on all sides by demanding sub-scribers, board members, and donors, with all their various interests. She will have to give them and other audiences reasons to come to her theater by engaging them, challenging them, provoking them, and maybe even, on occasion, entertaining them. She cannot cause a stir with every pro-duction, heaven knows—the Public has traditionally been the site of as many fiascoes as any other long-running theatrical institution—but with the sum of what must be diverse, searching, and professional seasons. It will take time, though how much time the increasingly pressed board of the Festival can or will give her is a fiscal and temperamental matter known only to them.

One hopes that JoAnne Akalaitis will be the producer that no less an authority than the man who appointed her thinks she can be. If she is, the New York theater will then only have to find a good half-dozen more like her if it is to begin to fill the almost unfathomable void in vision, en-ergy, and sheer guts left by the exit of Joseph Papp.

≡ *For the events surrounding this piece, see "Exit the Critic."*

MARCH OF THE FALSETTOS / FALSETTOLAND
HARTFORD STAGE, OCTOBER 15, 1991

It is not news that the history of American musicals in the 1980s be-gins and ends Off Broadway at Playwrights Horizons, with a pair of startling one-act musicals by William Finn that bracketed the decade, *March of the Falsettos* (1981) and *Falsettoland* (1990). But it was a se-cret, until now, that the two *Falsetto* shows, fused together on a single bill, form a whole that is not only larger than the sum of its parts but is also more powerful than any other American musical of its day.

For this discovery, audiences owe a huge thanks to the Hartford Stage. Under the artistic direction of Mark Lamos, it has the guts to produce these thorny musicals together at a time when few nonprofit theaters are willing to risk aggravating dwindling recession audiences by offering works that put homosexual passions (among many other passions in the *Falsetto* musicals' case) at center stage.

Just as important, Mr. Lamos had the intuition to entrust the produc-tion to Graciela Daniele, a director and choreographer (most recently of *Once on This Island*) who would not be the most obvious choice to direct a show about Marvin, a nice young neurotic Jewish man who leaves his wife, Trina, and bar-mitzvah-age son, Jason, for a male lover. "I was born in Argentina," Ms. Daniele writes in a program note. "I'm not Jewish, I'm not a gay man, I've never even been to a bar mitzvah!" Yet she has brought off an inspired, beautifully cast double bill that is true to its gay and Jewish characters—and to the spirit of the original James Lapine productions—even as it presents the evening's densely interwoven familial and romantic relationships through perspectives that perhaps only a woman and a choreographer could provide.

Seen through Ms. Daniele's eyes, and seen together so they can achieve both cumulative and symbiotic effect, the *Falsetto* shows seem even richer than before. Though *March of the Falsettos* and *Falsettoland* are set only a year apart—in 1980 and 1981, respectively—the nine years separating their creation makes them a de facto map of the giddy rise and tragic fall of a decade within one slice of middle-class New York life.

The first of the two, bright and fizzy in the style of a wisecracking revue, seems pulled from a time capsule now. Written without benefit of historical hindsight, it exuberantly bottles the joy of men (both hetero- and homosexual) who begin the 1980s gorging on the promise of sexual and emotional liberation, all achieved with the benediction of Marvin's friendly shrink, Mendel, who himself takes up with the abandoned Trina.

In *Falsettoland*, however, Mr. Finn's music has a wintry chill and his once buoyantly articulate lyrics are clouded by a literally nameless dread. "Something bad is happening," sings an internist puzzled by the "sick and frightened bachelors" passing "unenlightened" through her hospital. By the final curtain, no word has yet been found to name the virus in question, but the evening's clutch of friends and family has been reduced to "a teeny tiny band" huddling together in love and terror on a vast, darkened stage.

That vast stage, a feature of the Hartford playhouse, was not available in the theaters where the Finn shows played in New York. For her finale, Ms. Daniele exploits the spatial dimensions at her disposal with an overwhelming coup de théâtre [the unexpected revelation of Whizzer's square on an enormous AIDS quilt] that first reduces an audience to sobs and then raises it to its feet. Until that point, her staging is as lithe and uncluttered as the Lapine originals—movable cubes substitute for rolling chairs—without replicating them. Ms. Daniele uses the Hartford thrust stage's nearly basketball-court-size floor space to work out the constantly changing configuration of Marvin's family in bouncy, lightly drawn geometric dance terms. Nowhere is this more apparent than in the director's pointed exclusion of Trina (Barbara Walsh) from songs like "Four Jews in a Room" in which the swaggering male characters hold sway.

Ms. Daniele's most pronounced departure from the original productions overall is her treatment of Trina, who is no longer a resilient comedian with a belter's voice but, in Ms. Walsh's modestly sung but hugely affecting performance, a rueful figure who is allowed genuine as well as comic anger at all "the happy men who rule the world." Fittingly, in the evening's sole alteration of the original shows' text, Trina is given an additional song, adapted from *In Trousers,* an earlier Finn musical about Marvin's travails.

As the wife gains gravity through Ms. Walsh's acting, so the son, Jason, is enhanced simply by the linking of the two shows. The evening's dramatic thread becomes the boy's efforts to become a man even as his parents split up, his mother remarries, and his father moves in with his friend Whizzer. Jason's journey from his hilarious, innocently homophobic solo, "My Father's a Homo," early in Act 1 to his heroic Act 2 decision to celebrate his manhood by having his bar mitzvah in the dying Whizzer's hospital room gives the show its most inspiring burst of hope.

Not that the troubled love affair between Marvin and Whizzer is in any way shortchanged. Evan Pappas, who was so fine as another brand of selfish New Yorker in last season's Off Broadway revival of *I Can Get It for You Wholesale,* is equally striking here, bringing a savage edge (along with his strong voice) to Marvin's self-indulgence and emotional greed ("I want it all!") no matter who is hurt along the way. Roger Bart's Whizzer is as narcissistic a "pretty boy" as the lyrics claim, yet so ingenuously boyish that it is easy to see why he eventually earns the loyalty of his lover's son and why his example finally inspires a latently generous Marvin to embrace selfless love at last in the evening's final, searing duet, "What Would I Do?"

It is a tribute to both Mr. Finn's lyrics and his music, here played by Henry Aronson's sprightly band in the original Michael Starobin arrangements, that they can carry the depth of these characterizations and those by Adam Heller (as Mendel), Josh Ofrane and Etan Ofrane (identical twins who share Jason's role an act apiece), and Andrea Frierson and Joanne Baum (as the "spiky lesbians" who arrive after intermission). The eclectic musical-comedy melodies of Act 1 and the torrential lyricism of Act 2 still seem freshly minted, as do the many comic turns of phrase about matters as various as the methodology of psychotherapy and the plight of doting parents who must watch "Jewish boys who cannot play baseball play baseball."

The audience must experience grief along with the music and laughter, of course, for something bad is happening in Falsettoland, now no less than in the distant year of 1982 when the show's story ends. But surely there is solace to be had when the theater strikes back at something bad in life with a show that is this exhilaratingly good.

DANCING AT LUGHNASA
PLYMOUTH THEATRE, OCTOBER 25, 1991

Whenever an Irish dramatist writes a great play, or even a not-so-great one, habit demands that non-Irish audiences fall all over themselves praising the writer's poetic command of the English language. Those audiences may be in for a shock at *Dancing at Lughnasa,* Brian Friel's new play at the Plymouth Theatre, for its overwhelming power has almost nothing to do with beautiful words.

Just as living is not a literary experience, neither is theater at its fullest—theater that is at one with the buried yearnings and grave disappointments that are the inescapable drama of every life. In *Dancing at Lughnasa,* Mr. Friel and an extraordinary company of actors, most of whom originated their roles at the Abbey Theatre in Dublin, uncover that eternal drama in stolen glances, in bursts of unexpected laughter, in an idle fox trot to a big-band tune on the radio. That is the poetry of this play—its "dream music," in the narrator's phrase—and like the most fragrant music, it strikes deep chords that words cannot begin to touch.

Words are hardly scanted in *Dancing at Lughnasa,* but as Mr. Friel gradually reveals, they serve a different, less ethereal, more troubling function. Many of them are spoken by that narrator, a middle-aged autobiographical stand-in for the author named Michael (Gerard McSorley), who sets out to tell the audience about the "different kinds of memories" he has of three weeks in August 1936, when he was seven years old.

As Michael says at the outset, nothing of remarkable note happened over those weeks at the rural, financially straitened County Donegal house where he lived with five unmarried women, his mother, Chris (Catherine Byrne), and her four sisters. His little-seen father, a charming Welsh drifter named Gerry (Robert Gwilym), unexpectedly pops up for two brief visits. An old uncle, Jack (Donal Donnelly), returns to his sisters' home for keeps after twenty-five years in exile as a missionary priest at a Ugandan leper colony.

The only other red-letter event in the Mundy household is the arrival of its first wireless set, a clunky wooden box emblazoned with its brand name, Marconi. But the far-off music summoned by the radio, like the offstage village festival alluded to in Mr. Friel's title, exerts a tidal pull on the characters far stronger than any domestic occurrence. As the sisters go about their chores in Act 1, bickering and gossiping and joking in the kitchen, they are titillated by intermittent reports of the Lughnasa celebration, in which their neighbors honor the pagan god of the harvest, Lugh, with dancing and fires and other back-hills rituals well beyond the bounds of their own strictly enforced Christian propriety. Though the women's participation in the fun remains unlikely, an explosion of Celtic music on the new radio possesses them all, even the schoolmarmish Kate (Rosaleen Linehan), and leads them into a spontaneous, short-lived dance in which uninhibited leaps and cries of pure animalistic hunger momentarily throw off the monotony of a drab, impoverished existence for an incandescent explosion of joy.

What does the dancing mean? It is not our business to know, exactly, for as Michael later says, dancing is a language "to whisper private and sacred things"—the expression of a search for an "otherness," a passion that might be spiritual or romantic or uncategorizable but that in any case is an antidote to the harsh facts of an earthbound existence. It is typical of the production's delicacy that in the first, tumultuous dance, each sister's gestures, steps, and whoops have been precisely choreographed to raise the curtain, however briefly and enigmatically, on the individual passions of five contrasting private souls. It is typical of the play's own pagan force that that scene seems to yank the audience into communion with its own most private and sacred things, at a pre-intellectual gut level that leaves us full of personal feelings to which words can not be readily assigned.

Many of the other profoundly moving interludes in *Dancing at Lughnasa* grab the audience in the same way, by expressing the verbally inexpressible in gesture and music. The frustrated sexual affection between the young mother Chris and the ne'er-do-well Gerry is dramatized not in the dialogue of their tongue-tied reunion so much as in their Fred-and-Ginger spin to the radio's outpouring of "Dancing in the Dark," a song whose lyrics pointedly elude them. The unacknowledged longings of Uncle Jack, who seems to have left his heart back in Africa and has trouble retrieving his English vocabulary after twenty-five years of Swahili, can be articulated only when he walks toward the wheatfields beyond the Mundy garden and taps two sticks together in time with some Dionysian tribal rhythm banging about in his head. Almost as poignant are the faces of those characters who cannot hear the music or join in a dance: When the four other sisters watch Chris and Gerry two-step from afar, each of their expressions becomes a distinctive, haunting portrait in complex suppressed emotions.

As directed by Patrick Mason, *Dancing at Lughnasa* gets the brilliant acting it demands; no between-the-lines nuance is lost by the ensemble of eight performers. Among the more indelible images are those provided by Brid Brennan as the angriest and most secretive of the sisters and by Mr. Donnelly, whose aging, distracted, shuffling Uncle Jack adds a poignant perspective to a career that has been linked with Mr. Friel's since he starred as the sassy young protagonist in the playwright's first Broadway success, *Philadelphia, Here I Come!*, twenty-five years ago.

Such is Mr. Friel's generosity of spirit that every acting assignment in this play makes the actors stretch, starting with Mr. McSorley, who must act not only his present age but also fill in the voice of Michael as a wide-eyed and often lost child. Even seemingly unsympathetic characters like the irresponsible Gerry and the stern Kate are aware of their own limitations, and in the performances of Mr. Gwilym and Ms. Linehan, they concede their faults with a defenseless candor that makes one want to embrace them no less than the boisterous, good-humored Maggie (Dearbhla Molloy) and the simple, fragile Rose (Brid Ni Neachtain).

For all Mr. Friel's compassion toward the characters in *Dancing at Lughnasa*, he is not remotely sentimental. In a chilling device that recurs in his canon, he periodically has Michael step out of the past and jump-cut the narration to tell the audience what will happen to the characters long after the play's circumscribed action is over. It is giving away nothing to say that the dénouements are cruel, for Mr. Friel's people, no less than anyone else, are headed toward death, some by paths more circuitous and tragic than others.

Yet the play keeps going well after Michael has told the audience all the bad news its characters will some day learn. This is a memory play, after all, and as Michael says, in memory "atmosphere is more real than incident" and nothing is owed to fact. Even knowing what he knows and what everyone knows about life's inevitable end, he clings to his vision of his childhood, a golden end-of-summer landscape in this production's gorgeous design, for what other antidote than illusions is there to that inescapable final sadness? *Dancing at Lughnasa* does not dilute that sadness—the mean, cold facts of reality, finally, are what its words are for. But first this play does exactly what theater was born to do, carrying both its characters and audience aloft on those waves of distant music and ecstatic release that, in defiance of all language and logic, let us dance and dream just before night must fall.

MAD FOREST

New York Theatre Workshop, December 5, 1991

Three months after the 1989 fall of the Ceauşescus, a theatrical brigade including the British playwright Caryl Churchill, a director named Mark Wing-Davey, and ten of Mr. Wing-Davey's acting students went to Romania on what promised to be a preposterous mission. Their aim was to become instant experts on a nation in postrevolutionary turmoil and to make a play about what they had seen. Their visit was scarcely longer than a week.

Can you picture the results already? The acting students, being by definition romantics, would create a let-a-thousand-flowers-bloom pageant. Ms. Churchill, being an archetypal Royal Court Theatre ideologue of her day, would insist on equating Ilena Ceauşescu with Margaret Thatcher.

Or so one might reasonably imagine. But real artists—not to be confused with the cultural camp followers who have turned Prague into a chic tourist spot—are unpredictable. There is nothing knee-jerk about *Mad Forest,* as Ms. Churchill named her play, and it turns out to be just as surprising, inventive, and disturbing as the author's *Top Girls* and *Fen.* In its American premiere under the aegis of the New York Theatre Workshop, a full eighteen months after the London opening, the piece has not dated in the way that newspaper accounts of the same history already have. If anything, this "play from Romania," as it is subtitled, seems to seep beyond its specific events and setting to illuminate a broader nightmare of social collapse, especially in the insinuating production Mr. Wing-Davey has fashioned at the Perry Street Theatre with a crack American cast.

Mad Forest can penetrate beneath the surface of its well-chronicled story precisely because it is not journalism. Only in the second (and least successful) of the three acts, a Living Newspaper in which the company temporarily simulates Romanian accents to recite an anecdotal oral history of the tumultuous week after the massacre of demonstrators at Timişoara, does the play purport to traffic in documentary reality. The rest of *Mad Forest* forgets about the facts, which remain murky anyway in Romania, and exerts a theatrical imagination to capture the truth about people who remain in place no matter what regimes come and go.

Ms. Churchill achieves this by devoting her first and third acts to an examination of two Bucharest families, one of laborers and one of intellectuals, before and after the revolution. But if the two families give the evening a focus and a story of sorts—the households are to be linked by marriage—the technique of *Mad Forest* is elliptical and atmospheric, often in the manner of Eastern European fiction of the Kundera and Havel era. In Act 1, the double lives of people trapped in a totalitarian state are dramatized by gesture and image—the mute, dour figures waiting hopelessly in a meat queue, for instance—rather than by the dialogue, which is often oblique or insincere, lest the dread secret police, the Securitate, be eavesdropping. In Act 3, the liberated Romanians do little but talk, but they often talk over each other, screaming and arguing in paroxysms of xenophobia and paranoia that sometimes seem even more frightening than the sullen episodes of repression that precede them.

As is the playwright's style, some vignettes are meanly funny. A young woman (Calista Flockhart) seeking an abortion in Act 1 is told by a doctor (Joseph Siravo) that "there is no abortion in Romania" even as he pockets the bribe that will secure his illicit services. A teacher (Mary Shultz) who lauds the Ceauşescus in her classroom at the play's outset is wondering by Act 3 what strings can be pulled to keep her job in a new, upended Romania where "we don't know who we know." A rebellious art student (Jake Weber) turns on his parents for collaborating with the discredited dictatorship even as he finds the sloganeering of the new, Iliescu government chillingly interchangeable with that of the old.

But such conventional political satire is eventually overwhelmed by a more surreal form of theater. A nasty madman (Rob Campbell) roams through a hospital, challenging the official version of the December events by incanting such unanswered questions as "Did we have a revolution or a putsch?" and, "Were the Securitate disguised in army uniforms?" Mythological figures enter the action, among them an archangel who seemingly collaborated with the genocidal Iron Guard of the 1930s and an elegant Transylvanian vampire drawn by the smell of blood. As the phantasmagoric sequences thicken and grow more grotesque, Ms. Churchill gives poetic voice to the new crisis of a society in which the old totalitarian order has splintered into a no less malignant disorder. Abruptly the new democrats look suspiciously like the old fascists and a hunt for class and racial enemies becomes the pathological preoccupation of people who remain hungry and enraged.

By using a small cast to populate this large canvas, Ms. Churchill once again provides exceptional opportunities for actors to play multiple roles. What Mr. Wing-Davey achieves with his familiar but often unsung New York ensemble evokes memories of Tommy Tune's achievement with the American cast of Ms. Churchill's *Cloud 9* a decade ago. Everyone in *Mad Forest* is excellent, starting with Ms. Flockhart and Mr. Weber, though the showiest role-switching stunts belong to Lanny Flaherty (who plays both a proletarian lout and a tweedy translator), Randy Danson (representing several classes of Romanian womanhood), Mr. Siravo (as a variety of bloodsuckers), and Christopher McCann (doubling as an effete architect and a mangy street dog).

As designed by Marina Draghici (sets) and Christopher Akerlind (lighting), who turn a small stage into an ever-changing Chinese box of oppressively angled walls and shadowy, Kafkaesque cul-de-sacs, the evening's physical production also plays a major role. The staging often conjures up tableaux as evocative as the play's title, which refers to the dense forest that once stood where Bucharest is now and was, as a program note says, "impenetrable for the foreigner who did not know the paths."

Ms. Churchill does not pretend to know those paths, either—each scene is pointedly introduced by a banal sentence read from a tourist's Romanian phrasebook—but she does see the forest for the trees. Nowhere is this clearer than in the play's wedding finale, where every element of the production whirls together in an explosively choreographed panorama of drunken revelry and sadistic, retributive violence. Few lines can be heard over the ensuing pandemonium—"This country needs a strong man" is one—and the chaos that engulfs the small theater is terrifying. Surely I was not the only American in the audience who found the climax of *Mad Forest*, with its vision of an economically and racially inflamed populace on a rampage for scapegoats, a little too close to home.

MARVIN'S ROOM

Playwrights Horizons, December 6, 1991

The title character of *Marvin's Room,* who is seen only as a blurred shape behind the glass-brick wall of his sickroom, has been dying for twenty years. Eaten up by cancer and crippled by strokes, he turns for entertainment to the simple pleasure of watching his lamp's light bounce around the walls and ceiling when it is reflected at bedside from a compact mirror.

The heroine of *Marvin's Room* is the woman who takes care of Marvin, his forty-year-old daughter Bessie (Laura Esterman). She is dying of leukemia. The play's other characters include Marvin's aged sister and

Florida housemate, Aunt Ruth (Alice Drummond), who has electrodes in her brain to stop the pain of three collapsed vertebrae, and Bessie's sister, Lee (Lisa Emery), a cosmetician who is in good health but has two severely troubled teenage sons, the older of whom has been confined to a mental institution since burning down his own house and much of his neighborhood.

Is there any chance you will believe me when I tell you that *Marvin's Room,* which was written by Scott McPherson and opened at Playwrights Horizons last night, is one of the funniest plays of this year as well as one of the wisest and most moving? Maybe not. And that's how it should be. When the American theater gains a new voice this original, this unexpected, you really must hear it for yourself.

In bald outline, I know that *Marvin's Room* sounds like other things, from disease-of-the-week television movies to their more pretentious theatrical cousins, right-to-live and right-to-die plays like *The Shadow Box* and *Whose Life Is It, Anyway?* While its characters in fact watch soap operas to fill up their own afternoons, *Marvin's Room* is most decidedly not a soap itself. Nor is it a pitch-black gallows farce in the British mode of Joe Orton or Peter Nichols, though Mr. McPherson's ability to find laughter in such matters as bone marrow transplants, a doctor's fumbling attempts to draw blood, the strapping down of mental patients, and the disappearance of Monopoly hotels into a respirator are at least minor miracles of absurdist comedy. *Marvin's Room,* which was previously seen at the Goodman Theatre in Chicago and the Hartford Stage, is just too American to subscribe to European cynicism. It sees life as it is and how it could be, and it somewhat optimistically imagines how one might bridge that distance.

What separates *Marvin's Room* from so many synthetic American plays that cover its rough territory, however, is that even at its occasional sunniest, it never lies or sentimentalizes the truth. Mr. McPherson does not pretend that God has a divine plan for everyone. (As the dotty Aunt Ruth merrily puts it, the pain she has had since birth may be God's way of teaching her forbearance but may also be a less profound lesson in "how to dress without standing up.") Mr. McPherson does not pretend that people always die with dignity, either, or that everyone isn't dying. Instead he asks, What good can we do with the time, however much or little it is, that we have left before our inevitable harsh fate arrives?

For Bessie, the answer is never in doubt. She has taken care of her father and her aunt for her whole adult life, and she will continue to do so until they drop or she does. Both as written and as acted by Ms. Esterman, Bessie is the heart of *Marvin's Room* because she serves as a caretaker cheerfully, without complaint or self-pity or desire for thanks, without ever questioning or regretting a moment of it, even as her own terminal disease worsens.

"I can't imagine a better way to have spent my life," she says, and not only does Bessie mean it, but she also has trouble imagining how anyone might question her conviction that giving to others is its own reward, an end in itself. That she is a credible, ordinary person rather than a gooey fictive saint is a tribute to Ms. Esterman's extraordinary performance as well as to the writing. The actress has a gamin's features, a shade clownish with a touch of sadness tugging at her big, brimming eyes, and the airy, tickling comic voice of an Elaine May or Barbara Harris. She has a tough spine, which is revealed when facing down her selfish sister, and while she never married, she has a sexuality, which was once tapped by a carny worker who came to his own miserable end. Ms. Esterman always convinces us that Bessie's generosity is for real, not for show, a healthy choice rather than a neurotic need. We even laugh with her, not at her, when she can't stop herself from leaving coins in place of the candy her sister empties into her purse from the bowl in a nursing-home waiting room.

While Bessie's goodness cannot cure her physical ailments or those of her father and aunt, her impact on the psychological states of her selfish sister and her two antisocial nephews is the underlying story of *Marvin's Room*. In Ms. Emery's hilarious but never cheap portrayal, Lee is a white-trash vulgarian, a promiscuous and self-involved single mother of a sort who all too understandably could drive a child to pyromania. When she travels to Bessie's Gulf Coast household from her town in Ohio in the play's opening scenes, it is the first time she has bothered to see her sister, father, or aunt in years. She wouldn't mind making a fast escape after writing a guilt-easing check.

But Lee and the boys, wonderfully played by Mark Rosenthal and Karl Maschek, must hang around, and *Marvin's Room* finds its most powerful scenes as all three are inexorably transformed by the uncritical, guileless affection Bessie showers on them no less than on her dying elders. In one unforgettable scene, Lee finally musters some love for her sister in the only way she can—by offering her services as a budding beautician— and prompts Bessie to remove the wig used to hide the ravages of chemotherapy so that it might be styled into a "sophisticated, on-the-town evening" look. This intimate gesture of reconciliation, at once tender, funny, and mournful, is about as gripping as family drama gets. And it is matched by other moments, including one in which the dwindling Ms. Esterman, her thin wrists beating the air to express her incongruous joy, tells Ms. Emery how lucky she has been to have so much love in her life: not the love she has received but the love she has given to others.

Bessie's high spirits are bottled by the director, David Petrarca, whose seamless production is punctuated by buoyant, Claude Bollingesque jazz (by Rob Milburn), bright sets (by Linda Buchanan), and the bubbly comic turns contributed by Ms. Drummond's wired Aunt Ruth and Tim Monsion as a doctor with a bedside manner of burlesque-sketch vintage. *Marvin's Room* is so sure of its own, idiosyncratic tone that some of its most rending interludes unfold quite naturally during a visit to the cartoon-populated landscape of Disney World.

Even so, the evening's joy—that contained in the play and that prompted by the revelation of an exciting new playwright—is inevitably tempered by one's knowledge, hinted at in the author's *Playbill* note and expanded upon in an interview in this newspaper, that Mr. McPherson, who is thirty-two years old, has AIDS. *Marvin's Room* was written before Mr. McPherson became ill and in any case asks for sympathy no more than Bessie does. But like some other recent comedies that have nothing specifically to do with AIDS and everything to do with the force of self-less love in a world where life is short—plays like Craig Lucas's *Prelude to a Kiss* and Terrence McNally's *Frankie and Johnny in the Clair de Lune*—*Marvin's Room* wasn't conceived in a vacuum. It is a product of its time.

Like its peers, *Marvin's Room* reaches beyond its time. That isn't to say that Mr. McPherson's play is for everyone. Lee's tart-tongued sons concede in one youthful bedtime conversation that they never "think about actually dying," and one imagines that even the most worldly teenagers would not know what to make of this evening either. Nor, perhaps, would those adults fortunate enough never to have stood in a room and watched a loved one die.

But I can't speak for that audience. I can only speak for myself. My first impulse after seeing Mr. McPherson's play was to gather those I care about close to me and take them into *Marvin's Room*, so that they, too, could bask in its bouncing, healing light.

≡ *Scott McPherson didn't live to write another play, or to see this one made into a well-meaning but sentimentalized movie in which stars rubbed the edges off the characters that had given the play its bite on stage. Then again, he might have been powerless to stop the Hollywood nip-and-tuck machinery. With occasional exceptions—Milos Forman's rethinking of* Amadeus *being the best—the better plays of the eighties and nineties sank almost instantaneously on film, with* Plenty, 'night, Mother, Crimes of the Heart, Prelude to a Kiss, M. Butterfly, *and even a smooth enter-tainment like Neil Simon's* Brighton Beach Memoirs *faring much as the largely forgotten film versions of* Death of a Salesman, Long Day's Journey into Night, *and* The Glass Menagerie *had decades earlier.*

NICK AND NORA
Marquis Theatre, December 9, 1991

Leaving the Marquis Theatre after *Nick and Nora,* I kept hearing the same jaded comment from other members of the audience beside me on the escalator: "Well, it's not nearly as bad as they said it would be."

True, this comment is hard to evaluate if you have no way of knowing which "they" these people are referring to. After all, nearly 100,000 customers paid full price to see *Nick and Nora* during its nine weeks of previews before its official "opening" last night, and that's a lot of suspects, each, no doubt, bad-mouthing the show to a different degree. Even so, I bet the theatergoers I overheard on the Marquis escalator are right. *Nick and Nora,* in its finished form, is not as bad as they said, whoever the "they" might be.

Which is not to say that it is good.

Like the less-than-gifted celebrity who is famous for being famous, this musical will no doubt always be remembered, and not without fondness, for its troubled preview period, its much-postponed opening, its hassles with snooping journalists, and its conflict with the city's Consumer Affairs Commissioner. Indeed, the story of *Nick and Nora* in previews, should it ever be fully known, might in itself make for a riotous, 1930s-style screwball-comedy musical. But the plodding show that has emerged from all this tumult is, a few bright spots notwithstanding, an almost instantly forgettable mediocrity. As no one will confuse it with the hit musicals its authors have worked on in happier times—*Gypsy, West Side Story, Bye Bye Birdie, Annie,* and *Miss Saigon,* among many others—neither is *Nick and Nora* remotely in the calamitous league of such recent, excessively previewed fiascoes as, say, *Carrie* and *Legs Diamond.*

The distinguished authors—Arthur Laurents (book), Charles Strouse (music), Richard Maltby Jr. (lyrics)—began with a highly promising idea, a musical murder mystery prompted by the glamorous husband-and-wife detective team created by Dashiell Hammett in the Depression and immortalized on screen by William Powell, Myrna Loy, and Asta, their canine sidekick. The setting is Hollywoodland, the atmosphere is meant to be that of a glittering black-and-white Art Deco movie musical, and the whodunit plot aspires to be adult and ingenious. Yet one need not indulge in invidious comparisons with the old *Thin Man* movies (which were not all that wonderful to begin with) or legitimate comparisons with Broadway's current, similar, and far superior *City of Angels* to see that *Nick and Nora* was probably doomed before it played its first preview.

For starters, this production might have spent a little less time searching for the perfect Asta and a lot more time trying to find the right Nick and Nora. Barry Bostwick is a handsome leading man with an agreeable manner and sturdy voice, and Joanna Gleason, better still, is an astringent comic actress with impeccable timing and her own strong voice. But if either of these talents, together or separately, has the larger-than-life personality or all-around musical-comedy pizzazz it takes to ignite a star-centric Broadway musical, that incandescence is kept under a shroud in *Nick and Nora.* The heart sinks from their opening number, a low-key, charmingly written piece titled "Is There Anything Better Than Dancing?" Instead of setting the tone implied by its title, the song, as performed, reveals that Mr. Bostwick and Ms. Gleason have limited warmth and cannot really dance, and that their would-be Astaire-and-Rogers routines, wanly choreographed by Tina Paul, will have to be fudged all night. (As in fact they are, right through a finale that, if better executed, might have echoed "Rosie," the beguiling equivalent duet at the end of Mr. Strouse's *Bye Bye Birdie.*)

The other fatal drawback for a musical aspiring to the style of *Nick and Nora* is tipped off in the second number, in which the evening's second banana, Christine Baranski in the role of an egomaniacal movie queen, sings of how "Everybody Wants to Do a Musical." The song is set in a film studio and is redolent of the Busby Berkeley era, yet the campy fantasy of its lyric is never illustrated with chorus performers or even scenery. To put it another way, the sparsely appointed and underpopulated *Nick and Nora* looks from the start as if it were produced on the cheap—or as if its budget, however large, was not smartly spent—and that impression never dissipates. The final production number of Act 2, typically, is a Carmen Miranda send-up in which the singer (Yvette Lawrence) is backed up by two—count 'em, two—dancers.

All the other failures in *Nick and Nora* are secondary to its inability to deliver the glamorous stars and atmosphere promised by its title. (Such scenery as there is, by Douglas W. Schmidt, is bland, and Theoni V. Aldredge, in a rare lapse, has costumed all the women unbecomingly.) As director, Mr. Laurents must shoulder some of the blame for those central shortfalls, as well as for the sluggish, stop-and-go gait of the entire, nearly three-hour evening. His talky book is also not his sharpest, offering a murder puzzle that is ambitious and convoluted without being pleasurable and Hollywood repartee that for all its knowing allusions to Max Ophuls, Joseph Kennedy, and Louella Parsons is not especially funny. A subplot about Nick and Nora's marital travails seems to have been shredded into confusion during revision, so much so that the other man who briefly sours the couple's relationship (Chris Sarandon) is never coherently identified.

Though Mr. Strouse has written some rousing scores for frail shows (*It's a Bird It's a Plane It's Superman*, *All American*, *Rags*), that of *Nick and Nora* is not one of them. Yet there are some pretty tunes along the way, and one is always struck by how enthusiastically and professionally he and Mr. Maltby embrace and sometimes conquer the tough technical challenges of musical-theater writing. At their cleverest here, in one song in each act, they use witty music and lyrics to bring together all the suspects and motives in Nick and Nora's murder case so that the detectives and audience alike might weigh every conceivable scenario. At their worst, they give two of the most gifted comic actresses in town—Ms. Baranski and Debra Monk—flat would-be showstoppers that make the performers seem both unfunny and vocally uncomfortable.

A third supporting actress, Faith Prince, fares far better in the role of the evening's ubiquitous murder victim, Lorraine, a platinum-wigged film-industry bookkeeper who, among other attacks on her dubious character, is accused of trying to "play Barbara Stanwyck with Jean Harlow hair." Though Lorraine is already dead when the show begins, she keeps popping up again and again as her murder is reenacted in repeated flashbacks to the scene and night of the crime. The dizzy Ms. Prince not only takes a mean pratfall each time the gunshots ring out but also brings a brash, belting delivery to "Men," a musical diatribe that almost does to its satirical target what Miss Hannigan did to "Little Girls" in Mr. Strouse's *Annie*.

We can look forward to hearing a lot more from Ms. Prince. In the meantime, there is no escaping the unfortunate fact that the liveliest thing in *Nick and Nora* is a corpse.

≡ *As a columnist four years later I interviewed Arthur Laurents (the first time I'd met him, except through periodic testy correspondence) because of his efforts to bring the serious play back to Broadway as part of a "Broadway initiative" started by him and Stephen Sondheim. He put* Nick and Nora—*and certainly its reviews—behind him, crediting its failure with jolting him into a new burst of creativity: Since* Nick and Nora, *he's writ-*

ten several plays, including The Radical Mystique, Jolson Sings Again, *and* Two Friends, *and embarked on a memoir—even as he turned eighty. We became fast friends.*

Arthur doesn't look back much, his memoirs notwithstanding. And he's incapable of being sentimental. A theatergoing highpoint was a trip he, my wife, and my (then) twelve-year-old son, Simon, took to New Haven in 1997 to see a touring production of West Side Story. *Arthur was ruthless in finding fault with his own (and everyone else's) contributions to the show he'd written forty years earlier—much to the amusement of Simon, who had a spirited debate with him on what is and isn't "dated" in Arthur's script.*

TWO SHAKESPEAREAN ACTORS
Cort Theatre, January 17, 1992

Ham actors may be a horror, but fine actors playing ham actors are almost always a joy. Brian Bedford, cast as the nineteenth-century British tragedian William Charles Macready in Richard Nelson's new play, *Two Shakespearean Actors,* is no exception. Very grand, often pickled, and prone to forgetting the end of any sentence well before he has made it to the verb, Mr. Bedford's puffed-up Macready would be right at home in the hapless theatrical companies of *Nicholas Nickleby, The Dresser,* and *Noises Off.* Even his version of the actor's nightmare is egomaniacal: When Macready dreams this dream, he does not forget his lines but instead plays all the parts at once.

Mr. Bedford, a British actor who has been a mainstay of Broadway and Stratford, Ontario, over a thirty-odd-year stage career, pours a lifetime of both classical and boulevard-comedy experience into this role. In Mr. Nelson's play, Macready is a tired, fading figure who arrives to perform *Macbeth* in the New York City of 1849 only to find his supremacy challenged by a younger local upstart, the first great American Shakespearean, Edwin Forrest (Victor Garber), who is performing his own *Macbeth* elsewhere in town. It's an ugly situation. A symbolic target for enraged nationalistic forces beyond his comprehension, Macready suffers the indignity of less-than-full houses, a pelting with stones, and, finally, a full-scale Anglophobic riot that leaves more than a score dead outside the Astor Place Opera House.

Yet in Mr. Nelson's fictionalized retelling of this actual history, and in Mr. Bedford's meticulous performance, Macready never ceases to be human and never becomes the butt of the piece. Though he is always patronizing to his New York hosts (his idea of a compliment is to call Americans "intelligent in an instinctive sort of way"), Mr. Bedford cloaks the snobbery in a rheumy laugh, merry eyes, and a glinting smile. For all the outrageousness of Macready's Macbeth—performed in a kilt with a Lady Macbeth firmly consigned to the upstage shadows—this babbling ham actor is, finally and all too fleetingly, a tragic figure. When the mob boos and stones him, Mr. Bedford gives a stunned reading of the simple line "They have interrupted my performance!" that conveys the abject terror of another actor's nightmare, an audience's rejection. When the riots break out later, the spent, frightened Macready drifts into a passage from *King Lear* that Mr. Bedford plays for keeps, a fallen giant baring himself to an empty house as "a poor, infirm, weak, and despised old man."

People who love the theater will dote on Mr. Bedford, and they will be nearly as fond of Mr. Garber, who is just as good in a much less juicy role. But even if one does cherish the backstage lore and actors' shoptalk that are the currency of *Two Shakespearean Actors,* it's hard to shake the feeling that this evening, often diverting and sometimes more than that when Mr. Bedford is center stage, never lives up to its promise. And a lot is promised. The star turns, the fascinating premise, the huge cast that greets the audience in the play's opening moments, and the elegant staging by Jack O'Brien all imply that this production, a Lincoln Center Theater presentation at the Cort Theatre on Broadway, will have epic ambitions akin to *M. Butterfly* or *Amadeus,* or, perhaps more aptly, to the revisionist cultural-historical fictions of E. L. Doctorow. But Mr. Nelson's writing, as epitomized by the prosaic title, rises only sporadically to the scale of everything else.

This disappointment is unexpected, because *Two Shakespearean Actors* is poised to pick up where the author's savage previous comedy, *Some Americans Abroad,* left off. As in that play about American Anglophiles agog in present-day England, this one trades in Jamesian themes: the cultural clash between the Old World and the New, the declaration of an independent American artistic identity that is at once brave and vulgar, dynamic and insecure. Unfortunately, Mr. Nelson does not expand upon these points this time so much as reduce them to a simplistic, frequently reiterated duel of acting styles. Macready, representing England, stands for textual fidelity and outward sophistication while the rising American, anachronistically portrayed as an incipient Method Actor, stands for raw energy and the obsessive, inward study of subtext.

Even if this formulation were an accurate picture of the contrast between English and American actors of 1849—which it is not—it still would not be a big enough conflict, or, if you will, metaphor, to explain the bloody Astor Place riots. But no other explanation, real or imagined, is forthcoming in *Two Shakespearean Actors,* which consistently whets the audience's curiosity about its subject only to leave it unsatisfied. The political, economic, and xenophobic forces that lead to the evening's anticolonial conflagration—sentiments that have resurfaced, less violently, as recently as the Jonathan Pryce–*Miss Saigon* contretemps—remain hinted at but unexamined. Eventually the riots are all but forgotten, except as explosive noises off, while Mr. Nelson brings Macready and Forrest together for a sentimental, historically dubious display of noble theatrical fraternity that seems to belong to another play.

Since the personal stories of the title characters, notably Forrest's sad offstage juggling of a wife (Frances Conroy) and mistress (Jennifer Van Dyck), are also sketchily told, *Two Shakespearean Actors* often lacks emotional as well as intellectual bite. Anecdotal in structure, it is almost always at its best when it is dealing simply, parochially, and sometimes uproariously with the theater of missed cues, onstage mishaps, and offstage egos. The one conspicuous exception is a wildly overlong Act 1 sequence in which the rehearsals of the Forrest and Macready productions of *Macbeth* are supposedly contrasted but, accents and costumes aside, prove to be more alike than not.

There and elsewhere, Mr. Garber offers evidence that he can act Shakespeare at the same high level at which he acts everything else. (Having done a mock Otello in *Lend Me a Tenor* and a mock Macbeth here, maybe it's time for him to try the real thing.) His Forrest, a creature of the stage tortured by private demons Mr. Nelson never illuminates, is a commanding matinee idol who can make even self-pity and arrogance charming. In a company full of outstanding actors in cameo roles that never quite pay off, the better assignments, all executed superbly, belong to Zeljko Ivanek as a perennial understudy torn between two companies and countries, Eric Stoltz in a lecherous and opportunistic portrait of the Irish playwright Dion Boucicault, and Tom Lacy as a cynical supporting player nearing the farcical end of an unsung career.

Like Mr. Nelson's play, Mr. O'Brien's production evinces an overwhelming affection for the theater. As bathed in silken simulated gaslight by Jules Fisher, the simple, wood-beamed set by David Jenkins allows the action to swing gracefully from auditorium to backstage to dressing room to tavern; the sense of being taken into a hermetically sealed theatrical world of the Victorian age is completed by the Cort Theatre itself, a gilded relic closer in origin and spirit to 1849 than 1992. Though Mr. Nelson is an American writer, *Two Shakespearean Actors* was first produced two years ago with a different cast and director by the

Royal Shakespeare Company at Stratford-on-Avon. Rather than risk another riot, I will assume that the English production was far inferior to our own.

SIGHT UNSEEN
MANHATTAN THEATRE CLUB, JANUARY 21, 1992

In a theatrical space as intimate as the Manhattan Theatre Club Stage 2, you can tell when a play has gripped its audience, for no one seems to breathe, let alone shift in his seat. The phenomenon can be observed firsthand these nights at *Sight Unseen,* a smart and sad new comedy by Donald Margulies that has all sorts of unpleasant things to say about the 1980s art scene, the loss of love, and the price of assimilation, both ethnic and intellectual, in an America where authenticity often has little to do with an artist's—or anyone else's—rise to the top.

The scene that reduces the house to a dead hush is an Act 2 encounter set in a sleek London art gallery where a provocative American painter named Jonathan Waxman (Dennis Boutsikaris) is being honored with a retrospective. Jonathan, an intense, fashionably dressed young man who wears a pony tail and may or may not resemble Eric Fischl or Julian Schnabel, has been the subject of adulatory profiles in *Vanity Fair* and *The New York Times.* He has a long waiting list of patrons who have commissioned his future pictures, sight unseen, at outrageous prices. But to maintain his marketability, he must suffer through tedious interviews, like the one he is now giving to Grete (Laura Linney), a leggy, blond German woman who is a ferocious student of his work and tends to ask long, multiclause questions in impeccable, if strongly accented, English.

For all her flirtatious obsequiousness, Grete is a hostile interviewer. She demands that Jonathan reconcile his material success with his bleak paintings about the "emptiness and spiritual deadness of middle-class life." She asks why he employs a press agent. She traps him into spewing contempt for his own audience and for what she calls "the very system that made you what you are today." Worse, she attacks the content of his paintings from the politically correct left, reading sexual brutality and racism into a notorious canvas Jonathan regards as a celebration of physical love and a statement against bigotry.

Unsurprisingly, Jonathan squirms and grows defensive. But what holds the audience rapt is the double-edged drama Mr. Margulies has written into Grete's cross-examination. The more she closes in on

Jonathan, the more Jonathan begins (and not without reason) to suspect her of anti-Semitism. But is she in fact anti-Semitic? Or is Jonathan, who has strayed far from his Brooklyn Jewish roots, just exploiting the charge of anti-Semitism to deflect this German journalist's legitimate attacks on his work and integrity? The brilliance of the scene, aside from its stiletto language, is that Mr. Margulies answers yes to both questions, refusing to let anyone, least of all the audience, off the hook. Both Jonathan and Grete are right even as they are wrong, and the rest of us, left with no one to root for, must confront Mr. Margulies's own vision of a spiritual deadness he finds in middle-class intellectual life of the present day.

Not all of *Sight Unseen* is as bracing as this one confrontation, but the evening is almost always absorbing, especially as superbly acted by its cast of four in Michael Bloom's flawless production. As Mr. Margulies's daring last play, *The Loman Family Picnic,* toyed a bit with *Death of a Salesman,* so this one takes a leaf from *After the Fall,* its fractured time structure included. The narrative thread of *Sight Unseen,* told simultaneously in the present and in flashbacks, is the tale of Jonathan's midlife crisis: Spurred by his empty preeminence, his father's recent death, and the impending birth of his first child, the artist takes a journey into his past to find out how he lost his way. The quest leads him both to his bohemian student days and to a reunion with his first muse and lover, a self-described "sacrificial shiksa" named Patricia (Deborah Hedwall) who expatriated herself and married a British archeologist, Nick (Jon De Vries), after Jonathan abandoned her fifteen years earlier.

While the overall arc of Jonathan's path to self-discovery is predictable, Mr. Margulies makes the individual scenes crackle with biting dialogue, fully observed characterizations, and unexpected psychological complexities. In *Sight Unseen,* the metaphor of the title extends beyond a hollow painter's distant relationship to his art to a collection of long intertwined and emotionally dishonest personal relationships. The scenes in which Jonathan invites himself to Patricia and Nick's cottage in the English countryside have the lethal undercurrents of Harold Pinter's love-triangle plays, for the archeologist, a fount of malicious facetiousness in Mr. De Vries's unsettling performance, becomes almost unhinged in his esthetic and personal loathing for his unwelcome house guest. As the two men battle over the history of art (and obliquely over Patricia), the question is not who will be the victor but who is the unhappier man, the bigger self-deceiver and moral sham.

The play is less effective, even glib, when it jumps back to the Brooklyn home and art-school studio of Jonathan's youth to show when the painter was at his most authentic, as a painter and as a Jew. Jonathan's scantly described offstage parents carry more thematic weight than they can bear, and the whole juxtaposition between the jaded now and the idealistic then seems pat. That these scenes more or less work anyway is a tribute to Mr. Bloom's production: The shortcuts that eventually crop up in the script are camouflaged by the designer James Youmans's evocation of a Brooklyn boy's bedroom, Michael Roth's shimmering incidental music, and, most especially, the acting of the two principal players.

Mr. Boutsikaris, looking uncannily like Ron Silver, succeeds in keeping Jonathan from becoming unbearable in the present-day scenes without soft-pedaling his arrogance, then manages to find the frisky, likable artist as a young man in the flashbacks. As the woman he cannot forget, Ms. Hedwall is simply thrilling, and not just because of her technical mastery of abrupt time-leaping transitions that force her to jump from glassy-eyed middle-aged disappointment to youthful dewiness. In a play in which everyone, the older Patricia included, has made bad bargains with life and art, she is asked to embody the pure, direct human connection, the unclouded vision, that has been lost since the characters were young. This Ms. Hedwall achieves with a nakedness of spirit so incandescent that she adds a ray of hope to the otherwise angry brush strokes that dominate the canvas of *Sight Unseen*.

THE BALTIMORE WALTZ

CIRCLE REPERTORY COMPANY, FEBRUARY 12, 1992

To the memory of Carl—because I cannot sew," reads the *Playbill* dedication of Paula Vogel's new play, *The Baltimore Waltz*, at the Circle Repertory Company. Who Carl is we can only imagine, but can there be much doubt about what kind of memorial Ms. Vogel would like to sew for him? Her play is about an elementary-school teacher named Anna (Cherry Jones) who learns that her brother, a young San Francisco librarian named Carl (Richard Thompson), is terminally ill. Anna's response is to sweep her brother and herself into a fantasy world—a crazy-quilt patchwork of hyperventilating language, erotic jokes, movie kitsch, and medical nightmare—that spins before the audience in Viennese waltz time, replete with a dying fall.

The result is a dizzying evening at several levels, and the fact that *The Baltimore Waltz* is performed without an intermission did not prevent several Circle Rep subscribers from walking out at a critics' preview. This is not only a rare AIDS play written by a woman but also a rare AIDS play that rides completely off the rails of documentary reality, trying to rise above and even remake the world in which the disease exists.

Though ostensibly set in a Baltimore hospital, the actual landscape of Ms. Vogel's play is Anna's mind, which knows few imaginative bounds. Anna's powers of empathy are such that it is she, not her brother, who becomes the dying swan in her elaborate fantasies; she sees herself as the victim of a deadly malady that counts single teachers among its high-risk groups. Anna's dreams take her and Carl on a whirlwind tour through Europe that culminates in a macabre replay of the Carol Reed–Graham Greene thriller *The Third Man,* with its zither music, Ferris wheel, and a mad doctor (Joe Mantello) who usurps Orson Welles in the role of the mysterious Harry Lime.

"In art as in life, some things need no translation," says Carl. Some of *The Baltimore Waltz* too flagrantly defies translation, lacking the internal logic that can make some dream plays, including the preeminent Circle Rep dream play of recent vintage, Craig Lucas's *Reckless,* add up on their own idiosyncratic terms. Yet I respect what Ms. Vogel is up to and was steadily fascinated by it, even when her play seems too clever by half or less funny than it wants to be.

The fever pitch of *The Baltimore Waltz,* almost an oxygen rush at times, is always enlivened by the playwright's antic literacy and always justified by the tragedy at hand. "It's the language that terrifies me," says Anna when she first encounters the medical world, and it's language with which Ms. Vogel creates her heroine's strange wonderland. As the dialogue rifles several Berlitz phrase books or veers off into linguistic riffs (an extended declension of the sentence "There is nothing I can do," for instance), the play's words seem to splinter and finally metastasize in sync with the young bodies racked by an incurable epidemic.

The audience's irresistible human guide through the heady wordplay of Ms. Vogel's text is Ms. Jones, that wonderful actress last seen as a sullen eighteenth-century convict in *Our Country's Good.* A tall, big-boned woman with an incongruously pixieish face, she is credible as a devoted first-grade teacher, as an adoring sister, and, most important, as an improvisational artist desperately ransacking her soul to create something transporting, even beautiful out of the sadness life has dealt her. Ms. Jones makes Anna's generosity of spirit a matter of intellectual and emotional bravery rather than of sentimental outward show. Along the way, she provides a bravura display of seamless acting technique, most spectacularly when she demonstrates each of Elisabeth Kübler-Ross's stages of terminal illness in a rapid-fire series of vignettes that sand-wiches rage and heartbreak within the laughter of sketch comedy.

Ms. Jones's quicksilver changes of tone are matched by the supple production, which finds the director Anne Bogart treating a new script with a becoming delicacy and polish she does not always lavish upon the classics. *The Baltimore Waltz* is to be produced at several daring institu-tional theaters around the country this season, and one can only hope, for this brittle play's sake, that it is handled as sensitively elsewhere as it is here. With the help of Dennis Parichy's lighting, John Gromada's score, and Walker Hicklin's costumes, Loy Arcenas's sterile hospital set becomes a magical arena for Anna's tour around the world in ninety min-utes. Ms. Bogart also makes the most of the work's satirical interludes, with her principal accomplice being Mr. Mantello, who winningly per-forms a potpourri of burlesque turns in cameo roles of several national-ities and sexual dispositions.

While Mr. Thompson is likable in the role of Carl, it is one of the in-triguing aspects of *The Baltimore Waltz* that he is not an active charac-ter in his own drama: The play really is intended as a living memorial to him, a sister's loving, uninhibitedly sensuous, even lusty valentine to a brother whose private life away from her is represented only by a vague symbol, a child's stuffed toy rabbit, that floats benignly through the reveries. That Ms. Vogel has succeeded in creating that memorial is most apparent when she finally must burst the balloon, turning her enchanted accidental tourist back into a grieving schoolteacher, the rabbit back into a dying man's bedside totem, the mysteries of Vienna back into the cold, clammy realities of a hospital ward in Baltimore. Having turned up the volume and body heat of life so high with her dreamy theatrics, the au-thor makes us feel the loss all the more deeply when another young corpse is carted off the stage.

≡ *Paula Vogel went on to write one of the best American plays of the decade*—How I Learned to Drive (1997), *for which she received a Pulitzer Prize.*

CRAZY FOR YOU
SHUBERT THEATRE, FEBRUARY 20, 1992

When future historians try to find the exact moment at which Broadway finally rose up to grab the musical back from the British, they just may conclude that the revolution began last night. The shot was fired at the Shubert Theatre, where a riotously entertaining show called *Crazy for You* uncorked the American musical's classic blend of music, laughter, dancing, sentiment, and showmanship with a freshness and confidence rarely seen during the *Cats* decade.

Arriving within days of the enchanting production of *The Most Happy Fella,* its next-door neighbor in Shubert Alley, and a few weeks before three other eagerly anticipated American musicals promised for this season (*Guys and Dolls, Jelly's Last Jam,* and *Falsettos*), *Crazy for You* could not be a more celebratory expression of a long-awaited shift in Broadway's fortunes. And what more appropriate house could it play in than the Shubert, a theater too cozy to contain London's musical spectaculars, a theater that has been the sad symbol of the hole in Broadway's heart since *A Chorus Line* closed there two years ago?

Crazy for You calls itself a "new Gershwin musical comedy," and that's what it is: a musical comedy with songs by George and Ira Gershwin that makes everything old seem young again, the audience included. It is not a revival of *Girl Crazy,* the 1930 Gershwin hit with which it shares five of its eighteen numbers and a smidgen of plot, and it is not to be remotely confused with recent Broadway exercises in camp and nostalgia like *42nd Street, My One and Only,* and *Oh, Kay!* The miracle that has been worked here—most ingeniously, though not exclusively, by an extraordinary choreographer named Susan Stroman and the playwright Ken Ludwig—is to take some of the greatest songs ever written for Broadway and Hollywood and reawaken the impulse that first inspired them. *Crazy for You* scrapes away decades of cabaret and jazz and variety-show interpretations to reclaim the Gershwins' standards, in all their glorious youth, for the dynamism of the stage.

As soon as the overture begins, you know that the creators of this show have new and thrilling ideas, and are determined to make us hear familiar songs as if for the first time. William D. Brohn's orchestration acknowledges the standard treatment of "I Got Rhythm" but then reworks it, holding its full contour in smoldering check until finally it must erupt like a forest fire through the conductor Paul Gemignani's rollicking pit band. When the curtain rises, it is to the elevating opening bars of "Stairway to Paradise," a song that is never sung in *Crazy for You* but, in a typical example of the evening's cunning, is used more than once as an incidental motif to pump up the audience's pulse rate before springing the next theatrical surprise.

Those surprises are often the creations of Ms. Stroman, who, given a full corps of crack dancers, expands exponentially on the winning style she revealed in the revue *And the World Goes 'Round.* In *Crazy for You,* she works her magic with the plainest of stories. Mr. Ludwig's book is about nothing more than a wealthy Manhattan ne'er-do-well of the Depression, the stage-stuck Bobby Child (Harry Groener), who ends up in a broke Nevada mining town, where he rescues a bankrupt theater and wins the local girl, Polly Baker (Jodi Benson). Yet the choreographer reminds us that the well-worn imperatives of archetypal Astaire-and-Rogers, Mickey-and-Judy scenarios—boy meets girl, let's put on a show—can evoke untold joy when harnessed to movement, melodies, and words that spell them out with utter conviction in musical-comedy skywriting.

Ms. Stroman's dances do not comment on such apparent influences as Fred Astaire, Hermes Pan, and Busby Berkeley so much as reinvent them. Rather than piling on exhausting tap routines to steamroll the audience into enjoying itself, the choreographer uses the old forms in human proportion, to bring out specific feelings in the music and lyrics. When Mr. Groener leaps sideways on a thrice-repeated phrase in "Nice Work if You Can Get It"—to take just a throwaway bit—his legs are both punching out the notes in George Gershwin's tune and illustrating the sexual yearning in Ira Gershwin's verse. Ms. Stroman is not afraid of repose, either. In "Embraceable You," the embrace counts more than the steps, and the number reaches its consummation with a kiss that leaves the dance as dizzyingly unresolved as the newly acquainted couple's relationship.

Yet it is the big numbers in *Crazy for You* that people will be talking about, and in these, Ms. Stroman's signature is her use of homespun props, rather than an avalanche of spectacle, to turn her dances into theater. In "I Got Rhythm," the Act 1 finale, the regenerated hicks and drunks of Deadrock, Nev., whip up a torrent of music and merriment with washboards, corrugated tin roofing, and mining picks. "Slap That Bass" creates a visual jamboree out of pieces of rope, while "Stiff Upper Lip" finds the exhilarated populace erecting a house of chairs that figuratively parallels the accelerating spirits of their song and dance.

Short of George Balanchine's *Who Cares?* at the New York City Ballet, I have not seen a more imaginative choreographic response to the Gershwins onstage. That Ms. Stroman's numbers are theater dances that advance the show rather than bring it to repeated halts is also a tribute to Mr. Ludwig. His book has no intellectual content, and wants none, but is a model of old-school musical-comedy construction in its insistence on establishing a context, whether narrative, comic, or emotional, for every song. Mr. Ludwig also knows how to write jokes in the 1930s style, the funniest of which are reserved for such fine, acerbic clowns as Bruce Adler (a Florenz Ziegfeld stand-in), Jane Connell (the hero's meddling mother), and John Hillner and Michele Pawk as a pair of villains who fuse in a sadomasochistic dance (to the obscure "Naughty

Baby") that is the funniest of the several Stroman duets that turn seduction into an intricate, combative entanglement of limbs.

Mr. Ludwig is not above recycling mistaken-identity gags from his previous 1930s showbiz farce, *Lend Me a Tenor*—which had twin Otellos to match this script's twin Ziegfelds—but, as directed with a deep appreciation of slapstick by Mike Ockrent, the burlesque humor rarely flags. Mr. Ockrent, it must be said, is English, but, unsurprisingly, his hit West End musical of the 1980s was *Me and My Girl,* a knockoff of Broadway musicals of the Gershwin thirties.

Those looking to quibble with Mr. Ockrent's lithe production, which marches to a contemporary rhythm rather than that of a period piece, may question his choice of a leading lady. Ms. Benson's big voice (best known from the title role of the Disney film *The Little Mermaid*) and brash Mermanesque manner are fun, but she does not find the tenderness in "Someone to Watch Over Me." As for the exuberant Mr. Groener, a Jimmy Stewart who can hoof and sing, he typifies the kind of Broadway performer who has had too little work in our day; he has spent more time on television than onstage since his smash debut as Will Parker in the 1979 *Oklahoma!* Here he not only commands his numbers but also sets the cool tone required to make a complex theatrical undertaking look carefree.

Among the sophisticated complexities of *Crazy for You* is Robin Wagner's scenery, which, as backed by the starry Hollywood soundstage skies of the lighting designer, Paul Gallo, transport the company from a glittery old Times Square to a picture-book comic frontier reminiscent of *Destry Rides Again.* Since Mr. Ludwig's book largely unfolds in and around theaters, Mr. Wagner gets to re-create Joseph Urban's façade for the original Ziegfeld Theatre in New York as well as the gilded Victorian interiors of a mythical, reborn Gaiety Theatre in Deadrock.

The most startling of Mr. Wagner's theatrical settings, though, is the first, an angular vision of a Broadway theater's wings that specifically echoes the opening set of *Dreamgirls,* the last of this designer's collaborations with Michael Bennett. *Crazy for You* is not innovative, as the Bennett shows were, and it lacks the brand-new songs that must be the musical theater's lifeblood. But the evening is bursting with original talent that takes off on its own cocky path, pointedly mocking recent British musicals even as it sassily rethinks the American musical tradition stretching from the Gershwins to Bennett. "In two thousand years, there has been one resurrection, and it wasn't a theater," goes one of the evening's many showbiz one-liners. But in the secular land of Broadway, starved musical-theater audiences can't be blamed for at least dreaming that *Crazy for You* heralds a second coming.

MARCH 3, 1992

While Broadway is flush with the promise of the spring's new plays and musicals, the West End seems trapped in a wintry past.

The hottest ticket is a revival of the earliest Andrew Lloyd Webber hit, the 1972 *Joseph and the Amazing Technicolor Dreamcoat,* even as eight other brand-name musicals, some nearly as old and half of them also by Mr. Lloyd Webber, continue their immortal runs. These permanent fixtures are surrounded by no fewer than four other shows that anthologize American pop or rock and roll (from *A Swell Party* to *Good Rockin' Tonight*) and three more that merchandise vintage Harlem jazz and dance (or the British idea of it) to almost exclusively white audiences. *The Mousetrap,* anyone?

Only in one way does the current West End scene resemble Broadway: "Spare change?" is a ubiquitous line of dialogue. The recession, as much a factor in this British election year as it is in the American presidential race, is visible on every block. Makeshift encampments for the homeless abound, as do the vacant storefronts and marquees that often serve as their backdrops. London's commercial producers, like their New York counterparts, are frequently discounting their high-priced tickets, often reserving star billing in their newspaper advertisements for the phrase "seats available."

Even so, don't cry for the London audience. If the West End is largely a theatrical vacuum, the big subsidized companies, the Royal National Theatre and the Royal Shakespeare Company, easily compensate. Though the RSC's repertory of classics does not travel from Stratford-on-Avon to London's Barbican Centre until later this month, the National is in full roar, fielding a remarkably diverse array of critical and popular hits by authors of several nationalities (the Americans Tennessee Williams and Tony Kushner included) on its three stages. There are turn-away crowds for virtually all of its productions, and it could be argued that at this moment Richard Eyre, who took over the company's artistic leadership from Peter Hall in 1988, is the most successful producer, not to mention the most versatile, in the English-speaking theater.

One of Mr. Eyre's most important artistic allies this season is the playwright, actor, and sometime director Alan Bennett, who has two large-scale works in repertory at the National, a new play titled *The Madness of George III* and a long-running adaptation of the 1908 Kenneth Grahame children's classic, *The Wind in the Willows.* In a coup of Lloyd Webber proportions, Mr. Bennett is also responsible for *Talking Heads,* one of the very few serious dramas breaking up the musical monotony of the West End.

Actually, *Talking Heads* is an evening of monodramas, two performed by Patricia Routledge and one by Mr. Bennett himself, drawn in part from the television series of the same title, which has been seen on public television in the United States. Seeing the pieces on stage at the Comedy Theater is anything but a television experience, however. These riveting first-person accounts of lower-middle-class lives in Northern England are the dark side of monologues Mr. Bennett long ago performed in *Beyond the Fringe.* In their caustic humor and aching loneliness, they set an American to thinking of the forlorn small-town Midwestern voices of Edgar Lee Masters's *Spoon River Anthology* and Sherwood Anderson's *Winesburg, Ohio.*

In the first and most devastating of the Bennett soliloquies, titled *A Woman of No Importance,* Ms. Routledge sits in a chair, pocketbook firmly in hand, and gossips cheerily about the minutiae of her daily office machinations as a supposedly indispensable clerical worker in a large corporation. By the end of an hour, the chair has become a wheelchair, and the actress has seemingly melted from an animated busybody into a dying and solitary victim of an unidentified illness, her face distorted beyond recognition, her voice slurred, her body buried (in blankets) as if she were Samuel Beckett's Winnie in *Happy Days.*

But Mr. Bennett's real concern is not illness so much as the isolation and self-deception of a woman who does not realize that her colleagues never cared for her and who is soon abandoned and dismissed with get-well cards as anonymous as the hospital identification band on her wrist. Ms. Routledge, a hilarious comic actress distantly recalled by some New York audiences for her musical-comedy appearances (she won a Tony Award for *Darling of the Day* a quarter-century ago), is a large pudding of a woman whose delineation of her character's unwitting disintegration, as directed by the author, is harrowing to behold. I have never heard a restive Wednesday matinee audience, or at least one typically packed with women of the same late middle age as Ms. Routledge, grow so hushed as the one at the Comedy did during the terminal stages of this tour de force.

In the actress's concluding turn in *Talking Heads,* titled *A Lady of Letters,* another unmarried woman, a dour moral scold, comes to a perverse happy ending: She finds in jail the warm community and emotional liberation she never knew in the semidetached isolation of her mean little neighborhood. English life is also a prison in the middle monologue, *A Chip in the Sugar,* in which Mr. Bennett insinuatingly embodies Graham, a repressed, psychologically impaired homosexual whose narrow existence is jeopardized when his seventy-two-year-old widowed mother threatens to evict him to make room for her new "fancy man." Like the two women of *Talking Heads,* Graham and his unseen mother inhabit a fragmented and desolate human landscape in which an older generation is equally terrified of the T-shirt-wearing young, all racial minorities, and any glimmer of social change.

It would seem a long leap from the bleak, present-day interior worlds of *Talking Heads* to Mr. Bennett's highly populated period pieces at the National, both of which have been given extravagant, epic stagings by Nicholas Hytner, the director of *Miss Saigon.* Yet what most struck me about Mr. Bennett's version of *The Wind in the Willows* is that its hermetic vision of an eternal boyhood recalls Graham as much as Grahame.

Suffused with nostalgia for Edwardian England and its idyllic riverside vistas, this *Wind in the Willows* also cherishes the bygone boarding-school gentility and unarticulated gay crushes of Toad (Desmond Barrit), Rat (David Ross), Badger (Michael Bryant), and their new young protégé, Mole (Adrian Scarborough). If anything, they are reminiscent of the gentlemanly traitors Anthony Blunt and Guy Burgess, as much Cambridge as Marxist, that Mr. Bennett dramatized in his previous National Theatre work, *Single Spies.* For children, if not this impatient adult, *The Wind in the Willows* offers lush spectacle (designed by Mark Thompson), Christmas-pantomime-style burlesque comedy and, in the *Cats* manner, the frequent deployment of a large and musical chorus of anthropomorphic rabbits, hedgehogs, squirrels, and field mice.

The Madness of George III goes back to an even earlier Britain, that of 1788, when its title character, played by Nigel Hawthorne, was thought to have gone insane. Today George III is believed to have suffered from a metabolic rather than a psychological ailment, and much of Mr. Bennett's play is a nasty satire of the various quacks who torture the poor man with cruel and humiliating treatments in the name of advanced eighteenth-century medical science. The work's huge, gilt-framed canvas is filled out with lengthy recountings of Georgian political intrigues that add historical weight and plot to the evening without contributing much to either its dramatic force or intellectual passions.

It is when Mr. Hawthorne is at center stage that Mr. Bennett's play becomes highly charged, and not just because the actor is giving what may be the performance of his career as a quixotic monarch whose unpredictable behavior veers from clownish childishness to pathetic dementia to magisterial, Lear-like resignation, sometimes all in the same scene. *George III* is dominated by the image of its protagonist's illness, most horrifically realized at the Act 1 curtain, when he is strapped into a chair by his tormentors. As Handel's Coronation Anthem blares at top volume, the agonized, blistered Mr. Hawthorne howls defiantly, "I am the King of England!" only to be informed by his doctor: "No, sir. You are the patient."

As a suffering patient, this King is nothing if not a direct ancestor of the wheelchair-bound, middle-class woman of no importance played by Ms. Routledge in *Talking Heads*. Alan Bennett's comedies may be crowd-pleasers, but they are subversive ones, depicting lost souls who seem to emblemize an unhappy England that cannot diagnose, let alone cure, its ills.

≡ *Unlike Tom Stoppard, David Hare, Simon Gray, and Harold Pinter— but very much like Alan Ayckbourn—Alan Bennett has rarely received the productions of the quality he should have had in New York.*

ANGELS IN AMERICA: MILLENNIUM APPROACHES
ROYAL NATIONAL THEATRE, LONDON, MARCH 5, 1992

At the end of Tony Kushner's *Angels in America,* a new American play that has become a runaway sensation here, the theater rocks with deafening apocalyptic thunderclaps, a proscenium-size Old Glory explodes in a burst of lightning, and a beautiful angel descends from heaven to retrieve a young man who is dying of AIDS. "Very Steven Spielberg," says the awed young man. "The Great Work begins," announces the Angel. "The Messenger has arrived."

It says a lot about Mr. Kushner's huge talent that this outrageous finale, far from seeming as over-the-top as it sounds, is an appropriate, cathartic, and, yes, Spielbergian conclusion to the three and a half hours of provocative, witty, and deeply upsetting drama that have come before. Mr. Kushner, who is thirty-five years old and lives in Brooklyn, may well be creating a great work in *Angels in America,* a two-part epic of which this multilayered evening is only the first installment. Without question he is a messenger who demands to be heard.

Among many other things, this half of *Angels in America,* subtitled "Part 1: Millennium Approaches," is an idiosyncratically revisionist view of recent American political history in which Roy Cohn, the Joseph

McCarthy henchman who lived on to become the most politically incorrect of closeted AIDS victims, emerges as the totemic figure. As a piece of writing, the play is a searching and radical rethinking of the whole esthetic of American political drama in which far-flung hallucinations, explicit sexual encounters, and camp humor are given as much weight as erudite ideological argument.

The author labels his play "A Gay Fantasia on National Themes," and, pretentious as that may sound, he delivers on those ambitions, creating a modern answer to John Dos Passos's *U.S.A.* from the uncompromising yet undoctrinaire perspective of a gay American man of the early 1990s. *Angels in America* is the most extravagant and moving demonstration imaginable that even as the AIDS body count continues to rise, this tragedy has pushed some creative minds, many of them in the theater, to new and daring heights of imaginative expression.

Mr. Kushner's script ended up at the Royal National Theatre here—in the same intimate house, the Cottesloe, that was the site of the first production of David Mamet's groundbreaking *Glengarry Glen Ross*—by a circuitous route. The play was initially performed in a 1990 workshop at the Mark Taper Forum in Los Angeles, where part two (subtitled "Perestroika") will have its premiere next season, but its first full-fledged production was at the Eureka Theatre in San Francisco last year. It attracted the attention of the National's artistic director, Richard Eyre, who had the inspired idea of teaming Mr. Kushner with Declan Donnellan, a highly innovative director celebrated for the visual and sexual flamboyance he and his itinerant Cheek by Jowl company have brought to the classics.

Working with an ensemble cast that can be faulted only for the inevitable slippage of some of its American accents, Mr. Donnellan and his designer, Nick Ormerod, magically juggle overlapping scenes that whip among such diverse locales as a men's room in a Federal Court of Appeals, a middle-class home in Salt Lake City, the Ramble in Central Park, and a Valium addict's mystical vision of an ozone-depleted Antarctica. But the many fantastic flights of *Angels in America* are always tied to the real world of the mid-1980s by Mr. Kushner's principal characters, who include two young couples: a pair of gay lovers and a politically ambitious, rectitudinously Mormon lawyer and his wife. These couples are gradually brought into intersection by both their fantasy lives (sexual and otherwise) and their inadvertent proximity to the covert corridors of power ruled by Cohn in his latter-day incarnation as a Reagan-era Mr. Fixit.

Mr. Kushner, who likened the Reagan ethos to the Third Reich in a vapid previous agitprop drama (*A Bright Room Called Day*), certainly has some pointed things to say about the greed and selfishness of the Reagan decade. But *Angels in America* is more interested in looking ahead, in taking the spiritual temperature of the nation as it approaches the millennium, than in rehashing the political disputes, even those about AIDS, of the recent past. "AIDS shows us the limits of tolerance," says Louis Ironson (Marcus D'Amico), a Jewish clerical worker who has discovered that his lover of nearly five years, Prior Walter (Sean Chapman), is scarred by the lesions of Kaposi's sarcoma. Among the limits tested are those of the Jewish and Mormon religions and, less abstractly, those of Louis himself, a sweet, smart man who nonetheless abandons his longtime companion with a callousness a more limited playwright might ascribe exclusively to heterosexuals.

In the ecumenically depressed America of this play, everyone is running away from whoever he or she is, whether through sex, drugs, or betrayal, to dark destinations unknown. Yet for all his pessimism, Mr. Kushner sees many sides of every question. Nowhere is this more apparent than in his presentation of Cohn, who, in the demonic performance of Henry Goodman, is a dynamic American monster of Citizen Kane stature. True to fact, this Cohn, even at his most bullying and hypocritical, is neither stupid nor bereft of a sense of humor. In one typically arresting speech, he vehemently argues that he is not a homosexual but a heterosexual who has sex with men, for how could a man with his political influence be included among a constituency with "zero clout"? In Cohn's many fascinating self-contradictions, Mr. Kushner finds an ingenious vehicle for examining the twisted connections between power, sexuality, bigotry, and corruption in an America that has lost its moral bearings.

Such is the high-voltage theatricality achieved by both play and production that the English audience at *Angels in America* is totally gripped even as it must consult a program glossary to identify phenomena like Ethel Rosenberg (who materializes to call an ambulance for the stricken Cohn), Ed Meese, Shirley Booth, and the Yiddish expression "Feh!" Even a graphic simulation of rough, anonymous sex—brilliantly accomplished by two fully dressed actors miming their actions at opposite sides of the stage—becomes a funny and affecting metaphor for Mr. Kushner's larger, painful canvas of a country splintering at every public and private level. There are scenes of *Angels in America* that run on too long and thoughts that are not clear (though they may become so in part two). But the excitement never flags. Mr. Kushner has created an original theatrical world of his own, poetic and churning, that, once entered by an open-minded viewer of any political or sexual persuasion, simply cannot be escaped.

≡ *To say that this play caught me by surprise is an understatement. Reviewing Kushner's* A Bright Room Called Day *at the Public Theater a year earlier, I'd dismissed his writing as "fatuous." But I was so overwhelmed by* Angels *after a matinee in London that I canceled my theatergoing plans for that night; I needed time to think.*

Angels would have a circuitous route to New York. The British production was abandoned for another and inferior staging, which I reviewed at the Mark Taper Forum in Los Angeles. By the time the play arrived on Broadway, it would be in the hands of George C. Wolfe, whose production I liked (if perhaps not quite as much as this first, intimate version). Angels *would take to the road under the guidance of still another director, Michael Mayer, and has since been staged in different ways by many directors at resident theaters throughout the United States and well beyond.*

UNCLE VANYA/THE NIGHT OF THE IGUANA
ROYAL NATIONAL THEATRE, LONDON
HEARTBREAK HOUSE
GUILDFORD, MARCH 7, 1992

The only debate raging among London critics about the Royal National Theatre's new *Uncle Vanya* is this: Is the pairing of Ian McKellen and Antony Sher as Vanya and Astrov just as exciting as that of Michael Redgrave and Laurence Olivier thirty years ago, or is this merely the best *Uncle Vanya* since then? Either conclusion amounts to high praise, for Chekhov's play receives a major production every few seasons in London, and nearly every major British actor, from Michael Gambon to Michael Bryant to Peter O'Toole to Albert Finney, has undertaken it within fairly recent memory.

I cannot resolve the debate, but there's no denying the excitement at the Cottesloe, which is the National's most intimate house and which is where *Uncle Vanya,* performed at practically arm's length from the surrounding audience, is as hot a ticket as its repertory companion, *Angels in America.* Working with a lively new translation by the dramatist Pam Gems, the director Sean Mathias has taken a direct rather than an innovative approach to Chekhov, choosing to let his company dominate the spare, wintry scenic canvas with performances of an emotional intensity more reminiscent of American acting than British. The close-knit ensemble reflects the production's long gestation at the National Theatre Studio, a subsidized offshoot that allows actors, writers, and directors to experiment on pet projects without deadlines or even a requirement to give public performances.

The achievement is not always seamless. Mr. Sher's Astrov in particular has a tendency to leap out of the frame; his Dustin Hoffmanesque comic energy, which has earned him acclaim in epic plays like *Arturo Ui* and Peter Flannery's *Singer*, comes off as a star's showy self-infatuation rather than the country doctor's idealistic passion. Mr. McKellen, by contrast, subdues his usual bravura star presence, soon to be seen in an American tour of *Richard III*, to inhabit fully the defeated Vanya. Bespectacled and pale and looking not unlike the Chekhov of photographs, he provides a muted, life-size account of a middle-aged man awakening at every hapless turn to the futility of his existence in a stagnant provincial household. His crushed nobility of spirit—reflected in his embittered, inward mutterings and the winces of psychological self-flagellation in his eyes—sometimes recalls the fine-grained performances John Barrymore gave in his less flamboyant roles in films like *Topaze* and *Grand Hotel*.

This *Vanya* is at its most moving in those scenes that pair its title character with Lesley Sharp as Sonya, his niece. A stout, open-faced woman who really looks as if she was built to devote her life to hard, thankless work in the Russian boondocks, the actress often seems to be daughter and mother to Vanya as well as niece. Her self-knowledge is acute, whether she is contemplating her own plainness or paying unconvincing lip service to her doomed romantic designs on Astrov. The uncompromising final tableau, in which Ms. Sharp cradles the sobbing Mr. McKellen while promising him almost by rote the faint future reward of a peaceful afterlife, is a rending portrait of human endurance in the face of hopelessness, bathed by Mr. Mathias in the bleak glow of dying candlelight.

One of the production's other indelible performances, an exceptionally compassionate interpretation of Vanya's nemesis, the bullying old professor Serebryakov, comes from Eric Porter, who found similar depths in Big Daddy (opposite Ian Charleson's Brick) in Howard Davies's fine National Theatre production of *Cat on a Hot Tin Roof* a few years ago. The link between Chekhov and Tennessee Williams is being reinforced at the National this season by Richard Eyre's beautiful revival (on the Lyttelton's proscenium stage) of *The Night of the Iguana*, the 1961 play that was the author's last commercial hit but that is not usually counted among his major achievements.

"What writers influenced me as a young man? Chekhov! As a dramatist? Chekhov!" begins a famous Williams quotation that is reprinted in the National's program for *Iguana*. Set in a sleazy Mexican tourist hotel in 1940, the play charts the survival of two archetypal Williams misfits: a defrocked, sexually reckless priest named Shannon reduced to leading bargain-basement tour groups, and an impoverished New England spinster named Hannah Jelkes who carts around her ninety-seven-year-old grandfather, the world's "oldest living and practicing poet," and subsists by painting tacky portraits of tourists. Shannon and Hannah are thrown together, platonically and briefly, in a literal and figurative jungle where God is an "oblivious majesty," vulgar Bible Belt Americans turn treacherous, and German vacationers are celebrating the Nazi blitzkrieg of London.

Flaccidly structured and stuffed with overripe symbols, *Iguana* has its problems and languors, but with the aid of riveting performances by Alfred Molina and Eileen Atkins in the two key roles, Mr. Eyre has found more touching scenes (and humor) in this second-rank Williams play than many directors find in his masterworks. A long encounter on the veranda in which Shannon and Hannah try to help each other through the night with exchanged confessions is played with such plaintive understatement that one sees the bottom of the characters' souls as clearly as if one were staring through pristine water to the floor of the Caribbean. With a characteristic appreciation for Williams's theatricality, Mr. Eyre punctuates the veranda scene with the spectral, vaguely audible bedroom stumblings and mumblings of Hannah's grandfather (Robin Bailey) as he composes his dying poem.

The young and bearish Mr. Molina, the actor who played Joe Orton's lover, Kenneth Halliwell, in the film *Prick Up Your Ears,* is an ideal Williams protagonist. Dressed in a filthy white linen suit that announces his fragile hold on both his dignity and sanity, his Shannon conveys a voracious, self-destructive appetite for life as well as a hypersensitivity so vulnerable that it amounts to nudity. "Don't break human spirit!" he cries at one point to a tormentor who is threatening to drive him out of the job he must keep. Mr. Molina's ringing plea is pathetic, but when it is rejected, he strikes back at his antagonist with a bite that parallels Williams's own resilience in the face of suffering.

Though Ms. Atkins, unlike Mr. Molina, cannot reproduce a credible American accent, it hardly matters. Her penetrating intelligence, seen in New York last season in her Virginia Woolf monodrama, *A Room of One's Own,* is present here. But so is a spiritual inner calm—conveyed in a hushed delivery of lines like "Nothing human disgusts me unless it's unkind, violent"—that makes Hannah seem as unsentimental and wise as Emily Dickinson, from whom Williams took this play's epigraph.

For all the major British actors who hook up with either the National or the Royal Shakespeare Company to perform the classics, the West

End tradition of starry classic revivals under commercial auspices is still alive. The popular production of Jean Anouilh's *Becket* with Derek Jacobi and Robert Lindsay is ending its run at the Haymarket to be followed shortly by a Trevor Nunn revival of *Heartbreak House* with a dream cast: Vanessa Redgrave (Hesione Hushabye), Felicity Kendal (Ariadne Utterword), Daniel Massey (Hector Hushabye), Oliver Ford Davies (Mazzini Dunn), Joe Melia (the Burglar), and Paul Scofield (Captain Shotover).

Shaw's play, a majestic evocation of an England tottering into the apocalypse of World War I, acknowledges a debt to Chekhov (specifically *The Cherry Orchard*), but Captain Shotover, a crusty old man with two troublesome daughters, also echoes King Lear. Since Paul Scofield's Lear for Peter Brook in the early 1960s remains one of the most electrifying (and formative) experiences I have had in the theater, I could not resist going to the town of Guildford to see an early, inevitably embryonic preview of *Heartbreak House* in its pre-London tour. He is one of those great stage actors whose talent has never really come across on screen, the film version of the Brook *Lear* included.

Lean and baggy-eyed and bearded, Mr. Scofield is remarkably unchanged, still every bit the old monarch. To see him confront the aerial bombardments in the final act of *Heartbreak House* or to play his tender scene with young Ellie Dunn (Imogen Stubbs) is to flash back to his encounters with the storm and with Diana Rigg's Cordelia all those decades ago. And that voice! The dark woodwind rumble in Mr. Scofield's low, not particularly loud reading of Shotover's Act 1 curtain line—"Give me deeper darkness. Money is not made in the light"—is enough in itself to send Shaw's heartbreak house tumbling down. When this actor speaks, the universe seems to shiver.

DEATH AND THE MAIDEN
BROOKS ATKINSON THEATRE, MARCH 18, 1992

In *Death and the Maiden,* the new play at the Brooks Atkinson Theatre, the Chilean writer Ariel Dorfman tells the story of a Latin American woman, Paulina Salas, who is thrown together by chance with a man, Dr. Miranda, whom she believes to be the police-state thug who repeatedly raped and tortured her fifteen years earlier. Paulina ties up and gags Dr. Miranda in her living room, threatens him with a gun, then puts him on "trial" for his presumed crimes, not the least of which was pumping electric current through her body to the accompaniment of the Schubert quartet that gives Mr. Dorfman's play its double-barreled title.

Given this tale—one born of the author's own experiences as a witness to the horrors of the Pinochet dictatorship in Chile—it is no small feat that the director Mike Nichols has managed to transform *Death and the Maiden* into a fey domestic comedy. But what kind of feat, exactly? History should record that Mr. Nichols has given Broadway its first escapist entertainment about political torture. He has also allowed three terrific actors, welcome recruits to the stage, to practice artistic escapism of their own. Glenn Close (Paulina), Gene Hackman (Dr. Miranda), and Richard Dreyfuss (as Paulina's husband, Gerardo) all display their most charming star personae in lieu of acting, as if they were running for public office instead of animating characters locked in a harrowing struggle for survival.

So wide is the gap between the tense, life-and-death tenor of the play's text and the airy, bantering tone of the production that the packed house can only respond (and does) with absolute bewilderment. At the performance I attended, there was a severe coughing epidemic that might signal a public-health crisis were it not for the fact that the symptom was absent at the other plays I've seen this week. As for the laughter, it had a manic sound. The distinguished actors, not to mention the grave events in Mr. Dorfman's script, promise an audience that something of moment will happen onstage. When the drama never comes, theatergoers can hardly be blamed for overresponding to whatever stimulus they can find, even if that consolation amounts to small, bleak jokes incidental to the author's intentions.

Those intentions are not hard to decipher. *Death and the Maiden* is aimed at the jugular and devoid of the magical realism that has distinguished some of Mr. Dorfman's fiction. It's an unpretentious suspense melodrama, as slam-bang in its desired effects as *Wait Until Dark* or *Deathtrap* or even Ms. Close's most successful Hollywood vehicle, *Fatal Attraction.* Set in an isolated beach house in a country that has just overthrown its dictator for a fledgling democratic government, the play is meant to keep the audience guessing until (and even past) its dénouement. Is Dr. Miranda really the torturer who long ago harmed a blindfolded Paulina, or is Paulina simply indulging a paranoid fantasy symptomatic of the psychological damage caused by her ordeal? Does Paulina's husband, a human-rights lawyer, try to stop his wife from taking vengeance because he reveres legal justice, as he says, or does he have some hidden agenda?

Except for the contrived setup that lands Dr. Miranda in Gerardo and Paulina's house in the first place, *Death and the Maiden* is as tautly constructed as a mousetrap. And it's a mousetrap designed to catch the conscience of an international audience at a historic moment when many more nations than Chile are moving from totalitarian terror to fragile freedom. Underneath the questions in Mr. Dorfman's plot are more urgent ones not unlike those raised by Caryl Churchill's recent drama of post-Ceauşescu Romania, *Mad Forest*. If the victims of police-state crimes take the law into their own hands, do they sink to the level of their former oppressors and endanger their nation's new prospects for democracy? Yet if they fail to take that revenge, do they invite the historical amnesia that might allow fascism to take root again someday?

Mr. Dorfman does not patly resolve these conundrums any more than he does his plot. What makes *Death and the Maiden* ingenious is his ability to raise such complex issues within a thriller that is full of action and nearly devoid of preaching. But the play cannot say anything whatsoever if the dramatic vehicle for its ideas—the grueling high-stakes war of wills between Paulina and her captive—remains inert.

In Mr. Nichols's production, nothing seems at stake and no character has an ambiguous second or third dimension. Though all three stars are well cast in principle, they all give similarly superficial performances, ingratiating to a fault. Paulina is such a great role that it is hard to understand how an actress as smart, talented, and ambitious as Ms. Close could dribble it away. While her cheeks sometimes moisten with tears (in the immaculate Norma Shearer manner), and though she lowers her voice in rage and, more often, raises it to convey vaguely neurotic sarcasm, she is too genteel and controlled to suggest that Paulina might be teetering on the edge of madness or, more important, that she might be a true avenging fury, capable of actually using her gun.

Without those intense passions, she can neither move us with her remembrance of her unspeakable suffering nor, at the more primitive, *Jagged Edge* level, keep us guessing about what will happen next. Indeed, there's nothing in Ms. Close's performance here, a few guttural impersonations of her torturer's obscenities aside, that wouldn't serve equally well the temporarily distraught newlywed of *Barefoot in the Park*.

Mr. Hackman, an actor abundantly capable of conveying menace (and most anything else), is a gregarious, good-natured Dr. Miranda who never seems remotely guilty of having been a sadistic Dr. Mengele. In the least important role, Mr. Dreyfuss inherits the evening's laughs by default. When *Death and the Maiden* is stripped of its Costa-Gavras-style suspense, its secondary repartee about Gerardo's sexist treatment of his wife, the most wooden writing in the play, is thrust center stage. Mr. Dreyfuss soon finds himself performing a comic-book version of Torvald in *A Doll's*

House, driving Ms. Close at one slapstick juncture to drop a tray of dishes in a sink.

Although Mr. Nichols's choreography of the action is not dissimilar to that of Lindsay Posner's current and terrifying London production, he makes no effort to replicate its bloodcurdling, locked-room atmosphere. This version, unlike that one, is played with an intermission (oddly inserted one scene into Act 2) and in mostly bright lighting. Only in the play's coda, which is set before a proscenium-high mirror, does the staging achieve a chill, though the use of that mirror, both here and in London, owes a huge debt to Harold Prince's similar evocation of incipient totalitarianism in *Cabaret.*

No doubt Mr. Nichols would argue that his bouncy *Death and the Maiden* is not an incorrect interpretation of the play, just an unorthodox one, in the way that, say, his film version of *Who's Afraid of Virginia Woolf?* offered a funnier though still valid alternative to the Broadway original. But what exactly is the point of his jokey take on a play whose use of the word *death* in its title is anything but ironic? In this tedious trivialization of Ariel Dorfman's work, even the glamorous beach-house set and heavenly Technicolor lighting seem designed, like everything else, for no purpose greater than gazing at stars.

FOUR BABOONS ADORING THE SUN
Vivian Beaumont Theater, March 19, 1992

John Guare's *Six Degrees of Separation* may be best remembered as a postcrash bonfire of the vanities, a savagely funny unmasking of all kinds of Manhattan impostors of the late 1980s. But what made the play moving to me and timeless was its story of one woman's heroic search for authenticity—for love and rebirth—amid all that fraudulence. At evening's end Mr. Guare left us not with satirical laughter but with the image of a sadder but resolute Stockard Channing, in the role of the society wife Ouisa Kittredge, as she yearned to revisit the Sistine Chapel and reach once more toward the hand of God, as she desperately hoped to hold on to the real passion she had briefly tasted in an encounter with a vanished con artist.

Four Baboons Adoring the Sun, Mr. Guare's new play at the Vivian Beaumont and a fair bet to be the most controversial play of the season, puts the same great actress on the same stage in the same rending, do-or-die quest for some transcendent reason to go on living in a universe where there are too many degrees of separation between any two people. But everything else is wildly different, as if a beloved old folk tale had been set down in the middle of a mad dream. The least of the differences is Ms. Channing's new character, Penny McKenzie, a suburban house-wife who has left her husband to marry an old collegiate flame, an arche-ologist named Philip (James Naughton). The other shifts in the landscape are so dramatic that even before the houselights dim the au-dience knows it is being shoved into an alien world.

What greets us upon arrival in Peter Hall's commanding and poetic production is a classical set designed by Tony Walton, a mosaic-flecked disk that oozes smoke from a center stage opening and is surrounded by mysterious detritus redolent of the Bronze Age. When the play starts, the first character to arrive is Eros (Eugene Perry), an Ariel-like sprite who sings his dialogue to melancholy operatic fragments composed by Stephen Edwards. Though Ms. Channing's reassuringly familiar, con-temporary presence emerges soon after in Gap fashions, Mr. Guare re-moves her from the recognizable social circumstances of Manhattan, strips away all but a few jokes, abandons logical narrative, and piles on myths, dreams, and hallucinations, not to mention a quasi-Greek chorus of nine tart-tongued American children.

For the audience, it's a take-it-or-leave-it proposition. One either ac-cepts Mr. Guare's reverie on its own exotic terms from the start or is shut out entirely, with no clearly marked route back in. *Four Baboons* is cer-tain to produce what might be called the *Sunday in the Park with George* effect on any row of spectators: Some will be dozing at the end of its eighty minutes, others will be actively hostile, others will be sobbing.

I can understand all these points of view, but I can speak only from the perspective of someone who was deeply stirred by this play, not only esthetically by the bold risks of Mr. Guare's experiment but also at a cathartic level by the naked power of what he has to say about the risks of life itself. *Four Baboons* by its very definition demands a personal re-action, one way or another. It is not an intellectual work any more than any fable is. Those tempted to enter Mr. Guare's fantastical adventure need not bone up on mythology or opera or the meaning of antiquity. An open mind will help and so will an open heart. He demands that the au-dience, like his characters, leap from what the play calls Universe A, that of well-defended adulthood, to Universe B, the imaginative world of childhood to which one hungers to return.

"I'll die if I don't make a change and have love in my life," goes one of Penny's refrains in *Four Baboons*. The play's premise is prompted by the making of such a change. Penny and Philip ran off with each other—and have now run to Sicily, where they are conducting an archeological dig at a burial site—because they were tired of being the "same old, same old" people, tired of being like everybody else who ever lived off Exit 4 of the Connecticut Turnpike (in Penny's case) or was trapped in the stultifying academic bureaucracy of a large state university (in Philip's). Turned on by each other and their new freedom, the newlyweds bring the offspring of their previous marriages together for the first time in Italy, hoping that their liberated example will save their children from the drugs and alienation that are the lot of American adolescents.

Of course nothing turns out as planned, and some of the events that happen in *Four Baboons* echo those in *Six Degrees*. Brutally articulate children revolt against their parents. Philip and Penny are scandalized by an unorthodox sexual liaison in their household. A starry-eyed teenage boy leaps through the sky in what may be an accident or a suicide attempt or a spiritual if misguided flight to heaven in emulation of Icarus. A teenage girl is left inconsolable as she realizes that her idealistic dreams have been mutilated and she has been left a bitter, ordinary adult before her time.

There are more mystical and apocalyptic events, too—when the earth moves in this play, it really moves—but Mr. Guare's tale can only move in one inexorable direction. "Everything dies," sings Eros. "What's the big surprise?" As the mythological heroes whose tales Penny and Philip force on their children come to horrible endings, so in one way or another must the lives of the mere mortals who follow in their paths. Like *Six Degrees*, which had at least three deaths wrapped within its comic plot, *Four Baboons* embraces grief, then rises above it by offering the hope, however frail, of personal resurrection. Penny, like Ouisa, won't be deterred by tragedy from her conviction that her life might somehow be touched by grace, whether through the touch of a human hand or God.

What is technically impressive about *Four Baboons* is Mr. Guare's ability to work out his themes in spare, incantatory, and sometimes witty dialogue and metaphorical images that all merge in musical harmony by the final moments. He actually does create a modern mythological realm in which Alitalia Airlines, the Stanhope Hotel, and Bellini cocktails can play as large a role as the metamorphoses of ancient legend, in which the cynical realities of present-day divorce can coexist with an innocent faith in primal magic. As a two-sided Kandinsky painting set the esthetic terms of *Six Degrees*, so the titular artwork of this play, a favorite of Penny's and Philip's, dominates its imagery: a mysterious, 4,000-year-old granite sculpture in which four baboons stare into the sun, "their eyes running out of their heads with joy, their eyes burnt out because they've seen their God."

Mr. Hall's work in epic theater, both with classics of the stage and of opera, makes him an inspired choice for this piece, and he and his designers (of sounds and projections along with sets, costumes, and lighting) have given it the spectacular treatment, part Etruscan, part Magritte, that it demands. Mr. Hall has also done an impressive job with the daunting pack of children, led by Angela Goethals, who has the most adult acting assignment, and Wil Horneff, a boy who is asked to be enchanting and actually is.

As the attractive though somewhat limited Philip, Mr. Naughton conveys the sturdy intelligence and charm one expects. But when his character is severely tested by the fates, the actor rises higher, turning the husband's inability to respond and grow ("I hate emotions!" he shouts) into a pathetic, if not tragic, flaw. As for Ms. Channing, she seems to have become Mr. Guare's muse, as inseparable from his art as the love and loss and grief and hope that are his subject. Only those who hate emotions could be untouched by the sight of this woman rising from the ashes of unspeakable suffering to face a blinding new day's sun with eyes ablaze in joy.

≣ *I'm not sure there's anyone else in New York who liked this play— indeed, who didn't hate it. There's been no new Guare play since.*

THE MASTER BUILDER
BELASCO THEATRE, MARCH 20, 1991

Some theater companies take years to develop and refine a distinctive style, but the National Actors Theater has accomplished this feat in a single season. The latest example of its signature approach to the classics can be found in its production of *The Master Builder* at the Belasco Theatre.

The style might be called the esthetic equivalent of the Heimlich maneuver. The director, whoever he may be, assumes that the classic play at his disposal is near death, or at least thought so by the audience, and must be resuscitated by being pounded out by the actors, with waving arms and often at top volume. If the actors stand in place while declaiming (*The Crucible* and *The Master Builder*), you're at a drama. If they are jumping up and down (*A Little Hotel on the Side*), it's comedy tonight.

Though *The Master Builder* is the first of the productions directed by Tony Randall, the company's founder and artistic director—the *Playbill* lists no previous directing credits for him of any kind in New York—he is already a master of this method. The only way you can distinguish his *Master Builder* from Yossi Yzraely's *Crucible* is by the smaller size of the cast.

Ibsen's plays are not that often given major stagings in New York, and though *The Master Builder* received a decent Roundabout Theatre Company reading in 1983, the acclaimed and innovative productions of American directors like Robert Wilson and Mark Lamos and of British directors like Peter Hall and Adrian Noble remain only rumors here. The National Actors Theatre *Master Builder,* a passionless recital performed on dowdy realistic sets, could set the local Ibsen cause back a decade or two. In place of a psychologically tumultuous, at times mythic drama of an artist's self-inflicted decline and fall is one big slab of solid Norwegian wood.

Earle Hyman can be an interesting character actor, but his performance as Ibsen's autobiographical stand-in, Solness, is, like much of the production, beyond the purview of professional drama criticism. His voice, body, and jowls all quivering, he doesn't act the role so much as sing it, often, unaccountably, in falsetto. As Hilde Wangel, the mysterious young woman from the mountains who tempts him to both ecstasy and disaster, the perky Madeleine Potter is miscast, unless one assumes that Solness's erotic tastes run in the direction of the Trapp Family Singers. Among the others, Maryann Plunkett can be applauded for applying her fierce concentration to the small role of the bookkeeper, and Lynn Redgrave can be praised for bringing some genuine feeling (and a hint of a Norwegian tone) to Mrs. Solness, despite being made up to look like Cloris Leachman in Mel Brooks's *Young Frankenstein.*

In this *Master Builder,* when Solness falls from a great height, it is such an anticlimax that he might as well be stumbling from a footstool. Ms. Potter marks Solness's demise by waving her white shawl not once but three times in a manic windmill gesture that, depending on your point of view, is either the apotheosis of the National Actors Theatre style or a desperate plea of SOS.

≡ *Tony Randall certainly meant well, but his ill-conceived National Actors Theatre would lay waste to a wide repertory of classics before finding its identity (and some popular and critical success) with star-driven revivals of conventional Broadway warhorses* (Inherit the Wind, The Gin Game, The Odd Couple, The Sunshine Boys*).

CONVERSATIONS WITH MY FATHER
ROYALE THEATRE, MARCH 30, 1992

I wish I could tell you that he won my heart in that final chapter, but he did not," a successful novelist named Charlie (Tony Shalhoub) says of his aged father in the waning moments of *Conversations with My Father*. That line, at once brutally honest and clinically detached, seems to sum up just what is impressive and what is lacking in Herb Gardner's richly atmospheric new memory play at the Royale Theatre.

In Eddie Ross, the immigrant Canal Street bartender played by Judd Hirsch, Mr. Gardner has created, without apologies, a most disagreeable Jewish patriarch. An angry, remote, and abusive man who always lives "at the top of his voice and the edge of his nerves," Eddie is found yelling at a baby in his first scene and, a few joyous moments aside, rarely stops barking at all comers for two acts (and his thirty years of stage time) to follow. The sour realism of this portrait is not only uncompromising but is also a brave and unexpected feat from a writer whose *I'm Not Rappaport* offered the most adorable of cantankerous Jewish codgers, also played by Mr. Hirsch.

But if Eddie is too unlovable to win either his son's heart or an audience's by the final chapter, can he arouse any emotion deeper than irritation, whether pity or sorrow or rage? I wish I could tell you that he did, but *Conversations with My Father* may be honest to a fault. Mr. Gardner is so scrupulous about refusing to sentimentalize his title character that he hardly dramatizes him, leaving Eddie a distant figure changed by little but age from start to finish. No doubt that is how this stubborn father was in life, but after putting up with him all night, one hungers for some transcendent insight or conflict or catharsis that might strip him bare and deliver a knockout emotional punch. It says volumes about the evening's shortfall that Mr. Hirsch's two most wrenching moments find him with his back to the audience.

Mr. Gardner's play is far more satisfying in other departments, however incidental they sometimes seem to the father-son axis that is ostensibly its focus. Evocatively staged and superbly acted by a large cast, *Conversations with My Father* has some of its author's most flavorful writing. In telling the story of Eddie, Mr. Gardner also wishes to tell the saga of a first generation of American Jews who came of age in the Depression and assimilated at a high price during and after World War II. Although that history is dispiriting, the author's passionate affection for the Old World that Eddie wishes to disown gives the play a lot of warmth and more than a few piquant laughs.

Designed by Tony Walton with a poetic verve worthy of *The Iceman Cometh*, Eddie's saloon is an airless den of dark wood whose only consistent source of light is a brightly colored Wurlitzer jukebox. The first music we hear is a holdover from the old country, and as the play is a struggle between father and son, so it also proves to be a struggle between two cultures, as typified by the clashing songs on the jukebox. Eddie is so eager to melt into the melting pot and make big bucks that he gives his bar an "early American" decor, legally changes his family's name and, when all else fails, periodically renames the bar, too, in feeble emulation of the sophisticated uptown clubs he reads about in Walter Winchell's column. Yet the haunting melody of his old identity is not so easily silenced.

That melody prevails in the actual music and prayers of the evening and in Mr. Gardner's re-creation of a vanished Yiddish universe. In a delightful early speech, delivered by Mr. Shalhoub with priceless inflections and timing, sterile American vernacular is compared to Yiddish and found terribly wanting. For further enlightenment, the playwright sends on a little-employed Second Avenue actor named Zaretsky, "a dying man with a dead language and no place to go," who boards with Eddie and his family. In the wry, bantam figure of David Margulies, Zaretsky is a magical repository of his artistic and ethnic heritage, especially in a transporting scene in which he performs excerpts from all his shows, from *Hamlet* to *The Dybbuk,* while pulling props from a carpetbag. But he also lugs around a darker history. The old actor never stops reminding Eddie of the past pogroms and the gradually emerging Holocaust that the Americanized bartender would rather ignore.

Like the family relationships in this play, Eddie's battle with Zaretsky (and the themes it encapsulates) never comes to a resolution. A related and windy Act 1 subplot, in which Eddie and his older son, an aspiring pugilist named Joey, both must do battle against anti-Semitic toughs in their own neighborhood, also disappears abruptly. Depending on how you look at it, *Conversations* is either an impressionistic tapestry of flashbacks or an unfinished work that seems to have been hacked up and stitched together arbitrarily in a clumsy editing process. Too many major characters leave without saying good-bye. Too many supporting characters, starting with the various barflies, never amount to more than running gentile gags. Most grievously shortchanged is Eddie's blissfully unassimilated wife, Gusta, who is enlivened more by the actress Gordana Rashovich's radiant humor and frantic eyes than by anything in the text.

The play is directed by Daniel Sullivan with as much skill as he brought to New York's other current, if much different, play about an immigrant Jewish father at war with his heirs, *The Substance of Fire.* This production boasts two exceptional performances by children: Jason Biggs, who as the smart older brother recalls the precocious boy played by Barry Gordon in Mr. Gardner's *A Thousand Clowns,* and David Krumholtz, as the childhood incarnation of Mr. Shalhoub's Charlie. What even a director as deft as Mr. Sullivan cannot disguise are the play's strange dramatic omissions. Although there is a big and effective showdown between Mr. Hirsch and young Mr. Krumholtz, the final confrontation between the father and the grown Charlie proves to be one of the several anticlimaxes that make *Conversations* seem to drift off rather than arrive at a final curtain.

Whether this is the playwright's intention or a failure to come fully to terms with his characters is a question only he can answer. Either way, he has deprived Mr. Hirsch and Mr. Shalhoub of the payoff scene, that exorcism of personal dybbuks, that Arthur Miller or Neil Simon would have given them in their equivalent family dramas.

The play's many vignettes offer their own opportunities, all perfectly handled by the stars. Even in his few patches of benevolence, the fiercely energetic Mr. Hirsch acts with complete integrity here, never sugarcoating Eddie's bleak view of life as a constant boxing match in which each opponent, within or outside his family, is treated with derision. Mr. Shalhoub, who is onstage continuously, either narrating or participating in every flashback, conveys wisdom, warmth, and humor whether he is looking back with embarrassment at his awkward, horny adolescence or trying as an adult to have one conversation with his father that is not one-sided. It is hard to imagine how Mr. Gardner, or any other playwright, could be blessed with a better stand-in than this actor, who keeps you trusting, admiring, and enjoying the storyteller even when you spot the holes in his tale.

'TIS PITY SHE'S A WHORE
PUBLIC THEATER, APRIL 6, 1992

If you were trying to assemble the most invigorating production of a classic to be seen in New York City this season, would you mix the following elements?

An infrequently produced Jacobean revenge tragedy that ends with its hero ripping out the heroine's heart and carrying it aloft on a skewer.

("Enter Giovanni with a heart upon his dagger," reads the Grand Guignol stage direction.) A pair of young lead actors better known for their Hollywood roles in lubricious movies like *The Doors* and *Basic Instinct* than for their experience in speaking verse. A severely intellectual director whose previous encounters with another seventeenth-century author, Shakespeare, have been her least successful projects. A set designer, most recently of the Metropolitan Opera's *The Ghosts of Versailles,* who regards a classical text as an occasion for practicing the modern arts of deconstruction and collage.

No, the pieces of this jigsaw puzzle do not remotely begin to connect. But one of the great things about the theater is that logic does not necessarily have anything to do with how artistic collaborations play out on stage. As directed by JoAnne Akalaitis, acted by Val Kilmer and Jeanne Tripplehorn, and designed by John Conklin, *'Tis Pity She's a Whore* offers audiences at the Public Theater a fresh, contemporary encounter with a startling play written by John Ford in the 1630s. This is one of those evenings when you leave the theater convinced that the director must have rewritten the text, for how could a work with language so frank and nasty and sexual politics so sophisticated have been written almost four centuries ago? Yet Ms. Akalaitis has preserved Ford's words with an integrity one rarely finds at the New York Shakespeare Festival even as she weds those words to her own deeply personal vision of its author's themes.

For this director, *'Tis Pity She's a Whore* begins with its famously incestuous love affair between Giovanni and his sister, Annabella—a hot couple indeed in the form of Mr. Kilmer and Ms. Tripplehorn—but hardly ends there. Retaining the original setting, Parma, while shifting the time frame to the 1930s of Mussolini, Ms. Akalaitis at first presents Ford's play as many do, as a celebration of an outlaw erotic obsession that seems almost pure and idealistic next to the decadent society and corrupt religious establishment that are scandalized by it. What this production does not forget, however, is that in the end it is Giovanni, not society, who butchers Annabella. In Mr. Kilmer's impressively measured performance, the hero stealthily grows from a coltish Romeo into a Nietzschean megalomaniac, and he is not exempted from Ms. Akalaitis's withering indictment of a world in which most men treat most women as whores.

The director's slant on Giovanni is certainly supported by Ford, who shows the young man belittling Annabella's maidenhead as a "pretty toy" immediately after their first tryst. That this *'Tis Pity* billows into dreamy theater rather than settling into earthbound polemic can be attributed to the imaginative depth of the staging. The transposition of Ford's Parma to the 1930s amounts to much more than merely the literal-minded deployment of Brown Shirts and the interjected salutes to Il Duce. The director instead situates *'Tis Pity* in the hallucinatory 1930s of surrealistic art, a state of mind as much as a fascist state.

As stunningly visualized by Mr. Conklin and the lighting designer, Mimi Jordan Sherin, this Parma merges the eerily deserted piazzas of a Giorgio de Chirico canvas with the lunar dreamscapes of Yves Tanguy. As if to prefigure Annabella's eventual disembowelment, images of female body parts from Salvador Dalí and Man Ray proliferate after intermission. The point is not to offer a discourse on art history, but to do what the surrealists themselves did and bring a civilization's subconscious, forbidden emotions, including its sadistic sexual impulses, to the surface. The scheme even extends to the high-style Italian furnishings, among them twine-covered chairs that seem to be in bondage, and to Gabriel Berry's spectacular costumes, which put the men in oppressive evening clothes and turn the women into Schiaparelli-era fashion victims.

Ms. Akalaitis then adds ominous music (by Jan A. P. Kaczmarek) and sound design (by John Gromoda) worthy of Bertolucci and Visconti films, and fills in the canvas's intimate details. In the secretly pregnant Annabella's wedding of convenience to the proper nobleman Soranzo, the director orchestrates the actors' movements and expressions into an involuntary revelation of their hidden, coarse hungers. These grotesque human tableaux of stylized spasms and malevolent whispering, suggestive of Richard Foreman's Ontological-Hysteric theater pieces, raise the play's temperature to a fever pitch even as they imitate futurism, the aggressive school of art that actually formed a brief alliance with Mussolini's brutal school of fascism. The dramatic payoff arrives soon after when Soranzo, played with a terrifying mixture of aristocratic gentility and uncontrollable rage by Jared Harris, punishes Ms. Tripplehorn for cuckolding him by repeatedly slamming her against a blood-red wall.

Ms. Akalaitis has been energized by *'Tis Pity* in a way she was not by, say, the boys' universe of *Henry IV*. That may be because this play's esthetics anticipate the Jean Genet works she has directed around the country and because its content overlaps the Franz Xaver Kroetz plays about dehumanized women (*Request Concert* and *Through the Leaves*) that she staged so vividly in New York. This is not to say that her failings as a director have vanished. Once again Ms. Akalaitis, who has no apparent sense of humor, tries to finesse a classic's comic interludes by giving the clowns leaden burlesque shtick that prompts winces, not laughs. Her tin ear for comedy has also led her astray in setting a tone for the catalytic role of the servant Vasques, an Iago-like villain, who is more flip than sinister in Erick Avari's performance.

Nor can Ms. Akalaitis resist hitting her ideological points with a sledgehammer near evening's end, at which point Man Ray is left behind for a jolting descent into the misogynistic pornography of snuff films. But these lapses cannot destroy the artistry of the feminist statement that has come before. One hallmark of this production is that the men, a few irredeemable creeps excepted, are at times allowed to be appealing and human while the abused women, including those played by Ellen McElduff (Hippolita) and Deirdre O'Connell (Putana), are too self-possessed to devolve into abject victims. Even when Annabella is driven to paroxysms of sobbing by the horrors that befall her, Ms. Tripplehorn shows us a strong young woman with a fiery will rather than a trampled, helpless flower. True to its heroine, Ms. Akalaitis's *'Tis Pity She's a Whore* insists on insinuating its way into our minds rather than emulating its hero by lunging at our hearts.

FIVE GUYS NAMED MOE
EUGENE O'NEILL THEATRE, APRIL 9, 1992

Some Broadway musicals want to make you think. Some want to move you to tears. Some want to make you laugh. Some want to give you pure, mindless fun.

Five Guys Named Moe, the London hit that opened at the Eugene O'Neill Theatre last night, wants to sell you a drink.

This peculiar revue, ostensibly a celebration of songs made famous by the 1940s alto saxophone player and band leader Louis Jordan, has a specially designed restaurant called Moe's adjoining its auditorium, where you can eat, drink, and be merry before, during, or after the show—most notably during an extended intermission, when several extra bars are set up for your pleasure. If the management could only deliver alcohol intravenously, *Five Guys Named Moe* might actually convince its patrons that the joint is jumping at those moments when there is no option other than to watch the entertainment onstage.

That entertainment is unlikely to be confused by many New York audiences with this production's obvious prototypes, *Ain't Misbehavin'* and *One Mo' Time,* with which it shares its cast size, nostalgic musical ambitions, and intended saloon ambiance. *Five Guys* is instead a British tourist's view of a patch of black American pop music history when Jordan (1908–1975) and his Tympany Five served as a crossover from post–World War II jump and boogie to mid-1950s rhythm and blues with hits like "Choo, Choo Ch'boogie," "Caldonia," and "Saturday Night Fish Fry." Given that the show's creators are both American-born black men—Clarke Peters (book) and Charles Augins (direction and choreography)—the evening's synthetic tone is most surprising.

Perhaps the problem is that Mr. Peters and Mr. Augins have spent too much time in London (most of their careers, according to the *Playbill*). Or perhaps they have inflated or mutilated innocent original intentions in recruiting a new cast and restaging this piece for Broadway. I cannot say, since I did not see the London edition, which began at a theater half the size of the O'Neill before moving to the West End. Whatever the explanation, something has gone seriously, discomfortingly wrong.

The six men in the Broadway cast have decent voices. But they are asked to smile incessantly, and their musical delivery is so monotonously cheery (except in ballads, where completely expressionless crooning reigns) that their stage personalities are distinguishable only by such character names as Big Moe, Little Moe, and Four-Eyed Moe. This was hardly the case at a show like *Ain't Misbehavin'*, where each voice was an instantly recognizable, idiosyncratic original. In *Five Guys,* the goal seems to be a lowest-common-denominator, easy-listening, emotion-free version of the songs, and that impression is heightened by an onstage band that even Doc Severinsen might find lacking in funk.

Five Guys is closer to Shaftesbury Avenue than Fifty-second Street in other ways as well. The set, by Tim Goodchild, is a candied affair that looks like a Claymation version of a Harlem street scene. The modest choreography rips off the broad gestures of a jazz style—raised arms, shaking shoulders, finger snapping—without delivering much actual dancing. The humor is deeply British, male division: If the men aren't sashaying about in drag, they are dressing up in chicken feathers for "Ain't Nobody Here but Us Chickens." Further sexist humor and racial stereotyping comes from the book, a shameless bit of padding about the travails of a present-day lovesick swain (Jerry Dixon, with his belt unbuckled) whose blues are chased away by the five Moes once they burst out of his radio in a puff of smoke.

Stage smoke is a mainstay of British musicals, and so is the evening's dependence on a Disneyland theatrical gimmick and party-or-die audience participation. Moe's restaurant, which looks more like a chain franchise in a mall than an urban jazz club Louis Jordan might recognize, serves the same purpose for *Five Guys* as the feline junkyard of *Cats* and the roller-skating rink of *Starlight Express*. And as with *Cats*, the audience is invited onstage just before this show's intermission, in this case to participate in a mass conga line prompted by the incessant calypso "Push Ka Pi Shi Pie."

In fairness, I must report that many people, conspicuously including the former *Miss Saigon* star Jonathan Pryce, enthusiastically joined the conga line at the press performance I attended. I am sure, though I cannot prove it, that some participants in this spontaneous demonstration were not past or present employees of the *Five Guys Named Moe* producer, Cameron Mackintosh.

As the conga line heats up, one member of the cast yells out "Don't forget your pocketbooks!"—surely the most heartfelt dialogue of the evening. That's the cue for the conga line to turn toward the bar, where those who empty their pocketbooks will be rewarded with the good news that they can take their drinks back to their seats.

Bottoms up!

≡ *Although I'd never heard from Jonathan Pryce on all the other occasions I'd written about him—including the* Miss Saigon *flap—he faxed me a handwritten letter on this occasion to say that he was not at the show because he was employed by Cameron Mackintosh but as a regular ticket buyer. He was simply expressing his "genuine enthusiasm for fellow performers in a great show."*

A STREETCAR NAMED DESIRE
Ethel Barrymore Theatre, April 13, 1992

Depending on your feelings about *Long Day's Journey into Night, A Streetcar Named Desire* is either the greatest or second-greatest play ever written by an American. But actors have to be half-mad to star in Tennessee Williams's drama on Broadway, where the glare is unforgiving and the ghosts of Elia Kazan's original 1947 production, as magnified by the director's classic 1951 film version, are fierce. Stacked against Marlon Brando, the first Stanley Kowalski, and Jessica Tandy and Vivien Leigh, the stage and screen originators of Blanche DuBois, who can win?

The exciting news from the Ethel Barrymore Theatre, where Gregory Mosher's new Broadway staging of *Streetcar* arrived last night, is that Alec Baldwin has won. His Stanley is the first I've seen that doesn't leave one longing for Mr. Brando, even as his performance inevitably overlaps his predecessor's. Mr. Baldwin is simply fresh, dynamic, and true to his part as written and lets the echoes fall where they may. While his Stanley does not in the end ignite this play's explosive power, that limitation seems imposed not by his talent but by the production surrounding him and, especially, by his unequal partner in unhinged desire, Jessica Lange's Blanche DuBois.

Unsurprisingly, Mr. Baldwin imbues Stanley with an animalistic sexual energy that sends waves through the house every time he appears onstage. The audience responds with edgy delight from when he first removes his shirt and unself-consciously uses it to wipe the New Orleans sweat from his armpits and torso. Yet the actor's more important achievement is to bring a full palette to a man who is less than a hero but more than a brute. Cruel as Mr. Baldwin's Stanley is, and must be, he comes across as an ingenuous, almost-innocent working stiff until Blanche provokes him to move in for the kill. His Stanley is funny in a postadolescent, bowling buddy way as late as the rape scene, when he fondly emulates a cousin who was a "human bottle-opener." Even the famous interlude in which he screams for his wife, Stella (Amy Madigan), becomes pitiful as well as harrowing when Mr. Baldwin, a fallen, baffled beast, deposits himself in a sobbing heap at the bottom of a tenement's towering stairs.

Not the least of the actor's achievements is to remind us why Williams's play is so much more than the sum of its story of Stanley's battle with the sister-in-law who invades his and Stella's shabby French Quarter flat. "I am one hundred percent American, born and raised in the greatest country on earth," Stanley rightly bellows at one point, after Blanche has taunted him one time too many for being a "Polack." He fills the play with the America of big-shouldered urban industrialism, of can-do pragmatism, of brute strength and vulgar humors: the swaggering America that believes, as Stanley paraphrases Huey Long, that "every man is a king." Mr. Baldwin makes it easy to see how Blanche and the ambivalent, self-destructive author for whom she is a surrogate could find this simian, menacing man mesmerizing even as he embodies the very forces on a "dark march" to destroy them and their romantic old America of decaying plantations, kind strangers, and "tenderer feelings."

That destruction, which is the inexorable tragedy of *Streetcar*, remains untapped here because Ms. Lange's Blanche leaves the play pretty much as she enters it: as a weepy, uncertain yet resourceful woman who has endured some hard knocks rather than suffered a complete meltdown into madness. A terrific film actress who deserves credit for courageously making her Broadway debut in the most demanding of roles, Ms. Lange can easily be faulted for her lack of stage technique, including a voice that is not always audible and never sounds like that of a lapsed Mississippi belle. But she works harder and more intelligently than all three movie stars put together across the street in *Death and the Maiden,* and the real problem with her Blanche is less a matter of deficient stage experience than of emotional timidity.

"I don't want realism, I want magic!" goes one of Blanche's signature lines, but Ms. Lange insists on providing realism. She's not a moth facing disintegration as she flies into the flame but a spaced out, softer-spoken Frances Farmer in her cups. The diaphanous web of artifice that surrounds this heroine, the gauzy lies and fantasies that cloak her as surely as her paper Chinese lantern disguises her room's naked lightbulb, never materializes.

Without them, there are no layers of personality for Mr. Baldwin's Stanley to rip through and no chance for the audience to be shattered by the drama of a woman being stripped of illusion after illusion until there is nothing left but the faint, bruised memory of an existence torn between the poles of gentility and desire. In Ms. Lange's resilient characterization, which siphons off much of Blanche's fragility and sorrow into an omnipresent and much-twisted handkerchief, the heroine's wry English teacher's humor survives but the traumatic soliloquies, from the account of her husband's suicide to her late confession of promiscuity, seem thought-out rather than felt.

Mr. Mosher, an unerring director of David Mamet's plays, does not seem to be at his best directing women, in *Streetcar* anyway. Ms. Madigan, whose stage work has generally been as accomplished as her screen appearances, captures Stella's Southern gregariousness but not the erotic exuberance and divided loyalties of a young, pregnant wife caught between her husband and her sister.

As Mitch, the stolid suitor Blanche sees as a protector, Timothy Carhart still seems to be playing the coarse redneck of *Thelma and Louise.* He is physically wrong for the role and anachronistic in tone and appearance.

What Mr. Mosher does achieve in his production is an impressive display of a director's stagecraft. Except for the placement of intermission, this *Streetcar* is meticulous in its efforts to conform to the well-documented Kazan original, which played the same stage almost forty-five years ago. Ben Edwards's brooding and decaying indoor-outdoor set, Kevin Rigdon's poetic lighting, the floating fragments of music, and even the questionable dropping of the curtain at the end of each scene all respect tradition, to the cautious point of treating *Streetcar* as a museum piece.

While this approach does not permit many surprises, it does allow an audience to appreciate the baroque architecture and verdant language of a play that never ceases to fascinate, even in readings far inferior to this one. When the electric Mr. Baldwin is onstage, you can, for better and worse, imagine the bold new *Streetcar* that has been allowed to slip away.

GUYS AND DOLLS
MARTIN BECK THEATRE, APRIL 15, 1992

If you have ever searched Times Square to find that vanished Broad-way of lovable gangsters, wisecracking dolls, and neon-splashed dawns, you must not miss the *Guys and Dolls* that roared into the old neighborhood last night. As directed with a great eye and a big heart by Jerry Zaks and performed by a thrilling young company that even boasts, in Faith Prince, the rare sighting of a brand-new musical-comedy star, this is an enchanting rebirth of the show that defines Broadway dazzle.

It's hard to know which genius, and I do mean genius, to celebrate first while cheering the entertainment at the Martin Beck. Do we speak of Damon Runyon, who created the characters of *Guys and Dolls* in his stories and with them a whole new American language? Or of Frank Loesser, who in 1950 translated Runyon into songs with melodies by turns brash and melting and lyrics that are legend? This being the the-ater department, please forgive my tilt toward Loesser, whose musical setting of phrases like "I got the horse right here" and "a person could develop a cold" and "the oldest established permanent floating crap game in New York" are as much a part of our landscape as the Chrysler Building and Radio City Music Hall.

The thing to remember about Runyon is that he was born in Kansas and didn't reach Manhattan until he was twenty-six. His love for his adopted town is the helplessly romantic ardor of a pilgrim who finally found his Mecca. That romance is built into the text of *Guys and Dolls,* in which the hoods and chorus girls engage in no violence, never men-tion sex, and speak in an exaggeratedly polite argot that is as courtly as dese-and-dose vernacular can be.

Runyon's idyllic spirit informs every gesture in this production. Mr. Zaks, the choreographer Christopher Chadman, and an extraordinary design team led by Tony Walton give the audience a fantasy Broadway that, if it ever existed, is now as defunct as such *Guys and Dolls* land-marks as Klein's, Rogers Peet, and the Roxy. Yet it is the place we dream about whenever we think of Runyon and Loesser or anyone else who painted New York as a nocturnal paradise where ideas and emotions are spelled out sky-high on blinking signs and, to quote another lyric, "the street lamp light fills the gutter with gold."

Mr. Zaks, whose achievements include most relevantly the Lincoln Center revivals of *Anything Goes* and *The Front Page,* stages the book of *Guys and Dolls* for both its comedy and its emotions. That book was written by Abe Burrows from an abandoned first draft by the screenwriter Jo Swerling, and its solid construction reflects the influence of the original production's director, George S. Kaufman. But funny and fast-paced as the dialogue is, the show seems about more than Nathan Detroit's farcical route to a crap game and the calculating efforts of Sky Masterson to win a bet by bamboozling the puritanical Sarah Brown, of the Save-a-Soul Mission, into a dinner date in Cuba. This company turns up the temperature just enough to induce goose bumps in the guy-and-doll encounters of *Guys and Dolls.*

Peter Gallagher, who made an impression in one Broadway musical (the short-lived *A Doll's Life*) before moving on to heavier dramatic duties, is a heaven-sent Sky Masterson with brooding good looks, a voice that always remains both in mellow key and in gritty character, and a dark, commanding presence that is up to the high theatrical stakes of "Luck Be a Lady." Mr. Gallagher also has a shy smile that slowly breaks through his tough façade much as the Havana moon does through the clouds behind him. When he clasps the hands of his Sarah, Josie de Guzman, to his chest while she sings her half of "I've Never Been in Love Before," you feel the sweet infatuation typical of couples in Mr. Zaks's productions and you understand that the Loesser who wrote this ballad is indeed the same man who wrote "My Heart Is So Full of You" for *The Most Happy Fella.* Ms. de Guzman, whose refreshing mission doll is bemusedly prim rather than a schoolmarm, makes a lovely partner to Mr. Gallagher, with a voice that peals joyously as well as tipsily in "If I Were a Bell."

The evening's biggest laughs, of course, belong to Ms. Prince's Miss Adelaide, the Hot Box dancer and perennial fiancée who stops the show with her sneeze-laden lament in Act 1, then brings down the house in Act 2 with "Take Back Your Mink," surely the only striptease ever written as one long nasal kvetch. Ms. Prince, the only bright spot in the late *Nick and Nora,* here crosses into another dimension as she punctuates "A Bushel and a Peck" with Marilyn Monroe squeaks, roars a lifetime of frustration into the phrase "then they get off at Saratoga, for the fourteenth time" and turns the word "subsequently" (as in "Marry the man today and train him subsequently") into a one-word playlet that makes happily ever after sound a bit like boot camp.

With her big features, piled blond hair, and prematurely matronly sexuality, this wholly assured actress echoes Judy Holliday as much as she does her famous predecessor as Adelaide, Vivian Blaine. The combination, though, is a bracing original. As her eternal intended, that supremely gifted actor Nathan Lane does not remotely echo the first Nathan Detroit, Sam Levene, for whose New York Jewish cadences the role was written. Mr. Lane is more like a young Jackie Gleason and usually funny in his own right, though expressions like "all right, already" and "so nu?" do not fall trippingly from his tongue. But once he and Ms. Prince loudly lock vocal horns during "Sue Me," chances are you will forgive him anything.

In all his casting, Mr. Zaks seems to have followed the producer Cy Feuer's 1950 dictum of seeking "people with bumps." There are some classic gangster mugs on the mugs in this company, including those of J. K. Simmons (as Benny Southstreet), Ernie Sabella (Harry the Horse), and Herschel Sparber (the villain, Big Jule). Walter Bobbie nicely breaks the chubby mold established by Stubby Kaye in the part of Nicely-Nicely Johnson (the character is thin in Runyon) and leads an infectious "Sit Down, You're Rockin' the Boat" that is choreographed to a claustrophobic frenzy by Mr. Chadman, who has such spectacular dancers as Scott Wise and Gary Chryst stashed in his chorus.

Mr. Chadman's other dance routines, including the energizing "Crapshooters' Dance" led by Mr. Wise in the depths of a sewer, are in the spirit of Michael Kidd's wonderful originals (as re-created in the Sam Goldwyn film) but are not imprisoned by them. The same is true of the orchestrations, which preserve all the indelible passages of the Ted Royal–George Bassman originals but are helpfully amended by contributions from Michael Starobin and Michael Gibson.

The production's highly stylized design is in a class apart. William Ivey Long's boldly striped and extravagantly iridescent costumes pay an acknowledged debt to those first created by Alvin Colt and Irene Sharaff for Broadway and Hollywood, much as Mr. Walton's sets take a recognizable bow to Jo Mielziner and Oliver Smith, who respectively designed the original settings for stage and screen. The brilliant lighting, which offers a rainbow of hues for all times of day, is by Paul Gallo, who both here and in *Crazy for You* is setting a high standard for his art that would have been unimaginable, and technologically unattainable, in the days of Loesser or the Gershwins.

But Mr. Walton's achievement here goes beyond his nostalgic evocation of 1950s musicals, with his pointed use of the painted drops that dominated Broadway design mechanics of that time. In his *Guys and Dolls,* a black-and-white front curtain of an urban scene reminiscent of a Reginald Marsh drawing can pull up to reveal the same scene, now painted on a backdrop, that remakes New York in deeply saturated colors from the fantastic spectrums of Matisse and Dufy. A vintage pay phone can be splashed in sea green, as if rising up from an audience's buried collective fantasy of a distant past, and stacks of newspapers thrown on a Times Square pavement at daybreak can form a lonely composition worthy of Edward Hopper's New York.

Everything about Mr. Walton's design, like nearly everything about this production, demands that the audience look at *Guys and Dolls* again and see it fresh. The cherished Runyonland of memory is not altered, just felt and dreamt anew by intoxicated theater artists. No doubt another Broadway generation will one day find a different, equally exciting way to reimagine this classic. But in our lifetime? Don't bet on it.

METRO

MINSKOFF THEATRE, APRIL 17, 1992

What's the Polish word for fiasco? Whatever it is, I'm not sure even it is adequate to describe the unique experience that is *Metro,* the hit Warsaw musical that arrived on Broadway last night.

Here is a show that wants nothing more than to imitate *A Chorus Line,* and where is it playing? Not just in New York City, but at the cavernous Minskoff, right across Shubert Alley from the theater where the original *Chorus Line* ran for only about fifteen years! It's one thing to carry coals to Newcastle, but a whole coal mine?

Purportedly costing $5 million, this show is *A Chorus Line* as it might have been produced by the Festrunk brothers, those wild and crazy Eastern European swingers that Dan Aykroyd and Steve Martin used to play on *Saturday Night Live.* Gloomy and jerky, *Metro* often looks as if it is taking its cues from a faded tenth-generation bootleg videocassette of the film version of its Broadway prototype, with a reel of *Hair* thrown in by mistake. The score, by Janusz Stoklosa, mixes fragments of ersatz Hamlisch with heavily miked Europop, though the music, too, sounds muted and distorted, as if in imitation of West European radio stations in the days when their signals still battled Soviet jamming on their way East. Should *Metro* be indicative of how our mass-cultural debris is filtering into the new Europe, America has a lot more to answer for than just Euro Disneyland.

The show's book, as translated into less-than-colloquial English, has to do with several dozen ragtag young street performers variously dressed in torn jeans and tutus who audition for an autocratic director assembling a new musical. When they fail to get jobs, they stage a rival show in the subway, and it proves so successful that capitalists start throwing money at them. "I think things were easier under the Communists," says one of the characters who are torn between pure artistic principles and the Faustian prospect of selling out to showbiz commerce. Given *Metro* itself, the resolution of this moral drama is never in doubt.

The evening has a little bit of everything, including break dancing, a love story, gymnastics, laser-light displays, a tap routine, and, for a socko finish, a suicide. The spare black set is dominated by a large post-constructivist staircase that rotates on a turntable and by subway signs that spell out the alluring word *Exit* in a wide variety of languages. Periodically the cast pushes forward en masse and at the edge of the stage vehemently delivers a song that is the *Metro* answer to "Let the Sun Shine In." Though lyrics like "We are the children!" and "We are the people!" are repeatedly punctuated by loud cries of "Freedom!" the number does not significantly alter the audience's impression that it has landed in jail.

As Janis Joplin once sang, freedom's just another word for nothing left to lose. You have to feel sorry for the kids in *Metro,* who work extremely hard, singing and dancing with unflagging energy in pursuit of starry-eyed dreams. If only New York City had a heart, someone might treat them to a steak dinner and maybe even tickets to a Broadway show.

≡ *The doomed cast members of* Metro, *in the hands of some savvy show-biz exploiters, protested my review by bringing a pile of steaks from Sardi's to the lobby of the* Times *as local TV-news cameras paid eyewitness. This didn't save the universally panned show but the* Times's *security guards thanked me for weeks for the meat.*

JELLY'S LAST JAM
VIRGINIA THEATRE, APRIL 27, 1992

On the short list of people who have so much talent they hardly know what to do with it all, count Gregory Hines, the star, and George C. Wolfe, the author and director of the new Broadway musical *Jelly's Last Jam.*

Mr. Hines's brilliance is no secret. Few, if any, tap dancers in this world can match him for elegance, speed, grace, and musicianship, and, as if that weren't enough, he also happens to be a silken jazz crooner, supple in voice and plaintive in emotions. In the role of Jelly Roll Morton, Mr. Hines gets to display these gifts to the fullest, not to mention his relatively unsung prowess as an actor. Even when the band is taking a break, every note he hits rings true.

As for Mr. Wolfe, a visionary talent who is making his Broadway debut, he has given *Jelly's Last Jam* ambitions beyond the imagination of most Broadway musicals, many of the street's current hits included. The show at the Virginia Theatre is not merely an impressionistic biography of the man who helped ignite the twentieth-century jazz revolution, but it is also a sophisticated attempt to tell the story of the birth of jazz in general and, through that story, the edgy drama of being black in the tumultuous modern America that percolated to jazz's beat. And that's not all: *Jelly's Last Jam,* a show in part about what it means to be African American, is itself an attempt to remake the Broadway musical in a mythic, African American image. Mr. Wolfe wants nothing less than to do for popular theater what Morton and his peers once did for pop music.

Is the effort a complete success? No. But after watching the sizzling first act of *Jelly's Last Jam,* at once rollicking and excessive, roof-raising and overstuffed, you fly into intermission, high on the sensation that something new and exciting is happening, whatever the wrong turns along the way. The briefer Act 2 is another, deflating story, but one that should not be permitted to deface the memory of the adventurous Act 1.

That adventure begins the moment Mr. Hines makes an unorthodox star entrance that is the first of the show's many breaches of Broadway tradition. Elevated into view on a platform at the edge of the darkened, empty stage, Mr. Hines arrives without fanfare. His back is to the audience, his posture crestfallen. When he finally turns to look at us, he is unsmiling, mute, and shuddering. His baggy eyes are wide with the fright of someone who has just seen a ghost.

As it happens, the ghost he has seen is his own. *Jelly's Last Jam* takes place on the eve of its title character's death. It is conceived as a Judgment Day inquisition into the meaning of a life that began in turn-of-the-century New Orleans, where Ferdinand Le Menthe Morton was born into light-skinned Creole gentility, and is about to end in the "colored wing" of the Los Angeles hospital where he died, destitute and forgotten, in 1941. The elastic setting for this trial is "a lowdown club somewhere's 'tween Heaven 'n' Hell," and its chief jurist is a mysterious, raffish agent of the supernatural, Chimney Man (a majestic Keith David), who accuses Jelly of denying the black heritage that gave his music its syncopation and its pain.

While this conceit sounds heavy, the execution is often liberating. Mr. Wolfe brings on a high-voltage company of singers and dancers and a series of musical numbers in which biographical flashbacks, daring theatrical stylization, boisterous entertainment, and tragic inferences all mesh in repeated crescendos. The songs have been ingeniously crafted, mostly from Morton's own compositions, by the arranger and composer, Luther Henderson, and the lyricist, Susan Birkenhead, who have tailored this instrumental music to meet the demands of the theater and of singers without sacrificing its integrity.

In one remarkable sequence that seems to be Mr. Wolfe's pointed response to the vendors' scene in *Porgy and Bess,* the young Jelly, played by that exuberant dancer Savion Glover, leaves behind his straitlaced Creole upbringing to assimilate the authentic indigenous music of a diverse army of New Orleans street singers. This leads to a showstopping tap challenge between Mr. Glover and Mr. Hines—in which their heads, wrists, and elbows are choreographed (by Mr. Hines and Ted L. Levy) as tightly as their feet—and then into a galvanic blues belted out in a Storyland brothel by Mary Bond Davis. As Jelly moves on toward fame and fortune in 1920s Chicago, he passes through a dance hall in which a whirlwind of a chorus picks up his steps, much as his tinkling piano is echoed by the blast of horns. "That's How You Jazz," as the number is called, makes the invention of jazz a miraculous, eruptive theatrical event.

The intimate moments in Jelly's story are handled just as innovatively, with the young Jelly's banishment by his disapproving grandmother and the older Jelly's romance with a tough, independent nightclub proprietor named Anita being dramatized through wildly different blues songs. Ann Duquesnay and Tonya Pinkins bring big voices to these roles, but Ms. Pinkins's powerhouse Anita also has spicy, outspoken dialogue redolent of the strong women in Mr. Wolfe's Zora Neale Hurston adaptation, *Spunk.* Her first night in bed with Jelly, a war for dominance as funny as it is erotic, aims for a new adult standard in male-female encounters in Broadway musicals. It is soon followed by a bracing Act 1 finale, memorably choreographed by Hope Clarke and red-hot in rage, in which Jelly's racist denial of his own blackness spirals into a nightmarish explosion of the toadying minstrel mentality he cannot leave behind.

Mr. Wolfe's harsh view of Morton, touchingly leavened by Mr. Hines's sympathetic portrayal, will not surprise those who saw his *Colored Museum,* in which Josephine Baker and Michael Jackson were skewered for denying their pasts. *Jelly's Last Jam* is also consistent with that previous work's satirical assault on *A Raisin in the Sun,* for it regards white racism as an old-fashioned subject for drama. Except for one brief, flat Tin Pan

Alley sequence, Mr. Wolfe leaves whites offstage, choosing instead to examine schisms within black America from the inside. He is less concerned with whether Jelly can walk through doors labeled "whites only" than whether he will walk through a symbolic door, covered with tribal hieroglyphs, that leads to his African past. *Jelly's Last Jam* no more resembles old-time Broadway civil-rights musicals than it does those countless upbeat revues saluting Jelly Roll Morton's peers.

That this writer can paint his themes on a large, costly Broadway canvas without losing his own devilish voice and fabulist esthetics is doubly impressive. As director, Mr. Wolfe has also made an effortless leap, eliciting intense performances even from the ensemble and achieving a striking visual polish with the aid of such fine previous collaborators as the costume designer Toni-Leslie James and the mask and puppet designer Barbara Pollitt. The inventive sets are by Robin Wagner, whose sleek, abstract use of a black void and changing configurations of lights occasionally make a winking reference to the thematically related *Dreamgirls* that he designed for Michael Bennett.

When *Jelly's Last Jam* collapses in Act 2, as it does despite Mr. Hines's heartfelt efforts, it is because Mr. Wolfe has not imaginatively recast the banal material of Jelly's decline and fall. Having nothing to add to his overall point about his hero's racial denial, he settles instead for the conventions of showbiz biography. The hit songs, money, and women run out; a Freudian cliché is invoked to explain Jelly's lifelong inability to feel. And as the song-and-dance interludes dwindle, Chimney Man blows too much smoke by preachily repeating the evening's incantatory messages. The curtain finally falls on the show's one dishonest note, a Broadway happy button slapped on to a dénouement that is otherwise a downer.

The second act of Mr. Wolfe's career promises to be a lot more exciting than the second act of *Jelly's Last Jam*. In the meantime, anyone who cares about the future of the American musical will want to see and welcome his first.

CRITIC'S NOTEBOOK: FIRES IN THE MIRROR
MAY 15, 1992

Some actors create their own one-person shows because their souls are on fire. Some do so because the world around them is in flames.

Anna Deavere Smith falls into both camps. Ms. Smith, a Stanford University drama professor who is young and black, seems to pack all the inflammatory national passions rekindled by the Los Angeles riots into her piece at the Joseph Papp Public Theater, *Fires in the Mirror: Crown Heights, Brooklyn, and Other Identities.* It offers spectacular further proof, not that any more is needed this season, that the American theater is rising to illuminate these rancorous times with a vitality that may be equaled but is certainly not surpassed by any of our other native arts.

Fires in the Mirror is, quite simply, the most compelling and sophisticated view of urban racial and class conflict, up to date to this week, that one could hope to encounter in a swift ninety minutes. And it is ingenious in concept. An interwoven series of brief monologues by nearly thirty characters, ranging from the famous to the notorious to the nameless, the show consists entirely of verbatim excerpts from fresh interviews Ms. Smith conducted with her subjects. As an interviewer, she seems to have Studs Terkel's knack for gaining the confidence of a wide variety of people and inducing them to reveal themselves in haunting offhand anecdotes and reminiscences.

As if that isn't enough, Ms. Smith also has the talent to impersonate all her interviewees herself: black, white, men, women, young, old. Without pause and with a minimum of props, this slender, elegantly featured performer in white shirt and black slacks whips among characters as varied as the playwright George C. Wolfe (of *Jelly's Last Jam*) and the author Letty Cottin Pogrebin (of *Deborah, Golda, and Me*), as the Rabbi Joseph Spielman and the rapper Monique (Big Mo) Matthews. Ms. Smith can capture the eruptive humors of the Reverend Al Sharpton even as she summons the good-natured but skeptical Jewish woman who wonders aloud of Mr. Sharpton, "I'd like to know who ordained him."

Ms. Smith's performance abilities are impressive and fun, but what makes *Fires in the Mirror* so moving and provocative, so remarkably free of cant and polemics, is its creator's ability to find the unexpected and unguarded in nearly each speaker and her objective grasp of the troubling big picture. Mr. Sharpton's guileless explanation of his hair style (as his personal tribute to the singer James Brown) is set next to an equally sincere and telling discourse by a Hasidic graphic artist named Rivkah Siegel about her ambivalent attitude toward wearing a ritualistic wig. Minister Conrad Muhammad, of the Nation of Islam, offers a searing short history of slavery that is then matched in brevity and power by a Pogrebin anecdote about how her family learned of the Holocaust in 1940.

As Ms. Smith shifts her focus from general snapshots of blacks and Jews to the actual narrative of the tragedy of Crown Heights, her journalistic balance remains perfectly pitched, her command of detail meticulous. Black outrage at the accidental death of a black seven-year-old, Gavin Cato, who was hit by a runaway car in the motorcade of the leader of the Lubavitch movement, Rabbi Menachem M. Schneerson, is given full, articulate vent and context even as the anti-Semitic homicidal rampage that led to the subsequent mob killing of Yankel Rosenbaum, a Hasidic scholar visiting Crown Heights from Australia, courses through the theater in all its terrifying ugliness.

Among so many other memorable people, we meet a feral youth who condones Rosenbaum's murder, a black Episcopal minister who mischievously questions why Rebbe Schneerson has "to be whisked" about like a president, and a wise Jewish matron, Roz Malamud, who amusingly explains how glad she was that her son was visiting the relatively safe Soviet Union during the Crown Heights riots, even though the Soviet coup also occurred on that same fateful day. In a brilliant example of Ms. Smith's technique at revealing character, Yankel Rosenbaum's brother, Norman, is presented first as a roaring public figure demanding justice at a rally in New York and then as a modest private man, a soft-spoken Melbourne lawyer incredulously recalling how his wife first told him the unbelievable news that his brother had been stabbed in a strange neighborhood sixteen time zones away. Norman Rosenbaum is soon followed by the dignified, stricken figure of Gavin Cato's father, Carmel, whose grief is just as searing to witness and who knows as little about Rosenbaum's world as Rosenbaum does about his.

There are no villains in this piece, with the chilling exception of the CUNY professor Leonard Jeffries, who is found offering a megalomaniacal, name-dropping, and anti-Semitic account of how he single-handedly tried to preserve the integrity of the television adaptation of *Roots*. There are no answers to the questions raised by Ms. Smith's piece, either. Idiosyncratic thinkers as diverse as Angela Davis, now a University of California professor, and Robert Sherman, of the New York City Commission on Human Rights, question the very language (that of "healing" included) with which this country addresses issues of race and poverty. Richard Green, a resilient youth leader who founded a black and Lubavitch basketball team in Crown Heights, explains that most of the vigilantes yelling "Heil Hitler!" do not even know who Hitler was, so adrift is the ghetto underclass from any remaining outposts of school, family, or social order of any kind.

More than one observer in *Fires in the Mirror* promises a string of long, hot summers in which those powder kegs, our cities, are bound to explode. Though not offering any false hopes to the contrary, Ms. Smith herself represents some slender sort of hope. Her show is a self-contained example of what one person can accomplish, at the very least in disseminating accurate, unbiased inside reportage, simply by listening to all the warring occupants of the urban neighborhood. This puts Ms. Smith ahead of most politicians, and, indeed, she may be that rare actor who actually should be encouraged to run for public office.

FOURTEENTH SEASON

1992—93

The Who's *Tommy*

The week that the vice president began lecturing the country about family values, I decided to take my children—Nat, twelve, and Simon, eight—to a family musical on Broadway. Our options included:

- *The Secret Garden,* a show about an orphaned girl who is raised by her widowed uncle.
- *Les Misérables,* in which another orphan, the illegitimate daughter of a prostitute, is adopted by a bachelor who is never home.
- *Guys and Dolls,* the story of a compulsive gambler and a nightclub dancer who have had sex without benefit of marriage for more than a decade.
- *Cats,* which tells of a feline prostitute's aspirations to ascend to heaven.

All things considered, I decided that the most wholesome choice would be *Falsettos,* the William Finn musical in which the hero, Marvin, sings in his first number of his overwhelming desire to be part of "a tightknit family, a group that harmonizes."

The vice president might not agree. Though *Falsettos* offers such traditional family tableaux as a Little League baseball game and a bar mitzvah, it is set in an America where, as one song has it, "the rules keep changing" and "families aren't what they were." Marvin has left his wife, Trina, and his twelve-year-old son, Jason, for a male lover, Whizzer. When Jason's bar mitzvah arrives at evening's end, it is held in a hospital room where Whizzer is dying of AIDS. Those in attendance include a lesbian caterer of "nouvelle bar mitzvah cuisine."

Before I got the tickets, I told my children about all of the above except the one concept certain to defy their understanding, nouvelle cuisine. Did they still want to see *Falsettos*? Yes, they said, though Simon added that AIDS made him "very sad because it is an awful disease." Not so sad, however, that he would forgo the show. The boys' curiosity was piqued not only by my sketchy description but also by their knowledge that a relative of ours, my cousin's son Isaac, was playing Jason in a Washington production of *Falsettoland,* the second of the one-act musicals brought together in the Broadway *Falsettos*. If you like *Falsettos* in New York, I told Nat and Simon, we'll check out Isaac's *Falsettoland* in Washington as well.

When we took our seats at the Golden Theatre on a Friday night, the boys were amused to find that they were the subject of stares, given that they were the only children in the house. They weren't self-conscious, but I was. Waiting for the performance to start, I had second thoughts. Should I have taken the easy way out and joined most of the country's other families that weekend at *Lethal Weapon 3*?

Then again, I had chosen to take Nat and Simon to *Falsettos* in part as an antidote to the monolithic images of masculinity with which they are routinely assaulted by television and movies. I do not believe, as the vice president does, that role models in pop culture determine what kind of adults children will become; if that were the case, my entire generation would resemble Lucy and Ricky Ricardo. Yet I wanted to take my children to an entertainment, a musical no less, that reinforces the notion that there are many ways to be masculine, from selfish to generous, from brutal to brave, and that it is up to each boy to make a choice. In this sense, *Falsettos* has more to say about becoming a man than some contemporary bar mitzvahs do.

I was also grateful to take my children to a show that depicts homosexuals neither as abject victims of prejudice or disease nor campy figures of fun but as sometimes likable, sometimes smarmy, sometimes witty, sometimes fallible, sometimes juvenile, sometimes noble people no more or less extraordinary than the rest of us. In other words, gay people are just part of the family in *Falsettos,* and the values of Marvin's family are those of any other. Marvin and Whizzer and Trina and Jason fight and fight and fight—not for nothing is the first song titled "Four Jews in a Room Bitching"—only to unite when one of them is in desperate need.

Such domestic images of gay people, and of gay people lovingly connected to heterosexuals, almost never surface in Hollywood movies, or on network television, or in rock or rap music—the common cultural currencies of my children's (and most Americans') lives. They do exist frequently in the theater, but rarely in a piece so accessible to the young as *Falsettos*. As cowritten by James Lapine, whose other credits include the book of *Into the Woods*, *Falsettos* hooks the audience on its unorthodox story as deftly as that Stephen Sondheim musical lured children into its subversive retelling of Grimm fairy tales.

Nat and Simon were riveted from the start, laughing in some if not all of the places adults did and taking in stride the show's PG-13 depictions of romantic homosexual intimacy in and out of bed. In Act 2, they grew somber along with the characters, a change in key announced by the doctor's prognostic song, "Something Bad Is Happening." As kids tend to do, they bounced back from grief faster than the grown-ups around them, leaping to their feet at the curtain call.

What did my boys take away from *Falsettos*? They liked the acting, the story ("I could never make up a story like that," said Simon, a prolific tale spinner), the jokes, and the music. But they also responded to the show's family values. "Marvin tried to be a good father, and I think he was the best father he could be," said Nat, who added that he liked watching father and son work out their "adjustment" to a sudden change that was "hard to deal with at first."

Simon, who described the show as "very emotional," felt sorry for the "bummed-out" Trina but thought that Marvin had to leave her because, "if you're gay, you shouldn't be married." He liked the fact that Jason, who "thought it was kind of weird that his father was gay," ended up "liking his father better" at the final curtain. If Simon had been in Jason's place, would he have liked Marvin's gay lover? "If he was nice, like Whizzer." Was he surprised to discover that the gay characters in *Falsettos* were the same in most ways as heterosexuals? "They are the same, Dad."

Both Nat and Simon were disgruntled that *Falsettos* had lost the Tony Award for best musical to *Crazy for You*, which they dismissed as "corny." "*Falsettos* is really about something," said Nat.

A week later in Washington, we resumed our conversation about *Falsettos* with Isaac, who is thirteen. While *Falsettoland* is Isaac's first professional acting experience, rave reviews and several weeks of capacity audiences at the Studio Theatre have given him the self-assurance of a hardened theatrical veteran. He particularly delights in telling the story of the night the house was bought out by a gay and lesbian square-dancing group, prompting the stage manager to warn the cast in advance to expect a more idiosyncratic audience response. "We told him we could relate to the gay and lesbian," said Isaac, "but not the square dancing."

Inevitably, Isaac's eight-year-old sister, Lilly, had insisted on seeing the show her brother had been rehearsing night and day. Her mother found a way to explain the show's characters, once Lilly noticed the similarity between a word she had recently learned in the second grade, homophone, and homosexuals, which is the first word sung in *Falsettoland*. But "less than half" of Isaac's classmates had come to see him play Jason, and those who did were sometimes puzzled. One friend—"not my friend anymore"—told Isaac the next day in school that he had heard in the theater lobby that he was "a fag." Isaac chastised his friend for his language, then defiantly added, "I'm not a homosexual, but I work with numerous homosexuals!"

Isaac's own transformation into a knowing proselytizer for gay rights has been a fast one. Before *Falsettoland*, he had never met anyone who was openly homosexual. In this he is no different from my sons, who do not know who, if anyone, among their acquaintances is gay. And Nat and Simon are no different from their father at their age, who, in another era not as distant as it seems, did not meet anyone until college who identified himself as gay and did not have an honest conversation with an uncloseted gay man until a couple of years after that.

Will a show like *Falsettos*, or a dozen like it, sow tolerance, especially at a time when an exclusionary definition of "family values" is being wielded like a club in a divisive political campaign? I have my doubts. My children do not. While Nat and Simon were not sure if their friends would enjoy *Falsettos*—"they're not into plays"—they were, to my amazement, utterly certain that every boy they knew would be accepting of homosexuals whether encountered in theater or in life. (They were less optimistic about the vice president. Simon, who rated *Falsettos* 10 on a scale of 10, said he thought the vice president, in light of the *Murphy Brown* episode, would give it "a 2.")

Surely not everyone they knew was so tolerant and free of the old sexual stereotypes, I insisted, but my children would have none of my adult pessimism. "Kids are stereotyped," said Nat, with an exasperated adolescent roll of the eyes meant to terminate the conversation. Since I believe in preserving tightknit families as strenuously as both Marvin and Dan Quayle do, I conceded to my son that he was right.

LES ATRIDES
PARK SLOPE ARMORY, BROOKLYN, OCTOBER 6, 1992

Ariane Mnouchkine, the Parisian director, may or may not be one of the world's greatest theater artists, but who can doubt that even by France's high standards in the field she is a champion control freak?

Those attending *Les Atrides,* the four-play, ten-hour cycle of Greek tragedy with which Ms. Mnouchkine and her company, Théâtre du Soleil, are making their New York debut, will quickly learn that there are strict rules to be obeyed.

Latecomers are not admitted to the Park Slope Armory, where *Les Atrides* is being presented to audiences on punishing bleacher seats under the auspices of the Brooklyn Academy of Music. There are no intermissions. There are no reserved seats, a form of democracy that prompts some ticket-holders to line up hours before curtain time and that leads to picturesque shoving matches, some of them involving celebrities, once everyone gets indoors. During the on-site meal breaks that separate the matinee and evening plays during a weekend marathon, those who finish eating early find attendants blocking the passageway from the picnic tables (dimly lighted, also per Ms. Mnouchkine's orders) to the performance space.

"Didn't you hear? You're all part of the human sacrifice," said an usher to complaining patrons eager to escape captivity for a post-lunch, pre-*Eumenides* stroll. Not so many people laughed as you might think.

Given this militaristic atmosphere—which even extends to the director's choices of venue, whether an armory in Brooklyn or a former munitions factory outside Paris—it is easy to imagine the chilling authenticity she will bring to one of her pet projects for the future, a piece on Vichy France. But Ms. Mnouchkine's relentlessly tight leash on her theatrical realm, which in *Les Atrides* sometimes creates an onstage airlessness to match that in the auditorium, can also produce remarkable results.

This is certainly the case with *The Libation Bearers,* the middle play in Aeschylus' trilogy about the House of Atreus but the third play of Ms. Mnouchkine's quartet, in which Euripides' *Iphigenia in Aulis* is a prelude. For contemporary sensibilities, *The Libation Bearers* may be the most action-packed drama of the lot: As Orestes returns from exile to avenge the murder of his father, Agamemnon, he is propelled into a reunion with his sister, a grueling act of matricide, and finally a mad escape from the Furies. Yet in the Théâtre du Soleil rendition, the storytelling is neither modern nor archaic in the presumed manner of the fifth century B.C. but timeless. Ms. Mnouchkine fulfills her idea of a cosmopolitan, ritualistic theater that is beyond language, plot, or any kind of realism and that instead digs deep into the primordial passions, many of them ugly, that seem the eternal, inescapable legacy of the human race.

The director accomplishes this feat with the multicultural devices that typify the entire cycle. The playing area is a vast wooden corral, a neutral space reminiscent of the sandboxes used by that other Parisian theatrical visionary, Peter Brook. The performers appear in opulent ceremonial costumes of vaguely Asian provenance. The stagehands are Kabuki-ish while the chorus's choreography emulates the Kathakali dance dramas of Southern India. The musical accompaniment, composed by Jean-Jacques Lemetre and generally played by him in a rustic bandstand containing more than 140 exotic instruments, careers from eclectic Eastern folk improvisations to Kabuki percussion to recorded Indian music to what might be a hyperventilating Bernard Herrmann film score for Alfred Hitchcock. The acting, fiery and grand and never inward, is classical French (even if the actors themselves are not).

From the moment Orestes (Simon Abkarian) arrives at Agamemnon's tomb, *The Libation Bearers* exerts a subterranean, not easily articulated pull on a viewer's psyche. Some of this is a matter of ominous mood, whether created by the buzzing of Mr. Lemetre's strings or the cold blue lighting that shrouds Orestes' return. There are also arresting tableaux, including the tall, windblown altar that reveals the sleeping Clytemnestra (Juliana Carneiro da Cunha) on what will be her death bed. And there is the high-throttle confrontation between mother and son, as Clytemnestra runs but cannot hide from Orestes, whose monomaniacal pursuit of his prey turns the wooden arena into a bullring.

But the most impressive coup de théâtre in *The Libation Bearers*—and, for that matter, in *Les Atrides*—arrives after the blood is spilled: As the lights dim to black and the barking of approaching dogs rises to a terrifying pitch, individual attempts to remove the bloodied mattress bearing the mutilated corpses of Clytemnestra and her lover, Aegisthus, come to nothing. Finally the entire chorus must advance to do the macabre deed, and the apocalyptic spectacle leaves the anxious audience in dread of an unchanging world in which blood inexorably begets blood and evil forces are never tamed.

So upsetting is *The Libation Bearers* that the cycle's concluding play, *The Eumenides,* has a tough time evoking a persuasive vision of justice, peace, and reconciliation in its savage wake. Though Ms. Mnouchkine makes the most of her leaping chorus of Furies—snarling, mutated hellhounds, part canine, part simian, and reminiscent of the furious apes in Stanley Kubrick's *2001*—her staging becomes flat once the theater's first courtroom drama begins. When handed lengthy passages of discourse, the director tends to settle for static recitations of the text. Whether heard in French or through earphones in William M. Hoffman's able English rendering, the talk is numbing, not just in the debates of *The Eumenides* but also in the expository first hour of *Agamemnon*.

The text throughout is somewhat idiosyncratic, seemingly to further the feminist viewpoint that is the undisguised and at times fascinating ideological agenda of *Les Atrides.* By opening her cycle with the Euripides play in which Clytemnestra must sacrifice her daughter Iphigenia (a touching Nirupama Nityanandan) to the dubiously greater good of her husband's war machine, Ms. Mnouchkine makes her principal heroine a far more sympathetic (and dominant) figure in the Aeschylus trilogy to come. The director further shifts the gender balance by imprisoning most of the male characters behind masklike makeup while giving the women more literal and figurative freedom of expression. By the time *The Eumenides* arrives, this slant is more sentimental than provocative: Athena is presented as a syrupy guru (embodied by Ms. da Cunha, the previously mesmerizing Clytemnestra), and the three Brechtian bag ladies who lead the Furies are transformed into beaming automatons of saintly matriarchy.

Ms. Mnouchkine's artistic ideology shapes *Les Atrides* far more than her politics does, however. And the extraordinary payoff of her perfectionism, her lengthy rehearsal period, and her cultural crossbreeding can be found in all four plays. The dancing of the androgynous chorus, led and cochoreographed by the amazing Catherine Schaub (who also codesigned the costumes), has a fervor, precision, and ethereal lightness that cannot be matched by many dance companies, let alone theatrical troupes. Fierce dramatic images, often achieved with means as simple as the rushing forward of a platform or the tearing of a curtain, abound. The five principal actors, each playing multiple roles, may engage in old-fashioned histrionics, but they do so with a commitment and brilliant intensity that flirts with greatness in the case of Mr. Abkarian's portraits of Agamemnon, Achilles, and a finally feral Orestes.

What the director's controlling esthetic forbids, by definition, is unruliness, emotional or otherwise, that does not fit the precise meter of her neoclassicism. While early arrivals to *Les Atrides* are encouraged to watch the actors put on their makeup in an open but roped-off dressing-room area behind the bleachers, the spectators soon discover that even this ostensible backstage space is rigorously designed. The rugs underfoot are color-coordinated with the costume accessories hanging above, and every object is as neatly displayed as the goods in a department store window.

Are these impeccably sober, silent actors freely warming up in their own domain, or are they merely executing another one of Ms. Mnouchkine's meticulous illusions within the confines of a public cage? Either way, it is a beautiful, strangely antiseptic, and poignant sight that, like much of *Les*

Atrides, creates an elegant, hermetically sealed world of pure theater that is securely and safely cordoned off from the spontaneity of life.

≡ Nicholas Nickleby *left producers convinced that New Yorkers had a bottomless tolerance not only for high ticket prices but also for long, epic productions:* The Mahabharata, Angels in America, The Kentucky Cycle.

THE DESTINY OF ME
LUCILLE LORTEL THEATRE, OCTOBER 21, 1992

What do you do when you're dying from a disease you need not be dying from?" cries out Ned Weeks, the autobiographical hero of Larry Kramer's new play, *The Destiny of Me.* If you are Larry Kramer, a founder of the Gay Men's Health Crisis and Act-Up as well as the author of *The Normal Heart,* you keep crying out: in the streets, on *Nightline,* or, at this moment, from the stage of the Lucille Lortel Theatre, where the Circle Repertory Company is giving his blistering confessional drama its premiere. As the AIDS epidemic courses into its second decade, Mr. Kramer, weakened by the effects of HIV but still slugging, won't stop shouting at those in authority who he feels impede the search for a cure.

And where has it got him—or us? "When I started yelling there were forty-one cases of a mysterious disease," says Ned (Jonathan Hadary) as he checks into the National Institutes of Health for an experimental treatment. "Now they're talking about 150 million. And it's still mysterious. And the mystery isn't why they don't know anything, it's why they don't want to know anything."

No one can accuse Mr. Kramer of being a boy who cried wolf. History may judge this impossible, reflexively contentious man a patriot. But what makes *The Destiny of Me* so fascinating, and at times overwhelmingly powerful, is not so much its expected single-mindedness about AIDS as its unexpectedly relentless pursuit of the crusader at center stage. Mr. Kramer cannot solve the medical mystery of the virus or the psychological mystery of the world's tardy response to the peril. What he can try to crack is his own mystery: Why was he of all people destined to scream bloody murder with the aim of altering the destiny of the human race?

The writing in *The Destiny of Me* can fall short of Mr. Kramer's ambitions, but it is never less than scaldingly honest. There is nothing defensive or self-aggrandizing or self-martyring about the playwright's presentation of Ned Weeks: This character is every bit as difficult and loudmouthed as the Larry Kramer who has often angered his allies as much as his adversaries. And he is much more melancholy than an outsider might guess. Throughout the evening, Ned is haunted by "Make Believe" and "This Nearly Was Mine," a pair of songs from beloved Broadway musicals of his childhood, both with lyrics by Oscar Hammerstein II. They are songs about love imagined but not attained, blue anthems for a man whose loneliness long predates the isolation imposed by illness.

Though *The Destiny of Me* is set in a gleaming, if embattled, government hospital administered by a doctor named Anthony Della Vida (Bruce McCarty) who transparently evokes Anthony Fauci of the National Institutes of Health, the present is usually little more than a backdrop for Mr. Kramer's investigative sifting of his past. Flashbacks to the 1940s and fifties abound and sepia-tinged John Lee Beatty sets roll forward as Ned recalls a Jewish childhood lived in the shadows of the Depression, the Holocaust, and McCarthyism in the new suburban subdivisions of a rootless postwar Washington.

Ned, as it happens, is a name Mr. Kramer's hero took in later life (from the glittering Phillip Barry comedy *Holiday*). As a child, Ned was Alexander, a spindly, fluttery, incessantly chattering boy who is rendingly acted in *The Destiny of Me* by John Cameron Mitchell, a young actor who dominates the show with a performance at once ethereal and magnetic. In scenes that are almost too harrowing to watch, Mr. Hadary's affecting Ned, feisty yet frail, looks on from his hospital bed as Mr. Mitchell's Alexander is reviled and beaten by his father, Richard (David Spielberg), for being "different." A federal bureaucrat who never achieved the aspirations instilled by a Yale education, Richard not only attacks his son as a "sissy" but also coarsely wishes aloud that his wife, Rena (Piper Laurie), had aborted the pregnancy that spawned him. While Rena, a would-be radio actress and congenital community do-gooder, is far more sympathetic to the boy, she never protects or rescues him.

As Ned's rage and creativity alike are a product of these parents, so the fifty-seven-year-old Mr. Kramer, as a playwright, is very much a product of the theater of his formative years. Young Alexander, a habitué of the second balcony in Washington's National Theatre and prone to mimicking Mary Martin and Cornelia Otis Skinner, decorates his room with contemporaneous Broadway posters of *Mister Roberts* and *A Streetcar Named Desire*. Not by happenstance is *The Destiny of Me* a juicy, three-act memory play in the mode of that Arthur Miller–Tennessee Williams era, with occasional flashes of humor reminiscent of latter-day variations on the form by Neil Simon and Herb Gardner. Indeed, Mr. Kramer, like Mr. Simon and Mr. Miller, brackets his autobiographical stand-in with a pointedly contrasting brother: the resolutely straight Benjamin Weeks (Peter Frechette), a golden boy who grows up to become a star lawyer.

Given the conventionality of Mr. Kramer's dramatic format, one sometimes wishes the dialogue fleshing it out were finer. He has a good ear, but it is the ear of a journalist, not a poet. The passages in which Richard, Rena, and Ben are in repose, engaged in reminiscence or introspection rather than confrontation, do not always elevate them memorably above type. The performances of Ms. Laurie, whose robust maternal warmth is tempered by a withholding brusqueness, and Mr. Frechette, whose brother is warm and secure despite all his limitations, do a lot to help add nuances of character missing in the language. The same cannot be said, unfortunately, of Mr. Spielberg, who is the only serious shortcoming in the director Marshall W. Mason's otherwise fluent production. While it is to the actor's credit that he never sentimentalizes or caricatures the father's brutality, his acting nonetheless lacks the size and heft that might give this putative Willy Loman a tragic dimension.

Mr. Kramer's journalistic view of his family, though not esthetically transporting, does have its uses, for the reportage is remarkably objective. The play's archetypal familial constellation is enlivened by the fact that Alexander and Ben are allowed widely different but equally credible views of the same two parents; the author is always scrupulous in portraying the differences (not just sexual) in the psychological destinies of men raised in the same household. While the playwright does have an ideological agenda in telling Alexander's coming-out story—he settles the score with Freudian psychotherapists who commonly viewed homosexuality as a disease to be cured—he never leans on that message as a catchall rationalization for the angst of the adult Ned.

So evenhanded is Mr. Kramer here that in the play's present-day sequences, he stops short of vilifying the American medical establishment represented by Dr. Della Vida and by Ned's nurse (Oni Faida Lampley), who happens to be married to Della Vida. In this instance, the author may be fair-minded to a fault, for the interplay between Ned and the Della Vidas, sketchy and often unconvincing to begin with, ultimately produces the work's only contrived plot twist, an abrupt political conversion that belongs to a lesser breed of agitprop theater.

To be sure, *The Destiny of Me* is polemical when it wants to be, its rage about AIDS ultimately sending forth a seismic jolt of visceral theatricality that tops the similarly electric scene in which an inflamed Ned smashes a milk carton before his dying lover in *The Normal Heart*. But standing before the larger canvas of the epidemic—in the intimate twin image of the weary Mr. Hadary and the still-hopeful Mr. Mitchell—is a solitary man as tormented by the meaning of his unhappy life as he is by the meaningless-ness of millions of unnecessary deaths. It was Mr. Kramer's destiny, it turns out, to be blessed and cursed by a far larger than normal heart.

OLEANNA
ORPHEUM THEATRE, OCTOBER 26, 1992

A year later, a mere newspaper photograph of Anita Hill can revive those feelings of rage, confusion, shame, and revulsion that were the country's daily diet during the Senate hearings on Clarence Thomas. Sexual harassment remains such a hot button that even at the height of a raucous presidential and senatorial election campaign a new case in-volving a relatively obscure mayoral appointee threatens to sweep all other news and issues from center stage in New York City. What are the piddling disputes of Democrats and Republicans, after all, next to the blood feuds between men who supposedly "don't get it" and women who doubt they ever will?

Enter David Mamet, who with impeccable timing has marched right into the crossfire. *Oleanna*, the playwright's new drama at the Orpheum Theatre, is an impassioned response to the Thomas hearings. As if ripped right from the typewriter, it could not be more direct in its tech-nique or more incendiary in its ambitions. In Act 1, Mr. Mamet locks one man and one woman in an office where, depending on one's point of view, an act of sexual harassment does or does not occur. In Act 2, the antagonists, a middle-aged university professor (William H. Macy) and an undergraduate student (Rebecca Pidgeon), return to the scene of the alleged crime to try to settle their case without benefit of counsel, surro-gates, or, at times, common sense.

The result? During the pause for breath that separates the two scenes of Mr. Mamet's no-holds-barred second act, the audience seemed to be squirming and hyperventilating en masse, so nervous was the laughter and the low rumble of chatter that wafted through the house. The ensu-ing dénouement, which raised the drama's stakes still higher, does nothing to alter the impression that *Oleanna* is likely to provoke more ar-guments than any play this year.

Those arguments are more likely to involve the play's content than its esthetics. *Oleanna* can be seriously faulted as a piece of dramatic writing only for its first act, which, despite some funny asides about a *Glengarry Glen Ross*–like real-estate deal, is too baldly an expository setup for the real action to come. The evening's second half, however, is wholly absorbing—a typically virtuoso display of Mr. Mamet's gift for locking the audience inside the violent drama of his characters.

This playwright does not write sermonizing problem plays. John, the professor, and Carol, the student, do not talk around the issues that divide them or engage in pious philosophical debates that might eventually bring the audience to some logical, soothing resolution of the conflict. Instead, John and Carol go to it with hand-to-hand combat that amounts to a primal struggle for power. As usual with Mr. Mamet, the vehicle for that combat is crackling, highly distilled dialogue unencumbered by literary frills or phony theatrical ones. (The production, directed by the author, makes do with a few sticks of standard-issue office furniture for a set.) Imagine eavesdropping on a hypothetical, private Anita Hill–Clarence Thomas confrontation in an empty room, and you can get a sense of what the playwright is aiming for and sometimes achieves.

If it is hard to argue with Mr. Mamet's talent, it is also hard to escape his tendency to stack the play's ideological deck. To his credit, the incident of alleged sexual harassment that gives the play its premise is ambiguous: Both Carol and John win scattered points as they argue, Rashomon-style, that a particular physical gesture or a few lines of suggestive conversation in their first office encounter may have been either menacing or innocuous. But once Carol inflates her accusations for rhetorical purposes before a faculty committee, Mr. Mamet's sympathies often seem to reside with the defendant.

John, an intelligent if harried and pedantic man, is given an offstage life that he may lose if found guilty. He is up for tenure, has just made a deposit on a new house, and has an apparently loving wife and son. By contrast, Carol is presented alternately as a dunce and a zealot. Though she does not understand the meaning of some garden-variety twenty-five-cent words, she all too easily wields such malevolent jargon as "classist," "paternal prerogative," and "protected hierarchy" once her cause is taken up by an unnamed campus "group." She is given no offstage loved ones that might appeal to the audience's sympathy and is costumed in asexual outfits that come close to identifying her brand of rigid political correctness with the cultural police of totalitarian China.

Like any other playwright, Mr. Mamet has no obligation to be objective. To demand that he come out squarely and unequivocally on the side of women is to ask that he write a pandering (and no doubt tedious) play that would challenge no one and would subscribe to the exact intellectual conformity that *Oleanna* rightly condemns. Nor can one glibly reject his argument against fanatics like Carol who would warp the crusade against sexism, or any other worthy cause, into a reckless new McCarthyism that abridges freedom of speech and silences dissent. Yet *Oleanna* might be a meatier work if its female antagonist had more dimensions, even unpleasant ones, and if she were not so much of an interchangeable piece with the manipulative, monochromatic Mamet heroines of, say, *House of Games* and *Speed-the-Plow.*

Even so, it would be overstating the case—and surely it will be overstated by some—to suggest that *Oleanna* is sexist. By evening's end, Mr. Mamet has at least entertained the possibility that there is less to John and more to Carol than the audience has previously supposed. And the playwright is well supported by his able actors in this regard, for Mr. Macy's ostensibly benign professor and Ms. Pidgeon's humorless, vengeful student pass through a shocking final catharsis that throws any pat conclusions about either character into chaos.

The play's title, taken from a folk song, refers to a nineteenth-century escapist vision of utopia. *Oleanna* itself evokes, however crudely, what one might wish to escape from: a sexual battleground where trust and even rational human discourse between men and women are in grave jeopardy. No wonder *Oleanna* leaves us feeling much the way the Thomas hearings did: soiled and furious. If some of that fury is inevitably aimed at the author, no one can accuse him of failing to provoke an audience about a subject that matters. The wounds of a year ago have hardly healed. Mr. Mamet, true to his role of artist, rips open what may be his society's most virulent scab.

SPIC-O-RAMA
WESTSIDE THEATRE, OCTOBER 28, 1992

John Leguizamo arrives on stage in *Spic-o-Rama* like a hip-hop star, leaping and bouncing in the flash of strobe lights to thunderous music and the cheers of fans. Which makes it all the more amazing when the music fades, and the performer metamorphoses into the first of six characters in his new one-man show: nine-year-old Miggy, a bespectacled, geeky boy with a high-pitched voice, a serious overbite, and floppy hands. Mr. Leguizamo is a star, no question—he doesn't need a strobe to burn bright—but he also announces himself from that moment as an actor of phenomenal range. And there's a hundred minutes of his tour de force still to come.

Spic-o-Rama, which is at the Westside Theatre, picks up where his previous survey of Hispanic New Yorkers, *Mambo Mouth,* left off. This time Mr. Leguizamo's writing is more ambitious. The evening is not a series of sketches but a play of sorts, complete with a Loy Arcenas set that impressionistically evokes an entire neighborhood. All six characters in *Spic-o-Rama* belong to a Jackson Heights family that is preparing for the wedding of its oldest son. As each relative takes a turn at center stage, the audience pieces together the full psychological portrait of a household that may give new meaning to the Spanish word for dysfunctional.

Much of *Spic-o-Rama* is hilarious, with comic targets as various as Arnold Schwarzenegger, Telemundo, and *The Partridge Family.* The most compulsive wisecracker is Crazy Willie, the bridegroom and a veteran of the Persian Gulf war, during which he shot at "people who looked just like us but with towels on their heads." Stalled in life, Willie hangs out by his immobilized car, whose motor has been stolen, and shoots off both his gun and his mouth to kill time. Even before the fact, his marriage to Yvonne, a teenybopper with overheated Andy Garcia fantasies, seems doomed. Though Willie has a low regard for monogamy, he has magnanimously told Yvonne that "as a bonus" to their nuptials, "I'm going to let you have my babies."

His brother Raffi is just as funny but far sadder. Wearing a silk bathrobe, platform shoes, briefs overstuffed with Kleenex, and a thick mane of Clorox-bleached hair, Raffi imagines himself to be not only an actor but also the albino illegitimate son of Laurence Olivier. "It's hard to be Elizabethan in Jackson Heights," he says, but Mr. Leguizamo shows Raffi struggling to leap over that cultural divide by affecting a B-movie British accent and preening before the mirror to perfect his pose as an "occasional heterosexual." As he explains: "I don't know why people insist on knowing themselves. It's hard enough to know what to wear."

The biggest triumphs of *Spic-o-Rama,* both in the writing and in performance, are appropriately saved for last: the parents who produced these children. Mr. Leguizamo's portrayal of the mother, Gladyz, is, to be sure, an impressive, even sexy feat of sassy female impersonation, outfitted with cascading hair ("not a hair weave, a hair fusion") and a pink slash of a mouth to match a provocative wardrobe. Gladyz is also a survivor, a lifelong slave to child-rearing who dreams of something more. As she tends the baby who is the youngest of her five children and exchanges gossip and wisecracks with a friend in the Laundromat, she rebels impotently against her status as an "ornament." Gladyz has learned the hard way that when "you go for something you really want, then you're a bitch."

Gladyz's grievances, like those of her sons, are brought into sharpest relief when we meet her estranged, philandering husband, Felix, as he toasts the newlyweds at the wedding. Felix is a cad who feels that lies, half-truths, and "critical omissions" are "the key to all relationships." When he isn't belittling his children as misfits or disappointments, he is tipsily singing the theme from *The Godfather* into a hand mike or graphically describing the credo of male sexuality that has imprisoned him and his sons in eternal childhood and his wife at home. Yet Mr. Leguizamo has sympathy for Felix, as he does for Gladyz. There is pathos in this ridiculous but intelligent, even witty Colombian immigrant who does not have a clue about how to be better than he is.

Perhaps some will see the irresponsible, irrepressibly macho Felix as a stereotype. When Mr. Leguizamo had his first success with *Mambo Mouth,* he was attacked by some Hispanic critics for trading in ethnic clichés. To disarm the thought police this time, *Spic-o-Rama* carries an announced disclaimer: "This Latin family is not representative of all Latin families. It is a unique and individual case. If your family is like this one, please seek professional help." And one would have to be humorless indeed to read Felix or any of the precisely observed characters of *Spic-o-Rama* as noxious generalizations.

Still, there are places where the writing falls short. Another brother, wheelchair-bound, is sentimentally drawn (though well acted); his lines tug at the heartstrings too mechanically to engender real sympathy. Other segments also could lose passages in which the characters announce directly what the audience is supposed to think or feel, and nearly every soliloquy could be shortened. *Spic-o-Rama* lacks a real ending, too, settling for a jokey rather than a cathartic dénouement.

Perhaps Peter Askin, the director, might have helped solve these problems, but he has otherwise kept the production fleet. To vamp during the costume changes, there are antic video clips featuring the offstage characters, like Yvonne, described in the monologues. But it's the star, not the videos, that make good on the evening's title. In *Spic-o-Rama*, Mr. Leguizamo's huge presence and talent fill the theater so totally you feel he's everywhere at once.

≡ *John Leguizamo parlayed this success into a somewhat rocky movie career, then returned to New York with* Freak, *a triumph on Broadway in 1998.*

CAROUSEL
ROYAL NATIONAL THEATRE, LONDON, DECEMBER 17, 1992

Even in the age of Andrew Lloyd Webber, the British remain in awe of the Broadway musical. Only the most obviously disreputable of American imports and revivals fail to earn critical raves here, and on occasion local versions of New York shows are proclaimed superior to the originals. During the 1980s, this was most famously the case with Richard Eyre's staging of *Guys and Dolls* and Cameron Mackintosh's upbeat revision of Stephen Sondheim's *Follies,* though American visitors could see that both productions were far from fluent in Broadwayese. In *Guys and Dolls,* Damon Runyon's mugs sometimes spoke with Southern accents and tapped like Bojangles.

So it was with skepticism that I approached the new production of the 1945 Rodgers and Hammerstein *Carousel,* which opened last weekend to ecstatic reviews and turn-away crowds at the Royal National Theatre, the site of the Eyre *Guys and Dolls.* But for once the wild enthusiasm may be an understatement. This is without question the most revelatory, not to mention the most moving, revival I've seen of any Rodgers and Hammerstein musical. The National has recently found startling new ways of looking at the dramas of Tennessee Williams and Arthur Miller under both Peter Hall's and Mr. Eyre's leadership, and now it proves just as imaginative in sweeping away decades of clichés from an American musical classic of the same period.

Carousel was Richard Rodgers's own favorite show among his collaborations with Oscar Hammerstein II, but it is infrequently revived, in part because its vocally demanding lead role, the carousel barker, Billy Bigelow, is hard to cast, in part because its dark book (adapted from Ferenc Molnár's *Liliom*) asks audiences to stomach Billy's wife-beating and suicide. The last major New York production, a good one at Lincoln Center in which John Raitt re-created his original Billy, was nearly thirty years ago. Though almost everyone is familiar with *Carousel,* what most audiences have actually seen is the distorted, candied Hollywood film adaptation of 1956.

The National Theatre production is a collaboration by Nicholas Hytner, a director whose eclectic reach has extended from opera to *Miss Saigon* to Alan Bennett's *The Madness of George III,* and Kenneth MacMillan, the principal choreographer of the Royal Ballet, who died while *Carousel* was still in rehearsal but not before he had finished what a program note says was 85 percent of the dancing. From the very first bars of "The Carousel Waltz," they and the brilliant designer, Bob Crowley, aspire to an adult emotional purity that is devastating in its cumulative effect.

Surely this is the first staging of the piece in which the curtain does not rise to reveal a carousel. Instead the sinister opening bars of Rodgers's waltz are set in the grim late-nineteenth-century New England mill where the heroine, Julie Jordan, works absentmindedly at her loom. The stage is at first dominated by a large Victorian clock that ticks off the minutes until the closing time of six, at which point the clock flies away, the abruptly liberated mill laborers twirl out of the forbidding factory gates in mad abandon, and a full moon sweeps one and all to the fairground. There the drab colors of industrial servitude briefly give way to bright lights and raucous carnival sideshows while the carousel is slowly erected by roustabouts before the audience's eyes. Familiar as the music may be, it has never sounded so urgent or so troubling as it does when illustrated by this bittersweet cinematic panorama of oppression and release.

Without making a British fetish of class conflict, the National's *Carousel* is always conscious of the lowly economic status of its major characters. When Julie (Joanna Riding) and Billy (Michael Hayden) get together in "If I Loved You," the song's indirect expression of feeling comes across not as coy musical-comedy flirtation but as inarticulate, self-protective wariness. These incipient young lovers, aged by drudgery and snubbed by respectable society, are old and achingly lonely before their time, a mere "couple of specks" in the scheme of things, as Billy sadly puts it. The duet's sexual crescendo, so titillatingly elongated and then consummated in the tidal music, becomes Billy and Julie's thrilling defiance of both their own sense of defeat and their community's Puritan propriety. As designed by Mr. Crowley, the scene is set on an Andrew Wyeth hill that is painted in the vivid folk-art colors of Grandma Moses but is suffused with the solitude of Edward Hopper.

In this *Carousel*, the whalers' tavern is as dark as a saloon out of O'Neill, and the waterfront setting for Billy's attempt at armed robbery could be Steinbeck's Cannery Row. Yet the production is airy, fluid, and poetic, not heavy or realistic. Mr. Crowley, whose work has been seen in New York in *Les Liaisons Dangereuses* and the Ian McKellen *Richard III*, avoids the busy mechanics of contemporary English musicals, restricting himself to the drops and turntables of the Rodgers and Hammerstein era. His New England fishing village is in a cobalt blue box that doubles as heaven when Billy ascends there in the second act. The visual harmony is matched aurally: Amplification in the National's proscenium house, the Lyttelton, is slight, and the original Don Walker orchestrations are sumptuously served by a large pit orchestra.

What is remarkable about Mr. Hytner's direction, aside from its unorthodox faith in the virtues of simplicity and stillness, is its ability to make a 1992 audience believe in Hammerstein's vision of redemption, which has it that a dead sinner can return to Earth to do godly good. Mr. Hytner's principal accomplice in this feat is Mr. Hayden, a previously unknown American actor not long out of Juilliard who brings to Billy a Warren Beatty–like mixture of masculine belligerence, bewilderment, and tenderness and sings his marathon "Soliloquy" like an angel well before the character becomes one. Almost as important to the production is Patricia Routledge's Nettie, whose direct and understated delivery of "You'll Never Walk Alone" to the just-widowed Julie shakes the cobwebs from a song long synonymous with sentimental overkill.

The National *Carousel* is not without its sporadic, typically British lapses. Some of the singing is so-so (a flaw in Ms. Riding's otherwise fine Julie) and some of the casting is stock (the black Mr. Snow, Clive Rowe, happily excepted). The MacMillan choreography of the Act 1 ensemble numbers "June Is Busting Out All Over" and "Blow High, Blow Low!," while intended to salute the Agnes de Mille originals, looks like the West End's perennially warmed-over idea of Michael Kidd. But in the affectingly performed Act 2 pas de deux, in which Billy's unhappy teenage daughter (Bonnie Moore) searches for her dead father's love by taking up with a fairground boy (Stanislav Tchassov), MacMillan joins the hero in seeming to speak to a spellbound audience from beyond the grave.

≡ Carousel *traveled to Lincoln Center with Michael Hayden and a new (even better) supporting cast. The production was mainly well received— and paved the way for major Broadway revivals of other shows written by Rodgers and/or Hammerstein:* Show Boat, The King and I, The Sound of Music, *as well as a short-lived stage adaptation of their 1945 film,* State Fair.

ANNA CHRISTIE
ROUNDABOUT THEATRE, JANUARY 15, 1993

Maybe it's just the nature of Americans to rush forward, forever shedding their past. Whatever the reason, it is now British directors, far more often than our own, who dust off neglected American plays and startle audiences with their rediscoveries.

While prominent New York companies were boring theatergoers silly last month with mannered rehashes of Chekhov and Büchner, the air was electric in London, where the Royal National Theatre opened Nicholas Hytner's revelatory take on Rodgers and Hammerstein's *Carousel*. Last week, public television broadcast a feverish new version of Tennessee Williams's *Suddenly, Last Summer*, directed by Richard Eyre of the National.

And last night another British director who has worked at the National, David Leveaux, gave the Roundabout Theatre Company a thrilling staging of Eugene O'Neill's *Anna Christie*. Like *Carousel* and *Suddenly, Last Summer, Anna Christie* has been largely forgotten by the modern American theater that O'Neill, more than anyone else, willed into being.

Following the example of his peers, Mr. Leveaux seamlessly mixes actors from both sides of the Atlantic in his company. The astonishing Natasha Richardson, who was also brilliant in *Suddenly, Last Summer*, gives what may prove to be the performance of the season as Anna, turning a heroine who has long been portrayed (and reviled) as a whore with a heart of gold into a tough, ruthlessly unsentimental apostle of O'Neill's tragic understanding of life. Yet Ms. Richardson could not triumph without the sensitive partnering she receives from both Liam Neeson, the Irish actor recently seen courting Mia Farrow in *Husbands and Wives*, and Rip Torn, an actor's actor in the gritty New York style.

The production's style is one of utter simplicity, reflecting the passion of a director who has reached into the fragile heart of a work and wants the audience to share the depth of pure feeling he found there. Stripping away the excesses of O'Neill's labored New England waterfront patois and the fussy naturalism of the setting, Mr. Leveaux also strips down the characters until finally there are no illusions left for them to hide behind, only a harsh and crushing truth that unites them in their nakedness. Starkly painterly to the eye and merciless in its emotional attack, this *Anna Christie* is reminiscent of the Hytner *Carousel* to the point where one can see how the contemporaneous O'Neill and Oscar Hammerstein II, though antithetical in philosophical convictions, were allies in forcing the American theater of a still-young century to enter adulthood.

In this telling, *Anna Christie* is not so much the salty romantic yarn of a woman's redemption in the arms of a shipwrecked sailor as a compacted long day's journey into night. The story, such as it is, seems to end soon after the play begins: The battered twenty-year-old Anna, looking for peace, seeks out the seafaring father who deserted her as a child, Chris Christopherson (Mr. Torn), only to be condemned by him and her worshipful suitor, Mat Burke (Mr. Neeson), once she reveals her scarlet history. What follows is the play's notorious "happy" ending, whose happiness O'Neill vehemently denied when criticized for it after the 1921 Broadway premiere. Mr. Leveaux, keen to the text's black Irish wit, vindicates O'Neill's argument. Any happiness that attends to Anna, Mat, and Chris at the end of this nominal comedy is as ephemeral and illusory as the booze and morphine that anesthetize the tragic protagonists of O'Neill's late masterpieces.

Ms. Richardson, seeming more like a youthful incarnation of her mother, Vanessa Redgrave, than she has before, is riveting from her first entrance through a saloon doorway's ethereal shaft of golden light. Her face bruised, her eyelids heavy, her slender frame draped in the gaudy fabrics and cheap jewelry of her trade, she is the tattered repository of a thousand anonymous men's alcoholic lusts and fists. But the actress does not make Anna a victim deserving of abject pity. She forces the audience instead to see this woman's fiercely held point of view.

Anna hates men as much for their hypocrisy as for their wish to own her and treat her "like a piece of furniture." As her father and lover berate her for not subscribing to their moralistic notions of propriety, she reminds them it is "nice people," Chris and Mat included, who frequent whorehouses, that it was a "nice" cousin on a Minnesota farm who first raped her as a teenager. Within Ms. Richardson's bone-deep weariness there is a tight coil of anger—the word *nice* has rarely been spit out more lethally—and when the rage pours out after intermission, it shames and humbles Anna's men and the audience alike into examining what cruelties they have committed under the veil of decency. When Anna goes further still, begging that Mat end her misery by crushing her skull, the logic of her hunger for self-annihilation is so vivid that the audience seems to shrink from the certainty of a bloodbath.

What Mr. Neeson brings to that demanding scene and to the rest of his performance is the expected simian sexuality but also the interior, unarticulated contradictions of a sanctimonious Irish Catholic who condemns Anna's sins even as he searches his soul clandestinely for a compassion that might allow him to forgive her. ("There ain't nothing to forgive, anyway," says the always realistic Anna.) It is the drama of the baffled Mat, angrily confronting himself, not Anna, that makes the performance moving, especially in the morning-after scene in which his proper, sunny airs of courtship have given way to the blind, undirected venom of a mangy, injured dog.

Mr. Torn's father is another kind of cur. The perfectly pitched, bowlegged comic booziness of his first entrance is soon usurped by the pathetic regret of a man who knows he is responsible for the psychological maiming of both his daughter and the wife he abandoned in life and death. When Mr. Torn's Chris digs into himself to retrieve the Swedish endearment that is his only tender paternal memory of Anna's childhood, he seems to be clinging to this last tiny souvenir of his youth and humanity, much as the aged Mary Tyrone clutches her faded wedding gown in *Long Day's Journey into Night*.

Every detail in this *Anna Christie* has been supplely orchestrated, from the spare grace notes of Douglas J. Cuomo's incidental music to Anne Meara's finely shaded cameo of the doomed yet self-aware old mistress Chris dismisses in the opening scene. The dreamlike production design, with sets by John Lee Beatty and costumes by Martin Pakledinaz, is dominated by the lighting of Marc B. Weiss, who made a similarly memorable contribution to the production of O'Neill's *A Moon for the Misbegotten* that Mr. Leveaux directed with Kate Nelligan some Broadway seasons ago. The fog that O'Neill's people keep talking about, the fog that Anna says will cleanse her, becomes a poetic presence, as does the blackness of the old devil sea on which Chris blames all his woes.

O'Neill, of course, did not believe that the sea and the fog either cause or cure man's ills. O'Neill did believe, as Anna puts it, that "we're all poor nuts, and things happen, and we just get mixed in wrong." In *Anna Christie*, life is mean, familial and romantic love are both transient (if they exist at all), hope is a joke, and affixing blame is pointless. All these immutable facts are to be found in Mr. Leveaux's production. But Ms. Richardson's Anna, while "sick of the whole game," clings to life anyway, a sad and brave and indisputably American heroine who is last seen facing a frontier of pure fog.

CRITIC'S NOTEBOOK: PAUL RUDNICK'S JEFFREY
WPA THEATRE, FEBRUARY 3, 1993

People with AIDS are dying like clockwork in the Manhattan of Paul Rudnick's new play, *Jeffrey*. So how can it be that *Jeffrey* is the funniest play of this season and maybe last season, too?

There are two explanations for this phenomenon, one simple, one less so. The simple one is Mr. Rudnick's talent. An essayist, novelist (*Social Disease*), playwright (*I Hate Hamlet*), and unbilled Hollywood script doctor (*The Addams Family*), Mr. Rudnick is a born showbiz wit with perfect pitch for priceless one-liners. Though only thirty-four years old, he might be a household name by now had he not chosen to pour some of his most hilarious wisecracks into ramshackle vehicles about cartoonish subjects. (And had *I Hate Hamlet,* his Broadway debut, not been capsized by the onstage misbehavior of its star, Nicol Williamson.)

In *Jeffrey,* a runaway Off Broadway hit at the WPA Theatre, the dramaturgy is still ramshackle, but the subject is not remotely cartoonish. The title character, a scantly employed young actor played by John Michael Higgins, inhabits a particular present-day Manhattan where the most prevalent form of party is a memorial service ("each more creative and moving than the last"), where the sight of young men hobbling on canes is a commonplace, where red ribbons are nearly as plentiful as the condoms that are supposed to keep them at bay. Jeffrey, who stays afloat by working as a waiter for the tony catering services he likens to a "gay national guard," has a front-row seat for it all.

And through it all, through scenes of grotesque death at St. Vincent's Hospital and bloody gay bashing on mean streets nearby, Mr. Rudnick nails laugh after laugh.

To understand what the laughter means and why it offers so cathartic a release from the tragedy of AIDS, for a couple of hours in a theater at least, one must look beyond Mr. Rudnick's talent to the style that his talent serves. *Jeffrey* is not the expected blood-squirting black comedy prompted by disease and dying; there is no gallows medical humor in the vein of *Marvin's Room* or *Joe Egg* or *M*A*S*H.* Instead of writing about the bleak absurdity of meaningless death, Mr. Rudnick, with wicked honesty, focuses on the far more manic, at times bizarrely festive absurdity of those who survive.

He is a social critic, not a moralist or nihilist, and he is most emphatically an uncloseted gay writer. While *Jeffrey* is a direct descendant of Joe Orton's subversive play *Loot,* in which irreverent characters farcically treat a corpse and its coffin as props in a crime scheme, Mr. Rudnick can be forthright about his aims in a way Orton could not in the mid-1960s. *Jeffrey* is not a coded manifestation of gay humor but an open, intoxicated celebration of it, a concerted effort to induce laughter in the epidemic's darkness. The play seems to have been conceived less in rage against straight bigotry than in defiance of what its author fears is galloping defeatism among gay men in 1990s New York.

Just before *Jeffrey* opened last month, Mr. Rudnick explained his tack in a brief essay, "Laughing at AIDS," for the op-ed page of *The New York Times.* He described "uncontrollable laughter" as the "only possible release" after a hospital visit five years ago with a dying friend whose comically whiny, bitchy behavior made him more of "a huge pain" than "a

suitably noble dying person." Rejecting the notion that humor "can dilute and trivialize" real-life horrors, Mr. Rudnick argued that "gay writers, drawing on the repartee that is a form of gay soul, use camp, irony,
and epigram to, if not defeat the virus, at least scorn and contain it."

Packed with highly quotable epigrams (which I'll try not to quote,
however great the temptation), *Jeffrey* transforms Mr. Rudnick's op-ed
theory into a theatrical reality. The entire play is dedicated to mocking
the sober pieties of its gay protagonist, a newly reformed sexual hedonist
who has sworn off even fail-safe sex to keep his spirit and his health in
line with the grim verities of the AIDS era.

But as Mr. Rudnick propels his waiter through a series of burlesque
sketches depicting archetypal Manhattan milieus, from a gym to acting
auditions to a guru's lecture hall, Jeffrey obeys his pledge of abstinence
at the very high cost of losing his sense of humor and his humanity. Indeed, he stops living. Though attracted to a kind bartender named Steve
(Tom Hewitt) who more than reciprocates his affection, Jeffrey keeps
the suitor at an emotional as well as a sexual distance, and increases that
distance once he learns that Steve is HIV-positive. Jeffrey even divorces
himself from the lives of his closest platonic friends, whether he finds
them in sickness or in health.

Mr. Rudnick, however, is as fizzy and outspoken as Jeffrey is smug and
detached. He makes fun of a fund-raising "hoedown for AIDS" given by
lockjawed socialites at the Waldorf-Astoria, ecumenically portrays both
AIDS memorials and St. Patrick's Cathedral services as cruising opportunities for secular and clerical homosexuals alike, and makes his play's
principal AIDS patient, Darius (Bryan Batt), a spectacularly dumb *Cats*
chorus dancer who wears his costume offstage. Darius is not, in Mr.
Rudnick's phrase, "a suitably noble dying person." He wants his memorial staged at the Winter Garden with his fellow cats singing his praises
in doggerel to the tune of "Memory."

Given Mr. Rudnick's propensity for making jokes at funerals, it is easy
to accuse him of being trivial and escapist in the face of overwhelming despair. But to do so is to miss the point. In a succinct statement of the author's true position, Darius says: "Think of AIDS as the guest who won't
leave, the one we all hate. It's still our party." Mr. Rudnick acknowledges
the unwanted guest's presence but is determined to keep the party going.
And the party that he has in mind is far from frivolous: It is nothing less
than the gay culture and sense of community that have been threatened
not only by AIDS but also by the rising wave of gay-bashing and verbal ho-
mophobia that has greeted President Clinton's efforts to end the ban on
homosexuals in the armed forces.

To Mr. Rudnick, an integral part of that imperiled gay culture is the particular "gay soul" he described in his essay, a dazzling comic style whose underlying esthetic spirit he has inherited from Orton and Oscar Wilde and countless other artists, in and out of the theater, in and out of the closet. In *Jeffrey,* the playwright insists by example on his right to retain his pronounced gay artistic identity in the time of AIDS, no matter who might find his bright repartee out of sync with his grave subject. To relinquish his hard-won comic attack, he implies, is to become an "innocent bystander" like Jeffrey and, perhaps, to capitulate to the establishment culture that expects writers to enshrine suitably noble dying persons in AIDS soap operas. Should that happen, the party, as Mr. Rudnick defines it, will be over and the "gay soul" will be yet another of the virus's unnecessary casualties.

"Even Brecht wrote musicals," Mr. Rudnick notes in *Jeffrey.* The snappy comic tone of his own writing (far snappier than *The Rise and Fall of the City of Mahagonny,* to be sure) belies its intrinsic seriousness. Here is an AIDS play where HIV-positive characters can complain about being dehumanized by red ribbons, cheap pity, and even a sentimental square on the quilt. It's a play in which a decorator (the evening's conscience, now being brilliantly acted by a newcomer to the cast, Peter Bartlett), has the freedom of comic mind to attribute the failure of the revolt in Tiananmen Square to the Chinese students' inability to create snazzy graphics for their T-shirts. Mr. Rudnick prizes people who insist on being their whiny, picky, angry, sometimes ignoble gay selves no matter what the temptation to turn into a martyr, eunuch, or Mother Teresa (who is a cameo character in *Jeffrey*). Though Darius ultimately becomes an angel, he never does give up his tacky *Cats* costume.

Like Robert Plunket's recent comic novel *Love Junkie,* which concludes with an ironically "fabulous" all-star memorial service, and Tony Kushner's play *Angels in America,* a "gay fantasia" that has both its own angels and an unexpectedly entertaining gay devil in the form of Roy Cohn, *Jeffrey* is far more energizing than mournful. Not because it can conquer AIDS—"only money, rage, and science" can do that, as Mr. Rudnick has written—but because it clasps the audience to the heart of a heroic American community fighting fiercely to sustain its complex soul even as its body is imperiled.

Far from being escapist, the laughter along the way is a battle cry, a defiant expression of who these idiosyncratic characters were before AIDS arrived and who they will still be after it has gone. While sex must be safe in the meantime, Mr. Rudnick's sharp, uninhibited wit must, as a matter of life-and-death mission, remain anything but.

☰ *Rudnick steadily built a career as a New York wit both in his theater work (starting with* Poor Little Lambs *a decade earlier), his novels (*Social Disease*), his magazine pieces (including his film criticism under the name Libby Gelman-Waxner), and his screenplays (*Addams Family Values, In and Out*).*

Jeffrey was Rudnick's best play to date by far, and also an important one: It marked as much a change in theatrical sensibility in dealing with AIDS in its own way as did Angels in America. *A subject that had often lent itself to journalistic reportage and sometimes preachy melodrama was at last being dramatized as part of a broader canvas of American life (in* Angels*) and, in Rudnick's hands, with defiant humor.*

FOOL MOON
RICHARD RODGERS THEATRE, FEBRUARY 26, 1993

To that short list of unbeatable combinations that includes bacon and eggs, bourbon and soda, and Laurel and Hardy, you can now add Shiner and Irwin.

Fool Moon, the show that David Shiner and Bill Irwin have brought to the Richard Rodgers Theatre, proves that the whole can be greater than the sum of its parts even when the parts are as great as these two beloved clowns. Call the phenomenon comic combustion, or maybe fools' fission. Whatever the magic at play, *Fool Moon* is a meltdown for the audience, whose laughter pauses only long enough to permit the savoring of such emotions as wide-eyed wonder and sheer joy.

For those who have encountered Mr. Shiner at the Cirque du Soleil or Mr. Irwin in his shows *The Regard of Flight* and *Largely New York,* much of the material in *Fool Moon* will be fondly familiar. Here again Mr. Shiner walks through, on, and over the first few rows of spectators, demonically mussing hair, borrowing hats, and picking pockets along his Hellzapoppin path. Mr. Irwin shows off such signature routines as those featuring a bottomless trunk, an antic Harlequin, and the fierce pull of an imaginary offstage vacuum cleaner. But even the old tricks, all of them lovingly polished through time, are lifted higher by the alchemy of the new partnership.

The hard angles of Mr. Shiner, whose extraordinarily quick-witted humor is peppered with urban angst and aggression, adds the spice needed to balance Mr. Irwin, whose sweet comic personality is one of gentle, almost bland bemusement. Just as the dark and intense Mr.

Shiner can look like the conniving Chico Marx in his fool's cap, so the blond and pacific Mr. Irwin looks like Harpo in his. They were born to finish each other's thoughts, in body language if not in words. (Neither speaks a line in *Fool Moon*.) They were born to be in farcical conflict, as they are in a stunning Act 1 sketch in which Mr. Shiner, adopting the pose of a Chaplinesque, rose-bearing suitor, finds his date under siege from Mr. Irwin, as a swank nightclub captain with the nose of another Marx, Groucho. And they were born to be brothers, as they are by the final curtain, when a storybook crescent moon raises them and the audience to a starry heaven.

Both men are also master mimics, slapstick artists, and elastic comic dancers, but the enchantment cast by *Full Moon* cannot be summed up by a list of its stars' skills, jokes, and routines. The show has a pungent theatrical atmosphere that seems to embrace the old Broadway house in which it has landed. The gags of *Full Moon* fully exploit the velvet red-and-gold front curtain, the auditorium's antique boxes, the stage's trapdoors. The sly allusions to clown history, from commedia dell'arte to Bobby Clark and Buster Keaton and Jackie Gleason, are present in everything from the totemic costumes and props to the vintage burlesque of a demented soft-shoe performed in top hats and tails to "Tea for Two."

In his past shows, Mr. Irwin has made much of being a New Vaudevillian. Either he or his accomplices would use words to deconstruct the comedy as it was being performed, as if to put the humor in quotes. That postmodern self-consciousness has been dropped along with the verbiage in *Full Moon,* and his clowning breathes freer for it. This show isn't New Vaudeville. It's vaudeville, pure and simple: unpretentiously lowercase, timeless, and as exquisitely honed as vaudeville was purported to be in the day when it was a frontline American art.

The evening's retro mood is further enhanced by the Red Clay Ramblers, a musical group whose eclectic repertory is that of a fantasy roadhouse band from a vanished rural America. Bluegrass, New Orleans, classical, folk, and gospel sounds emerge in nutty profusion from these talented instrumentalists and singers, whose music making is perfection but whose personalities are authentically idiosyncratic. The Red Clay Ramblers give *Full Moon* an at times almost subliminal sound track that wafts through the night like a mysterious distant station pulled in by a car radio.

Perhaps the stars' most crucial collaborators, however, are the several audience members whom Mr. Shiner, with the eye of a virtuoso director, recruits from the first few rows for the most extended routines of the show. Because the amateurs are used not simply as patsies but as major players, a wrong choice or two could severely dent the fun. The draftees I saw at a preview, some of them required to engage in sexual clinches with strangers and to execute elaborate mime or dance routines, were so good they almost could be ringers. But I doubt they are. Mr. Shiner's most famous Cirque du Soleil stunt, in which he directs three men and a woman in an elaborate mock silent-movie melodrama, seems to succeed brilliantly no matter who the players, largely because of his forceful improvisational leadership. It also packs more punch in the intimacy of a theater than it does under a vast circus tent, bringing the evening to a climax that leaves the convulsed audience rocking like passengers on a wave-tossed ocean liner.

By using a fresh supporting cast every night, Mr. Shiner and Mr. Irwin no doubt keep *Full Moon* fresh, too. With time, they'll probably take their partnership even further as they find more new routines they can perform together to go with the old favorites they do apart. Although the differences in their personalities make them an ideal team, they share that spontaneous inventiveness that makes the best clowns seem like uninhibited kids. Their beautiful show passes by as dreamily as childhood, ending much too soon, but not before it touches us somewhere hidden and deep.

TOMMY

St. James Theatre, April 23, 1993

The Broadway musical has never been the same since rock and roll stole its audience and threw it into an identity crisis. For three decades, from the moment *Meet the Beatles* usurped the supremacy of such Broadway pop as *Hello, Dolly!*, the commercial theater has desperately tried to win back the young (without alienating their elders) by watering down rock music, simulating rock music, and ripping off rock music. A result has been a few scattered hits over the years, typified by *Hair* and *Jesus Christ Superstar,* most of which have tamed the rock-and-roll revolution rather than spread it throughout Times Square.

Until now.

Tommy, the stunning new stage adaptation of the 1969 rock opera by the British group the Who, is at long last the authentic rock musical that has eluded Broadway for two generations. A collaboration of its original principal author, Pete Townshend, and the director, Des McAnuff, this show is not merely an entertainment juggernaut, riding at full tilt on the visual and musical highs of its legendary pinball iconography and irresistible tunes, but also a surprisingly moving resuscitation of the disturbing passions that made *Tommy* an emblem of its era. In the apocalyptic year of 1969, *Tommy* was the unwitting background music for the revelation of the My Lai massacre, the Chicago Seven trial, the Charles Manson murders. Those cataclysmic associations still reverberate within the piece, there to be tapped for the Who's generation, even as the show at the St. James is so theatrically fresh and emotionally raw that newcomers to *Tommy* will think it was born yesterday.

In a way, it was. Though the voices and pit band of this *Tommy* faithfully reproduce the 1969 double album, adding merely one song ("I Believe My Own Eyes"), a few snippets of dialogue, and some extended passages of underscoring, the production bears no resemblance to the Who's own concert performances of the opera (which culminated in an appearance at the Metropolitan Opera House in 1970) or to Ken Russell's pious, gag-infested 1975 film adaptation. Instead of merely performing the songs or exploiting them as cues for general riffs of dance and psychedelia, the evening's creators, who also include the choreographer Wayne Cilento and some brilliant multimedia artists led by the set designer John Arnone, use their singing actors to flesh out the drama of *Tommy*. Better still, they excavate the fable's meaning until finally the opera's revised conclusion spreads catharsis like wildfire through the cheering house.

Both the story and its point are as simple as *Peter Pan* (with which *Tommy* shares its London setting and some flying stunts by Foy). The show's eponymous hero is a boy who is stricken deaf, dumb, and blind at the age of four after watching his father return from a World War II prisoners' camp to shoot his mother's lover. Tommy's only form of communication proves to be his latent wizardry at pinball, a talent that soon turns him into a media sensation. As played by Michael Cerveris with the sleek white outfit, dark shades, and narcissistic attitude of a rock star, the grown-up Tommy is nearly every modern child's revenge fantasy come true: the untouchable icon who gets the uncritical adulation from roaring crowds that his despised parents never gave him at home.

In this telling, Tommy is often played simultaneously by two child actors (representing him at ages four and ten) in addition to Mr. Cerveris. The isolated young Tommy's totemic, recurring cry of yearning—"See me, feel me, touch me, heal me"—flows repeatedly between inner child and grown man, giving piercing voice to the eternal childhood psychic aches of loneliness and lovelessness. It is this primal theme, expressed with devastating simplicity in Mr. Townshend's score and lyrics, that has made *Tommy* timeless, outlasting the Who itself (which more or less dis-banded in 1982). Yet it is the evil of the authority figures the hero must overcome—a distant father (Jonathan Dokuchitz), a dismissive mother (Marcia Mitzman), a sexually abusive Uncle Ernie (Paul Kandel), and various fascistic thugs—that also makes *Tommy* a poster-simple political statement reflecting the stark rage of the Vietnam era.

As staged by Mr. McAnuff, that anger is present but the story is kept firmly rooted in its own time, from the forties to the early sixties. The slide projections that drive the production design at first re-create in black-and-white the London of the blitz, then spill into the vibrant Pop Art imagery of pinball machines, early Carnaby Street, and Andy Warhol paintings before returning to black-and-white for televised crowd images that recall the early British rock explosion as witnessed on *The Ed Sulli-van Show*. Mr. Cilento's compact dances similarly advance from wartime jitterbugging to the fifties sock-hopping of early rock-and-roll movies to evocations of the mod antics of *A Hard Day's Night* and its imitators in the sixties.

But the highly sophisticated theatrical style of this *Tommy*, which co-alesces as a continuous wave of song, scenes, kaleidoscopic design, and dance, owes everything to musical-theater innovations unknown until the mid-1970s. Mr. McAnuff, whose past Broadway works include the relatively stodgy *Big River* and *A Walk in the Woods*, shrewdly turns to ex-amples set by such directors as Harold Prince, Michael Bennett, and Robert Wilson. Here and there are echoes of the mock-documentary su-perstar sequences of *Evita* and *Dreamgirls*, in which abstract scaffolding and bridges suggest a showbiz firmament and a surging mob. As in those cinematic Prince and Bennett shows, the entire company becomes an undulating organism that defines the stage space and is always on the fly.

From Mr. Wilson, whose theater experiments have sometimes in-volved autistic boys eerily resembling the fictive Tommy, Mr. McAnuff and his designers take the notion of threading a few repeated images ab-stractly through the action: floating chairs, mirrors, the Union Jack, air-plane propellers, and disembodied Man Ray eyes, not to mention doors and windows reminiscent of sixties rock-album cover art and the hallu-cinogenic mythology such art canonized. (Sometimes the new incidental scoring takes some hints from Mr. Wilson's occasional musical collabo-rator, Philip Glass.) These dreamy visual touchstones are constantly reshuffled and distorted throughout *Tommy* for subliminal effect, reach-ing their apotheosis in an inevitable (and superbly executed) set piece in which the entire theater becomes a gyrating pinball machine celebrating the rebellious hero's "amazing journey" to newfound freedom.

Even in that blowout sequence, *Tommy* eschews the heavy visual spectacle of recent West End rock operas (and Broadway musicals) to keep its effects lithe and to the point. Often the most evocative sequences are spare and intimate: a candlelit Christmas dinner haunted by the ghosts of family horrors past, an abandoned urban lot in which the Acid Queen (Cheryl Freeman, paying persuasive vocal homage to Tina Turner) is more a feral junkie than a phantasmagoric gypsy. Dominating the stage instead of being usurped by hardware, the performers can shine as well, from the dazzling Mr. Cerveris, who grows from melancholy youth to strutting pop belter, to Ms. Mitzman's powerfully sung mother, Mr. Kandel's sinister Uncle Ernie, and the tireless ensemble, its youngest members included.

When the time comes for the entire company to advance on the audience to sing the soaring final incantation—"Listening to you I get the music / Gazing at you I get the heat"—*Tommy* has done what rock and roll can do but almost never does in the theater: reawaken an audience's adolescent feelings of rebellion and allow them open-throated release. But reflecting the passage of time and Mr. Townshend's own mature age of forty-seven, this version takes a brave step further, concluding with a powerful tableau of reconciliation that lifts an audience of the 1990s out of its seats.

"Hope I die before I get old," sang the Who in "My Generation," its early hit single. A quarter-century or so later, Mr. Townshend hasn't got old so much as grown up, into a deeper view of humanity unthinkable in the late 1960s. Far from being another of Broadway's excursions into nostalgia, *Tommy* is the first musical in years to feel completely alive in its own moment. No wonder that for two hours it makes the world seem young.

ANGELS IN AMERICA: MILLENNIUM APPROACHES
WALTER KERR THEATRE, MAY 5, 1993

History is about to crack open," says Ethel Rosenberg, back from the dead, as she confronts a cadaverous Roy Cohn, soon to die of AIDS, in his East Side town house. "Something's going to give," says a Brooklyn housewife so addicted to Valium she thinks she is in Antarctica. The year is 1985. It is fifteen years until the next millennium. And a young man drenched in death fevers in his Greenwich Village bedroom hears a persistent throbbing, a thunderous heartbeat, as if the heavens were about to give birth to a miracle so that he might be born again.

This is the astonishing theatrical landscape, intimate and epic, of Tony Kushner's *Angels in America,* which made its much-awaited Broadway debut at the Walter Kerr Theatre last night. This play has already been talked about so much that you may feel you have already seen it, but believe me, you haven't, even if you actually have. The new New York production is the third I've seen of *Millennium Approaches,* as the first, self-contained, three-and-a-half-hour part of *Angels in America* is titled. (Part two, *Perestroika,* is to join it in repertory in the fall.) As directed with crystalline lucidity by George C. Wolfe and ignited by blood-churning performances by Ron Leibman and Stephen Spinella, this staging only adds to the impression that Mr. Kushner has written the most thrilling American play in years.

Angels in America is a work that never loses its wicked sense of humor or its wrenching grasp on such timeless dramatic matters as life, death, and faith even as it ranges through territory as far-flung as the complex, plague-ridden nation Mr. Kushner wishes both to survey and to address. Subtitled "A Gay Fantasia on National Themes," the play is a political call to arms for the age of AIDS, but it is no polemic. Mr. Kushner's convictions about power and justice are matched by his conviction that the stage, and perhaps the stage alone, is a space large enough to accommodate everything from precise realism to surrealistic hallucination, from black comedy to religious revelation. In *Angels in America,* a true American work in its insistence on embracing all possibilities in art and life, he makes the spectacular case that they can all be brought into fusion in one play.

At center stage, *Angels* is a domestic drama, telling the story of two very different but equally troubled young New York couples, one gay and one nominally heterosexual, who intersect by chance. But the story of these characters soon proves inseparable from the way Mr. Kushner tells it. His play opens with a funeral led by an Orthodox rabbi and reaches its culmination with what might be considered a Second Coming. In between, it travels to Salt Lake City in search of latter-day saints and spirals into dreams and dreams-within-dreams where the languages spoken belong to the minority American cultures of drag and jazz. Hovering above it all is not only an Angel (Ellen McLaughlin) but also an Antichrist, Mr. Leibman's Roy Cohn, an unreconstructed right-wing warrior who believes that "life is full of horror" from which no one can escape.

While Cohn is a villain, a hypocritical closet case and a corrupt paragon of both red-baiting and Reagan-era greed, his dark view of life is not immediately dismissed by Mr. Kushner. The America of *Angels in America* is riddled with cruelty. When a young WASP esthete named Prior Walter (Mr. Spinella) reveals his first lesions of Kaposi's sarcoma to his lover of four years, a Jewish clerical worker named Louis Ironson (Joe Mantello), he finds himself deserted in a matter of weeks. Harper Pitt (Marcia Gay Harden), pill-popping housewife and devout Mormon, has recurrent nightmares that a man with a knife is out to kill her; she also has real reason to fear that the man is her husband, Joe (David Marshall Grant), an ambitious young lawyer with a dark secret and aspirations to rise high in Ed Meese's Justice Department.

But even as Mr. Kushner portrays an America of lies and cowardice to match Cohn's cynical view, he envisions another America of truth and beauty, the paradise imagined by both his Jewish and Mormon characters' ancestors as they made their crossing to the new land. *Angels in America* not only charts the split of its two central couples but it also implicitly sets its two gay men with AIDS against each other in a battle over their visions of the future. While the fatalistic, self-loathing Cohn ridicules gay men as political weaklings with "zero clout" doomed to defeat, the younger, equally ill Prior sees the reverse. "I am a gay man, and I am used to pressure," he says from his sick bed. "I am tough and strong." Possessed by scriptural visions he describes as "very Steven Spielberg" even when in abject pain, Prior is Mr. Kushner's prophet of hope in the midst of apocalypse.

Though Cohn and Prior never have a scene together, they are the larger-than-life poles between which all of *Angels in America* swings. And they could not be more magnetically portrayed than they are in this production. Mr. Leibman, red-faced and cackling, is a demon of Shakespearean grandeur, an alternately hilarious and terrifying mixture of chutzpah and megalomania, misguided brilliance and relentless cunning. He turns the mere act of punching telephone buttons into a grotesque manipulation of the levers of power, and he barks out the most outrageous pronouncements ("I brought out something tender in him," he says of Joe McCarthy) with a shamelessness worthy of history's most indelible monsters.

Mr. Spinella is a boyish actor so emaciated that when he removes his clothes for a medical examination, some in the audience gasp. But he fluently conveys buoyant idealism and pungent drag-queen wit as well as the piercing, openmouthed cries of fear and rage that arrive with the graphically dramatized collapse of his health. Mr. Spinella is also blessed with a superb acting partner in Mr. Mantello, who as his callow lover is a combustible amalgam of puppyish Jewish guilt and self-serving intellectual piety.

The entire cast, which includes Kathleen Chalfant and Jeffrey Wright in a variety of crisply observed comic cameos, is first rate. Ms. Harden's shattered, sleepwalking housewife is pure pathos, a figure of slurred thought, voice and emotions, while Mr. Grant fully conveys the internal warfare of her husband, torn between Mormon rectitude and uncontrollable sexual heat. When Mr. Wolfe gets both of the play's couples on stage simultaneously to enact their parallel, overlapping domestic crack-ups, *Angels in America* becomes a wounding fugue of misunderstanding and recrimination committed in the name of love.

But *Angels in America* is an ideal assignment for Mr. Wolfe because of its leaps beyond the bedroom into the fabulous realms of myth and American archetypes, which have preoccupied this director and playwright in such works as *The Colored Museum* and *Spunk*. Working again with Robin Wagner, the designer who was an essential collaborator on *Jelly's Last Jam*, Mr. Wolfe makes the action fly through the delicate, stylized heaven that serves as the evening's loose scenic environment, yet he also manages to make some of the loopier scenes, notably those involving a real-estate agent in Salt Lake City and a homeless woman in the South Bronx, sharper and far more pertinent than they have seemed before.

What has really affected *Angels in America* during the months of its odyssey to New York, however, is not so much its change of directors as Washington's change of administrations. When first seen a year or so ago, the play seemed defined by its anger at the reigning political establishment, which tended to reward the Roy Cohns and ignore the Prior Walters. Mr. Kushner has not revised the text since—a crony of Cohn's still boasts of a Republican lock on the White House until the year 2000—but the shift in Washington has had the subliminal effect of making *Angels in America* seem more focused on what happens next than on the past.

This is why any debate about what this play means or does not mean for Broadway seems, in the face of the work itself, completely beside the point. *Angels in America* speaks so powerfully because something far larger and more urgent than the future of the theater is at stake. It really is history that Mr. Kushner intends to crack open. He sends his haunting messenger, a spindly, abandoned gay man with a heroic spirit and a ravaged body, deep into the audience's heart to ask just who we are and just what, as the plague continues and the millennium approaches, we intend this country to become.

FINAL SEASON

Autumn 1993

Tony Kushner's *Angels in America: Perestroika*

SUNSET BOULEVARD
ADELPHI THEATRE, LONDON, JUNE 14, 1993

In the narrow world of British show business, little short of an earthquake could upstage the opening of a new Andrew Lloyd Webber musical. But as it bizarrely happened, just such a tremor shook the West End on Monday. Hours before the opening of Mr. Lloyd Webber's *Sunset Boulevard*, the newspapers gave big play to the unexpected announcement that the West End production of the Broadway hit *City of Angels* would close after only a four-month run.

City of Angels received rave reviews, and its box-office collapse was blamed on the gravity of the recession and the declining sophistication of West End audiences. Since both *City of Angels* and *Sunset Boulevard* happen to be about Hollywood in the late 1940s, the abrupt failure of the American show cast a particular pall over Mr. Lloyd Webber's gala premiere. Although *Sunset* boasts the cushion of a large advance sale— at £4 million ($6 million), neck and neck with a new revival of *Grease*, starring Debbie Gibson—any visitor to its box office last week could discover that seats are readily available, as they are for virtually every West End attraction. No wonder, then, that *The Evening Standard* ran an editorial on Monday all but praying for the musical's success, reminding its readers that a "smash hit show" not only "lifts our thoughts from humdrum, everyday toils" but "also draws foreign visitors to London."

The paper was still on the stands when the curtain at the Adelphi Theatre rose on a show that, despite its occasional resemblance to Madame Tussaud's, is unlikely to be a perennial tourist attraction akin to the last new Lloyd Webber musical to become an international hit, the nearly seven-year-old *Phantom of the Opera*. The early reviews are supportively mixed, with some of the critics pointedly finding *Sunset Boulevard* wanting in comparison not so much with the 1950 Billy Wilder movie on which it is based but with *City of Angels*.

In truth, *Sunset* tries very hard, arguably to the point of artistic imprisonment, to be faithful to Mr. Wilder's acerbic masterpiece. Much of the film's plot, dialogue, and horror-movie mood are preserved, not to mention clips used to illustrate those sequences in which the faded silent-film star, Norma Desmond (Patti LuPone), and her kept young screenwriter, Joe Gillis (Kevin Anderson), travel by car. While a few anachronisms slip in, the co-librettists, the lyricist, Don Black (*Aspects of Love*), and the playwright, Christopher Hampton (*Les Liaisons Dangereuses*), smartly tailor their new jokes to the original screenplay's style.

At times even Mr. Lloyd Webber gets into the Wilder swing. Both acts open with joltingly angry diatribes about Hollywood, part exposition-packed recitative and part song, in which the surprisingly dark, jazz-accented music, the most interesting I've yet encountered from this composer, meshes perfectly with the cynical lyrics. Each of these numbers is led with bite, sexual swagger, and vocal force by Mr. Anderson, whose invaluable performance suggests a mixture of *Pal Joey* (which he once played at the Goodman Theatre in Chicago) and Tim Robbins's contemporary Hollywood shark in *The Player*. Like his screen predecessor in the part, William Holden, Mr. Anderson makes the sardonic Wilder voice an almost physical presence in *Sunset Boulevard*. But that voice is too often drowned out by both Ms. LuPone's Broadway belt and the mechanical efforts of Mr. Lloyd Webber and his director, Trevor Nunn, to stamp the proven formulas of *Phantom* and *Les Mis* on even an intimate tale.

Ms. LuPone is a gifted actress whose vocal pyrotechnics are especially idolized by the British, not least because their own musical-theater stars can rarely match them. Yet despite her uncanny mimicry of Gloria Swanson's speaking voice and her powerhouse delivery of the score's grand if predictable ballads, she is miscast and unmoving as Norma Desmond. Until the final scenes, when she is given a fright wig more suggestive of radiation treatment than of advancing years, Ms. LuPone acts and looks her own spry forty-something. Since Mr. Anderson appears to be only about five years younger—as opposed to the seeming two-to-three-decade gap between Swanson and Holden—the pathos and creepiness are drained from Norma's desperate attachment to Joe and, by extension, to her own vanished youth as the most glamorous star of a bygone day. Even in her showy, final mad scene, Ms. LuPone does not snap in the heartbreaking Blanche DuBois manner called for and instead finds her strenuous efforts vulgarized by one of many garish Anthony Powell costumes, the sudden and baffling appearance of a red ribbon as a maniacally waved prop, and echo-chamber sound effects.

An equally serious shortcoming is Ms. LuPone's inability, through no fault of her own, to convey the heroine's legendary status in the showbiz firmament. As Swanson was in real life a repository of a half-forgotten screen era at the time she made *Sunset Boulevard,* so the musical version would seem to need its own resonant equivalent, a Shirley MacLaine or an Angela Lansbury, generically speaking. But Mr. Lloyd Webber, who still puts his desire to write pop hits above the theatrical needs of his projects, has written himself into a corner with Norma. The major arias he has given her, designed as usual to be extracted and plugged by recording artists, are too vocally demanding to be sung by most older stars who might otherwise be plausible in the part. (One exception is Barbra Streisand, who has recorded two *Sunset* songs without, as yet, turning either into a hit of remotely "Memory" or "Music of the Night" proportions.)

Parts of the musical *Sunset,* notably the vivid staging of the scene in which Norma briefly finds herself in a spotlight while visiting a Cecil B. DeMille soundstage, might be thrilling with a more affecting figure center stage. Such is the story's tidal pull. But much of this production would still droop. While the show runs a standard two and a half hours or so, it feels heavily padded. Three supposedly comic numbers, occasioned by such trivial events as Joe's wardrobe shopping spree, are leaden, with one New Year's party routine for Hollywood's young crowd weirdly recalling Lincoln Center's ill-fated *My Favorite Year.* Much of Act 2, in which six of ten songs are reprises, is given over to an attenuated account of Joe's illicit romance with a fledgling screenwriter (the Nancy Olson role in the film), who is insipidly written and performed (by Meredith Braun) and must be ludicrously reduced to nearly jailbait age to make her a young alternative to Ms. LuPone's youthful Norma.

John Napier's scenery is, as expected, spectacular, with an artful rather than literal-minded swimming-pool effect for the famous opening scene and an evocative array of film noir shadows, some of them redolent of Mother Bates's homestead in *Psycho.* The eye-filling main set is the living room of Norma's mansion, which honors the film's vision of an old-time Hollywood palazzo even as it revives the gilt and glittering candelabra of *The Phantom of the Opera.* There are many more *Phantom* echoes in *Sunset Boulevard,* not all scenic or musical or innocent, from the broad premise (a lovesick, potentially lethal phantom haunting a Baroque palace) to the parody sequences (of spear-carrying movie epics instead of kitsch operas) to the final unmasking of its protagonist. Mr. Nunn, unfortunately, cannot muster the cinematic touch with which Harold Prince gave *Phantom* the illusion of continuous movement. The only fluid sequence in *Sunset* is the first, a tour of Hollywood that is choreographed by Bob Avian with a flair worthy of the stage montages on which he collaborated with Michael Bennett.

The occasional excursion into fresh air aside, *Sunset Boulevard* is usually a three-character piece encased in a lumbering environment large enough to accommodate *Aïda*, the third character being Daniel Benzali's waxworks replica of Erich von Stroheim's mysterious aide de camp, Max. At odd moments, sometimes for no apparent reason other than to exercise the stage machinery, the mammoth set advances like a glacier toward the audience or retreats or, most dramatically, rises partly up into the flies, actors in tow. Since *Sunset Boulevard* is not scheduled to open in Los Angeles (with Glenn Close as Norma) until December and on Broadway (with Ms. LuPone and Mr. Anderson) until the fall of 1994, its creators have the time and the increasingly rare West End luxury of presold audiences to search for means other than hydraulics to make their show lift off.

≡ Sunset Boulevard *eventually found its theatrical life as a continuing story in the tabloids—as Lloyd Webber dropped LuPone for the Broadway production, replaced her with Glenn Close after Close got great reviews in L.A. (including one from Vincent Canby in the* Times*), and then fired Close's L.A. successor, Faye Dunaway, in rehearsal. None of this hoopla, however, prevented* Sunset Boulevard *from achieving its final headlines as the costliest flop in Broadway history—the ultimate "hit" flop, since it ran more than two years. Given the financial settlements paid to LuPone and Dunaway, the extravagances of the production, and losses piled up by its road companies, Broadway hands estimated the total* Sunset *loss at a record $20 million. As a further sign the Lloyd Webber bubble was bursting, his first post-*Sunset *musical,* Whistle Down the Wind, *closed in Washington during its pre-Broadway tryout, and his production company, Really Useful, started downsizing. Lloyd Webber has not had a new hit since* Phantom *opened a decade ago.*

ARCADIA / AN INSPECTOR CALLS
ROYAL NATIONAL THEATRE, LONDON, JULY 8, 1993

Only an Englishman could write a play about sexual passion and sublimate it in three hours of witty discourse on the second law of thermodynamics, the history of British landscape gardening, the elu-

sive movements of Lord Byron, and the advent of the mathematical revolution known as chaos theory. And probably no Englishman could write
such a play better than Tom Stoppard, whose new comedy, *Arcadia,* is
his first London hit and only his second major work for the theater since
The Real Thing a decade ago.

At the Royal National Theatre, where *Arcadia* is playing in a glossy
Trevor Nunn production on the Lyttelton stage, the program is stuffed
with enough scholarly apparatus to support a cross-discipline seminar
jointly taught by Stephen Hawking and A. S. Byatt. Some English newspapers sent science correspondents along with their drama critics to
cover the play when it opened this spring.

Set on the same grand Derbyshire estate, Sidley Park, in both 1809
and the present, *Arcadia* is, ostensibly at least, a crash course on the
birth of the modern age. Mr. Stoppard's 1809 characters occupy a physical and mental landscape whose classical gardens, Newtonian scientific
principles, and matching codes of behavior are giving way to the unruly
Gothic urges of the Romantic era. His major present-day characters, two
rival historical researchers played by Felicity Kendal and Bill Nighy, are
trying to investigate what really went on with Byron and company at
Sidley Park in 1809 even as they stumble, with the rest of us, into an uncertain future of their own. In the contemporary scientific Arcadia of *Arcadia,* man is "better at predicting events on the edge of the galaxy . . .
than whether it'll rain on Auntie's garden party three weeks from now."

What is most unpredictable about *Arcadia,* however, is the powerful
emotional spin it achieves by its nocturnal final scene, in which past and
present collide in waltz time in an unexpected, disorienting fusion of
hearts, not minds. For all this densely packed play's jabbering about
every matter under the intellectual sun, it is that old devil moon, a lovers'
moon, that really moves Mr. Stoppard and the audience. The author
played by Ms. Kendal in *Arcadia,* like the writer at the center of *The Real
Thing,* is a chilly know-it-all who must learn what life's real thing is and
inexorably does. "What is carnal embrace?" a thirteen-year-old math
prodigy of 1809 (Emma Fielding) asks her hot-blooded tutor (Rufus
Sewell) in the evening's very first line, raising the only question in the
play to which the answer is not rhetorical.

This central thread of *Arcadia* is deeply felt but too often lost in the
work's vast tapestry. While Mr. Stoppard celebrates human "bodies in
heat" who practice with free will "the attraction that Newton left out,"
his play sometimes grinds along, however amusingly, in a deterministic
gear. There are a half-dozen or so secondary characters, from a naval
captain in 1809 to a mute teenage boy in the modern scenes, who exist

as integers in the evening's thematic and narrative equations but make no independent impressions as people. (By contrast, a couple of major figures in the action, including Byron, remain offstage.) While some of the shortfall can be attributed to the production's largely routine acting—Ms. Fielding and Mr. Sewell are the notable exceptions—even Ms. Kendal's role is so perfunctorily sketched that an actor can take it only so far.

There are some hilarious riffs along the way, many of them at the expense of academics (as in Mr. Stoppard's *Jumpers*) and English lit (as slyly embodied by Harriet Walter, in the role of a Sheridanesque queen bee). But like the repressed author played by Ms. Kendal, Mr. Stoppard does not always know when to leave well enough alone and muzzle the erudition with which he shields himself from the vagaries of feeling. It is the paradox of the fascinating but overwritten *Arcadia* that it is most rendingly alive when the mysteries of the past, present, and future elude the brilliant characters entirely and, for the duration of a waltz or a carnal embrace, strike them and their creator dumb.

Also to be found at the National is a 1945 play by J. B. Priestley (1894–1984) that's a match in hair-raising theatrical thrills for the other 1945 revival, of Rodgers and Hammerstein's *Carousel,* staged by the company last winter. The play is *An Inspector Calls,* a well-made, sometimes didactic old warhorse, which has been transformed by its director, Stephen Daldry, into a nonstop, 110-minute bolt of nightmarish hallucination with a guillotine-sharp political edge.

Priestley set his play in 1912 but conceived it as a call to arms for the end of World War II, as English voters had to choose between the Conservative status quo and Labor's promise of egalitarian social reform. The villains of the tightly told piece are the members of a selfish ruling-class family in industrial Yorkshire whose dinner party is interrupted by the mysterious arrival of an inspector investigating the suicide of a poor young local woman. As Inspector Goole (pronounced "ghoul" and acted accordingly by Kenneth Cranham) asks insinuating questions of the complacent, bourgeois revelers, it becomes clear that they all bear guilt for the destruction of a woman they have variously exploited for cheap labor, cheap sex, or worse. And then the plot thickens.

Mr. Daldry, collaborating with a most remarkable designer, Ian MacNeil, stages *An Inspector Calls* as if it were a hybrid of Orson Welles's shadowy expressionist film version of *The Trial,* Poe's "The Fall of the House of Usher," and a surreal canvas by Paul Delvaux, all set to a macabre incidental score echoing that of Alfred Hitchcock's *Vertigo.* Like the neighboring *Arcadia,* this production exists in two periods at once, pre–World War I and post–World War II, and to chilling effect. Although the family parlor is aglow in Edwardian finery, it is reduced to almost doll-house proportions, placed on stilts, and surrounded by an ominously gray, crater-pocked, postwar landscape that overwhelms it. The well-to-do characters in evening dress must occasionally step down into the proletarian gloom to play their scenes, and they are frequently shadowed by a silent, scurrying chorus of shell-shocked and starving refugees, many of them hollow-eyed children, who could be blitz victims or dispossessed miners' families or both.

It's only a matter of time before the privileged doll's house perched above the mass of humanity literally comes crashing down, but Mr. Daldry does not stop there. The entire staging is framed by an old-fashioned gilt proscenium, complete with red plush curtain, which proves a source of still other coups de théâtre. As Priestley makes his startlingly timeless statement about social responsibility in a world driven by greed for power and capital, so this thirty-two-year-old director makes his own revisionist statement, deconstructing and reinventing Priestley's stodgy theater before our astonished eyes even as he leaves the playwright's moral credos untouched.

≡ *Both these productions—both recast—eventually came to New York,* Inspector Calls *more successfully than* Arcadia.

IN THE SUMMER HOUSE

VIVIAN BEAUMONT THEATER, AUGUST 2, 1993

I'm Jewish, homosexual, alcoholic, a communist—and I'm a cripple!" Jane Bowles once bragged, winning a bout of one-upsmanship with a self-pitying fellow traveler on the literary fringe. Bowles, whose writing career was over by the time she had a stroke at the age of forty and who died in 1973 at fifty-six, was everything she said and more, including the wife of the novelist and composer Paul Bowles (*The Sheltering Sky*), with whom she fashioned a now-legendary open marriage in the sybaritic expatriates' colony of Tangier.

An original and independent woman, yet one who never escaped her demons or her husband's orbit, Jane Bowles was born to be a heroine for our time, if only a cult figure in her own. She'd be fascinating with or without her limp, as those who have read her letters, her biography (by Millicent Dillon), or Michelle Green's recent group portrait of the Tangier crowd (*The Dream at the End of the World*) can attest. Her own literary output, however, was tiny: one novel, seven short stories, and one full-length play, *In the Summer House,* which was revived at the Vivian Beaumont Theater last night.

This odd-duck drama about mothers and daughters, which received respectful reviews but scant audiences during its two-month run in the 1953–54 Broadway season, is just the sort of unjustly neglected piece a company like Lincoln Center Theater should be reexamining. As far as I can determine, it has received only one previous professional revival in New York, short-lived and Off Broadway thirty years ago. This production, directed by JoAnne Akalaitis, is faithful to the work's letter and spirit, but it is seriously compromised by some poor acting and by the vast expanse of the Beaumont stage, which the designer, George Tsypin, accentuates to serve the play's poetic subtext but not the performers who must deliver the text itself.

In the Summer House finds its life in the free spin of characters and language, not epic vistas or plot. Its 1950s Bohemian manner, in which the transitions and emotional key changes are as abrupt as those in a jazz improvisation, is typified by the opening monologue, spoken from a balcony by Dianne Wiest in a Judy Holliday voice and a flaming red wig. Ms. Wiest plays Gertrude Eastman Cuevas, a Southern California widow whose mind veers illogically from her acerbic memories of her dead husband to her deepest feelings of loss and isolation, with time out to browbeat her teenage daughter (Alina Arenal) and to plot her cynical next marriage to a moneyed Mexican (Jaime Tirelli). Forty years after its debut, the speech is still so tricky that Ms. Akalaitis feels compelled to negotiate it for the audience by underlining its gravest passages with such *Bell Jar* effects as portentous lighting cues and weeping Philip Glass music.

Mrs. Eastman Cuevas is a suffocating mother from hell, but so full of unexpected edges she defies cliché. She is soon matched in eccentricity by another widow, the visiting Mrs. Constable (Frances Conroy, in the evening's outstanding performance), and another problem daughter (Kali Rocha), who add their own tragic complications to the Eastman Cuevas ménage. In a program note comparing Bowles to a number of twentieth-century male playwrights, Ms. Akalaitis argues that these women are closer to Eugene O'Neill's than to those of Tennessee Williams, a Bowles friend. But despite a scene that echoes Mary Tyrone's mad descent in her wedding dress in *Long Day's Journey into Night,* the women of *In the Summer House* usually can be found replicating the struggles between the weak and the strong in Williams plays.

The one significant male intruder, a suitor (Liev Schreiber) for Mrs. Eastman Cuevas's daughter, pushes the filial struggles for dominance into overdrive.

Yet Bowles's uninhibited voice, distinguished by surreal humor and non sequiturs ("Whenever I think of a woman going wild, I always picture her with black hair"), is her own. A character in mid-breakdown forgets her sorrows the moment she retrieves a lost pocketbook. A drunken reverie includes a bizarre digression about the difficulty of registering to vote. Incongruous food imagery is ubiquitous: Sugar, rice, spaghetti and meatballs, hot dogs, chop suey, and oyster cocktails all play strange, sometimes dreamy, sometimes farcical roles in the action. One character fantasizes about opening an "odd" Restaurant Midnight; the entire second act takes place in a joint called the Lobster Bowl.

Ms. Akalaitis is at her most imaginative juggling such absurdities. Mr. Tsypin's set, a Dali landscape bathed in Georgia O'Keeffe light by Jennifer Tipton, allows the director to make ditsy spectacle out of the eating, singing, and dancing of the Mexican entourage surrounding Mrs. Eastman Cuevas's new husband. A beach scene opens with a striking tableau of catatonic sunbathers in shades; Act 1 ends with the spooky, silent business of a just-wed couple sitting at a table reading magazines. A sad image of drowning, seen through a gauzy haze, could be a classical icon.

It's the intimate moments and the nuances of acting that, as usual, too frequently elude this director. Both unstable daughters, one of them described as "dangerous" and "ready to explode," come across as collegiate ingenues; Mr. Schreiber's suitor offers a single dull note of wounded innocence, and Sheila Tousey, in the role of the chain-smoking, tattooed, loudmouthed Lobster Bowl proprietor, is a brassy hash-slinger as she might be imagined by an anthropologist who has yet to go out on a field trip. These inadequate performances are stretched thinner still by the large distances the open set and expansive staging require their flat voices and wan personalities to command.

For Ms. Wiest, an actress of brilliant technique, the challenges are in the text. Although she does wonderfully by Mrs. Eastman Cuevas's wit, she is not in the habit of playing unlovable characters and rarely conveys the requisite cruelty; in her final scene of nervous collapse, she reconciles the role's complex strands by blurring and sentimentalizing them in bouts of sobbing histrionics that do not devastate the audience as intended.

In the 1953 production, Judith Anderson's Mrs. Eastman Cuevas was widely thought to have been overshadowed by Mildred Dunnock's Mrs.

Constable, and history repeats itself here. Ms. Conroy's prim, patrician mother, forever trying to avoid "the black pit" by concentrating on "petty details," starts off a bit squeakily. But her extended drunk scene in the second act, in which the actress's ghostly pallor and aura of crumbling gentility belie her guttural alcoholic wisecracks, is a memorable ride through psychic hairpin turns. Alternately hilarious and desperate, in focus and utterly lost, Ms. Conroy embraces Mrs. Constable's mad contradictions without reining them in to form a conventional stage neurotic.

Is this character what Jane Bowles was like? So it seems. For all that is problematic in Ms. Akalaitis's *In the Summer House,* the rare bird that wrote it is still there to be heard, beating her bright and crippled wings.

BLOWN SIDEWAYS THROUGH LIFE
New York Theatre Workshop, September 22, 1993

Claudia Shear is a Brooklyn-born woman of uncertain age (the late thirties, perhaps?) who personifies two middle-class nightmares. She is fat, and she cannot keep a job. As she explains in *Blown Sideways Through Life,* her hour-long autobiographical monologue at the New York Theatre Workshop, to be fat is to be branded not merely unerotic but un-American. And to have had and lost sixty-four (count 'em, sixty-four) jobs—for employers as varied as Bear Stearns and a whorehouse operating clandestinely on East Forty-ninth Street—is to be seen as without character, class, or a place in the world.

But in this aptly titled piece, Ms. Shear has at last found a place: in the theater. Her show, drawn exclusively from her own true, sometimes hilarious misadventures, marks the debut of a born dramatist. Neither a stand-up routine nor a strictly journalistic memoir, the monologue mixes vividly observed anecdotes with a sly, poignant, and highly theatrical investigation of one woman's search for an identity deeper and more human than any job description. The questions Ms. Shear raises about her own hapless quest for personal fulfillment in the workplace end up implicating an audience that may have arrived at the theater smug in its identity as the gainfully employed.

Blown Sideways may not be a play, exactly, but it merits the elegant full-dress production that it has received from the director Christopher Ashley, whose recent credits include *Fires in the Mirror* and *Jeffrey.* Aside from the occasional tale in need of editing (notably an attenuated account of a baptism in film acting in Rome), the only real letdown in the hour is Ms. Shear's acting. She is wonderful at playing herself—or at least the frank, assertive, alternately hostile and dreamy misfit she presents as herself—but no one will confuse her mimicry of the many colorful characters she meets with the chameleon, quick-change guises of even a fledgling Eric Bogosian or Anna Deavere Smith.

The writing is so inventive that it supports the show even when the performance is routine. A few choice words in close proximity can summon up a social milieu (Raoul's, size 6, Barneys). A phrase can capture a setting ("the empty, quiet light" of an artist's studio where Ms. Shear modeled), a sentence an entire scene ("It's four-fifteen in the morning and I'm trying to take a nap in a bathroom on Wall Street balancing my head on the toilet paper roll"). Sometimes Ms. Shear free-associates, running through lists of outfits she's worn on the job, or obnoxious demands made by authoritarian bosses, or the many lines with which she has been canned. The poetic effect of these hallucinatory verbal résumés of her employment history is to create an encyclopedic whirlwind tour of a city in which any kind of labor is possible at any place, any time.

Ms. Shear makes us see New York City fresh even with her briefest glimpses of such stints as pushing Helena Rubinstein cosmetics at Bloomingdale's, handling mounds of processed turkey meat in a catering operation at Madison Square Garden, and serving as a "fake secretary for a guy pulling a con involving pens." Her extended stays in degrading jobs inspire her to whip up a Dante-ish extravagance of detail: A long account of her duties as phone receptionist and confidante to a den of East Side prostitutes proves an unforgettable mixture of low sexual farce, graphic professional secrets, and casual snapshots of a humiliating trade.

"The voice of the world says it's time to stop being stories," Ms. Shear eventually worries, wondering if maybe it is time "to have a life" instead of seeking out adventures that only leave her older and exhausted. But she just as quickly decides that her many disjointed stories do constitute a life after all. "Nobody is just a busboy," she says at evening's end, insistently reminding the audience that everyone they meet, including the seemingly faceless people in menial jobs, "has a story that will stop your heart."

By then, we feel we know Ms. Shear's story, which has reached a catharsis of sorts after a transforming adventure in the Maine wilderness with Outward Bound. Or do we? *Blown Sideways Through Life*, after all, is itself a job (number sixty-five), not its author's life. The show ends with Ms. Shear breaking into a dance that wordlessly reveals the even more intimate self hidden behind her autobiographical stage persona. It's a story that will stop your heart.

OCTOBER 10, 1993

It seems almost embarrassing now that on a crisp early winter night in 1964 I had nothing better to do in my young life than walk up to the box office of the Shubert Theatre and buy a ticket for *Bajour*.

Bajour: The title doesn't exactly roar down memory lane thirty years later, does it? In truth, even at the time, it was the kind of carefree Broadway musical designed to be forgotten during intermission. When Act 2 began, you counted on the characters to remind you of just what they were doing when the curtain fell fifteen minutes earlier. The show was so artificial, so hermetically sealed in the creakiest conventions of musical comedy, that its every line abhorred any cohesive connections to human experience as practiced beyond Shubert Alley.

But for an indiscriminately stagestruck fifteen-year-old who had seen every respectable play in town at least once, there seemed no plausible alternative to *Bajour*. For one thing, M.K. had raved it—M.K. being an anonymous but ubiquitous graffiti scribbler of the time, perhaps also fifteen, who specialized in scrawling his own critical pronouncements in quote-ese on the posters in the theater district. Although M.K. routinely wielded his Magic Marker to dismiss the street's reigning hits ("A big bore!—M.K." was the verdict on *Hello, Dolly!*), he had pronounced *Bajour* the "best musical in town!" Also to the point, for me anyway, was the fact that *Bajour* had just opened and, like most musicals of the time, had enough of a theater-party advance to assure sold-out performances early in the run. A sold-out house meant the liberation of standing-room tickets. I preferred standing room not only because it was cheap—still three bucks or less—but because I had a romantic attachment to watching plays from the rear of the house, a consequence of my part-time job as a ticket taker back home in Washington at the National Theatre, an active tryout house of the time.

Bajour. I hadn't thought about the show much since 1964 until last year when I was trolling the racks of my local record store and discovered, to my amazement, that its original-cast recording was abundantly displayed in a shiny new CD rerelease by Sony, its cover that same poster image that M.K. had merrily defaced all those years ago.

I had to laugh. What audience could there possibly be for *Bajour* in the 1990s? Chita Rivera fanatics? (She starred in it, as a Gypsy who sang a palm-reading ballad, "Love-Line.") Collectors of Michael Bennett juvenilia? (He danced in the chorus.) Students of the journalistic canon of Joseph Mitchell?

It was Mr. Mitchell's *New Yorker* magazine reportage about Gypsies in New York that inspired *Bajour,* though the show itself was less interested in ethnic verisimilitude than in the marital prospects of its heroine, an aspiring young anthropologist with a meddling Jewish mother. The mother was played by none other than Mae Questel, the original voice of Hollywood's animated Betty Boop. The anthropologist was Nancy Dussault, who finally embraced romance after singing the lyric:

> Love is a chance made to be taken
> Why should I take to my heels?
> Why run away from mayhem that may come?
> Maybe I'd like how it feels.
> Love is a chance flighty and fleeting
> Here like quicksilver, then gone.
> Hi ho quick Silver! I'm riding with you
> Whether it's hither or yon.
> See how my heart's open wide—hey there!
> Love, take a good seat inside—and stay there!

You had to be there.

As it turns out, the *Bajour* CD was only one example of a flood of Broadway kitsch that Sony, Angel, RCA, and MCA have been sending forth during the last two years. With considerable energy, technical expertise, and expense, these labels have revived the original-cast recordings of often unrevivable musicals from the mid-1940s to the mid-1970s. Shows that originally never made it as far as Cleveland now can be reconsidered with the aid of booklets offering elaborate scholarly apparatus, in some cases in German, French, and Italian as well as English. As a friend of mine from those teenage years recently wondered, "Is it possible that M.K. grew up to become the head of Sony records?"

To be sure, many of the new releases are of the expected hits, sonically remastered and sometimes expanded with alternate tracks retrieved from dusty vaults. (Particularly elegant among the retooled classics are MCA's restored original-cast recordings of *Oklahoma!* and *Carousel,*

Sony's of *South Pacific*.) But what fascinates me most are all the releases of recordings that might be classified as marginalia and trivia—in some cases recordings that had scant audiences in their initial airing, souvenirs of forgotten shows so routine that they cannot even aspire to the status of cult flops. Stephen Sondheim's *Anyone Can Whistle*, which ran nine performances at the Majestic Theatre in 1964 but whose cast recording has rarely been out of print since, is a cult flop. So are *Candide, House of Flowers*, and *She Loves Me* in their original productions. By contrast, *Bajour*, which ran 232 performances, or seven months, shortly after *Anyone Can Whistle* closed in a week, is merely a flop. Some of the shows in the tidal wave of Broadway reissues, like *Plain and Fancy* and *Golden Boy*, belong to an equally ignominious category—the forgotten hit.

Great artistic claims can be made for few, if any, of these second-rung recordings, although in almost all cases they are far superior to the shows themselves. As a group, however, they impale in digital sound what in retrospect was the last dying gasp of the Broadway musical as an abundant mainstream American entertainment industry.

True, Broadway musicals are not extinct today, and occasionally a new one comes along that can be discussed in the same sentence as the classics. But the economy and culture that allowed a dozen or more musicals to prosper on Broadway in a typical season—most of them neither smash hits nor overnight flops but middling shows of the type canonized in the new CDs—are long gone. Today, brand-new American musicals are so costly to mount that they threaten to become semiannual events on Broadway. The throwaway Broadway musical, which might recoup its investment with a one-season New York run and a subsequent tour, is extinct. A theater like the Shubert or Winter Garden, which might have housed a new show (or two) every season (or two) thirty years ago, is now tied up by a single show for a decade.

Yet even if Broadway's economics permitted a dozen new musicals a season, it is hard to imagine who would write them or see them. Few new songwriters have been welcomed to Broadway since rock music solidified its hold on mainstream American culture in the 1960s; many of the major American songwriters of Broadway 1993 (Sondheim, Styne, Kander and Ebb, Coleman, Strouse) were in place at the time of *Bajour*, just as this year's Tony-winning musical actress, Ms. Rivera, was. Similarly, the middle-class theatergoers, often roped in by theater parties and brokers, who would support a *Bajour* for a season—while waiting to get into the big hits—are dead, retired, no longer in New York, or unable or unwilling to spring for sixty-five-dollar tickets. They have not been replenished by a young audience, whose musical tastes are scantily represented on modern Broadway.

Listening to the lesser musicals of the fifties and sixties again in their new sonic packages, I realize that even at the time I should have known the genre as it then existed was doomed. The Broadway musical's last peak came in the late 1950s—*My Fair Lady, West Side Story, The Music Man, Gypsy, The Sound of Music*—with shows whose scores remain as much a part of the period's enduring pop culture as Elvis. But only a few years later, the gap between Broadway entertainment, an increasingly minority taste, and the rest of the culture was enormous. *Hello, Dolly!* (1964), a smash hit that actually piled up a longer run than *My Fair Lady,* seems to harken from a distant, different century than contemporaneous compositions by the Beatles and Bob Dylan.

By then, Broadway was well into its decadent phase, when silly, brassy musical comedies continued to roll off the assembly line even though their audiences, authors, and cultural rationale were disappearing. Though superior relics of this old school, like *Dolly* and *Funny Girl* and *Mame,* were still immensely popular in the sixties, the many also-rans in their style, shows like *Subways Are for Sleeping* and *High Spirits,* amounted to filler. None of them would be produced on the prohibitive Broadway of today, where the few fluffy new musicals attempted are re-cyclings of the past (*Crazy for You, Guys and Dolls*) and where most new musicals (also few) are musical dramas like *Les Misérables* and *Kiss of the Spider Woman* in the image of weightier sixties shows like *Fiddler on the Roof* and *Cabaret.*

The brainless, second-rate musicals of the late 1950s and early 1960s were still fun to watch, at least to a wide-eyed youth of the time. They aspired to nothing more than commercial entertainment and were professional of their kind. Since I had in part sought out the fantasy world of the theater, as so many adolescents do, to seek refuge from a real world that I found inhospitable, these colorful shows offered complete escape. They were not my first choices for a night at the theater, but they served honorably while I waited for those infrequent nights of higher art to come along.

What made these mediocre musicals theatrical was their vulgar energy, their brazen self-assurance (however unearned), their genetic trace memories of vaudeville and burlesque rituals (however diluted) dating back to before I was born. Their performers were committed to what they were doing, which was to sing and dance in a larger-than-life idiom that television and movies abhorred. The shows boasted heat and light and noise, a freneticism that echoed the neon-hued tumult of the Times

Square that spawned them. They made a boy trapped in what was then a provincial Southern town feel nearer to the distant theater capital of his hyperventilated, insomniacal imaginings. In that sense, a disposable show like *Bajour* was closer in spirit to the honky-tonk Broadway of its time than was *My Fair Lady,* which was and is timeless.

Yet nostalgia for these musicals must be held in check. Their kinetic energy, severed as it was from first-rate songwriting, produced a tinny sound. For the performers who strained to put them over, they were dead ends. By the early sixties, the stars of the Broadway musical's last vintage era, Merman and Martin and Raitt and Drake and Channing, were nearing the final stage of their careers. No matter how hard the new, younger Broadway musical talents worked, they had arrived too late to achieve the same magnitude of stardom.

The only real musical-comedy stars that Broadway produced in this period, Julie Andrews and Barbra Streisand, immediately decamped to Hollywood, never to return. [In 1995, Andrews would end her thirty-five-year exile with, alas, *Victor/Victoria.*] The others took what work they could. An ingenue like Nancy Dussault, proclaimed an overnight sensation (and instantly booked on *The Ed Sullivan Show*) after her debut in a Phil Silvers vehicle, *Do Re Mi,* in 1960, had no hope of finding the roles that might make her the next Mary Martin. Instead, she became Mary Martin's final replacement in the Broadway production of *The Sound of Music.* From there, it was on to *Bajour.*

To me, a paradigmatic musical of this period of decline was *Mr. President* (among the Sony reissues), which had a three-week tryout in Washington on its way to Broadway in 1962. The show marked Irving Berlin's emergence from his self-imposed retirement after *Call Me Madam* in 1950. Berlin's collaborators included the producer Leland Hayward (lately of *Gypsy* and *The Sound of Music*) and the director Joshua Logan (*South Pacific* and half the Broadway dramatic hits of the fifties). The authors of the book were Howard Lindsay and Russel Crouse, whose credits included signature Broadway hits of three decades—the thirties (*Anything Goes*), forties (*Life with Father*), and fifties (*The Sound of Music*).

What could go wrong? The pandemonium surrounding the production was such that the manager of the National Theatre refused to accept mail orders and returned 4,000 pieces of unsolicited mail, much of it containing blank checks. The advance-sale box office was opened on Labor Day to avoid jamming downtown Washington streets on a business day, and the entire run was sold out by noon two days later. The real Mr. President and his wife, who were lightly spoofed from the stage, presided over a charity-benefit opening night, though Kennedy missed the first act to watch a closed-circuit broadcast of the Liston-Patterson fight back at the White House.

He didn't miss much. *Mr. President* was accurately described as a "clinker" and "a timid bore" by the local press, and its creators seemed desperate in their efforts to keep up with the puzzling new audience of the New Frontier: As a sop to the young, the composer of "White Christmas" and "There's No Business Like Show Business" was reduced to writing a song titled "The Washington Twist."

On more nights than I care to recall, I stood at the back of the auditorium, where the show's creators lined up in a row behind the rail along with the standees, watching how a packed house was responding to whatever inane plot twist had been written into the second act that afternoon. No matter what revisions were made, the only number that ever got a rise out of the audience was a song sung by the president's daughter lamenting her fiercely chaperoned love life ("The Secret Service makes me nervous/And I can't").

One night at a gala performance heavily populated by congressmen and the diplomatic corps, the fresh young actress playing the daughter, Anita Gillette, got out the first line of the song only to raise her hand, silence the band, and abruptly squeal, "Oh, I forgot my words!" Given the exhausting hours of revision and rehearsal that preceded each night's performance, it was amazing she or anyone could perform at all. The audience ate up Ms. Gillette's attempts to jump-start "The Secret Service" as she repeatedly requested cues from Jay Blackton, the conductor. The mishap was, after all, the only spontaneous theatrical happening of the entire night.

But while the audience roared with laughter, the show's authors were not amused. Like horsemen of the apocalypse, Berlin, Lindsay, Crouse, Logan, and Peter Gennaro, the choreographer, stood impassively in the shadows, their tired faces set in stone.

Well, it was only a show. A couple of weeks earlier, a chapter in Broadway history had been turned when *My Fair Lady* finally ended its then-record six-and-a-half-year run at its final home, the Broadway. A couple of weeks later, *Mr. President* would move to the St. James, a few blocks down the street, and take its lumps, then run through its unheard-of $2.6 million advance sale (roughly $17 million at today's ticket prices) for eight months before closing, unmourned.

Berlin, Lindsay, and Crouse never wrote another Broadway musical; Logan never had another hit. If you listen to the CD of *Mr. President,* you'll hear why. But hindsight is easy. For a kid in the back of the house who was just discovering the theater, the travails of *Mr. President* seemed an exciting business. Only years later did I realize that what I had witnessed those nights in Washington was the quixotic last stand of show people whose long and illustrious day on Broadway had already passed.

SHOW BOAT

NORTH YORK PERFORMING ARTS CENTRE,
TORONTO, OCTOBER 20, 1993

Without *Show Boat,* there would have been no *Porgy and Bess,* no *Oklahoma!,* no *West Side Story.* Jerome Kern and Oscar Hammerstein's 1927 Broadway musical was the first to tell an adult story adapted from a sprawling novel (by Edna Ferber), the first to traffic in serious themes (miscegenation, marital collapse), the first to aspire to the epic size of classic nineteenth-century American literature. With its cracker-barrel humor, metaphorical use of the Mississippi River, and poignant attempts to bridge the vast American racial divide, *Show Boat* is the Broadway musical's answer to *The Adventures of Huckleberry Finn.* Or would be if Twain had had Florenz Ziegfeld's taste for soaring melodies and lavish spectacle.

In today's American theater, there may be no artist more indebted to *Show Boat* than Harold Prince, whose entire career, from the original production of *West Side Story* to the current *Kiss of the Spider Woman,* has been devoted to building on the serious musical that Kern and Hammerstein invented. So it is no surprise that Mr. Prince's staging of *Show Boat* here, as the opening attraction of the North York Performing Arts Centre, is a seismic event in the American musical theater. Given a huge budget, an enormous cast in which Broadway stalwarts vastly outnumber local recruits, and a house that resembles the mammoth Gershwin Theatre back home, Mr. Prince has approached the piece as if it were a new work that might have been submitted to him by Stephen Sondheim shortly after their collaboration on *Sweeney Todd.* The result is a continuously fascinating display of theatrical wizardry that, largely because of inadequate acting, still falls short of what must be its principal goal: to make *Show Boat* as powerful for contemporary audiences as it was for those of the late 1920s and thirties.

Mr. Prince has a lot of latitude in rethinking *Show Boat,* and he uses it to the fullest. The latitude is there because the show has never really had a fixed text. Even the original Broadway version was a partly compromised revision of the *Show Boat* presented during its pre–New York tryout. Kern and Hammerstein made further changes for subsequent tours and revivals as well as for the wonderful 1936 film version. To complicate matters further, some crucial *Show Boat* material was lost for a half-century; it was not until the musical-theater historian Miles Kreuger and the conductor John McGlinn pooled their knowledge and archival detective work on a nearly four-hour studio recording in 1988 that *Show Boat* in all its variations could be heard and judged in the original Robert Russell Bennett orchestrations.

In creating his own three-hour version, Mr. Prince has been as shrewd as you would expect. With the aid of William David Brohn, Bennett's heir among present-day orchestrators, he generally preserves the 1927 score. Two added songs, the atmospherically foreboding chorale "Mis'ry's Comin' Aroun'" (dropped during the 1927 tryout) and a charming lovers' duet, "I Have the Room Above Her" (from the 1936 film), are far superior to what has been cut ("At the Fair," most conspicuously).

To streamline Hammerstein's book, which maps the travails of five couples and four decades of American social and cultural history, Mr. Prince and his choreographer, the dazzling Susan Stroman of *Crazy for You,* have taken a cinematic view unknown to the Broadway theater of the 1920s. The rush of time and events during the Chicago passages of Act 2 is facilitated by montages in which music, movement, and costume changes spin the company from World War I into a Charleston-crazed Jazz Age reminiscent of *Jelly's Last Jam.*

With the further collaboration of the designers, this staging of *Show Boat* severs the work's clichéd ties to operetta. As was the case with his set for *Sweeney Todd,* Eugene Lee's design is huge and elaborate but uses a monochromatic (black, white, and sepia) palette. The entire stage becomes a levee that can accommodate everything that glides in, from the show boat's interior auditorium (with its gaslight stage and two levels of spectators) to the Chicago Loop's Palmer House. Hammerstein's liberal political sympathies are literally built into the environment, which captures both the oppression of black laborers in the segregated, post-Reconstruction South and the Dreiseresque indifference of the churning, industrialized city that swallows up the white characters who migrate there.

The stage is also set for a string of quintessential Prince moments. The stevedore Joe (Michel Bell), with his reprises of "Ol' Man River," stalks the racially torn America of *Show Boat* as a harbinger of unrest much as Joel Grey's Emcee stalked Weimar Germany in *Cabaret.* When Magnolia (Rebecca Luker), the innocent daughter of the show boat captain, and Ravenel (Mark Jacoby), the suave river lothario, rendezvous at night on the Cotton Blossom's top deck, both the inky, star-filled night and the tone of incipient doom recall the romantic assignations on the opera-house roof in *The Phantom of the Opera.* To watch a drop that depicts a grim eternity of cotton fields be violently torn to the ground while a black chorus sings of plantation drudgery is to recall a similar eruption of underclass rage in *Sweeney Todd.* (In fact, the anger this *Show Boat* directs against racism is far more caustic than the chants and signs of the polite, ill-informed local protesters who have accused the show of racism without bothering to see it.)

Such are the brilliance of the staging, the ingenuity of the dramatic restructuring, and the almost uniform plushness of the singing voices that Mr. Prince's *Show Boat* would seem to be all smooth sailing. Esthetically and intellectually, it is, but that's not good enough. If this *Show Boat* is to attract the large audiences it deserves beyond the musical-theater faithful, whether here or in its presumed destination of New York, there is hard work yet to be done to bring the performances up to the sophisticated level of the frame containing them. What is missing from this show is emotional punch.

There are some exceptions to the bland general rule. Robert Morse, obviously fighting a chest cold on opening night, should bring his customary comic panache to Captain Andy with better health and more guidance and playing time. Lonette McKee, a stunning Julie in the 1983 Houston Grand Opera revival seen on Broadway, continues to lead a rousing "Can't Help Lovin' Dat Man" and deliver a rending "Bill," despite some intervening vocal wear-and-tear. Gretha Boston's piquant Queenie so successfully liberates the role from the Aunt Jemima stereotype of a thousand stock productions that one hopes her cut song, "Hey, Feller!," will be reinstated. As Parthy, Captain Andy's battle-ax wife, Elaine Stritch is underused, and it says much about the evening that her one interjected line in "Life on the Wicked Stage" is funnier than the whole verses delivered by the production's earthbound Ellie (Dorothy Stanley). When Mr. Prince gives an incongruously maternal Ms. Stritch the present of a solo in "Why Do I Love You" after intermission—Parthy sings it to her baby granddaughter—the performer's busted whiskey voice is more moving than most of the night's perfect-pitch vocalizing.

Far less affecting is Mr. Bell's stentorian "Ol' Man River," which announces the song's greatness rather than communing with it. As Magnolia, the first American musical heroine to age and grow from scene to scene, Ms. Luker offers only dewy innocence (Act 1) and medicinal gloom (Act 2), while Mr. Jacoby's Ravenal seems more like a proper banker than a rakish gambler who once killed a man. The couple's singing of "Make Believe" and "You Are Love" is gorgeous to the ear, not the heart, as if they expect their wigs and costumes to fill in their characters.

Because of all the bad and adulterated productions it has received, the real *Show Boat,* with all its sunken treasures, is unknown to most modern theatergoers. For decades it has been unjustly thought of as a saccharine relic. This version finally restores the work to its authors' original intentions in every substantive theatrical and musical particular only to concede center stage to acting as dated in style as the hammy show-boat performances Kern and Hammerstein were sending up in 1927. As the Royal National Theatre demonstrated this year in its London revival of a later Hammerstein masterpiece, his collaboration with Richard Rodgers on *Carousel,* there are real adults with biting passions and sexual drives, not picture-postcard mannequins, singing the beautiful songs in our classic musical dramas. *Show Boat* needs them on board to complete its long and potentially triumphant voyage home.

≡ *This* Show Boat *did arrive on Broadway, where it flourished and launched several road companies.*

HOW TO WRITE A PLAY

RIDICULOUS THEATRICAL COMPANY, NOVEMBER 9, 1993

Things could not have been going much better for Charles Ludlam a decade ago, when he wrote *How to Write a Play. Le Bourgeois Avant-Garde* and *Galas,* his major endeavors as playwright, star, and director at the Ridiculous Theatrical Company in 1983, were artistic and popular successes. Next up was *The Mystery of Irma Vep,* a crowd-pleaser that repeatedly extended its run. So much so that *How to Write a Play,* which was originally intended to fill out the *Irma Vep* season, emerged from the wings for only a couple of in-house performances.

To see this lost play at last in 1993, in the authentically outrageous staging it receives from Everett Quinton, Ludlam's heir as star and director at the Ridiculous, is to be catapulted right back to an exuberant moment in the history of a groundbreaking theatrical company. For a couple of hours you can almost forget that Ludlam died in 1987 at the age of forty-four.

How to Write a Play is a casual, frankly autobiographical work that revels joyously in its author's professional and personal callings. Originally set in Ludlam's own apartment, which he shared with his lover, costar, and costume designer, Everett (roles that Mr. Quinton played in real life at the time), it is a Ridiculous version of the old burlesque bit about the man who sits down to do some work in peace and quiet only to find that the entire world is intent on interrupting him.

In adapting the original text for the current production, Mr. Quinton has changed the name of the playwright from Charles to Everett and taken the part himself, while giving his old role the new name of Michael (who is played by a young and eager Jimmy Szczepanek). There are a few other updatings, too, from a farcical sight gag about the World Trade Center bombing to the poignant display of some Ludlam memorabilia in Everett's Greenwich Village apartment.

What audiences new to the Charles Ludlam Theatre, as the company's home is named, will make of *How to Write a Play*, I couldn't tell you. "This is farce, not Sunday School," Ludlam once wrote in an artistic manifesto, and time has not dimmed the subversiveness of his humor. There is something here to offend humorless men (gay or straight), women, American and African blacks, Asians, and, most of all, anyone who believes that to be mature art must outgrow an artist's uncensored childish impulses. Ludlam was not afraid to be juvenile and silly even though he had a greater appreciation for theatrical classicism than most sober middlebrow playwrights of his time.

Constructed almost like a Jack Benny sketch, *How to Write a Play* has little plot beyond the one inevitable twist that propels Mr. Quinton into drag. There is, however, a steady parade of interlopers who insist on knocking on the exasperated hero's door as he tries and fails to write his play: a randy Federal Express delivery man, a psychotic stage mother and her tap-dancing child (twenty-six going on eight), a macrobiotic chef named Madame Wong, a would-be Cole Porter with the unfortunate name of Ima Poussy, and the Emperor and Empress of Humidia, a land whose weather is definitively summed up as "damp." A deposed Latin American dictator with a limited English vocabulary also appears, eager to invest his ill-gotten gains in the theater, and so does the enormous Katy Dierlam, a longtime Ridiculous regular. On this occasion, Ms. Dierlam plays a cleaning lady who terrorizes both the audience and Mr. Quinton by threatening to go all the way in her rendition of "I'm a G-String Girl."

Though there are some witty asides, including a wicked period zinger at the expense of *La Cage aux Folles* and all manner of politically intentioned sexual switches, *How to Write a Play* finds its greatest pleasure in celebrating the sheer artificiality of theater and the infinite ways its oldest and hoariest devices (mistaken identities, the reunion of long-lost spouses, purloined jewels) can be revivified by fresh inspiration. Ludlam even stoops to sending a man on stage in a gorilla suit, in a riotous, gender-bending variation on the subtext of *King Kong*.

Besides being the most hilariously and matter-of-factly masculine of drag performers, Mr. Quinton continues to be a born caretaker of the Ludlam directorial style. He pays keen attention to comic props, costumes, scenery, and wigs, as if a Ridiculous production were pulled together by rummaging through a warehouse full of theatrical trunks. He lets the many idiosyncratic comic personalities in the cast go their own ways.

At the end of *How to Write a Play*, when Everett finally reaches the conclusion that he should write a play "about all the distractions and interruptions" that have kept him from writing, the entire company reemerges in a brief and frenetic conga-line reprise of the evening's many shenanigans. The spectacle is not just funny but moving: Charles Ludlam's imagination unfurls as if by magic to fill up the tiny house on Sheridan Square and fold everyone on both sides of the footlights into its generous embrace.

THE KENTUCKY CYCLE

ROYALE THEATRE, NOVEMBER 15, 1993

Remember plot? In the often absorbing first half of *The Kentucky Cycle*, a six-hour, two-part saga about 200 years of Kentucky history, Robert Schenkkan delights in the kind of robust, jam-packed narrative that the modern theater long ago ceded to movies and television. Settlers battle with Injuns, parents with children, husbands with wives, families with their neighbors, the North with the South. No one hesitates to use a gun, on relatives and strangers alike. A character presumed dead can come back to life at the most dramatically exquisite moment. Two grown boys who seem to have no genealogy in common can abruptly turn out to be long-lost brothers.

As Thelma Ritter, playing a backstage dresser in *All About Eve*, once said of another tall Broadway tale: "What a story! Everything but the bloodhounds snapping at her rear end!"

Mr. Schenkkan's theatrical dreams are larger still. *The Kentucky Cycle*, which opened at the Royale yesterday, believes that the stage can still accommodate a work with scores of characters (played by twenty-one actors) and thematic ambitions that embrace the entire history of the country. By telling the story of three intersecting families in a small, impoverished patch of eastern Kentucky from the dawn of the Revolution in 1775 to 1975, the author wishes to erect an epic of the failure of the American dream. The beautiful, unsullied piece of land where an indentured Irishman, Michael Rowen (Stacy Keach), settles in the play's opening scene is steadily soiled by blood feuds and racial conflict, then pillaged by capitalist greed until finally it is nothing more than a polluted wasteland, a ghost town.

Given this noble purpose, not to mention the time and space the play occupies, I wish I could add that *The Kentucky Cycle* offered either one startling insight into American history, one original turn of phrase, one novel theatrical moment, or one character of tragic size who is deeply moving as an individual rather than as a generic representative of some sociopolitical development. But I can't. *The Kentucky Cycle* is best enjoyed as a melodramatic pageant, and an entertaining one until it turns pedagogical when its story reaches the twentieth century early in part two. The winner of a 1992 Pulitzer Prize, this work has less in common with those Pulitzer plays that try to stretch the imagination while taking the pulse of American civilization (from *Our Town* to *Buried Child*) than with those like *State of the Union* and *J.B.* that lend themselves to methodical parsing in the classroom.

The Kentucky Cycle is actually nine individually titled one-act plays related by bloodlines, a smart device that liberates Mr. Schenkkan to leap over decades when he wants, sometimes to delicious effect. It is fun to watch actors play their own grown children and grandchildren as the years fly by. The fun is not unalloyed, however, because the playwright is sincerely committed to his dark take on the corruption and despoilment of America. In some of the more powerful scenes, a husband (Mr. Keach) courts a Cherokee bride (Lillian Garrett-Groag) with racial and sexual violence, and a Confederate soldier (Tuck Milligan) joins the massacres led by William Clark Quantrill in Lawrence, Kansas. When Mr. Keach, as a later Rowen descendant, is villainously reduced to sharecropping his own ancestral land, or, as a still later Rowen, sells out cheaply to the barons of strip-mining, Mr. Schenkkan's long cycle of vengeance and betrayal achieves a true theatrical arc.

But it was more than a half-century ago on Broadway that Lillian Hellman in *The Little Foxes* divided America into "the people who eat the earth and eat all the people on it" and "other people who stand around and watch them eat it." Mr. Schenkkan has nothing to add in historical detail or unorthodox thought to that now-standard liberal view of the

American chronicle, yet he retails its most familiar points unadorned, with the naïveté of a virgin breathlessly recounting his first visit to a whorehouse. He seems to have discovered only yesterday that the white man's treatment of the Indians and their land can be equated with Standard Oil's rape of the same territory several generations later. Part two of *The Kentucky Cycle* presents the rise and fall of labor unions in dioramas as totemic as the panels on a WPA mural.

Even if one often agrees with Mr. Schenkkan's views, as I do and much of a New York audience will, the knee-jerk predictability with which he hammers them in flattens the play's drama into predictability as well. Once you realize that the cycle's men all tend to be ruthless scoundrels and the women mostly noble, that almost all white people and rich people are bad and all representatives of minority groups are victims, your mind shifts into P.C. autopilot. You sense where every scene is going well before it gets there, and guess the function of every pawn the second he first opens his mouth. (Typically, the moment a new character gives his name as Abe Steinman at the mining camp in the 1920s, we know he is the Jewish Labor Organizer, and we know exactly what will happen to him.)

If Mr. Schenkkan animated these types with arresting language, perhaps they would not pall so quickly. But the dialogue in *The Kentucky Cycle* is that of a high-grade miniseries. When the characters are not using prefab regional boilerplate (can all variations on the phrase "that dog won't hunt" be retired from American discourse?), they speak in intelligent, impersonal prose that lacks any distinctive voice and is more concerned with conveying the story and themes than revealing human intimacies. "It ain't just dirt," begins one characteristic signposting speech. "It's land. It's a living thing." Or: "I learned early blood is just the coin of the realm." Or: "I bring news. We're a state—a full member of the United States." The script's various biblical allusions and mechanically deployed metaphors (an old oak tree, a watch that is the Rowens' undying heirloom), like the author's quotes from Aeschylus, Frantz Fanon, and T. S. Eliot in the *Playbill*, do not lend the writing either epic mythos or psychological depth by osmosis.

In the entire play, only one character has an interior life beyond what he appears to be at first blush and behaves surprisingly, as if he had a free will untethered to the playwright's moral: a con man (superbly played by Gregory Itzin) who dominates *Tall Tales*, the lively play that opens part two on what proves to be a false high. (The anomalously spontaneous *Tall Tales* was, intriguingly, the first of the nine plays of the cycle that Mr. Schenkkan wrote.) At the other extreme are the stock black characters, symbolic ciphers one and all, who are as disenfranchised by their perfunctory lines as they are by slavery.

Because no one in the cast is required to sustain a single role for more than a hour or so, and because many of the roles are minor variations on their ancestral predecessors, *The Kentucky Cycle* is more of a showcase for its actors' energy than for their range. Mr. Keach, whose blunt masculine vigor increasingly recalls Robert Preston's, is particularly forceful, whether as a frontier varmint or the very image of a corrupt, overfed union official of the 1950s. Along with him and Mr. Itzin, the other standouts include Mr. Milligan, as a variety of young idealists, and Jeanne Paulsen, as a mine-country Ma Joad.

Warner Shook's staging, always swift and efficient, invites comparisons to *Nicholas Nickleby* with its bare-bones environmental setting, omnipresent cast, and occasional story-theater staging techniques. But the comparisons will be taken seriously only by those theatergoers who did not see or don't remember the magical, cinematic choreography with which Trevor Nunn and his company coursed through the entire house in that Dickensian marathon. In Mr. Shook's show, the action is often downstage front and center, with the impressive exception of the mine disaster sequences. Frances Kenny's brown and gray costumes are rigorously drab; Michael Olich's set, dominated by antiseptic industrial pipes, and James Ragland's ominous incidental music are both grimly utilitarian. Peter Maradudin's inventive lighting, by contrast, offers more ambiguous shades of gray than much of *The Kentucky Cycle* in delivering its author's passionately held vision of an American paradise lost.

ANGELS IN AMERICA: PERESTROIKA
WALTER KERR THEATRE, NOVEMBER 24, 1993

If you end the first half of an epic play with an angel crashing through a Manhattan ceiling to visit a young man ravaged by AIDS, what do you do for an encore?

If you are Tony Kushner, the author of *Angels in America,* you follow the angel up into the stratosphere, then come back home with a healing vision of heaven on Earth. *Perestroika,* the much awaited part two of Mr. Kushner's "Gay Fantasia on National Themes," is not only a stunning resolution of the rending human drama of part one, *Millennium Approaches,* but also a true millennial work of art, uplifting, hugely comic, and pantheistically religious in a very American style.

Set at once in New York City in the real plague year of 1986 and on a timeless, celestial threshold of revelation, it has the audacity to ask big questions in its opening moments: "Are we doomed? Will the past release us? Can we change? In time?" And then, even more dazzlingly, come the answers, delivered in three and a half hours of spellbinding theater embracing such diverse and compelling native legends as the Army-McCarthy hearings, the Mormon iconography of Joseph Smith, and the MGM film version of *The Wizard of Oz*.

The opening questions are asked by a character who never reappears: a blind Russian man who is the world's oldest living Bolshevik. *Perestroika* is aptly titled not because it has much to do with the former Soviet Union but because it burrows into that historical moment of change when all the old orders, from communism to Reaganism, are splintering, and no one knows what apocalypse or paradise the next millennium might bring. "How are we to proceed without theory?" asks the cross, aged Bolshevik. Not the least of Mr. Kushner's many achievements is his refusal to adhere to any theatrical or political theory. *Angels in America* expands in complexity as it moves forward, unwilling to replace gods that failed with new ones any more than it follows any textbook rules of drama.

Even so, Mr. Kushner does not neglect the intimate tales of the characters who captured the audience's imagination in part one. The show at the Walter Kerr Theatre, where both parts will now play in repertory, is still driven by two antithetical AIDS patients, the thirty-one-year-old free spirit Prior Walter (Stephen Spinella) and the closeted old right-wing cynic Roy Cohn (Ron Leibman). Louis Ironson (Joe Mantello), the leftist Jewish lover who deserted Prior, begins an affair with the Republican, Mormon lawyer Joe Pitt (David Marshall Grant) early in part two, even as Joe's wife, Harper (Marcia Gay Harden), continues to drift in a Valium-induced fantasy of Antarctica. Belize (Jeffrey Wright), the black former drag queen, turns up as Cohn's sassy hospital nurse while Joe's mother (Kathleen Chalfant), who has left Salt Lake City and now works at the Mormons' Visitor Center in New York, becomes an equally unlikely solace to Prior.

The collisions of these people are often more comic than you might expect. In classical terms, *Perestroika* is a comedy, for it brings all its characters' conflicts into more or less peaceful resolution, with much laughter along the way. When Louis and Joe go to bed, for instance, their irreconcilable political differences turn their coupling into a riotous ideological fistfight—"a sex scene in an Ayn Rand novel," in Louis's aghast summation—even though the utter selfishness of both men, guiltless conservative and guilty liberal alike, binds them closer than their knee-jerk party lines admit. When Ethel Rosenberg (Ms. Chalfant) returns from the grave to exchange wisecracks with Cohn and then say the kaddish for him, Mr. Kushner rebalances the scales of justice and revives the gallows humor of Lenny Bruce even as he blankets the scene with the reconciliatory poetic cadences of the prayer. How much more cosmically comic can you get?

Still more so, as it happens. The crux of *Perestroika* is the tying up of the greatest dangling thread from part one: that final-curtain arrival of the Angel who anoints Prior a prophet. As played by Ellen McLaughlin with down-to-earth puckishness, the Angel proves something of a comedian in part two. Up to a point. She is also, as Prior comes to realize, an angel of stasis and death. Pursuing a fever dream as vivid as the one that propelled Judy Garland to Munchkinland, Prior climbs to a heaven resembling the earthquake-shattered San Francisco of 1906. Given a red epistolary book and robe, if not red slippers, he encounters a conclave of angels on his way to deciding just what kind of prophet he will be when he returns to a home that God seems to have abandoned.

Prior's searching pilgrimage is echoed throughout *Perestroika* by the Mormon, Jewish, and black characters and implicitly by their pioneer, immigrant, and enslaved ancestors. As Prior journeys to heaven, so the Mormon mannequins in a wagon-train diorama come magically to life; Belize is possessed by the ghosts of Abolitionist days while Louis must wrestle with his discarded Jewishness. Only Cohn stays adamantly put, canonizing himself as "the heartbeat of modern conservatism" even as he consigns Henry Kissinger and George Schultz to history's dustbin along with the more expected names on his enemies' list.

It takes an artist of Mr. Kushner's talent and empathic powers to elevate Cohn, a mere scoundrel in real life, into a villain of such wit and cunning that he becomes mesmerizing theatrical company. Mr. Leibman, his face ashen, his eyes rimmed in red, his stooped posture wrapped in a demonic green robe, plays him with savage grandeur in *Perestroika,* as a sweaty pulp of rage and hatred and blasted nerves. A whirligig of malevolence, he barks "Find the vein, you moron!" to Belize one moment, then blackmails Iran-Contra conspirators for a supply of AZT the next. As always, his telephone serves as an extra appendage—his last word in *Angels in America,* like his first, is "Hold!"—but now the cord is entwined with the many tubes of his illness. This does not stop Mr. Leibman, in an absolutely terrifying scene, from ripping loose of his IV, his poisoned blood spurting everywhere, to make one last hypocritical plea that Joe, his gay protégé, return to his heterosexual marriage.

This patient from hell notwithstanding, George C. Wolfe, the director, and Robin Wagner, the designer, have slightly lowered the temperature of *Angels* for its second half, as befits a text in which hallucinations overwhelm any quarrelsome domestic or political reality. Much of the action takes place in a cool, dark limbo that, as lighted by Jules Fisher and flecked with jazz by the composer Anthony Davis, both captures the literal setting (largely New York City during a spring rain) and conveys the pregnant end-of-millennium mood. The roles that grow markedly in part two—Mr. Wright's agent provocateur of a nurse, Ms. Chalfant's nononsense yet strangely comforting matriarch, and especially Mr. Grant's Joe—are beautifully rendered. Like the impressive Mr. Mantello, Mr. Grant has an unusual knack for finding humor and shading in a character whose self-righteousness is matched only by his callousness to a partner in desperate need.

Yet the heart of the play is Prior Walter, as acted by the extraordinary Mr. Spinella. "I'm not a prophet," he protests early in part two. "I'm a sick, lonely man." Deserted by his lover, thin to the point of emaciation, covered with the lesions of Kaposi's sarcoma, Prior is the one who must bear the weight of the future on his slender shoulders. While Mr. Spinella looks like God's avenger in the quasiclerical black cape and hood he wears for much of the evening, his performance is the opposite of Mr. Leibman's Cohn. He is beyond anger.

"The worst thing about being sick in America is you are booted out of the parade," Cohn says. Prior, who has an "addiction to being alive," refuses to be booted. He wants to "live past hope," he tells the angel of death. "I want more life." Appropriately, *Angels in America* is one play of the AIDS era that does not end at a memorial service but with the characters gathered in expectation, on a brilliant day, before Bethesda Fountain in Central Park. The year of this epilogue is 1990, and though Prior is now leaning on a cane like the Bolshevik of the prologue and is nearly as blind, Mr. Spinella radiates joy. "This disease will be the end of many of us, but not nearly all," he says. "The world only spins forward."

People no longer build cathedrals, as they did a thousand years ago, to greet the next millennium, but *Angels in America* both spins forward and spirals upward in its own way, for its own time. If anything, Prior's description of statuary angels like the one in the fountain honoring the Civil War dead could stand for Mr. Kushner's fabulous play: "They commemorate death, but they suggest a world without dying."

"Bye now!" cries a smiling Mr. Spinella as this great epic draws to a close, raising his long arm and throwing it back in an ecstatic wave. His indelible gesture feels less like a good-bye than a benediction, less like a final curtain than a kiss that blesses everyone in the theater with the promise of more life.

EPILOGUE

My career as the chief drama critic of *The New York Times* began with a car crash and a death, and ended with another car crash and another death. But don't get me wrong: There was lots of life, onstage and off, along the way.

The first crash took place on a hot morning in the Berkshires in July 1980, shortly after I arrived at the *Times* to serve as a second-stringer to Walter Kerr. The previous night I had covered *Candida* at the Williamstown Theatre Festival. Driving back to New York, I lost control of the rental car, which skidded across the country road and flipped over on its roof.

I landed on an examination table back in Manhattan, where an orthopedist inspected my fractured collarbone. As the doctor manipulated my shoulder, making me writhe in pain, he looked solemnly into my eyes.

"Tell me something," he said. "Could you get me a pair for *Barnum* for Saturday night?"

This was my introduction to the omnipotence that strangers attach to the job of drama critic at *The New York Times*.

What would follow was a thirteen-year journey full of hairpin turns and plot twists. I would have far more than my share of wild journalistic adventures, be reviled as the Butcher of Broadway, and have a front-row seat for a seismic shift in the American theater.

But back in 1980, I realize now, I was still something of an innocent. For one thing, I believed that it was nothing to bounce back from a car crash. Even so, my injury slowed me down, ejecting me from my beat as abruptly as I had landed in it that spring, when Arthur Gelb recruited me from *Time* magazine, where I was a film and television critic. My torso was elaborately wrapped by the doctor, and I couldn't type easily.

I was still recuperating when Arthur called me with an urgent request. Defying Broadway practice, the producer David Merrick was mysteriously canceling previews of his new musical, *42nd Street*. Critics would have to cover the show the old-fashioned way—on deadline on opening night—rather than follow the standard practice of the past decade, attending a final preview and writing at a slightly more leisurely (and thoughtful) pace. Walter Kerr, who had been ailing himself, did not want the assignment under those conditions. Neither did I. This was the most high-profile Broadway show in years. I was still a novice theater critic, little known by *Times* readers and unsure of myself. Throw in the added pressure of a one-hour deadline and. . . .

"Are you crazy?" Arthur shouted, all but leaping out of the phone to dismiss my objections. He was a one-of-a-kind editor who exceeded even Ben Hecht and Charles MacArthur's newspapermen in chutzpah and verve. "How can you not cover it?"

When the big night arrived, I was a wreck. But as I saw the huge billboard above the Winter Garden marquee on Broadway, I also felt an undeniable rush of excitement. I thought of my first visit to the Winter Garden, as a teenager on the outside looking in: watching Barbra Streisand from the last row of the orchestra during her final weeks in *Funny Girl*, in a seat my stepfather had me fetch from an illegal broker in a dusty walk-up hovel near the old Gaiety Delicatessen on West Forty-seventh Street.

And I thought fondly of David Merrick. His shameless promotion of his productions, often at the expense of critics he baited through practical jokes and irrational public ravings, had always struck me as part of the essential romance of Broadway. As a child, I had read every article I could find about him.

Then again, once the theater became my chosen escape from a troubled home, I had read everything I could find on the subject. The stage was my obsession from age six—an idiosyncratic one, to put it mildly, for a child growing up in the sleepy provincial Washington of the 1950s.

By my early teens, I had become so conspicuous a Stage Door Johnny that the manager of the National Theatre, Washington's one Broadway tryout house in the pre–Kennedy Center era, took pity on me and hired me as a ticket taker, at four dollars a show. (Plus all the performances I could watch free of charge.) That's where I saw Merrick and the director Gower Champion put in an elaborate new number for Carol Channing at the end of Act 1 of *Hello, Dolly!* And Merrick, Lauren Bacall, and Abe Burrows frantically teaching Barry Nelson how not to bump into the turntable sets of *Cactus Flower,* Nelson having just arrived in

Washington to replace the leading man the producer had canned the night before.

If someone had told me then that someday I would not only be attending a David Merrick opening on Broadway, directed by Gower Champion no less, but sitting down front and writing about what I saw for the whole world to read in *The New York Times* the next morning, I would have sooner believed I'd win the Nobel Prize for my youthful stabs at poetry. For the *Times* was also inextricably bound up with my passion. From earliest memory, it was Al Hirschfeld's drawings of plays and the imposing full-page advertisements heralding them in the Sunday *Times* drama section—and then the Brooks Atkinson reviews the morning after—that had transported my imagination to the New York theater while I impatiently languished two hundred miles away.

Now here I was, at *42nd Street*, and high as could be—until the end of the opening number. Then the leaden dialogue commenced, and my heart sank: *42nd Street* was no match for *Hello, Dolly!*, *Oliver!*, *Carnival!*, or any other Merrick musical with an exclamation point in its title from my youth.

Anxiously, I started taking notes so I could illustrate with examples the disappointment I felt in my gut. I had a clear idea of my job—to report what I saw on stage honestly and pointedly, as I might in conversation with a friend—and it never occurred to me that someone might object to what I wrote.

When the show ended, I waited through one curtain call and ran up the aisle with my then wife, Gail, to make my deadline at the *Times*, seven blocks down Broadway. I hadn't reached the street when an acquaintance in the movie business stopped me.

"Frank, I have to talk to you," he said.

"I'm on deadline," I replied, annoyed, racing toward a cab.

"But I've got big news," he said. "Gower Champion is dead."

What? I had read that Champion had been elusive during the Washington tryout of *42nd Street*. But dead? He was fifty-nine and not rumored to be seriously ill.

Panic-stricken, I looked back toward the one open door leading into the theater. The sound of the ovation still thundered, but my informant had disappeared. This was big news. But I wasn't a reporter; I was a theater critic, and a fledgling one at that. Had I been handed the scoop of the century? Or was I the patsy in another fabled Merrick hoax? And how could I find out and still write my review by deadline?

As I slid into the cab beside Gail, I looked toward the theater one last desperate time and discovered a solitary couple emerging—Arthur Gelb and his wife, Barbara, who had stayed only long enough for the second curtain call.

I leaped back out and, from the middle of Broadway, started waving my sling and shrieking at them. Arthur looked at me as if I was having a breakdown, then ran over, yanking Barbara with him. I told them my news, and Arthur said: "Gower Champion dead! That's impossible!" But they piled into the jump seats, and the driver raced down Broadway to the *Times*.

When, a few minutes later, we emerged from the elevator on the third floor to enter the deserted culture department, every phone seemed to be ringing off the hook. Arthur picked one up to learn that Merrick had just announced Champion's abrupt death from the Winter Garden stage, saving the bulletin for the very end of the curtain calls.

Arthur dashed to the news desk as the first edition was about to close to break into the front page with a picture and caption announcing the news. (The caption carefully said that Merrick had announced Champion's death rather than that Champion was dead, lest the producer be up to no good.) I sat down to write my bittersweet mixed review for the second edition and proceeded to sweat right through my clothes. John Corry, the drama reporter, breathlessly arrived, and Arthur seated him a desk away from me to hammer out the page-one news story.

Big-time journalism! Big-time Broadway! What more could I want? I made my deadline. Once I had, I sat at the terminal alone, my shoulder suddenly throbbing again. Then I broke unexpectedly into tears, partly, perhaps, out of psychic release, now that the pressure had lifted, but also out of some sense of mourning for Champion. I had never met him, but I took the loss personally anyway, out of an inchoate sense that some of my old childhood fantasies about the theater had died with him that night.

Merrick got so much publicity from his brilliant stage management of the announcement of Champion's death—the director had actually died early that afternoon, but the producer suppressed the news—that it didn't matter what any review said. *42nd Street* was a smash.

And I was the living proof of its undying Broadway legend, the understudy who went out a nobody and came back a star. When I returned to work for real, minus the sling, after Labor Day, Abe Rosenthal, the executive editor, told me that Walter wanted to return to Sunday reviewing and that I was the new chief drama critic.

I called my mother. She had always indulged my twin passions for newspaper writing and the theater; it was she who took me to Broadway for the first time as a child, as an unspoken consolation for the pain of her and my father's divorce. By then my fate had been sealed, and now, twenty-odd years later, at age thirty-one, I was doing exactly what she said she always knew I was born to do. "I can't believe it," I told her. "I can," she said.

• • •

The first show I had to review as chief critic was an innocuous Off Broadway play, *An Act of Kindness,* about which I have forgotten everything except that it took me about eight hours to write the 800-word review, so heavily did the august responsibilities of my new job with its preposterously official-sounding title weigh on me.

But I soon loosened up. I found a method for preserving the spontaneity of theatergoing, so essential to the joy of the experience. I didn't read about new plays before seeing them (or read their scripts); I didn't listen to friends either. This allowed me to still feel that rush of anticipation and surprise when the curtain went up.

I gradually aspired to write reviews as stories evoking the play's impact rather than as merely report cards leaning on adjectives and plot. This, I felt, was a way to engage the majority of readers, who never went to the theater no matter what the reviews, and to reach those readers like my younger self, who wanted to go to the theater but couldn't, for reasons of finances or geography. I also learned that if I had anything positive to say, say it first, because the artists who do valiant work in a mediocre enterprise are, in the journalistic sense, the real news—the lead.

Just the same, I couldn't shake the sense that my calling was a bit arcane, that I had arrived at my dream job after the dream had ended. In college, friends had ridiculed my obsession with so obsolete an art form and had argued (correctly, as it turned out) that I was much more likely to find a job writing about movies than plays after graduation. As I looked around the theater in the early 1980s, I saw few critics who were remotely my contemporaries. When I had been a movie critic in the seventies, by contrast, most of my colleagues were roughly my age.

It wasn't difficult to see why. The seismic cultural events that happened in the theater in my youth now happened at the movies. No theatrical event was capable of creating the American earthquake that *Long Day's Journey into Night, My Fair Lady,* or *Marat/Sade* had in my formative years.

Yet the talent in the American theater was still considerable, if often young and not widely known. I found a mission in championing new voices—David Henry Hwang, Beth Henley, William Finn, Marsha Norman, Eric Bogosian, among others, early on—even as I delighted in charting established talents like Sam Shepard, Michael Bennett, David Mamet, Lanford Wilson, and Athol Fugard. Joseph Papp, in a surprising Anglophilic phase, was producing such invigorating works as the Kevin Kline–Linda Ronstadt *Pirates of Penzance* and David Hare's *Plenty,* starring Kate Nelligan. In a single week, an Off Broadway theatergoer could discover two sensational new young actresses: Laurie Metcalf (in *Balm in Gilead*) and Holly Hunter (in *The Miss Firecracker Contest*). Broadway's diversity could range from Michael Frayn's *Noises Off,* the single funniest play I ever saw on the job, to *Ma Rainey's Black Bottom,* in which the angry black playwright August Wilson introduced himself to a white, middle-class audience by having the fearsome actor Charles Dutton figuratively hold it at knifepoint.

The work and hours were daunting, but I could not disagree with friends who said that I had the best job in the world. When I was virtually alone among my colleagues in liking a show—Michael Bennett's *Dreamgirls,* for instance—it was a kick to buck the consensus. Even the occasional contretemps were fun. Displeased by both my review and other *Times* coverage of *42nd Street,* Merrick tried and failed to place a pair of agate-type ads at the bottom of the front page: "Every time I pass *The New York Times* building I get hit with a wave of pyromania—David Merrick" and "Anyone having the power of pyrokinesis, please contact me—David Merrick." When I once happened to walk past Merrick's table at Elaine's restaurant, he intercepted me, then dressed me down in a low, snide voice out of Victorian melodrama—as his stricken dinner guests, one of them Mary Tyler Moore, looked on.

He must have sensed that I was more titillated than insulted; critics may not be, as is generally presumed, frustrated actors or playwrights, but few of us mind playing our assigned role in the timeless sideshows of the rialto.

Arthur Gelb, who had been a drama critic and reporter in the Brooks Atkinson era at the *Times,* inculcated me from the start in my journalistic role: to serve the paper's readers, not the theater's public relations needs. A classic conflict between the *Times*'s view of my job and the theater's popped up early in my first full season. The Shubert Organization, perhaps emboldened by Merrick's successful ploy with *42nd Street,* announced that critics must cover its new import, *Amadeus,* on opening night, rather than at a preview. The Shuberts' theory, one of the many old wives' tales among aged Broadway hands, was that critics would write more favorable reviews with more quotable quotes if pumped full of deadline adrenaline and subjected to the cheers of a house full of backers.

In truth, a critic quickly learns to tune out any audience response in reaching his own judgment. The old opening-night system was deplored by many critics, who often had to miss the end of a show to make a deadline and felt it unfair to review artists' work as if it were a fire or sporting event. (Covering the opening night of *A Streetcar Named Desire* in 1947, Brooks Atkinson had to miss the last scene, which meant that he reviewed the play without having heard "the kindness of strangers.") The system's collapse was inevitable in any case once opening nights on Broadway ceased to be real opening nights in the late 1960s, when New York preview performances for paying audiences began to replace the out-of-town tryout and an "opening" became an artificially designated event.

Merrick had succeeded in getting critics to cover *42nd Street* on opening night because it was a bona fide event; at huge financial cost, he had canceled the final previews, leaving the press no option but to surrender to the promotional gala he wanted. The Shuberts, by contrast, were loath to waste money in pursuit of principle. They wanted critics to cover *Amadeus* at the so-called opening, which they could pack with cheerleaders, but they had no intention of canceling highly remunerative previews presold to theater parties.

Gerald Schoenfeld, the chairman of the Shubert Organization, called Arthur to plead his case. Arthur told Schoenfeld, "I promise you that Frank Rich will be at *Amadeus* on opening night." Which I would be. What Arthur did not tell him was that I would already have filed my review, since I would buy a ticket for a preview.

As it happened, I had met Gerry Schoenfeld in childhood when the Broadway trade organization, the League of New York Theatres, hired my stepfather, a Washington lawyer, to lobby the Johnson Administration for the removal of the excise tax on theater tickets. In the 1970s in New York, I had occasionally run into Gerry, who sometimes graciously passed me into the previews of Shubert shows. Neither he nor I could ever have imagined that I would someday end up as the *Times*'s drama critic.

But the day I went to see *Amadeus,* I walked right in front of Gerry, who seemed too busy counting the house to notice anything else and failed to recognize me as I went up the stairs to my seat in the Broadhurst mezzanine.

My mission accomplished, my review filed, I went to the *Amadeus* opening. True to form, Gerry sat right behind me to exert maximum influence on my thoughts. He apparently did not find it odd that I didn't take a single note and didn't hurry up the aisle at the final curtain. But, as I would later learn from a friend at the opening-night party, he had no sooner announced to the assembled that there would be no *Times* review until the following morning when someone ran in waving my first-edition review in his face. He was not amused.

It didn't seem to matter to him that the review was a rave, or that *Amadeus* was a hit. A few weeks after the opening, I was walking on Fifth Avenue with my friend Wendy Wasserstein, a playwright as yet unknown to the Shuberts, for whom she would later make a ton of money with *The Heidi Chronicles* and *The Sisters Rosensweig*. (With no help from me; I never reviewed plays written by her or by the few other friends I had in the theater before I became a critic.) In front of Tiffany's we ran smack into Gerry's wife, Pat, who berated me for a good twenty minutes, accusing me of betraying the friendship of our two families.

The *Amadeus* incident marked a surge in the Shuberts' paranoia about the *Times,* which dated back to the original Shubert brothers in 1915, who had barred the paper's critic, Alexander Woollcott, from one of its theaters. (The *Times's* publisher, Adolph S. Ochs, beat back the challenge by rejecting Shubert advertising, which proved to cost the Shuberts more business than it did the *Times.*) Arthur and I soon discovered that the Shuberts had canvassed the staff at the restaurant where we ate together during the dinner break of the eight-hour *Nicholas Nickleby* to ascertain advance word on my review. (In vain, since I was compulsive about never discussing any play before my review appeared.)

Rather more successfully, the Shuberts revived the old tradition of finding out reviews in advance through a *Times* mole with computer access. When Gerry Schoenfeld brazenly told Abe Rosenthal my review of the musical *Song & Dance* before the curtain went up on opening night and before Abe had read the review himself, the *Times* set out to find the culprit. Sherlock Holmes was not required—an obscure editor was discovered to be a conspicuous and frequent lunchtime guest of top theatrical executives at Sardi's—and the electronic leaks were plugged.

· · ·

Broadway was not all *Amadeus* and *Dreamgirls*. At a time when production costs were still low enough for first-time producers to indulge their most catastrophic theatrical whims, covering the theater was as madcap as going to the circus. It became a running gag with me and Wendy Wasserstein, who would accompany me to anything, that many of the biggest bombs on Broadway had titles beginning with the letter M. (*Macbeth* also fell into this category; every production of this play I covered, whether with Philip Anglim, Nicol Williamson, or Christopher Plummer, was a fiasco.) There was *Marlowe,* a rock musical in which the titular playwright joined Shakespeare and Richard Burbage to smoke dope backstage at the Globe Theater, and *Merlin,* in which the onstage animals outnumbered the audience at the Mark Hellinger Theatre on a snowy matinee day, and *Marilyn,* a musical biography of Marilyn Monroe that had sixteen producers. (Favorite line, spoken by Marilyn: "But you're Arthur Miller. How can you be so boring?")

Moose Murders was a special case. It is the worst play I've ever seen on a Broadway stage. A murder mystery set in a hunting lodge in the Adirondacks, it reached its climax when a mummified quadriplegic abruptly bolted out of his wheelchair to kick an intruder, dressed in a moose costume, in the groin.

Wendy and I saw *Moose Murders* at a Wednesday matinee. Hardly had the play started when the smell of vomit wafted through the orchestra at the Eugene O'Neill Theatre. Gradually, those seated in the first few rows starting taking refuge in empty seats at the back of the house, until finally we and the apparent source of the exodus, a voluminous man third-row center, were virtually the only members of the audience in the front rows. Yet I feared that if we moved back, I might be too far away to give the play a fair shake.

Finally, my sense of justice gave way. I bolted to the back of the theater, where the press agent and other staff members of the production inevitably hang out at critics' performances, to seek a solution. To my amazement, however, there was no one in the back of the house; this sinking ship had already been abandoned. I retrieved Wendy, and we moved to the back row, where we watched the unfolding horror with no less amazement than we had from close up. *Moose Murders* closed on opening night, but its gallant cast members still list the credit in their *Playbill* biographies, usually preceded by the word "legendary."

For all the frivolous Broadway amateur nights like *Moose Murders* or *Shogun* (in which flying scenery beaned the leading man) or *Into the Light* (the first and last musical about the Shroud of Turin), there would always be professional failures in which talented people, working under the burden of the commercial theater's costly and rushed production schedule, would stumble. The saddest "M" flop of the early eighties was *Merrily We Roll Along,* the last collaboration of the director Harold Prince and the songwriter Stephen Sondheim, both heroes of my youth. The show had first-rate songs—the overture quickened my pulse in false anticipation of a triumph—but what surrounded them was chaos. (Most critics didn't even like the songs.)

Or was I being too harsh? As I sat down to write I couldn't square my powerful emotional response to Sondheim's music with my disapproval of the soulless acting, ugly staging, and pale characters. I felt queasy.

While it can be fun to write a joke-strewn pan of a venal or lunatic the-atrical catastrophe, whether *Moose Murders* or *Carrie,* there is no plea-sure in writing about a failure in which artists commit no crime other than fallibility in pursuit of high theatrical ambitions. But neither was there any point in pulling punches for *Times* readers who know better. It was a no-win situation.

Haunted by *Merrily,* I went back to see it again at the final Saturday matinee. I bought a ticket at the half-price booth at Duffy Square, but only lasted an act. The show was at least as depressing as I remembered it, the audience was noisy and rude and what could I or any journalist do about any of it?

The antithesis of the *Merrily* experience was to feel that unmistakable sensation that something extraordinary was happening on a stage—best of all, something new—and that I would have the thrill of breaking the story.

Such nights, and they were not infrequent, made the job seem hopeful despite all the larger signs that the theater was collapsing as a business in New York. Ticket prices were rising; the Morosco and Helen Hayes the-atres were razed for the Marriott Marquis Hotel; even Merrick, who suf-fered a stroke during the run of *42nd Street,* had apparently retired. But a new and daring company like Steppenwolf in Chicago or an incendiary play like *Aunt Dan and Lemon,* by Wallace Shawn, or an original talent like George Wolfe would still come along (usually Off Broadway).

One show that exemplified my stubborn faith was the very next Sond-heim musical, *Sunday in the Park with George.* The night I reviewed it, people were walking out all around me, yet as the first act ended, with the re-creation of a Georges Seurat canvas, I felt that tickling sensation on the back of my neck that always arrives when the theater speaks to me at a level so deep that my spirit responds before my mind.

I didn't understand everything that I had seen on stage that night. When all the reviews came out and were mostly hostile, I was full of self-doubt and shaken by the loneliness of my stand, especially since I couldn't articulate my response to *Sunday* to my own satisfaction. So I went back and saw it again and again and again—and kept being moved and kept writing about it until I felt I had made my case. One conse-quence of my obsession was to dramatize the *Times*'s power, since my es-says kept alive a production that many others deemed worthy of a quick death.

I particularly angered the late Richard Hummler, of the trade publi-cation *Variety,* who despised the *Times*'s extensive coverage of the show nearly as much as he did the show itself. The theater's resentment of the iconoclastic Sondheim, always apparent in the anonymous and not-so-anonymous mail I perennially received from Broadway folk attacking him, eventually even surfaced on stage at the Tony Awards: Jerry Herman, who won the Tony for *La Cage aux Folles* over *Sunday in the Park,* took a swipe at his rival. And now some of the venom spilled over to me, Sondheim's champion (for this show anyway).

For the first time, I found people in the theater questioning my motives in a personal way. Though theater professionals had always heartily (and understandably) protested negative reviews—either with seriously argued letters or sly, Merrickesque stunts (a picket line of chorus performers materialized on Forty-third Street after I panned a stage version of *Seven Brides for Seven Brothers*)—the tone changed. Page Six of the *New York Post* called to confirm the rumors that I had liked *Sunday* so much because its director, James Lapine, was my college roommate. (In fact, I had never met Lapine, who didn't attend my college and wasn't even my age.) Another, equally scurrilous rumor had me in bed with the show's press agent.

Apparently no one in the theater could imagine that I might like *Sunday in the Park* for the reasons I stated in print. But as the season wore on, some other critics began to reverse their stands about the show. *Sunday in the Park* won the Drama Critics Circle Award and the Pulitzer Prize. The supposed clout of the *Times* and those awards notwithstanding, however, it did not become a financial success.

It was not until 1986, after *Sunday* closed, that I officially became the Butcher of Broadway. The traditional term was revived for my benefit by the British comedian Rowan Atkinson, who told London reporters that he held me responsible for the demise of a revue he brought to New York. I happened to be in London when Atkinson made his remarks. When I went to Heathrow a few days later to fly home, I was chased into a British Airways lounge by a couple of men in trench coats who turned out to be British tabloid reporters seeking a comment. It was a hilarious, surreal adventure, and in subsequent visits, almost anything I did was front-page news in the local tabloid press. Invitations to appear on British television rained down on me, to the point where the Savoy Hotel had to screen the avalanche of calls when I was in London. Only in England, where the theater is still center stage in the nation's cultural life as well as a major export industry, could a drama critic star in a farcical escapade right out of *A Hard Day's Night.*

Rowan Atkinson's battle cry was amplified by two other Brits as they passed through New York. One was David Hare, who was infuriated when I wrote that he had mutilated his own fine play *The Secret Rapture* by miscasting and misdirecting the New York production. (The play had been beautifully staged by Howard Davies in London.) Hare wrote an open letter to me that he distributed to the press, arguing that it was part of my job "to insure the survival of the theater" and "support . . . the continuance of the serious play on Broadway." I wrote back that "my responsibility" was "to be honest with the *Times's* readers," who were too smart to follow any critic with blind Pavlovian slavishness, but instead extrapolated according to their own tastes from a familiar critic's point of view.

The dispute made for great copy and landed me on the front page of publications ranging from *The Wall Street Journal* to *Variety* (where Hummler wrote a tendentious story with a classic headline, RUFFLED HARE AIRS RICH BITCH). Hare was seconded by Andrew Lloyd Webber, who, though I had never met him, told reporters that I had not liked the performance given by his wife, Sarah Brightman, in *The Phantom of the Opera,* because I was bitter about my own pending divorce. (Webber's divorce from Brightman was yet to come.) When *60 Minutes* did a segment about me, Hare and Lloyd Webber were both heard from, with the latter delivering, in the correspondent Morley Safer's words, an "unprintable tirade" off-camera, questioning my "integrity, sexuality, and sanity." Even the stroke-impaired Merrick made a cameo appearance, labeling me "a savage dog."

Merrick had come back to Broadway with *Oh, Kay!,* a feeble attempt to create a musical in the style of *42nd Street,* his last hit, now a decade old. At the critics' preview I attended, he pulled one of his old tricks: In the seat next to Alex Witchel, the *Times* theater columnist whom I was dating, he planted a loud, disruptive woman who talked and bounced in her seat throughout the show. After my negative review of *Oh, Kay!* came out, Merrick circulated a protesting letter to the *Times* in which he claimed Alex had talked through the performance. To heighten the public relations push, he then placed an ad in which a negative quote from my review and a news item from Alex's column about an Actors Equity dispute involving *Oh, Kay!* were contained within a cupid's heart. "At last, people are holding hands in the theatre again!" read the headline.

The stunt was a replay of a famous one he had pulled on Walter and Jean Kerr three decades earlier, when he publicly accused Jean of influencing Walter's reviews by dramatically "nudging" him at the theater. (Walter's answer to the charge in the *Herald Tribune*—"Surely, Mr. Merrick, someone, somewhere has liked you well enough to give you a little dig in the elbow. No? Ah, well"—is a journalism classic.) And by Merrick standards, the treatment I got was mild. In his prime, Merrick likened

Brooks Atkinson's successor, Howard Taubman, to Adolf Eichmann during a half-hour tirade on Johnny Carson's *Tonight* show, on which the producer also accused the critic of feeding poison nuts to the squirrels in Central Park and spraying pesticide at Hubert's Flea Circus. Those were the days! It's hard to imagine any theatrical producer even being booked on a network talk show now.

Merrick's ad ran for one edition in the *Times* and was reprinted widely. The publicity did not save *Oh, Kay!*, which died ignominiously in a welter of financial disputes pitting Merrick against his own employees. The great producer's career was over. But the notion Merrick perpetrated that Alex and I were in league either to reward or punish the New York theater hardly died with *Oh, Kay!* It became a mantra of New York theater people, who were dumbfounded as Alex got scoop after scoop in her Friday *Times* column: No one in the business seemed to remember that she wrote a theater column for the publication *7 Days* before the *Times* hired her. Or that she worked in the theater, both for the Shuberts and Joseph Papp, before entering journalism, and had developed countless sources throughout its infrastructure, many of whom knew more about what was going on in theatrical offices than the bosses did. The idea of an evil woman behind the throne also seemed to titillate the almost exclusively male theater establishment, and its members planted gossip items about Alex that, predictably, made the expected juvenile plays on her last name and, eventually, referred to her "Hillary headbands."

The *Times*'s editors, who by this point routinely had husbands and wives working in tandem on beats far more important than the theater, saw the attacks for the frequently misogynist whining they were. The biggest problem for Alex and me in this controversy was our loss of privacy. If we went looking for an apartment, it was in the papers. If we ate at a restaurant, a waiter might report our most innocuous conversation to a gossip column. Even our small wedding was infiltrated by a tabloid spy.

The juvenile tone of the gossip began to dispirit me. The Shubert Alley backbiting that had seemed romantic in *All About Eve,* Joseph Mankiewicz's brilliant film satire of the New York theater in its post–World War II heyday, now seemed to be a larger growth industry on Broadway than play production itself, reflecting the diminished size of the business and the spare time its managers had on their hands. As I turned forty, a world I had once seen as sophisticated no longer struck me as adult.

The constant carping also left me wondering whether my own standards were indeed too tough for the tourist arena the Broadway theater had become. Since those standards were inseparable from who I am, I couldn't have changed them even if I wanted to. But was it worth applying them to a Broadway where the apex of achievement in the 1980s was *Cats*?

Yet even in this period of intense criticism, most people in the theater were courteous in their dealings with Alex and me. Alex, as a reporter, had far more dealings than I did, since I had always tried to avoid meeting people I might review. Though the occasional ambitious actor would write me a pleading note—Glenn Close, for instance, who wrote asking that I return to *Barnum* eleven months into its run to see how she had deepened her performance as Barnum's wife—most people kept a polite distance. The only producer who repeatedly tried to hawk his shows to me by schmoozing was Gordon Davidson, of the Mark Taper Forum in Los Angeles; some major showmen (like James Nederlander, the second-largest Broadway theater owner, after the Shuberts) never contacted me for any reason throughout my career at the *Times*. I rarely had ugly confrontations with anyone in the theater, and my mail from theater people, even at its angriest, was civilized.

In thirteen years the few significant exceptions invariably involved Robert Brustein, the artistic director of the American Repertory Theatre at Harvard University, and the few contemporary playwrights who worked at his theater (a list that dwindled rapidly as the eighties went on). The nastiest encounter I ever had was with Arthur Kopit, whose play *End of the World*, to be produced later by Brustein in Cambridge, fared poorly in New York. One night after it opened I was passing under the marquee of the Music Box, where it was playing, and was buttonholed by Kopit, who, after telling me I was too stupid to appreciate his work, embarked on even more vitriolic tongue-lashings of three other plays, all praised by me, running on the same Forty-fifth Street block: *Sunday in the Park, The Real Thing*, by Tom Stoppard, and *Glengarry Glen Ross*, by David Mamet. (After Sondheim, no one seemed to arouse more jealousy and anger among theatrical rivals than Mamet.)

Brustein was smoother. He offered me a teaching position at Harvard weeks after I arrived at the paper, airfare to and from my weekly seminars included. I mentioned this offer to Arthur Gelb—I was naively mesmerized by the prospect—and he ended the fantasy right there. Not only was the offer unethical, Arthur elaborated, but Brustein had a tortured history with the paper. In his memoir, *Making Scenes*, Brustein had objected to the prominence of the *Times*'s 1978 news story about A. Bartlett Giamatti's decision to replace him as dean of the Yale School of Drama.

I turned Brustein's offer down. But I did not fall into his ill graces until a few years later, when I praised the work of August Wilson, who had been discovered by Brustein's successor at Yale, the director Lloyd Richards, and would eventually win two Pulitzer Prizes (for *Fences* and *The Piano Lesson*). In his theater column in *The New Republic,* which he routinely used to deride rivals and reward associates in the theater, Brustein savaged Wilson for writing exclusively about "the black experience in a relatively literalistic style." (Brustein's American Repertory Theatre was notorious among major American institutional theaters for never originating main-stage productions of plays by black Americans.) In a follow-up essay for *American Theatre* magazine, Brustein attacked Wilson's plays and a long list of others—among them, *M. Butterfly, Marvin's Room, As Is, The Normal Heart, Eastern Standard, Falsettoland, Lips Together, Teeth Apart*—that were conspicuous for having received favorable reviews in the *Times.* Many of these works were by gay writers, another sore spot for Brustein, who implied in print in 1983 that an "AIDS sympathy vote" had contributed to the Tony Award victory of *Torch Song Trilogy* over his production of *'night, Mother.*

But if Brustein was jealous of Lloyd Richards, and uncomfortable with minority playwrights, what drove him most crazy about me, it seemed, was my wife. Often he would stare conspicuously at Alex before the lights went down at a performance we both attended. Soon enough, he wrote a column titled "An Embarrassment of Riches," that attacked the intersection of our marital and professional lives. There was an odd twist to Brustein's attack, since a decade earlier he chastised the *Times* in his memoir for mentioning that the lead actress in one of his Yale productions was his own late wife. The Brusteins had argued that calling attention to "relationships between husbands and wives who worked in the same place" was irrelevant to evaluating their work.

His article started a new wave of publicity. The power of the *Times* drama critic, real or imagined, now seemed the most interesting story in the theater. And there was nothing I could do about it. The *Times*'s drama critic, whoever it was, had been the most influential in town before I was born, and would be after I'd gone. And the more publicity the drama critic got, the more powerful he seemed to become. When the Shuberts banned Woollcott seventy-five years earlier, they made both the paper and Woollcott more famous and powerful than they had been before. "They threw me out and now I'm basking in the fierce white light that beats upon the thrown," Woollcott said.

Like most of Woollcott's successors, I felt ambivalent about the paper's weight. If a review of mine could convince people to check out the work of an exciting new playwright, the *Times*'s influence seemed worthwhile. If it had the opposite effect, who could take pleasure in that? Yet was the alternative to write waffling reviews, imploring readers to go to some well-meaning mediocrity for the good of the theater and those who worked in it? If I did that, I'd become the boy who cried wolf: Those same readers would not believe me when I praised the really good play that came along. I was writing for the reader who did not want to waste a night or a hundred bucks on a dull evening—and who did not want a patronizing critic to trick him into doing so. I was hardly writing for the producer who might lose a million dollars on *Merlin*.

This was the way the *Times* wanted it, too, which is why the paper and I were well matched. Though the theater inevitably thought I was too tough, readers and some of my editors more often found me guilty of the reverse: I got far more mail from theatergoers who disliked plays I had praised than the other way around, and no wonder, given the fact that someone who loves the theater enough to be a theater critic is always going to be more charitable than the typical patron who might carefully pick out only a few plays to see each season. When looking through old reviews in retrospect I find that while I occasionally underpraised— *Nicholas Nickleby*, for instance—my biggest whoppers of critical judgment were mostly of overpraise, from Elizabeth Taylor in *The Little Foxes* to *La Cage aux Folles*. (Some other plays that I was accused of overpraising, and that few other critics liked, I still feel strongly about, like *Grown Ups*, by Jules Feiffer, *Eastern Standard*, by Richard Greenberg, and *Four Baboons Adoring the Sun*, by John Guare.)

The power of the job was not so vast as the Butcher of Broadway gags would have it, in any event. The huge, fast flops of my time, from *Moose Murders* to *Carrie* and *Nick and Nora*, invariably received unanimously poor press from all newspaper, magazine, and television critics; it would be hard to argue, as a Brustein or Hare might, that the *Times* review alone "closed" any of these shows. Similarly, many of the big hits, from *Amadeus* to *Angels in America*, received almost uniformly favorable reviews, which makes it difficult to argue that the *Times* alone carried the day. Commercial entertainments with true mass appeal, whether by Neil Simon or Andrew Lloyd Webber, are review-proof: Who in the standing-room-only audience at *The Phantom of the Opera* this week either knows or cares what I wrote about it? Does anyone remember that I didn't like *Brighton Beach Memoirs* or *Agnes of God*? Commercial shows that earn mixed or poor reviews can often survive if a producer is willing to do his job and promote it—as the histories of productions like *I'm Not Rappaport* and *Blood Brothers* attest. In the post-Merrick era, sadly, such producers are in perilously short supply. The only showman left on Broadway who matches Merrick is the British producer Cameron Mackintosh, but he stages only large musicals, and infrequently at that. Merrick would not only mount several productions a season, but for every *Hello, Dolly!* there would be a drama, whether Peter Brook's *Midsummer Night's Dream* or Brian Friel's *Philadelphia, Here I Come!* And he would sell them as hard as he would a musical cash cow.

While I would not dispute some areas of the *Times*'s influence—especially its critics' ability to encourage extended runs (or commercial transfers) of plays in Off Broadway or out-of-town venues—the power to control the fate of that most endangered species, the drama on Broadway, is close to nil. Serious dramas enthusiastically greeted by me and most other critics, whether *The Grapes of Wrath* or *Joe Turner's Come and Gone,* by August Wilson, or Royal Shakespeare Company imports like the Trevor Nunn *All's Well That Ends Well,* routinely fail on Broadway. The marketplace now only accommodates one drama per season—one *Dancing at Lughnasa* or *Angels in America*—unless there is a Madonna or Jessica Lange on another marquee.

But why should I even bother to argue my case? The myth will never die. As Brooks Atkinson wrote in the *Times* in 1953, when a musical he panned the year before (*Wish You Were Here*) became a hit while well-reviewed plays flopped, "Facts will not destroy the ancient legend that critics are dictators who arbitrarily permit some plays to succeed and haughtily consign most of them to the ash-can."

Or as Atkinson put it when his power was under attack in 1947: "What the theater needs is not the suppression of opinion but a sharp and drastic deflation in the cost of tickets and a sharp and drastic improvement in the quality of plays."

Some things, it's clear, never change.

. . .

What did change in the late 1980s and early 1990s was the quality and texture of American playwriting, which became more diverse in style, ethnic origin, and themes. As American theatrical production is now decentralized, with most new plays originating at institutional theaters Off Broadway and throughout the country rather than on Broadway, so American theatrical writing and performance reflect a far less homogenous society than they once did. A list of writers as varied as Jon Robin Baitz, Anna Deavere Smith, Craig Lucas, John Leguizamo, Paul Rudnick, Paula Vogel, Donald Margulies, José Rivera, Richard Greenberg, and Eduardo Machado just touches the surface of this explosive new talent pool. If the directorial visions of Robert Wilson and Peter Sellars have no wider an American following in the early nineties than they did in the early eighties, the edgy, stylized African American esthetic that the director George C. Wolfe brings to plays by black and white writers has caught on. Wolfe's staging and Tony Kushner's writing of *Angels in America* arguably brought more excitement to the American theater than any single work since *Who's Afraid of Virginia Woolf?* three decades earlier.

Yet, for all this creative flowering, the mood in the New York theater continued to turn sour as the millennium approached. Rising costs and ticket prices continued to erode Broadway, restricting its ability to present the American theater's large new creative bounty. The theater's old guard, which controls much of Broadway's bureaucracy and funds, resented the new generation that questioned its ways (much as it resented the taste of critics like myself who championed that new generation). Off Broadway theater companies, where most of the artistic action is, remain barred from the Tony Awards, a promotional event that increasingly seemed designed (like high ticket prices) to keep young talents and young audiences running in the opposite direction of Broadway. The Dramatists Guild, the playwrights organization that might have fought the establishment for revolutionary change, was under the thumb of Peter Stone, an old-line Broadway musical-theater book writer (*Woman of the Year, The Will Rogers Follies*) who, unlike much of the group's membership, never worked Off Broadway and was out of touch with the rising writers half his age working in nonprofit theaters.

But one reason for the growing gloom in the New York theater was beyond its control, and that, of course, was AIDS. The disease stepped out of the theater's closet in 1985 when it made its debut as a stage subject (in *As Is,* by William Hoffman, and *The Normal Heart,* by Larry Kramer). Two years later, two of New York's greatest theatrical leaders, Broadway's Michael Bennett and Off Broadway's Charles Ludlam, joined the long list of casualties. The deaths would have been shocking under any circumstance, but the tragedy was heightened by the fresh memories of their recent triumphs. Bennett's extravagant staging of the gala, record-breaking performance of *A Chorus Line* in 1983 and Ludlam's Ridiculous Theatrical Company tour de force, *The Mystery of Irma Vep,* in 1984, had suggested a limitless future for both men. They both died at forty-four.

"Sometimes you see death everywhere," went a totemic line in John Guare's brilliant theatrical summation of the 1980s in New York, *Six Degrees of Separation.*

. . .

In June 1991, however, I could not have been happier. A week after my forty-second birthday, Alex and I were married in New York. The joy proved short-lived. On July 4, we went to a cookout at the home of Janet Maslin, my close friend and colleague who had first introduced me to Arthur Gelb (and the *Times*) a dozen years earlier. When we returned to my apartment at nightfall, a phone message announced that my mother and stepfather had been in a grotesque car accident on Route 95 between Baltimore and Washington, on their way home from an Independence Day lunch.

For a month, I commuted back and forth by train between New York and Baltimore, where my mother languished in a shock trauma center. The weather was fetid, the train and Baltimore itself always seemed deserted. My mother was sixty-four years old and had been in perfect health. There was some chance she might survive her extensive injuries. My stepfather was released from the hospital in a couple of weeks. But hard as my mother fought—or I imagined her to fight, since she was sedated the entire time—it was not to be. She died exactly a month after the accident.

My grief was so overwhelming that more than two years later, my memories of that summer remain a blur. For the first time in my life, the theater offered no solace, no escape. My mother too abundantly haunted the theater for me: She had always told me how she listened to the newly issued cast recording of *South Pacific* when she was pregnant with me; it was she who had given me Moss Hart's inspiring *Act One* a decade later.

But just as I hit psychic bottom, one person in the theater reached out to me, as if to bring me back within its spell.

That person was Joseph Papp. Like every critic, especially every *Times* critic, I had always had an up-and-down relationship with him—and it had only been a professional relationship, largely in theater lobbies before a curtain went up. While he had never attempted to throw me out of his theater, as he had Walter Kerr, we had had our innings, the fracas over David Hare and *The Secret Rapture* included, once the New York Shakespeare Festival started to stumble in the late 1980s. The stumbling, I and others had not realized, was directly attributable to Papp's fight with cancer, the severity of which he successfully kept secret until the last year of his life.

By the time of my mother's death in August 1991, it was widely known that Papp was dying. No one had seen him in weeks. My last encounter with him, an atypical one, had been in March: He had phoned me to tell me how much he agreed with a favorable review I had written of a play he had read but not seen, Jon Robin Baitz's *The Substance of Fire*. When I encouraged him to go see the production at Playwrights Horizons, he gave vague excuses.

Now Papp was determined to give an extensive interview to the *Times*—his last—and, more specifically, to give it to Alex. She had worked for him in her college days, and they had hit it off. He had been a constant and reliable source for her column, even when the stories were not flattering to his own institution.

Alex's interview ran in the *Times* less than three weeks after my mother's death. A few mornings later, I picked up the phone in the kitchen and it was Papp's familiar voice, far stronger than I remembered it having been in March. He was calling to offer condolences. I told him how touched I was by his concern, then told him how sorry I had been to hear about his son, who had died of AIDS since our last conversation. Within moments, both of us were sobbing on the phone, knowing we were saying good-bye. "I want you to know," Joe said, "that even when I was angry at you I always knew you loved the theater." We expressed a desire to become the friends we had never been. Choosing my words delicately, I told him that he and his wife, Gail Merrifield, must come to our place for dinner when he felt well enough to do so. The conversation ended on a high note, the warmest embrace possible by phone, after which I felt more energized than I had since the accident—if only for a few minutes, until the weight of my grief about Papp kicked in. As Merrick was the impresario who sponsored much of the exciting American theater of my youth, Papp was the far more visionary producer who played that role (reinventing American theater in the process) during my adulthood. Who was left?

• • •

As Labor Day arrived, I realized that for the first time in memory, I was not looking forward to a new theater season. The only way I could get back to writing, and to reconnecting with my passion for the theater, was to write an essay summing up Papp's career. Five weeks after it was published Papp died. But then the emotional weather changed for me; the theater came to my rescue with an exceptionally fine season: *Dancing at Lughnasa, Angels in America* in London, *Jelly's Last Jam, Falsettos, Fires in the Mirror,* and *Marvin's Room,* a daffy yet devastating comedy about a woman who gives her life to caring for her terminally infirm father. My colleague and eventual successor as chief drama critic, David Richards, had written a profile of the young playwright, Scott McPherson, and invited me to join the two of them for breakfast the day after my review ran. This was unusual for me, but *Marvin's Room,* more than any play I'd seen before or since, had spoken directly to me about what life had been like at my mother's side in the hospital. And I didn't have to worry about my integrity being compromised: McPherson, who was thirty-two and sick with AIDS, was not going to write another play.

In the incongruously cheery setting of Sarabeth's Kitchen on Amsterdam Avenue, the elfin McPherson was much like the heroine, Bessie, in his play—funny, guileless, more concerned about others than himself. His lover, an AIDS activist named Daniel Sotomayor, was too sick to emerge from his hotel room; he died back home in Chicago two months later. McPherson talked buoyantly about his future writing plans. A year later, he, too, was dead.

The fact of the theater's dwindling was inescapable, yet, paradoxically, American plays continued to rise to a level far higher than had been typical of my beat in the early eighties. However gravely ill the economic and physical health of the American theater, its art was thriving against all odds, and its young artists (Tony Kushner, typically, was only thirty-six) promised a real future.

For me, the future increasingly seemed elsewhere. As election year arrived, and with it the prospect of both a political and generational turnover in American life, my journalistic focus widened; I found myself more interested in writing about the world itself rather than just the theater's vision of that world. A year after my mother's death, I took a leave from my beat to write columns about the Democratic and Republican conventions with my friend Maureen Dowd; the country was getting ready to elect a president only a couple of years older than I was. Though I returned to the theater for another season, I knew it would be my last. I started balancing my theater reviewing with a column about other matters for this magazine.

When the *Times* announced my appointment as an op-ed columnist, I heard from people in the theater, many of whom I had never met or communicated with before. My favorite send-off, however, turned up in a newspaper clipping from London. The *Sunday Telegraph* reported that David Merrick, ailing but still kicking, said through a lawyer that "Mr. Rich made many contributions to the American theater, none more great than to leave his post as theater critic."

The locution sounded suspiciously British for Merrick, but what the hell. For now at least, my career in the theater was complete; it seemed only right that the old fox who was there at the start would write my comic exit line.

There were still a few more plays to review. The very last, determined by the calendar, was *Perestroika,* the second half of *Angels in America.* I invited my oldest friend, Alan Brinkley, and his wife, Evangeline, to join me and Alex. My mother and Alan's had shared a hospital room in Washington on the day we were born forty-four years earlier. Now Alan gave me a *Playbill* from that summer of 1949 as a token of the occasion.

A couple of afternoons later, I was alone in my cubicle at the paper, finishing my review of the play. The image that had most stayed in my mind from Kushner's voluminous epic was one of its last: the almost festive farewell wave to the audience of a man with AIDS who is determined to go on living.

So I wrote about the frail young man's buoyant wave, and, after I did, I realized that his good-bye was also my own; I went back and changed a couple of words in my final sentence to reinforce that double meaning. When I finished, I found myself as tearful as I had been that long-ago night when Gower Champion's death had rung down the opening-night curtain on *42nd Street.* But I was older now, and this was a different catharsis. Rereading my final review one last time before sending it out into the world, I suddenly saw clearly why I so strongly identified with the character on stage. Death had been transfigured for me, too, into something that looked very much like hope.

The mail I (and the magazine) received in response to my memoir in the Sunday *Times Magazine,* "Exit the Critic," was voluminous, often warm but sometimes not, with many of the nicest letters coming from theater people I'd never met. Some of the most touching responses came from readers who followed the theater through the *Times* but could not, for either financial or geographical reasons, see any of the plays I reviewed, favorably or not.

Some theatrical correspondents filled in details I hadn't known about various events I described—especially David Merrick events. One of his lawyers wrote an amusing letter explaining that he was the author of the producer's London statement about my departure from the drama critic's job—and that the locution sounded British because the *Sunday Telegraph* reporter to whom he gave the quote "did change a few words, but as you say, what the hell." Marge Champion Sagal, Gower Champion's longtime professional partner and former wife, wrote a very touching and detailed account of the Merrick-Champion "love-hate relationship," revealing her own emergency role in the director's final medical drama.

The only poisonous letter was sent by a Broadway producer not mentioned in the piece, Emanuel Azenberg, who, though not a friend of Joseph Papp's, wrote on his own personal authority that Papp had nothing but "detestation" for me. Another point of view came from Gail Merrifield Papp, Papp's widow, who generously sent a Xerox of a handwritten note her husband had written her on the day of our final phone conversation, August 11, 1991. It read (in its entirety):

> Long talk with Frank Rich, whose mother died. With Rich, unprecedented expression of love betw. major drama critic of Times and producer, Me. *NO OPPORTUNISM.* Just free exchange of deep & tender feeling—sharing losses (Tony) (Rich's Mother) & commiserations. *UNHEARD* of such things, prod./critic.

Needless to say, Robert Brustein and Peter Stone begged to differ, strongly, with my comments about our various conflicts. As I began writing my op-ed column, which occasionally deals with the theater, Stone called me with some helpful news tips, thus beginning a chatty phone relationship. Brustein and I continued to squabble in print—especially after I wrote a column about his public debate with August Wilson about race and the theater—but at a small dinner to celebrate Rocco Landesman's fiftieth birthday in July 1997, he offered to "bury the hatchet" and I gladly agreed. The truth is that Bob and I had gotten along well before we came to blows—the record will even show that I wrote many more favorable reviews of his productions than negative ones—and I looked forward to retrieving our common ground. Also at that dinner were Gerald and Pat Schoenfeld, with whom I'd renewed a cordial relationship, not unlike the one I'd had with them in the sixties, long before I came to New York to do battle with the Shuberts over our conflicting visions of the theater.

The theater will, of course, survive all of us—and will continue to surprise all its critics and prognosticators. No one—not me, not the Shuberts, not the editors of the *Times* or *Variety*—anticipated the single biggest development to shake Broadway since my departure: the arrival of Disney as a producing and redevelopment force, leading to the revival of Forty-second Street and, with it, the rebirth of the entire Times Square neighborhood in which the Broadway theater lives. What remains unclear is whether there is any more hope for the survival of new American plays—as opposed to revivals, imported British dramas, tourist spectacles, and musicals, all happily booming—in this new Times Square than there was in the old one I covered. At the end of the exceptionally busy 1997–98 season, there were only three new American plays on Broadway. Only one of them was filling its relatively small Broadway house.

A year into my tenure as drama critic—in May 1981—I summed up the season by examining the Tony Award nominees: "All four of the nominated best plays were produced (and acclaimed) away from Broadway, and only one (*Fifth of July*) is the work of a native playwright. Of the four best musical nominees, only one (*Woman of the Year*) offers new songs instead of a score of old standards"—and then went on to list all the season's Off Broadway triumphs: *Request Concert, Cloud 9, March of the Falsettos, Crimes of the Heart, Dead End Kids, How I Got That Story, The Dance and the Railroad, Beyond Therapy, Penguin Touquet,* etc. Some seventeen years later, the picture for new musicals has brightened—though the most promising new songwriter, Jonathan Larson of *Rent*, died just as his career was born—but the most exciting new American plays (*How I Learned to Drive, Gross Indecency,* among many others) remain Off Broadway. The British magazine *The Economist* has argued that, if anything, Broadway is moving further away from doing new work, noting in 1996 that "nearly half the shows on Broadway are revivals; fifteen years ago only one in ten was."

The problem of the straight play on Broadway remains one of economics, not talent. Not one season during my years as drama critic lacked for an exciting new voice, nor has any season since. What's needed is a major revamping of an antiquated industry so that those voices, not just musicals and revivals, can be showcased in the country's premiere theatrical venue, in some of the most beautiful playhouses ever built: There's something seriously wrong when it's so financially prohibitive to run a drama on Broadway that the houses that once were home to Williams and Miller and O'Neill are booked with one-man shows from *Freak* to *Defending the Caveman* but are economically out of reach of any exciting new dramas containing more than a handful of characters. Should the remarkable resurgence of Forty-second Street at last trigger the long-awaited overhaul of the Broadway industry and reverse this thirty-year-plus trend, it will be a dénouement so far-fetched, and so exciting, it could only happen in the theater.

APPENDIX

"Best" and "Worst" lists are arbitrary, and certainly these are no exception. In each category except the last two, the items are listed in chronological order. (The dates in parentheses are the date the production was reviewed.)

MY FAVORITE NEW PLAYS

"Master Harold" . . . *and the Boys,* by Athol Fugard (March 17, 1982)
Plenty, by David Hare (October 22, 1982)
'night, Mother, by Marsha Norman (January 12, 1983)
Noises Off, by Michael Frayn (December 12, 1983)
Glengarry Glen Ross, by David Mamet (March 26, 1984)
Ma Rainey's Black Bottom, by August Wilson (October 12, 1984)
M. Butterfly, by David Henry Hwang (March 21, 1988)
Six Degrees of Separation, by John Guare (June 15, 1990)
Dancing at Lughnasa, by Brian Friel (October 25, 1991)
Marvin's Room, by Scott McPherson (December 6, 1991)
Angels in America, by Tony Kushner (March 5, 1992; May 5, 1993;
     November 24, 1993)

MY FAVORITE NEW MUSICALS

March of the Falsettos, by William Finn (April 10, 1981)
Dreamgirls, book and lyrics by Tom Eyen; music by Henry Krieger
     (December 12, 1981)
Sunday in the Park with George, book by James Lapine; music and
     lyrics by Stephen Sondheim (May 3, 1984)
City of Angels, book by Larry Gelbart; music by Cy Coleman; lyrics by
     David Zippel (December 12, 1989)

TEN ELECTRIFYING NIGHTS:
UNEXPECTED REVIVALS AND OTHERS

Lena Horne: The Lady and Her Music (May 13, 1981)
A Chorus Line No. 3,389 (October 1, 1983)

La Tragédie de Carmen (November 18, 1983)
Balm in Gilead (June 1, 1984)
Follies (September 15, 1985)
Let the Artists Die (October 15, 1985)
Les Liaisons Dangereuses (May 1, 1987)
The Cherry Orchard (January 25, 1988)
Juno and the Paycock (June 22, 1988)
Carousel (December 17, 1992)

TWENTY INDELIBLE PERFORMANCES

Kevin Kline, *The Pirates of Penzance* (July 30, 1980)
Ian McKellen, *Amadeus* (December 18, 1980)
Gregory Hines, *Sophisticated Ladies* (March 2, 1981)
Tom Courtenay, *The Dresser* (November 10, 1981)
Jennifer Holliday, *Dreamgirls* (December 21, 1981)
Christopher Plummer, *Othello* (February 4, 1982)
Kate Nelligan, *Plenty* (October 22, 1982)
Jessica Tandy, *Foxfire* (November 12, 1982)
Ralph Richardson, *Inner Voices* (June 20, 1983)
Billie Whitelaw, *Rockaby* (February 17, 1984)
Charles Dutton, *Ma Rainey's Black Bottom* (October 12, 1984)
Swoosie Kurtz, *House of Blue Leaves* (March 20, 1986)
Robert Lindsay, *Me and My Girl* (August 11, 1986)
Vanessa Redgrave, *Orpheus Descending* (December 15, 1988)
Tyne Daly, *Gypsy* (November 17, 1989)
Eric Bogosian, *Sex, Drugs, Rock & Roll* (February 9, 1990)
Pat Carroll, *The Merry Wives of Windsor* (May 30, 1990)
Stockard Channing, *Six Degrees of Separation* (June 15, 1990)
Jonathan Pryce, *Miss Saigon* (August 10, 1990; August 12, 1991)
Laura Esterman, *Marvin's Room* (December 6, 1991)

TWENTY MORE INDELIBLE PERFORMANCES: COUPLES

Anne Pitoniak and Kathy Bates, *'night, Mother* (January 12, 1983)
Charles Ludlam and Everett Quinton, *Galas* (September 16, 1983)
Bernadette Peters and Mandy Patinkin, *Sunday in the Park with George*
   (May 3, 1984)
Penn & Teller (April 19, 1985)
Donal McCann and John Kavanagh, *Juno and the Paycock*
   (June 22, 1988)
Alec Baldwin and Mary-Louise Parker, *Prelude to a Kiss*
   (March 15, 1990)

Nathan Lane and Faith Prince, *Guys and Dolls* (April 15, 1992)
Natasha Richardson and Liam Neeson, *Anna Christie*
  (January 15, 1993)
Bill Irwin and David Shiner, *Fool Moon* (February 26, 1993)
Joe Mantello and Stephen Spinella, *Angels in America* (May 5, 1993;
  November 24, 1993)

INDELIBLE ENSEMBLE CASTS

The Life and Adventures of Nicholas Nickleby (October 5, 1981)
Jerome Robbins' Broadway (February 27, 1989)
Dancing at Lughnasa (October 25, 1991)

FABULOUS FLOPS: THE MOST UNFORGETTABLE DISASTERS

Marlowe (October 13, 1981)
Moose Murders (February 23, 1983)
Private Lives (May 9, 1983)
Marilyn (November 21, 1983)
Carrie (May 13, 1988)

PRODUCTIONS I MOST UNDERRATED

The Life and Adventures of Nicholas Nickleby (October 5, 1981)
The Normal Heart (April 22, 1985)

PRODUCTIONS I MOST OVERRATED

La Cage aux Folles (August 22, 1983)
As Is (March 11, 1985)
The Mystery of Edwin Drood (August 23, 1985)
A Lie of the Mind (December 6, 1985)
Serious Money (December 4, 1987)
The Piano Lesson (April 17, 1990)

THE POWER OF THE *TIMES* REVISITED 1: RAVE REVIEWS, SHORT BROADWAY RUNS

All's Well That Ends Well—38 performances
The Iceman Cometh—55 performances
Grown Ups—83 performances
Plenty—92 performances
Eastern Standard—92 performances
Joe Turner's Come and Gone—105 performances
Les Liaisons Dangereuses—148 performances
La Tragédie de Carmen—187 performances

The Grapes of Wrath—188 performances
Benefactors—217 performances

THE POWER OF THE *TIMES* REVISITED 2:
MIXED TO NEGATIVE REVIEWS, LONG BROADWAY RUNS

42nd Street—3,486 performances
Brighton Beach Memoirs—1,530 performances
The Will Rogers Follies—963 performances
I'm Not Rappaport—890 performances
Into the Woods—765 performances
Starlight Express—761 performances
The Secret Garden—706 performances
Agnes of God—599 performances
On Your Toes—505 performances
Song & Dance—474 performances

ACKNOWLEDGMENTS

It was Arthur Gelb, then a managing editor, who wooed me to *The New York Times* without promising me any specific job, and it was his enthusiasm for the theater, for the *Times,* and for my work that gave me the confidence I needed to be drama critic. Arthur has played an inspirational role for many young writers at the paper, but it was my particular good fortune to be covering the beat that was nearest to his heart. In the 1950s and early sixties, before becoming an editor, he had been a second-string critic to my most fabled predecessor, Brooks Atkinson, as well as a drama reporter and the coauthor (with his wife, Barbara) of a major biography of Eugene O'Neill. Arthur's and my mutual love for the theater and newspapers—and ultimately for each other—led to the most exciting creative collaboration of my professional life. He also gave me the title for this book.

The institutional support Arthur gave me was matched by that of a remarkable series of *Times* executive editors—Abe Rosenthal, Max Frankel, and Joe Lelyveld—and by other top executives on Forty-third Street, including Sydney Gruson, Seymour Topping, and John Lee. Generous moral support was provided by Walter and Jean Kerr, childhood heroes who became great friends, and by my other friends among my critical colleagues: Michiko Kakutani, Janet Maslin, Vincent Canby, Benedict Nightingale, David Richards, and Ben Brantley. Without Carol Coburn—who deals with every press release, schedule change, and nut who turns up over the transom or the phone at the paper's drama desk—no *Times* drama critic could do the job; I benefited incalculably not just from her unflappable professionalism but from her warm friendship and unfailing wisdom during our years together. In a category by himself is the artist who showed me what Broadway looked like before I ever saw it and who remains to this day a sounding board for all matters theatrical and journalistic, Al Hirschfeld.

It would be impossible for any drama critic to function at the *Times* without the unflinching loyalty of the paper's management, even (or especially) when some of the biggest advertisers ask for his head. In my entire time as critic, I never heard a single discouraging word from the

Times's publisher, Punch Sulzberger, or, when he succeeded his father toward the end of my tenure, Arthur Sulzberger Jr. It is this family's bedrock insistence on editorial independence that has given the *Times* a reputation for integrity that bolsters all who work there and that few, if any, American journalistic institutions can match.

On a day-to-day basis, in the throes of deadline pressure, my copy and thoughts were inevitably sharpened by the *Times*'s deep ranks of editing talent. I can't thank these wonderful and often selfless men and women enough. In rough chronological order, they include: Seymour Peck, Robert Berkvist, William Honan, Mike Leahy, Marvin Siegel, Eva Hoffman, Constance Rosenblum, Andrea Stevens, John Montorio, Myra Forsberg, Donald Caswell, Martha Wilson, Wade Burkhart, Diane Nottle, Gladys Bourdain, Andrea Higbie, and John Storm. My friend Adam Moss, at *The New York Times Magazine,* was the editor who helped me conceive of my valedictory piece, "Exit the Critic," and with his typical creativity and perseverance led me through its various revisions. I also thank my current assistant at the *Times,* Carlos Briceno, for his patience while I was assembling this volume.

This book happened because of the generous enthusiasm and support of my editor at Random House, Ann Godoff, and my agent, Kathy Robbins. Without the tireless intelligence and hard work of Random House editor Sean Abbott, you wouldn't be reading it now. I am equally grateful to the many others at Random House whose professionalism not only added so much to the book but made the entire publishing process a joy: Benjamin Dreyer, Stacy Rockwood, J. K. Lambert, Gabrielle Bordwin, Robbin Schiff, Thomas Perry, Carol Schneider, and Stephen McNabb. Any errors in this book are mine, not theirs.

Finally, I thank my wife, Alex Witchel, who entered this book's narrative well into the second act and gave it an unexpectedly happy ending, as well as my sons, Nathaniel and Simon, who in these pages will learn perhaps more than they want to know about what their father was doing after they were tucked in bed.

INDEX

Page numbers in italics refer to illustrations.

FRANK RICH was born and raised in Washington, D.C., and educated at Harvard. He became an op-ed columnist for *The New York Times* in 1994, after having served since 1980 as the paper's chief drama critic. He has written about culture and politics for many publications, including *Time, Esquire,* and *The New Republic*. He lives in New York City with his wife, the writer Alex Witchel.

ABOUT THE TYPE

This book was set in Fairfield, the first typeface from the hand of the distinguished American artist and engraver Rudolph Ruzicka (1883–1978). Rudolph Ruzicka was born in Bohemia and came to America in 1894. He set up his own shop, devoted to wood engraving and printing, in New York in 1913 after a varied career working as a wood engraver, in photo-engraving and banknote printing plants, and as an art director and freelance artist. He designed and illustrated many books, and was the creator of a considerable list of individual prints—wood engravings, line engravings on copper, and aquatints.